Arvo

urbit/pkg/arvo/sys/

West Martian Limited Company
3rd Edition, April 2024

Contents

Arvo

Arvo 237K

```
=>  ..ride  =>
!:
|%
+|  %global
::
++  arvo  %237
::
::   $arch: node identity
::   $axal: fundamental node, recursive (trie)
::   $axil: fundamental node
::   $beak: global context
::   $beam: global name
::   $bone: opaque duct handle
::   $case: global version
::   $cage: marked vase
::   +cask: marked data builder
::   $desk: local workspace
::   $dock: message target
::   $gang: infinite set of peers
::   $mark: symbolic content type
::   $mien: orientation
::   $page: untyped cage
::   $omen: fully-qualified namespace path
::   $ship: network identity
::   $sink: subscription
::
+$  arch  (axil @uvI)
++  axal
  |$  [item]
  [fil=(unit item) dir=(map @ta $)]
++  axil
  |$  [item]
  [fil=(unit item) dir=(map @ta ~)]
::
+$  beak  (trel ship desk case)
+$  beam  [beak s=path]
+$  bone  @ud
+$  case
  $%  ::  %da:  date
      ::  %tas: label
      ::  %ud:  sequence
      ::  %uv:  hash
      ::
      [%da p=@da]
      [%tas p=@tas]
      [%ud p=@ud]
      [%uv p=@uv]
  ==
+$  cage  (cask vase)
++  cask  |$  [a]  (pair mark a)
+$  desk  @tas
+$  dock  (pair @p term)
+$  gang  (unit (set ship))
+$  mark  @tas
+$  mien  [our=ship now=@da eny=@uvJ]
```

```hoon
56  +$    page    (cask)
57  +$    omen    [vis=view bem=beam]
58  +$    ship    @p
59  +$    sink    (trel bone ship path)
60  ::
61  +|    %meta
62  ::
63  ::    +hypo: type-associated builder
64  ::    $meta: meta-vase
65  ::    $maze: vase, or meta-vase
66  ::
67  ++    hypo
68      |$  [a]
69      (pair type a)
70  +$    meta    (pair)
71  +$    maze    (each vase meta)
72  ::
73  +|    %interface
74  ::
75  ::    $ball: dynamic kernel action
76  ::    $card: tagged, untyped event
77  ::    $duct: causal history
78  ::    +hobo: %soft task builder
79  ::    $goof: crash label and trace XX fail/ruin/crud/flaw/lack/miss
80  ::    $mass: memory usage
81  ::    $move: cause and action
82  ::    $ovum: card with cause
83  ::    $roof: namespace
84  ::    $rook: meta-namespace (super advanced)
85  ::    +room: generic namespace
86  ::    +roon: partial namespace
87  ::    $root: raw namespace
88  ::    $view: namespace perspective
89  ::    +wind: kernel action builder
90  ::    $wire: event pretext
91  ::    +wite: kernel action/error builder
92  ::
93  +$    ball    (wite [vane=term task=maze] maze)
94  +$    card    (cask)
95  +$    duct    (list wire)
96  ++    hobo
97      |$  [a]
98      $?  $%  [%soft p=*]
99          ==
100         a
101     ==
102 +$    goof    [mote=term =tang]
103 +$    mass    $~   $+|+~
104             (pair cord (each * (list mass)))
105 +$    move    [=duct =ball]
106 +$    ovum    [=wire =card]
107 ::
108 +$    roof    (room vase)                        ::  namespace
109 +$    rook    (room meta)                        ::  meta-namespace
110 ++    room                                       ::  either namespace
111     |$  [a]
112     $~   =>(~ |~(* ~))
113     $~   $:  lyc=gang                             ::  leakset
```

```
114           pov=path                          ::  provenance
115         omen                                ::  perspective, path
116       ==                                    ::
117   %-  unit                                  ::  ~: unknown
118   %-  unit                                  ::  ~ ~: invalid
119   (cask a)                                  ::
120 +$  roon                                    ::  partial namespace
121   $~  =>(~ |-(* ~))
122   $-  [lyc=gang pov=path car=term bem=beam]
123   (unit (unit cage))
124 +$  root  $-(^ (unit (unit)))
125 +$  view  $@(term [way=term car=term])      ::  perspective
126 ::
127 ++  wind
128   |$  ::  a: forward
129       ::  b: reverse
130       ::
131       [a b]
132   $%  ::  %pass: advance
133       ::  %slip: lateral
134       ::  %give: retreat
135       ::
136       [%pass p=path q=a]
137       [%slip p=a]
138       [%give p=b]
139   ==
140 +$  wire  path
141 ++  wite
142   |$  ::  note: a routed $task
143       ::  gift: a reverse action
144       ::
145       ::    NB:  task: a forward action
146       ::         sign: a sourced $gift
147       ::
148       [note gift]
149   $%  ::  %hurl: action failed
150       ::  %pass: advance
151       ::  %slip: lateral
152       ::  %give: retreat
153       ::
154       [%hurl =goof wite=$;($>(?(%pass %give) $))]
155       [%pass =wire =note]
156       [%slip =note]
157       [%give =gift]
158   ==
159 ::
160 +|  %implementation
161 ::
162 ::  $debt: ephemeral state
163 ::  $grub: persistent state, larval stage
164 ::  $germ: worklist source and bar stack
165 ::  $heir: upgradeable state
166 ::  $plan: worklist
167 ::  $soul: persistent state
168 ::  $vane: kernel module
169 ::  $vere: runtime version
170 ::  $vile: reflexive constants
171 ::  $waif: arvo task, from anywhere
```

```
172  ::    $wasp: arvo task, from Outside
173  ::    $weft: kelvin version, tag and number
174  ::    $worm: compiler cache
175  ::    $wisp: arvo task, larval stage
176  ::    $wynn: kelvin stack
177  ::
178  +$  debt
179    $:  ::  run: list of worklists
180        ::  out: pending output
181        ::  kel: kernel files
182        ::  fil: pending files
183        ::
184        run=(list plan)
185        out=(list ovum)
186        kel=(list (pair path (cask)))
187        fil=(list (pair path (cask)))
188    ==
189  +$  germ   [vane=term bars=(list duct)]
190  +$  grub
191    $:  ::  who: identity once we know it
192        ::  eny: entropy once we learn it
193        ::  lac: laconicity as we want it
194        ::  ver: the Outside as we see it
195        ::  fat: source when we attain it
196        ::  lul: %lull when we acquire it
197        ::  zus: %zuse once we receive it
198        ::  van: vanes while we desire it
199        ::
200        who=(unit ship)
201        eny=(unit @)
202        lac=?
203        ver=(unit vere)
204        fat=(unit (axal (cask)))
205        lul=(unit (trap vase))
206        zus=(unit (trap vase))
207        van=(map term (trap vase))
208    ==
209  +$  heir
210    $%  $:  %grub
211            $%  [?(%240 %239 %238 %237) =grub]
212        ==  ==
213        [?(%240 %239 %238 %237) =debt =soul]
214    ==
215  +$  plan  (pair germ (list move))
216  +$  soul
217    $:  ::  identity, time, entropy
218        ::  fad: configuration
219        ::  zen: Outside knowledge
220        ::  mod: internal modules
221        ::
222        mien
223        $=  fad
224        $:  ::  lac: not verbose
225            ::
226            lac=?
227        ==
228        $=  zen
229        $:  ::  ver: runtime version
```

```
230              ::  lag: upgrade blocked
231              ::
232              ver=vere
233              lag=_|
234          ==
235      $=  mod
236      $:  ::  fat: filesystem
237          ::  lul: %lull
238          ::  zus: %zuse
239          ::  van: vanes
240          ::
241          fat=(axal (cask))
242          lul=vase
243          zus=vase
244          van=(map term vane)
245          ==
246      ==
247  +$  vane   [=vase =worm]
248  +$  vere   [[non=@ta rev=path] kel=wynn]
249  +$  vile
250      $:  typ=type     ::  -:!>(*type)
251          duc=type     ::  -:!>(*duct)
252          wir=type     ::  -:!>(*wire)
253          dud=type     ::  -:!>(*(unit goof))
254      ==
255  ::
256  +$  waif
257      ::  %trim: trim state, spam to all
258      ::  %what: update from files
259      ::  %whey: produce $mass               :: XX remove, scry
260      ::  %verb: toggle laconicity
261      ::  %whiz: prime vane caches
262      ::
263      $%  [%trim p=@ud]
264          [%what p=(list (pair path (cask)))]
265          [%whey ~]
266          [%verb p=(unit ?)]
267          [%whiz ~]
268      ==
269  +$  wasp
270      ::  %crud: reroute $ovum with $goof
271      ::  %wack: iterate entropy
272      ::  %wyrd: check/record runtime kelvin stack
273      ::
274      $%  [%crud =goof =ovum]
275          [%wack p=@uvJ]
276          [%wyrd p=vere]
277      ==
278  +$  weft   [lal=@tas num=@ud]
279  +$  worm
280      $:  ::  +nest, +play, and +mint
281          ::
282          nes=(set ^)
283          pay=(map (pair type hoon) type)
284          mit=(map (pair type hoon) (pair type nock))
285      ==
286  +$  wisp
287      $%  $>(?(%verb %what) waif)
```

```
288        $>(?(%wack %wyrd) wasp)
289        [%whom p=ship]
290    ==
291  +$  wynn  (list weft)
292  --  =>
293  ::
294  ~%  %hex  ..ut  ~
295  |%
296  ::::::::::::::::::::::::::::::::::::::::::::::::::::::::::::::::::
297  ::                    section 3bE, Arvo core                 ::
298  ::
299  ++  en-beam
300    |=(b=beam =*(s scot `path`[(s %p p.b) q.b (s r.b) s.b]))
301  ::
302  ++  de-beam
303    ~/  %de-beam
304    |=  p=path
305    ^-  (unit beam)
306    ?.  ?=([@ @ @ *] p)  ~
307    ?~  who=(slaw %p i.p)  ~
308    ?~  des=?~(i.t.p (some %$) (slaw %tas i.t.p))  ~  :: XX +sym ;~(pose low (easy %$))
309    ?~  ved=(de-case i.t.t.p)  ~
310    `[[`ship`u.who `desk`u.des u.ved] t.t.t.p]
311  ::
312  ++  de-case
313    ~/  %de-case
314    |=  =knot
315    ^-  (unit case)
316    ?^  num=(slaw %ud knot)  `[%ud u.num]
317    ?^  wen=(slaw %da knot)  `[%da u.wen]
318    ?^  hax=(slaw %uv knot)  `[%uv u.hax]
319    ?~  lab=(slaw %tas knot)  ~
320    `[%tas u.lab]
321  ::
322  ++  en-omen
323    |=  omen
324    ^-  path
325    :_  (en-beam bem)
326    ?@  vis  vis
327    ~(rent co [%many $/tas/way.vis $/tas/car.vis ~])
328  ::
329  ++  de-omen
330    ~/  %de-omen
331    |=  pax=path
332    ^-  (unit omen)
333    ?~  pax  ~
334    ?~  bem=(de-beam t.pax)  ~
335    ?:  ((sane %tas) i.pax)
336      `[i.pax u.bem]
337    =/  lot=(unit coin)  (rush i.pax ;~(pfix dot perd:so))
338    ?.  ?&  ?=(^ lot)
339            ?=([%many [%$ %tas @] [%$ %tas @] ~] u.lot)
340        ==
341      ~
342    `[[q.p.i q.p.i.t]:p.u.lot u.bem]
343  ::
344  ++  look
345    ~/  %look
```

```
346    |=  [rof=roof lyc=gang pov=path]
347    ^-  root
348    ~/  %in
349    |=  [ref=* raw=*]
350    ?~  pax=((soft path) raw)  ~
351    ?~  mon=(de-omen u.pax)  ~
352    ?~  dat=(rof lyc pov u.mon)  ~
353    ?~  u.dat  [~ ~]
354    =*  vax  q.u.u.dat
355    ?.  =>  [ref=ref vax=p=p.vax hoon-version=hoon-version wa=wa worm=worm]
356        ~>  %memo./arvo/look                     ::  with memoization
357        ?&  ?=(^ ref)
358            =(hoon-version -.ref)
359            -:(~(nets wa *worm) +.ref p.vax)
360        ==
361      ~>(%slog.[0 leaf+"arvo: scry-lost"] ~)
362    [~ ~ q.vax]
363  ::  |wyrd: kelvin negotiation
364  ::
365  ::    specified but unimplemented:
366  ::    arvo should produce a [wend/wynn] effect
367  ::    to signal downgrade
368  ::
369  ++  wyrd
370    |%
371    ::  +sane: kelvin stack for validity
372    ::
373    ++  sane
374      |=  kel=wynn
375      ^-  ?
376      ?:  =(~ kel)  &
377      =^  las=weft  kel  kel
378      |-  ^-  ?
379      ?~  kel  &
380      ?&  (gte num.las num.i.kel)
381          $(las i.kel, kel t.kel)
382      ==
383    ::  +need: require kelvins
384    ::
385    ++  need
386      |=  [run=wynn hav=wynn]
387      ::  wyr: ~: runtime supports all required kelvins
388      ::       ^: runtime support is missing or lagging
389      ::
390      =;  wyr  !.
391        ?~  wyr
392          same
393        ~&  wyrd=wyr
394        ~_  :+  %rose
395              [" " ~ ~]
396            :~  =+  p.u.wyr
397                leaf/"%{(trip lal)} %{(scow %ud num)} required;"
398                ?~  q.u.wyr
399                  leaf/"runtime missing support"
400                leaf/"runtime only supports %{(scow %ud u.q.u.wyr)}"
401            ==
402        ~>  %mean.'arvo: upgrade blocked'
403        ~>  %mean.'wyrd'
```

```
    !!
    ::
    |-  ^-  (unit (pair weft (unit @ud)))
    ?~  hav  ~
    ::
    ::  fel: %&: runtime kelvin for [i.hav]
    ::        %|: no specified runtime support
    ::
    =/  fel
      |-  ^-  (each @ud weft)
      ?~  run  |/i.hav
      ?:(=(lal.i.hav lal.i.run) &/num.i.run $(run t.run))
    ::
    ?-  -.fel
      %|  `[p.fel ~]
      %&  ?.((lte p.fel num.i.hav) `[i.hav `p.fel] $(hav t.hav))
    ==
  --
::
::  |of: axal engine
::
++  of
  =|  fat=(axal)
  |@
  ++  del
    |=  pax=path
    ^+  fat
    ?~  pax  [~ dir.fat]
    =/  kid  (~(get by dir.fat) i.pax)
    ?~  kid  fat
    fat(dir (~(put by dir.fat) i.pax $(fat u.kid, pax t.pax)))
  ::  Descend to the axal at this path
  ::
  ++  dip
    |=  pax=path
    ^+  fat
    ?~  pax  fat
    =/  kid  (~(get by dir.fat) i.pax)
    ?~  kid  [~ ~]
    $(fat u.kid, pax t.pax)
  ::
  ++  gas
    |=  lit=(list (pair path _?>(?=(^ fil.fat) u.fil.fat)))
    ^+  fat
    ?~  lit  fat
    $(fat (put p.i.lit q.i.lit), lit t.lit)
  ::
  ++  get
    |=  pax=path
    fil:(dip pax)
  ::  Fetch file at longest existing prefix of the path
  ::
  ++  fit
    |=  pax=path
    ^+  [pax fil.fat]
    ?~  pax  [~ fil.fat]
    =/  kid  (~(get by dir.fat) i.pax)
    ?~  kid  [pax fil.fat]
```

```
462      =/  low  $(fat u.kid, pax t.pax)
463      ?~  +.low
464        [pax fil.fat]
465      low
466    ::
467    ++  has
468      |=  pax=path
469      !=(~ (get pax))
470    ::  Delete subtree
471    ::
472    ++  lop
473      |=  pax=path
474      ^+  fat
475      ?~  pax  fat
476      |-
477      ?~  t.pax  fat(dir (~(del by dir.fat) i.pax))
478      =/  kid  (~(get by dir.fat) i.pax)
479      ?~  kid  fat
480      fat(dir (~(put by dir.fat) i.pax $(fat u.kid, pax t.pax)))
481    ::
482    ++  put
483      |*  [pax=path dat=*]
484      =>  .(dat `_?>(?=(^ fil.fat) u.fil.fat)`dat, pax `path`pax)
485      |-  ^+  fat
486      ?~  pax  fat(fil `dat)
487      =/  kid  (~(gut by dir.fat) i.pax ^+(fat [~ ~]))
488      fat(dir (~(put by dir.fat) i.pax $(fat kid, pax t.pax)))
489    ::
490    ++  tap
491      =|  pax=path
492      =|  out=(list (pair path _?>(?=(^ fil.fat) u.fil.fat)))
493      |-  ^+  out
494      =?  out  ?=(^ fil.fat)  :_(out [pax u.fil.fat])
495      =/  dir  ~(tap by dir.fat)
496      |-  ^+  out
497      ?~  dir  out
498      %=  $
499        dir  t.dir
500        out  ^$(pax (weld pax /[p.i.dir]), fat q.i.dir)
501      ==
502    ::  Serialize to map
503    ::
504    ++  tar
505      (~(gas by *(map path _?>(?=(^ fil.fat) u.fil.fat))) tap)
506    --
507  ::
508  ++  wa                                       :: cached compile
509    |_  worm
510    ++  nell  |=(ref=type (nest [%cell %noun %noun] ref)) :: nest in cell
511    ++  nest                                   :: nest:ut, cached
512      |=  [sut=type ref=type]
513      ^-  [? worm]
514      ?:  (~(has in nes) [sut ref])  [& +>+<]
515      ?.  (~(nest ut sut) | ref)
516        ~&  %nest-failed
517        =+  foo=(skol ref)
518        =+  bar=(skol sut)
519        ~&  %nest-need
```

```
520        ~>  %slog.[0 bar]
521        ~&  %nest-have
522        ~>  %slog.[0 foo]
523      [| +>+<.$]
524    [& +>+<(nes (~(put in nes) [sut ref]))]
525    ::
526    ++  call                                        ::  call gate
527      |=  [vax=vase nam=term som=(each vase ^)]
528      ^-  [vase worm]
529      =^  duf  +>+<.$  (open vax nam som)
530      (slap duf [%limb %$])
531    ::
532    ++  open                                        ::  assemble door
533      |=  [vax=vase nam=term som=(each vase ^)]
534      ^-  [vase worm]
535      =*  key  [%cncb [[%& 2] ~] [[[%& 6] ~] [%$ 3]] ~]
536      =^  dor  +>+<.$  (slap vax [%limb nam])
537      =^  mes  +>+<.$  (slot 6 dor)
538      =^  hip  +>+<.$
539        ?-  -.som
540          %&  (nest p.mes p.p.som)
541          %|  (nets p.mes -.p.som)
542        ==
543      ?>  hip
544      [[p.dor q.dor(+6 +7.som)] +>+<.$]
545    ::
546    ++  neat                                        ::  type compliance
547      |=  [typ=type som=(each vase ^)]
548      ^-  worm
549      =^  hip  +>+<.$
550        ?-  -.som
551          %&  (nest typ p.p.som)
552          %|  (nets typ -.p.som)
553        ==
554      ?>  hip
555      +>+<.$
556    ::
557    ++  nets                                        ::  typeless nest
558      |=  [sut=* ref=*]
559      ^-  [? worm]
560      ?:  (~(has in nes) [sut ref])  [& +>+<]
561      =+  gat=|=([a=type b=type] (~(nest ut a) | b))
562      ?.  (? (slum gat [sut ref]))
563        ~&  %nets-failed
564        =+  tag=`*`skol
565        =+  foo=(tank (slum tag ref))
566        =+  bar=(tank (slum tag sut))
567        ~&  %nets-need
568        ~>  %slog.[0 bar]
569        ~&  %nets-have
570        ~>  %slog.[0 foo]
571      [| +>+<.$]
572    [& +>+<.$(nes (~(put in nes) [sut ref]))]
573    ::  +play: +play:ut, cached
574    ::
575    ++  play
576      |=  [sut=type gen=hoon]
577      ^-  [type worm]
```

```
578      =+  old=(~(get by pay) [sut gen])
579      ?^  old  [u.old +>+<.$]
580      =+  new=(~(play ut sut) gen)
581      [new +>+<.$(pay (~(put by pay) [sut gen] new))]
582  ::  +mint: +mint:ut to noun, cached
583  ::
584  ++  mint
585    |=  [sut=type gen=hoon]
586    ^-  [(pair type nock) worm]
587    =+  old=(~(get by mit) [sut gen])
588    ?^  old  [u.old +>+<.$]
589    =+  new=(~(mint ut sut) %noun gen)
590    [new +>+<.$(mit (~(put by mit) [sut gen] new))]
591  ::  +slam: +slam:ut, cached
592  ::
593  ++  slam
594    |=  [gat=vase sam=vase]
595    =/  sut=type  [%cell p.gat p.sam]
596    =/  gen=hoon  [%cnsg [%$ ~] [%$ 2] [%$ 3] ~]
597    =^  new=type  +>+<.$  (play sut gen)
598    [[new (slum q.gat q.sam)] +>+<.$]
599  ::  +slap: +slap:ut, cached
600  ::
601  ++  slap
602    |=  [vax=vase gen=hoon]
603    ^-  [vase worm]
604    =^  gun  +>+<  (mint p.vax gen)
605    [[p.gun .*(q.vax q.gun)] +>+<.$]
606  ::  +slot: +slot:ut, cached
607  ::
608  ++  slot
609    |=  [axe=@ vax=vase]
610    ^-  [vase worm]
611    =^  gun  +>+<  (mint p.vax [%$ axe])
612    [[p.gun .*(q.vax [0 axe])] +>+<.$]
613  ::
614  ::  +slur: slam a vase with a maze
615  ::
616  ++  slur
617    |=  [gat=vase sam=maze]
618    ^-  [vase worm]
619    =^  cur  +>+<.$  (slot 6 gat)
620    =.  +>+<.$  (neat p.cur sam)
621    (slym gat q.p.sam)
622  ::  +slym: +slym:ut, cached
623  ::
624  ++  slym
625    |=  [gat=vase sam=*]
626    ^-  [vase worm]
627    (slap gat(+<.q sam) [%limb %$])
628  ::
629  ++  sped                                       ::  specialize vase
630    |=  vax=vase
631    ^-  [vase worm]
632    =+  ^=  gen  ^-  hoon
633      ?@  q.vax    [%wtts [%base [%atom %$]] [%& 1]~]
634      ?@  -.q.vax  [%wtts [%leaf %tas -.q.vax] [%& 2]~]
635      [%wtts [%base %cell] [%& 1]~]
```

```
636      =^  typ  +>+<.$  (play p.vax [%wtgr gen [%$ 1]])
637      [[typ q.vax] +>+<.$]
638    ::
639    ++  spot                                          ::  slot then sped
640      |=  [axe=@ vax=vase]
641      ^-  [vase worm]
642      =^  xav  +>+<  (slot axe vax)
643      (sped xav)
644    ::
645    ++  stop                                          ::  sped then slot
646      |=  [axe=@ vax=vase]
647      ^-  [vase worm]
648      =^  xav  +>+<  (sped vax)
649      (slot axe xav)
650    --
651  ::
652  ::  |part: arvo structures and engines
653  ::
654  ++  part
655    =>  |%
656        ::  $card: tagged, untyped event
657        ::  $ovum: card with cause
658        ::  $news: collated updates
659        ::  $oped: module updates
660        ::  $seed: next kernel source
661        ::
662        +$  news
663            $:  ::  sys: installs + replacements
664                ::  use: non-system files
665                ::
666                sys=(map path (cask))
667                use=(map path (cask))
668            ==
669        +$  oped
670          $:  lul=(unit cord)
671              zus=(unit cord)
672              van=(list (cask cord))
673          ==
674        +$  seed  [hun=(unit cord) arv=cord]
675        --
676    ::
677    ~%  %part  ..part  ~
678    |%
679    ::
680    +|  %engines
681    ::
682    ::  |eden: lifecycle and bootstrap formula generators
683    ::
684    ::    while unused by arvo itself, these nock formulas
685    ::    bootstrap arvo and define its lifecycle.
686    ::
687    ::    we're creating an event series E whose lifecycle can be computed
688    ::    with the urbit lifecycle formula L, `[2 [0 3] [0 2]]`.  that is:
689    ::    if E is the list of events processed by a computer in its life,
690    ::    its final state is S, where S is nock(E L).
691    ::
692    ::    in practice, the first five nouns in E are: two boot formulas,
693    ::    a hoon compiler as a nock formula, the same compiler as source,
```

```
694  ::    and the arvo kernel as source.
695  ::
696  ::    after the first five special events, we enter an iterative
697  ::    sequence of regular events which continues for the rest of the
698  ::    computer's life.  during this sequence, each state is a function
699  ::    that, passed the next event, produces the next state.
700  ::
701  ::    a regular event is an $ovum, or `[date wire type data]` tuple, where
702  ::    `date` is a 128-bit Urbit date; `wire` is an opaque path which
703  ::    output can match to track causality; `type` is a symbol describing
704  ::    the type of input; and `data` is input data specific to `type`.
705  ::
706  ::    in real life we don't actually run the lifecycle loop,
707  ::    since real life is updated incrementally and also cares
708  ::    about things like output.  we couple to the internal
709  ::    structure of the state machine and work directly with
710  ::    the underlying arvo engine.
711  ::
712  ::    this arvo core, which is at `+7` (Lisp `cddr`) of the state
713  ::    function (see its public interface in `sys/arvo`), gives us
714  ::    extra features, like output, which are relevant to running
715  ::    a real-life urbit vm, but don't affect the formal definition.
716  ::
717  ::    so a real-life urbit interpreter is coupled to the shape of
718  ::    the arvo core.  it becomes very hard to change this shape.
719  ::    fortunately, it is not a very complex interface.
720  ::
721  ++  eden
722    |%
723    ::    +aeon: arvo lifecycle loop
724    ::
725    ::    the first event in a ship's log,
726    ::    computing the final state from the rest of log
727    ::    when invoked via the lifecycle formula: [%2 [%0 3] %0 2]
728    ::
729    ::    the formal urbit state is always just a gate (function)
730    ::    which, passed the next event, produces the next state.
731    ::
732    ++  aeon
733      ^-  *
734      =>  ::  boot: kernel bootstrap, event 2
735          ::  tale: events 3-n
736          ::
737          *log=[boot=* tale=*]
738      !=  ::  arvo: bootstrapped kernel
739          ::  epic: remainder of the log
740          ::
741      =+  [arvo epic]=.*(tale.log boot.log)
742      |-  ^-  *
743      ?@  epic  arvo
744      %=  $
745        epic  +.epic
746        arvo  .*([arvo -.epic] [%9 2 %10 [6 %0 3] %0 2])
747      ==
748    ::
749    ::  +boot: event 2: bootstrap a kernel from source
750    ::
751    ++  boot
```

```
752        ^-  *
753        ::
754        ::  event 2 is the startup formula, which verifies the compiler
755        ::  and starts the main lifecycle.
756        ::
757    =>  ::  fate: event 3: a nock formula producing the hoon bootstrap compiler
758        ::  hoon: event 4: compiler source
759        ::  arvo: event 5: kernel source
760        ::  epic: event 6-n
761        ::
762        *log=[fate=* hoon=@ arvo=@ epic=*]
763    !=
764        ::
765        ::  activate the compiler gate.  the product of this formula
766        ::  is smaller than the formula.  so you might think we should
767        ::  save the gate itself rather than the formula producing it.
768        ::  but we have to run the formula at runtime, to register jets.
769        ::
770        ::  as always, we have to use raw nock as we have no type.
771        ::  the gate is in fact ++ride.
772        ::
773    ~>  %slog.[0 leaf+"1-b"]
774    =/  compiler-gate  .*(0 fate.log)
775        ::
776        ::  compile the compiler source, producing (pair span nock).
777        ::  the compiler ignores its input so we use a trivial span.
778        ::
779    ~>  %slog.[0 leaf+"1-c (compiling compiler, wait a few minutes)"]
780    =/  compiler-tool
781      ~>  %bout
782      .*([compiler-gate noun/hoon.log] [%9 2 %10 [6 %0 3] %0 2])
783        ::
784        ::  switch to the second-generation compiler.  we want to be
785        ::  able to generate matching reflection nouns even if the
786        ::  language changes -- the first-generation formula will
787        ::  generate last-generation spans for `!>`, etc.
788        ::
789    ~>  %slog.[0 leaf+"1-d"]
790    =.  compiler-gate  ~>(%bout .*(0 +.compiler-tool))
791        ::
792        ::  get the span (type) of the kernel core, which is the context
793        ::  of the compiler gate.  we just compiled the compiler,
794        ::  so we know the span (type) of the compiler gate.  its
795        ::  context is at tree address `+>` (ie, `+7` or Lisp `cddr`).
796        ::  we use the compiler again to infer this trivial program.
797        ::
798    ~>  %slog.[0 leaf+"1-e"]
799    =/  kernel-span
800      ~>  %bout
801      -:.*([compiler-gate -.compiler-tool '+>'] [%9 2 %10 [6 %0 3] %0 2])
802        ::
803        ::  compile the arvo source against the kernel core.
804        ::
805    ~>  %slog.[0 leaf+"1-f"]
806    =/  kernel-tool
807      ~>  %bout
808      .*([compiler-gate kernel-span arvo.log] [%9 2 %10 [6 %0 3] %0 2])
809        ::
```

```
810       ::    create the arvo kernel, whose subject is the kernel core.
811       ::
812       ~>    %slog.[0 leaf+"1-g"]
813       ~>    %bout
814       [.*(+>.compiler-gate +.kernel-tool) epic.log]
815       --
816   ::
817   ::  |adapt
818   ::
819   ++    adapt
820     =>    |%
821         ::    deep file as source
822         ::
823         ++    sole  |=(a=(cask) `cord`?>(?=([%hoon @t] a) q.a))
824         --
825     |_  fat=(axal (cask))
826     ::
827     ::  +group: collate changes
828     ::
829     ++  group
830       |=  fal=(list (pair path (cask)))
831       =|  del=news
832       |-  ^+    del
833       ?~  fal   del
834       ::  classify files, ignoring unchanged
835       ::
836       =*  pax   p.i.fal
837       =*  dat   q.i.fal
838       =/  hav   (~(get of fat) pax)
839       =?  del   |(?=(~ hav) !=(u.hav dat))
840         ?:    ?=([%sys *] pax)
841           del(sys (~(put by sys.del) pax dat))
842         del(use (~(put by use.del) pax dat))
843       $(fal t.fal)
844     ::  +usurp: consider self-replacement
845     ::
846     ++    usurp
847       |=  del=news
848       ^-  (unit (pair seed (list (pair path (cask)))))
849       =/  hun   (~(get by sys.del) /sys/hoon)
850       =/  arv   (~(get by sys.del) /sys/arvo)
851       ?~  hun
852         ?~    arv   ~
853         `[`(sole u.arv) [/sys/arvo u.arv] ~]
854       =/  rav
855         ~|  %usurp-hoon-no-arvo
856         ((bond |.((need (~(get of fat) /sys/arvo)))) arv)
857       ~!  rav
858       :+  ~
859         [`(sole u.hun) (sole rav)]
860       [[/sys/arvo rav] [/sys/hoon u.hun] ~]
861     ::  +adorn: augment capabilities
862     ::
863     ++    adorn
864       |=  [del=news all=?]
865       ^-  (pair oped _fat)
866       ::  lull: shared structures
867       ::
```

```
        =^    lul   fat
          ?^    hav=(~(get by sys.del) /sys/lull)
            :-    `(sole u.hav)
            (~(put of fat) /sys/lull u.hav)
          :_    fat
          ~|    %adorn-no-lull
          ?.(all ~ `(sole (need (~(get of fat) /sys/lull))))
        ::  zuse: shared library
        ::
        ::    %lull is the subject of %zuse; force all if we have a new %lull
        ::
        =.    all   |(all ?=(^ lul))
        =^    zus   fat
          ?^    hav=(~(get by sys.del) /sys/zuse)
            :-    `(sole u.hav)
            (~(put of fat) /sys/zuse u.hav)
          :_    fat
          ~|    %adorn-no-zuse
          ?.(all ~ `(sole (need (~(get of fat) /sys/zuse))))
        ::  kernel modules
        ::
        ::    %zuse is the subject of the vanes; force all if we have a new %zuse
        ::
        =.    all   |(all ?=(^ zus))
        =|    nav=(map term cord)
        =?    nav   all
          %-    ~(gas by nav)
          %+    turn
            ~(tap by dir:(~(dip of fat) /sys/vane))
          |=([name=@ta _fat] [`@tas`name (sole (need fil))])
        ::
        =^    new   fat
          %^    spin
              %+  skim  ~(tap by sys.del)
              |=([p=path *] ?=([%sys %vane @tas ~] p))
            fat
          |=  [[p=path q=(cask)] taf=_fat]
          ^-  (pair (cask cord) _fat)
          ?>  ?=([%sys %vane @tas ~] p)
          =*  nam  i.t.t.p
          ?>  ((sane %tas) nam)
          [[`@tas`nam (sole q)] (~(put of taf) p q)]
        ::
        =;  van
          [[lul zus van] fat]
        %+    sort  ~(tap by (~(gas by nav) new))
        |=([[a=@tas *] [b=@tas *]] (aor a b))
      --  :: adapt
    ::
    ::  |me: dynamic analysis
    ::
    ++  me
      ~/  %me
      |_  ::  sac: compiler cache
          ::  pyt: cached types
          ::
          [sac=worm vil=vile]
      ::  +refine-moves: move list from vase
```

```
    ::
++  refine-moves
  |=  vax=vase
  ^-  (pair (list move) worm)
  ?:  =(~ q.vax)  [~ sac]
  =^  hed  sac  (~(slot wa sac) 2 vax)
  =^  tal  sac  (~(slot wa sac) 3 vax)
  =^  mov  sac  (refine-move hed)
  =^  moz  sac  $(vax tal)
  [[mov moz] sac]
::  +refine-move: move from vase
::
++  refine-move
  |=  vax=vase
  ^-  (pair move worm)
  ~>  %mean.'bad-move'
  =^  hip  sac  (~(nell wa sac) p.vax)
  ?.  hip
    ~>(%mean.'not-cell' !!)
  =/  duc
    ~>  %mean.'bad-duct'
    ;;(duct -.q.vax)
  ::
  ::  yat: specialized ball vase
  ::
  =^  yat  sac  (~(spot wa sac) 3 vax)
  =^  del  sac  (refine-ball yat)
  [[duc del] sac]
::  +refine-ball: ball from vase
::
++  refine-ball
  |=  vax=vase
  ^-  (pair ball worm)
  ?+    q.vax
      ~>  %mean.'bad-ball'
      ~_  (sell vax)
      !!
  ::
      [%give card]
    ::  yed: vase containing card
    ::  hil: card as maze
    ::
    =^  yed  sac  (~(spot wa sac) 3 vax)
    =^  hil  sac  (refine-card yed)
    [[%give hil] sac]
  ::
      [%pass wire=* vane=term card]
    =/  =wire
      ~>  %mean.'bad-wire'
      ;;(wire wire.q.vax)
    =/  vane
      ~>  %mean.'bad-vane-label'
      ?>  ((sane %tas) vane.q.vax)
      vane.q.vax
    ::
    ::  yed: vase containing card
    ::  hil: card as maze
    ::
```

```
=^  xav   sac  (~(spot wa sac) 7 vax)
=^  yed   sac  (~(spot wa sac) 3 xav)
=^  hil   sac  (refine-card yed)
[[%pass wire vane hil] sac]
::
    [%slip vane=term card]
=/  vane
  ~>  %mean.'bad-vane-label'
  ?>  ((sane %tas) vane.q.vax)
  vane.q.vax
::
::  yed: vase containing card
::  hil: card as maze
::
=^  xav   sac  (~(spot wa sac) 3 vax)
=^  yed   sac  (~(spot wa sac) 3 xav)
=^  hil   sac  (refine-card yed)
[[%slip vane hil] sac]
::
    [%hurl goof=^ ball=*]
=/  =goof
  =/  mote  -.goof.q.vax
  ?>  ?&  ?=(@ mote)
          ((sane %tas) mote)
      ==
  [mote ;;(tang +.goof.q.vax)]
::
=^  bal  sac
  =^  lab   sac  (~(spot wa sac) 7 vax)
  $(vax lab)
::
?>  ?=(?(%pass %give) -.p.bal)
[[%hurl goof p.bal] sac]
  ==
::  +refine-card: card from vase
::
++  refine-card
  |=  vax=vase
  ^-  (pair maze worm)
  ~>  %mean.'bad-card'
  =^  hip  sac  (~(nell wa sac) p.vax)
  ?>  hip
  ?.  ?=(%meta -.q.vax)
    ::
    ::  for a non-meta card, the maze is the vase
    ::
    [[%& vax] sac]
  ~>  %mean.'bad-meta'
  ::
  ::  tiv: vase of vase of card
  ::  typ: vase of span
  ::
  =^  tiv  sac  (~(slot wa sac) 3 vax)
  =^  hip  sac  (~(nell wa sac) p.tiv)
  ?>  hip
  =^  typ  sac  (~(slot wa sac) 2 tiv)
  =.  sac  (~(neat wa sac) typ.vil [%& typ])
  ::
```

```
1042          ::   support for meta-meta-cards has been removed
1043          ::
1044          ?>   ?=(meta q.tiv)
1045          [[[%| q.tiv] sac]
1046      --
1047    ::
1048    ::  |va: vane engine
1049    ::
1050    ++  va
1051      =>  ~%  %va-ctx  ..va  ~
1052          |%
1053          +$  vane-sample  [now=@da eny=@uvJ rof=rook]
1054          ::
1055          ++  smit
1056            |=  [cap=tape sub=vase pax=path txt=@t]
1057            ^-  vase
1058            ~>  %slog.[0 leaf/"{cap}: {(scow uv+(mug txt))}"]
1059            ~>  %bout
1060            %-  road  |.
1061            ~_  leaf/"{cap}: build failed"
1062            (slap sub (rain pax txt))
1063          ::
1064          ++  create
1065            ~/  %create
1066            |=  [our=ship zus=vase lal=term pax=path txt=@t]
1067            ^-  vase
1068            =/  cap  "vane: %{(trip lal)}"
1069            (slym (smit cap zus pax txt) our)
1070          ::
1071          ++  settle
1072            ~/  %settle
1073            |=  van=vase
1074            ^-  (pair vase worm)
1075            =|  sac=worm
1076            =^  rig=vase  sac  (~(slym wa sac) van *vane-sample)
1077            =^  gat=vase  sac  (~(slap wa sac) rig [%limb %scry])
1078            =^  pro=vase  sac  (~(slap wa sac) gat [%limb %$])
1079            [van +:(~(mint wa sac) p.pro [%$ 7])]
1080          ::
1081          ::  XX pass identity to preserve behavior?
1082          ::
1083          ++  update
1084            ~/  %update
1085            |=  [las=vase nex=vase]
1086            ^-  vase
1087            =/  sam=vase  (slap (slym las *vane-sample) [%limb %stay])
1088            =/  gat=vase  (slap (slym nex *vane-sample) [%limb %load])
1089            (slam gat sam)
1090          --
1091      ::
1092      ~%  %va  ..va  ~
1093      |_  [vil=vile vax=vase sac=worm]
1094      ::
1095      ::  |plow:va: operate in time and space
1096      ::
1097      ++  plow
1098        ~/  %plow
1099        |=  [now=@da rok=rook]
```

```
1100      ~%  %plow-core  +  ~
1101      |%
1102      ::  +peek:plow:va: read from a local namespace
1103      ::
1104      ++  peek
1105        ~/  %peek
1106        ^-  rook
1107        |=  [lyc=gang pov=path omen]
1108        ^-  (unit (unit (cask meta)))
1109        ::  namespace reads receive no entropy
1110        ::
1111        =/  sam=vane-sample  [now *@uvJ rok]
1112        =^  rig  sac
1113          ~>  %mean.'peek: activation failed'
1114          (~(slym wa sac) vax sam)
1115        =^  gat  sac
1116          ~>  %mean.'peek: pull failed'
1117          (~(slap wa sac) rig [%limb %scry])
1118        ::
1119        =/  mas=[gang path view beam]  [lyc pov vis bem]
1120        ::
1121        =^  pro  sac
1122          ~>  %mean.'peek: call failed'
1123          (~(slym wa sac) gat mas)
1124        ?~  q.pro  ~
1125        ?~  +.q.pro  [~ ~]
1126        =^  dat  sac  (~(slot wa sac) 7 pro)
1127        ``[(,mark -.q.dat) (,^ +.q.dat)]
1128      ::
1129      ::  |spin:plow:va: move statefully
1130      ::
1131      ++  spin
1132        |=  [hen=duct eny=@uvJ dud=(unit goof)]
1133        =*  duc  [duc.vil hen]
1134        =*  err  [dud.vil dud]
1135        =/  sam=vane-sample  [now eny rok]
1136        =^  rig  sac
1137          ~>  %mean.'spin: activation failed'
1138          (~(slym wa sac) vax sam)
1139        ::
1140        =>  |%
1141            ::  +slid: cons a vase onto a maze
1142            ::
1143            ++  slid
1144              |=  [hed=vase tal=maze]
1145              ^-  maze
1146              ?-  -.tal
1147                %&  [%& (slop hed p.tal)]
1148                %|  [%| [%cell p.hed p.p.tal] [q.hed q.p.tal]]
1149              ==
1150            --
1151        |%
1152        ::  +peel:spin:plow:va: extract products, finalize vane
1153        ::
1154        ++  peel
1155          |=  pro=vase
1156          ^-  (pair [vase vase] worm)
1157          =^  moz  sac  (~(slot wa sac) 2 pro)
```

```
        =^  vem  sac  (~(slot wa sac) 3 pro)
        ::  replace vane sample with default to plug leak
        ::
        =.  +<.q.vem  *vane-sample
        [[moz vem] sac]
      ::  +call:spin:plow:va: advance statefully
      ::
      ++  call
        |=  task=maze
        ^-  (pair [vase vase] worm)
        ~>  %mean.'call: failed'
        =^  gat  sac
          (~(slap wa sac) rig [%limb %call])
        ::
        ::  sample is [duct (unit goof) (hobo task)]
        ::
        =/  sam=maze
          (slid duc (slid err task))
        =^  pro  sac  (~(slur wa sac) gat sam)
        (peel pro)
      ::  +take:spin:plow:va: retreat statefully
      ::
      ++  take
        |=  [=wire from=term gift=maze]
        ^-  (pair [vase vase] worm)
        ~>  %mean.'take: failed'
        =^  gat  sac
          (~(slap wa sac) rig [%limb %take])
        =/  src=vase
          [[%atom %tas `from] from]
        ::
        ::  sample is [wire duct (unit goof) sign=[term gift]]
        ::
        =/  sam=maze
          =*  tea  [wir.vil wire]
          (slid tea (slid duc (slid err (slid src gift))))
        =^  pro  sac  (~(slur wa sac) gat sam)
        (peel pro)
      --
    --
  --
::
:: |le: arvo event-loop engine
::
++  le
  ~%  %le  ..le  ~
  =|  $:  :: run: list of worklists
          :: out: pending output
          :: gem: worklist metadata
          :: dud: propagate error
          :: but: reboot signal
          ::
          ::
          run=(list plan)
          out=(list ovum)
          gem=germ
          dud=(unit goof)
          $=  but  %-  unit
```

```
1216                              $:  gat=$-(heir (trap ^))
1217                                  kel=(list (pair path (cask)))
1218                                  fil=(list (pair path (cask)))
1219                              ==
1220                  ==
1221          ::
1222          |_  [[pit=vase vil=vile] soul]
1223          +*  this  .
1224              sol   +<+
1225          ::
1226          ::  +abet: finalize loop
1227          ::
1228          ++  abet
1229            ^-  (each (pair (list ovum) soul) (trap ^))
1230            ?~  but
1231              ^-    [%& (pair (list ovum) soul)]
1232              &/[(flop out) sol]
1233            |/(gat.u.but [arvo [run out [kel fil]:u.but] sol])
1234          ::  +poke: prepare a worklist-of-one from outside
1235          ::
1236          ++  poke
1237            |=  =ovum
1238            ^+  this
1239            ~>  %mean.'arvo: poke crashed'
1240            ~?  !lac.fad  ["" %unix p.card.ovum wire.ovum now]
1241            (poke:pith ovum)
1242          ::
1243          ++  jump
1244            |=  =debt
1245            ^+  this
1246            =:  run   run.debt
1247                out   out.debt
1248                ==
1249            ::  apply remaining update
1250            ::
1251            =.  ..this  (~(lod what:pith fil.debt) kel.debt)
1252            ::  send upgrade notifications
1253            ::
1254            =+  [wir car]=[/arvo vega/~]
1255            =.  ..this  (xeno:pith $/wir car)
1256            (emit $/~ (spam:pith wir !>(car)))
1257          ::  +emit: enqueue a worklist with source
1258          ::
1259          ++  emit
1260            |=  pan=plan
1261            this(run [pan run])
1262          ::  +loop: until done
1263          ::
1264          ++  loop
1265            ^+  abet
1266            ?:  ?|  ?=(~ run)
1267                    ?=(^ but)
1268                ==
1269              abet
1270            ?:  =(~ q.i.run)      :: XX TMI
1271              loop(run t.run)
1272            =.  dud  ~
1273            =.  gem  p.i.run
```

```
1274        =^  mov=move  q.i.run  q.i.run
1275      loop:(step mov)
1276    ::  +step: advance the loop one step by routing a move
1277    ::
1278    ++  step
1279      |=  =move
1280      ^+  this
1281      ::
1282      ~?  &(!lac.fad ?=(^ dud))  %goof
1283      ::
1284      ?-  -.ball.move
1285      ::
1286      ::  %pass: forward move
1287      ::
1288          %pass
1289        =*  wire  wire.ball.move
1290        =*  duct  duct.move
1291        =*  vane  vane.note.ball.move
1292        =*  task  task.note.ball.move
1293        ::
1294        ~?  &(!lac.fad !=(%$ vane.gem))
1295          :-  (runt [(lent bars.gem) '|'] "")
1296          :^  %pass  [vane.gem vane]
1297            ?:  ?=(?(%deal %deal-gall) +>-.task)
1298              :-  :-  +>-.task
1299                ;;([[ship ship path] term term] [+>+< +>+>- +>+>+<]:task)
1300              wire
1301            [(symp +>-.task) wire]
1302          duct
1303        ::
1304        ::  cons source onto wire, and wire onto duct
1305        ::
1306        (call [[vane.gem wire] duct] vane task)
1307      ::
1308      ::  %slip: lateral move
1309      ::
1310          %slip
1311        =*  duct  duct.move
1312        =*  vane  vane.note.ball.move
1313        =*  task  task.note.ball.move
1314        ::
1315        ~?  !lac.fad
1316          :-  (runt [(lent bars.gem) '|'] "")
1317          [%slip [vane.gem vane] (symp +>-.task) duct]
1318        ::
1319        (call duct vane task)
1320      ::
1321      ::  %give: return move
1322      ::
1323          %give
1324        ?.  ?=(^ duct.move)
1325          ~>(%mean.'give-no-duct' !!)
1326        ::
1327        =/  wire  i.duct.move
1328        =/  duct  t.duct.move
1329        =*  gift  gift.ball.move
1330        ::
1331        =^  way=term  wire
```

```
1332            ~|   [%give duct.move (symp -.q.p.gift)]
1333            ?>(?=(^ wire) wire)
1334        ::
1335        ~?  &(!lac.fad !=(%$ way) |(!=(%blit +>-.gift) !=(%d vane.gem)))
1336          :-  (runt [(lent bars.gem) '|'] "")
1337          :^  %give  vane.gem
1338            ?:  ?=(%unto +>-.gift)
1339              [+>-.gift (symp +>+<.gift)]
1340            (symp +>-.gift)
1341          duct.move
1342        ::
1343      (take duct wire way gift)
1344      ::
1345      ::  %hurl: action with error
1346      ::
1347          %hurl
1348      %=  $
1349          dud        `goof.ball.move
1350          ball.move  wite.ball.move
1351      ==
1352    ==
1353  ::  +whey: measure memory usage
1354  ::
1355  ++  whey
1356    ^-  mass
1357    =;  sam=(list mass)
1358      :+  %arvo  %|
1359      :~  :+  %hoon  %|
1360          :~  one+&+..bloq
1361              two+&+..turn
1362              tri+&+..year
1363              qua+&+..sane
1364              pen+&+..ride
1365          ==
1366          hex+&+..part
1367          pit+&+pit
1368          lull+|+[dot+&+q typ+&+p ~]:lul.mod
1369          zuse+|+[dot+&+q typ+&+p ~]:zus.mod
1370          vane+|+sam
1371      ==
1372    ::
1373    %+  turn
1374      (sort ~(tap by van.mod) |=([[a=@tas *] [b=@tas *]] (aor a b)))
1375    =/  bem=beam  [[our %$ da+now] //whey]
1376    |=  [nam=term =vane]
1377    =;  mas=(list mass)
1378      nam^|+(welp mas [dot+&+q.vase typ+&+p.vase sac+&+worm ~]:vane)
1379    ?~  met=(peek [~ ~] / [nam %x] bem)  ~
1380    ?~  u.met  ~
1381    ~|  mass+nam
1382    ;;((list mass) q.q.u.u.met)
1383  ::  +peek: read from the entire namespace
1384  ::
1385  ++  peek
1386    ^-  rook
1387    |=  [lyc=gang pov=path omen]
1388    ^-  (unit (unit (cask meta)))
1389    ::  vane and care may be concatenated
```

```
1390      ::
1391      =/  [way=term car=term]
1392        ?^  vis  vis
1393        ?.  =(2 (met 3 vis))
1394          [vis %$]
1395        [(end 3 vis) (rsh 3 vis)]
1396      ::
1397      ?:  ?=(%$ way)
1398        (peek:pith lyc pov car bem)
1399      ::
1400      =.  way  (grow way)
1401      ?~  van=(~(get by van.mod) way)
1402        ~
1403      %.  [lyc pov car bem]
1404      peek:spin:(~(plow va [vil u.van]) now peek)
1405    ::  +call: advance to target
1406    ::
1407    ++  call
1408      |=  [=duct way=term task=maze]
1409      ^+  this
1410      ?:  ?=(%$ way)
1411        ~>  %mean.'arvo: call:pith failed'
1412        %-  call:pith
1413        ~>  %mean.'call: bad waif'
1414        ;;(waif q.p.task)
1415      ::
1416      =.  way  (grow way)
1417      %+  push  [way duct bars.gem]
1418      ~|  bar-stack=`(list ^duct)`[duct bars.gem]
1419      %.  task
1420      call:(spin:(plow way) duct eny dud)
1421    ::  +take: retreat along call-stack
1422    ::
1423    ++  take
1424      |=  [=duct =wire way=term gift=maze]
1425      ^+  this
1426      ?:  ?=(%$ way)
1427        ::
1428        ::  the caller was Outside
1429        ::
1430        ?>  ?=(~ duct)
1431        (xeno:pith wire ;;(card q.p.gift))
1432      ::  the caller was a vane
1433      ::
1434      =.  way  (grow way)
1435      %+  push  [way duct bars.gem]
1436      ::
1437      ::  cons source onto .gift to make a $sign
1438      ::
1439      ~|  wire=wire
1440      ~|  bar-stack=`(list ^duct)`[duct bars.gem]
1441      %.  [wire [vane.gem gift]]
1442      take:(spin:(plow way) duct eny dud)
1443    ::  +push: finalize an individual step
1444    ::
1445    ++  push
1446      |=  [gum=germ [zom=vase vax=vase] sac=worm]
1447      ^+  this
```

```
        =^  moz  sac
          (~(refine-moves me sac vil) zom)
        =.  van.mod  (~(put by van.mod) vane.gum [vax sac])
        (emit `plan`[`germ`gum `(list move)`moz])
    ::  +plow: operate on a vane, in time and space
    ::
    ++  plow
      |=  way=term
      ~|  [%plow-failed way]
      =/  =vane
        ~|  [%missing-vane way]
        (~(got by van.mod) way)
      (~(plow va [vil vane]) now peek)
    ::
    ::  |pith: operate on arvo internals
    ::
    ++  pith
      |%
      ++  gest
        |=  =ovum
        ^-  $>(%pass ball)
        =^  way=term  wire.ovum  wire.ovum
        ::
        ::  %$: default, routed to arvo-proper as trivial vase
        ::  @:  route to vane as $hobo
        ::
        =/  =vase
          ?-  way
            %$  noun/card.ovum
            @   [cell/[atom/tas/`%soft %noun] soft/card.ovum]
          ==
        [%pass wire.ovum way &/vase]
      ::
      ::  |what: update engine
      ::
      ::    +kel: (maybe) initiate a kernel update
      ::    +lod: continue with update after kernel +load
      ::    +mod: update the modules of the kernel
      ::
      ++  what
        |_  fil=(list (pair path (cask)))
        ::
        ++  kel
          ^+  ..pith
          =/  del  (~(group adapt fat.mod.sol) fil)
          =/  tub  (~(usurp adapt fat.mod.sol) del)
          ?~  tub
            (mod del |)
          =/  gat  (boot kel.ver.zen [hun arv]:p.u.tub)
          ..pith(but `[gat q.u.tub fil])
        ::
        ++  lod
          |=  kel=(list (pair path (cask)))
          ^+  ..pith
          =.  fat.mod.sol  (~(gas of fat.mod.sol) kel)
          %+  mod
            (~(group adapt fat.mod.sol) fil)
          %+  lien  kel
```

```
      |=  [p=path *]
      ?=([%sys ?(%arvo %hoon) *] p)
  ::
  ++  mod
    |=  [del=news all=?]
    ^+  ..pith
    =^  job=oped  fat.mod.sol  (~(adorn adapt fat.mod.sol) del all)
    =?  lul.mod.sol  ?=(^ lul.job)
      (smit:va "lull" pit /sys/lull/hoon u.lul.job)
    =?  zus.mod.sol  ?=(^ zus.job)
      (smit:va "zuse" lul.mod.sol /sys/zuse/hoon u.zus.job)
    %-  %+  need:wyrd   kel.ver.zen
        :~  lull/;;(@ud q:(slap lul.mod.sol limb/%lull))
            zuse/;;(@ud q:(slap zus.mod.sol limb/%zuse))
        ==
    %=    ..pith
      van.mod
        %+  roll  van.job
        |=  [[nam=term txt=cord] van=_van.mod.sol]
        ^+  van
        =/  nex  (create:va our zus.mod.sol nam /sys/vane/[nam]/hoon txt)
        =/  nav  (~(get by van) nam)
        =?  nex  ?=(^ nav)  (update:va vase.u.nav nex)
        (~(put by van) nam (settle:va nex))
    ==
  --
  ::
  ++  call
    |=  =waif
    ^+  ..pith
    ?^  dud  ~>(%mean.'pith: goof' !!)
    ?-  -.waif
      ::
      ::  %trim: clear state
      ::
      ::    clears compiler caches if high-priority
      ::    XX add separate $wasp if this should happen last
      ::
      %trim  =?  van.mod  =(0 p.waif)
               (~(run by van.mod) |=(=vane vane(worm *worm)))
             (emit $/~ (spam /arvo !>(waif)))
      ::
      %verb  ..pith(lac.fad ?~(p.waif !lac.fad u.p.waif))
      %what  ~(kel what p.waif)
      %whey  ..pith(out [[//arvo mass/whey] out])
      ::
          %whiz
      ..pith(van.mod (~(run by van.mod) |=(vane (settle:va:part vase))))
    ==
  ::
  ++  peek
    ^-  roon
    |=  [lyc=gang pov=path car=term bem=beam]
    ^-  (unit (unit cage))
    ?.  ?&  =(our p.bem)
            ?=(%$ q.bem)
            =([%da now] r.bem)
        ==
```

```
1564              ~
1565          ?+  s.bem  ~
1566            [%whey ~]      ``mass/!>(whey)
1567            [%fad %lac ~]  ``noun/!>(lac.fad)
1568            [%zen %lag ~]  ``noun/!>(lag.zen)
1569            [%zen %ver ~]  ``noun/!>(ver.zen)
1570            [%mod %fat *]  ``noun/!>((~(dip of fat.mod) t.t.s.bem))
1571          ==
1572      ::
1573      ++  poke
1574        |=  =ovum
1575        ^+  ..pith
1576        ?~  wire.ovum
1577          ~>(%mean.'pith: bad wire' !!)
1578        ::
1579        ?.  ?=(?(%crud %wack %wyrd) p.card.ovum)
1580          (emit $/~ [*duct (gest ovum)] ~)
1581        ::
1582        =/  buz  ~>  %mean.'pith: bad wasp'
1583                 ;;(wasp card.ovum)
1584        ?-  -.buz
1585        ::
1586        ::  %crud: forward error notification
1587        ::
1588          %crud  =?  lag.zen  ?&  ?=(%exit mote.goof.buz)
1589                                  ?=(^ tang.goof.buz)
1590                                  ?=([%leaf *] i.tang.goof.buz)
1591                                  ?=(%wyrd (crip p.i.tang.goof.buz))
1592                              ==
1593                 ~&(%lagging &)
1594                 (emit $/~ [*duct hurl/[goof.buz (gest ovum.buz)]] ~)
1595        ::
1596        ::  XX review
1597        ::
1598          %wack  ..pith(eny (shaz (cat 3 eny p.buz)))
1599        ::
1600        ::  %wyrd: check for runtime kelvin compatibility
1601        ::
1602          %wyrd  ?.  (sane:wyrd kel.p.buz)
1603                   ~>(%mean.'wyrd: insane' !!)
1604               %-  %+  need:wyrd  kel.p.buz
1605                   ^-  wynn
1606                   :~  hoon/hoon-version
1607                       arvo/arvo
1608                       lull/;;(@ud q:(slap lul.mod limb/%lull))
1609                       zuse/;;(@ud q:(slap zus.mod limb/%zuse))
1610                   ==
1611               =?  lag.zen  !=(rev.ver.zen rev.p.buz)  ~&(%unlagging |)
1612               ..pith(ver.zen p.buz)
1613        ==
1614      ::
1615      ++  spam
1616        |=  [=wire =vase]
1617        ^-  (list move)
1618        %+  turn
1619          %+  sort  ~(tap by van.mod)
1620          |=([[a=@tas *] [b=@tas *]] (aor a b))
1621        |=([way=term *] `move`[*duct %pass wire way `maze`&/vase])
```

```
        ::
++  xeno
   |=  =ovum
   ^+  ..pith
   ..pith(out [ovum out])
   --
--
--
::
++  symp                                            ::  symbol or empty
|=  a=*  ^-  @tas
?.(&(?=(@ a) ((sane %tas) a)) %$ a)
::
++  boot
|=  [kel=wynn hun=(unit @t) van=@t]
^-  $-(heir (trap ^))
~>  %mean.'arvo: upgrade failed'
~>  %slog.[0 'arvo: beginning upgrade']
?~  hun
  =/  gat
    ~>  %slog.[0 'arvo: compiling next arvo']
    ~>  %bout
    %-  road  |.
    (slap !>(..ride) (rain /sys/arvo/hoon van))
  =/  lod
  (slap (slot 7 gat) [%limb %load])
  |=  =heir
  |.  ~>  %slog.[0 'arvo: +load next']
  ;;(^ q:(slam lod !>(heir)))
::
:: hyp: hoon core type
:: hoc: hoon core
:: cop: compiler gate
::
=/  [hyp=* hoc=* cop=*]
  ::  compile new hoon.hoon source with the current compiler
  ::
  =/  raw
    ~>  %slog.[0 'arvo: compiling hoon']
    ~>  %bout
    (road |.((ride %noun u.hun)))
  ::  activate the new compiler gate, producing +ride
  ::
  =/  cop  .*(0 +.raw)
  ::  find the kelvin version number of the new compiler
  ::
  =/  nex
    ;;(@ .*(cop q:(~(mint ut p.raw) %noun [%limb %hoon-version]))))
  ::  require single-step upgrade
  ::
  ?.  |(=(nex hoon-version) =(+(nex) hoon-version))
    =*  ud  |=(a=@ (scow %ud a))
    ~_  leaf/"cannot upgrade to hoon %{(ud nex)} from %{(ud hoon-version)}"
    !!
  ::  require runtime compatibility
  ::
  %-  (need:wyrd kel [hoon/nex ~])
  ::
```

```
      ::  if we're upgrading language versions, recompile the compiler
      ::
    =^  hot=*  cop
      ?:  =(nex hoon-version)
        [raw cop]
      =/  hot
        ~>  %slog.[0 leaf/"arvo: recompiling hoon %{(scow %ud nex)}"]
        ~>  %bout
        (road |.((slum cop [%noun u.hun])))
      [hot .*(0 +.hot)]
    ::  extract the hoon core from the outer gate (+ride)
    ::
    =/  hoc  .*(cop [%0 7])
    ::  compute the type of the hoon.hoon core
    ::
    =/  hyp  -:(slum cop [-.hot '+>'])
    ::
    [hyp hoc cop]
  ::
  ::  compile arvo
  ::
  =/  rav
    ~>  %slog.[0 'arvo: compiling next arvo']
    ~>  %bout
    (road |.((slum cop [hyp van])))
  ::  activate arvo and extract the arvo core from the outer gate
  ::
  =/  voc  .*(hoc [%7 +.rav %0 7])
  ::
  ::  extract the upgrade gate +load
  ::
  =/  lod
    ::  vip: type of the arvo.hoon core
    ::  fol: formula for the +load gate
    ::
    =/  vip  -:(slum cop [-.rav '+>'])
    =/  fol  +:(slum cop [vip 'load'])
    ::  produce the upgrade gate
    ::
    .*(voc fol)
  ::
  |=  =heir
  |.  ~>  %slog.[1 'arvo: +load next']
  ;;(^ (slum lod heir))
::
++  viol                                              ::  vane tools
  |=  but=type
  ^-  vile
  =+  pal=|=(a=@t ^-(type (~(play ut but) (vice a))))
  :*  typ=(pal '$:type')
      duc=(pal '$:duct')
      wir=(pal '$:wire')
      dud=(pal '=<($ (unit goof))')  ::  XX misparse
  ==
::
++  grow
  |=  way=term
  ?+  way  way
```

```
%a    %ames
%b    %behn
%c    %clay
%d    %dill
%e    %eyre
%g    %gall
%i    %iris
%j    %jael
%k    %khan
%l    %lick
==
--  =>
::
::  cached reflexives
::
=/  pit=vase  !>(..part)
=/  vil=vile  (viol p.pit)
::
::  arvo state, as a discriminable sample
::
=|  [_arvo soul]
=*  sol  ->
|%
::  +load: upgrade from previous state
::
++  load                                            ::  +4
  |=  hir=$<(%grub heir)
  ^-  ^
  ~|  %load
  ::  store persistent state
  ::
  =.  sol
    ?-  -.hir
      ?(%240 %239 %238 %237)  soul.hir
    ==
  ::  clear compiler caches
  ::
  =.  van.mod  (~(run by van.mod) |=(=vane vane(worm *worm)))
  ::
  %-  %+  need:wyrd  kel.ver.zen
      ^-  wynn
      :~  hoon/hoon-version
          arvo/arvo
          lull/;;(@ud q:(slap lul.mod limb/%lull))
          zuse/;;(@ud q:(slap zus.mod limb/%zuse))
      ==
  ::  restore working state and resume
  ::
  =/  zef=(each (pair (list ovum) soul) (trap ^))
    loop:(~(jump le:part [pit vil] sol) debt.hir)
  ?-  -.zef
    %&  [p.p.zef ..load(sol q.p.zef)]
    %|  $:p.zef
  ==
::
::  +peek: external inspect
::
++  peek                                            ::  +22
```

```
|=  $:  lyc=gang
        $=  nom
        %+  each  path
        $%  [%once vis=view syd=desk tyl=spur]
            [%beam omen]  :: XX unfortunate naming
        ==
    ==
^-  (unit (cask))
=/  hap=(unit [pat=? omen])
  ?-  nom
    [%& *]          ?~(mon=(de-omen p.nom) ~ `[| u.mon])
    [%| %beam *]  `[| vis bem]:p.nom
    [%| %once *]  `[& vis.p.nom [our syd.p.nom da/now] tyl.p.nom]
  ==
::
?~  hap  ~
=/  pro  (~(peek le:part [pit vil] sol) lyc / [vis bem]:u.hap)
?:  |(?=(~ pro) ?=(~ u.pro))  ~
=/  dat=(cask)  [p q.q]:u.u.pro
?.  pat.u.hap  `dat
`[%omen (en-omen [vis bem]:u.hap) dat]
::
::  +poke: external apply
::
++  poke                                           ::  +23
  |=  [now=@da ovo=ovum]
  ^-  ^
  ::  this assertion is not yet viable, as vere's timestamps
  ::  are too unreliable. sad!
  ::
  ::  ?.  (gth now now.sol)
  ::    ~|  poke/[now=now last=now.sol wire.ovo p.card.ovo]
  ::    ~>(%mean.'time-marches-on' !!)
  ::
  =:  eny.sol  (shaz (cat 3 eny now))  ::  XX review
      now.sol  now
    ==
  ::
  ~|  poke/p.card.ovo
  =/  zef=(each (pair (list ovum) soul) (trap ^))
    loop:(~(poke le:part [pit vil] sol) ovo)
  ?-  -.zef
    %&  [p.p.zef ..poke(sol q.p.zef)]
    %|  $:p.zef
  ==
::
::  +wish: external compute
::
++  wish                                           ::  +10
  |=  txt=@
  q:(slap zus.mod (ream txt))
--  =>
::
::  larval stage
::
::    The true Arvo kernel knows who it is. It should not *maybe*
::    have an identity, nor should it contain multitudes. This outer
::    kernel exists to accumulate identity, entropy, and the
```

```
1854  ::    standard library. Upon having done so, it upgrades itself into
1855  ::    the true Arvo kernel. Subsequent upgrades will fall through
1856  ::    the larval stage directly into the actual kernel.
1857  ::
1858  ::    For convenience, this larval stage also supports hoon compilation
1859  ::    with +wish and vane installation with the %veer event.
1860  ::
1861  =>  |%
1862      ++  molt
1863      |=  [now=@da grub]
1864      ^-  (unit $>(_arvo heir))
1865      ?.  &(?=(^ who) ?=(^ eny) ?=(^ ver) ?=(^ fat) ?=(^ lul) ?=(^ zus))
1866        ~
1867      =/  lul  $:u.lul
1868      =/  zus  $:u.zus
1869      %-  %+  need:wyrd  kel.u.ver
1870          ^-  wynn
1871          :~  hoon/hoon-version
1872              arvo/arvo
1873              lull/;;(@ud q:(slap lul limb/%lull))
1874              zuse/;;(@ud q:(slap zus limb/%zuse))
1875          ==
1876      =/  nav  %-  ~(run by van)
1877              |=(a=(trap vase) (settle:va:part (slym $:a u.who)))
1878      :^  ~  arvo  *debt
1879      [[u.who now u.eny] [lac] [u.ver |] u.fat lul zus nav]
1880      ::
1881      ++  what
1882      =>  |%
1883          ++  smit
1884          |=  [cap=tape sub=(trap vase) pax=path txt=@t]
1885          ^-  (trap vase)
1886          ~>  %slog.[0 leaf/"{cap}: {(scow uv+(mug txt))}"]
1887          %-  road  |.
1888          ~_  leaf/"{cap}: build failed"
1889          (swat sub (rain pax txt))
1890          --
1891      ::
1892      |=  [grub fil=(list (pair path (cask)))]
1893      ^-  grub
1894      =*  gub  +<-
1895      =/  taf  (fall fat *(axal (cask)))
1896      =/  del  (~(group adapt:part taf) fil)
1897      =/  tub  (~(usurp adapt:part taf) del)
1898      ?:  &(?=(^ dir.taf) ?=(^ tub))
1899        ~>(%mean.'arvo: larval reboot' !!)      :: XX support
1900      ::
1901      :: require, and unconditionally adopt, initial kernel source
1902      ::
1903      =?  taf  =(~ dir.taf)      ::  XX TMI
1904        ~|  %larval-need-kernel
1905        ?>  &(?=(^ tub) ?=(^ hun.p.u.tub))
1906        (~(gas of taf) q.u.tub)
1907      ::
1908      =^  job=oped:part  taf  (~(adorn adapt:part taf) del |)
1909      =?  lul  ?=(^ lul.job)
1910        `(smit "lull" |.(pit) /sys/lull/hoon u.lul.job)
1911      =?  zus  ?=(^ zus.job)
```

```
1912          ?.  ?=(^ lul)
1913            ~|(%larval-need-lull !!)
1914            `(smit "zuse" u.lul /sys/zuse/hoon u.zus.job)
1915        =?  van  !=(~ van.job)     ::  XX TMI
1916          ?.  ?=(^ zus)
1917            ~|(%larval-need-zuse !!)
1918          %+  roll  van.job
1919          |=  [[nam=term txt=cord] =_van]
1920          ^+  van
1921          %+  ~(put by van)  nam
1922          (smit "vane: %{(trip nam)}" u.zus /sys/vane/[nam]/hoon txt)
1923        gub(fat `taf)
1924      --
1925  ::
1926  ::  larval state, as a discriminable sample
1927  ::
1928  =|  [%grub _arvo grub]
1929  =*  gub  ->+
1930  ::
1931  |%
1932  ++  load                                            ::    +4
1933    |=  hir=heir
1934    ?:  ?=(%grub -.hir)
1935      ~>(%mean.'arvo: larval reboot' !!)     ::  XX support
1936    (^load hir)
1937  ::
1938  ++  peek  _~                                        ::    +22
1939  ++  poke                                            ::    +23
1940    |=  [now=@da ovo=ovum]
1941    ^-  ^
1942    ~|  poke/p.card.ovo
1943    =/  wip
1944      ~>  %mean.'arvo: bad wisp'
1945      ;;(wisp card.ovo)
1946    ::
1947    =.  ..poke
1948      ?-    -.wip
1949        %verb  ..poke(lac ?~(p.wip !lac u.p.wip))
1950        %wack  ..poke(eny `p.wip)
1951        %what  ..poke(gub (what gub p.wip))
1952        %whom  ..poke(who ~|(%whom-once ?>(?=(~ who) `p.wip)))
1953        ::
1954        %wyrd  ?.  (sane:wyrd kel.p.wip)
1955                    ~>(%mean.'wyrd: insane' !!)
1956               %-  %+  need:wyrd  kel.p.wip
1957                   ^-  wynn
1958                   :*  hoon/hoon-version
1959                       arvo/arvo
1960                       ?~  lul  ~
1961                       :-  lull/;;(@ud q:(slap $:u.lul limb/%lull))
1962                       ?~  zus  ~
1963                       [zuse/;;(@ud q:(slap $:u.zus limb/%zuse)) ~]
1964                   ==
1965               ..poke(ver `p.wip)
1966      ==
1967    ::
1968    ::  upgrade once we've accumulated necessary state
1969    ::
```

```
1970    ?~  hir=(molt now gub)
1971      [~ ..poke]
1972    ~>  %slog.[0 leaf+"arvo: metamorphosis"]
1973    (load u.hir)
1974 ::
1975 ++  wish                                        ::  +10
1976    |=  txt=*
1977    q:(slap ?~(zus pit $:u.zus) (ream ;;(@t txt)))
1978 --
1979 ::
1980 ::  Arvo formal interface
1981 ::
1982 ::    this lifecycle wrapper makes the arvo door (multi-armed core)
1983 ::    look like a gate (function or single-armed core), to fit
1984 ::    urbit's formal lifecycle function (see aeon:eden:part).
1985 ::    a practical interpreter can and will ignore it.
1986 ::
1987 |=  [now=@da ovo=ovum]
1988 ^-  *
1989 .(+> +:(poke now ovo))
```

Hoon 138K

```
1  ::
2  ::::    /sys/hoon                                          ::
3    ::                                                        ::
4  =<  ride
5  =>  %138  =>
6  ::                                                          ::
7  ::::    0: version stub                                     ::
8    ::                                                        ::
9  ~%  %k.138  ~  ~                                            ::
10 |%
11 ++  hoon-version  +
12 --  =>
13 ~%  %one  +  ~
14 ::    layer-1
15 ::
16 ::  basic mathematical operations
17 |%
18 ::    unsigned arithmetic
19 +|  %math
20 ++  add
21   ~/  %add
22   ::    unsigned addition
23   ::
24   ::  a: augend
25   ::  b: addend
26   |=  [a=@ b=@]
27   ::  sum
28   ^-  @
29   ?:  =(0 a)  b
30   $(a (dec a), b +(b))
31 ::
32 ++  dec
33   ~/  %dec
34   ::    unsigned decrement by one.
35   |=  a=@
36   ~_  leaf+"decrement-underflow"
37   ?<  =(0 a)
38   =+  b=0
39   ::  decremented integer
40   |-  ^-  @
41   ?:  =(a +(b))  b
42   $(b +(b))
43 ::
44 ++  div
45   ~/  %div
46   ::    unsigned divide
47   ::
48   ::  a: dividend
49   ::  b: divisor
50   |:  [a=`@`1 b=`@`1]
51   ::  quotient
52   ^-  @
53   -:(dvr a b)
54 ::
55 ++  dvr
56   ~/  %dvr
```

```
57    ::      unsigned divide with remainder
58    ::
59    ::  a: dividend
60    ::  b: divisor
61    |:  [a=`@`1 b=`@`1]
62    ::  p: quotient
63    ::  q: remainder
64    ^-  [p=@ q=@]
65    ~_  leaf+"divide-by-zero"
66    ?<  =(0 b)
67    =+  c=0
68    |-
69    ?:  (lth a b)  [c a]
70    $(a (sub a b), c +(c))
71  ::
72  ++  gte
73    ~/  %gte
74    ::      unsigned greater than or equals
75    ::
76    ::  returns whether {a >= b}.
77    ::
78    ::  a: left hand operand (todo: name)
79    ::  b: right hand operand
80    |=  [a=@ b=@]
81    ::  greater than or equal to?
82    ^-  ?
83    !(lth a b)
84  ::
85  ++  gth
86    ~/  %gth
87    ::      unsigned greater than
88    ::
89    ::  returns whether {a > b}
90    ::
91    ::  a: left hand operand (todo: name)
92    ::  b: right hand operand
93    |=  [a=@ b=@]
94    ::  greater than?
95    ^-  ?
96    !(lte a b)
97  ::
98  ++  lte
99    ~/  %lte
100   ::      unsigned less than or equals
101   ::
102   ::  returns whether {a >= b}.
103   ::
104   ::  a: left hand operand (todo: name)
105   ::  b: right hand operand
106   |=  [a=@ b=@]
107   ::  less than or equal to?
108   |(=(a b) (lth a b))
109 ::
110 ++  lth
111   ~/  %lth
112   ::      unsigned less than
113   ::
114   ::  a: left hand operand (todo: name)
```

```
::  b: right hand operand
|=  [a=@ b=@]
::  less than?
^-  ?
?&  !=(a b)
    |-
    ?|  =(0 a)
        ?&  !=(0 b)
            $(a (dec a), b (dec b))
==  ==  ==
::
++  max
  ~/  %max
  ::    unsigned maximum
  |=  [a=@ b=@]
  ::  the maximum
  ^-  @
  ?:  (gth a b)  a
  b
::
++  min
  ~/  %min
  ::    unsigned minimum
  |=  [a=@ b=@]
  ::  the minimum
  ^-  @
  ?:  (lth a b)  a
  b
::
++  mod
  ~/  %mod
  ::    unsigned modulus
  ::
  ::  a: dividend
  ::  b: divisor
  |:  [a=`@`1 b=`@`1]
  ::  the remainder
  ^-  @
  +:(dvr a b)
::
++  mul
  ~/  %mul
  ::    unsigned multiplication
  ::
  ::  a: multiplicand
  ::  b: multiplier
  |:  [a=`@`1 b=`@`1]
  ::  product
  ^-  @
  =+  c=0
  |-
  ?:  =(0 a)  c
  $(a (dec a), c (add b c))
::
++  sub
  ~/  %sub
  ::    unsigned subtraction
  ::
```

```
173    ::  a: minuend
174    ::  b: subtrahend
175    |=  [a=@ b=@]
176    ~_  leaf+"subtract-underflow"
177    ::  difference
178    ^-  @
179    ?:  =(0 b)  a
180    $(a (dec a), b (dec b))
181  ::
182  ::    tree addressing
183  +|  %tree
184  ++  cap
185    ~/  %cap
186    ::    tree head
187    ::
188    ::  tests whether an `a` is in the head or tail of a noun. produces %2 if it
189    ::  is within the head, or %3 if it is within the tail.
190    |=  a=@
191    ^-  ?(%2 %3)
192    ?-  a
193      %2          %2
194      %3          %3
195      ?(%0 %1)  !!
196      *           $(a (div a 2))
197    ==
198  ::
199  ++  mas
200    ~/  %mas
201    ::    axis within head/tail
202    ::
203    ::  computes the axis of `a` within either the head or tail of a noun
204    ::  (depends whether `a` lies within the the head or tail).
205    |=  a=@
206    ^-  @
207    ?-  a
208      ?(%2 %3)  1
209      ?(%0 %1)  !!
210      *           (add (mod a 2) (mul $(a (div a 2)) 2))
211    ==
212  ::
213  ++  peg
214    ~/  %peg
215    ::    axis within axis
216    ::
217    ::  computes the axis of {b} within axis {a}.
218    |=  [a=@ b=@]
219    ?<  =(0 a)
220    ?<  =(0 b)
221    ::  a composed axis
222    ^-  @
223    ?-  b
224      %1  a
225      %2  (mul a 2)
226      %3  +((mul a 2))
227      *   (add (mod b 2) (mul $(b (div b 2)) 2))
228    ==
229  ::
230  ::  #  %containers
```

```
::
::      the most basic of data types
+|  %containers
::
+$  bite
  ::      atom slice specifier
  ::
  $@(bloq [=bloq =step])
::
+$  bloq
  ::      blocksize
  ::
  ::  a blocksize is the power of 2 size of an atom. ie, 3 is a byte as 2^3 is
  ::  8 bits.
  @
::
++  each
  |$  [this that]
  ::      either {a} or {b}, defaulting to {a}.
  ::
  ::  mold generator: produces a discriminated fork between two types,
  ::  defaulting to {a}.
  ::
  $%  [%| p=that]
      [%& p=this]
  ==
::
+$  gate
  ::      function
  ::
  ::  a core with one arm, `$`--the empty name--which transforms a sample noun
  ::  into a product noun. If used dryly as a type, the subject must have a
  ::  sample type of `*`.
  $-(* *)
::
++  list
  |$  [item]
  ::      null-terminated list
  ::
  ::  mold generator: produces a mold of a null-terminated list of the
  ::  homogeneous type {a}.
  $@(~ [i=item t=(list item)])
::
++  lone
  |$  [item]
  ::      single item tuple
  ::
  ::  mold generator: puts the face of `p` on the passed in mold.
  ::
  p=item
::
++  lest
  |$  [item]
  ::      null-terminated non-empty list
  ::
  ::  mold generator: produces a mold of a null-terminated list of the
  ::  homogeneous type {a} with at least one element.
```

```
289    [i=item t=(list item)]
290  ::
291  +$  mold
292    ::     normalizing gate
293    ::
294    ::  a gate that accepts any noun, and validates its shape, producing the
295    ::  input if it fits or a default value if it doesn't.
296    ::
297    ::  examples: * @ud  ,[p=time q=?(%a %b)]
298    $~(* $-(* *))
299  ::
300  ++  pair
301    |$  [head tail]
302    ::     dual tuple
303    ::
304    ::  mold generator: produces a tuple of the two types passed in.
305    ::
306    ::  a: first type, labeled {p}
307    ::  b: second type, labeled {q}
308    ::
309    [p=head q=tail]
310  ::
311  ++  pole
312    |$  [item]
313    ::     faceless list
314    ::
315    ::  like ++list, but without the faces {i} and {t}.
316    ::
317    $@(~ [item (pole item)])
318  ::
319  ++  qual
320    |$  [first second third fourth]
321    ::     quadruple tuple
322    ::
323    ::  mold generator: produces a tuple of the four types passed in.
324    ::
325    [p=first q=second r=third s=fourth]
326  ::
327  ++  quip
328    |$  [item state]
329    ::     pair of list of first and second
330    ::
331    ::  a common pattern in hoon code is to return a ++list of changes, along with
332    ::  a new state.
333    ::
334    ::  a: type of list item
335    ::  b: type of returned state
336    ::
337    [(list item) state]
338  ::
339  ++  step
340    ::     atom size or offset, in bloqs
341    ::
342    _`@u`1
343  ::
344  ++  trap
345    |$  [product]
346    ::     a core with one arm `$`
```

```hoon
    ::
    _|?($:product)
::
++  tree
  |$  [node]
    ::    tree mold generator
    ::
    ::  a `++tree` can be empty, or contain a node of a type and
    ::  left/right sub `++tree` of the same type. pretty-printed with `{}`.
    ::
  $@(~ [n=node l=(tree node) r=(tree node)])
::
++  trel
  |$  [first second third]
    ::    triple tuple
    ::
    ::  mold generator: produces a tuple of the three types passed in.
    ::
  [p=first q=second r=third]
::
++  unit
  |$  [item]
    ::    maybe
    ::
    ::  mold generator: either `~` or `[~ u=a]` where `a` is the
    ::  type that was passed in.
    ::
  $@(~ [~ u=item])
--  =>
::
~%  %two  +  ~
::    layer-2
::
|%
::    2a: unit logic
+|  %unit-logc
::
++  biff                                  ::  apply
  |*  [a=(unit) b=$-(* (unit))]
  ?~  a  ~
  (b u.a)
::
++  bind                                  ::  argue
  |*  [a=(unit) b=gate]
  ?~  a  ~
  [~ u=(b u.a)]
::
++  bond                                  ::  replace
  |*  a=(trap)
  |*  b=(unit)
  ?~  b  $:a
  u.b
::
++  both                                  ::  all the above
  |*  [a=(unit) b=(unit)]
  ?~  a  ~
  ?~  b  ~
  [~ u=[u.a u.b]]
```

```
405  ::
406  ++  clap                                          ::  combine
407    |*  [a=(unit) b=(unit) c=_=>(~ |=(^ +<-))]
408    ?~  a  b
409    ?~  b  a
410    [~ u=(c u.a u.b)]
411  ::
412  ++  clef                                          ::  compose
413    |*  [a=(unit) b=(unit) c=_=>(~ |=(^ `+<-))]
414    ?~  a  ~
415    ?~  b  ~
416    (c u.a u.b)
417  ::
418  ++  drop                                          ::  enlist
419    |*  a=(unit)
420    ?~  a  ~
421    [i=u.a t=~]
422  ::
423  ++  fall                                          ::  default
424    |*  [a=(unit) b=*]
425    ?~(a b u.a)
426  ::
427  ++  flit                                          ::  make filter
428    |*  a=$-(* ?)
429    |*  b=*
430    ?.((a b) ~ [~ u=b])
431  ::
432  ++  hunt                                          ::  first of units
433    |*  [ord=$-(^ ?) a=(unit) b=(unit)]
434    ^-  %-  unit
435        $?  _?>(?=(^ a) u.a)
436            _?>(?=(^ b) u.b)
437        ==
438    ?~  a  b
439    ?~  b  a
440    ?:((ord u.a u.b) a b)
441  ::
442  ++  lift                                          ::  lift mold (fmap)
443    |*  a=mold                                      ::  flipped
444    |*  b=(unit)                                    ::  curried
445    (bind b a)                                      ::  bind
446  ::
447  ++  mate                                          ::  choose
448    |*  [a=(unit) b=(unit)]
449    ?~  b  a
450    ?~  a  b
451    ?.(=(u.a u.b) ~>(%mean.'mate' !!) a)
452  ::
453  ++  need                                          ::  demand
454    ~/  %need
455    |*  a=(unit)
456    ?~  a  ~>(%mean.'need' !!)
457    u.a
458  ::
459  ++  some                                          ::  lift (pure)
460    |*  a=*
461    [~ u=a]
462  ::
```

```
::      2b: list logic
+|  %list-logic
::  +snoc: append an element to the end of a list
::
++  snoc
  |*  [a=(list) b=*]
  (weld a ^+(a [b]~))
::
::  +lure: List pURE
++  lure
  |*  a=*
  [i=a t=~]
::
++  fand                                    ::  all indices
  ~/  %fand
  |=  [nedl=(list) hstk=(list)]
  =|  i=@ud
  =|  fnd=(list @ud)
  |-  ^+  fnd
  =+  [n=nedl h=hstk]
  |-
  ?:  |(?=(~ n) ?=(~ h))
    (flop fnd)
  ?:  =(i.n i.h)
    ?~  t.n
      ^$(i +(i), hstk +.hstk, fnd [i fnd])
    $(n t.n, h t.h)
  ^$(i +(i), hstk +.hstk)
::
++  find                                    ::  first index
  ~/  %find
  |=  [nedl=(list) hstk=(list)]
  =|  i=@ud
  |-  ^-  (unit @ud)
  =+  [n=nedl h=hstk]
  |-
  ?:  |(?=(~ n) ?=(~ h))
    ~
  ?:  =(i.n i.h)
    ?~  t.n
      `i
    $(n t.n, h t.h)
  ^$(i +(i), hstk +.hstk)
::
++  flop                                    ::  reverse
  ~/  %flop
  |*  a=(list)
  =>  .(a (homo a))
  ^+  a
  =+  b=`_a`~
  |-
  ?~  a  b
  $(a t.a, b [i.a b])
::
++  gulf                                    ::  range inclusive
  |=  [a=@ b=@]
  ?>  (lte a b)
  |-  ^-  (list @)
```

```
521    ?:(=(a +(b))  ~  [a $(a +(a))])
522  ::
523  ++  homo                                          ::  homogenize
524    |*  a=(list)
525    ^+  =<  $
526      |@  ++  $  ?:(*? ~ [i=(snag 0 a) t=$])
527      --
528    a
529  ::  +join: construct a new list, placing .sep between every pair in .lit
530  ::
531  ++  join
532    |*  [sep=* lit=(list)]
533    =.  sep  `_?>(?=(^ lit) i.lit)`sep
534    ?~  lit  ~
535    =|  out=(list _?>(?=(^ lit) i.lit))
536    |-  ^+  out
537    ?~  t.lit
538      (flop [i.lit out])
539    $(out [sep i.lit out], lit t.lit)
540  ::
541  ::  +bake: convert wet gate to dry gate by specifying argument mold
542  ::
543  ++  bake
544    |*  [f=gate a=mold]
545    |=  arg=a
546    (f arg)
547  ::
548  ++  lent                                          ::  length
549    ~/  %lent
550    |=  a=(list)
551    ^-  @
552    =+  b=0
553    |-
554    ?~  a  b
555    $(a t.a, b +(b))
556  ::
557  ++  levy
558    ~/  %levy                                       ::  all of
559    |*  [a=(list) b=$-(* ?)]
560    |-  ^-  ?
561    ?~  a  &
562    ?.  (b i.a)  |
563    $(a t.a)
564  ::
565  ++  lien                                          ::  some of
566    ~/  %lien
567    |*  [a=(list) b=$-(* ?)]
568    |-  ^-  ?
569    ?~  a  |
570    ?:  (b i.a)  &
571    $(a t.a)
572  ::
573  ++  limo                                          ::  listify
574    |*  a=*
575    ^+  =<  $
576      |@  ++  $  ?~(a ~ ?:(*? [i=-.a t=$] $(a +.a)))
577      --
578    a
```

```
::
++  murn                                        ::  maybe transform
  ~/  %murn
  |*  [a=(list) b=$-(* (unit))]
  =>  .(a (homo a))
  |-  ^-  (list _?>(?=(^ a) (need (b i.a))))
  ?~  a  ~
  =/  c  (b i.a)
  ?~  c  $(a t.a)
  [+.c $(a t.a)]
::
++  oust                                        ::  remove
  ~/  %oust
  |*  [[a=@ b=@] c=(list)]
  (weld (scag +<-< c) (slag (add +<-< +<->) c))
::
++  reap                                        ::  replicate
  ~/  %reap
  |*  [a=@ b=*]
  |-  ^-  (list _b)
  ?~  a  ~
  [b $(a (dec a))]
::
++  rear                                        ::  last item of list
  ~/  %rear
  |*  a=(list)
  ^-  _?>(?=(^ a) i.a)
  ?>  ?=(^ a)
  ?:  =(~ t.a)  i.a  ::NOTE  avoiding tmi
  $(a t.a)
::
++  reel                                        ::  right fold
  ~/  %reel
  |*  [a=(list) b=_=>(~ |=([* *] +<+))]
  |-  ^+  ,.+<+.b
  ?~  a
    +<+.b
  (b i.a $(a t.a))
::
++  roll                                        ::  left fold
  ~/  %roll
  |*  [a=(list) b=_=>(~ |=([* *] +<+))]
  |-  ^+  ,.+<+.b
  ?~  a
    +<+.b
  $(a t.a, b b(+<+ (b i.a +<+.b)))
::
++  scag                                        ::  prefix
  ~/  %scag
  |*  [a=@ b=(list)]
  |-  ^+  b
  ?:  |(?=(~ b) =(0 a))  ~
  [i.b $(b t.b, a (dec a))]
::
++  skid                                        ::  separate
  ~/  %skid
  |*  [a=(list) b=$-(* ?)]
  |-  ^+  [p=a q=a]
```

```
637    ?~  a  [~ ~]
638    =+  c=$(a t.a)
639    ?:((b i.a) [[i.a p.c] q.c] [p.c [i.a q.c]])
640  ::
641  ++  skim                                    ::  only
642    ~/  %skim
643    |*  [a=(list) b=$-(* ?)]
644    |-
645    ^+  a
646    ?~  a  ~
647    ?:((b i.a) [i.a $(a t.a)] $(a t.a))
648  ::
649  ++  skip                                    ::  except
650    ~/  %skip
651    |*  [a=(list) b=$-(* ?)]
652    |-
653    ^+  a
654    ?~  a  ~
655    ?:((b i.a) $(a t.a) [i.a $(a t.a)])
656  ::
657  ++  slag                                    ::  suffix
658    ~/  %slag
659    |*  [a=@ b=(list)]
660    |-  ^+  b
661    ?:  =(0 a)  b
662    ?~  b  ~
663    $(b t.b, a (dec a))
664  ::
665  ++  snag                                    ::  index
666    ~/  %snag
667    |*  [a=@ b=(list)]
668    |-  ^+  ?>(?=(^ b) i.b)
669    ?~  b
670      ~_  leaf+"snag-fail"
671      !!
672    ?:  =(0 a)  i.b
673    $(b t.b, a (dec a))
674  ::
675  ++  snip                                    ::  drop tail off list
676    ~/  %snip
677    |*  a=(list)
678    ^+  a
679    ?~  a  ~
680    ?:  =(~ t.a)  ~
681    [i.a $(a t.a)]
682  ::
683  ++  sort  !.                                ::  quicksort
684    ~/  %sort
685    |*  [a=(list) b=$-([* *] ?)]
686    =>  .(a ^.(homo a))
687    |-  ^+  a
688    ?~  a  ~
689    =+  s=(skid t.a |:(c=i.a (b c i.a)))
690    %+  weld
691      $(a p.s)
692    ^+  t.a
693    [i.a $(a q.s)]
694  ::
```

```
695  ++  spin                                             ::  stateful turn
696    ::
697    ::  a: list
698    ::  b: state
699    ::  c: gate from list-item and state to product and new state
700    ~/  %spin
701    |*  [a=(list) b=* c=_|=(^ [** +<+])]
702    =>  .(c `$-([_?>(?=(^ a) i.a) _b] [_-:(c) _b])`c)
703    =/  acc=(list _-:(c))  ~
704    ::  transformed list and updated state
705    |-  ^-  (pair _acc _b)
706    ?~  a
707      [(flop acc) b]
708    =^  res  b  (c i.a b)
709    $(acc [res acc], a t.a)
710  ::
711  ++  spun                                             ::  internal spin
712    ::
713    ::  a: list
714    ::  b: gate from list-item and state to product and new state
715    ~/  %spun
716    |*  [a=(list) b=_|=(^ [** +<+])]
717    ::  transformed list
718    p:(spin a +<+.b b)
719  ::
720  ++  swag                                             ::  slice
721    |*  [[a=@ b=@] c=(list)]
722    (scag +<-> (slag +<-< c))
723  ::  +turn: transform each value of list :a using the function :b
724  ::
725  ++  turn
726    ~/  %turn
727    |*  [a=(list) b=gate]
728    =>  .(a (homo a))
729    ^-  (list _?>(?=(^ a) (b i.a)))
730    |-
731    ?~  a  ~
732    [i=(b i.a) t=$(a t.a)]
733  ::
734  ++  weld                                             ::  concatenate
735    ~/  %weld
736    |*  [a=(list) b=(list)]
737    =>  .(a ^.(homo a), b ^.(homo b))
738    |-  ^+  b
739    ?~  a  b
740    [i.a $(a t.a)]
741  ::
742  ++  snap                                             ::  replace item
743    ~/  %snap
744    |*  [a=(list) b=@ c=*]
745    ^+  a
746    (weld (scag b a) [c (slag +(b) a)])
747  ::
748  ++  into                                             ::  insert item
749    ~/  %into
750    |*  [a=(list) b=@ c=*]
751    ^+  a
752    (weld (scag b a) [c (slag b a)])
```

```
::
++  welp                                              ::  faceless weld
  ~/  %welp
  |*  [* *]
  ?~  +<-
    +<-(. +<+)
  +<-(+ $(+<- +<->))
::
++  zing                                              ::  promote
  ~/  %zing
  |*  *
  ?~  +<
    +<
  (welp +<- $(+< +<+))
::
::    2c: bit arithmetic
+|  %bit-arithmetic
::
++  bex                                               ::  binary exponent
  ~/  %bex
  |=  a=bloq
  ^-  @
  ?:  =(0 a)  1
  (mul 2 $(a (dec a)))
::
++  can                                               ::  assemble
  ~/  %can
  |=  [a=bloq b=(list [p=step q=@])]
  ^-  @
  ?~  b  0
  (add (end [a p.i.b] q.i.b) (lsh [a p.i.b] $(b t.b)))
::
++  cat                                               ::  concatenate
  ~/  %cat
  |=  [a=bloq b=@ c=@]
  (add (lsh [a (met a b)] c) b)
::
++  cut                                               ::  slice
  ~/  %cut
  |=  [a=bloq [b=step c=step] d=@]
  (end [a c] (rsh [a b] d))
::
++  end                                               ::  tail
  ~/  %end
  |=  [a=bite b=@]
  =/  [=bloq =step]  ?^(a a [a *step])
  (mod b (bex (mul (bex bloq) step)))
::
++  fil                                               ::  fill bloqstream
  ~/  %fil
  |=  [a=bloq b=step c=@]
  =|  n=@ud
  =.  c  (end a c)
  =/  d  c
  |-  ^-  @
  ?:  =(n b)
    (rsh a d)
  $(d (add c (lsh a d)), n +(n))
```

```
811  ::
812  ++  lsh                                           ::  left-shift
813    ~/  %lsh
814    |=  [a=bite b=@]
815    =/  [=bloq =step]  ?^(a a [a *step])
816  (mul b (bex (mul (bex bloq) step)))
817  ::
818  ++  met                                           ::  measure
819    ~/  %met
820    |=  [a=bloq b=@]
821    ^-  @
822    =+  c=0
823    |-
824    ?:  =(0 b)  c
825  $(b (rsh a b), c +(c))
826  ::
827  ++  rap                                           ::  assemble variable
828    ~/  %rap
829    |=  [a=bloq b=(list @)]
830    ^-  @
831    ?~  b  0
832  (cat a i.b $(b t.b))
833  ::
834  ++  rep                                           ::  assemble fixed
835    ~/  %rep
836    |=  [a=bite b=(list @)]
837    =/  [=bloq =step]  ?^(a a [a *step])
838    =|  i=@ud
839    |-  ^-  @
840    ?~  b  0
841    %+  add  $(i +(i), b t.b)
842  (lsh [bloq (mul step i)] (end [bloq step] i.b))
843  ::
844  ++  rev
845    ::      reverses block order, accounting for leading zeroes
846    ::
847    ::  boz: block size
848    ::  len: size of dat, in boz
849    ::  dat: data to flip
850    ~/  %rev
851    |=  [boz=bloq len=@ud dat=@]
852    ^-  @
853    =.  dat  (end [boz len] dat)
854    %+  lsh
855      [boz (sub len (met boz dat))]
856  (swp boz dat)
857  ::
858  ++  rip                                           ::  disassemble
859    ~/  %rip
860    |=  [a=bite b=@]
861    ^-  (list @)
862    ?:  =(0 b)  ~
863  [(end a b) $(b (rsh a b))]
864  ::
865  ++  rsh                                           ::  right-shift
866    ~/  %rsh
867    |=  [a=bite b=@]
868    =/  [=bloq =step]  ?^(a a [a *step])
```

```hoon
869    (div b (bex (mul (bex bloq) step)))
870  ::
871  ++  run                                           ::  +turn into atom
872    ~/  %run
873    |=  [a=bite b=@ c=$-(@ @)]
874    (rep a (turn (rip a b) c))
875  ::
876  ++  rut                                           ::  +turn into list
877    ~/  %rut
878    |*  [a=bite b=@ c=$-(@ *)]
879    (turn (rip a b) c)
880  ::
881  ++  sew                                           ::  stitch into
882    ~/  %sew
883    |=  [a=bloq [b=step c=step d=@] e=@]
884    ^-  @
885    %+  add
886      (can a b^e c^d ~)
887    =/  f  [a (add b c)]
888    (lsh f (rsh f e))
889  ::
890  ++  swp                                           ::  naive rev bloq order
891    ~/  %swp
892    |=  [a=bloq b=@]
893    (rep a (flop (rip a b)))
894  ::
895  ++  xeb                                           ::  binary logarithm
896    ~/  %xeb
897    |=  a=@
898    ^-  @
899    (met 0 a)
900  ::
901  ++  fe                                            ::  modulo bloq
902    |_  a=bloq
903    ++  dif                                         ::  difference
904      |=([b=@ c=@] (sit (sub (add out (sit b)) (sit c))))
905    ++  inv  |=(b=@ (sub (dec out) (sit b)))        ::  inverse
906    ++  net  |=  b=@  ^-  @                          ::  flip byte endianness
907             =>  .(b (sit b))
908             ?:  (lte a 3)
909               b
910             =+  c=(dec a)
911             %+  con
912               (lsh c $(a c, b (cut c [0 1] b)))
913             $(a c, b (cut c [1 1] b))
914    ++  out  (bex (bex a))                          ::  mod value
915    ++  rol  |=  [b=bloq c=@ d=@]  ^-  @             ::  roll left
916             =+  e=(sit d)
917             =+  f=(bex (sub a b))
918             =+  g=(mod c f)
919             (sit (con (lsh [b g] e) (rsh [b (sub f g)] e)))
920    ++  ror  |=  [b=bloq c=@ d=@]  ^-  @             ::  roll right
921             =+  e=(sit d)
922             =+  f=(bex (sub a b))
923             =+  g=(mod c f)
924             (sit (con (rsh [b g] e) (lsh [b (sub f g)] e)))
925    ++  sum  |=([b=@ c=@] (sit (add b c)))          ::  wrapping add
926    ++  sit  |=(b=@ (end a b))                      ::  enforce modulo
```

```
    --
::
::      2d: bit logic
+|    %bit-logic
::
++    con                                              ::  binary or
  ~/  %con
  |=  [a=@ b=@]
  =+  [c=0 d=0]
  |-  ^-  @
  ?:  ?&(=(0 a) =(0 b))  d
  %=  $
    a   (rsh 0 a)
    b   (rsh 0 b)
    c   +(c)
    d   %+  add  d
        %+  lsh  [0 c]
        ?&  =(0 (end 0 a))
            =(0 (end 0 b))
        ==
  ==
::
++    dis                                              ::  binary and
  ~/  %dis
  |=  [a=@ b=@]
  =|  [c=@ d=@]
  |-  ^-  @
  ?:  ?|(=(0 a) =(0 b))  d
  %=  $
    a   (rsh 0 a)
    b   (rsh 0 b)
    c   +(c)
    d   %+  add  d
        %+  lsh  [0 c]
        ?|  =(0 (end 0 a))
            =(0 (end 0 b))
        ==
  ==
::
++    mix                                              ::  binary xor
  ~/  %mix
  |=  [a=@ b=@]
  ^-  @
  =+  [c=0 d=0]
  |-
  ?:  ?&(=(0 a) =(0 b))  d
  %=  $
    a   (rsh 0 a)
    b   (rsh 0 b)
    c   +(c)
    d   (add d (lsh [0 c] =((end 0 a) (end 0 b))))
  ==
::
++    not  |=  [a=bloq b=@ c=@]                        ::  binary not (sized)
  (mix c (dec (bex (mul b (bex a)))))
::
::      2e: insecure hashing
+|    %insecure-hashing
```

```
985    ::
986    ++  muk                                              ::  standard murmur3
987      ~%  %muk  ..muk  ~
988      =+  ~(. fe 5)
989      |=  [syd=@ len=@ key=@]
990      =.  syd        (end 5 syd)
991      =/  pad        (sub len (met 3 key))
992      =/  data       (weld (rip 3 key) (reap pad 0))
993      =/  nblocks    (div len 4)  ::  intentionally off-by-one
994      =/  h1  syd
995      =+  [c1=0xcc9e.2d51 c2=0x1b87.3593]
996      =/  blocks  (rip 5 key)
997      =/  i  nblocks
998      =.  h1  =/  hi  h1  |-
999        ?:  =(0 i)  hi
1000       =/  k1  (snag (sub nblocks i) blocks)  ::  negative array index
1001       =.  k1  (sit (mul k1 c1))
1002       =.  k1  (rol 0 15 k1)
1003       =.  k1  (sit (mul k1 c2))
1004       =.  hi  (mix hi k1)
1005       =.  hi  (rol 0 13 hi)
1006       =.  hi  (sum (sit (mul hi 5)) 0xe654.6b64)
1007       $(i (dec i))
1008     =/  tail  (slag (mul 4 nblocks) data)
1009     =/  k1    0
1010     =/  tlen  (dis len 3)
1011     =.  h1
1012       ?+  tlen  h1  ::  fallthrough switch
1013         %3  =.  k1  (mix k1 (lsh [0 16] (snag 2 tail)))
1014             =.  k1  (mix k1 (lsh [0 8] (snag 1 tail)))
1015             =.  k1  (mix k1 (snag 0 tail))
1016             =.  k1  (sit (mul k1 c1))
1017             =.  k1  (rol 0 15 k1)
1018             =.  k1  (sit (mul k1 c2))
1019             (mix h1 k1)
1020         %2  =.  k1  (mix k1 (lsh [0 8] (snag 1 tail)))
1021             =.  k1  (mix k1 (snag 0 tail))
1022             =.  k1  (sit (mul k1 c1))
1023             =.  k1  (rol 0 15 k1)
1024             =.  k1  (sit (mul k1 c2))
1025             (mix h1 k1)
1026         %1  =.  k1  (mix k1 (snag 0 tail))
1027             =.  k1  (sit (mul k1 c1))
1028             =.  k1  (rol 0 15 k1)
1029             =.  k1  (sit (mul k1 c2))
1030             (mix h1 k1)
1031       ==
1032     =.  h1  (mix h1 len)
1033     |^  (fmix32 h1)
1034     ++  fmix32
1035       |=  h=@
1036       =.  h  (mix h (rsh [0 16] h))
1037       =.  h  (sit (mul h 0x85eb.ca6b))
1038       =.  h  (mix h (rsh [0 13] h))
1039       =.  h  (sit (mul h 0xc2b2.ae35))
1040       =.  h  (mix h (rsh [0 16] h))
1041       h
1042     --
```

```
1043  ::
1044  ++  mug                                              ::  mug with murmur3
1045    ~/  %mug
1046    |=  a=*
1047    |^  ?@  a  (mum 0xcafe.babe 0x7fff a)
1048        =/  b  (cat 5 $(a -.a) $(a +.a))
1049        (mum 0xdead.beef 0xfffe b)
1050    ::
1051    ++  mum
1052      |=  [syd=@uxF fal=@F key=@]
1053      =/  wyd  (met 3 key)
1054      =|  i=@ud
1055      |-  ^-  @F
1056      ?:  =(8 i)  fal
1057      =/  haz=@F  (muk syd wyd key)
1058      =/  ham=@F  (mix (rsh [0 31] haz) (end [0 31] haz))
1059      ?.(=(0 ham) ham $(i +(i), syd +(syd)))
1060    --
1061  ::                                                   ::
1062  ::    2f: noun ordering
1063  +|  %noun-ordering
1064  ::
1065  ::  +aor: alphabetical order
1066  ::
1067  ::    Orders atoms before cells, and atoms in ascending LSB order.
1068  ::
1069  ++  aor
1070    ~/  %aor
1071    |=  [a=* b=*]
1072    ^-  ?
1073    ?:  =(a b)  &
1074    ?.  ?=(@ a)
1075      ?:  ?=(@ b)  |
1076      ?:  =(-.a -.b)
1077        $(a +.a, b +.b)
1078      $(a -.a, b -.b)
1079    ?.  ?=(@ b)  &
1080    |-
1081    =+  [c=(end 3 a) d=(end 3 b)]
1082    ?:  =(c d)
1083      $(a (rsh 3 a), b (rsh 3 b))
1084    (lth c d)
1085  ::  +dor: depth order
1086  ::
1087  ::    Orders in ascending tree depth.
1088  ::
1089  ++  dor
1090    ~/  %dor
1091    |=  [a=* b=*]
1092    ^-  ?
1093    ?:  =(a b)  &
1094    ?.  ?=(@ a)
1095      ?:  ?=(@ b)  |
1096      ?:  =(-.a -.b)
1097        $(a +.a, b +.b)
1098      $(a -.a, b -.b)
1099    ?.  ?=(@ b)  &
1100    (lth a b)
```

```
1101  ::  +gor: mug order
1102  ::
1103  ::      Orders in ascending +mug hash order, collisions fall back to +dor.
1104  ::
1105  ++  gor
1106    ~/  %gor
1107    |=  [a=* b=*]
1108    ^-  ?
1109    =+  [c=(mug a) d=(mug b)]
1110    ?:  =(c d)
1111      (dor a b)
1112    (lth c d)
1113  ::  +mor: (more) mug order
1114  ::
1115  ::      Orders in ascending double +mug hash order, collisions fall back to +dor.
1116  ::
1117  ++  mor
1118    ~/  %mor
1119    |=  [a=* b=*]
1120    ^-  ?
1121    =+  [c=(mug (mug a)) d=(mug (mug b))]
1122    ?:  =(c d)
1123      (dor a b)
1124    (lth c d)
1125  ::
1126  ::      2g: unsigned powers
1127  +|  %unsigned-powers
1128  ::
1129  ++  pow                                             ::  unsigned exponent
1130    ~/  %pow
1131    |=  [a=@ b=@]
1132    ?:  =(b 0)   1
1133    |-  ?:  =(b 1)   a
1134    =+  c=$(b (div b 2))
1135    =+  d=(mul c c)
1136    ?~  (dis b 1)  d  (mul d a)
1137  ::
1138  ++  sqt                                             ::  unsigned sqrt/rem
1139    ~/  %sqt
1140    |=  a=@   ^-  [p=@ q=@]
1141    ?~  a  [0 0]
1142    =+  [q=(div (dec (xeb a)) 2) r=0]
1143    =-  [-.b (sub a +.b)]
1144    ^=  b  |-
1145    =+  s=(add r (bex q))
1146    =+  t=(mul s s)
1147    ?:  =(q 0)
1148      ?:((lte t a) [s t] [r (mul r r)])
1149    ?:  (lte t a)
1150      $(r s, q (dec q))
1151    $(q (dec q))
1152  ::
1153  ::      2h: set logic
1154  +|  %set-logic
1155  ::
1156  ++  in                                              ::  set engine
1157    ~/  %in
1158    =|  a=(tree)  ::  (set)
```

```
|@
++  all                                     ::  logical AND
  ~/  %all
  |*  b=$-(* ?)
  |-  ^-  ?
  ?~  a
    &
  ?&((b n.a) $(a l.a) $(a r.a))
::
++  any                                     ::  logical OR
  ~/  %any
  |*  b=$-(* ?)
  |-  ^-  ?
  ?~  a
    |
  ?|((b n.a) $(a l.a) $(a r.a))
::
++  apt                                     ::  check correctness
  =<  $
  ~/  %apt
  =|  [l=(unit) r=(unit)]
  |.  ^-  ?
  ?~  a  &
  ?&  ?~(l & &((gor n.a u.l) !=(n.a u.l)))
      ?~(r & &((gor u.r n.a) !=(u.r n.a)))
      ?~(l.a & ?&((mor n.a n.l.a) !=(n.a n.l.a) $(a l.a, l `n.a)))
      ?~(r.a & ?&((mor n.a n.r.a) !=(n.a n.r.a) $(a r.a, r `n.a)))
  ==
::
++  bif                                     ::  splits a by b
  ~/  %bif
  |*  b=*
  ^+  [l=a r=a]
  =<  +
  |-  ^+  a
  ?~  a
    [b ~ ~]
  ?:  =(b n.a)
    a
  ?:  (gor b n.a)
    =+  c=$(a l.a)
    ?>  ?=(^ c)
    c(r a(l r.c))
  =+  c=$(a r.a)
  ?>  ?=(^ c)
  c(l a(r l.c))
::
++  del                                     ::  b without any a
  ~/  %del
  |*  b=*
  |-  ^+  a
  ?~  a
    ~
  ?.  =(b n.a)
    ?:  (gor b n.a)
      a(l $(a l.a))
    a(r $(a r.a))
  |-  ^-  [$?(~ _a)]
```

```
1217      ?~  l.a  r.a
1218      ?~  r.a  l.a
1219      ?:  (mor n.l.a n.r.a)
1220        l.a(r $(l.a r.l.a))
1221      r.a(l $(r.a l.r.a))
1222    ::
1223    ++  dif                                       ::  difference
1224      ~/  %dif
1225      |*  b=_a
1226      |-  ^+  a
1227      ?~  b
1228        a
1229      =+  c=(bif n.b)
1230      ?>  ?=(^ c)
1231      =+  d=$(a l.c, b l.b)
1232      =+  e=$(a r.c, b r.b)
1233      |-  ^-  [$?(~ _a)]
1234      ?~  d  e
1235      ?~  e  d
1236      ?:  (mor n.d n.e)
1237        d(r $(d r.d))
1238      e(l $(e l.e))
1239    ::
1240    ++  dig                                       ::  axis of a in b
1241      |=  b=*
1242      =+  c=1
1243      |-  ^-  (unit @)
1244      ?~  a  ~
1245      ?:  =(b n.a)  [~ u=(peg c 2)]
1246      ?:  (gor b n.a)
1247        $(a l.a, c (peg c 6))
1248      $(a r.a, c (peg c 7))
1249    ::
1250    ++  gas                                       ::  concatenate
1251      ~/  %gas
1252      |=  b=(list _?>(?=(^ a) n.a))
1253      |-  ^+  a
1254      ?~  b
1255        a
1256      $(b t.b, a (put i.b))
1257    ::  +has: does :b exist in :a?
1258    ::
1259    ++  has
1260      ~/  %has
1261      |*  b=*
1262      ^-  ?
1263      ::    wrap extracted item type in a unit because bunting fails
1264      ::
1265      ::  If we used the real item type of _?^(a n.a !!) as the sample type,
1266      ::  then hoon would bunt it to create the default sample for the gate.
1267      ::
1268      ::  However, bunting that expression fails if :a is ~. If we wrap it
1269      ::  in a unit, the bunted unit doesn't include the bunted item type.
1270      ::
1271      ::  This way we can ensure type safety of :b without needing to perform
1272      ::  this failing bunt. It's a hack.
1273      ::
1274      %.  [~ b]
```

```
|=    b=(unit _?>(?=(^ a) n.a))
=>    .(b ?>(?=(^ b) u.b))
|-    ^-   ?
?~    a
      |
?:  =(b n.a)
    &
?:  (gor b n.a)
  $(a l.a)
$(a r.a)
::
++  int                                   ::  intersection
~/  %int
|*  b=_a
|-  ^+  a
?~  b
    ~
?~  a
    ~
?.  (mor n.a n.b)
  $(a b, b a)
?:  =(n.b n.a)
  a(l $(a l.a, b l.b), r $(a r.a, b r.b))
?:  (gor n.b n.a)
  %-  uni(a $(a l.a, r.b ~))  $(b r.b)
%-  uni(a $(a r.a, l.b ~))  $(b l.b)
::
++  put                                   ::  puts b in a, sorted
~/  %put
|*  b=*
|-  ^+  a
?~  a
  [b ~ ~]
?:  =(b n.a)
  a
?:  (gor b n.a)
  =+  c=$(a l.a)
  ?>  ?=(^ c)
  ?:  (mor n.a n.c)
    a(l c)
  c(r a(l r.c))
=+  c=$(a r.a)
?>  ?=(^ c)
?:  (mor n.a n.c)
  a(r c)
c(l a(r l.c))
::
++  rep                                   ::  reduce to product
~/  %rep
|*  b=_=>(~ |=([* *] +<+))
|-
?~  a  +<+.b
$(a r.a, +<+.b $(a l.a, +<+.b (b n.a +<+.b)))
::
++  run                                   ::  apply gate to values
~/  %run
|*  b=gate
=+  c=`(set _?>(?=(^ a) (b n.a)))`~
```

```
|-    ?~  a c
=.    c  (~(put in c) (b n.a))
=.    c  $(a l.a, c c)
$(a r.a, c c)
::
++  tap                                     ::  convert to list
=<  $
~/  %tap
=+  b=`(list _?>(?=(^ a) n.a))`~
|.  ^+  b
?~  a
  b
$(a r.a, b [n.a $(a l.a)])
::
++  uni                                     ::  union
~/  %uni
|*  b=_a
?:  =(a b)  a
|-  ^+  a
?~  b
  a
?~  a
  b
?:  =(n.b n.a)
  b(l $(a l.a, b l.b), r $(a r.a, b r.b))
?:  (mor n.a n.b)
  ?:  (gor n.b n.a)
    $(l.a $(a l.a, r.b ~), b r.b)
  $(r.a $(a r.a, l.b ~), b l.b)
?:  (gor n.a n.b)
  $(l.b $(b l.b, r.a ~), a r.a)
$(r.b $(b r.b, l.a ~), a l.a)
::
++  wyt                                     ::  size of set
=<  $
~%  %wyt  +  ~
|.  ^-  @
?~(a 0 +((add $(a l.a) $(a r.a))))
--
::
::    2i: map logic
+|  %map-logic
::
++  by                                      ::  map engine
~/  %by
=|  a=(tree (pair))  ::  (map)
|@
++  all                                     ::  logical AND
  ~/  %all
  |*  b=$-(* ?)
  |-  ^-  ?
  ?~  a
    &
  ?&((b q.n.a) $(a l.a) $(a r.a))
  ::
++  any                                     ::  logical OR
  ~/  %any
  |*  b=$-(* ?)
```

```
|-  ^-   ?
?~  a
   |
?|((b q.n.a) $(a l.a) $(a r.a))
::
++  bif                                ::  splits a by b
~/  %bif
|*  b=*
|-  ^+  [l=a r=a]
?~  a
  [~ ~]
?:  =(b p.n.a)
  +.a
?:  (gor b p.n.a)
  =+  d=$(a l.a)
  ?>  ?=(^ d)
  [l.d a(l r.d)]
=+  d=$(a r.a)
?>  ?=(^ d)
[a(r l.d) r.d]
::
++  del                                ::  delete at key b
~/  %del
|*  b=*
|-  ^+  a
?~  a
  ~
?.  =(b p.n.a)
  ?:  (gor b p.n.a)
    a(l $(a l.a))
  a(r $(a r.a))
|-  ^-  [$?(~ _a)]
?~  l.a  r.a
?~  r.a  l.a
?:  (mor p.n.l.a p.n.r.a)
  l.a(r $(l.a r.l.a))
r.a(l $(r.a l.r.a))
::
++  dif                                ::  difference
~/  %dif
|*  b=_a
|-  ^+  a
?~  b
  a
=+  c=(bif p.n.b)
?>  ?=(^ c)
=+  d=$(a l.c, b l.b)
=+  e=$(a r.c, b r.b)
|-  ^-  [$?(~ _a)]
?~  d  e
?~  e  d
?:  (mor p.n.d p.n.e)
  d(r $(d r.d))
e(l $(e l.e))
::
++  dig                                ::  axis of b key
|=  b=*
=+  c=1
```

```
1449      |-  ^-  (unit @)
1450      ?~  a   ~
1451      ?:  =(b p.n.a)  [~ u=(peg c 2)]
1452      ?:  (gor b p.n.a)
1453        $(a l.a, c (peg c 6))
1454      $(a r.a, c (peg c 7))
1455    ::
1456    ++  apt                                      ::  check correctness
1457      =<  $
1458      ~/  %apt
1459      =|  [l=(unit) r=(unit)]
1460      |.  ^-  ?
1461      ?~  a   &
1462      ?&  ?~(l & &((gor p.n.a u.l) !=(p.n.a u.l)))
1463          ?~(r & &((gor u.r p.n.a) !=(u.r p.n.a)))
1464          ?~  l.a   &
1465          &((mor p.n.a p.n.l.a) !=(p.n.a p.n.l.a) $(a l.a, l `p.n.a))
1466          ?~  r.a   &
1467          &((mor p.n.a p.n.r.a) !=(p.n.a p.n.r.a) $(a r.a, r `p.n.a))
1468      ==
1469    ::
1470    ++  gas                                       ::  concatenate
1471      ~/  %gas
1472      |*  b=(list [p=* q=*])
1473      =>  .(b `(list _?>(?=(^ a) n.a))`b)
1474      |-  ^+  a
1475      ?~  b
1476        a
1477      $(b t.b, a (put p.i.b q.i.b))
1478    ::
1479    ++  get                                       ::  grab value by key
1480      ~/  %get
1481      |*  b=*
1482      =>  .(b `_?>(?=(^ a) p.n.a)`b)
1483      |-  ^-  (unit _?>(?=(^ a) q.n.a))
1484      ?~  a
1485        ~
1486      ?:  =(b p.n.a)
1487        (some q.n.a)
1488      ?:  (gor b p.n.a)
1489        $(a l.a)
1490      $(a r.a)
1491    ::
1492    ++  got                                       ::  need value by key
1493      |*  b=*
1494      (need (get b))
1495    ::
1496    ++  gut                                       ::  fall value by key
1497      |*  [b=* c=*]
1498      (fall (get b) c)
1499    ::
1500    ++  has                                       ::  key existence check
1501      ~/  %has
1502      |*  b=*
1503      !=(~ (get b))
1504    ::
1505    ++  int                                       ::  intersection
1506      ~/  %int
```

```
|*  b=_a
|-  ^+  a
?~  b
  ~
?~  a
  ~
?:  (mor p.n.a p.n.b)
  ?:  =(p.n.b p.n.a)
    b(l $(a l.a, b l.b), r $(a r.a, b r.b))
  ?:  (gor p.n.b p.n.a)
    %-  uni(a $(a l.a, r.b ~))  $(b r.b)
  %-  uni(a $(a r.a, l.b ~))  $(b l.b)
?:  =(p.n.a p.n.b)
  b(l $(b l.b, a l.a), r $(b r.b, a r.a))
?:  (gor p.n.a p.n.b)
  %-  uni(a $(b l.b, r.a ~))  $(a r.a)
%-  uni(a $(b r.b, l.a ~))  $(a l.a)
::
++  jab
  ~/  %jab
  |*  [key=_?>(?=(^ a) p.n.a) fun=$-(_?>(?=(^ a) q.n.a) _?>(?=(^ a) q.n.a))]
  ^+  a
  ::
  ?~  a  !!
  ::
  ?:  =(key p.n.a)
    a(q.n (fun q.n.a))
  ::
  ?:  (gor key p.n.a)
    a(l $(a l.a))
  ::
  a(r $(a r.a))
::
++  mar                                       ::  add with validation
  |*  [b=* c=(unit *)]
  ?~  c
    (del b)
  (put b u.c)
::
++  put                                       ::  adds key-value pair
  ~/  %put
  |*  [b=* c=*]
  |-  ^+  a
  ?~  a
    [[b c] ~ ~]
  ?:  =(b p.n.a)
    ?:  =(c q.n.a)
      a
    a(n [b c])
  ?:  (gor b p.n.a)
    =+  d=$(a l.a)
    ?>  ?=(^ d)
    ?:  (mor p.n.a p.n.d)
      a(l d)
    d(r a(l r.d))
  =+  d=$(a r.a)
  ?>  ?=(^ d)
  ?:  (mor p.n.a p.n.d)
```

```
1565        a(r d)
1566      d(l a(r l.d))
1567    ::
1568    ++  rep                                      ::  reduce to product
1569      ~/  %rep
1570      |*  b=_=>(~ |=([* *] +<+))
1571      |-
1572      ?~  a  +<+.b
1573      $(a r.a, +<+.b $(a l.a, +<+.b (b n.a +<+.b)))
1574    ::
1575    ++  rib                                      ::  transform + product
1576      |*  [b=* c=gate]
1577      |-  ^+  [b a]
1578      ?~  a  [b ~]
1579      =+  d=(c n.a b)
1580      =.  n.a  +.d
1581      =+  e=$(a l.a, b -.d)
1582      =+  f=$(a r.a, b -.e)
1583      [-.f a(l +.e, r +.f)]
1584    ::
1585    ++  run                                      ::  apply gate to values
1586      ~/  %run
1587      |*  b=gate
1588      |-
1589      ?~  a  a
1590      [n=[p=p.n.a q=(b q.n.a)] l=$(a l.a) r=$(a r.a)]
1591    ::
1592    ++  tap                                      ::  listify pairs
1593      =<  $
1594      ~/  %tap
1595      =+  b=`(list _?>(?=(^ a) n.a))`~
1596      |.  ^+  b
1597      ?~  a
1598        b
1599      $(a r.a, b [n.a $(a l.a)])
1600    ::
1601    ++  uni                                      ::  union, merge
1602      ~/  %uni
1603      |*  b=_a
1604      |-  ^+  a
1605      ?~  b
1606        a
1607      ?~  a
1608        b
1609      ?:  =(p.n.b p.n.a)
1610        b(l $(a l.a, b l.b), r $(a r.a, b r.b))
1611      ?:  (mor p.n.a p.n.b)
1612        ?:  (gor p.n.b p.n.a)
1613          $(l.a $(a l.a, r.b ~), b r.b)
1614        $(r.a $(a r.a, l.b ~), b l.b)
1615      ?:  (gor p.n.a p.n.b)
1616        $(l.b $(b l.b, r.a ~), a r.a)
1617      $(r.b $(b r.b, l.a ~), a l.a)
1618    ::
1619    ++  uno                                      ::  general union
1620      |*  b=_a
1621      |*  meg=$-([* * *] *)
1622      |-  ^+  a
```

```
?~  b
  a
?~  a
  b
?:  =(p.n.b p.n.a)
  :+  [p.n.a `_?>(?=(^ a) q.n.a)`(meg p.n.a q.n.a q.n.b)]
    $(b l.b, a l.a)
  $(b r.b, a r.a)
?:  (mor p.n.a p.n.b)
  ?:  (gor p.n.b p.n.a)
    $(l.a $(a l.a, r.b ~), b r.b)
  $(r.a $(a r.a, l.b ~), b l.b)
?:  (gor p.n.a p.n.b)
  $(l.b $(b l.b, r.a ~), a r.a)
$(r.b $(b r.b, l.a ~), a l.a)
::
++  urn                                         ::  apply gate to nodes
  ~/  %urn
  |*  b=$-([* *] *)
  |-
  ?~  a  ~
  a(n n.a(q (b p.n.a q.n.a)), l $(a l.a), r $(a r.a))
::
++  wyt                                         ::  depth of map
  =<  $
  ~%  %wyt  +  ~
  |.  ^-  @
  ?~(a 0 +((add $(a l.a) $(a r.a))))
::
++  key                                         ::  set of keys
  =<  $
  ~/  %key
  =+  b=`(set _?>(?=(^ a) p.n.a))`~
  |.  ^+  b
  ?~  a  b
  $(a r.a, b $(a l.a, b (~(put in b) p.n.a)))
::
++  val                                         ::  list of vals
  =+  b=`(list _?>(?=(^ a) q.n.a))`~
  |-  ^+  b
  ?~  a  b
  $(a r.a, b [q.n.a $(a l.a)])
--
::
::    2j: jar and jug logic
+|  %jar-and-jug-logic
++  ja                                          ::  jar engine
  =|  a=(tree (pair * (list)))  ::  (jar)
  |@
  ++  get                                       ::  gets list by key
    |*  b=*
    =+  c=(~(get by a) b)
    ?~(c ~ u.c)
  ::
  ++  add                                       ::  adds key-list pair
    |*  [b=* c=*]
    =+  d=(get b)
    (~(put by a) b [c d])
```

```
1681      ::
1682      ++  zip                                          ::  listify jar
1683      =<  $
1684      ~/  %zip
1685      =+  b=`(list _?>(?=([[* ^] *] a) [p=p q=i.q]:n.a))`~
1686      |.  ^+  b
1687      ?~  a  b
1688      %=  $
1689        a  r.a
1690        b  |-  ^+  b
1691           ?~  q.n.a  ^$(a l.a)
1692           [[p i.q]:n.a $(q.n.a t.q.n.a)]
1693      ==
1694    --
1695  ++  ju                                            ::  jug engine
1696    =|  a=(tree (pair * (tree)))  ::  (jug)
1697    |@
1698    ++  del                                         ::  del key-set pair
1699    |*  [b=* c=*]
1700    ^+  a
1701    =+  d=(get b)
1702    =+  e=(~(del in d) c)
1703    ?~  e
1704      (~(del by a) b)
1705    (~(put by a) b e)
1706    ::
1707    ++  gas                                         ::  concatenate
1708    |*  b=(list [p=* q=*])
1709    =>  .(b `(list _?>(?=([[* ^] ^] a) [p=p q=n.q]:n.a))`b)
1710    |-  ^+  a
1711    ?~  b
1712      a
1713    $(b t.b, a (put p.i.b q.i.b))
1714    ::
1715    ++  get                                         ::  gets set by key
1716    |*  b=*
1717    =+  c=(~(get by a) b)
1718    ?~(c ~ u.c)
1719    ::
1720    ++  has                                         ::  existence check
1721    |*  [b=* c=*]
1722    ^-  ?
1723    (~(has in (get b)) c)
1724    ::
1725    ++  put                                         ::  add key-set pair
1726    |*  [b=* c=*]
1727    ^+  a
1728    =+  d=(get b)
1729    (~(put by a) b (~(put in d) c))
1730    --
1731  ::
1732  ::    2k: queue logic
1733  +|  %queue-logic
1734  ::
1735  ++  to                                            ::  queue engine
1736    =|  a=(tree)  ::  (qeu)
1737    |@
1738    ++  apt                                         ::  check correctness
```

```
|-  ^-  ?
?~  a  &
?&  ?~(l.a & ?&((mor n.a n.l.a) $(a l.a)))
    ?~(r.a & ?&((mor n.a n.r.a) $(a r.a)))
==
::
++  bal
  |-  ^+  a
  ?~  a  ~
  ?.  |(?=(~ l.a) (mor n.a n.l.a))
    $(a l.a(r $(a a(l r.l.a))))
  ?.  |(?=(~ r.a) (mor n.a n.r.a))
    $(a r.a(l $(a a(r l.r.a))))
  a
::
++  dep                                   ::  max depth of queue
  |-  ^-  @
  ?~  a  0
  +((max $(a l.a) $(a r.a)))
::
++  gas                                   ::  insert list to que
  |=  b=(list _?>(?=(^ a) n.a))
  |-  ^+  a
  ?~(b a $(b t.b, a (put i.b)))
::
++  get                                   ::  head-rest pair
  |-  ^+  ?>(?=(^ a) [p=n.a q=*(tree _n.a)])
  ?~  a
    !!
  ?~  r.a
    [n.a l.a]
  =+  b=$(a r.a)
  :-  p.b
  ?:  |(?=(~ q.b) (mor n.a n.q.b))
    a(r q.b)
  a(n n.q.b, l a(r l.q.b), r r.q.b)
::
++  nip                                   ::  removes root
  |-  ^+  a
  ?~  a  ~
  ?~  l.a  r.a
  ?~  r.a  l.a
  ?:  (mor n.l.a n.r.a)
    l.a(r $(l.a r.l.a))
  r.a(l $(r.a l.r.a))
::
++  nap                                   ::  removes root
  ?>  ?=(^ a)
  ?:  =(~ l.a)  r.a
  =+  b=get(a l.a)
  bal(n.a p.b, l.a q.b)
::
++  put                                   ::  insert new tail
  |*  b=*
  |-  ^+  a
  ?~  a
    [b ~ ~]
  bal(l.a $(a l.a))
```

```
1797      ::
1798      ++  run                                        :: apply gate to values
1799        |*  b=gate
1800        |-
1801        ?~  a  a
1802        [n=(b n.a) l=$(a l.a) r=$(a r.a)]
1803      ::
1804      ++  tap                                        :: adds list to end
1805        =+  b=`(list _?>(?=(^ a) n.a))`~
1806        |-  ^+  b
1807        =+  0                                        :: hack for jet match
1808        ?~  a
1809          b
1810        $(a r.a, b [n.a $(a l.a)])
1811      ::
1812      ++  top                                        :: produces head
1813        |-  ^-  (unit _?>(?=(^ a) n.a))
1814        ?~  a  ~
1815        ?~(r.a [~ n.a] $(a r.a))
1816      --
1817  ::
1818  ::    2l: container from container
1819  +|  %container-from-container
1820  ::
1821  ++  malt                                           :: map from list
1822    |*  a=(list)
1823    (molt `(list [p=_-<.a q=_->.a])`a)
1824  ::
1825  ++  molt                                           :: map from pair list
1826    |*  a=(list (pair))  ::  ^-  =,(i.-.a (map _p _q))
1827    (~(gas by `(tree [p=_p.i.-.a q=_q.i.-.a])`~) a)
1828  ::
1829  ++  silt                                           :: set from list
1830    |*  a=(list)  ::  ^-  (set _i.-.a)
1831    =+  b=*(tree _?>(?=(^ a) i.a))
1832    (~(gas in b) a)
1833  ::
1834  ::    2m: container from noun
1835  +|  %container-from-noun
1836  ::
1837  ++  ly                                             :: list from raw noun
1838    le:nl
1839  ::
1840  ++  my                                             :: map from raw noun
1841    my:nl
1842  ::
1843  ++  sy                                             :: set from raw noun
1844    si:nl
1845  ::
1846  ++  nl
1847    |%
1848    ::                                               ::
1849    ++  le                                           :: construct list
1850      |*  a=(list)
1851      ^+  =<  $
1852      |@  ++  $  ?:(*? ~ [i=(snag 0 a) t=$])
1853      --
1854      a
```

```
1855      ::                                        ::
1856      ++  my                                    ::  construct map
1857        |*  a=(list (pair))
1858        =>  .(a ^+((le a) a))
1859        (~(gas by `(map _p.i.-.a _q.i.-.a)`~) a)
1860      ::                                        ::
1861      ++  si                                    ::  construct set
1862        |*  a=(list)
1863        =>  .(a ^+((le a) a))
1864        (~(gas in `(set _i.-.a)`~) a)
1865      ::                                        ::
1866      ++  snag                                  ::  index
1867        |*  [a=@ b=(list)]
1868        ?~  b
1869          ~_  leaf+"snag-fail"
1870          !!
1871        ?:  =(0 a)  i.b
1872        $(b t.b, a (dec a))
1873      ::                                        ::
1874      ++  weld                                  ::  concatenate
1875        |*  [a=(list) b=(list)]
1876        =>  .(a ^+((le a) a), b ^+((le b) b))
1877        =+  42
1878        |-
1879        ?~  a  b
1880        [i=i.a t=$(a t.a)]
1881    --
1882  ::      2n: functional hacks
1883  +|  %functional-hacks
1884  ::
1885  ++  aftr  |*(a=$-(* *) |*(b=$-(* *) (pair b a)))   ::  pair after
1886  ++  cork  |*([a=$-(* *) b=$-(* *)] (corl b a))     ::  compose forward
1887  ++  corl                                           ::  compose backwards
1888    |*  [a=$-(* *) b=$-(* *)]
1889    =<  +:|.((a (b)))        ::  type check
1890    |*  c=_,.+<.b
1891    (a (b c))
1892  ::
1893  ++  cury                                           ::  curry left
1894    |*  [a=$-(^ *) b=*]
1895    |*  c=_,.+<+.a
1896    (a b c)
1897  ::
1898  ++  curr                                           ::  curry right
1899    |*  [a=$-(^ *) c=*]
1900    |*  b=_,.+<-.a
1901    (a b c)
1902  ::
1903  ++  fore  |*(a=$-(* *) |*(b=$-(* *) (pair a b)))   ::  pair before
1904  ::
1905  ++  head  |*(^ ,:+<-)                              ::  get head
1906  ++  same  |*(* +<)                                 ::  identity
1907  ::
1908  ++  succ  |=(@ +(+<))                              ::  successor
1909  ::
1910  ++  tail  |*(^ ,:+<+)                              ::  get tail
1911  ++  test  |=(^ =(+<- +<+))                         ::  equality
1912  ::
```

```
1913  ++  lead  |*(* |*(* [+>+< +<]))                    ::  put head
1914  ++  late  |*(* |*(* [+< +>+<]))                    ::  put tail
1915  ::
1916  ::    2o: containers
1917  +|  %containers
1918  ++  jar  |$  [key value]  (map key (list value))   ::  map of lists
1919  ++  jug  |$  [key value]  (map key (set value))     ::  map of sets
1920  ::
1921  ++  map
1922    |$  [key value]                                   ::  table
1923    $|  (tree (pair key value))
1924    |=(a=(tree (pair)) ?:(=(~ a) & ~(apt by a)))
1925  ::
1926  ++  qeu
1927    |$  [item]                                        ::  queue
1928    $|  (tree item)
1929    |=(a=(tree) ?:(=(~ a) & ~(apt to a)))
1930  ::
1931  ++  set
1932    |$  [item]                                        ::  set
1933    $|  (tree item)
1934    |=(a=(tree) ?:(=(~ a) & ~(apt in a)))
1935  ::
1936  ::    2p: serialization
1937  +|  %serialization
1938  ::
1939  ++  cue                                             ::  unpack
1940    ~/  %cue
1941    |=  a=@
1942    ^-  *
1943    =+  b=0
1944    =+  m=`(map @ *)`~
1945    =<  q
1946    |-  ^-  [p=@ q=* r=(map @ *)]
1947    ?:  =(0 (cut 0 [b 1] a))
1948      =+  c=(rub +(b) a)
1949      [+(p.c) q.c (~(put by m) b q.c)]
1950    =+  c=(add 2 b)
1951    ?:  =(0 (cut 0 [+(b) 1] a))
1952      =+  u=$(b c)
1953      =+  v=$(b (add p.u c), m r.u)
1954      =+  w=[q.u q.v]
1955      [(add 2 (add p.u p.v)) w (~(put by r.v) b w)]
1956    =+  d=(rub c a)
1957    [(add 2 p.d) (need (~(get by m) q.d)) m]
1958  ::
1959  ++  jam                                             ::  pack
1960    ~/  %jam
1961    |=  a=*
1962    ^-  @
1963    =+  b=0
1964    =+  m=`(map * @)`~
1965    =<  q
1966    |-  ^-  [p=@ q=@ r=(map * @)]
1967    =+  c=(~(get by m) a)
1968    ?~  c
1969      =>  .(m (~(put by m) a b))
1970      ?:  ?=(@ a)
```

```
=+  d=(mat a)
[(add 1 p.d) (lsh 0 q.d) m]
=>  .(b (add 2 b))
=+  d=$(a -.a)
=+  e=$(a +.a, b (add b p.d), m r.d)
[(add 2 (add p.d p.e)) (mix 1 (lsh [0 2] (cat 0 q.d q.e))) r.e]
?:  ?&(?=(@ a) (lte (met 0 a) (met 0 u.c)))
=+  d=(mat a)
[(add 1 p.d) (lsh 0 q.d) m]
=+  d=(mat u.c)
[(add 2 p.d) (mix 3 (lsh [0 2] q.d)) m]
::
++  mat                                         ::  length-encode
~/  %mat
|=  a=@
^-  [p=@ q=@]
?:  =(0 a)
  [1 1]
=+  b=(met 0 a)
=+  c=(met 0 b)
:-  (add (add c c) b)
(cat 0 (bex c) (mix (end [0 (dec c)] b) (lsh [0 (dec c)] a)))
::
++  rub                                         ::  length-decode
~/  %rub
|=  [a=@ b=@]
^-  [p=@ q=@]
=+  ^=  c
    =+  [c=0 m=(met 0 b)]
    |-  ?<  (gth c m)
    ?.  =(0 (cut 0 [(add a c) 1] b))
      c
    $(c +(c))
?:  =(0 c)
  [1 0]
=+  d=(add a +(c))
=+  e=(add (bex (dec c)) (cut 0 [d (dec c)] b))
[(add (add c c) e) (cut 0 [(add d (dec c)) e] b)]
::
++  fn  ::    float, infinity, or NaN
        ::
        ::    s=sign, e=exponent, a=arithmetic form
        ::    (-1)^s * a * 2^e
        $%  [%f s=? e=@s a=@u]
            [%i s=?]
            [%n ~]
        ==
::
++  dn  ::    decimal float, infinity, or NaN
        ::
        ::    (-1)^s * a * 10^e
        $%  [%d s=? e=@s a=@u]
            [%i s=?]
            [%n ~]
        ==
::
++  rn  ::    parsed decimal float
        ::
```

```
2029          $%  [%d a=? b=[c=@ [d=@ e=@] f=? i=@]]
2030              [%i a=?]
2031              [%n ~]
2032          ==
2033  ::
2034  ::    2q: molds and mold builders
2035  +|  %molds-and-mold-builders
2036  ::
2037  +$  axis  @                                       ::  tree address
2038  +$  bean  ?                                       ::  0=&=yes, 1=|=no
2039  +$  flag  ?
2040  +$  char  @t                                      ::  UTF8 byte
2041  +$  cord  @t                                      ::  UTF8, LSB first
2042  +$  byts  [wid=@ud dat=@]                         ::  bytes, MSB first
2043  +$  date  [[a=? y=@ud] m=@ud t=tarp]              ::  parsed date
2044  +$  knot  @ta                                     ::  ASCII text
2045  +$  noun  *                                       ::  any noun
2046  +$  path  (list knot)                             ::  like unix path
2047  +$  pith  (list iota)                             ::  typed urbit path
2048  +$  stud                                          ::  standard name
2049          $@  mark=@tas                             ::  auth=urbit
2050          $:  auth=@tas                             ::  standards authority
2051              type=path                             ::  standard label
2052          ==                                        ::
2053  +$  tang  (list tank)                             ::  bottom-first error
2054  ::                                                ::
2055  +$  iota                                          ::  typed path segment
2056    $~  [%n ~]
2057    $@  @tas
2058    $%  [%ub @ub]   [%uc @uc]   [%ud @ud]   [%ui @ui]
2059        [%ux @ux]   [%uv @uv]   [%uw @uw]
2060        [%sb @sb]   [%sc @sc]   [%sd @sd]   [%si @si]
2061        [%sx @sx]   [%sv @sv]   [%sw @sw]
2062        [%da @da]   [%dr @dr]
2063        [%f ?]      [%n ~]
2064        [%if @if]   [%is @is]
2065        [%t @t]     [%ta @ta]   ::   @tas
2066        [%p @p]     [%q @q]
2067        [%rs @rs]   [%rd @rd]   [%rh @rh]   [%rq @rq]
2068    ==
2069  ::
2070  ::  $tank: formatted print tree
2071  ::
2072  ::    just a cord, or
2073  ::    %leaf: just a tape
2074  ::    %palm: backstep list
2075  ::           flat-mid, open, flat-open, flat-close
2076  ::    %rose: flat list
2077  ::           flat-mid, open, close
2078  ::
2079  +$  tank
2080    $~  leaf/~
2081    $@  cord
2082    $%  [%leaf p=tape]
2083        [%palm p=(qual tape tape tape tape) q=(list tank)]
2084        [%rose p=(trel tape tape tape) q=(list tank)]
2085    ==
2086  ::
```

```
+$  tape  (list @tD)                                    ::  utf8 string as list
+$  tour  (list @c)                                     ::  utf32 clusters
+$  tarp  [d=@ud h=@ud m=@ud s=@ud f=(list @ux)]        ::  parsed time
+$  term  @tas                                          ::  ascii symbol
+$  wain  (list cord)                                   ::  text lines
+$  wall  (list tape)                                   ::  text lines
::
--  =>
::                                                      ::
~%  %tri  +
  ==
    %year  year
    %yore  yore
    %ob    ob
  ==
::    layer-3
::
|%
::    3a: signed and modular ints
+|  %signed-and-modular-ints
::
++  egcd                                                ::  schneier's egcd
  |=  [a=@ b=@]
  =+  si
  =+  [c=(sun a) d=(sun b)]
  =+  [u=[c=(sun 1) d=--0] v=[c=--0 d=(sun 1)]]
  |-  ^-  [d=@ u=@s v=@s]
  ?:  =(--0 c)
    [(abs d) d.u d.v]
  ::  ?>  ?&  =(c (sum (pro (sun a) c.u) (pro (sun b) c.v)))
  ::          =(d (sum (pro (sun a) d.u) (pro (sun b) d.v)))
  ::      ==
  =+  q=(fra d c)
  %=  $
    c  (dif d (pro q c))
    d  c
    u  [(dif d.u (pro q c.u)) c.u]
    v  [(dif d.v (pro q c.v)) c.v]
  ==
::
++  fo                                                  ::  modulo prime
  ^|
  |_  a=@
  ++  dif
    |=  [b=@ c=@]
    (sit (sub (add a b) (sit c)))
  ::
  ++  exp
    |=  [b=@ c=@]
    ?:  =(0 b)
      1
    =+  d=$(b (rsh 0 b))
    =+  e=(pro d d)
    ?:(=(0 (end 0 b)) e (pro c e))
  ::
  ++  fra
    |=  [b=@ c=@]
    (pro b (inv c))
```

```
2145      ::
2146      ++  inv
2147        |=  b=@
2148        =+  c=(dul:si u:(egcd b a) a)
2149        c
2150      ::
2151      ++  pro
2152        |=  [b=@ c=@]
2153        (sit (mul b c))
2154      ::
2155      ++  sit
2156        |=  b=@
2157        (mod b a)
2158      ::
2159      ++  sum
2160        |=  [b=@ c=@]
2161        (sit (add b c))
2162      --
2163  ::
2164  ++  si                                             ::  signed integer
2165      ^?
2166      |%
2167      ++  abs  |=(a=@s (add (end 0 a) (rsh 0 a)))     ::  absolute value
2168      ++  dif  |=  [a=@s b=@s]                        ::  subtraction
2169               (sum a (new !(syn b) (abs b)))
2170      ++  dul  |=  [a=@s b=@]                         ::  modulus
2171               =+(c=(old a) ?:(-.c (mod +.c b) (sub b +.c)))
2172      ++  fra  |=  [a=@s b=@s]                        ::  divide
2173               (new =(0 (mix (syn a) (syn b))) (div (abs a) (abs b)))
2174      ++  new  |=  [a=? b=@]                          ::  [sign value] to @s
2175               `@s`?:(a (mul 2 b) ?:(=(0 b) 0 +((mul 2 (dec b)))))
2176      ++  old  |=(a=@s [(syn a) (abs a)])             ::  [sign value]
2177      ++  pro  |=  [a=@s b=@s]                        ::  multiplication
2178               (new =(0 (mix (syn a) (syn b))) (mul (abs a) (abs b)))
2179      ++  rem  |=([a=@s b=@s] (dif a (pro b (fra a b))))  ::  remainder
2180      ++  sum  |=  [a=@s b=@s]                        ::  addition
2181               =+  [c=(old a) d=(old b)]
2182               ?:  -.c
2183                 ?:  -.d
2184                   (new & (add +.c +.d))
2185                 ?:  (gte +.c +.d)
2186                   (new & (sub +.c +.d))
2187                 (new | (sub +.d +.c))
2188               ?:  -.d
2189                 ?:  (gte +.c +.d)
2190                   (new | (sub +.c +.d))
2191                 (new & (sub +.d +.c))
2192               (new | (add +.c +.d))
2193      ++  sun  |=(a=@u (mul 2 a))                     ::  @u to @s
2194      ++  syn  |=(a=@s =(0 (end 0 a)))               ::  sign test
2195      ++  cmp  |=  [a=@s b=@s]                        ::  compare
2196               ^-  @s
2197               ?:  =(a b)
2198                 --0
2199               ?:  (syn a)
2200                 ?:  (syn b)
2201                   ?:  (gth a b)
2202                     --1
```

```
             -1
             --1
       ?:  (syn b)
          -1
       ?:  (gth a b)
           -1
           --1
    --
::
::     3b: floating point
+|  %floating-point
::
++  fl                                          :: arb. precision fp
  =/  [[p=@u v=@s w=@u] r=$?(%n %u %d %z %a) d=$?(%d %f %i)]
     [[113 -16.494 32.765] %n %d]
  ::  p=precision:    number of bits in arithmetic form; must be at least 2
  ::  v=min exponent: minimum value of e
  ::  w=width:        max - min value of e, 0 is fixed point
  ::  r=rounding mode: nearest (ties to even), up, down, to zero, away from zero
  ::  d=behavior:     return denormals, flush denormals to zero,
  ::                  infinite exponent range
  =>
    ~%  %cofl  +>  ~
    ::    cofl
    ::
    ::  internal functions; mostly operating on [e=@s a=@u], in other words
    ::  positive numbers. many of these error out if a=0.
    |%
    ++  rou
      |=  [a=[e=@s a=@u]]   ^-  fn   (rau a &)
    ::
    ++  rau
      |=  [a=[e=@s a=@u] t=?]   ^-  fn
      ?-  r
        %z  (lug %fl a t)  %d  (lug %fl a t)
        %a  (lug %ce a t)  %u  (lug %ce a t)
        %n  (lug %ne a t)
      ==
    ::
    ++  add                                     :: add; exact if e
      |=  [a=[e=@s a=@u] b=[e=@s a=@u] e=?]   ^-  fn
      =+  q=(dif:si e.a e.b)
      |-  ?.  (syn:si q)  $(b a, a b, q +(q))   :: a has larger exp
      ?:  e
        [%f & e.b (^add (lsh [0 (abs:si q)] a.a) a.b)]
      =+  [ma=(met 0 a.a) mb=(met 0 a.b)]
      =+  ^=  w  %+  dif:si  e.a  %-  sun:si     :: expanded exp of a
        ?:  (gth prc ma)  (^sub prc ma)  0
      =+  ^=  x  %+  sum:si  e.b  (sun:si mb)    :: highest exp for b
      ?:  =((cmp:si w x) --1)                    :: don't need to add
        ?-  r
          %z  (lug %fl a &)  %d  (lug %fl a &)
          %a  (lug %lg a &)  %u  (lug %lg a &)
          %n  (lug %na a &)
        ==
      (rou [e.b (^add (lsh [0 (abs:si q)] a.a) a.b)])
    ::
    ++  sub                                      :: subtract; exact if e
```

```
2261      |=  [a=[e=@s a=@u] b=[e=@s a=@u] e=?]   ^-  fn
2262      =+  q=(dif:si e.a e.b)
2263      |-  ?.  (syn:si q)
2264        (fli $(b a, a b, q +(q), r swr))
2265      =+  [ma=(met 0 a.a) mb=(met 0 a.b)]
2266      =+  ^=  w  %+  dif:si   e.a  %-  sun:si
2267        ?:  (gth prc ma)  (^sub prc ma)  0
2268      =+  ^=  x  %+  sum:si  e.b  (sun:si +(mb))
2269      ?:  &(!e =((cmp:si w x) --1))
2270        ?-  r
2271          %z  (lug %sm a &)  %d  (lug %sm a &)
2272          %a  (lug %ce a &)  %u  (lug %ce a &)
2273          %n  (lug %nt a &)
2274        ==
2275      =+  j=(lsh [0 (abs:si q)] a.a)
2276      |-  ?.  (gte j a.b)
2277        (fli $(a.b j, j a.b, r swr))
2278      =+  i=(^sub j a.b)
2279      ?~  i  [%f & zer]
2280      ?:  e  [%f & e.b i]  (rou [e.b i])
2281    ::
2282    ++  mul                                       ::  multiply
2283      |=  [a=[e=@s a=@u] b=[e=@s a=@u]]   ^-  fn
2284      (rou (sum:si e.a e.b) (^mul a.a a.b))
2285    ::
2286    ++  div                                       ::  divide
2287      |=  [a=[e=@s a=@u] b=[e=@s a=@u]]   ^-  fn
2288      =+  [ma=(met 0 a.a) mb=(met 0 a.b)]
2289      =+  v=(dif:si (sun:si ma) (sun:si +((^add mb prc))))
2290      =.  a  ?:  (syn:si v)  a
2291      a(e (sum:si v e.a), a (lsh [0 (abs:si v)] a.a))
2292      =+  [j=(dif:si e.a e.b) q=(dvr a.a a.b)]
2293      (rau [j p.q] =(q.q 0))
2294    ::
2295    ++  sqt                                       ::  square root
2296      |=  [a=[e=@s a=@u]]   ^-  fn
2297      =.  a
2298        =+  [w=(met 0 a.a) x=(^mul +(prc) 2)]
2299        =+  ?:((^lth w x) (^sub x w) 0)
2300        =+  ?:  =((dis - 1) (dis (abs:si e.a) 1))  -
2301          (^add - 1)
2302        a(e (dif:si e.a (sun:si -)), a (lsh [0 -] a.a))
2303      =+  [y=(^sqt a.a) z=(fra:si e.a --2)]
2304      (rau [z p.y] =(q.y 0))
2305    ::
2306    ++  lth                                       ::  less-than
2307      |=  [a=[e=@s a=@u] b=[e=@s a=@u]]   ^-  ?
2308      ?:  =(e.a e.b)  (^lth a.a a.b)
2309      =+  c=(cmp:si (ibl a) (ibl b))
2310      ?:  =(c -1)  &  ?:  =(c --1)  |
2311      ?:  =((cmp:si e.a e.b) -1)
2312        (^lth (rsh [0 (abs:si (dif:si e.a e.b))] a.a) a.b)
2313      (^lth (lsh [0 (abs:si (dif:si e.a e.b))] a.a) a.b)
2314    ::
2315    ++  equ                                       ::  equals
2316      |=  [a=[e=@s a=@u] b=[e=@s a=@u]]   ^-  ?
2317      ?.  =((ibl a) (ibl b))  |
2318      ?:  =((cmp:si e.a e.b) -1)
```

```
=((lsh [0 (abs:si (dif:si e.a e.b))] a.b) a.a)
=((lsh [0 (abs:si (dif:si e.a e.b))] a.a) a.b)
::
::    integer binary logarithm: 2^ibl(a) <= |a| < 2^(ibl(a)+1)
++  ibl
  |=  [a=[e=@s a=@u]]  ^-  @s
  (sum:si (sun:si (dec (met 0 a.a))) e.a)
::
::  +uni
::
::    change to a representation where a.a is odd
::    every fn has a unique representation of this kind
++  uni
  |=  [a=[e=@s a=@u]]
  |-  ?:  =((end 0 a.a) 1)  a
  $(a.a (rsh 0 a.a), e.a (sum:si e.a --1))
::
::  +xpd: expands to either full precision or to denormalized
++  xpd
  |=  [a=[e=@s a=@u]]
  =+  ma=(met 0 a.a)
  ?:  (gte ma prc)  a
  =+  ?:  =(den %i)  (^sub prc ma)
      =+  ^=  q
        =+  w=(dif:si e.a emn)
        ?:  (syn:si w)  (abs:si w)  0
      (min q (^sub prc ma))
  a(e (dif:si e.a (sun:si -)), a (lsh [0 -] a.a))
::
::  +lug: central rounding mechanism
::
::    can perform: floor, ceiling, smaller, larger,
::                 nearest (round ties to: even, away from 0, toward 0)
::    s is sticky bit: represents a value less than ulp(a) = 2^(e.a)
::
++  lug
  ~/  %lug
  |=  [t=$?(%fl %ce %sm %lg %ne %na %nt) a=[e=@s a=@u] s=?]  ^-  fn
  ?<  =(a.a 0)
  =-
    ?.  =(den %f)  -                            ::  flush denormals
    ?.  ?=([%f *] -)  -
    ?:  =((met 0 ->+>) prc)  -  [%f & zer]
  ::
  =+  m=(met 0 a.a)
  ?>  |(s (gth m prc))                          ::  require precision
  =+  ^=  q  %+  max
      ?:  (gth m prc)  (^sub m prc)  0          ::  reduce precision
    %-  abs:si  ?:  =(den %i)  --0              ::  enforce min. exp
    ?:  =((cmp:si e.a emn) -1)  (dif:si emn e.a)  --0
  =^  b  a  :-  (end [0 q] a.a)
  a(e (sum:si e.a (sun:si q)), a (rsh [0 q] a.a))
  ::
  ?~  a.a
    ?<  =(den %i)
    ?-  t
      %fl  [%f & zer]
      %sm  [%f & zer]
```

```
2377        %ce   [%f & spd]
2378        %lg   [%f & spd]
2379        %ne   ?:  s   [%f & ?:((lte b (bex (dec q))) zer spd)]
2380              [%f & ?:((^lth b (bex (dec q))) zer spd)]
2381        %nt   ?:  s   [%f & ?:((lte b (bex (dec q))) zer spd)]
2382              [%f & ?:((^lth b (bex (dec q))) zer spd)]
2383        %na   [%f & ?:((^lth b (bex (dec q))) zer spd)]
2384      ==
2385    ::
2386    =.  a  (xpd a)
2387    ::
2388    =.  a
2389      ?-  t
2390        %fl  a
2391        %lg  a(a +(a.a))
2392        %sm  ?.  &(=(b 0) s)  a
2393             ?:  &(=(e.a emn) !=(den %i))  a(a (dec a.a))
2394             =+  y=(dec (^mul a.a 2))
2395             ?.  (lte (met 0 y) prc)  a(a (dec a.a))
2396             [(dif:si e.a --1) y]
2397        %ce  ?:  &(=(b 0) s)  a  a(a +(a.a))
2398        %ne  ?~  b  a
2399             =+  y=(bex (dec q))
2400             ?:  &(=(b y) s)                          ::  round halfs to even
2401               ?~  (dis a.a 1)  a  a(a +(a.a))
2402             ?:  (^lth b y)  a  a(a +(a.a))
2403        %na  ?~  b  a
2404             =+  y=(bex (dec q))
2405             ?:  (^lth b y)  a  a(a +(a.a))
2406        %nt  ?~  b  a
2407             =+  y=(bex (dec q))
2408             ?:  =(b y)  ?:  s  a  a(a +(a.a))
2409             ?:  (^lth b y)  a  a(a +(a.a))
2410        ==
2411    ::
2412    =.  a  ?.  =((met 0 a.a) +(prc))  a
2413      a(a (rsh 0 a.a), e (sum:si e.a --1))
2414    ?~  a.a  [%f & zer]
2415    ::
2416    ?:  =(den %i)  [%f & a]
2417    ?:  =((cmp:si emx e.a) -1)  [%i &]  [%f & a]    ::  enforce max. exp
2418  ::
2419  ++  drg                                          ::  dragon4; get
2420    ~/  %drg                                        ::  printable decimal;
2421    |=  [a=[e=@s a=@u]]  ^-  [@s @u]                 ::  guaranteed accurate
2422    ?<  =(a.a 0)                                     ::  for rounded floats
2423    =.  a  (xpd a)
2424    =+  r=(lsh [0 ?:((syn:si e.a) (abs:si e.a) 0)] a.a)
2425    =+  s=(lsh [0 ?.((syn:si e.a) (abs:si e.a) 0)] 1)
2426    =+  mn=(lsh [0 ?:((syn:si e.a) (abs:si e.a) 0)] 1)
2427    =+  mp=mn
2428    =>  ?.
2429          ?&  =(a.a (bex (dec prc)))                 ::  if next smallest
2430              |(!=(e.a emn) =(den %i))               ::  float is half ULP,
2431          ==                                          ::  tighten lower bound
2432          .
2433      %=  .
2434        mp  (lsh 0 mp)
```

```
2435        r  (lsh 0 r)
2436        s  (lsh 0 s)
2437      ==
2438    =+  [k=--0 q=(^div (^add s 9) 10)]
2439    |-  ?:  (^lth r q)
2440      %=  $
2441      k  (dif:si k --1)
2442      r  (^mul r 10)
2443      mn  (^mul mn 10)
2444      mp  (^mul mp 10)
2445      ==
2446    |-  ?:  (gte (^add (^mul r 2) mp) (^mul s 2))
2447      $(s (^mul s 10), k (sum:si k --1))
2448    =+  [u=0 o=0]
2449    |-                                      ::  r/s+o = a*10^-k
2450    =+  v=(dvr (^mul r 10) s)
2451    =>  %=  .
2452      k  (dif:si k --1)
2453      u  p.v
2454      r  q.v
2455      mn  (^mul mn 10)
2456      mp  (^mul mp 10)
2457      ==
2458    =+  l=(^lth (^mul r 2) mn)              ::  in lower bound
2459    =+  ^=  h                               ::  in upper bound
2460      ?|  (^lth (^mul s 2) mp)
2461          (gth (^mul r 2) (^sub (^mul s 2) mp))
2462      ==
2463    ?:  &(!l !h)
2464      $(o (^add (^mul o 10) u))
2465    =+  q=&(h |(!l (gth (^mul r 2) s)))
2466    =.  o  (^add (^mul o 10) ?:(q +(u) u))
2467    [k o]
2468  ::
2469  ++  toj                                   ::  round to integer
2470    |=  [a=[e=@s a=@u]]  ^-  fn
2471    ?.  =((cmp:si e.a --0) -1)  [%f & a]
2472    =+  x=(abs:si e.a)
2473    =+  y=(rsh [0 x] a.a)
2474    ?:  |(=(r %d) =(r %z))  [%f & --0 y]
2475    =+  z=(end [0 x] a.a)
2476    ?:  |(=(r %u) =(r %a))  [%f & --0 ?~(z y +(y))]
2477    =+  i=(bex (dec x))
2478    ?:  &(=(z i) =((dis y 1) 0))  [%f & --0 y]
2479    ?:  (^lth z i)  [%f & --0 y]  [%f & --0 +(y)]
2480  ::
2481  ++  ned                                   ::  require ?=([%f *] a)
2482    |=  [a=fn]  ^-  [%f s=? e=@s a=@u]
2483    ?:  ?=([%f *] a)  a
2484    ~_  leaf+"need-float"
2485    !!
2486  ::
2487  ++  shf                                   ::  a * 2^b; no rounding
2488    |=  [a=fn b=@s]
2489    ?:  |(?=([%n *] a) ?=([%i *] a))  a
2490    a(e (sum:si e.a b))
2491  ::
2492  ++  fli                                    ::  flip sign
```

```
2493      |=  [a=fn]  ^-  fn
2494      ?-(-.a %f a(s !s.a), %i a(s !s.a), %n a)
2495    ::
2496    ++  swr  ?+(r r %d %u, %u %d)                ::  flipped rounding
2497    ++  prc  ?>((gth p 1) p)                     ::  force >= 2 precision
2498    ++  den  d                                   ::  denorm+flush+inf exp
2499    ++  emn  v                                   ::  minimum exponent
2500    ++  emx  (sum:si emn (sun:si w))             ::  maximum exponent
2501    ++  spd  [e=emn a=1]                         ::  smallest denormal
2502    ++  spn  [e=emn a=(bex (dec prc))]           ::  smallest normal
2503    ++  lfn  [e=emx a=(fil 0 prc 1)]             ::  largest
2504    ++  lfe  (sum:si emx (sun:si prc))           ::  2^lfe is > than all
2505    ++  zer  [e=--0 a=0]
2506    --
2507  |%
2508  ++  rou                                        ::  round
2509    |=  [a=fn]  ^-  fn
2510    ?.  ?=([%f *] a)  a
2511    ?~  a.a  [%f s.a zer]
2512    ?:  s.a  (^rou +>.a)
2513    =.(r swr (fli (^rou +>.a)))
2514  ::
2515  ++  syn                                        ::  get sign
2516    |=  [a=fn]  ^-  ?
2517    ?-(-.a %f s.a, %i s.a, %n &)
2518  ::
2519  ++  abs                                        ::  absolute value
2520    |=  [a=fn]  ^-  fn
2521    ?:  ?=([%f *] a)  [%f & e.a a.a]
2522    ?:  ?=([%i *] a)  [%i &]  [%n ~]
2523  ::
2524  ++  add                                        ::  add
2525    |=  [a=fn b=fn]  ^-  fn
2526    ?:  |(?=([%n *] a) ?=([%n *] b))  [%n ~]
2527    ?:  |(?=([%i *] a) ?=([%i *] b))
2528      ?:  &(?=([%i *] a) ?=([%i *] b))
2529        ?:  =(a b)  a  [%n ~]
2530      ?:  ?=([%i *] a)  a  b
2531    ?:  |(=(a.a 0) =(a.b 0))
2532      ?.  &(=(a.a 0) =(a.b 0))  %-  rou  ?-(a.a b a)
2533      [%f ?:(=(r %d) &(s.a s.b) |(s.a s.b)) zer]
2534    %-  |=  [a=fn]
2535        ?.  ?=([%f *] a)  a
2536        ?.  =(a.a 0)  a
2537        [%f !=(r %d) zer]
2538    ?:  =(s.a s.b)
2539      ?:  s.a  (^add +>.a +>.b |)
2540      =.(r swr (fli (^add +>.a +>.b |)))
2541    ?:  s.a  (^sub +>.a +>.b |)
2542    (^sub +>.b +>.a |)
2543  ::
2544  ++  ead                                        ::  exact add
2545    |=  [a=fn b=fn]  ^-  fn
2546    ?:  |(?=([%n *] a) ?=([%n *] b))  [%n ~]
2547    ?:  |(?=([%i *] a) ?=([%i *] b))
2548      ?:  &(?=([%i *] a) ?=([%i *] b))
2549        ?:  =(a b)  a  [%n ~]
2550      ?:  ?=([%i *] a)  a  b
```

```
2551      ?:  |(=(a.a 0) =(a.b 0))
2552        ?.  &(=(a.a 0) =(a.b 0))  ?~(a.a b a)
2553        [%f ?:(=(r %d) &(s.a s.b) |(s.a s.b)) zer]
2554      %-  |=  [a=fn]
2555        ?.  ?=([%f *] a)   a
2556        ?.  =(a.a 0)   a
2557        [%f !=(r %d) zer]
2558      ?:  =(s.a s.b)
2559        ?:  s.a  (^add +>.a +>.b &)
2560        (fli (^add +>.a +>.b &))
2561      ?:  s.a  (^sub +>.a +>.b &)
2562      (^sub +>.b +>.a &)
2563    ::
2564    ++  sub                                  ::  subtract
2565      |=  [a=fn b=fn]   ^-  fn  (add a (fli b))
2566    ::
2567    ++  mul                                  ::  multiply
2568      |=  [a=fn b=fn]   ^-  fn
2569      ?:  |(?=([%n *] a) ?=([%n *] b))  [%n ~]
2570      ?:  ?=([%i *] a)
2571        ?:  ?=([%i *] b)
2572        [%i =(s.a s.b)]
2573        ?:  =(a.b 0)  [%n ~]  [%i =(s.a s.b)]
2574      ?:  ?=([%i *] b)
2575        ?:  =(a.a 0)  [%n ~]  [%i =(s.a s.b)]
2576      ?:  |(=(a.a 0) =(a.b 0))  [%f =(s.a s.b) zer]
2577      ?:  =(s.a s.b)  (^mul +>.a +>.b)
2578      =.(r swr (fli (^mul +>.a +>.b)))
2579    ::
2580    ++  emu                                  ::  exact multiply
2581      |=  [a=fn b=fn]   ^-  fn
2582      ?:  |(?=([%n *] a) ?=([%n *] b))  [%n ~]
2583      ?:  ?=([%i *] a)
2584        ?:  ?=([%i *] b)
2585        [%i =(s.a s.b)]
2586        ?:  =(a.b 0)  [%n ~]  [%i =(s.a s.b)]
2587      ?:  ?=([%i *] b)
2588        ?:  =(a.a 0)  [%n ~]  [%i =(s.a s.b)]
2589      ?:  |(=(a.a 0) =(a.b 0))  [%f =(s.a s.b) zer]
2590      [%f =(s.a s.b) (sum:si e.a e.b) (^^mul a.a a.b)]
2591    ::
2592    ++  div                                  ::  divide
2593      |=  [a=fn b=fn]   ^-  fn
2594      ?:  |(?=([%n *] a) ?=([%n *] b))  [%n ~]
2595      ?:  ?=([%i *] a)
2596        ?:  ?=([%i *] b)  [%n ~]  [%i =(s.a s.b)]
2597      ?:  ?=([%i *] b)  [%f =(s.a s.b) zer]
2598      ?:  =(a.a 0)  ?:  =(a.b 0)  [%n ~]  [%f =(s.a s.b) zer]
2599      ?:  =(a.b 0)  [%i =(s.a s.b)]
2600      ?:  =(s.a s.b)  (^div +>.a +>.b)
2601      =.(r swr (fli (^div +>.a +>.b)))
2602    ::
2603    ++  fma                                  ::  fused multiply-add
2604      |=  [a=fn b=fn c=fn]   ^-  fn          ::  (a * b) + c
2605      (add (emu a b) c)
2606    ::
2607    ++  sqt                                  ::  square root
2608      |=  [a=fn]   ^-  fn
```

```
2609      ?:  ?=([%n *] a)  [%n ~]
2610      ?:  ?=([%i *] a)  ?:(s.a a [%n ~])
2611      ?~  a.a  [%f s.a zer]
2612      ?:  s.a  (^sqt +>.a)  [%n ~]
2613    ::
2614    ++  inv                                     ::  inverse
2615      |=  [a=fn]  ^-  fn
2616      (div [%f & --0 1] a)
2617    ::
2618    ++  sun                                     ::  uns integer to float
2619      |=  [a=@u]  ^-  fn
2620      (rou [%f & --0 a])
2621    ::
2622    ++  san                                     ::  sgn integer to float
2623      |=  [a=@s]  ^-  fn
2624      =+  b=(old:si a)
2625      (rou [%f -.b --0 +.b])
2626    ::
2627    ++  lth                                     ::  less-than
2628      ::     comparisons return ~ in the event of a NaN
2629      |=  [a=fn b=fn]  ^-  (unit ?)
2630      ?:  |(?=([%n *] a) ?=([%n *] b))  ~  :-  ~
2631      ?:  =(a b)  |
2632      ?:  ?=([%i *] a)  !s.a  ?:  ?=([%i *] b)  s.b
2633      ?:  |(=(a.a 0) =(a.b 0))
2634        ?:  &(=(a.a 0) =(a.b 0))  |
2635        ?:  =(a.a 0)  s.b  !s.a
2636      ?:  !=(s.a s.b)  s.b
2637      ?:  s.a  (^lth +>.a +>.b)  (^lth +>.b +>.a)
2638    ::
2639    ++  lte                                     ::  less-equal
2640      |=  [a=fn b=fn]  ^-  (unit ?)
2641      %+  bind  (lth b a)  |=  a=?  !a
2642    ::
2643    ++  equ                                     ::  equal
2644      |=  [a=fn b=fn]  ^-  (unit ?)
2645      ?:  |(?=([%n *] a) ?=([%n *] b))  ~  :-  ~
2646      ?:  =(a b)  &
2647      ?:  |(?=([%i *] a) ?=([%i *] b))  |
2648      ?:  |(=(a.a 0) =(a.b 0))
2649        ?:  &(=(a.a 0) =(a.b 0))  &  |
2650      ?:  |(=(e.a e.b) !=(s.a s.b))  |
2651      (^equ +>.a +>.b)
2652    ::
2653    ++  gte                                     ::  greater-equal
2654      |=  [a=fn b=fn]  ^-  (unit ?)  (lte b a)
2655    ::
2656    ++  gth                                     ::  greater-than
2657      |=  [a=fn b=fn]  ^-  (unit ?)  (lth b a)
2658    ::
2659    ++  drg                                     ::  float to decimal
2660      |=  [a=fn]  ^-  dn
2661      ?:  ?=([%n *] a)  [%n ~]
2662      ?:  ?=([%i *] a)  [%i s.a]
2663      ?~  a.a  [%d s.a --0 0]
2664      [%d s.a (^drg +>.a)]
2665    ::
2666    ++  grd                                     ::  decimal to float
```

```
      |=  [a=dn]  ^-  fn
      ?:  ?=([%n *] a)  [%n ~]
      ?:  ?=([%i *] a)  [%i s.a]
      =>  .(r %n)
      =+  q=(abs:si e.a)
      ?:  (syn:si e.a)
        (mul [%f s.a --0 a.a] [%f & e.a (pow 5 q)])
      (div [%f s.a --0 a.a] [%f & (sun:si q) (pow 5 q)])
    ::
    ++  toi                                     ::  round to integer @s
      |=  [a=fn]  ^-  (unit @s)
      =+  b=(toj a)
      ?.  ?=([%f *] b)  ~  :-  ~
      =+  c=(^^mul (bex (abs:si e.b)) a.b)
      (new:si s.b c)
    ::
    ++  toj                                     ::  round to integer fn
      |=  [a=fn]  ^-  fn
      ?.  ?=([%f *] a)  a
      ?~  a.a  [%f s.a zer]
      ?:  s.a  (^toj +>.a)
      =.(r swr (fli (^toj +>.a)))
    --
::      +ff
::
::  this core has no use outside of the functionality
::  provided to ++rd, ++rs, ++rq, and ++rh
::
::  w=width:        bits in exponent field
::  p=precision:    bits in fraction field
::  b=bias:         added to exponent when storing
::  r=rounding mode: same as in ++fl
++  ff                                          ::  ieee 754 format fp
  |_  [[w=@u p=@u b=@s] r=$?(%n %u %d %z %a)]
  ::
  ++  sb  (bex (^add w p))                       ::  sign bit
  ++  me  (dif:si (dif:si --1 b) (sun:si p))     ::  minimum exponent
  ::
  ++  pa
    %*(. fl p +(p), v me, w (^sub (bex w) 3), d %d, r r)
  ::
  ++  sea                                        ::  @r to fn
    |=  [a=@r]  ^-  fn
    =+  [f=(cut 0 [0 p] a) e=(cut 0 [p w] a)]
    =+  s=(sig a)
    ?:  =(e 0)
      ?:  =(f 0)  [%f s --0 0]  [%f s me f]
    ?:  =(e (fil 0 w 1))
      ?:  =(f 0)  [%i s]  [%n ~]
    =+  q=:(sum:si (sun:si e) me -1)
    =+  r=(^add f (bex p))
    [%f s q r]
  ::
  ++  bit  |=  [a=fn]  (bif (rou:pa a))          ::  fn to @r w+ rounding
  ::
  ++  bif                                        ::  fn to @r no rounding
    |=  [a=fn]  ^-  @r
    ?:  ?=([%i *] a)
```

```
2725        =+  q=(lsh [0 p] (fil 0 w 1))
2726        ?:  s.a  q  (^add q sb)
2727      ?:  ?=([%n *] a)  (lsh [0 (dec p)] (fil 0 +(w) 1))
2728      ?~  a.a  ?:  s.a  `@r`0  sb
2729      =+  ma=(met 0 a.a)
2730      ?.  =(ma +(p))
2731        ?>  =(e.a me)
2732        ?>  (^lth ma +(p))
2733        ?:  s.a  `@r`a.a  (^add a.a sb)
2734      =+  q=(sum:si (dif:si e.a me) --1)
2735      =+  r=(^add (lsh [0 p] (abs:si q)) (end [0 p] a.a))
2736      ?:  s.a  r  (^add r sb)
2737    ::
2738    ++  sig                                    ::  get sign
2739      |=  [a=@r]  ^-  ?
2740      =(0 (cut 0 [(^add p w) 1] a))
2741    ::
2742    ++  exp                                    ::  get exponent
2743      |=  [a=@r]  ^-  @s
2744      (dif:si (sun:si (cut 0 [p w] a)) b)
2745    ::
2746    ++  add                                    ::  add
2747      |=  [a=@r b=@r]
2748      (bif (add:pa (sea a) (sea b)))
2749    ::
2750    ++  sub                                    ::  subtract
2751      |=  [a=@r b=@r]
2752      (bif (sub:pa (sea a) (sea b)))
2753    ::
2754    ++  mul                                    ::  multiply
2755      |=  [a=@r b=@r]
2756      (bif (mul:pa (sea a) (sea b)))
2757    ::
2758    ++  div                                    ::  divide
2759      |=  [a=@r b=@r]
2760      (bif (div:pa (sea a) (sea b)))
2761    ::
2762    ++  fma                                    ::  fused multiply-add
2763      |=  [a=@r b=@r c=@r]
2764      (bif (fma:pa (sea a) (sea b) (sea c)))
2765    ::
2766    ++  sqt                                    ::  square root
2767      |=  [a=@r]
2768      (bif (sqt:pa (sea a)))
2769    ::
2770    ++  lth                                    ::  less-than
2771      |=  [a=@r b=@r]  (fall (lth:pa (sea a) (sea b)) |)
2772    ++  lte                                    ::  less-equals
2773      |=  [a=@r b=@r]  (fall (lte:pa (sea a) (sea b)) |)
2774    ++  equ                                    ::  equals
2775      |=  [a=@r b=@r]  (fall (equ:pa (sea a) (sea b)) |)
2776    ++  gte                                    ::  greater-equals
2777      |=  [a=@r b=@r]  (fall (gte:pa (sea a) (sea b)) |)
2778    ++  gth                                    ::  greater-than
2779      |=  [a=@r b=@r]  (fall (gth:pa (sea a) (sea b)) |)
2780    ++  sun                                    ::  uns integer to @r
2781      |=  [a=@u]  (bit [%f & --0 a])
2782    ++  san                                    ::  signed integer to @r
```

```
2783      |=  [a=@s]  (bit [%f (syn:si a) --0 (abs:si a)])
2784  ++  toi                                              ::  round to integer
2785      |=  [a=@r]  (toi:pa (sea a))
2786  ++  drg                                              ::  @r to decimal float
2787      |=  [a=@r]  (drg:pa (sea a))
2788  ++  grd                                              ::  decimal float to @r
2789      |=  [a=dn]  (bif (grd:pa a))
2790      --
2791  ::
2792  ++  rlyd  |=  a=@rd  ^-  dn  (drg:rd a)              ::  prep @rd for print
2793  ++  rlys  |=  a=@rs  ^-  dn  (drg:rs a)              ::  prep @rs for print
2794  ++  rlyh  |=  a=@rh  ^-  dn  (drg:rh a)              ::  prep @rh for print
2795  ++  rlyq  |=  a=@rq  ^-  dn  (drg:rq a)              ::  prep @rq for print
2796  ++  ryld  |=  a=dn  ^-  @rd  (grd:rd a)              ::  finish parsing @rd
2797  ++  ryls  |=  a=dn  ^-  @rs  (grd:rs a)              ::  finish parsing @rs
2798  ++  rylh  |=  a=dn  ^-  @rh  (grd:rh a)              ::  finish parsing @rh
2799  ++  rylq  |=  a=dn  ^-  @rq  (grd:rq a)              ::  finish parsing @rq
2800  ::
2801  ++  rd                                               ::  double precision fp
2802      ^|
2803      ~%  %rd  +>  ~
2804      |_  r=$?(%n %u %d %z)
2805      ::  round to nearest, round up, round down, round to zero
2806      ::
2807  ++  ma
2808      %*(. ff w 11, p 52, b --1.023, r r)
2809      ::
2810  ++  sea                                              ::  @rd to fn
2811      |=  [a=@rd]  (sea:ma a)
2812      ::
2813  ++  bit                                              ::  fn to @rd
2814      |=  [a=fn]  ^-  @rd  (bit:ma a)
2815      ::
2816  ++  add  ~/  %add                                    ::  add
2817      |=  [a=@rd b=@rd]  ^-  @rd
2818      ~_  leaf+"rd-fail"
2819      (add:ma a b)
2820      ::
2821  ++  sub  ~/  %sub                                    ::  subtract
2822      |=  [a=@rd b=@rd]  ^-  @rd
2823      ~_  leaf+"rd-fail"
2824      (sub:ma a b)
2825      ::
2826  ++  mul  ~/  %mul                                    ::  multiply
2827      |=  [a=@rd b=@rd]  ^-  @rd
2828      ~_  leaf+"rd-fail"
2829      (mul:ma a b)
2830      ::
2831  ++  div  ~/  %div                                    ::  divide
2832      |=  [a=@rd b=@rd]  ^-  @rd
2833      ~_  leaf+"rd-fail"
2834      (div:ma a b)
2835      ::
2836  ++  fma  ~/  %fma                                    ::  fused multiply-add
2837      |=  [a=@rd b=@rd c=@rd]  ^-  @rd
2838      ~_  leaf+"rd-fail"
2839      (fma:ma a b c)
2840      ::
```

```
2841    ++  sqt  ~/  %sqt                                        ::  square root
2842      |=  [a=@rd]  ^-  @rd  ~_  leaf+"rd-fail"
2843      (sqt:ma a)
2844    ::
2845    ++  lth  ~/  %lth                                        ::  less-than
2846      |=  [a=@rd b=@rd]
2847      ~_  leaf+"rd-fail"
2848      (lth:ma a b)
2849    ::
2850    ++  lte  ~/  %lte                                        ::  less-equals
2851      |=  [a=@rd b=@rd]
2852      ~_  leaf+"rd-fail"
2853      (lte:ma a b)
2854    ::
2855    ++  equ  ~/  %equ                                        ::  equals
2856      |=  [a=@rd b=@rd]
2857      ~_  leaf+"rd-fail"
2858      (equ:ma a b)
2859    ::
2860    ++  gte  ~/  %gte                                        ::  greater-equals
2861      |=  [a=@rd b=@rd]
2862      ~_  leaf+"rd-fail"
2863      (gte:ma a b)
2864    ::
2865    ++  gth  ~/  %gth                                        ::  greater-than
2866      |=  [a=@rd b=@rd]
2867      ~_  leaf+"rd-fail"
2868      (gth:ma a b)
2869    ::
2870    ++  sun  |=  [a=@u]    ^-  @rd  (sun:ma a)               ::  uns integer to @rd
2871    ++  san  |=  [a=@s]    ^-  @rd  (san:ma a)               ::  sgn integer to @rd
2872    ++  sig  |=  [a=@rd]   ^-  ?  (sig:ma a)                 ::  get sign
2873    ++  exp  |=  [a=@rd]   ^-  @s  (exp:ma a)                ::  get exponent
2874    ++  toi  |=  [a=@rd]   ^-  (unit @s)  (toi:ma a)         ::  round to integer
2875    ++  drg  |=  [a=@rd]   ^-  dn  (drg:ma a)                ::  @rd to decimal float
2876    ++  grd  |=  [a=dn]    ^-  @rd  (grd:ma a)               ::  decimal float to @rd
2877    --
2878  ::
2879  ++  rs                                                     ::  single precision fp
2880    ~%  %rs  +>  ~
2881    ^|
2882    ::    round to nearest, round up, round down, round to zero
2883    |_  r=$?(%n %u %d %z)
2884    ::
2885    ++  ma
2886      %*(. ff w 8, p 23, b --127, r r)
2887    ::
2888    ++  sea                                                  ::  @rs to fn
2889      |=  [a=@rs]  (sea:ma a)
2890    ::
2891    ++  bit                                                  ::  fn to @rs
2892      |=  [a=fn]  ^-  @rs  (bit:ma a)
2893    ::
2894    ++  add  ~/  %add                                        ::  add
2895      |=  [a=@rs b=@rs]  ^-  @rs
2896      ~_  leaf+"rs-fail"
2897      (add:ma a b)
2898    ::
```

```
++  sub  ~/  %sub                                      ::  subtract
  |=  [a=@rs b=@rs]  ^-  @rs
  ~_  leaf+"rs-fail"
  (sub:ma a b)
::
++  mul  ~/  %mul                                      ::  multiply
  |=  [a=@rs b=@rs]  ^-  @rs
  ~_  leaf+"rs-fail"
  (mul:ma a b)
::
++  div  ~/  %div                                      ::  divide
  |=  [a=@rs b=@rs]  ^-  @rs
  ~_  leaf+"rs-fail"
  (div:ma a b)
::
++  fma  ~/  %fma                                      ::  fused multiply-add
  |=  [a=@rs b=@rs c=@rs]  ^-  @rs
  ~_  leaf+"rs-fail"
  (fma:ma a b c)
::
++  sqt  ~/  %sqt                                      ::  square root
  |=  [a=@rs]  ^-  @rs
  ~_  leaf+"rs-fail"
  (sqt:ma a)
::
++  lth  ~/  %lth                                      ::  less-than
  |=  [a=@rs b=@rs]
  ~_  leaf+"rs-fail"
  (lth:ma a b)
::
++  lte  ~/  %lte                                      ::  less-equals
  |=  [a=@rs b=@rs]
  ~_  leaf+"rs-fail"
  (lte:ma a b)
::
++  equ  ~/  %equ                                      ::  equals
  |=  [a=@rs b=@rs]
  ~_  leaf+"rs-fail"
  (equ:ma a b)
::
++  gte  ~/  %gte                                      ::  greater-equals
  |=  [a=@rs b=@rs]
  ~_  leaf+"rs-fail"
  (gte:ma a b)
::
++  gth  ~/  %gth                                      ::  greater-than
  |=  [a=@rs b=@rs]
  ~_  leaf+"rs-fail"
  (gth:ma a b)
::
++  sun  |=  [a=@u]  ^-  @rs  (sun:ma a)               ::  uns integer to @rs
++  san  |=  [a=@s]  ^-  @rs  (san:ma a)               ::  sgn integer to @rs
++  sig  |=  [a=@rs]  ^-  ?  (sig:ma a)                ::  get sign
++  exp  |=  [a=@rs]  ^-  @s  (exp:ma a)               ::  get exponent
++  toi  |=  [a=@rs]  ^-  (unit @s)  (toi:ma a)        ::  round to integer
++  drg  |=  [a=@rs]  ^-  dn  (drg:ma a)               ::  @rs to decimal float
++  grd  |=  [a=dn]  ^-  @rs  (grd:ma a)               ::  decimal float to @rs
--
```

```
2957  ::
2958  ++  rq                                              ::  quad precision fp
2959    ~%  %rq  +>  ~
2960    ^|
2961    ::    round to nearest, round up, round down, round to zero
2962    |_  r=$?(%n %u %d %z)
2963    ::
2964    ++  ma
2965      %*(. ff w 15, p 112, b --16.383, r r)
2966    ::
2967    ++  sea                                           ::  @rq to fn
2968      |=  [a=@rq]  (sea:ma a)
2969    ::
2970    ++  bit                                           ::  fn to @rq
2971      |=  [a=fn]  ^-  @rq  (bit:ma a)
2972    ::
2973    ++  add  ~/  %add                                 ::  add
2974      |=  [a=@rq b=@rq]  ^-  @rq
2975      ~_  leaf+"rq-fail"
2976      (add:ma a b)
2977    ::
2978    ++  sub  ~/  %sub                                 ::  subtract
2979      |=  [a=@rq b=@rq]  ^-  @rq
2980      ~_  leaf+"rq-fail"
2981      (sub:ma a b)
2982    ::
2983    ++  mul  ~/  %mul                                 ::  multiply
2984      |=  [a=@rq b=@rq]  ^-  @rq
2985      ~_  leaf+"rq-fail"
2986      (mul:ma a b)
2987    ::
2988    ++  div  ~/  %div                                 ::  divide
2989      |=  [a=@rq b=@rq]  ^-  @rq
2990      ~_  leaf+"rq-fail"
2991      (div:ma a b)
2992    ::
2993    ++  fma  ~/  %fma                                 ::  fused multiply-add
2994      |=  [a=@rq b=@rq c=@rq]  ^-  @rq
2995      ~_  leaf+"rq-fail"
2996      (fma:ma a b c)
2997    ::
2998    ++  sqt  ~/  %sqt                                 ::  square root
2999      |=  [a=@rq]  ^-  @rq
3000      ~_  leaf+"rq-fail"
3001      (sqt:ma a)
3002    ::
3003    ++  lth  ~/  %lth                                 ::  less-than
3004      |=  [a=@rq b=@rq]
3005      ~_  leaf+"rq-fail"
3006      (lth:ma a b)
3007    ::
3008    ++  lte  ~/  %lte                                 ::  less-equals
3009      |=  [a=@rq b=@rq]
3010      ~_  leaf+"rq-fail"
3011      (lte:ma a b)
3012    ::
3013    ++  equ  ~/  %equ                                 ::  equals
3014      |=  [a=@rq b=@rq]
```

```
3015        ~_  leaf+"rq-fail"
3016      (equ:ma a b)
3017    ::
3018    ++  gte  ~/  %gte                                    ::  greater-equals
3019      |=  [a=@rq b=@rq]
3020        ~_  leaf+"rq-fail"
3021      (gte:ma a b)
3022    ::
3023    ++  gth  ~/  %gth                                    ::  greater-than
3024      |=  [a=@rq b=@rq]
3025        ~_  leaf+"rq-fail"
3026      (gth:ma a b)
3027    ::
3028    ++  sun  |=  [a=@u]   ^-  @rq  (sun:ma a)            ::  uns integer to @rq
3029    ++  san  |=  [a=@s]   ^-  @rq  (san:ma a)            ::  sgn integer to @rq
3030    ++  sig  |=  [a=@rq]  ^-  ?  (sig:ma a)              ::  get sign
3031    ++  exp  |=  [a=@rq]  ^-  @s  (exp:ma a)             ::  get exponent
3032    ++  toi  |=  [a=@rq]  ^-  (unit @s)  (toi:ma a)      ::  round to integer
3033    ++  drg  |=  [a=@rq]  ^-  dn  (drg:ma a)             ::  @rq to decimal float
3034    ++  grd  |=  [a=dn]   ^-  @rq  (grd:ma a)            ::  decimal float to @rq
3035    --
3036  ::
3037  ++  rh                                                 ::  half precision fp
3038    ~%  %rh  +>  ~
3039    ^|
3040    ::    round to nearest, round up, round down, round to zero
3041    |_  r=$?(%n %u %d %z)
3042    ::
3043    ++  ma
3044      %*(. ff w 5, p 10, b --15, r r)
3045    ::
3046    ++  sea                                              ::  @rh to fn
3047      |=  [a=@rh]  (sea:ma a)
3048    ::
3049    ++  bit                                              ::  fn to @rh
3050      |=  [a=fn]   ^-  @rh  (bit:ma a)
3051    ::
3052    ++  add  ~/  %add                                    ::  add
3053      |=  [a=@rh b=@rh]  ^-  @rh
3054        ~_  leaf+"rh-fail"
3055      (add:ma a b)
3056    ::
3057    ++  sub  ~/  %sub                                    ::  subtract
3058      |=  [a=@rh b=@rh]  ^-  @rh
3059        ~_  leaf+"rh-fail"
3060      (sub:ma a b)
3061    ::
3062    ++  mul  ~/  %mul                                    ::  multiply
3063      |=  [a=@rh b=@rh]  ^-  @rh
3064        ~_  leaf+"rh-fail"
3065      (mul:ma a b)
3066    ::
3067    ++  div  ~/  %div                                    ::  divide
3068      |=  [a=@rh b=@rh]  ^-  @rh
3069        ~_  leaf+"rh-fail"
3070      (div:ma a b)
3071    ::
3072    ++  fma  ~/  %fma                                    ::  fused multiply-add
```

```
3073      |=  [a=@rh b=@rh c=@rh]  ^-  @rh
3074      ~_  leaf+"rh-fail"
3075      (fma:ma a b c)
3076    ::
3077    ++  sqt  ~/  %sqt                              ::  square root
3078      |=  [a=@rh]  ^-  @rh
3079      ~_  leaf+"rh-fail"
3080      (sqt:ma a)
3081    ::
3082    ++  lth  ~/  %lth                              ::  less-than
3083      |=  [a=@rh b=@rh]
3084      ~_  leaf+"rh-fail"
3085      (lth:ma a b)
3086    ::
3087    ++  lte  ~/  %lte                              ::  less-equals
3088      |=  [a=@rh b=@rh]
3089      ~_  leaf+"rh-fail"
3090      (lte:ma a b)
3091    ::
3092    ++  equ  ~/  %equ                              ::  equals
3093      |=  [a=@rh b=@rh]
3094      ~_  leaf+"rh-fail"
3095      (equ:ma a b)
3096    ::
3097    ++  gte  ~/  %gte                              ::  greater-equals
3098      |=  [a=@rh b=@rh]
3099      ~_  leaf+"rh-fail"
3100      (gte:ma a b)
3101    ::
3102    ++  gth  ~/  %gth                              ::  greater-than
3103      |=  [a=@rh b=@rh]
3104      ~_  leaf+"rh-fail"
3105      (gth:ma a b)
3106    ::
3107    ++  tos                                        ::  @rh to @rs
3108      |=  [a=@rh]  (bit:rs (sea a))
3109    ::
3110    ++  fos                                        ::  @rs to @rh
3111      |=  [a=@rs]  (bit (sea:rs a))
3112    ::
3113    ++  sun  |=  [a=@u]   ^-  @rh  (sun:ma a)       ::  uns integer to @rh
3114    ++  san  |=  [a=@s]   ^-  @rh  (san:ma a)       ::  sgn integer to @rh
3115    ++  sig  |=  [a=@rh]  ^-  ?  (sig:ma a)         ::  get sign
3116    ++  exp  |=  [a=@rh]  ^-  @s  (exp:ma a)        ::  get exponent
3117    ++  toi  |=  [a=@rh]  ^-  (unit @s)  (toi:ma a) ::  round to integer
3118    ++  drg  |=  [a=@rh]  ^-  dn  (drg:ma a)        ::  @rh to decimal float
3119    ++  grd  |=  [a=dn]   ^-  @rh  (grd:ma a)       ::  decimal float to @rh
3120    --
3121  ::
3122  ::    3c: urbit time
3123  +|  %urbit-time
3124  ::
3125  ++  year                                         ::  date to @d
3126    |=  det=date
3127    ^-  @da
3128    =+  ^=  yer
3129      ?:  a.det
3130        (add 292.277.024.400 y.det)
```

```
    (sub 292.277.024.400 (dec y.det))
=+  day=(yawn yer m.det d.t.det)
(yule day h.t.det m.t.det s.t.det f.t.det)
::
++  yore                                          ::  @d to date
  |=  now=@da
  ^-  date
  =+  rip=(yell now)
  =+  ger=(yall d.rip)
  :-  ?:  (gth y.ger 292.277.024.400)
        [a=& y=(sub y.ger 292.277.024.400)]
      [a=| y=+((sub 292.277.024.400 y.ger))]
  [m.ger d.ger h.rip m.rip s.rip f.rip]
::
++  yell                                          ::  tarp from @d
  |=  now=@d
  ^-  tarp
  =+  sec=(rsh 6 now)
  =+  ^=  fan
    =+  [muc=4 raw=(end 6 now)]
    |-  ^-  (list @ux)
    ?:  |(=(0 raw) =(0 muc))
        ~
    =>  .(muc (dec muc))
    [(cut 4 [muc 1] raw) $(raw (end [4 muc] raw))]
  =+  day=(div sec day:yo)
  =>  .(sec (mod sec day:yo))
  =+  hor=(div sec hor:yo)
  =>  .(sec (mod sec hor:yo))
  =+  mit=(div sec mit:yo)
  =>  .(sec (mod sec mit:yo))
  [day hor mit sec fan]
::
++  yule                                          ::  time atom
  |=  rip=tarp
  ^-  @d
  =+  ^=  sec   ;:  add
                  (mul d.rip day:yo)
                  (mul h.rip hor:yo)
                  (mul m.rip mit:yo)
                    s.rip
                ==
  =+  ^=  fac   =+  muc=4
                |-  ^-  @
                ?~  f.rip
                    0
                =>  .(muc (dec muc))
                (add (lsh [4 muc] i.f.rip) $(f.rip t.f.rip))
  (con (lsh 6 sec) fac)
::
++  yall                                          ::  day / to day of year
  |=  day=@ud
  ^-  [y=@ud m=@ud d=@ud]
  =+  [era=0 cet=0 lep=*?]
  =>  .(era (div day era:yo), day (mod day era:yo))
  =>  ^+  .
    ?:  (lth day +(cet:yo))
      .(lep &, cet 0)
```

```
3189        =>  .(lep |, cet 1, day (sub day +(cet:yo)))
3190        .(cet (add cet (div day cet:yo)), day (mod day cet:yo))
3191    =+  yer=(add (mul 400 era) (mul 100 cet))
3192    |-  ^-  [y=@ud m=@ud d=@ud]
3193    =+  dis=?:(lep 366 365)
3194    ?.  (lth day dis)
3195      =+  ner=+(yer)
3196      $(yer ner, day (sub day dis), lep =(0 (end [0 2] ner)))
3197    |-  ^-  [y=@ud m=@ud d=@ud]
3198    =+  [mot=0 cah=?:(lep moy:yo moh:yo)]
3199    |-  ^-  [y=@ud m=@ud d=@ud]
3200    =+  zis=(snag mot cah)
3201    ?:  (lth day zis)
3202      [yer +(mot) +(day)]
3203    $(mot +(mot), day (sub day zis))
3204  ::
3205  ++  yawn                                      ::  days since Jesus
3206    |=  [yer=@ud mot=@ud day=@ud]
3207    ^-  @ud
3208    =>  .(mot (dec mot), day (dec day))
3209    =>  ^+  .
3210        %=    .
3211            day
3212          =+  cah=?:((yelp yer) moy:yo moh:yo)
3213          |-  ^-  @ud
3214          ?:  =(0 mot)
3215            day
3216          $(mot (dec mot), cah (slag 1 cah), day (add day (snag 0 cah)))
3217        ==
3218    |-  ^-  @ud
3219    ?.  =(0 (mod yer 4))
3220      =+  ney=(dec yer)
3221      $(yer ney, day (add day ?:((yelp ney) 366 365)))
3222    ?.  =(0 (mod yer 100))
3223      =+  nef=(sub yer 4)
3224      $(yer nef, day (add day ?:((yelp nef) 1.461 1.460)))
3225    ?.  =(0 (mod yer 400))
3226      =+  nec=(sub yer 100)
3227      $(yer nec, day (add day ?:((yelp nec) 36.525 36.524)))
3228    (add day (mul (div yer 400) (add 1 (mul 4 36.524))))
3229  ::
3230  ++  yelp                                      ::  leap year
3231    |=  yer=@ud  ^-  ?
3232    &(=(0 (mod yer 4)) |(!=(0 (mod yer 100)) =(0 (mod yer 400))))
3233  ::
3234  ++  yo                                        ::  time constants
3235    |%  ++  cet  36.524              ::  (add 24 (mul 100 365))
3236        ++  day  86.400              ::  (mul 24 hor)
3237        ++  era  146.097             ::  (add 1 (mul 4 cet))
3238        ++  hor  3.600               ::  (mul 60 mit)
3239        ++  jes  106.751.991.084.417   ::  (mul 730.692.561 era)
3240        ++  mit  60
3241        ++  moh  `(list @ud)`[31 28 31 30 31 30 31 31 30 31 30 31 ~]
3242        ++  moy  `(list @ud)`[31 29 31 30 31 30 31 31 30 31 30 31 ~]
3243        ++  qad  126.144.001         ::  (add 1 (mul 4 yer))
3244        ++  yer  31.536.000          ::  (mul 365 day)
3245    --
3246  ::
```

```
3247  ::    3d: SHA hash family
3248  +|  %sha-hash-family
3249  ::
3250  ++  shad  |=(ruz=@ (shax (shax ruz)))              ::  double sha-256
3251  ++  shaf                                           ::  half sha-256
3252    |=  [sal=@ ruz=@]
3253    =+  haz=(shas sal ruz)
3254    (mix (end 7 haz) (rsh 7 haz))
3255  ::
3256  ++  sham                                           ::  128bit noun hash
3257    |=  yux=*  ^-  @uvH  ^-  @
3258    ?@  yux
3259      (shaf %mash yux)
3260    (shaf %sham (jam yux))
3261  ::
3262  ++  shas                                           ::  salted hash
3263    ~/  %shas
3264    |=  [sal=@ ruz=@]
3265    =/  len  (max 32 (met 3 sal))
3266    (shay len (mix sal (shax ruz)))
3267  ::
3268  ++  shax                                           ::  sha-256
3269    ~/  %shax
3270    |=  ruz=@  ^-  @
3271    (shay [(met 3 ruz) ruz])
3272  ::
3273  ++  shay                                           ::  sha-256 with length
3274    ~/  %shay
3275    |=  [len=@u ruz=@]  ^-  @
3276    =>  .(ruz (cut 3 [0 len] ruz))
3277    =+  [few==>(fe .(a 5)) wac=|=([a=@ b=@] (cut 5 [a 1] b))]
3278    =+  [sum=sum.few ror=ror.few net=net.few inv=inv.few]
3279    =+  ral=(lsh [0 3] len)
3280    =+  ^=  ful
3281        %+  can  0
3282        :~  [ral ruz]
3283            [8 128]
3284            [(mod (sub 960 (mod (add 8 ral) 512)) 512) 0]
3285            [64 (~(net fe 6) ral)]
3286        ==
3287    =+  lex=(met 9 ful)
3288    =+  ^=  kbx  0xc671.78f2.bef9.a3f7.a450.6ceb.90be.fffa.
3289                   8cc7.0208.84c8.7814.78a5.636f.748f.82ee.
3290                   682e.6ff3.5b9c.ca4f.4ed8.aa4a.391c.0cb3.
3291                   34b0.bcb5.2748.774c.1e37.6c08.19a4.c116.
3292                   106a.a070.f40e.3585.d699.0624.d192.e819.
3293                   c76c.51a3.c24b.8b70.a81a.664b.a2bf.e8a1.
3294                   9272.2c85.81c2.c92e.766a.0abb.650a.7354.
3295                   5338.0d13.4d2c.6dfc.2e1b.2138.27b7.0a85.
3296                   1429.2967.06ca.6351.d5a7.9147.c6e0.0bf3.
3297                   bf59.7fc7.b003.27c8.a831.c66d.983e.5152.
3298                   76f9.88da.5cb0.a9dc.4a74.84aa.2de9.2c6f.
3299                   240c.a1cc.0fc1.9dc6.efbe.4786.e49b.69c1.
3300                   c19b.f174.9bdc.06a7.80de.b1fe.72be.5d74.
3301                   550c.7dc3.2431.85be.1283.5b01.d807.aa98.
3302                   ab1c.5ed5.923f.82a4.59f1.11f1.3956.c25b.
3303                   e9b5.dba5.b5c0.fbcf.7137.4491.428a.2f98
3304    =+  ^=  hax  0x5be0.cd19.1f83.d9ab.9b05.688c.510e.527f.
```

```
                          a54f.f53a.3c6e.f372.bb67.ae85.6a09.e667
    =+  i=0
    |-  ^-  @
    ?:  =(i lex)
      (run 5 hax net)
    =+  ^=  wox
        =+  dux=(cut 9 [i 1] ful)
        =+  wox=(run 5 dux net)
        =+  j=16
        |-  ^-  @
        ?:  =(64 j)
          wox
        =+  :*  l=(wac (sub j 15) wox)
                m=(wac (sub j 2) wox)
                n=(wac (sub j 16) wox)
                o=(wac (sub j 7) wox)
            ==
        =+  x=:(mix (ror 0 7 l) (ror 0 18 l) (rsh [0 3] l))
        =+  y=:(mix (ror 0 17 m) (ror 0 19 m) (rsh [0 10] m))
        =+  z=:(sum n x o y)
        $(wox (con (lsh [5 j] z) wox), j +(j))
    =+  j=0
    =+  :*  a=(wac 0 hax)
            b=(wac 1 hax)
            c=(wac 2 hax)
            d=(wac 3 hax)
            e=(wac 4 hax)
            f=(wac 5 hax)
            g=(wac 6 hax)
            h=(wac 7 hax)
        ==
    |-  ^-  @
    ?:  =(64 j)
      %=  ^$
        i  +(i)
        hax  %+  rep 5
             :~  (sum a (wac 0 hax))
                 (sum b (wac 1 hax))
                 (sum c (wac 2 hax))
                 (sum d (wac 3 hax))
                 (sum e (wac 4 hax))
                 (sum f (wac 5 hax))
                 (sum g (wac 6 hax))
                 (sum h (wac 7 hax))
             ==
      ==
    =+  l=:(mix (ror 0 2 a) (ror 0 13 a) (ror 0 22 a))       ::  s0
    =+  m=:(mix (dis a b) (dis a c) (dis b c))               ::  maj
    =+  n=(sum l m)                                          ::  t2
    =+  o=:(mix (ror 0 6 e) (ror 0 11 e) (ror 0 25 e))       ::  s1
    =+  p=(mix (dis e f) (dis (inv e) g))                    ::  ch
    =+  q=:(sum h o p (wac j kbx) (wac j wox))               ::  t1
    $(j +(j), a (sum q n), b a, c b, d c, e (sum d q), f e, g f, h g)
::
++  shaw                                                     ::  hash to nbits
  |=  [sal=@ len=@ ruz=@]
  (~(raw og (shas sal (mix len ruz))) len)
::
```

```
++  shaz                                              ::  sha-512
  |=  ruz=@  ^-  @
  (shal [(met 3 ruz) ruz])
::
++  shal                                              ::  sha-512 with length
  ~/  %shal
  |=  [len=@ ruz=@]  ^-  @
  =>  .(ruz (cut 3 [0 len] ruz))
  =+  [few==>(fe .(a 6)) wac=|=([a=@ b=@] (cut 6 [a 1] b))]
  =+  [sum=sum.few ror=ror.few net=net.few inv=inv.few]
  =+  ral=(lsh [0 3] len)
  =+  ^=  ful
      %+  can  0
      :~  [ral ruz]
          [8 128]
          [(mod (sub 1.920 (mod (add 8 ral) 1.024)) 1.024) 0]
          [128 (~(net fe 7) ral)]
      ==
  =+  lex=(met 10 ful)
  =+  ^=  kbx  0x6c44.198c.4a47.5817.5fcb.6fab.3ad6.faec.
                 597f.299c.fc65.7e2a.4cc5.d4be.cb3e.42b6.
                 431d.67c4.9c10.0d4c.3c9e.be0a.15c9.bebc.
                 32ca.ab7b.40c7.2493.28db.77f5.2304.7d84.
                 1b71.0b35.131c.471b.113f.9804.bef9.0dae.
                 0a63.7dc5.a2c8.98a6.06f0.67aa.7217.6fba.
                 f57d.4f7f.ee6e.d178.eada.7dd6.cde0.eb1e.
                 d186.b8c7.21c0.c207.ca27.3ece.ea26.619c.
                 c671.78f2.e372.532b.bef9.a3f7.b2c6.7915.
                 a450.6ceb.de82.bde9.90be.fffa.2363.1e28.
                 8cc7.0208.1a64.39ec.84c8.7814.a1f0.ab72.
                 78a5.636f.4317.2f60.748f.82ee.5def.b2fc.
                 682e.6ff3.d6b2.b8a3.5b9c.ca4f.7763.e373.
                 4ed8.aa4a.e341.8acb.391c.0cb3.c5c9.5a63.
                 34b0.bcb5.e19b.48a8.2748.774c.df8e.eb99.
                 1e37.6c08.5141.ab53.19a4.c116.b8d2.d0c8.
                 106a.a070.32bb.d1b8.f40e.3585.5771.202a.
                 d699.0624.5565.a910.d192.e819.d6ef.5218.
                 c76c.51a3.0654.be30.c24b.8b70.d0f8.9791.
                 a81a.664b.bc42.3001.a2bf.e8a1.4cf1.0364.
                 9272.2c85.1482.353b.81c2.c92e.47ed.aee6.
                 766a.0abb.3c77.b2a8.650a.7354.8baf.63de.
                 5338.0d13.9d95.b3df.4d2c.6dfc.5ac4.2aed.
                 2e1b.2138.5c26.c926.27b7.0a85.46d2.2ffc.
                 1429.2967.0a0e.6e70.06ca.6351.e003.826f.
                 d5a7.9147.930a.a725.c6e0.0bf3.3da8.8fc2.
                 bf59.7fc7.beef.0ee4.b003.27c8.98fb.213f.
                 a831.c66d.2db4.3210.983e.5152.ee66.dfab.
                 76f9.88da.8311.53b5.5cb0.a9dc.bd41.fbd4.
                 4a74.84aa.6ea6.e483.2de9.2c6f.592b.0275.
                 240c.a1cc.77ac.9c65.0fc1.9dc6.8b8c.d5b5.
                 efbe.4786.384f.25e3.e49b.69c1.9ef1.4ad2.
                 c19b.f174.cf69.2694.9bdc.06a7.25c7.1235.
                 80de.b1fe.3b16.96b1.72be.5d74.f27b.896f.
                 550c.7dc3.d5ff.b4e2.2431.85be.4ee4.b28c.
                 1283.5b01.4570.6fbe.d807.aa98.a303.0242.
                 ab1c.5ed5.da6d.8118.923f.82a4.af19.4f9b.
                 59f1.11f1.b605.d019.3956.c25b.f348.b538.
                 e9b5.dba5.8189.dbbc.b5c0.fbcf.ec4d.3b2f.
```

```
3421                       7137.4491.23ef.65cd.428a.2f98.d728.ae22
3422    =+  ^=  hax  0x5be0.cd19.137e.2179.1f83.d9ab.fb41.bd6b.
3423                       9b05.688c.2b3e.6c1f.510e.527f.ade6.82d1.
3424                       a54f.f53a.5f1d.36f1.3c6e.f372.fe94.f82b.
3425                       bb67.ae85.84ca.a73b.6a09.e667.f3bc.c908
3426    =+  i=0
3427    |-  ^-  @
3428    ?:  =(i lex)
3429      (run 6 hax net)
3430    =+  ^=  wox
3431        =+  dux=(cut 10 [i 1] ful)
3432        =+  wox=(run 6 dux net)
3433        =+  j=16
3434        |-  ^-  @
3435        ?:  =(80 j)
3436          wox
3437        =+  :*  l=(wac (sub j 15) wox)
3438                m=(wac (sub j 2) wox)
3439                n=(wac (sub j 16) wox)
3440                o=(wac (sub j 7) wox)
3441            ==
3442        =+  x=:(mix (ror 0 1 l) (ror 0 8 l) (rsh [0 7] l))
3443        =+  y=:(mix (ror 0 19 m) (ror 0 61 m) (rsh [0 6] m))
3444        =+  z=:(sum n x o y)
3445        $(wox (con (lsh [6 j] z) wox), j +(j))
3446    =+  j=0
3447    =+  :*  a=(wac 0 hax)
3448            b=(wac 1 hax)
3449            c=(wac 2 hax)
3450            d=(wac 3 hax)
3451            e=(wac 4 hax)
3452            f=(wac 5 hax)
3453            g=(wac 6 hax)
3454            h=(wac 7 hax)
3455        ==
3456    |-  ^-  @
3457    ?:  =(80 j)
3458      %=  ^$
3459        i  +(i)
3460        hax  %+  rep  6
3461             :~  (sum a (wac 0 hax))
3462                 (sum b (wac 1 hax))
3463                 (sum c (wac 2 hax))
3464                 (sum d (wac 3 hax))
3465                 (sum e (wac 4 hax))
3466                 (sum f (wac 5 hax))
3467                 (sum g (wac 6 hax))
3468                 (sum h (wac 7 hax))
3469             ==
3470      ==
3471    =+  l=:(mix (ror 0 28 a) (ror 0 34 a) (ror 0 39 a))    :: S0
3472    =+  m=:(mix (dis a b) (dis a c) (dis b c))             :: maj
3473    =+  n=(sum l m)                                        :: t2
3474    =+  o=:(mix (ror 0 14 e) (ror 0 18 e) (ror 0 41 e))    :: S1
3475    =+  p=(mix (dis e f) (dis (inv e) g))                  :: ch
3476    =+  q=:(sum h o p (wac j kbx) (wac j wox))             :: t1
3477    $(j +(j), a (sum q n), b a, c b, d c, e (sum d q), f e, g f, h g)
3478  ::
```

```
3479  ++  shan                                               ::  sha-1 (deprecated)
3480  |=  ruz=@
3481  =+  [few==>(fe .(a 5)) wac=|=([a=@ b=@] (cut 5 [a 1] b))]
3482  =+  [sum=sum.few ror=ror.few rol=rol.few net=net.few inv=inv.few]
3483  =+  ral=(lsh [0 3] (met 3 ruz))
3484  =+  ^=  ful
3485      %+  can  0
3486      :~  [ral ruz]
3487          [8 128]
3488          [(mod (sub 960 (mod (add 8 ral) 512)) 512) 0]
3489          [64 (~(net fe 6) ral)]
3490      ==
3491  =+  lex=(met 9 ful)
3492  =+  kbx=0xca62.c1d6.8f1b.bcdc.6ed9.eba1.5a82.7999
3493  =+  hax=0xc3d2.e1f0.1032.5476.98ba.dcfe.efcd.ab89.6745.2301
3494  =+  i=0
3495  |-
3496  ?:  =(i lex)
3497    (rep 5 (flop (rip 5 hax)))
3498  =+  ^=  wox
3499      =+  dux=(cut 9 [i 1] ful)
3500      =+  wox=(rep 5 (turn (rip 5 dux) net))
3501      =+  j=16
3502      |-  ^-  @
3503      ?:  =(80 j)
3504        wox
3505      =+  :*  l=(wac (sub j 3) wox)
3506              m=(wac (sub j 8) wox)
3507              n=(wac (sub j 14) wox)
3508              o=(wac (sub j 16) wox)
3509          ==
3510      =+  z=(rol 0 1 :(mix l m n o))
3511      $(wox (con (lsh [5 j] z) wox), j +(j))
3512  =+  j=0
3513  =+  :*  a=(wac 0 hax)
3514          b=(wac 1 hax)
3515          c=(wac 2 hax)
3516          d=(wac 3 hax)
3517          e=(wac 4 hax)
3518      ==
3519  |-  ^-  @
3520  ?:  =(80 j)
3521    %=  ^$
3522      i  +(i)
3523      hax  %+  rep  5
3524           :~
3525                (sum a (wac 0 hax))
3526                (sum b (wac 1 hax))
3527                (sum c (wac 2 hax))
3528                (sum d (wac 3 hax))
3529                (sum e (wac 4 hax))
3530           ==
3531    ==
3532  =+  fx=(con (dis b c) (dis (not 5 1 b) d))
3533  =+  fy=:(mix b c d)
3534  =+  fz=:(con (dis b c) (dis b d) (dis c d))
3535  =+  ^=  tem
3536      ?:  &((gte j 0) (lte j 19))
```

```
3537          :(sum (rol 0 5 a) fx e (wac 0 kbx) (wac j wox))
3538        ?:  &((gte j 20) (lte j 39))
3539          :(sum (rol 0 5 a) fy e (wac 1 kbx) (wac j wox))
3540        ?:  &((gte j 40) (lte j 59))
3541          :(sum (rol 0 5 a) fz e (wac 2 kbx) (wac j wox))
3542        :(sum (rol 0 5 a) fy e (wac 3 kbx) (wac j wox))
3543      $(j +(j), a tem, b a, c (rol 0 30 b), d c, e d)
3544  ::
3545  ++  og                                          ::  shax-powered rng
3546    ~/  %og
3547    |_  a=@
3548    ++  rad                                        ::  random in range
3549      |=  b=@  ^-  @
3550      ~_  leaf+"rad-zero"
3551      ?<  =(0 b)
3552      =+  c=(raw (met 0 b))
3553      ?:((lth c b) c $(a +(a)))
3554    ::
3555    ++  rads                                       ::  random continuation
3556      |=  b=@
3557      =+  r=(rad b)
3558      [r +>.$(a (shas %og-s (mix a r)))]
3559    ::
3560    ++  raw                                        ::  random bits
3561      ~/  %raw
3562      |=  b=@  ^-  @
3563      %+  can
3564          0
3565      =+  c=(shas %og-a (mix b a))
3566      |-  ^-  (list [@ @])
3567      ?:  =(0 b)
3568          ~
3569      =+  d=(shas %og-b (mix b (mix a c)))
3570      ?:  (lth b 256)
3571        [[b (end [0 b] d)] ~]
3572      [[256 d] $(c d, b (sub b 256))]
3573    ::
3574    ++  raws                                       ::  random bits
3575      |=  b=@                                       ::  continuation
3576      =+  r=(raw b)
3577      [r +>.$(a (shas %og-s (mix a r)))]
3578    --
3579  ::
3580  ++  sha                                          ::  correct byte-order
3581    ~%  %sha  ..sha  ~
3582    =>  |%
3583        ++  flin  |=(a=@ (swp 3 a))                 ::  flip input
3584        ++  flim  |=(byts [wid (rev 3 wid dat)])    ::  flip input w= length
3585        ++  flip  |=(w=@u (cury (cury rev 3) w))    ::  flip output of size
3586        ++  meet  |=(a=@ [(met 3 a) a])             ::  measure input size
3587        --
3588    |%
3589    ::
3590    ::  use with @
3591    ::
3592    ++  sha-1     (cork meet sha-1l)
3593    ++  sha-256   :(cork flin shax (flip 32))
3594    ++  sha-512   :(cork flin shaz (flip 64))
```

```
3595    ::
3596    ::  use with byts
3597    ::
3598    ++  sha-2561  :(cork flim shay (flip 32))
3599    ++  sha-5121  :(cork flim shal (flip 64))
3600    ::
3601    ++  sha-11
3602    ~/  %sha1
3603    |=  byts
3604    ^-  @
3605    =+  [few==>(fe .(a 5)) wac=|=([a=@ b=@] (cut 5 [a 1] b))]
3606    =+  [sum=sum.few ror=ror.few rol=rol.few net=net.few inv=inv.few]
3607    =+  ral=(lsh [0 3] wid)
3608    =+  ^=  ful
3609        %+  can  0
3610        :~  [ral (rev 3 wid dat)]
3611            [8 128]
3612            [(mod (sub 960 (mod (add 8 ral) 512)) 512) 0]
3613            [64 (~(net fe 6) ral)]
3614        ==
3615    =+  lex=(met 9 ful)
3616    =+  kbx=0xca62.c1d6.8f1b.bcdc.6ed9.eba1.5a82.7999
3617    =+  hax=0xc3d2.e1f0.1032.5476.98ba.dcfe.efcd.ab89.6745.2301
3618    =+  i=0
3619    |-
3620    ?:  =(i lex)
3621      (rep 5 (flop (rip 5 hax)))
3622    =+  ^=  wox
3623        =+  dux=(cut 9 [i 1] ful)
3624        =+  wox=(rep 5 (turn (rip 5 dux) net))
3625        =+  j=16
3626        |-  ^-  @
3627        ?:  =(80 j)
3628           wox
3629        =+  :*  l=(wac (sub j 3) wox)
3630                m=(wac (sub j 8) wox)
3631                n=(wac (sub j 14) wox)
3632                o=(wac (sub j 16) wox)
3633            ==
3634        =+  z=(rol 0 1 :(mix l m n o))
3635        $(wox (con (lsh [5 j] z) wox), j +(j))
3636    =+  j=0
3637    =+  :*  a=(wac 0 hax)
3638            b=(wac 1 hax)
3639            c=(wac 2 hax)
3640            d=(wac 3 hax)
3641            e=(wac 4 hax)
3642        ==
3643    |-  ^-  @
3644    ?:  =(80 j)
3645      %=  ^$
3646        i  +(i)
3647        hax  %+  rep  5
3648             :~
3649                (sum a (wac 0 hax))
3650                (sum b (wac 1 hax))
3651                (sum c (wac 2 hax))
3652                (sum d (wac 3 hax))
```

```
3653                        (sum e (wac 4 hax))
3654                   ==
3655          ==
3656      =+  fx=(con (dis b c) (dis (not 5 1 b) d))
3657      =+  fy=:(mix b c d)
3658      =+  fz=:(con (dis b c) (dis b d) (dis c d))
3659      =+  ^=  tem
3660          ?:  &((gte j 0) (lte j 19))
3661            :(sum (rol 0 5 a) fx e (wac 0 kbx) (wac j wox))
3662          ?:  &((gte j 20) (lte j 39))
3663            :(sum (rol 0 5 a) fy e (wac 1 kbx) (wac j wox))
3664          ?:  &((gte j 40) (lte j 59))
3665            :(sum (rol 0 5 a) fz e (wac 2 kbx) (wac j wox))
3666          :(sum (rol 0 5 a) fy e (wac 3 kbx) (wac j wox))
3667      $(j +(j), a tem, b a, c (rol 0 30 b), d c, e d)
3668    --
3669 ::    3f: scrambling
3670 +|  %scrambling
3671 ::
3672 ++  un                                         ::  =(x (wred (wren x)))
3673   |%
3674   ++  wren                                      ::  conceal structure
3675    |=  pyn=@  ^-  @
3676    =+  len=(met 3 pyn)
3677    ?:  =(0 len)
3678       0
3679    =>  .(len (dec len))
3680    =+  mig=(zaft (xafo len (cut 3 [len 1] pyn)))
3681    %+  can  3
3682    %-  flop  ^-  (list [@ @])
3683    :-  [1 mig]
3684    |-  ^-  (list [@ @])
3685    ?:  =(0 len)
3686        ~
3687    =>  .(len (dec len))
3688    =+  mog=(zyft :(mix mig (end 3 len) (cut 3 [len 1] pyn)))
3689    [[1 mog] $(mig mog)]
3690   ::
3691   ++  wred                                      ::  restore structure
3692    |=  cry=@  ^-  @
3693    =+  len=(met 3 cry)
3694    ?:  =(0 len)
3695       0
3696    =>  .(len (dec len))
3697    =+  mig=(cut 3 [len 1] cry)
3698    %+  can  3
3699    %-  flop  ^-  (list [@ @])
3700    :-  [1 (xaro len (zart mig))]
3701    |-  ^-  (list [@ @])
3702    ?:  =(0 len)
3703        ~
3704    =>  .(len (dec len))
3705    =+  mog=(cut 3 [len 1] cry)
3706    [[1 :(mix mig (end 3 len) (zyrt mog))] $(mig mog)]
3707   ::
3708   ++  xafo  |=([a=@ b=@] +((mod (add (dec b) a) 255)))
3709   ++  xaro  |=([a=@ b=@] +((mod (add (dec b) (sub 255 (mod a 255))) 255)))
3710   ::
```

```
3711  ++  zaft                                          ::  forward 255-sbox
3712    |=  a=@D
3713    =+  ^=  b
3714        0xcc.75bc.86c8.2fb1.9a42.f0b3.79a0.92ca.21f6.1e41.cde5.fcc0.
3715        7e85.51ae.1005.c72d.1246.07e8.7c64.a914.8d69.d9f4.59c2.8038.
3716        1f4a.dca2.6fdf.66f9.f561.a12e.5a16.f7b0.a39f.364e.cb70.7318.
3717        1de1.ad31.63d1.abd4.db68.6a33.134d.a760.edee.5434.493a.e323.
3718        930d.8f3d.3562.bb81.0b24.43cf.bea5.a6eb.52b4.0229.06b2.6704.
3719        78c9.45ec.d75e.58af.c577.b7b9.c40e.017d.90c3.87f8.96fa.1153.
3720        0372.7f30.1c32.ac83.ff17.c6e4.d36d.6b55.e2ce.8c71.8a5b.b6f3.
3721        9d4b.eab5.8b3c.e7f2.a8fe.9574.5de0.bf20.3f15.9784.9939.5f9c.
3722        e609.564f.d8a4.b825.9819.94aa.2c08.8e4c.9b22.477a.2840.3ed6.
3723        3750.6ef1.44dd.89ef.6576.d00a.fbda.9ed2.3b6c.7b0c.bde9.2ade.
3724        5c88.c182.481a.1b0f.2bfd.d591.2726.57ba
3725    (cut 3 [(dec a) 1] b)
3726  ::
3727  ++  zart                                          ::  reverse 255-sbox
3728    |=  a=@D
3729    =+  ^=  b
3730        0x68.4f07.ea1c.73c9.75c2.efc8.d559.5125.f621.a7a8.8591.5613.
3731        dd52.40eb.65a2.60b7.4bcb.1123.ceb0.1bd6.3c84.2906.b164.19b3.
3732        1e95.5fec.ffbc.f187.fbe2.6680.7c77.d30e.e94a.9414.fd9a.017d.
3733        3a7e.5a55.8ff5.8bf9.c181.e5b6.6ab2.35da.50aa.9293.3bc0.cdc6.
3734        f3bf.1a58.4130.f844.3846.744e.36a0.f205.789e.32d8.5e54.5c22.
3735        0f76.fce7.4569.0d99.d26e.e879.dc16.2df4.887f.1ffe.4dba.6f5d.
3736        bbcc.2663.1762.aed7.af8a.ca20.dbb4.9bc7.a942.834c.105b.c4d4.
3737        8202.3e61.a671.90e6.273d.bdab.3157.cfa4.0c2e.df86.2496.f7ed.
3738        2b48.2a9d.5318.a343.d128.be9c.a5ad.6bb5.6dfa.c5e1.3408.128d.
3739        2c04.0339.97a1.2ff0.49d0.eeb8.6c0a.0b37.b967.c347.d9ac.e072.
3740        e409.7b9f.1598.1d3f.33de.8ce3.8970.8e7a
3741    (cut 3 [(dec a) 1] b)
3742  ::
3743  ++  zyft                                          ::  forward 256-sbox
3744    |=  a=@D
3745    =+  ^=  b
3746        0xbb49.b71f.b881.b402.17e4.6b86.69b5.1647.115f.dddb.7ca5.
3747        8371.4bd5.19a9.b092.605d.0d9b.e030.a0cc.78ba.5706.4d2d.
3748        986a.768c.f8e8.c4c7.2f1c.effe.3cae.01c0.253e.65d3.3872.
3749        ce0e.7a74.8ac6.daac.7e5c.6479.44ec.4143.3d20.4af0.ee6c.
3750        c828.deca.0377.249f.ffcd.7b4f.eb7d.66f2.8951.042e.595a.
3751        8e13.f9c3.a79a.f788.6199.9391.7fab.6200.4ce5.0758.e2f1.
3752        7594.c945.d218.4248.afa1.e61a.54fb.1482.bea4.96a2.3473.
3753        63c2.e7cb.155b.120a.4ed7.bfd8.b31b.4008.f329.fca3.5380.
3754        9556.0cb2.8722.2bea.e96e.3ac5.d1bc.10e3.2c52.a62a.b1d6.
3755        35aa.d05e.f6a8.0f3b.31ed.559d.09ad.f585.6d21.fd1d.8d67.
3756        370b.26f4.70c1.b923.4684.6fbd.cf8b.5036.0539.9cdc.d93f.
3757        9068.1edf.8f33.b632.d427.97fa.9ee1
3758    (cut 3 [a 1] b)
3759  ::
3760  ++  zyrt                                          ::  reverse 256-sbox
3761    |=  a=@D
3762    =+  ^=  b
3763        0x9fc8.2753.6e02.8fcf.8b35.2b20.5598.7caa.c9a9.30b0.9b48.
3764        47ce.6371.80f6.407d.00dd.0aa5.ed10.ecb7.0f5a.5c3a.e605.
3765        c077.4337.17bd.9eda.62a4.79a7.ccb8.44cd.8e64.1ec4.5b6b.
3766        1842.ffd8.1dfb.fd07.f2f9.594c.3be3.73c6.2cb6.8438.e434.
3767        8d3d.ea6a.5268.72db.a001.2e11.de8c.88d3.0369.4f7a.87e2.
3768        860d.0991.25d0.16b9.978a.4bf4.2a1a.e96c.fa50.85b5.9aeb.
```

```
      9dbb.b2d9.a2d1.7bba.66be.e81f.1946.29a8.f5d2.f30c.2499.
      c1b3.6583.89e1.ee36.e0b4.6092.937e.d74e.2f6f.513e.9615.
      9c5d.d581.e7ab.fe74.f01b.78b1.ae75.af57.0ec2.adc7.3245.
      12bf.2314.3967.0806.31dc.cb94.d43f.493c.54a6.0421.c3a1.
      1c4a.28ac.fc0b.26ca.5870.e576.f7f1.616d.905f.ef41.33bc.
      df4d.225e.2d56.7fd6.1395.a3f8.c582
    (cut 3 [a 1] b)
  --
::
++  ob
  ~%  %ob  ..ob
    ==
      %fein  fein
      %fynd  fynd
    ==
  |%
  ::
  ::  +fein: conceal structure, v3.
  ::
  ::    +fein conceals planet-sized atoms.  The idea is that it should not be
  ::    trivial to tell which planet a star has spawned under.
  ::
  ++  fein
    ~/  %fein
    |=  pyn=@  ^-  @
    ?:  &((gte pyn 0x1.0000) (lte pyn 0xffff.ffff))
      (add 0x1.0000 (feis (sub pyn 0x1.0000)))
    ?:  &((gte pyn 0x1.0000.0000) (lte pyn 0xffff.ffff.ffff.ffff))
      =/  lo  (dis pyn 0xffff.ffff)
      =/  hi  (dis pyn 0xffff.ffff.0000.0000)
      %+  con  hi
      $(pyn lo)
    pyn
  ::
  ::  +fynd: restore structure, v3.
  ::
  ::    Restores obfuscated values that have been enciphered with +fein.
  ::
  ++  fynd
    ~/  %fynd
    |=  cry=@  ^-  @
    ?:  &((gte cry 0x1.0000) (lte cry 0xffff.ffff))
      (add 0x1.0000 (tail (sub cry 0x1.0000)))
    ?:  &((gte cry 0x1.0000.0000) (lte cry 0xffff.ffff.ffff.ffff))
      =/  lo  (dis cry 0xffff.ffff)
      =/  hi  (dis cry 0xffff.ffff.0000.0000)
      %+  con  hi
      $(cry lo)
    cry
  ::  +feis: a four-round generalised Feistel cipher over the domain
  ::         [0, 2^32 - 2^16 - 1].
  ::
  ::    See: Black & Rogaway (2002), Ciphers for arbitrary finite domains.
  ::
  ++  feis
    |=  m=@
    ^-  @
    (fee 4 0xffff 0x1.0000 (mul 0xffff 0x1.0000) eff m)
```

```
::
::  +tail: reverse +feis.
::
++  tail
  |=  m=@
  ^-  @
  (feen 4 0xffff 0x1.0000 (mul 0xffff 0x1.0000) eff m)
::
::  +fee: "Fe" in B&R (2002).
::
::    A Feistel cipher given the following parameters:
::
::    r:    number of Feistel rounds
::    a, b: parameters such that ab >= k
::    k:    value such that the domain of the cipher is [0, k - 1]
::    prf:  a gate denoting a family of pseudorandom functions indexed by
::          its first argument and taking its second argument as input
::    m:    an input value in the domain [0, k - 1]
::
++  fee
  |=  [r=@ a=@ b=@ k=@ prf=$-([j=@ r=@] @) m=@]
  ^-  @
  =/  c  (fe r a b prf m)
  ?:  (lth c k)
    c
  (fe r a b prf c)
::
::  +feen: "Fe^-1" in B&R (2002).
::
::    Reverses a Feistel cipher constructed with parameters as described in
::    +fee.
::
++  feen
  |=  [r=@ a=@ b=@ k=@ prf=$-([j=@ r=@] @) m=@]
  ^-  @
  =/  c  (fen r a b prf m)
  ?:  (lth c k)
    c
  (fen r a b prf c)
::
::  +fe:  "fe" in B&R (2002).
::
::    An internal function to +fee.
::
::    Note that this implementation differs slightly from the reference paper
::    to support some legacy behaviour.  See urbit/arvo#1105.
::
++  fe
  |=  [r=@ a=@ b=@ prf=$-([j=@ r=@] @) m=@]
  =/  j  1
  =/  ell  (mod m a)
  =/  arr  (div m a)
  |-  ^-  @
  ::
  ?:  (gth j r)
    ?.  =((mod r 2) 0)
      (add (mul arr a) ell)
    ::
```

```
3885        :: Note that +fe differs from B&R (2002)'s "fe" below, as a previous
3886        :: implementation of this cipher contained a bug such that certain inputs
3887        :: could encipher to the same output.
3888        ::
3889        :: To correct these problem cases while also preserving the cipher's
3890        :: legacy behaviour on most inputs, we check for a problem case (which
3891        :: occurs when 'arr' is equal to 'a') and, if detected, use an alternate
3892        :: permutation instead.
3893        ::
3894        ?:  =(arr a)
3895          (add (mul arr a) ell)
3896        (add (mul ell a) arr)
3897      ::
3898      =/  f  (prf (sub j 1) arr)
3899      ::
3900      =/  tmp
3901        ?.  =((mod j 2) 0)
3902          (mod (add f ell) a)
3903        (mod (add f ell) b)
3904      ::
3905      $(j +(j), ell arr, arr tmp)
3906    ::
3907    ::  +fen:  "fe^-1" in B&R (2002).
3908    ::
3909    ::    Note that this implementation differs slightly from the reference paper
3910    ::    to support some legacy behaviour.  See urbit/arvo#1105.
3911    ::
3912    ++  fen
3913    |=  [r=@ a=@ b=@ prf=$-([j=@ r=@] @) m=@]
3914    =/  j  r
3915    ::
3916    =/  ahh
3917      ?.  =((mod r 2) 0)
3918        (div m a)
3919      (mod m a)
3920    ::
3921    =/  ale
3922      ?.  =((mod r 2) 0)
3923        (mod m a)
3924      (div m a)
3925    ::
3926    :: Similar to the comment in +fe, +fen differs from B&R (2002)'s "fe^-1"
3927    :: here in order to preserve the legacy cipher's behaviour on most inputs.
3928    ::
3929    :: Here problem cases can be identified by 'ahh' equating with 'a'; we
3930    :: correct those cases by swapping the values of 'ahh' and 'ale'.
3931    ::
3932    =/  ell
3933      ?:  =(ale a)
3934        ahh
3935      ale
3936    ::
3937    =/  arr
3938      ?:  =(ale a)
3939        ale
3940      ahh
3941    ::
3942    |-  ^-  @
```

```
?:  (lth j 1)
  (add (mul arr a) ell)
=/  f  (prf (sub j 1) ell)
::
::  Note that there is a slight deviation here to avoid dealing with
::  negative values.  We add 'a' or 'b' to arr as appropriate and reduce
::  'f' modulo the same number before performing subtraction.
::
=/  tmp
  ?.  =((mod j 2) 0)
    (mod (sub (add arr a) (mod f a)) a)
  (mod (sub (add arr b) (mod f b)) b)
::
$(j (sub j 1), ell tmp, arr ell)
::
::  +eff: a murmur3-based pseudorandom function.  'F' in B&R (2002).
::
++  eff
|=  [j=@ r=@]
^-  @
(muk (snag j raku) 2 r)
::
::  +raku: seeds for eff.
::
++  raku
^-  (list @ux)
:~  0xb76d.5eed
    0xee28.1300
    0x85bc.ae01
    0x4b38.7af7
==
::
--
::
::    3g: molds and mold builders
+|  %molds-and-mold-builders
::
+$  coin  $~  [%$ %ud 0]                                ::  print format
          $%  [%$ p=dime]                               ::
              [%blob p=*]                               ::
              [%many p=(list coin)]                     ::
          ==                                            ::
+$  dime  [p=@ta q=@]                                   ::
+$  edge  [p=hair q=(unit [p=* q=nail])]                ::  parsing output
+$  hair  [p=@ud q=@ud]                                 ::  parsing trace
++  like  |*  a=$-(* *)                                 ::  generic edge
          |:  b=`*`[(hair) ~]                           ::
          :-  p=(hair -.b)                              ::
          ^=  q                                         ::
          ?@  +.b  ~                                    ::
          :-  ~                                         ::
          u=[p=(a +>-.b) q=[p=(hair -.b) q=(tape +.b)]] ::
+$  nail  [p=hair q=tape]                               ::  parsing input
+$  pint  [p=[p=@ q=@] q=[p=@ q=@]]                      ::  line+column range
+$  rule  _|:($:nail $:edge)                            ::  parsing rule
+$  spot  [p=path q=pint]                               ::  range in file
+$  tone  $%  [%0 product=*]                            ::  success
              [%1 block=*]                              ::  single block
```

```
            [%2 trace=(list [@ta *])]               ::  error report
          ==                                        ::
+$  toon  $%  [%0 p=*]                              ::  success
              [%1 p=*]                              ::  block
              [%2 p=(list tank)]                    ::  stack trace
          ==                                        ::
++  wonk  |*  veq=_$:edge                           ::  product from edge
          ?~(q.veq !! p.u.q.veq)           ::
--  =>
::
~%    %qua
    +
  ==
    %mure  mure
    %mute  mute
    %show  show
  ==
::    layer-4
::
|%
::
::    4a: exotic bases
+|  %exotic-bases
::
++  po                                              ::  phonetic base
  ~/  %po
  =+  :-  ^=  sis                                   ::  prefix syllables
      'dozmarbinwansamlitsighidfidlissogdirwacsabwissib\
      /rigsoldopmodfoglidhopdardorlorhodfolrintogsilmir\
      /holpaslacrovlivdalsatlibtabhanticpidtorbolfosdot\
      /losdilforpilramtirwintadbicdifrocwidbisdasmidlop\
      /rilnardapmolsanlocnovsitnidtipsicropwitnatpanmin\
      /ritpodmottamtolsavposnapnopsomfinfonbanmorworsip\
      /ronnorbotwicsocwatdolmagpicdavbidbaltimtasmallig\
      /sivtagpadsaldivdactansidfabtarmonranniswolmispal\
      /lasdismaprabtobrollatlonnodnavfignomnibpagsopral\
      /bilhaddocridmocpacravripfaltodtiltinhapmicfanpat\
      /taclabmogsimsonpinlomrictapfirhasbosbatpochactid\
      /havsaplindibhosdabbitbarracparloddosbortochilmac\
      /tomdigfilfasmithobharmighinradmashalraglagfadtop\
      /mophabnilnosmilfopfamdatnoldinhatnacrisfotribhoc\
      /nimlarfitwalrapsarnalmoslandondanladdovrivbacpol\
      /laptalpitnambonrostonfodponsovnocsorlavmatmipfip'
      ^=  dex                                       ::  suffix syllables
      'zodnecbudwessevpersutletfulpensytdurwepserwylsun\
      /rypsyxdyrnuphebpeglupdepdysputlughecryttyvsydnex\
      /lunmeplutseppesdelsulpedtemledtulmetwenbynhexfeb\
      /pyldulhetmevruttylwydtepbesdexsefwycburderneppur\
      /rysrebdennutsubpetrulsynregtydsupsemwynrecmegnet\
      /secmulnymtevwebsummutnyxrextebfushepbenmuswyxsym\
      /selrucdecwexsyrwetdylmynmesdetbetbeltuxtugmyrpel\
      /syptermebsetdutdegtexsurfeltudnuxruxrenwytnubmed\
      /lytdusnebrumtynseglyxpunresredfunrevrefmectedrus\
      /bexlebduxrynnumpyxrygryxfeptyrtustyclegnemfermer\
      /tenlusnussyltecmexpubrymtucfyllepdebbermughuttun\
      /bylsudpemdevlurdefbusbeprunmelpexdytbyttyplevmyl\
      /wedducfurfexnulluclennerlexrupnedlecrydlydfenwel\
      /nydhusrelrudneshesfetdesretdunlernyrsebhulryllud\
```

```
4059        /remlysfynwerrycsugnysnyllyndyndemluxfedsedbecmun\
4060        /lyrtesmudnytbyrsenwegfyrmurtelreptegpecnelnevfes'
4061    |%
4062    ++  ins  ~/  %ins                                   ::    parse prefix
4063            |=  a=@tas
4064            =+  b=0
4065            |-  ^-  (unit @)
4066            ?:(=(256 b) ~ ?:(=(a (tos b)) [~ b] $(b +(b))))
4067    ++  ind  ~/  %ind                                   ::    parse suffix
4068            |=  a=@tas
4069            =+  b=0
4070            |-  ^-  (unit @)
4071            ?:(=(256 b) ~ ?:(=(a (tod b)) [~ b] $(b +(b))))
4072    ++  tos  ~/  %tos                                   ::    fetch prefix
4073            |=(a=@ ?>((lth a 256) (cut 3 [(mul 3 a) 3] sis)))
4074    ++  tod  ~/  %tod                                   ::    fetch suffix
4075            |=(a=@ ?>((lth a 256) (cut 3 [(mul 3 a) 3] dex)))
4076    --
4077  ::
4078  ++  fa                                                ::    base58check
4079    =+  key='123456789ABCDEFGHJKLMNPQRSTUVWXYZabcdefghijkmnopqrstuvwxyz'
4080    =/  yek=@ux  ~+
4081      =-  yek:(roll (rip 3 key) -)
4082      =+  [a=*char b=*@ yek=`@ux`(fil 3 256 0xff)]
4083      |.
4084      [+(b) (mix yek (lsh [3 `@u`a] (~(inv fe 3) b)))]
4085    |%
4086    ++  cha  |=(a=char `(unit @uF)`=+(b=(cut 3 [`@`a 1] yek) ?:(=(b 0xff) ~ `b)))
4087    ++  tok
4088      |=  a=@ux  ^-  @ux
4089      =+  b=(pad a)
4090      =-  (~(net fe 5) (end [3 4] (shay 32 -)))
4091      (shay (add b (met 3 a)) (lsh [3 b] (swp 3 a)))
4092    ::
4093    ++  pad  |=(a=@ =+(b=(met 3 a) ?:((gte b 21) 0 (sub 21 b))))
4094    ++  enc  |=(a=@ux `@ux`(mix (lsh [3 4] a) (tok a)))
4095    ++  den
4096      |=  a=@ux  ^-  (unit @ux)
4097      =+  b=(rsh [3 4] a)
4098      ?.  =((tok b) (end [3 4] a))
4099        ~
4100      `b
4101    --
4102  ::     4b: text processing
4103  +|  %text-processing
4104  ::
4105  ++  at                                                ::    basic printing
4106    |_  a=@
4107    ++  r
4108      ?:  ?&  (gte (met 3 a) 2)
4109              |-
4110              ?:  =(0 a)
4111                &
4112              =+  vis=(end 3 a)
4113              ?&  ?|(=('-' vis) ?&((gte vis 'a') (lte vis 'z')))
4114                  $(a (rsh 3 a))
4115              ==
4116          ==
```

```
          rtam
      ?:  (lte (met 3 a) 2)
        rud
      rux
    ::
    ++  rf     `tape`[?-(a %& '&', %| '|', * !!) ~]
    ++  rn     `tape`[?>(=(0 a) '~') ~]
    ++  rt     `tape`['\'' (weld (mesc (trip a)) `tape`['\'' ~])]
    ++  rta    rt
    ++  rtam   `tape`['%' (trip a)]
    ++  rub    `tape`['0' 'b' (rum 2 ~ |=(b=@ (add '0' b)))]
    ++  rud    (rum 10 ~ |=(b=@ (add '0' b)))
    ++  rum
      |=  [b=@ c=tape d=$-(@ @)]
      ^-  tape
      ?:  =(0 a)
        [(d 0) c]
      =+  e=0
      |-  ^-  tape
      ?:  =(0 a)
        c
      =+  f=&(!=(0 e) =(0 (mod e ?:(=(10 b) 3 4))))
      %=  $
        a  (div a b)
        c  [(d (mod a b)) ?:(f [?:(=(10 b) ',' '-') c] c)]
        e  +(e)
      ==
    ::
    ++  rup
      =+  b=(met 3 a)
      ^-  tape
      :-  '-'
      |-  ^-  tape
      ?:  (gth (met 5 a) 1)
        %+  weld
          $(a (rsh 5 a), b (sub b 4))
        `tape`['-' '-' $(a (end 5 a), b 4)]
      ?:  =(0 b)
        ['~' ~]
      ?:  (lte b 1)
        (trip (tos:po a))
      |-  ^-  tape
      ?:  =(2 b)
        =+  c=(rsh 3 a)
        =+  d=(end 3 a)
        (weld (trip (tod:po c)) (trip (tos:po (mix c d))))
      =+  c=(rsh [3 2] a)
      =+  d=(end [3 2] a)
      (weld ^$(a c, b (met 3 c)) `tape`['-' $(a (mix c d), b 2)])
    ::
    ++  ruv
      ^-  tape
      :+  '0'
        'v'
      %^    rum
          64
        ~
      |=  b=@
```

```
    ?:  =(63 b)
      '+'
    ?:  =(62 b)
      '-'
    ?:((lth b 26) (add 65 b) ?:((lth b 52) (add 71 b) (sub b 4)))
  ::
  ++  rux   `tape`['0' 'x' (rum 16 ~ |=(b=@ (add b ?:((lth b 10) 48 87))))]
  --
++  cass                                    ::  lowercase
  |=  vib=tape
  ^-  tape
  (turn vib |=(a=@ ?.(&((gte a 'A') (lte a 'Z')) a (add 32 a))))
::
++  cuss                                    ::  uppercase
  |=  vib=tape
  ^-  tape
  (turn vib |=(a=@ ?.(&((gte a 'a') (lte a 'z')) a (sub a 32))))
::
++  crip  |=(a=tape `@t`(rap 3 a))          ::  tape to cord
::
++  mesc                                    ::  ctrl code escape
  |=  vib=tape
  ^-  tape
  ?~  vib
    ~
  ?:  =('\\' i.vib)
    ['\\' '\\' $(vib t.vib)]
  ?:  ?|((gth i.vib 126) (lth i.vib 32) =(`@`39 i.vib))
    ['\\' (welp ~(rux at i.vib) '/' $(vib t.vib))]
  [i.vib $(vib t.vib)]
::
++  runt                                    ::  prepend repeatedly
  |=  [[a=@ b=@] c=tape]
  ^-  tape
  ?:  =(0 a)
    c
  [b $(a (dec a))]
::
++  sand                                    ::  atom sanity
  |=  a=@ta
  (flit (sane a))
::
++  sane                                    ::  atom sanity
  |=  a=@ta
  |=  b=@   ^-  ?
  ?.  =(%t (end 3 a))
    ::  XX more and better sanity
    ::
    &
  =+  [inx=0 len=(met 3 b)]
  ?:  =(%tas a)
    |-  ^-  ?
    ?:  =(inx len)   &
    =+  cur=(cut 3 [inx 1] b)
    ?&  ?|  &((gte cur 'a') (lte cur 'z'))
            &(=('-' cur) !=(0 inx) !=(len inx))
            &(&((gte cur '0') (lte cur '9')) !=(0 inx))
        ==
```

```
        $(inx +(inx))
      ==
  ?:  =(%ta a)
    |-  ^-  ?
    ?:  =(inx len)  &
    =+  cur=(cut 3 [inx 1] b)
    ?&  ?|  &((gte cur 'a') (lte cur 'z'))
            &((gte cur '0') (lte cur '9'))
            |(=('-' cur) =('~' cur) =('_' cur) =('.' cur))
        ==
        $(inx +(inx))
    ==
  |-  ^-  ?
  ?:  =(inx len)  &
  =+  cur=(cut 3 [inx 1] b)
  ?:  &((lth cur 32) !=(10 cur))  |
  =+  tef=(teff cur)
  ?&  ?|  =(1 tef)
          =+  i=1
          |-  ^-  ?
          ?|  =(i tef)
              ?&  (gte (cut 3 [(add i inx) 1] b) 128)
                  $(i +(i))
      ==  ==  ==
      $(inx (add inx tef))
  ==
::
++  ruth                                        ::  biblical sanity
  |=  [a=@ta b=*]
  ^-  @
  ?^  b  !!
  ::  ?.  ((sane a) b)  !!
  b
::
++  trim                                        ::  tape split
  |=  [a=@ b=tape]
  ^-  [p=tape q=tape]
  ?~  b
    [~ ~]
  ?:  =(0 a)
    [~ b]
  =+  c=$(a (dec a), b t.b)
  [[i.b p.c] q.c]
::
++  trip                                        ::  cord to tape
  ~/  %trip
  |=  a=@  ^-  tape
  ?:  =(0 (met 3 a))
    ~
  [^-(@ta (end 3 a)) $(a (rsh 3 a))]
::
++  teff                                        ::  length utf8
  |=  a=@t  ^-  @
  =+  b=(end 3 a)
  ?:  =(0 b)
    ?>(=(`@`0 a) 0)
  ?>  |((gte b 32) =(10 b))
  ?:((lte b 127) 1 ?:((lte b 223) 2 ?:((lte b 239) 3 4)))
```

```
::
++  taft                                     ::  utf8 to utf32
  |=  a=@t
  ^-  @c
  %+  rap  5
  |-  ^-  (list @c)
  =+  b=(teff a)
  ?:  =(0 b)  ~
  =+  ^=  c
      %+  can  0
      %+  turn
        ^-  (list [p=@ q=@])
        ?+  b  !!
          %1  [[0 7] ~]
          %2  [[8 6] [0 5] ~]
          %3  [[16 6] [8 6] [0 4] ~]
          %4  [[24 6] [16 6] [8 6] [0 3] ~]
        ==
      |=([p=@ q=@] [q (cut 0 [p q] a)])
  ?>  =((tuft c) (end [3 b] a))
  [c $(a (rsh [3 b] a))]
::
++  tuba                                     ::  utf8 to utf32 tape
  |=  a=tape
  ^-  (list @c)
  (rip 5 (taft (rap 3 a)))                   ::  XX horrible
::
++  tufa                                     ::  utf32 to utf8 tape
  |=  a=(list @c)
  ^-  tape
  ?~  a  ""
  (weld (rip 3 (tuft i.a)) $(a t.a))
::
++  tuft                                     ::  utf32 to utf8 text
  |=  a=@c
  ^-  @t
  %+  rap  3
  |-  ^-  (list @)
  ?:  =(`@`0 a)
    ~
  =+  b=(end 5 a)
  =+  c=$(a (rsh 5 a))
  ?:  (lte b 0x7f)
    [b c]
  ?:  (lte b 0x7ff)
    :*  (mix 0b1100.0000 (cut 0 [6 5] b))
        (mix 0b1000.0000 (end [0 6] b))
        c
    ==
  ?:  (lte b 0xffff)
    :*  (mix 0b1110.0000 (cut 0 [12 4] b))
        (mix 0b1000.0000 (cut 0 [6 6] b))
        (mix 0b1000.0000 (end [0 6] b))
        c
    ==
  :*  (mix 0b1111.0000 (cut 0 [18 3] b))
      (mix 0b1000.0000 (cut 0 [12 6] b))
      (mix 0b1000.0000 (cut 0 [6 6] b))
```

```
4349          (mix 0b1000.0000 (end [0 6] b))
4350          c
4351      ==
4352  ::
4353  ++  wack                                              ::  knot escape
4354    |=  a=@ta
4355    ^-  @ta
4356    =+  b=(rip 3 a)
4357    %+  rap  3
4358    |-  ^-  tape
4359    ?~  b
4360        ~
4361    ?:  =('~' i.b)  ['~' '~' $(b t.b)]
4362    ?:  =('_' i.b)  ['~' '-' $(b t.b)]
4363    [i.b $(b t.b)]
4364  ::
4365  ++  wick                                              ::  knot unescape
4366    |=  a=@
4367    ^-  (unit @ta)
4368    =+  b=(rip 3 a)
4369    =-  ?^(b ~ (some (rap 3 (flop c))))
4370    =|  c=tape
4371    |-  ^-  [b=tape c=tape]
4372    ?~  b  [~ c]
4373    ?.  =('~' i.b)
4374      $(b t.b, c [i.b c])
4375    ?~  t.b  [b ~]
4376    ?-  i.t.b
4377      %'~'  $(b t.t.b, c ['~' c])
4378      %'-'  $(b t.t.b, c ['_' c])
4379      @     [b ~]
4380    ==
4381  ::
4382  ++  woad                                              ::  cord unescape
4383    |=  a=@ta
4384    ^-  @t
4385    %+  rap  3
4386    |-  ^-  (list @)
4387    ?:  =(`@`0 a)
4388        ~
4389    =+  b=(end 3 a)
4390    =+  c=(rsh 3 a)
4391    ?:  =('.' b)
4392      [' ' $(a c)]
4393    ?.  =('~' b)
4394      [b $(a c)]
4395    =>  .(b (end 3 c), c (rsh 3 c))
4396    ?+  b  =-  (weld (rip 3 (tuft p.d)) $(a q.d))
4397           ^=  d
4398           =+  d=0
4399           |-  ^-  [p=@ q=@]
4400           ?:  =('.' b)
4401             [d c]
4402           ?<  =(0 c)
4403           %=  $
4404             b  (end 3 c)
4405             c  (rsh 3 c)
4406             d  %+  add  (mul 16 d)
```

```
4407            %+  sub  b
4408            ?:  &((gte b '0') (lte b '9'))  48
4409            ?>(&((gte b 'a') (lte b 'z')) 87)
4410          ==
4411      %'.'  ['.' $(a c)]
4412      %'~'  ['~' $(a c)]
4413    ==
4414  ::
4415  ++  wood                                          ::  cord escape
4416    |=  a=@t
4417    ^-  @ta
4418    %+  rap  3
4419    |-  ^-  (list @)
4420    ?:  =(`@`0 a)
4421      ~
4422    =+  b=(teff a)
4423    =+  c=(taft (end [3 b] a))
4424    =+  d=$(a (rsh [3 b] a))
4425    ?:  ?|  &((gte c 'a') (lte c 'z'))
4426            &((gte c '0') (lte c '9'))
4427            =(`@`'-' c)
4428        ==
4429      [c d]
4430    ?+  c
4431      :-  '~'
4432      =+  e=(met 2 c)
4433      |-  ^-  tape
4434      ?:  =(0 e)
4435        ['.' d]
4436      =.  e  (dec e)
4437      =+  f=(rsh [2 e] c)
4438      [(add ?:((lte f 9) 48 87) f) $(c (end [2 e] c))]
4439    ::
4440      %' '  ['.' d]
4441      %'.'  ['~' '.' d]
4442      %'~'  ['~' '~' d]
4443    ==
4444  ::
4445  ::  4c: tank printer
4446  +|  %tank-printer
4447  ::
4448  ++  wash                                          ::  render tank at width
4449    |=  [[tab=@ edg=@] tac=tank]  ^-  wall
4450    (~(win re tac) tab edg)
4451  ::
4452  ::  +re: tank renderer
4453  ::
4454  ++  re
4455    |_  tac=tank
4456    ::  +ram: render a tank to one line (flat)
4457    ::
4458    ++  ram
4459      ^-  tape
4460      ?@  tac
4461        (trip tac)
4462      ?-  -.tac
4463        %leaf  p.tac
4464      ::
```

```
4465      ::   flat %palm rendered as %rose with welded openers
4466      ::
4467          %palm
4468        =*  mid  p.p.tac
4469        =*  for  (weld q.p.tac r.p.tac)
4470        =*  end  s.p.tac
4471        ram(tac [%rose [mid for end] q.tac])
4472      ::
4473      ::   flat %rose rendered with open/mid/close
4474      ::
4475          %rose
4476        =*  mid  p.p.tac
4477        =*  for  q.p.tac
4478        =*  end  r.p.tac
4479        =*  lit  q.tac
4480      %+  weld
4481          for
4482      |-  ^-  tape
4483      ?~  lit
4484          end
4485      %+  weld
4486          ram(tac i.lit)
4487        =*  voz  $(lit t.lit)
4488      ?~(t.lit voz (weld mid voz))
4489       ==
4490    ::  +win: render a tank to multiple lines (tall)
4491    ::
4492    ::     indented by .tab, soft-wrapped at .edg
4493    ::
4494    ++  win
4495    |=  [tab=@ud edg=@ud]
4496    ::  output stack
4497    ::
4498    =|  lug=wall
4499    |^  ^-  wall
4500        ?@  tac
4501          (rig (trip tac))
4502        ?-    -.tac
4503            %leaf  (rig p.tac)
4504        ::
4505            %palm
4506        =/  hom   ram
4507        ?:  (lte (lent hom) (sub edg tab))
4508          (rig hom)
4509        ::
4510        =*  for  q.p.tac
4511        =*  lit  q.tac
4512        ?~  lit
4513          (rig for)
4514        ?~  t.lit
4515          =:  tab  (add 2 tab)
4516              lug  $(tac i.lit)
4517          ==
4518          (rig for)
4519        ::
4520        =>  .(lit `(list tank)`lit)
4521        =/  lyn  (mul 2 (lent lit))
4522        =.  lug
```

```
          |-  ^-  wall
          ?~  lit
            lug
          =/  nyl  (sub lyn 2)
          %=  ^$
            tac  i.lit
            tab  (add tab nyl)
            lug  $(lit t.lit, lyn nyl)
          ==
      (wig for)
    ::
        %rose
      =/  hom  ram
      ?:  (lte (lent hom) (sub edg tab))
        (rig hom)
      ::
      =*  for  q.p.tac
      =*  end  r.p.tac
      =*  lit  q.tac
      =.  lug
        |-  ^-  wall
        ?~  lit
          ?~(end lug (rig end))
        %=  ^$
          tac  i.lit
          tab  (mod (add 2 tab) (mul 2 (div edg 3)))
          lug  $(lit t.lit)
        ==
      ?~(for lug (wig for))
    ==
::  +rig: indent tape and cons with output stack
::
++  rig
  |=  hom=tape
  ^-  wall
  [(runt [tab ' '] hom) lug]
::  +wig: indent tape and cons with output stack
::
::    joined with the top line if whitespace/indentation allow
::
++  wig
  |=  hom=tape
  ^-  wall
  ?~  lug
    (rig hom)
  =/  wug  :(add 1 tab (lent hom))
  ?.  =+  mir=i.lug
      |-  ^-  ?
      ?~  mir  |
      ?|  =(0 wug)
          ?&(=(' ' i.mir) $(mir t.mir, wug (dec wug)))
      ==
    (rig hom)        :: ^ XX regular form?
  :_  t.lug
  %+  runt  [tab ' ']
  (weld hom `tape`['  ' (slag wug i.lug)])
  --
--
```

```
4581  ++  show                                                  ::  XX deprecated!
4582    |=  vem=*
4583    |^  ^-  tank
4584      ?:  ?=(@ vem)
4585        [%leaf (mesc (trip vem))]
4586      ?-    vem
4587          [s=~ c=*]
4588        [%leaf '\'' (weld (mesc (tape +.vem)) `tape`['\'' ~])]
4589        ::
4590          [s=%a c=@]            [%leaf (mesc (trip c.vem))]
4591          [s=%b c=*]            (shop c.vem |=(a=@ ~(rub at a)))
4592          [s=[%c p=@] c=*]
4593        :+  %palm
4594          [['.' ~] ['-' ~] ~ ~]
4595        [[%leaf (mesc (trip p.s.vem))] $(vem c.vem) ~]
4596        ::
4597          [s=%d c=*]            (shop c.vem |=(a=@ ~(rud at a)))
4598          [s=%k c=*]            (tank c.vem)
4599          [s=%h c=*]
4600        :+  %rose
4601          [['/' ~] ['/' ~] ~]
4602        =+  yol=((list @ta) c.vem)
4603        (turn yol |=(a=@ta [%leaf (trip a)]))
4604        ::
4605          [s=%l c=*]            (shol c.vem)
4606          [s=%o c=*]
4607      %=    $
4608            vem
4609        :-  [%m '%h::[%d %d].[%d %d]>']
4610        [-.c.vem +<-.c.vem +<+.c.vem +>-.c.vem +>+.c.vem ~]
4611      ==
4612        ::
4613          [s=%p c=*]            (shop c.vem |=(a=@ ~(rup at a)))
4614          [s=%q c=*]            (shop c.vem |=(a=@ ~(r at a)))
4615          [s=%r c=*]            $(vem [[%r ' ' '{' '}'] c.vem])
4616          [s=%t c=*]            (shop c.vem |=(a=@ ~(rt at a)))
4617          [s=%v c=*]            (shop c.vem |=(a=@ ~(ruv at a)))
4618          [s=%x c=*]            (shop c.vem |=(a=@ ~(rux at a)))
4619          [s=[%m p=@] c=*]    (shep p.s.vem c.vem)
4620          [s=[%r p=@] c=*]
4621        $(vem [[%r ' ' (cut 3 [0 1] p.s.vem) (cut 3 [1 1] p.s.vem)] c.vem])
4622        ::
4623          [s=[%r p=@ q=@ r=@] c=*]
4624        :+  %rose
4625          :*  p=(mesc (trip p.s.vem))
4626              q=(mesc (trip q.s.vem))
4627              r=(mesc (trip r.s.vem))
4628          ==
4629        |-  ^-  (list tank)
4630        ?@  c.vem
4631          ~
4632        [^$(vem -.c.vem) $(c.vem +.c.vem)]
4633        ::
4634          [s=%z c=*]            $(vem [[%r %$ %$ %$] c.vem])
4635          *                    !!
4636      ==
4637  ++  shep
4638    |=  [fom=@ gar=*]
```

```
    ^-  tank
=+  l=(met 3 fom)
=+  i=0
:-  %leaf
|-  ^-  tape
?:  (gte i l)
    ~
=+  c=(cut 3 [i 1] fom)
?.  =(37 c)
  (weld (mesc [c ~]) $(i +(i)))
=+  d=(cut 3 [+(i) 1] fom)
?.  .?(gar)
  ['\\' '#' $(i (add 2 i))]
(weld ~(ram re (show d -.gar)) $(i (add 2 i), gar +.gar))
::
++  shop
|=  [aug=* vel=$-(a=@ tape)]
    ^-  tank
?:  ?=(@ aug)
  [%leaf (vel aug)]
:+  %rose
  [[' ' ~] ['[' ~] [']' ~]]
=>  .(aug `*`aug)
|-  ^-  (list tank)
?:  ?=(@ aug)
  [^$ ~]
[^$(aug -.aug) $(aug +.aug)]
::
++  shol
|=  lim=*
:+  %rose
  [['.' ~] ~ ~]
|-    ^-  (list tank)
?:  ?=(@ lim)  ~
:_  $(lim +.lim)
?+  -.lim  (show '#')
  ~  (show '$')
  c=@  (show c.lim)
  [%& %1]  (show '.')
  [%& c=@]
  [%leaf '+' ~(rud at c.lim)]
::
  [%| @ ~]  (show ',')
  [%| n=@ ~ c=@]
  [%leaf (weld (reap n.lim '^') ?~(c.lim "$" (trip c.lim)))]
==
--
::
::    4d: parsing (tracing)
+|  %parsing-tracing
::
++  last  |=  [zyc=hair naz=hair]              ::  farther trace
          ^-  hair
          ?:  =(p.zyc p.naz)
            ?:((gth q.zyc q.naz) zyc naz)
          ?:((gth p.zyc p.naz) zyc naz)
::
++  lust  |=  [weq=char naz=hair]              ::  detect newline
```

```
4697              ^-  hair
4698              ?:(=(`@`10 weq) [+(p.naz) 1] [p.naz +(q.naz)])
4699  ::
4700  ::    4e: parsing (combinators)
4701  +|  %parsing-combinators
4702  ::
4703  ++  bend                                        ::  conditional comp
4704    ~/  %bend
4705    |*  raq=_|*([a=* b=*] [~ u=[a b]])
4706    ~/  %fun
4707    |*  [vex=edge sab=rule]
4708    ?~  q.vex
4709      vex
4710    =+  yit=(sab q.u.q.vex)
4711    =+  yur=(last p.vex p.yit)
4712    ?~  q.yit
4713      [p=yur q=q.vex]
4714    =+  vux=(raq p.u.q.vex p.u.q.yit)
4715    ?~  vux
4716      [p=yur q=q.vex]
4717    [p=yur q=[~ u=[p=u.vux q=q.u.q.yit]]]
4718  ::
4719  ++  comp
4720    ~/  %comp
4721    |*  raq=_|*([a=* b=*] [a b])                   ::  arbitrary compose
4722    ~/  %fun
4723    |*  [vex=edge sab=rule]
4724    ~!  +<
4725    ?~  q.vex
4726      vex
4727    =+  yit=(sab q.u.q.vex)
4728    =+  yur=(last p.vex p.yit)
4729    ?~  q.yit
4730      [p=yur q=q.yit]
4731    [p=yur q=[~ u=[p=(raq p.u.q.vex p.u.q.yit) q=q.u.q.yit]]]
4732  ::
4733  ++  fail  |=(tub=nail [p=p.tub q=~])             ::  never parse
4734  ++  glue                                         ::  add rule
4735    ~/  %glue
4736    |*  bus=rule
4737    ~/  %fun
4738    |*  [vex=edge sab=rule]
4739    (plug vex ;~(pfix bus sab))
4740  ::
4741  ++  less                                         ::  no first and second
4742    |*  [vex=edge sab=rule]
4743    ?~  q.vex
4744      =+  roq=(sab)
4745      [p=(last p.vex p.roq) q=q.roq]
4746    (fail +<.sab)
4747  ::
4748  ++  pfix                                         ::  discard first rule
4749    ~/  %pfix
4750    |*  sam=[vex=edge sab=rule]
4751    %.  sam
4752    (comp |*([a=* b=*] b))
4753  ::
4754  ++  plug                                         ::  first then second
```

```
~/  %plug
|*  [vex=edge sab=rule]
?~  q.vex
  vex
=+  yit=(sab q.u.q.vex)
=+  yur=(last p.vex p.yit)
?~  q.yit
  [p=yur q=q.yit]
[p=yur q=[~ u=[p=[p.u.q.vex p.u.q.yit] q=q.u.q.yit]]]
::
++  pose                                    ::  first or second
~/  %pose
|*  [vex=edge sab=rule]
?~  q.vex
  =+  roq=(sab)
  [p=(last p.vex p.roq) q=q.roq]
vex
::
++  simu                                    ::  first and second
|*  [vex=edge sab=rule]
?~  q.vex
  vex
=+  roq=(sab)
roq
::
++  sfix                                    ::  discard second rule
~/  %sfix
|*  sam=[vex=edge sab=rule]
%.  sam
(comp |*([a=* b=*] a))
::
::    4f: parsing (rule builders)
+|  %parsing-rule-builders
::
++  bass                                    ::  leftmost base
|*  [wuc=@ tyd=rule]
%+  cook
  |=  waq=(list @)
  %+  roll
    waq
  =|([p=@ q=@] |.((add p (mul wuc q))))
tyd
::
++  boss                                    ::  rightmost base
|*  [wuc=@ tyd=rule]
%+  cook
  |=  waq=(list @)
  %+  reel
    waq
  =|([p=@ q=@] |.((add p (mul wuc q))))
tyd
::
++  cold                                    ::  replace w+ constant
~/  %cold
|*  [cus=* sef=rule]
~/  %fun
|=  tub=nail
=+  vex=(sef tub)
```

```
4813    ?~  q.vex
4814      vex
4815    [p=p.vex q=[~ u=[p=cus q=q.u.q.vex]]]
4816  ::
4817  ++  cook                                        ::  apply gate
4818    ~/  %cook
4819    |*  [poq=gate sef=rule]
4820    ~/  %fun
4821    |=  tub=nail
4822    =+  vex=(sef tub)
4823    ?~  q.vex
4824      vex
4825    [p=p.vex q=[~ u=[p=(poq p.u.q.vex) q=q.u.q.vex]]]
4826  ::
4827  ++  easy                                        ::  always parse
4828    ~/  %easy
4829    |*  huf=*
4830    ~/  %fun
4831    |=  tub=nail
4832    ^-  (like _huf)
4833    [p=p.tub q=[~ u=[p=huf q=tub]]]
4834  ::
4835  ++  fuss
4836    |=  [sic=@t non=@t]
4837    ;~(pose (cold %& (jest sic)) (cold %| (jest non)))
4838  ::
4839  ++  full                                        ::  has to fully parse
4840    |*  sef=rule
4841    |=  tub=nail
4842    =+  vex=(sef tub)
4843    ?~(q.vex vex ?:(=(~ q.q.u.q.vex) vex [p=p.vex q=~]))
4844  ::
4845  ++  funk                                        ::  add to tape first
4846    |*  [pre=tape sef=rule]
4847    |=  tub=nail
4848    (sef p.tub (weld pre q.tub))
4849  ::
4850  ++  here                                        ::  place-based apply
4851    ~/  %here
4852    |*  [hez=_|=([a=pint b=*] [a b]) sef=rule]
4853    ~/  %fun
4854    |=  tub=nail
4855    =+  vex=(sef tub)
4856    ?~  q.vex
4857      vex
4858    [p=p.vex q=[~ u=[p=(hez [p.tub p.q.u.q.vex] p.u.q.vex) q=q.u.q.vex]]]
4859  ::
4860  ++  inde  |*  sef=rule                          ::  indentation block
4861    |=  nail  ^+  (sef)
4862    =+  [har tap]=[p q]:+<
4863    =+  lev=(fil 3 (dec q.har) ' ')
4864    =+  eol=(just `@t`10)
4865    =+  =-  roq=((star ;~(pose prn ;~(sfix eol (jest lev)) -)) har tap)
4866        ;~(simu ;~(plug eol eol) eol)
4867    ?~  q.roq  roq
4868    =+  vex=(sef har(q 1) p.u.q.roq)
4869    =+  fur=p.vex(q (add (dec q.har) q.p.vex))
4870    ?~  q.vex  vex(p fur)
```

```
4871    =-  vex(p fur, u.q -)
4872    :+  &3.vex
4873      &4.vex(q.p (add (dec q.har) q.p.&4.vex))
4874    =+  res=|4.vex
4875    |-  ?~  res  |4.roq
4876    ?.  =(10 -.res)  [-.res $(res +.res)]
4877    (welp [`@t`10 (trip lev)] $(res +.res))
4878  ::
4879  ++  ifix
4880    |*  [fel=[rule rule] hof=rule]
4881    ~!  +<
4882    ~!  +<:-.fel
4883    ~!  +<:+.fel
4884    ;~(pfix -.fel ;~(sfix hof +.fel))
4885  ::
4886  ++  jest                                  ::  match a cord
4887    |=  daf=@t
4888    |=  tub=nail
4889    =+  fad=daf
4890    |-  ^-  (like @t)
4891    ?:  =(`@`0 daf)
4892      [p=p.tub q=[~ u=[p=fad q=tub]]]
4893    ?:  |(?=(~ q.tub) !=((end 3 daf) i.q.tub))
4894      (fail tub)
4895    $(p.tub (lust i.q.tub p.tub), q.tub t.q.tub, daf (rsh 3 daf))
4896  ::
4897  ++  just                                  ::  XX redundant, jest
4898    ~/  %just                               ::  match a char
4899    |=  daf=char
4900    ~/  %fun
4901    |=  tub=nail
4902    ^-  (like char)
4903    ?~  q.tub
4904      (fail tub)
4905    ?.  =(daf i.q.tub)
4906      (fail tub)
4907    (next tub)
4908  ::
4909  ++  knee                                  ::  callbacks
4910    |*  [gar=* sef=_|.(*rule)]
4911    |=  tub=nail
4912    ^-  (like _gar)
4913    ((sef) tub)
4914  ::
4915  ++  mask                                  ::  match char in set
4916    ~/  %mask
4917    |=  bud=(list char)
4918    ~/  %fun
4919    |=  tub=nail
4920    ^-  (like char)
4921    ?~  q.tub
4922      (fail tub)
4923    ?.  (lien bud |=(a=char =(i.q.tub a)))
4924      (fail tub)
4925    (next tub)
4926  ::
4927  ++  more                                  ::  separated, *
4928    |*  [bus=rule fel=rule]
```

```
4929      ;~(pose (most bus fel) (easy ~))
4930    ::
4931    ++  most                                          ::  separated, +
4932      |*  [bus=rule fel=rule]
4933      ;~(plug fel (star ;~(pfix bus fel)))
4934    ::
4935    ++  next                                          ::  consume a char
4936      |=  tub=nail
4937      ^-  (like char)
4938      ?~  q.tub
4939        (fail tub)
4940      =+  zac=(lust i.q.tub p.tub)
4941      [zac [~ i.q.tub [zac t.q.tub]]]
4942    ::
4943    ++  perk                                          ::  parse cube fork
4944      |*  a=(pole @tas)
4945      ?~  a  fail
4946      ;~  pose
4947        (cold -.a (jest -.a))
4948        $(a +.a)
4949      ==
4950    ::
4951    ++  pick                                          ::  rule for ++each
4952      |*  [a=rule b=rule]
4953      ;~  pose
4954        (stag %& a)
4955        (stag %| b)
4956      ==
4957    ++  plus  |*(fel=rule ;~(plug fel (star fel)))     ::
4958    ++  punt  |*([a=rule] ;~(pose (stag ~ a) (easy ~)))  ::
4959    ++  sear                                          ::  conditional cook
4960      |*  [pyq=$-(* (unit)) sef=rule]
4961      |=  tub=nail
4962      =+  vex=(sef tub)
4963      ?~  q.vex
4964        vex
4965      =+  gey=(pyq p.u.q.vex)
4966      ?~  gey
4967        [p=p.vex q=~]
4968      [p=p.vex q=[~ u=[p=u.gey q=q.u.q.vex]]]
4969    ::
4970    ++  shim                                          ::  match char in range
4971      ~/  %shim
4972      |=  [les=@ mos=@]
4973      ~/  %fun
4974      |=  tub=nail
4975      ^-  (like char)
4976      ?~  q.tub
4977        (fail tub)
4978      ?.  ?&((gte i.q.tub les) (lte i.q.tub mos))
4979        (fail tub)
4980      (next tub)
4981    ::
4982    ++  stag                                          ::  add a label
4983      ~/  %stag
4984      |*  [gob=* sef=rule]
4985      ~/  %fun
4986      |=  tub=nail
```

```
4987    =+  vex=(sef tub)
4988    ?~  q.vex
4989      vex
4990    [p=p.vex q=[~ u=[p=[gob p.u.q.vex] q=q.u.q.vex]]]
4991  ::
4992  ++  stet                                          ::
4993    |*  leh=(list [?(@ [@ @]) rule])
4994    |-
4995    ?~  leh
4996      ~
4997    [i=[p=-.i.leh q=+.i.leh] t=$(leh t.leh)]
4998  ::
4999  ++  stew                                          :: switch by first char
5000    ~/  %stew
5001    |*  leh=(list [p=?(@ [@ @]) q=rule])             :: char+range keys
5002    =+  ^=  wor                                      :: range complete lth
5003        |=  [ort=?(@ [@ @]) wan=?(@ [@ @])]
5004        ?@  ort
5005          ?@(wan (lth ort wan) (lth ort -.wan))
5006        ?@(wan (lth +.ort wan) (lth +.ort -.wan))
5007    =+  ^=  hel                                      :: build parser map
5008    =+  hel=`(tree _?>(?=(^ leh) i.leh))`~
5009    |-  ^+  hel
5010    ?~  leh
5011      ~
5012    =+  yal=$(leh t.leh)
5013    |-  ^+  hel
5014    ?~  yal
5015      [i.leh ~ ~]
5016    ?:  (wor p.i.leh p.n.yal)
5017      =+  nuc=$(yal l.yal)
5018      ?>  ?=(^ nuc)
5019      ?:  (mor p.n.yal p.n.nuc)
5020        [n.yal nuc r.yal]
5021      [n.nuc l.nuc [n.yal r.nuc r.yal]]
5022    =+  nuc=$(yal r.yal)
5023    ?>  ?=(^ nuc)
5024    ?:  (mor p.n.yal p.n.nuc)
5025      [n.yal l.yal nuc]
5026    [n.nuc [n.yal l.yal l.nuc] r.nuc]
5027    ~%  %fun  ..^$  ~
5028    |=  tub=nail
5029    ?~  q.tub
5030      (fail tub)
5031    |-
5032    ?~  hel
5033      (fail tub)
5034    ?:  ?@  p.n.hel
5035          =(p.n.hel i.q.tub)
5036        ?&((gte i.q.tub -.p.n.hel) (lte i.q.tub +.p.n.hel))
5037      ::  (q.n.hel [(lust i.q.tub p.tub) t.q.tub])
5038      (q.n.hel tub)
5039    ?:  (wor i.q.tub p.n.hel)
5040      $(hel l.hel)
5041    $(hel r.hel)
5042  ::
5043  ++  slug                                           ::
5044    |*  raq=_=>(~ |*([a=* b=*] [a b]))
```

```
|*  [bus=rule fel=rule]
;~((comp raq) fel (stir +<+.raq raq ;~(pfix bus fel)))
::
++  star                                          ::  0 or more times
|*  fel=rule
(stir `(list _(wonk *fel))`~ |*([a=* b=*] [a b]) fel)
::
++  stir
~/  %stir
|*  [rud=* raq=_=>(~ |*([a=* b=*] [a b])) fel=rule]
~/  %fun
|=  tub=nail
^-  (like _rud)
::
::  lef: successful interim parse results (per .fel)
::  wag: initial accumulator (.rud in .tub at farthest success)
::
=+  ^=  [lef wag]
  =|  lef=(list _(fel tub))
  |-  ^-  [_lef (pair hair [~ u=(pair _rud nail)])]
  =+  vex=(fel tub)
  ?~  q.vex
    :-  lef
    [p.vex [~ rud tub]]
  $(lef [vex lef], tub q.u.q.vex)
::
::  fold .lef into .wag, combining results with .raq
::
%+  roll  lef
|=  _[vex=(fel tub) wag=wag]  :: q.vex is always (some)
^+  wag
:-  (last p.vex p.wag)
[~ (raq p.u.+.q.vex p.u.q.wag) q.u.q.wag]
::
++  stun                                          ::  parse several times
~/  %stun
|*  [lig=[@ @] fel=rule]
|=  tub=nail
^-  (like (list _(wonk (fel))))
?:  =(0 +.lig)
  [p.tub [~ ~ tub]]
=+  vex=(fel tub)
?~  q.vex
  ?:  =(0 -.lig)
    [p.vex [~ ~ tub]]
  vex
=+  ^=  wag  %=  $
                -.lig  ?:(=(0 -.lig) 0 (dec -.lig))
                +.lig  ?:(=(0 +.lig) 0 (dec +.lig))
                tub  q.u.q.vex
              ==
?~  q.wag
  wag
[p.wag [~ [p.u.q.vex p.u.q.wag] q.u.q.wag]]
::
::    4g: parsing (outside caller)
+|  %parsing-outside-caller
::
```

```
5103 ++  rash  |*([naf=@ sab=rule] (scan (trip naf) sab))
5104 ++  rose  |*  [los=tape sab=rule]
5105          =+  vex=(sab [[1 1] los])
5106          =+  len=(lent los)
5107          ?.  =(+(len) q.p.vex)   [%| p=(dec q.p.vex)]
5108          ?~  q.vex
5109            [%& p=~]
5110          [%& p=[~ u=p.u.q.vex]]
5111 ++  rush  |*([naf=@ sab=rule] (rust (trip naf) sab))
5112 ++  rust  |*  [los=tape sab=rule]
5113          =+  vex=((full sab) [[1 1] los])
5114          ?~(q.vex ~ [~ u=p.u.q.vex])
5115 ++  scan  |*  [los=tape sab=rule]
5116          =+  vex=((full sab) [[1 1] los])
5117          ?~  q.vex
5118            ~_  (show [%m '{%d %d}'] p.p.vex q.p.vex ~)
5119            ~_(leaf+"syntax error" !!)
5120          p.u.q.vex
5121 ::
5122 ::      4h: parsing (ascii glyphs)
5123 +|  %parsing-ascii-glyphs
5124 ::
5125 ++  ace  (just ' ')              ::  spACE
5126 ++  bar  (just '|')              ::  vertical BAR
5127 ++  bas  (just '\\')             ::  Back Slash (escaped)
5128 ++  buc  (just '$')              ::  dollars BUCks
5129 ++  cab  (just '_')              ::  CABoose
5130 ++  cen  (just '%')              ::  perCENt
5131 ++  col  (just ':')              ::  COLon
5132 ++  com  (just ',')              ::  COMma
5133 ++  doq  (just '"')              ::  Double Quote
5134 ++  dot  (just '.')              ::  dot dot dot ...
5135 ++  fas  (just '/')              ::  Forward Slash
5136 ++  gal  (just '<')              ::  Greater Left
5137 ++  gar  (just '>')              ::  Greater Right
5138 ++  hax  (just '#')              ::  Hash
5139 ++  hep  (just '-')              ::  HyPhen
5140 ++  kel  (just '{')              ::  Curly Left
5141 ++  ker  (just '}')              ::  Curly Right
5142 ++  ket  (just '^')              ::  CareT
5143 ++  lus  (just '+')              ::  pLUS
5144 ++  mic  (just ';')              ::  seMIColon
5145 ++  pal  (just '(')              ::  Paren Left
5146 ++  pam  (just '&')              ::  AMPersand pampersand
5147 ++  par  (just ')')              ::  Paren Right
5148 ++  pat  (just '@')              ::  AT pat
5149 ++  sel  (just '[')              ::  Square Left
5150 ++  ser  (just ']')              ::  Square Right
5151 ++  sig  (just '~')              ::  SIGnature squiggle
5152 ++  soq  (just '\'')             ::  Single Quote
5153 ++  tar  (just '*')              ::  sTAR
5154 ++  tic  (just '`')              ::  backTiCk
5155 ++  tis  (just '=')              ::  'tis tis, it is
5156 ++  wut  (just '?')              ::  wut, what?
5157 ++  zap  (just '!')              ::  zap! bang! crash!!
5158 ::
5159 ::      4i: parsing (useful idioms)
5160 +|  %parsing-useful-idioms
```

```
5161  ::
5162  ++  alf  ;~(pose low hig)                                ::  alphabetic
5163  ++  aln  ;~(pose low hig nud)                            ::  alphanumeric
5164  ++  alp  ;~(pose low hig nud hep)                        ::  alphanumeric and -
5165  ++  bet  ;~(pose (cold 2 hep) (cold 3 lus))              ::  axis syntax - +
5166  ++  bin  (bass 2 (most gon but))                         ::  binary to atom
5167  ++  but  (cook |=(a=@ (sub a '0')) (shim '0' '1'))       ::  binary digit
5168  ++  cit  (cook |=(a=@ (sub a '0')) (shim '0' '7'))       ::  octal digit
5169  ++  dem  (bass 10 (most gon dit))                        ::  decimal to atom
5170  ++  dit  (cook |=(a=@ (sub a '0')) (shim '0' '9'))       ::  decimal digit
5171  ++  dog  ;~(plug dot gay)                                ::  .  number separator
5172  ++  dof  ;~(plug hep gay)                                ::  -  @q separator
5173  ++  doh  ;~(plug ;~(plug hep hep) gay)                   ::  --  phon separator
5174  ++  dun  (cold ~ ;~(plug hep hep))                       ::  -- (stop) to ~
5175  ++  duz  (cold ~ ;~(plug tis tis))                       ::  == (stet) to ~
5176  ++  gah  (mask [`@`10 ' ' ~])                            ::  newline or ace
5177  ++  gap  (cold ~ ;~(plug gaq (star ;~(pose vul gah))))   ::  plural space
5178  ++  gaq  ;~  pose                                        ::  end of line
5179            (just `@`10)
5180            ;~(plug gah ;~(pose gah vul))
5181            vul
5182        ==
5183  ++  gaw  (cold ~ (star ;~(pose vul gah)))                ::  classic white
5184  ++  gay  ;~(pose gap (easy ~))                           ::
5185  ++  gon  ;~(pose ;~(plug bas gay fas) (easy ~))          ::  long numbers \ /
5186  ++  gul  ;~(pose (cold 2 gal) (cold 3 gar))              ::  axis syntax < >
5187  ++  hex  (bass 16 (most gon hit))                        ::  hex to atom
5188  ++  hig  (shim 'A' 'Z')                                  ::  uppercase
5189  ++  hit  ;~  pose                                        ::  hex digits
5190            dit
5191            (cook |=(a=char (sub a 87)) (shim 'a' 'f'))
5192            (cook |=(a=char (sub a 55)) (shim 'A' 'F'))
5193        ==
5194  ++  iny                                                  ::  indentation block
5195    |*  sef=rule
5196    |=  nail  ^+  (sef)
5197    =+  [har tap]=[p q]:+<
5198    =+  lev=(fil 3 (dec q.har) ' ')
5199    =+  eol=(just `@t`10)
5200    =+  =-  roq=((star ;~(pose prn ;~(sfix eol (jest lev)) -)) har tap)
5201        ;~(simu ;~(plug eol eol) eol)
5202    ?~  q.roq  roq
5203    =+  vex=(sef har(q 1) p.u.q.roq)
5204    =+  fur=p.vex(q (add (dec q.har) q.p.vex))
5205    ?~  q.vex  vex(p fur)
5206    =-  vex(p fur, u.q -)
5207    :+  &3.vex
5208      &4.vex(q.p (add (dec q.har) q.p.&4.vex))
5209    =+  res=|4.vex
5210    |-  ?~  res  |4.roq
5211    ?.  =(10 -.res)  [-.res $(res +.res)]
5212    (welp [`@t`10 (trip lev)] $(res +.res))
5213  ::
5214  ++  low  (shim 'a' 'z')                                   ::  lowercase
5215  ++  mes  %+  cook                                        ::  hexbyte
5216          |=([a=@ b=@] (add (mul 16 a) b))
5217          ;~(plug hit hit)
5218  ++  nix  (boss 256 (star ;~(pose aln cab)))              ::
```

```
5219  ++  nud  (shim '0' '9')                                    ::  numeric
5220  ++  prn  ;~(less (just `@`127) (shim 32 256))              ::  non-control
5221  ++  qat  ;~  pose                                          ::  chars in blockcord
5222           prn
5223           ;~(less ;~(plug (just `@`10) soz) (just `@`10))
5224         ==
5225  ++  qit  ;~  pose                                          ::  chars in a cord
5226           ;~(less bas soq prn)
5227           ;~(pfix bas ;~(pose bas soq mes))                 ::  escape chars
5228         ==
5229  ++  qut  ;~  simu  soq                                     ::  cord
5230             ;~  pose
5231               ;~  less  soz
5232                 (ifix [soq soq] (boss 256 (more gon qit)))
5233               ==
5234               =+  hed=;~(pose ;~(plug (plus ace) vul) (just '\0a'))
5235               %-  iny  %+  ifix
5236                 :-  ;~(plug soz hed)
5237                 ;~(plug (just '\0a') soz)
5238               (boss 256 (star qat))
5239             ==
5240         ==
5241  ++  soz  ;~(plug soq soq soq)                              ::  delimiting '''
5242  ++  sym                                                    ::  symbol
5243    %+  cook
5244      |=(a=tape (rap 3 ^-((list @) a)))
5245    ;~(plug low (star ;~(pose nud low hep)))
5246  ::
5247  ++  mixed-case-symbol
5248    %+  cook
5249      |=(a=tape (rap 3 ^-((list @) a)))
5250    ;~(plug alf (star alp))
5251  ::
5252  ++  ven  ;~  (comp |=([a=@ b=@] (peg a b)))               ::  +>- axis syntax
5253           bet
5254           =+  hom=`?`|
5255           |=  tub=nail
5256           ^-  (like @)
5257           =+  vex=?:(hom (bet tub) (gul tub))
5258           ?~  q.vex
5259             [p.tub [~ 1 tub]]
5260           =+  wag=$(p.tub p.vex, hom !hom, tub q.u.q.vex)
5261           ?>  ?=(^ q.wag)
5262           [p.wag [~ (peg p.u.q.vex p.u.q.wag) q.u.q.wag]]
5263         ==
5264  ++  vit                                                    ::  base64 digit
5265    ;~  pose
5266    (cook |=(a=@ (sub a 65)) (shim 'A' 'Z'))
5267    (cook |=(a=@ (sub a 71)) (shim 'a' 'z'))
5268    (cook |=(a=@ (add a 4)) (shim '0' '9'))
5269    (cold 62 (just '-'))
5270    (cold 63 (just '+'))
5271    ==
5272  ++  vul  %+  cold   ~                                      ::  comments
5273           ;~  plug  col  col
5274             (star prn)
5275             (just `@`10)
5276           ==
```

```
5277  ::
5278  ::      4j: parsing (bases and base digits)
5279  +|  %parsing-bases-and-base-digits
5280  ::
5281  ++  ab
5282    |%
5283    ++  bix  (bass 16 (stun [2 2] six))
5284    ++  fem  (sear |=(a=@ (cha:fa a)) aln)
5285    ++  haf  (bass 256 ;~(plug tep tiq (easy ~)))
5286    ++  hef  %+  sear  |=(a=@ ?:(=(a 0) ~ (some a)))
5287             %+  bass  256
5288             ;~(plug tip tiq (easy ~))
5289    ++  hif  (bass 256 ;~(plug tip tiq (easy ~)))
5290    ++  hof  (bass 0x1.0000 ;~(plug hef (stun [1 3] ;~(pfix hep hif))))
5291    ++  huf  (bass 0x1.0000 ;~(plug hef (stun [0 3] ;~(pfix hep hif))))
5292    ++  hyf  (bass 0x1.0000 ;~(plug hif (stun [3 3] ;~(pfix hep hif))))
5293    ++  pev  (bass 32 ;~(plug sev (stun [0 4] siv)))
5294    ++  pew  (bass 64 ;~(plug sew (stun [0 4] siw)))
5295    ++  piv  (bass 32 (stun [5 5] siv))
5296    ++  piw  (bass 64 (stun [5 5] siw))
5297    ++  qeb  (bass 2 ;~(plug seb (stun [0 3] sib)))
5298    ++  qex  (bass 16 ;~(plug sex (stun [0 3] hit)))
5299    ++  qib  (bass 2 (stun [4 4] sib))
5300    ++  qix  (bass 16 (stun [4 4] six))
5301    ++  seb  (cold 1 (just '1'))
5302    ++  sed  (cook |=(a=@ (sub a '0')) (shim '1' '9'))
5303    ++  sev  ;~(pose sed sov)
5304    ++  sew  ;~(pose sed sow)
5305    ++  sex  ;~(pose sed sox)
5306    ++  sib  (cook |=(a=@ (sub a '0')) (shim '0' '1'))
5307    ++  sid  (cook |=(a=@ (sub a '0')) (shim '0' '9'))
5308    ++  siv  ;~(pose sid sov)
5309    ++  siw  ;~(pose sid sow)
5310    ++  six  ;~(pose sid sox)
5311    ++  sov  (cook |=(a=@ (sub a 87)) (shim 'a' 'v'))
5312    ++  sow  ;~  pose
5313               (cook |=(a=@ (sub a 87)) (shim 'a' 'z'))
5314               (cook |=(a=@ (sub a 29)) (shim 'A' 'Z'))
5315               (cold 62 (just '-'))
5316               (cold 63 (just '~'))
5317             ==
5318    ++  sox  (cook |=(a=@ (sub a 87)) (shim 'a' 'f'))
5319    ++  ted  (bass 10 ;~(plug sed (stun [0 2] sid)))
5320    ++  tep  (sear |=(a=@ ?:(=(a 'doz') ~ (ins:po a))) til)
5321    ++  tip  (sear |=(a=@ (ins:po a)) til)
5322    ++  tiq  (sear |=(a=@ (ind:po a)) til)
5323    ++  tid  (bass 10 (stun [3 3] sid))
5324    ++  til  (boss 256 (stun [3 3] low))
5325    ++  urs  %+  cook
5326               |=(a=tape (rap 3 ^-((list @) a)))
5327             (star ;~(pose nud low hep dot sig cab))
5328    ++  urt  %+  cook
5329               |=(a=tape (rap 3 ^-((list @) a)))
5330             (star ;~(pose nud low hep dot sig))
5331    ++  urx  %+  cook
5332               |=(a=tape (rap 3 ^-((list @) a)))
5333             %-  star
5334             ;~  pose
```

```
5335                    nud
5336                    low
5337                    hep
5338                    cab
5339                    (cold ' ' dot)
5340                    (cook tuft (ifix [sig dot] hex))
5341                    ;~(pfix sig ;~(pose sig dot))
5342                ==
5343    ++  voy  ;~(pfix bas ;~(pose bas soq bix))
5344    --
5345  ++  ag
5346    |%
5347    ++  ape  |*(fel=rule ;~(pose (cold `@`0 (just '0')) fel))
5348    ++  bay  (ape (bass 16 ;~(plug qeb:ab (star ;~(pfix dog qib:ab)))))
5349    ++  bip  =+  tod=(ape qex:ab)
5350             (bass 0x1.0000 ;~(plug tod (stun [7 7] ;~(pfix dog tod))))
5351    ++  dem  (ape (bass 1.000 ;~(plug ted:ab (star ;~(pfix dog tid:ab)))))
5352    ++  dim  (ape dip)
5353    ++  dip  (bass 10 ;~(plug sed:ab (star sid:ab)))
5354    ++  dum  (bass 10 (plus sid:ab))
5355    ++  fed  %+  cook  fynd:ob
5356             ;~  pose
5357               %+  bass  0x1.0000.0000.0000.0000        ::  oversized
5358                 ;~  plug
5359                   huf:ab
5360                   (plus ;~(pfix doh hyf:ab))
5361                 ==
5362               hof:ab                                   ::  planet or moon
5363               haf:ab                                   ::  star
5364               tiq:ab                                   ::  galaxy
5365             ==
5366    ++  feq  %+  cook  |=(a=(list @) (rep 4 (flop a)))
5367             ;~  plug
5368               ;~(pose hif:ab tiq:ab)
5369               (star ;~(pfix dof hif:ab))
5370             ==
5371    ++  fim  (sear den:fa (bass 58 (plus fem:ab)))
5372    ++  hex  (ape (bass 0x1.0000 ;~(plug qex:ab (star ;~(pfix dog qix:ab)))))
5373    ++  lip  =+  tod=(ape ted:ab)
5374             (bass 256 ;~(plug tod (stun [3 3] ;~(pfix dog tod))))
5375    ++  mot  ;~  pose
5376               ;~  pfix
5377                 (just '1')
5378                 (cook |=(a=@ (add 10 (sub a '0'))) (shim '0' '2'))
5379               ==
5380               sed:ab
5381             ==
5382    ++  viz  (ape (bass 0x200.0000 ;~(plug pev:ab (star ;~(pfix dog piv:ab)))))
5383    ++  vum  (bass 32 (plus siv:ab))
5384    ++  wiz  (ape (bass 0x4000.0000 ;~(plug pew:ab (star ;~(pfix dog piw:ab)))))
5385    --
5386  ++  mu
5387    |_  [top=@ bot=@]
5388    ++  zag  [p=(end 4 (add top bot)) q=bot]
5389    ++  zig  [p=(end 4 (add top (sub 0x1.0000 bot))) q=bot]
5390    ++  zug  (mix (lsh 4 top) bot)
5391    --
5392  ++  ne
```

```
5393      |_  tig=@
5394      ++  c  (cut 3 [tig 1] key:fa)
5395      ++  d  (add tig '0')
5396      ++  x  ?:((gte tig 10) (add tig 87) d)
5397      ++  v  ?:((gte tig 10) (add tig 87) d)
5398      ++  w  ?:(=(tig 63) '~' ?:(=(tig 62) '-' ?:((gte tig 36) (add tig 29) x)))
5399      --
5400  ::
5401  ::    4k: atom printing
5402  +|  %atom-printing
5403  ::
5404  ++  co
5405    !:
5406    ~%  %co  ..co  ~
5407    =<  |_  lot=coin
5408        ++  rear  |=(rom=tape rend(rep rom))
5409        ++  rent  ~+  `@ta`(rap 3 rend)
5410        ++  rend
5411        ^-  tape
5412        ~+
5413        ?:  ?=(%blob -.lot)
5414          ['~' '0' ((v-co 1) (jam p.lot))]
5415        ?:  ?=(%many -.lot)
5416          :-  '.'
5417          |-  ^-  tape
5418          ?~  p.lot
5419            ['_' '_' rep]
5420          ['_' (weld (trip (wack rent(lot i.p.lot))) $(p.lot t.p.lot))]
5421        =+  [yed=(end 3 p.p.lot) hay=(cut 3 [1 1] p.p.lot)]
5422        |-  ^-  tape
5423        ?+  yed  (z-co q.p.lot)
5424            %c  ['~' '-' (weld (rip 3 (wood (tuft q.p.lot))) rep)]
5425            %d
5426          ?+  hay  (z-co q.p.lot)
5427              %a
5428            =+  yod=(yore q.p.lot)
5429            =?  rep  ?=(^ f.t.yod)  ['.' (s-co f.t.yod)]
5430            =?  rep  !&(?=(~ f) =(0 h) =(0 m) =(0 s)):t.yod
5431              =.  rep  ['.' (y-co s.t.yod)]
5432              =.  rep  ['.' (y-co m.t.yod)]
5433              ['.' '.' (y-co h.t.yod)]
5434            =.  rep  ['.' (a-co d.t.yod)]
5435            =.  rep  ['.' (a-co m.yod)]
5436            =?  rep  !a.yod  ['-' rep]
5437            ['~' (a-co y.yod)]
5438          ::
5439              %r
5440            =+  yug=(yell q.p.lot)
5441            =?  rep  ?=(^ f.yug)  ['.' (s-co f.yug)]
5442            :-  '~'
5443            ?:  &(=(0 d.yug) =(0 m.yug) =(0 h.yug) =(0 s.yug))
5444              ['s' '0' rep]
5445            =?  rep  !=(0 s.yug)  ['.' 's' (a-co s.yug)]
5446            =?  rep  !=(0 m.yug)  ['.' 'm' (a-co m.yug)]
5447            =?  rep  !=(0 h.yug)  ['.' 'h' (a-co h.yug)]
5448            =?  rep  !=(0 d.yug)  ['.' 'd' (a-co d.yug)]
5449            +.rep
5450          ==
```

```
5451          ::
5452            %f
5453      ?:  =(& q.p.lot)
5454        ['.' 'y' rep]
5455      ?:(=(| q.p.lot) ['.' 'n' rep] (z-co q.p.lot))
5456          ::
5457        %n    ['~' rep]
5458        %i
5459      ?+  hay  (z-co q.p.lot)
5460        %f  ((ro-co [3 10 4] |=(a=@ ~(d ne a))) q.p.lot)
5461        %s  ((ro-co [4 16 8] |=(a=@ ~(x ne a))) q.p.lot)
5462      ==
5463          ::
5464            %p
5465      =+  sxz=(fein:ob q.p.lot)
5466      =+  dyx=(met 3 sxz)
5467      :-  '~'
5468      ?:  (lte dyx 1)
5469        (weld (trip (tod:po sxz)) rep)
5470      =+  dyy=(met 4 sxz)
5471      =|  imp=@ud
5472      |-  ^-  tape
5473      ?:  =(imp dyy)
5474        rep
5475      %=  $
5476        imp  +(imp)
5477        rep  =/  log  (cut 4 [imp 1] sxz)
5478             ;:  weld
5479               (trip (tos:po (rsh 3 log)))
5480               (trip (tod:po (end 3 log)))
5481               ?:(=((mod imp 4) 0) ?:(=(imp 0) "" "--") "-")
5482               rep
5483      ==        ==
5484          ::
5485            %q
5486      :+  '.'   '~'
5487      =;  res=(pair ? tape)
5488        (weld q.res rep)
5489      %+  roll
5490        =*  val  q.p.lot
5491        ?:(=(0 val) ~[0] (rip 3 val))
5492      |=  [q=@ s=? r=tape]
5493      :-  !s
5494      %+  weld
5495        (trip (?:(s tod:po tos:po) q))
5496      ?.(&(s !=(r "")) r ['-' r])
5497          ::
5498            %r
5499      ?+  hay  (z-co q.p.lot)
5500        %d  ['.' '~' (r-co (rlyd q.p.lot))]
5501        %h  ['.' '~' '~' (r-co (rlyh q.p.lot))]
5502        %q  ['.' '~' '~' '~' (r-co (rlyq q.p.lot))]
5503        %s  ['.' (r-co (rlys q.p.lot))]
5504      ==
5505          ::
5506            %u
5507      ?:  ?=(%c hay)
5508        %+  welp  ['0' 'c' (reap (pad:fa q.p.lot) '1')]
```

```
5509              (c-co (enc:fa q.p.lot))
5510          ::
5511          =;  gam=(pair tape tape)
5512            (weld p.gam ?:(=(0 q.p.lot) `tape`['0' ~] q.gam))
5513          ?+  hay  [~ ((ox-co [10 3] |=(a=@ ~(d ne a))) q.p.lot)]
5514            %b  [['0' 'b' ~] ((ox-co [2 4] |=(a=@ ~(d ne a))) q.p.lot)]
5515            %i  [['0' 'i' ~] ((d-co 1) q.p.lot)]
5516            %x  [['0' 'x' ~] ((ox-co [16 4] |=(a=@ ~(x ne a))) q.p.lot)]
5517            %v  [['0' 'v' ~] ((ox-co [32 5] |=(a=@ ~(x ne a))) q.p.lot)]
5518            %w  [['0' 'w' ~] ((ox-co [64 5] |=(a=@ ~(w ne a))) q.p.lot)]
5519          ==
5520        ::
5521          %s
5522        %+  weld
5523          ?:((syn:si q.p.lot) "--" "-")
5524        $(yed 'u', q.p.lot (abs:si q.p.lot))
5525        ::
5526          %t
5527        ?:  =('a' hay)
5528          ?:  =('s' (cut 3 [2 1] p.p.lot))
5529            (weld (rip 3 q.p.lot) rep)
5530          ['~' '.' (weld (rip 3 q.p.lot) rep)]
5531        ['~' '~' (weld (rip 3 (wood q.p.lot)) rep)]
5532        ==
5533      --
5534  =|  rep=tape
5535  =<  |%
5536      ::  rendering idioms, output zero-padded to minimum lengths
5537      ::
5538      ::  +a-co: decimal
5539      ::  +c-co: base58check
5540      ::  +d-co: decimal, takes minimum output digits
5541      ::  +r-co: floating point
5542      ::  +s-co: list of '.'-prefixed base16, 4 digit minimum
5543      ::  +v-co: base32, takes minimum output digits
5544      ::  +w-co: base64, takes minimum output digits
5545      ::  +x-co: base16, takes minimum output digits
5546      ::  +y-co: decimal, 2 digit minimum
5547      ::  +z-co: '0x'-prefixed base16
5548      ::
5549      ++  a-co  |=(dat=@ ((d-co 1) dat))
5550      ++  c-co  (em-co [58 1] |=([? b=@ c=tape] [~(c ne b) c]))
5551      ++  d-co  |=(min=@ (em-co [10 min] |=([? b=@ c=tape] [~(d ne b) c])))
5552      ::
5553      ++  r-co
5554        |=  a=dn
5555        ?:  ?=([%i *] a)  (weld ?:(s.a "inf" "-inf") rep)
5556        ?:  ?=([%n *] a)  (weld "nan" rep)
5557        =;  rep  ?:(s.a rep ['-' rep])
5558        =/  f  ((d-co 1) a.a)
5559        =^  e  e.a
5560          =/  e=@s  (sun:si (lent f))
5561          =/  sci  :(sum:si e.a e -1)
5562          ?:  (syn:si (dif:si e.a --3))  [--1 sci]  :: 12000 -> 12e3 e>+2
5563          ?:  !(syn:si (dif:si sci -2))  [--1 sci]  :: 0.001 -> 1e-3 e<-2
5564          [(sum:si sci --1) --0]  :: 1.234e2 -> '.'@3 -> 123 .4
5565        =?  rep  !=(--0 e.a)
5566          :(weld ?:((syn:si e.a) "e" "e-") ((d-co 1) (abs:si e.a)))
```

```
5567          (weld (ed-co e f) rep)
5568        ::
5569        ++  s-co
5570          |=  esc=(list @)   ^-  tape
5571          ?~  esc  rep
5572          ['.' =>(.(rep $(esc t.esc)) ((x-co 4) i.esc))]
5573        ::
5574        ++  v-co  |=(min=@ (em-co [32 min] |=([? b=@ c=tape] [~(v ne b) c])))
5575        ++  w-co  |=(min=@ (em-co [64 min] |=([? b=@ c=tape] [~(w ne b) c])))
5576        ++  x-co  |=(min=@ (em-co [16 min] |=([? b=@ c=tape] [~(x ne b) c])))
5577        ++  y-co  |=(dat=@ ((d-co 2) dat))
5578        ++  z-co  |=(dat=@ `tape`['0' 'x' ((x-co 1) dat)])
5579        --
5580    |%
5581    ::  +em-co: format in numeric base
5582    ::
5583    ::    in .bas, format .min digits of .hol with .par
5584    ::
5585    ::    - .hol is processed least-significant digit first
5586    ::    - all available digits in .hol will be processed, but
5587    ::      .min digits can exceed the number available in .hol
5588    ::    - .par handles all accumulated output on each call,
5589    ::      and can edit it, prepend or append digits, &c
5590    ::    - until .hol is exhausted, .par's sample is [| digit output],
5591    ::      subsequently, it's [& 0 output]
5592    ::
5593    ++  em-co
5594      |=  [[bas=@ min=@] par=$-([? @ tape] tape)]
5595      |=  hol=@
5596      ^-  tape
5597      ?:  &(=(0 hol) =(0 min))
5598        rep
5599      =/  [dar=@ rad=@]  (dvr hol bas)
5600      %=  $
5601        min  ?:(=(0 min) 0 (dec min))
5602        hol  dar
5603        rep  (par =(0 dar) rad rep)
5604      ==
5605    ::
5606    ::  +ed-co: format in numeric base, with output length
5607    ::
5608    ::    - like +em-co, but .par's sample will be [| digit output]
5609    ::      on the first call, regardless of the available digits in .hol
5610    ::    - used only for @r* floats
5611    ::
5612    ++  ed-co
5613      |=  [exp=@s int=tape]  ^-  tape
5614      =/  [pos=? dig=@u]  [=(--1 (cmp:si exp --0)) (abs:si exp)]
5615      ?.  pos
5616        (into (weld (reap +(dig) '0') int) 1 '.')
5617      =/  len  (lent int)
5618      ?:  (lth dig len)  (into int dig '.')
5619      (weld int (reap (sub dig len) '0'))
5620    ::
5621    ::  +ox-co: format '.'-separated digit sequences in numeric base
5622    ::
5623    ::    in .bas, format each digit of .hol with .dug,
5624    ::    with '.' separators every .gop digits.
```

```
5625    ::
5626    ::      - .hol is processed least-significant digit first
5627    ::      - .dug handles individual digits, output is prepended
5628    ::      - every segment but the last is zero-padded to .gop
5629    ::
5630    ++  ox-co
5631    |=  [[bas=@ gop=@] dug=$-(@ @)]
5632    %+  em-co
5633      [(pow bas gop) 0]
5634    |=  [top=? seg=@ res=tape]
5635    %+  weld
5636      ?:(top ~ `tape`['.' ~])
5637    %.  seg
5638    %+  em-co(rep res)
5639      [bas ?:(top 0 gop)]
5640    |=([? b=@ c=tape] [(dug b) c])
5641    ::
5642    ::  +ro-co: format '.'-prefixed bloqs in numeric base
5643    ::
5644    ::      in .bas, for .buz bloqs 0 to .dop, format at least one
5645    ::      digit of .hol, prefixed with '.'
5646    ::
5647    ::      - used only for @i* addresses
5648    ::
5649    ++  ro-co
5650    |=  [[buz=@ bas=@ dop=@] dug=$-(@ @)]
5651    |=  hol=@
5652    ^-  tape
5653    ?:  =(0 dop)
5654      rep
5655    :-  '.'
5656    =/  pod  (dec dop)
5657    %.  (cut buz [pod 1] hol)
5658    %+  em-co(rep $(dop pod))
5659      [bas 1]
5660    |=([? b=@ c=tape] [(dug b) c])
5661    --
5662  ::
5663  ::    41: atom parsing
5664  +|  %atom-parsing
5665  ::
5666  ++  so
5667    ~%  %so  +  ~
5668    |%
5669    ++  bisk
5670      ~+
5671      ;~  pose
5672        ;~  pfix  (just '0')
5673          ;~  pose
5674            (stag %ub ;~(pfix (just 'b') bay:ag))
5675            (stag %uc ;~(pfix (just 'c') fim:ag))
5676            (stag %ui ;~(pfix (just 'i') dim:ag))
5677            (stag %ux ;~(pfix (just 'x') hex:ag))
5678            (stag %uv ;~(pfix (just 'v') viz:ag))
5679            (stag %uw ;~(pfix (just 'w') wiz:ag))
5680          ==
5681        ==
5682        (stag %ud dem:ag)
```

```
5683        ==
5684    ++  crub
5685      ~+
5686      ;~  pose
5687        (cook |=(det=date `dime`[%da (year det)]) when)
5688        ::
5689        %+  cook
5690          |=  [a=(list [p=?(%d %h %m %s) q=@]) b=(list @)]
5691          =+  rop=`tarp`[0 0 0 0 b]
5692          |-  ^-  dime
5693          ?~  a
5694            [%dr (yule rop)]
5695          ?-  p.i.a
5696            %d  $(a t.a, d.rop (add q.i.a d.rop))
5697            %h  $(a t.a, h.rop (add q.i.a h.rop))
5698            %m  $(a t.a, m.rop (add q.i.a m.rop))
5699            %s  $(a t.a, s.rop (add q.i.a s.rop))
5700          ==
5701        ;~  plug
5702          %+  most
5703            dot
5704          ;~  pose
5705            ;~(pfix (just 'd') (stag %d dim:ag))
5706            ;~(pfix (just 'h') (stag %h dim:ag))
5707            ;~(pfix (just 'm') (stag %m dim:ag))
5708            ;~(pfix (just 's') (stag %s dim:ag))
5709          ==
5710          ;~(pose ;~(pfix ;~(plug dot dot) (most dot qix:ab)) (easy ~))
5711        ==
5712        ::
5713        (stag %p fed:ag)
5714        ;~(pfix dot (stag %ta urs:ab))
5715        ;~(pfix sig (stag %t urx:ab))
5716        ;~(pfix hep (stag %c (cook taft urx:ab)))
5717      ==
5718    ++  nuck
5719      ~/  %nuck  |=  a=nail  %.  a
5720      %+  knee  *coin  |.  ~+
5721      %-  stew
5722      ^.  stet  ^.  limo
5723      :~  :-  ['a' 'z']  (cook |=(a=@ta [%$ %tas a]) sym)
5724          :-  ['0' '9']  (stag %$ bisk)
5725          :-  '-'        (stag %$ tash)
5726          :-  '.'        ;~(pfix dot perd)
5727          :-  '~'        ;~(pfix sig ;~(pose twid (easy [%$ %n 0])))
5728      ==
5729    ++  nusk
5730      ~+
5731      :(sear |=(a=@ta (rush a nuck)) wick urt:ab)
5732    ++  perd
5733      ~+
5734      ;~  pose
5735        (stag %$ zust)
5736        (stag %many (ifix [cab ;~(plug cab cab)] (more cab nusk)))
5737      ==
5738    ++  royl
5739      ~+
5740      ;~  pose
```

```
5741        (stag %rh royl-rh)
5742        (stag %rq royl-rq)
5743        (stag %rd royl-rd)
5744        (stag %rs royl-rs)
5745      ==
5746    ::
5747    ++  royl-rh  (cook rylh ;~(pfix ;~(plug sig sig) (cook royl-cell royl-rn)))
5748    ++  royl-rq  (cook rylq ;~(pfix ;~(plug sig sig sig) (cook royl-cell royl-rn)))
5749    ++  royl-rd  (cook ryld ;~(pfix sig (cook royl-cell royl-rn)))
5750    ++  royl-rs  (cook ryls (cook royl-cell royl-rn))
5751    ::
5752    ++  royl-rn
5753      =/  moo
5754        |=  a=tape
5755        :-  (lent a)
5756        (scan a (bass 10 (plus sid:ab)))
5757      ;~  pose
5758        ;~  plug
5759          (easy %d)
5760          ;~(pose (cold | hep) (easy &))
5761          ;~  plug  dim:ag
5762            ;~  pose
5763              ;~(pfix dot (cook moo (plus (shim '0' '9'))))
5764              (easy [0 0])
5765            ==
5766            ;~  pose
5767              ;~  pfix
5768                (just 'e')
5769                ;~(plug ;~(pose (cold | hep) (easy &)) dim:ag)
5770              ==
5771              (easy [& 0])
5772            ==
5773          ==
5774        ==
5775        ::
5776        ;~  plug
5777          (easy %i)
5778          ;~  sfix
5779            ;~(pose (cold | hep) (easy &))
5780            (jest 'inf')
5781          ==
5782        ==
5783        ::
5784        ;~  plug
5785          (easy %n)
5786          (cold ~ (jest 'nan'))
5787        ==
5788      ==
5789    ::
5790    ++  royl-cell
5791      |=  rn
5792      ^-  dn
5793      ?.  ?=([%d *] +<)  +<
5794      =+  ^=  h
5795        (dif:si (new:si f.b i.b) (sun:si d.b))
5796      [%d a h (add (mul c.b (pow 10 d.b)) e.b)]
5797    ::
5798    ++  tash
```

```
5799      ~+
5800      =+  ^=  neg
5801          |=  [syn=? mol=dime]  ^-  dime
5802          ?>  =('u' (end 3 p.mol))
5803          [(cat 3 's' (rsh 3 p.mol)) (new:si syn q.mol)]
5804      ;~  pfix  hep
5805        ;~  pose
5806          (cook |=(a=dime (neg | a)) bisk)
5807          ;~(pfix hep (cook |=(a=dime (neg & a)) bisk))
5808        ==
5809      ==
5810  ::
5811  ++  twid
5812      ~+
5813      ;~  pose
5814        %+  stag  %blob
5815        %+  sear  |=(a=@ (mole |.((cue a))))
5816        ;~(pfix (just '0') vum:ag)
5817      ::
5818        (stag %$ crub)
5819      ==
5820  ::
5821  ++  when
5822      ~+
5823      ;~  plug
5824        %+  cook
5825          |=([a=@ b=?] [b a])
5826        ;~(plug dim:ag ;~(pose (cold | hep) (easy &)))
5827        ;~(pfix dot mot:ag)    ::   month
5828        ;~(pfix dot dip:ag)    ::   day
5829        ;~  pose
5830          ;~  pfix
5831            ;~(plug dot dot)
5832            ;~  plug
5833              dum:ag
5834              ;~(pfix dot dum:ag)
5835              ;~(pfix dot dum:ag)
5836              ;~(pose ;~(pfix ;~(plug dot dot) (most dot qix:ab)) (easy ~))
5837            ==
5838          ==
5839          (easy [0 0 0 ~])
5840        ==
5841      ==
5842  ::
5843  ++  zust
5844      ~+
5845      ;~  pose
5846        (stag %is bip:ag)
5847        (stag %if lip:ag)
5848        royl
5849        (stag %f ;~(pose (cold & (just 'y')) (cold | (just 'n'))))
5850        (stag %q ;~(pfix sig feq:ag))
5851      ==
5852  --
5853  ::
5854  ::    4m: formatting functions
5855  +|  %formatting-functions
5856  ++  scot
```

```
5857    ~/  %scot
5858    |=(mol=dime ~(rent co %$ mol))
5859  ++  scow
5860    ~/  %scow
5861    |=(mol=dime ~(rend co %$ mol))
5862  ++  slat  |=(mod=@tas |=(txt=@ta (slaw mod txt)))
5863  ++  slav  |=([mod=@tas txt=@ta] (need (slaw mod txt)))
5864  ++  slaw
5865    ~/  %slaw
5866    |=  [mod=@tas txt=@ta]
5867    ^-  (unit @)
5868    ?+    mod
5869        ::  slow fallback case to the full slay
5870        ::
5871        =+  con=(slay txt)
5872        ?.(&(?=([~ %$ @ @] con) =(p.p.u.con mod)) ~ [~ q.p.u.con])
5873      ::
5874        %da
5875      (rush txt ;~(pfix sig (cook year when:so)))
5876      ::
5877        %p
5878      (rush txt ;~(pfix sig fed:ag))
5879      ::
5880        %ud
5881      (rush txt dem:ag)
5882      ::
5883        %ux
5884      (rush txt ;~(pfix (jest '0x') hex:ag))
5885      ::
5886        %uv
5887      (rush txt ;~(pfix (jest '0v') viz:ag))
5888      ::
5889        %ta
5890      (rush txt ;~(pfix ;~(plug sig dot) urs:ab))
5891      ::
5892        %tas
5893      (rush txt sym)
5894    ==
5895  ::
5896  ++  slay
5897    |=  txt=@ta  ^-  (unit coin)
5898    =+  ^=  vex
5899        ?:  (gth 0x7fff.ffff txt)                     ::  XX  petty cache
5900          ~+  ((full nuck:so) [[1 1] (trip txt)])
5901        ((full nuck:so) [[1 1] (trip txt)])
5902    ?~  q.vex
5903      ~
5904    [~ p.u.q.vex]
5905  ::
5906  ++  smyt                                            ::  pretty print path
5907    |=  bon=path  ^-  tank
5908    :+  %rose  [['/' ~] ['/' ~] ~]
5909    (turn bon |=(a=@ [%leaf (trip a)]))
5910  ::
5911  ++  spat  |=(pax=path (crip (spud pax)))            ::  render path to cord
5912  ++  spud  |=(pax=path ~(ram re (smyt pax)))         ::  render path to tape
5913  ++  stab  |=(zep=@t `path`(rash zep stap))          ::  parse cord to path
5914  ++  stap                                            ::  path parser
```

```
%+  sear
  |=  p=path
  ^-  (unit path)
  ?:  ?=([~ ~] p)   `~
  ?.  =(~ (rear p))  `p
  ~
;~(pfix fas (most fas urs:ab))
::
++  stip                                        ::  typed path parser
  =<  swot
  |%
  ++  swot  |=(n=nail (;~(pfix fas (more fas spot)) n))
  ::
  ++  spot
    %+  sear  (soft iota)
    %-  stew
    ^.  stet  ^.  limo
    :~  :-  'a'^'z'  (stag %tas sym)
        :-  '$'      (cold [%tas %$] buc)
        :-  '0'^'9'  bisk:so
        :-  '-'      tash:so
        :-  '.'      zust:so
        :-  '~'      ;~(pfix sig ;~(pose crub:so (easy [%n ~])))
        :-  '\''     (stag %t qut)
    ==
  --
::
++  pout
  |=  =pith
  ^-  path
  %+  turn  pith
  |=  i=iota
  ?@(i i (scot i))
::
++  pave
  |=  =path
  ^-  pith
  %+  turn  path
  |=  i=@ta
  (fall (rush i spot:stip) [%ta i])
::
::    4n: virtualization
+|  %virtualization
::
::  +mack: untyped, scry-less, unitary virtualization
::
++  mack
  |=  [sub=* fol=*]
  ^-  (unit)
  =/  ton  (mink [sub fol] |~(^ ~))
  ?.(?=(%0 -.ton) ~ `product.ton)
::  +mink: raw virtual nock
::
++  mink  !.
  ~/  %mink
  |=  $:  [subject=* formula=*]
          scry=$-(^ (unit (unit)))
      ==
```

```
5973    =|  trace=(list [@ta *])
5974    |^  ^-  tone
5975        ?+  formula  [%2 trace]
5976          [^ *]
5977        =/  head  $(formula -.formula)
5978        ?.  ?=(%0 -.head)  head
5979        =/  tail  $(formula +.formula)
5980        ?.  ?=(%0 -.tail)  tail
5981        [%0 product.head product.tail]
5982      ::
5983          [%0 axis=@]
5984        =/  part  (frag axis.formula subject)
5985        ?~  part  [%2 trace]
5986        [%0 u.part]
5987      ::
5988          [%1 constant=*]
5989        [%0 constant.formula]
5990      ::
5991          [%2 subject=* formula=*]
5992        =/  subject  $(formula subject.formula)
5993        ?.  ?=(%0 -.subject)  subject
5994        =/  formula  $(formula formula.formula)
5995        ?.  ?=(%0 -.formula)  formula
5996        %=  $
5997          subject  product.subject
5998          formula  product.formula
5999        ==
6000      ::
6001          [%3 argument=*]
6002        =/  argument  $(formula argument.formula)
6003        ?.  ?=(%0 -.argument)  argument
6004        [%0 .?(product.argument)]
6005      ::
6006          [%4 argument=*]
6007        =/  argument  $(formula argument.formula)
6008        ?.  ?=(%0 -.argument)  argument
6009        ?^  product.argument  [%2 trace]
6010        [%0 .+(product.argument)]
6011      ::
6012          [%5 a=* b=*]
6013        =/  a  $(formula a.formula)
6014        ?.  ?=(%0 -.a)  a
6015        =/  b  $(formula b.formula)
6016        ?.  ?=(%0 -.b)  b
6017        [%0 =(product.a product.b)]
6018      ::
6019          [%6 test=* yes=* no=*]
6020        =/  result  $(formula test.formula)
6021        ?.  ?=(%0 -.result)  result
6022        ?+  product.result
6023            [%2 trace]
6024          %&  $(formula yes.formula)
6025          %|  $(formula no.formula)
6026        ==
6027      ::
6028          [%7 subject=* next=*]
6029        =/  subject  $(formula subject.formula)
6030        ?.  ?=(%0 -.subject)  subject
```

```
6031        %=  $
6032          subject  product.subject
6033          formula  next.formula
6034        ==
6035    ::
6036          [%8 head=* next=*]
6037      =/  head  $(formula head.formula)
6038      ?.  ?=(%0 -.head)  head
6039      %=  $
6040          subject  [product.head subject]
6041          formula  next.formula
6042        ==
6043    ::
6044          [%9 axis=@ core=*]
6045      =/  core  $(formula core.formula)
6046      ?.  ?=(%0 -.core)  core
6047      =/  arm  (frag axis.formula product.core)
6048      ?~  arm  [%2 trace]
6049      %=  $
6050          subject  product.core
6051          formula  u.arm
6052        ==
6053    ::
6054          [%10 [axis=@ value=*] target=*]
6055      ?:  =(0 axis.formula)  [%2 trace]
6056      =/  target  $(formula target.formula)
6057      ?.  ?=(%0 -.target)  target
6058      =/  value  $(formula value.formula)
6059      ?.  ?=(%0 -.value)  value
6060      =/  mutant=(unit *)
6061        (edit axis.formula product.target product.value)
6062      ?~  mutant  [%2 trace]
6063      [%0 u.mutant]
6064    ::
6065          [%11 tag=@ next=*]
6066      =/  next  $(formula next.formula)
6067      ?.  ?=(%0 -.next)  next
6068      :-  %0
6069      .*  subject
6070      [11 tag.formula 1 product.next]
6071    ::
6072          [%11 [tag=@ clue=*] next=*]
6073      =/  clue  $(formula clue.formula)
6074      ?.  ?=(%0 -.clue)  clue
6075      =/  next
6076        =?    trace
6077            ?=(?(%hunk %hand %lose %mean %spot) tag.formula)
6078          [[tag.formula product.clue] trace]
6079        $(formula next.formula)
6080      ?.  ?=(%0 -.next)  next
6081      :-  %0
6082      .*  subject
6083      [11 [tag.formula 1 product.clue] 1 product.next]
6084    ::
6085          [%12 ref=* path=*]
6086      =/  ref  $(formula ref.formula)
6087      ?.  ?=(%0 -.ref)  ref
6088      =/  path  $(formula path.formula)
```

```
6089        ?.  ?=(%0 -.path)  path
6090        =/  result  (scry product.ref product.path)
6091        ?~  result
6092          [%1 product.path]
6093        ?~  u.result
6094          [%2 [%hunk product.ref product.path] trace]
6095        [%0 u.u.result]
6096      ==
6097    ::
6098    ++  frag
6099      |=  [axis=@ noun=*]
6100      ^-  (unit)
6101      ?:  =(0 axis)  ~
6102      |-  ^-  (unit)
6103      ?:  =(1 axis)  `noun
6104      ?@  noun  ~
6105      =/  pick  (cap axis)
6106      %=  $
6107        axis  (mas axis)
6108        noun  ?-(pick %2 -.noun, %3 +.noun)
6109      ==
6110    ::
6111    ++  edit
6112      |=  [axis=@ target=* value=*]
6113      ^-  (unit)
6114      ?:  =(1 axis)  `value
6115      ?@  target  ~
6116      =/  pick  (cap axis)
6117      =/  mutant
6118        %=  $
6119          axis    (mas axis)
6120          target  ?-(pick %2 -.target, %3 +.target)
6121        ==
6122      ?~  mutant  ~
6123      ?-  pick
6124        %2  `[u.mutant +.target]
6125        %3  `[-.target u.mutant]
6126      ==
6127    --
6128  ::  +mock: virtual nock
6129  ::
6130  ++  mock
6131    |=  [[sub=* fol=*] gul=$-(^ (unit (unit)))]
6132    (mook (mink [sub fol] gul))
6133  ::  +mook: convert %tone to %toon, rendering stack frames
6134  ::
6135  ++  mook
6136    |=  ton=tone
6137    ^-  toon
6138    ?.  ?=([%2 *] ton)
6139      ton
6140    |^  [%2 (turn skip rend)]
6141    ::
6142    ++  skip
6143      ^+  trace.ton
6144      =/  yel  (lent trace.ton)
6145      ?.  (gth yel 1.024)  trace.ton
6146      %+  weld
```

```
        (scag 512 trace.ton)
      ^+  trace.ton
      :_  (slag (sub yel 512) trace.ton)
      :-  %lose
      (crip "[skipped {(scow %ud (sub yel 1.024))} frames]")
    ::
    ::  +rend: raw stack frame to tank
    ::
    ::      $%  [%hunk ref=* path]                ::  failed scry ([~ ~])
    ::          [%lose cord]                      ::  skipped frames
    ::          [%hand *]                         ::  mug any
    ::          [%mean $@(cord (trap tank))]      ::  ~_ et al
    ::          [%spot spot]                      ::  source location
    ::      ==
    ::
    ++  rend
      |=  [tag=@ta dat=*]
      ^-  tank
      ?+    tag
        ::
        leaf+"mook.{(rip 3 tag)}"
        ::
          %hunk
        ?@  dat  leaf+"mook.hunk"
        =/  sof=(unit path)  ((soft path) +.dat)
        ?~  sof  leaf+"mook.hunk"
        (smyt u.sof)
        ::
          %lose
        ?^  dat  leaf+"mook.lose"
        leaf+(rip 3 dat)
        ::
          %hand
        leaf+(scow %p (mug dat))
        ::
          %mean
        ?@  dat  leaf+(rip 3 dat)
        =/  mac  (mack dat -.dat)
        ?~  mac  leaf+"####"
        =/  sof  ((soft tank) u.mac)
        ?~  sof  leaf+"mook.mean"
        u.sof
        ::
          %spot
        =/  sof=(unit spot)  ((soft spot) dat)
        ?~  sof  leaf+"mook.spot"
        :+  %rose  [":" ~ ~]
        :~  (smyt p.u.sof)
            =*  l    p.q.u.sof
            =*  r    q.q.u.sof
            =/  ud  |=(a=@u (scow %ud a))
            leaf+"<[{(ud p.l)} {(ud q.l)}].[{(ud p.r)} {(ud q.r)}]>"
        ==
      ==
    --
    ::  +mole: typed unitary virtual
    ::
    ++  mole
```

```hoon
6205      ~/  %mole
6206      |*  tap=(trap)
6207      ^-  (unit _$:tap)
6208      =/  mur  (mure tap)
6209      ?~(mur ~ `$:tap)
6210  ::  +mong: virtual slam
6211  ::
6212  ++  mong
6213      |=  [[gat=* sam=*] gul=$-(^ (unit (unit)))]
6214      ^-  toon
6215      ?.  ?=([* ^] gat)  [%2 ~]
6216      (mock [gat(+< sam) %9 2 %0 1] gul)
6217  ::  +mule: typed virtual
6218  ::
6219  ++  mule
6220      ~/  %mule
6221      |*  tap=(trap)
6222      =/  mud  (mute tap)
6223      ?-  -.mud
6224        %&  [%& p=$:tap]
6225        %|  [%| p=p.mud]
6226      ==
6227  ::  +mure: untyped unitary virtual
6228  ::
6229  ++  mure
6230      |=  tap=(trap)
6231      ^-  (unit)
6232      =/  ton  (mink [tap %9 2 %0 1] |=(a=^ ``.*(a [%12 [%0 2] %0 3])))
6233      ?.(?=(%0 -.ton) ~ `product.ton)
6234  ::    +mute: untyped virtual
6235  ::
6236  ++  mute
6237      |=  tap=(trap)
6238      ^-  (each * (list tank))
6239      =/  ton  (mock [tap %9 2 %0 1] |=(a=^ ``.*(a [%12 [%0 2] %0 3])))
6240      ?-  -.ton
6241        %0  [%& p.ton]
6242        ::
6243        %1  =/  sof=(unit path)  ((soft path) p.ton)
6244            [%| ?~(sof leaf+"mute.hunk" (smyt u.sof)) ~]
6245        ::
6246        %2  [%| p.ton]
6247      ==
6248  ::  +slum: slam a gate on a sample using raw nock, untyped
6249  ::
6250  ++  slum
6251      ~/  %slum
6252      |=  sub=[gat=* sam=*]
6253      .*(sub [%9 2 %10 [6 %0 3] %0 2])
6254  ::  +soft: virtual clam
6255  ::
6256  ++  soft
6257      |*  han=$-(* *)
6258      |=(fud=* (mole |.((han fud))))
6259  ::
6260  ::      4o: molds and mold builders
6261  +|  %molds-and-mold-builders
6262  ::
```

```
6263  +$  abel   typo                                    ::  original sin: type
6264  +$  alas   (list (pair term hoon))                 ::  alias list
6265  +$  atom   @                                       ::  just an atom
6266  +$  aura   @ta                                     ::  atom format
6267  +$  base                                           ::  base mold
6268    $@  $?  %noun                                    ::  any noun
6269              %cell                                  ::  any cell
6270              %flag                                  ::  loobean
6271              %null                                  ::  ~ == 0
6272              %void                                  ::  empty set
6273            ==                                       ::
6274      [%atom p=aura]                                 ::  atom
6275  ::
6276  +$  woof   $@(@ [~ p=hoon])                         ::  simple embed
6277  +$  chum   $?  lef=term                            ::  jet name
6278              [std=term kel=@]                       ::  kelvin version
6279              [ven=term pro=term kel=@]              ::  vendor and product
6280              [ven=term pro=term ver=@ kel=@]        ::  all of the above
6281            ==                                       ::
6282  +$  coil   $:  p=garb                              ::  name, wet=dry, vary
6283              q=type                                 ::  context
6284              r=(pair seminoun (map term tome))      ::  chapters
6285            ==                                       ::
6286  +$  garb   (trel (unit term) poly vair)            ::  core
6287  +$  poly   ?(%wet %dry)                            ::  polarity
6288  +$  foot   $%  [%dry p=hoon]                       ::  dry arm, geometric
6289              [%wet p=hoon]                          ::  wet arm, generic
6290            ==                                       ::
6291  +$  link                                           ::  lexical segment
6292         $%  [%chat p=term]                          ::  |chapter
6293              [%cone p=aura q=atom]                  ::  %constant
6294              [%frag p=term]                         ::  .face
6295              [%funk p=term]                         ::  +arm
6296              [%plan p=term]                         ::  $spec
6297            ==                                       ::
6298  +$  cuff   (list link)                             ::  parsed lex segments
6299  +$  crib   [summary=cord details=(list sect)]      ::
6300  +$  help   [=cuff =crib]                           ::  documentation
6301  +$  limb   $@  term                                ::  wing element
6302         $%  [%& p=axis]                             ::  by geometry
6303              [%| p=@ud q=(unit term)]               ::  by name
6304            ==                                       ::
6305              ::  XX more and better sanity
6306              ::
6307  +$  null   ~                                       ::  null, nil, etc
6308  +$  onyx   (list (pair type foot))                 ::  arm activation
6309  +$  opal                                           ::  limb match
6310         $%  [%& p=type]                             ::  leg
6311              [%| p=axis q=(set [p=type q=foot])]    ::  arm
6312            ==                                       ::
6313  +$  pica   (pair ? cord)                            ::  & prose, | code
6314  +$  palo   (pair vein opal)                         ::  wing trace, match
6315  +$  pock   (pair axis nock)                         ::  changes
6316  +$  port   (each palo (pair type nock))            ::  successful match
6317  +$  spec                                           ::  structure definition
6318         $~  [%base %null]                           ::
6319         $%  [%base p=base]                          ::  base type
6320              [%dbug p=spot q=spec]                  ::  set debug
```

```
6321                    [%gist p=[%help p=help] q=spec]          ::  formal comment
6322                    [%leaf p=term q=@]                        ::  constant atom
6323                    [%like p=wing q=(list wing)]              ::  reference
6324                    [%loop p=term]                            ::  hygienic reference
6325                    [%made p=(pair term (list term)) q=spec]  ::  annotate synthetic
6326                    [%make p=hoon q=(list spec)]              ::  composed spec
6327                    [%name p=term q=spec]                     ::  annotate simple
6328                    [%over p=wing q=spec]                     ::  relative to subject
6329            ::                                                ::
6330                    [%bcgr p=spec q=spec]                     ::  $>, filter: require
6331                    [%bcbc p=spec q=(map term spec)]          ::  $$, recursion
6332                    [%bcbr p=spec q=hoon]                     ::  $|, verify
6333                    [%bccb p=hoon]                            ::  $_, example
6334                    [%bccl p=[i=spec t=(list spec)]]          ::  $:, tuple
6335                    [%bccn p=[i=spec t=(list spec)]]          ::  $%, head pick
6336                    [%bcdt p=spec q=(map term spec)]          ::  $., read-write core
6337                    [%bcgl p=spec q=spec]                     ::  $<, filter: exclude
6338                    [%bchp p=spec q=spec]                     ::  $-, function core
6339                    [%bckt p=spec q=spec]                     ::  $^, cons pick
6340                    [%bcls p=stud q=spec]                     ::  $+, standard
6341                    [%bcfs p=spec q=(map term spec)]          ::  $/, write-only core
6342                    [%bcmc p=hoon]                            ::  $;, manual
6343                    [%bcpm p=spec q=hoon]                     ::  $&, repair
6344                    [%bcsg p=hoon q=spec]                     ::  $~, default
6345                    [%bctc p=spec q=(map term spec)]          ::  $`, read-only core
6346                    [%bcts p=skin q=spec]                     ::  $=, name
6347                    [%bcpt p=spec q=spec]                     ::  $@, atom pick
6348                    [%bcwt p=[i=spec t=(list spec)]]          ::  $?, full pick
6349                    [%bczp p=spec q=(map term spec)]          ::  $!, opaque core
6350            ==                                                ::
6351  +$  tent                                                    ::  model builder
6352          $%  [%| p=wing q=tent r=(list spec)]                ::  ~(p q r...)
6353              [%& p=(list wing)]                              ::  a.b:c.d
6354          ==                                                  ::
6355  +$  tiki                                                    ::  test case
6356          $%  [%& p=(unit term) q=wing]                       ::  simple wing
6357              [%| p=(unit term) q=hoon]                       ::  named wing
6358          ==                                                  ::
6359  +$  skin                                                    ::  texture
6360          $@  =term                                           ::  name/~[term %none]
6361          $%  [%base =base]                                   ::  base match
6362              [%cell =skin =skin]                             ::  pair
6363              [%dbug =spot =skin]                             ::  trace
6364              [%leaf =aura =atom]                             ::  atomic constant
6365              [%help =help =skin]                             ::  describe
6366              [%name =term =skin]                             ::  apply label
6367              [%over =wing =skin]                             ::  relative to
6368              [%spec =spec =skin]                             ::  cast to
6369              [%wash depth=@ud]                               ::  strip faces
6370          ==                                                  ::
6371  +$  tome  (pair what (map term hoon))                       ::  core chapter
6372  +$  tope                                                    ::  topographic type
6373    $@  $?  %&                                                ::  cell or atom
6374            %|                                                ::  atom
6375        ==                                                    ::
6376    (pair tope tope)                                          ::  cell
6377  ++  hoot                                                    ::  hoon tools
6378    |%
```

```
+$  beer  $@(char [~ p=hoon])                          ::  simple embed
+$  mane  $@(@tas [@tas @tas])                         ::  XML name+space
+$  manx  $~([[%$ ~] ~] [g=marx c=marl])               ::  dynamic XML node
+$  marl  (list tuna)                                  ::  dynamic XML nodes
+$  mart  (list [n=mane v=(list beer)])                ::  dynamic XML attrs
+$  marx  $~([%$ ~] [n=mane a=mart])                   ::  dynamic XML tag
+$  mare  (each manx marl)                             ::  node or nodes
+$  maru  (each tuna marl)                             ::  interp or nodes
+$  tuna                                               ::  maybe interpolation
    $~  [[%$ ~] ~]
    $^  manx
    $:  ?(%tape %manx %marl %call)
        p=hoon
    ==
--                                                     ::
+$  hoon                                               ::  hoon AST
  $~  [%zpzp ~]                                        ::
  $^  [p=hoon q=hoon]                                  ::
  $%                                                   ::
    [%$ p=axis]                                        ::  simple leg
  ::                                                   ::
    [%base p=base]                                     ::  base spec
    [%bust p=base]                                     ::  bunt base
    [%dbug p=spot q=hoon]                              ::  debug info in trace
    [%eror p=tape]                                     ::  assembly error
    [%hand p=type q=nock]                              ::  premade result
    [%note p=note q=hoon]                              ::  annotate
    [%fits p=hoon q=wing]                              ::  underlying ?=
    [%knit p=(list woof)]                              ::  assemble string
    [%leaf p=(pair term @)]                            ::  symbol spec
    [%limb p=term]                                     ::  take limb
    [%lost p=hoon]                                     ::  not to be taken
    [%rock p=term q=*]                                 ::  fixed constant
    [%sand p=term q=*]                                 ::  unfixed constant
    [%tell p=(list hoon)]                              ::  render as tape
    [%tune p=$@(term tune)]                            ::  minimal face
    [%wing p=wing]                                     ::  take wing
    [%yell p=(list hoon)]                              ::  render as tank
    [%xray p=manx:hoot]                                ::  ;foo; templating
  ::                                                   :::::: cores
    [%brbc sample=(lest term) body=spec]               ::  |$
    [%brcb p=spec q=alas r=(map term tome)]            ::  |_
    [%brcl p=hoon q=hoon]                              ::  |:
    [%brcn p=(unit term) q=(map term tome)]            ::  |%
    [%brdt p=hoon]                                     ::  |.
    [%brkt p=hoon q=(map term tome)]                   ::  |^
    [%brhp p=hoon]                                     ::  |-
    [%brsg p=spec q=hoon]                              ::  |~
    [%brtr p=spec q=hoon]                              ::  |*
    [%brts p=spec q=hoon]                              ::  |=
    [%brpt p=(unit term) q=(map term tome)]            ::  |@
    [%brwt p=hoon]                                     ::  |?
  ::                                                   :::::: tuples
    [%clcb p=hoon q=hoon]                              ::  :_ [q p]
    [%clkt p=hoon q=hoon r=hoon s=hoon]                ::  :^ [p q r s]
    [%clhp p=hoon q=hoon]                              ::  :- [p q]
    [%clls p=hoon q=hoon r=hoon]                       ::  :+ [p q r]
    [%clsg p=(list hoon)]                              ::  :~ [p ~]
```

```
6437      [%cltr p=(list hoon)]                                    ::  :* p as a tuple
6438    ::                                                 :::::::  invocations
6439    [%cncb p=wing q=(list (pair wing hoon))]               ::  %_
6440    [%cndt p=hoon q=hoon]                                  ::  %.
6441    [%cnhp p=hoon q=hoon]                                  ::  %-
6442    [%cncl p=hoon q=(list hoon)]                           ::  %:
6443    [%cntr p=wing q=hoon r=(list (pair wing hoon))]        ::  %*
6444    [%cnkt p=hoon q=hoon r=hoon s=hoon]                    ::  %^
6445    [%cnls p=hoon q=hoon r=hoon]                           ::  %+
6446    [%cnsg p=wing q=hoon r=(list hoon)]                    ::  %~
6447    [%cnts p=wing q=(list (pair wing hoon))]               ::  %=
6448    ::                                                :::::::  nock
6449    [%dtkt p=spec q=hoon]                                  ::  .^  nock 11
6450    [%dtls p=hoon]                                         ::  .+  nock 4
6451    [%dttr p=hoon q=hoon]                                  ::  .*  nock 2
6452    [%dtts p=hoon q=hoon]                                  ::  .=  nock 5
6453    [%dtwt p=hoon]                                         ::  .?  nock 3
6454    ::                                                :::::::  type conversion
6455    [%ktbr p=hoon]                                         ::  ^|  contravariant
6456    [%ktdt p=hoon q=hoon]                                  ::  ^.  self-cast
6457    [%ktls p=hoon q=hoon]                                  ::  ^+  expression cast
6458    [%kthp p=spec q=hoon]                                  ::  ^-  structure cast
6459    [%ktpm p=hoon]                                         ::  ^&  covariant
6460    [%ktsg p=hoon]                                         ::  ^~  constant
6461    [%ktts p=skin q=hoon]                                  ::  ^=  label
6462    [%ktwt p=hoon]                                         ::  ^?  bivariant
6463    [%kttr p=spec]                                         ::  ^*  example
6464    [%ktcl p=spec]                                         ::  ^:  filter
6465    ::                                                :::::::  hints
6466    [%sgbr p=hoon q=hoon]                                  ::  ~|  sell on trace
6467    [%sgcb p=hoon q=hoon]                                  ::  ~_  tank on trace
6468    [%sgcn p=chum q=hoon r=tyre s=hoon]                    ::  ~%  general jet hint
6469    [%sgfs p=chum q=hoon]                                  ::  ~/  function j-hint
6470    [%sggl p=$@(term [p=term q=hoon]) q=hoon]              ::  ~<  backward hint
6471    [%sggr p=$@(term [p=term q=hoon]) q=hoon]              ::  ~>  forward hint
6472    [%sgbc p=term q=hoon]                                  ::  ~$  profiler hit
6473    [%sgls p=@ q=hoon]                                     ::  ~+  cache=memoize
6474    [%sgpm p=@ud q=hoon r=hoon]                            ::  ~&  printf=priority
6475    [%sgts p=hoon q=hoon]                                  ::  ~=  don't duplicate
6476    [%sgwt p=@ud q=hoon r=hoon s=hoon]                     ::  ~?  tested printf
6477    [%sgzp p=hoon q=hoon]                                  ::  ~!  type on trace
6478    ::                                                :::::::  miscellaneous
6479    [%mcts p=marl:hoot]                                    ::  ;=  list templating
6480    [%mccl p=hoon q=(list hoon)]                           ::  ;:  binary to nary
6481    [%mcfs p=hoon]                                         ::  ;/  [%$ [%$ p ~] ~]
6482    [%mcgl p=spec q=hoon r=hoon s=hoon]                    ::  ;<  bind
6483    [%mcsg p=hoon q=(list hoon)]                           ::  ;~  kleisli arrow
6484    [%mcmc p=spec q=hoon]                                  ::  ;;  normalize
6485    ::                                                :::::::  compositions
6486    [%tsbr p=spec q=hoon]                                  ::  =|  push bunt
6487    [%tscl p=(list (pair wing hoon)) q=hoon]               ::  =:  q w= p changes
6488    [%tsfs p=skin q=hoon r=hoon]                           ::  =/  typed variable
6489    [%tsmc p=skin q=hoon r=hoon]                           ::  =;  =/(q p r)
6490    [%tsdt p=wing q=hoon r=hoon]                           ::  =.  r with p as q
6491    [%tswt p=wing q=hoon r=hoon s=hoon]                    ::  =?  conditional =.
6492    [%tsgl p=hoon q=hoon]                                  ::  =<  =>(q p)
6493    [%tshp p=hoon q=hoon]                                  ::  =-  =+(q p)
6494    [%tsgr p=hoon q=hoon]                                  ::  =>  q w=subject p
```

```
6495        [%tskt p=skin q=wing r=hoon s=hoon]                  ::  =^   state machine
6496        [%tsls p=hoon q=hoon]                                ::  =+   q w=[p subject]
6497        [%tssg p=(list hoon)]                                ::  =~   hoon stack
6498        [%tstr p=(pair term (unit spec)) q=hoon r=hoon]      ::  =*   new style
6499        [%tscm p=hoon q=hoon]                                ::  =,   overload p in q
6500    ::                                                  ::::::: conditionals
6501        [%wtbr p=(list hoon)]                                ::  ?|   loobean or
6502        [%wthp p=wing q=(list (pair spec hoon))]             ::  ?-   pick case in q
6503        [%wtcl p=hoon q=hoon r=hoon]                         ::  ?:   if=then=else
6504        [%wtdt p=hoon q=hoon r=hoon]                         ::  ?.   ?:(p r q)
6505        [%wtkt p=wing q=hoon r=hoon]                         ::  ?^   if p is a cell
6506        [%wtgl p=hoon q=hoon]                                ::  ?<   ?:(p !! q)
6507        [%wtgr p=hoon q=hoon]                                ::  ?>   ?:(p q !!)
6508        [%wtls p=wing q=hoon r=(list (pair spec hoon))]      ::  ?+   ?-  w=default
6509        [%wtpm p=(list hoon)]                                ::  ?&   loobean and
6510        [%wtpt p=wing q=hoon r=hoon]                         ::  ?@   if p is atom
6511        [%wtsg p=wing q=hoon r=hoon]                         ::  ?~   if p is null
6512        [%wthx p=skin q=wing]                                ::  ?#   if q matches p
6513        [%wtts p=spec q=wing]                                ::  ?=   if q matches p
6514        [%wtzp p=hoon]                                       ::  ?!   loobean not
6515    ::                                                  ::::::: special
6516        [%zpcm p=hoon q=hoon]                                ::  !,
6517        [%zpgr p=hoon]                                       ::  !>
6518        [%zpgl p=spec q=hoon]                                ::  !<
6519        [%zpmc p=hoon q=hoon]                                ::  !;
6520        [%zpts p=hoon]                                       ::  !=
6521        [%zppt p=(list wing) q=hoon r=hoon]                  ::  !@
6522        [%zpwt p=$@(p=@ [p=@ q=@]) q=hoon]                   ::  !?
6523        [%zpzp ~]                                            ::  !!
6524    ==                                                   ::
6525 +$  tyre  (list [p=term q=hoon])                         ::
6526 +$  tyke  (list (unit hoon))                             ::
6527 ::                                                    ::::::: virtual nock
6528 +$  nock  $^  [p=nock q=nock]                           ::  autocons
6529           $%  [%1 p=*]                                  ::  constant
6530               [%2 p=nock q=nock]                        ::  compose
6531               [%3 p=nock]                               ::  cell test
6532               [%4 p=nock]                               ::  increment
6533               [%5 p=nock q=nock]                        ::  equality test
6534               [%6 p=nock q=nock r=nock]                 ::  if, then, else
6535               [%7 p=nock q=nock]                        ::  serial compose
6536               [%8 p=nock q=nock]                        ::  push onto subject
6537               [%9 p=@ q=nock]                           ::  select arm and fire
6538               [%10 p=[p=@ q=nock] q=nock]               ::  edit
6539               [%11 p=$@(@ [p=@ q=nock]) q=nock]         ::  hint
6540               [%12 p=nock q=nock]                       ::  grab data from sky
6541               [%0 p=@]                                  ::  axis select
6542           ==                                           ::
6543 +$  note                                               ::  type annotation
6544           $%  [%help p=help]                           ::  documentation
6545               [%know p=stud]                           ::  global standard
6546               [%made p=term q=(unit (list wing))]      ::  structure
6547           ==                                           ::
6548 +$  type  $~  %noun                                    ::
6549           $@  $?  %noun                                ::  any nouns
6550                   %void                                ::  no noun
6551               ==                                       ::
6552           $%  [%atom p=term q=(unit @)]                ::  atom / constant
```

```
6553                    [%cell p=type q=type]                  ::  ordered pair
6554                    [%core p=type q=coil]                  ::  object
6555                    [%face p=$@(term tune) q=type]         ::  namespace
6556                    [%fork p=(set type)]                   ::  union
6557                    [%hint p=(pair type note) q=type]      ::  annotation
6558                    [%hold p=type q=hoon]                  ::  lazy evaluation
6559                ==                                         ::
6560  +$   tony                                                ::  ++tone done right
6561            $%  [%0 p=tine q=*]                            ::  success
6562                [%1 p=(set)]                               ::  blocks
6563                [%2 p=(list [@ta *])]                      ::  error ~_s
6564                ==                                         ::
6565  +$   tine                                                ::  partial noun
6566            $@  ~                                          ::  open
6567            $%  [%& p=tine q=tine]                         ::  half-blocked
6568                [%| p=(set)]                               ::  fully blocked
6569                ==                                         ::
6570  +$   tool $@(term tune)                                  ::  type decoration
6571  +$   tune                                                ::  complex
6572            $~  [~ ~]                                      ::
6573            $:  p=(map term (unit hoon))                   ::  aliases
6574                q=(list hoon)                              ::  bridges
6575                ==                                         ::
6576  +$   typo  type                                          ::  old type
6577  +$   vase  [p=type q=*]                                  ::  type-value pair
6578  +$   vise  [p=typo q=*]                                  ::  old vase
6579  +$   vial  ?(%read %rite %both %free)                    ::  co/contra/in/bi
6580  +$   vair  ?(%gold %iron %lead %zinc)                    ::  in/contra/bi/co
6581  +$   vein  (list (unit axis))                            ::  search trace
6582  +$   sect  (list pica)                                   ::  paragraph
6583  +$   whit                                                ::  prefix docs parse
6584    $:  bat=(map cuff (pair cord (list sect)))             ::  batch comment
6585    ==                                                     ::
6586  +$   whiz  cord                                          ::  postfix doc parse
6587  +$   what  (unit (pair cord (list sect)))                ::  help slogan/section
6588  +$   wing  (list limb)                                   ::  search path
6589  ::
6590  ::  +block: abstract identity of resource awaited
6591  ::
6592  +$   block
6593    path
6594  ::
6595  ::  +result: internal interpreter result
6596  ::
6597  +$   result
6598    $@(~ seminoun)
6599  ::
6600  ::  +thunk: fragment constructor
6601  ::
6602  +$   thunk
6603    $-(@ud (unit noun))
6604  ::
6605  ::  +seminoun:
6606  ::
6607  +$   seminoun
6608    ::   partial noun; blocked subtrees are ~
6609    ::
6610    $~  [[%full / ~ ~] ~]
```

```
    [mask=stencil data=noun]
::
::    +stencil: noun knowledge map
::
+$  stencil
  $%  ::
      ::    %half: noun has partial block substructure
      ::
      [%half left=stencil rite=stencil]
      ::
      ::    %full: noun is either fully complete, or fully blocked
      ::
      [%full blocks=(set block)]
      ::
      ::    %lazy: noun can be generated from virtual subtree
      ::
      [%lazy fragment=axis resolve=thunk]
  ==
::
+$  output
  ::  ~: interpreter stopped
  ::
  %-  unit
  $%  ::
      ::    %done: output is complete
      ::
      [%done p=noun]
      ::
      ::    %wait: output is waiting for resources
      ::
      [%wait p=(list block)]
  ==
:: profiling
+$  doss
  $:  mon=moan                              ::  sample count
      hit=(map term @ud)                    ::  hit points
      cut=(map path hump)                   ::  cut points
  ==
+$  moan                                    ::  sample metric
  $:  fun=@ud                               ::  samples in C
      noc=@ud                               ::  samples in nock
      glu=@ud                               ::  samples in glue
      mal=@ud                               ::  samples in alloc
      far=@ud                               ::  samples in frag
      coy=@ud                               ::  samples in copy
      euq=@ud                               ::  samples in equal
  ==                                        ::
::
+$  hump
  $:  mon=moan                              ::  sample count
      out=(map path @ud)                    ::  calls out of
      inn=(map path @ud)                    ::  calls into
  ==
--
::
~%    %pen
    +
  ==
```

```
6669        %ap    ap
6670        %ut    ut
6671    ==
6672 ::    layer-5
6673 ::
6674 |%
6675 ::
6676 ::    5aa: new partial nock interpreter
6677 +|  %new-partial-nock-interpreter
6678 ::
6679 ++  musk  !.                                        :: nock with block set
6680   |%
6681   ++  abet
6682     ::    simplify raw result
6683     ::
6684     |=  $:  :: noy: raw result
6685             ::
6686             noy=result
6687         ==
6688     ^-  output
6689     ::  propagate stop
6690     ::
6691     ?~  noy  ~
6692     :-  ~
6693     ::  merge all blocking sets
6694     ::
6695     =/  blocks  (squash mask.noy)
6696     ?:  =(~ blocks)
6697       ::  no blocks, data is complete
6698       ::
6699       done/data.noy
6700     ::  reduce block set to block list
6701     ::
6702     wait/~(tap in blocks)
6703   ::
6704   ++  araw
6705     ::    execute nock on partial subject
6706     ::
6707     |=  $:  :: bus: subject, a partial noun
6708             :: fol: formula, a complete noun
6709             ::
6710             bus=seminoun
6711             fol=noun
6712         ==
6713     ::  interpreter loop
6714     ::
6715     |-  ^-  result
6716     ?@  fol
6717       ::  bad formula, stop
6718       ::
6719       ~
6720     ?:  ?=(^ -.fol)
6721       ::  hed: interpret head
6722       ::
6723       =+  hed=$(fol -.fol)
6724       ::  propagate stop
6725       ::
6726       ?~  hed  ~
```

```
6727        ::   tal: interpret tail
6728        ::
6729        =+   tal=$(fol +.fol)
6730        ::   propagate stop
6731        ::
6732        ?~   tal   ~
6733        ::   combine
6734        ::
6735        (combine hed tal)
6736      ?+    fol
6737      ::  bad formula; stop
6738      ::
6739            ~
6740      ::   0; fragment
6741      ::
6742          [%0 b=@]
6743      ::   if bad axis, stop
6744      ::
6745      ?:   =(0 b.fol)   ~
6746      ::   reduce to fragment
6747      ::
6748      (fragment b.fol bus)
6749    ::
6750    ::   1; constant
6751    ::
6752        [%1 b=*]
6753    ::   constant is complete
6754    ::
6755    [full/~ b.fol]
6756    ::
6757    ::   2; recursion
6758    ::
6759        [%2 b=* c=*]
6760    ::   require complete formula
6761    ::
6762    %+  require
6763        ::   compute formula with current subject
6764        ::
6765        $(fol c.fol)
6766    |=  ::   ryf: next formula
6767        ::
6768        ryf=noun
6769    ::   lub: next subject
6770    ::
6771    =+   lub=^$(fol b.fol)
6772    ::   propagate stop
6773    ::
6774    ?~   lub   ~
6775    ::   recurse
6776    ::
6777    ^$(fol ryf, bus lub)
6778    ::
6779    ::   3; probe
6780    ::
6781        [%3 b=*]
6782      %+  require
6783        $(fol b.fol)
6784      |=  ::   fig: probe input
```

```
6785          ::
6786          fig=noun
6787      ::  yes if cell, no if atom
6788      ::
6789      [full/~ .?(fig)]
6790  ::
6791  ::  4; increment
6792  ::
6793      [%4 b=*]
6794    %+  require
6795      $(fol b.fol)
6796    |=  ::  fig: increment input
6797        ::
6798        fig=noun
6799    ::  stop for cells, increment for atoms
6800    ::
6801    ?^(fig ~ [full/~ +(fig)])
6802  ::
6803  ::  5; compare
6804  ::
6805      [%5 b=* c=*]
6806    %+  require
6807      $(fol b.fol)
6808    |=  ::  hed: left input
6809        ::
6810        hed=noun
6811    %+  require
6812      ^$(fol c.fol)
6813    |=  ::  tal: right input
6814        ::
6815        tal=noun
6816    [full/~ =(hed tal)]
6817  ::
6818  ::  6; if-then-else
6819  ::
6820      [%6 b=* c=* d=*]
6821    ::  semantic expansion
6822    ::
6823    %+  require
6824      $(fol b.fol)
6825    |=  ::  fig: boolean
6826        ::
6827        fig=noun
6828    ::  apply proper booleans
6829    ::
6830    ?:  =(& fig)  ^$(fol c.fol)
6831    ?:  =(| fig)  ^$(fol d.fol)
6832    ::  stop on bad test
6833    ::
6834    ~
6835  ::
6836  ::  7; composition
6837  ::
6838      [%7 b=* c=*]
6839    ::  one: input
6840    ::
6841    =+  one=$(fol b.fol)
6842    ::  propagate stop
```

```
6843        ::
6844        ?~  one   ~
6845        ::  complete composition
6846        ::
6847        $(fol c.fol, bus one)
6848    ::
6849    ::  8; introduction
6850    ::
6851        [%8 b=* c=*]
6852        ::  one: input
6853        ::
6854        =+  one=$(fol b.fol)
6855        ::  propagate stop
6856        ::
6857        ?~  one   ~
6858        ::  complete introduction
6859        ::
6860        $(fol c.fol, bus (combine one bus))
6861    ::
6862    ::  9; invocation
6863    ::
6864        [%9 b=* c=*]
6865        ::  semantic expansion
6866        ::
6867        ?^  b.fol   ~
6868        ::  one: core
6869        ::
6870        =+  one=$(fol c.fol)
6871        ::  propagate stop
6872        ::
6873        ?~  one   ~
6874        ::  if core is constant
6875        ::
6876        ?:  ?=([[[%full ~] *] one)
6877          ::  then call virtual nock directly
6878          ::
6879          =+  (mack data.one [%9 b.fol %0 1])
6880          ::  propagate stop
6881          ::
6882          ?~  -   ~
6883          ::  produce result
6884          ::
6885          [[%full ~] u.-]
6886        ::  else complete call
6887        ::
6888        %+  require
6889          ::  retrieve formula
6890          ::
6891          (fragment b.fol one)
6892        ::  continue
6893        ::
6894        |=(noun ^$(bus one, fol +<))
6895    ::
6896    ::  10; edit
6897    ::
6898        [%10 [b=@ c=*] d=*]
6899        ::  tar:  target of edit
6900        ::
```

```
6901      =+  tar=$(fol d.fol)
6902      ::  propagate stop
6903      ::
6904      ?~  tar  ~
6905      ::  inn:  inner value
6906      ::
6907      =+  inn=$(fol c.fol)
6908      ::  propagate stop
6909      ::
6910      ?~  inn  ~
6911      (mutate b.fol inn tar)
6912    ::
6913    ::  11; static hint
6914    ::
6915        [%11 @ c=*]
6916      ::  ignore hint
6917      ::
6918      $(fol c.fol)
6919    ::
6920    ::  11; dynamic hint
6921    ::
6922        [%11 [b=* c=*] d=*]
6923      ::  noy: dynamic hint
6924      ::
6925      =+  noy=$(fol c.fol)
6926      ::  propagate stop
6927      ::
6928      ?~  noy  ~
6929      ::  if hint is a fully computed trace
6930      ::
6931      ?:  &(?=(%spot b.fol) ?=([[[%full ~] *] noy))
6932        ::  compute within trace
6933        ::
6934        ~_((show %o +.noy) $(fol d.fol))
6935      ::  else ignore hint
6936      ::
6937      $(fol d.fol)
6938    ==
6939  ::
6940  ++  apex
6941    ::     execute nock on partial subject
6942    ::
6943  |=  $:  ::  bus: subject, a partial noun
6944          ::  fol: formula, a complete noun
6945          ::
6946          bus=seminoun
6947          fol=noun
6948      ==
6949    ~+
6950    ^-  output
6951    ::  simplify result
6952    ::
6953    (abet (araw bus fol))
6954  ::
6955  ++  combine
6956    ::     combine a pair of seminouns
6957    ::
6958  |=  $:  ::  hed: head of pair
```

```
6959              ::  tal: tail of pair
6960              ::
6961              hed=seminoun
6962              tal=seminoun
6963          ==
6964      ^-  seminoun
6965      ?.  ?&  &(?=(%full -.mask.hed) ?=(%full -.mask.tal))
6966              =(=(~ blocks.mask.hed) =(~ blocks.mask.tal))
6967          ==
6968        ::  default merge
6969        ::
6970        [half/[mask.hed mask.tal] [data.hed data.tal]]
6971      ::  both sides total
6972      ::
6973      ?:  =(~ blocks.mask.hed)
6974        ::  both sides are complete
6975        ::
6976        [full/~ data.hed data.tal]
6977      ::  both sides are blocked
6978      ::
6979      [full/(~(uni in blocks.mask.hed) blocks.mask.tal) ~]
6980    ::
6981    ++  complete
6982      ::    complete any laziness
6983      ::
6984      |=  bus=seminoun
6985      ^-  seminoun
6986      ?-  -.mask.bus
6987        %full  bus
6988        %lazy  ::  fragment 1 is the whole thing
6989               ::
6990               ?:  =(1 fragment.mask.bus)
6991                 ::  blocked; we can't get fragment 1 while compiling it
6992                 ::
6993                 [[%full [~ ~ ~]] ~]
6994               ::  execute thunk
6995               ::
6996               =+  (resolve.mask.bus fragment.mask.bus)
6997               ::  if product is nil
6998               ::
6999               ?~  -
7000                 ::  then blocked
7001                 ::
7002                 [[%full [~ ~ ~]] ~]
7003               ::  else use value
7004               ::
7005               [[%full ~] u.-]
7006        %half  ::  recursive descent
7007               ::
7008               %+  combine
7009                 $(bus [left.mask.bus -.data.bus])
7010                 $(bus [rite.mask.bus +.data.bus])
7011      ==
7012    ::
7013    ++  fragment
7014      ::    seek to an axis in a seminoun
7015      ::
7016      |=  $:  ::  axe: tree address of subtree
```

```
7017              ::  bus: partial noun
7018              ::
7019              axe=axis
7020              bus=seminoun
7021          ==
7022      ^-  result
7023      ::  1 is the root
7024      ::
7025      ?:  =(1 axe)  bus
7026      ::  now: top of axis (2 or 3)
7027      ::  lat: rest of axis
7028      ::
7029      =+  [now=(cap axe) lat=(mas axe)]
7030      ?-  -.mask.bus
7031        %lazy  ::  propagate laziness
7032               ::
7033               bus(fragment.mask (peg fragment.mask.bus axe))
7034      ::
7035        %full  ::  if fully blocked, produce self
7036               ::
7037               ?^  blocks.mask.bus  bus
7038               ::  descending into atom, stop
7039               ::
7040               ?@  data.bus  ~
7041               ::  descend into complete cell
7042               ::
7043               $(axe lat, bus [full/~ ?:(=(2 now) -.data.bus +.data.bus)])
7044      ::
7045        %half  ::  descend into partial cell
7046               ::
7047               %=  $
7048                 axe  lat
7049                 bus  ?:  =(2 now)
7050                        [left.mask.bus -.data.bus]
7051                        [rite.mask.bus +.data.bus]
7052      ==        ==
7053    ::
7054    ++  mutate
7055    ::     change a single axis in a seminoun
7056    ::
7057    |=  $:  ::  axe: axis within big to change
7058            ::  lit: (little) seminoun to insert within big at axe
7059            ::  big: seminoun to mutate
7060            ::
7061            axe=@
7062            lit=seminoun
7063            big=seminoun
7064        ==
7065    ^-  result
7066    ::  stop on zero axis
7067    ::
7068    ?~  axe  ~
7069    ::  edit root of big means discard it
7070    ::
7071    ?:  =(1 axe)  lit
7072    ::  decompose axis into path of head-tail
7073    ::
7074    |-  ^-  result
```

```
7075    ?:  =(2 axe)
7076      ::  mutate head of cell
7077      ::
7078    =+  tal=(fragment 3 big)
7079    ::  propagate stop
7080    ::
7081    ?~  tal  ~
7082    (combine lit tal)
7083    ?:  =(3 axe)
7084      ::  mutate tail of cell
7085      ::
7086    =+  hed=(fragment 2 big)
7087    ::  propagate stop
7088    ::
7089    ?~  hed  ~
7090    (combine hed lit)
7091  ::  deeper axis: keep one side of big and
7092  ::  recurse into the other with smaller axe
7093  ::
7094  =+  mor=(mas axe)
7095  =+  hed=(fragment 2 big)
7096  ::  propagate stop
7097  ::
7098  ?~  hed  ~
7099  =+  tal=(fragment 3 big)
7100  ::  propagate stop
7101  ::
7102  ?~  tal  ~
7103    ?:  =(2 (cap axe))
7104    ::  recurse into the head
7105    ::
7106    =+  mut=$(big hed, axe mor)
7107    ::  propagate stop
7108    ::
7109    ?~  mut  ~
7110    (combine mut tal)
7111  ::  recurse into the tail
7112  ::
7113  =+  mut=$(big tal, axe mor)
7114  ::  propagate stop
7115  ::
7116  ?~  mut  ~
7117  (combine hed mut)
7118  ::
7119  ++  require
7120    ::    require complete intermediate step
7121    ::
7122  |=  $:  noy=result
7123          yen=$-(* result)
7124      ==
7125  ^-  result
7126  ::  propagate stop
7127  ::
7128  ?~  noy  ~
7129  ::  suppress laziness
7130  ::
7131  =/  bus=seminoun  (complete noy)
7132  ?<  ?=(%lazy -.mask.bus)
```

```
7133      ::    if partial block, squash blocks and stop
7134      ::
7135      ?:  ?=(%half -.mask.bus)  [full/(squash mask.bus) ~]
7136      ::    if full block, propagate block
7137      ::
7138      ?:  ?=(^ blocks.mask.bus)  [mask.bus ~]
7139      ::    otherwise use complete noun
7140      ::
7141      (yen data.bus)
7142    ::
7143    ++  squash
7144      ::      convert stencil to block set
7145      ::
7146      |=  tyn=stencil
7147      ^-  (set block)
7148      ?-  -.tyn
7149        %lazy  $(tyn -:(complete tyn ~))
7150        %full  blocks.tyn
7151        %half  (~(uni in $(tyn left.tyn)) $(tyn rite.tyn))
7152      ==
7153    --
7154  ::
7155  ::    5a: compiler utilities
7156  +|  %compiler-utilities
7157  ::
7158  ++  bool                                          ::  make loobean
7159    ^-  type
7160    (fork [%atom %f `%.y] [%atom %f `%.n] ~)
7161  ::
7162  ++  cell                                          ::  make %cell type
7163    ~/  %cell
7164    |=  [hed=type tal=type]
7165    ^-  type
7166    ?:(=(%void hed) %void ?:(=(%void tal) %void [%cell hed tal]))
7167  ::
7168  ++  core                                          ::  make %core type
7169    ~/  %core
7170    |=  [pac=type con=coil]
7171    ^-  type
7172    ?:(=(%void pac) %void [%core pac con])
7173  ::
7174  ++  hint
7175    |=  [p=(pair type note) q=type]
7176    ^-  type
7177    ?:  =(%void q)  %void
7178    ?:  =(%noun q)  %noun
7179    [%hint p q]
7180  ::
7181  ++  face                                          ::  make %face type
7182    ~/  %face
7183    |=  [giz=$@(term tune) der=type]
7184    ^-  type
7185    ?:  =(%void der)
7186      %void
7187    [%face giz der]
7188  ::
7189  ++  fork                                          ::  make %fork type
7190    ~/  %fork
```

```
7191    |=  yed=(list type)
7192    =|  lez=(set type)
7193    |-  ^-  type
7194    ?~  yed
7195      ?~  lez  %void
7196      ?:  ?=([* ~ ~] lez)  n.lez
7197      [%fork lez]
7198    %=    $
7199        yed  t.yed
7200        lez
7201      ?:  =(%void i.yed)  lez
7202      ?:  ?=([%fork *] i.yed)  (~(uni in lez) p.i.yed)
7203      (~(put in lez) i.yed)
7204    ==
7205  ::
7206  ++  cove                                          ::  extract [0 *] axis
7207    |=  nug=nock
7208    ?-    nug
7209        [%0 *]   p.nug
7210        [%11 *]  $(nug q.nug)
7211        *        ~_(leaf+"cove" !!)
7212    ==
7213  ++  comb                                          ::  combine two formulas
7214    ~/  %comb
7215    |=  [mal=nock buz=nock]
7216    ^-  nock
7217    ?:  ?&(?=([%0 *] mal) !=(0 p.mal))
7218      ?:  ?&(?=([%0 *] buz) !=(0 p.buz))
7219      [%0 (peg p.mal p.buz)]
7220    ?:  ?=([%2 [%0 *] [%0 *]] buz)
7221      [%2 [%0 (peg p.mal p.p.buz)] [%0 (peg p.mal p.q.buz)]]
7222    [%7 mal buz]
7223    ?:  ?=([^ [%0 %1]] mal)
7224      [%8 p.mal buz]
7225    ?:  =([%0 %1] buz)
7226      mal
7227    [%7 mal buz]
7228  ::
7229  ++  cond                                          ::  ?:  compile
7230    ~/  %cond
7231    |=  [pex=nock yom=nock woq=nock]
7232    ^-  nock
7233    ?:  =([%1 &] pex)  yom
7234    ?:  =([%1 |] pex)  woq
7235    ?:  =([%0 0] pex)  pex
7236    [%6 pex yom woq]
7237  ::
7238  ++  cons                                          ::  make formula cell
7239    ~/  %cons
7240    |=  [vur=nock sed=nock]
7241    ^-  nock
7242    ::  this optimization can remove crashes which are essential
7243    ::
7244    ::  ?:  ?=([[%0 *] [%0 *]] +<)
7245    ::  ?:  ?&(=(+(p.vur) p.sed) =((div p.vur 2) (div p.sed 2)))
7246    ::    [%0 (div p.vur 2)]
7247    ::  [vur sed]
7248    ?:  ?=([[%1 *] [%1 *]] +<)
```

```
7249        [%1 p.vur p.sed]
7250      [vur sed]
7251    ::
7252    ++  fitz                                          ::  odor compatibility
7253      ~/  %fitz
7254      |=  [yaz=term wix=term]
7255      =+  ^=  fiz
7256          |=  mot=@ta  ^-  [p=@ q=@ta]
7257          =+  len=(met 3 mot)
7258          ?:  =(0 len)
7259            [0 %$]
7260          =+  tyl=(rsh [3 (dec len)] mot)
7261          ?:  &((gte tyl 'A') (lte tyl 'Z'))
7262            [(sub tyl 64) (end [3 (dec len)] mot)]
7263          [0 mot]
7264      =+  [yoz=(fiz yaz) wux=(fiz wix)]
7265      ?&  ?|  =(0 p.yoz)
7266              =(0 p.wux)
7267              &(!=(0 p.wux) (lte p.wux p.yoz))
7268          ==
7269          |-  ?|  =(%$ q.yoz)
7270                  =(%$ q.wux)
7271                  ?&  =((end 3 q.yoz) (end 3 q.wux))
7272                      $(q.yoz (rsh 3 q.yoz), q.wux (rsh 3 q.wux))
7273                  ==
7274              ==
7275      ==
7276    ::
7277    ++  flan                                          ::  loobean  &
7278      ~/  %flan
7279      |=  [bos=nock nif=nock]
7280      ^-  nock
7281      ?:  ?|  =(bos nif)
7282              =([%1 |] bos)
7283              =([%1 &] nif)
7284              =([%0 0] bos)
7285          ==
7286        bos
7287      ?:  ?|  =([%1 &] bos)
7288              =([%1 |] nif)
7289              =([%0 0] nif)
7290          ==
7291        nif
7292      [%6 bos nif [%1 |]]
7293    ::
7294    ++  flip                                          ::  loobean negation
7295      ~/  %flip
7296      |=  dyr=nock
7297      ^-  nock
7298      ?:  =([%1 &] dyr)  [%1 |]
7299      ?:  =([%1 |] dyr)  [%1 &]
7300      ?:  =([%0 0] dyr)  dyr
7301      [%6 dyr [%1 |] %1 &]
7302    ::
7303    ++  flor                                          ::  loobean  |
7304      ~/  %flor
7305      |=  [bos=nock nif=nock]
7306      ^-  nock
```

```
7307      ?:  ?|  =(bos nif)
7308              =([%1 &] bos)
7309              =([%1 |] nif)
7310              =([%0 0] bos)
7311          ==
7312        bos
7313      ?:  ?|  =([%1 |] bos)
7314              =([%1 &] nif)
7315              =([%0 0] nif)
7316          ==
7317        nif
7318      [%6 bos [%1 &] nif]
7319    ::
7320    ++  hike
7321      ~/  %hike
7322      |=  [a=axis pac=(list (pair axis nock))]
7323      |^  =/  rel=(map axis nock)  (roll pac insert)
7324          =/  ord=(list axis)     (sort ~(tap in ~(key by rel)) gth)
7325          |-  ^-  nock
7326          ?~  ord
7327            [%0 a]
7328          =/  b=axis  i.ord
7329          =/  c=nock  (~(got by rel) b)
7330          =/  d=nock  $(ord t.ord)
7331          [%10 [b c] d]
7332      ::
7333      ++  contains
7334        |=  [container=axis contained=axis]
7335        ^-  ?
7336        =/  big=@    (met 0 container)
7337        =/  small=@  (met 0 contained)
7338        ?:  (lte small big)  |
7339        =/  dif=@  (sub small big)
7340        =(container (rsh [0 dif] contained))
7341      ::
7342      ++  parent
7343        |=  a=axis
7344        `axis`(rsh 0 a)
7345      ::
7346      ++  sibling
7347        |=  a=axis
7348        ^-  axis
7349        ?~  (mod a 2)
7350          +(a)
7351        (dec a)
7352      ::
7353      ++  insert
7354        |=  [e=[axe=axis fol=nock] n=(map axis nock)]
7355        ^-  (map axis nock)
7356        ?:  =/  a=axis  axe.e
7357            |-  ^-  ?
7358            ?:  =(1 a)  |
7359            ?:  (~(has by n) a)
7360               &
7361            $(a (parent a))
7362          ::  parent already in
7363          n
7364        =.  n
```

```
7365        ::   remove children
7366        %+   roll  ~(tap by n)
7367        |=  [[axe=axis fol=nock] m=_n]
7368        ?.  (contains axe.e axe)  m
7369        (~(del by m) axe)
7370      =/  sib  (sibling axe.e)
7371      =/  un   (~(get by n) sib)
7372      ?~  un   (~(put by n) axe.e fol.e)
7373      ::  replace sibling with parent
7374      %=  $
7375        n  (~(del by n) sib)
7376        e  :-  (parent sib)
7377          ?:  (gth sib axe.e)
7378            (cons fol.e u.un)
7379          (cons u.un fol.e)
7380        ==
7381      --
7382  ::
7383  ++  jock
7384    |=  rad=?
7385    |=  lot=coin  ^-  hoon
7386    ?-     -.lot
7387         ~
7388      ?:(rad [%rock p.lot] [%sand p.lot])
7389    ::
7390        %blob
7391      ?:  rad
7392        [%rock %$ p.lot]
7393      ?@(p.lot [%sand %$ p.lot] [$(p.lot -.p.lot) $(p.lot +.p.lot)])
7394    ::
7395        %many
7396      [%cltr (turn p.lot |=(a=coin ^$(lot a)))]
7397    ==
7398  ::
7399  ++  look
7400    ~/  %look
7401    |=  [cog=term dab=(map term hoon)]
7402    =+  axe=1
7403    |-  ^-  (unit [p=axis q=hoon])
7404    ?-  dab
7405          ~  ~
7406    ::
7407        [* ~ ~]
7408      ?:(=(cog p.n.dab) [~ axe q.n.dab] ~)
7409    ::
7410        [* ~ *]
7411      ?:  =(cog p.n.dab)
7412        [~ (peg axe 2) q.n.dab]
7413      ?:  (gor cog p.n.dab)
7414          ~
7415      $(axe (peg axe 3), dab r.dab)
7416    ::
7417        [* * ~]
7418      ?:  =(cog p.n.dab)
7419        [~ (peg axe 2) q.n.dab]
7420      ?:  (gor cog p.n.dab)
7421        $(axe (peg axe 3), dab l.dab)
7422          ~
```

```
7423      ::
7424          [* * *]
7425      ?:  =(cog p.n.dab)
7426        [~ (peg axe 2) q.n.dab]
7427      ?:  (gor cog p.n.dab)
7428        $(axe (peg axe 6), dab l.dab)
7429      $(axe (peg axe 7), dab r.dab)
7430    ==
7431  ::
7432  ++  loot
7433    ~/  %loot
7434    |=  [cog=term dom=(map term tome)]
7435    =+  axe=1
7436    |-  ^-  (unit [p=axis q=hoon])
7437    ?-  dom
7438        ~   ~
7439    ::
7440        [* ~ ~]
7441      %+  bind  (look cog q.q.n.dom)
7442      |=((pair axis hoon) [(peg axe p) q])
7443    ::
7444        [* ~ *]
7445      =+  yep=(look cog q.q.n.dom)
7446      ?^  yep
7447        [~ (peg (peg axe 2) p.u.yep) q.u.yep]
7448      $(axe (peg axe 3), dom r.dom)
7449    ::
7450        [* * ~]
7451      =+  yep=(look cog q.q.n.dom)
7452      ?^  yep
7453        [~ (peg (peg axe 2) p.u.yep) q.u.yep]
7454      $(axe (peg axe 3), dom l.dom)
7455    ::
7456        [* * *]
7457      =+  yep=(look cog q.q.n.dom)
7458      ?^  yep
7459        [~ (peg (peg axe 2) p.u.yep) q.u.yep]
7460      =+  pey=$(axe (peg axe 6), dom l.dom)
7461      ?^  pey  pey
7462      $(axe (peg axe 7), dom r.dom)
7463    ==
7464  ::
7465  ::    5b: macro expansion
7466  +|  %macro-expansions
7467  ::
7468  ++  ah                                              ::  tiki engine
7469    |_  tik=tiki
7470    ++  blue
7471      |=  gen=hoon
7472      ^-  hoon
7473      ?.  &(?=(%| -.tik) ?=(~ p.tik))  gen
7474      [%tsgr [%$ 3] gen]
7475    ::
7476    ++  teal
7477      |=  mod=spec
7478      ^-  spec
7479      ?:  ?=(%& -.tik)  mod
7480      [%over [%& 3]~ mod]
```

```
7481      ::
7482      ++  tele
7483        |=  syn=skin
7484        ^-  skin
7485        ?:  ?=(%& -.tik)  syn
7486        [%over [%& 3]~ syn]
7487      ::
7488      ++  gray
7489        |=  gen=hoon
7490        ^-  hoon
7491        ?-  -.tik
7492          %&  ?~(p.tik gen [%tstr [u.p.tik ~] [%wing q.tik] gen])
7493          %|  [%tsls ?~(p.tik q.tik [%ktts u.p.tik q.tik]) gen]
7494        ==
7495      ::
7496      ++  puce
7497        ^-  wing
7498        ?-  -.tik
7499          %&  ?~(p.tik q.tik [u.p.tik ~])
7500          %|  [[%& 2] ~]
7501        ==
7502      ::
7503      ++  wthp  |=  opt=(list (pair spec hoon))
7504                %+  gray  %wthp
7505                [puce (turn opt |=([a=spec b=hoon] [a (blue b)]))]
7506      ++  wtkt  |=([sic=hoon non=hoon] (gray [%wtkt puce (blue sic) (blue non)]))
7507      ++  wtls  |=  [gen=hoon opt=(list (pair spec hoon))]
7508                %+  gray  %wtls
7509                [puce (blue gen) (turn opt |=([a=spec b=hoon] [a (blue b)]))]
7510      ++  wtpt  |=([sic=hoon non=hoon] (gray [%wtpt puce (blue sic) (blue non)]))
7511      ++  wtsg  |=([sic=hoon non=hoon] (gray [%wtsg puce (blue sic) (blue non)]))
7512      ++  wthx  |=(syn=skin (gray [%wthx (tele syn) puce]))
7513      ++  wtts  |=(mod=spec (gray [%wtts (teal mod) puce]))
7514      --
7515  ::
7516  ++  ax
7517    =+  :*  ::  .dom: axis to home
7518            ::  .hay: wing to home
7519            ::  .cox: hygienic context
7520            ::  .bug: debug annotations
7521            ::  .nut: annotations
7522            ::  .def: default expression
7523            ::
7524            dom=`axis`1
7525            hay=*wing
7526            cox=*(map term spec)
7527            bug=*(list spot)
7528            nut=*(unit note)
7529            def=*(unit hoon)
7530        ==
7531    |_  mod=spec
7532    ::
7533    ++  autoname
7534      ::      derive name from spec
7535      ::
7536      |-  ^-  (unit term)
7537      ?-  -.mod
7538        %base  ?.(?=([%atom *] p.mod) ~ ?:(=(%$ p.p.mod) `%atom `p.p.mod))
```

```
7539        %dbug  $(mod q.mod)
7540        %gist  $(mod q.mod)
7541        %leaf  `p.mod
7542        %loop  `p.mod
7543        %like  ?~(p.mod ~ ?^(i.p.mod ?:(?=(%& -.i.p.mod) ~ q.i.p.mod) `i.p.mod))
7544        %make  ~(name ap p.mod)
7545        %made  $(mod q.mod)
7546        %over  $(mod q.mod)
7547        %name  $(mod q.mod)
7548      ::
7549        %bcbc  $(mod p.mod)
7550        %bcbr  $(mod p.mod)
7551        %bccb  ~(name ap p.mod)
7552        %bccl  $(mod i.p.mod)
7553        %bccn  $(mod i.p.mod)
7554        %bcdt  ~
7555        %bcgl  $(mod q.mod)
7556        %bcgr  $(mod q.mod)
7557        %bchp  $(mod p.mod)
7558        %bckt  $(mod q.mod)
7559        %bcls  $(mod q.mod)
7560        %bcfs  ~
7561        %bcmc  ~(name ap p.mod)
7562        %bcpm  $(mod p.mod)
7563        %bcsg  $(mod q.mod)
7564        %bctc  ~
7565        %bcts  $(mod q.mod)
7566        %bcpt  $(mod q.mod)
7567        %bcwt  $(mod i.p.mod)
7568        %bczp  ~
7569      ==
7570    ::
7571    ++  function
7572      ::    construct a function example
7573      ::
7574      |=  [fun=spec arg=spec]
7575      ^-  hoon
7576      ::  minimal context as subject
7577      ::
7578      :+  %tsgr
7579        ::  context is example of both specs
7580        ::
7581        [example:clear(mod fun) example:clear(mod arg)]
7582      ::  produce an %iron (contravariant) core
7583      ::
7584      :-  %ktbr
7585      ::  make an actual gate
7586      ::
7587      :+  %brcl
7588        [%$ 2]
7589      [%$ 15]
7590    ::
7591    ++  interface
7592      ::    construct a core example
7593      ::
7594      |=  [variance=vair payload=spec arms=(map term spec)]
7595      ^-  hoon
7596      ::  attach proper variance control
```

```
7597        ::
7598    =-  ?-  variance
7599          %gold  -
7600          %lead  [%ktwt -]
7601          %zinc  [%ktpm -]
7602          %iron  [%ktbr -]
7603        ==
7604    ^-  hoon
7605    :+  %tsgr  example:clear(mod payload)
7606    :+  %brcn  ~
7607    =-  [[%$ ~ -] ~ ~]
7608    %-  ~(gas by *(map term hoon))
7609    %+  turn
7610      ~(tap by arms)
7611    |=  [=term =spec]
7612    ::
7613    ::  note that we *don't* make arm specs in an interface
7614    ::  hygienic -- we leave them in context, to support
7615    ::  maximum programmer flexibility
7616    ::
7617    [term example:clear(mod spec)]
7618  ::
7619  ++  home
7620    ::    express a hoon against the original subject
7621    ::
7622    |=  gen=hoon
7623    ^-  hoon
7624    =/  ,wing
7625        ?:  =(1 dom)
7626          hay
7627        (weld hay `wing`[[%& dom] ~])
7628    ?~  - gen
7629    [%tsgr [%wing -] gen]
7630  ::
7631  ++  clear
7632    ::    clear annotations
7633    ^+  .
7634    .(bug ~, def ~, nut ~)
7635  ::
7636  ++  basal
7637    ::    example base case
7638    ::
7639    |=  bas=base
7640    ?-  bas
7641    ::
7642        [%atom *]
7643      ::  we may want sped
7644      ::
7645      [%sand p.bas ?:(=(%da p.bas) ~2000.1.1 0)]
7646    ::
7647        %noun
7648      ::  raw nock produces noun type
7649      ::
7650      =+([%rock %$ 0] [%ktls [%dttr - - [%rock %$ 1]] -])
7651    ::
7652        %cell
7653      ::  reduce to pair of nouns
7654        ::
```

```
      =+($(bas %noun) [- -])
   ::
        %flag
   ::  comparison produces boolean type
   ::
      =+([%rock %$ 0] [%ktls [%dtts - -] -])
   ::
        %null
      [%rock %n 0]
   ::
        %void
      [%zpzp ~]
   ==
::
++  unfold
   |=  [fun=hoon arg=(list spec)]
   ^-  hoon
   [%cncl fun (turn arg |=(spec ktcl/+<))]
::
++  unreel
   |=  [one=wing res=(list wing)]
   ^-  hoon
   ?~(res [%wing one] [%tsgl [%wing one] $(one i.res, res t.res)])
::
++  descend
   ::    record an axis to original subject
   ::
   |=  axe=axis
   +>(dom (peg axe dom))
::
++  decorate
   ::    apply documentation to expression
   ::
   |=  gen=hoon
   ^-  hoon
   =-  ?~(nut - [%note u.nut -])
   |-
   ?~(bug gen [%dbug i.bug $(bug t.bug)])
::
++  pieces
   ::    enumerate tuple wings
   ::
   |=  =(list term)
   ^-  (^list wing)
   (turn list |=(=term `wing`[term ~]))
::
++  spore
   ::    build default sample
   ::
   ^-  hoon
   ::  sample is always typeless
   ::
   :+  %ktls
   [%bust %noun]
   ::  consume debugging context
   ::
   %-  decorate
   ::  use home as subject
```

```
7713      ::
7714      %-  home
7715      ::  if default is set, use it
7716      ::
7717      ?^  def  u.def
7718      ::  else map structure to expression
7719      ::
7720      ~+
7721      |-  ^-  hoon
7722      ?-  mod
7723        [%base *]  ?:(=(%void p.mod) [%rock %n 0] (basal p.mod))
7724        [%bcbc *]  ::  track hygienic recursion points lexically
7725                   ::
7726                   %=  $
7727                     mod  p.mod
7728                     cox  ::  merge lexically and don't forget %$
7729                          ::
7730                          (~(put by ^+(cox (~(uni by cox) q.mod))) %$ p.mod)
7731                   ==
7732        [%dbug *]  [%dbug p.mod $(mod q.mod)]
7733        [%gist *]  $(mod q.mod)
7734        [%leaf *]  [%rock p.mod q.mod]
7735        [%loop *]  ~|([%loop p.mod] $(mod ~(got by cox) p.mod)))
7736        [%like *]  $(mod bcmc/(unreel p.mod q.mod))
7737        [%made *]  $(mod q.mod)
7738        [%make *]  $(mod bcmc/(unfold p.mod q.mod))
7739        [%name *]  $(mod q.mod)
7740        [%over *]  $(hay p.mod, mod q.mod)
7741      ::
7742        [%bcbr *]  $(mod p.mod)
7743        [%bccb *]  [%rock %n 0]
7744        [%bccl *]  |-  ^-  hoon
7745                   ?~  t.p.mod  ^$(mod i.p.mod)
7746                   :-  ^$(mod i.p.mod)
7747                   $(i.p.mod i.t.p.mod, t.p.mod t.t.p.mod)
7748        [%bccn *]  ::  use last entry
7749                   ::
7750                   |-  ^-  hoon
7751                   ?~  t.p.mod  ^$(mod i.p.mod)
7752                   $(i.p.mod i.t.p.mod, t.p.mod t.t.p.mod)
7753        [%bchp *]  ::  see under %bccb
7754                   ::
7755                   [%rock %n 0]
7756        [%bcgl *]  $(mod q.mod)
7757        [%bcgr *]  $(mod q.mod)
7758        [%bckt *]  $(mod q.mod)
7759        [%bcls *]  [%note [%know p.mod] $(mod q.mod)]
7760        [%bcmc *]  ::  borrow sample
7761                   ::
7762                   [%tsgl [%$ 6] p.mod]
7763        [%bcpm *]  $(mod p.mod)
7764        [%bcsg *]  [%kthp q.mod p.mod]
7765        [%bcts *]  [%ktts p.mod $(mod q.mod)]
7766        [%bcpt *]  $(mod p.mod)
7767        [%bcwt *]  ::  use last entry
7768                   ::
7769                   |-  ^-  hoon
7770                   ?~  t.p.mod  ^$(mod i.p.mod)
```

```
              $(i.p.mod i.t.p.mod, t.p.mod t.t.p.mod)
    [%bcdt *]   [%rock %n 0]
    [%bcfs *]   [%rock %n 0]
    [%bctc *]   [%rock %n 0]
    [%bczp *]   [%rock %n 0]
  ==
::
++  example
  ::    produce a correctly typed default instance
  ::
  ~+
  ^-  hoon
  ?+  mod
    ::  in the general case, make and analyze a spore
    ::
    :+  %tsls
      spore
    ~(relative analyze:(descend 3) 2)
  ::
    [%base *]   (decorate (basal p.mod))
    [%dbug *]   example(mod q.mod, bug [p.mod bug])
    [%gist *]   example(mod q.mod, nut `p.mod)
    [%leaf *]   (decorate [%rock p.mod q.mod])
    [%like *]   example(mod bcmc/(unreel p.mod q.mod))
    [%loop *]   [%limb p.mod]
    [%made *]   example(mod q.mod, nut `made/[p.p.mod `(pieces q.p.mod)])
    [%make *]   example(mod bcmc/(unfold p.mod q.mod))
    [%name *]   example(mod q.mod, nut `made/[p.mod ~])
    [%over *]   example(hay p.mod, mod q.mod)
  ::
    [%bccb *]   (decorate (home p.mod))
    [%bccl *]   %-  decorate
                |-  ^-  hoon
                ?~  t.p.mod
                  example:clear(mod i.p.mod)
                :-  example:clear(mod i.p.mod)
                example:clear(i.p.mod i.t.p.mod, t.p.mod t.t.p.mod)
    [%bchp *]   (decorate (function:clear p.mod q.mod))
    [%bcmc *]   (decorate (home [%tsgl [%limb %$] p.mod]))
    [%bcsg *]   [%ktls example(mod q.mod) (home p.mod)]
    [%bcls *]   (decorate [%note [%know p.mod] example(mod q.mod)])
    [%bcts *]   (decorate [%ktts p.mod example:clear(mod q.mod)])
    [%bcdt *]   (decorate (home (interface %gold p.mod q.mod)))
    [%bcfs *]   (decorate (home (interface %iron p.mod q.mod)))
    [%bczp *]   (decorate (home (interface %lead p.mod q.mod)))
    [%bctc *]   (decorate (home (interface %zinc p.mod q.mod)))
  ==
::
++  factory
  ::    make a normalizing gate (mold)
  ::
  ^-  hoon
  ::  process annotations outside construct, to catch default
  ::
  ::TODO: try seeing if putting %gist in here fixes %brbc
  ?:  ?=(%dbug -.mod)  factory(mod q.mod, bug [p.mod bug])
  ?:  ?=(%bcsg -.mod)  factory(mod q.mod, def `[%kthp q.mod p.mod])
  ^-  hoon
```

```hoon
7829      ::  if we recognize an indirection
7830      ::
7831      ?:  &(=(~ def) ?=(?(%bcmc %like %loop %make) -.mod))
7832        ::  then short-circuit it
7833        ::
7834        %-  decorate
7835        %-  home
7836        ?-  -.mod
7837          %bcmc  p.mod
7838          %like  (unreel p.mod q.mod)
7839          %loop  [%limb p.mod]
7840          %make  (unfold p.mod q.mod)
7841        ==
7842      ::  else build a gate
7843      ::
7844      :+  %brcl
7845        [%ktsg spore]
7846      :+  %tsls
7847        ~(relative analyze:(descend 7) 6)
7848      ::  trigger unifying equality
7849      ::
7850      :+  %tsls  [%dtts $/14 $/2]
7851      $/6
7852    ::
7853    ++  analyze
7854      ::    normalize a fragment of the subject
7855      ::
7856      |_  $:  ::  axe: axis to fragment
7857              ::
7858              axe=axis
7859          ==
7860      ++  basic
7861        |=  bas=base
7862        ^-  hoon
7863        ?-  bas
7864          [%atom *]
7865          :+  %ktls  example
7866          ^-  hoon
7867          :^    %zppt
7868              [[[%| 0 `%ruth] ~] ~]
7869            [%cnls [%limb %ruth] [%sand %ta p.bas] fetch]
7870          [%wtpt fetch-wing fetch [%zpzp ~]]
7871        ::
7872          %cell
7873          :+  %ktls  example
7874          =+  fetch-wing
7875          :-  [%wing [[%& %2] -]]
7876            [%wing [[%& %3] -]]
7877        ::
7878          %flag
7879          :^    %wtcl
7880              [%dtts [%rock %$ &] [%$ axe]]
7881            [%rock %f &]
7882          :+  %wtgr
7883            [%dtts [%rock %$ |] [%$ axe]]
7884          [%rock %f |]
7885        ::
7886          %noun
```

```
7887          fetch
7888      ::
7889            %null
7890      :+  %wtgr
7891          [%dtts [%bust %noun] [%$ axe]]
7892          [%rock %n ~]
7893      :::
7894            %void
7895          [%zpzp ~]
7896      ==
7897  ++  clear
7898    .(..analyze ^clear)
7899  ::
7900  ++  fetch
7901    ::    load the fragment
7902    ::
7903    ^-  hoon
7904    [%$ axe]
7905  ::
7906  ++  fetch-wing
7907    ::    load, as a wing
7908    ::
7909    ^-  wing
7910    [[%& axe] ~]
7911  ::
7912  ++  choice
7913    ::    match full models, by trying them
7914    ::
7915    |=  $:  ::  one: first option
7916            ::  rep: other options
7917            ::
7918            one=spec
7919            rep=(list spec)
7920        ==
7921    ^-  hoon
7922    ::  if no other choices, construct head
7923    ::
7924    ?~  rep  relative:clear(mod one)
7925    ::  build test
7926    ::
7927    :^    %wtcl
7928        ::  if we fit the type of this choice
7929        ::
7930        [%fits example:clear(mod one) fetch-wing]
7931      ::  build with this choice
7932      ::
7933      relative:clear(mod one)
7934    ::  continue through loop
7935    ::
7936    $(one i.rep, rep t.rep)
7937  ::
7938  ++  switch
7939    |=  $:  ::  one: first format
7940            ::  two: more formats
7941            ::
7942            one=spec
7943            rep=(list spec)
7944        ==
```

```
7945        |-  ^-  hoon
7946        ::  if no other choices, construct head
7947        ::
7948        ?~  rep  relative:clear(mod one)
7949        ::  fin: loop completion
7950        ::
7951        =/  fin=hoon  $(one i.rep, rep t.rep)
7952        ::  interrogate this instance
7953        ::
7954        :^    %wtcl
7955          ::  test if the head matches this wing
7956          ::
7957          :+  %fits
7958            [%tsgl [%$ 2] example:clear(mod one)]
7959          fetch-wing(axe (peg axe 2))
7960        ::  if so, use this form
7961        ::
7962      relative:clear(mod one)
7963      ::  continue in the loop
7964      ::
7965    fin
7966  ::
7967  ++  relative
7968      ::    local constructor
7969      ::
7970      ~+
7971      ^-  hoon
7972      ?-  mod
7973      ::
7974      ::  base
7975      ::
7976        [%base *]
7977      (decorate (basic:clear p.mod))
7978      ::
7979      ::  debug
7980      ::
7981        [%dbug *]
7982      relative(mod q.mod, bug [p.mod bug])
7983      ::
7984      ::  formal comment
7985      ::
7986        [%gist *]
7987      relative(mod q.mod, nut `p.mod)
7988      ::
7989      ::  constant
7990      ::
7991        [%leaf *]
7992      %-  decorate
7993      :+  %wtgr
7994        [%dtts fetch [%rock %$ q.mod]]
7995      [%rock p.mod q.mod]
7996      ::
7997      ::  composite
7998      ::
7999        [%make *]
8000      relative(mod bcmc/(unfold p.mod q.mod))
8001      ::
8002      ::  indirect
```

```
8003      ::
8004        [%like *]
8005      relative(mod bcmc/(unreel p.mod q.mod))
8006      ::
8007      ::  loop
8008      ::
8009        [%loop *]
8010      (decorate [%cnhp [%limb p.mod] fetch])
8011      ::
8012      ::  simple named structure
8013      ::
8014        [%name *]
8015      relative(mod q.mod, nut `made/[p.mod ~])
8016      ::
8017      ::  synthetic named structure
8018      ::
8019        [%made *]
8020      relative(mod q.mod, nut `made/[p.p.mod `(pieces q.p.mod)])
8021      ::
8022      ::  subjective
8023      ::
8024        [%over *]
8025      relative(hay p.mod, mod q.mod)
8026      ::
8027      ::  recursive, $$
8028      ::
8029        [%bcbc *]
8030      ::
8031      ::  apply semantically
8032      ::
8033      :+  %brkt
8034        relative(mod p.mod, dom (peg 3 dom))
8035      =-  [[%$ ~ -] ~ ~]
8036      %-  ~(gas by *(map term hoon))
8037      ^-  (list (pair term hoon))
8038      %+  turn
8039        ~(tap by q.mod)
8040      |=  [=term =spec]
8041      [term relative(mod spec, dom (peg 3 dom))]
8042      ::
8043      ::  normalize, $&
8044      ::
8045        [%bcpm *]
8046      ::  push the raw result
8047      ::
8048      :+  %tsls  relative(mod p.mod)
8049      ::  push repair function
8050      ::
8051      :+  %tsls
8052        [%tsgr $/3 q.mod]
8053      ::  push repaired product
8054      ::
8055      :+  %tsls
8056        [%cnhp $/2 $/6]
8057      ::  sanity-check repaired product
8058      ::
8059      :+  %wtgr
8060        ::  either
```

```
    ::
    :~  %wtbr
        ::  the repair did not change anything
        ::
        [%dtts $/14 $/2]
        ::  when we fix it again, it stays fixed
        ::
        [%dtts $/2 [%cnhp $/6 $/2]]
      ==
    $/2
  ::
  ::  verify, $|
  ::
      [%bcbr *]
    ^-  hoon
    ::  push the raw product
    ::
    :+  %tsls  relative(mod p.mod)
    ^-  hoon
    ::  assert
    ::
    :+  %wtgr
      ::  run the verifier
      ::
      [%cnhp [%tsgr $/3 q.mod] $/2]
    ::  produce verified product
    ::
    $/2
  ::
  ::  special, $_
  ::
      [%bccb *]
    (decorate (home p.mod))
  ::
  ::  switch, $%
  ::
      [%bccn *]
    (decorate (switch i.p.mod t.p.mod))
  ::
  ::  tuple, $:
  ::
      [%bccl *]
    %-  decorate
    |-  ^-  hoon
    ?~  t.p.mod
      relative:clear(mod i.p.mod)
    :-  relative:clear(mod i.p.mod, axe (peg axe 2))
    %=  relative
      i.p.mod  i.t.p.mod
      t.p.mod  t.t.p.mod
      axe      (peg axe 3)
    ==
  ::
  ::  exclude, $<
  ::
      [%bcgl *]
    :+  %tsls
      relative:clear(mod q.mod)
```

```
8119      :+  %wtgl
8120        [%wtts [%over ~[&/3] p.mod] ~[&/4]]
8121      $/2
8122    ::
8123    ::  require, $>
8124    ::
8125        [%bcgr *]
8126      :+  %tsls
8127      relative:clear(mod q.mod)
8128      :+  %wtgr
8129        [%wtts [%over ~[&/3] p.mod] ~[&/4]]
8130      $/2
8131    ::
8132    ::  function
8133    ::
8134        [%bchp *]
8135    %-  decorate
8136    =/  fun  (function:clear p.mod q.mod)
8137    ?^  def
8138      [%ktls fun u.def]
8139    fun
8140    ::
8141    ::  bridge, $^
8142    ::
8143        [%bckt *]
8144    %-  decorate
8145    :^    %wtcl
8146        [%dtwt fetch(axe (peg axe 2))]
8147      relative:clear(mod p.mod)
8148    relative:clear(mod q.mod)
8149    ::
8150    ::  synthesis, $;
8151    ::
8152        [%bcmc *]
8153    (decorate [%cncl (home p.mod) fetch ~])
8154    ::
8155    ::  default
8156    ::
8157        [%bcsg *]
8158    relative(mod q.mod, def `[%kthp q.mod p.mod])
8159    ::
8160    ::  choice, $?
8161    ::
8162        [%bcwt *]
8163    (decorate (choice i.p.mod t.p.mod))
8164    ::
8165    ::  name, $=
8166    ::
8167        [%bcts *]
8168    [%ktts p.mod relative(mod q.mod)]
8169    ::
8170    ::  branch, $@
8171    ::
8172        [%bcpt *]
8173    %-  decorate
8174    :^    %wtcl
8175        [%dtwt fetch]
8176      relative:clear(mod q.mod)
```

```
    relative:clear(mod p.mod)
::
    [%bcls *]   [%note [%know p.mod] relative(mod q.mod)]
    [%bcdt *]   (decorate (home (interface %gold p.mod q.mod)))
    [%bcfs *]   (decorate (home (interface %iron p.mod q.mod)))
    [%bczp *]   (decorate (home (interface %lead p.mod q.mod)))
    [%bctc *]   (decorate (home (interface %zinc p.mod q.mod)))
  ==
  --
--
::
++  ap                                                    ::  hoon engine
  ~%    %ap
      +>+
  ==
    %open  open
    %rake  rake
  ==
  |_  gen=hoon
  ::
  ++  grip
    |=  =skin
    =|  rel=wing
    |-  ^-  hoon
    ?-    skin
        @
      [%tsgl [%tune skin] gen]
        [%base *]
      ?:  ?=(%noun base.skin)
        gen
      [%kthp skin gen]
    ::
        [%cell *]
      =+  haf=~(half ap gen)
      ?^  haf
        :-  $(skin skin.skin, gen p.u.haf)
        $(skin ^skin.skin, gen q.u.haf)
      :+  %tsls
        gen
      :-  $(skin skin.skin, gen [%$ 4])
      $(skin ^skin.skin, gen [%$ 5])
    ::
        [%dbug *]
      [%dbug spot.skin $(skin skin.skin)]
    ::
        [%leaf *]
      [%kthp skin gen]
    ::
        [%help *]
      [%note [%help help.skin] $(skin skin.skin)]
    ::
        [%name *]
      [%tsgl [%tune term.skin] $(skin skin.skin)]
    ::
        [%over *]
      $(skin skin.skin, rel (weld wing.skin rel))
    ::
        [%spec *]
```

```
      :+  %kthp
        ?~(rel spec.skin [%over rel spec.skin])
      $(skin skin.skin)
    ::
        [%wash *]
      :+  %tsgl
        :-  %wing
        |-  ^-  wing
        ?:  =(0 depth.skin)  ~
        [[[%| 0 ~] $(depth.skin (dec depth.skin))]
      gen
    ==
  ::
++  name
    |-  ^-  (unit term)
    ?+  gen  ~
      [%wing *]  ?~  p.gen  ~
                 ?^  i.p.gen
                   ?:(?=(%& -.i.p.gen) ~ q.i.p.gen)
                 `i.p.gen
      [%limb *]  `p.gen
      [%dbug *]  $(gen ~(open ap gen))
      [%tsgl *]  $(gen ~(open ap gen))
      [%tsgr *]  $(gen q.gen)
    ==
  ::
++  feck
    |-  ^-  (unit term)
    ?-  gen
      [%sand %tas @]  [~ q.gen]
      [%dbug *]       $(gen q.gen)
      *               ~
    ==
  ::
  :: not used at present; see comment at %csng in ++open
::::
::++  hail
::  |=  axe=axis
::  =|  air=(list (pair wing hoon))
::  |-  ^+  air
::  =+  hav=half
::  ?~  hav  [[[[%| 0 ~] [%& axe] ~] gen] air]
::  $(gen p.u.hav, axe (peg axe 2), air $(gen q.u.hav, axe (peg axe 3)))
::
++  half
    |-  ^-  (unit (pair hoon hoon))
    ?+  gen  ~
      [^ *]      `[p.gen q.gen]
      [%dbug *]  $(gen q.gen)
      [%clcb *]  `[q.gen p.gen]
      [%clhp *]  `[p.gen q.gen]
      [%clkt *]  `[p.gen %clls q.gen r.gen s.gen]
      [%clsg *]  ?~(p.gen ~ `[i.p.gen %clsg t.p.gen])
      [%cltr *]  ?~  p.gen  ~
                 ?~(t.p.gen $(gen i.p.gen) `[i.p.gen %cltr t.p.gen])
    ==
::::
  :: +flay: hoon to skin
```

```
8293      ::
8294      ++  flay
8295        |-  ^-  (unit skin)
8296        ?+    gen
8297          =+(open ?:(=(- gen) ~ $(gen -)))
8298        ::
8299            [^ *]
8300          =+  [$(gen p.gen) $(gen q.gen)]
8301          ?~(-< ~ ?~(-> ~ `[%cell -<+ ->+]))
8302        ::
8303            [%base *]
8304          `gen
8305        ::
8306            [%rock *]
8307          ?@(q.gen `[%leaf p.gen q.gen] ~)
8308        ::
8309            [%cnts [@ ~] ~]
8310          `i.p.gen
8311        ::
8312            [%tsgr *]
8313          %+  biff  reek(gen p.gen)
8314          |=  =wing
8315          (bind ^$(gen q.gen) |=(=skin [%over wing skin]))
8316        ::
8317            [%limb @]
8318          `p.gen
8319        ::
8320            [%note [%help *] *]
8321          (bind $(gen q.gen) |=(=skin [%help p.p.gen skin]))
8322        ::
8323            [%wing *]
8324          ?:  ?=([@ ~] p.gen)
8325            `i.p.gen
8326          =/  depth  0
8327          |-  ^-  (unit skin)
8328          ?~  p.gen  `[%wash depth]
8329          ?.  =([%| 0 ~] i.p.gen)  ~
8330          $(p.gen t.p.gen)
8331        ::
8332            [%kttr *]
8333          `[%spec p.gen %base %noun]
8334        ::
8335            [%ktts *]
8336          %+  biff  $(gen q.gen)
8337          |=  =skin
8338          ?@  p.gen  `[%name p.gen skin]
8339          ?.  ?=([%name @ [%base %noun]] p.gen)  ~
8340          `[%name term.p.gen skin]
8341        ==
8342      ::
8343      ::  +open: desugarer
8344      ++  open
8345        ^-  hoon
8346        ?-    gen
8347          [~ *]        [%cnts [[%& p.gen] ~] ~]
8348        ::
8349          [%base *]  ~(factory ax `spec`gen)
8350          [%bust *]  ~(example ax %base p.gen)
```

```
    [%ktcl *]   ~(factory ax p.gen)
    [%dbug *]   q.gen
    [%eror *]   ~_((crip p.gen) !!)
::
    [%knit *]                                  ::
  :+  %tsgr  [%ktts %v %$ 1]                   ::  =>   v=.
  :-  %brhp                                    ::  |-
  :+  %ktls                                    ::  ^+
    :-  %brhp                                  ::  |-
    :^    %wtcl                                ::  ?:
      [%bust %flag]                            ::  ?
      [%bust %null]                            ::  ~
      :-  [%ktts %i [%sand 'tD' *@]]           ::  :-  i=~~
      [%ktts %t [%limb %$]]                    ::  t=$
    |-  ^-  hoon                               ::
    ?~  p.gen                                  ::
      [%bust %null]                            ::  ~
    =+  res=$(p.gen t.p.gen)                   ::
    ^-  hoon                                   ::
    ?@  i.p.gen                                ::
      [[%sand 'tD' i.p.gen] res]               ::  [~~{i.p.gen} {res}]
    :+  %tsls                                  ::
      :-  :+  %ktts                            ::  ^=
            %a                                 ::  a
          :+  %ktls                            ::  ^+
            [%limb %$]                         ::  $
            [%tsgr [%limb %v] p.i.p.gen]       ::  =>(v {p.i.p.gen})
      [%ktts %b res]                           ::  b=[res]
    ^-  hoon                                   ::
    :-  %brhp                                  ::  |-
    :^    %wtpt                                ::  ?@
      [%a ~]                                   ::  a
      [%limb %b]                               ::  b
    :-  [%tsgl [%$ 2] [%limb %a]]              ::  :-  -.a
    :+  %cnts                                  ::  %=
      [%$ ~]                                   ::  $
      [[[%a ~] [%tsgl [%$ 3] [%limb %a]]] ~]   ::  a  +.a
  ::
    [%leaf *]   ~(factory ax `spec`gen)
    [%limb *]   [%cnts [p.gen ~] ~]
    [%tell *]   [%cncl [%limb %noah] [%zpgr [%cltr p.gen]] ~]
    [%wing *]   [%cnts p.gen ~]
    [%yell *]   [%cncl [%limb %cain] [%zpgr [%cltr p.gen]] ~]
    [%note *]   q.gen
  ::
  ::TODO: does %gist need to be special cased here?
    [%brbc *]   =-  ?~  -  !!
                    :+  %brtr
                      [%bccl -]
                    |-
                    ?.  ?=([%gist *] body.gen)
                      [%ktcl body.gen]
                    [%note p.body.gen $(body.gen q.body.gen)]
                %+  turn  `(list term)`sample.gen
                |=  =term
                ^-  spec
                =/  tar  [%base %noun]
                [%bcts term [%bcsg tar [%bchp tar tar]]]
```

```
8409          [%brcb *]    :+  %tsls  [%kttr p.gen]
8410                       :+  %brcn  ~
8411                       %-  ~(run by r.gen)
8412                       |=  =tome
8413                       :-  p.tome
8414                       %-  ~(run by q.tome)
8415                       |=  =hoon
8416                       ?~  q.gen  hoon
8417                       [%tstr [p.i.q.gen ~] q.i.q.gen $(q.gen t.q.gen)]
8418          [%brcl *]    [%tsls p.gen [%brdt q.gen]]
8419          [%brdt *]    :+  %brcn  ~
8420                       =-  [[%$ ~ -] ~ ~]
8421                       (~(put by *(map term hoon)) %$ p.gen)
8422          [%brkt *]    :+  %tsgl  [%limb %$]
8423                       :+  %brcn  ~
8424                       =+  zil=(~(get by q.gen) %$)
8425                       ?~  zil
8426                         %+  ~(put by q.gen)  %$
8427                         [*what [[%$ p.gen] ~ ~]]
8428                       %+  ~(put by q.gen)  %$
8429                       [p.u.zil (~(put by q.u.zil) %$ p.gen)]
8430          [%brhp *]    [%tsgl [%limb %$] [%brdt p.gen]]
8431          [%brsg *]    [%ktbr [%brts p.gen q.gen]]
8432          [%brtr *]    :+  %tsls  [%kttr p.gen]
8433                       :+  %brpt  ~
8434                       =-  [[%$ ~ -] ~ ~]
8435                       (~(put by *(map term hoon)) %$ q.gen)
8436          [%brts *]    :+  %brcb  p.gen
8437                       =-  [~ [[%$ ~ -] ~ ~]]
8438                       (~(put by *(map term hoon)) %$ q.gen)
8439          [%brwt *]    [%ktwt %brdt p.gen]
8440      ::
8441          [%clkt *]    [p.gen q.gen r.gen s.gen]
8442          [%clls *]    [p.gen q.gen r.gen]
8443          [%clcb *]    [q.gen p.gen]
8444          [%clhp *]    [p.gen q.gen]
8445          [%clsg *]
8446        |-  ^-  hoon
8447        ?~  p.gen
8448          [%rock %n ~]
8449        [i.p.gen $(p.gen t.p.gen)]
8450      ::
8451          [%cltr *]
8452        |-  ^-  hoon
8453        ?~  p.gen
8454          [%zpzp ~]
8455        ?~  t.p.gen
8456          i.p.gen
8457        [i.p.gen $(p.gen t.p.gen)]
8458      ::
8459          [%kttr *]    [%ktsg ~(example ax p.gen)]
8460          [%cncb *]    [%ktls [%wing p.gen] %cnts p.gen q.gen]
8461          [%cndt *]    [%cncl q.gen [p.gen ~]]
8462          [%cnkt *]    [%cncl p.gen q.gen r.gen s.gen ~]
8463          [%cnls *]    [%cncl p.gen q.gen r.gen ~]
8464          [%cnhp *]    [%cncl p.gen q.gen ~]
8465          ::  this probably should work, but doesn't
8466          ::
```

```
8467      ::    [%cncl *]    [%cntr [%$ ~] p.gen [[[[%& 6] ~] [%cltr q.gen]] ~]]
8468            [%cncl *]    [%cnsg [%$ ~] p.gen q.gen]
8469            [%cnsg *]
8470      ::   this complex matching system is a leftover from the old
8471      ::   "electroplating" era.  %cnsg should be removed and replaced
8472      ::   with the commented-out %cncl above.  but something is broken.
8473      ::
8474      :^   %cntr  p.gen   q.gen
8475      =+   axe=6
8476      |-   ^-   (list [wing hoon])
8477      ?~   r.gen   ~
8478      ?~   t.r.gen  [[[[%| 0 ~] [%& axe] ~] i.r.gen] ~]
8479      :-   [[[%| 0 ~] [%& (peg axe 2)] ~] i.r.gen]
8480      $(axe (peg axe 3), r.gen t.r.gen)
8481  ::
8482        [%cntr *]
8483      ?:   =(~ r.gen)
8484        [%tsgr q.gen [%wing p.gen]]
8485      :+   %tsls
8486        q.gen
8487      :+   %cnts
8488        (weld p.gen `wing`[[%& 2] ~])
8489      (turn r.gen |=([p=wing q=hoon] [p [%tsgr [%$ 3] q]]))
8490  ::
8491        [%ktdt *]    [%ktls [%cncl p.gen q.gen ~] q.gen]
8492        [%kthp *]    [%ktls ~(example ax p.gen) q.gen]
8493        [%ktts *]    (grip(gen q.gen) p.gen)
8494  ::
8495        [%sgbr *]
8496      :+   %sggr
8497        :-   %mean
8498        =+   fek=~(feck ap p.gen)
8499        ?^   fek   [%rock %tas u.fek]
8500        [%brdt [%cncl [%limb %cain] [%zpgr [%tsgr [%$ 3] p.gen]] ~]]
8501      q.gen
8502  ::
8503        [%sgcb *]    [%sggr [%mean [%brdt p.gen]] q.gen]
8504        [%sgcn *]
8505      :+   %sggl
8506        :-   %fast
8507        :-   %clls
8508        :+   [%rock %$ p.gen]
8509          [%zpts q.gen]
8510        :-   %clsg
8511        =+   nob=`(list hoon)`~
8512        |-   ^-   (list hoon)
8513        ?~   r.gen
8514          nob
8515        [[[%rock %$ p.i.r.gen] [%zpts q.i.r.gen]] $(r.gen t.r.gen)]
8516      s.gen
8517  ::
8518        [%sgfs *]    [%sgcn p.gen [%$ 7] ~ q.gen]
8519        [%sggl *]    [%tsgl [%sggr p.gen [%$ 1]] q.gen]
8520        [%sgbc *]    [%sggr [%live [%rock %$ p.gen]] q.gen]
8521        [%sgls *]    [%sggr [%memo %rock %$ p.gen] q.gen]
8522        [%sgpm *]
8523      :+   %sggr
8524        [%slog [%sand %$ p.gen] [%cncl [%limb %cain] [%zpgr q.gen] ~]]
```

```
        r.gen
    ::
      [%sgts *]   [%sggr [%germ p.gen] q.gen]
      [%sgwt *]
    :+  %tsls  [%wtdt q.gen [%bust %null] [[%bust %null] r.gen]]
    :^  %wtsg  [%& 2]~
      [%tsgr [%$ 3] s.gen]
    [%sgpm p.gen [%$ 5] [%tsgr [%$ 3] s.gen]]
    ::
      [%mcts *]
    |-
    ?~  p.gen  [%bust %null]
    ?-  -.i.p.gen
      ^          [[%xray i.p.gen] $(p.gen t.p.gen)]
    %manx  [p.i.p.gen $(p.gen t.p.gen)]
    %tape  [[%mcfs p.i.p.gen] $(p.gen t.p.gen)]
    %call  [%cncl p.i.p.gen [$(p.gen t.p.gen)]~]
    %marl  =-  [%cndt [p.i.p.gen $(p.gen t.p.gen)] -]
             ^-  hoon
             :+  %tsbr  [%base %cell]
             :+  %brpt  ~
             ^-  (map term tome)
             =-  [[%$ ~ -] ~ ~]
             ^-  (map term hoon)
             :_  [~ ~]
             =+  sug=[[%& 12] ~]
             :-  %$
             :^  %wtsg  sug
               [%cnts sug [[[[%& 1] ~] [%$ 13]] ~]]
             [%cnts sug [[[[%& 3] ~] [%cnts [%$ ~] [[sug [%$ 25]] ~]]] ~]]
    ==
    ::
      [%mccl *]
    ?-    q.gen
      ~          [%zpzp ~]
      [* ~]  i.q.gen
      ^
    :+  %tsls
      p.gen
    =+  yex=`(list hoon)`q.gen
    |-  ^-  hoon
    ?-  yex
      [* ~]  [%tsgr [%$ 3] i.yex]
      [* ^]  [%cncl [%$ 2] [%tsgr [%$ 3] i.yex] $(yex t.yex) ~]
      ~          !!
    ==
    ==
    ::
      [%mcfs *]  =+(zoy=[%rock %ta %$] [%clsg [zoy [%clsg [zoy p.gen] ~]] ~])
      [%mcgl *]  [%cnls [%cnhp q ktcl+p] r [%brts p [%tsgr $+3 s]]]:gen
    ::
      [%mcsg *]                        ::                   ;~
    |-  ^-  hoon
    ?-  q.gen
      ~          ~_(leaf+"open-mcsg" !!)
      ^
    :+  %tsgr  [%ktts %v %$ 1]                   ::  =>  v=.
    |-  ^-  hoon                                 ::
```

```
8583        ?:  ?=(~ t.q.gen)                                  ::
8584          [%tsgr [%limb %v] i.q.gen]                        ::    =>(v {i.q.gen})
8585        :+  %tsls   [%ktts %a $(q.gen t.q.gen)]             ::    =+  ^=  a
8586        :+  %tsls                                           ::      {$(q.gen t.q.gen)}
8587          [%ktts %b [%tsgr [%limb %v] i.q.gen]]             ::    =+  ^=  b
8588        :+  %tsls                                           ::     =>(v {i.q.gen})
8589          :+  %ktts  %c                                     ::    =+  c=,.+6.b
8590          :+  %tsgl                                         ::
8591            [%wing [%| 0 ~] [%& 6] ~]                        ::
8592          [%limb %b]                                        ::
8593        :-  %brdt                                           ::    |.
8594        :^    %cnls                                         ::    %+
8595          [%tsgr [%limb %v] p.gen]                          ::      =>(v {p.gen})
8596          [%cncl [%limb %b] [%limb %c] ~]                   ::     (b c)
8597        :+  %cnts   [%a ~]                                  ::    a(,.+6 c)
8598        [[[[%| 0 ~] [%& 6] ~] [%limb %c]] ~]                ::
8599      ==                                                    ::
8600    ::
8601        [%mcmc *]                                           ::                    ;;
8602      [%cnhp ~(factory ax p.gen) q.gen]
8603    ::
8604        [%tsbr *]
8605      [%tsls ~(example ax p.gen) q.gen]
8606    ::
8607        [%tstr *]
8608      :+  %tsgl
8609        r.gen
8610      [%tune [[p.p.gen ~ ?~(q.p.gen q.gen [%kthp u.q.p.gen q.gen])] ~ ~] ~]
8611    ::
8612        [%tscl *]
8613      [%tsgr [%cncb [[%& 1] ~] p.gen] q.gen]
8614    ::
8615        [%tsfs *]
8616      [%tsls [%ktts p.gen q.gen] r.gen]
8617    ::
8618        [%tsmc *]    [%tsfs p.gen r.gen q.gen]
8619        [%tsdt *]
8620      [%tsgr [%cncb [[%& 1] ~] [[p.gen q.gen] ~]] r.gen]
8621        [%tswt *]                                           ::                    =?
8622      [%tsdt p.gen [%wtcl q.gen r.gen [%wing p.gen]] s.gen]
8623    ::
8624        [%tskt *]                                           ::                    =^
8625      =+  wuy=(weld q.gen `wing`[%v ~])                     ::
8626      :+  %tsgr   [%ktts %v %$ 1]                           ::   =>  v=.
8627      :+  %tsls   [%ktts %a %tsgr [%limb %v] r.gen]         ::   =+  a==>(v \r.gen)
8628      :^  %tsdt   wuy  [%tsgl [%$ 3] [%limb %a]]
8629      :+  %tsgr   :-  :+  %ktts  [%over [%v ~] p.gen]
8630                  [%tsgl [%$ 2] [%limb %a]]
8631              [%limb %v]
8632      s.gen
8633    ::
8634        [%tsgl *]    [%tsgr q.gen p.gen]
8635        [%tsls *]    [%tsgr [p.gen [%$ 1]] q.gen]
8636        [%tshp *]    [%tsls q.gen p.gen]
8637        [%tssg *]
8638      |-  ^-  hoon
8639      ?~  p.gen    [%$ 1]
8640      ?~  t.p.gen  i.p.gen
```

```
    [%tsgr i.p.gen $(p.gen t.p.gen)]
::
    [%wtbr *]
  |-
  ?~(p.gen [%rock %f 1] [%wtcl i.p.gen [%rock %f 0] $(p.gen t.p.gen)])
::
    [%wtdt *]    [%wtcl p.gen r.gen q.gen]
    [%wtgl *]    [%wtcl p.gen [%zpzp ~] q.gen]
    [%wtgr *]    [%wtcl p.gen q.gen [%zpzp ~]]
    [%wtkt *]    [%wtcl [%wtts [%base %atom %$] p.gen] r.gen q.gen]
::
    [%wthp *]
  |-
  ?~  q.gen
    [%lost [%wing p.gen]]
  :^    %wtcl
      [%wtts p.i.q.gen p.gen]
    q.i.q.gen
  $(q.gen t.q.gen)
::
    [%wtls *]
  [%wthp p.gen (weld r.gen `_r.gen`[[[%base %noun] q.gen] ~])]
::
    [%wtpm *]
  |-
  ?~(p.gen [%rock %f 0] [%wtcl i.p.gen $(p.gen t.p.gen) [%rock %f 1]])
::
    [%xray *]
  |^  :-  [(open-mane n.g.p.gen) %clsg (turn a.g.p.gen open-mart)]
      [%mcts c.p.gen]
  ::
  ++  open-mane
    |=  a=mane:hoot
    ?@(a [%rock %tas a] [[%rock %tas -.a] [%rock %tas +.a]])
  ::
  ++  open-mart
    |=  [n=mane:hoot v=(list beer:hoot)]
    [(open-mane n) %knit v]
  --
::
    [%wtpt *]    [%wtcl [%wtts [%base %atom %$] p.gen] q.gen r.gen]
    [%wtsg *]    [%wtcl [%wtts [%base %null] p.gen] q.gen r.gen]
    [%wtts *]    [%fits ~(example ax p.gen) q.gen]
    [%wtzp *]    [%wtcl p.gen [%rock %f 1] [%rock %f 0]]
    [%zpgr *]
  [%cncl [%limb %onan] [%zpmc [%kttr [%bcmc %limb %abel]] p.gen] ~]
::
    [%zpwt *]
  ?:  ?:  ?=(@ p.gen)
        (lte hoon-version p.gen)
      &((lte hoon-version p.p.gen) (gte hoon-version q.p.gen))
    q.gen
  ~_(leaf+"hoon-version" !!)
::
    *                gen
  ==
::
++  rake  ~>(%mean.'rake-hoon' (need reek))
```

```
++  reek
  ^-  (unit wing)
  ?+  gen  ~
    [~ *]          `[[%& p.gen] ~]
    [%limb *]      `[p.gen ~]
    [%wing *]      `p.gen
    [%cnts * ~]    `p.gen
    [%dbug *]      reek(gen q.gen)
  ==
++  rusk
  ^-  term
  =+  wig=rake
  ?.  ?=([@ ~] wig)
    ~>(%mean.'rusk-hoon' !!)
  i.wig
--
::
::    5c: compiler backend and prettyprinter
+|  %compiler-backend-and-prettyprinter
::
++  ut
  ~%    %ut
      +>+
    ==
      %ar     ar
      %fan    fan
      %rib    rib
      %vet    vet
      %blow   blow
      %burp   burp
      %busk   busk
      %buss   buss
      %crop   crop
      %duck   duck
      %dune   dune
      %dunk   dunk
      %epla   epla
      %emin   emin
      %emul   emul
      %feel   feel
      %felt   felt
      %fine   fine
      %fire   fire
      %fish   fish
      %fond   fond
      %fund   fund
      %funk   funk
      %fuse   fuse
      %gain   gain
      %lose   lose
      %mile   mile
      %mine   mine
      %mint   mint
      %moot   moot
      %mull   mull
      %nest   nest
      %peel   peel
      %play   play
```

```
8757          %peek    peek
8758          %repo    repo
8759          %rest    rest
8760          %sink    sink
8761          %tack    tack
8762          %toss    toss
8763          %wrap    wrap
8764      ==
8765    =+  :*  fan=*(set [type hoon])
8766            rib=*(set [type type hoon])
8767            vet=`?`&
8768        ==
8769    =+  sut=`type`%noun
8770    |%
8771    ++  clip
8772      |=  ref=type
8773      ?>  ?|(!vet (nest(sut ref) & sut))
8774      ref
8775    ::
8776    ::  +ar: texture engine
8777    ::
8778    ++  ar  !:
8779      ~%    %ar
8780          +>
8781        ==
8782          %fish  fish
8783          %gain  gain
8784          %lose  lose
8785        ==
8786      |_  [ref=type =skin]
8787      ::
8788      ::  +fish: make a $nock that tests a .ref at .axis for .skin
8789      ::
8790      ++  fish
8791        |=  =axis
8792        ^-  nock
8793        ?@  skin  $(skin spec+[[%like [skin]~ ~] [%base %noun]])
8794        ?-    -.skin
8795        ::
8796            %base
8797          ?-  base.skin
8798            %cell      $(skin [%cell [%base %noun] [%base %noun]])
8799            %flag      ?:  (~(nest ut bool) | ref)
8800                         [%1 &]
8801                       %+  flan
8802                         $(skin [%base %atom %$])
8803                       %+  flor
8804                         [%5 [%0 axis] [%1 &]]
8805                       [%5 [%0 axis] [%1 |]]
8806            %noun      [%1 &]
8807            %null      $(skin [%leaf %n ~])
8808            %void      [%1 |]
8809            [%atom *]  ?:  (~(nest ut [%atom %$ ~]) | ref)
8810                         [%1 &]
8811                       ?:  (~(nest ut [%cell %noun %noun]) | ref)
8812                         [%1 |]
8813                       (flip [%3 %0 axis])
8814          ==
```

```
    ::
        %cell
      ?:  (~(nest ut [%atom %$ ~]) | ref)  [%1 |]
      %+  flan
        ?:  (~(nest ut [%cell %noun %noun]) | ref)
          [%1 &]
        [%3 %0 axis]
      %+  flan
        $(ref (peek(sut ref) %free 2), axis (peg axis 2), skin skin.skin)
        $(ref (peek(sut ref) %free 3), axis (peg axis 3), skin ^skin.skin)
    ::
        %leaf
      ?:  (~(nest ut [%atom %$ `atom.skin]) | ref)
        [%1 &]
      [%5 [%1 atom.skin] [%0 axis]]
    ::
        %dbug   $(skin skin.skin)
        %help   $(skin skin.skin)
        %name   $(skin skin.skin)
        %over   ::NOTE  might need to guard with +feel, crashing is too strict
                =+  ~|  %oops-guess-you-needed-feel-after-all
                    fid=(fend %read wing.skin)
                $(sut p.fid, axis (peg axis q.fid), skin skin.skin)
        %spec  =/  hit  (~(play ut sut) ~(example ax spec.skin))
                ?>  (~(nest ut hit) & ref)
                $(skin skin.skin)
        %wash   [%1 &]
      ==
    ::
    ::  +gain: make a $type by restricting .ref to .skin
    ::
    ++  gain
      |-  ^-  type
      ?@  skin  $(skin spec+[[%like [skin]~ ~] [%base %noun]])
      ?-    -.skin
      ::
          %base
        ?-    base.skin
          %cell     $(skin [%cell [%base %noun] [%base %noun]])
          %flag     (fork $(skin [%leaf %f &]) $(skin [%leaf %f |]) ~)
          %null     $(skin [%leaf %n ~])
          %void     %void
          %noun     ?:((~(nest ut %void) | ref) %void ref)
          [%atom *]
        =|  gil=(set type)
        |-  ^-  type
        ?-    ref
          %void     %void
          %noun     [%atom p.base.skin ~]
          [%atom *]  ?.  (fitz p.base.skin p.ref)
                        ~>(%mean.'atom-mismatch' !!)
                     :+  %atom
                       (max p.base.skin p.ref)
                     q.ref
          [%cell *]  %void
          [%core *]  %void
          [%face *]  $(ref q.ref)
          [%fork *]  (fork (turn ~(tap in p.ref) |=(=type ^$(ref type))))
```

```
8873              [%hint *]  (hint p.ref $(ref q.ref))
8874              [%hold *]  ?:  (~(has in gil) ref)  %void
8875                         $(gil (~(put in gil) ref), ref repo(sut ref))
8876          ==
8877      ==
8878    ::
8879        %cell
8880    =|  gil=(set type)
8881    |-  ^-  type
8882    ?-    ref
8883        %void        %void
8884        %noun        =+  ^$(skin skin.skin)
8885                     ?:  =(%void -)  %void
8886                     (cell - ^$(skin ^skin.skin))
8887      [%atom *]  %void
8888      [%cell *]      =+  ^$(skin skin.skin, ref p.ref)
8889                     ?:  =(%void -)  %void
8890                     (cell - ^$(skin ^skin.skin, ref q.ref))
8891      [%core *]      =+  ^$(skin skin.skin, ref p.ref)
8892                     ?:  =(%void -)  %void
8893                     ?.  =(%noun ^skin.skin)
8894                       (cell - ^$(skin ^skin.skin, ref %noun))
8895                     [%core - q.ref]
8896      [%face *]  $(ref q.ref)
8897      [%fork *]  (fork (turn ~(tap in p.ref) |=(=type ^$(ref type))))
8898      [%hint *]  (hint p.ref $(ref q.ref))
8899      [%hold *]  ?:  (~(has in gil) ref)  %void
8900                 $(gil (~(put in gil) ref), ref repo(sut ref))
8901      ==
8902    ::
8903        %leaf
8904    =|  gil=(set type)
8905    |-  ^-  type
8906    ?-  ref
8907        %void        %void
8908        %noun        [%atom aura.skin `atom.skin]
8909      [%atom *]  ?:  &(?=(^ q.ref) !=(atom.skin u.q.ref))
8910                       %void
8911                 ?.  (fitz aura.skin p.ref)
8912                   ~>(%mean.'atom-mismatch' !!)
8913                 :+  %atom
8914                   (max aura.skin p.ref)
8915                 `atom.skin
8916      [%cell *]  %void
8917      [%core *]  %void
8918      [%face *]  $(ref q.ref)
8919      [%fork *]  (fork (turn ~(tap in p.ref) |=(=type ^$(ref type))))
8920      [%hint *]  (hint p.ref $(ref q.ref))
8921      [%hold *]  ?:  (~(has in gil) ref)  %void
8922                 $(gil (~(put in gil) ref), ref repo(sut ref))
8923      ==
8924    ::
8925        %dbug  $(skin skin.skin)
8926        %help  (hint [sut %help help.skin] $(skin skin.skin))
8927        %name  (face term.skin $(skin skin.skin))
8928        %over  $(skin skin.skin, sut (~(play ut sut) %wing wing.skin))
8929        %spec  =/  hit  (~(play ut sut) ~(example ax spec.skin))
8930               ?>  (~(nest ut hit) & $(skin skin.skin))
```

```
8931                    (~(fuse ut ref) hit)
8932          %wash  =-  $(ref (~(play ut ref) -))
8933                 :-  %wing
8934                 |-  ^-  wing
8935                 ?:  =(0 depth.skin)  ~
8936                 [[%| 0 ~] $(depth.skin (dec depth.skin))]
8937      ==
8938    ::
8939    ::  +lose: make a $type by restricting .ref to exclude .skin
8940    ::
8941    ++  lose
8942      |-  ^-  type
8943      ?@  skin  $(skin spec+[[%like [skin]~ ~] [%base %noun]])
8944      ?-    -.skin
8945      ::
8946          %base
8947        ?-    base.skin
8948          %cell      $(skin [%cell [%base %noun] [%base %noun]])
8949          %flag      $(ref $(skin [%leaf %f &]), skin [%leaf %f |])
8950          %null      $(skin [%leaf %n ~])
8951          %void      ref
8952          %noun      %void
8953          [%atom *]
8954        =|  gil=(set type)
8955        |-  ^-  type
8956        ?-    ref
8957          %void      %void
8958          %noun      [%cell %noun %noun]
8959          [%atom *]  %void
8960          [%cell *]  ref
8961          [%core *]  ref
8962          [%face *]  (face p.ref $(ref q.ref))
8963          [%fork *]  (fork (turn ~(tap in p.ref) |=(=type ^$(ref type))))
8964          [%hint *]  (hint p.ref $(ref q.ref))
8965          [%hold *]  ?:  (~(has in gil) ref)  %void
8966                     $(gil (~(put in gil) ref), ref repo(sut ref))
8967        ==
8968      ==
8969      ::
8970          %cell
8971        =|  gil=(set type)
8972        |-  ^-  type
8973        ?-    ref
8974          %void      %void
8975          %noun      ?.  =([%cell [%base %noun] [%base %noun]] skin)
8976                       ref
8977                     [%atom %$ ~]
8978          [%atom *]  ref
8979          [%cell *]  =/  lef  ^$(skin skin.skin, ref p.ref)
8980                     =/  rig  ^$(skin ^skin.skin, ref q.ref)
8981                     (fork (cell lef rig) (cell lef q.ref) (cell p.ref rig) ~)
8982          [%core *]  =+  ^$(skin skin.skin, ref p.ref)
8983                     ?:  =(%void -)  %void
8984                     ?.  =(%noun ^skin.skin)
8985                       (cell - ^$(skin ^skin.skin, ref %noun))
8986                     [%core - q.ref]
8987          [%face *]  $(ref q.ref)
8988          [%fork *]  (fork (turn ~(tap in p.ref) |=(=type ^$(ref type))))
```

```
            [%hint *]   (hint p.ref $(ref q.ref))
            [%hold *]   ?:  (~(has in gil) ref)  %void
                        $(gil (~(put in gil) ref), ref repo(sut ref))
        ==
      ::
          %leaf
      =|  gil=(set type)
      |-  ^-  type
      ?-  ref
        %void       %void
        %noun       %noun
        [%atom *]   ?:  =(q.ref `atom.skin)
                        %void
                    ref
        [%cell *]   ref
        [%core *]   ref
        [%face *]   (face p.ref $(ref q.ref))
        [%fork *]   (fork (turn ~(tap in p.ref) |=(=type ^$(ref type))))
        [%hint *]   (hint p.ref $(ref q.ref))
        [%hold *]   ?:  (~(has in gil) ref)  %void
                        $(gil (~(put in gil) ref), ref repo(sut ref))
        ==
      ::
        %dbug  $(skin skin.skin)
        %help  $(skin skin.skin)
        %name  $(skin skin.skin)
        %over  ::TODO  if we guard in +fish (+feel), we have to guard again here
               $(skin skin.skin, sut (~(play ut sut) %wing wing.skin))
        %spec  =/  hit  (~(play ut sut) ~(example ax spec.skin))
               ?>  (~(nest ut hit) & $(skin skin.skin))
               (~(crop ut ref) hit)
        %wash  ref
        ==
    --
  ::
  ++  blow
    |=  [gol=type gen=hoon]
    ^-  [type nock]
    =+  pro=(mint gol gen)
    =+  jon=(apex:musk bran q.pro)
    ?:  |(?=(~ jon) ?=(%wait -.u.jon))
      [p.pro q.pro]
    [p.pro %1 p.u.jon]
  ::
  ++  bran
    ~+
    =+  gil=*(set type)
    |-  ~+  ^-  seminoun:musk
    ?-  sut
      %noun       [full/[~ ~ ~] ~]
      %void       [full/[~ ~ ~] ~]
      [%atom *]   ?~(q.sut [full/[~ ~ ~] ~] [full/~ u.q.sut])
      [%cell *]   (combine:musk $(sut p.sut) $(sut q.sut))
      [%core *]   %+  combine:musk
                    p.r.q.sut
                  $(sut p.sut)
      [%face *]   $(sut repo)
      [%fork *]   [full/[~ ~ ~] ~]
```

```
9047        [%hint *]   $(sut repo)
9048        [%hold *]   ?:  (~(has in gil) sut)
9049                        [full/[~ ~ ~] ~]
9050                    $(sut repo, gil (~(put in gil) sut))
9051      ==
9052    ::
9053    ++  burp
9054      ::    expel undigested seminouns
9055      ::
9056      ^-  type
9057      ~+
9058      =-  ?.(=(sut -) - sut)
9059      ?+  sut        sut
9060        [%cell *]   [%cell burp(sut p.sut) burp(sut q.sut)]
9061        [%core *]   :+  %core
9062                      burp(sut p.sut)
9063                    :*  p.q.sut
9064                      burp(sut q.q.sut)
9065                      :_  q.r.q.sut
9066                      ?:  ?=([[%full ~] *] p.r.q.sut)
9067                        p.r.q.sut
9068                      [[%full ~ ~ ~] ~]
9069                    ==
9070        [%face *]   [%face p.sut burp(sut q.sut)]
9071        [%fork *]   [%fork (~(run in p.sut) |=(type burp(sut +<)))]
9072        [%hint *]   (hint [burp(sut p.p.sut) q.p.sut] burp(sut q.sut))
9073        [%hold *]   [%hold burp(sut p.sut) q.sut]
9074      ==
9075    ::
9076    ++  busk
9077      ~/  %busk
9078      |=  gen=hoon
9079      ^-  type
9080      [%face [~ [gen ~]] sut]
9081    ::
9082    ++  buss
9083      ~/  %buss
9084      |=  [cog=term gen=hoon]
9085      ^-  type
9086      [%face [[[cog ~ gen] ~ ~] ~] sut]
9087    ::
9088    ++  crop
9089      ~/  %crop
9090      |=  ref=type
9091      =+  bix=*(set [type type])
9092      =<  dext
9093      |%
9094      ++  dext
9095        ^-  type
9096        ~_  leaf+"crop"
9097        ::  ~_  (dunk 'dext: sut')
9098        ::  ~_  (dunk(sut ref) 'dext: ref')
9099        ?:  |(=(sut ref) =(%noun ref))
9100          %void
9101        ?:  =(%void ref)
9102          sut
9103        ?-    sut
9104            [%atom *]
```

```
9105            ?+  ref         sint
9106              [%atom *]  ?^  q.sut
9107                           ?^(q.ref ?:(=(q.ref q.sut) %void sut) %void)
9108                           ?^(q.ref sut %void)
9109              [%cell *]  sut
9110            ==
9111          ::
9112              [%cell *]
9113            ?+  ref         sint
9114              [%atom *]  sut
9115              [%cell *]  ?.  (nest(sut p.ref) | p.sut)  sut
9116                         (cell p.sut dext(sut q.sut, ref q.ref))
9117            ==
9118          ::
9119              [%core *]  ?:(?=(?([%atom *] [%cell *]) ref) sut sint)
9120              [%face *]  (face p.sut dext(sut q.sut))
9121              [%fork *]  (fork (turn ~(tap in p.sut) |=(type dext(sut +<))))
9122              [%hint *]  (hint p.sut dext(sut q.sut))
9123              [%hold *]  ?<  (~(has in bix) [sut ref])
9124                         dext(sut repo, bix (~(put in bix) [sut ref]))
9125              %noun      dext(sut repo)
9126              %void      %void
9127          ==
9128        ::
9129      ++  sint
9130        ^-  type
9131        ?+    ref    !!
9132          [%core *]  sut
9133          [%face *]  dext(ref repo(sut ref))
9134          [%fork *]  =+  yed=~(tap in p.ref)
9135                     |-  ^-  type
9136                     ?~  yed  sut
9137                     $(yed t.yed, sut dext(ref i.yed))
9138          [%hint *]  dext(ref repo(sut ref))
9139          [%hold *]  dext(ref repo(sut ref))
9140        ==
9141      --
9142    ::
9143    ++  cool
9144      |=  [pol=? hyp=wing ref=type]
9145      ^-  type
9146      =+  fid=(find %both hyp)
9147      ?-  -.fid
9148        %|  sut
9149        %&  =<  q
9150            %+  take  p.p.fid
9151            |=(a=type ?:(pol (fuse(sut a) ref) (crop(sut a) ref)))
9152      ==
9153    ::
9154    ++  duck  ^-(tank ~(duck us sut))
9155    ++  dune  |.(duck)
9156    ++  dunk
9157      |=  paz=term  ^-  tank
9158      :+  %palm
9159        [['.' ~] ['-' ~] ~ ~]
9160      [[%leaf (mesc (trip paz))] duck ~]
9161    ::
9162    ++  elbo
```

```
9163      |=  [lop=palo rig=(list (pair wing hoon))]
9164      ^-  type
9165      ?:  ?=(%& -.q.lop)
9166        |-  ^-  type
9167      ?~  rig
9168        p.q.lop
9169      =+  zil=(play q.i.rig)
9170      =+  dar=(tack(sut p.q.lop) p.i.rig zil)
9171      %=  $
9172        rig      t.rig
9173        p.q.lop  q.dar
9174      ==
9175      =+  hag=~(tap in q.q.lop)
9176      %-  fire
9177      |-  ^+  hag
9178      ?~  rig
9179        hag
9180      =+  zil=(play q.i.rig)
9181      =+  dix=(toss p.i.rig zil hag)
9182      %=  $
9183        rig  t.rig
9184        hag  q.dix
9185      ==
9186    ::
9187    ++  ergo
9188      |=  [lop=palo rig=(list (pair wing hoon))]
9189      ^-  (pair type nock)
9190      =+  axe=(tend p.lop)
9191      =|  hej=(list (pair axis nock))
9192      ?:  ?=(%& -.q.lop)
9193        =-  [p.- (hike axe q.-)]
9194        |-  ^-  (pair type (list (pair axis nock)))
9195      ?~  rig
9196        [p.q.lop hej]
9197      =+  zil=(mint %noun q.i.rig)
9198      =+  dar=(tack(sut p.q.lop) p.i.rig p.zil)
9199      %=  $
9200        rig      t.rig
9201        p.q.lop  q.dar
9202        hej      [[p.dar q.zil] hej]
9203      ==
9204      =+  hag=~(tap in q.q.lop)
9205      =-  [(fire p.-) [%9 p.q.lop (hike axe q.-)]]
9206      |-  ^-  (pair (list (pair type foot)) (list (pair axis nock)))
9207      ?~  rig
9208        [hag hej]
9209      =+  zil=(mint %noun q.i.rig)
9210      =+  dix=(toss p.i.rig p.zil hag)
9211      %=  $
9212        rig  t.rig
9213        hag  q.dix
9214        hej  [[p.dix q.zil] hej]
9215      ==
9216    ::
9217    ++  endo
9218      |=  [lop=(pair palo palo) dox=type rig=(list (pair wing hoon))]
9219      ^-  (pair type type)
9220      ?:  ?=(%& -.q.p.lop)
```

```
9221      ?>  ?=(%& -.q.q.lop)
9222      |-  ^-  (pair type type)
9223      ?~  rig
9224        [p.q.p.lop p.q.q.lop]
9225      =+  zil=(mull %noun dox q.i.rig)
9226      =+  ^=  dar
9227          :-  p=(tack(sut p.q.p.lop) p.i.rig p.zil)
9228              q=(tack(sut p.q.q.lop) p.i.rig q.zil)
9229      ?>  =(p.p.dar p.q.dar)
9230      %=  $
9231        rig         t.rig
9232        p.q.p.lop   q.p.dar
9233        p.q.q.lop   q.q.dar
9234      ==
9235    ?>  ?=(%| -.q.q.lop)
9236    ?>  =(p.q.p.lop p.q.q.lop)
9237    =+  hag=[p=~(tap in q.q.p.lop) q=~(tap in q.q.q.lop)]
9238    =-  [(fire p.-) (fire(vet |) q.-)]
9239    |-  ^-  (pair (list (pair type foot)) (list (pair type foot)))
9240    ?~  rig
9241      hag
9242    =+  zil=(mull %noun dox q.i.rig)
9243    =+  ^=  dix
9244        :-  p=(toss p.i.rig p.zil p.hag)
9245            q=(toss p.i.rig q.zil q.hag)
9246    ?>  =(p.p.dix p.q.dix)
9247    %=  $
9248      rig  t.rig
9249      hag  [q.p.dix q.q.dix]
9250    ==
9251  ::
9252  ++  et
9253    |_  [hyp=wing rig=(list (pair wing hoon))]
9254    ::
9255    ++  play
9256      ^-  type
9257      =+  lug=(find %read hyp)
9258      ?:  ?=(%| -.lug)  ~>(%mean.'hoon' ?>(?=(~ rig) p.p.lug))
9259      (elbo p.lug rig)
9260    ::
9261    ++  mint
9262      |=  gol=type
9263      =-  ?>(?|(!vet (nest(sut gol) & p.-)) -)
9264      ^-  (pair type nock)
9265      =+  lug=(find %read hyp)
9266      ?:  ?=(%| -.lug)  ~>(%mean.'hoon' ?>(?=(~ rig) p.lug))
9267      (ergo p.lug rig)
9268    ::
9269    ++  mull
9270      |=  [gol=type dox=type]
9271      =-  ?>(?|(!vet (nest(sut gol) & p.-)) -)
9272      ^-  (pair type type)
9273      =+  lug=[p=(find %read hyp) q=(find(sut dox) %read hyp)]
9274      ?:  ?=(%| -.p.lug)
9275        ?>  &(?=(%| -.q.lug) ?=(~ rig))
9276        [p.p.p.lug p.p.q.lug]
9277      ?>  ?=(%& -.q.lug)
9278      (endo [p.p.lug p.q.lug] dox rig)
```

```
9279        --
9280    ::
9281    ++  epla
9282      ~/  %epla
9283      |=  [hyp=wing rig=(list (pair wing hoon))]
9284      ^-  type
9285      ~(play et hyp rig)
9286    ::
9287    ++  emin
9288      ~/  %emin
9289      |=  [gol=type hyp=wing rig=(list (pair wing hoon))]
9290      ^-  (pair type nock)
9291      (~(mint et hyp rig) gol)
9292    ::
9293    ++  emul
9294      ~/  %emul
9295      |=  [gol=type dox=type hyp=wing rig=(list (pair wing hoon))]
9296      ^-  (pair type type)
9297      (~(mull et hyp rig) gol dox)
9298    ::
9299    ++  felt  !!
9300    ::                                              ::
9301    ++  feel                                        ::  detect existence
9302      |=  rot=(list wing)
9303      ^-  ?
9304      =.  rot  (flop rot)
9305      |-  ^-  ?
9306      ?~  rot  &
9307      =/  yep  (fond %free i.rot)
9308      ?~  yep  |
9309      ?-    -.yep
9310        %&  %=  $
9311              rot  t.rot
9312              sut  p:(fine %& p.yep)
9313            ==
9314        %|  ?-  -.p.yep
9315              %&  |
9316              %|  %=  $
9317                    rot  t.rot
9318                    sut  p:(fine %| p.p.yep)
9319                  ==
9320      ==    ==
9321    ::
9322    ++  fond
9323      ~/  %fond
9324      |=  [way=vial hyp=wing]
9325      =>  |%
9326          ++  pony                                 ::  raw match
9327                $@  ~                              ::  void
9328                %+  each                           ::  natural/abnormal
9329                  palo                             ::  arm or leg
9330                %+  each                           ::  abnormal
9331                  @ud                              ::  unmatched
9332                (pair type nock)                   ::  synthetic
9333          --
9334      ^-  pony
9335      ?~  hyp
9336        [%& ~ %& sut]
```

```
9337      =+  mor=$(hyp t.hyp)
9338      ?-     -.mor
9339          %|
9340        ?-     -.p.mor
9341            %&  mor
9342            %|
9343          =+  fex=(mint(sut p.p.p.mor) %noun [%wing i.hyp ~])
9344          [%| %| p.fex (comb q.p.p.mor q.fex)]
9345        ==
9346      ::
9347          %&
9348      =.  sut
9349        =*  lap  q.p.mor
9350        ?-  -.lap
9351          %&  p.lap
9352          %|  (fork (turn ~(tap in q.lap) head))
9353        ==
9354      =>  :_  +
9355          :*  axe=`axis`1
9356              lon=p.p.mor
9357              heg=?^(i.hyp i.hyp [%| p=0 q=(some i.hyp)])
9358          ==
9359      ?:  ?=(%& -.heg)
9360        [%& [`p.heg lon] %& (peek way p.heg)]
9361      =|  gil=(set type)
9362      =<  $
9363      |%  ++  here  ?:  =(0 p.heg)
9364                      [%& [~ `axe lon] %& sut]
9365                      [%| %& (dec p.heg)]
9366          ++  lose  [%| %& p.heg]
9367          ++  stop  ?~(q.heg here lose)
9368          ++  twin  |=  [hax=pony yor=pony]
9369                    ^-  pony
9370                    ~_  leaf+"find-fork"
9371                    ?:  =(hax yor)  hax
9372                    ?~  hax  yor
9373                    ?~  yor  hax
9374                    ?:  ?=(%| -.hax)
9375                      ?>  ?&  ?=(%| -.yor)
9376                              ?=(%| -.p.hax)
9377                              ?=(%| -.p.yor)
9378                              =(q.p.p.hax q.p.p.yor)
9379                          ==
9380                      :+  %|
9381                        %|
9382                      [(fork p.p.p.hax p.p.p.yor ~) q.p.p.hax]
9383                    ?>  ?=(%& -.yor)
9384                    ?>  =(p.p.hax p.p.yor)
9385                    ?:  &(?=(%& -.q.p.hax) ?=(%& -.q.p.yor))
9386                      :+  %&  p.p.hax
9387                      [%& (fork p.q.p.hax p.q.p.yor ~)]
9388                    ?>  &(?=(%| -.q.p.hax) ?=(%| -.q.p.yor))
9389                    ?>  =(p.q.p.hax p.q.p.yor)
9390                    =+  wal=(~(uni in q.q.p.hax) q.q.p.yor)
9391                    :+  %&  p.p.hax
9392                    [%| p.q.p.hax wal]
9393          ++  $
9394              ^-  pony
```

```
9395        ?-    sut
9396          %void        ~
9397          %noun        stop
9398          [%atom *]     stop
9399          [%cell *]
9400        ?~  q.heg  here
9401        =+  taf=$(axe (peg axe 2), sut p.sut)
9402        ?~  taf   ~
9403        ?:  |(?=(%& -.taf) ?=(%| -.p.taf))
9404          taf
9405        $(axe (peg axe 3), p.heg p.p.taf, sut q.sut)
9406      ::
9407          [%core *]
9408        ?~  q.heg  here
9409        =^  zem  p.heg
9410          =+  zem=(loot u.q.heg q.r.q.sut)
9411          ?~  zem  [~ p.heg]
9412          ?:(=(0 p.heg) [zem 0] [~ (dec p.heg)])
9413        ?^  zem
9414        :+  %&
9415          [`axe lon]
9416        =/  zut   ^-  foot
9417                 ?-  q.p.q.sut
9418                  %wet  [%wet q.u.zem]
9419                  %dry  [%dry q.u.zem]
9420                 ==
9421        [%| (peg 2 p.u.zem) [[sut zut] ~ ~]]
9422        =+  pec=(peel way r.p.q.sut)
9423        ?.  sam.pec  lose
9424        ?:  con.pec  $(sut p.sut, axe (peg axe 3))
9425        $(sut (peek(sut p.sut) way 2), axe (peg axe 6))
9426      ::
9427          [%hint *]
9428        $(sut repo)
9429      ::
9430          [%face *]
9431        ?:  ?=(~ q.heg)  here(sut q.sut)
9432        =*  zot  p.sut
9433        ?@  zot
9434          ?:(=(u.q.heg zot) here(sut q.sut) lose)
9435        =<  main
9436        |%
9437        ++  main
9438          ^-  pony
9439          =+  tyr=(~(get by p.zot) u.q.heg)
9440          ?~  tyr
9441            next
9442          ?~  u.tyr
9443            $(sut q.sut, lon [~ lon], p.heg +(p.heg))
9444          ?.  =(0 p.heg)
9445            next(p.heg (dec p.heg))
9446          =+  tor=(fund way u.u.tyr)
9447          ?-  -.tor
9448            %&  [%& (weld p.p.tor `vein`[~ `axe lon]) q.p.tor]
9449            %|  [%| %| p.p.tor (comb [%0 axe] q.p.tor)]
9450          ==
9451        ++  next
9452          |-  ^-  pony
```

```
?~  q.zot
  ^$(sut q.sut, lon [~ lon])
=+  tiv=(mint(sut q.sut) %noun i.q.zot)
=+  fid=^$(sut p.tiv, lon ~, axe 1, gil ~)
?~  fid  ~
?:  ?=([%| %& *] fid)
  $(q.zot t.q.zot, p.heg p.p.fid)
=/  vat=(pair type nock)
  ?-    -.fid
    %&  (fine %& p.fid)
    %|  (fine %| p.p.fid)
  ==
[%| %| p.vat (comb (comb [%0 axe] q.tiv) q.vat)]
    --
  ::
    [%fork *]
=+  wiz=(turn ~(tap in p.sut) |=(a=type ^$(sut a)))
?~  wiz  ~
|-  ^-  pony
?~  t.wiz  i.wiz
(twin i.wiz $(wiz t.wiz))
  ::
    [%hold *]
?:  (~(has in gil) sut)
    ~
$(gil (~(put in gil) sut), sut repo)
==
    --
  ==
::
++  find
  ~/  %find
  |=  [way=vial hyp=wing]
  ^-  port
  ~_  (show [%c %find] %l hyp)
  =-  ?@  -  !!
      ?-    -<
        %&  [%& p.-]
        %|  ?-  -.p.-
              %|  [%| p.p.-]
              %&  !!
      ==  ==
  (fond way hyp)
::
++  fend
  |=  [way=vial hyp=wing]
  ^-  (pair type axis)
  =+  fid=(find way hyp)
  ~>  %mean.'fend-fragment'
  ?>  &(?=(%& -.fid) ?=(%& -.q.p.fid))
  [p.q.p.fid (tend p.p.fid)]
::
++  fund
  ~/  %fund
  |=  [way=vial gen=hoon]
  ^-  port
  =+  hup=~(reek ap gen)
  ?~  hup
```

```
      [%| (mint %noun gen)]
    (find way u.hup)
::
++  fine
  ~/  %fine
  |=  tor=port
  ^-  (pair type nock)
  ?-  -.tor
    %|  p.tor
    %&  =+  axe=(tend p.p.tor)
        ?-  -.q.p.tor
          %&  [`type`p.q.p.tor %0 axe]
          %|  [(fire ~(tap in q.q.p.tor)) [%9 p.q.p.tor %0 axe]]
    ==      ==
::
++  fire
  |=  hag=(list [p=type q=foot])
  ^-  type
  ?:  ?=([[* [%wet ~ %1]] ~] hag)
    p.i.hag
  %-  fork
  %+  turn
    hag.$
  |=  [p=type q=foot]
  ?.  ?=([%core *] p)
    ~_  (dunk %fire-type)
    ~_  leaf+"expected-fork-to-be-core"
    ~_  (dunk(sut p) %fork-type)
    ~>(%mean.'fire-core' !!)
  :-  %hold
  =+  dox=[%core q.q.p q.p(r.p %gold)]
  ?:  ?=(%dry -.q)
    ::  ~_  (dunk(sut [%cell q.q.p p.p]) %fire-dry)
    ?>  ?|(!vet (nest(sut q.q.p) & p.p))
    [dox p.q]
  ?>  ?=(%wet -.q)
  ::  ~_  (dunk(sut [%cell q.q.p p.p]) %fire-wet)
  =.  p.p  (redo(sut p.p) q.q.p)
  ?>  ?|  !vet
          (~(has in rib) [sut dox p.q])
          !=(** (mull(sut p, rib (~(put in rib) sut dox p.q)) %noun dox p.q))
      ==
  [p p.q]
::
++  fish
  ~/  %fish
  |=  axe=axis
  =+  vot=*(set type)
  |-  ^-  nock
  ?-  sut
    %void       [%1 1]
    %noun       [%1 0]
    [%atom *]   ?~  q.sut
                  (flip [%3 %0 axe])
                [%5 [%1 u.q.sut] [%0 axe]]
    [%cell *]
  %+  flan
    [%3 %0 axe]
```

```
9569            (flan $(sut p.sut, axe (peg axe 2)) $(sut q.sut, axe (peg axe 3)))
9570        ::
9571            [%core *]    ~>(%mean.'fish-core' !!)
9572            [%face *]    $(sut q.sut)
9573            [%fork *]    =+  yed=~(tap in p.sut)
9574                         |-  ^-  nock
9575                         ?~(yed [%1 1] (flor ^$(sut i.yed) $(yed t.yed)))
9576            [%hint *]    $(sut q.sut)
9577            [%hold *]
9578        ?:  (~(has in vot) sut)
9579          ~>(%mean.'fish-loop' !!)
9580        =>  %=(. vot (~(put in vot) sut))
9581        $(sut repo)
9582      ==
9583    ::
9584    ++  fuse
9585      ~/  %fuse
9586      |=  ref=type
9587      =+  bix=*(set [type type])
9588      |-  ^-  type
9589      ?:  ?|(=(sut ref) =(%noun ref))
9590        sut
9591      ?-    sut
9592          [%atom *]
9593        ?-    ref
9594            [%atom *]    =+  foc=?:((fitz p.ref p.sut) p.sut p.ref)
9595                         ?^  q.sut
9596                           ?^  q.ref
9597                             ?:  =(q.sut q.ref)
9598                               [%atom foc q.sut]
9599                             %void
9600                           [%atom foc q.sut]
9601                         [%atom foc q.ref]
9602            [%cell *]    %void
9603            *            $(sut ref, ref sut)
9604        ==
9605          [%cell *]
9606        ?-  ref
9607            [%cell *]    (cell $(sut p.sut, ref p.ref) $(sut q.sut, ref q.ref))
9608            *            $(sut ref, ref sut)
9609        ==
9610        ::
9611            [%core *]  $(sut repo)
9612            [%face *]  (face p.sut $(sut q.sut))
9613            [%fork *]  (fork (turn ~(tap in p.sut) |=(type ^$(sut +<))))
9614            [%hint *]  (hint p.sut $(sut q.sut))
9615            [%hold *]
9616        ?:  (~(has in bix) [sut ref])
9617          ~>(%mean.'fuse-loop' !!)
9618        $(sut repo, bix (~(put in bix) [sut ref]))
9619      ::
9620          %noun       ref
9621          %void       %void
9622      ==
9623    ::
9624    ++  gain
9625      ~/  %gain
9626      |=  gen=hoon  ^-  type
```

```
(chip & gen)
::
++  hemp
  ::      generate formula from foot
  ::
  |=  [hud=poly gol=type gen=hoon]
  ^-  nock
  ~+
  =+  %hemp-141
  ?-  hud
    %dry  q:(mint gol gen)
    %wet  q:(mint(vet |) gol gen)
  ==
::
++  laze
  ::      produce lazy core generator for static execution
  ::
  |=  [nym=(unit term) hud=poly dom=(map term tome)]
  ~+
  ^-  seminoun
  =+  %hemp-141
  ::  tal: map from battery axis to foot
  ::
  =;  tal=(map @ud hoon)
    ::  produce lazy battery
    ::
    :_  ~
    :+  %lazy  1
    |=  axe=@ud
    ^-  (unit noun)
    %+  bind  (~(get by tal) axe)
    |=  gen=hoon
    %.  [hud %noun gen]
    hemp(sut (core sut [nym hud %gold] sut [[%lazy 1 ..^$] ~] dom))
  ::
  %-  ~(gas by *(map @ud hoon))
  =|  yeb=(list (pair @ud hoon))
  =+  axe=1
  |^  ?-  dom
        ~          yeb
        [* ~ ~]    (chapter q.q.n.dom)
        [* * ~]    %=  $
                     dom  l.dom
                     axe  (peg axe 3)
                     yeb  (chapter(axe (peg axe 2)) q.q.n.dom)
                   ==
        [* ~ *]    %=  $
                     dom  r.dom
                     axe  (peg axe 3)
                     yeb  (chapter(axe (peg axe 2)) q.q.n.dom)
                   ==
        [* * *]    %=  $
                     dom  r.dom
                     axe  (peg axe 7)
                     yeb  %=  $
                            dom  l.dom
                            axe  (peg axe 6)
                            yeb  (chapter(axe (peg axe 2)) q.q.n.dom)
```

```
9685           ==              ==        ==
9686     ++    chapter
9687      |=   dab=(map term hoon)
9688      ^+   yeb
9689      ?-   dab
9690        ~             yeb
9691      [* ~ ~]   [[axe q.n.dab] yeb]
9692      [* * ~]   %=   $
9693                      dab   l.dab
9694                      axe   (peg axe 3)
9695                      yeb   [[(peg axe 2) q.n.dab] yeb]
9696                ==
9697      [* ~ *]   %=   $
9698                      dab   r.dab
9699                      axe   (peg axe 3)
9700                      yeb   [[(peg axe 2) q.n.dab] yeb]
9701                ==
9702      [* * *]   %=   $
9703                      dab   r.dab
9704                      axe   (peg axe 7)
9705                      yeb   %=   $
9706                          dab   l.dab
9707                          axe   (peg axe 6)
9708                          yeb   [[(peg axe 2) q.n.dab] yeb]
9709           ==              ==        ==
9710      --
9711    ::
9712    ++    lose
9713     ~/   %lose
9714     |=   gen=hoon   ^-   type
9715    (chip | gen)
9716    ::
9717    ++    chip
9718     ~/   %chip
9719     |=   [how=? gen=hoon]   ^-   type
9720    ?:   ?=([%wtts *] gen)
9721      (cool how q.gen (play ~(example ax p.gen)))
9722    ?:   ?=([%wthx *] gen)
9723      =+   fid=(find %both q.gen)
9724      ?-   -.fid
9725        %|   sut
9726        %&   =<   q
9727             %+   take   p.p.fid
9728             |=(a=type ?:(how ~(gain ar a p.gen) ~(lose ar a p.gen)))
9729        ==
9730    ?:   ?&(how ?=([%wtpm *] gen))
9731      |-(?~(p.gen sut $(p.gen t.p.gen, sut ^$(gen i.p.gen))))
9732    ?:   ?&(!how ?=([%wtbr *] gen))
9733      |-(?~(p.gen sut $(p.gen t.p.gen, sut ^$(gen i.p.gen))))
9734    =+   neg=~(open ap gen)
9735    ?:(=(neg gen) sut $(gen neg))
9736    ::
9737    ++    bake
9738     |=   [dox=type hud=poly dab=(map term hoon)]
9739     ^-   *
9740    ?:   ?=(~ dab)
9741        ~
9742     =+   ^=   dov
```

```
9743        ::   this seems wrong but it's actually right
9744        ::
9745        ?-  hud
9746          %dry  (mull %noun dox q.n.dab)
9747          %wet  ~
9748        ==
9749     ?-  dab
9750       [* ~ ~]  dov
9751       [* ~ *]  [dov $(dab r.dab)]
9752       [* * ~]  [dov $(dab l.dab)]
9753       [* * *]  [dov $(dab l.dab) $(dab r.dab)]
9754     ==
9755   ::
9756   ++  balk
9757     |=  [dox=type hud=poly dom=(map term tome)]
9758     ^-  *
9759     ?:  ?=(~ dom)
9760       ~
9761     =+  dov=(bake dox hud q.q.n.dom)
9762     ?-  dom
9763       [* ~ ~]  dov
9764       [* ~ *]  [dov $(dom r.dom)]
9765       [* * ~]  [dov $(dom l.dom)]
9766       [* * *]  [dov $(dom l.dom) $(dom r.dom)]
9767     ==
9768   ::
9769   ++  mile
9770     ::    mull all chapters and feet in a core
9771     ::
9772     |=  [dox=type mel=vair nym=(unit term) hud=poly dom=(map term tome)]
9773     ^-  (pair type type)
9774     =+  yet=(core sut [nym hud %gold] sut (laze nym hud dom) dom)
9775     =+  hum=(core dox [nym hud %gold] dox (laze nym hud dom) dom)
9776     =+  (balk(sut yet) hum hud dom)
9777     [yet hum]
9778   ::
9779   ++  mine
9780     ::    mint all chapters and feet in a core
9781     ::
9782     |=  [gol=type mel=vair nym=(unit term) hud=poly dom=(map term tome)]
9783     ^-  (pair type nock)
9784     |^
9785     =/  log  (chapters-check (core-check gol))
9786     =/  dog  (get-tomes log)
9787     =-  :_  [%1 dez]
9788         (core sut [nym hud mel] sut [[%full ~] dez] dom)
9789     ^=  dez
9790     =.  sut  (core sut [nym hud %gold] sut (laze nym hud dom) dom)
9791     |-  ^-  ?(~ ^)
9792     ?:  ?=(~ dom)
9793       ~
9794     =/  dov=?(~ ^)
9795       =/  dab=(map term hoon)  q.q.n.dom
9796       =/  dag  (arms-check dab (get-arms dog p.n.dom))
9797       |-  ^-  ?(~ ^)
9798       ?:  ?=(~ dab)
9799         ~
9800       =/  gog  (get-arm-type log dag p.n.dab)
```

```
9801        =+  vad=(hemp hud gog q.n.dab)
9802        ?-    dab
9803        [* ~ ~]    vad
9804        [* ~ *]    [vad $(dab r.dab)]
9805        [* * ~]    [vad $(dab l.dab)]
9806        [* * *]    [vad $(dab l.dab) $(dab r.dab)]
9807        ==
9808      ?-    dom
9809      [* ~ ~]    dov
9810      [* ~ *]    [dov $(dom r.dom)]
9811      [* * ~]    [dov $(dom l.dom)]
9812      [* * *]    [dov $(dom l.dom) $(dom r.dom)]
9813      ==
9814      ::
9815      ::  all the below arms are used for gol checking and should have no
9816      ::  effect other than giving more specific errors
9817      ::
9818      ::  +gol-type: all the possible types we could be expecting.
9819      ::
9820      +$  gol-type
9821        $~  %noun
9822        $@  %noun
9823        $%  [%cell p=type q=type]
9824            [%core p=type q=coil]
9825            [%fork p=(set gol-type)]
9826        ==
9827      ::  +core-check: check that we're looking for a core
9828      ::
9829      ++  core-check
9830        |=  log=type
9831        |-  ^-  gol-type
9832        ?+    log  $(log repo(sut log))
9833          %noun      (nice log &)
9834          %void      (nice %noun |)
9835          [%atom *]  (nice %noun |)
9836          [%cell *]  (nice log (nest(sut p.log) & %noun))
9837          [%core *]  (nice log(r.p.q %gold) &)
9838          [%fork *]
9839        =/  tys  ~(tap in p.log)
9840        :-  %fork
9841        |-  ^-  (set gol-type)
9842        ?~  tys
9843          ~
9844        =/  a  ^$(log i.tys)
9845        =/  b  $(tys t.tys)
9846        (~(put in b) a)
9847        ==
9848      ::  +chapters-check: check we have the expected number of chapters
9849      ::
9850      ++  chapters-check
9851        |=  log=gol-type
9852        |-  ^-  gol-type
9853        ?-    log
9854          %noun      (nice log &)
9855          [%cell *]  (nice log &)
9856          [%core *]  ~_  leaf+"core-number-of-chapters"
9857                     (nice log =(~(wyt by dom) ~(wyt by q.r.q.log)))
9858          [%fork *]
```

```
9859        =/  tys  ~(tap in p.log)
9860        |-  ^-  gol-type
9861        ?~  tys
9862          log
9863        =/  a  ^$(log i.tys)
9864        =/  b  $(tys t.tys)
9865        log
9866      ==
9867    ::  +get-tomes: get map of tomes if exists
9868    ::
9869    ++  get-tomes
9870      |=  log=gol-type
9871      ^-  (unit (map term tome))
9872      ?-    log
9873        %noun       ~
9874        [%cell *]   ~
9875        [%fork *]   ~  ::  maybe could be more aggressive
9876        [%core *]  `q.r.q.log
9877      ==
9878    ::  +get-arms: get arms in tome
9879    ::
9880    ++  get-arms
9881      |=  [dog=(unit (map term tome)) nam=term]
9882      ^-  (unit (map term hoon))
9883      %+  bind  dog
9884      |=  a=(map term tome)
9885      ~_  leaf+"unexpcted-chapter.{(trip nam)}"
9886      q:(~(got by a) nam)
9887    ::  +arms-check: check we have the expected number of arms
9888    ::
9889    ++  arms-check
9890      |=  [dab=(map term hoon) dag=(unit (map term hoon))]
9891      ?~  dag
9892        dag
9893      =/  a
9894        =/  exp  ~(wyt by u.dag)
9895        =/  hav  ~(wyt by dab)
9896        ~_  =/  expt  (scow %ud exp)
9897            =/  havt  (scow %ud hav)
9898            leaf+"core-number-of-arms.exp={expt}.hav={havt}"
9899        ~_  =/  missing  ~(tap in (~(dif in ~(key by u.dag)) ~(key by dab)))
9900            leaf+"missing.{<missing>}"
9901        ~_  =/  extra  ~(tap in (~(dif in ~(key by dab)) ~(key by u.dag)))
9902            leaf+"extra.{<extra>}"
9903        ~_  =/  have  ~(tap in ~(key by dab))
9904            leaf+"have.{<have>}"
9905        (nice dag =(exp hav))
9906      a
9907    ::  +get-arm-type: get expected type of this arm
9908    ::
9909    ++  get-arm-type
9910      |=  [log=gol-type dag=(unit (map term hoon)) nam=term]
9911      ^-  type
9912      %-  fall  :_  %noun
9913      %+  bind  dag
9914      |=  a=(map term hoon)
9915      =/  gen=hoon
9916        ~_  leaf+"unexpected-arm.{(trip nam)}"
```

```
        (~(got by a) nam)
      (play(sut log) gen)
  ::
  ++  nice
    |*  [typ=* gud=?]
    ?:  gud
      typ
    ~_  leaf+"core-nice"
    !!
  --
::
++  mint
  ~/  %mint
  |=  [gol=type gen=hoon]
  ^-  [p=type q=nock]
  ::~&  %pure-mint
  |^  ^-  [p=type q=nock]
  ?:  ?&(=(%void sut) !?=([%dbug *] gen))
    ?.  |(!vet ?=([%lost *] gen) ?=([%zpzp *] gen))
      ~>(%mean.'mint-vain' !!)
    [%void %0 0]
  ?-    gen
  ::
      [^ *]
    =+  hed=$(gen p.gen, gol %noun)
    =+  tal=$(gen q.gen, gol %noun)
    [(nice (cell p.hed p.tal)) (cons q.hed q.tal)]
  ::
      [%brcn *]  (grow %gold p.gen %dry [%$ 1] q.gen)
      [%brpt *]  (grow %gold p.gen %wet [%$ 1] q.gen)
  ::
      [%cnts *]  (~(mint et p.gen q.gen) gol)
  ::
      [%dtkt *]
    =+  nef=$(gen [%kttr p.gen])
    [p.nef [%12 [%1 hoon-version p.nef] q:$(gen q.gen, gol %noun)]]
  ::
      [%dtls *]  [(nice [%atom %$ ~]) [%4 q:$(gen p.gen, gol [%atom %$ ~])]]
      [%sand *]  [(nice (play gen)) [%1 q.gen]]
      [%rock *]  [(nice (play gen)) [%1 q.gen]]
  ::
      [%dttr *]
    [(nice %noun) [%2 q:$(gen p.gen, gol %noun) q:$(gen q.gen, gol %noun)]]
  ::
      [%dtts *]
    [(nice bool) [%5 q:$(gen p.gen, gol %noun) q:$(gen q.gen, gol %noun)]]
  ::
      [%dtwt *]  [(nice bool) [%3 q:$(gen p.gen, gol %noun)]]
      [%hand *]  [p.gen q.gen]
      [%ktbr *]  =+(vat=$(gen p.gen) [(nice (wrap(sut p.vat) %iron)) q.vat])
  ::
      [%ktls *]
    =+(hif=(nice (play p.gen)) [hif q:$(gen q.gen, gol hif)])
  ::
      [%ktpm *]  =+(vat=$(gen p.gen) [(nice (wrap(sut p.vat) %zinc)) q.vat])
      [%ktsg *]  (blow gol p.gen)
      [%tune *]  [(face p.gen sut) [%0 %1]]
      [%ktwt *]  =+(vat=$(gen p.gen) [(nice (wrap(sut p.vat) %lead)) q.vat])
```

```
9975        ::
9976            [%note *]
9977         =+  hum=$(gen q.gen)
9978         [(hint [sut p.gen] p.hum) q.hum]
9979        ::
9980            [%sgzp *]   ~_(duck(sut (play p.gen)) $(gen q.gen))
9981            [%sggr *]
9982         =+  hum=$(gen q.gen)
9983         :: ?:  &(huz !?=(%|(@ [?(%sgcn %sgls) ^]) p.gen))
9984         ::  hum
9985         :-  p.hum
9986         :+  %11
9987          ?-    p.gen
9988            @    p.gen
9989            ^    [p.p.gen q:$(gen q.p.gen, gol %noun)]
9990          ==
9991        q.hum
9992        ::
9993            [%tsgr *]
9994         =+  fid=$(gen p.gen, gol %noun)
9995         =+  dov=$(sut p.fid, gen q.gen)
9996         [p.dov (comb q.fid q.dov)]
9997        ::
9998            [%tscm *]
9999         $(gen q.gen, sut (busk p.gen))
10000       ::
10001           [%wtcl *]
10002        =+  nor=$(gen p.gen, gol bool)
10003        =+  [fex=(gain p.gen) wux=(lose p.gen)]
10004        ::
10005        ::  if either branch is impossible, eliminate it
10006        ::  (placing the conditional in a dynamic hint to preserve crashes)
10007        ::
10008        =+  ^=  [ned duy]
10009          ?-  -
10010            [%void %void]   |+[%0 0]
10011            [%void *]       &+[%1 |]
10012            [* %void]       &+[%1 &]
10013            *               |+q.nor
10014          ==
10015        =+  hiq=$(sut fex, gen q.gen)
10016        =+  ran=$(sut wux, gen r.gen)
10017        =+  fol=(cond duy q.hiq q.ran)
10018        [(fork p.hiq p.ran ~) ?.(ned fol [%11 [%toss q.nor] fol])]
10019       ::
10020           [%wthx *]
10021        :-  (nice bool)
10022        =+  fid=(fend %read [[%& 1] q.gen])
10023        (~(fish ar `type`p.fid `skin`p.gen) q.fid)
10024       ::
10025           [%fits *]
10026        :-  (nice bool)
10027        =+  ref=(play p.gen)
10028        =+  fid=(find %read q.gen)
10029        ~|  [%test q.gen]
10030        |-  ^-  nock
10031        ?-  -.fid
10032          %&  ?-  -.q.p.fid
```

```
        %&  (fish(sut ref) (tend p.p.fid))
        %|  $(fid [%| (fine fid)])
      ==
    %|  [%7 q.p.fid (fish(sut ref) 1)]
  ==
::
    [%dbug *]
  ~_  (show %o p.gen)
  =+  hum=$(gen q.gen)
  [p.hum [%11 [%spot %1 p.gen] q.hum]]
::
    [%zpcm *]   [(nice (play p.gen)) [%1 q.gen]]   ::  XX validate!
    [%lost *]
  ?:  vet
    ~_  (dunk(sut (play p.gen)) 'lost')
    ~>(%mean.'mint-lost' !!)
  [%void [%0 0]]
::
    [%zpmc *]
  =+  vos=$(gol %noun, gen q.gen)
  =+  ref=p:$(gol %noun, gen p.gen)
  [(nice (cell ref p.vos)) (cons [%1 burp(sut p.vos)] q.vos)]
::
    [%zpgl *]
  =/  typ  (nice (play [%kttr p.gen]))
  =/  val
    =<  q
    %_    $
      gol  %noun
      gen
    :^    %wtcl
        :+  %cncl  [%limb %levi]
        :~  [%tsgr [%zpgr [%kttr p.gen]] [%$ 2]]
            [%tsgr q.gen [%$ 2]]
        ==
      [%tsgr q.gen [%$ 3]]
    [%zpzp ~]
  ==
  [typ val]
::
    [%zpts *]   [(nice %noun) [%1 q:$(vet |, gen p.gen)]]
    [%zppt *]   ?:((feel p.gen) $(gen q.gen) $(gen r.gen))
::
    [%zpzp ~]  [%void [%0 0]]
    *
  =+  doz=~(open ap gen)
  ?:  =(doz gen)
    ~_  (show [%c 'hoon'] [%q gen])
    ~>(%mean.'mint-open' !!)
  $(gen doz)
==
::
++  nice
  |=  typ=type
  ~_  leaf+"mint-nice"
  ?>  ?|(!vet (nest(sut gol) & typ))
  typ
::
```

```
10091      ++    grow
10092      |=    [mel=vair nym=(unit term) hud=poly ruf=hoon dom=(map term tome)]
10093      ^-    [p=type q=nock]
10094      =+    dan=^$(gen ruf, gol %noun)
10095      =+    pul=(mine gol mel nym hud dom)
10096      [(nice p.pul) (cons q.pul q.dan)]
10097      --
10098    ::
10099    ++   moot
10100      =+   gil=*(set type)
10101      |-   ^-   ?
10102      ?-   sut
10103      [%atom *]   |
10104      [%cell *]   |($(sut p.sut) $(sut q.sut))
10105      [%core *]   $(sut p.sut)
10106      [%face *]   $(sut q.sut)
10107      [%fork *]   (levy ~(tap in p.sut) |=(type ^$(sut +<)))
10108      [%hint *]   $(sut q.sut)
10109      [%hold *]   |((~(has in gil) sut) $(gil (~(put in gil) sut), sut repo))
10110      %noun        |
10111      %void        &
10112      ==
10113    ::
10114    ++   mull
10115      ~/   %mull
10116      |=   [gol=type dox=type gen=hoon]
10117      |^   ^-   [p=type q=type]
10118      ?:   =(%void sut)
10119        ~>(%mean.'mull-none' !!)
10120      ?-     gen
10121      ::
10122         [^ *]
10123      =+   hed=$(gen p.gen, gol %noun)
10124      =+   tal=$(gen q.gen, gol %noun)
10125      [(nice (cell p.hed p.tal)) (cell q.hed q.tal)]
10126      ::
10127         [%brcn *]   (grow %gold p.gen %dry [%$ 1] q.gen)
10128         [%brpt *]   (grow %gold p.gen %wet [%$ 1] q.gen)
10129         [%cnts *]   (~(mull et p.gen q.gen) gol dox)
10130         [%dtkt *]   =+($(gen q.gen, gol %noun) $(gen [%kttr p.gen]))
10131         [%dtls *]   =+($(gen p.gen, gol [%atom %$ ~]) (beth [%atom %$ ~]))
10132         [%sand *]   (beth (play gen))
10133         [%rock *]   (beth (play gen))
10134      ::
10135         [%dttr *]
10136      =+([$(gen p.gen, gol %noun) $(gen q.gen, gol %noun)] (beth %noun))
10137      ::
10138         [%dtts *]
10139      =+([$(gen p.gen, gol %noun) $(gen q.gen, gol %noun)] (beth bool))
10140      ::
10141         [%dtwt *]   =+($(gen p.gen, gol %noun) (beth bool)) ::  XX  =|
10142         [%hand *]   [p.gen p.gen]
10143         [%ktbr *]
10144      =+(vat=$(gen p.gen) [(wrap(sut p.vat) %iron) (wrap(sut q.vat) %iron)])
10145      ::
10146         [%ktls *]
10147      =+   hif=[p=(nice (play p.gen)) q=(play(sut dox) p.gen)]
10148      =+($(gen q.gen, gol p.hif) hif)
```

```
10149      ::
10150        [%ktpm *]
10151      =+(vat=$(gen p.gen) [(wrap(sut p.vat) %zinc) (wrap(sut q.vat) %zinc)])
10152      ::
10153        [%tune *]
10154      [(face p.gen sut) (face p.gen dox)]
10155      ::
10156        [%ktwt *]
10157      =+(vat=$(gen p.gen) [(wrap(sut p.vat) %lead) (wrap(sut q.vat) %lead)])
10158      ::
10159        [%note *]
10160    =+  vat=$(gen q.gen)
10161    [(hint [sut p.gen] p.vat) (hint [dox p.gen] q.vat)]
10162      ::
10163        [%ktsg *]  $(gen p.gen)
10164        [%sgzp *]  ~_(duck(sut (play p.gen)) $(gen q.gen))
10165        [%sggr *]  $(gen q.gen)
10166        [%tsgr *]
10167    =+  lem=$(gen p.gen, gol %noun)
10168    $(gen q.gen, sut p.lem, dox q.lem)
10169      ::
10170        [%tscm *]
10171    =/  boc  (busk p.gen)
10172    =/  nuf  (busk(sut dox) p.gen)
10173    $(gen q.gen, sut boc, dox nuf)
10174      ::
10175        [%wtcl *]
10176    =+  nor=$(gen p.gen, gol bool)
10177    =+  ^=  hiq  ^-  [p=type q=type]
10178        =+  fex=[p=(gain p.gen) q=(gain(sut dox) p.gen)]
10179        ?:  =(%void p.fex)
10180          :-  %void
10181          ?:  =(%void q.fex)
10182            %void
10183          ~>(%mean.'if-z' (play(sut q.fex) q.gen))
10184        ?:  =(%void q.fex)
10185          ~>(%mean.'mull-bonk-b' !!)
10186        $(sut p.fex, dox q.fex, gen q.gen)
10187    =+  ^=  ran  ^-  [p=type q=type]
10188        =+  wux=[p=(lose p.gen) q=(lose(sut dox) p.gen)]
10189        ?:  =(%void p.wux)
10190          :-  %void
10191          ?:  =(%void q.wux)
10192            %void
10193          ~>(%mean.'if-a' (play(sut q.wux) r.gen))
10194        ?:  =(%void q.wux)
10195          ~>(%mean.'mull-bonk-c' !!)
10196        $(sut p.wux, dox q.wux, gen r.gen)
10197    [(nice (fork p.hiq p.ran ~)) (fork q.hiq q.ran ~)]
10198      ::
10199        [%fits *]
10200    =+  waz=[p=(play p.gen) q=(play(sut dox) p.gen)]
10201    =+  ^=  syx  :-  p=(cove q:(mint %noun [%wing q.gen]))
10202                    q=(cove q:(mint(sut dox) %noun [%wing q.gen]))
10203    =+  pov=[p=(fish(sut p.waz) p.syx) q=(fish(sut q.waz) q.syx)]
10204    ?.  &(=(p.syx q.syx) =(p.pov q.pov))
10205      ~>(%mean.'mull-bonk-a' !!)
10206    (beth bool)
```

```
10207          ::
10208              [%wthx *]
10209          ~>  %mean.'mull-bonk-x'
10210          =+  :-  new=[type=p axis=q]:(fend %read [[%& 1] q.gen])
10211              old=[type=p axis=q]:(fend(sut dox) %read [[%& 1] q.gen])
10212          ?>  =(axis.old axis.new)
10213          ?>  (nest(sut type.old) & type.new)
10214          (beth bool)
10215          ::
10216              [%dbug *]  ~_((show %o p.gen) $(gen q.gen))
10217              [%zpcm *]  [(nice (play p.gen)) (play(sut dox) p.gen)]
10218              [%lost *]
10219          ?:  vet
10220            ::  ~_  (dunk(sut (play p.gen)) 'also')
10221            ~>(%mean.'mull-skip' !!)
10222          (beth %void)
10223          ::
10224              [%zpts *]  (beth %noun)
10225          ::
10226              [%zpmc *]
10227          =+  vos=$(gol %noun, gen q.gen)         ::  XX validate!
10228          [(nice (cell (play p.gen) p.vos)) (cell (play(sut dox) p.gen) q.vos)]
10229          ::
10230              [%zpgl *]
10231          ::  XX is this right?
10232          (beth (play [%kttr p.gen]))
10233          ::
10234              [%zppt *]
10235          =+  [(feel p.gen) (feel(sut dox) p.gen)]
10236          ?.  =(-< ->)
10237            ~>(%mean.'mull-bonk-f' !!)
10238          ?:  -<
10239            $(gen q.gen)
10240          $(gen r.gen)
10241          ::
10242              [%zpzp *]  (beth %void)
10243              *
10244          =+  doz=~(open ap gen)
10245          ?:  =(doz gen)
10246            ~_  (show [%c 'hoon'] [%q gen])
10247            ~>(%mean.'mull-open' !!)
10248          $(gen doz)
10249      ==
10250      ::
10251      ++  beth
10252        |=  typ=type
10253        [(nice typ) typ]
10254      ::
10255      ++  nice
10256        |=  typ=type
10257        ::  ~_  (dunk(sut gol) 'need')
10258        ::  ~_  (dunk(sut typ) 'have')
10259        ~_  leaf+"mull-nice"
10260        ?>  ?|(!vet (nest(sut gol) & typ))
10261        typ
10262      ::
10263      ++  grow
10264        |=  [mel=vair nym=(unit term) hud=poly ruf=hoon dom=(map term tome)]
```

```
10265        ::   make al
10266        ~_  leaf+"mull-grow"
10267        ^-  [p=type q=type]
10268        =+  dan=^$(gen ruf, gol %noun)
10269        =+  yaz=(mile(sut p.dan) q.dan mel nym hud dom)
10270        [(nice p.yaz) q.yaz]
10271        --
10272  ++  meet  |=(ref=type &((nest | ref) (nest(sut ref) | sut)))
10273  ::                                                  ::
10274  ++  miss                                            ::  nonintersection
10275    |=  $:  ::  ref: symmetric type
10276            ::
10277            ref=type
10278        ==
10279    ::  intersection of sut and ref is empty
10280    ::
10281    ^-  ?
10282    =|  gil=(set (set type))
10283    =<  dext
10284    |%
10285    ++  dext
10286      ^-  ?
10287      ::
10288      ?:  =(ref sut)
10289        (nest(sut %void) | sut)
10290      ?-  sut
10291        %void        &
10292        %noun        (nest(sut %void) | ref)
10293        [%atom *]  sint
10294        [%cell *]  sint
10295        [%core *]  sint(sut [%cell %noun %noun])
10296        [%fork *]  %+  levy  ~(tap in p.sut)
10297                   |=(type dext(sut +<))
10298        [%face *]  dext(sut q.sut)
10299        [%hint *]  dext(sut q.sut)
10300        [%hold *]  =+  (~(gas in *(set type)) `(list type)`[sut ref ~])
10301                   ?:  (~(has in gil) -)
10302                     &
10303                   %=  dext
10304                     sut  repo
10305                     gil  (~(put in gil) -)
10306      ==           ==
10307    ++  sint
10308      ?+  ref        dext(sut ref, ref sut)
10309        [%atom *]  ?.  ?=([%atom *] sut)  &
10310                   ?&  ?=(^ q.ref)
10311                       ?=(^ q.sut)
10312                       !=(q.ref q.sut)
10313                   ==
10314        [%cell *]  ?.  ?=([%cell *] sut)  &
10315                   ?|  dext(sut p.sut, ref p.ref)
10316                       dext(sut q.sut, ref q.ref)
10317      ==           ==
10318    --
10319  ++  mite  |=(ref=type |((nest | ref) (nest(sut ref) & sut)))
10320  ++  nest
10321    ~/  %nest
10322    |=  [tel=? ref=type]
```

```
10323      =|  $:  seg=(set type)                            ::  degenerate sut
10324             reg=(set type)                            ::  degenerate ref
10325             gil=(set [p=type q=type])                 ::  assume nest
10326          ==
10327      =<  dext
10328      ~%  %nest-in  ..$  ~
10329      |%
10330      ++  deem
10331        |=  [mel=vair ram=vair]
10332        ^-  ?
10333        ?.  |(=(mel ram) =(%lead mel) =(%gold ram))  |
10334        ?-  mel
10335          %lead  &
10336          %gold  meet
10337          %iron  dext(sut (peek(sut ref) %rite 2), ref (peek %rite 2))
10338          %zinc  dext(sut (peek %read 2), ref (peek(sut ref) %read 2))
10339        ==
10340      ::
10341      ++  deep
10342        |=  $:  dom=(map term tome)
10343                vim=(map term tome)
10344            ==
10345        ^-  ?
10346        ?:  ?=(~ dom)  =(vim ~)
10347        ?:  ?=(~ vim)  |
10348        ?&  =(p.n.dom p.n.vim)
10349            $(dom l.dom, vim l.vim)
10350            $(dom r.dom, vim r.vim)
10351        ::
10352            =+  [dab hem]=[q.q.n.dom q.q.n.vim]
10353            |-  ^-  ?
10354            ?:  ?=(~ dab)  =(hem ~)
10355            ?:  ?=(~ hem)  |
10356            ?&  =(p.n.dab p.n.hem)
10357                $(dab l.dab, hem l.hem)
10358                $(dab r.dab, hem r.hem)
10359                %=  dext
10360                  sut  (play q.n.dab)
10361                  ref  (play(sut ref) q.n.hem)
10362        ==  ==  ==
10363      ::
10364      ++  dext
10365        =<  $
10366        ~%  %nest-dext  +  ~
10367        |.
10368        ^-  ?
10369        =-  ?:  -  &
10370            ?.  tel  |
10371            ~_  (dunk %need)
10372            ~_  (dunk(sut ref) %have)
10373            ~>  %mean.'nest-fail'
10374            !!
10375        ?:  =(sut ref)  &
10376        ?-  sut
10377          %void      sint
10378          %noun      &
10379          [%atom *]  ?.  ?=([%atom *] ref)  sint
10380                     ?&  (fitz p.sut p.ref)
```

```
10381                           |(?=(~ q.sut) =(q.sut q.ref))
10382                     ==
10383       [%cell *]   ?.   ?=([%cell *] ref)   sint
10384                   ?&  dext(sut p.sut, ref p.ref, seg ~, reg ~)
10385                       dext(sut q.sut, ref q.ref, seg ~, reg ~)
10386                     ==
10387       [%core *]   ?.   ?=([%core *] ref)   sint
10388                   ?:  =(q.sut q.ref)  dext(sut p.sut, ref p.ref)
10389                   ?&  =(q.p.q.sut q.p.q.ref)   ::   same wet/dry
10390                       meet(sut q.q.sut, ref p.sut)
10391                       dext(sut q.q.ref, ref p.ref)
10392                       (deem(sut q.q.sut, ref q.q.ref) r.p.q.sut r.p.q.ref)
10393                       ?:  =(%wet q.p.q.sut)  =(q.r.q.sut q.r.q.ref)
10394                       ?|  (~(has in gil) [sut ref])
10395                           %.  [q.r.q.sut q.r.q.ref]
10396                           %=  deep
10397                             gil  (~(put in gil) [sut ref])
10398                             sut  sut(p q.q.sut, r.p.q %gold)
10399                             ref  ref(p q.q.ref, r.p.q %gold)
10400                       ==  ==
10401                     ==
10402       [%face *]   dext(sut q.sut)
10403       [%fork *]   ?.   ?=(?([%atom *] %noun [%cell *] [%core *]) ref)   sint
10404                   (lien ~(tap in p.sut) |=(type dext(tel |, sut +<)))
10405       [%hint *]   dext(sut q.sut)
10406       [%hold *]   ?:  (~(has in seg) sut)  |
10407                   ?:  (~(has in gil) [sut ref])  &
10408                   %=  dext
10409                     sut  repo
10410                     seg  (~(put in seg) sut)
10411                     gil  (~(put in gil) [sut ref])
10412       ==            ==
10413     ::
10414     ++  meet  &(dext dext(sut ref, ref sut))
10415     ++  sint
10416       ^-  ?
10417       ?-  ref
10418         %noun        |
10419         %void        &
10420         [%atom *]    |
10421         [%cell *]    |
10422         [%core *]   dext(ref repo(sut ref))
10423         [%face *]   dext(ref q.ref)
10424         [%fork *]   (levy ~(tap in p.ref) |=(type dext(ref +<)))
10425         [%hint *]   dext(ref q.ref)
10426         [%hold *]   ?:  (~(has in reg) ref)  &
10427                     ?:  (~(has in gil) [sut ref])  &
10428                     %=  dext
10429                       ref  repo(sut ref)
10430                       reg  (~(put in reg) ref)
10431                       gil  (~(put in gil) [sut ref])
10432       ==            ==
10433     --
10434   ::
10435   ++  peek
10436     ~/  %peek
10437     |=  [way=?(%read %rite %both %free) axe=axis]
10438     ^-  type
```

```
10439        ?:   =(1 axe)
10440          sut
10441      =+   [now=(cap axe) lat=(mas axe)]
10442      =+   gil=*(set type)
10443      |-   ^-  type
10444      ?-     sut
10445          [%atom *]    %void
10446          [%cell *]    ?:(=(2 now) ^$(sut p.sut, axe lat) ^$(sut q.sut, axe lat))
10447          [%core *]
10448        ?.   =(3 now)  %noun
10449        =+   pec=(peel way r.p.q.sut)
10450        =/   tow
10451          ?:   =(1 lat)  1
10452          (cap lat)
10453        %=     ^$
10454            axe   lat
10455            sut
10456          ?:   ?|  =([& &] pec)
10457                   &(sam.pec =(tow 2))
10458                   &(con.pec =(tow 3))
10459             ==
10460            p.sut
10461          ~_   leaf+"payload-block"
10462          ?.   =(way %read)  !!
10463          %+   cell
10464            ?.(sam.pec %noun ^$(sut p.sut, axe 2))
10465          ?.(con.pec %noun ^$(sut p.sut, axe 3))
10466        ==
10467      ::
10468          [%fork *]    (fork (turn ~(tap in p.sut) |=(type ^$(sut +<))))
10469          [%hold *]
10470        ?:   (~(has in gil) sut)
10471          %void
10472        $(gil (~(put in gil) sut), sut repo)
10473      ::
10474          %void         %void
10475          %noun         %noun
10476          *             $(sut repo)
10477        ==
10478    ::
10479    ++  peel
10480      |=  [way=vial met=?(%gold %iron %lead %zinc)]
10481      ^-  [sam=? con=?]
10482      ?:  ?=(%gold met)  [& &]
10483      ?-  way
10484        %both  [| |]
10485        %free  [& &]
10486        %read  [?=(%zinc met) |]
10487        %rite  [?=(%iron met) |]
10488      ==
10489    ::
10490    ++  play
10491      ~/  %play
10492      =>  .(vet |)
10493      |=  gen=hoon
10494      ^-  type
10495      ?-  gen
10496        [^ *]      (cell $(gen p.gen) $(gen q.gen))
```

```
10497        [%brcn *]   (core sut [p.gen %dry %gold] sut *seminoun q.gen)
10498        [%brpt *]   (core sut [p.gen %wet %gold] sut *seminoun q.gen)
10499        [%cnts *]   ~(play et p.gen q.gen)
10500        [%dtkt *]   $(gen [%kttr p.gen])
10501        [%dtls *]   [%atom %$ ~]
10502        [%rock *]   |-  ^-  type
10503                    ?@  q.gen  [%atom p.gen `q.gen]
10504                    [%cell $(q.gen -.q.gen) $(q.gen +.q.gen)]
10505        [%sand *]   ?@  q.gen
10506                      ?:  =(%n p.gen)  ?>(=(0 q.gen) [%atom p.gen `q.gen])
10507                      ?:  =(%f p.gen)  ?>((lte q.gen 1) bool)
10508                      [%atom p.gen ~]
10509                    $(-.gen %rock)
10510        [%tune *]   (face p.gen sut)
10511        [%dttr *]   %noun
10512        [%dtts *]   bool
10513        [%dtwt *]   bool
10514        [%hand *]   p.gen
10515        [%ktbr *]   (wrap(sut $(gen p.gen)) %iron)
10516        [%ktls *]   $(gen p.gen)
10517        [%ktpm *]   (wrap(sut $(gen p.gen)) %zinc)
10518        [%ktsg *]   $(gen p.gen)
10519        [%ktwt *]   (wrap(sut $(gen p.gen)) %lead)
10520        [%note *]   (hint [sut p.gen] $(gen q.gen))
10521        [%sgzp *]   ~_(duck(sut ^$(gen p.gen)) $(gen q.gen))
10522        [%sggr *]   $(gen q.gen)
10523        [%tsgr *]   $(gen q.gen, sut $(gen p.gen))
10524        [%tscm *]   $(gen q.gen, sut (busk p.gen))
10525        [%wtcl *]   =+  [fex=(gain p.gen) wux=(lose p.gen)]
10526                    %-  fork  :~
10527                      ?:(=(%void fex) %void $(sut fex, gen q.gen))
10528                      ?:(=(%void wux) %void $(sut wux, gen r.gen))
10529                    ==
10530        [%fits *]   bool
10531        [%wthx *]   bool
10532        [%dbug *]   ~_((show %o p.gen) $(gen q.gen))
10533        [%zpcm *]   $(gen p.gen)
10534        [%lost *]   %void
10535        [%zpmc *]   (cell $(gen p.gen) $(gen q.gen))
10536        [%zpgl *]   (play [%kttr p.gen])
10537        [%zpts *]   %noun
10538        [%zppt *]   ?:((feel p.gen) $(gen q.gen) $(gen r.gen))
10539        [%zpzp *]   %void
10540        *           =+  doz=~(open ap gen)
10541                    ?:  =(doz gen)
10542                      ~_  (show [%c 'hoon'] [%q gen])
10543                      ~>  %mean.'play-open'
10544                      !!
10545                    $(gen doz)
10546      ==
10547    ::                                                      ::
10548    ++  redo                                                ::  refurbish faces
10549    ~/  %redo
10550    |=  $:  ::  ref: raw payload
10551            ::
10552            ref=type
10553        ==
10554    ::  :type: subject refurbished to reference namespace
```

```
10555        ::
10556        ^-  type
10557        ::  hos: subject tool stack
10558        ::  wec: reference tool stack set
10559        ::  gil: repetition set
10560        ::
10561        =|  hos=(list tool)
10562        =/  wec=(set (list tool))  [~ ~ ~]
10563        =|  gil=(set (pair type type))
10564        =<  ::  errors imply subject/reference mismatch
10565            ::
10566            ~|  %redo-match
10567            ::  reduce by subject
10568            ::
10569            dext
10570        |%
10571        ::                                          ::
10572        ++  dear                                    ::  resolve tool stack
10573          ::  :(unit (list tool)): unified tool stack
10574          ::
10575          ^-  (unit (list tool))
10576          ::  empty implies void
10577          ::
10578          ?~  wec  `~
10579          ::  any reference faces must be clear
10580          ::
10581          ?.  ?=([* ~ ~] wec)
10582            ~&  [%dear-many wec]
10583            ~
10584          :-  ~
10585          ::  har: single reference tool stack
10586          ::
10587          =/  har  n.wec
10588          ::  len: lengths of [sut ref] face stacks
10589          ::
10590          =/  len  [p q]=[(lent hos) (lent har)]
10591          ::  lip: length of sut-ref face stack overlap
10592          ::
10593          ::     AB
10594          ::      BC
10595          ::
10596          ::     +lip is (lent B), where +hay is forward AB
10597          ::     and +liv is forward BC (stack BA and CB).
10598          ::
10599          ::     overlap is a weird corner case.  +lip is
10600          ::     almost always 0.  brute force is fine.
10601          ::
10602          =/  lip
10603            =|  lup=(unit @ud)
10604            =|  lip=@ud
10605            |-  ^-  @ud
10606            ?:  |((gth lip p.len) (gth lip q.len))
10607              (fall lup 0)
10608            ::  lep: overlap candidate: suffix of subject face stack
10609            ::
10610            =/  lep  (slag (sub p.len lip) hos)
10611            ::  lap: overlap candidate: prefix of reference face stack
10612            ::
```

```
10613          =/  lap  (scag lip har)
10614          ::  save any match and continue
10615          ::
10616          $(lip +(lip), lup ?.(=(lep lap) lup `lip))
10617      ::  ~&  [har+har hos+hos len+len lip+lip]
10618      ::  produce combined face stack (forward ABC, stack CBA)
10619      ::
10620      (weld hos (slag lip har))
10621  ::                                                      ::
10622  ++  dext                                                ::  subject traverse
10623      ::  :type: refurbished subject
10624      ::
10625      ^-  type
10626      ::  check for trivial cases
10627      ::
10628      ?:  ?|  =(sut ref)
10629              ?=(?(%noun %void [?(%atom %core) *]) ref)
10630          ==
10631        done
10632      ::  ~_  (dunk 'redo: dext: sut ')
10633      ::  ~_  (dunk(sut ref) 'redo: dext: ref ')
10634      ?-    sut
10635        ?(%noun %void [?(%atom %core) *])
10636      ::  reduce reference and reassemble leaf
10637      ::
10638      done:(sint &)
10639  ::
10640          [%cell *]
10641      ::  reduce reference to match subject
10642      ::
10643      =>  (sint &)
10644      ?>  ?=([%cell *] sut)
10645      ::  leaf with possible recursive descent
10646      ::
10647      %=    done
10648            sut
10649      ::  clear face stacks for descent
10650      ::
10651      =:  hos  ~
10652          wec  [~ ~ ~]
10653          ==
10654      ::  descend into cell
10655      ::
10656      :+  %cell
10657        dext(sut p.sut, ref (peek(sut ref) %free 2))
10658      dext(sut q.sut, ref (peek(sut ref) %free 3))
10659      ==
10660  ::
10661          [%face *]
10662      ::  push face on subject stack, and descend
10663      ::
10664      dext(hos [p.sut hos], sut q.sut)
10665  ::
10666          [%hint *]
10667      ::  work through hint
10668      ::
10669      (hint p.sut dext(sut q.sut))
10670  ::
```

```
        [%fork *]
    ::  reconstruct each case in fork
    ::
    (fork (turn ~(tap in p.sut) |=(type dext(sut +<))))
  ::
      [%hold *]
    ::  reduce to hard
    ::
    =>  (sint |)
    ?>  ?=([%hold *] sut)
    ?:  (~(has in fan) [p.sut q.sut])
      ::  repo loop; redo depends on its own product
      ::
      done:(sint &)
    ?:  (~(has in gil) [sut ref])
      ::  type recursion, stop renaming
      ::
      done:(sint |)
    ::  restore unchanged holds
    ::
    =+  repo
    =-  ?:(=(- +<) sut -)
    dext(sut -, gil (~(put in gil) sut ref))
  ==
::                                              ::
++  done                                        ::  complete assembly
  ^-  type
  ::  :type: subject refurbished
  ::
  ::  lov: combined face stack
  ::
  =/  lov
      =/  lov  dear
      ?~  lov
        ::  ~_  (dunk 'redo: dear: sut')
        ::  ~_  (dunk(sut ref) 'redo: dear: ref')
        ~&  [%wec wec]
        !!
      (need lov)
  ::  recompose faces
  ::
  |-  ^-  type
  ?~  lov  sut
  $(lov t.lov, sut (face i.lov sut))
::
++  sint                                        ::  reduce by reference
  |=  $:  ::  hod: expand holds
          ::
          hod=?
      ==
  ::  ::.: reference with face/fork/hold reduced
  ::
  ^+  .
  ::  =-  ~>  %slog.[0 (dunk 'sint: sut')]
  ::      ~>  %slog.[0 (dunk(sut ref) 'sint: ref')]
  ::      ~>  %slog.[0 (dunk(sut =>(- ref)) 'sint: pro')]
  ::      -
  ?+    ref  .
```

```
10729              [%hint *]  $(ref q.ref)
10730              [%face *]
10731          ::  extend all stacks in set
10732          ::
10733          %=  $
10734            ref  q.ref
10735            wec  (~(run in wec) |=((list tool) [p.ref +<]))
10736          ==
10737        ::
10738            [%fork *]
10739          ::  reconstruct all relevant cases
10740          ::
10741          =-  ::  ~>  %slog.[0 (dunk 'fork: sut')]
10742              ::  ~>  %slog.[0 (dunk(sut ref) 'fork: ref')]
10743              ::  ~>  %slog.[0 (dunk(sut (fork ->)) 'fork: pro')]
10744              +(wec -<, ref (fork ->))
10745          =/  moy  ~(tap in p.ref)
10746          |-  ^-  (pair (set (list tool)) (list type))
10747          ?~  moy  [~ ~]
10748          ::  head recurse
10749          ::
10750          =/  mor  $(moy t.moy)
10751          ::  prune reference cases outside subject
10752          ::
10753          ?:  (miss i.moy)  mor
10754          ::  unify all cases
10755          ::
10756          =/  dis  ^$(ref i.moy)
10757          [(~(uni in p.mor) wec.dis) [ref.dis q.mor]]
10758        ::
10759            [%hold *]
10760          ?.  hod  .
10761          $(ref repo(sut ref))
10762          ==
10763        --
10764    ::
10765    ++  repo
10766      ^-  type
10767      ?-  sut
10768      [%core *]    [%cell %noun p.sut]
10769      [%face *]    q.sut
10770      [%hint *]    q.sut
10771      [%hold *]    (rest [[p.sut q.sut] ~])
10772      %noun        (fork [%atom %$ ~] [%cell %noun %noun] ~)
10773      *            ~>(%mean.'repo-fltt' !!)
10774      ==
10775    ::
10776    ++  rest
10777      ~/  %rest
10778      |=  leg=(list [p=type q=hoon])
10779      ^-  type
10780      ?:  (lien leg |=([p=type q=hoon] (~(has in fan) [p q])))
10781        ~>(%mean.'rest-loop' !!)
10782      =>  .(fan (~(gas in fan) leg))
10783      %-  fork
10784      %~  tap  in
10785      %-  ~(gas in *(set type))
10786      (turn leg |=([p=type q=hoon] (play(sut p) q)))
```

```
10787      ::
10788      ++  sink
10789        ~/  %sink
10790        |^  ^-  cord
10791        ?-  sut
10792          %void        'void'
10793          %noun        'noun'
10794          [%atom *]  (rap 3 'atom ' p.sut ' ' ?~(q.sut '~' u.q.sut) ~)
10795          [%cell *]  (rap 3 'cell ' (mup p.sut) ' ' (mup q.sut) ~)
10796          [%face *]  (rap 3 'face ' ?@(p.sut p.sut (mup p.sut)) ' ' (mup q.sut) ~)
10797          [%fork *]  (rap 3 'fork ' (mup p.sut) ~)
10798          [%hint *]  (rap 3 'hint ' (mup p.sut) ' ' (mup q.sut) ~)
10799          [%hold *]  (rap 3 'hold ' (mup p.sut) ' ' (mup q.sut) ~)
10800        ::
10801            [%core *]
10802          %+  rap  3
10803          :~  'core '
10804              (mup p.sut)
10805              ' '
10806              ?~(p.p.q.sut '~' u.p.p.q.sut)
10807              ' '
10808              q.p.q.sut
10809              ' '
10810              r.p.q.sut
10811              ' '
10812              (mup q.q.sut)
10813              ' '
10814              (mup p.r.q.sut)
10815          ==
10816        ==
10817      ::
10818      ++  mup  |=(* (scot %p (mug +<)))
10819      --
10820    ::
10821    ++  take
10822      |=  [vit=vein duz=$-(type type)]
10823      ^-  (pair axis type)
10824      :-  (tend vit)
10825      =.  vit  (flop vit)
10826      |-  ^-  type
10827      ?~  vit  (duz sut)
10828      ?~  i.vit
10829        |-  ^-  type
10830        ?+  sut        ^$(vit t.vit)
10831          [%face *]  (face p.sut ^$(vit t.vit, sut q.sut))
10832          [%hint *]  (hint p.sut ^$(sut q.sut))
10833          [%fork *]  (fork (turn ~(tap in p.sut) |=(type ^$(sut +<))))
10834          [%hold *]  $(sut repo)
10835        ==
10836      =+  vil=*(set type)
10837      |-  ^-  type
10838      ?:  =(1 u.i.vit)
10839        ^$(vit t.vit)
10840      =+  [now lat]=(cap u.i.vit)^(mas u.i.vit)
10841      ?-  sut
10842        %noun        $(sut [%cell %noun %noun])
10843        %void        %void
10844        [%atom *]  %void
```

```
10845        [%cell *]   ?:  =(2 now)
10846                      (cell $(sut p.sut, u.i.vit lat) q.sut)
10847                      (cell p.sut $(sut q.sut, u.i.vit lat))
10848        [%core *]   ?:  =(2 now)
10849                      $(sut repo)
10850                      (core $(sut p.sut, u.i.vit lat) q.sut)
10851        [%face *]   (face p.sut $(sut q.sut))
10852        [%fork *]   (fork (turn ~(tap in p.sut) |=(type ^$(sut +<))))
10853        [%hint *]   (hint p.sut $(sut q.sut))
10854        [%hold *]   ?:  (~(has in vil) sut)
10855                      %void
10856                      $(sut repo, vil (~(put in vil) sut))
10857      ==
10858    ::
10859    ++  tack
10860    |=  [hyp=wing mur=type]
10861    ~_  (show [%c %tack] %l hyp)
10862    =+  fid=(find %rite hyp)
10863    ?>  ?=(%& -.fid)
10864    (take p.p.fid |=(type mur))
10865    ::
10866    ++  tend
10867    |=  vit=vein
10868    ^-  axis
10869    ?~(vit 1 (peg $(vit t.vit) ?~(i.vit 1 u.i.vit)))
10870    ::
10871    ++  toss
10872    ~/  %toss
10873    |=  [hyp=wing mur=type men=(list [p=type q=foot])]
10874    ^-  [p=axis q=(list [p=type q=foot])]
10875    =-  [(need p.wib) q.wib]
10876    ^=  wib
10877    |-  ^-  [p=(unit axis) q=(list [p=type q=foot])]
10878    ?~  men
10879      [*(unit axis) ~]
10880    =+  geq=(tack(sut p.i.men) hyp mur)
10881    =+  mox=$(men t.men)
10882    [(mate p.mox `_p.mox`[~ p.geq]) [[q.geq q.i.men] q.mox]]
10883    ::
10884    ++  wrap
10885    ~/  %wrap
10886    |=  yoz=?(%lead %iron %zinc)
10887    ~_  leaf+"wrap"
10888    ^-  type
10889    ?+  sut  sut
10890      [%cell *]   (cell $(sut p.sut) $(sut q.sut))
10891      [%core *]   ?>(|(=(%gold r.p.q.sut) =(%lead yoz)) sut(r.p.q yoz))
10892      [%face *]   (face p.sut $(sut q.sut))
10893      [%fork *]   (fork (turn ~(tap in p.sut) |=(type ^$(sut +<))))
10894      [%hint *]   (hint p.sut $(sut q.sut))
10895      [%hold *]   $(sut repo)
10896    ==
10897    --
10898 ++  us                                              ::  prettyprinter
10899   =>  |%
10900      +$  cape  [p=(map @ud wine) q=wine]             ::
10901      +$  wine                                        ::
10902              $@  $?  %noun                           ::
```

```
10903                        %path                           ::
10904                        %type                           ::
10905                        %void                           ::
10906                        %wall                           ::
10907                        %wool                           ::
10908                        %yarn                           ::
10909                    ==                                  ::
10910              $%  [%mato p=term]                        ::
10911                  [%core p=(list @ta) q=wine]           ::
10912                  [%face p=term q=wine]                 ::
10913                  [%list p=term q=wine]                 ::
10914                  [%pear p=term q=@]                    ::
10915                  [%bcwt p=(list wine)]                 ::
10916                  [%plot p=(list wine)]                 ::
10917                  [%stop p=@ud]                         ::
10918                  [%tree p=term q=wine]                 ::
10919                  [%unit p=term q=wine]                 ::
10920                  [%name p=stud q=wine]                 ::
10921              ==                                        ::
10922          --
10923      |_  sut=type
10924      ++  dash
10925        |=  [mil=tape lim=char lam=tape]
10926        ^-  tape
10927        =/  esc  (~(gas in *(set @tD)) lam)
10928        :-  lim
10929        |-  ^-  tape
10930        ?~  mil  [lim ~]
10931        ?:  ?|  =(lim i.mil)
10932                =('\\' i.mil)
10933                (~(has in esc) i.mil)
10934            ==
10935          ['\\' i.mil $(mil t.mil)]
10936        ?:  (lte ' ' i.mil)
10937          [i.mil $(mil t.mil)]
10938        ['\\' ~(x ne (rsh 2 i.mil)) ~(x ne (end 2 i.mil)) $(mil t.mil)]
10939      ::
10940      ++  deal  |=(lum=* (dish dole lum))
10941      ++  dial
10942        |=  ham=cape
10943        =+  gid=*(set @ud)
10944        =<  `tank`-:$
10945        |%
10946        ++  many
10947          |=  haz=(list wine)
10948          ^-  [(list tank) (set @ud)]
10949          ?~  haz  [~ gid]
10950          =^  mor  gid  $(haz t.haz)
10951          =^  dis  gid  ^$(q.ham i.haz)
10952          [[dis mor] gid]
10953        ::
10954        ++  $
10955          ^-  [tank (set @ud)]
10956          ?-    q.ham
10957              %noun      :_(gid [%leaf '*' ~])
10958              %path      :_(gid [%leaf '/' ~])
10959              %type      :_(gid [%leaf '#' 't' ~])
10960              %void      :_(gid [%leaf '#' '!' ~])
```

```
      %wool      :_(gid [%leaf '*' '"' '"' ~])
      %wall      :_(gid [%leaf '*' '\'' '\'' ~])
      %yarn      :_(gid [%leaf '"' '"' ~])
      [%mato *]  :_(gid [%leaf '@' (trip p.q.ham)])
      [%core *]
    =^  cox  gid  $(q.ham q.q.ham)
    :_  gid
    :+  %rose
    [[' ' ~] ['<' ~] ['>' ~]]
    |-  ^-  (list tank)
    ?~  p.q.ham  [cox ~]
    [[%leaf (rip 3 i.p.q.ham)] $(p.q.ham t.p.q.ham)]
  ::
      [%face *]
    =^  cox  gid  $(q.ham q.q.ham)
    :_(gid [%palm [['=' ~] ~ ~ ~] [%leaf (trip p.q.ham)] cox ~])
  ::
      [%list *]
    =^  cox  gid  $(q.ham q.q.ham)
    :_(gid [%rose [" " (weld (trip p.q.ham) "(") ")"] cox ~])
  ::
      [%bcwt *]
    =^  coz  gid  (many p.q.ham)
    :_(gid [%rose [[' ' ~] ['?' '(' ~] [')' ~]] coz])
  ::
      [%plot *]
    =^  coz  gid  (many p.q.ham)
    :_(gid [%rose [[' ' ~] ['[' ~] [']' ~]] coz])
  ::
      [%pear *]
    :_(gid [%leaf '%' ~(rend co [%$ p.q.ham q.q.ham])])
  ::
      [%stop *]
    =+  num=~(rend co [%$ %ud p.q.ham])
    ?:  (~(has in gid) p.q.ham)
      :_(gid [%leaf '#' num])
    =^  cox  gid
      %=  $
        gid      (~(put in gid) p.q.ham)
        q.ham    (~(got by p.ham) p.q.ham)
      ==
    :_(gid [%palm [['.' ~] ~ ~ ~] [%leaf ['^' '#' num]] cox ~])
  ::
      [%tree *]
    =^  cox  gid  $(q.ham q.q.ham)
    :_(gid [%rose [" " (weld (trip p.q.ham) "(") ")"] cox ~])
  ::
      [%unit *]
    =^  cox  gid  $(q.ham q.q.ham)
    :_(gid [%rose [" " (weld (trip p.q.ham) "(") ")"] cox ~])
  ::
      [%name *]
    :_  gid
    ?@  p.q.ham  (cat 3 '#' mark.p.q.ham)
    (rap 3 '#' auth.p.q.ham '+' (spat type.p.q.ham) ~)
    ==
  --
::
```

```
11019    ++  dish  !:
11020    |=   [ham=cape lum=*]   ^-   tank
11021    ~|   [%dish-h ?@(q.ham q.ham -.q.ham)]
11022    ~|   [%lump lum]
11023    ~|   [%ham ham]
11024    %-   need
11025    =|   gil=(set [@ud *])
11026    |-   ^-   (unit tank)
11027    ?-      q.ham
11028        %noun
11029      %=      $
11030          q.ham
11031        ?:   ?=(@ lum)
11032          [%mato %$]
11033        :-   %plot
11034        |-   ^-   (list wine)
11035        [%noun ?:(?=(@ +.lum) [[%mato %$] ~] $(lum +.lum))]
11036      ==
11037    ::
11038        %path
11039    :-   ~
11040    :+   %rose
11041      [['/' ~] ['/' ~] ~]
11042    |-   ^-   (list tank)
11043    ?~   lum   ~
11044    ?@   lum   !!
11045    ?>   ?=(@ -.lum)
11046    [[%leaf (rip 3 -.lum)] $(lum +.lum)]
11047    ::
11048        %type
11049    =+   tyr=|.((dial dole))
11050    =+   vol=tyr(sut lum)
11051    =+   cis=;;(tank .*(vol [%9 2 %0 1]))
11052    :^   ~    %palm
11053      [~ ~ ~ ~]
11054    [[%leaf '#' 't' '/' ~] cis ~]
11055    ::
11056        %wall
11057    :-   ~
11058    :+   %rose
11059      [[' ' ~] ['<' '|' ~] ['|' '>' ~]]
11060    |-   ^-   (list tank)
11061    ?~   lum   ~
11062    ?@   lum   !!
11063    [[%leaf (trip ;;(@ -.lum))] $(lum +.lum)]
11064    ::
11065        %wool
11066    :-   ~
11067    :+   %rose
11068      [[' ' ~] ['<' '<' ~] ['>' '>' ~]]
11069    |-   ^-   (list tank)
11070    ?~   lum   ~
11071    ?@   lum   !!
11072    [(need ^$(q.ham %yarn, lum -.lum)) $(lum +.lum)]
11073    ::
11074        %yarn
11075    [~ %leaf (dash (tape lum) '"' "\{")]
11076    ::
```

```
11077          %void
11078      ~
11079    ::
11080        [%mato *]
11081    ?.   ?=(@ lum)
11082        ~
11083    :+  ~
11084      %leaf
11085    ?+    (rash p.q.ham ;~(sfix (cook crip (star low)) (star hig)))
11086        ~(rend co [%$ p.q.ham lum])
11087      %$    ~(rend co [%$ %ud lum])
11088      %t    (dash (rip 3 lum) '\'' ~)
11089      %tas  ['%' ?.(=(0 lum) (rip 3 lum) ['$' ~])]
11090      ==
11091    ::
11092        [%core *]
11093    ::  XX  needs rethinking for core metal
11094    ::  ?.   ?=(^ lum)   ~
11095    ::  =>   .(lum `*`lum)
11096    ::  =-   ?~(tok ~ [~ %rose [['  ' ~] ['<' ~] ['>' ~]] u.tok])
11097    ::  ^=  tok
11098    ::  |-  ^-  (unit (list tank))
11099    ::  ?~   p.q.ham
11100    ::    =+  den=^$(q.ham q.q.ham)
11101    ::    ?~(den ~ [~ u.den ~])
11102    ::  =+  mur=$(p.q.ham t.p.q.ham, lum +.lum)
11103    ::  ?~(mur ~ [~ [[%leaf (rip 3 i.p.q.ham)] u.mur]])
11104    [~ (dial ham)]
11105  ::
11106      [%face *]
11107  =+  wal=$(q.ham q.q.ham)
11108  ?~  wal
11109      ~
11110  [~ %palm [['=' ~] ~ ~ ~] [%leaf (trip p.q.ham)] u.wal ~]
11111  ::
11112      [%list *]
11113  ?:  =(~ lum)
11114    [~ %leaf '~' ~]
11115  =-  ?~  tok
11116      ~
11117      [~ %rose [['  ' ~] ['~' '[' ~] [']' ~]] u.tok]
11118  ^=  tok
11119  |-  ^-  (unit (list tank))
11120  ?:  ?=(@ lum)
11121    ?.(=(~ lum) ~ [~ ~])
11122  =+  [for=^$(q.ham q.q.ham, lum -.lum) aft=$(lum +.lum)]
11123  ?.   &(?=(^ for) ?=(^ aft))
11124      ~
11125  [~ u.for u.aft]
11126  ::
11127      [%bcwt *]
11128  |-  ^-  (unit tank)
11129  ?~  p.q.ham
11130      ~
11131  =+  wal=^$(q.ham i.p.q.ham)
11132  ?~  wal
11133    $(p.q.ham t.p.q.ham)
11134    wal
```

```
::
    [%plot *]
  =-  ?~  tok
          ~
      [~ %rose [[' ' ~] ['[' ~] [']' ~]] u.tok]
  ^=  tok
  |-  ^-  (unit (list tank))
  ?~  p.q.ham
      ~
  ?:  ?=([* ~] p.q.ham)
    =+  wal=^$(q.ham i.p.q.ham)
    ?~(wal ~ [~ [u.wal ~]])
  ?@  lum
      ~
  =+  gim=^$(q.ham i.p.q.ham, lum -.lum)
  ?~  gim
      ~
  =+  myd=$(p.q.ham t.p.q.ham, lum +.lum)
  ?~  myd
      ~
  [~ u.gim u.myd]
::
    [%pear *]
  ?.  =(lum q.q.ham)
      ~
  =.  p.q.ham
    (rash p.q.ham ;~(sfix (cook crip (star low)) (star hig)))
  =+  fox=$(q.ham [%mato p.q.ham])
  ?>  ?=([~ %leaf ^] fox)
  ?:  ?=(?(%n %tas) p.q.ham)
    fox
  [~ %leaf '%' p.u.fox]
::
    [%stop *]
  ?:  (~(has in gil) [p.q.ham lum])  ~
  =+  kep=(~(get by p.ham) p.q.ham)
  ?~  kep
    ~|([%stop-loss p.q.ham] !!)
  $(gil (~(put in gil) [p.q.ham lum]), q.ham u.kep)
::
    [%tree *]
  =-  ?~  tok
          ~
      [~ %rose [[' ' ~] ['{' ~] ['}' ~]] u.tok]
  ^=  tok
  =+  tuk=*(list tank)
  |-  ^-  (unit (list tank))
  ?:  =(~ lum)
    [~ tuk]
  ?.  ?=([n=* l=* r=*] lum)
      ~
  =+  rol=$(lum r.lum)
  ?~  rol
      ~
  =+  tim=^$(q.ham q.q.ham, lum n.lum)
  ?~  tim
      ~
  $(lum l.lum, tuk [u.tim u.rol])
```

```
    ::
        [%unit *]
      ?@  lum
        ?.(=(~ lum) ~ [~ %leaf '~' ~])
        ?.  =(~ -.lum)
          ~
        =+  wal=$(q.ham q.q.ham, lum +.lum)
        ?~  wal
          ~
        [~ %rose [[' ' ~] ['[' ~] [']' ~]] [%leaf '~' ~] u.wal ~]
    ::
        [%name *]
      $(q.ham q.q.ham)
    ==
::
++  doge
  |=  ham=cape
  =-  ?+  woz  woz
        [%list * [%mato %'ta']]  %path
        [%list * [%mato %'t']]   %wall
        [%list * [%mato %'tD']]  %yarn
        [%list * %yarn]          %wool
      ==
  ^=  woz
  ^-  wine
  ?.  ?=([%stop *] q.ham)
    ?:  ?&  ?=  [%bcwt [%pear %n %0] [%plot [%pear %n %0] [%face *] ~] ~]
                q.ham
              =(1 (met 3 p.i.t.p.i.t.p.q.ham))
        ==
        [%unit =<([p q] i.t.p.i.t.p.q.ham)]
      q.ham
  =+  may=(~(get by p.ham) p.q.ham)
  ?~  may
    q.ham
  =+  nul=[%pear %n 0]
  ?.  ?&  ?=([%bcwt *] u.may)
          ?=([* * ~] p.u.may)
          |(=(nul i.p.u.may) =(nul i.t.p.u.may))
      ==
    q.ham
  =+  din=?:(=(nul i.p.u.may) i.t.p.u.may i.p.u.may)
  ?:  ?&  ?=([%plot [%face *] [%face * %stop *] ~] din)
          =(p.q.ham p.q.i.t.p.din)
          =(1 (met 3 p.i.p.din))
          =(1 (met 3 p.i.t.p.din))
      ==
    :+  %list
      (cat 3 p.i.p.din p.i.t.p.din)
    q.i.p.din
  ?:  ?&  ?=  $:  %plot
                  [%face *]
                  [%face * %stop *]
                  [[%face * %stop *] ~]
              ==
              din
          =(p.q.ham p.q.i.t.p.din)
          =(p.q.ham p.q.i.t.t.p.din)
```

```
11251            =(1 (met 3 p.i.p.din))
11252            =(1 (met 3 p.i.t.p.din))
11253            =(1 (met 3 p.i.t.t.p.din))
11254         ==
11255      :+  %tree
11256      %^     cat
11257             3
11258           p.i.p.din
11259         (cat 3 p.i.t.p.din p.i.t.t.p.din)
11260       q.i.p.din
11261     q.ham
11262  ::
11263  ++  dole
11264    ^-  cape
11265    =+  gil=*(set type)
11266    =+  dex=[p=*(map type @) q=*(map @ wine)]
11267    =<  [q.p q]
11268    |-  ^-  [p=[p=(map type @) q=(map @ wine)] q=wine]
11269    =-  [p.tez (doge q.p.tez q.tez)]
11270    ^=  tez
11271    ^-  [p=[p=(map type @) q=(map @ wine)] q=wine]
11272    ?:  (~(meet ut sut) -:!>(*type))
11273      [dex %type]
11274    ?-    sut
11275        %noun       [dex sut]
11276        %void       [dex sut]
11277        [%atom *]   [dex ?~(q.sut [%mato p.sut] [%pear p.sut u.q.sut])]
11278        [%cell *]
11279      =+  hin=$(sut p.sut)
11280      =+  yon=$(dex p.hin, sut q.sut)
11281      :-  p.yon
11282      :-  %plot
11283      ?:(?=([%plot *] q.yon) [q.hin p.q.yon] [q.hin q.yon ~])
11284      ::
11285        [%core *]
11286      =+  yad=$(sut p.sut)
11287      :-  p.yad
11288      =+  ^=  doy  ^-  [p=(list @ta) q=wine]
11289          ?:  ?=([%core *] q.yad)
11290            [p.q.yad q.q.yad]
11291          [~ q.yad]
11292      :-  %core
11293      :_  q.doy
11294      :_  p.doy
11295      %^  cat  3
11296        %~  rent  co
11297        :+  %$  %ud
11298        %-  ~(rep by (~(run by q.r.q.sut) |=(tome ~(wyt by q.+<))))
11299        |=([[@ a=@u] b=@u] (add a b))
11300      %^  cat  3
11301        ?-(r.p.q.sut %gold '.', %iron '|', %lead '?', %zinc '&')
11302      =+  gum=(mug q.r.q.sut)
11303      %+  can  3
11304      :~  [1 (add 'a' (mod gum 26))]
11305          [1 (add 'a' (mod (div gum 26) 26))]
11306          [1 (add 'a' (mod (div gum 676) 26))]
11307      ==
11308    ::
```

```
        [%hint *]
    =+  yad=$(sut q.sut)
    ?.  ?=(%know -.q.p.sut)  yad
    [p.yad [%name p.q.p.sut q.yad]]
  ::
        [%face *]
    =+  yad=$(sut q.sut)
    ?^(p.sut yad [p.yad [%face p.sut q.yad]])
  ::
        [%fork *]
    =+  yed=(sort ~(tap in p.sut) aor)
    =-  [p [%bcwt q]]
    |-  ^-  [p=[p=(map type @) q=(map @ wine)] q=(list wine)]
    ?~  yed
      [dex ~]
    =+  mor=$(yed t.yed)
    =+  dis=^$(dex p.mor, sut i.yed)
    [p.dis q.dis q.mor]
  ::
        [%hold *]
    =+  hey=(~(get by p.dex) sut)
    ?^  hey
      [dex [%stop u.hey]]
    ?:  (~(has in gil) sut)
      =+  dyr=+(~(wyt by p.dex))
      [[(~(put by p.dex) sut dyr) q.dex] [%stop dyr]]
    =+  rom=$(gil (~(put in gil) sut), sut ~(repo ut sut))
    =+  rey=(~(get by p.p.rom) sut)
    ?~  rey
      rom
    [[p.p.rom (~(put by q.p.rom) u.rey q.rom)] [%stop u.rey]]
      ==
  ::
  ++  duck  (dial dole)
  --
++  cain  sell                                ::  $-(vase tank)
++  noah  text                                ::  $-(vase tape)
++  onan  seer                                ::  $-(vise vase)
++  levi                                      ::  $-([type type] ?)
  |=  [a=type b=type]
  (~(nest ut a) & b)
::
++  text                                      ::  tape pretty-print
  |=  vax=vase  ^-  tape
  ~(ram re (sell vax))
::
++  seem  |=(toy=typo `type`toy)              ::  promote typo
++  seer  |=(vix=vise `vase`vix)              ::  promote vise
::
::  +sell: pretty-print a vase to a tank using +deal.
::
++  sell
  ~/  %sell
  |=  vax=vase
  ^-  tank
  ~|  %sell
  (~(deal us p.vax) q.vax)
::
```

```
11367  ::    +skol:  $-(type tank) using duck.
11368  ::
11369  ++    skol
11370    |=  typ=type
11371    ^-  tank
11372    ~(duck ut typ)
11373  ::
11374  ++    slam                                    ::  slam a gate
11375    |=  [gat=vase sam=vase]  ^-  vase
11376    =+  :-  ^=  typ  ^-  type
11377            [%cell p.gat p.sam]
11378        ^=  gen  ^-  hoon
11379        [%cnsg [%$ ~] [%$ 2] [%$ 3] ~]
11380    =+  gun=(~(mint ut typ) %noun gen)
11381    [p.gun (slum q.gat q.sam)]
11382  ::
11383  ::    +slab: states whether you can access an arm in a type.
11384  ::
11385  ::        .way: the access type ($vial): read, write, or read-and-write.
11386  ::        The fourth case of $vial, %free, is not permitted because it would
11387  ::        allow you to discover "private" information about a type,
11388  ::        information which you could not make use of in (law-abiding) hoon anyway.
11389  ::
11390  ++    slab                                    ::  test if contains
11391    |=  [way=?(%read %rite %both) cog=@tas typ=type]
11392    ?=  [%& *]
11393    (~(fond ut typ) way ~[cog])
11394  ::
11395  ++    slap
11396    |=  [vax=vase gen=hoon]  ^-  vase          ::  untyped vase .*
11397    =+  gun=(~(mint ut p.vax) %noun gen)
11398    [p.gun .*(q.vax q.gun)]
11399  ::
11400  ++    slog                                    ::  deify printf
11401    =|  pri=@                                  ::  priority level
11402    |=  a=tang  ^+  same                       ::  .=  ~&(%a 1)
11403    ?~(a same ~>(%slog.[pri i.a] $(a t.a)))    ::  ((slog ~[>%a<]) 1)
11404  ::                                            ::
11405  ++    mean                                    ::  crash with trace
11406    |=  a=tang
11407    ^+  !!
11408    ?~  a  !!
11409    ~_(i.a $(a t.a))
11410  ::
11411  ++    road
11412    |*  =(trap *)
11413    ^+  $:trap
11414    =/  res  (mule trap)
11415    ?-  -.res
11416      %&  p.res
11417      %|  (mean p.res)
11418    ==
11419  ::
11420  ++    slew                                    ::  get axis in vase
11421    |=  [axe=@ vax=vase]
11422    =/  typ  |.  (~(peek ut p.vax) %free axe)
11423    |-  ^-  (unit vase)
11424    ?:  =(1 axe)  `[$:typ q.vax]
```

```
11425    ?@  q.vax        ~
11426    $(axe (mas axe), q.vax ?-((cap axe) %2 -.q.vax, %3 +.q.vax))
11427  ::
11428  ++  slim                                        ::  identical to seer?
11429    |=  old=vise  ^-  vase
11430    old
11431  ::
11432  ++  slit                                        ::  type of slam
11433    |=  [gat=type sam=type]
11434    ?>  (~(nest ut (~(peek ut gat) %free 6)) & sam)
11435    (~(play ut [%cell gat sam]) [%cnsg [%$ ~] [%$ 2] [%$ 3] ~])
11436  ::
11437  ++  slob                                        ::  superficial arm
11438    |=  [cog=@tas typ=type]
11439    ^-  ?
11440    ?+  typ  |
11441      [%hold *]  $(typ ~(repo ut typ))
11442      [%hint *]  $(typ ~(repo ut typ))
11443      [%core *]
11444    |-  ^-  ?
11445    ?~  q.r.q.typ  |
11446    ?|  (~(has by q.q.n.q.r.q.typ) cog)
11447        $(q.r.q.typ l.q.r.q.typ)
11448        $(q.r.q.typ r.q.r.q.typ)
11449    ==
11450    ==
11451  ::
11452  ++  sloe                                        ::  get arms in core
11453    |=  typ=type
11454    ^-  (list term)
11455    ?+    typ  ~
11456      [%hold *]  $(typ ~(repo ut typ))
11457      [%hint *]  $(typ ~(repo ut typ))
11458      [%core *]
11459    %-  zing
11460    %+  turn  ~(tap by q.r.q.typ)
11461    |=  [* b=tome]
11462    %+  turn  ~(tap by q.b)
11463    |=  [a=term *]
11464    a
11465    ==
11466  ::
11467  ++  slop                                        ::  cons two vases
11468    |=  [hed=vase tal=vase]
11469    ^-  vase
11470    [[%cell p.hed p.tal] [q.hed q.tal]]
11471  ::
11472  ++  slot                                        ::  got axis in vase
11473    |=  [axe=@ vax=vase]  ^-  vase
11474    [(~(peek ut p.vax) %free axe) .*(q.vax [0 axe])]
11475  ::
11476  ++  slym                                        ::  slam w+o sample-type
11477    |=  [gat=vase sam=*]  ^-  vase
11478    (slap gat(+<.q sam) [%limb %$])
11479  ::
11480  ++  sped                                        ::  reconstruct type
11481    |=  vax=vase
11482    ^-  vase
```

```
11483    :_  q.vax
11484    ?@  q.vax  (~(fuse ut p.vax) [%atom %$ ~])
11485    ?@  -.q.vax
11486      ^=  typ
11487      %-  ~(play ut p.vax)
11488      [%wtgr [%wtts [%leaf %tas -.q.vax] [%& 2]~] [%$ 1]]
11489    (~(fuse ut p.vax) [%cell %noun %noun])
11490  ::  +swat: deferred +slap
11491  ::
11492  ++  swat
11493    |=  [tap=(trap vase) gen=hoon]
11494    ^-  (trap vase)
11495    =/  gun  (~(mint ut p:$:tap) %noun gen)
11496    |.  ~+
11497    [p.gun .*(q:$:tap q.gun)]
11498  ::
11499  ::    5d: parser
11500  +|  %parser
11501  ::
11502  ::    +vang: set +vast params
11503  ::
11504  ::    bug: debug mode
11505  ::    doc: doccord parsing
11506  ::    wer: where we are
11507  ::
11508  ++  vang
11509    |=  [f=$@(? [bug=? doc=?]) wer=path]
11510    %*(. vast bug ?@(f f bug.f), doc ?@(f & doc.f), wer wer)
11511  ::
11512  ++  vast                                         ::  main parsing core
11513    =+  [bug=`?`| wer=*path doc=`?`&]
11514    |%
11515    ++  gash  %+  cook                             ::  parse path
11516              |=  a=(list tyke)  ^-  tyke
11517              ?~(a ~ (weld i.a $(a t.a)))
11518          (more fas limp)
11519    ++  gasp  ;~  pose                             ::  parse =path= etc.
11520              %+  cook
11521              |=([a=tyke b=tyke c=tyke] :(weld a b c))
11522            ;~  plug
11523              (cook |=(a=(list) (turn a |=(b=* ~))) (star tis))
11524              (cook |=(a=hoon [[~ a] ~]) hasp)
11525              (cook |=(a=(list) (turn a |=(b=* ~))) (star tis))
11526            ==
11527              (cook |=(a=(list) (turn a |=(b=* ~))) (plus tis))
11528          ==
11529    ++  glam  ~+((glue ace))
11530    ++  hasp  ;~  pose                             ::  path element
11531            (ifix [sel ser] wide)
11532            (stag %cncl (ifix [pal par] (most ace wide)))
11533            (stag %sand (stag %tas (cold %$ buc)))
11534            (stag %sand (stag %t qut))
11535            %+  cook
11536            |=(a=coin [%sand ?:(?=([~ %tas *] a) %tas %ta) ~(rent co a)])
11537            nuck:so
11538          ==
11539    ++  limp  %+  cook
11540            |=  [a=(list) b=tyke]
```

```
11541                    ?~  a  b
11542                    $(a t.a, b [`[%sand %tas %$] b])
11543                ;~(plug (star fas) gasp)
11544    ++  mota  %+  cook
11545                |=([a=tape b=tape] (rap 3 (weld a b)))
11546                ;~(plug (star low) (star hig))
11547    ++  docs
11548     |%
11549     ::  +apex: prefix comment. may contain batch comments.
11550     ::
11551     ::    when a prefix doccord is parsed, it is possible that there is no +gap
11552     ::    afterward to be consumed, so we add an additional newline and
11553     ::    decrement the line number in the `hair` of the parser
11554     ::
11555     ::    the reason for this is that the whitespace parsing under +vast seems
11556     ::    to factor more cleanly this way, at least compared to the variations
11557     ::    tried without the extra newline. this doesn't mean there isn't a
11558     ::    better factorization without it, though.
11559     ++  apex
11560       ?.  doc  (easy *whit)
11561       %+  knee  *whit  |.  ~+
11562       ;~  plug
11563         |=  tub=nail
11564         =/  vex
11565           %.  tub
11566           %-  star
11567           %+  cook  |*([[a=* b=*] c=*] [a b c])
11568           ;~(pfix (punt leap) into ;~(pose larg smol))
11569         ?~  q.vex  vex
11570         :-  p=p.vex
11571         %-  some
11572         ?~  p.u.q.vex
11573           [p=~ q=q.u.q.vex]
11574         :-  p=(malt p.u.q.vex)
11575         q=`nail`[[(dec p.p.q.u.q.vex) q.p.q.u.q.vex] ['\0a' q.q.u.q.vex]]
11576       ==
11577     ::
11578     ::  +apse: postfix comment.
11579     ::
11580     ::    a one line comment at the end of a line (typically starting at column
11581     ::    57) that attaches to the expression starting at the beginning of the
11582     ::    current line. does not use a $link.
11583     ++  apse
11584       ?.  doc  (easy *whiz)
11585       %+  knee  *whiz  |.  ~+
11586       ;~  pose
11587         ;~(less ;~(plug into step en-link col ace) ;~(pfix into step line))
11588         ::
11589         (easy *whiz)
11590       ==
11591     ::
11592     ++  leap                                          :: whitespace w/o docs
11593       %+  cold  ~
11594       ;~  plug
11595         ;~  pose
11596         (just '\0a')
11597         ;~(plug gah ;~(pose gah skip))
11598         skip
```

```
11599        ==
11600      (star ;~(pose skip gah))
11601    ==
11602  ::
11603  ::  +smol: 2 aces then summary, 4 aces then paragraphs.
11604  ++  smol
11605    ;~  pfix
11606      step
11607      ;~  plug
11608        ;~  plug
11609        (plus en-link)
11610          ;~  pose
11611          (ifix [;~(plug col ace) (just '\0a')] (cook crip (plus prn)))
11612          (ifix [(star ace) (just '\0a')] (easy *cord))
11613          ==
11614        ==
11615      (rant ;~(pfix step step text))
11616      ==
11617    ==
11618  ::
11619  ::  +larg: 4 aces then summary, 2 aces then paragraphs.
11620  ++  larg
11621    ;~  pfix
11622      step  step
11623      ;~  plug
11624        ;~  sfix
11625          ;~  plug
11626            ;~  pose
11627            ;~(sfix (plus en-link) col ace)
11628            ;~(less ace (easy *cuff))
11629            ==
11630          ;~(less ace (cook crip (plus prn)))
11631          ==
11632        (just '\0a')
11633        ==
11634      (rant ;~(pfix step teyt))
11635      ==
11636    ==
11637  ::
11638  ++  rant
11639    |*  sec=rule
11640    %-  star
11641    ;~  pfix
11642    (ifix [into (just '\0a')] (star ace))
11643    (plus (ifix [into (just '\0a')] sec))
11644    ==
11645  ::
11646  ++  skip                                          ::  non-doccord comment
11647    ;~  plug
11648      col  col
11649      ;~(less ;~(pose larg smol) ;~(plug (star prn) (just '\0a')))
11650      ==
11651  ::
11652  ++  null  (cold ~ (star ace))
11653  ++  text  (pick line code)
11654  ++  teyt  (pick line ;~(pfix step code))
11655  ++  line  ;~(less ace (cook crip (star prn)))
11656  ++  code  ;~(pfix step ;~(less ace (cook crip (star prn))))
```

```
11657      ++  step  ;~(plug ace ace)
11658      ::
11659      ++  into
11660        ;~(plug (star ace) col col)
11661      ::
11662      ++  en-link
11663        |=  a=nail  %.  a
11664        %+  knee  *link  |.  ~+
11665        %-  stew
11666        ^.  stet  ^.  limo
11667        :~  :-  '|'  ;~(pfix bar (stag %chat sym))
11668            :-  '.'  ;~(pfix dot (stag %frag sym))
11669            :-  '+'  ;~(pfix lus (stag %funk sym))
11670            :-  '$'  ;~(pfix buc (stag %plan sym))
11671            :-  '%'  ;~(pfix cen (stag %cone bisk:so))
11672        ==
11673      --
11674    ::
11675    ++  clad                                      ::  hoon doccords
11676      |*  fel=rule
11677      %+  cook
11678        |=  [a=whit b=hoon c=whiz]
11679        =?  b  !=(c *whiz)
11680          [%note help/`[c]~ b]
11681        =+  docs=~(tap by bat.a)
11682        |-
11683        ?~  docs  b
11684        $(docs t.docs, b [%note help/i.docs b])
11685      (seam fel)
11686    ++  coat                                      ::  spec doccords
11687      |*  fel=rule
11688      %+  cook
11689        |=  [a=whit b=spec c=whiz]
11690        =?  b  !=(c *whiz)
11691          [%gist help/`[c]~ b]
11692        =+  docs=~(tap by bat.a)
11693        |-
11694        ?~  docs  b
11695        $(docs t.docs, b [%gist help/i.docs b])
11696      (seam fel)
11697    ++  scye                                      ::  with prefix doccords
11698      |*  fel=rule
11699      ;~(pose ;~(plug apex:docs ;~(pfix gap fel)) ;~(plug (easy *whit) fel))
11700    ++  seam                                      ::  with doccords
11701      |*  fel=rule
11702      (scye ;~(plug fel apse:docs))
11703    ::
11704    ++  plex                                      ::  reparse static path
11705      |=  gen=hoon  ^-  (unit path)
11706      ?:  ?=([%dbug *] gen)                        ::  unwrap %dbug
11707        $(gen q.gen)
11708      ?.  ?=([%clsg *] gen)  ~                     ::  require :~ hoon
11709      %+  reel  p.gen                              ::  build using elements
11710      |=  [a=hoon b=_`(unit path)`[~ u=/]]          ::  starting from just /
11711      ?~  b  ~
11712      ?.  ?=([%sand ?(%ta %tas) @] a)  ~            ::  /foo constants
11713      `[q.a u.b]
11714    ::
```

```
++  phax
  |=  ruw=(list (list woof))
  =+  [yun=*(list hoon) cah=*(list @)]
  =+  wod=|=([a=tape b=(list hoon)] ^+(b ?~(a b [[%mcfs %knit (flop a)] b])))
  |-  ^+  yun
  ?~  ruw
    (flop (wod cah yun))
  ?~  i.ruw  $(ruw t.ruw)
  ?@  i.i.ruw
    $(i.ruw t.i.ruw, cah [i.i.ruw cah])
  $(i.ruw t.i.ruw, cah ~, yun [p.i.i.ruw (wod cah yun)])
::
++  posh
  |=  [pre=(unit tyke) pof=(unit [p=@ud q=tyke])]
  ^-  (unit (list hoon))
  =-  ?^(- - ~&(%posh-fail -))
  =+  wom=(poof wer)
  %+  biff
    ?~  pre  `u=wom
    %+  bind  (poon wom u.pre)
    |=  moz=(list hoon)
    ?~(pof moz (weld moz (slag (lent u.pre) wom)))
  |=  yez=(list hoon)
  ?~  pof  `yez
  =+  zey=(flop yez)
  =+  [moz=(scag p.u.pof zey) gul=(slag p.u.pof zey)]
  =+  zom=(poon (flop moz) q.u.pof)
  ?~(zom ~ `(weld (flop gul) u.zom))
::
++  poof                                          :: path -> (list hoon)
  |=(pax=path ^-((list hoon) (turn pax |=(a=@ta [%sand %ta a]))))
::
:: tyke is =foo== as ~[~ `foo ~ ~]
:: interpolate '=' path components
++  poon                                          :: try to replace '='s
  |=  [pag=(list hoon) goo=tyke]                   ::   default to pag
  ^-  (unit (list hoon))                           ::   for null goo's
  ?~  goo  `~                                      :: keep empty goo
  %+  both                                         :: otherwise head comes
    ?^(i.goo i.goo ?~(pag ~ `u=i.pag))             ::   from goo or pag
  $(goo t.goo, pag ?~(pag ~ t.pag))                :: recurse on tails
::
++  poor
  %+  sear  posh
  ;~  plug
    (stag ~ gash)
    ;~(pose (stag ~ ;~(pfix cen porc)) (easy ~))
  ==
::
++  porc
  ;~  plug
    (cook |=(a=(list) (lent a)) (star cen))
    ;~(pfix fas gash)
  ==
::
++  rump
  %+  sear
    |=  [a=wing b=(unit hoon)]  ^-  (unit hoon)
```

```
11773      ?~(b [~ %wing a] ?.(?=([@ ~] a) ~ [~ [%rock %tas i.a] u.b]))
11774      ;~(plug rope ;~(pose (stag ~ wede) (easy ~)))
11775  ::
11776  ++  rood
11777    ;~  pfix  fas
11778      (stag %clsg poor)
11779    ==
11780  ::
11781  ++  reed
11782    ;~  pfix  fas
11783      (stag %clsg (more fas stem))
11784    ==
11785  ::
11786  ++  stem
11787    %+  knee  *hoon  |.  ~+
11788    %+  cook
11789      |=  iota=$%([%hoon =hoon] iota)
11790      ?@  iota  [%rock %tas iota]
11791      ?:  ?=(%hoon -.iota)  hoon.iota
11792      [%clhp [%rock %tas -.iota] [%sand iota]]
11793    |^  %-  stew
11794    ^.  stet  ^.  limo
11795    :~  :-  'a'^'z'  ;~  pose
11796                    (spit (stag %cncl (ifix [pal par] (most ace wide))))
11797                    (spit (ifix [sel ser] wide))
11798                    (slot sym)
11799                    ==
11800      :-  '$'      (cold %$ buc)
11801      :-  '0'^'9'  (slot bisk:so)
11802      :-  '-'      (slot tash:so)
11803      :-  '.'      ;~(pfix dot zust:so)
11804      :-  '~'      (slot ;~(pfix sig ;~(pose crub:so (easy [%n ~]))))
11805      :-  '\''     (stag %t qut)
11806      :-  '['      (slip (ifix [sel ser] wide))
11807      :-  '('      (slip (stag %cncl (ifix [pal par] (most ace wide))))
11808      ==
11809    ::
11810    ++  slip  |*(r=rule (stag %hoon r))
11811    ++  slot  |*(r=rule (sear (soft iota) r))
11812    ++  spit
11813    |*  r=rule
11814    %+  stag  %hoon
11815    %+  cook
11816      |*([a=term b=*] `hoon`[%clhp [%rock %tas a] b])
11817    ;~((glue lus) sym r)
11818    --
11819  ::
11820  ++  rupl
11821    %+  cook
11822      |=  [a=? b=(list hoon) c=?]
11823      ?:  a
11824        ?:  c
11825          [%clsg [%clsg b] ~]
11826        [%clsg b]
11827      ?:  c
11828        [%clsg [%cltr b] ~]
11829      [%cltr b]
11830    ;~  plug
```

```
11831      ;~  pose
11832      (cold | (just '['))
11833      (cold & (jest '~['))
11834    ==
11835  ::
11836    ;~  pose
11837    (ifix [ace gap] (most gap tall))
11838    (most ace wide)
11839    ==
11840  ::
11841    ;~  pose
11842    (cold & (jest ']~'))
11843    (cold | (just ']'))
11844    ==
11845  ==
11846  ::
11847  ::
11848  ++  sail                                  ::  xml template
11849  |=  in-tall-form=?  =|  lin=?
11850  |%
11851  ::
11852  ++  apex                                  ::  product hoon
11853    %+  cook
11854    |=  tum=(each manx:hoot marl:hoot)  ^-  hoon
11855    ?-  -.tum
11856      %&  [%xray p.tum]
11857      %|  [%mcts p.tum]
11858    ==
11859    top-level
11860  ::
11861  ++  top-level                             ::  entry-point
11862    ;~(pfix mic ?:(in-tall-form tall-top wide-top))
11863  ::
11864  ++  inline-embed                          ::  brace interpolation
11865    %+  cook  |=(a=tuna:hoot a)
11866    ;~  pose
11867      ;~(pfix mic bracketed-elem(in-tall-form |))
11868      ;~(plug tuna-mode sump)
11869      (stag %tape sump)
11870    ==
11871  ::
11872  ++  script-or-style                       ::  script or style
11873    %+  cook  |=(a=marx:hoot a)
11874    ;~  plug
11875      ;~(pose (jest %script) (jest %style))
11876      wide-attrs
11877    ==
11878  ::
11879  ++  tuna-mode                             ::  xml node(s) kind
11880    ;~  pose
11881      (cold %tape hep)
11882      (cold %manx lus)
11883      (cold %marl tar)
11884      (cold %call cen)
11885    ==
11886  ::
11887  ++  wide-top                              ::  wide outer top
11888    %+  knee  *(each manx:hoot marl:hoot)  |.  ~+
```

```
11889      ;~  pose
11890        (stag %| wide-quote)
11891        (stag %| wide-paren-elems)
11892        (stag %& ;~(plug tag-head wide-tail))
11893      ==
11894    ::
11895    ++  wide-inner-top                            ::  wide inner top
11896      %+  knee  *(each tuna:hoot marl:hoot)  |.  ~+
11897      ;~  pose
11898        wide-top
11899        (stag %& ;~(plug tuna-mode wide))
11900      ==
11901    ::
11902    ++  wide-attrs                                ::  wide attributes
11903      %+  cook  |=(a=(unit mart:hoot) (fall a ~))
11904      %-  punt
11905      %+  ifix  [pal par]
11906      %+  more  (jest ', ')
11907      ;~((glue ace) a-mane hopefully-quote)
11908    ::
11909    ++  wide-tail                                 ::  wide elements
11910      %+  cook  |=(a=marl:hoot a)
11911      ;~(pose ;~(pfix col wrapped-elems) (cold ~ mic) (easy ~))
11912    ::
11913    ++  wide-elems                                ::  wide elements
11914      %+  cook  |=(a=marl:hoot a)
11915      %+  cook  join-tops
11916      (star ;~(pfix ace wide-inner-top))
11917    ::
11918    ++  wide-paren-elems                          ::  wide flow
11919      %+  cook  |=(a=marl:hoot a)
11920      %+  cook  join-tops
11921      (ifix [pal par] (more ace wide-inner-top))
11922    ::
11923    ::+|
11924    ::
11925    ++  drop-top
11926      |=  a=(each tuna:hoot marl:hoot)  ^-  marl:hoot
11927      ?-  -.a
11928        %&  [p.a]~
11929        %|  p.a
11930      ==
11931    ::
11932    ++  join-tops
11933      |=  a=(list (each tuna:hoot marl:hoot))  ^-  marl:hoot
11934      (zing (turn a drop-top))
11935    ::
11936    ::+|
11937    ::
11938    ++  wide-quote                                ::  wide quote
11939      %+  cook  |=(a=marl:hoot a)
11940      ;~  pose
11941        ;~  less  (jest '"""')
11942          (ifix [doq doq] (cook collapse-chars quote-innards))
11943        ==
11944      ::
11945        %-  inde
11946        %+  ifix  [(jest '"""\0a') (jest '\0a"""')]
```

```
        (cook collapse-chars quote-innards(lin |))
      ==
    ::
++  quote-innards                               ::    wide+tall flow
  %+  cook   |=(a=(list $@(@ tuna:hoot)) a)
  %-  star
  ;~  pose
    ;~(pfix bas ;~(pose (mask "-+*%;\{") bas doq bix:ab))
    inline-embed
    ;~(less bas kel ?:(in-tall-form fail doq) prn)
    ?:(lin fail ;~(less (jest '\0a"""') (just '\0a')))
  ==
  ::
++  bracketed-elem                              ::    bracketed element
  %+  ifix  [kel ker]
  ;~(plug tag-head wide-elems)
  ::
++  wrapped-elems                               ::    wrapped tuna
  %+  cook   |=(a=marl:hoot a)
  ;~  pose
    wide-paren-elems
    (cook |=(@t `marl`[;/((trip +<))]~) qut)
    (cook drop-top wide-top)
  ==
  ::
++  a-mane                                      ::    mane as hoon
  %+  cook
    |=  [a=@tas b=(unit @tas)]
    ?~(b a [a u.b])
  ;~  plug
    mixed-case-symbol
    ;~  pose
      %+  stag  ~
        ;~(pfix cab mixed-case-symbol)
      (easy ~)
    ==
  ==
  ::
++  en-class
  |=  a=(list [%class p=term])
  ^-  (unit [%class tape])
  ?~  a  ~
  %-  some
  :-  %class
  |-
  %+  welp  (trip p.i.a)
  ?~  t.a  ~
  [' ' $(a t.a)]
  ::
++  tag-head                                    ::    tag head
  %+  cook
    |=  [a=mane:hoot b=mart:hoot c=mart:hoot]
    ^-  marx:hoot
    [a (weld b c)]
  ;~  plug
    a-mane
    ::
      %+  cook
```

```
|=  a=(list (unit [term (list beer:hoot)]))
^-  (list [term (list beer:hoot)])
:: discard nulls
(murn a same)
;~  plug
(punt ;~(plug (cold %id hax) (cook trip sym)))
(cook en-class (star ;~(plug (cold %class dot) sym)))
(punt ;~(plug ;~(pose (cold %href fas) (cold %src pat)) soil))
(easy ~)
==
::
wide-attrs
==
::
++  tall-top                                      ::  tall top
%+  knee  *(each manx:hoot marl:hoot)  |.  ~+
;~  pose
(stag %|  ;~(pfix (plus ace) (cook collapse-chars quote-innards)))
(stag %&  ;~(plug script-or-style script-style-tail))
(stag %&  tall-elem)
(stag %|  wide-quote)
(stag %|  ;~(pfix tis tall-tail))
(stag %&  ;~(pfix gar gap (stag [%div ~] cram)))
(stag %|  ;~(plug ;~((glue gap) tuna-mode tall) (easy ~)))
(easy %|  [;/("\0a")]~)
==
::
++  tall-attrs                                    ::  tall attributes
%-  star
;~  pfix  ;~(plug gap tis)
;~((glue gap) a-mane hopefully-quote)
==
::
++  tall-elem                                     ::  tall preface
%+  cook
|=  [a=[p=mane:hoot q=mart:hoot] b=mart:hoot c=marl:hoot]
^-  manx:hoot
[[p.a (weld q.a b)] c]
;~(plug tag-head tall-attrs tall-tail)
::
::REVIEW is there a better way to do this?
++  hopefully-quote                               ::  prefer "quote" form
%+  cook  |=(a=(list beer:hoot) a)
%+  cook  |=(a=hoon ?:(?=(%knit -.a) p.a [~ a]~))
wide
::
++  script-style-tail                             ::  unescaped tall tail
%+  cook  |=(a=marl:hoot a)
%+  ifix  [gap ;~(plug gap duz)]
%+  most  gap
;~  pfix  mic
%+  cook  |=(a=tape ;/(a))
;~  pose
;~(pfix ace (star prn))
(easy "\0a")
==
==
==
::
```

```
12063     ++  tall-tail                                   ::  tall tail
12064       ?>  in-tall-form
12065       %+  cook  |=(a=marl:hoot a)
12066       ;~  pose
12067         (cold ~ mic)
12068         ;~(pfix col wrapped-elems(in-tall-form |))
12069         ;~(pfix col ace (cook collapse-chars(in-tall-form |) quote-innards))
12070         (ifix [gap ;~(plug gap duz)] tall-kids)
12071       ==
12072     ::
12073     ++  tall-kids                                   ::  child elements
12074       %+  cook  join-tops
12075       ::  look for sail first, or markdown if not
12076       (most gap ;~(pose top-level (stag %| cram)))
12077     ::
12078     ++  collapse-chars                              ::  group consec chars
12079       |=  reb=(list $@(@ tuna:hoot))
12080       ^-  marl:hoot
12081       =|  [sim=(list @) tuz=marl:hoot]
12082       |-  ^-  marl:hoot
12083       ?~  reb
12084         =.  sim
12085           ?.  in-tall-form    sim
12086           [10 |-(?~(sim sim ?:(=(32 i.sim) $(sim t.sim) sim)))]
12087         ?~(sim tuz [;/((flop sim)) tuz])
12088       ?@  i.reb
12089         $(reb t.reb, sim [i.reb sim])
12090       ?~  sim  [i.reb $(reb t.reb, sim ~)]
12091       [;/((flop sim)) i.reb $(reb t.reb, sim ~)]
12092     --
12093   ++  cram                                         ::  parse unmark
12094     =>  |%
12095         ++  item  (pair mite marl:hoot)            ::  xml node generator
12096         ++  colm  @ud                              ::  column
12097         ++  tarp  marl:hoot                        ::  node or generator
12098         ++  mite                                   ::  context
12099           $?  %down                                ::  outer embed
12100               %lunt                                ::  unordered list
12101               %lime                                ::  list item
12102               %lord                                ::  ordered list
12103               %poem                                ::  verse
12104               %bloc                                ::  blockquote
12105               %head                                ::  heading
12106           ==                                       ::
12107         ++  trig                                    ::  line style
12108           $:  col=@ud                              ::  start column
12109              sty=trig-style                       ::  style
12110          ==                                       ::
12111         ++  trig-style                             ::  type of parsed line
12112           $%  $:  %end                             ::  terminator
12113               $?  %done                            ::  end of input
12114                   %stet                            ::    == end of markdown
12115                   %dent                            ::    outdent
12116              ==  ==                                ::
12117              $:  %one                              ::  leaf node
12118              $?  %rule                             ::    --- horz rule
12119                  %fens                             ::    ``` code fence
12120                  %expr                             ::    ;sail expression
```

```
12121            ==   ==                                        ::
12122            [%new p=trig-new]                              ::  open container
12123            [%old %text]                                   ::  anything else
12124         ==                                                ::
12125      ++  trig-new                                         ::  start a
12126        $?  %lite                                          ::    + line item
12127            %lint                                          ::    - line item
12128            %head                                          ::  # heading
12129            %bloc                                          ::  > block-quote
12130            %poem                                          ::    [ ]{8} poem
12131        ==                                                 ::
12132      ++  graf                                             ::  paragraph element
12133        $%  [%bold p=(list graf)]                          ::  *bold*
12134            [%talc p=(list graf)]                          ::  _italics_
12135            [%quod p=(list graf)]                          ::  "double quote"
12136            [%code p=tape]                                 ::  code literal
12137            [%text p=tape]                                 ::  text symbol
12138            [%link p=(list graf) q=tape]                   ::  URL
12139            [%mage p=tape q=tape]                          ::  image
12140            [%expr p=tuna:hoot]                            ::  interpolated hoon
12141        ==
12142      --
12143    =<  (non-empty:parse |=(nail `(like tarp)`~($ main +<)))
12144    |%
12145    ++  main
12146      ::
12147      ::    state of the parsing loop.
12148      ::
12149      ::  we maintain a construction stack for elements and a line
12150      ::  stack for lines in the current block.  a blank line
12151      ::  causes the current block to be parsed and thrown in the
12152      ::  current element.  when the indent column retreats, the
12153      ::  element stack rolls up.
12154      ::
12155      ::  .verbose: debug printing enabled
12156      ::  .err: error position
12157      ::  .ind: outer and inner indent level
12158      ::  .hac: stack of items under construction
12159      ::  .cur: current item under construction
12160      ::  .par: current "paragraph" being read in
12161      ::  .[loc txt]: parsing state
12162      ::
12163      =/  verbose  &
12164      =|  err=(unit hair)
12165      =|  ind=[out=@ud inr=@ud]
12166      =|  hac=(list item)
12167      =/  cur=item  [%down ~]
12168      =|  par=(unit (pair hair wall))
12169      |_  [loc=hair txt=tape]
12170      ::
12171      ++  $                                         ::  resolve
12172        ^-  (like tarp)
12173        =>  line
12174        ::
12175        ::  if error position is set, produce error
12176        ?.  =(~ err)
12177          ~&  err+err
12178          [+.err ~]
```

```
12179      ::
12180      ::  all data was consumed
12181      =-  [loc `[- [loc txt]]]
12182      =>  close-par
12183      |-  ^-  tarp
12184      ::
12185      ::  fold all the way to top
12186      ?~  hac  cur-to-tarp
12187      $(..^$ close-item)
12188    ::
12189    ::+|
12190    ::
12191    ++  cur-indent
12192      ?-  p.cur
12193        %down  2
12194        %head  0
12195        %lunt  0
12196        %lime  2
12197        %lord  0
12198        %poem  8
12199        %bloc  2
12200      ==
12201    ::
12202    ++  back                                    ::  column retreat
12203      |=  luc=@ud
12204      ^+  +>
12205      ?:  (gte luc inr.ind)  +>
12206      ::
12207      ::  nex: next backward step that terminates this context
12208      =/  nex=@ud  cur-indent  ::  REVIEW code and poem blocks are
12209                               ::  handled elsewhere
12210      ?:  (gth nex (sub inr.ind luc))
12211        ::
12212        ::  indenting pattern violation
12213        ~?  verbose  indent-pattern-violation+[p.cur nex inr.ind luc]
12214        ..^$(inr.ind luc, err `[p.loc luc])
12215      =.  ..^$  close-item
12216      $(inr.ind (sub inr.ind nex))
12217    ::
12218    ++  cur-to-tarp                             ::  item to tarp
12219      ^-  tarp
12220      ?:  ?=(?(%down %head %expr) p.cur)
12221        (flop q.cur)
12222      =-  [[- ~] (flop q.cur)]~
12223      ?-  p.cur
12224        %lunt  %ul
12225        %lord  %ol
12226        %lime  %li
12227        %poem  %div ::REVIEW actual container element?
12228        %bloc  %blockquote
12229      ==
12230    ::
12231    ++  close-item  ^+  .                        ::  complete and pop
12232      ?~  hac  .
12233      %=  .
12234        hac  t.hac
12235        cur  [p.i.hac (weld cur-to-tarp q.i.hac)]
12236      ==
```

```
      ::
      ++  read-line                                  ::  capture raw line
        =|  lin=tape
        |-  ^+  [[lin *(unit _err)] +<.^$]  ::  parsed tape and halt/error
        ::
        ::  no unterminated lines
        ?~  txt
          ~?  verbose  %unterminated-line
          [[~ ``loc] +<.^$]
        ?.  =(`@`10 i.txt)
          ?:  (gth inr.ind q.loc)
            ?.  =(' ' i.txt)
              ~?  verbose  expected-indent+[inr.ind loc txt]
              [[~ ``loc] +<.^$]
            $(txt t.txt, q.loc +(q.loc))
          ::
          ::  save byte and repeat
          $(txt t.txt, q.loc +(q.loc), lin [i.txt lin])
        =.  lin
        ::
        ::  trim trailing spaces
        |-  ^-  tape
          ?:  ?=([%' ' *] lin)
            $(lin t.lin)
          (flop lin)
        ::
        =/  eat-newline=nail  [[+(p.loc) 1] t.txt]
        =/  saw  look(+<.$ eat-newline)
        ::
        ?:  ?=([~ @ %end ?(%stet %dent)] saw)             ::  stop on == or dedent
          [[lin `~] +<.^$]
        [[lin ~] eat-newline]
      ::
      ++  look                                        ::  inspect line
        ^-  (unit trig)
        %+  bind  (wonk (look:parse loc txt))
        |=  a=trig  ^+  a
        ::
        ::  treat a non-terminator as a terminator
        ::  if it's outdented
        ?:  =(%end -.sty.a)  a
        ?:  (lth col.a out.ind)
          a(sty [%end %dent])
        a
      ::
      ++  close-par                                   ::  make block
        ^+  .
        ::
        ::  empty block, no action
        ?~  par  .
        ::
        ::  if block is verse
        ?:  ?=(%poem p.cur)
          ::
          ::  add break between stanzas
          =.  q.cur  ?~(q.cur q.cur [[[%br ~] ~] q.cur])
          =-  close-item(par ~, q.cur (weld - q.cur), inr.ind (sub inr.ind 8))
          %+  turn  q.u.par
```

```
12295       |=  tape  ^-  manx
12296       ::
12297       ::  each line is a paragraph
12298       :-  [%p ~]
12299       :_  ~
12300       ;/("{+<}\0a")
12301     ::
12302     ::  yex: block recomposed, with newlines
12303     =/  yex=tape
12304       %-  zing
12305       %+  turn  (flop q.u.par)
12306       |=  a=tape
12307       (runt [(dec inr.ind) ' '] "{a}\0a")
12308     ::
12309     ::  vex: parse of paragraph
12310     =/  vex=(like tarp)
12311       ::
12312       ::  either a one-line header or a paragraph
12313       %.  [p.u.par yex]
12314       ?:  ?=(%head p.cur)
12315        (full head:parse)
12316       (full para:parse)
12317     ::
12318     ::  if error, propagate correctly
12319     ?~  q.vex
12320      ~?  verbose  [%close-par p.cur yex]
12321      ..$(err `p.vex)
12322     ::
12323     ::  finish tag if it's a header
12324     =<  ?:(?=(%head p.cur) close-item ..$)
12325     ::
12326     ::  save good result, clear buffer
12327     ..$(par ~, q.cur (weld p.u.q.vex q.cur))
12328   ::
12329   ++  line  ^+  .                                ::  body line loop
12330     ::
12331     ::  abort after first error
12332     ?:  !=(~ err)  .
12333     ::
12334     ::  saw: profile of this line
12335     =/  saw  look
12336     ~?  [debug=|]  [%look ind=ind saw=saw txt=txt]
12337     ::
12338     ::  if line is blank
12339     ?~  saw
12340       ::
12341       ::  break section
12342       =^  a=[tape fin=(unit _err)]  +<.$  read-line
12343       ?^  fin.a
12344        ..$(err u.fin.a)
12345       =>(close-par line)
12346     ::
12347     ::  line is not blank
12348     =>  .(saw u.saw)
12349     ::
12350     ::  if end of input, complete
12351     ?:  ?=(%end -.sty.saw)
12352      ..$(q.loc col.saw)
```

```
12353              ::
12354              =.  ind  ?~(out.ind [col.saw col.saw] ind)        ::  init indents
12355              ::
12356              ?:  ?|  ?=(~ par)                              ::  if after a paragraph or
12357                      ?&  ?=(?(%down %lime %bloc) p.cur)  ::  unspaced new container
12358                          |(!=(%old -.sty.saw) (gth col.saw inr.ind))
12359                  ==  ==
12360                => .(..$ close-par)
12361                  ::
12362                ::  if column has retreated, adjust stack
12363                =.  ..$  (back col.saw)
12364                  ::
12365                =^  col-ok  sty.saw
12366                  ?+  (sub col.saw inr.ind)  [| sty.saw]       ::  columns advanced
12367                    %0  [& sty.saw]
12368                    %8  [& %new %poem]
12369                  ==
12370                ?.  col-ok
12371                  ~?  verbose  [%columns-advanced col.saw inr.ind]
12372                  ..$(err `[p.loc col.saw])
12373              ::
12374                =.  inr.ind  col.saw
12375          ::
12376                ::  unless adding a matching item, close lists
12377                =.  ..$
12378                  ?:  ?|  &(?=(%lunt p.cur) !?=(%lint +.sty.saw))
12379                          &(?=(%lord p.cur) !?=(%lite +.sty.saw))
12380                      ==
12381                    close-item
12382                  ..$
12383              ::
12384                =<  line(par `[loc ~])  ^+  ..$             ::  continue with para
12385                ?-    -.sty.saw
12386                  %one  (read-one +.sty.saw)               ::  parse leaves
12387                  %new  (open-item p.sty.saw)              ::  open containers
12388                  %old  ..$                                ::  just text
12389                ==
12390              ::
12391              ::
12392              ::- - - foo
12393              ::  detect bad block structure
12394              ?.  ::  first line of container is legal
12395                  ?~  q.u.par  &
12396                  ?-  p.cur
12397              ::
12398                  ::  can't(/directly) contain text
12399                    ?(%lord %lunt)  ~|(bad-leaf-container+p.cur !!)
12400              ::
12401                  ::  only one line in a header
12402                    %head  |
12403                ::
12404                  ::  indented literals need to end with a blank line
12405                    %poem  (gte col.saw inr.ind)
12406                ::
12407                  ::  text tarps must continue aligned
12408                    ?(%down %lunt %lime %lord %bloc)  =(col.saw inr.ind)
12409                  ==
12410                ~?  verbose  bad-block-structure+[p.cur inr.ind col.saw]
```

```
12411        ..$(err `[p.loc col.saw])
12412      ::
12413      ::  accept line and maybe continue
12414      =^  a=[lin=tape fin=(unit _err)]  +<.$  read-line
12415      =.  par  par(q.u [lin.a q.u.par])
12416      ?^  fin.a  ..$(err u.fin.a)
12417      line
12418    ++  parse-block                           ::  execute parser
12419      |=  fel=$-(nail (like tarp))  ^+  +>
12420      =/  vex=(like tarp)  (fel loc txt)
12421      ?~  q.vex
12422        ~?  verbose  [%parse-block txt]
12423        +>.$(err `p.vex)
12424      =+  [res loc txt]=u.q.vex
12425      %_  +>.$
12426        loc  loc
12427        txt  txt
12428        q.cur  (weld (flop `tarp`res) q.cur)   ::  prepend to the stack
12429      ==
12430    ::
12431    ++  read-one                              ::  read %one item
12432      |=  sty=?(%expr %rule %fens)  ^+  +>
12433      ?-  sty
12434        %expr  (parse-block expr:parse)
12435        %rule  (parse-block hrul:parse)
12436        %fens  (parse-block (fens:parse inr.ind))
12437      ==
12438    ::
12439    ++  open-item                             ::  enter list/quote
12440      |=  saw=trig-new
12441      =<  +>.$:apex
12442      |%
12443      ++  apex  ^+  .                         ::  open container
12444        ?-  saw
12445          %poem  (push %poem)                 ::  verse literal
12446          %head  (push %head)                 ::  heading
12447          %bloc  (entr %bloc)                 ::  blockquote line
12448          %lint  (lent %lunt)                 ::  unordered list
12449          %lite  (lent %lord)                 ::  ordered list
12450        ==
12451      ::
12452      ++  push                                ::  push context
12453        |=(mite +>(hac [cur hac], cur [+< ~]))
12454      ::
12455      ++  entr                                ::  enter container
12456        |=  typ=mite
12457        ^+  +>
12458        ::
12459        ::  indent by 2
12460        =.  inr.ind  (add 2 inr.ind)
12461        ::
12462        ::  "parse" marker
12463        =.  txt  (slag (sub inr.ind q.loc) txt)
12464        =.  q.loc  inr.ind
12465        ::
12466        (push typ)
12467      ::
12468      ++  lent                                ::  list entry
```

```
12469          |=  ord=?(%lord %lunt)
12470          ^+  +>
12471          =>  ?:(=(ord p.cur) +>.$ (push ord))          ::  push list if new
12472          (entr %lime)
12473        --
12474      --
12475    ::
12476    ++  parse                                           ::  individual parsers
12477      |%
12478      ++  look                                          ::  classify line
12479        %+  cook  |=(a=(unit trig) a)
12480        ;~  pfix  (star ace)
12481          %+  here                                      ::  report indent
12482          |=([a=pint b=?(~ trig-style)] ?~(b ~ `[q.p.a b]))
12483          ;~  pose
12484            (cold ~ (just `@`10))                       ::  blank line
12485          ::
12486            (full (easy [%end %done]))                  ::  end of input
12487            (cold [%end %stet] duz)                     ::  == end of markdown
12488          ::
12489            (cold [%one %rule] ;~(plug hep hep hep))    ::  --- horizontal ruler
12490            (cold [%one %fens] ;~(plug tic tic tic))    ::  ``` code fence
12491            (cold [%one %expr] mic)                     ::  ;sail expression
12492          ::
12493            (cold [%new %head] ;~(plug (star hax) ace)) ::  # heading
12494            (cold [%new %lint] ;~(plug hep ace))        ::  - line item
12495            (cold [%new %lite] ;~(plug lus ace))        ::  + line item
12496            (cold [%new %bloc] ;~(plug gar ace))        ::  > block-quote
12497          ::
12498            (easy [%old %text])                         ::  anything else
12499          ==
12500        ==
12501      ::
12502      ::
12503      ++  calf                                           ::  cash but for tic tic
12504        |*  tem=rule
12505        %-  star
12506        ;~  pose
12507          ;~(pfix bas tem)
12508          ;~(less tem prn)
12509        ==
12510      ++  cash                                           ::  escaped fence
12511        |*  tem=rule
12512        %-  echo
12513        %-  star
12514        ;~  pose
12515          whit
12516          ;~(plug bas tem)
12517          ;~(less tem prn)
12518        ==
12519      ::
12520      ++  cool                                           ::  reparse
12521        |*  $:  ::  fex: primary parser
12522                ::  sab: secondary parser
12523                ::
12524                fex=rule
12525                sab=rule
12526            ==
```

```
12527       |=  [loc=hair txt=tape]
12528       ^+  *sab
12529       ::
12530       ::  vex: fenced span
12531       =/  vex=(like tape)  (fex loc txt)
12532       ?~  q.vex  vex
12533       ::
12534       ::  hav: reparse full fenced text
12535       =/  hav  ((full sab) [loc p.u.q.vex])
12536       ::
12537       ::  reparsed error position is always at start
12538       ?~  q.hav  [loc ~]
12539       ::
12540       ::  the complete type with the main product
12541       :-  p.vex
12542       `[p.u.q.hav q.u.q.vex]
12543     ::
12544     ::REVIEW surely there is a less hacky "first or after space" solution
12545     ++  easy-sol                                 ::  parse start of line
12546       |*  a=*
12547       |=  b=nail
12548       ?:  =(1 q.p.b)  ((easy a) b)
12549       (fail b)
12550     ::
12551     ++  echo                                     ::  hoon literal
12552       |*  sab=rule
12553       |=  [loc=hair txt=tape]
12554       ^-  (like tape)
12555       ::
12556       ::  vex: result of parsing wide hoon
12557       =/  vex  (sab loc txt)
12558       ::
12559       ::  use result of expression parser
12560       ?~  q.vex  vex
12561       =-  [p.vex `[- q.u.q.vex]]
12562       ::
12563       ::  but replace payload with bytes consumed
12564       |-  ^-  tape
12565       ?:  =(q.q.u.q.vex txt)  ~
12566       ?~  txt  ~
12567       [i.txt $(txt +.txt)]
12568     ::
12569     ++  non-empty
12570       |*  a=rule
12571       |=  tub=nail  ^+  (a)
12572       =/  vex  (a tub)
12573       ~!  vex
12574       ?~  q.vex  vex
12575       ?.  =(tub q.u.q.vex)  vex
12576       (fail tub)
12577     ::
12578     ::
12579     ++  word                                     ::  tarp parser
12580       %+  knee  *(list graf)  |.  ~+
12581       %+  cook
12582       |=  a=$%(graf [%list (list graf)])
12583       ^-  (list graf)
12584       ?:(?=(%list -.a) +.a [a ~])
```

```
12585          ;~  pose
12586          ::
12587          ::  ordinary word
12588          ::
12589            %+  stag  %text
12590            ;~(plug ;~(pose low hig) (star ;~(pose nud low hig hep)))
12591          ::
12592          ::  naked \escape
12593          ::
12594            (stag %text ;~(pfix bas (cook trip ;~(less ace prn))))
12595          ::
12596          ::  trailing \ to add <br>
12597          ::
12598            (stag %expr (cold [[%br ~] ~] ;~(plug bas (just '\0a'))))
12599          ::
12600          ::  *bold literal*
12601          ::
12602            (stag %bold (ifix [tar tar] (cool (cash tar) werk)))
12603          ::
12604          ::  _italic literal_
12605          ::
12606            (stag %talc (ifix [cab cab] (cool (cash cab) werk)))
12607          ::
12608          ::  "quoted text"
12609          ::
12610            (stag %quod (ifix [doq doq] (cool (cash doq) werk)))
12611          ::
12612          ::  `classic markdown quote`
12613          ::
12614            (stag %code (ifix [tic tic] (calf tic)))
12615          ::
12616          ::  ++arm, +$arm, +*arm, ++arm:core, ...
12617          ::
12618            %+  stag  %code
12619            ;~  plug
12620              lus  ;~(pose lus buc tar)
12621              low  (star ;~(pose nud low hep col))
12622            ==
12623          ::
12624          ::  [arbitrary *content*](url)
12625          ::
12626            %+  stag  %link
12627            ;~  (glue (punt whit))
12628              (ifix [sel ser] (cool (cash ser) werk))
12629              (ifix [pal par] (cash par))
12630            ==
12631          ::
12632          ::  ![alt text](url)
12633          ::
12634            %+  stag  %mage
12635            ;~  pfix  zap
12636              ;~  (glue (punt whit))
12637                (ifix [sel ser] (cash ser))
12638                (ifix [pal par] (cash par))
12639              ==
12640            ==
12641          ::
12642          ::  #hoon
```

```
12643        ::
12644          %+  stag  %list
12645          ;~  plug
12646            (stag %text ;~(pose (cold " " whit) (easy-sol ~)))
12647            (stag %code ;~(pfix hax (echo wide)))
12648            ;~(simu whit (easy ~))
12649          ==
12650        ::
12651        ::  direct hoon constant
12652        ::
12653          %+  stag  %list
12654          ;~  plug
12655            (stag %text ;~(pose (cold " " whit) (easy-sol ~)))
12656            ::
12657            %+  stag  %code
12658            %-  echo
12659            ;~  pose
12660              ::REVIEW just copy in 0x... parsers directly?
12661              ;~(simu ;~(plug (just '0') alp) bisk:so)
12662            ::
12663              tash:so
12664              ;~(pfix dot perd:so)
12665              ;~(pfix sig ;~(pose twid:so (easy [%$ %n 0])))
12666              ;~(pfix cen ;~(pose sym buc pam bar qut nuck:so))
12667            ==
12668          ::
12669            ;~(simu whit (easy ~))
12670          ==
12671        ::
12672        ::  whitespace
12673        ::
12674          (stag %text (cold " " whit))
12675        ::
12676        ::  {interpolated} sail
12677        ::
12678          (stag %expr inline-embed:(sail |))
12679        ::
12680        ::  just a byte
12681        ::
12682          (stag %text (cook trip ;~(less ace prn)))
12683        ==
12684      ::
12685      ++  werk  (cook zing (star word))                  ::  indefinite tarp
12686      ::
12687      ++  down                                           ::  parse inline tarp
12688        %+  knee  *tarp  |.  ~+
12689        =-  (cook - werk)
12690        ::
12691        ::  collect raw tarp into xml tags
12692        |=  gaf=(list graf)
12693        ^-  tarp
12694        =<  main
12695        |%
12696        ++  main
12697          ^-  tarp
12698          ?~  gaf  ~
12699          ?.  ?=(%text -.i.gaf)
12700            (weld (item i.gaf) $(gaf t.gaf))
```

```
                    ::
                    ::   fip: accumulate text blocks
                    =/   fip=(list tape)  [p.i.gaf]~
                    |-   ^-  tarp
                    ?~   t.gaf   [;/((zing (flop fip))) ~]
                    ?.   ?=(%text -.i.t.gaf)
                      [;/((zing (flop fip))) ^$(gaf t.gaf)]
                    $(gaf t.gaf, fip :_(fip p.i.t.gaf))
                  ::
              ++  item
                |=  nex=graf
                ^-  tarp  ::CHECK can be tuna:hoot?
                ?-  -.nex
                  %text  !!  :: handled separately
                  %expr  [p.nex]~
                  %bold  [[%b ~] ^$(gaf p.nex)]~
                  %talc  [[%i ~] ^$(gaf p.nex)]~
                  %code  [[%code ~] ;/(p.nex) ~]~
                  %quod  ::
                            :: smart quotes
                         %=   ^$
                             gaf
                            :-  [%text (tufa ~-~201c. ~)]
                            %+  weld  p.nex
                            `(list graf)`[%text (tufa ~-~201d. ~)]~
                         ==
                  %link  [[%a [%href q.nex] ~] ^$(gaf p.nex)]~
                  %mage  [[%img [%src q.nex] ?~(p.nex ~ [%alt p.nex]~)] ~]~
                ==
              --
            ::
          ++  hrul                                        :: empty besides fence
            %+  cold  [[%hr ~] ~]~
            ;~(plug (star ace) hep hep hep (star hep) (just '\0a'))
          ::
          ++  tics
            ;~(plug tic tic tic (just '\0a'))
          ::
          ++  fens
            |=  col=@u  ~+
            =/  ind  (stun [(dec col) (dec col)] ace)
            =/  ind-tics  ;~(plug ind tics)
            %+  cook  |=(txt=tape `tarp`[[%pre ~] ;/(txt) ~]~)
            ::
            :: leading outdent is ok since container may
            :: have already been parsed and consumed
            %+  ifix  [;~(plug (star ace) tics) ind-tics]
            %^  stir  ""  |=([a=tape b=tape] "{a}\0a{b}")
            ;~  pose
              %+  ifix  [ind (just '\0a')]
              ;~(less tics (star prn))
            ::
              (cold "" ;~(plug (star ace) (just '\0a')))
            ==
          ::
          ++  para                                        :: paragraph
            %+  cook
              |=(a=tarp ?~(a ~ [[%p ~] a]~))
```

```
12759        ;~(pfix (punt whit) down)
12760      ::
12761      ++  expr                                       ::  expression
12762      =>  (sail &)                                   ::  tall-form
12763      %+  ifix  [(star ace) ;~(simu gap (easy))]     ::  look-ahead for gap
12764      (cook drop-top top-level)                      ::  list of tags
12765        ::
12766      ::
12767      ++  whit                                       ::  whitespace
12768      (cold ' ' (plus ;~(pose (just ' ') (just '\0a'))))
12769      ::
12770      ++  head                                       ::  parse heading
12771        %+  cook
12772          |=  [haxes=tape kids=tarp]  ^-  tarp
12773          =/  tag  (crip 'h' <(lent haxes)>)         ::  e.g. ### -> %h3
12774          =/  id  (contents-to-id kids)
12775          [[tag [%id id]~] kids]~
12776        ::
12777        ;~(pfix (star ace) ;~((glue whit) (stun [1 6] hax) down))
12778      ::
12779      ++  contents-to-id                             ::  # text into elem id
12780        |=  a=(list tuna:hoot)  ^-  tape
12781        =;  raw=tape
12782          %+  turn  raw
12783          |=  @tD
12784          ^-  @tD
12785          ?:  ?|  &((gte +< 'a') (lte +< 'z'))
12786                  &((gte +< '0') (lte +< '9'))
12787              ==
12788            +<
12789          ?:  &((gte +< 'A') (lte +< 'Z'))
12790            (add 32 +<)
12791          '_'
12792        ::
12793        ::  collect all text in header tarp
12794        |-  ^-  tape
12795        ?~  a  ~
12796        %+  weld
12797          ^-  tape
12798          ?-  i.a
12799            [[%$ [%$ *] ~] ~]                         ::  text node contents
12800          (murn v.i.a.g.i.a |=(a=beer:hoot ?^(a ~ (some a))))
12801            [^ *]  $(a c.i.a)                         ::  concatenate children
12802            [@ *]  ~                                  ::  ignore interpolation
12803          ==
12804        $(a t.a)
12805      --
12806    --
12807  ::
12808  ++  scad
12809    %+  knee  *spec  |.  ~+
12810    %-  stew
12811    ^.  stet  ^.  limo
12812    :~
12813      :-  '_'
12814      ;~(pfix cab (stag %bccb wide))
12815      :-  ','
12816      ;~(pfix com (stag %bcmc wide))
```

```
12817          :-   '$'
12818            (stag %like (most col rope))
12819          :-   '%'
12820            ;~  pose
12821              ;~  pfix   cen
12822                ;~  pose
12823                  (stag %leaf (stag %tas (cold %$ buc)))
12824                  (stag %leaf (stag %f (cold & pam)))
12825                  (stag %leaf (stag %f (cold | bar)))
12826                  (stag %leaf (stag %t qut))
12827                  (stag %leaf (sear |=(a=coin ?:(?=(%$ -.a) (some +.a) ~)) nuck:so))
12828                ==
12829              ==
12830            ==
12831          :-   '('
12832            %+  cook  |=(spec +<)
12833            %+  stag  %make
12834            %+  ifix  [pal par]
12835            ;~  plug
12836              wide
12837              ;~(pose ;~(pfix ace (most ace wyde)) (easy ~))
12838            ==
12839          :-   '['
12840            (stag %bccl (ifix [sel ser] (most ace wyde)))
12841          :-   '*'
12842            (cold [%base %noun] tar)
12843          :-   '/'
12844            ;~(pfix fas (stag %loop ;~(pose (cold %$ buc) sym)))
12845          :-   '@'
12846            ;~(pfix pat (stag %base (stag %atom mota)))
12847          :-   '?'
12848            ;~  pose
12849              %+  stag  %bcwt
12850              ;~(pfix wut (ifix [pal par] (most ace wyde)))
12851            ::
12852              (cold [%base %flag] wut)
12853            ==
12854          :-   '~'
12855            (cold [%base %null] sig)
12856          :-   '!'
12857            (cold [%base %void] ;~(plug zap zap))
12858          :-   '^'
12859            ;~  pose
12860              (stag %like (most col rope))
12861              (cold [%base %cell] ket)
12862            ==
12863          :-   '='
12864            ;~  pfix  tis
12865              %+  sear
12866              |=  [=(unit term) =spec]
12867              %+  bind
12868                ~(autoname ax spec)
12869              |=  =term
12870              =*  name  ?~(unit term (cat 3 u.unit (cat 3 '-' term)))
12871              [%bcts name spec]
12872              ;~  pose
12873              ;~(plug (stag ~ ;~(sfix sym tis)) wyde)
12874              (stag ~ wyde)
```

```
12875              ==
12876           ==
12877    :-   ['a' 'z']
12878       ;~  pose
12879         (stag %bcts ;~(plug sym ;~(pfix tis wyde)))
12880         (stag %like (most col rope))
12881           ==
12882       ==
12883  ::
12884  ++  scat
12885    %+  knee  *hoon  |.  ~+
12886    %-  stew
12887    ^.  stet  ^.  limo
12888    :~
12889      :-  ','
12890        ;~  pose
12891          (stag %ktcl ;~(pfix com wyde))
12892          (stag %wing rope)
12893        ==
12894      :-  '!'
12895        ;~  pose
12896          (stag %wtzp ;~(pfix zap wide))
12897          (stag %zpzp (cold ~ ;~(plug zap zap)))
12898        ==
12899      :-  '_'
12900        ;~(pfix cab (stag %ktcl (stag %bccb wide)))
12901      :-  '$'
12902        ;~  pose
12903          ;~  pfix  buc
12904            ;~  pose
12905              ::  XX: these are all obsolete in hoon 142
12906              ::
12907              (stag %leaf (stag %tas (cold %$ buc)))
12908              (stag %leaf (stag %t qut))
12909              (stag %leaf (sear |=(a=coin ?:(?=(%$ -.a) (some +.a) ~)) nuck:so))
12910            ==
12911          ==
12912          rump
12913        ==
12914      :-  '%'
12915        ;~  pfix  cen
12916          ;~  pose
12917            (stag %clsg (sear |~([a=@ud b=tyke] (posh ~ ~ a b)) porc))
12918            (stag %rock (stag %tas (cold %$ buc)))
12919            (stag %rock (stag %f (cold & pam)))
12920            (stag %rock (stag %f (cold | bar)))
12921            (stag %rock (stag %t qut))
12922            (cook (jock &) nuck:so)
12923            (stag %clsg (sear |=(a=(list) (posh ~ ~ (lent a) ~)) (star cen)))
12924          ==
12925        ==
12926      :-  '&'
12927        ;~  pose
12928          (cook |=(a=wing [%cnts a ~]) rope)
12929          (stag %wtpm ;~(pfix pam (ifix [pal par] (most ace wide))))
12930          ;~(plug (stag %rock (stag %f (cold & pam))) wede)
12931          (stag %sand (stag %f (cold & pam)))
12932        ==
```

```
:-  '\''
  (stag %sand (stag %t qut))
:-  '('
  (stag %cncl (ifix [pal par] (most ace wide)))
:-  '*'
  ;~  pose
    (stag %kttr ;~(pfix tar wyde))
    (cold [%base %noun] tar)
  ==
:-  '@'
  ;~(pfix pat (stag %base (stag %atom mota)))
:-  '+'
  ;~  pose
    (stag %dtls ;~(pfix lus (ifix [pal par] wide)))
    ::
      %+  cook
        |=  a=(list (list woof))
        :-  %mcfs
        [%knit |-(^-((list woof) ?~(a ~ (weld i.a $(a t.a)))))]
      (most dog ;~(pfix lus soil))
    ::
      (cook |=(a=wing [%cnts a ~]) rope)
  ==
:-  '-'
  ;~  pose
    (stag %sand tash:so)
    ::
      %+  cook
        |=  a=(list (list woof))
        [%clsg (phax a)]
      (most dog ;~(pfix hep soil))
    ::
      (cook |=(a=wing [%cnts a ~]) rope)
  ==
:-  '.'
  ;~  pose
    (cook (jock |) ;~(pfix dot perd:so))
    (cook |=(a=wing [%cnts a ~]) rope)
  ==
:-  ['0' '9']
  %+  cook
    |=  [a=dime b=(unit hoon)]
    ?~(b [%sand a] [[%rock a] u.b])
  ;~(plug bisk:so (punt wede))
:-  ':'
  ;~  pfix  col
    ;~  pose
      (stag %mccl (ifix [pal par] (most ace wide)))
      ;~(pfix fas (stag %mcfs wide))
    ==
  ==
:-  '='
  ;~  pfix  tis
    ;~  pose
      (stag %dtts (ifix [pal par] ;~(glam wide wide)))
      ::
        %+  sear
          ::  mainly used for +skin formation
```

```
12991              ::
12992              |=  =spec
12993              ^-  (unit hoon)
12994              %+  bind  ~(autoname ax spec)
12995              |=(=term `hoon`[%ktts term %kttr spec])
12996            wyde
12997          ==
12998        ==
12999      :-  '?'
13000        ;~  pose
13001          %+  stag  %ktcl
13002          (stag %bcwt ;~(pfix wut (ifix [pal par] (most ace wyde))))
13003        ::
13004          (cold [%base %flag] wut)
13005        ==
13006      :-  '['
13007        rupl
13008      :-  '^'
13009        ;~  pose
13010          (stag %wing rope)
13011          (cold [%base %cell] ket)
13012        ==
13013      :-  '`'
13014        ;~  pfix  tic
13015          ;~  pose
13016            %+  cook
13017            |=([a=@ta b=hoon] [%ktls [%sand a 0] [%ktls [%sand %$ 0] b]])
13018            ;~(pfix pat ;~(plug mota ;~(pfix tic wide)))
13019            ;~  pfix  tar
13020            (stag %kthp (stag [%base %noun] ;~(pfix tic wide)))
13021          ==
13022          (stag %kthp ;~(plug wyde ;~(pfix tic wide)))
13023          (stag %ktls ;~(pfix lus ;~(plug wide ;~(pfix tic wide))))
13024          (cook |=(a=hoon [[%rock %n ~] a]) wide)
13025        ==
13026      ==
13027      :-  '"'
13028        %+  cook
13029        |=  a=(list (list woof))
13030        [%knit |-(^-((list woof) ?~(a ~ (weld i.a $(a t.a)))))]
13031        (most dog soil)
13032      :-  ['a' 'z']
13033        rump
13034      :-  '|'
13035        ;~  pose
13036          (cook |=(a=wing [%cnts a ~]) rope)
13037          (stag %wtbr ;~(pfix bar (ifix [pal par] (most ace wide))))
13038          ;~(plug (stag %rock (stag %f (cold | bar))) wede)
13039          (stag %sand (stag %f (cold | bar)))
13040        ==
13041      :-  '~'
13042        ;~  pose
13043          rupl
13044        ::
13045          ;~  pfix  sig
13046            ;~  pose
13047              (stag %clsg (ifix [sel ser] (most ace wide)))
13048            ::
```

```
13049                    %+   stag   %cnsg
13050                    %+   ifix
13051                      [pal par]
13052                    ;~(glam rope wide (most ace wide))
13053                ::
13054                    (cook (jock |) twid:so)
13055                    (stag [%bust %null] wede)
13056                    (easy [%bust %null])
13057                ==
13058            ==
13059          ==
13060        :-  '/'
13061          rood
13062        :-  '<'
13063        (ifix [gal gar] (stag %tell (most ace wide)))
13064        :-  '>'
13065        (ifix [gar gal] (stag %yell (most ace wide)))
13066        :-  '#'
13067          ;~(pfix hax reed)
13068      ==
13069    ++  soil
13070      ;~  pose
13071        ;~  less  (jest '"""')
13072          %+  ifix   [doq doq]
13073          %-  star
13074          ;~  pose
13075            ;~(pfix bas ;~(pose bas doq kel bix:ab))
13076            ;~(less doq bas kel prn)
13077          (stag ~ sump)
13078          ==
13079        ==
13080        ::
13081          %-  iny  %+  ifix
13082          [(jest '"""\0a') (jest '\0a"""')]
13083          %-  star
13084          ;~  pose
13085            ;~(pfix bas ;~(pose bas kel bix:ab))
13086            ;~(less bas kel prn)
13087            ;~(less (jest '\0a"""') (just `@`10))
13088          (stag ~ sump)
13089          ==
13090      ==
13091    ++  sump  (ifix [kel ker] (stag %cltr (most ace wide)))
13092    ++  norm                                          ::  rune regular form
13093    |=  tol=?
13094    |%
13095    ++  structure
13096      %-  stew
13097      ^.  stet  ^.  limo
13098      :~  :-  '$'
13099            ;~  pfix  buc
13100            %-  stew
13101            ^.  stet  ^.  limo
13102            :~  [':' (rune col %bccl exqs)]
13103                ['%' (rune cen %bccn exqs)]
13104                ['<' (rune gal %bcgl exqb)]
13105                ['>' (rune gar %bcgr exqb)]
13106                ['^' (rune ket %bckt exqb)]
```

```
13107                       ['~' (rune sig %bcsg exqd)]
13108                       ['|' (rune bar %bcbr exqc)]
13109                       ['&' (rune pam %bcpm exqc)]
13110                       ['@' (rune pat %bcpt exqb)]
13111                       ['_' (rune cab %bccb expa)]
13112                       ['-' (rune hep %bchp exqb)]
13113                       ['=' (rune tis %bcts exqg)]
13114                       ['?' (rune wut %bcwt exqs)]
13115                       [';' (rune mic %bcmc expa)]
13116                       ['+' (rune lus %bcls exqg)]
13117                   ==
13118                 ==
13119         :-  '%'
13120           ;~  pfix  cen
13121             %-  stew
13122             ^.  stet  ^.  limo
13123             :~  :-  '^'
13124                 %+  cook
13125                 |=  [%cnkt a=hoon b=spec c=spec d=spec]
13126                 [%make a b c d ~]
13127                 (rune ket %cnkt exqy)
13128               ::
13129                 :-  '+'
13130                 %+  cook
13131                 |=  [%cnls a=hoon b=spec c=spec]
13132                 [%make a b c ~]
13133                 (rune lus %cnls exqx)
13134               ::
13135                 :-  '-'
13136                 %+  cook
13137                 |=  [%cnhp a=hoon b=spec]
13138                 [%make a b ~]
13139                 (rune hep %cnhp exqd)
13140               ::
13141                 :-  '.'
13142                 %+  cook
13143                 |=  [%cndt a=spec b=hoon]
13144                 [%make b a ~]
13145                 (rune dot %cndt exqc)
13146               ::
13147                 :-  ':'
13148                 %+  cook
13149                 |=  [%cncl a=hoon b=(list spec)]
13150                 [%make a b]
13151                 (rune col %cncl exqz)
13152             ==
13153           ==
13154         :-  '#'
13155           ;~  pfix  hax  fas
13156             %+  stag  %bccl
13157             %+  cook
13158             |=  [[i=spec t=(list spec)] e=spec]
13159             [i (snoc t e)]
13160             ;~  plug
13161             %+  most  ;~(less ;~(plug fas tar) fas)
13162             %-  stew
13163             ^.  stet  ^.  limo
13164             :~  :-  ['a' 'z']
```

```
13165                    ;~  pose
13166                    ::  /name=@aura
13167                    ::
13168                    %+  cook
13169                    |=  [=term =aura]
13170                    ^-  spec
13171                    :+  %bccl
13172                      [%leaf %tas aura]
13173                    :_  ~
13174                    :+  %bcts  term
13175                    ?+  aura  [%base %atom aura]
13176                      %f  [%base %flag]
13177                      %n  [%base %null]
13178                    ==
13179                    ;~(plug sym ;~(pfix tis pat mota))
13180                  ::
13181                    ::  /constant
13182                    ::
13183                    (stag %leaf (stag %tas ;~(pose sym (cold %$ buc))))
13184               ==
13185                ::
13186                  ::  /@aura
13187                  ::
13188                  :-  '@'
13189                  %+  cook
13190                    |=  =aura
13191                    ^-  spec
13192                    :+  %bccl
13193                      [%leaf %tas aura]
13194                    [%base %atom aura]~
13195                  ;~(pfix pat mota)
13196                ::
13197                  ::  /?
13198                  ::
13199                  :-  '?'
13200                  (cold [%bccl [%leaf %tas %f] [%base %flag] ~] wut)
13201                ::
13202                  ::  /~
13203                  ::
13204                  :-  '~'
13205                  (cold [%bccl [%leaf %tas %n] [%base %null] ~] sig)
13206             ==
13207          ::
13208          ::  open-ended or fixed-length
13209          ::
13210          ;~  pose
13211            (cold [%base %noun] ;~(plug fas tar))
13212            (easy %base %null)
13213          ==
13214        ==
13215      ==
13216    ==
13217  ++  expression
13218    %-  stew
13219    ^.  stet  ^.  limo
13220    :~  :-  '|'
13221        ;~  pfix  bar
13222          %-  stew
```

```
13223              ^.  stet   ^.  limo
13224              :~  ['_' (rune cab %brcb exqr)]
13225                  ['%' (runo cen %brcn ~ expe)]
13226                  ['@' (runo pat %brpt ~ expe)]
13227                  [':' (rune col %brcl expb)]
13228                  ['.' (rune dot %brdt expa)]
13229                  ['-' (rune hep %brhp expa)]
13230                  ['^' (rune ket %brkt expr)]
13231                  ['~' (rune sig %brsg exqc)]
13232                  ['*' (rune tar %brtr exqc)]
13233                  ['=' (rune tis %brts exqc)]
13234                  ['?' (rune wut %brwt expa)]
13235                  ['$' (rune buc %brbc exqe)]
13236                ==
13237            ==
13238          :-  '$'
13239            ;~  pfix  buc
13240              %-  stew
13241              ^.  stet   ^.  limo
13242              :~  ['@' (stag %ktcl (rune pat %bcpt exqb))]
13243                  ['_' (stag %ktcl (rune cab %bccb expa))]
13244                  [':' (stag %ktcl (rune col %bccl exqs))]
13245                  ['%' (stag %ktcl (rune cen %bccn exqs))]
13246                  ['<' (stag %ktcl (rune gal %bcgl exqb))]
13247                  ['>' (stag %ktcl (rune gar %bcgr exqb))]
13248                  ['|' (stag %ktcl (rune bar %bcbr exqc))]
13249                  ['&' (stag %ktcl (rune pam %bcpm exqc))]
13250                  ['^' (stag %ktcl (rune ket %bckt exqb))]
13251                  ['~' (stag %ktcl (rune sig %bcsg exqd))]
13252                  ['-' (stag %ktcl (rune hep %bchp exqb))]
13253                  ['=' (stag %ktcl (rune tis %bcts exqg))]
13254                  ['?' (stag %ktcl (rune wut %bcwt exqs))]
13255                  ['+' (stag %ktcl (rune lus %bcls exqg))]
13256                  ['.' (rune dot %kttr exqa)]
13257                  [',' (rune com %ktcl exqa)]
13258                ==
13259            ==
13260          :-  '%'
13261            ;~  pfix  cen
13262              %-  stew
13263              ^.  stet   ^.  limo
13264              :~  ['_' (rune cab %cncb exph)]
13265                  ['.' (rune dot %cndt expb)]
13266                  ['^' (rune ket %cnkt expd)]
13267                  ['+' (rune lus %cnls expc)]
13268                  ['-' (rune hep %cnhp expb)]
13269                  [':' (rune col %cncl expi)]
13270                  ['~' (rune sig %cnsg expn)]
13271                  ['*' (rune tar %cntr expm)]
13272                  ['=' (rune tis %cnts exph)]
13273                ==
13274            ==
13275          :-  ':'
13276            ;~  pfix  col
13277              %-  stew
13278              ^.  stet   ^.  limo
13279              :~  ['_' (rune cab %clcb expb)]
13280                  ['^' (rune ket %clkt expd)]
```

```
13281                      ['+' (rune lus %clls expc)]
13282                      ['-' (rune hep %clhp expb)]
13283                      ['~' (rune sig %clsg exps)]
13284                      ['*' (rune tar %cltr exps)]
13285              ==
13286            ==
13287          :-  '.'
13288            ;~  pfix  dot
13289              %-  stew
13290              ^.  stet  ^.  limo
13291              :~  ['+' (rune lus %dtls expa)]
13292                  ['*' (rune tar %dttr expb)]
13293                  ['=' (rune tis %dtts expb)]
13294                  ['?' (rune wut %dtwt expa)]
13295                  ['^' (rune ket %dtkt exqn)]
13296              ==
13297            ==
13298          :-  '^'
13299            ;~  pfix  ket
13300              %-  stew
13301              ^.  stet  ^.  limo
13302              :~  ['|' (rune bar %ktbr expa)]
13303                  ['.' (rune dot %ktdt expb)]
13304                  ['-' (rune hep %kthp exqc)]
13305                  ['+' (rune lus %ktls expb)]
13306                  ['&' (rune pam %ktpm expa)]
13307                  ['~' (rune sig %ktsg expa)]
13308                  ['=' (rune tis %ktts expj)]
13309                  ['?' (rune wut %ktwt expa)]
13310                  ['*' (rune tar %kttr exqa)]
13311                  [':' (rune col %ktcl exqa)]
13312              ==
13313            ==
13314          :-  '~'
13315            ;~  pfix  sig
13316              %-  stew
13317              ^.  stet  ^.  limo
13318              :~  ['|' (rune bar %sgbr expb)]
13319                  ['$' (rune buc %sgbc expf)]
13320                  ['_' (rune cab %sgcb expb)]
13321                  ['%' (rune cen %sgcn hind)]
13322                  ['/' (rune fas %sgfs hine)]
13323                  ['<' (rune gal %sggl hinb)]
13324                  ['>' (rune gar %sggr hinb)]
13325                  ['+' (rune lus %sgls hinc)]
13326                  ['&' (rune pam %sgpm hinf)]
13327                  ['?' (rune wut %sgwt hing)]
13328                  ['=' (rune tis %sgts expb)]
13329                  ['!' (rune zap %sgzp expb)]
13330              ==
13331            ==
13332          :-  ';'
13333            ;~  pfix  mic
13334              %-  stew
13335              ^.  stet  ^.  limo
13336              :~  [':' (rune col %mccl expi)]
13337                  ['/' (rune fas %mcfs expa)]
13338                  ['<' (rune gal %mcgl expz)]
```

```
13339                    ['~' (rune sig %mcsg expi)]
13340                    [';' (rune mic %mcmc exqc)]
13341                ==
13342            ==
13343        :-  '='
13344          ;~  pfix  tis
13345            %-  stew
13346            ^.  stet  ^.  limo
13347            :~  ['|' (rune bar %tsbr exqc)]
13348                ['.' (rune dot %tsdt expq)]
13349                ['?' (rune wut %tswt expw)]
13350                ['^' (rune ket %tskt expt)]
13351                [':' (rune col %tscl expp)]
13352                ['/' (rune fas %tsfs expo)]
13353                [';' (rune mic %tsmc expo)]
13354                ['<' (rune gal %tsgl expb)]
13355                ['>' (rune gar %tsgr expb)]
13356                ['-' (rune hep %tshp expb)]
13357                ['*' (rune tar %tstr expg)]
13358                [',' (rune com %tscm expb)]
13359                ['+' (rune lus %tsls expb)]
13360                ['~' (rune sig %tssg expi)]
13361            ==
13362          ==
13363        :-  '?'
13364          ;~  pfix  wut
13365            %-  stew
13366            ^.  stet  ^.  limo
13367            :~  ['|' (rune bar %wtbr exps)]
13368                [':' (rune col %wtcl expc)]
13369                ['.' (rune dot %wtdt expc)]
13370                ['<' (rune gal %wtgl expb)]
13371                ['>' (rune gar %wtgr expb)]
13372                ['-' ;~(pfix hep (toad txhp))]
13373                ['^' ;~(pfix ket (toad tkkt))]
13374                ['=' ;~(pfix tis (toad txts))]
13375                ['#' ;~(pfix hax (toad txhx))]
13376                ['+' ;~(pfix lus (toad txls))]
13377                ['&' (rune pam %wtpm exps)]
13378                ['@' ;~(pfix pat (toad tkvt))]
13379                ['~' ;~(pfix sig (toad tksg))]
13380                ['!' (rune zap %wtzp expa)]
13381            ==
13382          ==
13383        :-  '!'
13384          ;~  pfix  zap
13385            %-  stew
13386            ^.  stet  ^.  limo
13387            :~  [':' ;~(pfix col (toad expy))]
13388                ['.' ;~(pfix dot (toad |.(loaf(bug |))))]
13389                [',' (rune com %zpcm expb)]
13390                [';' (rune mic %zpmc expb)]
13391                ['>' (rune gar %zpgr expa)]
13392                ['<' (rune gal %zpgl exqc)]
13393                ['@' (rune pat %zppt expx)]
13394                ['=' (rune tis %zpts expa)]
13395                ['?' (rune wut %zpwt hinh)]
13396            ==
```

```
13397                 ==
13398           ==
13399         ::
13400         ++  boog  !:
13401           %+  knee  [p=*whit q=*term r=*help s=*hoon]
13402           |.(~+((scye ;~(pose bola boba))))
13403         ++  bola                                        ::  ++  arms
13404           %+  knee  [q=*term r=*help s=*hoon]  |.  ~+
13405           %+  cook
13406             |=  [q=term r=whiz s=hoon]
13407             ?:  =(r *whiz)
13408               [q *help s]
13409             [q [[%funk q]~ [r]~] s]
13410           ;~  pfix  (jest '++')
13411             ;~  plug
13412               ;~(pfix gap ;~(pose (cold %$ buc) sym))
13413               apse:docs
13414               ;~(pfix jump loaf)
13415             ==
13416           ==
13417         ::TODO consider special casing $%
13418         ++  boba                                        ::  +$  arms
13419           %+  knee  [q=*term r=*help s=*hoon]  |.  ~+
13420           %+  cook
13421             |=  [q=term r=whiz s=spec]
13422             ?:  =(r *whiz)
13423               [q *help [%ktcl %name q s]]
13424             [q [[%plan q]~ [r]~] [%ktcl %name q s]]
13425           ;~  pfix  (jest '+$')
13426             ;~  plug
13427               ;~(pfix gap sym)
13428               apse:docs
13429               ;~(pfix jump loan)
13430             ==
13431           ==
13432         ::
13433         ::  parses a or [a b c] or a  b  c  ==
13434         ++  lynx
13435           =/  wid  (ifix [sel ser] (most ace sym))
13436           =/  tal
13437             ;~  sfix
13438               (most gap sym)
13439               ;~(plug gap duz)
13440             ==
13441           =/  one
13442             %-  cook  :_  sym
13443             |=  a=term
13444             `(list term)`~[a]
13445           %-  cook
13446           :_  ;~(pose (runq wid tal) one)
13447           ::  lestify
13448           |=  a=(list term)
13449           ?~(a !! a)
13450         ::
13451         ++  whap  !:                                     ::  chapter
13452           %+  cook
13453             |=  a=(list (qual whit term help hoon))
13454             ::  separate $helps into their own list to be passed to +glow
```

```
=/  [duds=(list help) nude=(list (pair term hoon))]
  %+  roll  a
  |=  $:  $=  bog
          (qual whit term help hoon)
      ::
          $=  gob
          [duds=(list help) nude=(list (pair term hoon))]
      ==
  =/  [unt=(list help) tag=(list help)]
    %+  skid  ~(tap by bat.p.bog)  |=(=help =(~ cuff.help))
  :-  ?:  =(*help r.bog)
        (weld tag duds.gob)
      [r.bog (weld tag duds.gob)]
    |-
  ?~  unt  [[q.bog s.bog] nude.gob]
  =.  s.bog  [%note help/i.unt s.bog]
    $(unt t.unt)
  ::
  %+  glow  duds
  |-  ^-  (map term hoon)
  ?~  nude  ~
  =+  $(nude t.nude)
  %+  ~(put by -)
    p.i.nude
  ?:  (~(has by -) p.i.nude)
    [%eror (weld "duplicate arm: +" (trip p.i.nude))]
  q.i.nude
  ::
  (most mush boog)
::
::  +glow: moves batch comments to the correct arm
++  glow
  |=  [duds=(list help) nude=(map term hoon)]
  ^-  (map term hoon)
  |-
  ?~  duds  nude
  ::  if there is no link, its not part of a batch comment
  ?~  cuff.i.duds
    ::  this shouldn't happen yet until we look for cuffs of length >1
    ::  but we need to prove that cuff is nonempty anyways
    $(duds t.duds)
  ::
  ::TODO: look past the first link. this probably requires
  ::a major rethink on how batch comments work
  =/  nom=(unit term)
    ?+    i.cuff.i.duds  ~
    ::  we only support ++ and +$ batch comments right now
    ::
        ?([%funk *] [%plan *])
      `p.i.cuff.i.duds
    ==
  %=  $
    duds  t.duds
    nude  ?~  nom  nude
          ?.  (~(has by nude) u.nom)
            ::  ~>  %slog.[0 leaf+"glow: unmatched link"]
            nude
          (~(jab by nude) u.nom |=(a=hoon [%note help+i.duds a]))
```

```
13513          ==
13514        ::
13515        ++  whip                                          ::  chapter declare
13516          %+  cook
13517            |=  [[a=whit b=term c=whiz] d=(map term hoon)]
13518            ^-  [whit (pair term (map term hoon))]
13519            ?.  =(*whit a)
13520              [a b d]
13521            ?:  =(*whiz c)
13522              [*whit b d]
13523            [%*(. *whit bat (malt [[%chat b]~ [c]~]~)) b d]
13524          ;~(plug (seam ;~(pfix (jest '+|') gap cen sym)) whap)
13525        ::
13526        ++  wasp                                          ::  $brcb aliases
13527          ;~  pose
13528            %+  ifix
13529              [;~(plug lus tar muck) muck]
13530            (most muck ;~(gunk sym loll))
13531          ::
13532            (easy ~)
13533          ==
13534        ::
13535        ++  wisp  !:                                       ::  core tail
13536          ?.  tol  fail
13537          %+  cook
13538            |=  a=(list [wit=whit wap=(pair term (map term hoon))])
13539            ^-  (map term tome)
13540            =<  p
13541            |-  ^-  (pair (map term tome) (map term hoon))
13542            ?~  a  [~ ~]
13543            =/  mor  $(a t.a)
13544            =.  q.wap.i.a
13545              %-  ~(urn by q.wap.i.a)
13546              |=  b=(pair term hoon)  ^+  +.b
13547              ::  tests for duplicate arms between two chapters
13548              ?.  (~(has by q.mor) p.b)  +.b
13549              [%eror (weld "duplicate arm: +" (trip p.b))]
13550            :_  (~(uni by q.mor) q.wap.i.a)
13551            %+  ~(put by p.mor)
13552              p.wap.i.a
13553            :-  %-  ~(get by bat.wit.i.a)
13554                ?:  (~(has by bat.wit.i.a) [%chat p.wap.i.a]~)
13555                  [%chat p.wap.i.a]~
13556                ~
13557            ?.  (~(has by p.mor) p.wap.i.a)
13558              q.wap.i.a
13559            [[%$ [%eror (weld "duplicate chapter: |" (trip p.wap.i.a))]] ~ ~]
13560          ::
13561          ::TODO: allow cores with unnamed chapter as well as named chapters?
13562          ;~  pose
13563            dun
13564            ;~  sfix
13565              ;~  pose
13566                (most mush whip)
13567                ;~(plug (stag *whit (stag %$ whap)) (easy ~))
13568              ==
13569              gap
13570              dun
```

```
13571          ==
13572        ==
13573      ::
13574      ::TODO: check parser performance
13575      ++  toad                                      ::  untrap parser expr
13576        |*  har=_expa
13577        =+  dur=(ifix [pal par] $:har(tol |))
13578        ?.  tol
13579          dur
13580        ;~(pose ;~(pfix jump $:har(tol &)) ;~(pfix gap $:har(tol &)) dur)
13581      ::
13582      ++  rune                                      ::  build rune
13583        |*  [dif=rule tuq=* har=_expa]
13584        ;~(pfix dif (stag tuq (toad har)))
13585      ::
13586      ++  runo                                      ::  rune plus
13587        |*  [dif=rule hil=* tuq=* har=_expa]
13588        ;~(pfix dif (stag hil (stag tuq (toad har))))
13589      ::
13590      ++  runq                                      ::  wide or tall if tol
13591        |*  [wid=rule tal=rule]                     ::  else wide
13592        ?.  tol
13593          wid
13594        ;~(pose wid tal)
13595      ::
13596      ++  butt  |*  zor=rule                         ::  closing == if tall
13597                ?:(tol ;~(sfix zor ;~(plug gap duz)) zor)
13598      ++  ulva  |*  zor=rule                         ::  closing -- and tall
13599                ?.(tol fail ;~(sfix zor ;~(plug gap dun)))
13600      ++  glop  ~+((glue mash))                      ::  separated by space
13601      ++  gunk  ~+((glue muck))                      ::  separated list
13602      ++  goop  ~+((glue mush))                      ::  separator list & docs
13603      ++  hank  (most mush loaf)                     ::  gapped hoons
13604      ++  hunk  (most mush loan)                     ::  gapped specs
13605      ++  jump  ;~(pose leap:docs gap)               ::  gap before docs
13606      ++  loaf  ?:(tol tall wide)                    ::  hoon
13607      ++  loll  ?:(tol tall(doc |) wide(doc |))      ::  hoon without docs
13608      ++  loan  ?:(tol till wyde)                    ::  spec
13609      ++  lore  (sear |=(=hoon ~(flay ap hoon)) loaf) ::  skin
13610      ++  lomp  ;~(plug sym (punt ;~(pfix tis wyde))) ::  typeable name
13611      ++  mash  ?:(tol gap ;~(plug com ace))         ::  list separator
13612      ++  muss  ?:(tol jump ;~(plug com ace))        ::  list w/ doccords
13613      ++  muck  ?:(tol gap ace)                      ::  general separator
13614      ++  mush  ?:(tol jump ace)                     ::  separator w/ docs
13615      ++  teak  %+  knee  *tiki  |.  ~+              ::  wing or hoon
13616            =+  ^=  gub
13617                |=  [a=term b=$%([%& p=wing] [%| p=hoon])]
13618                ^-  tiki
13619            ?-(-.b %& [%& [~ a] p.b], %| [%| [~ a] p.b])
13620            =+  ^=  wyp
13621            ;~  pose
13622              %+  cook  gub
13623              ;~  plug
13624                sym
13625                ;~(pfix tis ;~(pose (stag %& rope) (stag %| wide)))
13626              ==
13627            ::
13628                (stag %& (stag ~ rope))
```

```
13629                      (stag %| (stag ~ wide))
13630                  ==
13631            ?.  tol  wyp
13632            ;~  pose
13633              wyp
13634            ::
13635              ;~  pfix
13636                ;~(plug ket tis gap)
13637                %+  cook  gub
13638                ;~  plug
13639                  sym
13640                  ;~(pfix gap ;~(pose (stag %& rope) (stag %| tall)))
13641                ==
13642              ==
13643            ::
13644              (stag %| (stag ~ tall))
13645            ==
13646  ++  rack  (most muss ;~(goop loaf loaf))          ::  list [hoon hoon]
13647  ++  ruck  (most muss ;~(goop loan loaf))          ::  list [spec hoon]
13648  ++  rick  (most mash ;~(goop rope loaf))          ::  list [wing hoon]
13649  ::  hoon contents
13650  ::
13651  ++  expa  |.(loaf)                                ::  one hoon
13652  ++  expb  |.(;~(goop loaf loaf))                  ::  two hoons
13653  ++  expc  |.(;~(goop loaf loaf loaf))             ::  three hoons
13654  ++  expd  |.(;~(goop loaf loaf loaf loaf))        ::  four hoons
13655  ++  expe  |.(wisp)                                ::  core tail
13656  ++  expf  |.(;~(goop ;~(pfix cen sym) loaf))      ::  %term and hoon
13657  ++  expg  |.(;~(gunk lomp loll loaf))             ::  term/spec, two hoons
13658  ++  exph  |.((butt ;~(gunk rope rick)))           ::  wing, [wing hoon]s
13659  ++  expi  |.((butt ;~(goop loaf hank)))           ::  one or more hoons
13660  ++  expj  |.(;~(goop lore loaf))                  ::  skin and hoon
13661  ::  ++  expk  |.(;~(gunk loaf ;~(plug loaf (easy ~))))::  list of two hoons
13662  ::  ++  expl  |.(;~(gunk sym loaf loaf))          ::  term, two hoons
13663  ++  expm  |.((butt ;~(gunk rope loaf rick)))      ::  several [spec hoon]s
13664  ++  expn  |.  ;~  gunk  rope  loaf                ::  wing, hoon,
13665                    ;~(plug loaf (easy ~))          ::  list of one hoon
13666            ==                                      ::
13667  ++  expo  |.(;~(goop wise loaf loaf))             ::  =;
13668  ++  expp  |.(;~(goop (butt rick) loaf))           ::  [wing hoon]s, hoon
13669  ++  expq  |.(;~(goop rope loaf loaf))             ::  wing and two hoons
13670  ++  expr  |.(;~(goop loaf wisp))                  ::  hoon and core tail
13671  ++  exps  |.((butt hank))                         ::  closed gapped hoons
13672  ++  expt  |.(;~(gunk wise rope loaf loaf))        ::  =^
13673  ++  expu  |.(;~(gunk rope loaf (butt hank)))      ::  wing, hoon, hoons
13674  ::  ++  expv  |.((butt rick))                     ::  just changes
13675  ++  expw  |.(;~(goop rope loaf loaf loaf))        ::  wing and three hoons
13676  ++  expx  |.(;~(goop ropa loaf loaf))             ::  wings and two hoons
13677  ++  expy  |.(loaf(bug &))                         ::  hoon with tracing
13678  ++  expz  |.(;~(goop loan loaf loaf loaf))        ::  spec and three hoons
13679  ::  spec contents
13680  ::
13681  ++  exqa  |.(loan)                                ::  one spec
13682  ++  exqb  |.(;~(goop loan loan))                  ::  two specs
13683  ++  exqc  |.(;~(goop loan loaf))                  ::  spec then hoon
13684  ++  exqd  |.(;~(goop loaf loan))                  ::  hoon then spec
13685  ++  exqe  |.(;~(goop lynx loan))                  ::  list of names then spec
13686  ++  exqs  |.((butt hunk))                         ::  closed gapped specs
```

```
13687    ++  exqg  |.(;~(goop sym loan))                        ::  term and spec
13688    ::++  exqk  |.(;~(goop loaf ;~(plug loan (easy ~))))::  hoon with one spec
13689    ++  exqn  |.(;~(gunk loan (stag %cltr (butt hank))))::  autoconsed hoons
13690    ++  exqr  |.(;~(gunk loan ;~(plug wasp wisp)))       ::  spec/aliases?/tail
13691    ::++  exqw  |.(;~(goop loaf loan))                    ::  hoon and spec
13692    ++  exqx  |.(;~(goop loaf loan loan))                ::  hoon, two specs
13693    ++  exqy  |.(;~(goop loaf loan loan loan))           ::  hoon, three specs
13694    ++  exqz  |.(;~(goop loaf (butt hunk)))              ::  hoon, n specs
13695    ::
13696    ::    tiki expansion for %wt runes
13697    ::
13698    ++  txhp  |.  %+  cook  |=  [a=tiki b=(list (pair spec hoon))]
13699                          (~(wthp ah a) b)
13700             (butt ;~(gunk teak ruck))
13701    ++  tkkt  |.  %+  cook  |=  [a=tiki b=hoon c=hoon]
13702                          (~(wtkt ah a) b c)
13703             ;~(gunk teak loaf loaf)
13704    ++  txls  |.  %+  cook  |=  [a=tiki b=hoon c=(list (pair spec hoon))]
13705                          (~(wtls ah a) b c)
13706             (butt ;~(gunk teak loaf ruck))
13707    ++  tkvt  |.  %+  cook  |=  [a=tiki b=hoon c=hoon]
13708                          (~(wtpt ah a) b c)
13709             ;~(gunk teak loaf loaf)
13710    ++  tksg  |.  %+  cook  |=  [a=tiki b=hoon c=hoon]
13711                          (~(wtsg ah a) b c)
13712             ;~(gunk teak loaf loaf)
13713    ++  txts  |.  %+  cook  |=  [a=spec b=tiki]
13714                          (~(wtts ah b) a)
13715             ;~(gunk loan teak)
13716    ++  txhx  |.  %+  cook  |=  [a=skin b=tiki]
13717                          (~(wthx ah b) a)
13718             ;~(gunk lore teak)
13719    ::
13720    ::  hint syntax
13721    ::
13722    ++  hinb  |.(;~(goop bont loaf))                       ::  hint and hoon
13723    ++  hinc  |.                                           ::  optional =en, hoon
13724          ;~(pose ;~(goop bony loaf) (stag ~ loaf)) ::
13725    ++  hind  |.(;~(gunk bonk loaf ;~(goop bonz loaf))) ::  jet hoon "bon"s hoon
13726    ++  hine  |.(;~(goop bonk loaf))                      ::  jet-hint and hoon
13727    ++  hinf  |.                                          ::  0-3 >s, two hoons
13728      ;~  pose
13729        ;~(goop (cook lent (stun [1 3] gar)) loaf loaf)
13730        (stag 0 ;~(goop loaf loaf))
13731      ==
13732    ++  hing  |.                                          ::  0-3 >s, three hoons
13733      ;~  pose
13734        ;~(goop (cook lent (stun [1 3] gar)) loaf loaf loaf)
13735        (stag 0 ;~(goop loaf loaf loaf))
13736      ==
13737    ++  bonk                                              ::  jet signature
13738      ;~  pfix  cen
13739        ;~  pose
13740          ;~(plug sym ;~(pfix col ;~(plug sym ;~(pfix dot ;~(pfix dot dem)))))
13741          ;~(plug sym ;~(pfix col ;~(plug sym ;~(pfix dot dem))))
13742          ;~(plug sym ;~(pfix dot dem))
13743          sym
13744        ==
```

```
          ==
    ++  hinh  |.                                        ::  1/2 numbers, hoon
      ;~  goop
        ;~  pose
          dem
          (ifix [sel ser] ;~(plug dem ;~(pfix ace dem)))
          ==
          loaf
        ==
    ++  bont  ;~  (bend)                                 ::  term, optional hoon
              ;~(pfix cen sym)
              ;~(pfix dot ;~(pose wide ;~(pfix muck loaf)))
          ==
    ++  bony  (cook |=(a=(list) (lent a)) (plus tis))    ::  base 1 =en count
    ++  bonz                                             ::  term-labelled hoons
      ;~  pose
      (cold ~ sig)
      %+  ifix
        ?:(tol [;~(plug duz gap) ;~(plug gap duz)] [pal par])
      (more mash ;~(gunk ;~(pfix cen sym) loaf))
        ==
    --
    ::
    ++  lang                                             ::  lung sample
      $:  ros=hoon
          $=  vil
          $%  [%tis p=hoon]
              [%col p=hoon]
              [%ket p=hoon]
              [%lit p=(list (pair wing hoon))]
          ==
      ==
    ::
    ++  lung
      ~+
      %-  bend
      |:  $:lang
      ^-  (unit hoon)
      ?-    -.vil
        %col  ?:(=([%base %flag] ros) ~ [~ %tsgl ros p.vil])
        %lit  (bind ~(reek ap ros) |=(hyp=wing [%cnts hyp p.vil]))
        %ket  [~ ros p.vil]
        %tis  =+  rud=~(flay ap ros)
              ?~(rud ~ `[%ktts u.rud p.vil])
      ==
    ::
    ++  long
      %+  knee  *hoon  |.  ~+
      ;~  lung
        scat
        ;~  pose
          ;~(plug (cold %tis tis) wide)
          ;~(plug (cold %col col) wide)
          ;~(plug (cold %ket ket) wide)
          ;~  plug
            (easy %lit)
            (ifix [pal par] lobo)
          ==
```

```
13803        ==
13804      ==
13805    ::
13806  ++  lobo  (most ;~(plug com ace) ;~(glam rope wide))
13807  ++  loon  (most ;~(plug com ace) ;~(glam wide wide))
13808  ++  lute                                        ::  tall [] noun
13809    ~+
13810  %+  cook  |=(hoon +<)
13811  %+  stag  %cltr
13812  %+  ifix
13813    [;~(plug sel gap) ;~(plug gap ser)]
13814  (most gap tall)
13815    ::
13816  ++  ropa  (most col rope)
13817  ++  rope                                        ::  wing form
13818    %+  knee  *wing
13819    |.  ~+
13820    %+  (slug |=([a=limb b=wing] [a b]))
13821      dot
13822    ;~  pose
13823      (cold [%| 0 ~] com)
13824      %+  cook
13825        |=([a=(list) b=term] ?~(a b [%| (lent a) `b]))
13826      ;~(plug (star ket) ;~(pose sym (cold %$ buc)))
13827    ::
13828      %+  cook
13829        |=(a=axis [%& a])
13830      ;~  pose
13831        ;~(pfix lus dim:ag)
13832        ;~(pfix pam (cook |=(a=@ ?:(=(0 a) 0 (mul 2 +($(a (dec a)))))) dim:ag))
13833        ;~(pfix bar (cook |=(a=@ ?:(=(0 a) 1 +((mul 2 $(a (dec a)))))) dim:ag))
13834        ven
13835        (cold 1 dot)
13836      ==
13837    ==
13838    ::
13839  ++  wise
13840    ;~  pose
13841      ;~  pfix  tis
13842        %+  sear
13843          |=  =spec
13844          ^-  (unit skin)
13845          %+  bind  ~(autoname ax spec)
13846          |=  =term
13847          [%name term %spec spec %base %noun]
13848        wyde
13849      ==
13850    ::
13851      %+  cook
13852        |=  [=term =(unit spec)]
13853        ^-  skin
13854        ?~  unit
13855          term
13856        [%name term %spec u.unit %base %noun]
13857      ;~  plug  sym
13858      (punt ;~(pfix ;~(pose fas tis) wyde))
13859      ==
13860    ::
```

```
          %+  cook
            |=  =spec
            ^-  skin
            [%spec spec %base %noun]
          wyde
        ==
      ::
      ++  tall                                        ::  full tall form
        %+  knee  *hoon
        |.(~+((wart (clad ;~(pose expression:(norm &) long lute apex:(sail &)))))))
      ++  till                                        ::  mold tall form
        %+  knee  *spec
        |.(~+((wert (coat ;~(pose structure:(norm &) scad)))))
      ++  wede                                        ::  wide bulb
        ::  XX: lus deprecated
        ::
        ;~(pfix ;~(pose lus fas) wide)
      ++  wide                                        ::  full wide form
        %+  knee  *hoon
        |.(~+((wart ;~(pose expression:(norm |) long apex:(sail |)))))
      ++  wyde                                        ::  mold wide form
        %+  knee  *spec
        |.(~+((wert ;~(pose structure:(norm |) scad))))
      ++  wart
        |*  zor=rule
        %+  here
          |=  [a=pint b=hoon]
          ?:(bug [%dbug [wer a] b] b)
        zor
      ++  wert
        |*  zor=rule
        %+  here
          |=  [a=pint b=spec]
          ?:(bug [%dbug [wer a] b] b)
        zor
      --
    ::
    ++  vest
      ~/  %vest
      |=  tub=nail
      ^-  (like hoon)
      %.  tub
      %-  full
      (ifix [gay gay] tall:vast)
    ::
    ++  vice
      |=  txt=@ta
      ^-  hoon
      (rash txt wide:vast)
    ::
    ++  make                                          ::  compile cord to nock
      |=  txt=@
      q:(~(mint ut %noun) %noun (ream txt))
    ::
    ++  rain                                          ::  parse with % path
      |=  [bon=path txt=@]
      ^-  hoon
      =+  vaz=vast
```

```
13919      ~|  bon
13920      (scan (trip txt) (full (ifix [gay gay] tall:vaz(wer bon))))
13921    ::
13922    ++  ream                                         ::  parse cord to hoon
13923      |=  txt=@
13924      ^-  hoon
13925      (rash txt vest)
13926    ::
13927    ++  reck                                         ::  parse hoon file
13928      |=  bon=path
13929      (rain bon .^(@t %cx (weld bon `path`[%hoon ~])))
13930    ::
13931    ++  ride                                         ::  end-to-end compiler
13932      |=  [typ=type txt=@]
13933      ^-  (pair type nock)
13934      ~>  %slog.[0 leaf/"ride: parsing"]
13935      =/  gen  (ream txt)
13936      ~>  %slog.[0 leaf/"ride: compiling"]
13937      ~<  %slog.[0 leaf/"ride: compiled"]
13938      (~(mint ut typ) %noun gen)
13939    ::
13940    ::    5e: molds and mold builders
13941    +|  %molds-and-mold-builders
13942    ::
13943    +$  mane  $@(@tas [@tas @tas])                   ::  XML name+space
13944    +$  manx  $~([[%$ ~] ~] [g=marx c=marl])         ::  dynamic XML node
13945    +$  marl  (list manx)                            ::  XML node list
13946    +$  mars  [t=[n=%$ a=[i=[n=%$ v=tape] t=~]] c=~]  ::  XML cdata
13947    +$  mart  (list [n=mane v=tape])                 ::  XML attributes
13948    +$  marx  $~([%$ ~] [n=mane a=mart])             ::  dynamic XML tag
13949    +$  mite  (list @ta)                             ::  mime type
13950    +$  pass  @                                      ::  public key
13951    +$  ring  @                                      ::  private key
13952    +$  ship  @p                                     ::  network identity
13953    +$  shop  (each ship (list @ta))                 ::  urbit/dns identity
13954    +$  spur  path                                   ::  ship desk case spur
13955    +$  time  @da                                    ::  galactic time
13956    ::
13957    ::    5f: profiling support (XX move)
13958    +|  %profiling-support
13959    ::
13960    ++  pi-heck
13961      |=  [nam=@tas day=doss]
13962      ^-  doss
13963      =+  lam=(~(get by hit.day) nam)
13964      day(hit (~(put by hit.day) nam ?~(lam 1 +(u.lam))))
13965    ::
13966    ++  pi-noon                                      ::  sample trace
13967      |=  [mot=term paz=(list path) day=doss]
13968      =|  lax=(unit path)
13969      |-  ^-  doss
13970      ?~  paz  day(mon (pi-mope mot mon.day))
13971      %=  $
13972        paz  t.paz
13973        lax  `i.paz
13974        cut.day
13975      %+  ~(put by cut.day)  i.paz
13976        ^-  hump
```

```
13977      =+  nax=`(unit path)`?~(t.paz ~ `i.t.paz)
13978      =+  hup=`hump`=+(hup=(~(get by cut.day) i.paz) ?^(hup u.hup [*moan ~ ~]))
13979      :+  (pi-mope mot mon.hup)
13980        ?~  lax   out.hup
13981        =+  hag=(~(get by out.hup) u.lax)
13982        (~(put by out.hup) u.lax ?~(hag 1 +(u.hag)))
13983      ?~  nax  inn.hup
13984      =+  hag=(~(get by inn.hup) u.nax)
13985      (~(put by inn.hup) u.nax ?~(hag 1 +(u.hag)))
13986    ==
13987 ++  pi-mope                                         ::  add sample
13988    |=  [mot=term mon=moan]
13989    ?+  mot  mon
13990      %fun  mon(fun +(fun.mon))
13991      %noc  mon(noc +(noc.mon))
13992      %glu  mon(glu +(glu.mon))
13993      %mal  mon(mal +(mal.mon))
13994      %far  mon(far +(far.mon))
13995      %coy  mon(coy +(coy.mon))
13996      %euq  mon(euq +(euq.mon))
13997    ==
13998 ++  pi-moth                                         ::  count sample
13999    |=  mon=moan   ^-  @ud
14000    :(add fun.mon noc.mon glu.mon mal.mon far.mon coy.mon euq.mon)
14001 ::
14002 ++  pi-mumm                                          ::  print sample
14003    |=  mon=moan   ^-  tape
14004    =+  tot=(pi-moth mon)
14005    ;:  welp
14006      ^-  tape
14007      ?:  =(0 noc.mon)  ~
14008      (welp (scow %ud (div (mul 100 noc.mon) tot)) "n ")
14009    ::
14010      ^-  tape
14011      ?:  =(0 fun.mon)  ~
14012      (welp (scow %ud (div (mul 100 fun.mon) tot)) "c ")
14013    ::
14014      ^-  tape
14015      ?:  =(0 glu.mon)  ~
14016      (welp (scow %ud (div (mul 100 glu.mon) tot)) "g ")
14017    ::
14018      ^-  tape
14019      ?:  =(0 mal.mon)  ~
14020      (welp (scow %ud (div (mul 100 mal.mon) tot)) "m ")
14021    ::
14022      ^-  tape
14023      ?:  =(0 far.mon)  ~
14024      (welp (scow %ud (div (mul 100 far.mon) tot)) "f ")
14025    ::
14026      ^-  tape
14027      ?:  =(0 coy.mon)  ~
14028      (welp (scow %ud (div (mul 100 coy.mon) tot)) "y ")
14029    ::
14030      ^-  tape
14031      ?:  =(0 euq.mon)  ~
14032      (welp (scow %ud (div (mul 100 euq.mon) tot)) "e ")
14033    ==
14034 ::
```

```
14035  ++  pi-tell                                        ::  produce dump
14036    |=  day=doss
14037    ^-  (list tape)
14038    ?:  =(day *doss)  ~
14039    =+  tot=(pi-moth mon.day)
14040    ;:  welp
14041      [(welp "events: " (pi-mumm mon.day)) ~]
14042    ::
14043      %+  turn
14044        %+  sort  ~(tap by hit.day)
14045        |=  [a=[* @] b=[* @]]
14046        (lth +.a +.b)
14047      |=  [nam=term num=@ud]
14048      :(welp (trip nam) ": " (scow %ud num))
14049      ["" ~]
14050    ::
14051      %-  zing
14052      ^-  (list (list tape))
14053      %+  turn
14054        %+  sort  ~(tap by cut.day)
14055        |=  [one=(pair path hump) two=(pair path hump)]
14056        (gth (pi-moth mon.q.one) (pi-moth mon.q.two))
14057      |=  [pax=path hup=hump]
14058      =+  ott=(pi-moth mon.hup)
14059      ;:  welp
14060        [(welp "label: " (spud pax)) ~]
14061        [(welp "price: " (scow %ud (div (mul 100 ott) tot))) ~]
14062        [(welp "shape: " (pi-mumm mon.hup)) ~]
14063      ::
14064        ?:  =(~ out.hup)  ~
14065        :-  "into:"
14066        %+  turn
14067          %+  sort  ~(tap by out.hup)
14068          |=([[* a=@ud] [* b=@ud]] (gth a b))
14069        |=  [pax=path num=@ud]
14070        ^-  tape
14071        :(welp "  " (spud pax) ": " (scow %ud num))
14072      ::
14073        ?:  =(~ inn.hup)  ~
14074        :-  "from:"
14075        %+  turn
14076          %+  sort  ~(tap by inn.hup)
14077          |=([[* a=@ud] [* b=@ud]] (gth a b))
14078        |=  [pax=path num=@ud]
14079        ^-  tape
14080        :(welp "  " (spud pax) ": " (scow %ud num))
14081      ::
14082        ["" ~]
14083        ~
14084      ==
14085    ==
14086  --
```

Lull 323K

```
1   ::  /sys/lull
2   ::  %lull: arvo structures
3   !:
4   =>  ..part
5   ~%  %lull  ..part  ~
6   |%
7   ++  lull  %323
8   ::                                                     ::  ::
9   ::::                                                   ::  ::  (1) models
10   ::                                                    ::  ::
11  ::  #  %misc
12  ::
13  ::  miscellaneous systems types
14  ::+|
15  ::  +capped-queue: a +qeu with a maximum number of entries
16  ::
17  ++  capped-queue
18    |$  [item-type]
19    $:  queue=(qeu item-type)
20        size=@ud
21        max-size=_64
22    ==
23  ::  +clock: polymorphic cache type for use with the clock replacement algorithm
24  ::
25  ::      The +by-clock core wraps interface arms for manipulating a mapping from
26  ::      :key-type to :val-type. Detailed docs for this type can be found there.
27  ::
28  ++  clock
29    |$  ::   key-type: mold of keys
30        ::   val-type: mold of values
31        ::
32        [key-type val-type]
33    $:  lookup=(map key-type [val=val-type fresh=@ud])
34        queue=(qeu key-type)
35        size=@ud
36        max-size=_2.048
37        depth=_1
38    ==
39  ::  +mop: constructs and validates ordered ordered map based on key,
40  ::  val, and comparator gate
41  ::
42  ++  mop
43    |*  [key=mold value=mold]
44    |=  ord=$-([key key] ?)
45    |=  a=*
46    =/  b  ;;((tree [key=key val=value]) a)
47    ?>  (apt:((on key value) ord) b)
48    b
49  ::
50  ::
51  ++  ordered-map  on
52  ::  +on: treap with user-specified horizontal order, ordered-map
53  ::
54  ::  WARNING: ordered-map will not work properly if two keys can be
55  ::  unequal under noun equality but equal via the compare gate
```

```
56  ::
57  ++  on
58    ~%  %on  ..part  ~
59    |*  [key=mold val=mold]
60    =>  |%
61        +$  item  [key=key val=val]
62        --
63    ::  +compare: item comparator for horizontal order
64    ::
65    ~%  %comp  +>+  ~
66    |=  compare=$-([key key] ?)
67    ~%  %core  +  ~
68    |%
69    ::  +all: apply logical AND boolean test on all values
70    ::
71    ++  all
72      ~/  %all
73      |=  [a=(tree item) b=$-(item ?)]
74      ^-  ?
75      |-
76      ?~  a
77        &
78      ?&((b n.a) $(a l.a) $(a r.a))
79    ::  +any: apply logical OR boolean test on all values
80    ::
81    ++  any
82      ~/  %any
83      |=  [a=(tree item) b=$-(item ?)]
84      |-  ^-  ?
85      ?~  a
86        |
87      ?|((b n.a) $(a l.a) $(a r.a))
88    ::  +apt: verify horizontal and vertical orderings
89    ::
90    ++  apt
91      ~/  %apt
92      |=  a=(tree item)
93      =|  [l=(unit key) r=(unit key)]
94      |-  ^-  ?
95      ::  empty tree is valid
96      ::
97      ?~  a  %.y
98      ::  nonempty trees must maintain several criteria
99      ::
100     ?&  ::  if .n.a is left of .u.l, assert horizontal comparator
101         ::
102         ?~(l %.y (compare key.n.a u.l))
103         ::  if .n.a is right of .u.r, assert horizontal comparator
104         ::
105         ?~(r %.y (compare u.r key.n.a))
106         ::  if .a is not leftmost element, assert vertical order between
107         ::  .l.a and .n.a and recurse to the left with .n.a as right
108         ::  neighbor
109         ::
110         ?~(l.a %.y &((mor key.n.a key.n.l.a) $(a l.a, l `key.n.a)))
111         ::  if .a is not rightmost element, assert vertical order
112         ::  between .r.a and .n.a and recurse to the right with .n.a as
113         ::  left neighbor
```

```
114      ::
115      ?~(r.a %.y &((mor key.n.a key.n.r.a) $(a r.a, r `key.n.a)))
116    ==
117  ::  +bap: convert to list, right to left
118  ::
119  ++  bap
120    ~/  %bap
121    |=  a=(tree item)
122    ^-  (list item)
123    =|  b=(list item)
124    |-  ^+  b
125    ?~  a  b
126    $(a r.a, b [n.a $(a l.a)])
127  ::  +del: delete .key from .a if it exists, producing value iff deleted
128  ::
129  ++  del
130    ~/  %del
131    |=  [a=(tree item) =key]
132    ^-  [(unit val) (tree item)]
133    ?~  a  [~ ~]
134    ::  we found .key at the root; delete and rebalance
135    ::
136    ?:  =(key key.n.a)
137      [`val.n.a (nip a)]
138    ::  recurse left or right to find .key
139    ::
140    ?:  (compare key key.n.a)
141      =+  [found lef]=$(a l.a)
142      [found a(l lef)]
143    =+  [found rig]=$(a r.a)
144    [found a(r rig)]
145  ::  +dip: stateful partial inorder traversal
146  ::
147  ::    Mutates .state on each run of .f.  Starts at .start key, or if
148  ::    .start is ~, starts at the head.  Stops when .f produces .stop=%.y.
149  ::    Traverses from left to right keys.
150  ::    Each run of .f can replace an item's value or delete the item.
151  ::
152  ++  dip
153    ~/  %dip
154    |*  state=mold
155    |=  $:  a=(tree item)
156            =state
157            f=$-([state item] [(unit val) ? state])
158        ==
159    ^+  [state a]
160    ::  acc: accumulator
161    ::
162    ::    .stop: set to %.y by .f when done traversing
163    ::    .state: threaded through each run of .f and produced by +abet
164    ::
165    =/  acc  [stop=`?`%.n state=state]
166    =<  abet  =<  main
167    |%
168    ++  this  .
169    ++  abet  [state.acc a]
170    ::  +main: main recursive loop; performs a partial inorder traversal
171    ::
```

```
172      ++  main
173        ^+  this
174        ::  stop if empty or we've been told to stop
175        ::
176        ?:  =(~ a)  this
177        ?:  stop.acc  this
178        ::  inorder traversal: left -> node -> right, until .f sets .stop
179        ::
180        =.  this  left
181        ?:  stop.acc  this
182        =^  del  this  node
183        =?  this  !stop.acc  right
184        =?  a  del  (nip a)
185        this
186      ::  +node: run .f on .n.a, updating .a, .state, and .stop
187      ::
188      ++  node
189        ^+  [del=*? this]
190        ::  run .f on node, updating .stop.acc and .state.acc
191        ::
192        ?>  ?=(^ a)
193        =^  res  acc  (f state.acc n.a)
194        ?~  res
195          [del=& this]
196        [del=| this(val.n.a u.res)]
197      ::  +left: recurse on left subtree, copying mutant back into .l.a
198      ::
199      ++  left
200        ^+  this
201        ?~  a  this
202        =/  lef  main(a l.a)
203        lef(a a(l a.lef))
204      ::  +right: recurse on right subtree, copying mutant back into .r.a
205      ::
206      ++  right
207        ^+  this
208        ?~  a  this
209        =/  rig  main(a r.a)
210        rig(a a(r a.rig))
211      --
212    ::  +gas: put a list of items
213    ::
214    ++  gas
215      ~/  %gas
216      |=  [a=(tree item) b=(list item)]
217      ^-  (tree item)
218      ?~  b  a
219      $(b t.b, a (put a i.b))
220    ::  +get: get val at key or return ~
221    ::
222    ++  get
223      ~/  %get
224      |=  [a=(tree item) b=key]
225      ^-  (unit val)
226      ?~  a  ~
227      ?:  =(b key.n.a)
228        `val.n.a
229      ?:  (compare b key.n.a)
```

```
      $(a l.a)
    $(a r.a)
::  +got: need value at key
::
++  got
  |=  [a=(tree item) b=key]
  ^-  val
  (need (get a b))
::  +has: check for key existence
::
++  has
  ~/  %has
  |=  [a=(tree item) b=key]
  ^-  ?
  !=(~ (get a b))
::  +lot: take a subset range excluding start and/or end and all elements
::  outside the range
::
++  lot
  ~/  %lot
  |=  $:  tre=(tree item)
          start=(unit key)
          end=(unit key)
      ==
  ^-  (tree item)
  |^
  ?:  ?&(?=(~ start) ?=(~ end))
    tre
  ?~  start
    (del-span tre %end end)
  ?~  end
    (del-span tre %start start)
  ?>  (compare u.start u.end)
  =.  tre  (del-span tre %start start)
  (del-span tre %end end)
  ::
  ++  del-span
    |=  [a=(tree item) b=?(%start %end) c=(unit key)]
    ^-  (tree item)
    ?~  a  a
    ?~  c  a
    ?-  b
        %start
      ::  found key
      ?:  =(key.n.a u.c)
        (nip a(l ~))
      ::  traverse to find key
      ?:  (compare key.n.a u.c)
        ::  found key to the left of start
        $(a (nip a(l ~)))
      ::  found key to the right of start
      a(l $(a l.a))
    ::
        %end
      ::  found key
      ?:  =(u.c key.n.a)
        (nip a(r ~))
      ::  traverse to find key
```

```
288        ?:  (compare key.n.a u.c)
289            ::  found key to the left of end
290          a(r $(a r.a))
291          ::  found key to the right of end
292          $(a (nip a(r ~)))
293        ==
294      --
295    ::  +nip: remove root; for internal use
296    ::
297    ++  nip
298      ~/  %nip
299      |=  a=(tree item)
300      ^-  (tree item)
301      ?>  ?=(^ a)
302      ::  delete .n.a; merge and balance .l.a and .r.a
303      ::
304      |-  ^-  (tree item)
305      ?~  l.a  r.a
306      ?~  r.a  l.a
307      ?:  (mor key.n.l.a key.n.r.a)
308        l.a(r $(l.a r.l.a))
309      r.a(l $(r.a l.r.a))
310    ::
311    ::  +pop: produce .head (leftmost item) and .rest or crash if empty
312    ::
313    ++  pop
314      ~/  %pop
315      |=  a=(tree item)
316      ^-  [head=item rest=(tree item)]
317      ?~  a     !!
318      ?~  l.a  [n.a r.a]
319      =/  l  $(a l.a)
320      :-  head.l
321      ::  load .rest.l back into .a and rebalance
322      ::
323      ?:  |(?=(~ rest.l) (mor key.n.a key.n.rest.l))
324        a(l rest.l)
325      rest.l(r a(r r.rest.l))
326    ::  +pry: produce head (leftmost item) or null
327    ::
328    ++  pry
329      ~/  %pry
330      |=  a=(tree item)
331      ^-  (unit item)
332      ?~  a    ~
333      |-
334      ?~  l.a  `n.a
335      $(a l.a)
336    ::  +put: ordered item insert
337    ::
338    ++  put
339      ~/  %put
340      |=  [a=(tree item) =key =val]
341      ^-  (tree item)
342      ::  base case: replace null with single-item tree
343      ::
344      ?~  a  [n=[key val] l=~ r=~]
345      ::  base case: overwrite existing .key with new .val
```

```
346      ::
347      ?:  =(key.n.a key)  a(val.n val)
348      ::  if item goes on left, recurse left then rebalance vertical order
349      ::
350      ?:  (compare key key.n.a)
351        =/  l  $(a l.a)
352        ?>  ?=(^ l)
353        ?:  (mor key.n.a key.n.l)
354          a(l l)
355        l(r a(l r.l))
356      ::  item goes on right; recurse right then rebalance vertical order
357      ::
358      =/  r  $(a r.a)
359      ?>  ?=(^ r)
360      ?:  (mor key.n.a key.n.r)
361        a(r r)
362      r(l a(r l.r))
363    ::  +ram: produce tail (rightmost item) or null
364    ::
365    ++  ram
366      ~/  %ram
367      |=  a=(tree item)
368      ^-  (unit item)
369      ?~  a      ~
370      |-
371      ?~  r.a  `n.a
372      $(a r.a)
373    ::  +run: apply gate to transform all values in place
374    ::
375    ++  run
376      ~/  %run
377      |*  [a=(tree item) b=$-(val *)]
378      |-
379      ?~  a  a
380      [n=[key.n.a (b val.n.a)] l=$(a l.a) r=$(a r.a)]
381    ::  +tab: tabulate a subset excluding start element with a max count
382    ::
383    ++  tab
384      ~/  %tab
385      |=  [a=(tree item) b=(unit key) c=@]
386      ^-  (list item)
387      |^
388      (flop e:(tabulate (del-span a b) b c))
389      ::
390      ++  tabulate
391        |=  [a=(tree item) b=(unit key) c=@]
392        ^-  [d=@ e=(list item)]
393        ?:  ?&(?=(~ b) =(c 0))
394          [0 ~]
395        =|  f=[d=@ e=(list item)]
396        |-  ^+  f
397        ?:  ?|(?=(~ a) =(d.f c))  f
398        =.  f  $(a l.a)
399        ?:  =(d.f c)  f
400        =.  f  [+(d.f) [n.a e.f]]
401        ?:(=(d.f c) f $(a r.a))
402      ::
403      ++  del-span
```

```
404      |=  [a=(tree item) b=(unit key)]
405      ^-  (tree item)
406      ?~  a  a
407      ?~  b  a
408      ?:  =(key.n.a u.b)
409        r.a
410      ?:  (compare key.n.a u.b)
411        $(a r.a)
412      a(l $(a l.a))
413    --
414  ::  +tap: convert to list, left to right
415  ::
416  ++  tap
417    ~/  %tap
418    |=  a=(tree item)
419    ^-  (list item)
420    =|  b=(list item)
421    |-  ^+  b
422    ?~  a  b
423    $(a l.a, b [n.a $(a r.a)])
424  ::  +uni: unify two ordered maps
425  ::
426  ::      .b takes precedence over .a if keys overlap.
427  ::
428  ++  uni
429    ~/  %uni
430    |=  [a=(tree item) b=(tree item)]
431    ^-  (tree item)
432    ?~  b  a
433    ?~  a  b
434    ?:  =(key.n.a key.n.b)
435      [n=n.b l=$(a l.a, b l.b) r=$(a r.a, b r.b)]
436    ?:  (mor key.n.a key.n.b)
437      ?:  (compare key.n.b key.n.a)
438        $(l.a $(a l.a, r.b ~), b r.b)
439      $(r.a $(a r.a, l.b ~), b l.b)
440    ?:  (compare key.n.a key.n.b)
441      $(l.b $(b l.b, r.a ~), a r.a)
442    $(r.b $(b r.b, l.a ~), a l.a)
443  ::  +wyt: measure size
444  ::
445  ++  wyt
446    ~/  %wyt
447    |=  a=(tree item)
448    ^-  @ud
449    ?~(a 0 +((add $(a l.a) $(a r.a))))
450    --
451  ::
452  +$  deco  ?(~ %bl %br %un)              ::  text decoration
453  +$  json                               ::  normal json value
454    $@  ~                                ::  null
455    $%  [%a p=(list json)]               ::  array
456        [%b p=?]                         ::  boolean
457        [%o p=(map @t json)]             ::  object
458        [%n p=@ta]                       ::  number
459        [%s p=@t]                        ::  string
460    ==                                   ::
461  +$  life  @ud                          ::  ship key revision
```

```
+$    rift    @ud                                      ::    ship continuity
+$    mime    (pair mite octs)                         ::    mimetyped data
+$    octs    (pair @ud @)                             ::    octet-stream
+$    sock    (pair ship ship)                         ::    outgoing [src dest]
+$    sack    (trel ship ship path)                    ::    $sock /w provenance
+$    stub    (list (pair stye (list @c)))             ::    styled unicode
+$    stye    (pair (set deco) (pair tint tint))       ::    decos/bg/fg
+$    styl    %+  pair  (unit deco)                    ::    cascading style
              (pair (unit tint) (unit tint))           ::
+$    styx    (list $@(@t (pair styl styx)))           ::    styled text
+$    tint    $@  ?(%r %g %b %c %m %y %k %w %~)         ::    text color
              [r=@uxD g=@uxD b=@uxD]                    ::    24bit true color
+$    turf    (list @t)                                ::    domain, tld first
::                                                     ::::
::::                          ++ethereum-types           ::    eth surs for jael
  ::                                                   ::::
++  ethereum-types
  |%
  ::    ethereum address, 20 bytes.
  ::
  ++    address   @ux
  ::    event location
  ::
  +$    event-id   [block=@ud log=@ud]
  ::
  ++    events   (set event-id)
  --
::                                                     ::::
::::                          ++azimuth-types            ::    az surs for jael
  ::                                                   ::::
++  azimuth-types
  =,  ethereum-types
  |%
  ++  point
    $:  ::  ownership
        ::
        $=  own
        $:  owner=address
            management-proxy=address
            voting-proxy=address
            transfer-proxy=address
        ==
      ::
        ::  networking
        ::
        $=  net
        %-  unit
        $:  =life
            =pass
            continuity-number=@ud
            sponsor=[has=? who=@p]
            escape=(unit @p)
        ==
      ::
        ::  spawning
        ::
        $=  kid
        %-  unit
```

```
        $:  spawn-proxy=address
            spawned=(set @p)  ::TODO  sparse range, pile, see old jael ++py
        ==
    ==
  ::
+$  dnses  [pri=@t sec=@t ter=@t]
  ::
++  diff-azimuth
  $%  [%point who=@p dif=diff-point]
      [%dns dnses]
  ==
  ::
++  diff-point
  $%  [%full new=point]                       ::
      [%owner new=address]                    ::  OwnerChanged
      [%activated who=@p]                     ::  Activated
      [%spawned who=@p]                       ::  Spawned
      [%keys =life =pass]                     ::  ChangedKeys
      [%continuity new=@ud]                   ::  BrokeContinuity
      [%sponsor new=[has=? who=@p]]           ::  EscapeAcc/LostSpons
      [%escape new=(unit @p)]                 ::  EscapeReq/Can
      [%management-proxy new=address]         ::  ChangedManagementPro
      [%voting-proxy new=address]             ::  ChangedVotingProxy
      [%spawn-proxy new=address]              ::  ChangedSpawnProxy
      [%transfer-proxy new=address]           ::  ChangedTransferProxy
    ==
  --
::  +vane-task: general tasks shared across vanes
::
+$  vane-task
  $~  [%born ~]
  $%  ::  i/o device replaced (reset state)
      ::
      [%born ~]
      ::  boot completed (XX legacy)
      ::
      [%init ~]
      ::  trim state (in response to memory pressure)
      ::
      [%trim p=@ud]
      ::  kernel upgraded
      ::
      [%vega ~]
      ::  receive message via %ames
      ::
      ::    TODO: move .vane from $plea to here
      ::
      [%plea =ship =plea:ames]
  ==
::                                            :::::
:::::                       ++http           ::
  ::                                          :::::
::  http: shared representations of http concepts
::
++  http  ^?
  |%
  ::  +header-list: an ordered list of http headers
  ::
```

```hoon
+$  header-list
  (list [key=@t value=@t])
::  +method: exhaustive list of http verbs
::
+$  method
  $?  %'CONNECT'
      %'DELETE'
      %'GET'
      %'HEAD'
      %'OPTIONS'
      %'PATCH'
      %'POST'
      %'PUT'
      %'TRACE'
  ==
::  +request: a single http request
::
+$  request
  $:  ::  method: http method
      ::
      method=method
      ::  url: the url requested
      ::
      ::    The url is not escaped. There is no escape.
      ::
      url=@t
      ::  header-list: headers to pass with this request
      ::
      =header-list
      ::  body: optionally, data to send with this request
      ::
      body=(unit octs)
  ==
::  +response-header: the status code and header list on an http request
::
::    We separate these away from the body data because we may not wait for
::    the entire body before we send a %progress to the caller.
::
+$  response-header
  $:  ::  status: http status code
      ::
      status-code=@ud
      ::  headers: http headers
      ::
      headers=header-list
  ==
::  +http-event: packetized http
::
::    Urbit treats Earth's HTTP servers as pipes, where Urbit sends or
::    receives one or more %http-events. The first of these will always be a
::    %start or an %error, and the last will always be %cancel or will have
::    :complete set to %.y to finish the connection.
::
::    Calculation of control headers such as 'Content-Length' or
::    'Transfer-Encoding' should be performed at a higher level; this structure
::    is merely for what gets sent to or received from Earth.
::
+$  http-event
```

```
636      $%  ::  %start: the first packet in a response
637          ::
638          $:  %start
639              ::  response-header: first event information
640              ::
641              =response-header
642              ::  data: data to pass to the pipe
643              ::
644              data=(unit octs)
645              ::  whether this completes the request
646              ::
647              complete=?
648          ==
649          ::  %continue: every subsequent packet
650          ::
651          $:  %continue
652              ::  data: data to pass to the pipe
653              ::
654              data=(unit octs)
655              ::  complete: whether this completes the request
656              ::
657              complete=?
658          ==
659          ::  %cancel: represents unsuccessful termination
660          ::
661          [%cancel ~]
662      ==
663  ::  +get-header: returns the value for :header, if it exists in :header-list
664  ::
665  ++  get-header
666    |=  [header=@t =header-list]
667    ^-  (unit @t)
668    ::
669    ?~  header-list
670        ~
671    ::
672    ?:  =(key.i.header-list header)
673      `value.i.header-list
674    ::
675    $(header-list t.header-list)
676  ::  +set-header: sets the value of an item in the header list
677  ::
678  ::    This adds to the end if it doesn't exist.
679  ::
680  ++  set-header
681    |=  [header=@t value=@t =header-list]
682    ^-  ^header-list
683    ::
684    ?~  header-list
685      ::  we didn't encounter the value, add it to the end
686      ::
687      [[header value] ~]
688    ::
689    ?:  =(key.i.header-list header)
690      [[header value] t.header-list]
691    ::
692    [i.header-list $(header-list t.header-list)]
693  ::  +delete-header: removes the first instance of a header from the list
```

```
694    ::
695    ++  delete-header
696      |=  [header=@t =header-list]
697      ^-  ^header-list
698      ::
699      ?~  header-list
700        ~
701      ::  if we see it in the list, remove it
702      ::
703      ?:  =(key.i.header-list header)
704        t.header-list
705      ::
706      [i.header-list $(header-list t.header-list)]
707    ::  +unpack-header: parse header field values
708    ::
709    ++  unpack-header
710      |^  |=  value=@t
711          ^-  (unit (list (map @t @t)))
712          (rust (cass (trip value)) values)
713      ::
714      ++  values
715        %+  more
716          (ifix [. .]:(star ;~(pose ace (just '\09'))) com)
717        pairs
718      ::
719      ++  pairs
720        %+  cook
721          ~(gas by *(map @t @t))
722        %+  most  (ifix [. .]:(star ace) mic)
723        ;~(plug token ;~(pose ;~(pfix tis value) (easy '')))
724      ::
725      ++  value
726        ;~(pose token quoted-string)
727      ::
728      ++  token                                  ::  7230 token
729        %+  cook  crip
730        ::NOTE  this is ptok:de-purl:html, but can't access that here
731        %-  plus
732        ;~  pose
733          aln  zap  hax  buc  cen  pam  soq  tar  lus
734          hep  dot  ket  cab  tic  bar  sig
735        ==
736      ::
737      ++  quoted-string                          ::  7230 quoted string
738        %+  cook  crip
739        %+  ifix  [. .]:;~(less (jest '\\"') doq)
740        %-  star
741        ;~  pose
742          ;~(pfix bas ;~(pose (just '\09') ace prn))
743          ;~(pose (just '\09') ;~(less (mask "\22\5c\7f") (shim 0x20 0xff)))
744        ==
745      --
746    ::  +simple-payload: a simple, one event response used for generators
747    ::
748    +$  simple-payload
749      $:  ::  response-header: status code, etc
750          ::
751          =response-header
```

```
    ::    data: the data returned as the body
    ::
        data=(unit octs)
    ==
  --
::                                                        ::::
::::                          ++ames                      ::  (1a) network
  ::                                                      ::::
++  ames  ^?
  |%
  ::  $task: job for ames
  ::
  ::    Messaging Tasks
  ::
  ::    %hear: packet from unix
  ::    %dear: lane from unix
  ::    %heed: track peer's responsiveness; gives %clog if slow
  ::    %jilt: stop tracking peer's responsiveness
  ::    %cork: request to delete message flow
  ::    %tame: request to delete route for ship
  ::    %kroc: request to delete specific message flows, from their bones
  ::    %plea: request to send message
  ::    %deep: deferred calls to %ames, from itself
  ::    %stun: STUN response (or failure), from unix
  ::
  ::    Remote Scry Tasks
  ::
  ::    %keen: peek: [ship /vane/care/case/spur]
  ::    %yawn: cancel request from arvo
  ::    %wham: cancels all scry request from any vane
  ::
  ::    System and Lifecycle Tasks
  ::
  ::    %born: process restart notification
  ::    %init: vane boot
  ::    %prod: re-send a packet per flow, to all peers if .ships is ~
  ::    %sift: limit verbosity to .ships
  ::    %snub: set packet blocklist to .ships
  ::    %spew: set verbosity toggles
  ::    %cong: adjust congestion control parameters
  ::    %stir: recover from timer desync and assorted debug commands
  ::    %trim: release memory
  ::    %vega: kernel reload notification
  ::
  +$  task
    $+  ames-task
    $%  [%hear =lane =blob]
        [%dear =ship =lane]
        [%heed =ship]
        [%jilt =ship]
        [%cork =ship]
        [%tame =ship]
        [%kroc bones=(list [ship bone])]
        $>(%plea vane-task)
        [%deep =deep]
        [%stun =stun]
    ::
        [%keen sec=(unit [idx=@ key=@]) spar]
```

```
            [%chum spar]
            [%yawn spar]
            [%wham spar]
            [%plug =path]
        ::
            $>(%born vane-task)
            $>(%init vane-task)
            [%prod ships=(list ship)]
            [%sift ships=(list ship)]
            [%snub form=?(%allow %deny) ships=(list ship)]
            [%spew veb=(list verb)]
            [%cong msg=@ud mem=@ud]
            [%stir arg=@t]
            $>(%trim vane-task)
            $>(%vega vane-task)
        ==
::  $gift: effect from ames
::
::    Messaging Gifts
::
::    %boon: response message from remote ship
::    %clog: notify vane that %boon's to peer are backing up locally
::    %done: notify vane that peer (n)acked our message
::    %lost: notify vane that we crashed on %boon
::    %send: packet to unix
::    %nail: lanes to unix
::
::    Remote Scry Gifts
::
::    %tune: peek result
::
::    System and Lifecycle Gifts
::
::    %turf: domain report, relayed from jael
::    %saxo: our sponsor list report
::
+$  gift
  $%  [%boon payload=*]
      [%clog =ship]
      [%done error=(unit error)]
      [%lost ~]
      [%send =lane =blob]
      [%nail =ship lanes=(list lane)]
    ::
      [%stub num=@ud key=@]
      [%near spar dat=(unit (unit page))]
      [%tune spar roar=(unit roar)]
    ::
      [%turf turfs=(list turf)]
      [%saxo sponsors=(list ship)]
    ==
::
::::                                                    ::  (1a2)
  ::
++  acru  $_  ^?                                        ::  asym cryptosuite
  |%                                                    ::  opaque object
  ++  as  ^?                                            ::  asym ops
    |%  ++  seal  |~([a=pass b=@] *@)                   ::  encrypt to a
```

```
868            ++    sign    |~(a=@ *@)                              ::  certify as us
869            ++    sigh    |~(a=@ *@)                              ::  certification only
870            ++    sure    |~(a=@ *(unit @))                       ::  authenticate from us
871            ++    safe    |~([a=@ b=@] *?)                        ::  authentication only
872            ++    tear    |~([a=pass b=@] *(unit @))              ::  accept from a
873       --  ::as                                                  ::
874     ++  de  |~([a=@ b=@] *(unit @))                             ::  symmetric de, soft
875     ++  dy  |~([a=@ b=@] *@)                                   ::  symmetric de, hard
876     ++  en  |~([a=@ b=@] *@)                                   ::  symmetric en
877     ++  ex  ^?                                                  ::  export
878       |%  ++  fig  *@uvH                                        ::  fingerprint
879           ++  pac  *@uvG                                        ::  default passcode
880           ++  pub  *pass                                        ::  public key
881           ++  sec  *ring                                        ::  private key
882       --  ::ex                                                  ::
883     ++  nu  ^?                                                  ::  reconstructors
884       |%  ++  pit  |~([a=@ b=@] ^?(..nu))                       ::  from [width seed]
885           ++  nol  |~(a=ring ^?(..nu))                          ::  from ring
886           ++  com  |~(a=pass ^?(..nu))                          ::  from pass
887       --  ::nu                                                  ::
888     --  ::acru                                                  ::
889  ::  +protocol-version: current version of the ames wire protocol
890  ::
891  ++  protocol-version  `?(%0 %1 %2 %3 %4 %5 %6 %7)`%0
892  ::  $address: opaque atomic transport address to or from unix
893  ::
894  +$  address  @uxaddress
895  ::  $verb: verbosity flag for ames
896  ::
897  +$  verb  ?(%snd %rcv %odd %msg %ges %for %rot %kay %fin %sun)
898  ::  $blob: raw atom to or from unix, representing a packet
899  ::
900  +$  blob  @uxblob
901  ::  $error: tagged diagnostic trace
902  ::
903  +$  error  [tag=@tas =tang]
904  ::  $lane: ship transport address; either opaque $address or galaxy
905  ::
906  ::    The runtime knows how to look up galaxies, so we don't need to
907  ::    know their transport addresses.
908  ::
909  +$  lane  (each @pC address)
910  ::  $plea: application-level message, as a %pass
911  ::
912  ::    vane: destination vane on remote ship
913  ::    path: internal route on the receiving ship
914  ::    payload: semantic message contents
915  ::
916  +$  plea  [vane=@tas =path payload=*]
917  ::
918  +$  message
919    $%  [%plea plea]
920        [%boon payload=*]
921        [%naxplanation =message-num =error]
922    ==
923  ::  $spar:  pair of $ship and $path
924  ::
925  ::    Instead of fully qualifying a scry path, ames infers rift and
```

```
926  ::      life based on the ship.
927  ::
928  +$  spar  [=ship =path]
929  ::  $deep: deferred %ames call, from self, to keep +abet cores pure
930  ::
931  +$  deep
932    $%  [%nack =ship =nack=bone =message]
933        [%sink =ship =target=bone naxplanation=[=message-num =error]]
934        [%drop =ship =nack=bone =message-num]
935        [%cork =ship =bone]
936        [%kill =ship =bone]
937    ==
938  ::  $stun: STUN notifications, from unix
939  ::
940  ::      .lane is the latest cached lane in vere, from the point of view of .ship
941  ::
942  +$  stun
943    $%  [%stop =ship =lane]  :: succesful STUN response, stop %ping app
944        [%fail =ship =lane]  :: failure to STUN, re-enable %ping app
945        [%once =ship =lane]  :: new lane discovered, notify ping %app
946    ==
947  ::  +|  %atomics
948  ::
949  +$  bone           @udbone
950  +$  fragment       @uwfragment
951  +$  fragment-num   @udfragmentnum
952  +$  message-blob   @udmessageblob
953  +$  message-num    @udmessagenum
954  +$  public-key     @uwpublickey
955  +$  symmetric-key  @uwsymmetrickey
956  ::
957  ::  $hoot: request packet payload
958  ::  $yowl: serialized response packet payload
959  ::  $hunk: a slice of $yowl fragments
960  ::  $lock: keys for remote scry
961  ::
962  +$  hoot           @uxhoot
963  +$  yowl           @uxyowl
964  +$  hunk           [lop=@ len=@]
965  +$  lock           [idx=@ key=@]
966  ::
967  ::  +|  %kinetics
968  ::  $dyad: pair of sender and receiver ships
969  ::
970  +$  dyad  [sndr=ship rcvr=ship]
971  ::  $shot: noun representation of an ames datagram packet
972  ::
973  ::      Roundtrips losslessly through atom encoding and decoding.
974  ::
975  ::      .origin is ~ unless the packet is being forwarded.  If present,
976  ::      it's an atom that encodes a route to another ship, such as an IPv4
977  ::      address.  Routes are opaque to Arvo and only have meaning in the
978  ::      interpreter. This enforces that Ames is transport-agnostic.
979  ::
980  ::      req: is a request
981  ::      sam: is using the ames protocol (not fine or another protocol)
982  ::
983  +$  shot
```

```
$:  dyad
    req=?
    sam=?
    sndr-tick=@ubC
    rcvr-tick=@ubC
    origin=(unit @uxaddress)
    content=@uxcontent
==
::  $ack: positive ack, nack packet, or nack trace
::
+$  ack
  $%  [%ok ~]
      [%nack ~]
      [%naxplanation =error]
  ==
::
::  +|  %statics
::  $ship-state: all we know about a peer
::
::      %alien: no PKI data, so enqueue actions to perform once we learn it
::      %known: we know their life and public keys, so we have a channel
::
+$  ship-state
  $+  ship-state
  $%  [%alien alien-agenda]
      [%known peer-state]
  ==
::  $alien-agenda: what to do when we learn a peer's life and keys
::
::      messages: pleas local vanes have asked us to send
::      packets: packets we've tried to send
::      heeds: local tracking requests; passed through into $peer-state
::
+$  alien-agenda
  $+  alien-agenda
  $:  messages=(list [=duct =plea])
      packets=(set =blob)
      heeds=(set duct)
      keens=(jug path duct)
      chums=(jug path duct)
  ==
+$  chain  ((mop ,@ ,[key=@ =path]) lte)
::  $peer-state: state for a peer with known life and keys
::
::      route: transport-layer destination for packets to peer
::      qos: quality of service; connection status to peer
::      ossuary: bone<->duct mapper
::      snd: per-bone message pumps to send messages as fragments
::      rcv: per-bone message sinks to assemble messages from fragments
::      nax: unprocessed nacks (negative acknowledgments)
::          Each value is ~ when we've received the ack packet but not a
::          nack-trace, or an error when we've received a nack-trace but
::          not the ack packet.
::
::          When we hear a nack packet or an explanation, if there's no
::          entry in .nax, we make a new entry. Otherwise, if this new
::          information completes the packet+nack-trace, we remove the
::          entry and emit a nack to the local vane that asked us to send
```

```
::          the message.
::      heeds: listeners for %clog notifications
::      closing: bones closed on the sender side
::      corked:  bones closed on both sender and receiver
::
+$  peer-state
  $+  peer-state
  $:  $:  =symmetric-key
          =life
          =rift
          =public-key
          sponsor=ship
      ==
      route=(unit [direct=? =lane])
      =qos
      =ossuary
      snd=(map bone message-pump-state)
      rcv=(map bone message-sink-state)
      nax=(set [=bone =message-num])
      heeds=(set duct)
      closing=(set bone)
      corked=(set bone)
      keens=(map path keen-state)
      =chain
  ==
+$  keen-state
  $+  keen-state
  $:  wan=((mop @ud want) lte)  ::  request packets, sent
      nex=(list want)           ::  request packets, unsent
      hav=(list have)           ::  response packets, backward
      num-fragments=@ud
      num-received=@ud
      next-wake=(unit @da)
      listeners=(set duct)
      metrics=pump-metrics
  ==
+$  want
  $:  fra=@ud
      =hoot
      packet-state
  ==
+$  have
  $:  fra=@ud
      meow
  ==
::
+$  meow  ::  response fragment
  $:  sig=@ux  ::  signature
      num=@ud  ::  number of fragments
      dat=@ux  ::  contents
  ==
::
+$  peep  ::  fragment request
  $:  =path
      num=@ud
  ==
::
+$  wail  ::  tagged request fragment
```

```
1100      $%  [%0 peep]  :: unsigned
1101        ==
1102    ::
1103    +$  roar  ::  response message
1104      (tale:pki:jael (pair path (unit (cask))))
1105    ::
1106    +$  purr  ::  response packet payload
1107      $:  peep
1108          meow
1109        ==
1110    ::
1111    ::  $qos: quality of service; how is our connection to a peer doing?
1112    ::
1113    ::      .last-contact: last time we heard from peer, or if %unborn, when
1114    ::      we first started tracking time
1115    ::
1116    +$  qos
1117      $~  [%unborn *@da]
1118      [?(%live %dead %unborn) last-contact=@da]
1119    ::  $ossuary: bone<->duct bijection and .next-bone to map to a duct
1120    ::
1121    ::      The first bone is 0. They increment by 4, since each flow includes
1122    ::      a bit for each message determining forward vs. backward and a
1123    ::      second bit for whether the message is on the normal flow or the
1124    ::      associated diagnostic flow (for naxplanations).
1125    ::
1126    ::      The least significant bit of a $bone is:
1127    ::      1 if "forward", i.e. we send %plea's on this flow, or
1128    ::      0 if "backward", i.e. we receive %plea's on this flow.
1129    ::
1130    ::      The second-least significant bit is 1 if the bone is a
1131    ::      naxplanation bone, and 0 otherwise.  Only naxplanation
1132    ::      messages can be sent on a naxplanation bone, as %boon's.
1133    ::
1134    +$  ossuary
1135      $:  =next=bone
1136          by-duct=(map duct bone)
1137          by-bone=(map bone duct)
1138        ==
1139    ::  $message-pump-state: persistent state for |message-pump
1140    ::
1141    ::      Messages queue up in |message-pump's .unsent-messages until they
1142    ::      can be packetized and fed into |packet-pump for sending.  When we
1143    ::      pop a message off .unsent-messages, we push as many fragments as
1144    ::      we can into |packet-pump, which sends every packet it eats.
1145    ::      Packets rejected by |packet-pump are placed in .unsent-fragments.
1146    ::
1147    ::      When we hear a packet ack, we send it to |packet-pump to be
1148    ::      removed from its queue of unacked packets.
1149    ::
1150    ::      When we hear a message ack (positive or negative), we treat that
1151    ::      as though all fragments have been acked.  If this message is not
1152    ::      .current, then this ack is for a future message and .current has
1153    ::      not yet been acked, so we place the ack in .queued-message-acks.
1154    ::
1155    ::      If we hear a message ack before we've sent all the fragments for
1156    ::      that message, clear .unsent-fragments and have |packet-pump delete
1157    ::      all sent fragments from the message. If this early message ack was
```

```
    ::     positive, print it out because it indicates the peer is not
    ::     behaving properly.
    ::
    ::     If the ack is for the current message, have |packet-pump delete
    ::     all packets from the message, give the message ack back
    ::     to the client vane, increment .current, and check if this next
    ::     message is in .queued-message-acks.  If it is, emit the message
    ::     (n)ack, increment .current, and check the next message.  Repeat
    ::     until .current is not fully acked.
    ::
    ::     The following equation is always true:
    ::     .next - .current == number of messages in flight
    ::
    ::     At the end of a task, |message-pump sends a %halt task to
    ::     |packet-pump, which can trigger a timer to be set or cleared based
    ::     on congestion control calculations. When the timer fires, it will
    ::     generally cause a packet to be re-sent.
    ::
    ::     Message sequence numbers start at 1 so that the first message will
    ::     be greater than .last-acked.message-sink-state on the receiver.
    ::
    ::     current: sequence number of earliest message sent or being sent
    ::     next: sequence number of next message to send
    ::     unsent-messages: messages to be sent after current message
    ::     unsent-fragments: fragments of current message waiting for sending
    ::     queued-message-acks: future message acks to be applied after current
    ::     packet-pump-state: state of corresponding |packet-pump
    ::
    +$  message-pump-state
      $+  message-pump-state
      $:  current=_`message-num`1
          next=_`message-num`1
          unsent-messages=(qeu message)
          unsent-fragments=(list static-fragment)
          queued-message-acks=(map message-num ack)
          =packet-pump-state
      ==
    +$  static-fragment
      $:  =message-num
          num-fragments=fragment-num
          =fragment-num
          =fragment
      ==
    ::  $packet-pump-state: persistent state for |packet-pump
    ::
    ::    next-wake: last timer we've set, or null
    ::    live: packets in flight; sent but not yet acked
    ::    metrics: congestion control information
    ::
    +$  packet-pump-state
      $+  packet-pump-state
      $:  next-wake=(unit @da)
          live=((mop live-packet-key live-packet-val) lte-packets)
          metrics=pump-metrics
      ==
    ::  +lte-packets: yes if a is before b
    ::
    ++  lte-packets
```

```
    |=  [a=live-packet-key b=live-packet-key]
    ^-  ?
    ::
    ?:  (lth message-num.a message-num.b)
      %.y
    ?:  (gth message-num.a message-num.b)
      %.n
    (lte fragment-num.a fragment-num.b)
::  $pump-metrics: congestion control state for a |packet-pump
::
::    This is an Ames adaptation of TCP's Reno congestion control
::    algorithm.  The information signals and their responses are
::    identical to those of the "NewReno" variant of Reno; the
::    implementation differs because Ames acknowledgments differ from
::    TCP's, because this code uses functional data structures, and
::    because TCP's sequence numbers reset when a peer becomes
::    unresponsive, whereas Ames sequence numbers only change when a
::    ship breaches.
::
::    A deviation from Reno is +fast-resend-after-ack, which re-sends
::    timed-out packets when a peer starts responding again after a
::    period of unresponsiveness.
::
::    If .skips reaches 3, we perform a fast retransmit and fast
::    recovery.  This corresponds to Reno's handling of "three duplicate
::    acks".
::
::    rto: retransmission timeout
::    rtt: roundtrip time estimate, low-passed using EWMA
::    rttvar: mean deviation of .rtt, also low-passed with EWMA
::    ssthresh: slow-start threshold
::    cwnd: congestion window; max unacked packets
::
+$  pump-metrics
  $:  rto=_~s1
      rtt=_~s1
      rttvar=_~s1
      ssthresh=_10.000
      cwnd=_1
      counter=@ud
  ==
+$  live-packet
  $:  key=live-packet-key
      val=live-packet-val
  ==
+$  live-packet-key
  $:  =message-num
      =fragment-num
  ==
+$  live-packet-val
  $:  packet-state
      num-fragments=fragment-num
      =fragment
  ==
+$  packet-state
  $:  last-sent=@da
      tries=_1
      skips=@ud
```

```
    ==
::    $message-sink-state: state of |message-sink to assemble messages
::
::      last-acked: highest $message-num we've fully acknowledged
::      last-heard: highest $message-num we've heard all fragments on
::      pending-vane-ack: heard but not processed by local vane
::      live-messages: partially received messages
::
+$  message-sink-state
  $+  message-sink-state
  $:  last-acked=message-num
      last-heard=message-num
      pending-vane-ack=(qeu [=message-num message=*])
      live-messages=(map message-num partial-rcv-message)
      nax=(set message-num)
    ==
::    $partial-rcv-message: message for which we've received some fragments
::
::      num-fragments: total number of fragments in this message
::      num-received: how many fragments we've received so far
::      fragments: fragments we've received, eventually producing a $message
::
+$  partial-rcv-message
  $:  num-fragments=fragment-num
      num-received=fragment-num
      fragments=(map fragment-num fragment)
    ==
::    $rank: which kind of ship address, by length
::
::      0b0: galaxy or star -- 2  bytes
::      0b1: planet          -- 4  bytes
::      0b10: moon           -- 8  bytes
::      0b11: comet          -- 16 bytes
::
+$  rank  ?(%0b0 %0b1 %0b10 %0b11)
::
::    +|  %coding
::    +sift-ship-size: decode a 2-bit ship type specifier into a byte width
::
::      Type 0: galaxy or star -- 2 bytes
::      Type 1: planet          -- 4 bytes
::      Type 2: moon            -- 8 bytes
::      Type 3: comet           -- 16 bytes
::
++  sift-ship-size
  |=  rank=@ubC
  ^-  @
  ::
  ?+  rank  !!
    %0b0   2
    %0b1   4
    %0b10  8
    %0b11  16
  ==
::    +is-valid-rank: does .ship match its stated .size?
::
++  is-valid-rank
  |=  [=ship size=@ubC]
```

```
1332      ^-  ?
1333      .=  size
1334      =/  wid  (met 3 ship)
1335      ?:  (lte wid 1)    2
1336      ?:  =(2 wid)       2
1337      ?:  (lte wid 4)    4
1338      ?:  (lte wid 8)    8
1339      ?>  (lte wid 16)  16
1340  ::  +sift-shot: deserialize packet from bytestream or crash
1341  ::
1342  ++  sift-shot
1343    |=  =blob
1344    ^-  shot
1345    ~|  %sift-shot-fail
1346    ::  first 32 (2^5) bits are header; the rest is body
1347    ::
1348    =/  header  (end 5 blob)
1349    =/  body    (rsh 5 blob)
1350    ::  read header; first two bits are reserved
1351    ::
1352    =/  req  =(& (cut 0 [2 1] header))
1353    =/  sam  =(& (cut 0 [3 1] header))
1354    ::
1355    =/  version  (cut 0 [4 3] header)
1356    ?.  =(protocol-version version)
1357      ~&  [%ames-protocol-version protocol-version version]
1358      ~|  ames-protocol-version+version  !!
1359    ::
1360    =/  sndr-size  (sift-ship-size (cut 0 [7 2] header))
1361    =/  rcvr-size  (sift-ship-size (cut 0 [9 2] header))
1362    =/  checksum   (cut 0 [11 20] header)
1363    =/  relayed    (cut 0 [31 1] header)
1364    ::  origin, if present, is 6 octets long, at the end of the body
1365    ::
1366    =^  origin=(unit @)  body
1367      ?:  =(| relayed)
1368        [~ body]
1369      =/  len  (sub (met 3 body) 6)
1370      [`(end [3 6] body) (rsh [3 6] body)]
1371    ::  .checksum does not apply to the origin
1372    ::
1373    ?.  =(checksum (end [0 20] (mug body)))
1374      ~&  >>>  %ames-checksum
1375      ~|  %ames-checksum  !!
1376    ::  read fixed-length sndr and rcvr life data from body
1377    ::
1378    ::    These represent the last four bits of the sender and receiver
1379    ::    life fields, to be used for quick dropping of honest packets to
1380    ::    or from the wrong life.
1381    ::
1382    =/  sndr-tick  (cut 0 [0 4] body)
1383    =/  rcvr-tick  (cut 0 [4 4] body)
1384    ::  read variable-length .sndr and .rcvr addresses
1385    ::
1386    =/  off   1
1387    =^  sndr  off  [(cut 3 [off sndr-size] body) (add off sndr-size)]
1388    ?.  (is-valid-rank sndr sndr-size)
1389      ~&  >>>  [%ames-sender-imposter sndr sndr-size]
```

```
1390      ~|  ames-sender-impostor+[sndr sndr-size]  !!
1391    ::
1392    =^  rcvr  off  [(cut 3 [off rcvr-size] body) (add off rcvr-size)]
1393    ?.  (is-valid-rank rcvr rcvr-size)
1394      ~&  >>>  [%ames-receiver-imposter rcvr rcvr-size]
1395      ~|  ames-receiver-impostor+[rcvr rcvr-size]  !!
1396    ::  read variable-length .content from the rest of .body
1397    ::
1398    =/  content  (cut 3 [off (sub (met 3 body) off)] body)
1399    [[sndr rcvr] req sam sndr-tick rcvr-tick origin content]
1400  ::
1401  ++  sift-wail
1402    |=  =hoot
1403    ^-  wail
1404    ?>  =(0 (end 3 hoot))
1405    [%0 +:(sift-peep (rsh 3 hoot))]
1406  ::
1407  ++  sift-purr
1408    |=  =hoot
1409    ^-  purr
1410    =+  [wid peep]=(sift-peep hoot)
1411    [peep (sift-meow (rsh [3 wid] hoot))]
1412  ::
1413  ++  sift-peep
1414    |=  =hoot
1415    ^-  [wid=@ =peep]
1416    =+  num=(cut 3 [0 4] hoot)
1417    =+  len=(cut 3 [4 2] hoot)
1418    =+  pat=(cut 3 [6 len] hoot)
1419    ~|  pat=pat
1420    :-  (add 6 len)
1421    :_  num
1422    (rash pat ;~(pfix fas (most fas (cook crip (star ;~(less fas prn)))))))
1423  ::
1424  ++  sift-meow
1425    |=  =yowl
1426    :*  sig=(cut 3 [0 64] yowl)
1427        num=(cut 3 [64 4] yowl)
1428        dat=(rsh 3^68 yowl)
1429    ==
1430  ::  +etch-shot: serialize a packet into a bytestream
1431  ::
1432  ++  etch-shot
1433    |=  shot
1434    ^-  blob
1435    ::
1436    =/  sndr-meta  (ship-meta sndr)
1437    =/  rcvr-meta  (ship-meta rcvr)
1438    ::
1439    =/  body=@
1440      ;:  mix
1441        sndr-tick
1442        (lsh 2 rcvr-tick)
1443        (lsh 3 sndr)
1444        (lsh [3 +(size.sndr-meta)] rcvr)
1445        (lsh [3 +((add size.sndr-meta size.rcvr-meta))] content)
1446      ==
1447    =/  checksum  (end [0 20] (mug body))
```

```
=?  body  ?=(^ origin)  (mix u.origin (lsh [3 6] body))
::
=/  header=@
  %+  can  0
  :~  [2 reserved=0]
      [1 req]
      [1 sam]
      [3 protocol-version]
      [2 rank.sndr-meta]
      [2 rank.rcvr-meta]
      [20 checksum]
      [1 relayed=.?(origin)]
  ==
(mix header (lsh 5 body))
::
::  +ship-meta: produce size (in bytes) and address rank for .ship
::
::    0: galaxy or star
::    1: planet
::    2: moon
::    3: comet
::
++  ship-meta
  |=  =ship
  ^-  [size=@ =rank]
  ::
  =/  size=@  (met 3 ship)
  ::
  ?:  (lte size 2)  [2 %0b0]
  ?:  (lte size 4)  [4 %0b1]
  ?:  (lte size 8)  [8 %0b10]
  [16 %0b11]
--  ::ames
::                                                            ::::
::::                            ++behn                        ::  (1b) timekeeping
::                                                            ::::
++  behn  ^?
  |%
  +$  gift                                                    ::  out result <-$
    $%  [%doze p=(unit @da)]                                  ::  next alarm
        [%wake error=(unit tang)]                            ::  wakeup or failed
        [%meta p=vase]
        [%heck syn=sign-arvo]                                ::  response to %huck
    ==
  +$  task                                                    ::  in request ->$
    $~  [%vega ~]                                             ::
    $%  $>(%born vane-task)                                   ::  new unix process
        [%rest p=@da]                                         ::  cancel alarm
        [%drip p=vase]                                        ::  give in next event
        [%huck syn=sign-arvo]                                 ::  give back
        $>(%trim vane-task)                                   ::  trim state
        $>(%vega vane-task)                                   ::  report upgrade
        [%wait p=@da]                                         ::  set alarm
        [%wake ~]                                             ::  timer activate
    ==
  --  ::behn
::                                                            ::::
::::                            ++clay                        ::  (1c) versioning
```

```
1506    ::                                          :::::
1507  ++  clay  ^?
1508    |%
1509    +$  gift                                  ::  out result <-$
1510      $%  [%boon payload=*]                   ::  ames response
1511          [%croz rus=(map desk [r=regs w=regs])]  ::  rules for group
1512          [%cruz cez=(map @ta crew)]          ::  permission groups
1513          [%dirk p=@tas]                      ::  mark mount dirty
1514          [%ergo p=@tas q=mode]               ::  version update
1515          [%hill p=(list @tas)]               ::  mount points
1516          [%done error=(unit error:ames)]     ::  ames message (n)ack
1517          [%mere p=(each (set path) (pair term tang))]  ::  merge result
1518          [%ogre p=@tas]                      ::  delete mount point
1519          [%rule red=dict wit=dict]           ::  node r+w permissions
1520          [%tire p=(each rock:tire wave:tire)]  ::  app state
1521          [%writ p=riot]                      ::  response
1522          [%wris p=[%da p=@da] q=(set (pair care path))]  ::  many changes
1523      ==                                      ::
1524    +$  task                                  ::  in request ->$
1525      $~  [%vega ~]                           ::
1526      $%  [%boat ~]                           ::  pier rebooted
1527          [%cred nom=@ta cew=crew]            ::  set permission group
1528          [%crew ~]                           ::  permission groups
1529          [%crow nom=@ta]                     ::  group usage
1530          [%drop des=desk]                    ::  cancel pending merge
1531          [%info des=desk dit=nori]           ::  internal edit
1532          $>(%init vane-task)                 ::  report install
1533          [%into des=desk all=? fis=mode]     ::  external edit
1534          $:  %merg                           ::  merge desks
1535              des=desk                        ::  target
1536              her=@p  dem=desk  cas=case      ::  source
1537              how=germ                        ::  method
1538          ==                                  ::
1539          $:  %fuse                           ::  merge many
1540              des=desk                        ::  target desk
1541              bas=beak                        ::  base desk
1542              con=(list [beak germ])          ::  merges
1543          ==                                  ::
1544          [%mont pot=term bem=beam]           ::  mount to unix
1545          [%dirk pot=term]                    ::  mark mount dirty
1546          [%ogre pot=$@(term beam)]           ::  delete mount point
1547          [%park des=desk yok=yoki ran=rang]  ::  synchronous commit
1548          [%perm des=desk pax=path rit=rite]  ::  change permissions
1549          [%pork ~]                           ::  resume commit
1550          [%prep lat=(map lobe page)]         ::  prime clay store
1551          [%rein des=desk ren=rein]           ::  extra apps
1552          [%stir arg=*]                       ::  debug
1553          [%tire p=(unit ~)]                  ::  app state subscribe
1554          [%tomb =clue]                       ::  tombstone specific
1555          $>(%trim vane-task)                 ::  trim state
1556          $>(%vega vane-task)                 ::  report upgrade
1557          [%warp wer=ship rif=riff]           ::  internal file req
1558          [%werp who=ship wer=ship rif=riff-any]  ::  external file req
1559          [%wick ~]                           ::  try upgrade
1560          [%zeal lit=(list [=desk =zest])]    ::  batch zest
1561          [%zest des=desk liv=zest]           ::  live
1562          $>(%plea vane-task)                 ::  ames request
1563      ==                                      ::
```

```
      ::                                              ::
      ::::                                            ::  (1c2)
        ::                                            ::
  +$  aeon  @ud                                       ::  version number
  +$  beam  [[p=ship q=desk r=case] s=path]           ::  global name
  +$  beak  [p=ship q=desk r=case]                    ::  path prefix
  +$  cable                                           ::  lib/sur/mark ref
    $:  face=(unit term)                              ::
        file-path=term                                ::
    ==                                                ::
  +$  care                                            ::  clay submode
    $?  %a  %b  %c  %d  %e  %f                         ::
        %p  %q  %r  %s  %t  %u                         ::
        %v  %w  %x  %y  %z                             ::
    ==                                                ::
  +$  cash                                            ::  case or tako
    $%  [%tako p=tako]                                ::
        case                                          ::
    ==                                                ::
  +$  cass  [ud=@ud da=@da]                           ::  cases for revision
  +$  clue                                            ::  murder weapon
    $%  [%lobe =lobe]                                 ::  specific lobe
        [%all ~]                                      ::  all safe targets
        [%pick ~]                                     ::  collect garbage
        [%norm =ship =desk =norm]                     ::  set default norm
        [%worn =ship =desk =tako =norm]               ::  set commit norm
        [%seek =ship =desk =cash]                     ::  fetch source blobs
    ==                                                ::
  +$  cone  (map [ship desk] dome)                    ::  domes
  ::
  ::  Desk state.
  ::
  ::  Includes a checked-out ankh with current content, most recent version, map
  ::  of all version numbers to commit hashes (commits are in hut.rang), and map
  ::  of labels to version numbers.
  ::
  ::  `mim` is a cache of the content in the directories that are mounted
  ::  to unix.  Often, we convert to/from mime without anything really
  ::  having changed; this lets us short-circuit that in some cases.
  ::  Whenever you give an `%ergo`, you must update this.
  ::
  +$  dome
    $:  let=aeon                                      ::  top id
        hit=(map aeon tako)                           ::  versions by id
        lab=(map @tas aeon)                           ::  labels
        tom=(map tako norm)                           ::  tomb policies
        nor=norm                                      ::  default policy
        mim=(map path mime)                           ::  mime cache
        fod=flue                                      ::  ford cache
        wic=(map weft yoki)                           ::  commit-in-waiting
        liv=zest                                      ::  running agents
        ren=rein                                      ::  force agents on/off
    ==                                                ::
  +$  crew  (set ship)                                ::  permissions group
  +$  dict  [src=path rul=real]                       ::  effective permission
  +$  domo                                            ::  project state
    $:  let=@ud                                       ::  top id
        hit=(map @ud tako)                            ::  changes by id
```

```
      lab=(map @tas @ud)                        ::  labels
  ==                                            ::
+$  germ                                        ::  merge style
  $?  %init                                     ::  new desk
      %fine                                     ::  fast forward
      %meet                                     ::  orthogonal files
      %mate                                     ::  orthogonal changes
      %meld                                     ::  force merge
      %only-this                                ::  ours with parents
      %only-that                                ::  hers with parents
      %take-this                                ::  ours unless absent
      %take-that                                ::  hers unless absent
      %meet-this                                ::  ours if conflict
      %meet-that                                ::  hers if conflict
  ==                                            ::
+$  lobe  @uvI                                  ::  blob ref
+$  miso                                        ::  file delta
  $%  [%del ~]                                  ::  delete
      [%ins p=cage]                             ::  insert
      [%dif p=cage]                             ::  mutate from diff
      [%mut p=cage]                             ::  mutate from raw
  ==                                            ::
+$  misu                                        ::  computed delta
  $%  [%del ~]                                  ::  delete
      [%ins p=cage]                             ::  insert
      [%dif p=lobe q=cage]                      ::  mutate from diff
  ==                                            ::
+$  mizu  [p=@u q=(map @ud tako) r=rang]        ::  new state
+$  moar  [p=@ud q=@ud]                         ::  normal change range
+$  moat  [from=case to=case =path]             ::  change range
+$  mode  (list [path (unit mime)])             ::  external files
+$  mood  [=care =case =path]                   ::  request in desk
+$  mool  [=case paths=(set (pair care path))]  ::  requests in desk
+$  nori                                        ::  repository action
  $%  [%& p=soba]                               ::  delta
      [%| p=@tas q=(unit aeon)]                 ::  label
  ==                                            ::
+$  nuri                                        ::  repository action
  $%  [%& p=suba]                               ::  delta
      [%| p=@tas]                               ::  label
  ==                                            ::
+$  norm  (axal ?)                              ::  tombstone policy
+$  open  $-(path vase)                         ::  get prelude
+$  page  ^page                                 ::  export for compat
+$  pour                                        ::  ford build w/content
  $%  [%file =path]
      [%nave =mark]
      [%dais =mark]
      [%cast =mars]
      [%tube =mars]
      ::  leafs
      ::
      [%vale =path =lobe]
      [%arch =path =(map path lobe)]
  ==
+$  rang                                        ::  repository
  $+  rang
  $:  hut=(map tako yaki)                       ::  changes
```

```
1680          lat=(map lobe page)                        ::  data
1681      ==                                             ::
1682  +$  rant                                           ::  response to request
1683    $:  p=[p=care q=case r=desk]                     ::  clade release book
1684        q=path                                       ::  spur
1685        r=cage                                       ::  data
1686    ==                                               ::
1687  +$  rave                                           ::  general request
1688    $%  [%sing =mood]                                ::  single request
1689        [%next =mood]                                ::  await next version
1690        [%mult =mool]                                ::  next version of any
1691        [%many track=? =moat]                        ::  track range
1692    ==                                               ::
1693  +$  real                                           ::  resolved permissions
1694    $:  mod=?(%black %white)                         ::
1695        who=(pair (set ship) (map @ta crew))         ::
1696    ==                                               ::
1697  +$  regs  (map path rule)                          ::  rules for paths
1698  +$  rein  (map dude:gall ?)                        ::  extra apps
1699  +$  riff  [p=desk q=(unit rave)]                   ::  request+desist
1700  +$  riff-any                                       ::
1701    $%  [%1 =riff]                                   ::
1702    ==                                               ::
1703  +$  rite                                           ::  new permissions
1704    $%  [%r red=(unit rule)]                         ::  for read
1705        [%w wit=(unit rule)]                         ::  for write
1706        [%rw red=(unit rule) wit=(unit rule)]        ::  for read and write
1707    ==                                               ::
1708  +$  riot  (unit rant)                              ::  response+complete
1709  +$  rule  [mod=?(%black %white) who=(set whom)]    ::  node permission
1710  +$  rump  [p=care q=case r=@tas s=path]            ::  relative path
1711  +$  saba  [p=ship q=@tas r=moar s=dome]            ::  patch+merge
1712  +$  soak                                           ::  ford result
1713    $%  [%cage =cage]                                ::
1714        [%vase =vase]                                ::
1715        [%arch dir=(map @ta vase)]                   ::
1716        [%dais =dais]                                ::
1717        [%tube =tube]                                ::
1718    ==                                               ::
1719  +$  soba  (list [p=path q=miso])                   ::  delta
1720  +$  suba  (list [p=path q=misu])                   ::  delta
1721  +$  tako  @uvI                                     ::  yaki ref
1722  +$  toro  [p=@ta q=nori]                           ::  general change
1723  ++  unce                                           ::  change part
1724    |*  a=mold                                       ::
1725    $%  [%& p=@ud]                                   ::  skip[copy]
1726        [%| p=(list a) q=(list a)]                   ::  p -> q[chunk]
1727    ==                                               ::
1728  ++  urge  |*(a=mold (list (unce a)))               ::  list change
1729  +$  waft                                           ::  kelvin range
1730    $^  [[%1 ~] p=(set weft)]                        ::
1731    weft                                             ::
1732  +$  whom  (each ship @ta)                          ::  ship or named crew
1733  +$  yoki  (each yuki yaki)                         ::  commit
1734  +$  yuki                                           ::  proto-commit
1735    $:  p=(list tako)                                ::  parents
1736        q=(map path (each page lobe))                ::  namespace
1737    ==                                               ::
```

```
+$  yaki                                       ::  commit
  $:  p=(list tako)                            ::  parents
      q=(map path lobe)                        ::  namespace
      r=tako                                   ::  self-reference
      t=@da                                    ::  date
  ==                                           ::
+$  zest  $~(%dead ?(%dead %live %held))       ::  how live
::                                             ::
++  tire                                       ::  app state
  |%
  +$  rock  (map desk [=zest wic=(set weft)])  ::
  +$  wave                                     ::
    $%  [%wait =desk =weft]                    ::  blocked
        [%warp =desk =weft]                    ::  unblocked
        [%zest =desk =zest]                    ::  running
    ==                                         ::
  ::
  ++  wash                                     ::  patch
    |=  [=rock =wave]
    ^+  rock
    ?-    -.wave
        %wait
      =/  got=[=zest wic=(set weft)]
        (~(gut by rock) desk.wave *zest ~)
      (~(put by rock) desk.wave got(wic (~(put in wic.got) weft.wave)))
    ::
        %warp
      %-  ~(run by rock)
      |=  [=zest wic=(set weft)]
      [zest (~(del in wic) weft.wave)]
    ::
        %zest
      ?:  ?=(%dead zest.wave)
        (~(del by rock) desk.wave)
      =/  got=[=zest wic=(set weft)]
        (~(gut by rock) desk.wave *zest ~)
      (~(put by rock) desk.wave got(zest zest.wave))
    ==
  ::
  ++  walk                                     ::  diff
    |=  [a=rock b=rock]
    ^-  (list wave)
    =/  adds  (~(dif by b) a)
    =/  dels  (~(dif by a) b)
    =/  bots  (~(int by a) b)
    ;:  welp
      ^-  (list wave)
      %-  zing
      %+  turn  ~(tap by adds)
      |=  [=desk =zest wic=(set weft)]
      ^-  (list wave)
      :-  [%zest desk zest]
      %+  turn  ~(tap in wic)
      |=  =weft
      [%wait desk weft]
    ::
      ^-  (list wave)
      %+  turn  ~(tap by dels)
```

```
1796          |=  [=desk =zest wic=(set weft)]
1797          ^-  wave
1798          [%zest desk %dead]
1799      ::
1800          ^-  (list wave)
1801          %-  zing
1802          %+  turn  ~(tap by bots)
1803          |=  [=desk * *]
1804          ^-  (list wave)
1805          =/  aa  (~(got by a) desk)
1806          =/  bb  (~(got by b) desk)
1807          =/  wadds  (~(dif in wic.bb) wic.aa)
1808          =/  wdels  (~(dif in wic.aa) wic.bb)
1809          ;:  welp
1810            ?:  =(zest.aa zest.bb)
1811              ~
1812            [%zest desk zest.bb]~
1813          ::
1814            %+  turn  ~(tap by wadds)
1815            |=  =weft
1816            ^-  wave
1817            [%wait desk weft]
1818          ::
1819            %+  turn  ~(tap by wdels)
1820            |=  =weft
1821            ^-  wave
1822            [%warp desk weft]
1823          ==
1824        ==
1825      --
1826  ::
1827  ::  +page-to-lobe: hash a page to get a lobe.
1828  ::
1829  ++  page-to-lobe  |=(page (shax (jam +<)))
1830  ::
1831  ++  cord-to-waft
1832    |=  =cord
1833    ^-  waft
1834    =/  wefts=(list weft)
1835      %+  turn  (rash cord (star (ifix [gay gay] tall:vast)))
1836      |=  =hoon
1837      !<(weft (slap !>(~) hoon))
1838    ?:  ?=([* ~] wefts)
1839      i.wefts
1840    [[%1 ~] (sy wefts)]
1841  ::
1842  ++  waft-to-wefts
1843    |=  kal=waft
1844    ^-  (set weft)
1845    ?^  -.kal
1846      p.kal
1847    [kal ~ ~]
1848  ::
1849  ::  +make-yaki: make commit out of a list of parents, content, and date.
1850  ::
1851  ++  make-yaki
1852    |=  [p=(list tako) q=(map path lobe) t=@da]
1853    ^-  yaki
```

```
=+  ^=  has
    %^  cat  7  (sham [%yaki (roll p add) q t])
    (sham [%tako (roll p add) q t])
  [p q has t]
::
::  $leak: ford cache key
::
::    This includes all build inputs, including transitive dependencies,
::    recursively.
::
+$  leak
  $~  [*pour ~]
  $:  =pour
      deps=(set leak)
  ==
::
::  $flow: global ford cache
::
::    Refcount includes references from other items in the cache, and
::    from spills in each desk
::
::    This is optimized for minimizing the number of rebuilds, and given
::    that, minimizing the amount of memory used.  It is relatively slow
::    to lookup, because generating a cache key can be fairly slow (for
::    files, it requires parsing; for tubes, it even requires building
::    the marks).
::
+$  flow  (map leak [refs=@ud =soak])
::
::  Per-desk ford cache
::
::    Spill is the set of "roots" we have into the global ford cache.
::    We add a root for everything referenced directly or indirectly on
::    a desk, then invalidate them on commit only if their dependencies
::    change.
::
::    Sprig is a fast-lookup index over the global ford cache.  The only
::    goal is to make cache hits fast.
::
+$  flue  [spill=(set leak) sprig=(map mist [=leak =soak])]
::
::  Ford build without content.
::
+$  mist
  $%  [%file =path]
      [%nave =mark]
      [%dais =mark]
      [%cast =mars]
      [%tube =mars]
      [%vale =path]
      [%arch =path]
  ==
::
::  $pile: preprocessed hoon source file
::
::    /-  sur-file          ::  surface imports from /sur
::    /+  lib-file          ::  library imports from /lib
::    /=  face  /path       ::  imports built hoon file at path
```

```
::      /~  face  type   /path  ::  imports built hoon files from directory
::      /%  face  %mark          ::  imports mark definition from /mar
::      /$  face  %from  %to     ::  imports mark converter from /mar
::      /*  face  %mark  /path   ::  unbuilt file imports, as mark
::
+$  pile
  $:  sur=(list taut)
      lib=(list taut)
      raw=(list [face=term =path])
      raz=(list [face=term =spec =path])
      maz=(list [face=term =mark])
      caz=(list [face=term =mars])
      bar=(list [face=term =mark =path])
      =hoon
  ==
::  $taut: file import from /lib or /sur
::
+$  taut  [face=(unit term) pax=term]
::  $mars: mark conversion request
::  $tube: mark conversion gate
::  $nave: typed mark core
::
+$  mars  [a=mark b=mark]
+$  tube  $-(vase vase)
++  nave
  |$  [typ dif]
  $_
  ^?
  |%
  ++  diff  |~([old=typ new=typ] *dif)
  ++  form  *mark
  ++  join  |~([a=dif b=dif] *(unit (unit dif)))
  ++  mash
    |~  [a=[ship desk dif] b=[ship desk dif]]
    *(unit dif)
  ++  pact  |~([typ dif] *typ)
  ++  vale  |~(noun *typ)
  --
::  $dais: processed mark core
::
+$  dais
  $_  ^|
  |_  sam=vase
  ++  diff  |~(new=_sam *vase)
  ++  form  *mark
  ++  join  |~([a=vase b=vase] *(unit (unit vase)))
  ++  mash
    |~  [a=[ship desk diff=vase] b=[ship desk diff=vase]]
    *(unit vase)
  ++  pact  |~(diff=vase sam)
  ++  vale  |~(noun sam)
  --
::
++  get-fit
  |=  [bek=beak pre=@tas pax=@tas]
  ^-  (unit path)
  =/  paz  (segments pax)
  |-  ^-  (unit path)
```

```
    ?~  paz
      ~
    =/  puz=path  (snoc `path`[pre i.paz] %hoon)
    =+  .^(=arch cy+[(scot %p p.bek) q.bek (scot r.bek) puz])
    ?^  fil.arch
      `puz
    $(paz t.paz)
  ::  +segments: compute all paths from :path-part, replacing some `/`s with `-`s
  ::
  ::    For example, when passed a :path-part of 'foo-bar-baz',
  ::    the product will contain:
  ::    ```
  ::    dojo> (segments 'foo-bar-baz')
  ::    ~[/foo-bar-baz /foo-bar/baz /foo/bar-baz /foo/bar/baz]
  ::    ```
  ::
  ++  segments
    |=  suffix=@tas
    ^-  (list path)
    =/  parser
      (most hep (cook crip ;~(plug ;~(pose low nud) (star ;~(pose low nud)))))
    =/  torn=(list @tas)  (fall (rush suffix parser) ~[suffix])
    %-  flop
    |-  ^-  (list (list @tas))
    ?<  ?=(~ torn)
    ?:  ?=([@ ~] torn)
      ~[torn]
    %-  zing
    %+  turn  $(torn t.torn)
    |=  s=(list @tas)
    ^-  (list (list @tas))
    ?>  ?=(^ s)
    ~[[i.torn s] [(crip "{(trip i.torn)}-{(trip i.s)}") t.s]]
  --  ::clay
::                                                          ::::
::::                    ++dill                              ::  (1d) console
  ::                                                        ::::
++  dill  ^?
  |%
  +$  gift                                  ::  out result <-$
    $%  [%blit p=(list blit)]               ::  terminal output
        [%logo ~]                           ::  logout
        [%meld ~]                           ::  unify memory
        [%pack ~]                           ::  compact memory
        [%trim p=@ud]                       ::  trim kernel state
        [%logs =told]                       ::  system output
    ==                                      ::
  +$  task                                  ::  in request ->$
    $~  [%vega ~]                           ::
    $%  [%boot lit=? p=*]                   ::  weird %dill boot
        [%crop p=@ud]                       ::  trim kernel state
        [%flog p=flog]                      ::  wrapped error
        [%heft ~]                           ::  memory report
        $>(%init vane-task)                 ::  after gall ready
        [%logs p=(unit ~)]                  ::  watch system output
        [%meld ~]                           ::  unify memory
        [%pack ~]                           ::  compact memory
        [%seat =desk]                       ::  install desk
```

```hoon
2028        [%shot ses=@tas task=session-task]        ::  task for session
2029        $>(%trim vane-task)                        ::  trim state
2030        $>(%vega vane-task)                        ::  report upgrade
2031        [%verb ~]                                  ::  verbose mode
2032        [%knob tag=term level=?(%hush %soft %loud)] ::  deprecated removeme
2033        session-task                               ::  for default session
2034        told                                       ::  system output
2035    ==                                             ::
2036  ::                                               ::
2037  +$  session-task                                 ::  session request
2038    $%  [%belt p=belt]                             ::  terminal input
2039        [%blew p=blew]                             ::  terminal config
2040        [%flee ~]                                  ::  unwatch session
2041        [%hail ~]                                  ::  terminal refresh
2042        [%open p=dude:gall q=(list gill:gall)]     ::  setup session
2043        [%shut ~]                                  ::  close session
2044        [%view ~]                                  ::  watch session blits
2045    ==                                             ::
2046  ::                                               ::
2047  +$  told                                         ::  system output
2048    $%  [%crud p=@tas q=tang]                      ::  error
2049        [%talk p=(list tank)]                      ::  tanks (in order)
2050        [%text p=tape]                             ::  tape
2051    ==                                             ::
2052  ::                                               ::
2053  ::::                                             ::  (1d2)
2054    ::                                             ::
2055  +$  blew  [p=@ud q=@ud]                          ::  columns rows
2056  +$  belt                                         ::  client input
2057    $?  bolt                                       ::  simple input
2058        [%mod mod=?(%ctl %met %hyp) key=bolt]      ::  w/ modifier
2059        [%txt p=(list @c)]                         ::  utf32 text
2060        ::TODO  consider moving %hey, %rez, %yow here ::
2061    ==                                             ::
2062  +$  bolt                                         ::  simple input
2063    $@  @c                                         ::  simple keystroke
2064    $%  [%aro p=?(%d %l %r %u)]                    ::  arrow key
2065        [%bac ~]                                   ::  true backspace
2066        [%del ~]                                   ::  true delete
2067        [%hit x=@ud y=@ud]                         ::  mouse click
2068        [%ret ~]                                   ::  return
2069    ==                                             ::
2070  +$  blit                                         ::  client output
2071    $%  [%bel ~]                                   ::  make a noise
2072        [%clr ~]                                   ::  clear the screen
2073        [%hop p=$@(@ud [x=@ud y=@ud])]             ::  set cursor col/pos
2074        [%klr p=stub]                              ::  put styled
2075        [%mor p=(list blit)]                       ::  multiple blits
2076        [%nel ~]                                   ::  newline
2077        [%put p=(list @c)]                         ::  put text at cursor
2078        [%sag p=path q=*]                          ::  save to jamfile
2079        [%sav p=path q=@]                          ::  save to file
2080        [%url p=@t]                                ::  activate url
2081        [%wyp ~]                                   ::  wipe cursor line
2082    ==                                             ::
2083  +$  dill-belt                                    ::  arvo input
2084    $%  belt                                       ::  client input
2085        [%cru p=@tas q=(list tank)]                ::  errmsg (deprecated)
```

```
2086            [%hey ~]                                ::  refresh
2087            [%rez p=@ud q=@ud]                      ::  resize, cols, rows
2088            [%yow p=gill:gall]                      ::  connect to app
2089        ==                                          ::
2090    +$  dill-blit                                   ::  arvo output
2091      $%  blit                                      ::  client output
2092            [%qit ~]                                ::  close console
2093        ==                                          ::
2094    +$  flog                                        ::  sent to %dill
2095      $%  [%crop p=@ud]                             ::  trim kernel state
2096          $>(%crud told)                            ::
2097          [%heft ~]                                 ::
2098          [%meld ~]                                 ::  unify memory
2099          [%pack ~]                                 ::  compact memory
2100          $>(%text told)                            ::
2101          [%verb ~]                                 ::  verbose mode
2102        ==                                          ::
2103    ::                                              ::
2104    +$  poke                                        ::  dill to userspace
2105      $:  ses=@tas                                  ::  target session
2106          dill-belt                                 ::  input
2107        ==                                          ::
2108    --  ::dill                                      ::
2109  ::                                                ::::
2110  ::::                        ++eyre                 ::  (1e) http-server
2111    ::                                              ::::
2112 ++  eyre  ^?
2113    |%
2114    +$  cache-entry
2115      $:  auth=?
2116          $=  body
2117          $%  [%payload =simple-payload:http]
2118        ==  ==
2119    +$  gift
2120      $%  ::  ames responses
2121          ::
2122          $>(?(%boon %done) gift:ames)
2123          ::  set-config: configures the external http server
2124          ::
2125          ::    TODO: We need to actually return a (map (unit @t) http-config)
2126          ::    so we can apply configurations on a per-site basis
2127          ::
2128          [%set-config =http-config]
2129          ::  sessions: valid authentication cookie strings
2130          ::
2131          [%sessions ses=(set @t)]
2132          ::  response: response to an event from earth
2133          ::
2134          [%response =http-event:http]
2135          ::  response to a %connect or %serve
2136          ::
2137          ::    :accepted is whether :binding was valid. Duplicate bindings are
2138          ::    not allowed.
2139          ::
2140          [%bound accepted=? =binding]
2141          ::  notification that a cache entry has changed
2142          ::
2143          [%grow =path]
```

```
    ==
  ::
+$  task
  $~  [%vega ~]
  $%  ::  initializes ourselves with an identity
      ::
      $>(%init vane-task)
      ::  new unix process
      ::
      $>(%born vane-task)
      ::  network request
      ::
      $>(%plea vane-task)
      ::  trim state (in response to memory pressure)
      ::
      $>(%trim vane-task)
      ::  report upgrade
      ::
      $>(%vega vane-task)
      ::  notifies us of the ports of our live http servers
      ::
      [%live insecure=@ud secure=(unit @ud)]
      ::  update http configuration
      ::
      [%rule =http-rule]
      ::  set a base url for eauth, like `'https://sampel.com'
      ::
      ::    eyre will append /~/eauth to it internally to redirect into eauth
      ::
      [%eauth-host host=(unit @t)]
      ::  starts handling an inbound http request
      ::
      [%request secure=? =address =request:http]
      ::  starts handling an backdoor http request
      ::
      [%request-local secure=? =address =request:http]
      ::  cancels a previous request
      ::
      [%cancel-request ~]
      ::  connects a binding to an app
      ::
      [%connect =binding app=term]
      ::  connects a binding to a generator
      ::
      [%serve =binding =generator]
      ::  disconnects a binding
      ::
      ::    This must be called with the same duct that made the binding in
      ::    the first place.
      ::
      [%disconnect =binding]
      ::  notifies us that web login code changed
      ::
      [%code-changed ~]
      ::  start responding positively to cors requests from origin
      ::
      [%approve-origin =origin]
      ::  start responding negatively to cors requests from origin
```

```
        ::
        [%reject-origin =origin]
        ::  %spew: set verbosity toggle
        ::
        [%spew veb=@]
        ::  remember (or update) a cache mapping
        ::
        [%set-response url=@t entry=(unit cache-entry)]
    ==
::  +origin: request origin as specified in an Origin header
::
+$  origin  @torigin
::  +cors-registry: origins categorized by approval status
::
+$  cors-registry
  $:  requests=(set origin)
      approved=(set origin)
      rejected=(set origin)
  ==
::  +outstanding-connection: open http connections not fully complete:
::
::    This refers to outstanding connections where the connection to
::    outside is opened and we are currently waiting on an app to
::    produce the results.
::
+$  outstanding-connection
  $:  ::  action: the action that had matched
      ::
      =action
      ::  inbound-request: the original request which caused this connection
      ::
      =inbound-request
      ::  session-id: the session associated with this connection
      ::  identity:   the identity associated with this connection
      ::
      ::NOTE  technically the identity is associated with the session (id),
      ::       but we may still need to know the identity that was used
      ::       after the session proper expires.
      ::
      [session-id=@uv =identity]
      ::  response-header: set when we get our first %start
      ::
      response-header=(unit response-header:http)
      ::  bytes-sent: the total bytes sent in response
      ::
      bytes-sent=@ud
  ==
::  +authentication-state: state used in the login system
::
+$  authentication-state
  $:  ::  sessions: a mapping of session cookies to session information
      ::
      sessions=(map @uv session)
      ::  visitors: in-progress incoming eauth flows
      ::
      visitors=(map @uv visitor)
      ::  visiting: outgoing eauth state per ship
      ::
```

```
2260          visiting=(map ship logbook)
2261      ::   endpoint: hardcoded local eauth endpoint for %syn and %ack
2262      ::
2263      ::      user-configured or auth-o-detected, with last-updated timestamp.
2264      ::      both shaped like 'prot://host'
2265      ::
2266          endpoint=[user=(unit @t) auth=(unit @t) =time]
2267      ==
2268  ::  +session: server side data about a session
2269  ::
2270  +$  session
2271    $:  ::   identity: authentication level & id of this session
2272        ::
2273        =identity
2274        ::  expiry-time: when this session expires
2275        ::
2276        ::     We check this server side, too, so we aren't relying on the browser
2277        ::     to properly handle cookie expiration as a security mechanism.
2278        ::
2279        expiry-time=@da
2280        ::  channels: channels opened by this session
2281        ::
2282        channels=(set @t)
2283        ::
2284        ::  TODO: We should add a system for individual capabilities; we should
2285        ::  mint some sort of long lived cookie for mobile apps which only has
2286        ::  access to a single application path.
2287      ==
2288  ::   +visitor: completed or in-progress incoming eauth flow
2289  ::
2290  ::     duct: boon duct
2291  ::       and
2292  ::     sesh: login completed, session exists
2293  ::       or
2294  ::     pend: awaiting %tune for %keen sent at time, for initial eauth http req
2295  ::     ship: the @p attempting to log in
2296  ::     base: local protocol+hostname the attempt started on, if any
2297  ::     last: the url to redirect to after log-in
2298  ::     toke: authentication secret received over ames or offered by visitor
2299  ::
2300  +$  visitor
2301    $:  duct=(unit duct)
2302    $@  sesh=@uv
2303    $:  pend=(unit [http=duct keen=time])
2304        ship=ship
2305        base=(unit @t)
2306        last=@t
2307        toke=(unit @uv)
2308      ==  ==
2309  ::  +logbook: record of outgoing eauth comms & state
2310  ::
2311  ::     qeu: a queue of nonces for to-be-n/acked pleas
2312  ::     map: per nonce, completed or pending eauth session
2313  ::
2314  +$  logbook  [=(qeu @uv) =(map @uv portkey)]
2315  ::  +portkey: completed or in-progress outgoing eauth flow
2316  ::
2317  ::     made: live since
```

```
2318  ::        or
2319  ::      duct: confirm request awaiting redirect
2320  ::      toke: secret to include in redirect, unless aborting
2321  ::
2322  +$  portkey
2323    $@  made=@da            ::  live since
2324    $:  pend=(unit duct)   ::  or await redir
2325        toke=(unit @uv)    ::  with secret
2326    ==
2327  ::  +eauth-plea: client talking to host
2328  ::
2329  +$  eauth-plea
2330    $:  %0
2331    $%  ::  %open: client decided on an attempt, wants to return to url
2332        ::  %shut: client wants the attempt or session closed
2333        ::
2334        [%open nonce=@uv token=(unit @uv)]
2335        [%shut nonce=@uv]
2336    ==  ==
2337  ::  +eauth-boon: host responding to client
2338  ::
2339  +$  eauth-boon
2340    $:  %0
2341    $%  ::  %okay: attempt heard, client to finish auth through url
2342        ::  %shut: host has expired the session
2343        ::
2344        [%okay nonce=@uv url=@t]
2345        [%shut nonce=@uv]
2346    ==  ==
2347  ::  $identity: authentication method & @p
2348  ::
2349  +$  identity
2350    $~  [%ours ~]
2351    $%  [%ours ~]                                    ::  local, root
2352        [%fake who=@p]                              ::  guest id
2353        [%real who=@p]                              ::  authed cross-ship
2354    ==
2355  ::  channel-state: state used in the channel system
2356  ::
2357  +$  channel-state
2358    $:  ::  session: mapping between an arbitrary key to a channel
2359        ::
2360        session=(map @t channel)
2361        ::  by-duct: mapping from ducts to session key
2362        ::
2363        duct-to-key=(map duct @t)
2364    ==
2365  ::  +timer: a reference to a timer so we can cancel or update it.
2366  ::
2367  +$  timer
2368    $:  ::  date: time when the timer will fire
2369        ::
2370        date=@da
2371        ::  duct: duct that set the timer so we can cancel
2372        ::
2373        =duct
2374    ==
2375  ::  channel-event: unacknowledged channel event, vaseless sign
```

```hoon
::
+$  channel-event
  $%  $>(%poke-ack sign:agent:gall)
      $>(%watch-ack sign:agent:gall)
      $>(%kick sign:agent:gall)
      [%fact =desk =mark =noun]
  ==
:: channel: connection to the browser
::
::    Channels are the main method where a webpage communicates with Gall
::    apps. Subscriptions and pokes are issues with PUT requests on a path,
::    while GET requests on that same path open a persistent EventSource
::    channel.
::
::    The EventSource API is a sequence number based API that browser provide
::    which allow the server to push individual events to the browser over a
::    connection held open. In case of reconnection, the browser will send a
::    'Last-Event-Id: ' header to the server; the server then resends all
::    events since then.
::
+$  channel
  $:  mode=?(%json %jam)
      =identity
      ::  channel-state: expiration time or the duct currently listening
      ::
      ::    For each channel, there is at most one open EventSource
      ::    connection. A 400 is issues on duplicate attempts to connect to the
      ::    same channel. When an EventSource isn't connected, we set a timer
      ::    to reap the subscriptions. This timer shouldn't be too short
      ::    because the
      ::
      state=(each timer duct)
      ::  next-id: next sequence number to use
      ::
      next-id=@ud
      ::  last-ack: time of last client ack
      ::
      ::    used for clog calculations, in combination with :unacked
      ::
      last-ack=@da
      ::  events: unacknowledged events
      ::
      ::    We keep track of all events where we haven't received a
      ::    'Last-Event-Id: ' response from the client or a per-poke {'ack':
      ::    ...} call. When there's an active EventSource connection on this
      ::    channel, we send the event but we still add it to events because we
      ::    can't assume it got received until we get an acknowledgment.
      ::
      events=(qeu [id=@ud request-id=@ud =channel-event])
      ::  unacked: unacknowledged event counts by request-id
      ::
      ::    used for clog calculations, in combination with :last-ack
      ::
      unacked=(map @ud @ud)
      ::  subscriptions: gall subscriptions by request-id
      ::
      ::    We maintain a list of subscriptions so if a channel times out, we
      ::    can cancel all the subscriptions we've made.
```

```
2434        ::
2435        subscriptions=(map @ud [ship=@p app=term =path duc=duct])
2436        ::  heartbeat: sse heartbeat timer
2437        ::
2438        heartbeat=(unit timer)
2439    ==
2440  ::  +binding: A rule to match a path.
2441  ::
2442  ::    A +binding is a system unique mapping for a path to match. A +binding
2443  ::    must be system unique because we don't want two handlers for a path;
2444  ::    what happens if there are two different actions for [~ /]?
2445  ::
2446  +$  binding
2447    $:  ::  site: the site to match.
2448        ::
2449        ::    A ~ will match the Urbit's identity site (your.urbit.org). Any
2450        ::    other value will match a domain literal.
2451        ::
2452        site=(unit @t)
2453        ::  path: matches this prefix path
2454        ::
2455        ::    /~myapp will match /~myapp or /~myapp/longer/path
2456        ::
2457        path=(list @t)
2458    ==
2459  ::  +action: the action to take when a binding matches an incoming request
2460  ::
2461  +$  action
2462    $%  ::  dispatch to a generator
2463        ::
2464        [%gen =generator]
2465        ::  dispatch to an application
2466        ::
2467        [%app app=term]
2468        ::  internal authentication page
2469        ::
2470        [%authentication ~]
2471        ::  cross-ship authentication handling
2472        ::
2473        [%eauth ~]
2474        ::  internal logout page
2475        ::
2476        [%logout ~]
2477        ::  gall channel system
2478        ::
2479        [%channel ~]
2480        ::  gall scry endpoint
2481        ::
2482        [%scry ~]
2483        ::  respond with the @p the requester is authenticated as
2484        ::
2485        [%name ~]
2486        ::  respond with the @p of the ship serving the response
2487        ::
2488        [%host ~]
2489        ::  respond with the default file not found page
2490        ::
2491        [%four-oh-four ~]
```

```
2492      ==
2493  ::  +generator: a generator on the local ship that handles requests
2494  ::
2495  ::    This refers to a generator on the local ship, run with a set of
2496  ::    arguments. Since http requests are time sensitive, we require that the
2497  ::    generator be on the current ship.
2498  ::
2499  +$  generator
2500    $:  ::  desk: desk on current ship that contains the generator
2501        ::
2502        =desk
2503        ::  path: path on :desk to the generator's hoon file
2504        ::
2505        path=(list @t)
2506        ::  args: arguments passed to the gate
2507        ::
2508        args=*
2509    ==
2510  ::  +http-config: full http-server configuration
2511  ::
2512  +$  http-config
2513    $:  ::  secure: PEM-encoded RSA private key and cert or cert chain
2514        ::
2515        secure=(unit [key=wain cert=wain])
2516        ::  proxy: reverse TCP proxy HTTP(s)
2517        ::
2518        proxy=_|
2519        ::  log: keep HTTP(s) access logs
2520        ::
2521        log=?
2522        ::  redirect: send 301 redirects to upgrade HTTP to HTTPS
2523        ::
2524        ::    Note: requires certificate.
2525        ::
2526        redirect=?
2527    ==
2528  ::  +http-rule: update configuration
2529  ::
2530  +$  http-rule
2531    $%  ::  %cert: set or clear certificate and keypair
2532        ::
2533        [%cert cert=(unit [key=wain cert=wain])]
2534        ::  %turf: add or remove established dns binding
2535        ::
2536        [%turf action=?(%put %del) =turf]
2537    ==
2538  ::  +address: client IP address
2539  ::
2540  +$  address
2541    $%  [%ipv4 @if]
2542        [%ipv6 @is]
2543        ::  [%ames @p]
2544    ==
2545  ::  +inbound-request: +http-request and metadata
2546  ::
2547  +$  inbound-request
2548    $:  ::  authenticated: has a valid session cookie
2549        ::
```

```
2550          authenticated=?
2551          ::    secure: whether this request was encrypted (https)
2552          ::
2553          secure=?
2554          ::    address: the source address of this request
2555          ::
2556          =address
2557          ::    request: the http-request itself
2558          ::
2559          =request:http
2560      ==
2561  ::
2562  +$  cred                                      ::  credential
2563    $:  hut=hart                               ::  client host
2564        aut=(jug @tas @t)                       ::  client identities
2565        orx=oryx                                ::  CSRF secret
2566        acl=(unit @t)                           ::  accept-language
2567        cip=(each @if @is)                      ::  client IP
2568        cum=(map @tas *)                        ::  custom dirt
2569    ==                                          ::
2570  +$  epic                                      ::  FCGI parameters
2571    $:  qix=(map @t @t)                         ::  query
2572        ced=cred                                ::  client credentials
2573        bem=beam                                ::  original path
2574    ==                                          ::
2575  ::
2576  +$  hart  [p=? q=(unit @ud) r=host]           ::  http sec+port+host
2577  +$  hate  [p=purl q=@p r=moth]                ::  semi-cooked request
2578  +$  hiss  [p=purl q=moth]                     ::  outbound request
2579  +$  host  (each turf @if)                     ::  http host
2580  +$  hoke  %+  each  [%localhost ~]            ::  local host
2581            ?(%.0.0.0.0 %.127.0.0.1)            ::
2582  +$  httq                                      ::  raw http request
2583    $:  p=meth                                  ::  method
2584        q=@t                                    ::  unparsed url
2585        r=(list [p=@t q=@t])                    ::  headers
2586        s=(unit octs)                           ::  body
2587    ==                                          ::
2588  +$  httr  [p=@ud q=mess r=(unit octs)]        ::  raw http response
2589  +$  math  (map @t (list @t))                  ::  semiparsed headers
2590  +$  mess  (list [p=@t q=@t])                  ::  raw http headers
2591  +$  meth                                      ::  http methods
2592    $?  %conn                                   ::  CONNECT
2593        %delt                                   ::  DELETE
2594        %get                                    ::  GET
2595        %head                                   ::  HEAD
2596        %opts                                   ::  OPTIONS
2597        %post                                   ::  POST
2598        %put                                    ::  PUT
2599        %trac                                   ::  TRACE
2600    ==                                          ::
2601  +$  moth  [p=meth q=math r=(unit octs)]       ::  http operation
2602  +$  oryx  @t                                  ::  CSRF secret
2603  +$  pork  [p=(unit @ta) q=(list @t)]          ::  fully parsed url
2604  ::  +prox: proxy notification
2605  ::
2606  ::    Used on both the proxy (ward) and upstream sides for
2607  ::    sending/receiving proxied-request notifications.
```

```
::
+$  prox
  $:  :: por: tcp port
      ::
      por=@ud
      :: sek: secure?
      ::
      sek=?
      :: non: authentication nonce
      ::
      non=@uvJ
  ==
+$  purf  (pair purl (unit @t))                      ::  url with fragment
+$  purl  [p=hart q=pork r=quay]                     ::  parsed url
+$  quay  (list [p=@t q=@t])                         ::  parsed url query
++  quer  |-($@(~ [p=@t q=@t t=$]))                  ::  query tree
+$  quri                                             ::  request-uri
  $%  [%& p=purl]                                    ::  absolute
      [%| p=pork q=quay]                             ::  relative
  ==                                                 ::
::  +reserved: check if an ipv4 address is in a reserved range
::
++  reserved
  |=  a=@if
  ^-  ?
  =/  b  (flop (rip 3 a))
  ::  0.0.0.0/8 (software)
  ::
  ?.  ?=([@ @ @ @ ~] b)  &
  ?|  ::  10.0.0.0/8 (private)
      ::
      =(10 i.b)
      ::  100.64.0.0/10 (carrier-grade NAT)
      ::
      &(=(100 i.b) (gte i.t.b 64) (lte i.t.b 127))
      ::  127.0.0.0/8 (localhost)
      ::
      =(127 i.b)
      ::  169.254.0.0/16 (link-local)
      ::
      &(=(169 i.b) =(254 i.t.b))
      ::  172.16.0.0/12 (private)
      ::
      &(=(172 i.b) (gte i.t.b 16) (lte i.t.b 31))
      ::  192.0.0.0/24 (protocol assignment)
      ::
      &(=(192 i.b) =(0 i.t.b) =(0 i.t.t.b))
      ::  192.0.2.0/24 (documentation)
      ::
      &(=(192 i.b) =(0 i.t.b) =(2 i.t.t.b))
      ::  192.18.0.0/15 (reserved, benchmark)
      ::
      &(=(192 i.b) |(=(18 i.t.b) =(19 i.t.b)))
      ::  192.51.100.0/24 (documentation)
      ::
      &(=(192 i.b) =(51 i.t.b) =(100 i.t.t.b))
      ::  192.88.99.0/24 (reserved, ex-anycast)
      ::
```

```
2666        &(=(192 i.b) =(88 i.t.b) =(99 i.t.t.b))
2667        ::   192.168.0.0/16 (private)
2668        ::
2669        &(=(192 i.b) =(168 i.t.b))
2670        ::   203.0.113/24 (documentation)
2671        ::
2672        &(=(203 i.b) =(0 i.t.b) =(113 i.t.t.b))
2673        ::   224.0.0.0/8 (multicast)
2674        ::   240.0.0.0/4 (reserved, future)
2675        ::   255.255.255.255/32 (broadcast)
2676        ::
2677        (gte i.b 224)
2678      ==
2679  ::  +ipa: parse ip address
2680  ::
2681  ++  ipa
2682    ;~(pose (stag %ipv4 ip4) (stag %ipv6 ip6))
2683  ::  +ip4: parse ipv4 address
2684  ::
2685  ++  ip4
2686    =+  byt=(ape:ag ted:ab)
2687    (bass 256 ;~(plug byt (stun [3 3] ;~(pfix dot byt))))
2688  ::  +ip6: parse ipv6 address
2689  ::
2690  ++  ip6
2691    %+  bass  0x1.0000
2692    %+  sear
2693      |=  hexts=(list $@(@ [~ %zeros]))
2694      ^-  (unit (list @))
2695      ::  not every list of hextets is an ipv6 address
2696      ::
2697      =/  legit=?
2698        =+  l=(lent hexts)
2699        =+  c=|=(a=* ?=([~ %zeros] a))
2700        ?|  &((lth l 8) ?=([* ~] (skim hexts c)))
2701            &(=(8 l) !(lien hexts c))
2702        ==
2703      ?.  legit  ~
2704      %-  some
2705      ::  expand zeros
2706      ::
2707      %-  zing
2708      %+  turn  hexts
2709      |=  hext=$@(@ [~ %zeros])
2710      ?@  hext  [hext]~
2711      (reap (sub 9 (lent hexts)) 0)
2712    ::  parse hextets, producing cell for shorthand zeroes
2713    ::
2714    |^  %+  cook
2715        |=  [a=(list @) b=(list [~ %zeros]) c=(list @)]
2716        :(welp a b c)
2717      ;~  plug
2718        (more col het)
2719        (stun [0 1] cel)
2720        (more col het)
2721      ==
2722    ++  cel  (cold `%zeros ;~(plug col col))
2723    ++  het  (bass 16 (stun [1 4] six:ab))
```

```
2724        --
2725      ::
2726      +$  rout  [p=(list host) q=path r=oryx s=path]        ::  http route (new)
2727      +$  user  knot                                       ::  username
2728      --  ::eyre
2729  ::                                                        ::::
2730  ::::                        ++gall                        ::  (1g) extensions
2731    ::                                                      ::::
2732  ++  gall  ^?
2733    |%
2734    +$  gift                                                ::  outgoing result
2735      $%  [%boon payload=*]                                 ::  ames response
2736          [%done error=(unit error:ames)]                   ::  ames message (n)ack
2737          [%flub ~]                                         ::  not ready to handle plea
2738          [%unto p=unto]                                    ::
2739      ==                                                    ::
2740    +$  task                                                ::  incoming request
2741      $~  [%vega ~]                                         ::
2742      $%  [%deal p=sack q=term r=deal]                      ::  full transmission
2743          [%sear =ship]                                     ::  clear pending queues
2744          [%jolt =desk =dude]                               ::  (re)start agent
2745          [%idle =dude]                                     ::  suspend agent
2746          [%load =load]                                     ::  load agent
2747          [%nuke =dude]                                     ::  delete agent
2748          [%doff dude=(unit dude) ship=(unit ship)]         ::  kill subscriptions
2749          [%rake dude=(unit dude) all=?]                    ::  reclaim old subs
2750          $>(%init vane-task)                               ::  set owner
2751          $>(%trim vane-task)                               ::  trim state
2752          $>(%vega vane-task)                               ::  report upgrade
2753          $>(%plea vane-task)                               ::  network request
2754          [%spew veb=(list verb)]                           ::  set verbosity
2755          [%sift dudes=(list dude)]                         ::  per agent
2756      ==                                                    ::
2757    +$  bitt  (map duct (pair ship path))                   ::  incoming subs
2758    +$  boat  (map [=wire =ship =term] [acked=? =path])     ::  outgoing subs
2759    +$  boar  (map [=wire =ship =term] nonce=@)             ::  and their nonces
2760    ::
2761    +$  fans  ((mop @ud (pair @da (each page @uvI))) lte)
2762    +$  plot
2763      $:  bob=(unit @ud)
2764          fan=fans
2765      ==
2766    +$  stats                                               ::  statistics
2767      $:  change=@ud                                        ::  processed move count
2768          eny=@uvJ                                          ::  entropy
2769          time=@da                                          ::  current event time
2770      ==
2771    +$  hutch  [rev=@ud idx=@ud key=@]
2772    ::
2773    +$  farm
2774      $+  farm
2775      $~  [%plot ~ ~]
2776      $%  [%coop p=hutch q=(map path plot)]
2777          [%plot p=(unit plot) q=(map @ta farm)]
2778      ==
2779    ::
2780    +$  egg                                                 ::  migratory agent state
2781      $%  [%nuke sky=(map spur @ud) cop=(map coop hutch)]   ::  see /sys/gall $yoke
```

```hoon
      $:  %live
          control-duct=duct
          run-nonce=@t
          sub-nonce=@
          =stats
          =bitt
          =boat
          =boar
          code=~
          old-state=[%| vase]
          =beak
          marks=(map duct mark)
          sky=farm
          ken=(jug spar:ames wire)
          pen=(jug spar:ames wire)
          gem=(jug coop [path page])
    ==  ==
+$  egg-any  $%([%15 egg-15] [%16 egg])
+$  egg-15
  $%  [%nuke sky=(map spur @ud)]
      $:  %live
          control-duct=duct
          run-nonce=@t
          sub-nonce=@
          =stats
          =bitt
          =boat
          =boar
          code=~
          old-state=[%| vase]
          =beak
          marks=(map duct mark)
          sky=(map spur plot)
          ken=(jug spar:ames wire)
    ==  ==
::
+$  bowl                                          ::  standard app state
  $:  $:  our=ship                                ::  host
          src=ship                                ::  guest
          dap=term                                ::  agent
          sap=path                                ::  provenance
      ==                                          ::
      $:  wex=boat                                ::  outgoing subs
          sup=bitt                                ::  incoming subs
          sky=(map path fans)                     ::  scry bindings
      ==                                          ::
      $:  act=@ud                                 ::  change number
          eny=@uvJ                                ::  entropy
          now=@da                                 ::  current time
          byk=beak                                ::  load source
  ==  ==                                          ::                      ::
+$  dude  term                                    ::  server identity
+$  gill  (pair ship term)                        ::  general contact
+$  load  (list [=dude =beak =agent])             ::  loadout
+$  scar                                          ::  opaque duct
  $:  p=@ud                                       ::  bone sequence
      q=(map duct bone)                           ::  by duct
      r=(map bone duct)                           ::  by bone
```

```hoon
          ==                                        ::
+$  suss  (trel dude @tas @da)                      ::  config report
+$  well  (pair desk term)                          ::
+$  deal
  $%  [%raw-poke =mark =noun]
      task:agent
  ==
+$  unto
  $%  [%raw-fact =mark =noun]
      sign:agent
  ==
::  TODO: add more flags?
::
+$  verb  ?(%odd)
+$  coop  spur
::
::  +agent: app core
::
++  agent
  =<  form
  |%
  +$  step  (quip card form)
  +$  card  (wind note gift)
  +$  note
    $%  [%agent [=ship name=term] =task]
        [%arvo note-arvo]
        [%pyre =tang]
    ::
        [%grow =spur =page]
        [%tomb =case =spur]
        [%cull =case =spur]
    ::
        [%tend =coop =path =page]
        [%germ =coop]
        [%snip =coop]
    ::
        [%keen secret=? spar:ames]
    ==
  +$  task
    $%  [%watch =path]
        [%watch-as =mark =path]
        [%leave ~]
        [%poke =cage]
        [%poke-as =mark =cage]
    ==
  +$  gift
    $%  [%fact paths=(list path) =cage]
        [%kick paths=(list path) ship=(unit ship)]
        [%watch-ack p=(unit tang)]
        [%poke-ack p=(unit tang)]
    ==
  +$  sign
    $%  [%poke-ack p=(unit tang)]
        [%watch-ack p=(unit tang)]
        [%fact =cage]
        [%kick ~]
    ==
  ++  form
```

```
          $_  ^|
          |_  bowl
          ++  on-init
            *(quip card _^|(..on-init))
          ::
          ++  on-save
            *vase
          ::
          ++  on-load
            |~  old-state=vase
            *(quip card _^|(..on-init))
          ::
          ++  on-poke
            |~  [mark vase]
            *(quip card _^|(..on-init))
          ::
          ++  on-watch
            |~  path
            *(quip card _^|(..on-init))
          ::
          ++  on-leave
            |~  path
            *(quip card _^|(..on-init))
          ::
          ++  on-peek
            |~  path
            *(unit (unit cage))
          ::
          ++  on-agent
            |~  [wire sign]
            *(quip card _^|(..on-init))
          ::
          ++  on-arvo
            |~  [wire sign-arvo]
            *(quip card _^|(..on-init))
          ::
          ++  on-fail
            |~  [term tang]
            *(quip card _^|(..on-init))
          --
      --
  --  ::gall
::  %iris http-client interface
::
++  iris  ^?
  |%
  ::  +gift: effects the client can emit
  ::
  +$  gift
    $%  ::  %request: outbound http-request to earth
        ::
        ::    TODO: id is sort of wrong for this interface; the duct should
        ::    be enough to identify which request we're talking about?
        ::
        [%request id=@ud request=request:http]
        ::  %cancel-request: tell earth to cancel a previous %request
        ::
        [%cancel-request id=@ud]
```

```
2956          ::    %response: response to the caller
2957          ::
2958          [%http-response =client-response]
2959      ==
2960    ::
2961    +$  task
2962      $~  [%vega ~]
2963      $%  ::  system started up; reset open connections
2964          ::
2965          $>(%born vane-task)
2966          ::  trim state (in response to memory pressure)
2967          ::
2968          $>(%trim vane-task)
2969          ::  report upgrade
2970          ::
2971          $>(%vega vane-task)
2972          ::  fetches a remote resource
2973          ::
2974          [%request =request:http =outbound-config]
2975          ::  cancels a previous fetch
2976          ::
2977          [%cancel-request ~]
2978          ::  receives http data from outside
2979          ::
2980          [%receive id=@ud =http-event:http]
2981      ==
2982    ::  +client-response: one or more client responses given to the caller
2983    ::
2984    +$  client-response
2985      $%  ::  periodically sent as an update on the duct that sent %fetch
2986          ::
2987          $:  %progress
2988              ::  http-response-header: full transaction header
2989              ::
2990              ::    In case of a redirect chain, this is the target of the
2991              ::    final redirect.
2992              ::
2993              =response-header:http
2994              ::  bytes-read: bytes fetched so far
2995              ::
2996              bytes-read=@ud
2997              ::  expected-size: the total size if response had a content-length
2998              ::
2999              expected-size=(unit @ud)
3000              ::  incremental: data received since the last %http-progress
3001              ::
3002              incremental=(unit octs)
3003          ==
3004          ::  final response of a download, parsed as mime-data if successful
3005          ::
3006          [%finished =response-header:http full-file=(unit mime-data)]
3007          ::  canceled by the runtime system
3008          ::
3009          [%cancel ~]
3010      ==
3011    ::  mime-data: externally received but unvalidated mimed data
3012    ::
3013    +$  mime-data
```

```
[type=@t data=octs]
:: +outbound-config: configuration for outbound http requests
::
+$  outbound-config
  $:  :: number of times to follow a 300 redirect before erroring
      ::
      ::   Common values for this will be 3 (the limit most browsers use), 5
      ::   (the limit recommended by the http standard), or 0 (let the
      ::   requester deal with 300 redirects).
      ::
      redirects=_5
      :: number of times to retry before failing
      ::
      ::   When we retry, we'll automatically try to use the 'Range' header
      ::   to resume the download where we left off if we have the
      ::   'Accept-Range: bytes' in the original response.
      ::
      retries=_3
  ==
:: +to-httr: adapts to old eyre interface
::
++  to-httr
  |=  [header=response-header:http full-file=(unit mime-data)]
  ^-  httr:eyre
  ::
  =/  data=(unit octs)
    ?~(full-file ~ `data.u.full-file)
  ::
  [status-code.header headers.header data]
  --
::                                                          ::::
::::                      ++jael                            ::  (1h) security
  ::                                                        ::::
++  jael  ^?
  |%
  +$  public-keys-result
    $%  [%full points=(map ship point)]
        [%diff who=ship =diff:point]
        [%breach who=ship]
    ==
  ::                                                  ::
  +$  gift                                            ::  out result <-$
    $%  [%done error=(unit error:ames)]               ::  ames message (n)ack
        [%boon payload=*]                             ::  ames response
        [%private-keys =life vein=(map life ring)]    ::  private keys
        [%public-keys =public-keys-result]            ::  ethereum changes
        [%turf turf=(list turf)]                      ::  domains
    ==                                                ::
  :: +feed: potential boot parameters
  ::
  +$  feed
    $^  [[%1 ~] who=ship kyz=(list [lyf=life key=ring])]
    seed
  :: +seed: individual boot parameters
  ::
  +$  seed  [who=ship lyf=life key=ring sig=(unit oath:pki)]
  ::
  +$  task                                            ::  in request ->$
```

```hoon
      $~  [%vega ~]                                 ::
      $%  [%dawn dawn-event]                         ::  boot from keys
          [%fake =ship]                              ::  fake boot
          [%listen whos=(set ship) =source]          ::  set ethereum source
          ::TODO  %next for generating/putting new private key
          [%meet =ship =life =pass]                  ::  met after breach
          [%moon =ship =udiff:point]                 ::  register moon keys
          [%nuke whos=(set ship)]                    ::  cancel tracker from
          [%private-keys ~]                          ::  sub to privates
          [%public-keys ships=(set ship)]            ::  sub to publics
          [%rekey =life =ring]                       ::  update private keys
          [%resend ~]                                ::  resend private key
          [%ruin ships=(set ship)]                   ::  pretend breach
          $>(%trim vane-task)                        ::  trim state
          [%turf ~]                                  ::  view domains
          $>(%vega vane-task)                        ::  report upgrade
          $>(%plea vane-task)                        ::  ames request
          [%step ~]                                  ::  reset web login code
      ==                                             ::
  ::
  +$  dawn-event
    $:  =seed
        spon=(list [=ship point:azimuth-types])
        czar=(map ship [=rift =life =pass])
        turf=(list turf)
        bloq=@ud
        node=(unit purl:eyre)
    ==
  ::
  ++  block
    =<  block
    |%
    +$  hash    @uxblockhash
    +$  number  @udblocknumber
    +$  id      [=hash =number]
    +$  block   [=id =parent=hash]
    --
  ::
  ::  Azimuth points form a groupoid, where the objects are all the
  ::  possible values of +point and the arrows are the possible values
  ::  of (list point-diff).  Composition of arrows is concatenation,
  ::  and you can apply the diffs to a +point with +apply.
  ::
  ::  It's simplest to consider +point as the coproduct of three
  ::  groupoids, Rift, Keys, and Sponsor.  Recall that the coproduct
  ::  of monoids is the free monoid (Kleene star) of the coproduct of
  ::  the underlying sets of the monoids.  The construction for
  ::  groupoids is similar.  Thus, the objects of the coproduct are
  ::  the product of the objects of the underlying groupoids.  The
  ::  arrows are a list of a sum of the diff types of the underlying
  ::  groupoids.  Given an arrow=(list diff), you can project to the
  ::  underlying arrows with +skim filtering on the head of each diff.
  ::
  ::  The identity element is ~.  Clearly, composing this with any
  ::  +diff gives the original +diff.  Since this is a category,
  ::  +compose must be associative (true, because concatenation is
  ::  associative).  This is a groupoid, so we must further have that
  ::  every +point-diff has an inverse.  These are given by the
```

```
3130      ::    +inverse operation.
3131      ::
3132      ++  point
3133        =<  point
3134        |%
3135        +$  point
3136          $:  =rift
3137              =life
3138              keys=(map life [crypto-suite=@ud =pass])
3139              sponsor=(unit @p)
3140          ==
3141        ::
3142        +$  key-update  [=life crypto-suite=@ud =pass]
3143        ::
3144        ::  Invertible diffs
3145        ::
3146        +$  diffs  (list diff)
3147        +$  diff
3148          $%  [%rift from=rift to=rift]
3149              [%keys from=key-update to=key-update]
3150              [%spon from=(unit @p) to=(unit @p)]
3151          ==
3152        ::
3153        ::  Non-invertible diffs
3154        ::
3155        +$  udiffs  (list [=ship =udiff])
3156        +$  udiff
3157          $:  =id:block
3158          $%  [%rift =rift boot=?]
3159              [%keys key-update boot=?]
3160              [%spon sponsor=(unit @p)]
3161              [%disavow ~]
3162          ==  ==
3163        ::
3164        ++  udiff-to-diff
3165          |=  [=a=udiff =a=point]
3166          ^-  (unit diff)
3167          ?-    +<.a-udiff
3168              %disavow  ~|(%udiff-to-diff-disavow !!)
3169              %spon     `[%spon sponsor.a-point sponsor.a-udiff]
3170              %rift
3171            ?.  (gth rift.a-udiff rift.a-point)
3172              ~
3173            ~?  &(!=(rift.a-udiff +(rift.a-point)) !boot.a-udiff)
3174              [%udiff-to-diff-skipped-rift a-udiff a-point]
3175            `[%rift rift.a-point rift.a-udiff]
3176          ::
3177              %keys
3178            ?.  (gth life.a-udiff life.a-point)
3179              ~
3180            ~?  &(!=(life.a-udiff +(life.a-point)) !boot.a-udiff)
3181              [%udiff-to-diff-skipped-life a-udiff a-point]
3182            :^  ~  %keys
3183              [life.a-point (~(gut by keys.a-point) life.a-point *[@ud pass])]
3184            [life crypto-suite pass]:a-udiff
3185          ==
3186        ::
3187        ++  inverse
```

```
3188        |=  diffs=(list diff)
3189        ^-  (list diff)
3190        %-  flop
3191        %+  turn  diffs
3192        |=  =diff
3193        ^-  ^diff
3194        ?-  -.diff
3195          %rift  [%rift to from]:diff
3196          %keys  [%keys to from]:diff
3197          %spon  [%spon to from]:diff
3198        ==
3199      ::
3200      ++  compose
3201        (bake weld ,[(list diff) (list diff)])
3202      ::
3203      ++  apply
3204        |=  [diffs=(list diff) =a=point]
3205        (roll diffs (apply-diff a-point))
3206      ::
3207      ++  apply-diff
3208        |=  a=point
3209        |:  [*=diff a-point=a]
3210        ^-  point
3211        ?-    -.diff
3212            %rift
3213          ?>  =(rift.a-point from.diff)
3214          a-point(rift to.diff)
3215        ::
3216            %keys
3217          ?>  =(life.a-point life.from.diff)
3218          ?>  =((~(get by keys.a-point) life.a-point) `+.from.diff)
3219          %_  a-point
3220            life  life.to.diff
3221            keys  (~(put by keys.a-point) life.to.diff +.to.diff)
3222          ==
3223        ::
3224            %spon
3225          ?>  =(sponsor.a-point from.diff)
3226          a-point(sponsor to.diff)
3227        ==
3228      --
3229  ::                                                          ::
3230  ::::                                                        ::
3231    ::                                                        ::
3232  +$  source  (each ship term)
3233  +$  source-id  @udsourceid
3234  ::
3235  ::  +state-eth-node: state of a connection to an ethereum node
3236  ::
3237  +$  state-eth-node                            ::  node config + meta
3238    $:  top-source-id=source-id
3239        sources=(map source-id source)
3240        sources-reverse=(map source source-id)
3241        default-source=source-id
3242        ship-sources=(map ship source-id)
3243        ship-sources-reverse=(jug source-id ship)
3244    ==                                                        ::
3245  ::                                                          ::
```

```
3246    ::::                    ++pki:jael              ::  (1h2) certificates
3247    ::                                              ::::
3248  ++  pki  ^?
3249    |%
3250    ::TODO  update to fit azimuth-style keys
3251    ::  the urbit meta-certificate (++will) is a sequence
3252    ::  of certificates (++cert).  each cert in a will
3253    ::  revokes and replaces the previous cert.  the
3254    ::  version number of a ship is a ++life.
3255    ::
3256    ::  the deed contains an ++arms, a definition
3257    ::  of cosmetic identity; a semi-trusted parent,
3258    ::  which signs the initial certificate and provides
3259    ::  routing services; and a dirty bit.  if the dirty
3260    ::  bit is set, the new life of this ship may have
3261    ::  lost information that the old life had.
3262    ::
3263    +$  hand  @uvH                                  ::  128-bit hash
3264    +$  mind  [who=ship lyf=life]                   ::  key identifier
3265    +$  name  (pair @ta @t)                         ::  ascii / unicode
3266    +$  oath  @                                     ::  signature
3267    ++  tale                                        ::  urbit-signed *
3268      |$  [typ]                                     ::  payload mold
3269      $:  dat=typ                                   ::  data
3270          syg=(map ship (pair life oath))          ::  signatures
3271      ==                                            ::
3272    --  ::  pki
3273  --  ::  jael
3274  ::                                                ::::
3275  ::::                    ++khan                    ::  (1i) threads
3276  ::                                                ::::
3277  ++  khan  ^?
3278  |%
3279  +$  gift                                          ::  out result <-$
3280    $%  [%arow p=(avow cage)]                       ::  in-arvo result
3281        [%avow p=(avow page)]                       ::  external result
3282    ==                                              ::
3283  +$  task                                          ::  in request ->$
3284    $~  [%vega ~]                                   ::
3285    $%  $>(%born vane-task)                         ::  new unix process
3286        [%done ~]                                   ::  socket closed
3287        ::  TODO  mark ignored                      ::
3288        ::                                          ::
3289        [%fard p=(fyrd cage)]                       ::  in-arvo thread
3290        [%fyrd p=(fyrd cast)]                       ::  external thread
3291        [%lard =bear =shed]                         ::  inline thread
3292        $>(%trim vane-task)                         ::  trim state
3293        $>(%vega vane-task)                         ::  report upgrade
3294    ==                                              ::
3295  ::                                                ::
3296  ++  avow  |$  [a]  (each a goof)                  ::  $fyrd result
3297  +$  bear  $@(desk beak)                           ::  partial $beak
3298  +$  cast  (pair mark page)                        ::  output mark + input
3299  ++  fyrd  |$  [a]  [=bear name=term args=a]       ::  thread run request
3300  ::                                                ::
3301  +$  shed  _*form:(strand:rand ,vase)             ::  compute vase
3302  --  ::khan
3303  ::                                                ::::
```

```
::::                        ++lick                          ::  (1j) IPC
::                                                          ::::
++  lick  ^?
  |%
  +$  gift                                                 ::  out result <-$
    $%  [%spin =name]                                      ::  open an IPC port
        [%shut =name]                                      ::  close an IPC port
        [%spit =name =mark =noun]                          ::  spit a noun to the IPC port
        [%soak =name =mark =noun]                          ::  soak a noun from the IPC port
    ==
  +$  task                                                 ::  in request ->$
    $~  [%vega ~]                                          ::
    $%  $>(%born vane-task)                                ::  new unix process
        $>(%trim vane-task)                                ::  trim state
        $>(%vega vane-task)                                ::  report upgrade
        [%spin =name]                                      ::  open an IPC port
        [%shut =name]                                      ::  close an IPC port
        [%spit =name =mark =noun]                          ::  spit a noun to the IPC port
        [%soak =name =mark =noun]                          ::  soak a noun from the IPC port
    ==
  ::
  +$  name  path
  --  ::lick
::
++  rand                                                   ::  computation
  |%
  +$  card  card:agent:gall
  +$  input
    $%  [%poke =cage]
        [%sign =wire =sign-arvo]
        [%agent =wire =sign:agent:gall]
        [%watch =path]
    ==
  +$  strand-input  [=bowl in=(unit input)]
  +$  tid   @tatid
  +$  bowl
    $:  our=ship
        src=ship
        tid=tid
        mom=(unit tid)
        wex=boat:gall
        sup=bitt:gall
        eny=@uvJ
        now=@da
        byk=beak
    ==
  ::
  ::  cards:  cards to send immediately.  These will go out even if a
  ::          later stage of the computation fails, so they shouldn't have
  ::          any semantic effect on the rest of the system.
  ::          Alternately, they may record an entry in contracts with
  ::          enough information to undo the effect if the computation
  ::          fails.
  ::  wait:   don't move on, stay here.  The next sign should come back
  ::          to this same callback.
  ::  skip:   didn't expect this input; drop it down to be handled
  ::          elsewhere
  ::  cont:   continue computation with new callback.
```

```
::  fail:    abort computation; don't send effects
::  done:    finish computation; send effects
::
++  strand-output-raw
  |*  a=mold
  $~  [~ %done *a]
  $:  cards=(list card)
      $=  next
      $%  [%wait ~]
          [%skip ~]
          [%cont self=(strand-form-raw a)]
          [%fail err=(pair term tang)]
          [%done value=a]
      ==
  ==
::
++  strand-form-raw
  |*  a=mold
  $-(strand-input (strand-output-raw a))
::
::  Abort strand computation with error message
::
++  strand-fail
  |=  err=(pair term tang)
  |=  strand-input
  [~ %fail err]
::
::  Asynchronous transcaction monad.
::
::  Combo of four monads:
::  - Reader on input
::  - Writer on card
::  - Continuation
::  - Exception
::
++  strand
  |*  a=mold
  |%
  ++  output  (strand-output-raw a)
  ::
  ::  Type of an strand computation.
  ::
  ++  form  (strand-form-raw a)
  ::
  ::  Monadic pure.  Identity computation for bind.
  ::
  ++  pure
    |=  arg=a
    ^-  form
    |=  strand-input
    [~ %done arg]
  ::
  ::  Monadic bind.  Combines two computations, associatively.
  ::
  ++  bind
    |*  b=mold
    |=  [m-b=(strand-form-raw b) fun=$-(b form)]
    ^-  form
```

```
3420      |=  input=strand-input
3421      =/  b-res=(strand-output-raw b)
3422        (m-b input)
3423      ^-  output
3424      :-  cards.b-res
3425      ?-    -.next.b-res
3426        %wait  [%wait ~]
3427        %skip  [%skip ~]
3428        %cont  [%cont ..$(m-b self.next.b-res)]
3429        %fail  [%fail err.next.b-res]
3430        %done  [%cont (fun value.next.b-res)]
3431      ==
3432    ::
3433    ::  The strand monad must be evaluted in a particular way to maintain
3434    ::  its monadic character.  +take:eval implements this.
3435    ::
3436    ++  eval
3437      |%
3438      ::  Indelible state of a strand
3439      ::
3440      +$  eval-form
3441        $:  =form
3442        ==
3443      ::
3444      ::  Convert initial form to eval-form
3445      ::
3446      ++  from-form
3447        |=  =form
3448        ^-  eval-form
3449        form
3450      ::
3451      ::  The cases of results of +take
3452      ::
3453      +$  eval-result
3454        $%  [%next ~]
3455            [%fail err=(pair term tang)]
3456            [%done value=a]
3457        ==
3458      ::
3459      ++  validate-mark
3460        |=  [in=* =mark =bowl]
3461        ^-  cage
3462        =+  .^  =dais:clay  %cb
3463                /(scot %p our.bowl)/[q.byk.bowl]/(scot %da now.bowl)/[mark]
3464            ==
3465        =/  res  (mule |.((vale.dais in)))
3466        ?:  ?=(%| -.res)
3467          ~|  %spider-mark-fail
3468          (mean leaf+"spider: ames vale fail {<mark>}" p.res)
3469        [mark p.res]
3470      ::
3471      ::  Take a new sign and run the strand against it
3472      ::
3473      ++  take
3474        ::  cards: accumulate throughout recursion the cards to be
3475        ::         produced now
3476        =|  cards=(list card)
3477        |=  [=eval-form =strand-input]
```

```
^-  [[(list card) =eval-result] _eval-form]
=*  take-loop  $
=.  in.strand-input
  ?~  in.strand-input  ~
  =/  in  u.in.strand-input
  ?.  ?=(%agent -.in)        `in
  ?.  ?=(%fact -.sign.in)   `in
  ::
  :-  ~
  :^  %agent  wire.in  %fact
  (validate-mark q.q.cage.sign.in p.cage.sign.in bowl.strand-input)
::  run the strand callback
::
=/  =output  (form.eval-form strand-input)
::  add cards to cards
::
=.  cards
  %+  welp
    cards
  ::  XX add tag to wires?
  cards.output
::  case-wise handle next steps
::
?-  -.next.output
  %wait  [[cards %next ~] eval-form]
  %skip  [[cards %next ~] eval-form]
  %fail  [[cards %fail err.next.output] eval-form]
  %done  [[cards %done value.next.output] eval-form]
  %cont
::  recurse to run continuation with initialization input
::
%_  take-loop
  form.eval-form  self.next.output
  strand-input    [bowl.strand-input ~]
==
    ==
  --
  --
--  ::strand
::
+$  gift-arvo                              ::  out result <-$
  $~  [%doze ~]
  $%  gift:ames
      gift:behn
      gift:clay
      gift:dill
      gift:eyre
      gift:gall
      gift:iris
      gift:jael
      gift:khan
      gift:lick
  ==
+$  task-arvo                              ::  in request ->$
  $%  task:ames
      task:clay
      task:behn
      task:dill
```

```
3536          task:eyre
3537          task:gall
3538          task:iris
3539          task:jael
3540          task:khan
3541          task:lick
3542      ==
3543  +$  note-arvo                                    ::  out request $->
3544    $~  [%b %wake ~]
3545    $%  [%a task:ames]
3546        [%b task:behn]
3547        [%c task:clay]
3548        [%d task:dill]
3549        [%e task:eyre]
3550        [%g task:gall]
3551        [%i task:iris]
3552        [%j task:jael]
3553        [%k task:khan]
3554        [%l task:lick]
3555        [%$ %whiz ~]
3556        [@tas %meta vase]
3557      ==
3558  ::  full vane names are required in vanes
3559  ::
3560  +$  sign-arvo                                    ::  in result $<-
3561    $%  [%ames gift:ames]
3562        $:  %behn
3563            $%  gift:behn
3564                $>(%wris gift:clay)
3565                $>(%writ gift:clay)
3566                $>(%mere gift:clay)
3567                $>(%unto gift:gall)
3568            ==
3569        ==
3570        [%clay gift:clay]
3571        [%dill gift:dill]
3572        [%eyre gift:eyre]
3573        [%gall gift:gall]
3574        [%iris gift:iris]
3575        [%jael gift:jael]
3576        [%khan gift:khan]
3577        [%lick gift:lick]
3578      ==
3579  ::  $unix-task: input from unix
3580  ::
3581  +$  unix-task                                    ::  input from unix
3582    $~  [%wake ~]
3583    $%  ::  %dill: keyboard input
3584        ::
3585        $>(%belt task:dill)
3586        ::  %dill: configure terminal (resized)
3587        ::
3588        $>(%blew task:dill)
3589        ::  %clay: new process
3590        ::
3591        $>(%boat task:clay)
3592        ::  %behn/%eyre/%iris: new process
3593        ::
```

```
$>(%born vane-task)
::  %eyre: cancel request
::
[%cancel-request ~]
::  %dill: reset terminal configuration
::
$>(%hail task:dill)
::  %ames: hear packet
::
$>(%hear task:ames)
::  %clay: external edit
::
$>(%into task:clay)
::  %clay: synchronous commit
::
::    TODO: make $yuki an option for %into?
::
$>(%park task:clay)
::  %clay: load blob store
::
$>(%prep task:clay)
::  %eyre: learn ports of live http servers
::
$>(%live task:eyre)
::  %iris: hear (partial) http response
::
$>(%receive task:iris)
::  %eyre: starts handling an inbound http request
::
$>(%request task:eyre)
::  %eyre: starts handling an backdoor http request
::
$>(%request-local task:eyre)
::  %dill: close session
::
$>(%shut task:dill)
::  %behn: wakeup
::
$>(%wake task:behn)
==
--  ::
```

Zuse 411K

```
1   ::  /sys/zuse
2   ::  %zuse: arvo library
3   ::
4   =>  ..lull
5   ~%  %zuse  ..part  ~
6   |%
7   ++  zuse  %411
8   ::                                                      ::  ::
9   ::::                                                    ::  ::  (2) engines
10    ::                                                    ::  ::
11  ::                                                      ::::
12  ::::                          ++number                 ::  (2a) number theory
13    ::                                                    ::::
14  ++  number  ^?
15    |%
16    ::                                                    ::  ++fu:number
17    ++  fu                                                ::  modulo (mul p q)
18      |=  a=[p=@ q=@]
19      =+  b=?:(=([0 0] a) 0 (~(inv fo p.a) (~(sit fo p.a) q.a)))
20      |%
21      ::                                                  ::  ++dif:fu:number
22      ++  dif                                             ::  subtract
23        |=  [c=[@ @] d=[@ @]]
24        [(~(dif fo p.a) -.c -.d) (~(dif fo q.a) +.c +.d)]
25      ::                                                  ::  ++exp:fu:number
26      ++  exp                                             ::  exponent
27        |=  [c=@ d=[@ @]]
28        :-  (~(exp fo p.a) (mod c (dec p.a)) -.d)
29        (~(exp fo q.a) (mod c (dec q.a)) +.d)
30      ::                                                  ::  ++out:fu:number
31      ++  out                                             ::  garner's formula
32        |=  c=[@ @]
33        %+  add  +.c
34        %+  mul  q.a
35        %+  ~(pro fo p.a)  b
36        (~(dif fo p.a) -.c (~(sit fo p.a) +.c))
37      ::                                                  ::  ++pro:fu:number
38      ++  pro                                             ::  multiply
39        |=  [c=[@ @] d=[@ @]]
40        [(~(pro fo p.a) -.c -.d) (~(pro fo q.a) +.c +.d)]
41      ::                                                  ::  ++sum:fu:number
42      ++  sum                                             ::  add
43        |=  [c=[@ @] d=[@ @]]
44        [(~(sum fo p.a) -.c -.d) (~(sum fo q.a) +.c +.d)]
45      ::                                                  ::  ++sit:fu:number
46      ++  sit                                             ::  represent
47        |=  c=@
48        [(mod c p.a) (mod c q.a)]
49      --  ::fu
50    ::                                                    ::  ++pram:number
51    ++  pram                                              ::  rabin-miller
52      |=  a=@  ^-  ?
53      ?:  ?|  =(0 (end 0 a))
54              =(1 a)
55          =+  b=1
```

```
56          |-  ^-  ?
57          ?:  =(512 b)
58          |
59          ?|(=+(c=+((mul 2 b)) &(!=(a c) =(a (mul c (div a c))))) $(b +(b)))
60      ==
61    |
62  =+  ^=  b
63      =+  [s=(dec a) t=0]
64      |-  ^-  [s=@ t=@]
65      ?:  =(0 (end 0 s))
66        $(s (rsh 0 s), t +(t))
67      [s t]
68  ?>  =((mul s.b (bex t.b)) (dec a))
69  =+  c=0
70  |-  ^-  ?
71  ?:  =(c 64)
72    &
73  =+  d=(~(raw og (add c a)) (met 0 a))
74  =+  e=(~(exp fo a) s.b d)
75  ?&  ?|  =(1 e)
76          =+  f=0
77          |-  ^-  ?
78          ?:  =(e (dec a))
79            &
80          ?:  =(f (dec t.b))
81          |
82          $(e (~(pro fo a) e e), f +(f))
83      ==
84      $(c +(c))
85  ==
86  ::                                              ::  ++ramp:number
87  ++  ramp                                        ::  make r-m prime
88  |=  [a=@ b=(list @) c=@]  ^-  @ux              ::  [bits snags seed]
89  =>  .(c (shas %ramp c))
90  =+  d=*@
91  |-
92  ?:  =((mul 100 a) d)
93    ~|(%ar-ramp !!)
94  =+  e=(~(raw og c) a)
95  ?:  &((levy b |=(f=@ !=(1 (mod e f)))) (pram e))
96    e
97  $(c +(c), d (shax d))
98  ::                                              ::  ++curt:number
99  ++  curt                                        ::  curve25519
100  |=  [a=@ b=@]
101  =>  %=    .
102        +
103      =>  +
104      =+  =+  [p=486.662 q=(sub (bex 255) 19)]
105          =+  fq=~(. fo q)
106          [p=p q=q fq=fq]
107      |%
108      ::                                          ::  ++cla:curt:number
109      ++  cla                                     ::
110        |=  raw=@
111      =+  low=(dis 248 (cut 3 [0 1] raw))
112      =+  hih=(con 64 (dis 127 (cut 3 [31 1] raw)))
113      =+  mid=(cut 3 [1 30] raw)
```

```
            (can 3 [[1 low] [30 mid] [1 hih] ~])
      ::                                              ::  ++sqr:curt:number
    ++  sqr                                           ::
      |=(a=@ (mul a a))
      ::                                              ::  ++inv:curt:number
    ++  inv                                           ::
      |=(a=@ (~(exp fo q) (sub q 2) a))
      ::                                              ::  ++cad:curt:number
    ++  cad                                           ::
      |=  [n=[x=@ z=@] m=[x=@ z=@] d=[x=@ z=@]]
      =+  ^=  xx
          ;:  mul  4  z.d
            %-  sqr  %-  abs:si
            %+  dif:si
              (sun:si (mul x.m x.n))
              (sun:si (mul z.m z.n))
          ==
      =+  ^=  zz
          ;:  mul  4  x.d
            %-  sqr  %-  abs:si
            %+  dif:si
              (sun:si (mul x.m z.n))
              (sun:si (mul z.m x.n))
          ==
      [(sit.fq xx) (sit.fq zz)]
      ::                                              ::  ++cub:curt:number
    ++  cub                                           ::
      |=  [x=@ z=@]
      =+  ^=  xx
        %+  mul
          %-  sqr  %-  abs:si
          (dif:si (sun:si x) (sun:si z))
        (sqr (add x z))
      =+  ^=  zz
          ;:  mul  4  x  z
          :(add (sqr x) :(mul p x z) (sqr z))
          ==
      [(sit.fq xx) (sit.fq zz)]
      --  ::
    ==
  =+  one=[b 1]
  =+  i=253
  =+  r=one
  =+  s=(cub one)
  |-
  ?:  =(i 0)
    =+  x=(cub r)
    (sit.fq (mul -.x (inv +.x)))
  =+  m=(rsh [0 i] a)
  ?:  =(0 (mod m 2))
    $(i (dec i), s (cad r s one), r (cub r))
  $(i (dec i), r (cad r s one), s (cub s))
  ::                                                  ::  ++ga:number
++  ga                                                ::  GF (bex p.a)
  |=  a=[p=@ q=@ r=@]                                 ::  dim poly gen
  =+  si=(bex p.a)
  =+  ma=(dec si)
  =>  |%
```

```
172           ::                                          ::  ++dif:ga:number
173           ++  dif                                      ::  add and sub
174             |=  [b=@ c=@]
175             ~|  [%dif-ga a]
176             ?>  &((lth b si) (lth c si))
177             (mix b c)
178           ::                                          ::  ++dub:ga:number
179           ++  dub                                      ::  mul by x
180             |=  b=@
181             ~|  [%dub-ga a]
182             ?>  (lth b si)
183             ?:  =(1 (cut 0 [(dec p.a) 1] b))
184               (dif (sit q.a) (sit (lsh 0 b)))
185             (lsh 0 b)
186           ::                                          ::  ++pro:ga:number
187           ++  pro                                      ::  slow multiply
188             |=  [b=@ c=@]
189             ?:  =(0 b)
190               0
191             ?:  =(1 (dis 1 b))
192               (dif c $(b (rsh 0 b), c (dub c)))
193             $(b (rsh 0 b), c (dub c))
194           ::                                          ::  ++toe:ga:number
195           ++  toe                                      ::  exp+log tables
196             =+  ^=  nu
197                 |=  [b=@ c=@]
198                 ^-  (map @ @)
199                 =+  d=*(map @ @)
200                 |-
201                 ?:  =(0 c)
202                   d
203                 %=  $
204                   c  (dec c)
205                   d  (~(put by d) c b)
206                 ==
207             =+  [p=(nu 0 (bex p.a)) q=(nu ma ma)]
208             =+  [b=1 c=0]
209             |-  ^-  [p=(map @ @) q=(map @ @)]
210             ?:  =(ma c)
211               [(~(put by p) c b) q]
212             %=  $
213               b  (pro r.a b)
214               c  +(c)
215               p  (~(put by p) c b)
216               q  (~(put by q) b c)
217             ==
218           ::                                          ::  ++sit:ga:number
219           ++  sit                                      ::  reduce
220             |=  b=@
221             (mod b (bex p.a))
222           --  ::
223       =+  toe
224       |%
225       ::                                          ::  ++fra:ga:number
226       ++  fra                                      ::  divide
227         |=  [b=@ c=@]
228         (pro b (inv c))
229       ::                                          ::  ++inv:ga:number
```

```
      ++  inv                                         ::  invert
        |=  b=@
        ~|  [%inv-ga a]
        =+  c=(~(get by q) b)
        ?~  c  !!
        =+  d=(~(get by p) (sub ma u.c))
        (need d)
      ::                                              ::  ++pow:ga:number
      ++  pow                                         ::  exponent
        |=  [b=@ c=@]
        =+  [d=1 e=c f=0]
        |-
        ?:  =(p.a f)
          d
        ?:  =(1 (cut 0 [f 1] b))
          $(d (pro d e), e (pro e e), f +(f))
        $(e (pro e e), f +(f))
      ::                                              ::  ++pro:ga:number
      ++  pro                                         ::  multiply
        |=  [b=@ c=@]
        ~|  [%pro-ga a]
        =+  d=(~(get by q) b)
        ?~  d  0
        =+  e=(~(get by q) c)
        ?~  e  0
        =+  f=(~(get by p) (mod (add u.d u.e) ma))
        (need f)
      --  ::ga
    --  ::number
::                                                    ::::
::::                        ++crypto                  ::  (2b) cryptography
  ::                                                  ::::
++  crypto  ^?
  =,  ames
  =,  number
  |%
  ::                                                  ::
  ::::                        ++aes:crypto            ::  (2b1) aes, all sizes
    ::                                                ::::
  ++  aes    !.
    ~%  %aes  ..part  ~
    |%
    ::                                                ::  ++ahem:aes:crypto
    ++  ahem                                          ::  kernel state
      |=  [nnk=@ nnb=@ nnr=@]
      =>
        =+  =>  [gr=(ga 8 0x11b 3) few==>(fe .(a 5))]
            [pro=pro.gr dif=dif.gr pow=pow.gr ror=ror.few]
        =>  |%                                        ::
            ++  cipa  $_  ^?                          ::  AES params
              |%
              ++  co  *[p=@ q=@ r=@ s=@]              ::  column coefficients
              ++  ix  |~(a=@ *@)                      ::  key index
              ++  ro  *[p=@ q=@ r=@ s=@]              ::  row shifts
              ++  su  *@                              ::  s-box
              --  ::cipa
            --  ::
        |%
```

```
288      ::                                     ::  ++pen:ahem:aes:
289      ++  pen                                ::  encrypt
290        ^-  cipa
291        |%
292        ::                                   ::  ++co:pen:ahem:aes:
293        ++  co                               ::  column coefficients
294        [0x2 0x3 1 1]
295        ::                                   ::  ++ix:pen:ahem:aes:
296        ++  ix                               ::  key index
297        |~(a=@ a)
298        ::                                   ::  ++ro:pen:ahem:aes:
299        ++  ro                               ::  row shifts
300        [0 1 2 3]
301        ::                                   ::  ++su:pen:ahem:aes:
302        ++  su                               ::  s-box
303        0x16bb.54b0.0f2d.9941.6842.e6bf.0d89.a18c.
304          df28.55ce.e987.1e9b.948e.d969.1198.f8e1.
305          9e1d.c186.b957.3561.0ef6.0348.66b5.3e70.
306          8a8b.bd4b.1f74.dde8.c6b4.a61c.2e25.78ba.
307          08ae.7a65.eaf4.566c.a94e.d58d.6d37.c8e7.
308          79e4.9591.62ac.d3c2.5c24.0649.0a3a.32e0.
309          db0b.5ede.14b8.ee46.8890.2a22.dc4f.8160.
310          7319.5d64.3d7e.a7c4.1744.975f.ec13.0ccd.
311          d2f3.ff10.21da.b6bc.f538.9d92.8f40.a351.
312          a89f.3c50.7f02.f945.8533.4d43.fbaa.efd0.
313          cf58.4c4a.39be.cb6a.5bb1.fc20.ed00.d153.
314          842f.e329.b3d6.3b52.a05a.6e1b.1a2c.8309.
315          75b2.27eb.e280.1207.9a05.9618.c323.c704.
316          1531.d871.f1e5.a534.ccf7.3f36.2693.fdb7.
317          c072.a49c.afa2.d4ad.f047.59fa.7dc9.82ca.
318          76ab.d7fe.2b67.0130.c56f.6bf2.7b77.7c63
319        --
320      ::                                     ::  ++pin:ahem:aes:
321      ++  pin                                ::  decrypt
322        ^-  cipa
323        |%
324        ::                                   ::  ++co:pin:ahem:aes:
325        ++  co                               ::  column coefficients
326        [0xe 0xb 0xd 0x9]
327        ::                                   ::  ++ix:pin:ahem:aes:
328        ++  ix                               ::  key index
329        |~(a=@ (sub nnr a))
330        ::                                   ::  ++ro:pin:ahem:aes:
331        ++  ro                               ::  row shifts
332        [0 3 2 1]
333        ::                                   ::  ++su:pin:ahem:aes:
334        ++  su                               ::  s-box
335        0x7d0c.2155.6314.69e1.26d6.77ba.7e04.2b17.
336          6199.5383.3cbb.ebc8.b0f5.2aae.4d3b.e0a0.
337          ef9c.c993.9f7a.e52d.0d4a.b519.a97f.5160.
338          5fec.8027.5910.12b1.31c7.0788.33a8.dd1f.
339          f45a.cd78.fec0.db9a.2079.d2c6.4b3e.56fc.
340          1bbe.18aa.0e62.b76f.89c5.291d.711a.f147.
341          6edf.751c.e837.f9e2.8535.ade7.2274.ac96.
342          73e6.b4f0.cecf.f297.eadc.674f.4111.913a.
343          6b8a.1301.03bd.afc1.020f.3fca.8f1e.2cd0.
344          0645.b3b8.0558.e4f7.0ad3.bc8c.00ab.d890.
345          849d.8da7.5746.155e.dab9.edfd.5048.706c.
```

```
          92b6.655d.cc5c.a4d4.1698.6886.64f6.f872.
          25d1.8b6d.49a2.5b76.b224.d928.66a1.2e08.
          4ec3.fa42.0b95.4cee.3d23.c2a6.3294.7b54.
          cbe9.dec4.4443.8e34.87ff.2f9b.8239.e37c.
          fbd7.f381.9ea3.40bf.38a5.3630.d56a.0952
        --
    ::                                          ::  ++mcol:ahem:aes:
    ++  mcol                                    ::
      |=  [a=(list @) b=[p=@ q=@ r=@ s=@]]
      ^-  (list @)
      =+  c=[p=*@ q=*@ r=*@ s=*@]
      |-  ^-  (list @)
      ?~  a  ~
      =>  .(p.c (cut 3 [0 1] i.a))
      =>  .(q.c (cut 3 [1 1] i.a))
      =>  .(r.c (cut 3 [2 1] i.a))
      =>  .(s.c (cut 3 [3 1] i.a))
      :_  $(a t.a)
      %+  rep  3
      %+  turn
        %-  limo
        :~  [[p.c p.b] [q.c q.b] [r.c r.b] [s.c s.b]]
            [[p.c s.b] [q.c p.b] [r.c q.b] [s.c r.b]]
            [[p.c r.b] [q.c s.b] [r.c p.b] [s.c q.b]]
            [[p.c q.b] [q.c r.b] [r.c s.b] [s.c p.b]]
        ==
      |=  [a=[@ @] b=[@ @] c=[@ @] d=[@ @]]
      :(dif (pro a) (pro b) (pro c) (pro d))
    ::                                          ::  ++pode:ahem:aes:
    ++  pode                                    ::  explode to block
      |=  [a=bloq b=@ c=@]  ^-  (list @)
      =+  d=(rip a c)
      =+  m=(met a c)
      |-
      ?:  =(m b)
        d
      $(m +(m), d (weld d (limo [0 ~])))
    ::                                          ::  ++sube:ahem:aes:
    ++  sube                                    ::  s-box word
      |=  [a=@ b=@]  ^-  @
      (rep 3 (turn (pode 3 4 a) |=(c=@ (cut 3 [c 1] b))))
    --  ::
  |%
  ::                                            ::  ++be:ahem:aes:crypto
  ++  be                                        ::  block cipher
    |=  [a=? b=@ c=@H]  ^-  @uxH
    ~|  %be-aesc
    =>  %=    .
            +
          =>  +
          |%
          ::                                    ::  ++ankh:be:ahem:aes:
          ++  ankh                              ::
            |=  [a=cipa b=@ c=@]
            (pode 5 nnb (cut 5 [(mul (ix.a b) nnb) nnb] c))
          ::                                    ::  ++sark:be:ahem:aes:
          ++  sark                              ::
            |=  [c=(list @) d=(list @)]
```

```
404          ^-  (list @)
405          ?~  c  ~
406          ?~  d  !!
407          [(mix i.c i.d) $(c t.c, d t.d)]
408        ::                                          ::  ++srow:be:ahem:aes:
409        ++  srow                                    ::
410          |=  [a=cipa b=(list @)]  ^-  (list @)
411          =+  [c=0 d=~ e=ro.a]
412          |-
413          ?:  =(c nnb)
414            d
415          :_  $(c +(c))
416          %+  rep  3
417          %+  turn
418            (limo [0 p.e] [1 q.e] [2 r.e] [3 s.e] ~)
419          |=  [f=@ g=@]
420          (cut 3 [f 1] (snag (mod (add g c) nnb) b))
421        ::                                          ::  ++subs:be:ahem:aes:
422        ++  subs                                    ::
423          |=  [a=cipa b=(list @)]  ^-  (list @)
424          ?~  b  ~
425          [(sube i.b su.a) $(b t.b)]
426          --
427      ==
428    =+  [d=?:(a pen pin) e=(pode 5 nnb c) f=1]
429    =>  .(e (sark e (ankh d 0 b)))
430    |-
431    ?.  =(nnr f)
432      =>  .(e (subs d e))
433      =>  .(e (srow d e))
434      =>  .(e (mcol e co.d))
435      =>  .(e (sark e (ankh d f b)))
436      $(f +(f))
437    =>  .(e (subs d e))
438    =>  .(e (srow d e))
439    =>  .(e (sark e (ankh d nnr b)))
440    (rep 5 e)
441  ::                                          ::  ++ex:ahem:aes:crypto
442  ++  ex                                      ::  key expand
443    |=  a=@I  ^-  @
444    =+  [b=a c=0 d=su:pen i=nnk]
445    |-
446    ?:  =(i (mul nnb +(nnr)))
447      b
448    =>  .(c (cut 5 [(dec i) 1] b))
449    =>  ?:  =(0 (mod i nnk))
450        =>  .(c (ror 3 1 c))
451        =>  .(c (sube c d))
452        .(c (mix c (pow (dec (div i nnk)) 2)))
453      ?:  &((gth nnk 6) =(4 (mod i nnk)))
454        .(c (sube c d))
455        .
456    =>  .(c (mix c (cut 5 [(sub i nnk) 1] b)))
457    =>  .(b (can 5 [i b] [1 c] ~))
458    $(i +(i))
459  ::                                          ::  ++ix:ahem:aes:crypto
460  ++  ix                                      ::  key expand, inv
461    |=  a=@  ^-  @
```

```
=+  [i=1 j=*@ b=*@ c=co:pin]
|-
?:  =(nnr i)
  a
=>  .(b (cut 7 [i 1] a))
=>  .(b (rep 5 (mcol (pode 5 4 b) c)))
=>  .(j (sub nnr i))
%=    $
  i  +(i)
  a
%+  can  7
:~  [i (cut 7 [0 i] a)]
    [1 b]
    [j (cut 7 [+(i) j] a)]
==
==
--
::                                         ::  ++ecba:aes:crypto
++  ecba                                   ::  AES-128 ECB
~%  %ecba  +>  ~
|_  key=@H
::                                         ::  ++en:ecba:aes:crypto
++  en                                     ::  encrypt
~/  %en
|=  blk=@H  ^-  @uxH
=+  (ahem 4 4 10)
=:
  key  (~(net fe 7) key)
  blk  (~(net fe 7) blk)
==
%-  ~(net fe 7)
(be & (ex key) blk)
::                                         ::  ++de:ecba:aes:crypto
++  de                                     ::  decrypt
~/  %de
|=  blk=@H  ^-  @uxH
=+  (ahem 4 4 10)
=:
  key  (~(net fe 7) key)
  blk  (~(net fe 7) blk)
==
%-  ~(net fe 7)
(be | (ix (ex key)) blk)
--  ::ecba
::                                         ::  ++ecbb:aes:crypto
++  ecbb                                   ::  AES-192 ECB
~%  %ecbb  +>  ~
|_  key=@I
::                                         ::  ++en:ecbb:aes:crypto
++  en                                     ::  encrypt
~/  %en
|=  blk=@H  ^-  @uxH
=+  (ahem 6 4 12)
=:
  key  (rsh 6 (~(net fe 8) key))
  blk  (~(net fe 7) blk)
==
%-  ~(net fe 7)
```

```
520        (be & (ex key) blk)
521      ::                                            ::  ++de:ecbb:aes:crypto
522      ++  de                                        ::  decrypt
523        ~/  %de
524        |=  blk=@H   ^-  @uxH
525        =+  (ahem 6 4 12)
526        =:
527          key  (rsh 6 (~(net fe 8) key))
528          blk  (~(net fe 7) blk)
529        ==
530        %-  ~(net fe 7)
531        (be | (ix (ex key)) blk)
532      --  ::ecbb
533    ::                                              ::  ++ecbc:aes:crypto
534    ++  ecbc                                        ::  AES-256 ECB
535      ~%  %ecbc  +>  ~
536      |_  key=@I
537      ::                                            ::  ++en:ecbc:aes:crypto
538      ++  en                                        ::  encrypt
539        ~/  %en
540        |=  blk=@H   ^-  @uxH
541        =+  (ahem 8 4 14)
542        =:
543          key  (~(net fe 8) key)
544          blk  (~(net fe 7) blk)
545        ==
546        %-  ~(net fe 7)
547        (be & (ex key) blk)
548      ::                                            ::  ++de:ecbc:aes:crypto
549      ++  de                                        ::  decrypt
550        ~/  %de
551        |=  blk=@H   ^-  @uxH
552        =+  (ahem 8 4 14)
553        =:
554          key  (~(net fe 8) key)
555          blk  (~(net fe 7) blk)
556        ==
557        %-  ~(net fe 7)
558        (be | (ix (ex key)) blk)
559      --  ::ecbc
560    ::                                              ::  ++cbca:aes:crypto
561    ++  cbca                                        ::  AES-128 CBC
562      ~%  %cbca  +>  ~
563      |_  [key=@H prv=@H]
564      ::                                            ::  ++en:cbca:aes:crypto
565      ++  en                                        ::  encrypt
566        ~/  %en
567        |=  txt=@   ^-  @ux
568        =+  pts=?:(=(txt 0) `(list @)`~[0] (flop (rip 7 txt)))
569        =|  cts=(list @)
570        %+  rep  7
571        ::  logically, flop twice here
572        |-  ^-  (list @)
573        ?~  pts
574          cts
575        =+  cph=(~(en ecba key) (mix prv i.pts))
576        %=  $
577          cts  [cph cts]
```

```
        pts  t.pts
        prv  cph
      ==
    ::                                        ::  ++de:cbca:aes:crypto
    ++  de                                    ::  decrypt
      ~/  %de
      |=  txt=@  ^-  @ux
      =+  cts=?:(=(txt 0) `(list @)`~[0] (flop (rip 7 txt)))
      =|  pts=(list @)
      %+  rep  7
      ::  logically, flop twice here
      |-  ^-  (list @)
      ?~  cts
        pts
      =+  pln=(mix prv (~(de ecba key) i.cts))
      %=  $
        pts  [pln pts]
        cts  t.cts
        prv  i.cts
      ==
    --  ::cbca
  ::                                          ::  ++cbcb:aes:crypto
  ++  cbcb                                    ::  AES-192 CBC
    ~%  %cbcb  +>  ~
    |_  [key=@I prv=@H]
    ::                                        ::  ++en:cbcb:aes:crypto
    ++  en                                    ::  encrypt
      ~/  %en
      |=  txt=@  ^-  @ux
      =+  pts=?:(=(txt 0) `(list @)`~[0] (flop (rip 7 txt)))
      =|  cts=(list @)
      %+  rep  7
      ::  logically, flop twice here
      |-  ^-  (list @)
      ?~  pts
        cts
      =+  cph=(~(en ecbb key) (mix prv i.pts))
      %=  $
        cts  [cph cts]
        pts  t.pts
        prv  cph
      ==
    ::                                        ::  ++de:cbcb:aes:crypto
    ++  de                                    ::  decrypt
      ~/  %de
      |=  txt=@  ^-  @ux
      =+  cts=?:(=(txt 0) `(list @)`~[0] (flop (rip 7 txt)))
      =|  pts=(list @)
      %+  rep  7
      ::  logically, flop twice here
      |-  ^-  (list @)
      ?~  cts
        pts
      =+  pln=(mix prv (~(de ecbb key) i.cts))
      %=  $
        pts  [pln pts]
        cts  t.cts
        prv  i.cts
```

```
636          ==
637        --  ::cbcb
638      ::                                              ::  ++cbcc:aes:crypto
639      ++  cbcc                                         ::  AES-256 CBC
640      ~%  %cbcc  +>  ~
641      |_  [key=@I prv=@H]
642        ::                                            ::  ++en:cbcc:aes:crypto
643        ++  en                                        ::  encrypt
644        ~/  %en
645        |=  txt=@  ^-  @ux
646        =+  pts=?:(=(txt 0) `(list @)`~[0] (flop (rip 7 txt)))
647        =|  cts=(list @)
648        %+  rep  7
649        ::  logically, flop twice here
650        |-  ^-  (list @)
651        ?~  pts
652           cts
653        =+  cph=(~(en ecbc key) (mix prv i.pts))
654        %=  $
655          cts  [cph cts]
656          pts  t.pts
657          prv  cph
658        ==
659        ::                                            ::  ++de:cbcc:aes:crypto
660        ++  de                                        ::  decrypt
661        ~/  %de
662        |=  txt=@  ^-  @ux
663        =+  cts=?:(=(txt 0) `(list @)`~[0] (flop (rip 7 txt)))
664        =|  pts=(list @)
665        %+  rep  7
666        ::  logically, flop twice here
667        |-  ^-  (list @)
668        ?~  cts
669           pts
670        =+  pln=(mix prv (~(de ecbc key) i.cts))
671        %=  $
672          pts  [pln pts]
673          cts  t.cts
674          prv  i.cts
675        ==
676      --  ::cbcc
677    ::                                                ::  ++inc:aes:crypto
678    ++  inc                                           ::  inc. low bloq
679    |=  [mod=bloq ctr=@H]
680    ^-  @uxH
681    =+  bqs=(rip mod ctr)
682    ?~  bqs  0x1
683    %+  rep  mod
684    [(~(sum fe mod) i.bqs 1) t.bqs]
685    ::                                                ::  ++ctra:aes:crypto
686    ++  ctra                                          ::  AES-128 CTR
687    ~%  %ctra  +>  ~
688    |_  [key=@H mod=bloq len=@ ctr=@H]
689      ::                                              ::  ++en:ctra:aes:crypto
690      ++  en                                          ::  encrypt
691      ~/  %en
692      |=  txt=@
693      ^-  @ux
```

```
694      =/   encrypt   ~(en ecba key)
695      =/   blocks   (add (div len 16) ?:(=((^mod len 16) 0) 0 1))
696      ?>   (gte len (met 3 txt))
697      %+   mix   txt
698      %+   rsh   [3 (sub (mul 16 blocks) len)]
699      %+   rep   7
700      =|   seed=(list @ux)
701      |-   ^+   seed
702      ?:   =(blocks 0)   seed
703      %=   $
704        seed      [(encrypt ctr) seed]
705        ctr       (inc mod ctr)
706        blocks    (dec blocks)
707      ==
708    ::                                          ::  ++de:ctra:aes:crypto
709    ++   de                                     ::  decrypt
710      en
711    --   ::ctra
712  ::                                            ::  ++ctrb:aes:crypto
713  ++   ctrb                                     ::  AES-192 CTR
714    ~%   %ctrb   +>   ~
715    |_   [key=@I mod=bloq len=@ ctr=@H]
716    ::                                          ::  ++en:ctrb:aes:crypto
717    ++   en
718      ~/   %en
719      |=   txt=@
720      ^-   @ux
721      =/   encrypt   ~(en ecbb key)
722      =/   blocks   (add (div len 16) ?:(=((^mod len 16) 0) 0 1))
723      ?>   (gte len (met 3 txt))
724      %+   mix   txt
725      %+   rsh   [3 (sub (mul 16 blocks) len)]
726      %+   rep   7
727      =|   seed=(list @ux)
728      |-   ^+   seed
729      ?:   =(blocks 0)   seed
730      %=   $
731        seed      [(encrypt ctr) seed]
732        ctr       (inc mod ctr)
733        blocks    (dec blocks)
734      ==
735    ::                                          ::  ++de:ctrb:aes:crypto
736    ++   de                                     ::  decrypt
737      en
738    --   ::ctrb
739  ::                                            ::  ++ctrc:aes:crypto
740  ++   ctrc                                     ::  AES-256 CTR
741    ~%   %ctrc   +>   ~
742    |_   [key=@I mod=bloq len=@ ctr=@H]
743    ::                                          ::  ++en:ctrc:aes:crypto
744    ++   en                                     ::  encrypt
745      ~/   %en
746      |=   txt=@
747      ^-   @ux
748      =/   encrypt   ~(en ecbc key)
749      =/   blocks   (add (div len 16) ?:(=((^mod len 16) 0) 0 1))
750      ?>   (gte len (met 3 txt))
751      %+   mix   txt
```

```
752        %+  rsh  [3 (sub (mul 16 blocks) len)]
753        %+  rep  7
754        =|  seed=(list @ux)
755        |-  ^+  seed
756        ?:  =(blocks 0)  seed
757        %=  $
758          seed    [(encrypt ctr) seed]
759          ctr     (inc mod ctr)
760          blocks  (dec blocks)
761        ==
762      ::                                         ::  ++de:ctrc:aes:crypto
763    ++  de                                       ::  decrypt
764      en
765    --  ::ctrc
766  ::                                             ::  ++doub:aes:crypto
767  ++  doub                                       ::  double 128-bit
768    |=  ::  string mod finite
769        ::
770        str=@H
771    ::
772    ::  field (see spec)
773    ::
774    ^-  @uxH
775    %-  ~(sit fe 7)
776    ?.  =((xeb str) 128)
777      (lsh 0 str)
778    (mix 0x87 (lsh 0 str))
779  ::                                             ::  ++mpad:aes:crypto
780  ++  mpad                                       ::
781    |=  [oct=@ txt=@]
782    ::
783    ::  pad message to multiple of 128 bits
784    ::  by appending 1, then 0s
785    ::  the spec is unclear, but it must be octet based
786    ::  to match the test vectors
787    ::
788    ^-  @ux
789    =+  pad=(mod oct 16)
790    ?:  =(pad 0)  0x8000.0000.0000.0000.0000.0000.0000.0000
791    (lsh [3 (sub 15 pad)] (mix 0x80 (lsh 3 txt)))
792  ::                                             ::  ++suba:aes:crypto
793  ++  suba                                       ::  AES-128 subkeys
794    |=  key=@H
795    =+  l=(~(en ecba key) 0)
796    =+  k1=(doub l)
797    =+  k2=(doub k1)
798    ^-  [@ux @ux]
799    [k1 k2]
800  ::                                             ::  ++subb:aes:crypto
801  ++  subb                                       ::  AES-192 subkeys
802    |=  key=@I
803    =+  l=(~(en ecbb key) 0)
804    =+  k1=(doub l)
805    =+  k2=(doub k1)
806    ^-  [@ux @ux]
807    [k1 k2]
808  ::                                             ::  ++subc:aes:crypto
809  ++  subc                                       ::  AES-256 subkeys
```

```
810      |=  key=@I
811      =+  l=(~(en ecbc key) 0)
812      =+  k1=(doub l)
813      =+  k2=(doub k1)
814      ^-  [@ux @ux]
815      [k1 k2]
816    ::                                          ::  ++maca:aes:crypto
817    ++  maca                                     ::  AES-128 CMAC
818      ~/  %maca
819      |=  [key=@H oct=(unit @) txt=@]
820      ^-  @ux
821      =+  [sub=(suba key) len=?~(oct (met 3 txt) u.oct)]
822      =+  ^=  pdt
823        ?:  &(=((mod len 16) 0) !=(len 0))
824          [& txt]
825        [| (mpad len txt)]
826      =+  ^=  mac
827        %-  ~(en cbca key 0)
828        %+  mix  +.pdt
829        ?-  -.pdt
830          %&  -.sub
831          %|  +.sub
832        ==
833      ::  spec says MSBs, LSBs match test vectors
834      ::
835      (~(sit fe 7) mac)
836    ::                                          ::  ++macb:aes:crypto
837    ++  macb                                     ::  AES-192 CMAC
838      ~/  %macb
839      |=  [key=@I oct=(unit @) txt=@]
840      ^-  @ux
841      =+  [sub=(subb key) len=?~(oct (met 3 txt) u.oct)]
842      =+  ^=  pdt
843        ?:  &(=((mod len 16) 0) !=(len 0))
844          [& txt]
845        [| (mpad len txt)]
846      =+  ^=  mac
847        %-  ~(en cbcb key 0)
848        %+  mix  +.pdt
849        ?-  -.pdt
850          %&  -.sub
851          %|  +.sub
852        ==
853      ::  spec says MSBs, LSBs match test vectors
854      ::
855      (~(sit fe 7) mac)
856    ::                                          ::  ++macc:aes:crypto
857    ++  macc                                     ::  AES-256 CMAC
858      ~/  %macc
859      |=  [key=@I oct=(unit @) txt=@]
860      ^-  @ux
861      =+  [sub=(subc key) len=?~(oct (met 3 txt) u.oct)]
862      =+  ^=  pdt
863        ?:  &(=((mod len 16) 0) !=(len 0))
864          [& txt]
865        [| (mpad len txt)]
866      =+  ^=  mac
867        %-  ~(en cbcc key 0)
```

```
868      %+  mix  +.pdt
869      ?-  -.pdt
870        %&  -.sub
871        %|  +.sub
872      ==
873    ::  spec says MSBs, LSBs match test vectors
874    ::
875    (~(sit fe 7) mac)
876  ::                                          ::  ++s2va:aes:crypto
877  ++  s2va                                    ::  AES-128 S2V
878    ~/  %s2va
879    |=  [key=@H ads=(list @)]
880    ?~  ads  (maca key `16 0x1)
881    =/  res  (maca key `16 0x0)
882    %+  maca  key
883    |-  ^-  [[~ @ud] @uxH]
884    ?~  t.ads
885      =/  wyt  (met 3 i.ads)
886      ?:  (gte wyt 16)
887        [`wyt (mix i.ads res)]
888      [`16 (mix (doub res) (mpad wyt i.ads))]
889    %=  $
890      ads  t.ads
891      res  (mix (doub res) (maca key ~ i.ads))
892    ==
893  ::                                          ::  ++s2vb:aes:crypto
894  ++  s2vb                                    ::  AES-192 S2V
895    ~/  %s2vb
896    |=  [key=@I ads=(list @)]
897    ?~  ads  (macb key `16 0x1)
898    =/  res  (macb key `16 0x0)
899    %+  macb  key
900    |-  ^-  [[~ @ud] @uxH]
901    ?~  t.ads
902      =/  wyt  (met 3 i.ads)
903      ?:  (gte wyt 16)
904        [`wyt (mix i.ads res)]
905      [`16 (mix (doub res) (mpad wyt i.ads))]
906    %=  $
907      ads  t.ads
908      res  (mix (doub res) (macb key ~ i.ads))
909    ==
910  ::                                          ::  ++s2vc:aes:crypto
911  ++  s2vc                                    ::  AES-256 S2V
912    ~/  %s2vc
913    |=  [key=@I ads=(list @)]
914    ?~  ads  (macc key `16 0x1)
915    =/  res  (macc key `16 0x0)
916    %+  macc  key
917    |-  ^-  [[~ @ud] @uxH]
918    ?~  t.ads
919      =/  wyt  (met 3 i.ads)
920      ?:  (gte wyt 16)
921        [`wyt (mix i.ads res)]
922      [`16 (mix (doub res) (mpad wyt i.ads))]
923    %=  $
924      ads  t.ads
925      res  (mix (doub res) (macc key ~ i.ads))
```

```
926        ==
927      ::                                              ::  ++siva:aes:crypto
928      ++  siva                                        ::  AES-128 SIV
929        ~%  %siva  +>  ~
930        |_  [key=@I vec=(list @)]
931        ::                                            ::  ++en:siva:aes:crypto
932        ++  en                                        ::  encrypt
933          ~/  %en
934          |=  txt=@
935          ^-  (trel @uxH @ud @ux)
936          =+  [k1=(rsh 7 key) k2=(end 7 key)]
937          =+  iv=(s2va k1 (weld vec (limo ~[txt])))
938          =+  len=(met 3 txt)
939          =*  hib  (dis iv 0xffff.ffff.ffff.ffff.7fff.ffff.7fff.ffff)
940          :+
941            iv
942            len
943          (~(en ctra k2 7 len hib) txt)
944        ::                                            ::  ++de:siva:aes:crypto
945        ++  de                                        ::  decrypt
946          ~/  %de
947          |=  [iv=@H len=@ txt=@]
948          ^-  (unit @ux)
949          =+  [k1=(rsh 7 key) k2=(end 7 key)]
950          =*  hib  (dis iv 0xffff.ffff.ffff.ffff.7fff.ffff.7fff.ffff)
951          =+  ^=  pln
952            (~(de ctra k2 7 len hib) txt)
953          ?.  =((s2va k1 (weld vec (limo ~[pln]))) iv)
954            ~
955          `pln
956        --  ::siva
957      ::                                              ::  ++sivb:aes:crypto
958      ++  sivb                                        ::  AES-192 SIV
959        ~%  %sivb  +>  ~
960        |_  [key=@J vec=(list @)]
961        ::                                            ::  ++en:sivb:aes:crypto
962        ++  en                                        ::  encrypt
963          ~/  %en
964          |=  txt=@
965          ^-  (trel @uxH @ud @ux)
966          =+  [k1=(rsh [6 3] key) k2=(end [6 3] key)]
967          =+  iv=(s2vb k1 (weld vec (limo ~[txt])))
968          =*  hib  (dis iv 0xffff.ffff.ffff.ffff.7fff.ffff.7fff.ffff)
969          =+  len=(met 3 txt)
970          :+  iv
971            len
972          (~(en ctrb k2 7 len hib) txt)
973        ::                                            ::  ++de:sivb:aes:crypto
974        ++  de                                        ::  decrypt
975          ~/  %de
976          |=  [iv=@H len=@ txt=@]
977          ^-  (unit @ux)
978          =+  [k1=(rsh [6 3] key) k2=(end [6 3] key)]
979          =*  hib  (dis iv 0xffff.ffff.ffff.ffff.7fff.ffff.7fff.ffff)
980          =+  ^=  pln
981            (~(de ctrb k2 7 len hib) txt)
982          ?.  =((s2vb k1 (weld vec (limo ~[pln]))) iv)
983            ~
```

```
      `pln
  --   ::sivb
::                                              ::   ++sivc:aes:crypto
++   sivc                                        ::   AES-256 SIV
  ~%  %sivc  +>  ~
  |_  [key=@J vec=(list @)]
  ::                                              ::   ++en:sivc:aes:crypto
  ++   en                                        ::   encrypt
    ~/  %en
    |=  txt=@
    ^-  (trel @uxH @ud @ux)
    =+  [k1=(rsh 8 key) k2=(end 8 key)]
    =+  iv=(s2vc k1 (weld vec (limo ~[txt])))
    =*  hib  (dis iv 0xffff.ffff.ffff.ffff.7fff.ffff.7fff.ffff)
    =+  len=(met 3 txt)
    :+
      iv
      len
    (~(en ctrc k2 7 len hib) txt)
  ::                                              ::   ++de:sivc:aes:crypto
  ++   de                                        ::   decrypt
    ~/  %de
    |=  [iv=@H len=@ txt=@]
    ^-  (unit @ux)
    =+  [k1=(rsh 8 key) k2=(end 8 key)]
    =*  hib  (dis iv 0xffff.ffff.ffff.ffff.7fff.ffff.7fff.ffff)
    =+  ^=  pln
      (~(de ctrc k2 7 len hib) txt)
    ?.  =((s2vc k1 (weld vec (limo ~[pln]))) iv)
      ~
      `pln
  --   ::sivc
  --
::                                              ::
::::                     ++ed:crypto            ::   ed25519
  ::                                            ::::
++   ed
  =>
    =+  =+  [b=256 q=(sub (bex 255) 19)]
        =+  fq=~(. fo q)
        =+  ^=  l
            %+  add
              (bex 252)
            27.742.317.777.372.353.535.851.937.790.883.648.493
        =+  d=(dif.fq 0 (fra.fq 121.665 121.666))
        =+  ii=(exp.fq (div (dec q) 4) 2)
        [b=b q=q fq=fq l=l d=d ii=ii]
    ~%  %coed  ..part  ~
    |%
    ::                                          ::   ++norm:ed:crypto
    ++   norm                                   ::
      |=(x=@ ?:(=(0 (mod x 2)) x (sub q x)))
    ::                                          ::   ++xrec:ed:crypto
    ++   xrec                                   ::   recover x-coord
      |=  y=@  ^-  @
      =+  ^=  xx
          %+  mul  (dif.fq (mul y y) 1)
                  (inv.fq +:(mul d y y)))
```

```
=+  x=(exp.fq (div (add 3 q) 8) xx)
?:  !=(0 (dif.fq (mul x x) (sit.fq xx)))
  (norm (pro.fq x ii))
(norm x)
::                                          ::  ++ward:ed:crypto
++  ward                                    ::  edwards multiply
|=  [pp=[@ @] qq=[@ @]]  ^-  [@ @]
=+  dp=:(pro.fq d -.pp -.qq +.pp +.qq)
=+  ^=  xt
  %+  pro.fq
    %+  sum.fq
      (pro.fq -.pp +.qq)
    (pro.fq -.qq +.pp)
  (inv.fq (sum.fq 1 dp))
=+  ^=  yt
  %+  pro.fq
    %+  sum.fq
      (pro.fq +.pp +.qq)
    (pro.fq -.pp -.qq)
  (inv.fq (dif.fq 1 dp))
[xt yt]
::                                          ::  ++scam:ed:crypto
++  scam                                    ::  scalar multiply
|=  [pp=[@ @] e=@]  ^-  [@ @]
?:  =(0 e)
  [0 1]
=+  qq=$(e (div e 2))
=>  .(qq (ward qq qq))
?:  =(1 (dis 1 e))
  (ward qq pp)
qq
::                                          ::  ++etch:ed:crypto
++  etch                                    ::  encode point
|=  pp=[@ @]  ^-  @
(can 0 ~[[(sub b 1) +.pp] [1 (dis 1 -.pp)]])
::                                          ::  ++curv:ed:crypto
++  curv                                    ::  point on curve?
|=  [x=@ y=@]  ^-  ?
.=  0
  %+  dif.fq
    %+  sum.fq
      (pro.fq (sub q (sit.fq x)) x)
    (pro.fq y y)
  (sum.fq 1 :(pro.fq d x x y y))
::                                          ::  ++deco:ed:crypto
++  deco                                    ::  decode point
|=  s=@  ^-  (unit [@ @])
=+  y=(cut 0 [0 (dec b)] s)
=+  si=(cut 0 [(dec b) 1] s)
=+  x=(xrec y)
=>  .(x ?:(!=(si (dis 1 x)) (sub q x) x))
=+  pp=[x y]
?.  (curv pp)
  ~
[~ pp]
::                                          ::  ++bb:ed:crypto
++  bb                                      ::
=+  bby=(pro.fq 4 (inv.fq 5))
```

```
1100        [(xrec bby) bby]
1101      --  ::
1102    ~%  %ed   +   ~
1103    |%
1104    ::
1105    ++  point-add
1106      ~/  %point-add
1107      |=  [a-point=@udpoint b-point=@udpoint]
1108      ^-  @udpoint
1109      ::
1110      =/  a-point-decoded=[@ @]  (need (deco a-point))
1111      =/  b-point-decoded=[@ @]  (need (deco b-point))
1112      ::
1113      %-  etch
1114      (ward a-point-decoded b-point-decoded)
1115    ::
1116    ++  scalarmult
1117      ~/  %scalarmult
1118      |=  [a=@udscalar a-point=@udpoint]
1119      ^-  @udpoint
1120      ::
1121      =/  a-point-decoded=[@ @]  (need (deco a-point))
1122      ::
1123      %-  etch
1124      (scam a-point-decoded a)
1125    ::
1126    ++  scalarmult-base
1127      ~/  %scalarmult-base
1128      |=  scalar=@udscalar
1129      ^-  @udpoint
1130      %-  etch
1131      (scam bb scalar)
1132    ::
1133    ++  add-scalarmult-scalarmult-base
1134      ~/  %add-scalarmult-scalarmult-base
1135      |=  [a=@udscalar a-point=@udpoint b=@udscalar]
1136      ^-  @udpoint
1137      ::
1138      =/  a-point-decoded=[@ @]  (need (deco a-point))
1139      ::
1140      %-  etch
1141      %+  ward
1142        (scam bb b)
1143      (scam a-point-decoded a)
1144    ::
1145    ++  add-double-scalarmult
1146      ~/  %add-double-scalarmult
1147      |=  [a=@udscalar a-point=@udpoint b=@udscalar b-point=@udpoint]
1148      ^-  @udpoint
1149      ::
1150      =/  a-point-decoded=[@ @]  (need (deco a-point))
1151      =/  b-point-decoded=[@ @]  (need (deco b-point))
1152      ::
1153      %-  etch
1154      %+  ward
1155        (scam a-point-decoded a)
1156      (scam b-point-decoded b)
1157    ::                                                    ::  ++puck:ed:crypto
```

```
++  puck                                     ::  public key
  ~/  %puck
  |=  sk=@I  ^-  @
  ?:  (gth (met 3 sk) 32)  !!
  =+  h=(shal (rsh [0 3] b) sk)
  =+  ^=  a
      %+  add
        (bex (sub b 2))
      (lsh [0 3] (cut 0 [3 (sub b 5)] h))
  =+  aa=(scam bb a)
  (etch aa)
::                                           ::  ++suck:ed:crypto
++  suck                                     ::  keypair from seed
  |=  se=@I  ^-  @uJ
  =+  pu=(puck se)
  (can 0 ~[[b se] [b pu]])
::                                           ::  ++shar:ed:crypto
++  shar                                     ::  curve25519 secret
  ~/  %shar
  |=  [pub=@ sek=@]
  ^-  @ux
  =+  exp=(shal (rsh [0 3] b) (suck sek))
  =.  exp  (dis exp (can 0 ~[[3 0] [251 (fil 0 251 1)]]))
  =.  exp  (con exp (lsh [3 31] 0b100.0000))
  =+  prv=(end 8 exp)
  =+  crv=(fra.fq (sum.fq 1 pub) (dif.fq 1 pub))
  (curt prv crv)
::                                           ::  ++sign:ed:crypto
++  sign                                     ::  certify
  ~/  %sign
  |=  [m=@ se=@]  ^-  @
  =+  sk=(suck se)
  =+  pk=(cut 0 [b b] sk)
  =+  h=(shal (rsh [0 3] b) sk)
  =+  ^=  a
      %+  add
        (bex (sub b 2))
      (lsh [0 3] (cut 0 [3 (sub b 5)] h))
  =+  ^=  r
      =+  hm=(cut 0 [b b] h)
      =+  ^=  i
          %+  can  0
          :~  [b hm]
              [(met 0 m) m]
          ==
      (shaz i)
  =+  rr=(scam bb r)
  =+  ^=  ss
      =+  er=(etch rr)
      =+  ^=  ha
          %+  can  0
          :~  [b er]
              [b pk]
              [(met 0 m) m]
          ==
      (~(sit fo l) (add r (mul (shaz ha) a)))
  (can 0 ~[[b (etch rr)] [b ss]])
::                                           ::  ++veri:ed:crypto
```

```
1216      ++  veri                                          ::  validate
1217        ~/  %veri
1218        |=  [s=@ m=@ pk=@]  ^-  ?
1219        ?:  (gth (div b 4) (met 3 s))  |
1220        ?:  (gth (div b 8) (met 3 pk))  |
1221        =+  cb=(rsh [0 3] b)
1222        =+  rr=(deco (cut 0 [0 b] s))
1223        ?~  rr  |
1224        =+  aa=(deco pk)
1225        ?~  aa  |
1226        =+  ss=(cut 0 [b b] s)
1227        =+  ha=(can 3 ~[[cb (etch u.rr)] [cb pk] [(met 3 m) m]])
1228        =+  h=(shaz ha)
1229        =((scam bb ss) (ward u.rr (scam u.aa h)))
1230      --  ::ed
1231    ::                                                  ::
1232    ::::                      ++scr:crypto              ::  (2b3) scrypt
1233      ::                                                ::::
1234    ++  scr
1235      ~%  %scr  ..part  ~
1236      |%
1237      ::                                                ::  ++sal:scr:crypto
1238      ++  sal                                           ::  salsa20 hash
1239        |=  [x=@ r=@]                                   ::  with r rounds
1240        ?>  =((mod r 2) 0)                              ::
1241        =+  few==>(fe .(a 5))
1242        =+  ^=  rot
1243          |=  [a=@ b=@]
1244          (mix (end 5 (lsh [0 a] b)) (rsh [0 (sub 32 a)] b))
1245        =+  ^=  lea
1246          |=  [a=@ b=@]
1247          (net:few (sum:few (net:few a) (net:few b)))
1248        =>  |%
1249            ::                                          ::  ++qr:sal:scr:crypto
1250            ++  qr                                      ::  quarterround
1251              |=  y=[@ @ @ @ ~]
1252              =+  zb=(mix &2.y (rot 7 (sum:few &1.y &4.y)))
1253              =+  zc=(mix &3.y (rot 9 (sum:few zb &1.y)))
1254              =+  zd=(mix &4.y (rot 13 (sum:few zc zb)))
1255              =+  za=(mix &1.y (rot 18 (sum:few zd zc)))
1256              ~[za zb zc zd]
1257            ::                                          ::  ++rr:sal:scr:crypto
1258            ++  rr                                      ::  rowround
1259              |=  [y=(list @)]
1260              =+  za=(qr ~[&1.y &2.y &3.y &4.y])
1261              =+  zb=(qr ~[&6.y &7.y &8.y &5.y])
1262              =+  zc=(qr ~[&11.y &12.y &9.y &10.y])
1263              =+  zd=(qr ~[&16.y &13.y &14.y &15.y])
1264              ^-  (list @)  :~
1265                &1.za  &2.za  &3.za  &4.za
1266                &4.zb  &1.zb  &2.zb  &3.zb
1267                &3.zc  &4.zc  &1.zc  &2.zc
1268                &2.zd  &3.zd  &4.zd  &1.zd  ==
1269            ::                                          ::  ++cr:sal:scr:crypto
1270            ++  cr                                      ::  columnround
1271              |=  [x=(list @)]
1272              =+  ya=(qr ~[&1.x &5.x &9.x &13.x])
1273              =+  yb=(qr ~[&6.x &10.x &14.x &2.x])
```

```
1274        =+  yc=(qr ~[&11.x &15.x &3.x &7.x])
1275        =+  yd=(qr ~[&16.x &4.x &8.x &12.x])
1276        ^-  (list @)  :~
1277          &1.ya  &4.yb  &3.yc  &2.yd
1278          &2.ya  &1.yb  &4.yc  &3.yd
1279          &3.ya  &2.yb  &1.yc  &4.yd
1280          &4.ya  &3.yb  &2.yc  &1.yd  ==
1281        ::                                      :: ++dr:sal:scr:crypto
1282      ++  dr                                    :: doubleround
1283        |=  [x=(list @)]
1284        (rr (cr x))
1285        ::                                      :: ++al:sal:scr:crypto
1286      ++  al                                    :: add two lists
1287        |=  [a=(list @) b=(list @)]
1288        |-  ^-  (list @)
1289        ?~  a  ~  ?~  b  ~
1290        [i=(sum:few -.a -.b) t=$(a +.a, b +.b)]
1291        --  ::
1292    =+  xw=(rpp 5 16 x)
1293    =+  ^=  ow  |-  ^-  (list @)
1294              ?~  r  xw
1295              $(xw (dr xw), r (sub r 2))
1296      (rep 5 (al xw ow))
1297  ::                                            :: ++rpp:scr:crypto
1298  ++  rpp                                       :: rip+filler blocks
1299    |=  [a=bloq b=@ c=@]
1300    =+  q=(rip a c)
1301    =+  w=(lent q)
1302    ?.  =(w b)
1303      ?.  (lth w b)  (slag (sub w b) q)
1304      ^+  q  (weld q (reap (sub b (lent q)) 0))
1305    q
1306  ::                                            :: ++bls:scr:crypto
1307  ++  bls                                       :: split to sublists
1308    |=  [a=@ b=(list @)]
1309    ?>  =((mod (lent b) a) 0)
1310    |-  ^-  (list (list @))
1311    ?~  b  ~
1312    [i=(scag a `(list @)`b) t=$(b (slag a `(list @)`b))]
1313  ::                                            :: ++slb:scr:crypto
1314  ++  slb                                       ::
1315    |=  [a=(list (list @))]
1316    |-  ^-  (list @)
1317    ?~  a  ~
1318    (weld `(list @)`-.a $(a +.a))
1319  ::                                            :: ++sbm:scr:crypto
1320  ++  sbm                                       :: scryptBlockMix
1321    |=  [r=@ b=(list @)]
1322    ?>  =((lent b) (mul 2 r))
1323    =+  [x=(snag (dec (mul 2 r)) b) c=0]
1324    =|  [ya=(list @) yb=(list @)]
1325    |-  ^-  (list @)
1326    ?~  b  (flop (weld yb ya))
1327    =.  x  (sal (mix x -.b) 8)
1328    ?~  (mod c 2)
1329      $(c +(c), b +.b, ya [i=x t=ya])
1330    $(c +(c), b +.b, yb [i=x t=yb])
1331  ::                                            :: ++srm:scr:crypto
```

```
1332      ++  srm                                              ::  scryptROMix
1333        |=  [r=@ b=(list @) n=@]
1334        ?>  ?&  =((lent b) (mul 2 r))
1335                =(n (bex (dec (xeb n))))
1336                (lth n (bex (mul r 16)))
1337            ==
1338        =+  [v=*(list (list @)) c=0]
1339        =.  v
1340          |-  ^-  (list (list @))
1341          =+  w=(sbm r b)
1342          ?:  =(c n)  (flop v)
1343          $(c +(c), v [i=[b] t=v], b w)
1344        =+  x=(sbm r (snag (dec n) v))
1345        |-  ^-  (list @)
1346        ?:  =(c n)  x
1347        =+  q=(snag (dec (mul r 2)) x)
1348        =+  z=`(list @)`(snag (mod q n) v)
1349        =+  ^=  w  |-  ^-  (list @)
1350                  ?~  x  ~  ?~  z  ~
1351                  [i=(mix -.x -.z) t=$(x +.x, z +.z)]
1352        $(x (sbm r w), c +(c))
1353      ::                                               ::  ++hmc:scr:crypto
1354      ++  hmc                                          ::  HMAC-SHA-256
1355        |=  [k=@ t=@]
1356        (hml k (met 3 k) t (met 3 t))
1357      ::                                               ::  ++hml:scr:crypto
1358      ++  hml                                          ::  w+length
1359        |=  [k=@ kl=@ t=@ tl=@]
1360        =>  .(k (end [3 kl] k), t (end [3 tl] t))
1361        =+  b=64
1362        =?  k  (gth kl b)  (shay kl k)
1363        =+  ^=  q  %+  shay  (add b tl)
1364        (add (lsh [3 b] t) (mix k (fil 3 b 0x36)))
1365        %+  shay  (add b 32)
1366        (add (lsh [3 b] q) (mix k (fil 3 b 0x5c)))
1367      ::                                               ::  ++pbk:scr:crypto
1368      ++  pbk                                          ::  PBKDF2-HMAC-SHA256
1369        ~/  %pbk
1370        |=  [p=@ s=@ c=@ d=@]
1371        (pbl p (met 3 p) s (met 3 s) c d)
1372      ::                                               ::  ++pbl:scr:crypto
1373      ++  pbl                                          ::  w+length
1374        ~/  %pbl
1375        |=  [p=@ pl=@ s=@ sl=@ c=@ d=@]
1376        =>  .(p (end [3 pl] p), s (end [3 sl] s))
1377        =+  h=32
1378        ::
1379        ::  max key length 1GB
1380        ::  max iterations 2^28
1381        ::
1382        ?>  ?&  (lte d (bex 30))
1383                (lte c (bex 28))
1384                !=(c 0)
1385            ==
1386        =+  ^=  l  ?~  (mod d h)
1387          (div d h)
1388        +((div d h))
1389        =+  r=(sub d (mul h (dec l)))
```

```
1390      =+  [t=0 j=1 k=1]
1391      =.  t  |-  ^-  @
1392        ?:  (gth j l)  t
1393        =+  u=(add s (lsh [3 sl] (rep 3 (flop (rpp 3 4 j)))))
1394        =+  f=0  =.  f  |-  ^-  @
1395          ?:  (gth k c)  f
1396          =+  q=(hml p pl u ?:(=(k 1) (add sl 4) h))
1397          $(u q, f (mix f q), k +(k))
1398        $(t (add t (lsh [3 (mul (dec j) h)] f)), j +(j))
1399      (end [3 d] t)
1400    ::                                              ::  ++hsh:scr:crypto
1401    ++  hsh                                         ::  scrypt
1402      ~/  %hsh
1403      |=  [p=@ s=@ n=@ r=@ z=@ d=@]
1404      (hsl p (met 3 p) s (met 3 s) n r z d)
1405    ::                                              ::  ++hsl:scr:crypto
1406    ++  hsl                                         ::  w+length
1407      ~/  %hsl
1408      |=  [p=@ pl=@ s=@ sl=@ n=@ r=@ z=@ d=@]
1409      =|  v=(list (list @))
1410      =>  .(p (end [3 pl] p), s (end [3 sl] s))
1411      =+  u=(mul (mul 128 r) z)
1412      ::
1413      ::  n is power of 2; max 1GB memory
1414      ::
1415      ?>  ?&  =(n (bex (dec (xeb n))))
1416              !=(r 0)   !=(z 0)
1417              %+  lte
1418                (mul (mul 128 r) (dec (add n z)))
1419              (bex 30)
1420              (lth pl (bex 31))
1421              (lth sl (bex 31))
1422          ==
1423      =+  ^=  b  =+  (rpp 3 u (pbl p pl s sl 1 u))
1424        %+  turn  (bls (mul 128 r) -)
1425        |=(a=(list @) (rpp 9 (mul 2 r) (rep 3 a)))
1426      ?>  =((lent b) z)
1427      =+  ^=  q
1428        =+  |-  ?~  b  (flop v)
1429            $(b +.b, v [i=(srm r -.b n) t=v])
1430        %+  turn  `(list (list @))`-
1431        |=(a=(list @) (rpp 3 (mul 128 r) (rep 9 a)))
1432      (pbl p pl (rep 3 (slb q)) u 1 d)
1433    ::                                              ::  ++ypt:scr:crypto
1434    ++  ypt                                         ::  256bit {salt pass}
1435      |=  [s=@ p=@]
1436      ^-  @
1437      (hsh p s 16.384 8 1 256)
1438    --  ::scr
1439  ::                                                ::
1440  ::::                    ++crub:crypto             ::  (2b4) suite B, Ed
1441    ::                                              ::::
1442  ++  crub  !:
1443    ^-  acru
1444    =|  [pub=[cry=@ sgn=@] sek=(unit [cry=@ sgn=@])]
1445    |%
1446    ::                                              ::  ++as:crub:crypto
1447    ++  as                                          ::
```

```
1448        |%
1449        ::                                          ::  ++sign:as:crub:
1450        ++    sign                                  ::
1451          |=    msg=@
1452          ^-    @ux
1453          (jam [(sigh msg) msg])
1454        ::                                          ::  ++sigh:as:crub:
1455        ++    sigh                                  ::
1456          |=    msg=@
1457          ^-    @ux
1458          ?~    sek   ~|  %pubkey-only  !!
1459          (sign:ed msg sgn.u.sek)
1460        ::                                          ::  ++sure:as:crub:
1461        ++    sure                                  ::
1462          |=    txt=@
1463          ^-    (unit @ux)
1464          =+    ;;([sig=@ msg=@] (cue txt))
1465          ?.    (safe sig msg)   ~
1466          (some msg)
1467        ::                                          ::  ++safe:as:crub:
1468        ++    safe
1469          |=    [sig=@ msg=@]
1470          ^-    ?
1471          (veri:ed sig msg sgn.pub)
1472        ::                                          ::  ++seal:as:crub:
1473        ++    seal                                  ::
1474          |=    [bpk=pass msg=@]
1475          ^-    @ux
1476          ?~    sek   ~|  %pubkey-only  !!
1477          ?>    =('b' (end 3 bpk))
1478          =+    pk=(rsh 8 (rsh 3 bpk))
1479          =+    shar=(shax (shar:ed pk cry.u.sek))
1480          =+    smsg=(sign msg)
1481          (jam (~(en siva:aes shar ~) smsg))
1482        ::                                          ::  ++tear:as:crub:
1483        ++    tear                                  ::
1484          |=    [bpk=pass txt=@]
1485          ^-    (unit @ux)
1486          ?~    sek   ~|  %pubkey-only  !!
1487          ?>    =('b' (end 3 bpk))
1488          =+    pk=(rsh 8 (rsh 3 bpk))
1489          =+    shar=(shax (shar:ed pk cry.u.sek))
1490          =+    ;;([iv=@ len=@ cph=@] (cue txt))
1491          =+    try=(~(de siva:aes shar ~) iv len cph)
1492          ?~    try   ~
1493          (sure:as:(com:nu:crub bpk) u.try)
1494        --  ::as
1495      ::                                            ::  ++de:crub:crypto
1496      ++  de                                        ::  decrypt
1497        |=    [key=@J txt=@]
1498        ^-    (unit @ux)
1499        =+    ;;([iv=@ len=@ cph=@] (cue txt))
1500        %^    ~(de sivc:aes (shaz key) ~)
1501          iv
1502        len
1503      cph
1504      ::                                            ::  ++dy:crub:crypto
1505      ++  dy                                        ::  need decrypt
```

```
      |=  [key=@J cph=@]
      (need (de key cph))
    ::                                              ::  ++en:crub:crypto
    ++  en                                          ::  encrypt
      |=  [key=@J msg=@]
      ^-  @ux
      (jam (~(en sivc:aes (shaz key) ~) msg))
    ::                                              ::  ++ex:crub:crypto
    ++  ex                                          ::  extract
      |%
      ::                                            ::  ++fig:ex:crub:crypto
      ++  fig                                       ::  fingerprint
        ^-  @uvH
        (shaf %bfig pub)
      ::                                            ::  ++pac:ex:crub:crypto
      ++  pac                                       ::  private fingerprint
        ^-  @uvG
        ?~  sek  ~|  %pubkey-only  !!
        (end 6 (shaf %bcod sec))
      ::                                            ::  ++pub:ex:crub:crypto
      ++  pub                                       ::  public key
        ^-  pass
        (cat 3 'b' (cat 8 sgn.^pub cry.^pub))
      ::                                            ::  ++sec:ex:crub:crypto
      ++  sec                                       ::  private key
        ^-  ring
        ?~  sek  ~|  %pubkey-only  !!
        (cat 3 'B' (cat 8 sgn.u.sek cry.u.sek))
      --  ::ex
    ::                                              ::  ++nu:crub:crypto
    ++  nu                                          ::
      |%
      ::                                            ::  ++pit:nu:crub:crypto
      ++  pit                                       ::  create keypair
        |=  [w=@ seed=@]
        =+  wid=(add (div w 8) ?:(=((mod w 8) 0) 0 1))
        =+  bits=(shal wid seed)
        =+  [c=(rsh 8 bits) s=(end 8 bits)]
        ..nu(pub [cry=(puck:ed c) sgn=(puck:ed s)], sek `[cry=c sgn=s])
      ::                                            ::  ++nol:nu:crub:crypto
      ++  nol                                       ::  activate secret
        |=  a=ring
        =+  [mag=(end 3 a) bod=(rsh 3 a)]
        ~|  %not-crub-seckey  ?>  =('B' mag)
        =+  [c=(rsh 8 bod) s=(end 8 bod)]
        ..nu(pub [cry=(puck:ed c) sgn=(puck:ed s)], sek `[cry=c sgn=s])
      ::                                            ::  ++com:nu:crub:crypto
      ++  com                                       ::  activate public
        |=  a=pass
        =+  [mag=(end 3 a) bod=(rsh 3 a)]
        ~|  %not-crub-pubkey  ?>  =('b' mag)
        ..nu(pub [cry=(rsh 8 bod) sgn=(end 8 bod)], sek ~)
      --  ::nu
    --  ::crub
  ::                                                ::
  ::::                    ++crua:crypto            ::  (2b5) suite B, RSA
    ::                                              ::::
  ++  crua  !!
```

```
1564      ::                                                                ::
1565      ::::                         ++test:crypto                        ::  (2b6) test crypto
1566       ::                                                               ::::
1567      ++  test  ^?
1568      |%
1569       ::                                                               ::  ++trub:test:crypto
1570      ++  trub                                                          ::  test crub
1571      |=  msg=@t
1572      ::
1573      ::  make acru cores
1574      ::
1575      =/  ali       (pit:nu:crub 512 (shaz 'Alice'))
1576      =/  ali-pub   (com:nu:crub pub:ex.ali)
1577      =/  bob       (pit:nu:crub 512 (shaz 'Robert'))
1578      =/  bob-pub   (com:nu:crub pub:ex.bob)
1579      ::
1580      ::  alice signs and encrypts a symmetric key to bob
1581      ::
1582      =/  secret-key  %-  shaz
1583          'Let there be no duplicity when taking a stand against him.'
1584      =/  signed-key   (sign:as.ali secret-key)
1585      =/  crypted-key  (seal:as.ali pub:ex.bob-pub signed-key)
1586      ::  bob decrypts and verifies
1587      =/  decrypt-key-attempt  (tear:as.bob pub:ex.ali-pub crypted-key)
1588      =/  decrypted-key    ~|  %decrypt-fail  (need decrypt-key-attempt)
1589      =/  verify-key-attempt   (sure:as.ali-pub decrypted-key)
1590      =/  verified-key     ~|  %verify-fail  (need verify-key-attempt)
1591      ::  bob encrypts with symmetric key
1592      =/  crypted-msg (en.bob verified-key msg)
1593      ::  alice decrypts with same key
1594      `@t`(dy.ali secret-key crypted-msg)
1595      --  ::test
1596      ::                                                                ::
1597      ::::                         ++keccak:crypto                      ::  (2b7) keccak family
1598       ::                                                               ::::
1599      ++  keccak
1600      ~%  %kecc  ..part  ~
1601      |%
1602      ::
1603      ::  keccak
1604      ::
1605      ++  keccak-224  ~/  %k224  |=(a=octs (keccak 1.152 448 224 a))
1606      ++  keccak-256  ~/  %k256  |=(a=octs (keccak 1.088 512 256 a))
1607      ++  keccak-384  ~/  %k384  |=(a=octs (keccak 832 768 384 a))
1608      ++  keccak-512  ~/  %k512  |=(a=octs (keccak 576 1.024 512 a))
1609      ::
1610      ++  keccak  (cury (cury hash keccak-f) padding-keccak)
1611      ::
1612      ++  padding-keccak  (multirate-padding 0x1)
1613      ::
1614      ::  sha3
1615      ::
1616      ++  sha3-224  |=(a=octs (sha3 1.152 448 224 a))
1617      ++  sha3-256  |=(a=octs (sha3 1.088 512 256 a))
1618      ++  sha3-384  |=(a=octs (sha3 832 768 384 a))
1619      ++  sha3-512  |=(a=octs (sha3 576 1.024 512 a))
1620      ::
1621      ++  sha3  (cury (cury hash keccak-f) padding-sha3)
```

```
::
++  padding-sha3  (multirate-padding 0x6)
::
::  shake
::
++  shake-128  |=([o=@ud i=octs] (shake 1.344 256 o i))
++  shake-256  |=([o=@ud i=octs] (shake 1.088 512 o i))
::
++  shake  (cury (cury hash keccak-f) padding-shake)
::
++  padding-shake  (multirate-padding 0x1f)
::
::  rawshake
::
++  rawshake-128  |=([o=@ud i=octs] (rawshake 1.344 256 o i))
++  rawshake-256  |=([o=@ud i=octs] (rawshake 1.088 512 o i))
::
++  rawshake  (cury (cury hash keccak-f) padding-rawshake)
::
++  padding-rawshake  (multirate-padding 0x7)
::
::  core
::
++  hash
  ::  per:  permutation function with configurable width.
  ::  pad:  padding function.
  ::  rat:  bitrate, size in bits of blocks to operate on.
  ::  cap:  capacity, bits of sponge padding.
  ::  out:  length of desired output, in bits.
  ::  inp:  input to hash.
  |=  $:  per=$-(@ud $-(@ @))
          pad=$-([octs @ud] octs)
          rat=@ud
          cap=@ud
          out=@ud
          inp=octs
      ==
  ^-  @
  ::  urbit's little-endian to keccak's big-endian.
  =.  q.inp  (rev 3 inp)
  %.  [inp out]
  (sponge per pad rat cap)
::
::NOTE  if ++keccak ever needs to be made to operate
::        on bits rather than bytes, all that needs to
::        be done is updating the way this padding
::        function works. (and also "octs" -> "bits")
++  multirate-padding
  ::  dsb:  domain separation byte, reverse bit order.
  |=  dsb=@ux
  ?>  (lte dsb 0xff)
  |=  [inp=octs mut=@ud]
  ^-  octs
  =.  mut  (div mut 8)
  =+  pal=(sub mut (mod p.inp mut))
  =?  pal  =(pal 0)  mut
  =.  pal  (dec pal)
  :-  (add p.inp +(pal))
```

```hoon
1680        ::  padding is provided in lane bit ordering,
1681        ::  ie, LSB = left.
1682        (cat 3 (con (lsh [3 pal] dsb) 0x80) q.inp)
1683    ::
1684    ++  sponge
1685        ::  sponge construction
1686        ::
1687        ::  preperm:  permutation function with configurable width.
1688        ::  padding:  padding function.
1689        ::  bitrate:  size of blocks to operate on.
1690        ::  capacity:  sponge padding.
1691        |=  $:  preperm=$-(@ud $-(@ @))
1692                padding=$-([octs @ud] octs)
1693                bitrate=@ud
1694                capacity=@ud
1695            ==
1696        ::
1697        ::  preparing
1698        =+  bitrate-bytes=(div bitrate 8)
1699        =+  blockwidth=(add bitrate capacity)
1700        =+  permute=(preperm blockwidth)
1701        ::
1702        |=  [input=octs output=@ud]
1703        |^    ^-  @
1704          ::
1705          ::  padding
1706          =.  input  (padding input bitrate)
1707          ::
1708          ::  absorbing
1709          =/  pieces=(list @)
1710            ::  amount of bitrate-sized blocks.
1711            ?>  =(0 (mod p.input bitrate-bytes))
1712            =+  i=(div p.input bitrate-bytes)
1713            |-
1714            ?:  =(i 0)   ~
1715            :_  $(i (dec i))
1716            ::  get the bitrate-sized block of bytes
1717            ::  that ends with the byte at -.
1718            =-  (cut 3 [- bitrate-bytes] q.input)
1719            (mul (dec i) bitrate-bytes)
1720          =/  state=@
1721            ::  for every piece,
1722            %+  roll  pieces
1723            |=  [p=@ s=@]
1724            ::  pad with capacity,
1725            =.  p  (lsh [0 capacity] p)
1726            ::  xor it into the state and permute it.
1727            (permute (mix s (bytes-to-lanes p)))
1728          ::
1729          ::  squeezing
1730          =|  res=@
1731          =|  len=@ud
1732          |-
1733          ::  append a bitrate-sized head of state to the
1734          ::  result.
1735          =.  res
1736            %+  con  (lsh [0 bitrate] res)
1737            (rsh [0 capacity] (lanes-to-bytes state))
```

```
=.  len  (add len bitrate)
?:  (gte len output)
  ::  produce the requested bits of output.
  (rsh [0 (sub len output)] res)
$(res res, state (permute state))
::
++  bytes-to-lanes
  ::  flip byte order in blocks of 8 bytes.
  |=  a=@
  %^  run  6  a
  |=(b=@ (lsh [3 (sub 8 (met 3 b))] (swp 3 b)))
::
++  lanes-to-bytes
  ::  unflip byte order in blocks of 8 bytes.
  |=  a=@
  %+  can  6
  %+  turn
    =+  (rip 6 a)
    (weld - (reap (sub 25 (lent -)) 0x0))
  |=  a=@
  :-  1
  %+  can  3
  =-  (turn - |=(a=@ [1 a]))
  =+  (flop (rip 3 a))
  (weld (reap (sub 8 (lent -)) 0x0) -)
--
::
++  keccak-f
  ::  keccak permutation function
  |=  [width=@ud]
  ::  assert valid blockwidth.
  ?>  =-  (~(has in -) width)
      (sy 25 50 100 200 400 800 1.600 ~)
  ::  assumes 5x5 lanes state, as is the keccak
  ::  standard.
  =+  size=5
  =+  lanes=(mul size size)
  =+  lane-bloq=(dec (xeb (div width lanes)))
  =+  lane-size=(bex lane-bloq)
  =+  rounds=(add 12 (mul 2 lane-bloq))
  |=  [input=@]
  ^-  @
  =*  a  input
  =+  round=0
  |^
    ?:  =(round rounds)  a
    ::
    ::  theta
    =/  c=@
      %+  roll  (gulf 0 (dec size))
      |=  [x=@ud c=@]
      %+  con  (lsh [lane-bloq 1] c)
      %+  roll  (gulf 0 (dec size))
      |=  [y=@ud c=@]
      (mix c (get-lane x y a))
    =/  d=@
      %+  roll  (gulf 0 (dec size))
      |=  [x=@ud d=@]
```

```
%+  con  (lsh [lane-bloq 1] d)
%+  mix
  =-  (get-word - size c)
  ?:(=(x 0) (dec size) (dec x))
%^  ~(rol fe lane-bloq)  0  1
(get-word (mod +(x) size) size c)
=.  a
%+  roll  (gulf 0 (dec lanes))
|=  [i=@ud a=_a]
%+  mix  a
%+  lsh
  [lane-bloq (sub lanes +(i))]
(get-word i size d)
::
::  rho and pi
=/  b=@
%+  roll  (gulf 0 (dec lanes))
|=  [i=@ b=@]
=+  x=(mod i 5)
=+  y=(div i 5)
%+  con  b
%+  lsh
  :-  lane-bloq
  %+  sub  lanes
  %+  add  +(y)
  %+  mul  size
  (mod (add (mul 2 x) (mul 3 y)) size)
%^  ~(rol fe lane-bloq)  0
  (rotation-offset i)
(get-word i lanes a)
::
::  chi
=.  a
%+  roll  (gulf 0 (dec lanes))
|=  [i=@ud a=@]
%+  con  (lsh lane-bloq a)
=+  x=(mod i 5)
=+  y=(div i 5)
%+  mix  (get-lane x y b)
%+  dis
  =-  (get-lane - y b)
  (mod (add x 2) size)
%^  not  lane-bloq  1
(get-lane (mod +(x) size) y b)
::
::  iota
=.  a
=+  (round-constant round)
(mix a (lsh [lane-bloq (dec lanes)] -))
::
::  next round
$(round +(round))
::
++  get-lane
  ::  get the lane with coordinates
  |=  [x=@ud y=@ud a=@]
  =+  i=(add x (mul size y))
  (get-word i lanes a)
```

```
    ::
++  get-word
  ::  get word {n} from atom {a} of {m} words.
  |=  [n=@ud m=@ud a=@]
  (cut lane-bloq [(sub m +((mod n m))) 1] a)
::
++  round-constant
  |=  c=@ud
  =-  (snag (mod c 24) -)
  ^-  (list @ux)
  :~  0x1
      0x8082
      0x8000.0000.0000.808a
      0x8000.0000.8000.8000
      0x808b
      0x8000.0001
      0x8000.0000.8000.8081
      0x8000.0000.0000.8009
      0x8a
      0x88
      0x8000.8009
      0x8000.000a
      0x8000.808b
      0x8000.0000.0000.008b
      0x8000.0000.0000.8089
      0x8000.0000.0000.8003
      0x8000.0000.0000.8002
      0x8000.0000.0000.0080
      0x800a
      0x8000.0000.8000.000a
      0x8000.0000.8000.8081
      0x8000.0000.0000.8080
      0x8000.0001
      0x8000.0000.8000.8008
  ==
::
++  rotation-offset
  |=  x=@ud
  =-  (snag x -)
  ^-  (list @ud)
  :~   0   1  62  28  27
      36  44   6  55  20
       3  10  43  25  39
      41  45  15  21   8
      18   2  61  56  14
  ==
--
--  ::keccak
::                                                  ::
::::                        ++hmac:crypto           ::  (2b8) hmac family
  ::                                                ::::
++  hmac
  ~%  %hmac  ..part  ~
  =,  sha
  =>  |%
      ++  meet  |=([k=@ m=@] [[(met 3 k) k] [(met 3 m) m]])
      ++  flip  |=([k=@ m=@] [(swp 3 k) (swp 3 m)])
      --
```

```
1912      |%
1913      ::
1914      ::    use with @
1915      ::
1916      ++    hmac-sha1       (cork meet hmac-sha11)
1917      ++    hmac-sha256     (cork meet hmac-sha2561)
1918      ++    hmac-sha512     (cork meet hmac-sha5121)
1919      ::
1920      ::    use with @t
1921      ::
1922      ++    hmac-sha1t      (cork flip hmac-sha1)
1923      ++    hmac-sha256t    (cork flip hmac-sha256)
1924      ++    hmac-sha512t    (cork flip hmac-sha512)
1925      ::
1926      ::    use with byts
1927      ::
1928      ++    hmac-sha11      (cury hmac sha-11 64 20)
1929      ++    hmac-sha2561    (cury hmac sha-2561 64 32)
1930      ++    hmac-sha5121    (cury hmac sha-5121 128 64)
1931      ::
1932      ::    main logic
1933      ::
1934      ++    hmac
1935        ~/  %hmac
1936        ::  boq: block size in bytes used by haj
1937        ::  out: bytes output by haj
1938        |*  [[haj=$-([@u @] @) boq=@u out=@u] key=byts msg=byts]
1939        ::  ensure key and message fit signaled lengths
1940        =.  dat.key  (end [3 wid.key] dat.key)
1941        =.  dat.msg  (end [3 wid.msg] dat.msg)
1942        ::  keys longer than block size are shortened by hashing
1943        =?  dat.key  (gth wid.key boq)  (haj wid.key dat.key)
1944        =?  wid.key  (gth wid.key boq)  out
1945        ::  keys shorter than block size are right-padded
1946        =?  dat.key  (lth wid.key boq)  (lsh [3 (sub boq wid.key)] dat.key)
1947        ::  pad key, inner and outer
1948        =+  kip=(mix dat.key (fil 3 boq 0x36))
1949        =+  kop=(mix dat.key (fil 3 boq 0x5c))
1950        ::  append inner padding to message, then hash
1951        =+  (haj (add wid.msg boq) (add (lsh [3 wid.msg] kip) dat.msg))
1952        ::  prepend outer padding to result, hash again
1953        (haj (add out boq) (add (lsh [3 out] kop) -))
1954      --  ::  hmac
1955    ::                                                  ::
1956    ::::                      ++secp:crypto              ::  (2b9) secp family
1957      ::                                                ::::
1958  ++  secp  !.
1959    ::  TODO: as-octs and hmc are outside of jet parent
1960    =>  :+  ..part
1961        hmc=hmac-sha2561:hmac:crypto
1962        as-octs=as-octs:mimes:html
1963    ~%  %secp  +<  ~
1964    |%
1965    +$  jacobian    [x=@ y=@ z=@]                  ::  jacobian point
1966    +$  point       [x=@ y=@]                      ::  curve point
1967    +$  domain
1968      $:  p=@                                       ::  prime modulo
1969          a=@                                       ::  y^2=x^3+ax+b
```

```
            b=@                             ::
            g=point                         ::  base point
            n=@                             ::  prime order of g
        ==
    ++  secp
    |_  [bytes=@ =domain]
    ++  field-p  ~(. fo p.domain)
    ++  field-n  ~(. fo n.domain)
    ++  compress-point
      |=  =point
      ^-  @
      %+  can  3
      :~  [bytes x.point]
          [1 (add 2 (cut 0 [0 1] y.point))]
      ==
    ::
    ++  serialize-point
      |=  =point
      ^-  @
      %+  can  3
      :~  [bytes y.point]
          [bytes x.point]
          [1 4]
      ==
    ::
    ++  decompress-point
      |=  compressed=@
      ^-  point
      =/  x=@  (end [3 bytes] compressed)
      ?>  =(3 (mod p.domain 4))
      =/  fop  field-p
      =+  [fadd fmul fpow]=[sum.fop pro.fop exp.fop]
      =/  y=@  %+  fpow  (rsh [0 2] +(p.domain))
               %+  fadd  b.domain
               %+  fadd  (fpow 3 x)
          (fmul a.domain x)
      =/  s=@  (rsh [3 bytes] compressed)
      ~|  [`@ux`s `@ux`compressed]
      ?>  |(=(2 s) =(3 s))
      ::  check parity
      ::
      =?  y  !=((sub s 2) (mod y 2))
        (sub p.domain y)
      [x y]
    ::
    ++  jc                                  ::  jacobian math
      |%
      ++  from
        |=  a=jacobian
        ^-  point
        =/  fop   field-p
        =+  [fmul fpow finv]=[pro.fop exp.fop inv.fop]
        =/  z  (finv z.a)
        :-  (fmul x.a (fpow 2 z))
        (fmul y.a (fpow 3 z))
      ::
      ++  into
        |=  point
```

```
^-  jacobian
[x y 1]
::
++  double
|=  jacobian
^-  jacobian
?:  =(0 y)  [0 0 0]
=/  fop  field-p
=+  [fadd fsub fmul fpow]=[sum.fop dif.fop pro.fop exp.fop]
=/  s    :(fmul 4 x (fpow 2 y))
=/  m    %+  fadd
             (fmul 3 (fpow 2 x))
             (fmul a.domain (fpow 4 z))
=/  nx   %+  fsub
             (fpow 2 m)
             (fmul 2 s)
=/  ny   %+  fsub
             (fmul m (fsub s nx))
             (fmul 8 (fpow 4 y))
=/  nz   :(fmul 2 y z)
[nx ny nz]
::
++  add
|=  [a=jacobian b=jacobian]
^-  jacobian
?:  =(0 y.a)  b
?:  =(0 y.b)  a
=/  fop  field-p
=+  [fadd fsub fmul fpow]=[sum.fop dif.fop pro.fop exp.fop]
=/  u1   :(fmul x.a z.b z.b)
=/  u2   :(fmul x.b z.a z.a)
=/  s1   :(fmul y.a z.b z.b z.b)
=/  s2   :(fmul y.b z.a z.a z.a)
?:  =(u1 u2)
  ?.  =(s1 s2)
    [0 0 1]
  (double a)
=/  h     (fsub u2 u1)
=/  r     (fsub s2 s1)
=/  h2    (fmul h h)
=/  h3    (fmul h2 h)
=/  u1h2  (fmul u1 h2)
=/  nx   %+  fsub
             (fmul r r)
             :(fadd h3 u1h2 u1h2)
=/  ny   %+  fsub
             (fmul r (fsub u1h2 nx))
             (fmul s1 h3)
=/  nz   :(fmul h z.a z.b)
[nx ny nz]
::
++  mul
|=  [a=jacobian scalar=@]
^-  jacobian
?:  =(0 y.a)
  [0 0 1]
?:  =(0 scalar)
  [0 0 1]
```

```
          ?:  =(1 scalar)
            a
          ?:  (gte scalar n.domain)
            $(scalar (mod scalar n.domain))
          ?:  =(0 (mod scalar 2))
            (double $(scalar (rsh 0 scalar)))
          (add a (double $(scalar (rsh 0 scalar))))
        --
    ++  add-points
      |=  [a=point b=point]
      ^-  point
      =/  j  jc
      (from.j (add.j (into.j a) (into.j b)))
    ++  mul-point-scalar
      |=  [p=point scalar=@]
      ^-  point
      =/  j  jc
      %-  from.j
      %+  mul.j
        (into.j p)
      scalar
    ::
    ++  valid-hash
      |=  has=@
      (lte (met 3 has) bytes)
    ::
    ++  in-order
      |=  i=@
      ?&  (gth i 0)
          (lth i n.domain)
      ==
    ++  priv-to-pub
      |=  private-key=@
      ^-  point
      ?>  (in-order private-key)
      (mul-point-scalar g.domain private-key)
    ::
    ++  make-k
      |=  [hash=@ private-key=@]
      ^-  @
      ?>  (in-order private-key)
      ?>  (valid-hash hash)
      =/  v  (fil 3 bytes 1)
      =/  k  0
      =.  k  %+  hmc  [bytes k]
             %-  as-octs
             %+  can  3
             :~  [bytes hash]
                 [bytes private-key]
                 [1 0]
                 [bytes v]
             ==
      =.  v  (hmc bytes^k bytes^v)
      =.  k  %+  hmc  [bytes k]
             %-  as-octs
             %+  can  3
             :~  [bytes hash]
                 [bytes private-key]
```

```
2144                      [1 1]
2145                      [bytes v]
2146              ==
2147          =.  v  (hmc bytes^k bytes^v)
2148        (hmc bytes^k bytes^v)
2149      ::
2150      ++  ecdsa-raw-sign
2151      |=  [hash=@ private-key=@]
2152      ^-  [r=@ s=@ y=@]
2153      ::  make-k and priv-to pub will validate inputs
2154      =/  k   (make-k hash private-key)
2155      =/  rp  (priv-to-pub k)
2156      =*  r   x.rp
2157      ?<  =(0 r)
2158      =/  fon   field-n
2159      =+  [fadd fmul finv]=[sum.fon pro.fon inv.fon]
2160      =/  s  %+  fmul  (finv k)
2161             %+  fadd  hash
2162             %+  fmul  r
2163             private-key
2164      ?<  =(0 s)
2165      [r s y.rp]
2166      ::  general recovery omitted, but possible
2167      --
2168    ++  secp256k1
2169    ~%  %secp256k1  +  ~
2170    |%
2171    ++  t  :: in the battery for jet matching
2172      ^-  domain
2173      :*  0xffff.ffff.ffff.ffff.ffff.ffff.ffff.ffff.
2174          ffff.ffff.ffff.ffff.ffff.fffe.ffff.fc2f
2175          0
2176          7
2177          :-  0x79be.667e.f9dc.bbac.55a0.6295.ce87.0b07.
2178              029b.fcdb.2dce.28d9.59f2.815b.16f8.1798
2179          0x483a.da77.26a3.c465.5da4.fbfc.0e11.08a8.
2180              fd17.b448.a685.5419.9c47.d08f.fb10.d4b8
2181        0xffff.ffff.ffff.ffff.ffff.ffff.ffff.fffe.
2182          baae.dce6.af48.a03b.bfd2.5e8c.d036.4141
2183      ==
2184    ::
2185    ++  curve              ~(. secp 32 t)
2186    ++  serialize-point    serialize-point:curve
2187    ++  compress-point     compress-point:curve
2188    ++  decompress-point   decompress-point:curve
2189    ++  add-points         add-points:curve
2190    ++  mul-point-scalar   mul-point-scalar:curve
2191    ++  make-k
2192      ~/  %make
2193      |=  [hash=@uvI private-key=@]
2194      ::  checks sizes
2195      (make-k:curve hash private-key)
2196    ++  priv-to-pub
2197      |=  private-key=@
2198      ::  checks sizes
2199      (priv-to-pub:curve private-key)
2200    ::
2201    ++  ecdsa-raw-sign
```

```
      ~/    %sign
      |=    [hash=@uvI private-key=@]
      ^-    [v=@ r=@ s=@]
      =/    c   curve
      ::    raw-sign checks sizes
      =+    (ecdsa-raw-sign.c hash private-key)
      =/    rp=point  [r y]
      =/    s-high  (gte (mul 2 s) n.domain.c)
      =?    s    s-high
        (sub n.domain.c s)
      =?    rp   s-high
        [x.rp (sub p.domain.c y.rp)]
      =/    v    (end 0 y.rp)
      =?    v    (gte x.rp n.domain.c)
        (add v 2)
      [v x.rp s]
    ::
    ++  ecdsa-raw-recover
      ~/    %reco
      |=    [hash=@ sig=[v=@ r=@ s=@]]
      ^-    point
      ?>    (lte v.sig 3)
      =/    c    curve
      ?>    (valid-hash.c hash)
      ?>    (in-order.c r.sig)
      ?>    (in-order.c s.sig)
      =/    x   ?:  (gte v.sig 2)
                  (add r.sig n.domain.c)
                r.sig
      =/    fop   field-p.c
      =+    [fadd fmul fpow]=[sum.fop pro.fop exp.fop]
      =/    ysq   (fadd (fpow 3 x) b.domain.c)
      =/    beta  (fpow (rsh [0 2] +(p.domain.c)) ysq)
      =/    y   ?:  =((end 0 v.sig) (end 0 beta))
                  beta
                (sub p.domain.c beta)
      ?>    =(0 (dif.fop ysq (fmul y y)))
      =/    nz   (sub n.domain.c hash)
      =/    j    jc.c
      =/    gz   (mul.j (into.j g.domain.c) nz)
      =/    xy   (mul.j (into.j x y) s.sig)
      =/    qr   (add.j gz xy)
      =/    qj   (mul.j qr (inv:field-n.c x))
      =/    pub  (from.j qj)
      ?<    =([0 0] pub)
      pub
    ++  schnorr
      ~%  %schnorr  ..schnorr  ~
      =>  |%
          ++  tagged-hash
            |=  [tag=@ [l=@ x=@]]
            =+  hat=(sha-256:sha (swp 3 tag))
            %-  sha-2561:sha
            :-  (add 64 l)
            (can 3 ~[[l x] [32 hat] [32 hat]])
          ++  lift-x
            |=  x=@I
            ^-  (unit point)
```

```hoon
2260        =/  c  curve
2261        ?.  (lth x p.domain.c)
2262          ~
2263        =/  fop  field-p.c
2264        =+  [fadd fpow]=[sum.fop exp.fop]
2265        =/  cp  (fadd (fpow 3 x) 7)
2266        =/  y  (fpow (rsh [0 2] +(p.domain.c)) cp)
2267        ?.  =(cp (fpow 2 y))
2268          ~
2269        %-  some  :-  x
2270        ?:  =(0 (mod y 2))
2271          y
2272        (sub p.domain.c y)
2273        --
2274      |%
2275      ::
2276      ++  sign                                  ::  schnorr signature
2277        ~/  %sosi
2278        |=  [sk=@I m=@I a=@I]
2279        ^-  @J
2280        ?>  (gte 32 (met 3 m))
2281        ?>  (gte 32 (met 3 a))
2282        =/  c  curve
2283        ::  implies (gte 32 (met 3 sk))
2284        ::
2285        ?<  |(=(0 sk) (gte sk n.domain.c))
2286        =/  pp
2287          (mul-point-scalar g.domain.c sk)
2288        =/  d
2289          ?:  =(0 (mod y.pp 2))
2290            sk
2291          (sub n.domain.c sk)
2292        =/  t
2293          %+  mix  d
2294          (tagged-hash 'BIP0340/aux' [32 a])
2295        =/  rand
2296          %+  tagged-hash  'BIP0340/nonce'
2297          :-  96
2298          (rep 8 ~[m x.pp t])
2299        =/  kp  (mod rand n.domain.c)
2300        ?<  =(0 kp)
2301        =/  rr  (mul-point-scalar g.domain.c kp)
2302        =/  k
2303          ?:  =(0 (mod y.rr 2))
2304            kp
2305          (sub n.domain.c kp)
2306        =/  e
2307          %-  mod
2308          :_  n.domain.c
2309          %+  tagged-hash  'BIP0340/challenge'
2310          :-  96
2311          (rep 8 ~[m x.pp x.rr])
2312        =/  sig
2313          %^  cat  8
2314          (mod (add k (mul e d)) n.domain.c)
2315          x.rr
2316        ?>  (verify x.pp m sig)
2317        sig
```

```
            ::
            ++  verify                                  ::  schnorr verify
            ~/  %sove
            |=  [pk=@I m=@I sig=@J]
            ^-  ?
            ?>  (gte 32 (met 3 pk))
            ?>  (gte 32 (met 3 m))
            ?>  (gte 64 (met 3 sig))
            =/  c  curve
            =/  pup  (lift-x pk)
            ?~  pup
              %.n
            =/  pp  u.pup
            =/  r  (cut 8 [1 1] sig)
            ?:  (gte r p.domain.c)
              %.n
            =/  s  (end 8 sig)
            ?:  (gte s n.domain.c)
              %.n
            =/  e
              %-  mod
              :_  n.domain.c
              %+  tagged-hash  'BIP0340/challenge'
              :-  96
              (rep 8 ~[m x.pp r])
            =/  aa
              (mul-point-scalar g.domain.c s)
            =/  bb
              (mul-point-scalar pp (sub n.domain.c e))
            ?:  &(=(x.aa x.bb) !=(y.aa y.bb))          ::  infinite?
              %.n
            =/  rr  (add-points aa bb)
            ?.  =(0 (mod y.rr 2))
              %.n
            =(r x.rr)
          --
        --
      --
    ::
    ++  blake
      ~%  %blake  ..part  ~
      |%
      ::TODO  generalize for both blake2 variants
      ++  blake2b
        ~/  %blake2b
        |=  [msg=byts key=byts out=@ud]
        ^-  @
        ::  initialization vector
        =/  iv=@
          0x6a09.e667.f3bc.c908.
            bb67.ae85.84ca.a73b.
            3c6e.f372.fe94.f82b.
            a54f.f53a.5f1d.36f1.
            510e.527f.ade6.82d1.
            9b05.688c.2b3e.6c1f.
            1f83.d9ab.fb41.bd6b.
            5be0.cd19.137e.2179
        ::  per-round constants
```

```
2376        =/  sigma=(list (list @ud))
2377          :~
2378          :~   0   1   2   3   4   5   6   7   8   9  10  11  12  13  14  15  ==
2379          :~  14  10   4   8   9  15  13   6   1  12   0   2  11   7   5   3  ==
2380          :~  11   8  12   0   5   2  15  13  10  14   3   6   7   1   9   4  ==
2381          :~   7   9   3   1  13  12  11  14   2   6   5  10   4   0  15   8  ==
2382          :~   9   0   5   7   2   4  10  15  14   1  11  12   6   8   3  13  ==
2383          :~   2  12   6  10   0  11   8   3   4  13   7   5  15  14   1   9  ==
2384          :~  12   5   1  15  14  13   4  10   0   7   6   3   9   2   8  11  ==
2385          :~  13  11   7  14  12   1   3   9   5   0  15   4   8   6   2  10  ==
2386          :~   6  15  14   9  11   3   0   8  12   2  13   7   1   4  10   5  ==
2387          :~  10   2   8   4   7   6   1   5  15  11   9  14   3  12  13   0  ==
2388          :~   0   1   2   3   4   5   6   7   8   9  10  11  12  13  14  15  ==
2389          :~  14  10   4   8   9  15  13   6   1  12   0   2  11   7   5   3  ==
2390          ==
2391        =>  |%
2392            ++  get-word-list
2393            |=  [h=@ w=@ud]
2394            ^-  (list @)
2395            %-  flop
2396            =+  l=(rip 6 h)
2397            =-  (weld - l)
2398            (reap (sub w (lent l)) 0)
2399            ::
2400            ++  get-word
2401            |=  [h=@ i=@ud w=@ud]
2402            ^-  @
2403            %+  snag  i
2404            (get-word-list h w)
2405            ::
2406            ++  put-word
2407            |=  [h=@ i=@ud w=@ud d=@]
2408            ^-  @
2409            %+  rep  6
2410            =+  l=(get-word-list h w)
2411            %-  flop
2412            %+  weld  (scag i l)
2413            [d (slag +(i) l)]
2414            ::
2415            ++  mod-word
2416            |*  [h=@ i=@ud w=@ud g=$-(@ @)]
2417            (put-word h i w (g (get-word h i w)))
2418            ::
2419            ++  pad
2420            |=  [byts len=@ud]
2421            (lsh [3 (sub len wid)] dat)
2422            ::
2423            ++  compress
2424            |=  [h=@ c=@ t=@ud l=?]
2425            ^-  @
2426            ::  set up local work vector
2427            =+  v=(add (lsh [6 8] h) iv)
2428            ::  xor the counter t into v
2429            =.  v
2430              %-  mod-word
2431              :^  v  12  16
2432            (cury mix (end [0 64] t))
2433            =.  v
```

```
        %-  mod-word
        :^  v   13   16
        (cury mix (rsh [0 64] t))
    ::  for the last block, invert v14
    =?  v  1
        %-  mod-word
        :^  v   14   16
        (cury mix 0xffff.ffff.ffff.ffff)
    ::  twelve rounds of message mixing
    =+  i=0
    =|  s=(list @)
    |^
      ?:  =(i 12)
        ::  xor upper and lower halves of v into state h
        =.  h  (mix h (rsh [6 8] v))
        (mix h (end [6 8] v))
      ::  select message mixing schedule and mix v
      =.  s  (snag (mod i 10) sigma)
      =.  v  (do-mix 0 4 8 12 0 1)
      =.  v  (do-mix 1 5 9 13 2 3)
      =.  v  (do-mix 2 6 10 14 4 5)
      =.  v  (do-mix 3 7 11 15 6 7)
      =.  v  (do-mix 0 5 10 15 8 9)
      =.  v  (do-mix 1 6 11 12 10 11)
      =.  v  (do-mix 2 7 8 13 12 13)
      =.  v  (do-mix 3 4 9 14 14 15)
      $(i +(i))
    ::
    ++  do-mix
      |=  [na=@ nb=@ nc=@ nd=@ nx=@ ny=@]
      ^-  @
      =-  =.  v  (put-word v na 16 a)
          =.  v  (put-word v nb 16 b)
          =.  v  (put-word v nc 16 c)
              (put-word v nd 16 d)
      %-  b2mix
      :*  (get-word v na 16)
          (get-word v nb 16)
          (get-word v nc 16)
          (get-word v nd 16)
          (get-word c (snag nx s) 16)
          (get-word c (snag ny s) 16)
      ==
    --
  ::
  ++  b2mix
    |=  [a=@ b=@ c=@ d=@ x=@ y=@]
    ^-  [a=@ b=@ c=@ d=@]
    =.  x  (rev 3 8 x)
    =.  y  (rev 3 8 y)
    =+  fed=~(. fe 6)
    =.  a  :(sum:fed a b x)
    =.  d  (ror:fed 0 32 (mix d a))
    =.  c  (sum:fed c d)
    =.  b  (ror:fed 0 24 (mix b c))
    =.  a  :(sum:fed a b y)
    =.  d  (ror:fed 0 16 (mix d a))
    =.  c  (sum:fed c d)
```

```
2492              =.  b  (ror:fed 0 63 (mix b c))
2493              [a b c d]
2494            --
2495        ::  ensure inputs adhere to contraints
2496        =.  out  (max 1 (min out 64))
2497        =.  wid.msg  (min wid.msg (bex 128))
2498        =.  wid.key  (min wid.key 64)
2499        =.  dat.msg  (end [3 wid.msg] dat.msg)
2500        =.  dat.key  (end [3 wid.key] dat.key)
2501        ::  initialize state vector
2502        =+  h=iv
2503        ::  mix key length and output length into h0
2504        =.  h
2505          %-  mod-word
2506          :^  h  0  8
2507          %+  cury  mix
2508          %+  add  0x101.0000
2509          (add (lsh 3 wid.key) out)
2510        ::  keep track of how much we've compressed
2511        =*  mes  dat.msg
2512        =+  com=0
2513        =+  rem=wid.msg
2514        ::  if we have a key, pad it and prepend to msg
2515        =?  mes  (gth wid.key 0)
2516          (can 3 ~[rem^mes 128^(pad key 128)])
2517        =?  rem  (gth wid.key 0)
2518          (add rem 128)
2519        |-
2520        ::  compress 128-byte chunks of the message
2521        ?:  (gth rem 128)
2522          =+  c=(cut 3 [(sub rem 128) 128] mes)
2523          =.  com    (add com 128)
2524          %_  $
2525            rem    (sub rem 128)
2526            h      (compress h c com |)
2527          ==
2528        ::  compress the final bytes of the msg
2529        =+  c=(cut 3 [0 rem] mes)
2530        =.  com  (add com rem)
2531        =.  c  (pad [rem c] 128)
2532        =.  h  (compress h c com &)
2533        ::  produce output of desired length
2534        %+  rsh  [3 (sub 64 out)]
2535        ::  do some word
2536        %+  rep  6
2537        %+  turn  (flop (gulf 0 7))
2538        |=  a=@
2539        (rev 3 8 (get-word h a 8))
2540      --  ::blake
2541  ::
2542  ++  argon2
2543    ~%  %argon  ..part  ~
2544    |%
2545    ::
2546    ::  structures
2547    ::
2548    +$  argon-type  ?(%d %i %id %u)
2549    ::
```

```
2550      ::  shorthands
2551      ::
2552      ++  argon2-urbit
2553        |=  out=@ud
2554        (argon2 out %u 0x13 4 512.000 1 *byts *byts)
2555      ::
2556      ::  argon2 proper
2557      ::
2558      ::  main argon2 operation
2559      ++  argon2
2560        ::  out:       desired output size in bytes
2561        ::  typ:       argon2 type
2562        ::  version:   argon2 version (0x10/v1.0 or 0x13/v1.3)
2563        ::  threads:   amount of threads/parallelism
2564        ::  mem-cost:  kb of memory to use
2565        ::  time-cost: iterations to run
2566        ::  key:       optional secret
2567        ::  extra:     optional arbitrary data
2568        |=  $:  out=@ud
2569                typ=argon-type
2570                version=@ux
2571            ::
2572                threads=@ud
2573                mem-cost=@ud
2574                time-cost=@ud
2575            ::
2576                key=byts
2577                extra=byts
2578            ==
2579        ^-  $-([msg=byts sat=byts] @)
2580        ::
2581        ::  check configuration sanity
2582        ::
2583        ?:  =(0 threads)
2584          ~|  %parallelism-must-be-above-zero
2585          !!
2586        ?:  =(0 time-cost)
2587          ~|  %time-cost-must-be-above-zero
2588          !!
2589        ?:  (lth mem-cost (mul 8 threads))
2590          ~|  :-  %memory-cost-must-be-at-least-threads
2591              [threads %times 8 (mul 8 threads)]
2592          !!
2593        ?.  |(=(0x10 version) =(0x13 version))
2594          ~|  [%unsupported-version version %want [0x10 0x13]]
2595          !!
2596        ::
2597        ::  calculate constants and initialize buffer
2598        ::
2599        ::  for each thread, there is a row in the buffer.
2600        ::  the amount of columns depends on the memory-cost.
2601        ::  columns are split into groups of four.
2602        ::  a single such quarter section of a row is a segment.
2603        ::
2604        ::  blocks:     (m_prime)
2605        ::  columns:    row length (q)
2606        ::  seg-length: segment length
2607        =/  blocks=@ud
```

```
2608      ::  round mem-cost down to the nearest multiple of 4*threads
2609      =+  (mul 4 threads)
2610      (mul (div mem-cost -) -)
2611    =+  columns=(div blocks threads)
2612    =+  seg-length=(div columns 4)
2613    ::
2614    =/  buffer=(list (list @))
2615      (reap threads (reap columns 0))
2616    ::
2617    ::  main function
2618    ::
2619    ::  msg: the main input
2620    ::  sat: optional salt
2621    ~%  %argon2  ..argon2  ~
2622    |=  [msg=byts sat=byts]
2623    ^-  @
2624    ?:  (lth wid.sat 8)
2625      ~|  [%min-salt-length-is-8 wid.sat]
2626      !!
2627    ::
2628    ::  h0: initial 64-byte block
2629    =/  h0=@
2630      =-  (blake2b:blake - 0^0 64)
2631      :-  :(add 40 wid.msg wid.sat wid.key wid.extra)
2632      %+  can  3
2633      =+  (cury (cury rev 3) 4)
2634      :~  (prep-wid extra)
2635          (prep-wid key)
2636          (prep-wid sat)
2637          (prep-wid msg)
2638          4^(- (type-to-num typ))
2639          4^(- version)
2640          4^(- time-cost)
2641          4^(- mem-cost)
2642          4^(- out)
2643          4^(- threads)
2644      ==
2645    ::
2646    ::  do time-cost passes over the buffer
2647    ::
2648    =+  t=0
2649    |-
2650    ?:  (lth t time-cost)
2651      ::
2652      ::  process all four segments in the columns...
2653      ::
2654      =+  s=0
2655      |-
2656      ?.  (lth s 4)  ^$(t +(t))
2657      ::
2658      ::  ...of every row/thread
2659      ::
2660      =+  r=0
2661      |-
2662      ?.  (lth r threads)  ^$(s +(s))
2663      =;  new=_buffer
2664        $(buffer new, r +(r))
2665      %-  fill-segment
```

```
        :*  buffer    h0
            t         s            r
            blocks    columns      seg-length
            threads   time-cost    typ          version
        ==
    ::
    ::  mix all rows together and hash the result
    ::
    =+  r=0
    =|  final=@
    |-
    ?:  =(r threads)
      (hash 1.024^final out)
    =-  $(final -, r +(r))
    %+  mix   final
    (snag (dec columns) (snag r buffer))
  ::
  ::  per-segment computation
  ++  fill-segment
    |=  $:  buffer=(list (list @))
            h0=@
            ::
            itn=@ud
            seg=@ud
            row=@ud
            ::
            blocks=@ud
            columns=@ud
            seg-length=@ud
            ::
            threads=@ud
            time-cost=@ud
            typ=argon-type
            version=@ux
        ==
    ::
    ::  fill-segment utilities
    ::
    =>  |%
        ++  put-word
          |=  [rob=(list @) i=@ud d=@]
          %+  weld  (scag i rob)
          [d (slag +(i) rob)]
        --
    ^+  buffer
    ::
    ::  rob:   row buffer to operate on
    ::  do-i:  whether to use prns from input rather than state
    ::  rands: prns generated from input, if we do-i
    =+  rob=(snag row buffer)
    =/  do-i=?
      ?|  ?=(%i typ)
          &(?=(%id typ) =(0 itn) (lte seg 1))
          &(?=(%u typ) =(0 itn) (lte seg 2))
      ==
    =/  rands=(list (pair @ @))
      ?.  do-i  ~
      ::
```

```
2724          ::   keep going until we have a list of :seg-length prn pairs
2725          ::
2726          =+   l=0
2727          =+   counter=1
2728          |-   ^-  (list (pair @ @))
2729          ?:   (gte l seg-length)  ~
2730          =-   (weld - $(counter +(counter), l (add l 128)))
2731          ::
2732          ::   generate pseudorandom block by compressing metadata
2733          ::
2734          =/   random-block=@
2735            %+  compress  0
2736            %+  compress  0
2737            %+  lsh   [3 968]
2738            %+  rep  6
2739            =+  (cury (cury rev 3) 8)
2740            :~  (- counter)
2741                (- (type-to-num typ))
2742                (- time-cost)
2743                (- blocks)
2744                (- seg)
2745                (- row)
2746                (- itn)
2747              ==
2748          ::
2749          ::   split the random-block into 64-bit sections,
2750          ::   then extract the first two 4-byte sections from each.
2751          ::
2752          %+  turn  (flop (rip 6 random-block))
2753          |=  a=@
2754          ^-  (pair @ @)
2755          :-  (rev 3 4 (rsh 5 a))
2756          (rev 3 4 (end 5 a))
2757        ::
2758        ::   iterate over the entire segment length
2759        ::
2760        =+   sin=0
2761        |-
2762        ::
2763        ::   when done, produce the updated buffer
2764        ::
2765        ?:   =(sin seg-length)
2766          %+  weld  (scag row buffer)
2767          [rob (slag +(row) buffer)]
2768        ::
2769        ::   col: current column to process
2770        =/   col=@ud
2771          (add (mul seg seg-length) sin)
2772        ::
2773        ::   first two columns are generated from h0
2774        ::
2775        ?:   &(=(0 itn) (lth col 2))
2776          =+  (app-num (app-num 64^h0 col) row)
2777          =+  (hash - 1.024)
2778          $(rob (put-word rob col -), sin +(sin))
2779        ::
2780        ::   c1, c2: prns for picking reference block
2781        =/   [c1=@ c2=@]
```

```
2782      ?:  do-i  (snag sin rands)
2783      =+  =-  (snag - rob)
2784          ?:  =(0 col)  (dec columns)
2785          (mod (dec col) columns)
2786      :-  (rev 3 4 (cut 3 [1.020 4] -))
2787      (rev 3 4 (cut 3 [1.016 4] -))
2788      ::
2789      ::  ref-row: reference block row
2790      =/  ref-row=@ud
2791        ?:  &(=(0 itn) =(0 seg))  row
2792        (mod c2 threads)
2793      ::
2794      ::  ref-col: reference block column
2795      =/  ref-col=@ud
2796        =-  (mod - columns)
2797        %+  add
2798          ::  starting index
2799          ?:  |(=(0 itn) =(3 seg))  0
2800          (mul +(seg) seg-length)
2801        ::  pseudorandom offset
2802        =-  %+  sub  (dec -)
2803            %+  rsh  [0 32]
2804            %+  mul  -
2805            (rsh [0 32] (mul c1 c1))
2806        ::  reference area size
2807        ?:  =(0 itn)
2808          ?:  |(=(0 seg) =(row ref-row))  (dec col)
2809          ?:  =(0 sin)  (dec (mul seg seg-length))
2810          (mul seg seg-length)
2811        =+  sul=(sub columns seg-length)
2812        ?:  =(ref-row row)   (dec (add sul sin))
2813        ?:  =(0 sin)  (dec sul)
2814        sul
2815      ::
2816      ::  compress the previous and reference block
2817      ::  to create the new block
2818      ::
2819      =/  new=@
2820        %+  compress
2821          =-  (snag - rob)
2822          ::  previous index, wrap-around
2823          ?:  =(0 col)  (dec columns)
2824          (mod (dec col) columns)
2825        ::  get reference block
2826        %+  snag  ref-col
2827        ?:  =(ref-row row)  rob
2828        (snag ref-row buffer)
2829      ::
2830      ::  starting from v1.3, we xor the new block in,
2831      ::  rather than directly overwriting the old block
2832      ::
2833      =?  new  &(!=(0 itn) =(0x13 version))
2834        (mix new (snag col rob))
2835      $(rob (put-word rob col new), sin +(sin))
2836    ::
2837    ::  compression function (g)
2838    ++  compress
2839      ::  x, y: assumed to be 1024 bytes
```

```
|=  [x=@ y=@]
^-  @
::
=+  r=(mix x y)
=|  q=(list @)
::
::  iterate over rows of r to get q
::
=+  i=0
|-
?:  (lth i 8)
  =;  p=(list @)
    $(q (weld q p), i +(i))
  %-  permute
  =-  (weld (reap (sub 8 (lent -)) 0) -)
  %-  flop
  %+  rip  7
  (cut 10 [(sub 7 i) 1] r)
::
::  iterate over columns of q to get z
::
=/  z=(list @)  (reap 64 0)
=.  i  0
|-
::
::  when done, assemble z and xor it with r
::
?.  (lth i 8)
  (mix (rep 7 (flop z)) r)
::
::  permute the column
::
=/  out=(list @)
  %-  permute
  :~  (snag i q)
      (snag (add i 8) q)
      (snag (add i 16) q)
      (snag (add i 24) q)
      (snag (add i 32) q)
      (snag (add i 40) q)
      (snag (add i 48) q)
      (snag (add i 56) q)
  ==
::
::  put the result into z per column
::
=+  j=0
|-
?:  =(8 j)  ^$(i +(i))
=-  $(z -, j +(j))
=+  (add i (mul j 8))
%+  weld  (scag - z)
[(snag j out) (slag +(-) z)]
::
::  permutation function (p)
++  permute
  ::NOTE  this function really just takes and produces
  ::      8 values, but taking and producing them as
```

```
2898    ::       lists helps clean up the code significantly.
2899    |=  s=(list @)
2900    ?>  =(8 (lent s))
2901    ^-  (list @)
2902    ::
2903    ::  list inputs as 16 8-byte values
2904    ::
2905    =/  v=(list @)
2906      %-  zing
2907      ^-  (list (list @))
2908      %+  turn  s
2909      |=  a=@
2910      ::  rev for endianness
2911      =+  (rip 6 (rev 3 16 a))
2912    (weld - (reap (sub 2 (lent -)) 0))
2913    ::
2914    ::  do permutation rounds
2915    ::
2916    =.  v  (do-round v 0 4 8 12)
2917    =.  v  (do-round v 1 5 9 13)
2918    =.  v  (do-round v 2 6 10 14)
2919    =.  v  (do-round v 3 7 11 15)
2920    =.  v  (do-round v 0 5 10 15)
2921    =.  v  (do-round v 1 6 11 12)
2922    =.  v  (do-round v 2 7 8 13)
2923    =.  v  (do-round v 3 4 9 14)
2924    ::  rev for endianness
2925    =.  v  (turn v (cury (cury rev 3) 8))
2926    ::
2927    ::  cat v back together into 8 16-byte values
2928    ::
2929    %+  turn  (gulf 0 7)
2930    |=  i=@
2931    =+  (mul 2 i)
2932    (cat 6 (snag +(-) v) (snag - v))
2933    ::
2934    ::  perform a round and produce updated value list
2935    ++  do-round
2936      |=  [v=(list @) na=@ nb=@ nc=@ nd=@]
2937      ^+  v
2938      =>  |%
2939          ++  get-word
2940            |=  i=@ud
2941          (snag i v)
2942          ::
2943          ++  put-word
2944            |=  [i=@ud d=@]
2945            ^+  v
2946          %+  weld  (scag i v)
2947          [d (slag +(i) v)]
2948          --
2949      =-  =.  v  (put-word na a)
2950          =.  v  (put-word nb b)
2951          =.  v  (put-word nc c)
2952              (put-word nd d)
2953      %-  round
2954      :*  (get-word na)
2955          (get-word nb)
```

```
2956              (get-word nc)
2957              (get-word nd)
2958          ==
2959        ::
2960        ::  perform a round (bg) and produce updated values
2961        ++  round
2962          |=  [a=@ b=@ c=@ d=@]
2963          ^-  [a=@ b=@ c=@ d=@]
2964          ::  operate on 64 bit words
2965          =+  fed=~(. fe 6)
2966          =*  sum  sum:fed
2967          =*  ror  ror:fed
2968          =+  end=(cury end 5)
2969          =.  a  :(sum a b :(mul 2 (end a) (end b)))
2970          =.  d  (ror 0 32 (mix d a))
2971          =.  c  :(sum c d :(mul 2 (end c) (end d)))
2972          =.  b  (ror 0 24 (mix b c))
2973          =.  a  :(sum a b :(mul 2 (end a) (end b)))
2974          =.  d  (ror 0 16 (mix d a))
2975          =.  c  :(sum c d :(mul 2 (end c) (end d)))
2976          =.  b  (ror 0 63 (mix b c))
2977          [a b c d]
2978        ::
2979        ::  argon2 wrapper around blake2b (h')
2980        ++  hash
2981          =,  blake
2982          |=  [byts out=@ud]
2983          ^-  @
2984          ::
2985          ::  msg: input with byte-length prepended
2986          =+  msg=(prep-num [wid dat] out)
2987          ::
2988          ::  if requested size is low enough, hash directly
2989          ::
2990          ?:  (lte out 64)
2991            (blake2b msg 0^0 out)
2992          ::
2993          ::  build up the result by hashing and re-hashing
2994          ::  the input message, adding the first 32 bytes
2995          ::  of the hash to the result, until we have the
2996          ::  desired output size.
2997          ::
2998          =+  tmp=(blake2b msg 0^0 64)
2999          =+  res=(rsh [3 32] tmp)
3000          =.  out  (sub out 32)
3001          |-
3002          ?:  (gth out 64)
3003            =.  tmp  (blake2b 64^tmp 0^0 64)
3004            =.  res  (add (lsh [3 32] res) (rsh [3 32] tmp))
3005            $(out (sub out 32))
3006          %+  add  (lsh [3 out] res)
3007          (blake2b 64^tmp 0^0 out)
3008        ::
3009        ::  utilities
3010        ::
3011        ++  type-to-num
3012          |=  t=argon-type
3013          ?-  t
```

```
%d    0
%i    1
%id   2
%u    10
==
::
++  app-num
  |=  [byts num=@ud]
  ^-  byts
  :-  (add wid 4)
  %+  can  3
  ~[4^(rev 3 4 num) wid^dat]
::
++  prep-num
  |=  [byts num=@ud]
  ^-  byts
  :-  (add wid 4)
  %+  can  3
  ~[wid^dat 4^(rev 3 4 num)]
::
++  prep-wid
  |=  a=byts
  (prep-num a wid.a)
--
::
++  ripemd
  ~%  %ripemd  ..part  ~
  |%
  ++  ripemd-160
    ~/  %ripemd160
    |=  byts
    ^-  @
    ::  we operate on bits rather than bytes
    =.  wid  (mul wid 8)
    ::  add padding
    =+  (md5-pad wid dat)
    ::  endianness
    =.  dat  (run 5 dat |=(a=@ (rev 3 4 a)))
    =*  x  dat
    =+  blocks=(div wid 512)
    =+  fev=~(. fe 5)
    ::  initial register values
    =+  h0=0x6745.2301
    =+  h1=0xefcd.ab89
    =+  h2=0x98ba.dcfe
    =+  h3=0x1032.5476
    =+  h4=0xc3d2.e1f0
    ::  i: current block
    =+  [i=0 j=0]
    =+  *[a=@ b=@ c=@ d=@ e=@]         ::  a..e
    =+  *[aa=@ bb=@ cc=@ dd=@ ee=@]  ::  a'..e'
    |^
      ?:  =(i blocks)
        %+  rep  5
        %+  turn  `(list @)`~[h4 h3 h2 h1 h0]
        ::  endianness
        |=(h=@ (rev 3 4 h))
      =:  a  h0      aa  h0
```

```
      b   h1      bb  h1
      c   h2      cc  h2
      d   h3      dd  h3
      e   h4      ee  h4
  ==
  ::  j: current word
  =+  j=0
  |-
  ?:  =(j 80)
    %=  ^$
      i   +(i)
      h1  :(sum:fev h2 d ee)
      h2  :(sum:fev h3 e aa)
      h3  :(sum:fev h4 a bb)
      h4  :(sum:fev h0 b cc)
      h0  :(sum:fev h1 c dd)
    ==
  %=  $
    j   +(j)
    ::
    a   e
    b   (fn j a b c d e (get (r j)) (k j) (s j))
    c   b
    d   (rol 10 c)
    e   d
    ::
    aa  ee
    bb  (fn (sub 79 j) aa bb cc dd ee (get (rr j)) (kk j) (ss j))
    cc  bb
    dd  (rol 10 cc)
    ee  dd
  ==
  ::
++  get  ::  word from x in block i
  |=  j=@ud
  =+  (add (mul i 16) +(j))
  (cut 5 [(sub (mul blocks 16) -) 1] x)
::
++  fn
  |=  [j=@ud a=@ b=@ c=@ d=@ e=@ m=@ k=@ s=@]
  =-  (sum:fev (rol s :(sum:fev a m k -)) e)
  =.  j  (div j 16)
  ?:  =(0 j)  (mix (mix b c) d)
  ?:  =(1 j)  (con (dis b c) (dis (not 0 32 b) d))
  ?:  =(2 j)  (mix (con b (not 0 32 c)) d)
  ?:  =(3 j)  (con (dis b d) (dis c (not 0 32 d)))
  ?:  =(4 j)  (mix b (con c (not 0 32 d)))
  !!
::
++  rol  (cury rol:fev 0)
::
++  k
  |=  j=@ud
  =.  j  (div j 16)
  ?:  =(0 j)  0x0
  ?:  =(1 j)  0x5a82.7999
  ?:  =(2 j)  0x6ed9.eba1
  ?:  =(3 j)  0x8f1b.bcdc
```

```
      ?:  =(4 j)  0xa953.fd4e
      !!
  ::
  ++  kk   ::  k'
    |=  j=@ud
    =.  j  (div j 16)
    ?:  =(0 j)  0x50a2.8be6
    ?:  =(1 j)  0x5c4d.d124
    ?:  =(2 j)  0x6d70.3ef3
    ?:  =(3 j)  0x7a6d.76e9
    ?:  =(4 j)  0x0
    !!
  ::
  ++  r
    |=  j=@ud
    %+  snag  j
    ^-  (list @)
    :~  0  1  2  3  4  5  6  7  8  9  10  11  12  13  14  15
        7  4  13  1  10  6  15  3  12  0  9  5  2  14  11  8
        3  10  14  4  9  15  8  1  2  7  0  6  13  11  5  12
        1  9  11  10  0  8  12  4  13  3  7  15  14  5  6  2
        4  0  5  9  7  12  2  10  14  1  3  8  11  6  15  13
    ==
  ::
  ++  rr  ::  r'
    |=  j=@ud
    %+  snag  j
    ^-  (list @)
    :~  5  14  7  0  9  2  11  4  13  6  15  8  1  10  3  12
        6  11  3  7  0  13  5  10  14  15  8  12  4  9  1  2
        15  5  1  3  7  14  6  9  11  8  12  2  10  0  4  13
        8  6  4  1  3  11  15  0  5  12  2  13  9  7  10  14
        12  15  10  4  1  5  8  7  6  2  13  14  0  3  9  11
    ==
  ::
  ++  s
    |=  j=@ud
    %+  snag  j
    ^-  (list @)
    :~  11  14  15  12  5  8  7  9  11  13  14  15  6  7  9  8
        7  6  8  13  11  9  7  15  7  12  15  9  11  7  13  12
        11  13  6  7  14  9  13  15  14  8  13  6  5  12  7  5
        11  12  14  15  14  15  9  8  9  14  5  6  8  6  5  12
        9  15  5  11  6  8  13  12  5  12  13  14  11  8  5  6
    ==
  ::
  ++  ss  ::  s'
    |=  j=@ud
    %+  snag  j
    ^-  (list @)
    :~  8  9  9  11  13  15  15  5  7  7  8  11  14  14  12  6
        9  13  15  7  12  8  9  11  7  7  12  7  6  15  13  11
        9  7  15  11  8  6  6  14  12  13  5  14  13  13  7  5
        15  5  8  11  14  14  6  14  6  9  12  9  12  5  15  8
        8  5  12  9  12  5  14  6  8  13  6  5  15  13  11  11
    ==
    --
  ::
```

```
3188      ++  md5-pad
3189        |=  byts
3190        ^-  byts
3191        =+  (sub 511 (mod (add wid 64) 512))
3192        :-  :(add 64 +(-) wid)
3193        %+  can  0
3194        ~[64^(rev 3 8 wid) +(-)^(lsh [0 -] 1) wid^dat]
3195      --
3196    ::
3197    ++  pbkdf
3198      =>  |%
3199          ++  meet  |=([p=@ s=@ c=@ d=@] [[(met 3 p) p] [(met 3 s) s] c d])
3200          ++  flip  |=  [p=byts s=byts c=@ d=@]
3201                    [wid.p^(rev 3 p) wid.s^(rev 3 s) c d]
3202          --
3203      |%
3204      ::
3205      ::  use with @
3206      ::
3207      ++  hmac-sha1      (cork meet hmac-sha1l)
3208      ++  hmac-sha256    (cork meet hmac-sha256l)
3209      ++  hmac-sha512    (cork meet hmac-sha512l)
3210      ::
3211      ::  use with @t
3212      ::
3213      ++  hmac-sha1t     (cork meet hmac-sha1d)
3214      ++  hmac-sha256t   (cork meet hmac-sha256d)
3215      ++  hmac-sha512t   (cork meet hmac-sha512d)
3216      ::
3217      ::  use with byts
3218      ::
3219      ++  hmac-sha1l     (cork flip hmac-sha1d)
3220      ++  hmac-sha256l   (cork flip hmac-sha256d)
3221      ++  hmac-sha512l   (cork flip hmac-sha512d)
3222      ::
3223      ::  main logic
3224      ::
3225      ++  hmac-sha1d     (cury pbkdf hmac-sha1l:hmac 20)
3226      ++  hmac-sha256d   (cury pbkdf hmac-sha256l:hmac 32)
3227      ++  hmac-sha512d   (cury pbkdf hmac-sha512l:hmac 64)
3228      ::
3229      ++  pbkdf
3230        ::TODO  jet me! ++hmac:hmac is an example
3231        |*  [[prf=$-([byts byts] @) out=@u] p=byts s=byts c=@ d=@]
3232        =>  .(dat.p (end [3 wid.p] dat.p), dat.s (end [3 wid.s] dat.s))
3233        ::
3234        ::  max key length 1GB
3235        ::  max iterations 2^28
3236        ::
3237        ~|  [%invalid-pbkdf-params c d]
3238        ?>  ?&  (lte d (bex 30))
3239                (lte c (bex 28))
3240                !=(c 0)
3241            ==
3242        =/  l
3243          ?~  (mod d out)
3244            (div d out)
3245          +((div d out))
```

```
3246      =+   r=(sub d (mul out (dec 1)))
3247      =+   [t=0 j=1 k=1]
3248      =.   t
3249        |-   ^-   @
3250      ?:   (gth j l)   t
3251      =/   u
3252        %+   add   dat.s
3253        %+   lsh   [3 wid.s]
3254        %+   rep   3
3255        (flop (rpp:scr 3 4 j))
3256      =+   f=0
3257      =.   f
3258          |-   ^-   @
3259        ?:   (gth k c)   f
3260        =/   q
3261          %^   rev   3   out
3262          =+   ?:(=(k 1) (add wid.s 4) out)
3263          (prf [wid.p (rev 3 p)] [- (rev 3 - u)])
3264        $(u q, f (mix f q), k +(k))
3265      $(t (add t (lsh [3 (mul (dec j) out)] f)), j +(j))
3266      (rev 3 d (end [3 d] t))
3267      --
3268    --   ::crypto
3269  ::                                                   ::::
3270  ::::                            ++unity              ::   (2c) unit promotion
3271    ::                                                 ::::
3272  ++  unity   ^?
3273  |%
3274    ::                                                 ::   ++drop-list:unity
3275    ++  drop-list                                      ::   collapse unit list
3276      |*  lut=(list (unit))
3277      ?.  |-  ^-  ?
3278          ?~(lut & ?~(i.lut | $(lut t.lut)))
3279          ~
3280      %-  some
3281      |-
3282      ?~  lut   ~
3283      [i=u:+.i.lut t=$(lut t.lut)]
3284    ::                                                 ::   ++drop-map:unity
3285    ++  drop-map                                       ::   collapse unit map
3286      |*  lum=(map term (unit))
3287      ?:  (~(rep by lum) |=([[@ a=(unit)] b=_|] |(b ?=(~ a))))
3288          ~
3289      (some (~(run by lum) need))
3290    ::                                                 ::   ++drop-pole:unity
3291    ++  drop-pole                                      ::   collapse to tuple
3292      |^  |*  pul=(pole (unit))
3293          ?:  (test-pole pul)   ~
3294      (some (need-pole pul))
3295      ::
3296      ++  test-pole
3297        |*  pul=(pole (unit))
3298        ^-  ?
3299      ?~  pul  &
3300      ?|  ?=(~ -.pul)
3301          ?~(+.pul | (test-pole +.pul))
3302          ==
3303      ::
```

```
3304      ++  need-pole
3305        |*  pul=(pole (unit))
3306        ?~  pul  !!
3307        ?~  +.pul
3308          u:->.pul
3309        [u:->.pul (need-pole +.pul)]
3310        --
3311      --
3312  ::                                                  :::::
3313  :::::                           ++format            ::  (2d) common formats
3314    ::                                                :::::
3315  ++  format  ^?
3316    |%
3317    ::  0 ending a line (invalid @t) is not preserved  ::  ++to-wain:format
3318    ++  to-wain                                        ::  cord to line list
3319    ~%  %leer  ..part  ~
3320    |=  txt=cord
3321    ^-  wain
3322    ?~  txt  ~
3323    =/  len=@  (met 3 txt)
3324    =/  cut  =+(cut -(a 3, c 1, d txt))
3325    =/  sub  sub
3326    =|  [i=@ out=wain]
3327    |-  ^+  out
3328    =+  |-  ^-  j=@
3329        ?:  ?|  =(i len)
3330                =(10 (cut(b i)))
3331            ==
3332          i
3333        $(i +(i))
3334    =.  out  :_  out
3335      (cut(b i, c (sub j i)))
3336    ?:  =(j len)
3337      (flop out)
3338    $(i +(j))
3339    ::                                                ::  ++of-wain:format
3340    ++  of-wain                                        ::  line list to cord
3341    |=  tez=wain  ^-  cord
3342    (rap 3 (join '\0a' tez))
3343    ::                                                ::  ++of-wall:format
3344    ++  of-wall                                        ::  line list to tape
3345    |=  a=wall  ^-  tape
3346    ?~(a ~ "{i.a}\0a{$(a t.a)}")
3347    ::
3348    ++  json-rn                                        ::  json to rn parser
3349    %+  knee  *rn  |.
3350    ;~  plug
3351      (easy %d)
3352      ;~(pose (cold | hep) (easy &))
3353      ;~  plug  dim:ag
3354        ;~  pose
3355          ;~  pfix  dot
3356            %+  sear
3357              |=  a=tape
3358              =/  b  (rust a dum:ag)
3359              ?~  b  ~
3360              (some [(lent a) u.b])
3361            (plus (shim '0' '9'))
```

```
3362                  ==
3363                (easy [0 0])
3364              ==
3365            ;~  pose
3366              ;~  pfix
3367                (mask "eE")
3368                ;~  plug
3369                  ;~(pose (cold | hep) (cold & lus) (easy &))
3370                  ;~  pose
3371                    ;~(pfix (plus (just '0')) dim:ag)
3372                    dim:ag
3373                  ==
3374                ==
3375              ==
3376            (easy [& 0])
3377          ==
3378        ==
3379      ==
3380    ::                                          ::  ++enjs:format
3381    ++  enjs  ^?                                 ::  json encoders
3382      |%
3383      ::                                          ::  ++frond:enjs:format
3384      ++  frond                                   ::  object from k-v pair
3385        |=  [p=@t q=json]
3386        ^-  json
3387        [%o [[p q] ~ ~]]
3388      ::                                          ::  ++pairs:enjs:format
3389      ++  pairs                                   ::  object from k-v list
3390        |=  a=(list [p=@t q=json])
3391        ^-  json
3392        [%o (~(gas by *(map @t json)) a)]
3393      ::                                          ::  ++tape:enjs:format
3394      ++  tape                                    ::  string from tape
3395        |=  a=^tape
3396        ^-  json
3397        [%s (crip a)]
3398      ::                                          ::  ++wall:enjs:format
3399      ++  wall                                    ::  string from wall
3400        |=  a=^wall
3401        ^-  json
3402        (tape (of-wall a))
3403      ::                                          ::  ++ship:enjs:format
3404      ++  ship                                    ::  string from ship
3405        |=  a=^ship
3406        ^-  json
3407        [%n (rap 3 '"' (rsh [3 1] (scot %p a)) '"' ~)]
3408      ::                                          ::  ++numb:enjs:format
3409      ++  numb                                    ::  number from unsigned
3410        |=  a=@u
3411        ^-  json
3412        :-  %n
3413        ?:  =(0 a)  '0'
3414        %-  crip
3415        %-  flop
3416        |-  ^-  ^tape
3417        ?:(=(0 a) ~ [(add '0' (mod a 10)) $(a (div a 10))])
3418      ::                                          ::  ++sect:enjs:format
3419      ++  sect                                    ::  s timestamp
```

```
3420        |=  a=^time
3421        (numb (unt:chrono:userlib a))
3422    ::                                          ::  ++time:enjs:format
3423    ++  time                                    ::  ms timestamp
3424        |=  a=^time
3425        (numb (unm:chrono:userlib a))
3426    ::                                          ::  ++path:enjs:format
3427    ++  path                                    ::  string from path
3428        |=  a=^path
3429        ^-  json
3430        [%s (spat a)]
3431    ::                                          ::  ++tank:enjs:format
3432    ++  tank                                    ::  tank as string arr
3433        |=  a=^tank
3434        ^-  json
3435        [%a (turn (wash [0 80] a) tape)]
3436    --  ::enjs
3437  ::                                            ::  ++dejs:format
3438  ++  dejs                                      ::  json reparser
3439    =>  |%  ++  grub  *                         ::  result
3440            ++  fist  $-(json grub)             ::  reparser instance
3441        --  ::
3442    |%
3443    ::                                          ::  ++ar:dejs:format
3444    ++  ar                                      ::  array as list
3445      |*  wit=fist
3446      |=  jon=json  ^-  (list _(wit *json))
3447      ?>  ?=([%a *] jon)
3448      (turn p.jon wit)
3449    ::                                          ::  ++as:dejs:format
3450    ++  as                                      ::  array as set
3451      |*  a=fist
3452      (cu ~(gas in *(set _$:a)) (ar a))
3453    ::                                          ::  ++at:dejs:format
3454    ++  at                                      ::  array as tuple
3455      |*  wil=(pole fist)
3456      |=  jon=json
3457      ?>  ?=([%a *] jon)
3458      ((at-raw wil) p.jon)
3459    ::                                          ::  ++at-raw:dejs:format
3460    ++  at-raw                                  ::  array as tuple
3461      |*  wil=(pole fist)
3462      |=  jol=(list json)
3463      ?~  jol  !!
3464      ?-    wil                                 ::  mint-vain on empty
3465          ::  [wit=* t=*]
3466          [* t=*]
3467        =>  .(wil [wit *]=wil)
3468        ?~  t.wil  ?^(t.jol !! (wit.wil i.jol))
3469        [(wit.wil i.jol) ((at-raw t.wil) t.jol)]
3470      ==
3471    ::                                          ::  ++bo:dejs:format
3472    ++  bo                                      ::  boolean
3473      |=(jon=json ?>(?=([%b *] jon) p.jon))
3474    ::                                          ::  ++bu:dejs:format
3475    ++  bu                                      ::  boolean not
3476      |=(jon=json ?>(?=([%b *] jon) !p.jon))
3477    ::                                          ::  ++ci:dejs:format
```

```
3478      ++  ci                                          ::  maybe transform
3479        |*  [poq=gate wit=fist]
3480        |=  jon=json
3481        (need (poq (wit jon)))
3482      ::                                              ::  ++cu:dejs:format
3483      ++  cu                                          ::  transform
3484        |*  [poq=gate wit=fist]
3485        |=  jon=json
3486        (poq (wit jon))
3487      ::                                              ::  ++di:dejs:format
3488      ++  di                                          ::  millisecond date
3489        (cu from-unix-ms:chrono:userlib ni)
3490      ::                                              ::  ++du:dejs:format
3491      ++  du                                          ::  second date
3492        (cu from-unix:chrono:userlib ni)
3493      ::                                              ::  ++mu:dejs:format
3494      ++  mu                                          ::  true unit
3495        |*  wit=fist
3496        |=  jon=json
3497        ?~(jon ~ (some (wit jon)))
3498      ::                                              ::  ++ne:dejs:format
3499      ++  ne                                          ::  number as real
3500        |=  jon=json
3501        ^-  @rd
3502        ?>  ?=([%n *] jon)
3503        (rash p.jon (cook ryld (cook royl-cell:^so json-rn)))
3504      ::                                              ::  ++ni:dejs:format
3505      ++  ni                                          ::  number as integer
3506        |=  jon=json
3507        ?>  ?=([%n *] jon)
3508        (rash p.jon dem)
3509      ::                                              ::  ++ns:dejs:format
3510      ++  ns                                          ::  number as signed
3511        |=  jon=json
3512        ^-  @s
3513        ?>  ?=([%n *] jon)
3514        %+  rash  p.jon
3515        %+  cook  new:si
3516        ;~(plug ;~(pose (cold %| (jest '-')) (easy %&)) dem)
3517      ::                                              ::  ++no:dejs:format
3518      ++  no                                          ::  number as cord
3519        |=(jon=json ?>(?=([%n *] jon) p.jon))
3520      ::                                              ::  ++nu:dejs:format
3521      ++  nu                                          ::  parse number as hex
3522        |=  jon=json
3523        ?>  ?=([%s *] jon)
3524        (rash p.jon hex)
3525      ::                                              ::  ++of:dejs:format
3526      ++  of                                          ::  object as frond
3527        |*  wer=(pole [cord fist])
3528        |=  jon=json
3529        ?>  ?=([%o [@ *] ~ ~] jon)
3530        |-
3531        ?-    wer                                     ::  mint-vain on empty
3532            ::  [[key=@t wit=*] t=*]
3533            [[key=@t *] t=*]
3534          =>  .(wer [[* wit] *]=wer)
3535          ?:  =(key.wer p.n.p.jon)
```

```
3536        [key.wer ~|(key+key.wer (wit.wer q.n.p.jon))]
3537      ?~  t.wer  ~|(bad-key+p.n.p.jon !!)
3538      ((of t.wer) jon)
3539    ==
3540  ::                                          ::  ++ot:dejs:format
3541  ++  ot                                      ::  object as tuple
3542    |*  wer=(pole [cord fist])
3543    |=  jon=json
3544    ?>  ?=([%o *] jon)
3545    ((ot-raw wer) p.jon)
3546  ::                                          ::  ++ot-raw:dejs:format
3547  ++  ot-raw                                  ::  object as tuple
3548    |*  wer=(pole [cord fist])
3549    |=  jom=(map @t json)
3550    ?-    wer                                 ::  mint-vain on empty
3551        ::  [[key=@t wit=*] t=*]
3552        [[key=@t *] t=*]
3553      =>  .(wer [[* wit] *]=wer)
3554      =/  ten  ~|(key+key.wer (wit.wer (~(got by jom) key.wer)))
3555      ?~(t.wer ten [ten ((ot-raw t.wer) jom)])
3556    ==
3557  ::
3558  ++  ou                                      ::  object of units
3559    |*  wer=(pole [cord fist])
3560    |=  jon=json
3561    ?>  ?=([%o *] jon)
3562    ((ou-raw wer) p.jon)
3563  ::                                          ::  ++ou-raw:dejs:format
3564  ++  ou-raw                                  ::  object of units
3565    |*  wer=(pole [cord fist])
3566    |=  jom=(map @t json)
3567    ?-    wer                                 ::  mint-vain on empty
3568        ::  [[key=@t wit=*] t=*]
3569        [[key=@t *] t=*]
3570      =>  .(wer [[* wit] *]=wer)
3571      =/  ten  ~|(key+key.wer (wit.wer (~(get by jom) key.wer)))
3572      ?~(t.wer ten [ten ((ou-raw t.wer) jom)])
3573    ==
3574  ::                                          ::  ++oj:dejs:format
3575  ++  oj                                      ::  object as jug
3576    |*  =fist
3577    ^-  $-(json (jug cord _(fist *json)))
3578    (om (as fist))
3579  ::                                          ::  ++om:dejs:format
3580  ++  om                                      ::  object as map
3581    |*  wit=fist
3582    |=  jon=json
3583    ?>  ?=([%o *] jon)
3584    (~(run by p.jon) wit)
3585  ::                                          ::  ++op:dejs:format
3586  ++  op                                      ::  parse keys of map
3587    |*  [fel=rule wit=fist]
3588    |=  jon=json  ^-  (map _(wonk *fel) _*wit)
3589    =/  jom  ((om wit) jon)
3590    %-  malt
3591    %+  turn  ~(tap by jom)
3592    |*  [a=cord b=*]
3593    =>  .(+< [a b]=+<)
```

```
        [(rash a fel) b]
    ::                                          ::  ++pa:dejs:format
    ++  pa                                       ::  string as path
      (su stap)
    ::                                          ::  ++pe:dejs:format
    ++  pe                                       ::  prefix
      |*  [pre=* wit=fist]
      (cu |*(* [pre +<]) wit)
    ::                                          ::  ++sa:dejs:format
    ++  sa                                       ::  string as tape
      |=(jon=json ?>(?=([%s *] jon) (trip p.jon)))
    ::                                          ::  ++sd:dejs:format
    ++  sd                                       ::  string @ud as date
      |=  jon=json
      ^-  @da
      ?>  ?=(%s -.jon)
      `@da`(rash p.jon dem:ag)
    ::                                          ::  ++se:dejs:format
    ++  se                                       ::  string as aura
      |=  aur=@tas
      |=  jon=json
      ?>(?=([%s *] jon) (slav aur p.jon))
    ::                                          ::  ++so:dejs:format
    ++  so                                       ::  string as cord
      |=(jon=json ?>(?=([%s *] jon) p.jon))
    ::                                          ::  ++su:dejs:format
    ++  su                                       ::  parse string
      |*  sab=rule
      |=  jon=json  ^+  (wonk *sab)
      ?>  ?=([%s *] jon)
      (rash p.jon sab)
    ::                                          ::  ++uf:dejs:format
    ++  uf                                       ::  unit fall
      |*  [def=* wit=fist]
      |=  jon=(unit json)
      ?~(jon def (wit u.jon))
    ::                                          ::  ++un:dejs:format
    ++  un                                       ::  unit need
      |*  wit=fist
      |=  jon=(unit json)
      (wit (need jon))
    ::                                          ::  ++ul:dejs:format
    ++  ul                                       ::  null
      |=(jon=json ?~(jon ~ !!))
    ::
    ++  za                                       ::  full unit pole
      |*  pod=(pole (unit))
      ?~  pod  &
      ?~  -.pod  |
      (za +.pod)
    ::
    ++  zl                                       ::  collapse unit list
      |*  lut=(list (unit))
      ?.  |-  ^-  ?
          ?~(lut & ?~(i.lut | $(lut t.lut)))
        ~
      %-  some
      |-
```

```
    ?~  lut  ~
    [i=u:+.i.lut t=$(lut t.lut)]
  ::
++  zp                                            ::  unit tuple
  |*  but=(pole (unit))
  ?~  but  !!
  ?~  +.but
    u:->.but
  [u:->.but (zp +.but)]
  ::
++  zm                                            ::  collapse unit map
  |*  lum=(map term (unit))
  ?:  (~(rep by lum) |=([[@ a=(unit)] b=_|] |(b ?=(~ a))))
      ~
  (some (~(run by lum) need))
  --  ::dejs
::                                                ::  ++dejs-soft:format
++  dejs-soft                                     ::  json reparse to unit
  =,  unity
  =>  |%  ++  grub  (unit *)                       ::  result
          ++  fist  $-(json grub)                  ::  reparser instance
      --  ::
  ::
  ::  XX: this is old code that replaced a rewritten dejs.
  ::      the rewritten dejs rest-looped with ++redo.  the old
  ::      code is still in revision control -- revise and replace.
  ::
  |%
  ++  ar                                          ::  array as list
    |*  wit=fist
    |=  jon=json
    ?.  ?=([%a *] jon)  ~
    %-  zl
    |-
    ?~  p.jon  ~
    [i=(wit i.p.jon) t=$(p.jon t.p.jon)]
  ::
  ++  at                                          ::  array as tuple
    |*  wil=(pole fist)
    |=  jon=json
    ?.  ?=([%a *] jon)  ~
    ?.  =((lent wil) (lent p.jon))  ~
    =+  raw=((at-raw wil) p.jon)
    ?.((za raw) ~ (some (zp raw)))
  ::
  ++  at-raw                                      ::  array as tuple
    |*  wil=(pole fist)
    |=  jol=(list json)
    ?~  wil  ~
    :-  ?~(jol ~ (-.wil i.jol))
    ((at-raw +.wil) ?~(jol ~ t.jol))
  ::
  ++  bo                                          ::  boolean
    |=(jon=json ?.(?=([%b *] jon) ~ [~ u=p.jon]))
  ::
  ++  bu                                          ::  boolean not
    |=(jon=json ?.(?=([%b *] jon) ~ [~ u=!p.jon]))
  ::
```

```
++  ci                                          ::  maybe transform
  |*  [poq=gate wit=fist]
  |=  jon=json
  (biff (wit jon) poq)
::
++  cu                                          ::  transform
  |*  [poq=gate wit=fist]
  |=  jon=json
  (bind (wit jon) poq)
::
++  da                                          ::  UTC date
  |=  jon=json
  ?.  ?=([%s *] jon)  ~
  (bind (stud:chrono:userlib p.jon) |=(a=date (year a)))
::
++  dank                                        ::  tank
  ^-  $-(json (unit tank))
  %+  re  *tank  |.  ~+
  %-  of  :~
    leaf+sa
    palm+(ot style+(ot mid+sa cap+sa open+sa close+sa ~) lines+(ar dank) ~)
    rose+(ot style+(ot mid+sa open+sa close+sa ~) lines+(ar dank) ~)
  ==
::
++  di                                          ::  millisecond date
  (cu from-unix-ms:chrono:userlib ni)
::
++  mu                                          ::  true unit
  |*  wit=fist
  |=  jon=json
  ?~(jon (some ~) (bind (wit jon) some))
::
++  ne                                          ::  number as real
  |=  jon=json
  ^-  (unit @rd)
  ?.  ?=([%n *] jon)  ~
  (rush p.jon (cook ryld (cook royl-cell:^so json-rn)))
::
++  ni                                          ::  number as integer
  |=  jon=json
  ?.  ?=([%n *] jon)  ~
  (rush p.jon dem)
::
++  no                                          ::  number as cord
  |=  jon=json
  ?.  ?=([%n *] jon)  ~
  (some p.jon)
::
++  of                                          ::  object as frond
  |*  wer=(pole [cord fist])
  |=  jon=json
  ?.  ?=([%o [@ *] ~ ~] jon)  ~
  |-
  ?~  wer  ~
  ?:  =(-.-.wer p.n.p.jon)
    ((pe -.-.wer +.-.wer) q.n.p.jon)
  ((of +.wer) jon)
::
```

```
3768    ++  ot                                         ::  object as tuple
3769      |*  wer=(pole [cord fist])
3770      |=  jon=json
3771      ?.  ?=([%o *] jon)  ~
3772      =+  raw=((ot-raw wer) p.jon)
3773      ?.((za raw) ~ (some (zp raw)))
3774      ::
3775    ++  ot-raw                                     ::  object as tuple
3776      |*  wer=(pole [cord fist])
3777      |=  jom=(map @t json)
3778      ?~  wer  ~
3779      =+  ten=(~(get by jom) -.-.wer)
3780      [?~(ten ~ (+.-.wer u.ten)) ((ot-raw +.wer) jom)]
3781      ::
3782    ++  om                                         ::  object as map
3783      |*  wit=fist
3784      |=  jon=json
3785      ?.  ?=([%o *] jon)  ~
3786      (zm (~(run by p.jon) wit))
3787      ::
3788    ++  op                                         ::  parse keys of map
3789      |*  [fel=rule wit=fist]
3790      %+  cu
3791        |=  a=(list (pair _(wonk *fel) _(need *wit)))
3792        (my:nl a)
3793      %-  ci  :_  (om wit)
3794      |=  a=(map cord _(need *wit))
3795      ^-  (unit (list _[(wonk *fel) (need *wit)]))
3796      %-  zl
3797      %+  turn  ~(tap by a)
3798      |=  [a=cord b=_(need *wit)]
3799      =+  nit=(rush a fel)
3800      ?~  nit  ~
3801      (some [u.nit b])
3802      ::
3803    ++  pe                                         ::  prefix
3804      |*  [pre=* wit=fist]
3805      (cu |*(* [pre +<]) wit)
3806      ::
3807    ++  re                                         ::  recursive reparsers
3808      |*  [gar=* sef=_|.(fist)]
3809      |=  jon=json
3810      ^-  (unit _gar)
3811      ((sef) jon)
3812      ::
3813    ++  sa                                         ::  string as tape
3814      |=  jon=json
3815      ?.(?=([%s *] jon) ~ (some (trip p.jon)))
3816      ::
3817    ++  so                                         ::  string as cord
3818      |=  jon=json
3819      ?.(?=([%s *] jon) ~ (some p.jon))
3820      ::
3821    ++  su                                         ::  parse string
3822      |*  sab=rule
3823      |=  jon=json
3824      ?.  ?=([%s *] jon)  ~
3825      (rush p.jon sab)
```

```
      ::
      ++  ul  |=(jon=json ?~(jon (some ~) ~))              ::  null
      ++  za                                               ::  full unit pole
        |*  pod=(pole (unit))
        ?~  pod  &
        ?~  -.pod  |
        (za +.pod)
      ::
      ++  zl                                               ::  collapse unit list
        |*  lut=(list (unit))
        ?.  |-  ^-  ?
            ?~(lut & ?~(i.lut | $(lut t.lut)))
          ~
        %-  some
        |-
        ?~  lut  ~
        [i=u:+.i.lut t=$(lut t.lut)]
      ::
      ++  zp                                               ::  unit tuple
        |*  but=(pole (unit))
        ?~  but  !!
        ?~  +.but
          u:->.but
        [u:->.but (zp +.but)]
      ::
      ++  zm                                               ::  collapse unit map
        |*  lum=(map term (unit))
        ?:  (~(rep by lum) |=([[@ a=(unit)] b=_|] |(b ?=(~ a))))
          ~
        (some (~(run by lum) need))
      --  ::dejs-soft
    ::
    ++  klr                                                ::  styx/stub engine
      =,  dill
      |%
      ++  make                                             ::  stub from styx
        |=  a=styx  ^-  stub
        =|  b=stye
        %+  reel
          |-  ^-  stub
          %-  zing  %+  turn  a
          |=  a=$@(@t (pair styl styx))
          ?@  a  [b (tuba (trip a))]~
          ^$(a q.a, b (styd p.a b))
        ::
        |=  [a=(pair stye (list @c)) b=stub]
        ?~  b  [a ~]
        ?.  =(p.a p.i.b)  [a b]
        [[p.a (weld q.a q.i.b)] t.b]
      ::
      ++  styd                                             ::  stye from styl
        |=  [a=styl b=stye]  ^+  b                         ::  with inheritance
        :+  ?~  p.a  p.b
            ?~  u.p.a  ~
            (~(put in p.b) u.p.a)
          (fall p.q.a p.q.b)
        (fall q.q.a q.q.b)
      ::
```

```
3884      ++  lent-char
3885        |=  a=stub  ^-  @
3886        (roll (lnts-char a) add)
3887      ::
3888      ++  lnts-char                             ::  stub text lengths
3889        |=  a=stub  ^-  (list @)
3890        %+  turn  a
3891        |=  a=(pair stye (list @c))
3892        (lent q.a)
3893      ::
3894      ++  brek                                  ::  index + incl-len of
3895        |=  [a=@ b=(list @)]                     ::  stub pair w/ idx a
3896        =|  [c=@ i=@]
3897        |-  ^-  (unit (pair @ @))
3898        ?~  b  ~
3899        =.  c  (add c i.b)
3900        ?:  (gte c a)
3901          `[i c]
3902        $(i +(i), b t.b)
3903      ::
3904      ++  pact                                  ::  condense stub
3905        |=  a=stub
3906        ^-  stub
3907        ?~  a  ~
3908        ?~  t.a  a
3909        ?.  =(p.i.a p.i.t.a)  [i.a $(a t.a)]
3910        =.  q.i.t.a  (weld q.i.a q.i.t.a)
3911        $(a t.a)
3912      ::
3913      ++  slag                                  ::  slag stub
3914        |=  [a=@ b=stub]
3915        ^-  stub
3916        ?:  =(0 a)  b
3917        ?~  b  ~
3918        =+  c=(lent q.i.b)
3919        ?:  =(c a)  t.b
3920        ?:  (gth c a)
3921          [[p.i.b (^slag a q.i.b)] t.b]
3922        $(a (sub a c), b t.b)
3923      ::
3924      ++  scag                                  ::  scag stub
3925        |=  [a=@ b=stub]
3926        ^-  stub
3927        ?:  =(0 a)  ~
3928        ?~  b  ~
3929        =+  c=(lent q.i.b)
3930        ?:  (gth c a)
3931          [p.i.b (^scag a q.i.b)]~
3932        :-  i.b
3933        $(a (sub a c), b t.b)
3934      ::
3935      ++  swag                                  ::  swag stub
3936        |=  [[a=@ b=@] c=stub]
3937        (scag b (slag a c))
3938      ::
3939      ++  wail                                  ::  overlay stub
3940        |=  [a=stub b=@ c=stub d=@c]
3941        ^-  stub
```

```
3942      ;:   weld
3943       (scag b a)
3944      ::
3945       =+  e=(lent-char a)
3946       ?:  (lte b e)   ~
3947       [*stye (reap (sub b e) d)]~
3948      ::
3949       c
3950       (slag (add b (lent-char c)) a)
3951     ==
3952    --  ::  klr
3953  --
3954  ::  |cloy: clay helpers
3955  ::
3956  ++  cloy
3957   =,  clay
3958   |%
3959   ++  new-desk
3960    |=  [=desk tako=(unit tako) files=(map path page)]
3961    [%c %park desk &/[(drop tako) (~(run by files) (lead %&))] *rang]
3962   --
3963  ::                                                   ::
3964  ::::                         ++differ               ::  (2d) hunt-mcilroy
3965   ::                                                  ::::
3966  ++  differ  ^?
3967   =,  clay
3968   =,  format
3969   |%
3970   ::                                                  ::  ++berk:differ
3971   ++  berk                                            ::  invert diff patch
3972    |*  bur=(urge)
3973    |-  ^+  bur
3974    ?~  bur   ~
3975    :_  $(bur t.bur)
3976    ?-  -.i.bur
3977      %&  i.bur
3978      %|  [%| q.i.bur p.i.bur]
3979    ==
3980   ::                                                  ::  ++loss:differ
3981   ++  loss                                            ::  longest subsequence
3982    ~%  %loss  ..part  ~
3983    |*  [hel=(list) hev=(list)]
3984    |-  ^+  hev
3985    =+  ^=  sev
3986        =+  [inx=0 sev=*(map _i.-.hev (list @ud))]
3987        |-  ^+  sev
3988        ?~  hev  sev
3989        =+  guy=(~(get by sev) i.hev)
3990        %=  $
3991          hev  t.hev
3992          inx  +(inx)
3993          sev  (~(put by sev) i.hev [inx ?~(guy ~ u.guy)])
3994        ==
3995    =|  gox=[p=@ud q=(map @ud [p=@ud q=_hev])]
3996    =<  abet
3997    =<  main
3998    |%
3999    ::                                                  ::  ++abet:loss:differ
```

```
++  abet                                          ::  subsequence
  ^+  hev
  ?:  =(0 p.gox)  ~
  (flop q:(need (~(get by q.gox) (dec p.gox))))
::                                                ::  ++hink:loss:differ
++  hink                                          ::  extend fits top
  |=  [inx=@ud goy=@ud]  ^-  ?
  ?|  =(p.gox inx)
      (lth goy p:(need (~(get by q.gox) inx)))
  ==
::                                                ::  ++lonk:loss:differ
++  lonk                                          ::  extend fits bottom
  |=  [inx=@ud goy=@ud]  ^-  ?
  ?|  =(0 inx)
      (gth goy p:(need (~(get by q.gox) (dec inx))))
  ==
::                                                ::  ++luna:loss:differ
++  luna                                          ::  extend
  |=  [inx=@ud goy=@ud]
  ^+  +>
  %_    +>.$
      gox
    :-  ?:(=(inx p.gox) +(p.gox) p.gox)
    %+  ~(put by q.gox)  inx
    :+  goy
      (snag goy hev)
    ?:(=(0 inx) ~ q:(need (~(get by q.gox) (dec inx))))
  ==
::                                                ::  ++merg:loss:differ
++  merg                                          ::  merge all matches
  |=  gay=(list @ud)
  ^+  +>
  =+  ^=  zes
      =+  [inx=0 zes=*(list [p=@ud q=@ud])]
      |-  ^+  zes
      ?:  |(?=(~ gay) (gth inx p.gox))  zes
      ?.  (lonk inx i.gay)  $(gay t.gay)
      ?.  (hink inx i.gay)  $(inx +(inx))
      $(inx +(inx), gay t.gay, zes [[inx i.gay] zes])
  |-  ^+  +>.^$
  ?~(zes +>.^$ $(zes t.zes, +>.^$ (luna i.zes)))
::                                                ::  ++main:loss:differ
++  main                                          ::
  =+  hol=hel
  |-  ^+  +>
  ?~  hol  +>
  =+  guy=(~(get by sev) i.hol)
  $(hol t.hol, +> (merg (flop `(list @ud)`?~(guy ~ u.guy))))
  --  ::
::                                                ::  ++lurk:differ
++  lurk                                          ::  apply list patch
  |*  [hel=(list) rug=(urge)]
  ^+  hel
  =+  war=`_hel`~
  |-  ^+  hel
  ?~  rug  (flop war)
  ?-    -.i.rug
      %&
```

```
4058          %=    $
4059            rug  t.rug
4060            hel  (slag p.i.rug hel)
4061            war  (weld (flop (scag p.i.rug hel)) war)
4062          ==
4063        ::
4064          %|
4065        %=    $
4066            rug  t.rug
4067            hel  =+  gur=(flop p.i.rug)
4068                 |-  ^+  hel
4069                 ?~  gur  hel
4070                 ?>(&(?=(^ hel) =(i.gur i.hel)) $(hel t.hel, gur t.gur))
4071            war  (weld q.i.rug war)
4072        ==
4073      ==
4074  ::                                              ::  ++lusk:differ
4075  ++  lusk                                        ::  lcs to list patch
4076    |*  [hel=(list) hev=(list) lcs=(list)]
4077    =+  ^=  rag
4078        ^-  [$%([%& p=@ud] [%| p=_lcs q=_lcs])]
4079        [%& 0]
4080    =>  .(rag [p=rag q=*(list _rag)])
4081    =<  abet  =<  main
4082    |%
4083    ::                                            ::  ++abet:lusk:differ
4084    ++  abet                                      ::
4085      =?  q.rag  !=([& 0] p.rag)  [p.rag q.rag]
4086      (flop q.rag)
4087    ::                                            ::  ++done:lusk:differ
4088    ++  done                                      ::
4089      |=  new=_p.rag
4090      ^+  rag
4091      ?-  -.p.rag
4092        %|  ?-  -.new
4093              %|  [[%| (weld p.new p.p.rag) (weld q.new q.p.rag)] q.rag]
4094              %&  [new [p.rag q.rag]]
4095            ==
4096        %&  ?-  -.new
4097              %|  [new ?:(=(0 p.p.rag) q.rag [p.rag q.rag])]
4098              %&  [[%& (add p.p.rag p.new)] q.rag]
4099            ==
4100      ==
4101    ::                                            ::  ++main:lusk:differ
4102    ++  main                                      ::
4103      |-  ^+  +
4104      ?~  hel
4105        ?~  hev
4106          ?>(?=(~ lcs) +)
4107        $(hev t.hev, rag (done %| ~ [i.hev ~]))
4108      ?~  hev
4109        $(hel t.hel, rag (done %| [i.hel ~] ~))
4110      ?~  lcs
4111        +(rag (done %| (flop hel) (flop hev)))
4112      ?:  =(i.hel i.lcs)
4113        ?:  =(i.hev i.lcs)
4114          $(lcs t.lcs, hel t.hel, hev t.hev, rag (done %& 1))
4115        $(hev t.hev, rag (done %| ~ [i.hev ~]))
```

```hoon
          ?:  =(i.hev i.lcs)
            $(hel t.hel, rag (done %| [i.hel ~] ~))
          $(hel t.hel, hev t.hev, rag (done %| [i.hel ~] [i.hev ~]))
        --  ::
      --  ::differ
    ::                                                      ::
    ::::                        ++html                      ::  (2e) text encodings
      ::                                                    ::::
++  html  ^?  ::  XX rename to web-txt
  =,  eyre
  |%
    ::                                                      ::
    ::::                        ++mimes:html                ::  (2e1) MIME
      ::                                                    ::::
  ++  mimes  ^?
    ~%  %mimes  ..part  ~
    |%
    ::                                              ::  ++as-octs:mimes:html
    ++  as-octs                                     ::  atom to octstream
      |=  tam=@  ^-  octs
      [(met 3 tam) tam]
    ::                                              ::  ++as-octt:mimes:html
    ++  as-octt                                     ::  tape to octstream
      |=  tep=tape  ^-  octs
      (as-octs (rap 3 tep))
    ::                                              ::  ++en-mite:mimes:html
    ++  en-mite                                     ::  mime type to text
      |=  myn=mite
      %-  crip
      |-  ^-  tape
      ?~  myn  ~
      ?:  =(~ t.myn)  (trip i.myn)
      (weld (trip i.myn) `tape`['/' $(myn t.myn)])
    ::
    ::  |base16: en/decode arbitrary MSB-first hex strings
    ::
    ++  base16
      ~%  %base16  +  ~
      |%
      ++  en
        ~/  %en
        |=  a=octs  ^-  cord
        (crip ((x-co:co (mul p.a 2)) (end [3 p.a] q.a)))
      ::
      ++  de
        ~/  %de
        |=  a=cord  ^-  (unit octs)
        (rush a rule)
      ::
      ++  rule
        %+  cook
          |=  a=(list @)  ^-  octs
          [(add (dvr (lent a) 2)) (rep [0 4] (flop a))]
        (star hit)
      --
    ::  |base64: flexible base64 encoding for little-endian atoms
    ::
    ++  base64
```

```
=>  |%
    +$  byte    @D
    +$  word24  @
    ::
    ++  div-ceil
      ::  divide, rounding up.
      |=  [x=@ y=@]  ^-  @
      ?:  =(0 (mod x y))
        (div x y)
      +((div x y))
    ::
    ++  explode-bytes
      ::  Explode a bytestring into list of bytes. Result is in LSB order.
      |=  =octs  ^-  (list byte)
      =/  atom-byte-width  (met 3 q.octs)
      =/  leading-zeros    (sub p.octs atom-byte-width)
      (weld (reap leading-zeros 0) (rip 3 q.octs))
    ::
    ++  explode-words
      ::  Explode a bytestring to words of bit-width `wid`. Result is in LSW order.
      |=  [wid=@ =octs]
      ^-  (list @)
      =/  atom-bit-width   (met 0 q.octs)
      =/  octs-bit-width   (mul 8 p.octs)
      =/  atom-word-width  (div-ceil atom-bit-width wid)
      =/  rslt-word-width  (div-ceil octs-bit-width wid)
      =/  pad              (sub rslt-word-width atom-word-width)
      =/  x  (rip [0 wid] q.octs)
      %+  weld  x
      (reap pad 0)
    --
  ::
  ::  pad: include padding when encoding, require when decoding
  ::  url: use url-safe characters '-' for '+' and '_' for '/'
  ::
  =+  [pad=& url=|]
  |%
  ::  +en:base64: encode +octs to base64 cord
  ::
  ::  Encode an `octs` into a base64 string.
  ::
  ::  First, we break up the input into a list of 24-bit words. The input
  ::  might not be a multiple of 24-bits, so we add 0-2 padding bytes at
  ::  the end (to the least-significant side, with a left-shift).
  ::
  ::  Then, we encode each block into four base64 characters.
  ::
  ::  Finally we remove the padding that we added at the beginning: for
  ::  each byte that was added, we replace one character with an = (unless
  ::  `pad` is false, in which case we just remove the extra characters).
  ::
  ++  en
    ^-  $-(octs cord)
    ::
    =/  cha
      ?:  url
        'ABCDEFGHIJKLMNOPQRSTUVWXYZabcdefghijklmnopqrstuvwxyz0123456789-_'
      'ABCDEFGHIJKLMNOPQRSTUVWXYZabcdefghijklmnopqrstuvwxyz0123456789+/'
```

```
4232      ::
4233      |^  |=  bs=octs  ^-  cord
4234        =/  [padding=@ blocks=(list word24)]
4235          (octs-to-blocks bs)
4236        (crip (flop (unpad padding (encode-blocks blocks))))
4237      ::
4238      ++  octs-to-blocks
4239        |=  bs=octs  ^-  [padding=@ud (list word24)]
4240        =/  padding=@ud  (~(dif fo 3) 0 p.bs)
4241        =/  padded=octs  [(add padding p.bs) (lsh [3 padding] (rev 3 bs))]
4242        [padding (explode-words 24 padded)]
4243      ::
4244      ++  unpad
4245        |=  [extra=@ t=tape]  ^-  tape
4246        =/  without  (slag extra t)
4247        ?.  pad  without
4248        (weld (reap extra '=') without)
4249      ::
4250      ++  encode-blocks
4251        |=  ws=(list word24)  ^-  tape
4252        (zing (turn ws encode-block))
4253      ::
4254      ++  encode-block
4255        |=  w=word24  ^-  tape
4256        =/  a  (cut 3 [(cut 0 [0 6] w) 1] cha)
4257        =/  b  (cut 3 [(cut 0 [6 6] w) 1] cha)
4258        =/  c  (cut 3 [(cut 0 [12 6] w) 1] cha)
4259        =/  d  (cut 3 [(cut 0 [18 6] w) 1] cha)
4260        ~[a b c d]
4261      --
4262    ::
4263    ::  +de:base64: decode base64 cord to (unit @)
4264    ::
4265    ++  de
4266      |=  a=cord
4267      ^-  (unit octs)
4268      (rush a parse)
4269    ::  +parse:base64: parse base64 cord to +octs
4270    ::
4271    ++  parse
4272      =<  ^-  $-(nail (like octs))
4273          %+  sear  reduce
4274          ;~  plug
4275            %-  plus  ;~  pose
4276              (cook |=(a=@ (sub a 'A')) (shim 'A' 'Z'))
4277              (cook |=(a=@ (sub a 'G')) (shim 'a' 'z'))
4278              (cook |=(a=@ (add a 4)) (shim '0' '9'))
4279              (cold 62 (just ?:(url '-' '+')))
4280              (cold 63 (just ?:(url '_' '/')))
4281            ==
4282            (stun 0^2 (cold %0 tis))
4283          ==
4284      |%
4285      ::  +reduce:parse:base64: reduce, measure, and swap base64 digits
4286      ::
4287      ++  reduce
4288        |=  [dat=(list @) dap=(list @)]
4289        ^-  (unit octs)
```

```
=/  lat  (lent dat)
=/  lap  (lent dap)
=/  dif  (~(dif fo 4) 0 lat)
?:  &(pad !=(dif lap))
    ::  padding required and incorrect
  ~&(%base-64-padding-err-one ~)
?:  &(!pad !=(0 lap))
    ::  padding not required but present
  ~&(%base-64-padding-err-two ~)
=/  len  (sub (mul 3 (div (add lat dif) 4)) dif)
:+  ~  len
=/  res  (rsh [1 dif] (rep [0 6] (flop dat)))
=/  amt  (met 3 res)
::  left shift trailing zeroes in after byte swap
=/  trl  ?:  (lth len amt)  0  (sub len amt)
(lsh [3 trl] (swp 3 res))
    --
  --
::
++  en-base58
  |=  dat=@
  =/  cha
    '123456789ABCDEFGHJKLMNPQRSTUVWXYZabcdefghijkmnopqrstuvwxyz'
  %-  flop
  |-  ^-  tape
  ?:  =(0 dat)  ~
  :-  (cut 3 [(mod dat 58) 1] cha)
  $(dat (div dat 58))
::
++  de-base58
  |=  t=tape
  =-  (scan t (bass 58 (plus -)))
  ;~  pose
    (cook |=(a=@ (sub a 56)) (shim 'A' 'H'))
    (cook |=(a=@ (sub a 57)) (shim 'J' 'N'))
    (cook |=(a=@ (sub a 58)) (shim 'P' 'Z'))
    (cook |=(a=@ (sub a 64)) (shim 'a' 'k'))
    (cook |=(a=@ (sub a 65)) (shim 'm' 'z'))
    (cook |=(a=@ (sub a 49)) (shim '1' '9'))
  ==
--  ::mimes
::                                              ::
::::                    ++json:html            ::  (2e2) JSON
  ::                                            ::::
++  json  ^?
  ~%  %json  ..part  ~
  |%
  ::                                            ::  ++en:json:html
  ++  en                                        ::  encode JSON to cord
    ~%  %en  +>+  ~
    |^  |=  jon=^json
        ^-  cord
        (rap 3 (flop (onto jon ~)))
    ::                                          ::  ++onto:en:json:html
    ++  onto
      |=  [val=^json out=(list @t)]
      ^+  out
      ?~  val  ['null' out]
```

```hoon
4348        ?-    -.val
4349          %a
4350        ?~  p.val  ['[]' out]
4351        =.  out    ['[' out]
4352        !.
4353        |-  ^+  out
4354        =.  out  ^$(val i.p.val)
4355        ?~(t.p.val [']' out] $(p.val t.p.val, out [',' out]))
4356      ::
4357          %b
4358        [?:(p.val 'true' 'false') out]
4359      ::
4360          %n
4361        [p.val out]
4362      ::
4363          %s
4364        [(scap p.val) out]
4365      ::
4366          %o
4367        =/  viz  ~(tap by p.val)
4368        ?~  viz  ['{}' out]
4369        =.  out  ['{' out]
4370        !.
4371        |-  ^+  out
4372        =.  out  ^$(val q.i.viz, out [':' [(scap p.i.viz) out]])
4373        ?~(t.viz ['}' out] $(viz t.viz, out [',' out]))
4374        ==
4375      ::                                          :: ++scap:en:json:html
4376      ++  scap
4377        |=  val=@t
4378        ^-  @t
4379        =/  out=(list @t)  ['"' ~]
4380        =/  len  (met 3 val)
4381        =|  [i=@ud pos=@ud]
4382        |-  ^-  @t
4383        ?:  =(len i)
4384          (rap 3 (flop ['"' (rsh [3 pos] val) out]))
4385        =/  car  (cut 3 [i 1] val)
4386        ?:  ?&  (gth car 0x1f)
4387                !=(car 0x22)
4388                !=(car 0x5C)
4389                !=(car 0x7F)
4390            ==
4391          $(i +(i))
4392        =/  cap
4393          ?+  car  (crip '\\' 'u' ((x-co 4):co car))
4394            %10    '\\n'
4395            %'"'   '\\"'
4396            %'\\'  '\\\\'
4397          ==
4398        $(i +(i), pos +(i), out [cap (cut 3 [pos (sub i pos)] val) out])
4399      --  ::en
4400    ::                                          :: ++de:json:html
4401    ++  de                                      :: parse cord to JSON
4402      ~%  %de  +>+  ~
4403      |^  |=  txt=cord
4404          ^-  (unit ^json)
4405          (rush txt apex)
```

```
4406      ::                                              ::    ++abox:de:json:html
4407      ++  abox                                         ::    array
4408       %+  stag  %a
4409       (ifix [sel (wish ser)] (more (wish com) apex))
4410      ::                                              ::    ++apex:de:json:html
4411      ++  apex                                         ::    any value
4412       %+  knee  *^json  |.  ~+
4413       %+  ifix  [spac spac]
4414       ;~  pose
4415         (cold ~ (jest 'null'))
4416         (stag %b bool)
4417         (stag %s stri)
4418         (cook |=(s=tape [%n p=(rap 3 s)]) numb)
4419         abox
4420         obox
4421       ==
4422      ::                                              ::    ++bool:de:json:html
4423      ++  bool                                         ::    boolean
4424       ;~  pose
4425         (cold & (jest 'true'))
4426         (cold | (jest 'false'))
4427       ==
4428      ::                                              ::    ++esca:de:json:html
4429      ++  esca                                         ::    escaped character
4430       ;~  pfix  bas
4431         =*  loo
4432           =*  lip
4433             ^-  (list (pair @t @))
4434             [b+8 t+9 n+10 f+12 r+13 ~]
4435           =*  wow
4436             ^~
4437             ^-  (map @t @)
4438             (malt lip)
4439         (sear ~(get by wow) low)
4440       ;~(pose doq fas bas loo unic)
4441       ==
4442      ::                                              ::    ++expo:de:json:html
4443      ++  expo                                         ::    exponent
4444       ;~  (comp weld)
4445         (piec (mask "eE"))
4446         (mayb (piec (mask "+-")))
4447         (plus nud)
4448       ==
4449      ::                                              ::    ++frac:de:json:html
4450      ++  frac                                         ::    fraction
4451       ;~(plug dot (plus nud))
4452      ::                                              ::    ++jcha:de:json:html
4453      ++  jcha                                         ::    string character
4454       ;~(pose ;~(less doq bas (shim 32 255)) esca)
4455      ::                                              ::    ++mayb:de:json:html
4456      ++  mayb                                         ::    optional
4457       |*(bus=rule ;~(pose bus (easy ~)))
4458      ::                                              ::    ++numb:de:json:html
4459      ++  numb                                         ::    number
4460       ;~  (comp weld)
4461         (mayb (piec hep))
4462         ;~  pose
4463           (piec (just '0'))
```

```
4464          ;~(plug (shim '1' '9') (star nud))
4465        ==
4466        (mayb frac)
4467        (mayb expo)
4468      ==
4469    ::                                              ::  ++obje:de:json:html
4470    ++  obje                                        ::  object list
4471      %+  ifix  [(wish kel) (wish ker)]
4472      (more (wish com) pear)
4473    ::                                              ::  ++obox:de:json:html
4474    ++  obox                                        ::  object
4475      (stag %o (cook malt obje))
4476    ::                                              ::  ++pear:de:json:html
4477    ++  pear                                        ::  key-value
4478      ;~(plug ;~(sfix (wish stri) (wish col)) apex)
4479    ::                                              ::  ++piec:de:json:html
4480    ++  piec                                        ::  listify
4481      |*  bus=rule
4482      (cook |=(a=@ [a ~]) bus)
4483    ::                                              ::  ++stri:de:json:html
4484    ++  stri                                        ::  string
4485      %+  sear
4486        |=  a=cord
4487        ?.  (sune a)  ~
4488        (some a)
4489      (cook crip (ifix [doq doq] (star jcha)))
4490    ::                                              ::  ++spac:de:json:html
4491    ++  spac                                        ::  whitespace
4492      (star (mask [`@`9 `@`10 `@`13 ' ' ~]))
4493    ::                                              ::  ++unic:de:json:html
4494    ++  unic                                        ::  escaped UTF16
4495      =*  lob  0x0
4496      =*  hsb  0xd800
4497      =*  lsb  0xdc00
4498      =*  hib  0xe000
4499      =*  hil  0x1.0000
4500      |^
4501        %+  cook
4502          |=  a=@
4503          ^-  @t
4504          (tuft a)
4505        ;~  pfix  (just 'u')
4506          ;~(pose solo pair)
4507        ==
4508      ++  quad                                      ::  parse num from 4 hex
4509        (bass 16 (stun [4 4] hit))
4510      ++  meat                                      ::  gen gate for sear:
4511        |=  [bot=@ux top=@ux flp=?]                 ::  accept num in range,
4512        |=  sur=@ux                                 ::  optionally reduce
4513        ^-  (unit @)
4514        ?.  &((gte sur bot) (lth sur top))
4515          ~
4516        %-  some
4517        ?.  flp  sur
4518        (sub sur bot)
4519      ++  solo                                      ::  single valid UTF16
4520        ;~  pose
4521          (sear (meat lob hsb |) quad)
```

```
4522              (sear (meat hib hil |) quad)
4523          ==
4524      ++  pair                                  ::  UTF16 surrogate pair
4525        %+  cook
4526        |=  [hig=@ low=@]
4527          ^-  @t
4528          :(add hil low (lsh [1 5] hig))
4529        ;~  plug
4530          (sear (meat hsb lsb &) quad)
4531          ;~  pfix  (jest '\\u')
4532            (sear (meat lsb hib &) quad)
4533        ==
4534      ==
4535      --
4536    ::                                          ::  ++utfe:de:json:html
4537    ++  utfe                                    ::  UTF-8 sequence
4538      ;~  less  doq  bas
4539        =*  qua
4540        %+  cook
4541        |=  [a=@ b=@ c=@ d=@]
4542          (rap 3 a b c d ~)
4543        ;~  pose
4544          ;~  plug
4545            (shim 241 243)
4546            (shim 128 191)
4547            (shim 128 191)
4548            (shim 128 191)
4549          ==
4550          ;~  plug
4551            (just '\F0')
4552            (shim 144 191)
4553            (shim 128 191)
4554            (shim 128 191)
4555          ==
4556          ;~  plug
4557            (just '\F4')
4558            (shim 128 143)
4559            (shim 128 191)
4560            (shim 128 191)
4561          ==
4562        ==
4563        =*  tre
4564        %+  cook
4565        |=  [a=@ b=@ c=@]
4566          (rap 3 a b c ~)
4567        ;~  pose
4568          ;~  plug
4569            ;~  pose
4570              (shim 225 236)
4571              (shim 238 239)
4572          ==
4573          (shim 128 191)
4574          (shim 128 191)
4575        ==
4576          ;~  plug
4577            (just '\E0')
4578            (shim 160 191)
4579            (shim 128 191)
```

```
          ==
        ;~  plug
          (just '\ED')
          (shim 128 159)
          (shim 128 191)
        ==
      ==
    =*  dos
      %+  cook
      |=  [a=@ b=@]
      (cat 3 a b)
      ;~  plug
        (shim 194 223)
        (shim 128 191)
      ==
    ;~(pose qua tre dos)
  ==
::                                              ::  ++wish:de:json:html
++  wish                                        ::  with whitespace
  |*(sef=rule ;~(pfix spac sef))
::  XX: These gates should be moved to hoon.hoon
::                                              ::  ++sune:de:json:html
++  sune                                        ::  cord UTF-8 sanity
  |=  b=@t
  ^-  ?
  ?:  =(0 b)  &
  ?.  (sung b)  |
  $(b (rsh [3 (teff b)] b))
::                                              ::  ++sung:de:json:html
++  sung                                        ::  char UTF-8 sanity
  |^  |=  b=@t
      ^-  ?
      =+  len=(teff b)
      ?:  =(4 len)  (quad b)
      ?:  =(3 len)  (tres b)
      ?:  =(2 len)  (dos b)
      (lte (end 3 b) 127)
  ::
  ++  dos
    |=  b=@t
    ^-  ?
    =+  :-  one=(cut 3 [0 1] b)
            two=(cut 3 [1 1] b)
    ?&  (rang one 194 223)
        (cont two)
    ==
  ::
  ++  tres
    |=  b=@t
    ^-  ?
    =+  :+  one=(cut 3 [0 1] b)
            two=(cut 3 [1 1] b)
            tre=(cut 3 [2 1] b)
    ?&
      ?|
        ?&  |((rang one 225 236) (rang one 238 239))
            (cont two)
        ==
```

```
            ::
            ?&  =(224 one)
                (rang two 160 191)
            ==
            ::
            ?&  =(237 one)
                (rang two 128 159)
            ==
          ==
          ::
        (cont tre)
      ==
    ::
    ++  quad
      |=  b=@t
      ^-  ?
      =+  :^  one=(cut 3 [0 1] b)
              two=(cut 3 [1 1] b)
              tre=(cut 3 [2 1] b)
              for=(cut 3 [3 1] b)
        ?&
          ?|
            ?&  (rang one 241 243)
                (cont two)
            ==
            ::
            ?&  =(240 one)
                (rang two 144 191)
            ==
            ::
            ?&  =(244 one)
                (rang two 128 143)
            ==
          ==
          ::
        (cont tre)
        (cont for)
      ==
    ::
    ++  cont
      |=  a=@
      ^-  ?
      (rang a 128 191)
    ::
    ++  rang
      |=  [a=@ bot=@ top=@]
      ^-  ?
      ?>  (lte bot top)
      &((gte a bot) (lte a top))
    --
  ::  XX: This +teff should overwrite the existing +teff
  ::                                            ::  ++teff:de:json:html
  ++  teff                                      ::  UTF-8 length
    |=  a=@t
    ^-  @
    =+  b=(end 3 a)
    ?:  =(0 b)
      ?>  =(`@`0 a)  0
```

```
4696        ?:  (lte b 127)  1
4697        ?:  (lte b 223)  2
4698        ?:  (lte b 239)  3
4699        4
4700      --  ::de
4701    --  ::json
4702  ::                                              ::  ++en-xml:html
4703  ++  en-xml                                       ::  xml printer
4704  =<  |=(a=manx `tape`(apex a ~))
4705  |_  _[unq=`?`| cot=`?`|]
4706    ::                                            ::  ++apex:en-xml:html
4707    ++  apex                                       ::  top level
4708    |=  [mex=manx rez=tape]
4709    ^-  tape
4710    ?:  ?=([%$ [[%$ *] ~]] g.mex)
4711      (escp v.i.a.g.mex rez)
4712    =+  man=`mane`n.g.mex
4713    =.  unq  |(unq =(%script man) =(%style man))
4714    =+  tam=(name man)
4715    =+  att=`mart`a.g.mex
4716    :-  '<'
4717    %+  welp  tam
4718    =-  ?~(att rez [' ' (attr att rez)])
4719    ^-  rez=tape
4720    ?:  &(?=(~ c.mex) |(cot ?^(man | (clot man))))
4721      [' ' '/' '>' rez]
4722    :-  '>'
4723    (many c.mex :(weld "</" tam ">" rez))
4724    ::                                            ::  ++attr:en-xml:html
4725    ++  attr                                       ::  attributes to tape
4726    |=  [tat=mart rez=tape]
4727    ^-  tape
4728    ?~  tat  rez
4729    =.  rez  $(tat t.tat)
4730    ;:  weld
4731      (name n.i.tat)
4732      "=\""
4733      (escp(unq |) v.i.tat '"' ?~(t.tat rez [' ' rez]))
4734    ==
4735    ::                                            ::  ++escp:en-xml:html
4736    ++  escp                                       ::  escape for xml
4737    |=  [tex=tape rez=tape]
4738    ?:  unq
4739      (weld tex rez)
4740    =+  xet=`tape`(flop tex)
4741    !.
4742    |-  ^-  tape
4743    ?~  xet  rez
4744    %=    $
4745      xet  t.xet
4746      rez  ?-  i.xet
4747             %34  ['&' 'q' 'u' 'o' 't' ';' rez]
4748             %38  ['&' 'a' 'm' 'p' ';' rez]
4749             %39  ['&' '#' '3' '9' ';' rez]
4750             %60  ['&' 'l' 't' ';' rez]
4751             %62  ['&' 'g' 't' ';' rez]
4752             *    [i.xet rez]
4753           ==
```

```
4754      ==
4755    ::                                              ::  ++many:en-xml:html
4756    ++  many                                        ::  nodelist to tape
4757    |=  [lix=(list manx) rez=tape]
4758    |-  ^-  tape
4759    ?~  lix  rez
4760    (apex i.lix $(lix t.lix))
4761    ::                                              ::  ++name:en-xml:html
4762    ++  name                                        ::  name to tape
4763    |=  man=mane  ^-  tape
4764    ?@  man  (trip man)
4765    (weld (trip -.man) `tape`['.' (trip +.man)])
4766    ::                                              ::  ++clot:en-xml:html
4767    ++  clot  ~+                                    ::  self-closing tags
4768    %~  has  in
4769    %-  silt  ^-  (list term)  :~
4770      %area  %base  %br  %col  %command  %embed  %hr  %img  %inputt
4771      %keygen  %link  %meta  %param    %source   %track  %wbr
4772    ==
4773    --  ::en-xml
4774  ::                                                ::  ++de-xml:html
4775  ++  de-xml                                        ::  xml parser
4776  =<  |=(a=cord (rush a apex))
4777  |_  ent=_`(map term @t)`[[%apos '\''] ~ ~]
4778    ::                                              ::  ++apex:de-xml:html
4779    ++  apex                                        ::  top level
4780    =+  spa=;~(pose comt whit)
4781    %+  knee  *manx  |.  ~+
4782    %+  ifix
4783      [;~(plug (more spa decl) (star spa)) (star spa)]
4784    ;~  pose
4785      %+  sear  |=([a=marx b=marl c=mane] ?.(=(c n.a) ~ (some [a b])))
4786        ;~(plug head many tail)
4787      empt
4788    ==
4789    ::                                              ::  ++attr:de-xml:html
4790    ++  attr                                        ::  attributes
4791    %+  knee  *mart  |.  ~+
4792    %-  star
4793    ;~  plug
4794      ;~(pfix (plus whit) name)
4795      ;~  pose
4796        %+  ifix
4797          :_  doq
4798          ;~(plug (ifix [. .]:(star whit) tis) doq)
4799        (star ;~(less doq escp))
4800      ::
4801        %+  ifix
4802          :_  soq
4803          ;~(plug (ifix [. .]:(star whit) tis) soq)
4804        (star ;~(less soq escp))
4805      ::
4806        (easy ~)
4807      ==
4808    ==
4809    ::                                              ::  ++cdat:de-xml:html
4810    ++  cdat                                        ::  CDATA section
4811    %+  cook
```

```hoon
4812        |=(a=tape ^-(mars ;/(a)))
4813      %+  ifix
4814      [(jest '<![CDATA[') (jest ']]>')]
4815      %-  star
4816      ;~(less (jest ']]>') next)
4817    ::                                              ::  ++chrd:de-xml:html
4818    ++  chrd                                        ::  character data
4819      %+  cook  |=(a=tape ^-(mars ;/(a)))
4820      (plus ;~(pose (just `@`10) escp))
4821    ::                                              ::  ++comt:de-xml:html
4822    ++  comt                                        ::  comments
4823      =-  (ifix [(jest '<!--') (jest '-->')] (star -))
4824      ;~  pose
4825        ;~(less hep prn)
4826        whit
4827        ;~(less (jest '-->') hep)
4828      ==
4829    ::
4830    ++  decl                                        ::  ++decl:de-xml:html
4831      %+  ifix                                      ::  XML declaration
4832      [(jest '<?xml') (jest '?>')]
4833      %-  star
4834      ;~(less (jest '?>') prn)
4835    ::                                              ::  ++escp:de-xml:html
4836    ++  escp                                        ::
4837      ;~(pose ;~(less gal gar pam prn) enty)
4838    ::                                              ::  ++enty:de-xml:html
4839    ++  enty                                        ::  entity
4840      %+  ifix  pam^mic
4841      ;~  pose
4842        =+  def=^+(ent (my:nl [%gt '>'] [%lt '<'] [%amp '&'] [%quot '"'] ~))
4843        %+  sear  ~(get by (~(uni by def) ent))
4844        (cook crip ;~(plug alf (stun 1^31 aln)))
4845        %+  cook  |=(a=@c ?:((gth a 0x10.ffff) '' (tuft a)))
4846        =<  ;~(pfix hax ;~(pose - +))
4847        :-  (bass 10 (stun 1^8 dit))
4848        (bass 16 ;~(pfix (mask "xX") (stun 1^8 hit)))
4849      ==
4850    ::                                              ::  ++empt:de-xml:html
4851    ++  empt                                        ::  self-closing tag
4852      %+  ifix  [gal (jest '/>')]
4853      ;~(plug ;~(plug name attr) (cold ~ (star whit)))
4854    ::                                              ::  ++head:de-xml:html
4855    ++  head                                        ::  opening tag
4856      (ifix [gal gar] ;~(plug name attr))
4857    ::                                              ::  ++many:de-xml:html
4858    ++  many                                        ::  contents
4859      ;~(pfix (star comt) (star ;~(sfix ;~(pose apex chrd cdat) (star comt))))
4860    ::                                              ::  ++name:de-xml:html
4861    ++  name                                        ::  tag name
4862      =+  ^=  chx
4863          %+  cook  crip
4864          ;~  plug
4865            ;~(pose cab alf)
4866            (star ;~(pose cab dot alp))
4867          ==
4868      ;~(pose ;~(plug ;~(sfix chx col) chx) chx)
4869    ::                                              ::  ++tail:de-xml:html
```

```
4870      ++  tail                                         ::  closing tag
4871        (ifix [(jest '</') gar] name)
4872      ::                                              ::  ++whit:de-xml:html
4873      ++  whit                                        ::  whitespace
4874        (mask ~[' ' `@`0x9 `@`0xa])
4875      --  ::de-xml
4876    ::                                                ::  ++en-urlt:html
4877    ++  en-urlt                                       ::  url encode
4878      |=  tep=tape
4879      ^-  tape
4880      %-  zing
4881      %+  turn  tep
4882      |=  tap=char
4883      =+  xen=|=(tig=@ ?:((gte tig 10) (add tig 55) (add tig '0')))
4884      ?:  ?|  &((gte tap 'a') (lte tap 'z'))
4885              &((gte tap 'A') (lte tap 'Z'))
4886              &((gte tap '0') (lte tap '9'))
4887              =('.' tap)
4888              =('-' tap)
4889              =('~' tap)
4890              =('_' tap)
4891          ==
4892        [tap ~]
4893      ['%' (xen (rsh [0 4] tap)) (xen (end [0 4] tap)) ~]
4894    ::                                                ::  ++de-urlt:html
4895    ++  de-urlt                                       ::  url decode
4896      |=  tep=tape
4897      ^-  (unit tape)
4898      ?~  tep  [~ ~]
4899      ?:  =('%' i.tep)
4900        ?.  ?=([@ @ *] t.tep)  ~
4901        =+  nag=(mix i.t.tep (lsh 3 i.t.t.tep))
4902        =+  val=(rush nag hex:ag)
4903        ?~  val  ~
4904        =+  nex=$(tep t.t.t.tep)
4905        ?~(nex ~ [~ [`@`u.val u.nex]])
4906      =+  nex=$(tep t.tep)
4907      ?~(nex ~ [~ i.tep u.nex])
4908    ::                                                ::  ++en-purl:html
4909    ++  en-purl                                       ::  print purl
4910      =<  |=(pul=purl `tape`(apex %& pul))
4911      |%
4912      ::                                              ::  ++apex:en-purl:html
4913      ++  apex                                        ::
4914        |=  qur=quri  ^-  tape
4915        ?-  -.qur
4916          %&  (weld (head p.p.qur) `tape`$(qur [%| +.p.qur]))
4917          %|  ['/' (weld (body p.qur) (tail q.qur))]
4918        ==
4919      ::                                              ::  ++apix:en-purl:html
4920      ++  apix                                        ::  purf to tape
4921        |=  purf
4922        (weld (apex %& p) ?~(q "" `tape`['#' (trip u.q)]))
4923      ::                                              ::  ++body:en-purl:html
4924      ++  body                                        ::
4925        |=  pok=pork  ^-  tape
4926        ?~  q.pok  ~
4927        |-
```

```
4928      =+  seg=(en-urlt (trip i.q.pok))
4929      ?~  t.q.pok
4930        ?~(p.pok seg (welp seg '.' (trip u.p.pok)))
4931      (welp seg '/' $(q.pok t.q.pok))
4932    ::                                              ::  ++head:en-purl:html
4933    ++  head                                        ::
4934      |=  har=hart
4935      ^-  tape
4936      ;:  weld
4937        ?:(&(p.har !?=(hoke r.har)) "https://" "http://")
4938        ::
4939        ?-  -.r.har
4940          %|  (trip (rsh 3 (scot %if p.r.har)))
4941          %&  =+  rit=(flop p.r.har)
4942              |-  ^-  tape
4943              ?~  rit  ~
4944              (weld (trip i.rit) ?~(t.rit "" `tape`['.' $(rit t.rit)]))
4945        ==
4946        ::
4947        ?~(q.har ~ `tape`[':' ((d-co:co 1) u.q.har)])
4948      ==
4949    ::                                              ::  ++tail:en-purl:html
4950    ++  tail                                        ::
4951      |=  kay=quay
4952      ^-  tape
4953      ?:  =(~ kay)  ~
4954      :-  '?'
4955      |-  ^-  tape
4956      ?~  kay  ~
4957      ;:  welp
4958        (en-urlt (trip p.i.kay))
4959        ?~(q.i.kay ~ ['=' (en-urlt (trip q.i.kay))])
4960        ?~(t.kay ~ `tape`['&' $(kay t.kay)])
4961      ==
4962    --  ::
4963  ::                                                ::  ++de-purl:html
4964  ++  de-purl                                       ::  url+header parser
4965    =<  |=(a=cord `(unit purl)`(rush a auri))
4966    |%
4967    ::                                              ::  ++deft:de-purl:html
4968    ++  deft                                        ::  parse url extension
4969      |=  rax=(list @t)
4970      |-  ^-  pork
4971      ?~  rax
4972        [~ ~]
4973      ?^  t.rax
4974        [p.pok [ire q.pok]]:[pok=$(rax t.rax) ire=i.rax]
4975      =/  raf=(like term)
4976        %-  ;~  sfix
4977              %+  sear
4978                |=(a=@ ((sand %ta) (crip (flop (trip a)))))
4979              (cook |=(a=tape (rap 3 ^-((list @) a))) (star aln))
4980              dot
4981            ==
4982        [1^1 (flop (trip i.rax))]
4983      ?~  q.raf
4984        [~ [i.rax ~]]
4985      =+  `[ext=term [@ @] fyl=tape]`u.q.raf
```

```
    :-   `ext
    ?:(=(~ fyl) ~ [(crip (flop fyl)) ~])
  ::                                          ::  ++apat:de-purl:html
  ++  apat                                    ::  2396 abs_path
    %+  cook  deft
    ;~(pfix fas (more fas smeg))
  ::                                          ::  ++aurf:de-purl:html
  ++  aurf                                    ::  2396 with fragment
    %+  cook  |~(a=purf a)
    ;~(plug auri (punt ;~(pfix hax (cook crip (star pque)))))
  ::                                          ::  ++auri:de-purl:html
  ++  auri                                    ::  2396 URL
    ;~  plug
      ;~(plug htts thor)
      ;~(plug ;~(pose apat (easy *pork)) yque)
    ==
  ::                                          ::  ++auru:de-purl:html
  ++  auru                                    ::  2396 with maybe user
    %+  cook
      |=  $:  a=[p=? q=(unit user) r=[(unit @ud) host]]
              b=[pork quay]
          ==
      ^-  (pair (unit user) purl)
      [q.a [[p.a r.a] b]]
    ::
    ;~  plug
      ;~(plug htts (punt ;~(sfix urt:ab pat)) thor)
      ;~(plug ;~(pose apat (easy *pork)) yque)
    ==
  ::                                          ::  ++htts:de-purl:html
  ++  htts                                    ::  scheme
    %+  sear  ~(get by (malt `(list (pair term ?))`[http+| https+& ~]))
    ;~(sfix scem ;~(plug col fas fas))
  ::                                          ::  ++cock:de-purl:html
  ++  cock                                    ::  cookie
    %+  most  ;~(plug mic ace)
    ;~(plug toke ;~(pfix tis tosk))
  ::                                          ::  ++dlab:de-purl:html
  ++  dlab                                    ::  2396 domainlabel
    %+  sear
      |=  a=@ta
      ?.(=('-' (rsh [3 (dec (met 3 a))] a)) [~ u=a] ~)
    %+  cook  |=(a=tape (crip (cass a)))
    ;~(plug aln (star alp))
  ::                                          ::  ++fque:de-purl:html
  ++  fque                                    ::  normal query field
    (cook crip (plus pquo))
  ::                                          ::  ++fquu:de-purl:html
  ++  fquu                                    ::  optional query field
    (cook crip (star pquo))
  ::                                          ::  ++pcar:de-purl:html
  ++  pcar                                    ::  2396 path char
    ;~(pose pure pesc psub col pat)
  ::                                          ::  ++pcok:de-purl:html
  ++  pcok                                    ::  cookie char
    ;~(less bas mic com doq prn)
  ::                                          ::  ++pesc:de-purl:html
  ++  pesc                                    ::  2396 escaped
```

```
5044      ;~(pfix cen mes)
5045    ::                                        ::  ++pold:de-purl:html
5046    ++  pold                                  ::
5047    (cold ' ' (just '+'))
5048    ::                                        ::  ++pque:de-purl:html
5049    ++  pque                                  ::  3986 query char
5050      ;~(pose pcar fas wut)
5051    ::                                        ::  ++pquo:de-purl:html
5052    ++  pquo                                  ::  normal query char
5053      ;~(pose pure pesc pold fas wut col com)
5054    ::                                        ::  ++pure:de-purl:html
5055    ++  pure                                  ::  2396 unreserved
5056      ;~(pose aln hep cab dot zap sig tar soq pal par)
5057    ::                                        ::  ++psub:de-purl:html
5058    ++  psub                                  ::  3986 sub-delims
5059      ;~  pose
5060        zap  buc  pam  soq  pal  par
5061        tar  lus  com  mic  tis
5062      ==
5063    ::                                        ::  ++ptok:de-purl:html
5064    ++  ptok                                  ::  2616 token
5065      ;~  pose
5066        aln  zap  hax  buc  cen  pam  soq  tar  lus
5067        hep  dot  ket  cab  tic  bar  sig
5068      ==
5069    ::                                        ::  ++scem:de-purl:html
5070    ++  scem                                  ::  2396 scheme
5071      %+  cook  |=(a=tape (crip (cass a)))
5072      ;~(plug alf (star ;~(pose aln lus hep dot)))
5073    ::                                        ::  ++smeg:de-purl:html
5074    ++  smeg                                  ::  2396 segment
5075    (cook crip (star pcar))
5076    ::                                        ::  ++tock:de-purl:html
5077    ++  tock                                  ::  6265 raw value
5078    (cook crip (plus pcok))
5079    ::                                        ::  ++tosk:de-purl:html
5080    ++  tosk                                  ::  6265 quoted value
5081      ;~(pose tock (ifix [doq doq] tock))
5082    ::                                        ::  ++toke:de-purl:html
5083    ++  toke                                  ::  2616 token
5084    (cook crip (plus ptok))
5085    ::                                        ::  ++thor:de-purl:html
5086    ++  thor                                  ::  2396 host+port
5087      %+  cook  |*([* *] [+<+ +<-])
5088      ;~  plug
5089        thos
5090        ;~((bend) (easy ~) ;~(pfix col dim:ag))
5091      ==
5092    ::                                        ::  ++thos:de-purl:html
5093    ++  thos                                  ::  2396 host, no local
5094      ;~  plug
5095        ;~  pose
5096          %+  stag  %&
5097          %+  sear                            ::  LL parser weak here
5098            |=  a=(list @t)
5099            =+  b=(flop a)
5100            ?>  ?=(^ b)
5101            =+  c=(end 3 i.b)
```

```
          ?.(&((gte c 'a') (lte c 'z')) ~ [~ u=b])
        (most dot dlab)
      ::
      %+  stag  %|
      =+  tod=(ape:ag ted:ab)
      %+  bass  256
      ;~(plug tod (stun [3 3] ;~(pfix dot tod)))
    ==
  ==
  ::                                              ::  ++yque:de-purl:html
  ++  yque                                        ::  query ending
    ;~  pose
    ;~(pfix wut yquy)
    (easy ~)
  ==
  ::                                              ::  ++yquy:de-purl:html
  ++  yquy                                        ::  query
    ;~  pose
      ::  proper query
      ::
      %+  more
        ;~(pose pam mic)
      ;~(plug fque ;~(pose ;~(pfix tis fquu) (easy '')))
      ::
      ::  funky query
      ::
      %+  cook
        |=(a=tape [[%$ (crip a)] ~])
      (star pque)
    ==
  ::                                              ::  ++zest:de-purl:html
  ++  zest                                        ::  2616 request-uri
    ;~  pose
    (stag %& (cook |=(a=purl a) auri))
    (stag %| ;~(plug apat yque))
  ==
  --  ::de-purl
::  +en-turf: encode +turf as a TLD-last domain string
::
++  en-turf
  |=  =turf
  ^-  @t
  (rap 3 (flop (join '.' turf)))
::  +de-turf: parse a TLD-last domain string into a TLD first +turf
::
++  de-turf
  |=  host=@t
  ^-  (unit turf)
  %+  rush  host
  %+  sear
    |=  =host:eyre
    ?.(?=(%& -.host) ~ (some p.host))
  thos:de-purl:html
::
::  MOVEME
::                                                ::  ++fuel:html
++  fuel                                          ::  parse urbit fcgi
    |=  [bem=beam ced=noun:cred quy=quer]
```

```
5160        ^-  epic
5161        =+  qix=|-(`quay`?~(quy quy [[p q]:quy $(quy t.quy)]))
5162        [(malt qix) ;;(cred ced) bem]
5163    ::
5164    ++  hiss-to-request
5165      |=  =hiss
5166      ^-  request:http
5167      ::
5168      :*  ?-  p.q.hiss
5169            %conn  %'CONNECT'
5170            %delt  %'DELETE'
5171            %get   %'GET'
5172            %head  %'HEAD'
5173            %opts  %'OPTIONS'
5174            %post  %'POST'
5175            %put   %'PUT'
5176            %trac  %'TRACE'
5177          ==
5178      ::
5179        (crip (en-purl:html p.hiss))
5180      ::
5181        ^-  header-list:http
5182        ~!  q.q.hiss
5183        %+  turn  ~(tap by q.q.hiss)
5184        |=  [a=@t b=(list @t)]
5185        ^-  [@t @t]
5186        ?>  ?=(^ b)
5187        [a i.b]
5188      ::
5189        r.q.hiss
5190      ==
5191    --  ::  html
5192  ::                                                          ::
5193  ::::                              ++wired                    ::  wire formatting
5194    ::                                                        ::::
5195  ++  wired  ^?
5196    |%
5197    ::                                                        ::  ++dray:wired
5198    ++  dray                                                  ::  load tuple in path
5199      ::
5200      ::  .=  ~[p=~.ack q=~.~sarnel r=~..y]
5201      ::  (dray ~[p=%tas q=%p r=%f] %ack ~sarnel &)
5202      ::
5203      =-  |*  [a=[@tas (pole @tas)] b=*]  ^-  (paf a)
5204          =>  .(b `,(tup -.a +.a)`b)
5205          ?~  +.a  [(scot -.a b) ~]
5206          [(scot -.a -.b) `,(paf +.a)`(..$ +.a +.b)]
5207      :-  paf=|*(a=(pole) ?~(a ,~ ,[(odo:raid ,-.a(. %ta)) ,(..$ +.a)]))
5208      ^=  tup
5209      |*  [a=@tas b=(pole @tas)]
5210      =+  c=(odo:raid a)
5211      ?~(b c ,[c (..$ ,-.b ,+.b)])
5212    ::                                                        ::  ++raid:wired
5213    ++  raid                                                  ::  demand path odors
5214      ::
5215      ::  .=  [p=%ack q=~sarnel r=&]
5216      ::  (raid /ack/~sarnel+.y p=%tas q=%p r=%f ~)
5217      ::
```

```
5218      |*  [a=path b=[@tas (pole @tas)]]
5219      =*  fog  (odo -.b)
5220      ?-  +.b  `fog`(slav -.b -.a)
5221      [`fog`(slav -.b -.a) (..$ +.a +.b)]
5222    ^=  odo
5223    |*  a=@tas
5224    |=  b=*
5225    =-  a(, (- b))                       ::  preserve face
5226    ?+  a    @
5227      %c  @c  %da  @da  %dr  @dr  %f   @f   %if  @if  %is  @is  %p   @p
5228      %u  @u  %uc  @uc  %ub  @ub  %ui  @ui  %ux  @ux  %uv  @uv  %uw  @uw
5229      %s  @s  %t   @t   %ta  @ta  %tas @tas
5230    ==
5231  ::  ::                                 ::  ++read:wired
5232  ::  ++  read                           ::  parse odored path
5233  ::    =<  |*([a=path b=[@tas (pole @tas)]] ((+> b) a))
5234  ::    |*  b=[@tas (pole @tas)]
5235  ::    |=  a=path
5236  ::    ?~  a  ~
5237  ::    =+  hed=(slaw -.b i.a)
5238  ::    =*  fog  (odo:raid -.b)
5239  ::    ?~  +.b
5240  ::      ^-  (unit fog)
5241  ::      ?^(+.a ~ hed)
5242  ::    ^-  (unit [fog _(need *(..^$ +.b))])
5243  ::    (both hed ((..^$ +.b) +.a))
5244    --  ::wired
5245  ::                                     ::
5246  ::::                 ++title           ::  (2j) identity
5247  ::                                     ::::
5248  ++  title
5249    ::  deep core: for vane use, with $roof for scrying
5250    ::
5251    ::    TODO: refactor to share high-level gates like +saxo
5252    ::          among the three cores
5253    ::
5254    =>  |%
5255      ++  sein
5256      |=  [rof=roof pov=path our=ship now=@da who=ship]
5257      ;;  ship
5258      =<  q.q  %-  need  %-  need
5259      (rof [~ ~] pov %j `beam`[[our %sein %da now] /(scot %p who)])
5260      --
5261    ::  middle core: stateless queries for default numeric sponsorship
5262    ::
5263    =>  |%
5264      ::                                 ::  ++clan:title
5265      ++  clan                           ::  ship to rank
5266      |=  who=ship
5267      ^-  rank
5268      =/  wid  (met 3 who)
5269      ?:  (lte wid 1)    %czar
5270      ?:  =(2 wid)       %king
5271      ?:  (lte wid 4)    %duke
5272      ?:  (lte wid 8)    %earl
5273      ?>  (lte wid 16)   %pawn
5274      ::                                 ::  ++rank:title
5275      +$  rank  ?(%czar %king %duke %earl %pawn)   ::  ship width class
```

```
5276        ::                                              ::  ++name:title
5277        ++  name                                        ::  identity
5278        |=  who=ship
5279        ^-  ship
5280        ?.  ?=(%earl (clan who))  who
5281        (sein who)
5282        ::                                              ::  ++saxo:title
5283        ++  saxo                                        ::  autocanon
5284        |=  who=ship
5285        ^-  (list ship)
5286        =/  dad  (sein who)
5287        [who ?:(=(who dad) ~ $(who dad))]
5288        ::                                              ::  ++sein:title
5289        ++  sein                                        ::  autoboss
5290        |=  who=ship
5291        ^-  ship
5292        =/  mir  (clan who)
5293        ?-  mir
5294          %czar  who
5295          %king  (end 3 who)
5296          %duke  (end 4 who)
5297          %earl  (end 5 who)
5298          %pawn  (end 4 who)
5299        ==
5300      --
5301  ::  surface core: for userspace use, with .^
5302  ::
5303  |%
5304  ::                                                    ::  ++cite:title
5305  ++  cite                                              ::  render ship
5306    |=  who=@p
5307    ^-  tape
5308    =/  wid  (met 4 who)
5309    ?:  (lte wid 2)  (scow %p who)
5310    ?:  (lte wid 4)
5311      =/  nom  (scow %p (end 5 who))
5312      :(weld (scag 7 nom) "^" (slag 8 nom))
5313    %-  trip
5314    %+  rap  3
5315    :~  '~'
5316        (tos:po (cut 3 [(dec (mul wid 2)) 1] who))
5317        (tod:po (cut 3 [(mul (dec wid) 2) 1] who))
5318        '_'
5319        (tos:po (cut 3 [1 1] who))
5320        (tod:po (end 3 who))
5321    ==
5322  ::                                                    ::  ++saxo:title
5323  ++  saxo                                              ::  autocanon
5324    |=  [our=ship now=@da who=ship]
5325    .^  (list ship)
5326        %j
5327        /(scot %p our)/saxo/(scot %da now)/(scot %p who)
5328    ==
5329  ::                                                    ::  ++sein:title
5330  ++  sein                                              ::  autoboss
5331    |=  [our=ship now=@da who=ship]
5332    .^  ship
5333        %j
```

```
          /(scot %p our)/sein/(scot %da now)/(scot %p who)
     ==
::   +team was created with two meanings:
::      A. her / her moon
::      B. whoever should be able to control her ship
::
::   these two things aren't obviously equal anymore,
::   and it's more important for +team to satisfy B than A,
::   so now +team just means "her".
::
::   (ships can definitely be trusted to control themselves)
::                                                  ::  ++team:title
++   team                                           ::  her
   |=  [her=ship who=ship]
   ^-  ?
   =(her who)
::                                                  ::  ++moon:title
++   moon                                           ::  her moon
   |=  [her=ship who=ship]
   ^-  ?
   &(=(%earl (clan who)) =(her (^sein who)))
   --  ::title
::                                                  ::
::::                            ++milly             ::  (2k) milliseconds
   ::                                               ::::
++  milly  ^|
   |_  now=@da
   ::                                               ::  ++around:milly
   ++   around                                      ::  relative msec
      |=  wen=@da
      ^-  @tas
      ?:  =(wen now)   %now
      ?:  (gth wen now)
        (cat 3 (scot %ud (msec (sub wen now))) %ms)
      (cat 3 '-' $(now wen, wen now))
   ::
   ++  about                                        ::  ++about:milly
      |=  wun=(unit @da)                            ::  unit relative msec
      ^-  @tas
      ?~(wun %no (around u.wun))
   ::                                               ::  ++mill:milly
   ++  mill                                         ::  msec diff
      |=  one=@dr
      ^-  @tas
      ?:  =(`@`0 one)   '0ms'
      (cat 3 (scot %ud (msec one)) %ms)
   ::                                               ::  ++msec:milly
   ++  msec                                         ::  @dr to @ud ms
      |=(a=@dr `@ud`(div a (div ~s1 1.000)))
   ::                                               ::  ++mull:milly
   ++  mull                                         ::  unit msec diff
      |=  une=(unit @dr)
      ^-  @tas
      ?~(une %no (mill u.une))
   --
::
::::
   ::
```

```
5392  ++  contain  ^?
5393    |%
5394    ::  +by-clock: interface core for a cache using the clock replacement algorithm
5395    ::
5396    ::    Presents an interface for a mapping, but somewhat specialized, and with
5397    ::    stateful accessors. The clock's :depth parameter is used as the maximum
5398    ::    freshness that an entry can have. The standard clock algorithm has a depth
5399    ::    of 1, meaning that a single sweep of the arm will delete the entry. For
5400    ::    more scan resistance, :depth can be set to a higher number.
5401    ::
5402    ::    Internally, :clock maintains a :lookup of type
5403    ::    `(map key-type [val=val-type fresh=@ud])`, where :depth.clock is the
5404    ::    maximum value of :fresh. Looking up a key increments its freshness, and a
5405    ::    sweep of the clock arm decrements its freshness.
5406    ::
5407    ::    The clock arm is stored as :queue, which is a `(qeu key-type)`. The head
5408    ::    of the queue represents the position of the clock arm. New entries are
5409    ::    inserted at the tail of the queue. When the clock arm sweeps, it
5410    ::    pops the head off the queue. If the :fresh of the head's entry in :lookup
5411    ::    is 0, remove the entry from the mapping and replace it with the new entry.
5412    ::    Otherwise, decrement the entry's freshness, put it back at the tail of
5413    ::    the queue, and pop the next head off the queue and try again.
5414    ::
5415    ::    Cache entries must be immutable: a key cannot be overwritten with a new
5416    ::    value. This property is enforced for entries currently stored in the
5417    ::    cache, but it is not enforced for previously deleted entries, since we
5418    ::    no longer remember what that key's value was supposed to be.
5419    ::
5420    ++  by-clock
5421    |*  [key-type=mold val-type=mold]
5422    |_  clock=(clock key-type val-type)
5423    ::  +get: looks up a key, marking it as fresh
5424    ::
5425    ++  get
5426    |=  key=key-type
5427    ^-  [(unit val-type) _clock]
5428    ::
5429    =+  maybe-got=(~(get by lookup.clock) key)
5430    ?~  maybe-got
5431      [~ clock]
5432    ::
5433    =.  clock  (freshen key)
5434    ::
5435    [`val.u.maybe-got clock]
5436    ::  +put: add a new cache entry, possibly removing an old one
5437    ::
5438    ++  put
5439    |=  [key=key-type val=val-type]
5440    ^+  clock
5441    ::  do nothing if our size is 0 so we don't decrement-underflow
5442    ::
5443    ?:  =(0 max-size.clock)
5444      clock
5445    ::  no overwrite allowed, but allow duplicate puts
5446    ::
5447    ?^  existing=(~(get by lookup.clock) key)
5448      ::  val must not change
5449      ::
```

```
    ?>  =(val val.u.existing)
    ::
    (freshen key)
  ::
  =?  clock  =(max-size.clock size.clock)
    evict
  ::
  %_  clock
    size    +(size.clock)
    lookup  (~(put by lookup.clock) key [val 1])
    queue   (~(put to queue.clock) key)
  ==
::  +freshen: increment the protection level on an entry
::
++  freshen
  |=  key=key-type
  ^+  clock
  %_    clock
      lookup
    %+  ~(jab by lookup.clock)  key
    |=  entry=[val=val-type fresh=@ud]
    entry(fresh (min +(fresh.entry) depth.clock))
  ==
::  +resize: changes the maximum size, removing entries if needed
::
++  resize
  |=  new-max=@ud
  ^+  clock
  ::
  =.  max-size.clock  new-max
  ::
  ?:  (gte new-max size.clock)
    clock
  ::
  (trim (sub size.clock new-max))
::  +evict: remove an entry from the cache
::
++  evict
  ^+  clock
  ::
  =.  size.clock  (dec size.clock)
  ::
  |-
  ^+  clock
  ::
  =^  old-key  queue.clock  ~(get to queue.clock)
  =/  old-entry  (~(got by lookup.clock) old-key)
  ::
  ?:  =(0 fresh.old-entry)
    clock(lookup (~(del by lookup.clock) old-key))
  ::
  %_    $
      lookup.clock
    (~(put by lookup.clock) old-key old-entry(fresh (dec fresh.old-entry)))
  ::
      queue.clock
    (~(put to queue.clock) old-key)
  ==
```

```hoon
5508      ::  +trim: remove :count entries from the cache
5509      ::
5510      ++  trim
5511        |=  count=@ud
5512        ^+  clock
5513        ?:  =(0 count)
5514          clock
5515        $(count (dec count), clock evict)
5516      ::  +purge: removes all cache entries
5517      ::
5518      ++  purge
5519        ^+  clock
5520        %_  clock
5521          lookup  ~
5522          queue   ~
5523          size    0
5524        ==
5525      --
5526  ::  +to-capped-queue: interface door for +capped-queue
5527  ::
5528  ::    Provides a queue of a limited size where pushing additional items will
5529  ::    force pop the items at the front of the queue.
5530  ::
5531  ++  to-capped-queue
5532    |*  item-type=mold
5533    |_  queue=(capped-queue item-type)
5534    ::  +put: enqueue :item, possibly popping and producing an old item
5535    ::
5536    ++  put
5537      |=  item=item-type
5538      ^-  [(unit item-type) _queue]
5539      ::   are we already at max capacity?
5540      ::
5541      ?.  =(size.queue max-size.queue)
5542        ::  we're below max capacity, so push and increment size
5543        ::
5544        =.  queue.queue  (~(put to queue.queue) item)
5545        =.  size.queue   +(size.queue)
5546        ::
5547        [~ queue]
5548      ::  max is zero, the oldest item to return is the one which just went in.
5549      ::
5550      ?:  =(~ queue.queue)
5551        [`item queue]
5552      ::  we're at max capacity, so pop before pushing; size is unchanged
5553      ::
5554      =^  oldest  queue.queue  ~(get to queue.queue)
5555      =.  queue.queue          (~(put to queue.queue) item)
5556      ::
5557      [`oldest queue]
5558    ::  +get: pop an item off the queue, adjusting size
5559    ::
5560    ++  get
5561      ^-  [item-type _queue]
5562      ::
5563      =.  size.queue           (dec size.queue)
5564      =^  oldest  queue.queue  ~(get to queue.queue)
5565      ::
```

```
5566       [oldest queue]
5567    ::  change the :max-size of the queue, popping items if necessary
5568    ::
5569    ++  resize
5570      =|  pops=(list item-type)
5571      |=  new-max=@ud
5572      ^+  [pops queue]
5573      ::  we're not overfull, so no need to pop off more items
5574      ::
5575      ?:  (gte new-max size.queue)
5576        [(flop pops) queue(max-size new-max)]
5577      ::  we're above capacity; pop an item off and recurse
5578      ::
5579      =^  oldest  queue  get
5580      ::
5581      $(pops [oldest pops])
5582    --
5583  --
5584  ::                                                      ::
5585  ::::                      ++userlib            ::  (2u) non-vane utils
5586    ::                                                  ::::
5587  ++  userlib  ^?
5588    |%
5589    ::                                                  ::
5590    ::::                    ++chrono:userlib       ::  (2uB) time
5591      ::                                                ::::
5592    ++  chrono  ^?
5593      |%
5594      ::  +from-unix: unix seconds to @da
5595      ::
5596      ++  from-unix
5597        |=  timestamp=@ud
5598        ^-  @da
5599        %+  add  ~1970.1.1
5600        (mul timestamp ~s1)
5601      ::  +from-unix-ms: unix milliseconds to @da
5602      ::
5603      ++  from-unix-ms
5604        |=  timestamp=@ud
5605        ^-  @da
5606        %+  add  ~1970.1.1
5607        (div (mul ~s1 timestamp) 1.000)
5608      ::                                            ::  ++dawn:chrono:
5609      ++  dawn                                      ::  Jan 1 weekday
5610        |=  yer=@ud
5611        =+  yet=(sub yer 1)
5612        %-  mod  :_  7
5613        ;:  add
5614          1
5615          (mul 5 (mod yet 4))
5616          (mul 4 (mod yet 100))
5617          (mul 6 (mod yet 400))
5618        ==
5619      ::                                            ::  ++daws:chrono:
5620      ++  daws                                      ::  date weekday
5621        |=  yed=date
5622        %-  mod  :_  7
5623        %+  add
```

```
5624          (dawn y.yed)
5625          (sub (yawn [y.yed m.yed d.t.yed]) (yawn y.yed 1 1))
5626      ::                                          ::  ++deal:chrono:
5627      ++  deal                                    ::  to leap sec time
5628        |=  yer=@da
5629        =+  n=0
5630        =+  yud=(yore yer)
5631        |-  ^-  date
5632        ?:  (gte yer (add (snag n lef:yu) ~s1))
5633          (yore (year yud(s.t (add n s.t.yud))))
5634        ?:  &((gte yer (snag n lef:yu)) (lth yer (add (snag n lef:yu) ~s1)))
5635          yud(s.t (add +(n) s.t.yud))
5636        ?:  =(+(n) (lent lef:yu))
5637          (yore (year yud(s.t (add +(n) s.t.yud))))
5638        $(n +(n))
5639      ::                                          ::  ++lead:chrono:
5640      ++  lead                                    ::  from leap sec time
5641        |=  ley=date
5642        =+  ler=(year ley)
5643        =+  n=0
5644        |-  ^-  @da
5645        =+  led=(sub ler (mul n ~s1))
5646        ?:  (gte ler (add (snag n les:yu) ~s1))
5647          led
5648        ?:  &((gte ler (snag n les:yu)) (lth ler (add (snag n les:yu) ~s1)))
5649          ?:  =(s.t.ley 60)
5650            (sub led ~s1)
5651          led
5652        ?:  =(+(n) (lent les:yu))
5653          (sub led ~s1)
5654        $(n +(n))
5655      ::                                          ::  ++dust:chrono:
5656      ++  dust                                    ::  print UTC format
5657        |=  yed=date
5658        ^-  tape
5659        =+  wey=(daws yed)
5660        =/  num  (d-co:co 1)  :: print as decimal without dots
5661        =/  pik  |=([n=@u t=wall] `tape`(scag 3 (snag n t)))
5662        ::
5663        "{(pik wey wik:yu)}, ".
5664        "{(num d.t.yed)} {(pik (dec m.yed) mon:yu)} {(num y.yed)} ".
5665        "{(num h.t.yed)}:{(num m.t.yed)}:{(num s.t.yed)} +0000"
5666      ::                                          ::  ++stud:chrono:
5667      ++  stud                                    ::  parse UTC format
5668        =<  |=  a=cord                            ::  expose parsers
5669            %+  biff  (rush a (more sepa elem))
5670            |=  b=(list _(wonk *elem))  ^-  (unit date)
5671            =-  ?.((za:dejs:format -) ~ (some (zp:dejs:format -)))
5672            ^+  =+  [*date u=unit]
5673              *[(u _[a y]) (u _m) (u _d.t) (u _+.t) ~]
5674            :~
5675              |-(?~(b ~ ?.(?=(%y -.i.b) $(b t.b) `+.i.b)))
5676              |-(?~(b ~ ?.(?=(%m -.i.b) $(b t.b) `+.i.b)))
5677              |-(?~(b ~ ?.(?=(%d -.i.b) $(b t.b) `+.i.b)))
5678              |-(?~(b ~ ?.(?=(%t -.i.b) $(b t.b) `+.i.b)))
5679            ==
5680        |%
5681        ::                                          ::  ++snug:stud:chrono:
```

```
5682      ++    snug                                  ::  position in list
5683       |=  a=(list tape)
5684       |=  b=tape
5685       =+  [pos=1 len=(lent b)]
5686       |-  ^-  (unit @u)
5687       ?~  a   ~
5688       ?:  =(b (scag len i.a))
5689         `pos
5690       $(pos +(pos), a t.a)
5691     ::                                            ::  ++sepa:stud:chrono:
5692     ++    sepa                                    ::  separator
5693      ;~(pose ;~(plug com (star ace)) (plus ace))
5694     ::                                            ::  ++elem:stud:chrono:
5695     ++    elem                                    ::  date element
5696      ;~   pose
5697        (stag %t t)  (stag %y y)  (stag %m m)  (stag %d d)
5698        (stag %w w)  (stag %z z)
5699      ==
5700     ::                                            ::  ++y:stud:chrono:
5701     ++  y                                         ::  year
5702      (stag %& (bass 10 (stun 3^4 dit)))
5703     ::                                            ::  ++m:stud:chrono:
5704     ++  m                                         ::  month
5705      (sear (snug mon:yu) (plus alf))
5706     ::                                            ::  ++d:stud:chrono:
5707     ++  d                                         ::  day
5708      (bass 10 (stun 1^2 dit))
5709     ::                                            ::  ++t:stud:chrono:
5710     ++  t                                         ::  hours:minutes:secs
5711       %+  cook  |=([h=@u @ m=@u @ s=@u] ~[h m s])
5712       ;~(plug d col d col d)
5713     ::
5714     ::  XX day of week is currently unchecked, and
5715     ::  timezone outright ignored.
5716     ::                                            ::  ++w:stud:chrono:
5717     ++  w                                         ::  day of week
5718      (sear (snug wik:yu) (plus alf))
5719     ::                                            ::  ++z:stud:chrono:
5720     ++  z                                         ::  time zone
5721      ;~(plug (mask "-+") dd dd)
5722     ::                                            ::  ++dd:stud:chrono:
5723     ++  dd                                        ::  two digits
5724      (bass 10 (stun 2^2 dit))
5725     --  ::
5726   ::                                              ::  ++unm:chrono:userlib
5727   ++  unm                                         ::  Urbit to Unix ms
5728    |=  a=@da
5729    =-  (div (mul - 1.000) ~s1)
5730    (sub (add a (div ~s1 2.000)) ~1970.1.1)
5731   ::                                              ::  ++unt:chrono:userlib
5732   ++  unt                                         ::  Urbit to Unix time
5733    |=  a=@da
5734    (div (sub a ~1970.1.1) ~s1)
5735   ::                                              ::  ++yu:chrono:userlib
5736   ++  yu                                          ::  UTC format constants
5737    |%
5738     ::                                            ::  ++mon:yu:chrono:
5739     ++    mon                                     ::  months
```

```
5740              ^-  (list tape)
5741              :~  "January"  "February"  "March"  "April"  "May"  "June"  "July"
5742                  "August"  "September"  "October"  "November"  "December"
5743              ==
5744          ::                                              ::  ++wik:yu:chrono:
5745          ++  wik                                         ::  weeks
5746              ^-  (list tape)
5747              :~  "Sunday"  "Monday"  "Tuesday"  "Wednesday"  "Thursday"
5748                  "Friday"  "Saturday"
5749              ==
5750          ::                                              ::  ++lef:yu:chrono:
5751          ++  lef                                         ::  leapsecond dates
5752              ^-  (list @da)
5753              :~  ~2016.12.31..23.59.59   ~2015.6.30..23.59.59
5754                  ~2012.6.30..23.59.59    ~2008.12.31..23.59.58
5755                  ~2005.12.31..23.59.57   ~1998.12.31..23.59.56
5756                  ~1997.6.30..23.59.55    ~1995.12.31..23.59.54
5757                  ~1994.6.30..23.59.53    ~1993.6.30..23.59.52
5758                  ~1992.6.30..23.59.51    ~1990.12.31..23.59.50
5759                  ~1989.12.31..23.59.49   ~1987.12.31..23.59.48
5760                  ~1985.6.30..23.59.47    ~1983.6.30..23.59.46
5761                  ~1982.6.30..23.59.45    ~1981.6.30..23.59.44
5762                  ~1979.12.31..23.59.43   ~1978.12.31..23.59.42
5763                  ~1977.12.31..23.59.41   ~1976.12.31..23.59.40
5764                  ~1975.12.31..23.59.39   ~1974.12.31..23.59.38
5765                  ~1973.12.31..23.59.37   ~1972.12.31..23.59.36
5766                  ~1972.6.30..23.59.35
5767              ==
5768          ::
5769          ::  +les:yu:chrono: leapsecond days
5770          ::
5771          ::      https://www.ietf.org/timezones/data/leap-seconds.list
5772          ::
5773          ++  les
5774              ^-  (list @da)
5775              :~  ~2017.1.1  ~2015.7.1  ~2012.7.1  ~2009.1.1  ~2006.1.1  ~1999.1.1
5776                  ~1997.7.1  ~1996.1.1  ~1994.7.1  ~1993.7.1  ~1992.7.1  ~1991.1.1
5777                  ~1990.1.1  ~1988.1.1  ~1985.7.1  ~1983.7.1  ~1982.7.1  ~1981.7.1
5778                  ~1980.1.1  ~1979.1.1  ~1978.1.1  ~1977.1.1  ~1976.1.1  ~1975.1.1
5779                  ~1974.1.1  ~1973.1.1  ~1972.7.1
5780              ==
5781          --  ::yu
5782        --  ::chrono
5783  ::                                                      ::
5784  ::::                        ++space:userlib             ::  (2uC) file utils
5785    ::                                                    ::::
5786  ++  space  ^?
5787    =,  clay
5788    |%
5789    ::                                                    ::  ++feel:space:userlib
5790    ++  feel                                              ::  simple file write
5791    |=  [pax=path val=cage]
5792    ^-  miso
5793    =+  dir=.^(arch %cy pax)
5794    ?~  fil.dir  [%ins val]
5795    [%mut val]
5796    ::                                                    ::  ++file:space:userlib
5797    ++  file                                              ::  simple file load
```

```
      |=  pax=path
      ^-  (unit)
      =+  dir=.^(arch %cy pax)
      ?~(fil.dir ~ [~ .^(* %cx pax)])
    ::                                      ::  ++foal:space:userlib
    ++  foal                                ::  high-level write
      |=  [pax=path val=cage]
      ^-  toro
      ?>  ?=([* * * *] pax)
      [i.t.pax [%& [[[t.t.t.pax (feel pax val)] ~]]]]
    ::                                      ::  ++fray:space:userlib
    ++  fray                                ::  high-level delete
      |=  pax=path
      ^-  toro
      ?>  ?=([* * * *] pax)
      [i.t.pax [%& [[[t.t.t.pax [%del ~]] ~]]]]
    ::                                      ::  ++furl:space:userlib
    ++  furl                                ::  unify changes
      |=  [one=toro two=toro]
      ^-  toro
      ~|  %furl
      ?>  ?&  =(p.one p.two)                ::  same path
              &(?=(%& -.q.one) ?=(%& -.q.two))   ::  both deltas
          ==
      [p.one [%& (weld p.q.one p.q.two)]]
    --  ::space
::                                          ::
::::                    ++unix:userlib      ::  (2uD) unix line-list
  ::                                        ::::
++  unix  ^?
  |%
    ::                                      ::  ++lune:unix:userlib
    ++  lune                                ::  cord by unix line
      ~%  %lune  ..part  ~
      |=  txt=@t
      ?~  txt
        ^-  (list @t)  ~
      =+  [byt=(rip 3 txt) len=(met 3 txt)]
      =|  [lin=(list @t) off=@]
      ^-  (list @t)
      %-  flop
      |-  ^+  lin
      ?:  =(off len)
        ~|  %noeol  !!
      ?:  =((snag off byt) 10)
        ?:  =(+(off) len)
          [(rep 3 (scag off byt)) lin]
        %=  $
          lin  [(rep 3 (scag off byt)) lin]
          byt  (slag +(off) byt)
          len  (sub len +(off))
          off  0
        ==
      $(off +(off))
    ::                                      ::  ++nule:unix:userlib
    ++  nule                                ::  lines to unix cord
      ~%  %nule  ..part  ~
      |=  lin=(list @t)
```

```
      ^-  @t
      %+  can  3
      %+  turn  lin
      |=  t=@t
      [+((met 3 t)) (cat 3 t 10)]
      --
  ::                                              ::
  ::::                      ++scanf:userlib        ::  (2uF) exterpolation
    ::                                            ::::
  ++  scanf
    =<  |*  [tape (pole _;/(*[$^(rule tape)]))]    ::  formatted scan
        =>  .(+< [a b]=+<)
        (scan a (parsf b))
    |%
    ::                                            ::  ++parsf:scanf:
    ++  parsf                                      ::  make parser from:
      |*  a=(pole _;/(*[$^(rule tape)]))           ::  ;"chars{rule}chars"
      =-  (cook - (boil (norm a)))
      |*  (list)
      ?~  +<  ~
      ?~  t  i
      [i $(+< t)]
    ::
    ::  .=  (boil ~[[& dim] [| ", "] [& dim]]:ag)
    ::  ;~(plug dim ;~(pfix com ace ;~(plug dim (easy)))):ag
    ::
    ::                                            ::  ++boil:scanf:userlib
    ++  boil                                       ::
      |*  (list (each rule tape))
      ?~  +<  (easy ~)
      ?:  ?=(%| -.i)  ;~(pfix (jest (crip p.i)) $(+< t))
      %+  cook  |*([* *] [i t]=+<)
      ;~(plug p.i $(+< t))
    ::
    ::  .=  (norm [;"{n}, {n}"]:n=dim:ag)  ~[[& dim] [| ", "] [& dim]]:ag
    ::
    ::                                            ::  ++norm:scanf:userlib
    ++  norm                                       ::
      |*  (pole _;/(*[$^(rule tape)]))
      ?~  +<  ~
      =>  .(+< [i=+<- t=+<+])
      :_  t=$(+< t)
      =+  rul=->->.i
      ^=  i
      ?~  rul      [%| p=rul]
      ?~  +.rul    [%| p=rul]
      ?@  &2.rul   [%| p=;;(tape rul)]
      [%& p=rul]
    --  ::scanf
  --
  ::  +harden: coerce %soft $hobo or pass-through
  ::
  ++  harden
    |*  task=mold
    |=  wrapped=(hobo task)
    ^-  task
    ?.  ?=(%soft -.wrapped)
      wrapped
```

```
;;(task +.wrapped)
::
::
++  balk
  =<  bulk
  !:
  |%
  +$  bulk
    $:  [her=ship rif=rift lyf=life]
        [van=@ta car=@ta cas=case]
        spr=spur
    ==
  ::
  ++  de-part
    |=  [=ship =rift =life =(pole knot)]
    ^-  (unit bulk)
    ?.  ?=([van=@ car=@ cas=@ spr=*] pole)  ~
    ?~  cas=(de-case cas.pole)   ~
    :-  ~
    :*  [ship rift life]
        [van.pole car.pole u.cas]
        spr.pole
    ==
  ::
  ++  de-path-soft
    |=  =(pole knot)
    ^-  (unit bulk)
    ::  [ship rift life vane care case path]
    ?.  ?=([her=@ rif=@ lyf=@ van=@ car=@ cas=@ spr=*] pole)
        ~
    ?~  her=(slaw %p her.pole)   ~
    ?~  rif=(slaw %ud rif.pole)  ~
    ?~  lyf=(slaw %ud lyf.pole)  ~
    ?~  cas=(de-case cas.pole)   ~
    :-  ~
    :*  [u.her u.rif u.lyf]
        [van.pole car.pole u.cas]
        spr.pole
    ==
  ::
  ++  de-path
    |=  =path
    ^-  bulk
    (need (de-path-soft +<))
  ::
  ++  en-path
    |=  =bulk
    ^-  path
    :*  (scot %p her.bulk)
        (scot %ud rif.bulk)
        (scot %ud lyf.bulk)
        van.bulk
        car.bulk
        (scot cas.bulk)
        spr.bulk
    ==
  ::
  ++  as-omen
```

```
5972      |=  =bulk
5973      ^-  omen
5974      =/  [des=desk pax=path]
5975        ?^  spr.bulk  spr.bulk
5976        [%$ ~]
5977      =/  bem=beam  =,(bulk [[her des cas] pax])
5978      =+  vis=(cat 3 van.bulk car.bulk)
5979      [vis bem]
5980    --
5981  --
```

Ames

```
::    Ames extends Arvo's %pass/%give move semantics across the network.
::
::    Ames receives packets as Arvo events and emits packets as Arvo
::    effects.  The runtime is responsible for transferring the bytes in
::    an Ames packet across a physical network to another ship.
::
::    The runtime tells Ames which physical address a packet came from,
::    represented as an opaque atom.  Ames can emit a packet effect to
::    one of those opaque atoms or to the Urbit address of a galaxy
::    (root node), which the runtime is responsible for translating to a
::    physical address.  One runtime implementation sends UDP packets
::    using IPv4 addresses for ships and DNS lookups for galaxies, but
::    other implementations may overlay over other kinds of networks.
::
::    A local vane can pass Ames a %plea request message.  Ames
::    transmits the message over the wire to the peer ship's Ames, which
::    passes the message to the destination vane.
::
::    Once the peer has processed the %plea message, it sends a
::    message-acknowledgment packet over the wire back to the local
::    Ames.  This ack can either be positive to indicate the request was
::    processed, or negative to indicate the request failed, in which
::    case it's called a "nack".  (Don't confuse Ames nacks with TCP
::    nacks, which are a different concept).
::
::    When the local Ames receives either a positive message-ack or a
::    combination of a nack and naxplanation (explained in more detail
::    below), it gives an %done move to the local vane that had
::    requested the original %plea message be sent.
::
::    A local vane can give Ames zero or more %boon response messages in
::    response to a %plea, on the same duct that Ames used to pass the
::    %plea to the vane.  Ames transmits a %boon over the wire to the
::    peer's Ames, which gives it to the destination vane on the same
::    duct the vane had used to pass the original %plea to Ames.
::
::    %boon messages are acked automatically by the receiver Ames.  They
::    cannot be nacked, and Ames only uses the ack internally, without
::    notifying the client vane that gave Ames the %boon.
::
::    If the Arvo event that completed receipt of a %boon message
::    crashes, Ames instead sends the client vane a %lost message
::    indicating the %boon was missed.
::
::    %plea messages can be nacked, in which case the peer will send
::    both a message-nack packet and a naxplanation message, which is
::    sent in a way that does not interfere with normal operation.  The
::    naxplanation is sent as a full Ames message, instead of just a
::    packet, because the contained error information can be arbitrarily
::    large.  A naxplanation can only give rise to a positive ack --
::    never ack an ack, and never nack a naxplanation.
::
::    Ames guarantees a total ordering of messages within a "flow",
::    identified in other vanes by a duct and over the wire by a "bone":
::    an opaque number.  Each flow has a FIFO queue of %plea requests
::    from the requesting ship to the responding ship and a FIFO queue
```

```
57  ::      of %boon's in the other direction.
58  ::
59  ::      Message order across flows is not specified and may vary based on
60  ::      network conditions.
61  ::
62  ::      Ames guarantees that a message will only be delivered once to the
63  ::      destination vane.
64  ::
65  ::      Ames encrypts every message using symmetric-key encryption by
66  ::      performing an elliptic curve Diffie-Hellman using our private key
67  ::      and the public key of the peer.  For ships in the Jael PKI
68  ::      (public-key infrastructure), Ames looks up the peer's public key
69  ::      from Jael.  Comets (128-bit ephemeral addresses) are not
70  ::      cryptographic assets and must self-attest over Ames by sending a
71  ::      single self-signed packet containing their public key.
72  ::
73  ::      When a peer suffers a continuity breach, Ames removes all
74  ::      messaging state related to it.  Ames does not guarantee that all
75  ::      messages will be fully delivered to the now-stale peer.  From
76  ::      Ames's perspective, the newly restarted peer is a new ship.
77  ::      Ames's guarantees are not maintained across a breach.
78  ::
79  ::      A vane can pass Ames a %heed $task to request Ames track a peer's
80  ::      responsiveness.  If our %boon's to it start backing up locally,
81  ::      Ames will give a %clog back to the requesting vane containing the
82  ::      unresponsive peer's urbit address.  This interaction does not use
83  ::      ducts as unique keys.  Stop tracking a peer by sending Ames a
84  ::      %jilt $task.
85  ::
86  ::      Debug output can be adjusted using %sift and %spew $task's.
87  ::
88  !:
89  =,  ames
90  =*  point                   point:jael
91  =*  public-keys-result  public-keys-result:jael
92  ::  veb: verbosity flags
93  ::
94  =/  veb-all-off
95    :*  snd=`?`%.n  ::  sending packets
96        rcv=`?`%.n  ::  receiving packets
97        odd=`?`%.n  ::  unusual events
98        msg=`?`%.n  ::  message-level events
99        ges=`?`%.n  ::  congestion control
100       for=`?`%.n  ::  packet forwarding
101       rot=`?`%.n  ::  routing attempts
102       kay=`?`%.n  ::  is ok/not responding
103       fin=`?`%.n  ::  remote-scry
104       sun=`?`%.n  ::  STUN
105   ==
106 =/  packet-size  13
107 =>
108 ~%  %ames  ..part  ~
109 |%
110 +|  %helpers
111 ::  +get-forward-lanes: get all lanes to send to when forwarding to peer
112 ::
113 ++  get-forward-lanes
114   |=  [our=@p peer=peer-state peers=(map ship ship-state)]
```

```
115    ^-  (list lane)
116    =;  zar=(trap (list lane))
117      ?~  route.peer  $:zar
118      =*  rot  u.route.peer
119      ?:(direct.rot [lane.rot ~] [lane.rot $:zar])
120    ::
121    |.  ^-  (list lane)
122    ?:  ?=(%czar (clan:title sponsor.peer))
123      ?:  =(our sponsor.peer)
124        ~
125      [%& sponsor.peer]~
126    =/  next  (~(get by peers) sponsor.peer)
127    ?.  ?=([~ %known *] next)
128      ~
129    $(peer +.u.next)
130  ::
131  ++  chain
132    =<  mop
133    |%
134    ++  on    ((^on ,@ ,[key=@ =path]) lte)
135    +$  mop   ^chain
136    --
137  ::
138  ::  +trace: print if .verb is set and we're tracking .ship
139  ++  trace
140    |=  [mode=?(%ames %fine) verb=? =ship ships=(set ship) print=(trap tape)]
141    ^+  same
142    ?.  verb
143      same
144    ?.  =>  [ship=ship ships=ships in=in]
145        ~+  |(=(~ ships) (~(has in ships) ship))
146      same
147    (slog leaf/"{(trip mode)}: {(scow %p ship)}: {(print)}" ~)
148  ::  +qos-update-text: notice text for if connection state changes
149  ::
150  ++  qos-update-text
151    |=  [=ship mode=?(%ames %fine) old=qos new=qos k=? ships=(set ship)]
152    ^-  (unit tape)
153    ::
154    =+  trace=(cury trace mode)
155    ?+  [-.old -.new]  ~
156      [%unborn %live]   `"; {(scow %p ship)} is your neighbor"
157      [%dead %live]     ((trace k ship ships |.("is ok")) ~)
158      [%live %dead]     ((trace k ship ships |.("not responding still trying")) ~)
159      [%unborn %dead]   ((trace k ship ships |.("not responding still trying")) ~)
160      [%live %unborn]   `"; {(scow %p ship)} has sunk"
161      [%dead %unborn]   `"; {(scow %p ship)} has sunk"
162    ==
163  ::  +split-message: split message into kilobyte-sized fragments
164  ::
165  ::    We don't literally split it here since that would allocate many
166  ::    large atoms with no structural sharing.  Instead, each
167  ::    static-fragment has the entire message and a counter.  In
168  ::    +encrypt, we interpret this to get the actual fragment.
169  ::
170  ++  split-message
171    ~/  %split-message
172    |=  [=message-num =message-blob]
```

```
173    ^-  (list static-fragment)
174    ::
175    =/  num-fragments=fragment-num  (met packet-size message-blob)
176    =|  counter=@
177    ::
178    |-  ^-  (list static-fragment)
179    ?:  (gte counter num-fragments)
180      ~
181    ::
182    :-  [message-num num-fragments counter `@`message-blob]
183    $(counter +(counter))
184 ::  +assemble-fragments: concatenate fragments into a $message
185 ::
186 ++  assemble-fragments
187   ~/  %assemble-fragments
188   |=  [num-fragments=fragment-num fragments=(map fragment-num fragment)]
189   ^-  *
190   ::
191   =|  sorted=(list fragment)
192   =.  sorted
193     =/  index=fragment-num  0
194     |-  ^+  sorted
195     ?:  =(index num-fragments)
196       sorted
197     $(index +(index), sorted [(~(got by fragments) index) sorted])
198   ::
199   (cue (rep packet-size (flop sorted)))
200 ::  +jim: caching +jam
201 ::
202 ++  jim   |=(n=* ~>(%memo./ames/jam (jam n)))
203 ++  spit
204   |=  =path
205   ^-  [pat=@t wid=@ud]
206   =+  pat=(spat path)
207   =+  wid=(met 3 pat)
208   ?>  (lte wid 384)
209   [pat wid]
210 ::  +make-bone-wire: encode ship, rift and bone in wire for sending to vane
211 ::
212 ++  make-bone-wire
213   |=  [her=ship =rift =bone]
214   ^-  wire
215   ::
216   /bone/(scot %p her)/(scot %ud rift)/(scot %ud bone)
217 ::  +parse-bone-wire: decode ship, bone and rift from wire from local vane
218 ::
219 ++  parse-bone-wire
220   |=  =wire
221   ^-  %-  unit
222     $%  [%old her=ship =bone]
223         [%new her=ship =rift =bone]
224     ==
225   ?.  ?|  ?=([%bone @ @ @ ~] wire)
226           ?=([%bone @ @ ~] wire)
227       ==
228     ::  ignore malformed wires
229     ::
230     ~
```

```
231    ?+    wire  ~
232        [%bone @ @ ~]
233      `[%old `@p`(slav %p i.t.wire) `@ud`(slav %ud i.t.t.wire)]
234    ::
235        [%bone @ @ @ ~]
236    %-  some
237    :^      %new
238        `@p`(slav %p i.t.wire)
239      `@ud`(slav %ud i.t.t.wire)
240    `@ud`(slav %ud i.t.t.t.wire)
241    ==
242  ::    +make-pump-timer-wire: construct wire for |packet-pump timer
243  ::
244  ++   make-pump-timer-wire
245    |=  [her=ship =bone]
246    ^-  wire
247    /pump/(scot %p her)/(scot %ud bone)
248  ::    +parse-pump-wire: parse .her and .bone from |packet-pump wire
249  ::
250  ++   parse-pump-wire
251    |=  [ship=@ bone=@]
252    ^-  (unit [%pump her=^ship =^bone])
253    ?~  ship=`(unit @p)`(slaw %p ship)
254      ~
255    ?~  bone=`(unit @ud)`(slaw %ud bone)
256      ~
257    `pump/[u.ship u.bone]
258  ::
259  ++   parse-fine-wire
260    |=  [ship=@ =wire]
261    ^-  (unit [%fine her=^ship =^wire])
262    ?~  ship=`(unit @p)`(slaw %p ship)
263      ~
264    `fine/[u.ship wire]
265  ::    +derive-symmetric-key: $symmetric-key from $private-key and $public-key
266  ::
267  ::    Assumes keys have a tag on them like the result of the |ex:crub core.
268  ::
269  ++   derive-symmetric-key
270    ~/  %derive-symmetric-key
271    |=  [=public-key =private-key]
272    ^-  symmetric-key
273    ::
274    ?>  =('b' (end 3 public-key))
275    =.  public-key  (rsh 8 (rsh 3 public-key))
276    ::
277    ?>  =('B' (end 3 private-key))
278    =.  private-key  (rsh 8 (rsh 3 private-key))
279    ::
280    `@`(shar:ed:crypto public-key private-key)
281  ::    +encode-keys-packet: create key request $packet
282  ::
283  ++   encode-keys-packet
284    ~/  %encode-keys-packet
285    |=  [sndr=ship rcvr=ship sndr-life=life]
286    ^-  shot
287    :*  [sndr rcvr]
288        &
```

```
289        &
290        (mod sndr-life 16)
291        `@`1
292        origin=~
293        content=`@`%keys
294    ==
295  ::
296  ++  response-size  13  ::  1kb
297  ::  +sift-roar: assemble scry response fragments into full message
298  ::
299  ++  sift-roar
300    |=  [total=@ud hav=(list have)]
301    ^-  [sig=@ux dat=$@(~ (cask))]
302    =/  mes=@
303      %+  rep  response-size
304      (roll hav |=([=have dat=(list @ux)] [dat.have dat]))
305    =+  sig=(end 9 mes)
306    :-  sig
307    =+  dat=(rsh 9 mes)
308    ?~  dat  ~
309    =/  non  ~|(%fine-cue (cue dat))
310    ~|  [%fine %response-not-cask]
311    ;;((cask) non)
312  ::  +etch-hunk: helper core to serialize a $hunk
313  ::
314  ++  etch-hunk
315    |=  [=ship =life =acru:ames]
316    |%
317    ::
318    +|  %helpers
319    ::  +show-meow: prepare $meow for printing
320    ::
321    ++  show-meow
322      |=  =meow
323      :*  sig=`@q`(mug sig.meow)
324          num=num.meow
325          dat=`@q`(mug dat.meow)
326      ==
327    ::
328    ++  make-meow
329      |=  [=path mes=@ num=@ud]
330      ^-  meow
331      =/  tot  (met 13 mes)
332      =/  dat  (cut 13 [(dec num) 1] mes)
333      =/  wid  (met 3 dat)
334      :*  sig=(sign-fra path num dat)        ::  fragment signature
335          num=tot                            ::  number of fragments
336          dat=dat                            ::  response data fragment
337      ==
338    ::
339    ++  etch-meow
340      |=  =meow
341      ^-  yowl
342      %+  can  3
343      :~  64^sig.meow
344          4^num.meow
345          (met 3 dat.meow)^dat.meow
346      ==
```

```
347    ::
348    +|    %keys
349    ::
350    ++  sign  sigh:as:acru
351    ++  sign-fra
352      |=  [=path fra=@ud dat=@ux]
353      ::~>  %bout.[1 %sign-fra]
354      (sign (jam path fra dat))
355    ::
356    ++  full
357      |=  [=path data=$@(~ (cask))]
358      =/  buf  (jam ship life path data)
359      ::=/  nam  (crip "sign-full {<(met 3 buf)>}")
360      ::~>  %bout.[1 nam]
361      (sign buf)
362    ::
363    +|    %serialization
364    ::
365    ++  etch-data
366      |=  [=path data=$@(~ (cask))]
367      =/  sig=@  (full path data)
368      ?~  data  sig
369      (mix sig (lsh 9 (jam data)))
370    ++  etch-open
371      |=  [=path =hunk data=$@(~ (cask))]
372      (etch path hunk (etch-data path data))
373    ::
374    ++  etch
375      |=  [=path =hunk mes=@]
376      ^-  (list yowl)
377      ::
378      =/  las  (met 13 mes)
379      =/  tip  (dec (add [lop len]:hunk))
380      =/  top  (min las tip)
381      =/  num  lop.hunk
382      ?>  (lte num top)
383      =|  res=(list yowl)
384      |-  ^+  res
385      ?:  =(num top)
386        =-  (flop - res)
387        (etch-meow (make-meow path mes num))
388      $(num +(num), res :_(res (etch-meow (make-meow path mes num))))
389    --
390  ::  +etch-open-packet: convert $open-packet attestation to $shot
391  ::
392  ++  etch-open-packet
393    ~/  %etch-open-packet
394    |=  [pac=open-packet =acru:ames]
395    ^-  shot
396    :*  [sndr rcvr]:pac
397        req=&  sam=&
398        (mod sndr-life.pac 16)
399        (mod rcvr-life.pac 16)
400        origin=~
401        content=`@`(sign:as:acru (jam pac))
402    ==
403  ::  +sift-open-packet: decode comet attestation into an $open-packet
404  ::
```

```hoon
++  sift-open-packet
  ~/  %sift-open-packet
  |=  [=shot our=ship our-life=@]
  ^-  open-packet
  ::  deserialize and type-check packet contents
  ::
  =+  ;;  [signature=@ signed=@]  (cue content.shot)
  =+  ;;  =open-packet            (cue signed)
  ::  assert .our and .her and lives match
  ::
  ?>  .=        sndr.open-packet  sndr.shot
  ?>  .=        rcvr.open-packet  our
  ?>  .=  sndr-life.open-packet  1
  ?>  .=  rcvr-life.open-packet  our-life
  ::  only a star can sponsor a comet
  ::
  ?>  =(%king (clan:title (^sein:title sndr.shot)))
  =/  crub  (com:nu:crub:crypto public-key.open-packet)
  ::  comet public-key must hash to its @p address
  ::
  ?>  =(sndr.shot fig:ex:crub)
  ::  verify signature
  ::
  ?>  (safe:as:crub signature signed)
  open-packet
::  +etch-shut-packet: encrypt and packetize a $shut-packet
::
++  etch-shut-packet
  ~/  %etch-shut-packet
  ::  TODO add rift to signed messages to prevent replay attacks?
  ::
  |=  $:  =shut-packet
          =symmetric-key
          sndr=ship
          rcvr=ship
          sndr-life=@
          rcvr-life=@
      ==
  ^-  shot
  ::
  =?    meat.shut-packet
      ?&  ?=(%& -.meat.shut-packet)
          (gth (met packet-size fragment.p.meat.shut-packet) 1)
      ==
    %_    meat.shut-packet
      fragment.p
      (cut packet-size [[fragment-num 1] fragment]:p.meat.shut-packet)
    ==
  ::
  =/  vec  ~[sndr rcvr sndr-life rcvr-life]
  =/  [siv=@uxH len=@ cyf=@ux]
    (~(en sivc:aes:crypto (shaz symmetric-key) vec) (jam shut-packet))
  ::
  :*  ^=        dyad  [sndr rcvr]
      ^=        req  ?=(%& -.meat.shut-packet)
      ^=        sam  &
      ^=  sndr-tick  (mod sndr-life 16)
      ^=  sndr-tick  (mod rcvr-life 16)
```

```hoon
463        ^=        origin  ~
464        ^=        content  :(mix siv (lsh 7 len) (lsh [3 18] cyf))
465    ==
466  ::  +sift-shut-packet: decrypt a $shut-packet from a $shot
467  ::
468  ++  sift-shut-packet
469    ~/  %sift-shut-packet
470    |=  [=shot =symmetric-key sndr-life=@ rcvr-life=@]
471    ^-  (unit shut-packet)
472    ?.  ?&  =(sndr-tick.shot (mod sndr-life 16))
473            =(rcvr-tick.shot (mod rcvr-life 16))
474        ==
475      ~
476    =/  siv  (end 7 content.shot)
477    =/  len  (end 4 (rsh 7 content.shot))
478    =/  cyf  (rsh [3 18] content.shot)
479    ~|  ames-decrypt+[[sndr rcvr origin]:shot len siv]
480    =/  vec  ~[sndr.shot rcvr.shot sndr-life rcvr-life]
481    %-  some  ;;  shut-packet  %-  cue  %-  need
482    (~(de sivc:aes:crypto (shaz symmetric-key) vec) siv len cyf)
483  ::
484  ++  is-our-bulk
485    |=  [our=ship =ames-state =balk]
486    ^-  ?
487    =-  ~?  =(| -)
488        [%fine-mismatch our=[rift life]:ames-state her=[her rif lyf]:balk]
489        -
490    ?&  =(our her.balk)
491        =(rift.ames-state rif.balk)
492        =(life.ames-state lyf.balk)
493    ==
494  ::
495  ++  check-fine-key
496    |=  [=ames-state =balk key-idx=@]
497    ^-  ?
498    ?~  link=(get:on:chain chain.ames-state key-idx)
499      |
500    =/  gol  path.u.link
501    =/  =path  [van.balk car.balk spr.balk]
502    |-  ^-  ?
503    ?~  gol   &
504    ?~  path  |
505    ?.  =(i.path i.gol)
506      |
507    $(path t.path, gol t.gol)
508  ::
509  ++  is-peer-dead
510    |=  [now=@da =peer-state]
511    ^+  peer-state
512    =/  expiry=@da  (add ~s30 last-contact.qos.peer-state)
513    =?  -.qos.peer-state  (gte now expiry)
514      %dead
515    peer-state
516  ::
517  ++  update-peer-route
518    |=  [peer=ship =peer-state]
519    ^+  peer-state
520    ::  If the peer is not responding, mark the .lane.route as
```

```hoon
::    indirect.  The next packets we emit will be sent to the
::    receiver's sponsorship chain in case the receiver's
::    transport address has changed and this lane is no longer
::    valid.
::
::    If .peer is a galaxy, the lane will always remain direct.
::
?.    ?&  ?=(%dead -.qos.peer-state)
          ?=(^ route.peer-state)
          direct.u.route.peer-state
          !=(%czar (clan:title peer))
      ==
    peer-state
  peer-state(direct.u.route %.n)
::
++  poke-ping-app
  |=  [=duct our=ship poke=?(%stop %once [%kick fail=?])]
  ^-  move
  [duct %pass /ping %g %deal [our our /ames] %ping %poke noun+!>(poke)]
::
+|  %atomics
::
+$  private-key     @uwprivatekey
+$  signature       @uwsignature
::
+|  %kinetics
::  $channel: combined sender and receiver identifying data
::
+$  channel
  $:  [our=ship her=ship]
      now=@da
      ::  our data, common to all dyads
      ::
      $:  =our=life
          crypto-core=acru:ames
          =bug
      ==
      ::  her data, specific to this dyad
      ::
      $:  =symmetric-key
          =her=life
          =her=rift
          =her=public-key
          her-sponsor=ship
  ==  ==
::  $open-packet: unencrypted packet payload, for comet self-attestation
::
::    This data structure gets signed and jammed to form the .contents
::    field of a $packet.
::
::  TODO add rift to prevent replay attacks
::
+$  open-packet
  $:  =public-key
      sndr=ship
      =sndr=life
      rcvr=ship
      =rcvr=life
```

```
579      ==
580  ::  $shut-packet: encrypted packet payload
581  ::
582  +$  shut-packet
583    $:  =bone
584        =message-num
585        meat=(each fragment-meat ack-meat)
586      ==
587  ::  $fragment-meat: contents of a message-fragment packet
588  ::
589  +$  fragment-meat
590    $:  num-fragments=fragment-num
591        =fragment-num
592        =fragment
593      ==
594  ::  $ack-meat: contents of an acknowledgment packet; fragment or message
595  ::
596  ::    Fragment acks reference the $fragment-num of the target packet.
597  ::
598  ::    Message acks contain a success flag .ok, which is %.n in case of
599  ::    negative acknowledgment (nack), along with .lag that describes the
600  ::    time it took to process the message. .lag is zero if the message
601  ::    was processed during a single Arvo event. At the moment, .lag is
602  ::    always zero.
603  ::
604  +$  ack-meat  (each fragment-num [ok=? lag=@dr])
605  ::  $naxplanation: nack trace; explains which message failed and why
606  ::
607  +$  naxplanation  [=message-num =error]
608  ::
609  +|  %statics
610  ::
611  ::  $ames-state: state for entire vane
612  ::
613  ::    peers:       states of connections to other ships
614  ::    unix-duct:   handle to give moves to unix
615  ::    life:        our $life; how many times we've rekeyed
616  ::    crypto-core: interface for encryption and signing
617  ::    bug:         debug printing configuration
618  ::    snub:        blocklist for incoming packets
619  ::    cong:        parameters for marking a flow as clogged
620  ::    dead:        dead flow consolidation timer and recork timer, if set
621  ::
622  +$  ames-state
623    $+  ames-state-20
624    $:  peers=(map ship ship-state)
625        =unix=duct
626        =life
627        =rift
628        crypto-core=acru:ames
629        =bug
630        snub=[form=?(%allow %deny) ships=(set ship)]
631        cong=[msg=_5 mem=_100.000]
632        ::
633        $=  dead
634        $:  flow=[%flow (unit dead-timer)]
635            cork=[%cork (unit dead-timer)]
636          ==
```

```
637       ::
638         =chain
639       ==
640 ::
641 +$  dead-timer        [=duct =wire date=@da]
642 +$  azimuth-state     [=symmetric-key =life =rift =public-key sponsor=ship]
643 +$  azimuth-state-6   [=symmetric-key =life =public-key sponsor=ship]
644 +$  ames-state-4    ames-state-5
645 +$  ames-state-5
646   $+  ames-state-5
647   $:  peers=(map ship ship-state-5)
648       =unix=duct
649       =life
650       crypto-core=acru-12
651       bug=bug-9
652   ==
653 ::
654 +$  ship-state-4   ship-state-5
655 +$  ship-state-5
656   $+  ship-state-5
657   $%  [%alien alien-agenda-12]
658       [%known peer-state-5]
659   ==
660 ::
661 +$  peer-state-5
662   $+  peer-state-5
663   $:  azimuth-state-6
664       route=(unit [direct=? =lane])
665       =qos
666       =ossuary
667       snd=(map bone message-pump-state-16)
668       rcv=(map bone message-sink-state)
669       nax=(set [=bone =message-num])
670       heeds=(set duct)
671   ==
672 ::
673 +$  bug-9
674   $+  bug-9
675   $:  veb=_[`?`%.n `?`%.n `?`%.n `?`%.n `?`%.n `?`%.n `?`%.n]
676       ships=(set ship)
677   ==
678 ::
679 +$  ames-state-6
680   $+  ames-state-6
681   $:  peers=(map ship ship-state-6)
682       =unix=duct
683       =life
684       crypto-core=acru-12
685       bug=bug-9
686   ==
687 ::
688 +$  ship-state-6
689   $+  ship-state-6
690   $%  [%alien alien-agenda-12]
691       [%known peer-state-6]
692   ==
693 ::
694 +$  peer-state-6
```

```
695    $+  peer-state-6
696    $:  azimuth-state
697        route=(unit [direct=? =lane])
698        =qos
699        =ossuary
700        snd=(map bone message-pump-state-16)
701        rcv=(map bone message-sink-state)
702        nax=(set [=bone =message-num])
703        heeds=(set duct)
704    ==
705  ::
706  +$  ames-state-7
707    $+  ames-state-7
708    $:  peers=(map ship ship-state-7)
709        =unix=duct
710        =life
711        crypto-core=acru-12
712        bug=bug-9
713    ==
714  ::
715  +$  ames-state-8
716    $+  ames-state-8
717    $:  peers=(map ship ship-state-7)
718        =unix=duct
719        =life
720        crypto-core=acru-12
721        bug=bug-9
722        corks=(set wire)
723    ==
724  ::
725  +$  ames-state-9
726    $+  ames-state-9
727    $:  peers=(map ship ship-state-7)
728        =unix=duct
729        =life
730        crypto-core=acru-12
731        bug=bug-9
732        corks=(set wire)
733        snub=(set ship)
734    ==
735  ::
736  +$  ames-state-10
737    $+  ames-state-10
738    $:  peers=(map ship ship-state-7)
739        =unix=duct
740        =life
741        crypto-core=acru-12
742        bug=bug-12
743        corks=(set wire)
744        snub=(set ship)
745    ==
746  ::
747  +$  ship-state-7
748    $+  ship-state-7
749    $%  [%alien alien-agenda-12]
750        [%known peer-state-7]
751    ==
752  ::
```

```
753  +$  peer-state-7
754    $+  peer-state-7
755    $:  azimuth-state
756        route=(unit [direct=? =lane])
757        =qos
758        =ossuary
759        snd=(map bone message-pump-state-16)
760        rcv=(map bone message-sink-state)
761        nax=(set [=bone =message-num])
762        heeds=(set duct)
763        closing=(set bone)
764        corked=(set bone)
765        krocs=(set bone)
766    ==
767  ::
768  +$  ames-state-11
769    $+  ames-state-11
770    $:  peers=(map ship ship-state-7)
771        =unix=duct
772        =life
773        crypto-core=acru-12
774        bug=bug-12
775        corks=(set wire)
776        snub=(set ship)
777        cong=[msg=@ud mem=@ud]
778    ==
779  ::
780  +$  ames-state-12
781    $+  ames-state-12
782    $:  peers=(map ship ship-state-12)
783        =unix=duct
784        =life
785        crypto-core=acru-12
786        bug=bug-12
787        snub=[form=?(%allow %deny) ships=(set ship)]
788        cong=[msg=@ud mem=@ud]
789    ==
790  ::
791  +$  ship-state-12
792    $+  ship-state-12
793    $%  [%alien alien-agenda-12]
794        [%known peer-state-12]
795    ==
796  ::
797  +$  alien-agenda-12
798    $+  alien-agenda-12
799    $:  messages=(list [=duct =plea])
800        packets=(set =blob)
801        heeds=(set duct)
802    ==
803  ::
804  +$  peer-state-12
805    $+  peer-state-12
806    $:  azimuth-state
807        route=(unit [direct=? =lane])
808        =qos
809        =ossuary
810        snd=(map bone message-pump-state-16)
```

```hoon
      rcv=(map bone message-sink-state)
      nax=(set [=bone =message-num])
      heeds=(set duct)
      closing=(set bone)
      corked=(set bone)
  ==
::
+$  bug-12
  $:  veb=_[`?`%.n `?`%.n `?`%.n `?`%.n `?`%.n `?`%.n `?`%.n `?`%.n]
      ships=(set ship)
  ==
::
++  acru-12  $_  ^?
  |%
  ++  as  ^?
    |%  ++  seal  |~([a=pass b=@] *@)
        ++  sign  |~(a=@ *@)
        ++  sure  |~(a=@ *(unit @))
        ++  tear  |~([a=pass b=@] *(unit @))
    --
  ++  de  |~([a=@ b=@] *(unit @))
  ++  dy  |~([a=@ b=@] *@)
  ++  en  |~([a=@ b=@] *@)
  ++  ex  ^?
    |%  ++  fig  *@uvH
        ++  pac  *@uvG
        ++  pub  *pass
        ++  sec  *ring
    --
  ++  nu  ^?
    |%  ++  pit  |~([a=@ b=@] ^?(..nu))
        ++  nol  |~(a=ring ^?(..nu))
        ++  com  |~(a=pass ^?(..nu))
    --
  --
::
+$  ames-state-13
  $+  ames-state-13
  $:  peers=(map ship ship-state-13)
      =unix=duct
      =life
      =rift
      crypto-core=acru:ames
      bug=bug-19
      snub=[form=?(%allow %deny) ships=(set ship)]
      cong=[msg=@ud mem=@ud]
  ==
::
+$  ship-state-13
  $+  ship-state-13
  $%  [%alien alien-agenda-17]
      [%known peer-state-13]
  ==
::
+$  peer-state-13
  $+  peer-state-13
  $:  $:  =symmetric-key
          =life
```

```
869          =rift
870          =public-key
871          sponsor=ship
872        ==
873      route=(unit [direct=? =lane])
874      =qos
875      =ossuary
876      snd=(map bone message-pump-state-16)
877      rcv=(map bone message-sink-state)
878      nax=(set [=bone =message-num])
879      heeds=(set duct)
880      closing=(set bone)
881      corked=(set bone)
882      keens=(map path keen-state-13)
883    ==
884  ::
885  ++  keen-state-13
886    =<  $+  keen-state-13
887      $:  wan=(pha want)   ::  request packts, sent
888          nex=(list want)  ::  request packets, unsent
889          hav=(list have)  ::  response packets, backward
890          num-fragments=@ud
891          num-received=@ud
892          next-wake=(unit @da)
893          listeners=(set duct)
894          metrics=pump-metrics-16
895      ==
896    |%
897    ::  +afx: polymorphic node type for finger trees
898    ::
899    ++  afx
900      |$  [val]
901      $%  [%1 p=val ~]
902          [%2 p=val q=val ~]
903          [%3 p=val q=val r=val ~]
904          [%4 p=val q=val r=val s=val ~]
905      ==
906    ::  +pha: finger tree
907    ::
908    ::    DO NOT USE THIS
909    ::    It's wrong and only kept around for state migration purposes.
910    ::
911    ++  pha
912      |$  [val]
913      $~  [%nul ~]
914      $%  [%nul ~]
915          [%one p=val]
916          [%big p=(afx val) q=(pha val) r=(afx val)]
917      ==
918    ::  +deq: deque
919    ::
920    ::    DO NOT USE THIS
921    ::    It's wrong and only kept around for state migration purposes.
922    ::
923    ++  deq
924      |*  val=mold
925      |%
926  ::      ::
```

```
927  ::      ::  +|  %utilities
928  ::      ::
929  ::      ++  make-afx
930  ::        |=  ls=(list val)
931  ::        ?+  ls  ~|(bad-finger/(lent ls) !!)
932  ::          [* ~]          [%1 ls]
933  ::          [* * ~]        [%2 ls]
934  ::          [* * * ~]      [%3 ls]
935  ::          [* * * * ~]    [%4 ls]
936  ::        ==
937  ::      ++  afx-to-pha
938  ::        |=  =(afx val)
939  ::        ^-  (pha val)
940  ::        (apl *(pha val) +.afx)
941  ::      ::
942  ::      ::  +|  %left-biased-operations
943  ::      ::
944  ::      ::  +pop-left: remove leftmost value from tree
945  ::      ::
946  ::      ++  pop-left
947  ::        |=  a=(pha val)
948  ::        ^-  [val=(unit val) pha=(pha val)]
949  ::        ?-  -.a
950  ::          %nul  ~^a
951  ::        ::
952  ::          %one  [`p.a nul/~]
953  ::        ::
954  ::            %big
955  ::        [`p.p.a (big-left +.+.p.a q.a r.a)]
956  ::      ==
957  ::      ++  apl
958  ::        |=  [a=(pha val) vals=(list val)]
959  ::        ^-  (pha val)
960  ::        =.  vals  (flop vals)
961  ::        |-
962  ::        ?~  vals  a
963  ::        $(a (cons a i.vals), vals t.vals)
964  ::      ::
965  ::      ::
966  ::      ++  dip-left
967  ::        |*  state=mold
968  ::        |=  $:  a=(pha val)
969  ::                =state
970  ::                f=$-([state val] [(unit val) ? state])
971  ::            ==
972  ::        ^+  [state a]
973  ::        =/  acc  [stop=`?`%.n state=state]
974  ::        =|  new=(pha val)
975  ::        |-
976  ::        ?:  stop.acc
977  ::          ::  cat new and old
978  ::          [state.acc (weld a new)]
979  ::        =^  val=(unit val)  a
980  ::          (pop-left a)
981  ::        ?~  val
982  ::          [state.acc new]
983  ::        =^  res=(unit ^val)  acc
984  ::          (f state.acc u.val)
```

```
985  ::       ?~  res  $
986  ::       $(new (snoc new u.res))
987  ::     ::
988  ::     ++  big-left
989  ::       |=  [ls=(list val) a=(pha val) sf=(afx val)]
990  ::       ^-  (pha val)
991  ::       ?.  =(~ ls)
992  ::         [%big (make-afx ls) a sf]
993  ::       =/  [val=(unit val) inner=_a]
994  ::         (pop-left a)
995  ::       ?~  val
996  ::         (afx-to-pha sf)
997  ::       [%big [%1 u.val ~] inner sf]
998  ::     ::
999  ::     ++  cons
1000 ::       =|  b=(list val)
1001 ::       |=  [a=(pha val) c=val]
1002 ::       ^-  (pha val)
1003 ::       =.  b  [c b]
1004 ::       |-
1005 ::       ?~  b  a
1006 ::       ?-  -.a
1007 ::         ::
1008 ::           %nul
1009 ::         $(a [%one i.b], b t.b)
1010 ::         ::
1011 ::           %one
1012 ::         %=  $
1013 ::           b  t.b
1014 ::           a  [%big [%1 i.b ~] [%nul ~] [%1 p.a ~]]
1015 ::         ==
1016 ::         ::
1017 ::           %big
1018 ::         ?.  ?=(%4 -.p.a)
1019 ::           %=  $
1020 ::             b  t.b
1021 ::             ::
1022 ::               a
1023 ::             ?-  -.p.a
1024 ::               %1  big/[[%2 i.b p.p.a ~] q.a r.a]
1025 ::               %2  big/[[%3 i.b p.p.a q.p.a ~] q.a r.a]
1026 ::               %3  big/[[%4 i.b p.p.a q.p.a r.p.a ~] q.a r.a]
1027 ::             ==
1028 ::           ==
1029 ::         =/  inner
1030 ::           $(a q.a, b ~[s.p.a r.p.a q.p.a])
1031 ::         =.  inner
1032 ::           $(a inner, b t.b)
1033 ::         big/[[%2 i.b p.p.a ~] inner r.a]
1034 ::       ==
1035 ::     ::
1036 ::     ::  +|  %right-biased-operations
1037 ::     ::
1038 ::     ::  +snoc: append to end (right) of tree
1039 ::     ::
1040 ::     ++  snoc
1041 ::       |=  [a=(pha val) b=val]
1042 ::       ^+  a
```

```
1043  ::          ?-  -.a
1044  ::            %nul  [%one b]
1045  ::          ::
1046  ::              %one
1047  ::          :-  %big
1048  ::          :*  [%1 p.a ~]
1049  ::              [%nul ~]
1050  ::              [%1 b ~]
1051  ::          ==
1052  ::          ::
1053  ::              %big
1054  ::          ?-  -.r.a
1055  ::          ::
1056  ::              %1
1057  ::          :-  %big
1058  ::          [p.a q.a [%2 p.r.a b ~]]
1059  ::          ::
1060  ::              %2
1061  ::          :-  %big
1062  ::          [p.a q.a [%3 p.r.a q.r.a b ~]]
1063  ::          ::
1064  ::              %3
1065  ::          :-  %big
1066  ::          [p.a q.a [%4 p.r.a q.r.a r.r.a b ~]]
1067  ::          ::
1068  ::              %4
1069  ::          =/  inner
1070  ::            $(a q.a, b p.r.a)
1071  ::          =.  inner
1072  ::            $(a inner, b q.r.a)
1073  ::          =.  inner
1074  ::            $(a inner, b r.r.a)
1075  ::          :-  %big
1076  ::          :*  p.a
1077  ::              inner
1078  ::              [%2 s.r.a b ~]
1079  ::          ==
1080  ::          ==
1081  ::          ==
1082  ::  ::  +apr: append list to end (right) of tree
1083  ::  ::
1084  ::  ++  apr
1085  ::    |=  [a=(pha val) vals=(list val)]
1086  ::    ^-  (pha val)
1087  ::    ?~  vals  a
1088  ::    $(a (snoc a i.vals), vals t.vals)
1089  ::  ::  +|  %manipulation
1090  ::  ::
1091  ::  ::  +weld: concatenate two trees
1092  ::  ::
1093  ::  ::      O(log n)
1094  ::  ++  weld
1095  ::    =|  c=(list val)
1096  ::    |=  [a=(pha val) b=(pha val)]
1097  ::    ^-  (pha val)
1098  ::    ?-  -.b
1099  ::      %nul  (apr a c)
1100  ::      %one  (snoc (apr a c) p.b)
```

```
::          ::
::            %big
::          ?-  -.a
::            %nul  (apl b c)
::            %one  (cons (apl b c) p.a)
::          ::
::              %big
::            :-  %big
::            =-  [p.a - r.b]
::            $(a q.a, b q.b, c :(welp +.r.a c +.p.b))
::          ==
::        ==
    ::  +tap: transform tree to list
    ::
    ++  tap
      =|  res=(list val)
      |=  a=(pha val)
      !.
      |^  ^+  res
      ?-  -.a
        %nul  ~
        %one  ~[p.a]
        ::
            %big
        =/  fst=_res
          (tap-afx p.a)
        =/  lst=_res
          (tap-afx r.a)
        =/  mid=_res
          $(a q.a)
        :(welp fst mid lst)
      ==
      ++  tap-afx
        |=  ax=(afx val)
        ^+  res
        ?-  -.ax
          %1  +.ax
          %2  +.ax
          %3  +.ax
          %4  +.ax
        ==
      --
    --
  --
::
+$  ames-state-18  ames-state-17
+$  ames-state-17
  $+  ames-state-17
  $:  peers=(map ship ship-state-17)
      =unix=duct
      =life
      =rift
      crypto-core=acru:ames
      bug=bug-19
      snub=[form=?(%allow %deny) ships=(set ship)]
      cong=[msg=_5 mem=_100.000]
      ::
      $=  dead
```

```
1159              $:  flow=[%flow (unit dead-timer)]
1160                  cork=[%cork (unit dead-timer)]
1161          ==  ==
1162  ::
1163  +$  ship-state-17
1164      $+  ship-state-17
1165      $%  [%alien alien-agenda-17]
1166          [%known peer-state-17]
1167      ==
1168  ::
1169  +$  peer-state-17
1170      $+  peer-state-17
1171      $:  $:  =symmetric-key
1172                  =life
1173                  =rift
1174                  =public-key
1175                  sponsor=ship
1176          ==
1177          route=(unit [direct=? =lane])
1178          =qos
1179          =ossuary
1180          snd=(map bone message-pump-state-17)
1181          rcv=(map bone message-sink-state)
1182          nax=(set [=bone =message-num])
1183          heeds=(set duct)
1184          closing=(set bone)
1185          corked=(set bone)
1186          keens=(map path keen-state)
1187      ==
1188  ::
1189  +$  message-pump-state-17
1190      $+  message-pump-state-17
1191      $:  current=_`message-num`1
1192          next=_`message-num`1
1193          unsent-messages=(qeu message-blob)
1194          unsent-fragments=(list static-fragment)
1195          queued-message-acks=(map message-num ack)
1196          =packet-pump-state
1197      ==
1198  ::
1199  +$  ames-state-14  ames-state-16
1200  +$  ames-state-15  ames-state-16
1201  +$  ames-state-16
1202      $+  ames-state-16
1203      $:  peers=(map ship ship-state-16)
1204          =unix=duct
1205          =life
1206          =rift
1207          crypto-core=acru:ames
1208          bug=bug-19
1209          snub=[form=?(%allow %deny) ships=(set ship)]
1210          cong=[msg=@ud mem=@ud]
1211      ==
1212  ::
1213  +$  alien-agenda-17
1214      $+  alien-agenda
1215      $:  messages=(list [=duct =plea])
1216          packets=(set =blob)
```

```
1217        heeds=(set duct)
1218        keens=(jug path duct)
1219    ==
1220  ::
1221  +$  ship-state-16
1222    $+  ship-state-16
1223    $%  [%alien alien-agenda-17]
1224        [%known peer-state-16]
1225    ==
1226  ::
1227  +$  peer-state-16
1228    $+  peer-state-16
1229    $:  azimuth-state
1230        route=(unit [direct=? =lane])
1231        =qos
1232        =ossuary
1233        snd=(map bone message-pump-state-16)
1234        rcv=(map bone message-sink-state)
1235        nax=(set [=bone =message-num])
1236        heeds=(set duct)
1237        closing=(set bone)
1238        corked=(set bone)
1239        keens=(map path keen-state-16)
1240    ==
1241  ::
1242  +$  keen-state-14  keen-state-16
1243  +$  keen-state-16
1244    $+  keen-state-16
1245    $:  wan=((mop @ud want) lte)
1246        nex=(list want)
1247        hav=(list have)
1248        num-fragments=@ud
1249        num-received=@ud
1250        next-wake=(unit @da)
1251        listeners=(set duct)
1252        metrics=pump-metrics-16
1253    ==
1254  ::
1255  +$  message-pump-state-16
1256    $+  message-pump-state-16
1257    $:  current=_`message-num`1
1258        next=_`message-num`1
1259        unsent-messages=(qeu message-blob)
1260        unsent-fragments=(list static-fragment)
1261        queued-message-acks=(map message-num ack)
1262        packet-pump-state=packet-pump-state-16
1263    ==
1264  ::
1265  +$  packet-pump-state-16
1266    $+  packet-pump-state-16
1267    $:  next-wake=(unit @da)
1268        live=((mop live-packet-key live-packet-val) lte-packets)
1269        metrics=pump-metrics-16
1270    ==
1271  ::
1272  +$  pump-metrics-16
1273    $+  pump-metrics-16
1274    $:  rto=_~s1
```

```
rtt=_~s1
rttvar=_~s1
ssthresh=_10.000
cwnd=_1
num-live=@ud
counter=@ud
==
::
+$  queued-event-9-til-11
  $+  queued-event-9-til-11
  $%  [%call =duct wrapped-task=(hobo task-9-til-11)]
      [%take =wire =duct =sign]
  ==
::
+$  task-9-til-11
  $+  task-9-til-11
  $%  [%kroc dry=?]                  ::  introduced in state %10, modified in %17
      [%snub ships=(list ship)]      ::  introduced in state %9,  modified in %11
      $<(?(%snub %kroc %deep %keen) task) ::  %deep/%keen introduced later
  ==
::
+$  queued-event-12-til-16
  $+  queued-event-12-til-16
  $%  [%call =duct wrapped-task=(hobo task-12-til-16)]
      [%take =wire =duct =sign]
  ==
::
+$  task-12-til-16
  $+  task-12-til-16
  $%  [%kroc dry=?]                  ::  introduced in state %10, modified in %17
      [%keen spar]                   ::  introduced in state %13, modified in %19
      deep-task-14                   ::  introduced in state %14, modified in %19
      $<(?(%kroc %keen %deep) task)
  ==
::
+$  deep-task-14
  $:  %deep
      $%  [%nack =ship =nack=bone =message-blob]
          [%sink =ship =target=bone naxplanation=[=message-num =error]]
          [%drop =ship =nack=bone =message-num]
          [%cork =ship =bone]
          [%kill =ship =bone]
      ==  ==
::
+$  queued-event-17-and-18
  $+  queued-event-17-and-18
  $%  [%call =duct wrapped-task=(hobo task-16-and-18)]
      [%take =wire =duct =sign]
  ==
::
+$  task-16-and-18
  $+  task-16-and-18
  $%  [%keen spar]                   ::  introduced in state %13, modified in %19
      deep-task-14                   ::  introduced in state %14, modified in %19
      $<(?(%keen %deep) task)
  ==
::
+$  bug-19
```

```
$:  veb=_[`?`%.n `?`%.n `?`%.n `?`%.n `?`%.n `?`%.n `?`%.n `?`%.n `?`%.n]
    ships=(set ship)
  ==
::
+$  ames-state-19
  $+  ames-state-19
  $:  peers=(map ship ship-state)
      =unix=duct
      =life
      =rift
      crypto-core=acru:ames
      bug=bug-19
      snub=[form=?(%allow %deny) ships=(set ship)]
      cong=[msg=@ud mem=@ud]
      $=  dead
      $:  flow=[%flow (unit dead-timer)]
          cork=[%cork (unit dead-timer)]
      ==
  ::
      =chain
  ==
::  $bug: debug printing configuration
::
::    veb: verbosity toggles
::    ships: identity filter; if ~, print for all
::
+$  bug
  $:  veb=_veb-all-off
      ships=(set ship)
  ==
::
+|  %dialectics
::
::  $move: output effect; either request or response
::
+$  move  [=duct card=(wind note gift)]
::  $queued-event: event to be handled after initial boot completes
::
+$  queued-event
  $+  queued-event
  $%  [%call =duct wrapped-task=(hobo task)]
      [%take =wire =duct =sign]
  ==
::  $note: request to other vane
::
::    Ames passes a %plea note to another vane when it receives a
::    message on a "forward flow" from a peer, originally passed from
::    one of the peer's vanes to the peer's Ames.
::
::    Ames passes a %deep task to itself to handle deferred calls
::    Ames passes a %private-keys to Jael to request our private keys.
::    Ames passes a %public-keys to Jael to request a peer's public
::    keys.
::
+$  note
  $~  [%b %wait *@da]
  $%  $:  %a
          $>(?(%deep %keen) task:ames)
```

```
==
$:  %b
    $>(?(%wait %rest) task:behn)
==
$:  %c
    $>(%warp task:clay)
==
$:  %d
    $>(%flog task:dill)
==
$:  %g
    $>(%deal task:gall)
==
$:  %j
    $>  $?  %private-keys
            %public-keys
            %turf
            %ruin
        ==
    task:jael
==
$:  @tas
    $>(%plea vane-task)
==  ==
::  $sign: response from other vane
::
+$  sign
  $~  [%behn %wake ~]
  $%  $:  %ames
          $>(%tune gift:ames)
      ==
      $:  %behn
          $>(%wake gift:behn)
      ==
      $:  %gall
          $>(?(%flub %unto) gift:gall)
      ==
      $:  %jael
          $>  $?  %private-keys
                  %public-keys
                  %turf
              ==
          gift:jael
      ==
      $:  @tas
          $>(?(%boon %done) gift:ames)
  ==  ==
::
::  $message-pump-task: job for |message-pump
::
::    %memo: packetize and send application-level message
::    %hear: handle receipt of ack on fragment or message
::    %near: handle receipt of naxplanation
::    $prod: reset congestion control
::    %wake: handle timer firing
::
+$  message-pump-task
  $%  [%memo =message]
```

```
      [%hear =message-num =ack-meat]
      [%near =naxplanation]
      [%prod ~]
      [%wake ~]
  ==
::    $packet-pump-task: job for |packet-pump
::
::      %hear: deal with a packet acknowledgment
::      %done: deal with message acknowledgment
::      %halt: finish event, possibly updating timer
::      %wake: handle timer firing
::      %prod: reset congestion control
::
+$  packet-pump-task
  $%  [%hear =message-num =fragment-num]
      [%done =message-num lag=@dr]
      [%halt ~]
      [%wake current=message-num]
      [%prod ~]
  ==
::    $message-sink-task: job for |message-sink
::
::      %done: receive confirmation from vane of processing or failure
::      %drop: clear .message-num from .nax.state
::      %hear: handle receiving a message fragment packet
::        .ok: %.y unless previous failed attempt
::
+$  message-sink-task
  $%  [%done ok=?]
      [%flub ~]
      [%drop =message-num]
      [%hear =lane =shut-packet ok=?]
  ==
--
::  external vane interface
::
|=  our=ship
::  larval ames, before %born sets .unix-duct; wraps adult ames core
::
=<  =*  adult-gate  .
    =|  queued-events=(qeu queued-event)
    =|  $=  cached-state
        %-  unit
        $%  [%5 ames-state-5]
            [%6 ames-state-6]
            [%7 ames-state-7]
            [%8 ames-state-8]
            [%9 ames-state-9]
            [%10 ames-state-10]
            [%11 ames-state-11]
            [%12 ames-state-12]
            [%13 ames-state-13]
            [%14 ames-state-14]
            [%15 ames-state-15]
            [%16 ames-state-16]
            [%17 ames-state-17]
            [%18 ames-state-17]
            [%19 ames-state-19]
```

```
1507                [%20 ^ames-state]
1508          ==
1509      ::
1510      |=  [now=@da eny=@ rof=roof]
1511      =*  larval-gate  .
1512      =*  adult-core   (adult-gate +<)
1513      =<  |%
1514          ++  call  ^call
1515          ++  load  ^load
1516          ++  scry  ^scry
1517          ++  stay  ^stay
1518          ++  take  ^take
1519          --
1520      |%
1521      ++  larval-core  .
1522      ::  +call: handle request $task
1523      ::
1524      ++  call
1525        |=  [=duct dud=(unit goof) wrapped-task=(hobo task)]
1526        ::
1527        =/  =task  ((harden task) wrapped-task)
1528        ::  reject larval error notifications
1529        ::
1530        ?^  dud
1531          ~|(%ames-larval-call-dud (mean tang.u.dud))
1532        ::  before processing events, make sure we have state loaded
1533        ::
1534        =^  molt-moves  larval-core  molt
1535        ::
1536        ?:  &(!=(~ unix-duct.ames-state.adult-gate) =(~ queued-events))
1537          =^  moves  adult-gate  (call:adult-core duct dud task)
1538          ~>  %slog.0^leaf/"ames: metamorphosis"
1539          [(weld molt-moves moves) adult-gate]
1540        ::  drop incoming packets until we metamorphose
1541        ::
1542        ?:  ?=(%hear -.task)
1543          [~ larval-gate]
1544        ::  %born: set .unix-duct and start draining .queued-events
1545        ::
1546        ?:  ?=(%born -.task)
1547          ::  process %born using wrapped adult ames
1548          ::
1549          =^  moves  adult-gate  (call:adult-core duct dud task)
1550          =.  moves  (weld molt-moves moves)
1551          ::  kick off a timer to process the first of .queued-events
1552          ::
1553          =.  moves  :_(moves [duct %pass /larva %b %wait now])
1554          [moves larval-gate]
1555        ::  any other event: enqueue it until we have a .unix-duct
1556        ::
1557        ::     XX what to do with errors?
1558        ::
1559        =.  queued-events  (~(put to queued-events) %call duct task)
1560        [~ larval-gate]
1561      ::  +take: handle response $sign
1562      ::
1563      ++  take
1564        |=  [=wire =duct dud=(unit goof) =sign]
```

```
1565    ?^  dud
1566      ~|(%ames-larval-take-dud (mean tang.u.dud))
1567    ::
1568    =^  molt-moves  larval-core  molt
1569    ::
1570    ?:  &(!=(~ unix-duct.ames-state.adult-gate) =(~ queued-events))
1571      =^  moves  adult-gate  (take:adult-core wire duct dud sign)
1572      ~>  %slog.0^leaf/"ames: metamorphosis"
1573      [(weld molt-moves moves) adult-gate]
1574    ::  enqueue event if not a larval drainage timer
1575    ::
1576    ?.  =(/larva wire)
1577      =.  queued-events  (~(put to queued-events) %take wire duct sign)
1578      [~ larval-gate]
1579    ::  larval event drainage timer; pop and process a queued event
1580    ::
1581    ?.  ?=([%behn %wake *] sign)
1582      ~>  %slog.0^leaf/"ames: larva: strange sign"
1583      [~ larval-gate]
1584    ::  if crashed, print, dequeue, and set next drainage timer
1585    ::
1586    ?^  error.sign
1587      ::  .queued-events should never be ~ here, but if it is, don't crash
1588      ::
1589      ?:  =(~ queued-events)
1590        =/  =tang  [leaf/"ames: cursed metamorphosis" u.error.sign]
1591        =/  moves  [duct %pass /larva-crash %d %flog %crud %larva tang]~
1592        [moves adult-gate]
1593      ::  dequeue and discard crashed event
1594      ::
1595      =.  queued-events  +:~(get to queued-events)
1596      ::  .queued-events has been cleared; metamorphose
1597      ::
1598      ?~  queued-events
1599        ~>  %slog.0^leaf/"ames: metamorphosis"
1600        [~ adult-gate]
1601      ::  set timer to drain next event
1602      ::
1603      =/  moves
1604        =/  =tang  [leaf/"ames: larva: drain crash" u.error.sign]
1605        :~  [duct %pass /larva-crash %d %flog %crud %larva tang]
1606            [duct %pass /larva %b %wait now]
1607        ==
1608      [moves larval-gate]
1609    ::  normal drain timer; dequeue and run event
1610    ::
1611    =^  first-event  queued-events  ~(get to queued-events)
1612    =^  moves  adult-gate
1613      ?-  -.first-event
1614        %call  (call:adult-core [duct ~ wrapped-task]:+.first-event)
1615        %take  (take:adult-core [wire duct ~ sign]:+.first-event)
1616      ==
1617    =.  moves  (weld molt-moves moves)
1618    ::  .queued-events has been cleared; done!
1619    ::
1620    ?~  queued-events
1621      ~>  %slog.0^leaf/"ames: metamorphosis"
1622      [moves adult-gate]
```

```
1623          ::  set timer to drain next event
1624          ::
1625          =.  moves  :_(moves [duct %pass /larva %b %wait now])
1626          [moves larval-gate]
1627      ::  lifecycle arms; mostly pass-throughs to the contained adult ames
1628      ::
1629      ++  scry  scry:adult-core
1630      ++  stay  [%20 %larva queued-events ames-state.adult-gate]
1631      ++  load
1632        |=  $=  old
1633            $%  $:  %4
1634                $%  $:  %larva
1635                        events=(qeu queued-event)
1636                        state=ames-state-4
1637                    ==
1638                    [%adult state=ames-state-4]
1639                ==  ==
1640                $:  %5
1641                $%  $:  %larva
1642                        events=(qeu queued-event)
1643                        state=ames-state-5
1644                    ==
1645                    [%adult state=ames-state-5]
1646                ==  ==
1647                $:  %6
1648                $%  $:  %larva
1649                        events=(qeu queued-event)
1650                        state=ames-state-6
1651                    ==
1652                    [%adult state=ames-state-6]
1653                ==  ==
1654                $:  %7
1655                $%  $:  %larva
1656                        events=(qeu queued-event)
1657                        state=ames-state-7
1658                    ==
1659                    [%adult state=ames-state-7]
1660                ==  ==
1661                $:  %8
1662                $%  $:  %larva
1663                        events=(qeu queued-event)
1664                        state=ames-state-8
1665                    ==
1666                    [%adult state=ames-state-8]
1667                ==  ==
1668                $:  %9                               :: %snub introduced
1669                $%  $:  %larva
1670                        events=(qeu queued-event-9-til-11)
1671                        state=ames-state-9
1672                    ==
1673                    [%adult state=ames-state-9]
1674                ==  ==
1675                $:  %10                              :: %kroc introduced
1676                $%  $:  %larva
1677                        events=(qeu queued-event-9-til-11)
1678                        state=ames-state-10
1679                    ==
1680                    [%adult state=ames-state-10]
```

```
==  ==
$:  %11
$%  $:  %larva
        events=(qeu queued-event-9-til-11)
        state=ames-state-11
    ==
    [%adult state=ames-state-11]
==  ==
$:  %12                                    :: %snub modified
$%  $:  %larva
        events=(qeu queued-event-12-til-16)
        state=ames-state-12
    ==
    [%adult state=ames-state-12]
==  ==
$:  %13
$%  $:  %larva                             :: %keen introduced
        events=(qeu queued-event-12-til-16)
        state=ames-state-13
    ==
    [%adult state=ames-state-13]
==  ==
$:  %14                                    :: %deep introduced
$%  $:  %larva
        events=(qeu queued-event-12-til-16)
        state=ames-state-14
    ==
    [%adult state=ames-state-14]
==  ==
$:  %15
$%  $:  %larva
        events=(qeu queued-event-12-til-16)
        state=ames-state-15
    ==
    [%adult state=ames-state-15]
==  ==
$:  %16
$%  $:  %larva
        events=(qeu queued-event-12-til-16)
        state=ames-state-16
    ==
    [%adult state=ames-state-16]
==  ==
$:  %17                                    :: %kroc modified
$%  $:  %larva
        events=(qeu queued-event-17-and-18)
        state=ames-state-17
    ==
    [%adult state=ames-state-17]
==  ==
$:  %18
$%  $:  %larva
        events=(qeu queued-event-17-and-18)
        state=ames-state-18
    ==
    [%adult state=ames-state-18]
==  ==
$:  %19                                    :: %keen & %deep modified
```

```
              $%  $:  %larva
                      events=(qeu queued-event)
                      state=ames-state-19
                  ==
                  [%adult state=ames-state-19]
              ==  ==
              $:  %20                                  :: start informal %ping
              $%  $:  %larva
                      events=(qeu queued-event)
                      state=_ames-state.adult-gate
                  ==
                  [%adult state=_ames-state.adult-gate]
          ==  ==  ==

      |^  ?-  old
          [%4 %adult *]
        $(old [%5 %adult (state-4-to-5:load:adult-core state.old)])
      ::
          [%4 %larva *]
        =.  state.old  (state-4-to-5:load:adult-core state.old)
        $(-.old %5)
      ::
          [%5 %adult *]
        =.  cached-state  `[%5 state.old]
        ~>  %slog.0^leaf/"ames: larva %5 reload"
        larval-gate
      ::
          [%5 %larva *]
        ~>  %slog.0^leaf/"ames: larva %5 load"
        =.  cached-state  `[%5 state.old]
        =.  queued-events  events.old
        larval-gate
      ::
          [%6 %adult *]
        =.  cached-state  `[%6 state.old]
        ~>  %slog.0^leaf/"ames: larva %6 reload"
        larval-gate
      ::
          [%6 %larva *]
        ~>  %slog.0^leaf/"ames: larva %6 load"
        =.  cached-state  `[%6 state.old]
        =.  queued-events  events.old
        larval-gate
      ::
          [%7 %adult *]
        =.  cached-state  `[%7 state.old]
        ~>  %slog.0^leaf/"ames: larva %7 reload"
        larval-gate
      ::
          [%7 %larva *]
        ~>  %slog.0^leaf/"ames: larva %7 load"
        =.  queued-events  events.old
        =.  cached-state  `[%7 state.old]
        larval-gate
      ::
          [%8 %adult *]
        =.  cached-state  `[%8 state.old]
        ~>  %slog.0^leaf/"ames: larva %8 reload"
```

```
    larval-gate
::
    [%8 %larva *]
~>  %slog.0^leaf/"ames: larva %8 load"
=.  cached-state  `[%8 state.old]
=.  queued-events  events.old
    larval-gate
::
    [%9 %adult *]
=.  cached-state  `[%9 state.old]
~>  %slog.0^leaf/"ames: larva %9 reload"
    larval-gate
::
    [%9 %larva *]
~>  %slog.0^leaf/"ames: larva %9 load"
=.  cached-state  `[%9 state.old]
=.  queued-events  %-  event-17-and-18-to-last
                   %-  event-12-til-16-to-17
                   %-  event-9-til-11-to-12
                   events.old
    larval-gate
::
    [%10 %adult *]
=.  cached-state  `[%10 state.old]
~>  %slog.0^leaf/"ames: larva %10 reload"
    larval-gate
::
    [%10 %larva *]
~>  %slog.1^leaf/"ames: larva %10 load"
=.  cached-state  `[%10 state.old]
=.  queued-events  %-  event-17-and-18-to-last
                   %-  event-12-til-16-to-17
                   %-  event-9-til-11-to-12
                   events.old
    larval-gate
::
    [%11 %adult *]
=.  cached-state  `[%11 state.old]
~>  %slog.0^leaf/"ames: larva %11 reload"
    larval-gate
::
    [%11 %larva *]
~>  %slog.1^leaf/"ames: larva %11 load"
=.  cached-state  `[%11 state.old]
=.  queued-events  %-  event-17-and-18-to-last
                   %-  event-12-til-16-to-17
                   %-  event-9-til-11-to-12
                   events.old
    larval-gate
::
    [%12 %adult *]
=.  cached-state  `[%12 state.old]
~>  %slog.0^leaf/"ames: larva %12 reload"
    larval-gate
::
    [%12 %larva *]
~>  %slog.1^leaf/"ames: larva %12 load"
=.  cached-state  `[%12 state.old]
```

```
=.  queued-events  %-  event-17-and-18-to-last
                   %-  event-12-til-16-to-17
                   events.old
  larval-gate
::
    [%13 %adult *]
  =.  cached-state  `[%13 state.old]
  ~>  %slog.0^leaf/"ames: larva %13 reload"
  larval-gate
::
    [%13 %larva *]
  ~>  %slog.1^leaf/"ames: larva %13 load"
  =.  cached-state  `[%13 state.old]
  =.  queued-events  %-  event-17-and-18-to-last
                     %-  event-12-til-16-to-17
                     events.old
  larval-gate
::
    [%14 %adult *]
  =.  cached-state  `[%14 state.old]
  ~>  %slog.0^leaf/"ames: larva %14 reload"
  larval-gate
::
    [%14 %larva *]
  ~>  %slog.1^leaf/"ames: larva %14 load"
  =.  cached-state  `[%14 state.old]
  =.  queued-events  %-  event-17-and-18-to-last
                     %-  event-12-til-16-to-17
                     events.old
  larval-gate
::
    [%15 %adult *]
  =.  cached-state  `[%15 state.old]
  ~>  %slog.0^leaf/"ames: larva %15 reload"
  larval-gate
::
    [%15 %larva *]
  ~>  %slog.1^leaf/"ames: larva %15 load"
  =.  cached-state  `[%15 state.old]
  =.  queued-events  %-  event-17-and-18-to-last
                     %-  event-12-til-16-to-17
                     events.old
  larval-gate
::
    [%16 %adult *]
  =.  cached-state  `[%16 state.old]
  ~>  %slog.0^leaf/"ames: larva %16 reload"
  larval-gate
::
    [%16 %larva *]
  ~>  %slog.1^leaf/"ames: larva %16 load"
  =.  cached-state  `[%16 state.old]
  =.  queued-events  %-  event-17-and-18-to-last
                     %-  event-12-til-16-to-17
                     events.old
  larval-gate
::
    [%17 %adult *]
```

```
=.    cached-state   `[%17 state.old]
~>    %slog.0^leaf/"ames: larva %17 reload"
larval-gate
::
    [%17 %larva *]
~>    %slog.1^leaf/"ames: larva %17 load"
=.    cached-state   `[%17 state.old]
=.    queued-events  (event-17-and-18-to-last events.old)
larval-gate
::
    [%18 %adult *]
=.    cached-state   `[%18 state.old]
~>    %slog.0^leaf/"ames: larva %18 reload"
larval-gate
::
    [%18 %larva *]
~>    %slog.1^leaf/"ames: larva %18 load"
=.    cached-state   `[%18 state.old]
=.    queued-events  (event-17-and-18-to-last events.old)
larval-gate
::
    [%19 %adult *]
=.    cached-state   `[%19 state.old]
~>    %slog.0^leaf/"ames: larva %19 reload"
larval-gate
::
    [%19 %larva *]
~>    %slog.1^leaf/"ames: larva %19 load"
=.    cached-state   `[%19 state.old]
=.    queued-events  events.old
larval-gate
::
    [%20 %adult *]   (load:adult-core %20 state.old)
::
    [%20 %larva *]
~>    %slog.1^leaf/"ames: larva %20 load"
=.    queued-events  events.old
=.    adult-gate      (load:adult-core %20 state.old)
larval-gate
==
::
++  event-9-til-11-to-12
  |=  events=(qeu queued-event-9-til-11)
  ^-  (qeu queued-event-12-til-16)
  %-  ~(rep in events)
  |=  [e=queued-event-9-til-11 q=(qeu queued-event-12-til-16)]
  %-  ~(put to q)  ^-  queued-event-12-til-16
  ?.  ?=(%call -.e)  e
  =/  task=task-9-til-11  ((harden task-9-til-11) wrapped-task.e)
  %=    e
      wrapped-task
    ^-  task-12-til-16
    ?+  -.task  task
      %snub  [%snub %deny ships.task]
    ==
  ==
::
++  event-12-til-16-to-17
```

```
1971      |=  events=(qeu queued-event-12-til-16)
1972      ^-  (qeu queued-event-17-and-18)
1973      %-  ~(rep in events)
1974      |=  [e=queued-event-12-til-16 q=(qeu queued-event-17-and-18)]
1975      %-  ~(put to q)  ^-  queued-event-17-and-18
1976      ?.  ?=(%call -.e)  e
1977      =/  task=task-12-til-16  ((harden task-12-til-16) wrapped-task.e)
1978      %=    e
1979          wrapped-task
1980        ^-  task-16-and-18
1981        ?.  ?=(%kroc -.task)  task
1982        [%kroc ~]
1983        ==
1984    ::
1985    ++  event-17-and-18-to-last
1986      |=  events=(qeu queued-event-17-and-18)
1987      ^-  (qeu queued-event)
1988      %-  ~(rep in events)
1989      |=  [e=queued-event-17-and-18 q=(qeu queued-event)]
1990      %-  ~(put to q)  ^-  queued-event
1991      ?.  ?=(%call -.e)  e
1992      =/  task=task-16-and-18  ((harden task-16-and-18) wrapped-task.e)
1993      %=    e
1994          wrapped-task
1995        ^-  ^task
1996        ?:  ?=(%keen -.task)
1997        [%keen ~ +.task]
1998        ?.  ?=([%deep %nack *] task)  task
1999        =/  msg  =>([cue=cue arg=message-blob.task] ~+((cue arg)))
2000        =/  hed
2001          ?.  =(1 (end 0 nack-bone.task))
2002            %plea
2003          ?:  =(0 (end 0 (rsh 0 nack-bone.task)))
2004            %boon
2005          %naxplanation
2006        [%deep %nack ship.task nack-bone.task ;;(message [hed msg])]
2007        ==
2008      --
2009    ::  +molt: re-evolve to adult-ames
2010    ::
2011    ++  molt
2012      ^-  (quip move _larval-core)
2013      ?~  cached-state  [~ larval-core]
2014      ~>  %slog.0^leaf/"ames: molt"
2015      =?  u.cached-state  ?=(%5 -.u.cached-state)
2016        6+(state-5-to-6:load:adult-core +.u.cached-state)
2017      =?  u.cached-state  ?=(%6 -.u.cached-state)
2018        7+(state-6-to-7:load:adult-core +.u.cached-state)
2019      =^  moz  u.cached-state
2020        ?.  ?=(%7 -.u.cached-state)  [~ u.cached-state]
2021        ~>  %slog.0^leaf/"ames: init daily recork timer"
2022        :-  [[/ames]~ %pass /recork %b %wait `@da`(add now ~d1)]~
2023        8+(state-7-to-8:load:adult-core +.u.cached-state)
2024      =?  u.cached-state  ?=(%8 -.u.cached-state)
2025        9+(state-8-to-9:load:adult-core +.u.cached-state)
2026      =?  u.cached-state  ?=(%9 -.u.cached-state)
2027        10+(state-9-to-10:load:adult-core +.u.cached-state)
2028      =?  u.cached-state  ?=(%10 -.u.cached-state)
```

```
2029          11+(state-10-to-11:load:adult-core +.u.cached-state)
2030      =?  u.cached-state  ?=(%11 -.u.cached-state)
2031          12+(state-11-to-12:load:adult-core +.u.cached-state)
2032      =?  u.cached-state  ?=(%12 -.u.cached-state)
2033          13+(state-12-to-13:load:adult-core +.u.cached-state)
2034      =?  u.cached-state  ?=(%13 -.u.cached-state)
2035          14+(state-13-to-14:load:adult-core +.u.cached-state)
2036      =?  u.cached-state  ?=(%14 -.u.cached-state)
2037          15+(state-14-to-15:load:adult-core +.u.cached-state)
2038      =?  u.cached-state  ?=(%15 -.u.cached-state)
2039          16+(state-15-to-16:load:adult-core +.u.cached-state)
2040      =^  moz  u.cached-state
2041        ?.  ?=(%16 -.u.cached-state)  [~ u.cached-state]
2042        :_  17+(state-16-to-17:load:adult-core +.u.cached-state)
2043        ?^  moz  moz  ::  if we have just added the timer in state-7-to-8, skip
2044        =;  recork-timer=(list [@da duct])
2045          ?^  recork-timer  ~
2046          ~>  %slog.0^leaf/"ames: init daily recork timer"
2047          [[/ames]~ %pass /recork %b %wait `@da`(add now ~d1)]~
2048        %+  skim
2049          ;;  (list [@da duct])
2050          =<  q.q  %-  need  %-  need
2051          (rof [~ ~] /ames %bx [[our %$ da+now] /debug/timers])
2052        |=([@da =duct] ?=([[%ames %recork *] *] duct))
2053      ::
2054      =^  moz  u.cached-state
2055        ?.  ?=(%17 -.u.cached-state)  [~ u.cached-state]
2056        :_  [%18 +.u.cached-state]
2057        ~>  %slog.0^leaf/"ames: fetching our public keys"
2058        ^-  (list move)
2059        [[[/ames]~ %pass /public-keys %j %public-keys [n=our ~ ~]] moz]
2060      ::
2061      =?  u.cached-state  ?=(%18 -.u.cached-state)
2062          19+(state-18-to-19:load:adult-core +.u.cached-state)
2063      =^  moz  u.cached-state
2064        ?.  ?=(%19 -.u.cached-state)  [~ u.cached-state]
2065        :_  20+(state-19-to-20:load:adult-core +.u.cached-state)
2066        ::  if we didn't have a unix-duct, the larval stage will be expecting
2067        ::  a %born task from unix, which will in turn emit the %saxo that will
2068        ::  start sending informal pings to the sponsorship chain
2069        ::
2070        ?~  unix-duct.+.u.cached-state
2071          moz
2072        ~>  %slog.0^leaf/"ames: retrieving sponsorship chain"
2073        ^-  (list move)
2074        :_  moz
2075        =+  ev-core=(ev [now eny rof] [/saxo]~ ames-state.adult-gate)
2076        [unix-duct.+.u.cached-state %give %saxo get-sponsors:ev-core]
2077      ::
2078      ?>  ?=(%20 -.u.cached-state)
2079      =.  ames-state.adult-gate  +.u.cached-state
2080      [moz larval-core(cached-state ~)]
2081      --
2082  ::
2083  =>  ::  |ev: inner event-handling core
2084      ::
2085      ~%  %per-event  ..trace  ~
2086      |%
```

```
2087        ++  ev
2088        =|  moves=(list move)
2089        ~%  %event-gate  ..ev  ~
2090        |=  [[now=@da eny=@ rof=roof] =duct =ames-state]
2091        =*  veb  veb.bug.ames-state
2092        =|  cork-bone=(unit bone)  ::  modified by +on-kroc
2093        ~%  %event-core  ..$  ~
2094        |%
2095        +|  %helpers
2096        ::
2097        ++  event-core  .
2098        ++  abet  [(flop moves) ames-state]
2099        ++  emit  |=(=move event-core(moves [move moves]))
2100        ++  emil  |=(mos=(list move) event-core(moves (weld (flop mos) moves)))
2101        ++  channel-state  [life crypto-core bug]:ames-state
2102        ++  trace-fine    (cury trace %fine)
2103        ++  trace-ames    (cury trace %ames)
2104        ++  ev-trace
2105          |=  [verb=? =ship print=(trap tape)]
2106          ^+  same
2107          (trace-ames verb ship ships.bug.ames-state print)
2108        ::  +get-peer-state: lookup .her state or ~
2109        ::
2110        ++  get-peer-state
2111          |=  her=ship
2112          ^-  (unit peer-state)
2113          ::
2114          =-  ?.(?=([~ %known *] -) ~ `+.u)
2115          (~(get by peers.ames-state) her)
2116        ::  +got-peer-state: lookup .her state or crash
2117        ::
2118        ++  got-peer-state
2119          |=  her=ship
2120          ^-  peer-state
2121          ::
2122          ~|  %freaky-alien^her
2123          =-  ?>(?=(%known -<) ->)
2124          (~(got by peers.ames-state) her)
2125        ::  +gut-peer-state: lookup .her state or default
2126        ::
2127        ++  gut-peer-state
2128          |=  her=ship
2129          ^-  peer-state
2130          =/  ship-state  (~(get by peers.ames-state) her)
2131          ?.  ?=([~ %known *] ship-state)
2132            *peer-state
2133          +.u.ship-state
2134        ::
2135        ++  get-sponsors
2136          ;;  (list ship)
2137          =<  q.q  %-  need  %-  need
2138          (rof [~ ~] /ames %j `beam`[[our %saxo %da now] /(scot %p our)])
2139        ::
2140        +|  %tasks
2141        ::  +on-take-flub: vane not ready to process message, pretend it
2142        ::                 was never delivered
2143        ::
2144        ++  on-take-flub
```

```
2145      |=  =wire
2146      ^+  event-core
2147      ?~  parsed=(parse-bone-wire wire)
2148        ::  no-op
2149        ::
2150        ~>  %slog.0^leaf/"ames: dropping malformed wire: {(spud wire)}"
2151      event-core
2152      ?>  ?=([@ her=ship *] u.parsed)
2153      =*  her  her.u.parsed
2154      =/  peer-core  (abed-got:pe her)
2155      ?:  ?&  ?=([%new *] u.parsed)
2156              (lth rift.u.parsed rift.peer-state.peer-core)
2157          ==
2158        ::  ignore events from an old rift
2159        ::
2160        %-  %^  ev-trace  odd.veb  her
2161            |.("dropping old rift wire: {(spud wire)}")
2162      event-core
2163      =/  =bone
2164        ?-(u.parsed [%new *] bone.u.parsed, [%old *] bone.u.parsed)
2165      abet:(on-flub:peer-core bone)
2166    ::  +on-take-done: handle notice from vane that it processed a message
2167    ::
2168    ++  on-take-done
2169      |=  [=wire error=(unit error)]
2170      ^+  event-core
2171      ?~  parsed=(parse-bone-wire wire)
2172        ::  no-op
2173        ::
2174        ~>  %slog.0^leaf/"ames: dropping malformed wire: {(spud wire)}"
2175      event-core
2176      ?>  ?=([@ her=ship *] u.parsed)
2177      =*  her       her.u.parsed
2178      =/  peer-core  (abed-got:pe her)
2179      |^
2180      ?:  ?&  ?=([%new *] u.parsed)
2181              (lth rift.u.parsed rift.peer-state.peer-core)
2182          ==
2183        ::  ignore events from an old rift
2184        ::
2185        %-  %^  ev-trace  odd.veb  her
2186            |.("dropping old rift wire: {(spud wire)}")
2187      event-core
2188      =/  =bone
2189        ?-(u.parsed [%new *] bone.u.parsed, [%old *] bone.u.parsed)
2190      =?  peer-core  ?=([%old *] u.parsed)
2191        %-  %^  ev-trace  odd.veb  her
2192            |.("parsing old wire: {(spud wire)}")
2193      peer-core
2194      ::  relay the vane ack to the foreign peer
2195      ::
2196      =<  abet
2197      ?~(error (send-ack bone) (send-nack bone u.error))
2198      ::
2199      ::  if processing succeded, send positive ack packet and exit
2200      ::
2201      ++  send-ack
2202        |=  =bone
```

```
2203            ^+  peer-core
2204            ::  handle cork only deals with bones that are in closing
2205            ::
2206            %.  bone
2207            handle-cork:abet:(call:(abed:mi:peer-core bone) %done ok=%.y)
2208        ::  failed; send message nack packet
2209        ::
2210      ++  send-nack
2211        |=  [=bone =^error]
2212        ^+  peer-core
2213        =.  peer-core  abet:(call:(abed:mi:peer-core bone) %done ok=%.n)
2214        ::  construct nack-trace message, referencing .failed $message-num
2215        ::
2216        =/  failed=message-num
2217          last-acked:(~(got by rcv.peer-state.peer-core) bone)
2218        =/  =message  [%naxplanation failed error]
2219        ::  send nack-trace message on associated .nack-bone
2220        ::
2221        =/  nack-bone=^bone  (mix 0b10 bone)
2222        abet:(call:(abed:mu:peer-core nack-bone) %memo message)
2223        --
2224    ::  +on-sift: handle request to filter debug output by ship
2225    ::
2226    ++  on-sift
2227      |=  ships=(list ship)
2228      ^+  event-core
2229      =.  ships.bug.ames-state  (sy ships)
2230      event-core
2231    ::  +on-snub: handle request to change ship blacklist
2232    ::
2233    ++  on-snub
2234      |=  [form=?(%allow %deny) ships=(list ship)]
2235      ^+  event-core
2236      =.  snub.ames-state  [form (sy ships)]
2237      event-core
2238    ::  +on-spew: handle request to set verbosity toggles on debug output
2239    ::
2240    ++  on-spew
2241      |=  verbs=(list verb)
2242      ^+  event-core
2243      ::  start from all %.n's, then flip requested toggles
2244      ::
2245      =.  veb.bug.ames-state
2246        %+  roll  verbs
2247        |=  [=verb acc=_veb-all-off]
2248        ^+  veb.bug.ames-state
2249        ?-  verb
2250          %snd  acc(snd %.y)
2251          %rcv  acc(rcv %.y)
2252          %odd  acc(odd %.y)
2253          %msg  acc(msg %.y)
2254          %ges  acc(ges %.y)
2255          %for  acc(for %.y)
2256          %rot  acc(rot %.y)
2257          %kay  acc(kay %.y)
2258          %fin  acc(fin %.y)
2259          %sun  acc(sun %.y)
2260        ==
```

```
2261        event-core
2262    ::  +on-prod: re-send a packet per flow to each of .ships
2263    ::
2264    ++  on-prod
2265      |=  ships=(list ship)
2266      ^+  event-core
2267      =?  ships  =(~ ships)  ~(tap in ~(key by peers.ames-state))
2268      |^  ^+  event-core
2269      ?~  ships  event-core
2270      $(ships t.ships, event-core (prod-peer i.ships))
2271      ::
2272      ++  prod-peer
2273        |=  her=ship
2274        ^+  event-core
2275        =/  par  (get-peer-state her)
2276        ?~  par  event-core
2277        =/  peer-core  (abed-peer:pe her u.par)
2278        =/  bones  ~(tap in ~(key by snd.u.par))
2279        |-  ^+  event-core
2280        ?~  bones      abet:peer-core
2281        =.  peer-core  abet:(call:(abed:mu:peer-core i.bones) %prod ~)
2282        $(bones t.bones)
2283      --
2284    ::  +on-cong: adjust congestion control parameters
2285    ::
2286    ++  on-cong
2287      |=  [msg=@ud mem=@ud]
2288      ^+  event-core
2289      =.  cong.ames-state  msg^mem
2290      event-core
2291    ::  +on-stir: recover from timer desync, setting new timers as needed
2292    ::
2293    ::      .arg can be %rift or %dead
2294    ::
2295    ++  on-stir
2296      |=  arg=@t
2297      ^+  event-core
2298      |^  ?+  arg  do-stir
2299            %rift  do-rift
2300            %dead  do-dead
2301          ==
2302      ::
2303      ++  do-dead
2304        =/  ded=(unit dead-timer)  +.flow.dead.ames-state
2305        ?^  ded
2306          %-  (slog leaf+"ames: turning off dead flow consolidation" ~)
2307          =.  event-core
2308            (emit:event-core duct.u.ded %pass wire.u.ded %b %rest date.u.ded)
2309          =.  flow.dead.ames-state.event-core  [%flow ~]
2310          (wake-dead-flows:event-core ~)
2311        ::
2312        %-  (slog leaf+"ames: switching to dead flow consolidation" ~)
2313        =;  cor=event-core
2314          set-dead-flow-timer:cor
2315        %-  ~(rep by peers.ames-state:event-core)
2316        |=  [[=ship =ship-state] core=_event-core]
2317        ^+  event-core
2318        =/  peer-state=(unit peer-state)  (get-peer-state:core ship)
```

```
2319          ?~  peer-state  core
2320          %-  ~(rep by snd.u.peer-state)
2321          |=  [[=bone =message-pump-state] cor=_core]
2322          ^+  event-core
2323          =/  next-wake  next-wake.packet-pump-state.message-pump-state
2324          ?.  ?&  =(~m2 rto.metrics.packet-pump-state.message-pump-state)
2325                  ?=(^ next-wake)
2326              ==
2327            cor
2328          =/  peer-core  (abed-peer:pe:cor ship u.peer-state)
2329          =/  message-pump  (abed:mu:peer-core bone)
2330          abet:(pu-emit:packet-pump:message-pump %b %rest u.next-wake)
2331        ::
2332        ++  do-rift
2333          =/  =rift
2334          =-  ~|(%no-rift (,@ q.q:(need (need -))))
2335          (rof [~ ~] /ames %j `beam`[[our %rift %da now] /(scot %p our)])
2336          ?:  =(rift rift.ames-state)
2337            event-core
2338          ~&  "ames: fixing rift from {<rift.ames-state>} to {<rift>}"
2339          event-core(ames-state ames-state(rift rift))
2340        ::
2341        ++  do-stir
2342          =/  want=(set [@da ^duct])
2343            %-  ~(rep by peers.ames-state)
2344            |=  [[who=ship s=ship-state] acc=(set [@da ^duct])]
2345            ?.  ?=(%known -.s)  acc
2346            %-  ~(rep by snd.+.s)
2347            |=  [[b=bone m=message-pump-state] acc=_acc]
2348            =*  tim  next-wake.packet-pump-state.m
2349            ?~  tim  acc
2350            %-  ~(put in acc)
2351            [u.tim `^duct`~[ames+(make-pump-timer-wire who b) /ames]]
2352          =.  want
2353            (~(put in want) (add now ~d1) ~[/ames/recork /ames])
2354          ::
2355          =/  have
2356            %-  ~(gas in *(set [@da ^duct]))
2357            =/  tim
2358              ;;  (list [@da ^duct])
2359              =<  q.q  %-  need  %-  need
2360              (rof [~ ~] /ames %bx [[our %$ da+now] /debug/timers])
2361            (skim tim |=([@da hen=^duct] ?=([[%ames ?(%pump %recork) *] *] hen)))
2362          ::
2363          ::  set timers for flows that should have one set but don't
2364          ::
2365          =.  event-core
2366            %-  ~(rep in (~(dif in want) have))
2367            |=  [[wen=@da hen=^duct] this=_event-core]
2368            ?>  ?=([^ *] hen)
2369            (emit:this ~[/ames] %pass t.i.hen %b %wait wen)
2370          ::
2371          ::  cancel timers for flows that have one set but shouldn't
2372          ::
2373          %-  ~(rep in (~(dif in have) want))
2374          |=  [[wen=@da hen=^duct] this=_event-core]
2375          ?>  ?=([^ *] hen)
2376          (emit:this t.hen %pass t.i.hen %b %rest wen)
```

```
2377       --
2378    ::  +on-crud: handle event failure; print to dill
2379    ::
2380    ++  on-crud
2381      |=  =error
2382      ^+  event-core
2383      (emit duct %pass /crud %d %flog %crud error)
2384    ::  +on-heed: handle request to track .ship's responsiveness
2385    ::
2386    ++  on-heed
2387      |=  =ship
2388      ^+  event-core
2389      =/  ship-state  (~(get by peers.ames-state) ship)
2390      ?:  ?=([~ %known *] ship-state)
2391        abet:on-heed:(abed-peer:pe ship +.u.ship-state)
2392      %^  enqueue-alien-todo  ship  ship-state
2393      |=  todos=alien-agenda
2394      todos(heeds (~(put in heeds.todos) duct))
2395    ::  +on-jilt: handle request to stop tracking .ship's responsiveness
2396    ::
2397    ++  on-jilt
2398      |=  =ship
2399      ^+  event-core
2400      =/  ship-state  (~(get by peers.ames-state) ship)
2401      ?:  ?=([~ %known *] ship-state)
2402        abet:on-jilt:(abed-peer:pe ship +.u.ship-state)
2403      %^  enqueue-alien-todo  ship  ship-state
2404      |=  todos=alien-agenda
2405      todos(heeds (~(del in heeds.todos) duct))
2406    ::  +on-dear: handle lane from unix
2407    ::
2408    ++  on-dear
2409      |=  [=ship =lane]
2410      ^+  event-core
2411      ?:  ?=(%.y -.lane)
2412        event-core
2413      =/  ip=@if  (end [0 32] p.lane)
2414      =/  pt=@ud  (cut 0 [32 16] p.lane)
2415      ?:  =(%czar (clan:title ship))
2416        %-  %^  ev-trace  odd.veb  ship
2417            |.("ignoring %dear lane {(scow %if ip)}:{(scow %ud pt)} for galaxy")
2418        event-core
2419      =/  peer-state=(unit peer-state)  (get-peer-state ship)
2420      ?~  peer-state
2421        %-  %^  ev-trace  odd.veb  ship
2422            |.("no peer-state for ship, ignoring %dear")
2423        event-core
2424      %-  %^  ev-trace  rcv.veb  ship
2425          |.("incoming %dear lane {(scow %if ip)}:{(scow %ud pt)}")
2426      abet:(on-dear:(abed-peer:pe ship u.peer-state) lane)
2427    ::  +on-hear: handle raw packet receipt
2428    ::
2429    ++  on-hear
2430      |=  [l=lane b=blob d=(unit goof)]
2431      ^+  event-core
2432      =/  =shot      (sift-shot b)
2433      ?:  sam.shot  (on-hear-packet l shot d)
2434      ?:  req.shot  ~|([%fine %request-events-forbidden] !!)
```

```
        ::  TODO no longer true
        ::NOTE  we only send requests to ships we know,
        ::        so we should only get responses from ships we know.
        ::        below we assume sndr.shot is a known peer.
    =*  her  sndr.shot
    =+  ?~  d  ~
        %.  ~
        =*  mot  mote.u.d
        %+  slog  leaf+"ames: fine from {<her>} on {<l>} crashed {<mot>}"
        ?.  msg.veb  ~
        tang.u.d
    abet:(on-hear-fine:(abed-got:pe her) l shot)
  ::  +on-hear-packet: handle mildly processed packet receipt
  ::
  ++  on-hear-packet
    ~/  %on-hear-packet
    |=  [=lane =shot dud=(unit goof)]
    ^+  event-core
    %-  (ev-trace rcv.veb sndr.shot |.("received packet"))
    ::
    ?:  =(our sndr.shot)
      event-core
    ?:  .=  =(%deny form.snub.ames-state)
        (~(has in ships.snub.ames-state) sndr.shot)
      %-  (ev-trace rcv.veb sndr.shot |.("snubbed"))
      event-core
    ::
    %.  +<
    ::
    ?.  =(our rcvr.shot)
      on-hear-forward
    ::
    ?:  =(%keys content.shot)
      on-hear-keys
    ?:  ?&  ?=(%pawn (clan:title sndr.shot))
            !?=([~ %known *] (~(get by peers.ames-state) sndr.shot))
        ==
      on-hear-open
    on-hear-shut
  ::  +on-hear-forward: maybe forward a packet to someone else
  ::
  ::    Note that this performs all forwarding requests without
  ::    filtering.  Any protection against DDoS amplification will be
  ::    provided by Vere.
  ::
  ++  on-hear-forward
    ~/  %on-hear-forward
    |=  [=lane =shot dud=(unit goof)]
    ^+  event-core
    %-  %^  ev-trace  for.veb  sndr.shot
        |.("forward: {<sndr.shot>} -> {<rcvr.shot>}")
    ::  set .origin.shot if it doesn't have one, re-encode, and send
    ::
    =?  origin.shot
        &(?=(~ origin.shot) !=(%czar (clan:title sndr.shot)))
      ?:  ?=(%& -.lane)
        ~
      ?.  (lte (met 3 p.lane) 6)
```

```
2493              ~|  ames-lane-size+p.lane   !!
2494            `p.lane
2495        ::
2496        =/  =blob  (etch-shot shot)
2497        (send-blob for=& rcvr.shot blob (~(get by peers.ames-state) rcvr.shot))
2498      ::  +on-hear-keys: handle receipt of attestion request
2499      ::
2500      ++  on-hear-keys
2501        ~/  %on-hear-keys
2502        |=  [=lane =shot dud=(unit goof)]
2503        =+  %^  ev-trace  msg.veb  sndr.shot
2504            |.("requested attestation")
2505        ?.  =(%pawn (clan:title our))
2506          event-core
2507        =/  =blob  (attestation-packet sndr.shot 1)
2508        (send-blob for=| sndr.shot blob (~(get by peers.ames-state) sndr.shot))
2509      ::  +on-hear-open: handle receipt of plaintext comet self-attestation
2510      ::
2511      ++  on-hear-open
2512        ~/  %on-hear-open
2513        |=  [=lane =shot dud=(unit goof)]
2514        ^+  event-core
2515        =+  %^  ev-trace  msg.veb  sndr.shot
2516            |.("got attestation")
2517        ::  assert the comet can't pretend to be a moon or other address
2518        ::
2519        ?>  ?=(%pawn (clan:title sndr.shot))
2520        ::  if we already know .sndr, ignore duplicate attestation
2521        ::
2522        =/  ship-state  (~(get by peers.ames-state) sndr.shot)
2523        ?:  ?=([~ %known *] ship-state)
2524          event-core
2525        ::
2526        =/  =open-packet  (sift-open-packet shot our life.ames-state)
2527        ::  add comet as an %alien if we haven't already
2528        ::
2529        =?  peers.ames-state  ?=(~ ship-state)
2530          (~(put by peers.ames-state) sndr.shot %alien *alien-agenda)
2531        ::  upgrade comet to %known via on-publ-full
2532        ::
2533        =.  event-core
2534          =/  crypto-suite=@ud  1
2535          =/  keys
2536            (my [sndr-life.open-packet crypto-suite public-key.open-packet]~)
2537          =/  =point
2538            :*  ^=      rift  0
2539                ^=      life  sndr-life.open-packet
2540                ^=      keys  keys
2541                ^=  sponsor  `(^sein:title sndr.shot)
2542            ==
2543          (on-publ / [%full (my [sndr.shot point]~)])
2544        ::  manually add the lane to the peer state
2545        ::
2546        =/  =peer-state  (gut-peer-state sndr.shot)
2547        =.  route.peer-state  `[direct=%.n lane]
2548        =.  peers.ames-state
2549          (~(put by peers.ames-state) sndr.shot %known peer-state)
2550        ::
```

```
2551          =.  event-core
2552            %-  emit
2553            :*  unix-duct.ames-state  %give  %nail  sndr.shot
2554                (get-forward-lanes our peer-state peers.ames-state)
2555            ==
2556          ::
2557          event-core
2558      ::  +on-hear-shut: handle receipt of encrypted packet
2559      ::
2560      ++  on-hear-shut
2561        ~/  %on-hear-shut
2562        |=  [=lane =shot dud=(unit goof)]
2563        ^+  event-core
2564        =/  sndr-state  (~(get by peers.ames-state) sndr.shot)
2565        ::  If we don't know them, ask Jael for their keys. If they're a
2566        ::  comet, this will also cause us to request a self-attestation
2567        ::  from the sender. The packet itself is dropped; we can assume it
2568        ::  will be resent.
2569        ::
2570        ?.  ?=([~ %known *] sndr-state)
2571          (enqueue-alien-todo sndr.shot sndr-state |=(alien-agenda +<))
2572        ::  decrypt packet contents using symmetric-key.channel
2573        ::
2574        ::    If we know them, we have a $channel with them, which we've
2575        ::    populated with a .symmetric-key derived from our private key
2576        ::    and their public key using elliptic curve Diffie-Hellman.
2577        ::
2578        =/  =peer-state   +.u.sndr-state
2579        =/  =channel      [[our sndr.shot] now channel-state -.peer-state]
2580        =?  event-core  !=(sndr-tick.shot (mod her-life.channel 16))
2581          %.  event-core
2582          %^  ev-trace  odd.veb  sndr.shot
2583          |.  ^-  tape
2584          =/  sndr  [sndr-tick=sndr-tick.shot her-life=her-life.channel]
2585          "sndr-tick mismatch {<sndr>}"
2586        =?  event-core  !=(rcvr-tick.shot (mod our-life.channel 16))
2587          %.  event-core
2588          %^  ev-trace  odd.veb  sndr.shot
2589          |.  ^-  tape
2590          =/  rcvr  [rcvr-tick=rcvr-tick.shot our-life=our-life.channel]
2591          "rcvr-tick mismatch {<rcvr>}"
2592        ~|  %ames-crash-on-packet-from^her.channel
2593        =/  shut-packet=(unit shut-packet)
2594          (sift-shut-packet shot [symmetric-key her-life our-life]:channel)
2595        ?~  shut-packet
2596          event-core
2597        =/  old-route  route.peer-state
2598        ::  non-galaxy: update route with heard lane or forwarded lane
2599        ::
2600        =?  route.peer-state  !=(%czar (clan:title her.channel))
2601          ::  if new packet is direct, use that.  otherwise, if the new new
2602          ::  and old lanes are indirect, use the new one.  if the new lane
2603          ::  is indirect but the old lane is direct, then if the lanes are
2604          ::  identical, don't mark it indirect; if they're not identical,
2605          ::  use the new lane and mark it indirect.
2606          ::
2607          ::  if you mark lane as indirect because you got an indirect
2608          ::  packet even though you already had a direct identical lane,
```

```
      ::  then delayed forwarded packets will come later and reset to
      ::  indirect, so you're unlikely to get a stable direct route
      ::  (unless the forwarder goes offline for a while).
      ::
      ::  conversely, if you don't accept indirect routes with different
      ::  lanes, then if your lane is stale and they're trying to talk
      ::  to you, your acks will go to the stale lane, and you'll never
      ::  time it out unless you reach out to them.  this manifests as
      ::  needing to |hi or dotpost to get a response when the other
      ::  ship has changed lanes.
      ::
      ?:  ?=(~ origin.shot)
        `[direct=%.y lane]
      ?:  ?=([~ %& *] route.peer-state)
        ?:  =(lane.u.route.peer-state |+u.origin.shot)
          route.peer-state
        `[direct=%.n |+u.origin.shot]
      `[direct=%.n |+u.origin.shot]
    ::
    =?  event-core  !=(old-route route.peer-state)
      %-  emit
      :*  unix-duct.ames-state  %give  %nail  sndr.shot
          (get-forward-lanes our peer-state peers.ames-state)
      ==
    ::  perform peer-specific handling of packet
    ::
    =<  abet
    (~(on-hear-shut-packet pe peer-state channel) [lane u.shut-packet dud])
  ::  +on-take-boon: receive request to give message to peer
  ::
  ++  on-take-boon
    |=  [=wire payload=*]
    ^+  event-core
    ?~  parsed=(parse-bone-wire wire)
      ~>  %slog.0^leaf/"ames: dropping malformed wire: {(spud wire)}"
      event-core
    ::
    ?>  ?=([@ her=ship *] u.parsed)
    =*  her         her.u.parsed
    =/  peer-core   (abed-got:pe her)
    ::
    ?:  ?&  ?=([%new *] u.parsed)
            (lth rift.u.parsed rift.peer-state.peer-core)
        ==
      ::  ignore events from an old rift
      ::
      %-  %^  ev-trace  odd.veb  her
          |.("dropping old rift wire: {(spud wire)}")
      event-core
    =/  =bone
      ?-(u.parsed [%new *] bone.u.parsed, [%old *] bone.u.parsed)
    =?  peer-core  ?=([%old *] u.parsed)
      %-  %^  ev-trace  odd.veb  her
          |.("parsing old wire: {(spud wire)}")
      peer-core
    abet:(on-memo:peer-core bone [%boon payload])
  ::  +on-plea: handle request to send message
  ::
```

```
2667        ++  on-plea
2668          |=  [=ship =plea]
2669          ^+  event-core
2670          =/  ship-state  (~(get by peers.ames-state) ship)
2671          ::
2672          ?.  ?=([~ %known *] ship-state)
2673            %^  enqueue-alien-todo  ship  ship-state
2674            |=  todos=alien-agenda
2675            todos(messages [[duct plea] messages.todos])
2676          ::
2677          =+  peer-core=(abed-peer:pe ship +.u.ship-state)
2678          ::  .plea is from local vane to foreign ship
2679          ::
2680          =^  =bone  peer-core  (bind-duct:peer-core duct)
2681          %-  %^  ev-trace  msg.veb  ship
2682            |.  ^-  tape
2683            =/  sndr  [our our-life.channel.peer-core]
2684            =/  rcvr  [ship her-life.channel.peer-core]
2685            "plea {<sndr rcvr bone=bone vane.plea path.plea>}"
2686          abet:(on-memo:peer-core bone [%plea plea])
2687        ::  +on-tame: handle request to delete a route
2688        ::
2689        ++  on-tame
2690          |=  =ship
2691          ^+  event-core
2692          ?:  =(%czar (clan:title ship))
2693            %-  %+  slog
2694            leaf+"ames: bad idea to %tame galaxy {(scow %p ship)}, ignoring"
2695            ~
2696            event-core
2697          =/  peer-state=(unit peer-state)  (get-peer-state ship)
2698          ?~  peer-state
2699            %-  (slog leaf+"ames: no peer-state for {(scow %p ship)}, ignoring" ~)
2700            event-core
2701          abet:on-tame:(abed-peer:pe ship u.peer-state)
2702        ::
2703        ::
2704        ++  on-tune
2705          |=  [=wire s=[=ship path=(pole knot)] roar=(unit roar)]
2706          ^+  event-core
2707          ::  XX save or decrypt path?
2708          ::  XX crash in decryption/cue indicates misbehaving peer
2709          ::
2710          =/  per  (~(get by peers.ames-state) ship.s)
2711          ?>  ?=([~ %known *] per)
2712          ?>  ?=([%a %x @ %$ rest=*] path.s)
2713          ?.  ?=([%chum her=@ lyf=@ cyf=@ ~] rest.path.s)
2714            =>  .(wire `(pole knot)`wire)
2715            ~|  bad-wire/wire
2716            ?>  ?=([%fine %shut idx=@ ~] wire)
2717            ~|  bad-path/rest.path.s
2718            ?>  ?=([%fine %shut kef=@ cyf=@ ~] rest.path.s)
2719          =/  [key=@ ,path]  (~(got by chain.u.per) (slav %ud idx.wire))
2720          =/  raw=@t
2721            (dy:crub:crypto key (slav %uv cyf.rest.path.s))
2722          =/  pax=path
2723            (stab raw)
2724          =;  dat=(unit (unit page))
```

```
2725          (emit duct [%give %near [ship.s pax] dat])
2726      ?:  ?|  ?=(~ roar)
2727              ?=(~ q.dat.u.roar)
2728          ==
2729      ~  :: XX weird
2730      ?>  ?=([%atom @] u.q.dat.u.roar)
2731      =-  ``;;(page (cue -))
2732      (dy:crub:crypto key q.u.q.dat.u.roar)
2733    ?>  ?=([%chum *] wire)
2734    =/  pax
2735      %-  stab
2736      (dy:crub:crypto symmetric-key.u.per (slav %uv cyf.rest.path.s))
2737    =/  dat=(unit (unit page))
2738      ?:  ?|  ?=(~ roar)
2739              ?=(~ q.dat.u.roar)
2740          ==
2741      ~  :: XX weird
2742      ?>  ?=([%atom @] u.q.dat.u.roar)
2743      =-  `?~(- ~ `(,page (cue -)))
2744      (dy:crub:crypto symmetric-key.u.per q.u.q.dat.u.roar)
2745    (emit duct [%give %near [ship.s pax] dat])
2746  ::  +on-cork: handle request to kill a flow
2747  ::
2748  ++  on-cork
2749    |=  =ship
2750    ^+  event-core
2751    =/  =plea        [%$ /flow [%cork ~]]
2752    =/  ship-state  (~(get by peers.ames-state) ship)
2753    ?.  ?=([~ %known *] ship-state)
2754      %^  enqueue-alien-todo  ship  ship-state
2755      |=  todos=alien-agenda
2756      todos(messages [[duct plea] messages.todos])
2757    ::
2758    =+  peer-core=(abed-peer:pe ship +.u.ship-state)
2759    =^  =bone  peer-core
2760      ?^  cork-bone  [u.cork-bone peer-core]
2761      (bind-duct:peer-core duct)
2762    ::
2763    ?.  (~(has by by-bone.ossuary.peer-state.peer-core) bone)
2764      %.  event-core
2765      %^  ev-trace  odd.veb  ship
2766      |.("trying to cork {<bone=bone>}, not in the ossuary, ignoring")
2767    ::
2768    %-  %^  ev-trace  msg.veb  ship
2769        |.  ^-  tape
2770        =/  sndr  [our our-life.channel.peer-core]
2771        =/  rcvr  [ship her-life.channel.peer-core]
2772        "cork plea {<sndr rcvr bone=bone vane.plea path.plea>}"
2773    abet:(on-memo:(on-cork-flow:peer-core bone) bone [%plea plea])
2774  ::  +on-kroc: cork all stale flows from failed subscriptions
2775  ::
2776  ++  on-kroc
2777    |=  bones=(list [ship bone])
2778    ^+  event-core
2779    %+  roll  bones
2780    |=  [[=ship =bone] co=_event-core]
2781    (%*(on-cork co cork-bone `bone) ship)
2782  ::  +on-deep: deferred %ames calls from itself
```

```
2783          ::
2784          ++  on-deep
2785            |=  =deep
2786            ^+  event-core
2787            ::  currently $deep tasks are all focused on a
2788            ::  particular ship but future ones might not
2789            ::
2790            ?>  ?=([@ =ship *] deep)
2791            =/  ship-state  (~(get by peers.ames-state) ship.deep)
2792            ?>  ?=([~ %known *] ship-state)
2793            =+  peer-core=(abed-peer:pe ship.deep +.u.ship-state)
2794            |^  ?-  -.deep
2795              %nack  abet:(send-nack-trace [nack-bone message]:deep)
2796              %sink  abet:(sink-naxplanation [target-bone naxplanation]:deep)
2797              %drop  abet:(clear-nack [nack-bone message-num]:deep)
2798              %cork  =~((cork-bone bone.deep) (emit duct %give %done ~))
2799              %kill  (kill-bone bone.deep)
2800            ==
2801          ::
2802          ++  send-nack-trace
2803            |=  [=nack=bone =message]
2804            abet:(call:(abed:mu:peer-core nack-bone) %memo message)
2805          ::
2806          ++  sink-naxplanation
2807            |=  [=target=bone =naxplanation]
2808            abet:(call:(abed:mu:peer-core target-bone) %near naxplanation)
2809          ::
2810          ++  clear-nack
2811            |=  [=nack=bone =message-num]
2812            abet:(call:(abed:mi:peer-core nack-bone) %drop message-num)
2813          ::  client ames [%cork as plea] ->  server ames [sinks %cork plea],
2814          ::                                   pass %deep %cork task to self
2815          ::                                   put flow in closing (+cork-bone),
2816          ::                                   and give %done
2817          ::  sink %ack, pass %deep %kill <-  after +on-take-done, ack %cork plea
2818          ::  task to self, and delete the   and delete the flow in +handle-cork
2819          ::  flow (+kill-bone)
2820          ::
2821          ::
2822          ++  cork-bone  |=(=bone abet:(on-cork-flow:peer-core bone))
2823          ++  kill-bone  |=(=bone abet:(on-kill-flow:peer-core bone))
2824          --
2825        ::  +on-stun: poke %ping app when hearing a STUN response
2826        ::
2827        ++  on-stun
2828          |=  =stun
2829          ^+  event-core
2830          %-  %^  ev-trace  sun.veb  ship.stun
2831              =/  lane=tape
2832                ?:  &
2833                  ::  turn off until correct parsing ip/port in ames.c
2834                  ::  (see https://github.com/urbit/vere/pull/623)
2835                  ""
2836                ?:  ?=(%& -.lane.stun)
2837                  "from {<p.lane.stun>}"
2838                =,  lane.stun
2839                =/  ip=@if  (end [0 32] p)
2840                =/  pt=@ud  (cut 0 [32 16] p)
```

```
2841          "lane {(scow %if ip)}:{((d-co:co 1) pt)} ({(scow %ux p)})"
2842          |.("inject %stun {<-.stun>} {lane}")
2843      %-  emit
2844      %^  poke-ping-app  unix-duct.ames-state  our
2845      ?.  ?=(%fail -.stun)  -.stun
2846      [%kick fail=%.y]
2847  ::  +set-dead-flow-timer: set dead flow timer and corresponding ames state
2848  ::
2849  ++  set-dead-flow-timer
2850    ^+  event-core
2851    =.  flow.dead.ames-state.event-core
2852      flow/`[~[/ames] /dead-flow `@da`(add now ~m2)]
2853    (emit ~[/ames] %pass /dead-flow %b %wait `@da`(add now ~m2))
2854  ::  +wake-dead-flows: call on-wake on all dead flows, discarding any
2855  ::                    ames-state changes
2856  ::
2857  ++  wake-dead-flows
2858    |=  error=(unit tang)
2859    ^+  event-core
2860    %-  ~(rep by peers.ames-state:event-core)
2861    |=  [[=ship =ship-state] core=_event-core]
2862    ^+  event-core
2863    =/  peer-state=(unit peer-state)  (get-peer-state:core ship)
2864    ?~  peer-state  core
2865    =/  peer-core  (abed-peer:pe:core ship u.peer-state)
2866    =<  abort
2867    ^+  peer-core
2868    %-  ~(rep by snd.u.peer-state)
2869    |=  [[=bone =message-pump-state] cor=_peer-core]
2870    ?.  ?&  =(~m2 rto.metrics.packet-pump-state.message-pump-state)
2871            ?=(^ next-wake.packet-pump-state.message-pump-state)
2872        ==
2873      cor
2874    (on-wake:cor bone error)
2875  ::  +on-take-wake: receive wakeup or error notification from behn
2876  ::
2877  ++  on-take-wake
2878    |=  [=wire error=(unit tang)]
2879    ^+  event-core
2880    ?:  ?=([%alien @ ~] wire)
2881      ::  if we haven't received an attestation, ask again
2882      ::
2883      ?^  error
2884        %-  (slog 'ames: attestation timer failed' u.error)
2885        event-core
2886      ?~  ship=`(unit @p)`(slaw %p i.t.wire)
2887        %-  (slog leaf+"ames: got timer for strange wire: {<wire>}" ~)
2888        event-core
2889      =/  ship-state  (~(get by peers.ames-state) u.ship)
2890      ?:  ?=([~ %known *] ship-state)
2891        event-core
2892      (request-attestation u.ship)
2893    ::
2894    ?:  ?=([%dead-flow ~] wire)
2895      set-dead-flow-timer:(wake-dead-flows error)
2896    ::
2897    ?.  ?=([%recork ~] wire)
2898      =/  res=(unit ?([%fine her=ship =^wire] [%pump her=ship =bone]))
```

```
2899              ?+  wire  ~
2900                [%pump ship=@ bone=@ ~]  (parse-pump-wire &2.wire &3.wire)
2901                [%fine %behn %wake @ *]  (parse-fine-wire &4.wire t.t.t.t.wire)
2902              ==
2903            ?~  res
2904              %-  (slog leaf+"ames: got timer for strange wire: {<wire>}" ~)
2905              event-core
2906            ::
2907            =/  state=(unit peer-state)  (get-peer-state her.u.res)
2908            ?~  state
2909              %.  event-core
2910              %-  slog
2911              [leaf+"ames: got timer for strange ship: {<her.u.res>}, ignoring" ~]
2912            ::
2913            =/  peer-core  (abed-peer:pe her.u.res u.state)
2914            ?-  -.u.res
2915              %pump  abet:(on-wake:peer-core bone.u.res error)
2916              ::
2917                %fine
2918              ?.  (~(has by keens.peer-state.peer-core) wire.u.res)
2919                event-core
2920              abet:fi-abet:fi-take-wake:(abed:fi:peer-core wire.u.res)
2921            ==
2922          ::
2923          =.  event-core  (emit duct %pass /recork %b %wait `@da`(add now ~d1))
2924          =.  cork.dead.ames-state
2925            cork/`[~[/ames] /recork `@da`(add now ~d1)]
2926          ::
2927          ?^  error
2928            %-  (slog 'ames: recork timer failed' u.error)
2929            event-core
2930          ::  recork up to one bone per peer
2931          ::
2932          =/  pez  ~(tap by peers.ames-state)
2933          |-  ^+  event-core
2934          ?~  pez  event-core
2935          =+  [her sat]=i.pez
2936          ?.  ?=(%known -.sat)
2937            $(pez t.pez)
2938          $(pez t.pez, event-core abet:recork-one:(abed-peer:pe her +.sat))
2939        ::  +on-init: first boot; subscribe to our info from jael
2940        ::
2941        ++  on-init
2942          ^+  event-core
2943          ::
2944          =~  (emit duct %pass /turf %j %turf ~)
2945              (emit duct %pass /private-keys %j %private-keys ~)
2946              (emit duct %pass /public-keys %j %public-keys [n=our ~ ~])
2947          ==
2948        ::  +on-priv: set our private key to jael's response
2949        ::
2950        ++  on-priv
2951          |=  [=life vein=(map life private-key)]
2952          ^+  event-core
2953          ::
2954          =/  =private-key            (~(got by vein) life)
2955          =.  life.ames-state         life
2956          =.  crypto-core.ames-state  (nol:nu:crub:crypto private-key)
```

```
::  recalculate each peer's symmetric key
::
=/  our-private-key  sec:ex:crypto-core.ames-state
=.  peers.ames-state
  %-  ~(run by peers.ames-state)
  |=  =ship-state
  ^+  ship-state
  ::
  ?.  ?=(%known -.ship-state)
    ship-state
  ::
  =/  =peer-state  +.ship-state
  =.  symmetric-key.peer-state
    (derive-symmetric-key public-key.+.ship-state our-private-key)
  ::
  [%known peer-state]
::
event-core
::  +on-publ: update pki data for peer or self
::
++  on-publ
  |=  [=wire =public-keys-result]
  ^+  event-core
  ::
  |^  ^+  event-core
      ::
      ?-    public-keys-result
          [%diff @ %rift *]
        (on-publ-rift [who to.diff]:public-keys-result)
      ::
          [%diff @ %keys *]
        (on-publ-rekey [who to.diff]:public-keys-result)
      ::
          [%diff @ %spon *]
        (on-publ-sponsor [who to.diff]:public-keys-result)
      ::
          [%full *]
        (on-publ-full points.public-keys-result)
      ::
          [%breach *]
        (on-publ-breach who.public-keys-result)
      ==
  ::  +on-publ-breach: handle continuity breach of .ship; wipe its state
  ::
  ::    Abandon all pretense of continuity and delete all messaging state
  ::    associated with .ship, including sent and unsent messages.
  ::    Also cancel all timers related to .ship.
  ::
  ++  on-publ-breach
    |=  =ship
    ^+  event-core
    ?:  =(our ship)
      event-core
    ::
    =/  ship-state  (~(get by peers.ames-state) ship)
    ::  we shouldn't be hearing about ships we don't care about
    ::
    ?~  ship-state
```

```
3015          ~>  %slog.0^leaf/"ames: breach unknown {<our ship>}"
3016          event-core
3017      ::  if an alien breached, this doesn't affect us
3018      ::
3019      ?:  ?=([~ %alien *] ship-state)
3020          ~>  %slog.0^leaf/"ames: breach alien {<our ship>}"
3021          event-core
3022      ~>  %slog.0^leaf/"ames: breach peer {<our ship>}"
3023      ::  a peer breached; drop messaging state
3024      ::
3025      =/  =peer-state  +.u.ship-state
3026      =/  old-qos=qos  qos.peer-state
3027      ::  cancel all timers related to .ship
3028      ::
3029      =.  event-core
3030        %+  roll  ~(tap by snd.peer-state)
3031        |=  [[=snd=bone =message-pump-state] core=_event-core]
3032        ^+  core
3033        ::
3034        ?~  next-wake=next-wake.packet-pump-state.message-pump-state
3035          core
3036        ::  note: copies +on-pump-rest:message-pump
3037        ::
3038        =/  wire  (make-pump-timer-wire ship snd-bone)
3039        =/  duct  ~[/ames]
3040        (emit:core duct %pass wire %b %rest u.next-wake)
3041      ::  reset all peer state other than pki data
3042      ::
3043      =.  +.peer-state  +:*^peer-state
3044      ::  print change to quality of service, if any
3045      ::
3046      =/  text=(unit tape)
3047        %^  qos-update-text  ship  %ames
3048        [old-qos qos.peer-state kay.veb ships.bug.ames-state]
3049      ::
3050      =?  event-core  ?=(^ text)
3051        (emit duct %pass /qos %d %flog %text u.text)
3052      ::  reinitialize galaxy route if applicable
3053      ::
3054      =?  route.peer-state  =(%czar (clan:title ship))
3055        `[direct=%.y lane=[%& ship]]
3056      ::
3057      =.  peers.ames-state
3058        (~(put by peers.ames-state) ship [%known peer-state])
3059      ::
3060      =.  event-core
3061        %-  emit
3062        :*  unix-duct.ames-state  %give  %nail  ship
3063            (get-forward-lanes our peer-state peers.ames-state)
3064        ==
3065      ::  if one of our sponsors breached, give the updated list to vere
3066      ::
3067      =/  sponsors  (~(gas in *(set ^ship)) get-sponsors)
3068      =?  event-core  (~(has in sponsors) ship)
3069        (emit unix-duct.ames-state %give %saxo ~(tap in sponsors))
3070      ::
3071      event-core
3072    ::  +on-publ-rekey: handle new key for peer
```

```
3073      ::
3074      ::    TODO: assert .crypto-suite compatibility
3075      ::
3076      ++  on-publ-rekey
3077        |=  $:  =ship
3078                =life
3079                crypto-suite=@ud
3080                =public-key
3081            ==
3082      ^+  event-core
3083      ?:  =(our ship)
3084        event-core
3085      ::
3086      =/  ship-state  (~(get by peers.ames-state) ship)
3087      ?.  ?=([~ %known *] ship-state)
3088        =|  =point
3089        =.  life.point      life
3090        =.  keys.point      (my [life crypto-suite public-key]~)
3091        =.  sponsor.point   `(^^sein:title rof /ames our now ship)
3092        ::
3093        (on-publ-full (my [ship point]~))
3094      ::
3095      =/  =peer-state    +.u.ship-state
3096      =/  =private-key   sec:ex:crypto-core.ames-state
3097      =.  symmetric-key.peer-state
3098        (derive-symmetric-key public-key private-key)
3099      ::
3100      =.  life.peer-state        life
3101      =.  public-key.peer-state  public-key
3102      ::
3103      =.  peers.ames-state
3104        (~(put by peers.ames-state) ship %known peer-state)
3105      event-core
3106    ::  +on-publ-sponsor: handle new or lost sponsor for peer
3107    ::
3108    ::    TODO: really handle sponsor loss
3109    ::
3110    ++  on-publ-sponsor
3111      |=  [=ship sponsor=(unit ship)]
3112      ^+  event-core
3113      ::
3114      ?:  =(our ship)
3115        (emit unix-duct.ames-state %give %saxo get-sponsors)
3116      ::
3117      ?~  sponsor
3118        %-  (slog leaf+"ames: {(scow %p ship)} lost sponsor, ignoring" ~)
3119        event-core
3120      ::
3121      =/  state=(unit peer-state)  (get-peer-state ship)
3122      ?~  state
3123        %-  (slog leaf+"ames: missing peer-state, ignoring" ~)
3124        event-core
3125      =.  sponsor.u.state    u.sponsor
3126      =.  peers.ames-state  (~(put by peers.ames-state) ship %known u.state)
3127      =.  event-core
3128        %-  emit
3129        :*  unix-duct.ames-state  %give  %nail  ship
3130            (get-forward-lanes our u.state peers.ames-state)
```

```hoon
3131                  ==
3132              ::
3133          event-core
3134      ::  +on-publ-full: handle new pki data for peer(s)
3135      ::
3136      ++  on-publ-full
3137        |=  points=(map ship point)
3138        ^+  event-core
3139        ::
3140        =>  .(points ~(tap by points))
3141        |^  ^+  event-core
3142            ?~  points  event-core
3143            ::
3144            =+  ^-  [=ship =point]  i.points
3145            ::
3146            =?  rift.ames-state  =(our ship)
3147              rift.point
3148            ::
3149            ::  XX not needed?
3150            ::  =?  event-core  =(our ship)
3151            ::    (emit unix-duct.ames-state %give %saxo get-sponsors)
3152            ?.  (~(has by keys.point) life.point)
3153              $(points t.points)
3154            ::
3155            =/  old-ship-state  (~(get by peers.ames-state) ship)
3156            ::
3157            =.  event-core  (insert-peer-state ship point)
3158            ::
3159            =?  event-core  ?=([~ %alien *] old-ship-state)
3160              (meet-alien ship point +.u.old-ship-state)
3161            ::
3162            $(points t.points)
3163        ::
3164        ++  meet-alien
3165          |=  [=ship =point todos=alien-agenda]
3166          |^  ^+  event-core
3167          ::  if we're a comet, send self-attestation packet first
3168          ::
3169          =?  event-core  =(%pawn (clan:title our))
3170            =/  =blob  (attestation-packet ship life.point)
3171            (send-blob for=| ship blob (~(get by peers.ames-state) ship))
3172          ::  save current duct
3173          ::
3174          =/  original-duct  duct
3175          ::  apply heeds
3176          ::
3177          =.  event-core
3178            %+  roll  ~(tap in heeds.todos)
3179            |=  [=^duct core=_event-core]
3180            (on-heed:core(duct duct) ship)
3181          ::  apply outgoing messages, reversing for FIFO order
3182          ::
3183          =.  event-core
3184            %+  reel  messages.todos
3185            |=  [[=^duct =plea] core=_event-core]
3186            ?:  ?=(%$ -.plea)
3187              (on-cork:core(duct duct) ship)
3188            (on-plea:core(duct duct) ship plea)
```

```
3189            ::    apply outgoing packet blobs
3190            ::
3191            =.    event-core
3192              %+  roll  ~(tap in packets.todos)
3193              |=  [=blob core=_event-core]
3194              (send-blob:core for=| ship blob (~(get by peers.ames-state) ship))
3195            ::    apply remote scry requests
3196            ::
3197            =.    event-core  (meet-alien-fine keens.todos)
3198            ::
3199            event-core(duct original-duct)
3200            ::
3201            ++    meet-alien-fine
3202              |=  peens=(jug path ^duct)
3203              ^+  event-core
3204              =+  peer-core=(abed:pe ship)
3205              =<  abet  ^+  peer-core
3206              %-  ~(rep by peens)
3207              |=  [[=path ducts=(set ^duct)] cor=_peer-core]
3208              (~(rep in ducts) |=([=^duct c=_cor] (on-keen:c path duct)))
3209            --
3210          --
3211      ::  on-publ-rift: XX
3212      ::
3213      ++  on-publ-rift
3214        |=  [=ship =rift]
3215        ^+  event-core
3216        =?  rift.ames-state  =(our ship)
3217          rift
3218        ?~  ship-state=(~(get by peers.ames-state) ship)
3219          ::  print error here? %rift was probably called before %keys
3220          ::
3221          ~>  %slog.1^leaf/"ames: missing peer-state on-publ-rift"
3222          event-core
3223        ?:  ?=([%alien *] u.ship-state)
3224          ::  ignore aliens
3225          ::
3226          event-core
3227        =/  =peer-state      +.u.ship-state
3228        =.  rift.peer-state  rift
3229        =.  peers.ames-state
3230          (~(put by peers.ames-state) ship %known peer-state)
3231        event-core
3232      ::
3233      ++  insert-peer-state
3234        |=  [=ship =point]
3235        ^+  event-core
3236        ::
3237        =/  =peer-state      (gut-peer-state ship)
3238        =/  =public-key      pass:(~(got by keys.point) life.point)
3239        =/  =private-key     sec:ex:crypto-core.ames-state
3240        =/  =symmetric-key   (derive-symmetric-key public-key private-key)
3241        ::
3242        =.  qos.peer-state            [%unborn now]
3243        =.  life.peer-state           life.point
3244        =.  rift.peer-state           rift.point
3245        =.  public-key.peer-state     public-key
3246        =.  symmetric-key.peer-state  symmetric-key
```

```
3247          =.  sponsor.peer-state
3248            ?^  sponsor.point
3249              u.sponsor.point
3250            (^^sein:title rof /ames our now ship)
3251          ::  automatically set galaxy route, since unix handles lookup
3252          ::
3253          =?  route.peer-state  ?=(%czar (clan:title ship))
3254            `[direct=%.y lane=[%& ship]]
3255          ::
3256          =.  peers.ames-state
3257            (~(put by peers.ames-state) ship %known peer-state)
3258          ::
3259          =?  event-core  ?=(%czar (clan:title ship))
3260            %-  emit
3261            :*  unix-duct.ames-state  %give  %nail  ship
3262                (get-forward-lanes our peer-state peers.ames-state)
3263            ==
3264        event-core
3265      --
3266    ::  +on-take-turf: relay %turf move from jael to unix
3267    ::
3268    ++  on-take-turf
3269      |=  turfs=(list turf)
3270      ^+  event-core
3271      ::
3272      (emit unix-duct.ames-state %give %turf turfs)
3273    ::  +on-born: handle unix process restart
3274    ::
3275    ++  on-born
3276      ^+  event-core
3277      ::
3278      =.  unix-duct.ames-state  duct
3279      ::
3280      =/  turfs
3281        ;;  (list turf)
3282        =<  q.q  %-  need  %-  need
3283        (rof [~ ~] /ames %j `beam`[[our %turf %da now] /])
3284      ::
3285      =*  duct  unix-duct.ames-state
3286      ::
3287      =^  cork-moves  cork.dead.ames-state
3288        ?.  ?=(~ +.cork.dead.ames-state)
3289          `cork.dead.ames-state
3290        :-  [~[/ames] %pass /recork %b %wait `@da`(add now ~d1)]~
3291        cork/`[~[/ames] /recork `@da`(add now ~d1)]
3292      ::
3293      %-  emil
3294      %+  weld
3295        cork-moves
3296      ^-  (list move)
3297      :~  [duct %give %turf turfs]
3298          [duct %give %saxo get-sponsors]
3299          (poke-ping-app duct our %kick fail=%.n)
3300      ==
3301    ::  +on-vega: handle kernel reload
3302    ::
3303    ++  on-vega  event-core
3304    ::  +on-plug: handle key reservation
```

```
3305    ++  on-plug
3306     |=  =path
3307     ^+  event-core
3308     =/  key=@  (shaz eny) :: TODO: check key width
3309     =/  num=@ud
3310       ?~  latest=(ram:on:chain chain.ames-state)
3311         1
3312       .+(key.u.latest)
3313     =.  chain.ames-state
3314       (put:on:chain chain.ames-state num [key path])
3315     (emit duct %give %stub num key)
3316  ::  +on-trim: handle request to free memory
3317  ::
3318  ::  %ruin comets not seen for six months
3319  ::
3320  ++  on-trim    ::TODO  trim fine parts on high prio
3321     ^+  event-core
3322     =;  rui=(set @p)
3323       (emit duct %pass /ruin %j %ruin rui)
3324     =-  (silt (turn - head))
3325     %+  skim
3326       ~(tap by peers.ames-state)
3327     |=  [=ship s=ship-state]
3328     ?.  &(?=(%known -.s) =(%pawn (clan:title ship)))  %.n
3329     ?&  (gth (sub now ~d180) last-contact.qos.s)
3330         ::
3331         %-  ~(any by snd.s)
3332         |=  m=message-pump-state
3333         !=(~ unsent-fragments.m)
3334     ==
3335  ::
3336  +|  %fine-entry-points
3337  ::
3338  ++  on-keen
3339     |=  [sec=(unit [idx=@ key=@]) spar]
3340     ^+  event-core
3341     =+  ~:(spit path)  ::  assert length
3342     =/  ship-state  (~(get by peers.ames-state) ship)
3343     ?:  ?=([~ %known *] ship-state)
3344       ?~  sec
3345         abet:(on-keen:(abed-peer:pe ship +.u.ship-state) path duct)
3346       =.  chain.u.ship-state  (put:on:chain chain.u.ship-state [idx key /]:u.sec)
3347       =.  peers.ames-state  (~(put by peers.ames-state) ship u.ship-state)
3348       =/  enc
3349         (scot %uv (en:crub:crypto key.u.sec (spat path)))
3350       =/  lav  /a/x/1//fine/shut/(scot %ud idx.u.sec)/[enc]
3351       =/  wir  /fine/shut/(scot %ud idx.u.sec)
3352       (emit duct %pass wir %a %keen ~ ship lav)
3353     :: XX: key exchange over ames forces all encrypted scries to be
3354     :: to a known peer
3355     ?>  ?=(~ sec)
3356     %^  enqueue-alien-todo  ship  ship-state
3357     |=  todos=alien-agenda
3358     todos(keens (~(put ju keens.todos) path duct))
3359  ::
3360  ++  on-chum
3361     |=  spar
3362     ^+  event-core
```

```
3363        =/  ship-state  (~(get by peers.ames-state) ship)
3364        ?.  ?=([~ %known *] ship-state)
3365          %^  enqueue-alien-todo  ship  ship-state
3366          |=  todos=alien-agenda
3367          todos(chums (~(put ju chums.todos) path duct))
3368        =/  cyf
3369        (scot %uv (en:crub:crypto symmetric-key.u.ship-state (spat path)))
3370        =/  lav
3371        /a/x/1//chum/(scot %p our)/(scot %ud life.ames-state)/[cyf]
3372        (emit duct [%pass /chum %a %keen ~ ship lav])
3373      ::
3374      ++  on-cancel-scry
3375        |=  [all=? spar]
3376        ^+  event-core
3377        ?~  ship-state=(~(get by peers.ames-state) ship)
3378          ~|(%cancel-scry-missing-peer^ship^path !!)
3379        ?.  ?=([~ %known *] ship-state)
3380          :: XX delete from alien agenda?
3381          %.  event-core
3382          %^  trace-fine  fin.veb  ship
3383          [ships.bug.ames-state |.("peer still alien, skip cancel-scry")]
3384        =+  peer=(abed:pe ship)
3385        ?.  (~(has by keens.peer-state.peer) path)
3386          event-core
3387        abet:fi-abet:(fi-unsub:(abed:fi:peer path) duct all)
3388      ::
3389      +|  %implementation
3390      ::  +enqueue-alien-todo: helper to enqueue a pending request
3391      ::
3392      ::    Also requests key and life from Jael on first request.
3393      ::    If talking to a comet, requests attestation packet.
3394      ::
3395      ++  enqueue-alien-todo
3396        |=  $:  =ship
3397                ship-state=(unit ship-state)
3398                mutate=$-(alien-agenda alien-agenda)
3399            ==
3400        ^+  event-core
3401        ::  create a default $alien-agenda on first contact
3402        ::
3403        =+  ^-  [already-pending=? todos=alien-agenda]
3404          ?~  ship-state
3405            [%.n *alien-agenda]
3406          [%.y ?>(?=(%alien -.u.ship-state) +.u.ship-state)]
3407        ::  mutate .todos and apply to permanent state
3408        ::
3409        =.  todos            (mutate todos)
3410        =.  peers.ames-state  (~(put by peers.ames-state) ship %alien todos)
3411        ?:  already-pending
3412          event-core
3413        ::
3414        ?:  =(%pawn (clan:title ship))
3415          (request-attestation ship)
3416        ::  NB: we specifically look for this wire in +public-keys-give in
3417        ::  Jael.  if you change it here, you must change it there.
3418        ::
3419        (emit duct %pass /public-keys %j %public-keys [n=ship ~ ~])
3420      ::  +request-attestation: helper to request attestation from comet
```

```
3421      ::
3422      ::    Also sets a timer to resend the request every 30s.
3423      ::
3424      ++  request-attestation
3425        |=  =ship
3426        ^+  event-core
3427        =+  (ev-trace msg.veb ship |.("requesting attestion"))
3428        =.  event-core
3429          =/  =blob  (sendkeys-packet ship)
3430          (send-blob for=| ship blob (~(get by peers.ames-state) ship))
3431        =/  =wire  /alien/(scot %p ship)
3432        (emit duct %pass wire %b %wait (add now ~s30))
3433      ::  +send-blob: fire packet at .ship and maybe sponsors
3434      ::
3435      ::    Send to .ship and sponsors until we find a direct lane,
3436      ::    skipping .our in the sponsorship chain.
3437      ::
3438      ::    If we have no PKI data for a recipient, enqueue the packet and
3439      ::    request the information from Jael if we haven't already.
3440      ::
3441      ++  send-blob
3442        ~/  %send-blob
3443        |=  [for=? =ship =blob ship-state=(unit ship-state)]
3444        ::
3445        =/  final-ship  ship
3446        %-  (ev-trace rot.veb final-ship |.("send-blob: to {<ship>}"))
3447        |-
3448        |^  ^+  event-core
3449          ?.  ?=([~ %known *] ship-state)
3450            ?:  ?=(%pawn (clan:title ship))
3451              (try-next-sponsor (^sein:title ship))
3452            %^  enqueue-alien-todo  ship  ship-state
3453            |=  todos=alien-agenda
3454            todos(packets (~(put in packets.todos) blob))
3455          ::
3456          =/  =peer-state  +.u.ship-state
3457          ::
3458          ::  XX  routing hack to mimic old ames.
3459          ::
3460          ::    Before removing this, consider: moons when their planet is
3461          ::    behind a NAT; a planet receiving initial acknowledgment
3462          ::    from a star; a planet talking to another planet under
3463          ::    another galaxy.
3464          ::
3465          ?:  ?|  =(our ship)
3466                  ?&  !=(final-ship ship)
3467                      !=(%czar (clan:title ship))
3468                  ==
3469              ==
3470            (try-next-sponsor sponsor.peer-state)
3471          ::
3472          ?:  =(our ship)
3473            ::  if forwarding, don't send to sponsor to avoid loops
3474            ::
3475            ?:  for
3476              event-core
3477            (try-next-sponsor sponsor.peer-state)
3478          ::
```

```
3479            ?~  route=route.peer-state
3480              %-  (ev-trace rot.veb final-ship |.("no route to:  {<ship>}"))
3481              (try-next-sponsor sponsor.peer-state)
3482            ::
3483            %-  (ev-trace rot.veb final-ship |.("trying route: {<ship>}"))
3484            =.  event-core
3485              (emit unix-duct.ames-state %give %send lane.u.route blob)
3486            ::
3487            ?:  direct.u.route
3488              event-core
3489            (try-next-sponsor sponsor.peer-state)
3490          ::
3491        ++  try-next-sponsor
3492          |=  sponsor=^ship
3493          ^+  event-core
3494          ::
3495        ?:  =(ship sponsor)
3496          event-core
3497        ^$(ship sponsor, ship-state (~(get by peers.ames-state) sponsor))
3498          --
3499      ::  +attestation-packet: generate signed self-attestation for .her
3500      ::
3501      ::  Sent by a comet on first contact with a peer.  Not acked.
3502      ::
3503      ++  attestation-packet
3504        |=  [her=ship =her=life]
3505        ^-  blob
3506        %-  etch-shot
3507        %-  etch-open-packet
3508        :_  crypto-core.ames-state
3509        :*  ^=  public-key  pub:ex:crypto-core.ames-state
3510            ^=        sndr  our
3511            ^=   sndr-life  life.ames-state
3512            ^=        rcvr  her
3513            ^=   rcvr-life  her-life
3514        ==
3515      ::  +sendkeys-packet: generate a request for a self-attestation.
3516      ::
3517      ::  Sent by non-comets to comets.  Not acked.
3518      ::
3519      ++  sendkeys-packet
3520        |=  her=ship
3521        ^-  blob
3522        ?>  ?=(%pawn (clan:title her))
3523        %-  etch-shot
3524        (encode-keys-packet our her life.ames-state)
3525      ::
3526      +|  %internals
3527      ::  +pe: create nested |peer-core for per-peer processing
3528      ::
3529      ++  pe
3530        |_  [=peer-state =channel]
3531        +*  veb     veb.bug.channel
3532            her     her.channel
3533            keens   keens.peer-state
3534        ::
3535        +|  %helpers
3536        ::
```

```
3537      ++    peer-core   .
3538      ++    pe-emit     |=(move peer-core(event-core (emit +<)))
3539      ++    abed        |=(=ship (abed-peer ship (gut-peer-state ship)))
3540      ++    abed-got    |=(=ship (abed-peer ship (got-peer-state ship)))
3541      ++    abed-peer
3542        |=  [=ship peer=^peer-state]
3543        %_  peer-core
3544          peer-state  peer
3545            channel  [[our ship] now channel-state -.peer]
3546        ==
3547      ::
3548      ++    abort  event-core  :: keeps moves, discards state changes
3549      ++    abet
3550        ^+  event-core
3551        =.  peers.ames-state
3552          (~(put by peers.ames-state) her %known peer-state)
3553        event-core
3554      ::
3555      ++    pe-trace
3556        |=  [verb=? print=(trap tape)]
3557        ^+  same
3558        (ev-trace verb her print)
3559      ::
3560      ::  +got-duct: look up $duct by .bone, asserting already bound
3561      ::
3562      ++    got-duct
3563        |=  =bone
3564        ^-  ^duct
3565        ~|  %dangling-bone^her^bone
3566        (~(got by by-bone.ossuary.peer-state) bone)
3567      ::
3568      ::  +bind-duct: find or make new $bone for .duct in .ossuary
3569      ::
3570      ++    bind-duct
3571        |=  =^duct
3572        =*  ossa  ossuary.peer-state
3573        ^+  [next-bone.ossa peer-core]
3574        ?^  existing=(~(get by by-duct.ossa) duct)
3575          [u.existing peer-core]
3576        :-  next-bone.ossa
3577        =.  ossa
3578          :+  (add 4 next-bone.ossa)
3579            (~(put by by-duct.ossa) duct next-bone.ossa)
3580          (~(put by by-bone.ossa) next-bone.ossa duct)
3581        peer-core
3582      ::
3583      ++    is-corked
3584        |=  =bone
3585        ?|  (~(has in corked.peer-state) bone)
3586            ?&  =(1 (end 0 bone))
3587                =(1 (end 0 (rsh 0 bone)))
3588                (~(has in corked.peer-state) (mix 0b10 bone))
3589        ==  ==
3590      ::
3591      +|  %tasks
3592      ::
3593      ++    on-heed
3594        peer-core(heeds.peer-state (~(put in heeds.peer-state) duct))
```

```
3595          ::
3596      ++  on-jilt
3597        peer-core(heeds.peer-state (~(del in heeds.peer-state) duct))
3598      ::  +update-qos: update and maybe print connection status
3599      ::
3600      ++  update-qos
3601        |=  [mode=?(%ames %fine) =new=qos]
3602        ^+  peer-core
3603        ::
3604        =^  old-qos  qos.peer-state  [qos.peer-state new-qos]
3605        ::  if no update worth reporting, we're done
3606        ::
3607        =/  text
3608          %^  qos-update-text  her  mode
3609          [old-qos new-qos kay.veb ships.bug.ames-state]
3610        ?~  text
3611          peer-core
3612        ::  print message
3613        ::
3614        =.  peer-core  (pe-emit duct %pass /qos %d %flog %text u.text)
3615        ::  if peer has stopped responding, check if %boon's are backing up
3616        ::
3617        ?.  ?=(?(%dead %unborn) -.qos.peer-state)
3618          peer-core
3619        check-clog
3620      ::  +on-hear-shut-packet: handle receipt of ack or message fragment
3621      ::
3622      ++  on-hear-shut-packet
3623        |=  [=lane =shut-packet dud=(unit goof)]
3624        ^+  peer-core
3625        ::  update and print connection status
3626        ::
3627        =.  peer-core  (update-qos %ames %live last-contact=now)
3628        ::
3629        =/  =bone  bone.shut-packet
3630        ::
3631        ?:  ?=(%& -.meat.shut-packet)
3632          =+  ?.  &(?=(^ dud) msg.veb)  ~
3633              %.  ~
3634              %-  slog
3635              :_  tang.u.dud
3636              leaf+"ames: {<her>} fragment crashed {<mote.u.dud>}"
3637          abet:(call:(abed:mi bone) %hear lane shut-packet ?=(~ dud))
3638        ::  benign ack on corked bone
3639        ::
3640        ?:  (is-corked bone)  peer-core
3641        ::  Just try again on error, printing trace
3642        ::
3643        ::    Note this implies that vanes should never crash on %done,
3644        ::    since we have no way to continue using the flow if they do.
3645        ::
3646        =+  ?~  dud  ~
3647            %.  ~
3648            %+  slog  leaf+"ames: {<her>} ack crashed {<mote.u.dud>}"
3649            ?.  msg.veb  ~
3650            :-  >[bone=bone message-num=message-num meat=meat]:shut-packet<
3651            tang.u.dud
3652        abet:(call:(abed:mu bone) %hear [message-num +.meat]:shut-packet)
```

```
3653      ::
3654      ++  on-flub
3655        |=  =bone
3656        ^+  peer-core
3657        abet:(call:(abed:mi:peer-core bone) %flub ~)
3658      ::  +on-memo: handle request to send message
3659      ::
3660      ++  on-memo
3661        |=  [=bone =message]
3662        ^+  peer-core
3663        ?:  ?&  (~(has in closing.peer-state) bone)
3664                !=(message [%plea %$ /flow %cork ~])
3665            ==
3666          ~>  %slog.0^leaf/"ames: ignoring message on closing bone {<bone>}"
3667          peer-core
3668        ?:  (~(has in corked.peer-state) bone)
3669          ~>  %slog.0^leaf/"ames: ignoring message on corked bone {<bone>}"
3670          peer-core
3671        ::
3672        =.  peer-core  abet:(call:(abed:mu bone) %memo message)
3673        ::
3674        ?:  ?&  ?=(%boon -.message)
3675                (gte now (add ~s30 last-contact.qos.peer-state))
3676            ==
3677          check-clog
3678        peer-core
3679      ::  +on-wake: handle timer expiration
3680      ::
3681      ++  on-wake
3682        |=  [=bone error=(unit tang)]
3683        ^+  peer-core
3684        ::  if we previously errored out, print and reset timer for later
3685        ::
3686        ::    This really shouldn't happen, but if it does, make sure we
3687        ::    don't brick either this messaging flow or Behn.
3688        ::
3689        ?^  error
3690          =.  peer-core
3691            (pe-emit duct %pass /wake-fail %d %flog %crud %ames-wake u.error)
3692          ::
3693          ?~  message-pump-state=(~(get by snd.peer-state) bone)
3694            peer-core
3695          =*  packet-state  packet-pump-state.u.message-pump-state
3696          ?~  next-wake.packet-state  peer-core
3697          ::  If we crashed because we woke up too early, assume another
3698          ::  timer is already set.
3699          ::
3700          ?:  (lth now.channel u.next-wake.packet-state)
3701            peer-core
3702          ::
3703          =/  =wire  (make-pump-timer-wire her bone)
3704          (pe-emit duct %pass wire %b %wait (add now.channel ~s30))
3705        ::  update and print connection state
3706        ::
3707        =.  peer-core  (update-qos %ames qos:(is-peer-dead now peer-state))
3708        ::  expire direct route if the peer is not responding
3709        ::
3710        =/  old-route  route.peer-state
```

```
3711        =.  peer-state  (update-peer-route her peer-state)
3712        =?  peer-core  !=(old-route route.peer-state)
3713          %-  pe-emit
3714          :*  unix-duct.ames-state  %give  %nail  her
3715              (get-forward-lanes our peer-state peers.ames-state)
3716          ==
3717        ::  resend comet attestation packet if first message times out
3718        ::
3719        ::    The attestation packet doesn't get acked, so if we tried to
3720        ::    send a packet but it timed out, maybe they didn't get our
3721        ::    attestation.
3722        ::
3723        ::    Only resend on timeout of packets in the first message we
3724        ::    send them, since they should remember forever.
3725        ::
3726        =?    event-core
3727          ?&  ?=(%pawn (clan:title our))
3728              =(1 current:(~(got by snd.peer-state) bone))
3729          ==
3730        =/  =blob  (attestation-packet [her her-life]:channel)
3731        (send-blob for=| her blob `known/peer-state)
3732      ?:  (is-corked bone)
3733        ::  no-op if the bone (or, if a naxplanation, the reference bone)
3734        ::  was corked, because the flow doesn't exist anymore
3735        ::  TODO: clean up corked bones?
3736        ::
3737        peer-core
3738      ::  maybe resend some timed out packets
3739      ::
3740      abet:(call:(abed:mu bone) %wake ~)
3741    ::
3742    ++  on-hear-fine
3743      |=  [=lane =shot]
3744      ^+  peer-core
3745      ?>  =(sndr-tick.shot (mod life.peer-state 16))
3746      ::  TODO what if the error happened in sift-purr?
3747      ::      does vere discard malformed packets?
3748      =/  [=peep =meow]  (sift-purr `@ux`content.shot)
3749      =/  =path  (slag 3 path.peep)
3750      ::
3751      ?.  (~(has by keens) path)
3752        ~&(dead-response/peep peer-core)
3753      fi-abet:(fi-rcv:(abed:fi path) peep meow lane)
3754    ::
3755    ++  on-keen
3756      |=  [=path =^duct]
3757      ^+  peer-core
3758      ?:  (~(has by keens) path)
3759        ::  TODO use fi-trace
3760        ~>  %slog.0^leaf/"fine: dupe {(spud path)}"
3761        fi-abet:(fi-sub:(abed:fi path) duct)
3762      =.  keens  (~(put by keens) path *keen-state)
3763      fi-abet:(fi-start:(abed:fi path) duct)
3764    ::
3765    ++  on-dear
3766      |=  =lane
3767      ^+  peer-core
3768      %-  pe-emit:peer-core(route.peer-state `[%.y lane])
```

```
3769            [unix-duct.ames-state %give %nail her ~[lane]]
3770          ::
3771          ++  on-tame
3772            ^+  peer-core
3773            %-  pe-emit:peer-core(route.peer-state ~)
3774            [unix-duct.ames-state %give %nail her ~]
3775          ::  +on-cork-flow: mark .bone as closing
3776          ::
3777          ++  on-cork-flow
3778            |=  =bone
3779            ^+  peer-core
3780            peer-core(closing.peer-state (~(put in closing.peer-state) bone))
3781          ::  +on-kill-flow: delete flow on cork sender side
3782          ::
3783          ++  on-kill-flow
3784            |=  =bone
3785            ^+  peer-core
3786            ?:  (~(has in corked.peer-state) bone)
3787              ~>  %slog.0^leaf/"ames: ignoring kill on corked bone {<bone>}"
3788            peer-core
3789          =.  peer-state
3790            =,  peer-state
3791            %_  peer-state
3792              ::  if the publisher was behind, preemptively remove any nacks
3793              ::
3794              rcv                (~(del by (~(del by rcv) bone)) (mix 0b10 bone))
3795              snd                (~(del by snd) bone)
3796              corked             (~(put in corked) bone)
3797              closing            (~(del in closing) bone)
3798              by-duct.ossuary    (~(del by by-duct.ossuary) (got-duct bone))
3799              by-bone.ossuary    (~(del by by-bone.ossuary) bone)
3800            ==
3801          ::  since we got one cork ack, try the next one
3802          ::
3803          recork-one
3804        ::
3805        +|  %implementation
3806        ::  +check-clog: notify clients if peer has stopped responding
3807        ::
3808        ++  check-clog
3809          ^+  peer-core
3810          ::
3811          ::    Only look at response bones.  Request bones are unregulated,
3812          ::    since requests tend to be much smaller than responses.
3813          ::
3814        =/  pumps=(list message-pump-state)
3815          %+  murn  ~(tap by snd.peer-state)
3816          |=  [=bone =message-pump-state]
3817          ?:  =(0 (end 0 bone))
3818            ~
3819          `u=message-pump-state
3820        ::  if clogged, notify client vane
3821        ::
3822        |^  ?.  &(nuf-messages nuf-memory)  peer-core
3823            %+  roll  ~(tap in heeds.peer-state)
3824            |=([d=^duct core=_peer-core] (pe-emit:core d %give %clog her))
3825        ::  +nuf-messages: are there enough messages to mark as clogged?
3826        ::
```

```
3827            ++  nuf-messages
3828              =|  num=@ud
3829              |-  ^-  ?
3830              ?~  pumps  |
3831              =.  num
3832                ;:  add  num
3833                  (sub [next current]:i.pumps)
3834                  ~(wyt in unsent-messages.i.pumps)
3835                ==
3836              ?:  (gte num msg.cong.ames-state)
3837                &
3838              $(pumps t.pumps)
3839            ::  +nuf-memory: is enough memory used to mark as clogged?
3840            ::
3841            ++  nuf-memory
3842              =|  mem=@ud
3843              |-  ^-  ?
3844              ?~  pumps  |
3845              =.  mem
3846                %+  add
3847                  %-  ~(rep in unsent-messages.i.pumps)
3848                  |=([m=message b=_mem] (add b (met 3 (jim m))))
3849                ?~  unsent-fragments.i.pumps  0
3850                (met 3 fragment.i.unsent-fragments.i.pumps)
3851              ?:  (gte mem mem.cong.ames-state)
3852                &
3853              $(pumps t.pumps)
3854            --
3855          ::  +send-shut-packet: fire encrypted packet at rcvr and maybe sponsors
3856          ::
3857          ++  send-shut-packet
3858            |=  =shut-packet
3859            ^+  peer-core
3860            ::  swizzle last bone bit before sending
3861            ::
3862            ::    The peer has the opposite perspective from ours about what
3863            ::    kind of flow this is (forward/backward), so flip the bit
3864            ::    here.
3865            ::
3866            =.  event-core
3867              %:  send-blob  for=|  her
3868                %-  etch-shot
3869                %:  etch-shut-packet
3870                  shut-packet(bone (mix 1 bone.shut-packet))
3871                  symmetric-key.channel
3872                  our                her
3873                  our-life.channel  her-life.channel
3874                ==
3875              ::
3876                ship-state=`known/peer-state
3877              ==
3878            peer-core
3879          ::  +recork-one: re-send the next %cork to the peer
3880          ::
3881          ++  recork-one
3882            ^+  peer-core
3883            =/  boz  (sort ~(tap in closing.peer-state) lte)
3884            |-  ^+  peer-core
```

```
3885          ?~  boz  peer-core
3886          =/  pum=message-pump-state  (~(got by snd.peer-state) i.boz)
3887          ?.  =(next current):pum
3888            $(boz t.boz)
3889          ::  sanity check on the message pump state
3890          ::
3891          ?.  ?&  =(~ unsent-messages.pum)
3892                  =(~ unsent-fragments.pum)
3893                  =(~ live.packet-pump-state.pum)
3894              ==
3895            ~>  %slog.0^leaf/"ames: bad pump state {<her i.boz>}"
3896            $(boz t.boz)
3897          ::  no outstanding messages, so send a new %cork
3898          ::
3899          ::  TODO use +trace
3900          ~>  %slog.0^leaf/"ames: recork {<her i.boz>}"
3901          =/  =plea      [%$ /flow [%cork ~]]
3902          =/  =message   [%plea plea]
3903          (on-memo i.boz message)
3904      ::  +handle-cork: handle flow kill after server ames has taken %done
3905      ::
3906      ++  handle-cork
3907        |=  =bone
3908        |^  ^+  peer-core
3909        ?.  (~(has in closing.peer-state) bone)  peer-core
3910        =/  pump=message-pump-state
3911          (~(gut by snd.peer-state) bone *message-pump-state)
3912        =?  event-core  ?=(^ next-wake.packet-pump-state.pump)
3913          ::  reset-timer for boons
3914          ::
3915          (reset-timer her bone u.next-wake.packet-pump-state.pump)
3916        =/  nax-bone=^bone  (mix 0b10 bone)
3917        =/  nax-pump=message-pump-state
3918          (~(gut by snd.peer-state) nax-bone *message-pump-state)
3919        =?  event-core  ?=(^ next-wake.packet-pump-state.nax-pump)
3920          %-  %^  ev-trace  odd.veb  her
3921              |.("remove naxplanation flow {<[her bone=nax-bone]>}")
3922          ::  reset timer for naxplanations
3923          ::
3924          (reset-timer her nax-bone u.next-wake.packet-pump-state.nax-pump)
3925        =.  peer-state
3926          =,  peer-state
3927          %_  peer-state
3928            ::  preemptively delete nax flows (e.g. nacks for %watches)
3929            ::
3930            snd      (~(del by (~(del by snd) bone)) nax-bone)
3931            rcv      (~(del by rcv) bone)
3932            corked   (~(put in corked) bone)
3933            closing  (~(del in closing) bone)
3934          ==
3935        peer-core
3936        ::
3937        ++  reset-timer
3938          |=  [=ship =^bone wake=@da]
3939          (emit [/ames]~ %pass (make-pump-timer-wire ship bone) %b %rest wake)
3940        --
3941      ::
3942      +|  %internals
```

```
3943          ::  +mu: constructor for |pump message sender core
3944          ::
3945        ++  mu
3946          |_  [=bone state=message-pump-state]
3947          ::
3948          +|  %helpers
3949          ::
3950          ++  pump  .
3951          ++  abed
3952            |=  b=^bone
3953            pump(bone b, state (~(gut by snd.peer-state) b *message-pump-state))
3954          ++  abet
3955            ::  if the bone was corked, it's been removed from the state,
3956            ::  so we avoid adding it again.
3957            ::
3958            =?  snd.peer-state  !corked  (~(put by snd.peer-state) bone state)
3959            peer-core
3960          ::
3961          ++  packet-pump  (pu packet-pump-state.state)
3962          ++  closing      (~(has in closing.peer-state) bone)
3963          ++  corked       (~(has in corked.peer-state) bone)
3964          ::  +is-message-num-in-range: %.y unless duplicate or future ack
3965          ::
3966          ++  is-message-num-in-range
3967            |=  =message-num
3968            ^-  ?
3969            ::
3970            ?:  (gte message-num next.state)
3971              %.n
3972            ?:  (lth message-num current.state)
3973              %.n
3974            !(~(has by queued-message-acks.state) message-num)
3975          ::
3976          +|  %entry-points
3977          ::  +call: handle a $message-pump-task
3978          ::
3979          ++  call
3980            |=  task=message-pump-task
3981            ^+  pump
3982            ::
3983            =.  pump  =~((dispatch-task task) feed-packets)
3984            =+  top=top-live:packet-pump
3985            ::  sanity check to isolate error cases
3986            ::
3987            ?.  |(?=(~ top) (lte current.state message-num.key.u.top))
3988              ~|([%strange-current current=current.state key.u.top] !!)
3989            ::  maybe trigger a timer based on congestion control calculations
3990            ::
3991            abet:(call:packet-pump %halt ~)
3992          ::
3993          +|  %tasks
3994          ::  +dispatch-task: perform task-specific processing
3995          ::
3996          ++  dispatch-task
3997            |=  task=message-pump-task
3998            ^+  pump
3999            ::
4000            ?-  -.task
```

```
    %memo  (on-memo message.task)
    %prod  abet:(call:packet-pump %prod ~)
    %wake  abet:(call:packet-pump %wake current.state)
    %near  %-  on-done
           [[message-num %naxplanation error]:naxplanation.task %&]
    %hear
      ?-    -.ack-meat.task
          %&
      (on-hear [message-num fragment-num=p.ack-meat]:task)
      ::
          %|
     =/  cork=?
        =+  top=top-live:packet-pump
        ::  If we send a %cork and get an ack, we can know by
        ::  sequence number that the ack is for the %cork message
        ::
        ?&  closing
            ?=(^ top)
            =(0 ~(wyt in unsent-messages.state))
            =(0 (lent unsent-fragments.state))
            =(1 ~(wyt by live.packet-pump-state.state))
            =(message-num:task message-num.key.u.top)
        ==
      =+  [ack msg]=[p.ack-meat message-num]:task
      =.  pump
        %-  on-done
        [[msg ?:(ok.ack [%ok ~] [%nack ~])] cork]
      ?.  &(!ok.ack cork)  pump
      %.  pump
      %+  pe-trace  odd.veb
      |.("got nack for %cork {<bone=bone message-num=msg>}")
  ==  ==
::  +on-memo: handle request to send a message
::
++  on-memo
  |=  =message
  pump(unsent-messages.state (~(put to unsent-messages.state) message))
::  +on-hear: handle packet acknowledgment
::
++  on-hear
  |=  [=message-num =fragment-num]
  ^+  pump
  ::  pass to |packet-pump unless duplicate or future ack
  ::
  ?.  (is-message-num-in-range message-num)
    %.  pump
    (pe-trace snd.veb |.("hear pump out of range"))
  abet:(call:packet-pump %hear message-num fragment-num)
::  +on-done: handle message acknowledgment
::
::    A nack-trace message counts as a valid message nack on the
::    original failed message.
::
::    This prevents us from having to wait for a message nack packet,
::    which would mean we couldn't immediately ack the nack-trace
::    message, which would in turn violate the semantics of backward
::    flows.
::
```

```
4059              ++  on-done
4060              |=  [[=message-num =ack] cork=?]
4061              ^+  pump
4062              ::  unsent messages from the future should never get acked
4063              ::
4064              ~|  :*  bone=bone
4065                      mnum=message-num
4066                      next=next.state
4067                      unsent-messages=~(wyt in unsent-messages.state)
4068                      unsent-fragments=(lent unsent-fragments.state)
4069                      any-live=!=(~ live.packet-pump-state.state)
4070                  ==
4071              ?>  (lth message-num next.state)
4072              ::  ignore duplicate message acks
4073              ::
4074              ?:  (lth message-num current.state)
4075                %.  pump
4076                %+  pe-trace  snd.veb  |.
4077                "duplicate done {<current=current.state message-num=message-num>}"
4078              ::  ignore duplicate and future acks
4079              ::
4080              ?.  (is-message-num-in-range message-num)
4081                pump
4082              ::  clear and print .unsent-fragments if nonempty
4083              ::
4084              =?    unsent-fragments.state
4085                  &(=(current next) ?=(^ unsent-fragments)):state
4086                ::
4087                ~>  %slog.0^leaf/"ames: early message ack {<her>}"
4088                ~
4089              ::  clear all packets from this message from the packet pump
4090              ::
4091              =.  pump  abet:(call:packet-pump %done message-num lag=*@dr)
4092              ::  enqueue this ack to be sent back to local client vane
4093              ::
4094              ::    Don't clobber a naxplanation with just a nack packet.
4095              ::
4096              =?    queued-message-acks.state
4097                  =/  old  (~(get by queued-message-acks.state) message-num)
4098                  !?=(([~ %naxplanation *] old)
4099                (~(put by queued-message-acks.state) message-num ack)
4100              ::  emit local acks from .queued-message-acks until incomplete
4101              ::
4102              |-  ^+  pump
4103              ::  if .current hasn't been fully acked, we're done
4104              ::
4105              ?~  cur=(~(get by queued-message-acks.state) current.state)
4106                pump
4107              ::  .current is complete; pop, emit local ack, and try next message
4108              ::
4109              =.  queued-message-acks.state
4110                (~(del by queued-message-acks.state) current.state)
4111              ::  clear all packets from this message from the packet pump
4112              ::
4113              ::    Note we did this when the original packet came in, a few lines
4114              ::    above.  It's not clear why, but it doesn't always clear the
4115              ::    packets when it's not the current message.  As a workaround,
4116              ::    we clear the packets again when we catch up to this packet.
```

```
4117      ::
4118      ::      This is slightly inefficient because we run this twice for
4119      ::      each packet and it may emit a few unnecessary packets, but
4120      ::      it's not incorrect.  pump-metrics are updated only once,
4121      ::      at the time when we actually delete the packet.
4122      ::
4123      =.  pump  abet:(call:packet-pump %done current.state lag=*@dr)
4124      :: give %done to vane if we're ready
4125      ::
4126      ?-    -.u.cur
4127        %ok
4128      =.  peer-core
4129        ::  don't give %done for corks
4130        ::
4131        ?:  cork  (pump-cork current.state)
4132        (pump-done current.state ~)
4133      $(current.state +(current.state))
4134      ::
4135        %nack  pump
4136      ::
4137        %naxplanation
4138      =.  peer-core  (pump-done current.state `error.u.cur)
4139      $(current.state +(current.state))
4140      ==
4141    ::
4142    +|  %implementation
4143    :: +feed-packets: give packets to |packet-pump until full
4144    ::
4145    ++  feed-packets
4146      ::  if nothing to send, no-op
4147      ::
4148      ?:  &(=(~ unsent-messages) =(~ unsent-fragments)):state
4149        pump
4150      ::  we have unsent fragments of the current message; feed them
4151      ::
4152      ?.  =(~ unsent-fragments.state)
4153        ::  we have unsent fragments of the current message; feed them
4154        ::
4155        =^  unsent  pump  abut:(feed:packet-pump unsent-fragments.state)
4156        =.  unsent-fragments.state  unsent
4157        ::  if it sent all of them, feed it more; otherwise, we're done
4158        ::
4159        ?~(unsent feed-packets pump)
4160      ::  .unsent-messages is nonempty; pop a message off and feed it
4161      ::
4162      =^  =message  unsent-messages.state
4163        ~(get to unsent-messages.state)
4164      ::  break .message into .chunks and set as .unsent-fragments
4165      ::
4166      =.  unsent-fragments.state  (split-message next.state (jim +.message))
4167      ::  try to feed packets from the next message
4168      ::
4169      =.  next.state  +(next.state)
4170      feed-packets
4171    :: +pump-done: handle |message-pump's report of message (n)ack
4172    ::
4173    ++  pump-done
4174      |=  [=message-num error=(unit error)]
```

```
4175            ^+  peer-core
4176        ?:  ?&  =(1 (end 0 bone))
4177                =(1 (end 0 (rsh 0 bone)))
4178                (~(has in corked.peer-state) (mix 0b10 bone))
4179            ==
4180          %-  %+  pe-trace  msg.veb
4181              =/  dat  [her bone=bone message-num=message-num -.task]
4182              |.("remove naxplanation flow {<dat>}")
4183          ::  we avoid re-adding the bone in abet:mu
4184          ::
4185          =.  snd.peer-state  (~(del by snd.peer-state) bone)
4186        peer-core
4187      ?:  =(1 (end 0 bone))
4188          ::  ack is on "subscription update" message; no-op
4189          ::
4190          ?:  =(0 (end 0 (rsh 0 bone)))  peer-core
4191          ::  nack-trace bone; assume .ok, clear nack from |sink
4192          ::
4193          %+  pe-emit  duct
4194          [%pass /clear-nack %a %deep %drop her (mix 0b10 bone) message-num]
4195        ::  if the bone belongs to a closing flow and we got a
4196        ::  naxplanation, don't relay ack to the client vane
4197        ::
4198        ?:  &(closing ?=(%near -.task))  peer-core
4199        ::  not a nack-trace bone; relay ack to client vane
4200        ::
4201        (pe-emit (got-duct bone) %give %done error)
4202      ::  +pump-cork: handle %cork on the publisher
4203      ::
4204      ++  pump-cork
4205        |=  =message-num
4206        ^+  peer-core
4207        ::  clear all packets from this message from the packet pump
4208        ::
4209        =.  pump  abet:(call:packet-pump %done message-num lag=*@dr)
4210        ?:  corked
4211          %-  %+  pe-trace  odd.veb
4212              |.("trying to delete a corked bone={<bone>}")
4213          peer-core
4214        =/  =wire  (make-bone-wire her her-rift.channel bone)
4215        (pe-emit duct %pass wire %a %deep %kill her bone)
4216      ::  +pu: construct |packet-pump core
4217      ::
4218      ++  pu
4219        |=  state=packet-pump-state
4220        ::
4221        =|  unsent=(list static-fragment)
4222        |%
4223        +|  %helpers
4224        ++  pack  .
4225        ::  +abut: abet with gifts
4226        ::
4227        ++  abut  [unsent abet]
4228        ++  abet  pump(packet-pump-state.state state)
4229        ++  pu-trace
4230          |=  [verb=? print=(trap tape)]
4231          ^+  same
4232          (trace %ames verb her ships.bug.channel print)
```

```
4233      ::
4234      ++  pu-wire  (make-pump-timer-wire her bone)
4235      ++  pu-emit  |=(=note (pe-emit pump-duct %pass pu-wire note))
4236      ::  +packet-queue: type for all sent fragments (order: seq number)
4237      ::
4238      ++  packet-queue
4239        %-  (ordered-map live-packet-key live-packet-val)
4240        lte-packets
4241      ::  +gauge: inflate a |pump-gauge to track congestion control
4242      ::
4243      ++  gauge  (ga metrics.state ~(wyt by live.state))
4244      ::  +to-static-fragment: convenience function for |packet-pump
4245      ::
4246      ++  to-static-fragment
4247        |=  [live-packet-key live-packet-val]
4248        ^-  static-fragment
4249        [message-num num-fragments fragment-num fragment]
4250      ::
4251      ++  pump-duct  ~[/ames]
4252      ++  top-live   (pry:packet-queue live.state)
4253      ::
4254      +|  %entry-points
4255      ::
4256      ++  call
4257        |=  task=packet-pump-task
4258        ^+  pack
4259        ?-  -.task
4260          %hear  (on-hear [message-num fragment-num]:task)
4261          %done  (on-done message-num.task)
4262          %wake  (on-wake current.task)
4263          %prod  on-prod
4264          %halt  set-wake
4265        ==
4266      ::  +feed: try to send a list of packets, returning unsent ones
4267      ::
4268      ++  feed
4269        |=  fragments=(list static-fragment)
4270        ^+  pack
4271        ::  bite off as many fragments as we can send
4272        ::
4273        =/  num-slots  num-slots:gauge
4274        =/  sent       (scag num-slots fragments)
4275        =.  unsent     (slag num-slots fragments)
4276        ::  if nothing to send, we're done
4277        ::
4278        ?~  sent  pack
4279        ::  convert $static-fragment's into +ordered-set [key val] pairs
4280        ::
4281        =/  send-list
4282          %+  turn  sent
4283          |=  static-fragment
4284          ^-  [key=live-packet-key val=live-packet-val]
4285          ::
4286          :-  [message-num fragment-num]
4287          :-  [sent-date=now.channel tries=1 skips=0]
4288          [num-fragments fragment]
4289        ::  update .live and .metrics
4290        ::
```

```
4291            =.  live.state  (gas:packet-queue live.state send-list)
4292            ::  TMI
4293            ::
4294            =>  .(sent `(list static-fragment)`sent)
4295            ::  emit a $shut-packet for each packet to send
4296            ::
4297            =.  peer-core
4298              %+  roll  sent
4299              |=  [packet=static-fragment core=_peer-core]
4300              (send-shut-packet bone [message-num %& +]:packet)
4301            pack
4302          ::
4303          +|  %tasks
4304          ::  +on-prod: reset congestion control, re-send packets
4305          ::
4306          ++  on-prod
4307            ^+  pack
4308            ?:  =(~ next-wake.state)
4309              pack
4310            ::
4311            =.  metrics.state
4312              %*(. *pump-metrics counter counter.metrics.state)
4313            =.  live.state
4314              %+  run:packet-queue  live.state
4315              |=(p=live-packet-val p(- *packet-state))
4316            ::
4317            =/  sot  (max 1 num-slots:gauge)
4318            =/  liv  live.state
4319            |-  ^+  pack
4320            ?:  =(0 sot)  pack
4321            ?:  =(~ liv)  pack
4322            =^  hed  liv  (pop:packet-queue liv)
4323            =.  peer-core
4324              %+  send-shut-packet  bone
4325              [message-num %& +]:(to-static-fragment hed)
4326            $(sot (dec sot))
4327          ::  +on-wake: handle packet timeout
4328          ::
4329          ++  on-wake
4330            |=  current=message-num
4331            ^+  pack
4332            ::  assert temporal coherence
4333            ::
4334            ?<  =(~ next-wake.state)
4335            =.  next-wake.state  ~
4336            ::  tell congestion control a packet timed out
4337            ::
4338            =.  metrics.state  on-timeout:gauge
4339            =|  acc=(unit static-fragment)
4340            ::  re-send first packet and update its state in-place
4341            ::
4342            =;  [static-fragment=_acc live=_live.state]
4343                =.  live.state    live
4344                =?  peer-core  ?=(^ static-fragment)
4345                  %-  %+  pu-trace  snd.veb
4346                      =/  nums  [message-num fragment-num]:u.static-fragment
4347                      |.("dead {<nums show:gauge>}")
4348                  (send-shut-packet bone [message-num %& +]:u.static-fragment)
```

```
4349              pack
4350          ::
4351          %^  (dip:packet-queue _acc)  live.state  acc
4352          |=  $:  acc=_acc
4353                  key=live-packet-key
4354                  val=live-packet-val
4355              ==
4356          ^-  [new-val=(unit live-packet-val) stop=? _acc]
4357          ::  if already acked later message, don't resend
4358          ::
4359          ?:  (lth message-num.key current)
4360            %.  [~ stop=%.n ~]
4361            %-  slog  :_  ~  :-  %leaf
4362            "ames: strange wake queue, expected {<current>}, got {<key>}"
4363          ::  packet has expired; update it in-place, stop, and produce it
4364          ::
4365          =.  last-sent.val  now.channel
4366          =.  tries.val      +(tries.val)
4367          ::
4368          [`val stop=%.y `(to-static-fragment key val)]
4369      ::  +fast-resend-after-ack: resend timed out packets
4370      ::
4371      ::    After we finally receive an ack, we want to resend all the
4372      ::    live packets that have been building up.
4373      ::
4374      ++  fast-resend-after-ack
4375        |=  [=message-num =fragment-num]
4376        ^+  pack
4377        =;  res=[resends=(list static-fragment) live=_live.state]
4378          =.  live.state  live.res
4379          =.  peer-core
4380            %+  reel  resends.res
4381            |=  [packet=static-fragment core=_peer-core]
4382            (send-shut-packet bone [message-num %& +]:packet)
4383          pack
4384        ::
4385        =/  acc
4386          resends=*(list static-fragment)
4387        ::
4388        %^  (dip:packet-queue _acc)  live.state  acc
4389        |=  $:  acc=_acc
4390                key=live-packet-key
4391                val=live-packet-val
4392            ==
4393        ^-  [new-val=(unit live-packet-val) stop=? _acc]
4394        ?:  (lte-packets key [message-num fragment-num])
4395          [new-val=`val stop=%.n acc]
4396        ::
4397        ?:  (gth (next-expiry:gauge -.val) now.channel)
4398          [new-val=`val stop=%.y acc]
4399        ::
4400        =.  last-sent.val  now.channel
4401        =.  resends.acc  [(to-static-fragment key val) resends.acc]
4402        [new-val=`val stop=%.n acc]
4403    ::  +on-hear: handle ack on a live packet
4404    ::
4405    ::    If the packet was in our queue, delete it and update our
4406    ::    metrics, possibly re-sending skipped packets. Otherwise, no-op
```

```
4407          ::
4408          ++  on-hear
4409          |=  [=message-num =fragment-num]
4410          ^+  pack
4411          ::
4412          =-  ::  if no sent packet matches the ack,
4413              ::  don't apply mutations or effects
4414              ::
4415              ?.  found.-
4416                %-  (pu-trace snd.veb |.("miss {<show:gauge>}"))
4417                pack
4418              ::
4419              =.  metrics.state  metrics.-
4420              =.  live.state     live.-
4421              %-  ?.  ?|  =(0 fragment-num)
4422                          =(0 (mod counter.metrics.state 20))
4423                      ==
4424                    same
4425                  %+  pu-trace  snd.veb
4426                  |.("send: {<fragment=fragment-num show:gauge>}")
4427              ::  .resends is backward, so fold backward and emit
4428              ::
4429              =.  peer-core
4430                %+  reel  resends.-
4431                |=  [packet=static-fragment core=_peer-core]
4432                (send-shut-packet bone [message-num %& +]:packet)
4433              (fast-resend-after-ack message-num fragment-num)
4434          ::
4435          =/  acc
4436            :*  found=`?`%.n
4437                resends=*(list static-fragment)
4438                metrics=metrics.state
4439                num-live=~(wyt by live.state)
4440            ==
4441          ::
4442          ^+  [acc live=live.state]
4443          ::
4444          %^  (dip:packet-queue _acc)  live.state  acc
4445          |=  $:  acc=_acc
4446                  key=live-packet-key
4447                  val=live-packet-val
4448              ==
4449          ^-  [new-val=(unit live-packet-val) stop=? _acc]
4450          ::
4451          =/  gauge  (ga [metrics num-live]:acc)
4452          ::  is this the acked packet?
4453          ::
4454          ?:  =(key [message-num fragment-num])
4455            ::  delete acked packet, update metrics, and stop traversal
4456            ::
4457            =.    found.acc  %.y
4458            =.  metrics.acc  (on-ack:gauge -.val)
4459            =.  num-live.acc  (dec num-live.acc)
4460            [new-val=~ stop=%.y acc]
4461          ::  is this a duplicate ack?
4462          ::
4463          ?.  (lte-packets key [message-num fragment-num])
4464            ::  stop, nothing more to do
```

```
      ::
      [new-val=`val stop=%.y acc]
  ::  ack was on later packet; mark skipped, tell gauge, & continue
  ::
  =.  skips.val  +(skips.val)
  =^  resend  metrics.acc  (on-skipped-packet:gauge -.val)
  ?.  resend
    [new-val=`val stop=%.n acc]
  ::
  =.  last-sent.val  now.channel
  =.  tries.val      +(tries.val)
  =.  resends.acc    [(to-static-fragment key val) resends.acc]
  [new-val=`val stop=%.n acc]
::  +on-done: apply ack to all packets from .message-num
::
++  on-done
  |=  =message-num
  ^+  pack
  ::
  =-  =.  metrics.state  metrics.-
      =.  live.state     live.-
      ::
      %.  (fast-resend-after-ack message-num `fragment-num`0)
      (pu-trace snd.veb |.("done {<num=message-num show:gauge>}"))
  ::
  =/  acc  [metrics=metrics.state num-live=~(wyt by live.state)]
  ::
  ^+  [acc live=live.state]
  ::
  %^  (dip:packet-queue _acc)  live.state  acc
  |=  $:  acc=_acc
          key=live-packet-key
          val=live-packet-val
      ==
  ^-  [new-val=(unit live-packet-val) stop=? _acc]
  ::
  =/  gauge  (ga [metrics num-live]:acc)
  ::  if we get an out-of-order ack for a message, skip until it
  ::
  ?:  (lth message-num.key message-num)
    [new-val=`val stop=%.n acc]
  ::  if packet was from acked message, delete it and continue
  ::
  ?:  =(message-num.key message-num)
    =.  metrics.acc   (on-ack:gauge -.val)
    =.  num-live.acc  (dec num-live.acc)
    [new-val=~ stop=%.n acc]
  ::  we've gone past the acked message; we're done
  ::
  [new-val=`val stop=%.y acc]
::  +set-wake: set, unset, or reset timer, emitting moves
::
++  set-wake
  ^+  pack
  ::  if nonempty .live, pry at head to get next wake time
  ::
  =/  new-wake=(unit @da)
    ?~  head=(pry:packet-queue live.state)
```

```hoon
4523                          ~
4524                        `(next-expiry:gauge -.val.u.head)
4525              ::  no-op if no change
4526              ::
4527              ?:  =(new-wake next-wake.state)  pack
4528              ::  unset old timer if non-null
4529              ::
4530              =?  peer-core  !=(~ next-wake.state)
4531                (pu-emit %b %rest (need next-wake.state))
4532              ::  set new timer if non-null and not at at max-backoff
4533              ::
4534              ::  we are using the ~m2 literal instead of max-backoff:gauge
4535              ::  because /app/ping has a special cased maximum backoff of ~s25
4536              ::  and we don't want to consolidate that
4537              ::
4538              =?  peer-core  ?=(^ new-wake)
4539                ?:  ?&(?=(^ +.flow.dead.ames-state) =(~m2 rto.metrics.state))
4540                  peer-core
4541                (pu-emit %b %wait u.new-wake)
4542              ::
4543              =?  next-wake.state  !=(~ next-wake.state)   ~  ::  unset
4544              =?  next-wake.state  ?=(^ new-wake)   new-wake  ::  reset
4545              ::
4546            pack
4547          --
4548        --
4549    ::  +mi: constructor for |sink message receiver core
4550    ::
4551    ++  mi
4552      |_  [=bone state=message-sink-state]
4553      ::
4554      +|  %helpers
4555      ::
4556      ++  sink  .
4557      ++  abed
4558        |=  b=^bone
4559        sink(bone b, state (~(gut by rcv.peer-state) b *message-sink-state))
4560      ++  abet
4561        ::  if the bone was corked, it's been removed from the state,
4562        ::  so we avoid adding it again.
4563        ::
4564        =?  rcv.peer-state  !corked  (~(put by rcv.peer-state) bone state)
4565        peer-core
4566      ::
4567      ++  closing  (~(has in closing.peer-state) bone)
4568      ++  corked   (~(has in corked.peer-state) bone)
4569      ++  received
4570        |=  =^bone
4571        ::    odd bone:                 %plea request message
4572        ::    even bone, 0 second bit:  %boon response message
4573        ::    even bone, 1 second bit:  nack-trace %boon message
4574        ::
4575        ?:  =(1 (end 0 bone))          %plea
4576        ?:  =(0 (end 0 (rsh 0 bone)))  %boon
4577        %nack
4578      ::
4579      +|  %entry-points
4580      ::  +call: handle a $message-sink-task
```

```
4581          ::
4582          ++  call
4583            |=  task=message-sink-task
4584            ^+  sink
4585            ?-    -.task
4586                %drop  sink(nax.state (~(del in nax.state) message-num.task))
4587                %done  (done ok.task)
4588                %flub
4589              %=  sink
4590                last-heard.state         (dec last-heard.state)
4591                pending-vane-ack.state   ~(nap to pending-vane-ack.state)
4592              ==
4593                ::
4594                %hear
4595              |^  ?:  ?|  corked
4596                        ?&  %*(corked sink bone (mix 0b10 bone))
4597                            =(%nack (received bone))
4598                  ==  ==
4599              ack-on-corked-bone
4600            ::
4601            ?>  ?=(%& -.meat.shut-packet.task)
4602            =+  [num-fragments fragment-num fragment]=+.meat.shut-packet.task
4603            ?:  &(=(num-fragments 1) =(fragment-num 0))
4604              (check-pending-acks fragment)
4605            (hear [lane shut-packet ok]:task)
4606            ::
4607            ++  ack-on-corked-bone
4608              ::  if we %hear a fragment on a corked bone, always ack
4609              ::
4610              =.  peer-core
4611                %+  send-shut-packet  bone
4612                [message-num.shut-packet.task %| %| ok=& lag=*@dr]
4613              %.  sink
4614              %+  pe-trace  odd.veb
4615              |.("hear {<(received bone)>} on corked bone={<bone>}")
4616            ::
4617            ++  check-pending-acks
4618              ::  if this is a %cork %plea and we are still waiting to
4619              ::  hear %acks for previous naxplanations we sent, no-op
4620              ::
4621              |=  frag=@uw
4622              ^+  sink
4623              =/  blob=*  (cue (rep packet-size [frag]~))
4624              =+  pump=(abed:mu (mix 0b10 bone))
4625              ?.  ?&  ?=(^ ;;((soft [%$ path %cork ~]) blob))
4626                      ?=(^ live.packet-pump-state.state.pump)
4627                  ==
4628                (hear [lane shut-packet ok]:task)
4629              %.  sink
4630              %+  pe-trace  odd.veb
4631              |.("pending ack for naxplanation, skip %cork bone={<bone>}")
4632              --
4633            ==
4634          ::
4635          +|  %tasks
4636          ::  +hear: receive message fragment, possibly completing message
4637          ::
4638          ++  hear
```

```
4639    |=  [=lane =shut-packet ok=?]
4640    ^+  sink
4641    ::  we know this is a fragment, not an ack; expose into namespace
4642    ::
4643    ?>  ?=(%& -.meat.shut-packet)
4644    =+  [num-fragments fragment-num fragment]=+.meat.shut-packet
4645    ::  seq: message sequence number, for convenience
4646    ::
4647    =/  seq  message-num.shut-packet
4648    ::  ignore messages from far future; limit to 10 in progress
4649    ::
4650    ?:  (gte seq (add 10 last-acked.state))
4651      %-  %+  pe-trace  odd.veb
4652          |.("future %hear {<seq=seq last-acked=last-acked.state>}")
4653      sink
4654    ::
4655    =/  is-last-fragment=?  =(+(fragment-num) num-fragments)
4656    ::  always ack a dupe!
4657    ::
4658    ?:  (lte seq last-acked.state)
4659      ?.  is-last-fragment
4660        ::  single packet ack
4661        ::
4662        =.  peer-core  (send-shut-packet bone seq %| %& fragment-num)
4663        %.  sink
4664        %+  pe-trace  rcv.veb
4665        |.("send dupe ack {<seq=seq^fragment-num=fragment-num>}")
4666      ::  whole message (n)ack
4667      ::
4668      =/      ok=?  !(~(has in nax.state) seq)
4669      =.  peer-core  (send-shut-packet bone seq %| %| ok lag=`@dr`0)
4670      %.  sink
4671      %+  pe-trace  rcv.veb
4672      |.("send dupe message ack {<seq=seq>} ok={<ok>}")
4673    ::  last-acked<seq<=last-heard; heard message, unprocessed
4674    ::
4675    ::    Only true if we've heard some packets we haven't acked, which
4676    ::    doesn't happen for boons.
4677    ::
4678    ?:  (lte seq last-heard.state)
4679      ?:  &(is-last-fragment !closing)
4680        ::  if not from a closing bone, drop last packet,
4681        ::  since we don't know whether to ack or nack
4682        ::
4683        %-  %+  pe-trace  rcv.veb
4684            |.  ^-  tape
4685            =/  data
4686              :*  her  seq=seq  bone=bone.shut-packet
4687                  fragment-num  num-fragments
4688                  la=last-acked.state  lh=last-heard.state
4689              ==
4690            "hear last in-progress {<data>}"
4691        sink
4692      ::  ack all other packets
4693      ::
4694      =.  peer-core  (send-shut-packet bone seq %| %& fragment-num)
4695      %-  %+  pe-trace  rcv.veb  |.
4696          =/  data
```

```
4697                :*  seq=seq  fragment-num=fragment-num
4698                    num-fragments=num-fragments  closing=closing
4699                ==
4700            "send ack-1 {<data>}"
4701          sink
4702      ::  last-heard<seq<10+last-heard; this is a packet in a live message
4703      ::
4704      =/  =partial-rcv-message
4705        ::  create default if first fragment
4706        ::
4707        ?~  existing=(~(get by live-messages.state) seq)
4708          [num-fragments num-received=0 fragments=~]
4709        ::  we have an existing partial message; check parameters match
4710        ::
4711        ?>  (gth num-fragments.u.existing fragment-num)
4712        ?>  =(num-fragments.u.existing num-fragments)
4713        ::
4714        u.existing
4715      ::
4716      =/  already-heard-fragment=?
4717        (~(has by fragments.partial-rcv-message) fragment-num)
4718      ::  ack dupes except for the last fragment, in which case drop
4719      ::
4720      ?:  already-heard-fragment
4721        ?:  is-last-fragment
4722          %-  %+  pe-trace  rcv.veb  |.
4723              =/  data
4724                [her seq=seq lh=last-heard.state la=last-acked.state]
4725              "hear last dupe {<data>}"
4726          sink
4727        =.  peer-core  (send-shut-packet bone seq %| %& fragment-num)
4728        %.  sink
4729        %+  pe-trace  rcv.veb
4730        |.("send dupe ack {<her^seq=seq^fragment-num=fragment-num>}")
4731      ::  new fragment; store in state and check if message is done
4732      ::
4733      =.  num-received.partial-rcv-message
4734        +(num-received.partial-rcv-message)
4735      ::
4736      =.  fragments.partial-rcv-message
4737        (~(put by fragments.partial-rcv-message) fragment-num fragment)
4738      ::
4739      =.  live-messages.state
4740        (~(put by live-messages.state) seq partial-rcv-message)
4741      ::  ack any packet other than the last one, and continue either way
4742      ::
4743      =?  peer-core  !is-last-fragment
4744        %-  %+  pe-trace  rcv.veb  |.
4745            =/  data
4746              [seq=seq fragment-num=fragment-num fragments=num-fragments]
4747            "send ack-2 {<data>}"
4748        (send-shut-packet bone seq %| %& fragment-num)
4749      ::  enqueue all completed messages starting at +(last-heard.state)
4750      ::
4751      |-  ^+  sink
4752      ::  if this is not the next message to ack, we're done
4753      ::
4754      ?.  =(seq +(last-heard.state))
```

```hoon
4755            sink
4756        ::  if we haven't heard anything from this message, we're done
4757        ::
4758        ?~  live=(~(get by live-messages.state) seq)
4759          sink
4760        ::  if the message isn't done yet, we're done
4761        ::
4762        ?.  =(num-received num-fragments):u.live
4763          sink
4764        ::  we have whole message; update state, assemble, and send to vane
4765        ::
4766        =.  last-heard.state    +(last-heard.state)
4767        =.  live-messages.state  (~(del by live-messages.state) seq)
4768        ::
4769        %-  %+  pe-trace  msg.veb
4770            |.("hear {<her>} {<seq=seq>} {<num-fragments.u.live>}kb")
4771        =/  message=*  (assemble-fragments [num-fragments fragments]:u.live)
4772        =/  empty=?    =(~ pending-vane-ack.state)
4773        ::  enqueue message to be sent to local vane
4774        ::
4775        =.  pending-vane-ack.state
4776          (~(put to pending-vane-ack.state) seq message)
4777        ::
4778        =?  sink  empty  (handle-sink seq message ok)
4779        ::
4780        $(seq +(seq))
4781    ::  +done: handle confirmation of message processing from vane
4782    ::
4783    ++  done
4784      |=  ok=?
4785      ^+  sink
4786      ::
4787      =^  pending  pending-vane-ack.state
4788        ~(get to pending-vane-ack.state)
4789      =/  =message-num  message-num.p.pending
4790      ::
4791      =.  last-acked.state  +(last-acked.state)
4792      =?  nax.state  !ok  (~(put in nax.state) message-num)
4793      ::
4794      =.  peer-core
4795        (send-shut-packet bone message-num %| %| ok lag=`@dr`0)
4796      ?~  next=~(top to pending-vane-ack.state)  sink
4797      (handle-sink message-num.u.next message.u.next ok)
4798    ::
4799    +|  %implementation
4800    ::  +handle-sink: dispatch message
4801    ::
4802    ++  handle-sink
4803      |=  [=message-num message=* ok=?]
4804      ^+  sink
4805      |^  ?-((received bone) %plea ha-plea, %boon ha-boon, %nack ha-nack)
4806      ::
4807      ++  ha-plea
4808        ^+  sink
4809        ?:  |(closing corked)  sink
4810        %-  %+  pe-trace  msg.veb
4811            =/  dat  [her bone=bone message-num=message-num]
4812            |.("sink plea {<dat>}")
```

```
4813        ?.  ok
4814          =/  nack-bone=^bone  (mix 0b10 bone)
4815          =/  =^message        [%naxplanation message-num *error]
4816          =/  =wire  (make-bone-wire her her-rift.channel nack-bone)
4817          ::  send nack-trace with blank .error for security
4818          ::
4819          =.  peer-core
4820            %+  pe-emit  duct
4821            [%pass wire %a %deep %nack her nack-bone message]
4822          ::
4823          (done ok=%.n)
4824        ::
4825        =/  =wire  (make-bone-wire her her-rift.channel bone)
4826        =.  peer-core
4827          =+  ;;  =plea  message
4828          ?.  =(vane.plea %$)
4829            ?+  vane.plea  ~|  %ames-evil-vane^our^her^vane.plea  !!
4830              %c  (pe-emit duct %pass wire %c %plea her plea)
4831              %e  (pe-emit duct %pass wire %e %plea her plea)
4832              %g  (pe-emit duct %pass wire %g %plea her plea)
4833              %j  (pe-emit duct %pass wire %j %plea her plea)
4834            ==
4835          ::  a %cork plea is handled using %$ as the recipient vane to
4836          ::  account for publishers that still handle ames-to-ames %pleas
4837          ::
4838          ?>  &(?=([%cork *] payload.plea) ?=(%flow -.path.plea))
4839          (pe-emit duct %pass wire %a %deep %cork her bone)
4840        sink
4841      ::
4842      ::  +ha-boon: handle response message, acking unconditionally
4843      ::
4844      ::    .bone must be mapped in .ossuary.peer-state, or we crash.
4845      ::    This means a malformed message will kill a flow.  We
4846      ::    could change this to a no-op if we had some sort of security
4847      ::    reporting.
4848      ::
4849      ::    Note that if we had several consecutive packets in the queue
4850      ::    and crashed while processing any of them, the %hole card
4851      ::    will turn *all* of them into losts/nacks.
4852      ::
4853      ::    TODO: This handles a previous crash in the client vane, but
4854      ::    not in %ames itself.
4855      ::
4856      ++  ha-boon
4857        ^+  sink
4858        ?:  |(closing corked)  sink
4859        %-  %+  pe-trace  msg.veb  |.
4860            ::  XX -.task not visible, FIXME
4861            ::
4862            =/  dat  [her bone=bone message-num=message-num]
4863            ?:(ok "sink boon {<dat>}" "crashed on sink boon {<dat>}")
4864        =.  peer-core  (pe-emit (got-duct bone) %give %boon message)
4865        =?  moves  !ok
4866          ::  we previously crashed on this message; notify client vane
4867          ::
4868          %+  turn  moves
4869          |=  =move
4870          ?.  ?=([* %give %boon *] move)  move
```

```
4871                  [duct.move %give %lost ~]
4872              ::  send ack unconditionally
4873              ::
4874              (done ok=%.y)
4875          ::
4876          ++  ha-nack
4877            ^+  sink
4878            ::  if we get a naxplanation for a %cork, the publisher hasn't
4879            ::  received the OTA. The /recork timer will retry eventually.
4880            ::
4881            %-  %+  pe-trace  msg.veb
4882                =/  dat  [her bone=bone message-num=message-num]
4883                |.("sink naxplanation {<dat>}")
4884            ::  flip .bone's second bit to find referenced flow
4885            ::
4886            =/  target=^bone  (mix 0b10 bone)
4887            =.  peer-core
4888              ::  will notify |message-pump that this message got naxplained
4889              ::
4890              =/  =wire  (make-bone-wire her her-rift.channel target)
4891              %+  pe-emit  duct
4892              [%pass wire %a %deep %sink her target ;;(naxplanation message)]
4893            ::  ack nack-trace message (only applied if we don't later crash)
4894            ::
4895            (done ok=%.y)
4896          --
4897        --
4898      ::  +fi: constructor for |fine remote scry core
4899      ::
4900      ++  fi
4901        =>  |%
4902            ::  TODO: move +etch-peep/+etch-wail to %lull?
4903            ::
4904            ++  etch-peep
4905              |=  peep
4906              ^-  @
4907              ?>  (lth num ^~((bex 32)))
4908              =+  (spit path)
4909              %+  can  3
4910              :~  4^num       ::  fragment number
4911                  2^wid       ::  path size
4912                  wid^^@`pat  ::  namespace path
4913              ==
4914            ::
4915            ++  etch-wail
4916              |=  w=wail
4917              ^-  @
4918              ?-  -.w
4919                %0  (lsh 3 (etch-peep +.w))  :: tag byte
4920              ==
4921            ::
4922            ++  make-shot
4923              |=  w=wail
4924              ^-  shot
4925              =/  sic  (mod life.ames-state 16)
4926              =/  ric  (mod life.peer-state 16)
4927              [[our her] req=& sam=| sic ric ~ (etch-wail w)]
4928            ::
```

```
    ::
    ++  keys
      |%
      ++  mess
        |=  [=ship life=@ud =path dat=$@(~ (cask))]
        (jam +<)
      ::
      ++  sign  sigh:as:crypto-core.ames-state
      ::
      ++  veri-fra
        |=  [=path fra=@ud dat=@ux sig=@]
        (veri sig (jam path fra dat))
      ::
      ++  veri
        |=  [sig=@ dat=@]
        ^-  ?
        (safe:as:(com:nu:crub:crypto public-key.peer-state) sig dat)
      ::
      ++  meri
        |=  [pax=path sig=@ dat=$@(~ (cask))]
        (veri sig (mess her life.peer-state pax dat))
      --
    --
  ::
  |_  [=path keen=keen-state]
  ::
  +|  %helpers
  ::
  ++  fine  .
  ++  abed
    |=  p=^path
    ~|  no-keen-for-path/p
    fine(path p, keen (~(got by keens) p))
  ::
  ++  fi-abet
    ^+  peer-core
    ?.  =,  keen
        ::  num-fragments is 0 when unknown (i.e. no response yet)
        ::  if no-one is listening, kill request
        ::
        ?|  =(~ listeners.keen)
            &(!=(0 num-fragments) =(num-fragments num-received))
        ==
      =.  fine  fi-set-wake
      peer-core(keens.peer-state (~(put by keens) path keen))  :: XX tack.keens
    ::
    =?  fine  ?=(^ next-wake.keen)
      (fi-rest u.next-wake.keen)
    peer-core(keens.peer-state (~(del by keens) path))  :: XX tack.keens
  ::
  ++  fi-full-path
    :^    (scot %p her)
        (scot %ud rift.peer-state)
      (scot %ud life.peer-state)
    path
  ::
  ++  fi-show
    =,  keen
```

```
:*  nex=(lent nex)
    hav=(lent hav)
    num-fragments=num-fragments
    num-received=num-received
    next-wake=next-wake
    metrics=metrics
==
::
++  fi-trace
  |=  [verb=? print=(trap tape)]
  ^+  same
  (trace %fine verb her ships.bug.ames-state print)
::
++  fi-emit        |=(move fine(event-core (emit +<)))
++  fi-mop         ((on @ud want) lte)
++  fi-gauge       (ga metrics.keen (wyt:fi-mop wan.keen))
++  fi-wait        |=(tim=@da (fi-pass-timer %b %wait tim))
++  fi-rest        |=(tim=@da (fi-pass-timer %b %rest tim))
::
++  fi-etch-wail
  |=(frag=@ud `hoot``@`(etch-shot (make-shot %0 fi-full-path frag)))
::
++  fi-send
  |=  =blob
  fine(event-core (send-blob for=| her blob `known/peer-state))
::
++  fi-give-tune
  |=  dat=(unit roar)
  |=([=^duct =_fine] (fi-emit:fine duct %give %tune [her path] dat))
::
+|  %entry-points
::
++  fi-start
  |=  =^duct
  %-  (fi-trace fin.veb |.("keen {(spud fi-full-path)}"))
  =.  fine  (fi-sub duct)
  ?>  =(num-fragments.keen 0)
  =/  fra=@       1
  =/  req=hoot  (fi-etch-wail fra)
  =/    =want  [fra req last=now tries=1 skips=0]
  =.  wan.keen  (put:fi-mop ~ [fra .]:want)
  (fi-send `@ux`req)
::
++  fi-rcv
  |=  [[=full=^path num=@ud] =meow =lane:ames]
  ^+  fine
  =/  og  fine
  =.  peer-core  (update-qos %fine %live last-contact=now)
  ::  handle empty
  ?:  =(0 num.meow)
    ?>  =(~ dat.meow)
    (fi-done sig.meow ~)
  ::  update congestion, or fill details
  ::
  =?  fine  =(0 num-fragments.keen)
    ?>  =(num 1)
    (fi-first-rcv meow)
  ::
```

```
5045        ?.  ?=([@ @ @ *] full-path)
5046        ~|  fine-path-too-short+full-path
5047        !!
5048        ?.  =(`her (slaw %p i.full-path))
5049        ~|  fine-path-bunk-ship+[full-path her]
5050        !!
5051        ?.  =(`rift.peer-state (slaw %ud i.t.full-path))
5052        ~|  fine-path-bunk-rift+[full-path rift.peer-state]
5053        !!
5054        ?.  =(`life.peer-state (slaw %ud i.t.t.full-path))
5055        ~|  fine-path-bunk-life+[full-path life.peer-state]
5056        !!
5057        ?.  (veri-fra:keys [full-path num [dat sig]:meow])
5058        ~|  fine-purr-fail-signature/num^`@ux`sig.meow
5059        ~|  life.peer-state
5060        !!
5061      ::
5062      =^  found=?  fine  (fi-on-ack num)
5063      ?.  found
5064        (fi-fast-retransmit:og num)
5065      =.  num-received.keen  +(num-received.keen)
5066      =.  hav.keen
5067        ::  insert in reverse order
5068        ::
5069        |-  ^-  (list have)
5070        ?~  hav.keen
5071          [num meow]~
5072        ?:  (lth num fra.i.hav.keen)
5073          [i.hav.keen $(hav.keen t.hav.keen)]
5074        [[num meow] hav.keen]
5075      ?.  =(num-fragments num-received):keen
5076        fi-continue
5077      (fi-done [sig dat]:fi-sift-full)
5078    ::
5079    ++  fi-sub
5080      |=(=^duct fine(listeners.keen (~(put in listeners.keen) duct)))
5081    ::  scry is autocancelled in +abet if no more listeners
5082    ::
5083    ++  fi-unsub
5084      |=  [=^duct all=?]
5085      ^+  fine
5086      ?:  all
5087        %-  (fi-trace fin.veb |.("unsub all {<fi-full-path>}"))
5088        =.  fine  (~(rep in listeners.keen) (fi-give-tune ~))
5089        fine(listeners.keen ~)
5090      ::
5091      ?:  (~(has in listeners.keen) duct)
5092        %-  (fi-trace fin.veb |.("unsub {<fi-full-path>} on {<duct>}"))
5093        fine(listeners.keen (~(del in listeners.keen) duct))
5094      ::
5095      %.  fine
5096      (fi-trace fin.veb |.("unknown {<fi-full-path>} {<duct>}"))
5097    ::
5098    +|  %implementation
5099    ::
5100    ++  fi-on-ack
5101      =|  marked=(list want)
5102      |=  fra=@ud
```

```
5103          ^-  [found=? cor=_fine]
5104          =.  fine
5105            =/  first  (pry:fi-mop wan.keen)
5106            ?~  first
5107              fine
5108            ?:  =(fra fra.val.u.first)
5109              fine
5110            =^  resend=?  metrics.keen
5111              (on-skipped-packet:fi-gauge +>.val.u.first)
5112            ?:  !resend
5113              fine
5114            =.  tries.val.u.first  +(tries.val.u.first)
5115            =.  last-sent.val.u.first  now
5116            =.  wan.keen  (put:fi-mop wan.keen u.first)
5117            =.  fine  (fi-send `@ux`hoot.val.u.first)
5118            fine
5119          ::
5120          =/  found  (get:fi-mop wan.keen fra)
5121          ?~  found
5122            [| fine]
5123          =.  metrics.keen  (on-ack:fi-gauge +>.u.found)
5124          =.  wan.keen  +:(del:fi-mop wan.keen fra)
5125          [& fine]
5126        ::
5127        ++  fi-done
5128          |=  [sig=@ data=$@(~ (cask))]
5129          =/  ful  fi-full-path
5130          =/  roar=(unit roar)
5131            ?.  (meri:keys ful sig data)
5132              ~
5133            :+  ~  [ful ?~(data ~ `data)]
5134            [[her [life.peer-state sig]] ~ ~]
5135          ::
5136          %-  (fi-trace fin.veb |.("done {(spud ful)}"))
5137          (~(rep in listeners.keen) (fi-give-tune roar))
5138        ::
5139        ++  fi-first-rcv
5140          |=  =meow
5141          ^+  fine
5142          ::
5143          =;  paz=(list want)
5144            fine(keen keen(num-fragments num.meow, nex (tail paz)))
5145          %+  turn  (gulf 1 num.meow)
5146          |=  fra=@ud
5147          ^-  want
5148          [fra (fi-etch-wail fra) now 0 0]
5149        ::  +fi-continue: send packets based on normal congestion flow
5150        ::
5151        ++  fi-continue
5152          =|  inx=@ud
5153          =|  sent=(list @ud)
5154          =/  max  num-slots:fi-gauge
5155          |-  ^+  fine
5156          ?:  |(=(~ nex.keen) =(inx max))
5157            fine
5158          =^  =want  nex.keen  nex.keen
5159          =.  last-sent.want  now
5160          =.     tries.want  +(tries.want)
```

```
=.        wan.keen   (put:fi-mop wan.keen [fra .]:want)
=.             fine  (fi-send `@ux`hoot.want)
$(inx +(inx))
::
++  fi-sift-full
  =,  keen
  ?.  ?&  =(num-fragments num-received)
          =((lent hav) num-received)
      ==
    ~|  :-  %frag-mismatch
        [have/num-received need/num-fragments path/path]
    !!
  (sift-roar num-fragments hav)
::
++  fi-fast-retransmit
  |=  fra=@ud
  =;  [cor=_fine wants=_wan.keen]
    cor(wan.keen wants)
  %^  (dip:fi-mop ,cor=_fine)  wan.keen
    fine
  |=  [cor=_fine @ud =want]
  ^-  [(unit ^want) stop=? cor=_fine]
  ?.  (lte fra.want fra)
    [`want & cor]
  ?:  (gth (next-expiry:fi-gauge:cor +>.want) now)
    [`want & cor]
  =.  last-sent.want  now
  =.  cor  (fi-send:cor `@ux`hoot.want)
  [`want | cor]
::
++  fi-pass-timer
  |=  =note
  =/  =wire  (welp /fine/behn/wake/(scot %p her) path)
  (fi-emit unix-duct.ames-state %pass wire note)
::
++  fi-set-wake
  ^+  fine
  =/  next-wake=(unit @da)
    ?~  want=(pry:fi-mop wan.keen)
      ~
    `(next-expiry:fi-gauge +>:val.u.want)
  ?:  =(next-wake next-wake.keen)
    fine
  =?  fine  !=(~ next-wake.keen)
    =/  old  (need next-wake.keen)
    =.  next-wake.keen  ~
    (fi-rest old)
  =?  fine  ?=(^ next-wake)
    =.  next-wake.keen  next-wake
    (fi-wait u.next-wake)
  fine
::  +fi-take-wake: handle request packet timeout
::
++  fi-take-wake
  ^+  fine
  =.  next-wake.keen  ~
  =.  peer-core  (update-qos %fine qos:(is-peer-dead now peer-state))
  ::  has the direct route expired?
```

```hoon
      ::
      =/  old-route  route.peer-state
      =.  peer-state  (update-peer-route her peer-state)
      =?  peer-core  !=(old-route route.peer-state)
        %-  pe-emit
        :*  unix-duct.ames-state  %give  %nail  her
            (get-forward-lanes our peer-state peers.ames-state)
        ==
      =.  metrics.keen  on-timeout:fi-gauge
      =^  want=(unit want)  wan.keen
        ?~  res=(pry:fi-mop wan.keen)  `wan.keen
        (del:fi-mop wan.keen key.u.res)
      ~|  %took-wake-for-empty-want
      ?>  ?=(^ want)
      =:      tries.u.want  +(tries.u.want)
          last-sent.u.want  now
        ==
      =.  wan.keen  (put:fi-mop wan.keen [fra .]:u.want)
      (fi-send `@ux`hoot.u.want)
    --
  ::  +ga: constructor for |pump-gauge congestion control core
  ::
  ++  ga
    |=  [pump-metrics live-packets=@ud]
    =*  ship      her
    =*  now       now.channel
    =*  metrics   +<-
    |%
    +|  %helpers
    ::
    ++  ga-trace
      |=  [verb=? print=(trap tape)]
      ^+  same
      (trace %ames verb ship ships.bug.channel print)
    ::  +next-expiry: when should a newly sent fresh packet time out?
    ::
    ::    Use rtt + 4*sigma, where sigma is the mean deviation of rtt.
    ::    This should make it unlikely that a packet would time out
    ::    from a delay, as opposed to an actual packet loss.
    ::
    ++  next-expiry
      |=  packet-state
      ^-  @da
      (add last-sent rto)
    ::  +num-slots: how many packets can we send right now?
    ::
    ++  num-slots
      ^-  @ud
      (sub-safe cwnd live-packets)
    ::
    ::  +clamp-rto: apply min and max to an .rto value
    ::
    ++  clamp-rto
      |=  rto=@dr
      ^+  rto
      (min max-backoff (max ^~((div ~s1 5)) rto))
    ::  +max-backoff: calculate highest re-send interval
    ::
```

```
5277      ::      Keeps pinhole to sponsors open by inspecting the duct (hack).
5278      ::
5279      ++  max-backoff
5280        ^-  @dr
5281        ?:(?=([[%gall %use %ping *] *] duct) ~s25 ~m2)
5282      ::  +in-slow-start: %.y if we're in "slow-start" mode
5283      ::
5284      ++  in-slow-start
5285        ^-  ?
5286        (lth cwnd ssthresh)
5287      ::  +in-recovery: %.y if we're recovering from a skipped packet
5288      ::
5289      ::      We finish recovering when .live-packets finally dips back
5290      ::      down to .cwnd.
5291      ::
5292      ++  in-recovery
5293        ^-  ?
5294        (gth live-packets cwnd)
5295      ::  +sub-safe: subtract with underflow protection
5296      ::
5297      ++  sub-safe
5298        |=  [a=@ b=@]
5299        ^-  @
5300        ?:((lte a b) 0 (sub a b))
5301      ::  +show: produce a printable version of .metrics
5302      ::
5303      ++  show
5304        =/  ms  (div ~s1 1.000)
5305        ::
5306        :*  rto=(div rto ms)
5307            rtt=(div rtt ms)
5308            rttvar=(div rttvar ms)
5309            ssthresh=ssthresh
5310            cwnd=cwnd
5311            num-live=live-packets
5312            counter=counter
5313        ==
5314      ::
5315      +|  %entry-points
5316      ::  +on-ack: adjust metrics based on a packet getting acknowledged
5317      ::
5318      ++  on-ack
5319        |=  =packet-state
5320        ^-  pump-metrics
5321        ::
5322        =.  counter  +(counter)
5323        ::  if below congestion threshold, add 1; else, add avg 1 / cwnd
5324        ::
5325        =.  cwnd
5326          ?:  in-slow-start
5327            +(cwnd)
5328          (add cwnd !=(0 (mod (mug now) cwnd)))
5329        ::  if this was a re-send, don't adjust rtt or downstream state
5330        ::
5331        ?:  (gth tries.packet-state 1)
5332          metrics(rto (clamp-rto (add rtt (mul 4 rttvar))))
5333        ::  rtt-datum: new rtt measurement based on packet roundtrip
5334        ::
```

```
              =/  rtt-datum=@dr  (sub-safe now last-sent.packet-state)
              ::  rtt-error: difference between this measurement and expected
              ::
              =/  rtt-error=@dr
                ?:  (gte rtt-datum rtt)
                  (sub rtt-datum rtt)
                (sub rtt rtt-datum)
              ::  exponential weighting ratio for .rtt and .rttvar
              ::
              =.  rtt     (div (add rtt-datum (mul rtt 7)) 8)
              =.  rttvar  (div (add rtt-error (mul rttvar 7)) 8)
              =.  rto     (clamp-rto (add rtt (mul 4 rttvar)))
              ::
              %.  metrics
              %+  ga-trace  ges.veb  |.
              "ack update {<show rtt-datum=rtt-datum rtt-error=rtt-error>}"
            ::  +on-skipped-packet: handle misordered ack
            ::
            ++  on-skipped-packet
              |=  packet-state
              ^-  [resend=? pump-metrics]
              ::
              =/  resend=?  &((lte tries 1) |(in-recovery (gte skips 3)))
              :-  resend
              ::
              =?  cwnd  !in-recovery  (max 2 (div cwnd 2))
              %-  %+  ga-trace  snd.veb
                  |.("skip {<resend=resend in-recovery=in-recovery show>}")
              metrics
            ::  +on-timeout: (re)enter slow-start mode on packet loss
            ::
            ++  on-timeout
              ^-  pump-metrics
              ::
              %-  (ga-trace ges.veb |.("timeout update {<show>}"))
              =:  ssthresh  (max 1 (div cwnd 2))
                  cwnd  1
                  rto   (clamp-rto (mul rto 2))
                ==
              metrics
            --
          --
        --
      --
::  adult ames, after metamorphosis from larva
::
=|  =ames-state
|=  [now=@da eny=@ rof=roof]
=*  ames-gate   .
=*  veb  veb.bug.ames-state
|%
::  +call: handle request $task
::
++  call
  |=  [=duct dud=(unit goof) wrapped-task=(hobo task)]
  ^-  [(list move) _ames-gate]
  ::
  =/  =task         ((harden task) wrapped-task)
```

```
5393    =/  event-core  (ev [now eny rof] duct ames-state)
5394    ::
5395    =^  moves  ames-state
5396      =<  abet
5397      ::  handle error notifications
5398      ::
5399      ?^  dud
5400        ?+  -.task
5401            (on-crud:event-core -.task tang.u.dud)
5402          %hear  (on-hear:event-core lane.task blob.task dud)
5403        ==
5404      ::
5405      ?-  -.task
5406        %born  on-born:event-core
5407        %hear  (on-hear:event-core [lane blob ~]:task)
5408        %dear  (on-dear:event-core +.task)
5409        %heed  (on-heed:event-core ship.task)
5410        %init  on-init:event-core
5411        %jilt  (on-jilt:event-core ship.task)
5412        %prod  (on-prod:event-core ships.task)
5413        %sift  (on-sift:event-core ships.task)
5414        %snub  (on-snub:event-core [form ships]:task)
5415        %spew  (on-spew:event-core veb.task)
5416        %cong  (on-cong:event-core [msg mem]:task)
5417        %stir  (on-stir:event-core arg.task)
5418        %trim  on-trim:event-core
5419        %vega  on-vega:event-core
5420        %plea  (on-plea:event-core [ship plea]:task)
5421        %cork  (on-cork:event-core ship.task)
5422        %tame  (on-tame:event-core ship.task)
5423        %kroc  (on-kroc:event-core bones.task)
5424        %deep  (on-deep:event-core deep.task)
5425        %stun  (on-stun:event-core stun.task)
5426        %plug  (on-plug:event-core +.task)
5427      ::
5428        %keen  (on-keen:event-core +.task)
5429        %chum  (on-chum:event-core +.task)
5430        %yawn  (on-cancel-scry:event-core | +.task)
5431        %wham  (on-cancel-scry:event-core & +.task)
5432      ==
5433    ::
5434    [moves ames-gate]
5435  ::  +take: handle response $sign
5436  ::
5437  ++  take
5438    |=  [=wire =duct dud=(unit goof) =sign]
5439    ^-  [(list move) _ames-gate]
5440    ?^  dud
5441      ~|(%ames-take-dud (mean tang.u.dud))
5442    ::
5443    =/  event-core  (ev [now eny rof] duct ames-state)
5444    ::
5445    =^  moves  ames-state
5446      ?:  ?=([%gall %unto *] sign)
5447        `ames-state
5448      ::
5449      =<  abet
5450      ?-  sign
```

```
5451        [@ %done *]   (on-take-done:event-core wire error.sign)
5452        [@ %boon *]   (on-take-boon:event-core wire payload.sign)
5453    ::
5454        [%ames %tune *]  (on-tune:event-core wire [[ship path] roar]:sign)
5455    ::
5456        [%behn %wake *]  (on-take-wake:event-core wire error.sign)
5457    ::
5458        [%gall %flub ~]  (on-take-flub:event-core wire)
5459    ::
5460        [%jael %turf *]        (on-take-turf:event-core turf.sign)
5461        [%jael %private-keys *]  (on-priv:event-core [life vein]:sign)
5462        [%jael %public-keys *]   (on-publ:event-core wire public-keys-result.sign)
5463      ==
5464    ::
5465    [moves ames-gate]
5466  ::  +stay: extract state before reload
5467  ::
5468  ++  stay   [%20 %adult ames-state]
5469  ::  +load: load in old state after reload
5470  ::
5471  ++  load
5472    =<  |=  $=  old-state
5473            $%  [%20 ^ames-state]
5474            ==
5475        ^+  ames-gate
5476        ?>  ?=(%20 -.old-state)
5477        ames-gate(ames-state +.old-state)
5478    ::  all state transitions are called from larval ames
5479    ::
5480    |%
5481    ++  our-beam  `beam`[[our %rift %da now] /(scot %p our)]
5482    ++  state-4-to-5
5483      |=  ames-state=ames-state-4
5484      ^-  ames-state-5
5485      =.  peers.ames-state
5486        %-  ~(run by peers.ames-state)
5487        |=  ship-state=ship-state-4
5488        ?.  ?=(%known -.ship-state)
5489          ship-state
5490        =.  snd.ship-state
5491          %-  ~(run by snd.ship-state)
5492          |=  pump=message-pump-state-16
5493          =.  num-live.metrics.packet-pump-state.pump
5494            ~(wyt in live.packet-pump-state.pump)
5495          pump
5496        ship-state
5497      ames-state
5498    ::
5499    ++  state-5-to-6
5500      |=  ames-state=ames-state-5
5501      ^-  ames-state-6
5502      :_  +.ames-state
5503      %-  ~(urn by peers.ames-state)
5504      |=  [=ship ship-state=ship-state-5]
5505      ^-  ship-state-6
5506      ?.  ?=(%known -.ship-state)
5507        ship-state
5508      =/  peer-state=peer-state-5  +.ship-state
```

```
=/  =rift
    ::  harcoded because %jael doesn't have data about comets
    ::
    ?:  ?=(%pawn (clan:title ship))  0
    ;;  @ud
    =<  q.q  %-  need  %-  need
    (rof [~ ~] /ames %j `beam`[[our %rift %da now] /(scot %p ship)])
  :-  -.ship-state
  :_  +.peer-state
  =,  -.peer-state
  [symmetric-key life rift public-key sponsor]
::
++  state-6-to-7
  |=  ames-state=ames-state-6
  ^-  ames-state-7
  :_  +.ames-state
  %-  ~(run by peers.ames-state)
  |=  ship-state=ship-state-6
  ^-  ship-state-7
  ?.  ?=(%known -.ship-state)
    ship-state
  :-  %known
  ^-  peer-state-7
  :-  +<.ship-state
  [route qos ossuary snd rcv nax heeds ~ ~ ~]:ship-state
::
++  state-7-to-8
  |=  ames-state=ames-state-7
  ^-  ames-state-8
  =,  ames-state
  :*  peers  unix-duct  life  crypto-core  bug
      *(set wire)
  ==
::
++  state-8-to-9
  |=  ames-state=ames-state-8
  ^-  ames-state-9
  =,  ames-state
  :*  peers  unix-duct  life  crypto-core  bug  corks
      *(set ship)
  ==
::
++  state-9-to-10
  |=  ames-state=ames-state-9
  ^-  ames-state-10
  =,  ames-state
  :*  peers  unix-duct  life  crypto-core
      %=  bug.ames-state
        veb  [&1 &2 &3 &4 &5 &6 |6 %.n]:veb.bug
      ==
      corks  snub
  ==
::
++  state-10-to-11
  |=  ames-state=ames-state-10
  ^-  ames-state-11
  =,  ames-state
  :*  peers  unix-duct  life  crypto-core  bug  corks  snub
```

```
5567              ::  5 messages and 100Kb of data outstanding
5568              ::
5569              [msg=5 mem=100.000]
5570          ==
5571      ::
5572      ++  state-11-to-12
5573        |=  ames-state=ames-state-11
5574        ^-  ames-state-12
5575        :_  =,  ames-state
5576            :*  unix-duct
5577                life
5578                crypto-core
5579                bug
5580                [%deny snub]
5581                cong
5582            ==
5583        ^-  (map ship ship-state-12)
5584        %-  ~(run by peers.ames-state)
5585        |=  ship-state=ship-state-7
5586        ^-  ship-state-12
5587        ?.  ?=(%known -.ship-state)
5588          ship-state
5589        %=  ship-state
5590          +>  [route qos ossuary snd rcv nax heeds closing corked]:+>.ship-state
5591        ==
5592      ::
5593      ++  state-12-to-13
5594        |=  old=ames-state-12
5595        ^-  ames-state-13
5596        =+  !<(=rift q:(need (need (rof [~ ~] /ames %j our-beam))))
5597        =+  pk=sec:ex:crypto-core.old
5598        :*  peers=(~(run by peers.old) ship-state-12-to-13)
5599            unix-duct.old
5600            life.old
5601            rift
5602            ?:(=(*ring pk) *acru:ames (nol:nu:crub:crypto pk))
5603            %=  bug.old
5604              veb  [&1 &2 &3 &4 &5 &6 &7 |7 %.n]:veb.bug.old
5605            ==
5606            snub.old
5607            cong.old
5608        ==
5609      ::
5610      ++  ship-state-12-to-13
5611        |=  old=ship-state-12
5612        ^-  ship-state-13
5613        ?:  ?=(%alien -.old)
5614          old(heeds [heeds.old ~])
5615        old(corked [corked.old ~])
5616      ::
5617      ++  state-13-to-14
5618        |=  old=ames-state-13
5619        ^-  ames-state-14
5620        =-  old(peers -)
5621        %-  ~(run by peers.old)
5622        |=  old=ship-state-13
5623        |^  ?:  ?=(%alien -.old)  old
5624        old(keens (~(run by keens.old) keen-state-13-to-14))
```

```
    ::
    ++  keen-state-13-to-14
      |=  old=keen-state-13
      ^-  keen-state-14
      =-  old(wan -)
      %+  gas:((on @ud want) lte)  ~
      %+  turn  (tap:(deq:keen-state-13 want) wan.old)
      |=  =want  [fra .]:want
    --
  ::
  ++  state-14-to-15
    |=  old=ames-state-14
    ^-  ames-state-15
    old(rift !<(=rift q:(need (need (rof [~ ~] /ames %j our-beam)))))
  ::
  ++  state-15-to-16
    |=  old=ames-state-15
    ^-  ames-state-16
    ::  re-initialize default congestion control values, if bunted
    ::
    old(cong ?.(=(cong.old [0 0]) cong.old [5 100.000]))
  ::
  ++  state-16-to-17
    |=  old=ames-state-16
    ^-  ames-state-17
    %=    old
        cong
      :+  cong.old
        flow/~
      cork/`[~[/ames] /recork `@da`(add now ~d1)]
      ::
        peers
      %-  ~(run by peers.old)
      |=  ship-state=ship-state-16
      ^-  ship-state-17
      ?.  ?=(%known -.ship-state)
        ship-state
      |^
      %=    ship-state
        snd    (~(run by snd.ship-state) message-pump-16-to-17)
        keens  (~(run by keens.ship-state) keen-state-16-to-17)
        rcv    (~(urn by rcv.ship-state) remove-outbound-naxplanations)
      ==
      ::
      ++  message-pump-16-to-17
        |=  pump=message-pump-state-16
        ^-  message-pump-state-17
        %=    pump
            metrics.packet-pump-state
          [rto rtt rttvar ssthresh cwnd counter]:metrics.packet-pump-state.pump
        ==
      ::
      ++  keen-state-16-to-17
        |=  keen-state=keen-state-16
        ^-  ^keen-state
        %=    keen-state
          metrics  [rto rtt rttvar ssthresh cwnd counter]:metrics.keen-state
        ==
```

```
5683        ::
5684        ++  remove-outbound-naxplanations
5685          |=  [=bone sink=message-sink-state]
5686          ^+  sink
5687          =/  target=^bone  (mix 0b10 bone)
5688          ?.  =(%3 (mod target 4))
5689            sink
5690          ?~  pump=(~(get by snd.ship-state) target)
5691            sink
5692          %_    sink
5693              nax
5694            %-  ~(rep in nax.sink)
5695            |=  [=message-num nax=(set message-num)]
5696            ::  we keep messages in the queue that have not been acked.
5697            ::  if the message-num for the naxplanation we sent is
5698            ::  less than the current message, +pump-done:mu had been called,
5699            ::  so the message-num can be safely removed
5700            ::
5701            =?  nax  (gte message-num current.u.pump)
5702              (~(put in nax) message-num)
5703            nax
5704          ==
5705        --
5706      ==
5707    ::
5708    ++  state-18-to-19
5709      |=  old=ames-state-18
5710      ^-  ames-state-19
5711      %=  old
5712      ::
5713          dead  [dead.old ~]
5714      ::
5715          peers
5716        %-  ~(run by peers.old)
5717        |=  s=ship-state-17
5718        ^-  ship-state
5719        ?:  ?=(%alien -.s)
5720          %=  s
5721            keens  [keens.s ~]
5722          ==
5723        %=    s
5724        ::
5725            keens  [keens.s ~]
5726        ::
5727            snd.+
5728          %-  ~(urn by snd.+.s)
5729          |=  [=bone m=message-pump-state-17]
5730          =/  hed
5731            ?.  =(1 (end 0 bone))
5732              %plea
5733            ?:  =(0 (end 0 (rsh 0 bone)))
5734              %boon
5735            %naxplanation
5736          %=    m
5737              unsent-messages
5738            =*  um  unsent-messages.m
5739            =>  [..message hed=hed um=um ..cue]
5740            ~+  %-  ~(run to um)
```

```
|=  b=message-blob
^-  message
=>  [..message hed=hed ..cue arg=b]
~+  ;;(message [hed (cue arg)])
      ==
    ==
  ==
::
++  state-19-to-20
  |=  old=ames-state-19
  ^-  ^ames-state
  %=  old
    veb.bug  [&1 &2 &3 &4 &5 &6 &7 &8 |8 %.n]:veb.bug.old
  ==
--
::  +scry: dereference namespace
::
++  scry
  ^-  roon
  |=  [lyc=gang pov=path car=term bem=beam]
  ^-  (unit (unit cage))
  =*  ren  car
  =*  why=shop  &/p.bem
  =*  syd  q.bem
  =*  lot=coin  $/r.bem
  =*  tyl  s.bem
  ::
  ?:  ?&  =(&+our why)
          =([%ud 1] r.bem)
          =(%$ syd)
          =(%x ren)
      ==
    =>  .(tyl `(pole knot)`tyl)
    ?+  tyl  ~
    ::
      [%fine %shut kef=@ enc=@ ~]
    =/  key-idx  (slav %ud kef.tyl)
    =/  key  (got:on:chain chain.ames-state (slav %ud kef.tyl))
    =/  pat=(unit path)
    (rush `@t`(dy:crub:crypto key.key (slav %uv enc.tyl)) stap)
    ?~  pat
      [~ ~]
    ?~  blk=(de-part:balk our rift.ames-state life.ames-state u.pat)
      [~ ~]
    ?.  (check-fine-key ames-state u.blk key-idx)
      ~&  key-validation-failed/[u.pat key-idx chain.ames-state]
      [~ ~]
    =/  res  (rof [~ ~] /ames (as-omen:balk u.blk))
    ?~  res
      ~&  %bailing-close
      [~ ~]
    ?~  u.res
      ``atom+!>(~)
    ?~  key=(get:on:chain chain.ames-state key-idx)
        ~
    =-  ``atom+!>(-)
    `@uv`(en:crub:crypto -.u.key (jam [p q.q]:u.u.res))
    ::
```

```hoon
5799          [%chum her=@ lyf=@ cyf=@ ~]
5800      =/  who  (slaw %p her.tyl)
5801      =/  lyf  (slaw %ud lyf.tyl)
5802      =/  cyf  (slaw %uv cyf.tyl)
5803      ?:  |(?=(~ who) ?=(~ lyf) ?=(~ cyf))
5804        [~ ~]
5805      =/  per  (~(get by peers.ames-state) u.who)
5806      ?.  &(?=([~ %known *] per) =(life.u.per u.lyf))
5807        ~
5808      =/  bal=(unit balk)
5809        ?~  tex=(de:crub:crypto symmetric-key.u.per u.cyf)  ~
5810        ?~  pax=(rush u.tex stap)                           ~
5811        (de-part:balk our 0 0 u.pax)
5812      ?~  bal
5813        [~ ~]
5814      ?~  res=(rof `[u.who ~ ~] /ames (as-omen:balk u.bal))
5815          ~
5816      =-  ``atom+!>(`@ux`-)
5817      %+  en:crub:crypto  symmetric-key.u.per
5818      ?~(u.res ~ (jam [p q.q]:u.u.res))
5819    ==
5820    ::
5821    :: only respond for the local identity, %$ desk, current timestamp
5822    ::
5823    ?.  ?&  =(&+our why)
5824            =([%$ %da now] lot)
5825            =(%$ syd)
5826        ==
5827      ?.  for.veb.bug.ames-state  ~
5828      ~>  %slog.0^leaf/"ames: scry-fail {<why=why lot=lot now=now syd=syd>}"
5829        ~
5830    :: /ax//whey                     (list mass)
5831    :: /ax/protocol/version          @
5832    :: /ax/chain/[idx]               [idx=@ud key=@uvJ]
5833    :: /ax/chain/latest              [idx=@ud key=@uvJ]
5834    :: /ax/peers                     (map ship ?(%alien %known))
5835    :: /ax/peers/[ship]              ship-state
5836    :: /ax/peers/[ship]/last-contact (unit @da)
5837    :: /ax/peers/[ship]/forward-lane (list lane)
5838    :: /ax/bones/[ship]              [snd=(set bone) rcv=(set bone)]
5839    :: /ax/snd-bones/[ship]/[bone]   vase
5840    :: /ax/snubbed                   (?(%allow %deny) (list ship))
5841    :: /ax/fine/hunk/[path/...]      (list @ux) scry response fragments
5842    :: /ax/fine/ducts/[path/]        (list duct)
5843    :: /ax/fine/shut/[path/]         @ux encrypted response
5844    :: /ax/rift                      @
5845    :: /ax/corked/[ship]             (set bone)
5846    :: /ax/closing/[ship]            (set bone)
5847    ::
5848    ?.  ?=(%x ren)  ~
5849    =>  .(tyl `(pole knot)`tyl)
5850    :: public endpoints
5851    ?:  ?=([%fine %hunk lop=@t len=@t pax=^] tyl)
5852      ::TODO  separate endpoint for the full message (instead of packet list)
5853      :: .pax is expected to be a scry path of the shape /vc/desk/rev/etc,
5854      :: so we need to give it the right shape
5855      ::
5856      ?~  blk=(de-path-soft:balk pax.tyl)  ~
```

```
5857        ::
5858        ?.  (is-our-bulk our ames-state u.blk)
5859          ~
5860        =+  nom=(as-omen:balk u.blk)
5861        ~|  nom
5862        |^
5863        =/  van  ?@(vis.nom (end 3 vis.nom) way.vis.nom)
5864        =/  kyr  ?@(vis.nom (rsh 3 vis.nom) car.vis.nom)
5865        ?.  =(%c van)
5866          (en-hunk (rof ~ /ames nom))
5867        =+  pem=(rof [~ ~] /ames nom(vis %cp))
5868        ?.  ?=(^ pem)      ~
5869        ?.  ?=(^ u.pem)    ~
5870        ~|  u.u.pem
5871        =+  per=!<([r=dict:clay w=dict:clay] q.u.u.pem)
5872        ?.  =([%black ~ ~] rul.r.per)  ~
5873        (en-hunk (rof [~ ~] /ames nom))
5874        ::
5875        ++  en-hunk
5876          |=  res=(unit (unit cage))
5877          ^+  res
5878          ?~  res  ~
5879          =/  =hunk  [(slav %ud lop.tyl) (slav %ud len.tyl)]
5880          ::
5881          =/  hu-co  (etch-hunk our [life crypto-core]:ames-state)
5882          ?-  res
5883            [~ ~]     ``noun+!>((etch-open:hu-co pax.tyl hunk ~))
5884            [~ ~ *]   ``noun+!>((etch-open:hu-co pax.tyl hunk [p q.q]:u.u.res))
5885          ==
5886      --
5887    ::  private endpoints
5888    ?.  =([~ ~] lyc)  ~
5889      ?+    tyl  ~
5890        [%$ %whey ~]
5891      =/  maz=(list mass)
5892        =+  [known alien]=(skid ~(val by peers.ames-state) |=(^ =(%known +<-)))
5893        :~  peers-known+&+known
5894            peers-alien+&+alien
5895        ==
5896      ``mass+!>(maz)
5897      ::
5898        [%chain %latest ~]
5899      ``noun+!>(`[idx=@ key=@ =path]`(need (ram:on:chain chain.ames-state)))
5900      ::
5901        [%chain idx=@ ~]
5902      ?~  idx=(slaw %ud idx.tyl)
5903        [~ ~]
5904      ?~  key=(get:on:chain chain.ames-state u.idx)
5905        [~ ~]
5906      ``noun+!>(`[idx=@ key=@]`[u.idx key.u.key])
5907      ::
5908        [%peers ~]
5909      :^  ~  ~  %noun
5910      !>  ^-  (map ship ?(%alien %known))
5911      (~(run by peers.ames-state) head)
5912      ::
5913        [%peers her=@ req=*]
5914      =/  who  (slaw %p her.tyl)
```

```
5915        ?~  who  [~ ~]
5916        =/  peer  (~(get by peers.ames-state) u.who)
5917        ?+    req.tyl  [~ ~]
5918            ~
5919          ?~  peer
5920            [~ ~]
5921          ``noun+!>(u.peer)
5922        ::
5923            [%last-contact ~]
5924          :^    ~   ~   %noun
5925          !>  ^-  (unit @da)
5926          ?.  ?=([~ %known *] peer)
5927            ~
5928          `last-contact.qos.u.peer
5929        ::
5930            [%forward-lane ~]
5931          ::
5932          ::  this duplicates the routing hack from +send-blob:event-core
5933          ::  so long as neither the peer nor the peer's sponsoring galaxy is us,
5934          ::  and the peer has been reached recently:
5935          ::
5936          ::    - no route to the peer, or peer has not been contacted recently:
5937          ::      send to the peer's sponsoring galaxy
5938          ::    - direct route to the peer: use that
5939          ::    - indirect route to the peer: send to both that route and the
5940          ::      the peer's sponsoring galaxy
5941          ::
5942          :^    ~   ~   %noun
5943          !>  ^-  (list lane)
5944          ?:  =(our u.who)
5945            ~
5946          ?:  ?=([~ %known *] peer)
5947            (get-forward-lanes our +.u.peer peers.ames-state)
5948          =/  sax  (rof ~ /ames %j `beam`[[our %saxo %da now] /(scot %p u.who)])
5949          ?.  ?=([~ ~ *] sax)
5950            ~
5951          =/  gal  (rear ;;((list ship) q.q.u.u.sax))
5952          ?:  =(our gal)
5953            ~
5954          [%& gal]~
5955        ==
5956    ::
5957        [%bones her=@ ~]
5958      =/  who  (slaw %p her.tyl)
5959      ?~  who  [~ ~]
5960      =/  per  (~(get by peers.ames-state) u.who)
5961      ?.  ?=([~ %known *] per)  [~ ~]
5962      =/  res
5963        =,  u.per
5964        [snd=~(key by snd) rcv=~(key by rcv)]
5965      ``noun+!>(res)
5966    ::
5967        [%snd-bones her=@ bon=@ ~]
5968      =/  who  (slaw %p her.tyl)
5969      ?~  who  [~ ~]
5970      =/  ost  (slaw %ud bon.tyl)
5971      ?~  ost  [~ ~]
5972      =/  per  (~(get by peers.ames-state) u.who)
```

```
    ?.  ?=([~ %known *] per)  [~ ~]
    =/  mps  (~(get by snd.u.per) u.ost)
    ?~  mps  [~ ~]
    =/  res
      u.mps
    ``noun+!>(!>(res))
  ::
      [%snubbed ~]
    ``noun+!>([form.snub.ames-state ~(tap in ships.snub.ames-state)])
  ::
      [%fine %ducts pax=^]
    ?~  bulk=(de-path-soft:balk pax.tyl)  ~
    ?~  peer=(~(get by peers.ames-state) her.u.bulk)
      [~ ~]
    ?.  ?=([~ %known *] peer)
      [~ ~]  :: TODO handle aliens
    ?~  spr.u.bulk  [~ ~]
    =/  =path  =,(u.bulk [van car (scot cas) spr])
    ?~  keen=(~(get by keens.u.peer) path)
      [~ ~]
    ``noun+!>(listeners:u.keen)
  ::
      [%rift ~]
    ``noun+!>(rift.ames-state)
  ::
      [%corked her=@ ~]
    =/  who  (slaw %p her.tyl)
    ?~  who  [~ ~]
    =/  per  (~(get by peers.ames-state) u.who)
    ?.  ?=([~ %known *] per)  [~ ~]
    ``noun+!>(corked.u.per)
  ::
      [%closing her=@ ~]
    =/  who  (slaw %p her.tyl)
    ?~  who  [~ ~]
    =/  per  (~(get by peers.ames-state) u.who)
    ?.  ?=([~ %known *] per)  [~ ~]
    ``noun+!>(closing.u.per)
  ::
      [%protocol %version ~]
    ``noun+!>(protocol-version)
  ::
  ==
::
--
```

Behn

```
1   ::    %behn, just a timer
2   !:
3   !?  164
4   ::
5   =,  behn
6   |=  our=ship
7   =>  |%
8     +$  move   [p=duct q=(wite note gift)]
9     +$  note                                        ::  out request $->
10     $~  [%b %wait *@da]                             ::
11     $%  $:  %b                                      ::    to self
12             $>(%wait task)                 ::  set timer
13         ==                                          ::
14         $:  %d                                      ::    to %dill
15             $>(%flog task:dill)            ::  log output
16     ==  ==                                          ::
17     +$  sign
18     $~  [%behn %wake ~]
19     $%  [%behn $>(%wake gift)]
20     ==
21     ::
22     +$  behn-state
23     $:  %2
24         timers=(tree [key=@da val=(qeu duct)])
25         unix-duct=duct
26         next-wake=(unit @da)
27         drips=drip-manager
28     ==
29     ::
30     ++  timer-map  ((ordered-map ,@da ,(qeu duct)) lte)
31     ::
32     +$  drip-manager
33     $:  count=@ud
34         movs=(map @ud vase)
35     ==
36     ::
37     +$  timer  [date=@da =duct]
38     --
39   ::
40   =>
41   ~%  %behn  ..part  ~
42   |%
43   ++  per-event
44     =|  moves=(list move)
45     |=  [[now=@da =duct] state=behn-state]
46     ::
47     |%
48     ::
49     +|  %helpers
50     ::
51     ++  this  .
52     ++  emit  |=(m=move this(moves [m moves]))
53     ++  abet
54       ^+  [moves state]
55       ::  moves are statefully pre-flopped to ensure that
56       ::  any prepended %doze is emitted first
```

```hoon
::
=.  moves  (flop moves)
=/  new=(unit @da)  (bind (pry:timer-map timers.state) head)
::  emit %doze if needed
::
=?    ..this
    ?~  unix-duct.state  |
    =/  dif=[old=(unit @da) new=(unit @da)]  [next-wake.state new]
    ?+  dif  ~|([%unpossible dif] !!)
      [~ ~]  |                          :: no-op
      [~ ^]  &                          :: set
      [^ ~]  &                          :: clear
      [^ ^]  !=(u.old.dif u.new.dif)    :: set if changed
    ==
  (emit(next-wake.state new) [unix-duct.state %give %doze new])
::
[moves state]
::
+|  %entry-points
::
++  call
  |=  [=task error=(unit tang)]
  ^+  this
  ?:  ?&  ?=(^ error)
          !?=(%wake -.task)
      ==
    ::  XX more and better error handling
    ::
    ~&  %behn-crud-not-wake^-.task
    (emit [duct %slip %d %flog %crud -.task u.error])
  ::
  ?-  -.task
    %born  this(next-wake.state ~, unix-duct.state duct)
    %drip  (drip p.task)
    %huck  (emit [duct %give %heck syn.task])
    %rest  this(timers.state (unset-timer [p.task duct]))
    %trim  this
    %vega  this
    %wait  this(timers.state (set-timer [p.task duct]))
    %wake  (wake(next-wake.state ~) error)
  ==
::
::  +take-drip: the future is now, %give the deferred move
::
++  take-drip
  |=  [num=@ud error=(unit tang)]
  ^+  this
  =/  drip  (~(got by movs.drips.state) num)
  %-  emit(movs.drips.state (~(del by movs.drips.state) num))
  =/  card  [%give %meta drip]
  ?~  error
    [duct card]
  =/  =tang
    (weld u.error `tang`[leaf/"drip failed" ~])
  ::  XX we don't know the mote due to the %wake pattern
  ::
  [duct %hurl fail/tang card]
::
```

```
115  +|  %tasks
116  ::
117  ::  +drip: enqueue a future gift (as a vase), %pass ourselves a %wait
118  ::
119  ++  drip
120    |=  vax=vase
121    ^+  this
122    %.  [duct %pass /drip/(scot %ud count.drips.state) %b %wait +(now)]
123    %=  emit
124      movs.drips.state   (~(put by movs.drips.state) count.drips.state vax)
125      count.drips.state  +(count.drips.state)
126    ==
127  ::
128  ::  +wake: unix says wake up; process the elapsed timer (or forward error)
129  ::
130  ++  wake
131    |=  error=(unit tang)
132    ^+  this
133    ?:  =(~ timers.state)
134      ::  no-op on spurious but innocuous unix wakeups
135      ::
136      ~?  ?=(^ error)  %behn-wake-no-timer^u.error
137      this
138    =/  [=timer later-timers=_timers.state]  pop-timer
139    ?:  (gth date.timer now)
140      ::  no-op if timer is early, (+abet will reset)
141      ::
142      this
143    ::  pop the first timer and notify client vane,
144    ::  forwarding error if present
145    ::
146    ::    XX %wake errors should be signaled out-of-band
147    ::    [duct.timer %hurl goof %give %wake ~]
148    ::
149    (emit(timers.state later-timers) [duct.timer %give %wake error])
150  ::
151  +|  %implementation
152  ::
153  ::  +pop-timer: dequeue and produce earliest timer
154  ::
155  ++  pop-timer
156    ^+  [*timer timers.state]
157    =^  [date=@da dux=(qeu ^duct)]  timers.state  (pop:timer-map timers.state)
158    =^  dut  dux  ~(get to dux)
159    :-  [date dut]
160    ?:  =(~ dux)
161      timers.state
162    (put:timer-map timers.state date dux)
163  ::  +set-timer: set a timer, maintaining order
164  ::
165  ++  set-timer
166    ~%  %set-timer  ..part  ~
167    |=  t=timer
168    ^+  timers.state
169    =/  found  (find-ducts date.t)
170    (put:timer-map timers.state date.t (~(put to found) duct.t))
171  ::  +find-ducts: get timers at date
172  ::
```

```hoon
173  ::    TODO: move to +ordered-map
174  ::
175  ++  find-ducts
176    |=  date=@da
177    ^-  (qeu ^duct)
178    ?~  timers.state  ~
179    ?:  =(date key.n.timers.state)
180      val.n.timers.state
181    ?:  (lte date key.n.timers.state)
182      $(timers.state l.timers.state)
183    $(timers.state r.timers.state)
184  ::  +unset-timer: cancel a timer; if it already expired, no-op
185  ::
186  ++  unset-timer
187    |=  t=timer
188    ^+  timers.state
189    =/  [found=? dux=(qeu ^duct)]
190      =/  dux  (find-ducts date.t)
191      |-  ^-  [found=? dux=(qeu ^duct)]
192      ?~  dux  |+~
193      ?:  =(duct.t n.dux)  &+~(nip to `(qeu ^duct)`dux)
194      =^  found-left=?  l.dux  $(dux l.dux)
195      ?:  found-left  &+dux
196      =^  found-rite=?  r.dux  $(dux r.dux)
197      [found-rite dux]
198    ?.  found  timers.state
199    ?:  =(~ dux)
200      +:(del:timer-map timers.state date.t)
201    (put:timer-map timers.state date.t dux)
202    --
203  --
204  ::
205  =|  behn-state
206  =*  state  -
207  |=  [now=@da eny=@uvJ rof=roof]
208  =*  behn-gate  .
209  ^?
210  |%
211  ::  +call: handle a +task:behn request
212  ::
213  ++  call
214    ~%  %behn-call  ..part  ~
215    |=  $:  hen=duct
216            dud=(unit goof)
217            wrapped-task=(hobo task)
218        ==
219    ^-  [(list move) _behn-gate]
220    =/  =task  ((harden task) wrapped-task)
221    =/  event-core  (per-event [now hen] state)
222    =^  moves  state
223      abet:(call:event-core task ?~(dud ~ `tang.u.dud))
224    [moves behn-gate]
225  ::  +load: migrate an old state to a new behn version
226  ::
227  ++  load
228    |=  old=behn-state
229    ^+  behn-gate
230    behn-gate(state old)
```

```
231  ::    +scry: view timer state
232  ::
233  ::       TODO: not referentially transparent w.r.t. elapsed timers,
234  ::       which might or might not show up in the product
235  ::
236  ++  scry
237    ^-  roon
238    |=  [lyc=gang pov=path car=term bem=beam]
239    ^-  (unit (unit cage))
240    =*  ren   car
241    =*  why=shop  &/p.bem
242    =*  syd   q.bem
243    =*  lot=coin  $/r.bem
244    =*  tyl   s.bem
245    ::
246    ::  only respond for the local identity, %$ desk, current timestamp, root gang
247    ::
248    ?.  ?&  =(&+our why)
249            =([%$ %da now] lot)
250            =(%$ syd)
251            =([~ ~] lyc)
252        ==
253      ~
254    ::  /bx//whey          (list mass)        memory usage labels
255    ::  /bx/debug/timers   (list [@da duct])  all timers and their ducts
256    ::  /bx/timers         (list @da)         all timer timestamps
257    ::  /bx/timers/next    (unit @da)         the very next timer to fire
258    ::  /bx/timers/[da]    (list @da)         all timers up to and including da
259    ::
260    ?.  ?=(%x ren)   ~
261    ?+  tyl  [~ ~]
262        [%$ %whey ~]
263      =/  maz=(list mass)
264        :~  timers+&+timers.state
265        ==
266      ``mass+!>(maz)
267    ::
268        [%debug %timers ~]
269      :^  ~  ~  %noun
270      !>  ^-  (list [@da duct])
271      %-  zing
272      %+  turn  (tap:timer-map timers)
273      |=  [date=@da q=(qeu duct)]
274      %+  turn  ~(tap to q)
275      |=(d=duct [date d])
276    ::
277        [%timers ~]
278      :^  ~  ~  %noun
279      !>  ^-  (list @da)
280      %-  zing
281      %+  turn  (tap:timer-map timers)
282      |=  [date=@da q=(qeu duct)]
283      (reap ~(wyt in q) date)
284    ::
285        [%timers %next ~]
286      :^  ~  ~  %noun
287      !>  ^-  (unit @da)
288      (bind (pry:timer-map timers) head)
```

```hoon
289    ::
290        [%timers @ ~]
291      ?~  til=(slaw %da i.t.tyl)
292        [~ ~]
293      :^  ~  ~  %noun
294      !>  ^-  (list @da)
295      =/  tiz=(list [date=@da q=(qeu duct)])
296        (tap:timer-map timers)
297      |-  ^-  (list @da)
298      ?~  tiz  ~
299      ?:  (gth date.i.tiz u.til)  ~
300      %+  weld
301        (reap ~(wyt in q.i.tiz) date.i.tiz)
302      $(tiz t.tiz)
303    ==
304  ::
305  ++  stay  state
306  ++  take
307    |=  [tea=wire hen=duct dud=(unit goof) hin=sign]
308    ^-  [(list move) _behn-gate]
309    ?^  dud
310      ~|(%behn-take-dud (mean tang.u.dud))
311    ::
312    ?>  ?=([%drip @ ~] tea)
313    =/  event-core  (per-event [now hen] state)
314    =^  moves  state
315      abet:(take-drip:event-core (slav %ud i.t.tea) error.hin)
316    [moves behn-gate]
317  --
```

Clay

```
1  ::  clay (4c), revision control
2  ::
3  ::  The way to understand Clay is to take it section-by-section:
4  ::
5  ::  - Data structures.  You *must* start here; make sure you understand
6  ::  the entire contents of +raft.
7  ::
8  ::  - Individual reads.  +aver is the entry point, follow it through
9  ::  +read-at-tako to understand each kind of read.
10 ::
11 ::  - Subscriptions.  +wake is the center of this mechanism; nothing
12 ::  else responds to subscriptions.  +wake has no arguments, which means
13 ::  every subscription response happens when something in Clay's *state*
14 ::  has changed.  No edge-triggered responses.
15 ::
16 ::  - Receiving foreign data.  For individual requests, this is
17 ::  +take-foreign-answer.  For sync requests (%many, which is %sing %v
18 ::  for a foreign desk), this is +foreign-update.
19 ::
20 ::  - Ford.  +ford builds hoon files and gives files their types.
21 ::  Read +build-file for the first, and +read-file is the second.
22 ::
23 ::  - Writing to a desk.  Every write to a desk goes through +park, read
24 ::  it thoroughly.
25 ::
26 ::  - Merges.  Control flow starts at +start-merge, then +merge, but
27 ::  everything is scaffolding for +merge-by-germ, which is the ideal of
28 ::  a merge function: it takes two commits and a merge strategy and
29 ::  produces a new commit.
30 ::
31 ::  - Tombstoning.  This is in +tomb.
32 ::
33 ::::::::::::::::::::::::::::::::::::::::::::::::::::::::::::::::::::::::::::::
34 ::
35 ::  We use a system of "invariant footnotes", where nonlocal invariants
36 ::  are tagged with notes to construct a distributed argument that the
37 ::  invariant is maintained.  For example, see [wake].
38 ::
39 ::  Each one should be described somewhere, and then it should be
40 ::  referenced any time it's touched.  For example, any code which might
41 ::  fill a subscription should be tagged with [wake], and if +wake is
42 ::  not called by the end of that function, the function itself should
43 ::  be tagged with [wake].
44 ::
45 ::  The tagged code should constitute an argument that the invariant is
46 ::  maintained everywhere.  While this is vulnerable to omission ("I
47 ::  forgot that X could fill a subscription", it provides a good minimum
48 ::  bar.
49 ::
50 ::  Tag the specific line of code which affects the invariant.  You do
51 ::  not need to tag every function in a call stack if the invariant is
52 ::  guaranteed to be maintained by the time the function returns.
53 ::
54 ::  Some invariant references get tagged with whether they "open" or
55 ::  "close" the invariant.  For example, adding a commit to the dome
56 ::  "opens" the [wake] invariant, while calling +wake closes it.  When
```

```
57  ::    an invariant opens, you should be able to scan down and find why it
58  ::    closes in each possible flow of control.  For wake, these are
59  ::    labeled like this:
60  ::
61  ::      open: [wake] <
62  ::      close: [wake] >
63  ::      open and almost immediately close: [wake] <>
64  ::
65  ::    This system is best used for nonlocal invariants and is not
66  ::    necessary when a function can guarantee its own invariants.  For
67  ::    example, consider a set alongside a @ud representing its size.
68  ::    There is an invariant that any time you add or remove an item from
69  ::    the set you must update its size.  If you're operating on these
70  ::    directly, it could be beneficial to tag each line of code which
71  ::    might modify the set and make it clear where the size is modified.
72  ::
73  ::    Sometimes code can be restructured so that many fewer tags are
74  ::    needed.  In the above example, if the set is modified in many
75  ::    places, it may be worth factoring out set+size into a data structure
76  ::    with its own arms for put, del, uni, int, etc.  Then the invariant
77  ::    only needs to be maintained within that data structure, and call
78  ::    sites do not need to be tagged.
79  ::
80  ::::::::::::::::::::::::::::::::::::::::::::::::::::::::::::::::::::::::::::::
81  ::
82  ::    Here are the structures.  `++raft` is the formal arvo state.  It's
83  ::    also worth noting that many of the clay-related structures are
84  ::    defined in lull.
85  ::
86  ::::::::::::::::::::::::::::::::::::::::::::::::::::::::::::::::::::::::::::::
87  =/  bud
88    ^~
89    =/  zuse  !>(..zuse)
90    :*  zuse=zuse
91        nave=(slap zuse !,(*hoon nave:clay))
92        cork=(slap zuse !,(*hoon cork))
93        same=(slap zuse !,(*hoon same))
94        mime=(slap zuse !,(*hoon mime))
95        cass=(slap zuse !,(*hoon cass:clay))
96    ==
97  ::
98  |=  our=ship
99  =,  clay
100 =>  |%
101 +$  aeon  @ud                                      :: version number
102 ::
103 ::    Part of ++mery, representing the set of changes between the mergebase and
104 ::    one of the desks being merged.
105 ::
106 ::    --  `new` is the set of files in the new desk and not in the mergebase.
107 ::    --  `cal` is the set of changes in the new desk from the mergebase except
108 ::        for any that are also in the other new desk.
109 ::    --  `can` is the set of changes in the new desk from the mergebase and that
110 ::        are also in the other new desk (potential conflicts).
111 ::    --  `old` is the set of files in the mergebase and not in the new desk.
112 ::
113 +$  cane
114   $:  new=(map path lobe)
```

```
115          cal=(map path lobe)
116          can=(map path cage)
117          old=(map path ~)
118      ==
119  ::
120  ::    Type of request.
121  ::
122  ::    %d produces a set of desks, %p gets file permissions, %t gets all paths
123  ::    with the specified prefix, %u checks for existence, %v produces a ++dome
124  ::    of all desk data, %w gets @ud and @da variants for the given case, %x
125  ::    gets file contents, %y gets a directory listing, and %z gets a recursive
126  ::    hash of the file contents and children.
127  ::
128  ::    ++  care  ?(%d %p %t %u %v %w %x %y %z)
129  ::
130  ::    Keeps track of subscribers.
131  ::
132  ::    A map of requests to a set of all the subscribers who should be notified
133  ::    when the request is filled/updated.
134  ::
135  +$  cult   (jug wove duct)
136  ::
137  ::    State for ongoing %fuse merges. `con` maintains the ordering,
138  ::    `sto` stores the data needed to merge, and `bas` is the base
139  ::    beak for the merge.
140  ::
141  +$  melt   [bas=beak con=(list [beak germ]) sto=(map beak (unit domo))]
142  ::
143  ::    Domestic desk state.
144  ::
145  ::    Includes subscriber list, dome (desk content), possible commit state (for
146  ::    local changes), possible merge state (for incoming merges), and permissions.
147  ::
148  +$  dojo
149    $:  qyx=cult                                   ::  subscribers
150        dom=dome                                   ::  desk state
151        per=regs                                   ::  read perms per path
152        pew=regs                                   ::  write perms per path
153        fiz=melt                                   ::  state for mega merges
154    ==
155  ::
156  ::    Over-the-wire backfill request/response
157  ::
158  +$  fill
159    $%  [%0 =desk =lobe]
160        [%1 =desk =lobe]
161    ==
162  ::
163  ::    All except %1 are deprecated
164  ::
165  +$  fell
166    $%  [%direct p=lobe q=page]
167        [%delta p=lobe q=[p=mark q=lobe] r=page]
168        [%dead p=lobe ~]
169        [%1 peg=(unit page)]
170    ==
171  ::
172  ::    New desk data.
```

```
173  ::
174  ::  Sent to other ships to update them about a particular desk.
175  ::  Includes a map of all new aeons to hashes of their commits, the most
176  ::  recent aeon, and sets of all new commits and data.  `bar` is always
177  ::  empty now because we expect you to request any data you don't have
178  ::  yet
179  ::
180  +$  nako                                          ::  subscription state
181    $:  gar=(map aeon tako)                         ::  new ids
182        let=aeon                                    ::  next id
183        lar=(set yaki)                              ::  new commits
184        bar=~                                       ::  new content
185    ==                                              ::
186  ::
187  ::
188  ::  Formal vane state.
189  ::
190  ::  --  `rom` is our domestic state.
191  ::  --  `hoy` is a collection of foreign ships where we know something about
192  ::      their clay.
193  ::  --  `ran` is the object store.
194  ::  --  `mon` is a collection of mount points (mount point name to urbit
195  ::      location).
196  ::  --  `hez` is the unix duct that %ergo's should be sent to.
197  ::  --  `cez` is a collection of named permission groups.
198  ::  --  `pud` is an update that's waiting on a kernel upgrade
199  ::
200  +$  raft                                          ::  filesystem
201    $:  rom=room                                    ::  domestic
202        hoy=(map ship rung)                         ::  foreign
203        ran=rang                                    ::  hashes
204        fad=flow                                    ::  ford cache
205        mon=(map term beam)                         ::  mount points
206        hez=(unit duct)                             ::  sync duct
207        cez=(map @ta crew)                          ::  permission groups
208        tyr=(set duct)                              ::  app subs
209        tur=rock:tire                               ::  last tire
210        pud=(unit [=desk =yoki])                    ::  pending update
211        sad=(map ship @da)                          ::  scry known broken
212        bug=[veb=@ mas=@]                           ::  verbosity
213    ==                                              ::
214  ::
215  ::  Unvalidated response to a request.
216  ::
217  ::  Like a +$rant, but with a page of data rather than a cage of it.
218  ::
219  +$  rand                                          ::  unvalidated rant
220          $:  p=[p=care q=case r=@tas]              ::  clade release book
221              q=path                                ::  spur
222              r=page                                ::  data
223          ==                                        ::
224  ::
225  ::  Generic desk state.
226  ::
227  ::  --  `lim` is the most recent date we're confident we have all the
228  ::      information for.  For local desks, this is always `now`.  For foreign
229  ::      desks, this is the last time we got a full update from the foreign
230  ::      urbit.
```

```hoon
231 ::      --  `ref` is a possible request manager.  For local desks, this is null.
232 ::          For foreign desks, this keeps track of all pending foreign requests
233 ::          plus a cache of the responses to previous requests.
234 ::      --  `qyx` is the set of subscriptions, with listening ducts. These
235 ::          subscriptions exist only until they've been filled.
236 ::      --  `dom` is the actual state of the filetree.  Since this is used almost
237 ::          exclusively in `++ze`, we describe it there.
238 ::
239 +$  rede                                           ::  universal project
240         $:  lim=@da                                ::  complete to
241             ref=(unit rind)                        ::  outgoing requests
242             qyx=cult                               ::  subscribers
243             dom=dome                               ::  revision state
244             per=regs                               ::  read perms per path
245             pew=regs                               ::  write perms per path
246             fiz=melt                               ::  domestic mega merges
247         ==                                         ::
248 ::
249 ::  Foreign request manager.
250 ::
251 ::  When we send a request to a foreign ship, we keep track of it in here.  This
252 ::  includes a request counter, a map of request numbers to requests, a reverse
253 ::  map of requesters to request numbers, a simple cache of common %sing
254 ::  requests, and a possible nako if we've received data from the other ship and
255 ::  are in the process of validating it.
256 ::
257 +$  rind                                           ::  request manager
258   $:  nix=@ud                                       ::  request index
259       bom=(map @ud update-state)                   ::  outstanding
260       fod=(map duct @ud)                           ::  current requests
261       haw=(map mood (unit cage))                   ::  simple cache
262   ==                                               ::
263 ::
264 +$  bill  (list dude:gall)
265 ::
266 ::  Active downloads
267 ::
268 +$  update-state
269   $:  =duct
270       =rave
271       have=(map lobe fell)
272       need=(list $@(lobe [=tako =path =lobe]))     ::  opt deets for scry
273       nako=(qeu (unit nako))
274       busy=(unit $@(%ames [kind=@ta =time =path]))  ::  pending request
275   ==
276 ::
277 ::  Domestic ship.
278 ::
279 ::  `hun` is the duct to dill, and `dos` is a collection of our desks.
280 ::
281 +$  room                                           ::  fs per ship
282         $:  hun=duct                               ::  terminal duct
283             dos=(map desk dojo)                    ::  native desk
284         ==                                         ::
285 ::
286 ::  Stored request.
287 ::
288 ::  Like a +$rave but with caches of current versions for %next and %many.
```

```
289  ::  Generally used when we store a request in our state somewhere.
290  ::
291  ::  TODO: remove lobes from %many
292  ::
293  +$  cach  (unit (unit cage))                          ::  cached result
294  +$  wove  [for=(unit [=ship ver=@ud]) =rove]          ::  stored source + req
295  +$  rove                                              ::  stored request
296        $%  [%sing =mood]                               ::  single request
297            [%next =mood aeon=(unit aeon) =cach]        ::  next version of one
298            $:  %mult                                   ::  next version of any
299                =mool                                   ::  original request
300                aeon=(unit aeon)                        ::  checking for change
301                old-cach=(map [=care =path] cach)       ::  old version
302                new-cach=(map [=care =path] cach)       ::  new version
303            ==                                          ::
304            [%many track=? =moat lobes=(map path lobe)] ::  change range
305        ==                                              ::
306  ::
307  ::  Foreign desk data.
308  ::
309  +$  rung
310        $:  rus=(map desk rede)                         ::  neighbor desks
311        ==
312  ::
313  +$  card  (wind note gift)                            ::  local card
314  +$  move  [p=duct q=card]                             ::  local move
315  +$  note                                              ::  out request $->
316      $~  [%b %wait *@da]                               ::
317      $%  $:  %$                                        ::  to arvo
318              $>(%what waif)                            ::
319          ==                                            ::
320          $:  %a                                        ::  to %ames
321              $>(?(%plea %keen %yawn) task:ames)        ::
322          ==                                            ::
323          $:  %b                                        ::  to %behn
324              $>  $?  %drip                             ::
325                      %rest                             ::
326                      %wait                             ::
327                  ==                                    ::
328              task:behn                                 ::
329          ==                                            ::
330          $:  %c                                        ::  to %clay
331              $>  $?  %info                             ::  internal edit
332                      %merg                             ::  merge desks
333                      %fuse                             ::  merge many
334                      %park                             ::
335                      %perm                             ::
336                      %pork                             ::
337                      %warp                             ::
338                      %werp                             ::
339                  ==                                    ::
340              task                                      ::
341          ==                                            ::
342          $:  %d                                        ::  to %dill
343              $>  $?  %flog                             ::
344                      %text                             ::
345                  ==                                    ::
346              task:dill                                 ::
```

```hoon
        ==                                            ::
    $:  %g                                            :: to %gall
        $>  $?  %deal
                %jolt
                %load
            ==
        task:gall
    ==                                                ::
    $:  %j                                            :: by %jael
        $>(%public-keys task:jael)                    ::
==  ==                                                ::
+$  riot  (unit rant)                                 :: response+complete
+$  sign                                              :: in result $<-
    $~  [%behn %wake ~]                               ::
    $%  $:  %ames                                     ::
            $>  $?  %boon                              :: response
                    %done                             :: (n)ack
                    %lost                             :: lost boon
                    %tune                             :: scry response
                ==                                    ::
            gift:ames                                 ::
        ==                                            ::
        $:  %behn                                     ::
            $%  $>(%wake gift:behn)                    :: timer activate
                $>(%writ gift)                         ::
        ==  ==                                         ::
        $:  %clay                                     ::
            $>  $?  %mere                              ::
                    %writ                              ::
                    %wris                              ::
                ==                                    ::
            gift                                      ::
        ==                                            ::
        $:  %gall                                     ::
            $>  $?  %unto
                ==
            gift:gall
        ==
        $:  %jael                                     ::
            $>(%public-keys gift:jael)                 ::
==  ==                                                ::
--  =>
~%  %clay-utilities  ..part  ~
::  %utilities
::
|%
++  scry-timeout-time  ~m5
++  scry-retry-time    ~h1
::  +sort-by-head: sorts alphabetically using the head of each element
::
++  sort-by-head
  |=([a=(pair path *) b=(pair path *)] (aor p.a p.b))
::
::  By convention: paf == (weld pax pat)
::
++  mode-to-commit
  |=  [hat=(map path lobe) pax=path all=? mod=mode]
  ^-  [deletes=(set path) changes=(map path cage)]
```

```
405    =/  deletes
406      %-  silt
407      %+  turn
408        ^-  (list path)
409        %+  weld
410          ^-  (list path)
411          %+  murn  mod
412          |=  [pat=path mim=(unit mime)]
413          ^-  (unit path)
414          ?^  mim
415            ~
416          `pat
417        ^-  (list path)
418        ?.  all
419          ~
420        =+  mad=(malt mod)
421        =+  len=(lent pax)
422        =/  descendants=(list path)
423          %+  turn
424            %+  skim  ~(tap by hat)
425            |=  [paf=path lob=lobe]
426            =(pax (scag len paf))
427          |=  [paf=path lob=lobe]
428          (slag len paf)
429        %+  skim
430          descendants
431        |=  pat=path
432        (~(has by mad) pat)
433      |=  pat=path
434      (weld pax pat)
435    ::
436    =/  changes
437      %-  malt
438      %+  murn  mod
439      |=  [pat=path mim=(unit mime)]
440      ^-  (unit [path cage])
441      ?~  mim
442        ~
443      `[(weld pax pat) %mime !>(u.mim)]
444    ::
445    [deletes changes]
446  ::
447  ++  pour-to-mist
448    |=  =pour
449    ^-  mist
450    ?+    -.pour  pour
451        %vale  [%vale path.pour]
452        %arch  [%arch path.pour]
453    ==
454  ::
455  ++  fell-to-page
456    |=  =fell
457    ^-  (unit page)
458    ?-  -.fell
459      %dead    ~
460      %direct  `q.fell
461      %delta   ~
462      %1       peg.fell
```

```
463     ==
464 ::
465 ++  rave-to-rove
466   |=  rav=rave
467   ^-  rove
468   ?-  -.rav
469     %sing  rav
470     %next  [- mood ~ ~]:rav
471     %mult  [- mool ~ ~ ~]:rav
472     %many  [- track moat ~]:rav
473     ==
474 ::
475 ++  rove-to-rave
476   |=  rov=rove
477   ^-  rave
478   ?-  -.rov
479     %sing  rov
480     %next  [- mood]:rov
481     %mult  [- mool]:rov
482     %many  [- track moat]:rov
483     ==
484 --  =>
485 ~%  %clay  +  ~
486 |%
487 ::  Printable form of a wove; useful for debugging
488 ::
489 ++  print-wove
490   |=  =wove
491   :-  for.wove
492   ?-  -.rove.wove
493     %sing  [%sing mood.rove.wove]
494     %next  [%next [mood aeon]:rove.wove]
495     %mult  [%mult [mool aeon]:rove.wove]
496     %many  [%many [track moat]:rove.wove]
497     ==
498 ::
499 ::  Printable form of a cult; useful for debugging
500 ::
501 ++  print-cult
502   |=  =cult
503   %+  turn  ~(tap by cult)
504   |=  [=wove ducts=(set duct)]
505   [ducts (print-wove wove)]
506 ::
507 ++  fusion
508   ~%  %fusion  ..fusion  ~
509   |%
510   ::  +wrap: external wrapper
511   ::
512   ++  wrap
513     |*  [* state:ford]
514     [+<- +<+< +<+>-]  ::  [result cache.state flue]
515   ::
516   ++  with-face  |=([face=@tas =vase] vase(p [%face face p.vase]))
517   ++  with-faces
518     =|  res=(unit vase)
519     |=  vaz=(list [face=@tas =vase])
520     ^-  vase
```

```
?~  vaz  (need res)
=/  faz  (with-face i.vaz)
=.  res  `?~(res faz (slop faz u.res))
$(vaz t.vaz)
::
++  ford
  !.
  =>  |%
      +$  state
        $:  cache=flow
            flue
            cycle=(set mist)
            drain=(map mist leak)
            stack=(list (set leak))
        ==
      +$  args
        $:  files=(map path (each page lobe))
            file-store=(map lobe page)
            verb=@
            cache=flow
            flue
        ==
      --
  ~%  %ford-gate  ..ford  ~
  |=  args
  ::  nub: internal mutable state for this computation
  ::
  =|  nub=state
  =.  cache.nub  cache
  =.  spill.nub  spill
  =.  sprig.nub  sprig
  ~%  %ford-core  ..$  ~
  |%
  ::  +read-file: retrieve marked, validated file contents at path
  ::
  ++  read-file
    ~/  %read-file
    |=  =path
    ^-  [cage state]
    ~|  %error-validating^path
    %-  soak-cage
    %+  gain-sprig  vale+path  |.
    =.  stack.nub  [~ stack.nub]
    ?:  (~(has in cycle.nub) vale+path)
      ~|(cycle+vale+path^cycle.nub !!)
    =.  cycle.nub  (~(put in cycle.nub) vale+path)
    %+  gain-leak  vale+path
    |=  nob=state
    =.  nub  nob
    %-  (trace 1 |.("read file {(spud path)}"))
    =/  file
      ~|  %file-not-found^path
      (~(got by files) path)
    =/  page
      ?:  ?=(%& -.file)
        p.file
      ~|  %tombstoned-file^path^p.file
      (~(got by file-store) p.file)
```

```
579      =^  =cage  nub  (validate-page path page)
580      [[%cage cage] nub]
581  ::
582  ::  +build-nave: build a statically typed mark core
583  ::
584  ++  build-nave
585    ~/  %build-nave
586    |=  mak=mark
587    ^-  [vase state]
588    ~|  %error-building-mark^mak
589    %-  soak-vase
590    %+  gain-sprig  nave+mak  |.
591    =.  stack.nub  [~ stack.nub]
592    ?:  (~(has in cycle.nub) nave+mak)
593      ~|(cycle+nave+mak^cycle.nub !!)
594    =.  cycle.nub  (~(put in cycle.nub) nave+mak)
595    %-  (trace 1 |.("make mark {<mak>}"))
596    =^  cor=vase  nub  (build-fit %mar mak)
597    =/  gad=vase  (slap cor limb/%grad)
598    ?@  q.gad
599      =+  !<(mok=mark gad)
600      =^  deg=vase  nub  ^$(mak mok)
601      =^  tub=vase  nub  (build-cast mak mok)
602      =^  but=vase  nub  (build-cast mok mak)
603      %+  gain-leak  nave+mak
604      |=  nob=state
605      =.  nub  nob
606      :_  nub  :-  %vase
607      ^-  vase  ::  vase of nave
608      %+  slap
609        (with-faces deg+deg tub+tub but+but cor+cor nave+nave.bud ~)
610      !,  *hoon
611      =/  typ  _+<.cor
612      =/  dif  _*diff:deg
613      ^-  (nave typ dif)
614      |%
615      ++  diff
616        |=  [old=typ new=typ]
617        ^-  dif
618        (diff:deg (tub old) (tub new))
619      ++  form  form:deg
620      ++  join  join:deg
621      ++  mash  mash:deg
622      ++  pact
623        |=  [v=typ d=dif]
624        ^-  typ
625        (but (pact:deg (tub v) d))
626      ++  vale  noun:grab:cor
627      --
628    %+  gain-leak  nave+mak
629    |=  nob=state
630    =.  nub  nob
631    :_  nub  :-  %vase
632    ^-  vase  ::  vase of nave
633    %+  slap  (slop (with-face cor+cor) zuse.bud)
634    !,  *hoon
635    =/  typ  _+<.cor
636    =/  dif  _*diff:grad:cor
```

```
637      ^-  (nave:clay typ dif)
638      |%
639      ++  diff  |=([old=typ new=typ] (diff:~(grad cor old) new))
640      ++  form  form:grad:cor
641      ++  join
642        |=  [a=dif b=dif]
643        ^-  (unit (unit dif))
644        ?:  =(a b)
645            ~
646        `(join:grad:cor a b)
647      ++  mash
648        |=  [a=[=ship =desk =dif] b=[=ship =desk =dif]]
649        ^-  (unit dif)
650        ?:  =(dif.a dif.b)
651            ~
652        `(mash:grad:cor a b)
653      ++  pact  |=([v=typ d=dif] (pact:~(grad cor v) d))
654      ++  vale  noun:grab:cor
655      --
656    ::  +build-dais: build a dynamically typed mark definition
657    ::
658    ++  build-dais
659      ~/  %build-dais
660      |=  mak=mark
661      ^-  [dais state]
662      ~|  %error-building-dais^mak
663      %-  soak-dais
664      %+  gain-sprig  dais+mak  |.
665      =.  stack.nub  [~ stack.nub]
666      ?:  (~(has in cycle.nub) dais+mak)
667        ~|(cycle+dais+mak^cycle.nub !!)
668      =.  cycle.nub  (~(put in cycle.nub) dais+mak)
669      =^  nav=vase  nub  (build-nave mak)
670      %+  gain-leak  dais+mak
671      |=  nob=state
672      =.  nub  nob
673      %-  (trace 1 |.("make dais {<mak>}"))
674      :_  nub  :-  %dais
675      ^-  dais
676      =>  [nav=nav ..zuse]
677      |_  sam=vase
678      ++  diff
679        |=  new=vase
680        (slam (slap nav limb/%diff) (slop sam new))
681      ++  form  !<(mark (slap nav limb/%form))
682      ++  join
683        |=  [a=vase b=vase]
684        ^-  (unit (unit vase))
685        =/  res=vase  (slam (slap nav limb/%join) (slop a b))
686        ?~  q.res      ~
687        ?~  +.q.res  [~ ~]
688        ``(slap res !,(*hoon ?>(?=([~ ~ *] .) u.u)))
689      ++  mash
690        |=  [a=[=ship =desk diff=vase] b=[=ship =desk diff=vase]]
691        ^-  (unit vase)
692        =/  res=vase
693          %+  slam  (slap nav limb/%mash)
694          %+  slop
```

```
695              :(slop [[%atom %p ~] ship.a] [[%atom %tas ~] desk.a] diff.a)
696               :(slop [[%atom %p ~] ship.b] [[%atom %tas ~] desk.b] diff.b)
697          ?~  q.res
698            ~
699          `(slap res !,(*hoon ?>((^ .) u)))
700      ++  pact
701        |=  diff=vase
702        (slam (slap nav limb/%pact) (slop sam diff))
703      ++  vale
704        |:  noun=q:(slap nav !,(*hoon *vale))
705        (slam (slap nav limb/%vale) noun/noun)
706      --
707  ::  +build-cast: produce gate to convert mark .a to, statically typed
708  ::
709  ++  build-cast
710    ~/  %build-cast
711    |=  [a=mark b=mark]
712    ^-  [vase state]
713    ~|  error-building-cast+[a b]
714    %-  soak-vase
715    %+  gain-sprig  cast+a^b  |.
716    =.  stack.nub  [~ stack.nub]
717    ?:  (~(has in cycle.nub) cast+[a b])
718      ~|(cycle+cast+[a b]^cycle.nub !!)
719    ?:  =(a b)
720      %+  gain-leak  cast+a^b
721      |=  nob=state
722      %-  (trace 4 |.("identity shortcircuit"))
723      =.  nub  nob
724      :_(nub vase+same.bud)
725    ?:  =([%mime %hoon] [a b])
726      %-  (trace 4 |.("%mime -> %hoon shortcircuit"))
727      :_(nub [%vase =>(..zuse !>(|=(m=mime q.q.m)))])
728    ::  try +grow; is there a +grow core with a .b arm?
729    ::
730    %-  (trace 1 |.("make cast {<a>} -> {<b>}"))
731    =^  old=vase  nub  (build-fit %mar a)
732    ?:  (has-arm %grow b old)
733      ::  +grow core has .b arm; use that
734      ::
735      %+  gain-leak  cast+a^b
736      |=  nob=state
737      %-  (trace 4 |.("{<a>} -> {<b>}: +{(trip b)}:grow:{(trip a)}"))
738      =.  nub  nob
739      :_  nub  :-  %vase
740      %+  slap  (with-faces cor+old ~)
741      ^-  hoon
742      :+  %brcl  !,(*hoon v=+<.cor)
743      :+  %tsgl  limb/b
744      !,(*hoon ~(grow cor v))
745    ::  try direct +grab
746    ::
747    =^  new=vase  nub  (build-fit %mar b)
748    =/  arm=?  (has-arm %grab a new)
749    =/  rab  (mule |.((slap new tsgl/[limb/a limb/%grab])))
750    ?:  &(arm ?=(%& -.rab) ?=(^ q.p.rab))
751      %+  gain-leak  cast+a^b
752      |=  nob=state
```

```
753      %-  (trace 4 |.("{<a>} -> {<b>}: +{(trip a)}:grab:{(trip b)}"))
754      =.  nub  nob
755      :_(nub vase+p.rab)
756    ::  try +jump
757    ::
758    =/  jum  (mule |.((slap old tsgl/[limb/b limb/%jump]))))
759    ?:  &((has-arm %jump a old) ?=(%& -.jum))
760      =/  via  !<(mark p.jum)
761      %-  (trace 4 |.("{<a>} -> {<b>}: via {<via>} per +jump:{(trip a)}"))
762      (compose-casts a via b)
763    ?:  &(arm ?=(%& -.rab))
764      =/  via  !<(mark p.rab)
765      %-  (trace 4 |.("{<a>} -> {<b>}: via {<via>} per +grab:{(trip b)}"))
766      (compose-casts a via b)
767    ?:  ?=(%noun b)
768      %+  gain-leak  cast+a^b
769      |=  nob=state
770      %-  (trace 4 |.("{<a>} -> {<b>} default"))
771      =.  nub  nob
772      :_(nub vase+same.bud)
773    ~|(no-cast-from+[a b] !!)
774  ::
775  ++  compose-casts
776    |=  [x=mark y=mark z=mark]
777    ^-  [soak state]
778    =^  uno=vase  nub  (build-cast x y)
779    =^  dos=vase  nub  (build-cast y z)
780    %+  gain-leak  cast+x^z
781    |=  nob=state
782    =.  nub  nob
783    :_  nub  :-  %vase
784    %+  slap
785      (with-faces uno+uno dos+dos ~)
786    !,(*hoon |=(_+<.uno (dos (uno +<))))
787  ::
788  ++  has-arm
789    |=  [arm=@tas =mark core=vase]
790    ^-  ?
791    =/  rib  (mule |.((slap core [%wing ~[arm]])))
792    ?:  ?=(%| -.rib)  %.n
793    =/  lab  (mule |.((slob mark p.p.rib)))
794    ?:  ?=(%| -.lab)  %.n
795    p.lab
796  ::  +build-tube: produce a $tube mark conversion gate from .a to .b
797  ::
798  ++  build-tube
799    |=  [a=mark b=mark]
800    ^-  [tube state]
801    ~|  error-building-tube+[a b]
802    %-  soak-tube
803    %+  gain-sprig  tube+a^b  |.
804    =.  stack.nub  [~ stack.nub]
805    ?:  (~(has in cycle.nub) tube+[a b])
806      ~|(cycle+tube+[a b]^cycle.nub !!)
807    =^  gat=vase  nub  (build-cast a b)
808    %+  gain-leak  tube+a^b
809    |=  nob=state
810    =.  nub  nob
```

```
%-  (trace 1 |.("make tube {<a>} -> {<b>}"))
:_(nub [%tube =>([gat=gat ..zuse] |=(v=vase (slam gat v)))])
::
++  validate-page
  |=  [=path =page]
  ^-  [cage state]
  ~|  validate-page-fail+path^from+p.page
  =/  mak=mark  (head (flop path))
  ?:  =(mak p.page)
    (page-to-cage page)
  =^  [mark vax=vase]  nub  (page-to-cage page)
  =^  =tube  nub  (build-tube p.page mak)
  :_(nub [mak (tube vax)])
::
++  page-to-cage
  |=  =page
  ^-  [cage state]
  ?:  =(%hoon p.page)
    :_(nub [%hoon [%atom %t ~] q.page])
  ?:  =(%mime p.page)
    :_(nub [%mime =>([;;(mime q.page) ..zuse] !>(-))])
  =^  =dais  nub  (build-dais p.page)
  :_(nub [p.page (vale:dais q.page)])
::
++  cast-path
  |=  [=path mak=mark]
  ^-  [cage state]
  =/  mok  (head (flop path))
  ~|  error-casting-path+[path mok mak]
  =^  cag=cage  nub  (read-file path)
  ?:  =(mok mak)
    [cag nub]
  =^  =tube  nub  (build-tube mok mak)
  ~|  error-running-cast+[path mok mak]
  :_(nub [mak (tube q.cag)])
::
++  run-pact
  |=  [old=page diff=page]
  ^-  [cage state]
  ?:  ?=(%hoon p.old)
    =/  txt=wain  (to-wain:format ;;(@t q.old))
    =+  ;;(dif=(urge cord) q.diff)
    =/  new=@t  (of-wain:format (lurk:differ txt dif))
    :_(nub [%hoon =>([new ..zuse] !>(-))])
  =^  dys=dais  nub  (build-dais p.old)
  =^  syd=dais  nub  (build-dais p.diff)
  :_(nub [p.old (~(pact dys (vale:dys q.old)) (vale:syd q.diff))])
::
++  prelude
  |=  =path
  ^-  vase
  =^  cag=cage  nub  (read-file path)
  ?>  =(%hoon p.cag)
  =/  tex=tape  (trip !<(@t q.cag))
  =/  =pile  (parse-pile path tex)
  =.  hoon.pile  !,(*hoon .)
  =^  res=vase  nub  (run-prelude pile)
  res
```

```
    ::
    ++  build-dependency
      ~/  %build-dep
      |=  dep=(each [dir=path fil=path] path)
      ^-  [vase state]
      =/  =path
        ?:(?=(%| -.dep) p.dep fil.p.dep)
      ~|  %error-building^path
      %-  soak-vase
      %+  gain-sprig  file+path  |.
      =.  stack.nub  [~ stack.nub]
      %-  (trace 1 |.("make file {(spud path)}"))
      ?:  (~(has in cycle.nub) file+path)
        ~|(cycle+file+path^cycle.nub !!)
      =.  cycle.nub  (~(put in cycle.nub) file+path)
      =^  cag=cage  nub  (read-file path)
      ?>  =(%hoon p.cag)
      =/  tex=tape  (trip !<(@t q.cag))
      =/  =pile  (parse-pile path tex)
      =^  sut=vase  nub  (run-prelude pile)
      %+  gain-leak  file+path
      |=  nob=state
      =.  nub  nob
      =/  res=vase  (slap sut hoon.pile)
      [[%vase res] nub]
    ::
    ++  build-file
      |=  =path
      (build-dependency |+path)
    ::  +build-directory: builds files in top level of a directory
    ::
    ::    this excludes files directly at /path/hoon,
    ::    instead only including files in the unix-style directory at /path,
    ::    such as /path/file/hoon, but not /path/more/file/hoon.
    ::
    ++  build-directory
      |=  =path
      ^-  [(map @ta vase) state]
      %-  soak-arch
      %+  gain-sprig  arch+path  |.
      =.  stack.nub  [~ stack.nub]
      %+  gain-leak  arch+path
      |=  nob=state
      =.  nub  nob
      =/  fiz=(list @ta)
        =/  len  (lent path)
        %+  murn  ~(tap by files)
        |=  [pax=^path *]
        ^-  (unit @ta)
        ?.  =(path (scag len pax))
          ~
        =/  pat  (slag len pax)
        ?:  ?=([@ %hoon ~] pat)
          `i.pat
        ~
      ::
      =|  rez=(map @ta vase)
      |-
```

```
927        ?~  fiz
928          [[%arch rez] nub]
929        =*  nom=@ta    i.fiz
930        =/  pax=^path  (weld path nom %hoon ~)
931        =^  res  nub   (build-dependency &+[path pax])
932        $(fiz t.fiz, rez (~(put by rez) nom res))
933      ::
934      ++  run-prelude
935        |=  =pile
936        =/  sut=vase  zuse.bud
937        =^  sut=vase  nub  (run-tauts sut %sur sur.pile)
938        =^  sut=vase  nub  (run-tauts sut %lib lib.pile)
939        =^  sut=vase  nub  (run-raw sut raw.pile)
940        =^  sut=vase  nub  (run-raz sut raz.pile)
941        =^  sut=vase  nub  (run-maz sut maz.pile)
942        =^  sut=vase  nub  (run-caz sut caz.pile)
943        =^  sut=vase  nub  (run-bar sut bar.pile)
944        [sut nub]
945      ::
946      ++  parse-pile
947        ~/  %parse-pile
948        |=  [pax=path tex=tape]
949        ^-  pile
950        =/  [=hair res=(unit [=pile =nail])]
951          %-  road  |.
952          ((pile-rule pax) [1 1] tex)
953        ?^  res  pile.u.res
954        %-  mean
955        =/  lyn  p.hair
956        =/  col  q.hair
957        ^-  (list tank)
958        :~  leaf+"syntax error at [{<lyn>} {<col>}] in {<pax>}"
959            ::
960            =/  =wain  (to-wain:format (crip tex))
961            ?:  (gth lyn (lent wain))
962              '<<end of file>>'
963            (snag (dec lyn) wain)
964            ::
965            leaf+(runt [(dec col) '-'] "^")
966        ==
967      ::
968      ++  pile-rule
969        |=  pax=path
970        %-  full
971        %+  ifix
972          :_  gay
973          ::  parse optional /? and ignore
974          ::
975          ;~(plug gay (punt ;~(plug fas wut gap dem gap)))
976        |^
977        ;~  plug
978          %+  cook  (bake zing (list (list taut)))
979          %+  rune  hep
980          (most ;~(plug com gaw) taut-rule)
981          ::
982          %+  cook  (bake zing (list (list taut)))
983          %+  rune  lus
984          (most ;~(plug com gaw) taut-rule)
```

```
    ::
      %+  rune  tis
      ;~(plug sym ;~(pfix gap stap))
    ::
      %+  rune  sig
      ;~((glue gap) sym wyde:vast stap)
    ::
      %+  rune  cen
      ;~(plug sym ;~(pfix gap ;~(pfix cen sym)))
    ::
      %+  rune  buc
      ;~  (glue gap)
        sym
        ;~(pfix cen sym)
        ;~(pfix cen sym)
      ==
    ::
      %+  rune  tar
      ;~  (glue gap)
        sym
        ;~(pfix cen sym)
        ;~(pfix stap)
      ==
    ::
      %+  stag  %tssg
      (most gap tall:(vang & pax))
    ==
    ::
    ++  pant
      |*  fel=^rule
      ;~(pose fel (easy ~))
    ::
    ++  mast
      |*  [bus=^rule fel=^rule]
      ;~(sfix (more bus fel) bus)
    ::
    ++  rune
      |*  [bus=^rule fel=^rule]
      %-  pant
      %+  mast  gap
      ;~(pfix fas bus gap fel)
    --
::
++  taut-rule
  %+  cook  |=(taut +<)
  ;~  pose
    (stag ~ ;~(pfix tar sym))
    ;~(plug (stag ~ sym) ;~(pfix tis sym))
    (cook |=(a=term [`a a]) sym)
  ==
::
++  run-tauts
  |=  [sut=vase wer=?(%lib %sur) taz=(list taut)]
  ^-  [vase state]
  ?~  taz  [sut nub]
  =^  pin=vase  nub  (build-fit wer pax.i.taz)
  =?  p.pin  ?=(^ face.i.taz)  [%face u.face.i.taz p.pin]
  $(sut (slop pin sut), taz t.taz)
```

```
1043      ::
1044      ++  run-raw
1045        |=  [sut=vase raw=(list [face=term =path])]
1046        ^-  [vase state]
1047        ?~  raw  [sut nub]
1048        =^  pin=vase  nub  (build-file (snoc path.i.raw %hoon))
1049        =.  p.pin  [%face face.i.raw p.pin]
1050        $(sut (slop pin sut), raw t.raw)
1051      ::
1052      ++  run-raz
1053        |=  [sut=vase raz=(list [face=term =spec =path])]
1054        ^-  [vase state]
1055        ?~  raz  [sut nub]
1056        =^  res=(map @ta vase)  nub
1057          (build-directory path.i.raz)
1058        =;  pin=vase
1059          =.  p.pin  [%face face.i.raz p.pin]
1060          $(sut (slop pin sut), raz t.raz)
1061        ::
1062        =/  =type  (~(play ut p.sut) [%kttr spec.i.raz])
1063        ::  ensure results nest in the specified type,
1064        ::  and produce a homogenous map containing that type.
1065        ::
1066        :-  %-  ~(play ut p.sut)
1067            [%kttr %make [%wing ~[%map]] ~[[%base %atom %ta] spec.i.raz]]
1068        |-
1069        ?~  res  ~
1070        ?.  (~(nest ut type) | p.q.n.res)
1071          ~|  [%nest-fail path.i.raz p.n.res]
1072          !!
1073        :-  [p.n.res q.q.n.res]
1074        [$(res l.res) $(res r.res)]
1075      ::
1076      ++  run-maz
1077        |=  [sut=vase maz=(list [face=term =mark])]
1078        ^-  [vase state]
1079        ?~  maz  [sut nub]
1080        =^  pin=vase  nub  (build-nave mark.i.maz)
1081        =.  p.pin  [%face face.i.maz p.pin]
1082        $(sut (slop pin sut), maz t.maz)
1083      ::
1084      ++  run-caz
1085        |=  [sut=vase caz=(list [face=term =mars])]
1086        ^-  [vase state]
1087        ?~  caz  [sut nub]
1088        =^  pin=vase  nub  (build-cast mars.i.caz)
1089        =.  p.pin  [%face face.i.caz p.pin]
1090        $(sut (slop pin sut), caz t.caz)
1091      ::
1092      ++  run-bar
1093        |=  [sut=vase bar=(list [face=term =mark =path])]
1094        ^-  [vase state]
1095        ?~  bar  [sut nub]
1096        =^  =cage  nub  (cast-path [path mark]:i.bar)
1097        =.  p.q.cage  [%face face.i.bar p.q.cage]
1098        $(sut (slop q.cage sut), bar t.bar)
1099      ::
1100      ::  +build-fit: build file at path, maybe converting '-'s to '/'s in path
```

```
1101        ::
1102        ++  build-fit
1103          |=  [pre=@tas pax=@tas]
1104          ^-  [vase state]
1105          (build-file (fit-path pre pax))
1106        ::
1107        ::  +fit-path: find path, maybe converting '-'s to '/'s
1108        ::
1109        ::    Try '-' before '/', applied left-to-right through the path,
1110        ::    e.g. 'a-foo/bar' takes precedence over 'a/foo-bar'.
1111        ::
1112        ++  fit-path
1113          |=  [pre=@tas pax=@tas]
1114          ^-  path
1115          =/  paz  (segments pax)
1116          |-  ^-  path
1117          ?~  paz
1118            ~_(leaf/"clay: no files match /{(trip pre)}/{(trip pax)}/hoon" !!)
1119          =/  pux=path  pre^(snoc i.paz %hoon)
1120          ?:  (~(has by files) pux)
1121            pux
1122          $(paz t.paz)
1123        ::
1124        ++  all-fits
1125          |=  [=term suf=term]
1126          ^-  (list path)
1127          %+  turn  (segments suf)
1128          |=  seg=path
1129          [term (snoc seg %hoon)]
1130        ::
1131        ::  Gets a map of the data at the given path and all children of it.
1132        ::
1133        ::    i.e. +dip:of for a map, except doesn't shorten paths
1134        ::
1135        ++  dip-hat
1136          |=  pax=path
1137          ^-  (map path (each page lobe))
1138          %-  malt
1139          %+  skim  ~(tap by files)
1140          |=  [p=path *]
1141          ?|  ?=(~ pax)
1142              ?&  !?=(~ p)
1143                  =(-.pax -.p)
1144                  $(p +.p, pax +.pax)
1145          ==  ==
1146        ::
1147        ++  trace
1148          |=  [pri=@ print=(trap tape)]
1149          (^trace verb pri print)
1150        ::
1151        ++  mist-to-pour
1152          |=  =mist
1153          ^-  pour
1154          ?+    -.mist  mist
1155              %vale
1156            :+  %vale  path.mist
1157            ~|  %file-not-found-mist^path.mist
1158            =/  lob  (~(got by files) path.mist)
```

```
?-  -.lob
  %&  (page-to-lobe p.lob)
  %|  p.lob
==

    %arch
=/  dip  (dip-hat path.mist)
:+  %arch  path.mist
%-  ~(run by dip)
|=  file=(each page lobe)
?-  -.file
  %&  (page-to-lobe p.file)
  %|  p.file
==

==
::
++  soak-cage  |=([s=soak n=state] ?>(?=(%cage -.s) [cage.s n]))
++  soak-vase  |=([s=soak n=state] ?>(?=(%vase -.s) [vase.s n]))
++  soak-dais  |=([s=soak n=state] ?>(?=(%dais -.s) [dais.s n]))
++  soak-tube  |=([s=soak n=state] ?>(?=(%tube -.s) [tube.s n]))
++  soak-arch  |=([s=soak n=state] ?>(?=(%arch -.s) [dir.s n]))
::
++  gain-sprig
  |=  [=mist next=(trap [soak state])]
  ^-  [soak state]
  ?~  got=(~(get by sprig.nub) mist)
    $:next
  =?  stack.nub  ?=(^ stack.nub)
    stack.nub(i (~(put in i.stack.nub) leak.u.got))
  [soak.u.got nub]
::
++  gain-leak
  |=  [=mist next=$-(state [soak state])]
  ^-  [soak state]
  =^  top=(set leak)  stack.nub  stack.nub
  =/  =leak  [(mist-to-pour mist) top]
  =.  cycle.nub  (~(del in cycle.nub) mist)
  =?  stack.nub  ?=(^ stack.nub)
    stack.nub(i (~(put in i.stack.nub) leak))
  =/  spilt  (~(has in spill.nub) leak)
  =^  =soak  nub
    ?^  got=(~(get by cache.nub) leak)
      %-  %+  trace  3  |.
          =/  refs    ?:(spilt 0 1)
          %+  welp  "cache {<pour.leak>}: adding {<refs>}, "
          "giving {<(add refs refs.u.got)>}"
      =?  cache.nub  !spilt
      (~(put by cache.nub) leak [+(refs.u.got) soak.u.got])
      [soak.u.got nub]
    %-  (trace 2 |.("cache {<pour.leak>}: creating"))
    =^  =soak  nub  (next nub)
    =.  cache.nub  (~(put by cache.nub) leak [1 soak])
    ::  If we're creating a cache entry, add refs to our dependencies
    ::
    =/  deps  ~(tap in deps.leak)
    |-
    ?~  deps
      [soak nub]
```

```
1217        =/  got   (~(got by cache.nub) i.deps)
1218        %-  %+  trace  3  |.
1219            %+  welp  "cache {<pour.leak>} for {<pour.i.deps>}"
1220            ": bumping to ref {<refs.got>}"
1221        =.  cache.nub  (~(put by cache.nub) i.deps got(refs +(refs.got)))
1222        $(deps t.deps)
1223      ?:  spilt
1224      [soak nub]
1225      %-  (trace 3 |.("spilt {<mist>}"))
1226      =:  spill.nub  (~(put in spill.nub) leak)
1227          sprig.nub  (~(put by sprig.nub) mist leak soak)
1228          ==
1229      [soak nub]
1230    --
1231  ::
1232  ++  lose-leak
1233    |=  [verb=@ fad=flow =leak]
1234    ^-  flow
1235    ?~  got=(~(get by fad) leak)
1236      %-  (trace verb 0 |.("lose missing leak {<leak>}"))
1237      fad
1238    ?:  (lth 1 refs.u.got)
1239      %-  (trace verb 3 |.("cache {<pour.leak>}: decrementing from {<refs.u.got>}"))
1240      =.  fad  (~(put by fad) leak u.got(refs (dec refs.u.got)))
1241      fad
1242    =+  ?.  =(0 refs.u.got)  ~
1243        ((trace verb 0 |.("lose zero leak {<leak>}")) ~)
1244    %-  (trace verb 2 |.("cache {<pour.leak>}: freeing"))
1245    =.  fad  (~(del by fad) leak)
1246    =/  leaks  ~(tap in deps.leak)
1247    |-  ^-  flow
1248    ?~  leaks
1249      fad
1250    =.  fad  ^$(leak i.leaks)
1251    $(leaks t.leaks)
1252  ::
1253  ++  lose-leaks
1254    |=  [verb=@ fad=flow leaks=(set leak)]
1255    ^-  flow
1256    =/  leaks  ~(tap in leaks)
1257    |-
1258    ?~  leaks
1259      fad
1260    $(fad (lose-leak verb fad i.leaks), leaks t.leaks)
1261  ::
1262  ++  trace
1263    |=  [verb=@ pri=@ print=(trap tape)]
1264    ?:  (lth verb pri)
1265      same
1266    (slog leaf+"ford: {(print)}" ~)
1267  --
1268  ::::::::::::::::::::::::::::::::::::::::::::::::::::::::::::::::::::::::::::::
1269  ::  section 4cA, filesystem logic
1270  ::
1271  ::  This core contains the main logic of clay.  Besides `++ze`, this directly
1272  ::  contains the logic for commiting new revisions (local urbits), managing
1273  ::  and notifying subscribers (reactivity), and pulling and validating content
1274  ::  (remote urbits).
```

```
1275  ::
1276  ::    The state includes:
1277  ::
1278  ::    --  local urbit `our`
1279  ::    --  current time `now`
1280  ::    --  current duct `hen`
1281  ::    --  scry handler `ski`
1282  ::    --  all vane state `++raft` (rarely used, except for the object store)
1283  ::    --  target urbit `her`
1284  ::    --  target desk `syd`
1285  ::
1286  ::    For local desks, `our` == `her` is one of the urbits on our pier.  For
1287  ::    foreign desks, `her` is the urbit the desk is on and `our` is the local
1288  ::    urbit that's managing the relationship with the foreign urbit.  Don't mix
1289  ::    up those two, or there will be wailing and gnashing of teeth.
1290  ::
1291  ::    While setting up `++de`, we check if `our` == `her`. If so, we get
1292  ::    the desk information from `dos.rom`.  Otherwise, we get the rung from
1293  ::    `hoy` and get the desk information from `rus` in there.  In either case,
1294  ::    we normalize the desk information to a `++rede`, which is all the
1295  ::    desk-specific data that we utilize in `++de`.  Because it's effectively
1296  ::    a part of the `++de` state, let's look at what we've got:
1297  ::
1298  ::    --  `lim` is the most recent date we're confident we have all the
1299  ::        information for.  For local desks, this is always `now`.  For foreign
1300  ::        desks, this is the last time we got a full update from the foreign
1301  ::        urbit.
1302  ::    --  `ref` is a possible request manager.  For local desks, this is null.
1303  ::        For foreign desks, this keeps track of all pending foreign requests
1304  ::        plus a cache of the responses to previous requests.
1305  ::    --  `qyx` is the set of subscriptions, with listening ducts. These
1306  ::        subscriptions exist only until they've been filled.
1307  ::    --  `dom` is the actual state of the filetree.  Since this is used almost
1308  ::        exclusively in `++ze`, we describe it there.
1309  ::
1310  :::::::::::::::::::::::::::::::::::::::::::::::::::::::::::::::::::::::::::::::
1311  ++  de                                                      :: per desk
1312    ~%  %de  ..de  ~
1313    |=  [now=@da rof=roof hen=duct raft]
1314    ~/  %de-in
1315    |=  [her=ship syd=desk]
1316    :: NB: ruf=raft crashes in the compiler
1317    ::
1318    =*  ruf  |3.+6.^$
1319    =|  [mow=(list move) hun=(unit duct) rede]
1320    =*  red=rede  ->+
1321    =<  apex
1322    ~%  %de-core  ..$  ~
1323    |%
1324    ++  abet                                                  :: resolve
1325      ^-  [(list move) raft]
1326      :-  (flop mow)
1327      ?.  =(our her)
1328        :: save foreign +rede
1329        ::
1330      =/  run  (~(gut by hoy.ruf) her *rung)
1331      =/  rug  (~(put by rus.run) syd red)
1332      ruf(hoy (~(put by hoy.ruf) her run(rus rug)))
```

```
1333      ::  save domestic +room
1334      ::
1335      %=  ruf
1336        hun.rom  (need hun)
1337        dos.rom  (~(put by dos.rom.ruf) syd [qyx dom per pew fiz]:red)
1338      ==
1339    ::
1340    ++  apex
1341      ^+  ..park
1342      ?.  =(our her)
1343        ::  no duct, foreign +rede or default
1344        ::
1345        =.  mow
1346          ?:  (~(has by hoy.ruf) her)
1347            ~
1348          [hun.rom.ruf %pass /sinks %j %public-keys (silt her ~)]~
1349        =.  hun  ~
1350        =.  |2.+6.park
1351          =/  rus  rus:(~(gut by hoy.ruf) her *rung)
1352          %+  ~(gut by rus)  syd
1353          [lim=~2000.1.1 ref=`*rind qyx=~ dom=*dome per=~ pew=~ fiz=*melt]
1354        ..park
1355      ::  administrative duct, domestic +rede
1356      ::
1357      =.  mow  ~
1358      =.  hun  `hun.rom.ruf
1359      =.  |2.+6.park
1360        =/  jod  (~(gut by dos.rom.ruf) syd *dojo)
1361        [lim=now ref=*(unit rind) [qyx dom per pew fiz]:jod]
1362      ..park
1363    ::
1364    ::  Handle `%sing` requests
1365    ::
1366    ++  aver
1367      |=  [for=(unit ship) mun=mood]
1368      ^-  [(unit (unit cage)) _..park]
1369      =+  ezy=?~(ref ~ (~(get by haw.u.ref) mun))
1370      ?^  ezy
1371        [`u.ezy ..park]
1372      ?:  ?=([%s [%ud *] %late *] mun)
1373        :_  ..park
1374        ^-  (unit (unit cage))
1375        :+  ~  ~
1376        ^-  cage
1377        :-  %cass
1378        ?~  let.dom
1379          !>([0 *@da])
1380        !>([let.dom t:(~(got by hut.ran) (~(got by hit.dom) let.dom))])
1381      =+  tak=(case-to-tako case.mun)
1382      ?:  ?=([%s case %case ~] mun)
1383        ::  case existence check
1384        [``[%flag !>(!=(~ tak))] ..park]
1385      ?~(tak [~ ..park] (read-at-tako:ze for u.tak mun))
1386    ::
1387    ::  Queue a move.
1388    ::
1389    ++  emit
1390      |=  mof=move
```

```hoon
      %_(+> mow [mof mow])
    ::
    ::  Queue a list of moves
    ::
    ++  emil
      |=  mof=(list move)
      %_(+> mow (weld (flop mof) mow))
    ::
    ::  Queue a list of moves, to be emitted before the rest
    ::
    ++  lime
      |=  mof=(list move)
      %_(+> mow (weld mow (flop mof)))
    ::
    ::  Set timer.
    ::
    ++  bait
      |=  [hen=duct tym=@da]
      (emit hen %pass /tyme/(scot %p her)/[syd] %b %wait tym)
    ::
    ::  Cancel timer.
    ::
    ++  best
      |=  [hen=duct tym=@da]
      (emit hen %pass /tyme/(scot %p her)/[syd] %b %rest tym)
    ::
    ::  Give %writ, or slip a drip if foreign desk
    ::
    ++  writ
      |=  res=(unit [=mood =cage])
      ^-  card
      =/  =riot
        ?~  res
          ~
        `[[care.mood case.mood syd] path.mood cage]:[u.res syd=syd]
      ?~  ref
        [%give %writ riot]
      [%pass /drip %b %drip !>([%writ riot])]
    ::
    ++  case-to-date
      |=  =case
      ^-  @da
      ::  if the case is already a date, use it.
      ::
      ?:  ?=([%da *] case)
        p.case
      ::  translate other cases to dates
      ::
      =/  aey  (case-to-aeon-before lim case)
      ?~  aey  `@da`0
      ?:  =(0 u.aey)  `@da`0
      t:(aeon-to-yaki:ze u.aey)
    ::
    ++  case-to-aeon  (cury case-to-aeon-before lim)
    ::
    ::  Reduce a case to an aeon (version number)
    ::
    ::  We produce null if we can't yet reduce the case for whatever
```

```
1449    ::  resaon (usually either the time or aeon hasn't happened yet or
1450    ::  the label hasn't been created).
1451    ::
1452    ++  case-to-aeon-before
1453      |=  [lim=@da lok=case]
1454      ^-  (unit aeon)
1455      ?-    -.lok
1456          %tas  (~(get by lab.dom) p.lok)
1457          %ud   ?:((gth p.lok let.dom) ~ [~ p.lok])
1458          %uv   `(tako-to-aeon:ze p.lok)
1459          %da
1460        ?:  (gth p.lok lim)  ~
1461        |-  ^-  (unit aeon)
1462        ?:  =(0 let.dom)  [~ 0]                            ::  avoid underflow
1463        ?:  %+  gte  p.lok
1464            =<  t
1465            ~|  [%letdom let=let.dom hit=hit.dom hut=~(key by hut.ran)]
1466            ~|  [%getdom (~(get by hit.dom) let.dom)]
1467            %-  aeon-to-yaki:ze
1468            let.dom
1469          [~ let.dom]
1470        $(let.dom (dec let.dom))
1471      ==
1472    ::
1473    ++  case-to-tako
1474      |=  lok=case
1475      ^-  (unit tako)
1476      ?:  ?=(%uv -.lok)
1477        ?:((~(has by hut.ran) p.lok) `p.lok ~)
1478      (bind (case-to-aeon-before lim lok) aeon-to-tako:ze)
1479    ::
1480    ::  Create a ford appropriate for the aeon
1481    ::
1482    ::  Don't forget to call +tako-flow!
1483    ::
1484    ++  tako-ford
1485      |=  tak=tako
1486      %-  ford:fusion
1487      :-  (~(run by q:(tako-to-yaki:ze tak)) |=(=lobe |+lobe))
1488      [lat.ran veb.bug fad ?:(=(tak (aeon-to-tako:ze let.dom)) fod.dom [~ ~])]
1489    ::  Produce ford cache appropriate for the aeon
1490    ::
1491    ++  tako-flow
1492      |*  [tak=tako res=* fud=flow fod=flue]
1493      :-  res
1494      ^+  ..park
1495      ?:  &(?=(~ ref) =((aeon-to-tako:ze let.dom) tak))
1496        ..park(fad fud, fod.dom fod)
1497      ::  if in the past, don't update ford cache, since any results have
1498      ::  no roots
1499      ::
1500      ..park
1501    ::
1502    ++  request-wire
1503      |=  [kind=@ta =ship =desk index=@ud]
1504      /[kind]/(scot %p ship)/[desk]/(scot %ud index)
1505    ::
1506    ::  Transfer a request to another ship's clay.
```

```hoon
    ::
    ++  send-over-ames
      |=  [=duct =ship index=@ud =riff]
      ^+  +>
      ::
      =/  =desk  p.riff
      =/  =wire  (request-wire %warp-index ship desk index)
      =/  =path  [%question desk (scot %ud index) ~]
      (emit duct %pass wire %a %plea ship %c path `riff-any`[%1 riff])
    ::
    ++  send-over-scry
      |=  [kind=@ta =duct =ship index=@ud =desk =mood]
      ^-  [[timeout=@da =path] _..send-over-scry]
      =/  =time  (add now scry-timeout-time)
      =/  =wire  (request-wire kind ship desk index)
      =/  =path
        =,  mood
        [%c care (scot case) desk path]
      :-  [time path]
      %-  emil
      :~  [hen %pass wire %a %keen ~ ship path]
          [hen %pass wire %b %wait time]
      ==
    ::
    ++  cancel-scry-timeout
      |=  inx=@ud
      ~|  [%strange-timeout-cancel-no-scry-request her syd inx]
      ?>  ?=(^ ref)
      =/  sat=update-state  (~(got by bom.u.ref) inx)
      ?>  ?=([~ ^] busy.sat)
      =/  =wire  (request-wire kind.u.busy.sat her syd inx)
      (emit hen %pass wire %b %rest time.u.busy.sat)
    ::
    ++  foreign-capable
      |=  =rave
      |^
      ?-    -.rave
        %many  &
        %sing  (good-care care.mood.rave)
        %next  (good-care care.mood.rave)
        %mult
      %-  ~(all in paths.mool.rave)
      |=  [=care =path]
      (good-care care)
      ==
      ::
      ++  good-care
        |=  =care
        (~(has in ^~((silt `(list ^care)`~[%q %u %w %x %y %z]))) care)
      --
    ::
    ::  Build and send agents to gall
    ::
    ::  Must be called at the end of a commit, but only while Clay is in a
    ::  fully-consistent state (eg not in the middle of a kelvin upgrade).
    ::
    ++  goad
      ^+  ..park
```

```
1565      =^  moves-1  ruf  abet
1566      =^  moves-2  ruf  abet:goad:(lu now rof hen ruf)
1567      =.  ..park  apex
1568      (emil (weld moves-1 moves-2))
1569      ::
1570      ::  Notify subscribers of changes to tire
1571      ::
1572      ::  Must be called any time tire could have changed, unless you called
1573      ::  goad (which calls tare internally).
1574      ::
1575      ++  tare
1576        ^+  ..park
1577        =^  moves-1  ruf  abet
1578        =^  moves-2  ruf  abet:tare:(lu now rof hen ruf)
1579        =.  ..park  apex
1580        (emil (weld moves-1 moves-2))
1581      ::
1582      ::  Create a request that cannot be filled immediately.
1583      ::
1584      ::  If it's a local request, we just put in in `qyx`, setting a timer if it's
1585      ::  waiting for a particular time.  If it's a foreign request, we add it to
1586      ::  our request manager (ref, which is a ++rind) and make the request to the
1587      ::  foreign ship.
1588      ::
1589      ++  duce                                          ::  produce request
1590        |=  wov=wove
1591        ^+  +>
1592        =.  wov  (dedupe wov)
1593        =.  qyx  (~(put ju qyx) wov hen)
1594        ?~  ref
1595          ::  [wake] at @da must check if subscription was fulfilled
1596          ::
1597          (run-if-future rove.wov |=(@da (bait hen +<)))
1598        |-  ^+  +>+.$
1599        =/  =rave  (rove-to-rave rove.wov)
1600        =?  rave  ?=([%sing %v *] rave)
1601          [%many %| [%ud let.dom] case.mood.rave path.mood.rave]
1602        ::
1603        ?.  (foreign-capable rave)
1604          ~|([%clay-bad-foreign-request-care rave] !!)
1605        ::
1606        =+  inx=nix.u.ref
1607        =.  +>+.$
1608          =<  ?>(?=(^ ref) .)
1609          (send-over-ames hen her inx syd `rave)
1610        %=  +>+.$
1611          nix.u.ref  +(nix.u.ref)
1612          bom.u.ref  (~(put by bom.u.ref) inx [hen rave ~ ~ ~ ~])
1613          fod.u.ref  (~(put by fod.u.ref) hen inx)
1614        ==
1615      ::
1616      ::  If a similar request exists, switch to the existing request.
1617      ::
1618      ::  "Similar" requests are those %next and %many requests which are the same
1619      ::  up to starting case, but we're already after the starting case.  This
1620      ::  stacks later requests for something onto the same request so that they
1621      ::  all get filled at once.
1622      ::
```

```hoon
++  dedupe                                      ::  find existing alias
  |=  wov=wove
  ^-  wove
  =;  won=(unit wove)  (fall won wov)
  =*  rov  rove.wov
  ?-    -.rov
      %sing  ~
      %next
    =+  aey=(case-to-aeon case.mood.rov)
    ?~  aey  ~
    %-  ~(rep in ~(key by qyx))
    |=  [haw=wove res=(unit wove)]
    ?^  res  res
    ?.  =(for.wov for.haw)  ~
    =*  hav  rove.haw
    =-  ?:(- `haw ~)
    ?&  ?=(%next -.hav)
        =(mood.hav mood.rov(case case.mood.hav))
      ::
      ::  only a match if this request is before
      ::  or at our starting case.
      =+  hay=(case-to-aeon case.mood.hav)
      ?~(hay | (lte u.hay u.aey))
    ==
  ::
      %mult
    =+  aey=(case-to-aeon case.mool.rov)
    ?~  aey  ~
    %-  ~(rep in ~(key by qyx))
    |=  [haw=wove res=(unit wove)]
    ?^  res  res
    ?.  =(for.wov for.haw)  ~
    =*  hav  rove.haw
    =-  ?:(- `haw ~)
    ?&  ?=(%mult -.hav)
        =(mool.hav mool.rov(case case.mool.hav))
      ::
      ::  only a match if this request is before
      ::  or at our starting case, and it has been
      ::  tested at least that far.
      =+  hay=(case-to-aeon case.mool.hav)
      ?&  ?=(^ hay)
          (lte u.hay u.aey)
          ?=(^ aeon.hav)
          (gte u.aeon.hav u.aey)
      ==
    ==
  ::
      %many
    =+  aey=(case-to-aeon from.moat.rov)
    ?~  aey  ~
    %-  ~(rep in ~(key by qyx))
    |=  [haw=wove res=(unit wove)]
    ?^  res  res
    ?.  =(for.wov for.haw)  ~
    =*  hav  rove.haw
    =-  ?:(- `haw ~)
    ?&  ?=(%many -.hav)
```

```
1681            =(hav rov(from.moat from.moat.hav))
1682          ::
1683          ::   only a match if this request is before
1684          ::   or at our starting case.
1685          =+   hay=(case-to-aeon from.moat.hav)
1686          ?~(hay | (lte u.hay u.aey))
1687        ==
1688      ==
1689    ::
1690    ++   set-norm
1691      |=  =norm
1692      =.  nor.dom  norm
1693      ..park
1694    ::
1695    ++   set-worn
1696      |=  [=tako =norm]
1697      ?:  &(=(our her) =(tako (aeon-to-tako:ze let.dom)))
1698        (mean leaf+"clay: can't set norm for current commit in {<syd>}" ~)
1699      =.  tom.dom  (~(put by tom.dom) tako norm)
1700      ..park
1701    ::
1702    ::  Attach label to aeon
1703    ::
1704    ++   label
1705      |=  [bel=@tas aey=(unit aeon)]
1706      ^+  ..park
1707      =/  yon  ?~(aey let.dom u.aey)
1708      =/  yen  (~(get by lab.dom) bel)  :: existing aeon?
1709      ::  no existing aeon is bound to this label
1710      ::
1711      ?~  yen
1712        =.  lab.dom  (~(put by lab.dom) bel yon)          ::  [wake] <>
1713        wake
1714      ::  an aeon is bound to this label,
1715      ::  but it is the same as the existing one, so we no-op
1716      ::
1717      ?:  =(u.yen yon)
1718        ~&  "clay: tried to rebind existing label {<bel>} to equivalent aeon {<yon>}"
1719        ..park
1720      ::  an existing aeon bound to the label
1721      ::  that is distinct from the requested one.
1722      ::  rewriting would violate referential transparency
1723      ::
1724      ~|  %tried-to-rewrite-existing-label
1725      ~|  "requested aeon: {<yon>}, existing aeon: {<u.yen>}"
1726      !!
1727    ::
1728    ::  Porcelain commit
1729    ::
1730    ++   info
1731      ~/  %info
1732      |=  [deletes=(set path) changes=(map path cage)]
1733      ^+  ..park
1734      ?:  =(0 let.dom)
1735        ?>  ?=(~ deletes)
1736        =/  data=(map path (each page lobe))
1737          (~(run by changes) |=(=cage &+[p q.q]:cage))
1738        (park | & &+[~ data] *rang)
```

```
1739        ::
1740        =/  parent-tako=tako  (aeon-to-tako:ze let.dom)
1741        =/  data=(map path (each page lobe))
1742          =/  parent-yaki  (tako-to-yaki:ze parent-tako)
1743          =/  after-deletes
1744            %-  ~(dif by q.parent-yaki)
1745            (malt (turn ~(tap in deletes) |=(=path [path *lobe])))
1746          =/  after=(map path (each page lobe))
1747            (~(run by after-deletes) |=(=lobe |+lobe))
1748          %-  ~(uni by after)
1749          ^-  (map path (each page lobe))
1750          (~(run by changes) |=(=cage &+[p q.q]:cage))
1751        ::
1752        =/  =yuki  [~[parent-tako] data]
1753        (park | & &+yuki *rang)
1754      ::
1755      ::  Unix commit
1756      ::
1757      ++  into
1758        ~/  %into
1759        |=  [pax=path all=? mod=(list [pax=path mim=(unit mime)])]
1760        ^+  ..park
1761        ::  filter out unchanged, cached %mime values
1762        ::
1763        =.  mod
1764          %+  skip  mod
1765          |=  [pax=path mim=(unit mime)]
1766          ?~  mim
1767            |
1768          ?~  mum=(~(get by mim.dom) pax)
1769            |
1770          ::  TODO: check mimetype
1771          ::
1772          =(q.u.mim q.u.mum)
1773        =/  =yaki
1774          ?:  =(0 let.dom)
1775            *yaki
1776          (~(got by hut.ran) (~(got by hit.dom) let.dom))
1777        (info (mode-to-commit q.yaki pax all mod))
1778      ::
1779      ::  Plumbing commit
1780      ::
1781      ::    Guaranteed to finish in one event.
1782      ::
1783      ::    updated: whether we've already completed sys upgrade
1784      ::    goat: whether we should call +goad at the end.  Only false
1785      ::      during kelvin upgrade so that all commits can happen before
1786      ::      the +goad.
1787      ::    yoki: new commit
1788      ::    rang: any additional objects referenced
1789      ::
1790      ::    [goad] < if goat is false, then the caller is responsible to
1791      ::    call +goad.
1792      ::
1793      ::    TODO: needs to check tako in rang
1794      ::
1795      ++  park
1796        =/  check-sane  |
```

```
1797    |^
1798    |=  [updated=? goat=? =yoki =rang]
1799    ^+  ..park
1800    =:  hut.ran  (~(uni by hut.rang) hut.ran)
1801        lat.ran  (~(uni by lat.rang) lat.ran)
1802      ==
1803    =/  new-data=(map path (each page lobe))
1804      ?-  -.yoki
1805        %&  q.p.yoki
1806        %|  (~(run by q.p.yoki) |=(=lobe |+lobe))
1807      ==
1808    ?.  %-  ~(all in new-data)  ::  use +all:in so we get the key
1809        |=  [=path tum=(each page lobe)]
1810        ?:  |(?=(%& -.tum) (~(has by lat.ran) p.tum))
1811          &
1812        =-  (mean leaf/- ~)
1813        "clay: commit failed, file tombstoned: {<path>} {<`@uv`p.tum>}"
1814      !!
1815    ::  find desk kelvin
1816    ::
1817    =/  kel=(set weft)  (waft-to-wefts (get-kelvin yoki))
1818    ?.  ?|  (~(has in kel) zuse+zuse)                  ::  kelvin match
1819            ?&  !=(%base syd)                          ::  best-effort compat
1820                %-  ~(any in kel)
1821                |=  =weft
1822                &(=(%zuse lal.weft) (gth num.weft zuse))
1823            ==
1824            ?&  =(%base syd)                           ::  ready to upgrade
1825                %+  levy  ~(tap by tore:(lu now rof hen ruf))
1826                |=  [=desk =zest wic=(set weft)]
1827                ?|  =(%base desk)
1828                    !?=(%live zest)
1829                    !=(~ (~(int in wic) kel))
1830                ==
1831            ==
1832        ==
1833      ?:  (~(all in kel) |=(=weft (gth num.weft zuse)))
1834        %-  (slog leaf+"clay: old-kelvin, {<[need=zuse/zuse have=kel]>}" ~)
1835        ..park
1836      =.  wic.dom                                      ::  [tare] <
1837        %+  roll  ~(tap in kel)
1838        |:  [weft=*weft wic=wic.dom]
1839        (~(put by wic) weft yoki)
1840      =?  ..park  !?=(%base syd)  wick              ::  [wick]
1841      %-  (slog leaf+"clay: wait-for-kelvin, {<[need=zuse/zuse have=kel]>}" ~)
1842      tare                                            ::  [tare] >
1843    =.  wic.dom
1844      %-  ~(gas by *(map weft ^yoki))
1845      %+  skip  ~(tap by wic.dom)
1846      |=  [w=weft ^yoki]
1847      (gte num.w zuse)
1848    ::
1849    =/  old-yaki
1850      ?:  =(0 let.dom)
1851        *yaki
1852      (aeon-to-yaki:ze let.dom)
1853    =/  old-kel=(set weft)
1854      ?:  =(0 let.dom)
```

```
      [zuse+zuse ~ ~]
    (waft-to-wefts (get-kelvin %| old-yaki))
=/  [deletes=(set path) changes=(map path (each page lobe))]
    (get-changes q.old-yaki new-data)
~|  [from=let.dom deletes=deletes changes=~(key by changes)]
::
::  promote ford cache
::  promote and fill in mime cache
::
=/  invalid  (~(uni in deletes) ~(key by changes))
::  if /sys updated in %base, defer to arvo and return early
::
?:  &(=(%base syd) !updated (~(any in invalid) is-kernel-path))
  (sys-update yoki new-data)
::  after this point, there must be no early return except if it's a
::  complete no-op.  any error conditions must crash.  since we're
::  changing state, we may need to call +wake, +goad, etc, which
::  happens at the end of the function.
::
::  [wick] if this commit added compatibility to a future kelvin,
::  then we might have unblocked a kelvin upgrade.
::
::  or, if *this* is a kelvin upgrade, it's possible that another
::  kelvin upgrade will immediately be ready.  for example, this
::  could be the case if all desks but one are ready for the next
::  two kelvins, and then that desk is suspended or receives a
::  commit with compatiblity with both kelvins.
::
::  in any of these cases, we finish the current commit but call
::  +wick so that we try to execute the kelvin upgrade afterward.
::  we want this commit to persist even if the subsequent kelvin
::  upgrade fails.
::
=.  ..park  wick
=.  wic.dom                                   ::  [tare] <
  %+  roll  ~(tap in kel)
  |:  [weft=*weft wic=wic.dom]
  ?:  (gte num.weft zuse)
    wic
  (~(put by wic) weft yoki)
::
=+  ?.  (did-kernel-update invalid)  ~
    ((slog 'clay: kernel updated' ~) ~)
=?  updated  updated  (did-kernel-update invalid)
=>  ?.  updated  .
    ~>(%slog.0^leaf/"clay: rebuilding {<syd>} after kernel update" .)
::  clear caches if zuse reloaded
::
=/  old-fod  fod.dom
=.  fod.dom
  ?:  updated  [~ ~]
  (promote-ford fod.dom invalid)
=.  fad
  (lose-leaks:fusion veb.bug fad (~(dif in spill.old-fod) spill.fod.dom))
=?  changes  updated  (changes-for-upgrade q.old-yaki deletes changes)
::
=/  files
  =/  original=(map path (each page lobe))
```

```
1913        (~(run by q.old-yaki) |=(=lobe |+lobe))
1914    %-  ~(dif by (~(uni by original) changes))
1915    %-  ~(gas by *(map path (each page lobe)))
1916    (turn ~(tap in deletes) |=(=path [path |+*lobe]))
1917  =/  =args:ford:fusion  [files lat.ran veb.bug fad fod.dom]
1918  ::
1919  =^  change-cages  args  (checkout-changes args changes)
1920  =/  sane-continuation  (sane-changes changes change-cages)
1921  =/  new-pages=(map lobe page)
1922    %-  malt
1923    %+  turn  ~(tap by change-cages)
1924    |=  [=path =lobe =cage]
1925    [lobe [p q.q]:cage]
1926  =/  data=(map path lobe)
1927    %-  ~(urn by new-data)
1928    |=  [=path value=(each page lobe)]
1929    ?-  -.value
1930      %|  p.value
1931      %&  lobe:(~(got by change-cages) path)
1932    ==
1933  ::  if we didn't change the data and it's not a merge commit, abort
1934  ::
1935  ?:  &(=([r.old-yaki ~] p.p.yoki) =(data q.old-yaki))
1936    ::  [tare] > if no changes, then commits-in-waiting could not have
1937    ::  changed.
1938    ::
1939    ..park
1940  =/  =yaki
1941    ?-  -.yoki
1942      %&  (make-yaki p.p.yoki data now)
1943      %|  ?>  =(data q.p.yoki)
1944          p.yoki
1945    ==
1946  ::  [wake] < [ergo] < [goad] <
1947  ::
1948  =:  let.dom  +(let.dom)
1949      hit.dom  (~(put by hit.dom) +(let.dom) r.yaki)
1950      hut.ran  (~(put by hut.ran) r.yaki yaki)
1951      lat.ran  (~(uni by new-pages) lat.ran)
1952    ==
1953  =.  file-store.args  lat.ran
1954  ::
1955  =/  mem  (want-mime 0)
1956  =/  res=[mum=(map path (unit mime)) mim=_mim.dom args=_args]
1957    ?.  mem  [~ ~ args]
1958    =^  mum  args  (checkout-mime args deletes ~(key by changes))
1959    [mum (apply-changes-to-mim mim.dom mum) args]
1960  =.  mim.dom  mim.res
1961  =.  args      args.res
1962  ::
1963  =.  fod.dom  [spill sprig]:args
1964  =.  fad      cache.args
1965  =.  ..park  (emil (print q.old-yaki data))
1966  ::  if upgrading kelvin and there's a commit-in-waiting, use that
1967  ::
1968  =?  ..park  &(=(%base syd) !=(old-kel kel))
1969    =/  desks=(list [=desk =dojo])  ~(tap by dos.rom)
1970    =^  moves-1  ruf  abet
```

```
1971      =|  moves-2=(list move)
1972      |-  ^+  ..park
1973      ?~  desks
1974        =.  ..park  apex
1975        (emil (weld moves-1 moves-2))
1976      ?.  ?=(%live liv.dom.dojo.i.desks)
1977        $(desks t.desks)
1978      ?:  ?=(%base desk.i.desks)
1979        $(desks t.desks)
1980      ?~  wat=(~(get by wic.dom.dojo.i.desks) zuse+zuse)
1981        (mean (cat 3 'clay: missing commit-in-waiting on ' desk.i.desks) ~)
1982      =/  den  ((de now rof hen ruf) our desk.i.desks)
1983      ::  [goad] < call without goading so that we apply all the commits
1984      ::  before trying to compile all desks to send to gall.
1985      ::
1986      =^  moves-3  ruf  abet:(park:den | | u.wat *^rang)
1987      =.  moves-2  (weld moves-2 moves-3)
1988      $(desks t.desks)
1989    ::  tell gall to try to run agents if %held
1990    ::
1991    ::  [goad] > if goat or desk not running.  %held uses park-held to
1992    ::  defer the goad into a new event, to attempt to revive the desk.
1993    ::  Note that %base will always be %live.
1994    ::
1995    =.  ..park
1996      ?-  liv.dom
1997        %held  (emit hen %pass /park-held/[syd] %b %wait now)
1998        %dead  ..park
1999        %live  ?:(goat goad ..park)
2000      ==
2001    ::  notify unix and subscribers
2002    ::
2003    =?  ..park  mem  (ergo 0 mum.res)                      ::  [ergo] >
2004    wake:tare                                              ::  [wake] > [tare] >
2005    ::
2006    ::  +is-kernel-path: should changing .pax cause a kernel or vane reload?
2007    ::
2008    ++  is-kernel-path  |=(pax=path ?=([%sys *] pax))
2009    ::
2010    ++  did-kernel-update
2011      |=  invalid=(set path)
2012      ?.  =(%base syd)
2013          |
2014      %-  ~(any in invalid)
2015      |=(p=path &((is-kernel-path p) !?=([%sys %vane *] p)))
2016    ::
2017    ::  +get-kelvin: read the desk's kernel version from /sys/kelvin
2018    ::
2019    ++  get-kelvin
2020      |=  =yoki
2021      ^-  waft
2022      |^  ?-    -.yoki
2023              %|
2024            %-  lobe-to-waft
2025            ~>  %mean.(cat 3 'clay: missing /sys/kelvin on ' syd)
2026            ~|  ~(key by q.p.yoki)
2027            (~(got by q.p.yoki) /sys/kelvin)
2028              ::
```

```
              %&
          =/  fil=(each page lobe)
            ~>  %mean.(cat 3 'clay: missing /sys/kelvin on ' syd)
            ~|  ~(key by q.p.yoki)
            (~(got by q.p.yoki) /sys/kelvin)
          ?-    -.fil
              %&  (page-to-waft p.fil)
              %|  (lobe-to-waft p.fil)
          ==
        ==
    ::
    ++  lobe-to-waft
      |=  =lobe
      ^-  waft
      =/  peg=(unit page)  (~(get by lat.ran) lobe)
      ?~  peg  ~|([%sys-kelvin-tombstoned syd] !!)
      (page-to-waft u.peg)
    ::
    ++  page-to-waft
      |=  =page
      ^-  waft
      ?+    p.page  ~|(clay-bad-kelvin-mark/p.page !!)
          %kelvin  ;;(waft q.page)
          %mime    (cord-to-waft q.q:;;(mime q.page))
      ==
    --
  ::
  ::  Find which files changed or were deleted
  ::
  ++  get-changes
    |=  [old=(map path lobe) new=(map path (each page lobe))]
    ^-  [deletes=(set path) changes=(map path (each page lobe))]
    =/  old=(map path (each page lobe))
      (~(run by old) |=(=lobe |+lobe))
    :*  %-  silt  ^-  (list path)
        %+  murn  ~(tap by (~(uni by old) new))
        |=  [=path *]
        ^-  (unit ^path)
        =/  a  (~(get by new) path)
        =/  b  (~(get by old) path)
        ?:  |(=(a b) !=(~ a))
          ~
        `path
      ::
        %-  malt  ^-  (list [path (each page lobe)])
        %+  murn  ~(tap by (~(uni by old) new))
        |=  [=path *]
        ^-  (unit [^path (each page lobe)])
        =/  a  (~(get by new) path)
        =/  b  (~(get by old) path)
        ?:  |(=(a b) ?=(~ a))
          ~
        `[path u.a]
    ==
  ::  Find all files for full desk rebuild
  ::
  ++  changes-for-upgrade
    |=  $:  old=(map path lobe)
```

```
2087              deletes=(set path)
2088              changes=(map path (each page lobe))
2089          ==
2090      ^+  changes
2091      =.  old
2092        %+  roll  ~(tap in deletes)
2093        |=  [pax=path old=_old]
2094        (~(del by old) pax)
2095      =/  pre=_changes  (~(run by old) |=(lob=lobe |+lob))
2096      (~(uni by pre) changes)
2097    ::
2098    ++  promote-ford
2099      |=  [fod=flue invalid=(set path)]
2100      ^-  flue
2101      =/  old=(list leak)  ~(tap in spill.fod)
2102      =|  new=flue
2103      |-  ^-  flue
2104      ?~  old
2105        new
2106      =/  invalid
2107        |-  ^-  ?
2108        ?|  ?+    -.pour.i.old  %|
2109              %vale  (~(has in invalid) path.pour.i.old)
2110              %arch
2111            ::  TODO: overly conservative, should be only direct hoon
2112            ::  children
2113            ::
2114            =/  len  (lent path.pour.i.old)
2115            %-  ~(any in invalid)
2116            |=  =path
2117            =(path.pour.i.old (scag len path))
2118          ==
2119        ::
2120            =/  deps  ~(tap in deps.i.old)
2121            |-  ^-  ?
2122            ?~  deps
2123            %|
2124            ?|  ^$(i.old i.deps)
2125                $(deps t.deps)
2126            ==
2127        ==
2128      =?  new  !invalid
2129        :-  (~(put in spill.new) i.old)
2130        =/  =mist  (pour-to-mist pour.i.old)
2131        ?~  got=(~(get by sprig.fod) mist)
2132          sprig.new
2133        (~(put by sprig.new) mist u.got)
2134      $(old t.old)
2135    ::
2136    ++  page-to-cord
2137      |=  =page
2138      ^-  @t
2139      ?+  p.page  ~|([%sys-bad-mark p.page] !!)
2140        %hoon  ;;(@t q.page)
2141        %mime  q.q:;;(mime q.page)
2142      ==
2143    ::
2144    ++  lobe-to-cord
```

```
2145      |=  =lobe
2146      ^-  @t
2147      =/  peg=(unit page)  (~(get by lat.ran) lobe)
2148      ?~  peg
2149        ~|([%lobe-to-cord-tombstoned syd lobe] !!)
2150      ;;(@t q.u.peg)
2151    ::
2152    ::  Updated q.yaki
2153    ::
2154    ++  checkout-changes
2155      |=  [=ford=args:ford:fusion changes=(map path (each page lobe))]
2156      ^-  [(map path [=lobe =cage]) args:ford:fusion]
2157      %+  roll  `(list [path (each page lobe)])`~(tap by changes)
2158      |=  $:  [=path change=(each page lobe)]
2159              [built=(map path [lobe cage]) cache=_ford-args]
2160          ==
2161      ^+  [built ford-args]
2162      =.  ford-args  cache
2163      =/  [=cage fud=flow fod=flue]
2164        ::  ~>  %slog.[0 leaf/"clay: validating {(spud path)}"]
2165        %-  wrap:fusion
2166        (read-file:(ford:fusion ford-args) path)
2167      =.  cache.ford-args  fud
2168      =.  spill.ford-args  spill.fod
2169      =.  sprig.ford-args  sprig.fod
2170      =/  =lobe
2171        ?-  -.change
2172          %|  p.change
2173          ::  Don't use p.change.i.cans because that's before casting to
2174          ::  the correct mark.
2175          ::
2176          %&  (page-to-lobe [p q.q]:cage)
2177        ==
2178      [(~(put by built) path [lobe cage]) ford-args]
2179    ::
2180    ::  Print notification to console
2181    ::
2182    ++  print
2183      |=  [old=(map path lobe) new=(map path lobe)]
2184      ^-  (list move)
2185      =/  [deletes=(set path) upserts=(map path (each page lobe))]
2186        (get-changes old (~(run by new) |=(=lobe |+lobe)))
2187      =/  upsert-set  ~(key by upserts)
2188      =/  old-set     ~(key by old)
2189      =/  changes=(set path)    (~(int in upsert-set) old-set)
2190      =/  additions=(set path)  (~(dif in upsert-set) old-set)
2191      ?~  hun
2192          ~
2193      ?:  (lte let.dom 1)
2194          ~
2195      |^
2196      ;:  weld
2197        (paths-to-notes '-' deletes)
2198        (paths-to-notes ':' changes)
2199        (paths-to-notes '+' additions)
2200      ==
2201      ::
2202      ++  paths-to-notes
```

```
2203        |=  [prefix=@tD paths=(set path)]
2204        %+  turn  ~(tap in paths)
2205        |=  =path
2206        ^-  move
2207        [u.hun %pass /note %d %text prefix ' ' ~(ram re (path-to-tank path))]
2208      ::
2209    ++  path-to-tank
2210      |=  =path
2211      =/  pre=^path  ~[(scot %p our) syd (scot %ud let.dom)]
2212      :+  %rose  ["/" "/" ~]
2213      %+  turn  (weld pre path)
2214      |=  a=cord
2215      ^-  tank
2216      ?:  ((sane %ta) a)
2217        [%leaf (trip a)]
2218      [%leaf (dash:us (trip a) '\'' ~)]
2219    --
2220    ::
2221    ::  Check sanity
2222    ::
2223    ++  sane-changes
2224      |=  $:  changes=(map path (each page lobe))
2225              change-cages=(map path [lobe cage])
2226          ==
2227      ^-  (unit [(map path [lobe cage]) args:ford:fusion])
2228      ?.  check-sane
2229        ~
2230      =/  tak=(unit tako)  (~(get by hit.dom) let.dom)
2231      ?~  tak
2232        ~
2233      =/  =yaki  (~(got by hut.ran) u.tak)
2234      ::  Assert all pages hash to their lobe
2235      ::
2236      =/  foo
2237        %-  ~(urn by lat.ran)
2238        |=  [=lobe =page]
2239        =/  actual-lobe=^lobe  `@uv`(page-to-lobe page)
2240        ~|  [%bad-lobe have=lobe need=actual-lobe]
2241        ?>  =(lobe actual-lobe)
2242        ~
2243      ::  Assert we calculated the same change-cages w/o cache
2244      ::
2245      ::  ? remove deletes
2246      ::
2247      =/  all-changes=(map path (each page lobe))
2248        =/  original=(map path (each page lobe))
2249          (~(run by q.yaki) |=(=lobe |+lobe))
2250        (~(uni by original) changes)
2251      =/  =args:ford:fusion  [all-changes lat.ran veb.bug ~ ~ ~]
2252      =^  all-change-cages  args  (checkout-changes args all-changes)
2253      =/  ccs=(list [=path =lobe =cage])  ~(tap by change-cages)
2254      |-  ^+  *sane-changes
2255      ?^  ccs
2256        ?.  =(`[lobe cage]:i.ccs (~(get by all-change-cages) path.i.ccs))
2257          ~|  not-same-cages+path.i.ccs
2258          !!
2259        $(ccs t.ccs)
2260      `[all-change-cages args]
```

```
2261      ::
2262      ::  Delay current update until sys update is complete
2263      ::
2264      ++  sys-update
2265        |=  $:  =yoki
2266                data=(map path (each page lobe))
2267            ==
2268        ^+  ..park
2269        ?>  =(~ pud)
2270        =.  pud  `[syd yoki]
2271        |^  %.  [hen %slip %c %pork ~]
2272            emit:(pass-what files)
2273        ::
2274        ++  files
2275          ^-  (list (pair path (cask)))
2276          %+  murn
2277            ~(tap by data)
2278          |=  [pax=path dat=(each page lobe)]
2279          ^-  (unit (pair path (cask)))
2280          =/  xap  (flop pax)
2281          ?>  ?=(^ xap)
2282          ?.  ?=(%hoon i.xap)  ~
2283          :^  ~  (flop t.xap)  %hoon
2284          ~|  [pax=pax p.dat]
2285          ?-  -.dat
2286            %&  (page-to-cord p.dat)
2287            %|  (lobe-to-cord p.dat)
2288          ==
2289        ::
2290        ++  pass-what
2291          |=  fil=(list (pair path (cask)))
2292          ^+  ..park
2293          (emit hen %pass /what %$ what/fil)
2294        --
2295      --
2296    ::
2297    ::  [goad] Try to revive desk, but if it fails crash the event.
2298    ::
2299    ++  take-park-held
2300      |=  err=(unit tang)
2301      ^+  ..park
2302      ?^  err
2303      ((slog leaf+"clay: desk {<syd>} failed to unsuspend" u.err) ..park)
2304      =.  liv.dom  %live
2305      goad
2306    ::
2307    ::  We always say we're merging from 'ali' to 'bob'.  The basic steps,
2308    ::  not all of which are always needed, are:
2309    ::
2310    ::  --  fetch ali's desk, async in case it's remote
2311    ::  --  diff ali's desk against the mergebase
2312    ::  --  diff bob's desk against the mergebase
2313    ::  --  merge the diffs
2314    ::  --  commit
2315    ::
2316    ++  start-merge
2317      |=  [=ali=ship =ali=desk =case =germ]
2318      ^+  ..start-merge
```

```
=/  =wire  /merge/[syd]/(scot %p ali-ship)/[ali-desk]/[germ]
(emit hen %pass wire %c %warp ali-ship ali-desk `[%sing %v case /])
::
++  make-melt
  |=  [bas=beak con=(list [beak germ])]
  ^-  melt
  :+  bas  con
  %-  ~(gas by *(map beak (unit domo)))
  :-  [bas *(unit domo)]
  (turn con |=(a=[beak germ] [-.a *(unit domo)]))
::
++  start-fuse
  |=  [bas=beak con=(list [beak germ])]
  ^+  ..start-fuse
  =/  moves=(list move)
    %+  turn
      [[bas *germ] con]
    |=  [bec=beak germ]
    ^-  move
    =/  wir=wire  /fuse/[syd]/(scot %p p.bec)/[q.bec]/(scot r.bec)
    [hen %pass wir %c %warp p.bec q.bec `[%sing %v r.bec /]]
  ::
  ::  We also want to clear the state (fiz) associated with this
  ::  merge and print a warning if it's non trivial i.e. we're
  ::  starting a new fuse before the previous one terminated.
  ::
  =/  err=tang
    ?~  con.fiz
      ~
    =/  discarded=tang
      %+  turn
        ~(tap in sto.fiz)
      |=  [k=beak v=(unit domo)]
      ^-  tank
      =/  received=tape  ?~(v "missing" "received")
      leaf+"{<(en-beam k ~)>} {received}"
    :_  discarded
    leaf+"fusing into {<syd>} from {<bas>} {<con>} - overwriting prior fuse"
  =.  fiz  (make-melt bas con)
  ((slog err) (emil moves))
::
++  take-fuse
  |^
  ::
  |=  [bec=beak =riot]
  ^+  ..take-fuse
  ?~  riot
    ::
    ::  By setting fiz to *melt the merge is aborted - any further
    ::  responses we get for the merge will cause take-fuse to crash
    ::
    =.  fiz  *melt
    =/  msg=tape  <(en-beam bec ~)>
    ((slog [leaf+"clay: fuse failed, missing {msg}"]~) ..take-fuse)
  ?.  (~(has by sto.fiz) bec)
    =/  msg=tape  <(en-beam bec ~)>
    ((slog [leaf+"clay: got strange fuse response {<msg>}"]~) ..take-fuse)
  =.  fiz
```

```
2377          :+  bas.fiz  con.fiz
2378          (~(put by sto.fiz) bec `!<(domo q.r.u.riot))
2379      =/  all-done=flag
2380        %-  ~(all by sto.fiz)
2381        |=  res=(unit domo)
2382        ^-  flag
2383        !=(res ~)
2384      ?.  all-done
2385        ..take-fuse
2386      =|  rag=rang
2387      =/  clean-state  ..take-fuse
2388      =/  initial-dome=domo  (need (~(got by sto.fiz) bas.fiz))
2389      =/  next-yaki=yaki
2390        (~(got by hut.ran) (~(got by hit.initial-dome) let.initial-dome))
2391      =/  parents=(list tako)  ~[(~(got by hit.initial-dome) let.initial-dome)]
2392      =/  merges  con.fiz
2393      |-
2394      ^+  ..take-fuse
2395      ?~  merges
2396        =.  ..take-fuse  (done-fuse clean-state %& ~)
2397        (park | & [%| next-yaki(p (flop parents))] rag)
2398      =/  [bec=beak g=germ]  i.merges
2399      =/  ali-dom=domo  (need (~(got by sto.fiz) bec))
2400      =/  result  (merge-helper p.bec q.bec g ali-dom `next-yaki)
2401      ?-    -.result
2402          %|
2403        =/  failing-merge=tape  "{<bec>} {<g>}"
2404        (done-fuse clean-state %| %fuse-merge-failed leaf+failing-merge p.result)
2405      ::
2406          %&
2407        =/  merge-result=(unit merge-result)  +.result
2408        ?~  merge-result
2409          ::
2410          ::  This merge was a no-op, just continue
2411          ::
2412          $(merges t.merges)
2413        ?^  conflicts.u.merge-result
2414          ::
2415          ::  If there are merge conflicts send the error and abort the merge
2416          ::
2417          (done-fuse clean-state %& conflicts.u.merge-result)
2418        =/  merged-yaki=yaki
2419          ?-    -.new.u.merge-result
2420              %|  +.new.u.merge-result
2421              %&
2422            ::
2423            ::  Convert the yuki to yaki
2424            ::
2425            =/  yuk=yuki  +.new.u.merge-result
2426            =/  lobes=(map path lobe)
2427              %-  ~(run by q.yuk)
2428              |=  val=(each page lobe)
2429              ^-  lobe
2430              ?-  -.val
2431                %&  (page-to-lobe +.val)
2432                %|  +.val
2433              ==
2434            (make-yaki p.yuk lobes now)
```

```
2435          ==
2436        %=  $
2437          next-yaki  merged-yaki
2438          merges     t.merges
2439          hut.ran    (~(put by hut.ran) r.merged-yaki merged-yaki)
2440          lat.rag    (~(uni by lat.u.merge-result) lat.rag)
2441          lat.ran    (~(uni by lat.u.merge-result) lat.ran)
2442          parents    [(~(got by hit.ali-dom) let.ali-dom) parents]
2443        ==
2444      ==
2445      ::  +done-fuse: restore state after a fuse is attempted, whether it
2446      ::  succeeds or fails.
2447      ::
2448      ++  done-fuse
2449        |=  [to-restore=_..take-fuse result=(each (set path) (pair term tang))]
2450        ^+  ..take-fuse
2451        =.  fiz.to-restore  *melt
2452        (done:to-restore result)
2453      --
2454    ::
2455    ++  done
2456      |=  result=(each (set path) (pair term tang))
2457      ^+  ..merge
2458      (emit hen %give %mere result)
2459    ::
2460    ++  merge
2461      |=  [=ali=ship =ali=desk =germ =riot]
2462      ^+  ..merge
2463      ?~  riot
2464        (done %| %ali-unavailable ~[>[ali-ship ali-desk germ]<])
2465      =/  ali-dome=domo
2466        ?:  &(?=(@ -.q.q.r.u.riot) !=(~ -.q.q.r.u.riot))
2467          !<(domo q.r.u.riot)
2468        +:!<([* domo] q.r.u.riot)
2469      =/  result=(each (unit merge-result) (pair term tang))
2470        (merge-helper ali-ship ali-desk germ ali-dome ~)
2471      ?-    -.result
2472          %|  (done %| +.result)
2473          %&
2474        =/  mr=(unit merge-result)  +.result
2475        ?~  mr
2476          (done %& ~)
2477        =.  ..merge  (done %& conflicts.u.mr)
2478        (park | & new.u.mr ~ lat.u.mr)
2479      ==
2480    ::
2481    +$  merge-result  [conflicts=(set path) new=yoki lat=(map lobe page)]
2482    ::
2483    ++  merge-helper
2484      |=  [=ali=ship =ali=desk =germ ali-dome=domo next-yaki=(unit yaki)]
2485      ^-  (each (unit merge-result) [term tang])
2486      |^
2487      ^-  (each (unit merge-result) [term tang])
2488      =/  ali-yaki=yaki  (~(got by hut.ran) (~(got by hit.ali-dome) let.ali-dome))
2489      =/  bob-yaki=(unit yaki)
2490        ?~  next-yaki
2491          ?~  let.dom
2492            ~
```

```
      (~(get by hut.ran) (~(got by hit.dom) let.dom))
    next-yaki
=/  res   (mule |.((merge-by-germ ali-yaki bob-yaki)))
?-  -.res
  %&  &+p.res
  %|  |+merge-failed+p.res
==
::
++  merge-by-germ
  |=  [=ali=yaki bob-yaki=(unit yaki)]
  ^-  (unit merge-result)
  ::
  ::  If this is an %init merge, we set the ali's commit to be
  ::  bob's.
  ::
  ?:  ?=(%init germ)
    ?>  ?=(~ bob-yaki)
    `[conflicts=~ new=|+ali-yaki lat=~]
  ::
  =/  bob-yaki  (need bob-yaki)
  |^
  ^-  (unit merge-result)
  ?-    germ
  ::
  ::  If this is a %only-this merge, we check to see if ali's and bob's
  ::  commits are the same, in which case we're done.
  ::  Otherwise, we create a new commit with bob's data plus ali and
  ::  bob as parents.
  ::
      %only-this
    ?:  =(r.ali-yaki r.bob-yaki)
      ~
    :*  ~
        conflicts=~
        new=&+[[r.bob-yaki r.ali-yaki ~] (to-yuki q.bob-yaki)]
        lat=~
    ==
  ::
  ::  If this is a %only-that merge, we check to see if ali's and bob's
  ::  commits are the same, in which case we're done.  Otherwise, we
  ::  create a new commit with ali's data plus ali and bob as
  ::  parents.
  ::
      %only-that
    ?:  =(r.ali-yaki r.bob-yaki)
      ~
    :*  ~
        conflicts=~
        new=&+[[r.bob-yaki r.ali-yaki ~] (to-yuki q.ali-yaki)]
        lat=~
    ==
  ::
  ::  Create a merge commit with exactly the contents of the
  ::  destination desk except take any files from the source commit
  ::  which are not in the destination desk.
  ::
      %take-this
    ?:  =(r.ali-yaki r.bob-yaki)
```

```
2551            ~
2552        =/  new-data  (~(uni by q.ali-yaki) q.bob-yaki)
2553        :*  ~
2554            conflicts=~
2555            new=&+[[r.bob-yaki r.ali-yaki ~] (to-yuki new-data)]
2556            lat=~
2557        ==
2558      ::
2559      ::  Create a merge commit with exactly the contents of the source
2560      ::  commit except preserve any files from the destination desk
2561      ::  which are not in the source commit.
2562      ::
2563          %take-that
2564      ?:  =(r.ali-yaki r.bob-yaki)
2565          ~
2566        =/  new-data  (~(uni by q.bob-yaki) q.ali-yaki)
2567        :*  ~
2568            conflicts=~
2569            new=&+[[r.bob-yaki r.ali-yaki ~] (to-yuki new-data)]
2570            lat=~
2571        ==
2572      ::
2573      ::  If this is a %fine merge, we check to see if ali's and bob's
2574      ::  commits are the same, in which case we're done.  Otherwise, we
2575      ::  check to see if ali's commit is in the ancestry of bob's, in
2576      ::  which case we're done.  Otherwise, we check to see if bob's
2577      ::  commit is in the ancestry of ali's.  If not, this is not a
2578      ::  fast-forward merge, so we error out.  If it is, we add ali's
2579      ::  commit to bob's desk and checkout.
2580      ::
2581          %fine
2582      ?:  =(r.ali-yaki r.bob-yaki)
2583          ~
2584      ?:  (~(has in (reachable-takos:ze r.bob-yaki)) r.ali-yaki)
2585          ~
2586      ?.  (~(has in (reachable-takos:ze r.ali-yaki)) r.bob-yaki)
2587        ~_  %bad-fine-merge
2588        ~|  "tried fast-forward but is not ancestor or descendant"
2589        !!
2590      `[conflicts=~ new=|+ali-yaki lat=~]
2591      ::
2592          ?(%meet %mate %meld %meet-this %meet-that)
2593      ?:  =(r.ali-yaki r.bob-yaki)
2594          ~
2595      ?:  (~(has in (reachable-takos:ze r.bob-yaki)) r.ali-yaki)
2596          ~
2597      ?:  (~(has in (reachable-takos:ze r.ali-yaki)) r.bob-yaki)
2598        $(germ %fine)
2599      =/  merge-points  (find-merge-points ali-yaki bob-yaki)
2600      ?~  merge-points
2601        ~_  %merge-no-merge-base
2602        ~|  "consider a %this or %that merge to get a mergebase"
2603        !!
2604      =/  merge-point=yaki  n.merge-points
2605      ?:  ?=(?(%mate %meld) germ)
2606        =/  ali-diffs=cane  (diff-base ali-yaki bob-yaki merge-point)
2607        =/  bob-diffs=cane  (diff-base bob-yaki ali-yaki merge-point)
2608        =/  bof=(map path (unit cage))
```

```
      (merge-conflicts can.ali-diffs can.bob-diffs)
      (build ali-yaki bob-yaki merge-point ali-diffs bob-diffs bof)
=/  ali-diffs=cane  (calc-diffs ali-yaki merge-point)
=/  bob-diffs=cane  (calc-diffs bob-yaki merge-point)
=/  both-diffs=(map path *)
  %-  %~  int  by
      %-  ~(uni by `(map path *)`new.ali-diffs)
      %-  ~(uni by `(map path *)`cal.ali-diffs)
      %-  ~(uni by `(map path *)`can.ali-diffs)
      `(map path *)`old.ali-diffs
  %-  ~(uni by `(map path *)`new.bob-diffs)
  %-  ~(uni by `(map path *)`cal.bob-diffs)
  %-  ~(uni by `(map path *)`can.bob-diffs)
  `(map path *)`old.bob-diffs
?:  &(?=(%meet germ) !=(~ both-diffs))
  ~_  %meet-conflict
  ~|  [~(key by both-diffs) "consider a %mate merge"]
  !!
=/  both-done=(map path lobe)
  |^
  ?-  germ
    %meet       ~
    %meet-this  (resolve (~(uni by new.bob-diffs) cal.bob-diffs))
    %meet-that  (resolve (~(uni by new.ali-diffs) cal.ali-diffs))
  ==
  ++  resolve
    |=  news=(map path lobe)
    %-  malt   ^-  (list [path lobe])
    %+  murn  ~(tap by both-diffs)
    |=  [=path *]
    ^-  (unit [^path lobe])
    =/  new  (~(get by news) path)
    ?~  new
      ~
    `[path u.new]
    --
  ::
=/  deleted
  %-  ~(dif by (~(uni by old.ali-diffs) old.bob-diffs))
  (~(run by both-done) |=(* ~))
=/  not-deleted=(map path lobe)
  %+  roll  ~(tap by deleted)
  =<  .(not-deleted q.merge-point)
  |=  [[pax=path ~] not-deleted=(map path lobe)]
  (~(del by not-deleted) pax)
=/  hat=(map path lobe)
  %-  ~(uni by not-deleted)
  %-  ~(uni by new.ali-diffs)
  %-  ~(uni by new.bob-diffs)
  %-  ~(uni by cal.ali-diffs)
  cal.bob-diffs
:*  ~
    conflicts=~
    new=&+[[r.bob-yaki r.ali-yaki ~] (to-yuki hat)]
    lat=~
==
==
::
```

```
2667      ++  to-yuki
2668        |=  m=(map path lobe)
2669        ^-  (map path (each page lobe))
2670        (~(run by m) |=(=lobe |+lobe))
2671      ::
2672      ::  The set of changes between the mergebase and one of the desks
2673      ::  being merged
2674      ::
2675      ::  -- `new` is the set of files in the new desk and not in the
2676      ::  mergebase.
2677      ::  -- `cal` is the set of changes in the new desk from the
2678      ::  mergebase except for any that are also in the other new desk.
2679      ::  -- `can` is the set of changes in the new desk from the
2680      ::  mergebase that are also in the other new desk (potential
2681      ::  conflicts).
2682      ::  -- `old` is the set of files in the mergebase and not in the
2683      ::  new desk.
2684      ::
2685      +$  cane
2686        $:  new=(map path lobe)
2687            cal=(map path lobe)
2688            can=(map path cage)
2689            old=(map path ~)
2690        ==
2691      ::
2692      ::  Calculate cane knowing there are no files changed by both
2693      ::  desks
2694      ::
2695      ++  calc-diffs
2696        |=  [hed=yaki bas=yaki]
2697        ^-  cane
2698        :*  %-  molt
2699            %+  skip  ~(tap by q.hed)
2700            |=  [pax=path lob=lobe]
2701            (~(has by q.bas) pax)
2702          ::
2703            %-  molt
2704            %+  skip  ~(tap by q.hed)
2705            |=  [pax=path lob=lobe]
2706            =+  (~(get by q.bas) pax)
2707            |(=(~ -) =([~ lob] -))
2708          ::
2709            ~
2710          ::
2711            %-  malt  ^-  (list [path ~])
2712            %+  murn  ~(tap by q.bas)
2713            |=  [pax=path lob=lobe]
2714            ^-  (unit (pair path ~))
2715            ?.  =(~ (~(get by q.hed) pax))
2716              ~
2717            `[pax ~]
2718        ==
2719      ::
2720      ::  Diff yak against bas where different from yuk
2721      ::
2722      ++  diff-base
2723        |=  [yak=yaki yuk=yaki bas=yaki]
2724        ^-  cane
```

```
=/  new=(map path lobe)
  %-  malt
  %+  skip  ~(tap by q.yak)
  |=  [=path =lobe]
  (~(has by q.bas) path)
::
=/  cal=(map path lobe)
  %-  malt  ^-  (list [path lobe])
  %+  murn  ~(tap by q.bas)
  |=  [pax=path lob=lobe]
  ^-  (unit (pair path lobe))
  =+  a=(~(get by q.yak) pax)
  =+  b=(~(get by q.yuk) pax)
  ?.  ?&  ?=(^ a)
          !=([~ lob] a)
          =([~ lob] b)
      ==
    ~
  `[pax +.a]
::
=/  can=(map path cage)
  %-  malt
  %+  murn  ~(tap by q.bas)
  |=  [=path =lobe]
  ^-  (unit [^path cage])
  =/  in-yak  (~(get by q.yak) path)
  ?~  in-yak
    ~
  ?:  =(lobe u.in-yak)
    ~
  =/  in-yuk  (~(get by q.yuk) path)
  ?~  in-yuk
    ~
  ?:  =(lobe u.in-yuk)
    ~
  ?:  =(u.in-yak u.in-yuk)
    ~
  =/  cug=(unit cage)  (diff-lobes lobe u.in-yak)
  ?~  cug
    ~_  %tombstoned-mergebase
    ~|  path
    ~|  "consider a 2-way merge such as %only-this or %only-that"
    !!
  `[path u.cug]
::
=/  old=(map path ~)
  %-  malt  ^-  (list [path ~])
  %+  murn  ~(tap by q.bas)
  |=  [pax=path lob=lobe]
  ?.  =(~ (~(get by q.yak) pax))
    ~
  (some pax ~)
::
[new cal can old]
::
::  These can/should save their caches
::
++  lobe-to-cage
```

```
2783      |=  =lobe
2784      ^-  (unit cage)
2785      =/  peg=(unit page)  (~(get by lat.ran) lobe)
2786      ?~  peg
2787        ~
2788      =/  [=cage *]
2789        %-  wrap:fusion
2790        (page-to-cage:(tako-ford (~(got by hit.dom) let.dom)) u.peg)
2791      `cage
2792    ::
2793    ++  get-dais
2794      |=  =mark
2795      ^-  dais
2796      =/  [=dais *]
2797        %-  wrap:fusion
2798        (build-dais:(tako-ford (~(got by hit.dom) let.dom)) mark)
2799      dais
2800    ::
2801    ::  Diff two files on bob-desk
2802    ::
2803    ++  diff-lobes
2804      |=  [=a=lobe =b=lobe]
2805      ^-  (unit cage)
2806      =/  a-cage  (lobe-to-cage a-lobe)
2807      =/  b-cage  (lobe-to-cage b-lobe)
2808      ?:  |(?=(~ a-cage) ?=(~ b-cage))
2809        ~
2810      ?>  =(p.u.a-cage p.u.b-cage)
2811      =/  =dais  (get-dais p.u.a-cage)
2812      `[form:dais (~(diff dais q.u.a-cage) q.u.b-cage)]
2813    ::
2814    ::  Merge diffs that are on the same file.
2815    ::
2816    ++  merge-conflicts
2817      |=  [ali-conflicts=(map path cage) bob-conflicts=(map path cage)]
2818      ^-  (map path (unit cage))
2819      %-  ~(urn by (~(int by ali-conflicts) bob-conflicts))
2820      |=  [=path *]
2821      ^-  (unit cage)
2822      =/  cal=cage  (~(got by ali-conflicts) path)
2823      =/  cob=cage  (~(got by bob-conflicts) path)
2824      =/  =mark
2825        =+  (slag (dec (lent path)) path)
2826        ?~(- %$ i.-)
2827      =/  =dais  (get-dais mark)
2828      =/  res=(unit (unit vase))  (~(join dais *vale:dais) q.cal q.cob)
2829      ?~  res
2830        `[form:dais q.cob]
2831      ?~  u.res
2832        ~
2833      `[form:dais u.u.res]
2834    ::
2835    ::  Apply the patches in bof to get the new merged content.
2836    ::
2837    ::  Gather all the changes between ali's and bob's commits and the
2838    ::  mergebase.  This is similar to the %meet of ++merge, except
2839    ::  where they touch the same file, we use the merged versions.
2840    ::
```

```
++  build
  |=  $:  ali=yaki
          bob=yaki
          bas=yaki
          dal=cane
          dob=cane
          bof=(map path (unit cage))
      ==
  ^-  (unit merge-result)
  =/  both-patched=(map path cage)
    %-  malt
    %+  murn  ~(tap by bof)
    |=  [=path cay=(unit cage)]
    ^-  (unit [^path cage])
    ?~  cay
      ~
    :+  ~  path
    =+  (~(get by q.bas) path)
    ?~  -
      ~|  %mate-strange-diff-no-base
      !!
    ::  +need ok because we would have crashed in +diff-base
    ::
    =/  =cage  ~|([%build-need path] (need (lobe-to-cage u.-)))
    =/  =dais  (get-dais p.cage)
    ?>  =(p.u.cay form.dais)
    :-  p.cage
    (~(pact dais q.cage) q.u.cay)
  =/  con=(map path *)                          ::  2-change conflict
    %-  molt
    %+  skim  ~(tap by bof)
    |=([pax=path cay=(unit cage)] ?=(~ cay))
  =/  cab=(map path lobe)                        ::  conflict base
    %-  ~(urn by con)
    |=  [pax=path *]
    (~(got by q.bas) pax)
  =.  con                                        ::  change+del conflict
    %-  ~(uni by con)
    %-  malt  ^-  (list [path *])
    %+  skim  ~(tap by old.dal)
    |=  [pax=path ~]
    ?:  (~(has by new.dob) pax)
      ~|  %strange-add-and-del
      !!
    (~(has by can.dob) pax)
  =.  con                                        ::  change+del conflict
    %-  ~(uni by con)
    %-  malt  ^-  (list [path *])
    %+  skim  ~(tap by old.dob)
    |=  [pax=path ~]
    ?:  (~(has by new.dal) pax)
      ~|  %strange-del-and-add
      !!
    (~(has by can.dal) pax)
  =.  con                                        ::  add+add conflict
    %-  ~(uni by con)
    %-  malt  ^-  (list [path *])
    %+  skim  ~(tap by (~(int by new.dal) new.dob))
```

```
2899            |=  [pax=path *]
2900            =((~(got by new.dal) pax) (~(got by new.dob) pax))
2901          ?:  &(?=(%mate germ) ?=(^ con))
2902            =+  (turn ~(tap by `(map path *)`con) |=([path *] >[+<-]<))
2903            ~_  %mate-conflict
2904            ~|  (turn ~(tap by `(map path *)`con) |=([path *] +<-))
2905            !!
2906        =/  old=(map path lobe)                          ::  oldies but goodies
2907          %+  roll  ~(tap by (~(uni by old.dal) old.dob))
2908          =<  .(old q.bob)
2909          |=  [[pax=path ~] old=(map path lobe)]
2910          (~(del by old) pax)
2911        =/  [hot=(map path lobe) lat=(map lobe page)]   ::  new content
2912          %+  roll  ~(tap by both-patched)
2913          |=  [[pax=path cay=cage] hat=(map path lobe) lat=(map lobe page)]
2914          =/  =page  [p q.q]:cay
2915          =/  =lobe  (page-to-lobe page)
2916          :-  (~(put by hat) pax lobe)
2917          ?:  (~(has by lat) lobe)
2918            lat
2919          (~(uni by (malt [lobe page] ~)) lat)
2920        =/  hat=(map path lobe)                          ::  all the content
2921          %-  ~(uni by old)
2922          %-  ~(uni by new.dal)
2923          %-  ~(uni by new.dob)
2924          %-  ~(uni by cal.dal)
2925          %-  ~(uni by cal.dob)
2926          %-  ~(uni by hot)
2927          cab
2928        =/  del=(map path ?)
2929          (~(run by (~(uni by old.dal) old.dob)) |=(~ %|))
2930        =/  new  &+[[r.bob r.ali ~] (~(run by hat) |=(=lobe |+lobe))]
2931        :*  ~
2932            (silt (turn ~(tap by con) head))
2933            new
2934            lat
2935        ==
2936      --
2937    --
2938  ::
2939  ::  Find the most recent common ancestor(s).
2940  ::
2941  ::    For performance, this depends on +reachable-takos being
2942  ::    memoized.
2943  ::
2944  ++  find-merge-points
2945    |=  [=ali=yaki =bob=yaki]
2946    ^-  (set yaki)
2947    ::  Loop through ancestors breadth-first, lazily generating ancestry
2948    ::
2949    =/  ali-takos  (reachable-takos:ze r.ali-yaki)
2950    ::  Tako worklist
2951    ::
2952    =/  takos=(qeu tako)  [r.bob-yaki ~ ~]
2953    ::  Mergebase candidates.  Have proven they're common ancestors, but
2954    ::  not that they're a most recent
2955    ::
2956    =|  bases=(set tako)
```

```
2957      ::  Takos we've already checked or are in our worklist
2958      ::
2959      =|  done=(set tako)
2960      |-  ^-  (set yaki)
2961      =*  outer-loop  $
2962      ::  If we've finished our worklist, convert to yakis and return
2963      ::
2964      ?:  =(~ takos)
2965        (silt (turn ~(tap in bases) ~(got by hut.ran)))
2966      =^  =tako  takos  ~(get to takos)
2967      =.  done  (~(put in done) tako)
2968      ::  If this is a common ancestor, stop recursing through our
2969      ::  parentage.  Check if it's comparable to any existing candidate.
2970      ::
2971      ?:  (~(has in ali-takos) tako)
2972        =/  base-list  ~(tap in bases)
2973        |-  ^-  (set yaki)
2974        =*  bases-loop  $
2975        ?~  base-list
2976          ::  Proven it's not an ancestor of any previous candidate.
2977          ::  Remove all ancestors of new candidate and add it to the
2978          ::  candidate list.
2979          ::
2980          =.  bases
2981            =/  new-reachable  (reachable-takos:ze tako)
2982            (~(put in (~(dif in bases) new-reachable)) tako)
2983          outer-loop
2984        ::  If it's an ancestor of another candidate, this is not most
2985        ::  recent, so skip and try next in worklist.
2986        ::
2987        =/  base-reachable  (reachable-takos:ze i.base-list)
2988        ?:  (~(has in base-reachable) tako)
2989          outer-loop
2990        bases-loop(base-list t.base-list)
2991      ::  Append parents to list and recurse
2992      ::
2993      =/  bob-yaki  (~(got by hut.ran) tako)
2994      =/  new-candidates  (skip p.bob-yaki ~(has in done))
2995      %_  outer-loop
2996        done   (~(gas in done) new-candidates)
2997        takos  (~(gas to takos) new-candidates)
2998      ==
2999    ::
3000    ++  want-mime
3001      |=  yon=aeon
3002      %-  ~(any by mon)
3003      |=  =beam
3004      &(=(p.beam her) =(q.beam syd) =(r.beam ud+yon))
3005    ::
3006    ::  Update mime cache
3007    ::
3008    ++  checkout-mime
3009      |=  $:  =ford=args:ford:fusion
3010              deletes=(set path)
3011              changes=(set path)
3012          ==
3013      ^-  [(map path (unit mime)) args:ford:fusion]
3014      =/  mim=(map path (unit mime))
```

```
3015      =/  dels=(list path)  ~(tap by deletes)
3016      |-  ^-  (map path (unit mime))
3017      ?~  dels
3018        ~
3019      (~(put by $(dels t.dels)) i.dels ~)
3020    =/  cans=(list path)  ~(tap by changes)
3021    |-  ^-  [(map path (unit mime)) args:ford:fusion]
3022    ?~  cans
3023      [mim ford-args]
3024    =/  [=cage fud=flow fod=flue]
3025      ~|  mime-cast-fail+i.cans
3026      (wrap:fusion (cast-path:(ford:fusion ford-args) i.cans %mime))
3027    =.  cache.ford-args  fud
3028    =.  spill.ford-args  spill.fod
3029    =.  sprig.ford-args  sprig.fod
3030    =^  mim  ford-args  $(cans t.cans)
3031    [(~(put by mim) i.cans `!<(mime q.cage)) ford-args]
3032  ::
3033  ::  Add or remove entries to the mime cache
3034  ::
3035  ++  apply-changes-to-mim
3036    |=  [mim=(map path mime) changes=(map path (unit mime))]
3037    ^-  (map path mime)
3038    =/  changes-l=(list [pax=path change=(unit mime)])
3039      ~(tap by changes)
3040    |-  ^-  (map path mime)
3041    ?~  changes-l
3042      mim
3043    ?~  change.i.changes-l
3044      $(changes-l t.changes-l, mim (~(del by mim) pax.i.changes-l))
3045    $(changes-l t.changes-l, mim (~(put by mim) [pax u.change]:i.changes-l))
3046  ::
3047  ::  Emit update to unix sync
3048  ::
3049  ::  [ergo] Must be called any time the set of files changes that must
3050  ::  be mirrored to unix.  +want-mime may optionally be used to cheaply
3051  ::  check if a version of a desk is mirrored to unix (and so +ergo
3052  ::  must be called).
3053  ::
3054  ++  ergo
3055    |=  [yon=aeon mim=(map path (unit mime))]
3056    ^+  ..park
3057    =/  must  (must-ergo yon mon (turn ~(tap by mim) head))
3058    %-  emil
3059    %+  turn  ~(tap by must)
3060    |=  [pot=term len=@ud pak=(set path)]
3061    :*  (need hez)  %give  %ergo  pot
3062        %+  turn  ~(tap in pak)
3063        |=  pax=path
3064        [(slag len pax) (~(got by mim) pax)]
3065    ==
3066  ::
3067  ::  Output is a map of mount points to {length-of-mounted-path set-of-paths}.
3068  ::
3069  ++  must-ergo
3070    |=  [yon=aeon mon=(map term beam) can=(list path)]
3071    ^-  (map term (pair @ud (set path)))
3072    %-  malt  ^-  (list (trel term @ud (set path)))
```

```
3073      %+    murn   ~(tap by mon)
3074      |=    [nam=term bem=beam]
3075      ^-    (unit (trel term @ud (set path)))
3076      =-    ?~(- ~ `[nam (lent s.bem) (silt `(list path)`-)])
3077      %+    skim   can
3078      |=    pax=path
3079      &(=(p.bem her) =(q.bem syd) =(r.bem ud+yon) =(s.bem (scag (lent s.bem) pax)))
3080    ::
3081    ::    Mount a beam to unix
3082    ::
3083    ++    mount
3084      |=    [pot=term =case =spur]
3085      ^+    ..mount
3086      =/    old-mon   (~(get by mon) pot)
3087      ?^    old-mon
3088        %-    (slog >%already-mounted< >u.old-mon< ~)
3089        ..mount
3090      =/    yon   (case-to-aeon case)
3091      ?~    yon
3092        %-    (slog >%unknown-case< >[her syd case spur]< ~)
3093        ..mount
3094      =/    for-yon   ?:(=(let.dom u.yon) 0 u.yon)
3095      =.    mon                                          ::  [ergo]
3096        (~(put by mon) pot [her syd ud+for-yon] spur)
3097      =/    =yaki   (~(got by hut.ran) (~(got by hit.dom) u.yon))
3098      =/    files   (~(run by q.yaki) |=(=lobe |+lobe))
3099      =/    =args:ford:fusion
3100        [files lat.ran veb.bug fad ?:(=(yon let.dom) fod.dom [~ ~])]
3101      =^    mim   args
3102        (checkout-mime args ~ ~(key by files))
3103      =.    mim.dom   (apply-changes-to-mim mim.dom mim)
3104      (ergo for-yon mim)
3105    ::
3106    ::    Unmount a beam
3107    ::
3108    ++    unmount
3109      |=    [pot=term =case =spur]
3110      ^+    ..unmount
3111      ?>    ?=(^ hez.ruf)
3112      =.    mon   (~(del by mon) pot)                    ::  [ergo]
3113      =?    mim.dom   !(want-mime 0)   ~
3114      (emit u.hez.ruf %give %ogre pot)
3115    ::
3116    ::    Set permissions for a node.
3117    ::
3118    ++    perm
3119      |=    [pax=path rit=rite]
3120      ^+    +>
3121      =/    mis=(set @ta)
3122        %+    roll
3123          =-    ~(tap in -)
3124          ?-    -.rit
3125            %r    who:(fall red.rit *rule)
3126            %w    who:(fall wit.rit *rule)
3127            %rw   (~(uni in who:(fall red.rit *rule)) who:(fall wit.rit *rule))
3128          ==
3129        |=    [w=whom s=(set @ta)]
3130        ?:    |(?=(%& -.w) (~(has by cez) p.w))   s
```

```
3131        (~(put in s) p.w)
3132      ?^  mis
3133      ::  TODO remove this nasty hack
3134      ::
3135      ?.  ?=([[%a *] *] hen)
3136        +>.$
3137      =-  (emit hen %give %done `[%perm-fail [%leaf "No such group(s): {-}"]~])
3138      %+  roll  ~(tap in `(set @ta)`mis)
3139      |=  [g=@ta t=tape]
3140      ?~  t  (trip g)
3141      :(weld t ", " (trip g))
3142      ::  TODO remove this nasty hack
3143      ::
3144      =<  ?.  ?=([[%a *] *] hen)
3145            .
3146          (emit hen %give %done ~)
3147      ::
3148      ?-  -.rit                                  ::  [wake] <>
3149        %r   wake(per (put-perm per pax red.rit))
3150        %w   wake(pew (put-perm pew pax wit.rit))
3151        %rw  wake(per (put-perm per pax red.rit), pew (put-perm pew pax wit.rit))
3152      ==
3153    ::
3154    ++  put-perm
3155    |=  [pes=regs pax=path new=(unit rule)]
3156    ?~  new  (~(del by pes) pax)
3157    (~(put by pes) pax u.new)
3158    ::
3159    ::  Remove a group from all rules.
3160    ::
3161    ::  [wake] <
3162    ::
3163    ++  forget-crew
3164    |=  nom=@ta
3165    %=  +>                                      ::  [wake] < +call
3166      per  (forget-crew-in nom per)
3167      pew  (forget-crew-in nom pew)
3168    ==
3169    ::
3170    ++  forget-crew-in
3171    |=  [nom=@ta pes=regs]
3172    %-  ~(run by pes)
3173    |=  r=rule
3174    r(who (~(del in who.r) |+nom))
3175    ::
3176    ++  set-rein                                ::  [goad] <
3177    |=  [ren=(map dude:gall ?)]
3178    ^+  ..park
3179    ..park(ren.dom ren)
3180    ::
3181    ++  set-zest                                ::  [goad] <
3182    |=  liv=zest
3183    =?  liv  =(%base syd)  %live
3184    ..park(liv.dom liv)
3185    ::
3186    ++  rise                                    ::  [goad] <
3187    |=  [=dude:gall on=(unit ?)]
3188    ?<  =(%base syd)
```

```
3189      %_    ..park
3190        ren.dom
3191      ?~  on
3192        (~(del by ren.dom) dude)
3193      (~(put by ren.dom) dude u.on)
3194      ==
3195  ::
3196  ++  stay
3197    |=  ver=(unit weft)
3198    ^+  ..park
3199    =.  wic.dom                                    ::  [tare] <>
3200      ?~  ver
3201        ~
3202      (~(del by wic.dom) u.ver)
3203    tare
3204  ::
3205  ::  Try to apply highest-versioned %base commit-in-waiting
3206  ::
3207  ::  [wick] Must be called whenever we might have unblocked a kelvin
3208  ::  upgrade.  This is move-order agnostic because it defers the
3209  ::  upgrade into a new event.
3210  ::
3211  ++  wick
3212    ^+  ..park
3213    (emit hen %pass /wick %b %wait now)
3214  ::
3215  ++  take-wick
3216    |=  err=(unit tang)
3217    ^+  ..park
3218    ?^  err
3219      ((slog leaf+"clay: failed to upgrade kelvin (wick)" u.err) ..park)
3220    ?>  ?=(%base syd)
3221    =/  wis=(list [weft =yoki])
3222      %+  sort  ~(tap by wic.dom)
3223      |=  [a=[weft yoki] b=[weft yoki]]
3224      (gth num.a num.b)
3225    =.  wis  (skip wis |=([[* a=@ud] *] (gte a zuse)))
3226    ?~  wis  ::  Every commit bottoms out here ?
3227      ..park
3228    (park | & yoki.i.wis *rang)
3229  ::
3230  ::  Cancel a request.
3231  ::
3232  ::  For local requests, we just remove it from `qyx`.  For foreign requests,
3233  ::  we remove it from `ref` and tell the foreign ship to cancel as well.
3234  ::
3235  ++  cancel-request                                :: release request
3236    ^+  ..cancel-request
3237    =^  wos=(list wove)  qyx
3238      :_  (~(run by qyx) |=(a=(set duct) (~(del in a) hen)))
3239      %-  ~(rep by qyx)
3240      |=  [[a=wove b=(set duct)] c=(list wove)]
3241      ?:((~(has in b) hen) [a c] c)
3242    ::
3243    ?~  ref
3244      =>  .(ref `(unit rind)`ref)
3245      ?:  =(~ wos)  ..cancel-request            ::  TODO handle?
3246      |-  ^+  ..cancel-request
```

```
3247        ?~  wos  ..cancel-request
3248        =.  ..cancel-request  (run-if-future rove.i.wos |=(@da (best hen +<)))
3249        $(wos t.wos)
3250      ::
3251      ?~  nux=(~(get by fod.u.ref) hen)
3252        ..cancel-request(ref `(unit rind)`ref)  ::  XX TMI
3253      =/  sat  (~(got by bom.u.ref) u.nux)
3254      =:  fod.u.ref  (~(del by fod.u.ref) hen)
3255          bom.u.ref  (~(del by bom.u.ref) u.nux)
3256        ==
3257      ::  cancel the request as appropriate
3258      ::
3259      ?.  ?=([~ ^] busy.sat)
3260        %.  [hen her u.nux [syd ~]]
3261        send-over-ames(ref `(unit rind)`ref)    ::  XX TMI
3262      %-  emil
3263      =*  bus  u.busy.sat
3264      =/  =wire  (request-wire kind.bus her syd u.nux)
3265      ~&  %cancel-request-yawn
3266      :~  [hen %pass wire %a %yawn her path.bus]
3267          [hen %pass wire %b %rest time.bus]
3268        ==
3269    ::
3270    ::  Handles a request.
3271    ::
3272    ::  `%sing` requests are handled by ++aver.  `%next` requests are handled by
3273    ::  running ++aver at the given case, and then subsequent cases until we find
3274    ::  a case where the two results aren't equivalent.  If it hasn't happened
3275    ::  yet, we wait.  `%many` requests are handled by producing as much as we can
3276    ::  and then waiting if the subscription range extends into the future.
3277    ::
3278    ++  start-request
3279      |=  [for=(unit [ship @ud]) rav=rave]
3280      ^+  ..start-request
3281      ?:  &(?=(^ for) !(foreign-capable rav))
3282        ~&  [%bad-foreign-request-care from=for rav]
3283        ..start-request
3284      =^  [new-sub=(unit rove) cards=(list card)]  ..start-request
3285        (try-fill-sub for (rave-to-rove rav))
3286      =.  ..start-request  (send-cards cards [hen ~ ~])
3287      ?~  new-sub
3288        ..start-request
3289      (duce for u.new-sub)
3290    ::
3291    ::  +retry-with-ames: we tried scrying. now try with ames instead.
3292    ::
3293    ++  retry-with-ames
3294      |=  [kind=@ta inx=@ud]
3295      ^+  ..retry-with-ames
3296      ~|  [%retry-with-ames kind]
3297      ?>  ?=(%back-index kind)
3298      ~|  [%strange-retry-no-request her syd inx]
3299      ?>  ?=(^ ref)
3300      =/  sat=update-state  (~(got by bom.u.ref) inx)
3301      ::  mark her as having broken scry comms
3302      ::
3303      =.  sad  (~(put by sad) her now)
3304      ::  clean up scry request & timer
```

```
    ::
    =.    ..retry-with-ames
      =<    ?>(?=(^ ref) .)
      ~|    [%strange-retry-not-scry her syd inx busy.sat -.rave.sat]
      =/    bus    ?>(?=([~ ^] busy.sat) u.busy.sat)
      =/    =wire  (request-wire kind her syd inx)
      %-    emil
      ~&    %retry-with-ames-yawn
      :~    [hen %pass wire %b %rest time.bus]
            [hen %pass wire %a %yawn her path.bus]
      ==
    ::  re-send over ames
    ::
    =.    bom.u.ref  (~(put by bom.u.ref) inx sat(busy ~))
    abet:work:(foreign-update inx)
  ::
  ::  Called when a foreign ship answers one of our requests.
  ::
  ::  If it's a `%many` request, process in +take-foreign-update
  ::
  ::  After updating ref (our request manager), we handle %x, %w, and %y
  ::  responses.  For %x, we call ++validate-x to validate the type of
  ::  the response.  For %y, we coerce the result to an arch.
  ::
  ++    take-foreign-answer                                 ::    external change
    |=  [inx=@ud rut=(unit rand)]
    ^+  +>
    ?>  ?=(^ ref)
    =+  ruv=(~(get by bom.u.ref) inx)
    ?~  ruv
      ~&  %bad-answer
       +>.$
    =/  rav=rave  rave.u.ruv
    ?:  ?=(%many -.rav)
      abet:(apex:(foreign-update inx) rut)
    ?~  rut
      ::  nothing here, so cache that
      ::
      %_    wake                                            ::  [wake] <>
          haw.u.ref
        ?.  ?=(%sing -.rav)  haw.u.ref
        (~(put by haw.u.ref) mood.rav ~)
      ==
    |^
    =/  result=(unit cage)  (validate u.rut)
    =/  =mood  [p.p q.p q]:u.rut
    =:  haw.u.ref  (~(put by haw.u.ref) mood result)    ::  [wake] <>
        bom.u.ref  (~(del by bom.u.ref) inx)
        fod.u.ref  (~(del by fod.u.ref) hen)
      ==
    wake
    ::  something here, so validate
    ::
    ++    validate
      |=  =rand
      ^-  (unit cage)
      ?-    p.p.rand
          %a  ~|  %no-big-ford-builds-across-network-for-now  !!
```

```
3363        %b  ~|  %i-guess-you-ought-to-build-your-own-marks   !!
3364        %c  ~|  %casts-should-be-compiled-on-your-own-ship    !!
3365        %d  ~|  %totally-temporary-error-please-replace-me     !!
3366        %e  ~|  %yes-naves-also-shouldnt-cross-the-network     !!
3367        %f  ~|  %even-static-casts-should-be-built-locally     !!
3368        %p  ~|  %requesting-foreign-permissions-is-invalid     !!
3369        %r  ~|  %no-cages-please-they-are-just-way-too-big     !!
3370        %s  ~|  %please-dont-get-your-takos-over-a-network     !!
3371        %t  ~|  %requesting-foreign-directory-is-vaporware     !!
3372        %v  ~|  %weird-shouldnt-get-v-request-from-network     !!
3373        %q  `[p %noun q]:r.rand
3374        %u  `(validate-u r.rand)
3375        %w  `(validate-w r.rand)
3376        %x  (validate-x [p.p q.p q r]:rand)
3377        %y  `[p.r.rand !>(;;(arch q.r.rand))]
3378        %z  `(validate-z r.rand)
3379      ==
3380    ::
3381    ::  Make sure the incoming data is a %u response
3382    ::
3383    ++  validate-u
3384      |=  =page
3385      ^-  cage
3386      ?>  ?=(%flag p.page)
3387      :-  p.page
3388      !>  ;;(? q.page)
3389    ::
3390    ::  Make sure the incoming data is a %w response
3391    ::
3392    ++  validate-w
3393      |=  =page
3394      ^-  cage
3395      :-  p.page
3396      ?+  p.page  ~|  %strange-w-over-nextwork  !!
3397        %cass  !>(;;(cass q.page))
3398        %null  [[%atom %n ~] ~]
3399        %nako  !>(~|([%molding [&1 &2 &3]:q.page] ;;(nako q.page)))
3400      ==
3401    ::
3402    ::  Make sure that incoming data is of the mark it claims to be.
3403    ::
3404    ++  validate-x
3405      |=  [car=care cas=case pax=path peg=page]
3406      ^-  (unit cage)
3407      =/  vale-result
3408        %-  mule  |.
3409        %-  wrap:fusion
3410        ::  Use %base's marks to validate, so we don't have to build the
3411        ::  foreign marks
3412        ::
3413        =/  base-dome  dom:(~(got by dos.rom) %base)
3414        =/  f
3415          %-  %*(. tako-ford dom base-dome)
3416          (~(got by hit.base-dome) let.base-dome)
3417        (page-to-cage:f peg)
3418      ?:  ?=(%| -.vale-result)
3419        %-  (slog >%validate-x-failed< p.vale-result)
3420        ~
```

```
3421        `-.p.vale-result
3422      ::
3423      ::  Make sure the incoming data is a %z response
3424      ::
3425      ++  validate-z
3426        |=  =page
3427        ^-  cage
3428        ?>  ?=(%uvi p.page)
3429        :-  p.page
3430        !>  ;;(@uvI q.page)
3431      --
3432    ::
3433    ::  Respond to backfill request
3434    ::
3435    ::  Maybe should verify the requester is allowed to access this lobe?
3436    ::
3437    ++  give-backfill
3438      |=  [ver=?(%0 %1) =lobe]
3439      ^+  ..give-backfill
3440      =/  peg=(unit page)  (~(get by lat.ran) lobe)
3441      =/  res
3442        ?-  ver
3443          %0  ?~(peg [%1 ~] [%direct lobe u.peg])
3444          %1  [%1 peg]
3445        ==
3446      (emit hen %give %boon res)
3447    ::
3448    ::  Ingest foreign update, requesting missing lobes if necessary
3449    ::
3450    ++  foreign-update
3451      |=  inx=@ud
3452      ?>  ?=(^ ref)
3453      =/  [sat=update-state lost=?]
3454        =/  ruv  (~(get by bom.u.ref) inx)
3455        ?~  ruv
3456          ~&  [%clay-foreign-update-lost her syd inx]
3457          [*update-state &]
3458        [u.ruv |]
3459      =/  done=?  |
3460      =.  hen  duct.sat
3461      |%
3462      ++  abet
3463        ^+  ..foreign-update
3464        ?:  lost
3465          ..foreign-update
3466        ?:  done
3467          =:  bom.u.ref  (~(del by bom.u.ref) inx)
3468              fod.u.ref  (~(del by fod.u.ref) hen)
3469          ==
3470          =<(?>(?=(^ ref) .) wake)
3471        =.  bom.u.ref  (~(put by bom.u.ref) inx sat)
3472        ..foreign-update
3473      ::
3474      ++  apex
3475        |=  rut=(unit rand)
3476        ^+  ..abet
3477        ?:  lost  ..abet
3478        ?~  rut
```

```hoon
3479        =.  nako.sat  (~(put to nako.sat) ~)
3480      work
3481    ?>  ?=(%nako p.r.u.rut)
3482    =/  nako  ;;(nako q.r.u.rut)
3483    ::  must be appended because we delete off front
3484    ::
3485    =.  need.sat  (welp need.sat (missing-lobes nako))
3486    =.  nako.sat  (~(put to nako.sat) ~ nako)
3487    work
3488  ::
3489  ++  missing-lobes
3490    |=  =nako
3491    ^-  (list [tako path lobe])
3492    =|  miss=(set lobe)
3493    =/  let-tako  (~(got by gar.nako) let.nako)
3494    =/  yakis  ~(tap in lar.nako)
3495    |-  ^-  (list [tako path lobe])
3496    =*  yaki-loop  $
3497    ?~  yakis
3498        ~
3499    =/  =norm
3500      ::  Always try to fetch the entire last commit, because often we
3501      ::  want to merge from it.
3502      ::
3503      ?:  =(let-tako r.i.yakis)
3504        *norm:clay
3505      (~(gut by tom.dom) r.i.yakis nor.dom)
3506    =/  lobes=(list [=path =lobe])  ~(tap by q.i.yakis)
3507    |-  ^-  (list [tako path lobe])
3508    =*  blob-loop  $
3509    ?~  lobes
3510      yaki-loop(yakis t.yakis)
3511    =*  lobe  lobe.i.lobes
3512    ?:  ?|  (~(has by lat.ran) lobe)
3513            =([~ %|] +:(~(fit of norm) path.i.lobes))
3514            (~(has in miss) lobe)
3515        ==
3516      blob-loop(lobes t.lobes)
3517    :-  [r.i.yakis i.lobes]
3518    blob-loop(lobes t.lobes, miss (~(put in miss) lobe))
3519  ::
3520  ::  Receive backfill response
3521  ::
3522  ++  take-backfill
3523    |=  =fell
3524    ^+  ..abet
3525    ?:  lost  ..abet
3526    =?  need.sat  ?=(^ need.sat)  t.need.sat
3527    =.  ..park  =>((take-fell fell) ?>(?=(^ ref) .))
3528    work(busy.sat ~)
3529  ::
3530  ::  Fetch next lobe
3531  ::
3532  ++  work
3533    ^+  ..abet
3534    ?.  =(~ busy.sat)  ::NOTE  tmi
3535      ..abet
3536    |-  ^+  ..abet
```

```
?~  need.sat
  ::  NB: if you change to release nakos as we get enough lobes
  ::  for them instead of all at the end, you *must* store the
  ::  `lim` that should be applied after the nako is complete and
  ::  not use the one in the rave, since that will apply to the
  ::  end of subscription.
  ::
  |-  ^+  ..abet
  ?:  =(~ nako.sat)
    ..abet
  =^  next=(unit nako)  nako.sat  ~(get to nako.sat)
  ?~  next
    ..abet(done &)
  =.  ..abet  =>((apply-foreign-update u.next) ?>(?=(~ need.sat) .))
  =.  ..foreign-update  =<(?>(?=(^ ref) .) wake)  ::  [wake] >
  $
::  This used to be what always removed an item from `need`.  Now,
::  we remove in +take-backfill, but in the meantime we could have
::  received the next data from elsewhere (such as another desk
::  updating).  Additionally, this is needed for backward
::  compatibility with old /backfill wires.
::
=/  =lobe
  ?@  i.need.sat  i.need.sat
  lobe.i.need.sat
?:  (~(has by lat.ran) lobe)
  $(need.sat t.need.sat)
::  otherwise, fetch the next blob (aka fell)
::
=^  scry=(unit [@ta @da path])  ..foreign-update
  =<  ?>(?=(^ ref) .)
  ::  if we know a revision & path for the blob,
  ::  and :ship's remote scry isn't known to be broken,
  ::  or we learned it was broken more than an hour ago,
  ::
  ?:  ?&  ?=(^ i.need.sat)
          ?|  !(~(has by sad) her)
              (gth now (add scry-retry-time (~(got by sad) her)))
          ==  ==
    ::  make the request over remote scry
    ::
    =/  =mood  [%q uv+tako path]:i.need.sat
    =<  [`[%back-index -] +]
    (send-over-scry %back-index hen her inx syd mood)
  ::  otherwise, request over ames
  ::
  :-  ~
  =/  =wire  (request-wire %back-index her syd inx)
  =/  =path  [%backfill syd (scot %ud inx) ~]
  ::  TODO: upgrade to %1 when most ships have upgaded
  =/  =fill  [%0 syd lobe]
  (emit hen %pass wire %a %plea her %c path fill)
..abet(busy.sat ?~(scry `%ames scry))
::
::  When we get a %w foreign update, store this in our state.
::
::  We get the commits from the nako and add them to our object
::  store, then we update the map of aeons to commits and the latest
```

```
3595      ::  aeon.
3596      ::
3597      ::  [wake] <
3598      ::
3599      ++  apply-foreign-update
3600        |=  =nako
3601        ^+  ..abet
3602        ::  hit: updated commit-hashes by @ud case
3603        ::  nut: new commit-hash/commit pairs
3604        ::  hut: updated commits by hash
3605        ::
3606        =/  hit  (~(uni by hit.dom) gar.nako)
3607        =/  nut  (turn ~(tap in lar.nako) |=(=yaki [r.yaki yaki]))
3608        =/  hut  (~(uni by (malt nut)) hut.ran)
3609        ::  traverse updated state and sanity check
3610        ::
3611        =+  ~|  :*  %bad-foreign-update
3612                   [gar=gar.nako let=let.nako nut=(turn nut head)]
3613                   [hitdom=hit.dom letdom=let.dom]
3614              ==
3615          ?:  =(0 let.nako)
3616            ~
3617          =/  =aeon  1
3618          |-  ^-  ~
3619          =/  =tako
3620            ~|  [%missing-aeon aeon]  (~(got by hit) aeon)
3621          =/  =yaki
3622            ~|  [%missing-tako tako]  (~(got by hut) tako)
3623          ?:  =(let.nako aeon)
3624            ~
3625          $(aeon +(aeon))
3626        ::  produce updated state
3627        ::
3628        =/  =rave  rave:(~(got by bom.u.ref) inx)
3629        ?>  ?=(%many -.rave)
3630        ::  [ergo] We do not call +ergo here, but if we wanted to support
3631        ::  keeping a foreign mounted desk up-to-date, this would open
3632        ::  that invariant.
3633        ::
3634        ::  [goad] Same for +goad -- if we supported running agents off
3635        ::  foreign desks at an up-to-date revision, we would need to call
3636        ::  +goad here.
3637        ::
3638        =:  let.dom   (max let.nako let.dom)              ::  [wake] < +work
3639            hit.dom    hit
3640            hut.ran    hut
3641            ::  Is this correct?  Seeems like it should only go to `to` if
3642            ::  we've gotten all the way to the end.  Leaving this
3643            ::  behavior unchanged for now, but I believe it's wrong.
3644            ::
3645            lim        ?.(?=(%da -.to.moat.rave) lim p.to.moat.rave)
3646          ==
3647        ..abet
3648      --
3649    ::
3650    ++  seek
3651      |=  =cash
3652      ^+  ..park
```

```
?>   ?=(^ ref)
=/   =tako
  ?:   ?=(%tako -.cash)
    p.cash
  (aeon-to-tako:ze (need (case-to-aeon cash)))
=/   =yaki   (tako-to-yaki:ze tako)
=/   lobes=(list lobe)
  %+   murn   ~(tap by q.yaki)
  |=   [=path =lobe]
  ?:   (~(has by lat.ran) lobe)
    ~
  `lobe
%-   emil
%+   turn   lobes
|=   =lobe
::   TODO: upgrade to %1 when most ships have upgaded
::
=/   =fill   [%0 syd lobe]
=/   =wire   /seek/(scot %p her)/[syd]
=/   =path   [%backfill syd ~]
[hen %pass wire %a %plea her %c path fill]
::
++   take-fell
  |=   =fell
  ^+   ..park
  ?>   ?=(^ ref)
  =/   peg=(unit page)   (fell-to-page fell)
  =?   lat.ran   ?=(^ peg)
    (~(uni by (malt [(page-to-lobe u.peg) u.peg] ~)) lat.ran)
  ..park
::
::   fire function if request is in future
::
++   run-if-future
  |=   [rov=rove fun=$-(@da _.)]
  ^+   +>.$
  =/   date=(unit @da)
    ?-      -.rov
        %sing
      ?.   ?=(%da -.case.mood.rov)   ~
      `p.case.mood.rov
    ::
        %next   ~
        %mult   ~
        %many
      %^   hunt   lth
        ?.   ?=(%da -.from.moat.rov)     ~
        ?.   (lth now p.from.moat.rov)   ~
        [~ p.from.moat.rov]
      ?.   ?=(%da -.to.moat.rov)   ~
      `(max now p.to.moat.rov)
    ==
  ?~   date
    +>.$
  (fun u.date)
::
++   send-cards
  |=   [cards=(list card) ducts=(set duct)]
```

```
3711      ^+    ..park
3712      %-    emil
3713      %-    zing
3714      %+    turn   cards
3715      |=  =card
3716      %+    turn   ~(tap by ducts)
3717      |=  =duct
3718      [duct card]
3719    ::
3720    ::  Loop through open subscriptions and check if we can fill any of
3721    ::  them.
3722    ::
3723    ::  [wake] This must be called any time something might have changed
3724    ::  which fills a subscription or changes the set of subscriptions.
3725    ::
3726    ::  It is safe to call this multiple times, because it updates the
3727    ::  subscription state to reflect that it's responded.  Usually this
3728    ::  means deleting the subscription, but %many can respond multiple
3729    ::  times.
3730    ::
3731    ::  One way of describing this invariant is that if you called +wake
3732    ::  on every desk at the end of every +call/+take, it would always
3733    ::  no-op.
3734    ::
3735    ++  wake
3736      ^+  .
3737      =/  subs=(list [=wove ducts=(set duct)])  ~(tap by qyx)
3738      =|  qux=cult
3739      |-  ^+  ..wake
3740      ?~  subs
3741        ..wake(qyx qux)
3742      ?:  =(~ ducts.i.subs)
3743        $(subs t.subs)
3744      =^  [new-sub=(unit rove) cards=(list card)]  ..park
3745        (try-fill-sub wove.i.subs)
3746      =.  ..wake  (send-cards cards ducts.i.subs)
3747      =?  qux  ?=(^ new-sub)
3748        =/  =wove  [for.wove.i.subs u.new-sub]
3749        %+  ~(put by qux)  wove
3750        (~(uni in ducts.i.subs) (~(get ju qux) wove))
3751      $(subs t.subs)
3752    ::
3753    ::  Try to fill a subscription
3754    ::
3755    ++  try-fill-sub
3756      |=  [far=(unit [=ship ver=@ud]) rov=rove]
3757      ^-  [[(unit rove) (list card)] _..park]
3758      =/  for=(unit ship)  ?~(far ~ `ship.u.far)
3759      ?-    -.rov
3760          %sing
3761        =/  cache-value=(unit (unit cage))
3762          ?~(ref ~ (~(get by haw.u.ref) mood.rov))
3763        ?^  cache-value
3764          ::  if we have a result in our cache, produce it
3765          ::
3766          :_  ..park  :-  ~  :_  ~
3767          (writ ?~(u.cache-value ~ `[mood.rov u.u.cache-value]))
3768        ::  else, check to see if rove is for an aeon we know
```

```
::
=/  tako=(unit tako)  (case-to-tako case.mood.rov)
?~  tako
  [[`rov ~] ..park]
::  we have the appropriate tako, so read in the data
::
=^  value=(unit (unit cage))  ..park
  (read-at-tako:ze for u.tako mood.rov)
?~  value
  ::  we don't have the data directly.  how can we fetch it?
  ::
  ?:  =(0v0 u.tako)
    ~&  [%clay-sing-indirect-data-0 `path`[syd '0' path.mood.rov]]
    [[~ ~] ..park]
  ~&  [%clay-sing-indirect-data desk=syd mood=mood.rov tako=u.tako]
  [[`rov ~] ..park]
::  we have the data, so produce the results
::
:_  ..park  :-  ~  :_  ~
%-  writ
?~  u.value
   ~
`[mood.rov u.u.value]
::
:: %next is just %mult with one path, so we pretend %next = %mult here.
::
  ?(%next %mult)
?.  ?=(~ for)
::  reject if foreign (doesn't work over the network)
::
  [[~ ~] ..park]
::  because %mult requests need to wait on multiple files for each
::  revision that needs to be checked for changes, we keep two
::  cache maps.  {old} is the revision at {(dec aeon)}, {new} is
::  the revision at {aeon}.  if we have no {aeon} yet, that means
::  it was still unknown last time we checked.
::
=*  vor  rov
|^
=/  rov=rove
  ?:  ?=(%mult -.vor)  vor
  :*  %mult
      [case [[care path] ~ ~]]:mood.vor
      aeon.vor
      [[[care.mood.vor path.mood.vor] cach.vor] ~ ~]
      ~
  ==
?>  ?=(%mult -.rov)
::  recurse here on next aeon if possible/needed.
::
|-
::  if we don't have an aeon yet, see if we have one now.
::
?~  aeon.rov
  =/  aeon=(unit aeon)  (case-to-aeon case.mool.rov)
  ::  if we still don't, wait.
  ::
  ?~  aeon  [(store rov) ..park]
```

```
3827        ::  if we do, update the request and retry.
3828        ::
3829        $(aeon.rov `+(u.aeon), old-cach.rov ~, new-cach.rov ~)
3830    ::  if old isn't complete, try filling in the gaps.
3831    ::
3832    =^  o  ..park
3833      ?:  (complete old-cach.rov)
3834        [old-cach.rov ..park]
3835      (read-unknown mool.rov(case [%ud (dec u.aeon.rov)]) old-cach.rov)
3836    =.  old-cach.rov  o
3837    ::  if the next aeon we want to compare is in the future, wait again.
3838    ::
3839    =/  next-aeon=(unit aeon)  (case-to-aeon [%ud u.aeon.rov])
3840    ?~  next-aeon  [(store rov) ..park]
3841    ::  if new isn't complete, try filling in the gaps.
3842    ::
3843    =^  n  ..park
3844      ?:  (complete new-cach.rov)
3845        [new-cach.rov ..park]
3846      (read-unknown mool.rov(case [%ud u.aeon.rov]) new-cach.rov)
3847    =.  new-cach.rov  n
3848    ::  if new still isn't complete, wait again.
3849    ::
3850    ?.  (complete new-cach.rov)
3851      [(store rov) ..park]
3852    ::  if old not complete, give a result (possible false positive).
3853    ::
3854    ?:  !(complete old-cach.rov)
3855      :_  ..park
3856      %-  respond
3857      %-  malt
3858      %+  murn  ~(tap in paths.mool.rov)
3859      |=  [=care =path]
3860      ^-  (unit [mood (unit cage)])
3861      =/  cached  (~(get by new-cach.rov) [care path])
3862      ?.  ?=([~ ~ *] cached)
3863        %-  (slog 'clay: strange new-cache' >[care path cached]< ~)
3864        ~
3865      `u=[[care [%ud let.dom] path] u.u.cached]
3866    ::  both complete, so check if anything has changed
3867    ::
3868    =/  changes=(map mood (unit cage))
3869      %+  roll  ~(tap by old-cach.rov)
3870      |=  $:  [[car=care pax=path] old-cach=cach]
3871              changes=(map mood (unit cage))
3872          ==
3873      =/  new-cach=cach  (~(got by new-cach.rov) car pax)
3874      ?<  |(?=(~ old-cach) ?=(~ new-cach))
3875      =/  new-entry=(unit (pair mood (unit cage)))
3876        =/  =mood  [car [%ud u.aeon.rov] pax]
3877        ?~  u.new-cach
3878          ::  if new does not exist, always notify
3879          ::
3880          `[mood ~]
3881        ?~  u.old-cach
3882          ::  added
3883          ::
3884          `[mood `u.u.new-cach]
```

```
3885        ?:  =([p q.q]:u.u.new-cach [p q.q]:u.u.old-cach)
3886          ::   unchanged
3887          ::
3888          ~
3889        ::   changed
3890        ::
3891        `[mood `u.u.new-cach]
3892      ::  if changed, save the change
3893      ::
3894      ?~  new-entry
3895        changes
3896      (~(put by changes) u.new-entry)
3897    ::  if there are any changes, send response. if none, move on to
3898    ::  next aeon.
3899    ::
3900    ?^  changes  [(respond changes) ..park]
3901    $(u.aeon.rov +(u.aeon.rov), new-cach.rov ~)
3902    ::
3903    ::  check again later
3904    ::
3905    ++  store
3906      |=  rov=rove
3907      ^-  [(unit rove) (list card)]
3908      =/  new-rove=rove
3909        ?>  ?=(%mult -.rov)
3910        ?:  ?=(%mult -.vor)  rov
3911        ?>  ?=([* ~ ~] old-cach.rov)
3912        =*  one  n.old-cach.rov
3913        [%next [care.p.one case.mool.rov path.p.one] aeon.rov q.one]
3914      [`new-rove ~]
3915    ::
3916    ::  send changes
3917    ::
3918    ++  respond
3919      |=  res=(map mood (unit cage))
3920      ^-  [(unit rove) (list card)]
3921      :-  ~
3922      ?:  ?=(%mult -.vor)
3923        :_  ~
3924        =/  moods  ~(key by res)
3925        =/  cas
3926          ?>  ?=(^ moods)
3927          [%da (case-to-date case.n.moods)]
3928        =/  res
3929          (~(run in moods) |=(m=mood [care.m path.m]))
3930        =/  gift  [%wris cas res]
3931        ?:  ?=(^ ref)
3932          [%pass /drip %b %drip !>(gift)]   :: XX s/b [%behn %wris ...] in $sign?
3933        [%give gift]
3934      ?>  ?=([* ~ ~] res)
3935      :_  ~
3936      %-  writ
3937      ?~  q.n.res
3938        ~
3939      `[p u.q]:n.res
3940    ::
3941    ::  no unknowns
3942    ::
```

```
3943        ++  complete
3944          |=  hav=(map (pair care path) cach)
3945          ?&  !=(~ hav)
3946              (levy ~(tap by hav) know)
3947            ==
3948        ::
3949        ::  know about file in cach
3950        ::
3951        ++  know  |=([(pair care path) c=cach] ?=(^ c))
3952        ::
3953        ::  fill in the blanks
3954        ::
3955        ++  read-unknown
3956          |=  [=mool hav=(map (pair care path) cach)]
3957          ^-  [_hav _..park]
3958          =?  hav  ?=(~ hav)
3959            %-  malt  ^-  (list (pair (pair care path) cach))
3960            %+  turn
3961              ~(tap in paths.mool)
3962            |=  [c=care p=path]
3963            ^-  [[care path] cach]
3964            [[c p] ~]
3965          |-  ^+  [hav ..park]
3966          ?~  hav  [hav ..park]
3967          =^  lef  ..park  $(hav l.hav)
3968          =.  l.hav  lef
3969          =^  rig  ..park  $(hav r.hav)
3970          =.  r.hav  rig
3971          =/  [[=care =path] =cach]  n.hav
3972          ?^  cach
3973            [hav ..park]
3974          =^  q  ..park  (aver for care case.mool path)
3975          =.  q.n.hav  q
3976          [hav ..park]
3977        --
3978    ::
3979        %many
3980      :_  ..park
3981      ?.  |(?=(~ for) (allowed-by:ze u.for path.moat.rov per.red))
3982        [~ ~]
3983      =/  from-aeon  (case-to-aeon from.moat.rov)
3984      ?~  from-aeon
3985        ::  haven't entered the relevant range, so do nothing
3986        ::
3987        [`rov ~]
3988      =/  to-aeon  (case-to-aeon to.moat.rov)
3989      ::  TODO: shouldn't skip if tracking
3990      ::
3991      =/  up-to  ?~(to-aeon let.dom u.to-aeon)
3992      =/  ver  ?~(far %1 ver.u.far)
3993      =.  from.moat.rov  [%ud +(let.dom)]
3994      =/  =card
3995        =/  =cage
3996          ?:  track.rov
3997            [%null [%atom %n ~] ~]
3998          [%nako !>((make-nako:ze ver u.from-aeon up-to))]
3999        (writ ~ [%w ud+let.dom /] cage)
4000      ?~  to-aeon
```

```
    ::  we're in the middle of the range, so produce what we can,
    ::  but don't end the subscription
    ::
  [`rov card ~]
::  we're past the end of the range, so end subscription
::
[~ [card (writ ~) ~]]
==
::
::::::::::::::::::::::::::::::::::::::::::::::::::::::::::::::::::::::::::
::
::  This core has no additional state, and the distinction exists purely for
::  documentation.  The overarching theme is that `++de` directly contains
::  logic for metadata about the desk, while `++ze` is composed primarily
::  of helper functions for manipulating the desk state (`++dome`) itself.
::  Functions include:
::
::  --  converting between cases, commit hashes, commits, content hashes,
::      and content
::  --  creating commits and content and adding them to the tree
::  --  finding which data needs to be sent over the network to keep the
::      other urbit up-to-date
::  --  reading from the file tree through different `++care` options
::  --  the `++me` core for merging.
::
::  The dome is composed of the following:
::
::  --  `let` is the number of the most recent revision.
::  --  `hit` is a map of revision numbers to commit hashes.
::  --  `lab` is a map of labels to revision numbers.
::
::::::::::::::::::::::::::::::::::::::::::::::::::::::::::::::::::::::::::
::
::
::  Other utility functions
::
++  ze
  |%
  ::  These convert between aeon (version number), tako (commit hash),
  ::  and yaki (commit data structure)
  ::
  ++  aeon-to-tako  |=(=aeon ?:(=(0 aeon) 0v0 (~(got by hit.dom) aeon)))
  ++  aeon-to-yaki  |=(=aeon (tako-to-yaki (aeon-to-tako aeon)))
  ++  tako-to-yaki  ~(got by hut.ran)
  ::
  ++  tako-to-aeon
    |=  tak=tako
    ^-  aeon  ~+
    ?:  =(0v0 tak)  0
    =/  a=aeon  1
    |-
    ?:  (gth a let.dom)  ~|([%tako-mia tak] !!)
    ?:  (~(has in (reachable-takos (~(got by hit.dom) a))) tak)  a
    $(a +(a))
  ::
  ::  Creates a nako of all the changes between a and b.
  ::
  ++  make-nako
```

```
4059      |=  [ver=@ud a=aeon b=aeon]
4060      ^-  nako
4061      :+  ?>  (lte b let.dom)
4062          |-
4063          ?:  =(b let.dom)
4064            hit.dom
4065            ::  del everything after b
4066          $(hit.dom (~(del by hit.dom) let.dom), let.dom (dec let.dom))
4067        b
4068      ?:  =(0 b)
4069        [~ ~]
4070      =/  excludes=(set tako)
4071          =|  acc=(set tako)
4072          =/  lower=@ud  1
4073          |-
4074          ::  a should be excluded, so wait until we're past it
4075          ?:  (gte lower +(a))
4076            acc
4077          =/  res=(set tako)  (reachable-takos (~(got by hit.dom) lower))
4078          $(acc (~(uni in acc) res), lower +(lower))
4079      =/  includes=(set tako)
4080          =|  acc=(set tako)
4081          =/  upper=@ud  b
4082          |-
4083          ?:  (lte upper a)
4084            acc
4085          =/  res=(set tako)  (reachable-takos (~(got by hit.dom) upper))
4086          $(acc (~(uni in acc) res), upper (dec upper))
4087      [(~(run in (~(dif in includes) excludes)) tako-to-yaki) ~]
4088    ::  Traverse parentage and find all ancestor hashes
4089    ::
4090    ++  reachable-takos                                    ::  reachable
4091      |=  p=tako
4092      ^-  (set tako)
4093      ~+
4094      =|  s=(set tako)
4095      |-  ^-  (set tako)
4096      =.  s  (~(put in s) p)
4097      =+  y=(tako-to-yaki p)
4098      |-  ^-  (set tako)
4099      ?~  p.y
4100        s
4101      ?:  (~(has in s) i.p.y)
4102        $(p.y t.p.y)
4103      =.  s  ^$(p i.p.y)
4104      $(p.y t.p.y)
4105    ::
4106    ++  read-a
4107      !.
4108      |=  [=tako =path]
4109      ^-  [(unit (unit cage)) _..park]
4110      =^  =vase  ..park
4111        ~_  leaf/"clay: %a build failed {<[syd tako path]>}"
4112        %+  tako-flow  tako
4113        %-  wrap:fusion
4114        (build-file:(tako-ford tako) path)
4115      :_(..park [~ ~ %vase !>(vase)])
4116    ::
```

```
4117      ++  read-b
4118        !.
4119        |=  [=tako =path]
4120        ^-  [(unit (unit cage)) _..park]
4121        ?.  ?=([@ ~] path)
4122          [[~ ~] ..park]
4123        =^  =dais  ..park
4124          %+  tako-flow  tako
4125          %-  wrap:fusion
4126          (build-dais:(tako-ford tako) i.path)
4127        :_(..park [~ ~ %dais !>(dais)])
4128      ::
4129      ++  read-c
4130        !.
4131        |=  [=tako =path]
4132        ^-  [(unit (unit cage)) _..park]
4133        ?.  ?=([@ @ ~] path)
4134          [[~ ~] ..park]
4135        =^  =tube  ..park
4136          %+  tako-flow  tako
4137          %-  wrap:fusion
4138          (build-tube:(tako-ford tako) [i i.t]:path)
4139        :_(..park [~ ~ %tube !>(tube)])
4140      ::
4141      ++  read-e
4142        !.
4143        |=  [=tako =path]
4144        ^-  [(unit (unit cage)) _..park]
4145        ?.  ?=([@ ~] path)
4146          [[~ ~] ..park]
4147        =^  =vase  ..park
4148          %+  tako-flow  tako
4149          %-  wrap:fusion
4150          (build-nave:(tako-ford tako) i.path)
4151        :_(..park [~ ~ %nave vase])
4152      ::
4153      ++  read-f
4154        !.
4155        |=  [=tako =path]
4156        ^-  [(unit (unit cage)) _..park]
4157        ?.  ?=([@ @ ~] path)
4158          [[~ ~] ..park]
4159        =^  =vase  ..park
4160          %+  tako-flow  tako
4161          %-  wrap:fusion
4162          (build-cast:(tako-ford tako) [i i.t]:path)
4163        :_(..park [~ ~ %cast vase])
4164      ::
4165      ::  TODO move to +read-buc
4166      ::
4167      ++  read-d
4168        !.
4169        |=  [=tako =path]
4170        ^-  (unit (unit cage))
4171        ~&  [%clay %d-on-desk-deprecated desk=syd %use-empty-desk]
4172        ?.  =(our her)
4173          [~ ~]
4174        ?^  path
```

```
      ~&(%no-cd-path [~ ~])
      [~ ~ %noun !>(~(key by dos.rom.ruf))]
  ::
  ::  Gets the permissions that apply to a particular node.
  ::
  ::  If the node has no permissions of its own, we use its parent's.
  ::  If no permissions have been set for the entire tree above the node,
  ::  we default to fully private (empty whitelist).
  ::
  ++  read-p
    |=  pax=path
    ^-  (unit (unit cage))
    =-  [~ ~ %noun !>(-)]
    :-  (read-p-in pax per.red)
    (read-p-in pax pew.red)
  ::
  ++  read-p-in
    |=  [pax=path pes=regs]
    ^-  dict
    =/  rul=(unit rule)  (~(get by pes) pax)
    ?^  rul
      :+  pax  mod.u.rul
      %-  ~(rep in who.u.rul)
      |=  [w=whom out=(pair (set ship) (map @ta crew))]
      ?:  ?=([%& @p] w)
        [(~(put in p.out) +.w) q.out]
      =/  cru=(unit crew)  (~(get by cez.ruf) +.w)
      ?~  cru  out
      [p.out (~(put by q.out) +.w u.cru)]
    ?~  pax  [/ %white ~ ~]
    $(pax (scag (dec (lent pax)) `path`pax))
  ::
  ++  may-read
    |=  [who=ship car=care tak=tako pax=path]
    ^-  ?
    ?+  car
      (allowed-by who pax per.red)
    ::
        %p
      =(who our)
    ::
        ?(%y %z)
      =+  yak=(tako-to-yaki tak)
      =+  len=(lent pax)
      =-  (levy ~(tap in -) |=(p=path (allowed-by who p per.red)))
      %+  roll  ~(tap in (~(del in ~(key by q.yak)) pax))
      |=  [p=path s=(set path)]
      ?.  =(pax (scag len p))  s
      %-  ~(put in s)
      ?:  ?=(%z car)  p
      (scag +(len) p)
    ==
  ::
  ++  may-write
    |=  [w=ship p=path]
    (allowed-by w p pew.red)
  ::
  ++  allowed-by
```

```
4233      |=  [who=ship pax=path pes=regs]
4234      ^-  ?
4235      =/  rul=real  rul:(read-p-in pax pes)
4236      =/  in-list/?
4237        ?|  (~(has in p.who.rul) who)
4238            ::
4239            %-  ~(rep by q.who.rul)
4240            |=  [[@ta cru=crew] out=_|]
4241            ?:  out  &
4242            (~(has in cru) who)
4243        ==
4244      ?:  =(%black mod.rul)
4245        !in-list
4246      in-list
4247    ::  +content-hash: get hash of contents (%cz hash)
4248    ::
4249    ++  content-hash
4250      |=  [=yaki pax=path]
4251      ^-  @uvI
4252      =+  len=(lent pax)
4253      =/  descendants=(list (pair path lobe))
4254          %+  turn
4255            %+  skim  ~(tap by (~(del by q.yaki) pax))
4256            |=  [paf=path lob=lobe]
4257            =(pax (scag len paf))
4258          |=  [paf=path lob=lobe]
4259          [(slag len paf) lob]
4260      =+  us=(~(get by q.yaki) pax)
4261      ?:  &(?=(~ descendants) ?=(~ us))
4262        *@uvI
4263      %+  roll
4264        ^-  (list (pair path lobe))
4265        [[~ ?~(us *lobe u.us)] descendants]
4266      |=([[path lobe] @uvI] (shax (jam +<)))
4267    ::  +read-q: typeless %x
4268    ::
4269    ::  useful if the marks can't be built (eg for old marks built
4270    ::  against an incompatible standard library).  also useful if you
4271    ::  don't need the type (eg for remote scry) because it's faster.
4272    ::
4273    ++  read-q
4274      |=  [tak=tako pax=path]
4275      ^-  (unit (unit cage))
4276      ?:  =(0v0 tak)
4277        [~ ~]
4278      =+  yak=(tako-to-yaki tak)
4279      =+  lob=(~(get by q.yak) pax)
4280      ?~  lob
4281        [~ ~]
4282      =/  peg=(unit page)  (~(get by lat.ran) u.lob)
4283      ::  if tombstoned, nothing to return
4284      ::
4285      ?~  peg
4286        ~
4287      ``[p.u.peg %noun q.u.peg]
4288    ::  +read-r: %x wrapped in a vase
4289    ::
4290    ++  read-r
```

```
4291        |=  [tak=tako pax=path]
4292        ^-  [(unit (unit cage)) _..park]
4293        =^  x  ..park  (read-x tak pax)
4294        :_  ..park
4295        ?~  x    ~
4296        ?~  u.x  [~ ~]
4297        ``[p.u.u.x !>(q.u.u.x)]
4298    ::  +read-s: produce miscellaneous
4299    ::
4300    ++  read-s
4301        |=  [tak=tako pax=path =case]
4302        ^-  (unit (unit cage))
4303      ?:  ?=([%subs ~] pax)
4304        ?.  =([%da now] case)  ~
4305        =|  sus=(set ship)
4306        =/  doj=(unit dojo)  (~(get by dos.rom) syd)
4307        ?~  doj
4308          ``noun+!>(sus)
4309        =/  wos  ~(tap in ~(key by qyx.u.doj))
4310        |-
4311        ?~  wos
4312          ``noun+!>(sus)
4313        ?~  for.i.wos
4314          $(wos t.wos)
4315        %=  $
4316          wos  t.wos
4317          sus  (~(put in sus) ship.u.for.i.wos)
4318        ==
4319      ?:  ?=([%bloc ~] pax)
4320        :^  ~  ~  %noun
4321        :-  -:!>(*(map lobe page))
4322        ^-  (map lobe page)
4323        %-  %~  rep  in
4324            |-  ^-  (set tako)
4325            =/  ts=(set tako)
4326              %-  reachable-takos
4327              (~(got by hit.dom) let.dom)
4328            ?:  (lte let.dom 1)  ts
4329            (~(uni in ts) $(let.dom (dec let.dom)))
4330        |=  [t=tako o=(map lobe page)]
4331        %-  ~(gas by o)
4332        %+  turn
4333          ~(val by q:(~(got by hut.ran) t))
4334        |=(l=lobe [l (~(got by lat.ran) l)])
4335      ?.  ?=([@ * *] pax)
4336        `~
4337      ?+  i.pax  `~
4338          %tako
4339        ``tako+[-:!>(*tako) tak]
4340      ::
4341          %yaki
4342        =/  yak=(unit yaki)  (~(get by hut.ran) (slav %uv i.t.pax))
4343        ?~  yak
4344          ~
4345        ``yaki+[-:!>(*yaki) u.yak]
4346      ::
4347          %blob
4348        =/  peg=(unit page)  (~(get by lat.ran) (slav %uv i.t.pax))
```

```
?~  peg
  ~
``blob+[-:!>(*page) u.peg]
::
    %hash
=/  yak=(unit yaki)  (~(get by hut.ran) (slav %uv i.t.pax))
?~  yak
    ~
``uvi+[-:!>(*@uvI) (content-hash u.yak /)]
::
    %cage
::  should save ford cache
::
=/  =lobe  (slav %uv i.t.pax)
=/  peg=(unit page)  (~(get by lat.ran) lobe)
?~  peg
    ~
=/  [=cage *]
  %-  wrap:fusion
  (page-to-cage:(tako-ford tak) u.peg)
``cage+[-:!>(*^cage) cage]
::
    %open  ``open+!>(prelude:(tako-ford tak))
    %late  !!  :: handled in +aver
    %case  !!  :: handled in +aver
    %base-tako
::  TODO this ignores the given beak
::  maybe move to +aver?
?>  ?=(^ t.t.pax)
:^  ~  ~  %uvs  !>
^-  (list @uv)
=/  tako-a  (slav %uv i.t.pax)
=/  tako-b  (slav %uv i.t.t.pax)
=/  yaki-a  (~(got by hut.ran) tako-a)
=/  yaki-b  (~(got by hut.ran) tako-b)
%+  turn    ~(tap in (find-merge-points yaki-a yaki-b))
|=  =yaki
r.yaki
::
    %base
?>  ?=(^ t.t.pax)
:^  ~  ~  %uvs  !>
^-  (list @uv)
=/  him  (slav %p i.t.pax)
=/  other  dom:((de now rof hen ruf) him i.t.t.pax)
?:  =(0 let.other)
    ~
=/  our-yaki  (~(got by hut.ran) tak)
=/  other-yaki  (~(got by hut.ran) (~(got by hit.other) let.other))
%+  turn  ~(tap in (find-merge-points other-yaki our-yaki))
|=  =yaki
r.yaki
==
::  +read-t: produce the list of paths within a yaki with :pax as prefix
::
++  read-t
|=  [tak=tako pax=path]
^-  (unit (unit [%file-list (hypo (list path))]))
```

```
4407      ::  if asked for version 0, produce an empty list of files
4408      ::
4409      ?:  =(0v0 tak)
4410        ``[%file-list -:!>(*(list path)) *(list path)]
4411      ::  look up the yaki snapshot based on the version
4412      ::
4413      =/  yak=yaki  (tako-to-yaki tak)
4414      ::  calculate the path length once outside the loop
4415      ::
4416      =/  path-length  (lent pax)
4417      ::
4418      :^    ~    ~    %file-list
4419      :-  -:!>(*(list path))
4420      ^-  (list path)
4421      ::  sort the matching paths alphabetically
4422      ::
4423      =-  (sort - aor)
4424      ::  traverse the filesystem, filtering for paths with :pax as prefix
4425      ::
4426      %+  skim  ~(tap in ~(key by q.yak))
4427      |=(paf=path =(pax (scag path-length paf)))
4428    ::
4429    ::  Checks for existence of a node at an aeon.
4430    ::
4431    ::  This checks for existence of content at the node, and does *not* look
4432    ::  at any of its children.
4433    ::
4434    ++  read-u
4435      |=  [tak=tako pax=path]
4436      ^-  (unit (unit [%flag (hypo ?)]))
4437      ::  if asked for version 0, that never exists, so always give false
4438      ::
4439      ?:  =(0v0 tak)
4440        ``[%flag -:!>(*?) |]
4441      ::  look up the yaki snapshot based on the version
4442      ::
4443      =/  yak=yaki  (tako-to-yaki tak)
4444      ::  produce the result based on whether or not there's a file at :pax
4445      ::
4446      ``[%flag -:!>(*?) (~(has by q.yak) pax)]
4447    ::
4448    ::  Gets the dome (desk state) at a particular aeon.
4449    ::
4450    ++  read-v
4451      |=  [tak=tako pax=path]
4452      ^-  (unit (unit [%dome (hypo domo:clay)]))
4453      =/  yon=aeon  (tako-to-aeon:ze tak)
4454      ?:  (lth yon let.dom)
4455        :*  ~    ~    %dome  -:!>(*domo)
4456              ^-  domo
4457            :*  let=yon
4458                hit=(molt (skim ~(tap by hit.dom) |=([p=@ud *] (lte p yon))))
4459                lab=(molt (skim ~(tap by lab.dom) |=([* p=@ud] (lte p yon))))
4460        ==  ==
4461      ?:  (gth yon let.dom)
4462        ~
4463      ``[%dome -:!>(*domo) [let hit lab]:dom]
4464    ::
```

```
4465    ::  Gets all cases refering to the same revision as the given case.
4466    ::
4467    ::  For the %da case, we give just the canonical timestamp of the revision.
4468    ::
4469    ++  read-w
4470      |=  tak=tako
4471      ^-  (unit (unit cage))
4472      =-  [~ ~ %cass !>(-)]
4473      ^-  cass  ::TODO  should include %uv case
4474      :-  (tako-to-aeon tak)
4475      ?:  =(0v0 tak)  `@da`0
4476      t:(tako-to-yaki tak)
4477    ::
4478    ::  Get the data at a node.
4479    ::
4480    ::  Use ford to read the file.  Note this special-cases the hoon
4481    ::  mark for bootstrapping purposes.
4482    ::
4483    ++  read-x
4484      |=  [tak=tako pax=path]
4485      ^-  [(unit (unit cage)) _..park]
4486      =/  q  (read-q tak pax)
4487      ?~  q     `..park
4488      ?~  u.q  [[~ ~] ..park]
4489      ::  should convert any lobe to cage
4490      ::
4491      =^  =cage  ..park
4492        %+  tako-flow  tak
4493        %-  wrap:fusion
4494        (page-to-cage:(tako-ford tak) p.u.u.q q.q.u.u.q)
4495      [``cage ..park]
4496    ::
4497    ::  Gets an arch (directory listing) at a node.
4498    ::
4499    ++  read-y
4500      |=  [tak=tako pax=path]
4501      ^-  (unit (unit [%arch (hypo arch)]))
4502      ?:  =(0v0 tak)
4503        ``[%arch -:!>(*arch) *arch]
4504      =+  yak=(tako-to-yaki tak)
4505      =+  len=(lent pax)
4506      :^  ~  ~  %arch
4507      ::  ~&  cy+pax
4508      :-  -:!>(*arch)
4509      ^-  arch
4510      :-  (~(get by q.yak) pax)
4511      ^-  (map knot ~)
4512      %-  molt  ^-  (list (pair knot ~))
4513      %+  turn
4514        ^-  (list (pair path lobe))
4515        %+  skim  ~(tap by (~(del by q.yak) pax))
4516        |=  [paf=path lob=lobe]
4517        =(pax (scag len paf))
4518      |=  [paf=path lob=lobe]
4519      =+  pat=(slag len paf)
4520      [?>(?=(^ pat) i.pat) ~]
4521    ::
4522    ::  Gets a recursive hash of a node and all its children.
```

```
4523        ::
4524        ++  read-z
4525          |=  [tak=tako pax=path]
4526          ^-  (unit (unit [%uvi (hypo @uvI)]))
4527          ?:  =(0v0 tak)
4528            ``uvi+[-:!>(*@uvI) *@uvI]
4529          [~ ~ %uvi [%atom %'uvI' ~] (content-hash (tako-to-yaki tak) pax)]
4530        ::
4531        :: Get a value at an aeon.
4532        ::
4533        :: Value can be either null, meaning we don't have it yet, [null null],
4534        :: meaning we know it doesn't exist, or [null null cage],
4535        :: meaning we either have the value directly or a content hash of the
4536        :: value.
4537        ::
4538        ++  read-at-tako                                ::    read-at-tako:ze
4539          |=  [for=(unit ship) tak=tako mun=mood]       ::  seek and read
4540          ^-  [(unit (unit cage)) _..park]
4541          :: non-zero commits must be known, and reachable from within this desk
4542          ::
4543          ?.  ?|  =(0v0 tak)
4544              ?&  (~(has by hut.ran) tak)
4545                  ?|  (~(any by hit.dom) |=(=tako =(tak tako)))  ::  fast-path
4546                      |-  ^-  ?
4547                      ?:  (lte let.dom 1)
4548                        %.n
4549                      ?|  (~(has in (reachable-takos (aeon-to-tako:ze let.dom))) tak)
4550                          $(let.dom (dec let.dom))
4551                      ==
4552              ==
4553                  |(?=(~ for) (may-read u.for care.mun tak path.mun))
4554          ==  ==
4555            [~ ..park]
4556          :: virtualize to catch and produce deterministic failures
4557          ::
4558          |^  =/  res  (mule |.(read))
4559          ?:  ?=(%& -.res)  p.res
4560          %.  [[~ ~] ..park]
4561          (slog leaf+"clay: read-at-tako fail {<[desk=syd mun]>}" p.res)
4562          ::
4563          ++  read
4564            ^-  [(unit (unit cage)) _..park]
4565            ?-  care.mun
4566              %a  (read-a tak path.mun)
4567              %b  (read-b tak path.mun)
4568              %c  (read-c tak path.mun)
4569              %d  [(read-d tak path.mun) ..park]
4570              %e  (read-e tak path.mun)
4571              %f  (read-f tak path.mun)
4572              %p  [(read-p path.mun) ..park]
4573              %q  [(read-q tak path.mun) ..park]
4574              %r  (read-r tak path.mun)
4575              %s  [(read-s tak path.mun case.mun) ..park]
4576              %t  [(read-t tak path.mun) ..park]
4577              %u  [(read-u tak path.mun) ..park]
4578              %v  [(read-v tak path.mun) ..park]
4579              %w  [(read-w tak) ..park]
4580              %x  (read-x tak path.mun)
```

```
      %y  [(read-y tak path.mun) ..park]
      %z  [(read-z tak path.mun) ..park]
    ==
  --
--
::  userspace agent management
::
++  lu
  |=  [now=@da rof=roof hen=duct raft]
  =*  ruf  |3.+<.$
  =|  mow=(list move)
  |%
  ++  abet
    ^-  [(list move) raft]
    [(flop mow) ruf]
  ::
  ++  emit
    |=  mof=move
    %_(+> mow [mof mow])
  ::
  ++  emil
    |=  mof=(list move)
    %_(+> mow (weld (flop mof) mow))
  ::  +ford: init ford
  ::
  ++  ford
    |=  [her=ship syd=desk yon=(unit aeon)]
    =/  den  ((de now rof hen ruf) her syd)
    %-  tako-ford:den
    ::TODO  is this +got after +got semantically correct?
    (~(got by hit.dom:(~(got by dos.rom) syd)) ?~(yon let.dom:den u.yon))
  ::  +wrap: save ford cache
  ::
  ++  wrap
    |*  [her=ship syd=desk yon=(unit aeon) res=* =state:ford:fusion]
    =^  moves  ruf
      =/  den  ((de now rof hen ruf) her syd)
      =/  tak  (aeon-to-tako:ze:den ?~(yon let.dom:den u.yon))
      abet:+:(tako-flow:den tak res cache.state &2.state)
    [res (emil moves)]
  ::
  ++  trace
    |=  [pri=@ print=(trap tape)]
    ?:  (lth veb.bug pri)
      same
    (slog leaf+"goad: {(print)}" ~)
  ::  +goad: emit %load move for all desks, applying $rein's
  ::
  ::  [goad] Must be called any time the set of running agents changes.
  ::  This is whenever an agent is started, stopped, or updated.
  ::
  ::  This is not move-order agnostic -- you must be careful of
  ::  reentrancy as long as arvo's move order is depth-first.
  ::
  ::  [tare] >
  ::
  ++  goad
```

```
^+  ..abet
=^  sat=(list [=desk =bill])  ..abet
  =/  desks=(list desk)  ~(tap in ~(key by dos.rom))
  |-  ^-  [(list [desk bill]) _..abet]
  ?~  desks
    [~ ..abet]
  =/  den  ((de now rof hen ruf) our i.desks)
  ?.  =(%live liv.dom.den)
    %-  (trace 2 |.("{<i.desks>} is not live"))
    $(desks t.desks)
  =^  res  den  (aver:den ~ %x da+now /desk/bill)
  =.  ruf  +:abet:den
  =/  bill
    ?.  ?=([~ ~ *] res)  *bill
    ~|([%building-bill i.desks] !<(bill q.u.u.res))
  ?~  rid=(override bill ren.dom.den)
    %-  (trace 2 |.("{<i.desks>} has no dudes"))
    $(desks t.desks)
  %-  %+  trace  2  |.
      "{<i.desks>} has bill {<bill>} and rein {<ren.dom.den>}, so {<rid>}"
  =^  sats  ..abet  $(desks t.desks)
  [[[i.desks rid] sats] ..abet]
  ::
=.  sat  (apply-precedence sat)
=+  ?:  (lth veb.bug 1)  ~
    %.  ~  %-  slog
    %+  turn  sat
    |=  [=desk =bill]
    leaf+"goad: output: {<desk>}: {<bill>}"
=^  agents  ..abet  (build-agents sat)
::  TODO: enable if we can reduce memory usage
::
::  =.  ..abet
::    (build-marks (turn (skip sat |=([desk =bill] =(bill ~))) head))
::
=.  ..abet  tare                                        ::  [tare] >
(emit hen %pass /lu/load %g %load agents)
::  +override: apply rein to bill
::
++  override
  |=  [duz=bill ren=(map dude:gall ?)]  ^-  bill
  =/  out=bill  (skip duz ~(has by ren))
  (~(rep by ren) |=([[d=dude:gall r=?] =_out] ?.(r out [d out])))
::  +apply-precedence: resolve conflicts between $bill's
::
::    policy is to crash if multiple desks are trying to run the same
::    agent.
::
++  apply-precedence
  |=  sat=(list [=desk =bill])
  ^+  sat
  ::  sort desks in alphabetical order with %base first
  ::
  =.  sat  (sort sat sort-desks)
  ::  for each desk
  ::
  =|  done=(set dude:gall)
  |-  ^+  sat
```

```
4697      ?~  sat
4698        ~
4699      ::  for each agent
4700      ::
4701      =/  bil  bill.i.sat
4702      =^  this  done
4703        |-  ^-  [bill (set dude:gall)]
4704        ?~  bil
4705          [~ done]
4706        ::
4707        ?:  (~(has in done) i.bil)
4708          ~>  %mean.(cat 3 'clay: cannot run app from two desks: %' i.bil)
4709          !!
4710        =.  done  (~(put in done) i.bil)
4711        =^  next  done  $(bil t.bil)
4712        [[i.bil next] done]
4713      [[desk.i.sat this] $(sat t.sat)]
4714    ::
4715    ++  sort-desks
4716      |=  [a=[=desk *] b=[=desk *]]
4717      ^-  ?
4718      ?:  =(%base desk.a)  &
4719      ?:  =(%base desk.b)  |
4720      (aor desk.a desk.b)
4721    ::  build-file for each dude
4722    ::
4723    ++  build-agents
4724      |=  sat=(list [=desk =bill])
4725      ^-  [load:gall _..abet]
4726      =|  lad=load:gall
4727      |-  ^-  [load:gall _..abet]
4728      ?~  sat
4729        [lad ..abet]
4730      =/  f  (ford our desk.i.sat ~)
4731      =^  new=load:gall  ..abet
4732        %-  wrap  :^  our  desk.i.sat  ~
4733        |-  ^-  [load:gall state:ford:fusion]
4734        ?~  bill.i.sat
4735          [~ nub.f]
4736        =^  =vase  nub.f  (build-file:f /app/[i.bill.i.sat]/hoon)
4737        =/  agent  ~|  [%building-app bill.i.sat]  !<(agent:gall vase)
4738        =^  lid  nub.f  $(bill.i.sat t.bill.i.sat)
4739        [[[i.bill.i.sat [our desk.i.sat da+now] agent] lid] nub.f]
4740      =.  lad  (weld lad new)
4741      $(sat t.sat)
4742    ::  build-dais for each mark
4743    ::
4744    ++  build-marks
4745      |=  desks=(list desk)
4746      ^+  ..abet
4747      ?~  desks
4748        ..abet
4749      =/  f  (ford our i.desks ~)
4750      =^  null  ..abet
4751        %-  wrap  :^  our  i.desks  ~
4752        =^  marks=(list mark)  nub.f
4753          =/  pax=path  /
4754          |-  ^-  [(list mark) _nub.f]
```

```hoon
=/  den  ((de now rof hen ruf) our i.desks)
=^  res  den  (aver:den ~ %y da+now mar+pax)
?.  ?=([~ ~ *] res)
  [~ nub.f]
=/  arch  ~|  [%building-arch i.desks]  !<(arch q.u.u.res)
=/  m1=(list mark)
  ?.  ?&  ?=(^ fil.arch)
          ?=(^ pax)
          =(/hoon (slag (dec (lent pax)) `path`pax))
      ==
      ~
  :_  ~
  ?~  t.pax
    ''
  |-  ^-  mark
  ?~  t.t.pax
    i.pax
  (rap 3 i.pax '-' $(pax t.pax) ~)
::
=^  m2  nub.f
  |-  ^-  [(list mark) _nub.f]
  ?~  dir.arch
    [~ nub.f]
  =^  n1  nub.f  ^$(pax (weld pax /[p.n.dir.arch]))
  =^  n2  nub.f  $(dir.arch l.dir.arch)
  =^  n3  nub.f  $(dir.arch r.dir.arch)
  [:(weld n1 n2 n3) nub.f]
[(weld m1 m2) nub.f]
::
|-  ^-  [~ state:ford:fusion]
?~  marks
  [~ nub.f]
=^  =dais  nub.f  (build-dais:f i.marks)
$(marks t.marks)
$(desks t.desks)
::
++  tore
  ^-  rock:tire
  %-  ~(run by dos.rom)
  |=  =dojo
  [liv.dom.dojo ~(key by wic.dom.dojo)]
::
::  [tare] Must be called any time the zest or commits-in-waiting
::  might have changed for a desk.  +goad calls this uncondtionally,
::  but if you're not calling +goad, you may need to call this.
::
++  tare
  ?:  =(~ tyr)
    ..abet
  =/  tor  tore
  =/  waves=(list wave:tire)  (walk:tire tur tor)
  ?~  waves
    ..abet
  =.  tur  tor
  %-  emil
  %-  zing
  %+  turn  ~(tap in tyr)
  |=  =duct
```

```
    ^-  (list move)
    %+  turn  waves
    |=  =wave:tire
    ^-  move
    [duct %give %tire %| wave]
  --
--
::::::::::::::::::::::::::::::::::::::::::::::::::::::::::::::::::::::::::
::                  section 4cA, filesystem vane
::
::  This is the arvo interface vane.  Our formal state is a `++raft`, which
::  has five components:
::
::  --  `rom` is the state for all local desks.
::  --  `hoy` is the state for all foreign desks.
::  --  `ran` is the global, hash-addressed object store.
::  --  `mon` is the set of mount points in unix.
::  --  `hez` is the duct to the unix sync.
::
::::::::::::::::::::::::::::::::::::::::::::::::::::::::::::::::::::::::::
=|                                              ::  instrument state
    $:  ver=%14                                 ::  vane version
        ruf=raft                                ::  revision tree
    ==                                          ::
|=  [now=@da eny=@uvJ rof=roof]                 ::  current invocation
~%  %clay-top  ..part  ~
|%                                              ::
++  call                                        ::  handle request
  ~/  %clay-call
  |=  $:  hen=duct
          dud=(unit goof)
          wrapped-task=(hobo task)
      ==
  ^-  [(list move) _..^$]
  ::
  =/  req=task  ((harden task) wrapped-task)
  ::
  ::  TODO handle error notifications
  ::
  ?^  dud
    [[[hen %slip %d %flog %crud [-.req tang.u.dud]] ~] ..^$]
  ::
  ?-    -.req
      %boat
    :_    ..^$
    [hen %give %hill (turn ~(tap by mon.ruf) head)]~
  ::
      %cred
    =.  cez.ruf
      ?~  cew.req  (~(del by cez.ruf) nom.req)
      (~(put by cez.ruf) nom.req cew.req)
    ::  wake all desks, a request may have been affected.
    =|  mos=(list move)
    =/  des  ~(tap in ~(key by dos.rom.ruf))
    |-
    ?~  des  [[[hen %give %done ~] mos] ..^^$]
    =/  den  ((de now rof hen ruf) our i.des)
    =^  mor  ruf
```

```
4871        =<  abet:wake                                    ::  [wake] >
4872        ?:  ?=(^ cew.req)  den
4873        (forget-crew:den nom.req)
4874      $(des t.des, mos (weld mos mor))
4875    ::
4876        %crew
4877      [[hen %give %cruz cez.ruf]~ ..^$]
4878    ::
4879        %crow
4880      =/  des  ~(tap by dos.rom.ruf)
4881      =|  rus=(map desk [r=regs w=regs])
4882      |^
4883        ?~  des  [[hen %give %croz rus]~ ..^^$]
4884        =+  per=(filter-rules per.q.i.des)
4885        =+  pew=(filter-rules pew.q.i.des)
4886        =?  rus  |(?=(^ per) ?=(^ pew))
4887          (~(put by rus) p.i.des per pew)
4888        $(des t.des)
4889      ::
4890      ++  filter-rules
4891        |=  pes=regs
4892        ^+  pes
4893        =-  (~(gas in *regs) -)
4894        %+  skim  ~(tap by pes)
4895        |=  [p=path r=rule]
4896        (~(has in who.r) |+nom.req)
4897      --
4898    ::
4899        %drop
4900      ~&  %clay-idle
4901      [~ ..^$]
4902    ::
4903        %info
4904      ?:  ?=(%| -.dit.req)
4905        =/  bel=@tas        p.dit.req
4906        =/  aey=(unit aeon)  q.dit.req
4907        =^  mos  ruf
4908          =/  den  ((de now rof hen ruf) our des.req)
4909          abet:(label:den bel aey)
4910        [mos ..^$]
4911      =/  [deletes=(set path) changes=(map path cage)]
4912        =/  =soba  p.dit.req
4913        =|  deletes=(set path)
4914        =|  changes=(map path cage)
4915        |-  ^+  [deletes changes]
4916        ?~  soba
4917          [deletes changes]
4918        ?-  -.q.i.soba
4919          %del  $(soba t.soba, deletes (~(put in deletes) p.i.soba))
4920          %ins  $(soba t.soba, changes (~(put by changes) [p p.q]:i.soba))
4921          %mut  $(soba t.soba, changes (~(put by changes) [p p.q]:i.soba))
4922          %dif  ~|(%dif-not-implemented !!)
4923        ==
4924      =^  mos  ruf
4925        =/  den  ((de now rof hen ruf) our des.req)
4926        abet:(info:den deletes changes)
4927      [mos ..^$]
4928    ::
```

```
    %init
  [~ ..^$(hun.rom.ruf hen)]
::
    %into
  =.  hez.ruf  `hen
  =+  bem=(~(get by mon.ruf) des.req)
  ?:  &(?=(~ bem) !=(%$ des.req))
    ~|([%bad-mount-point-from-unix des.req] !!)
  =/  bem=beam
    ?^  bem
      u.bem
    [[our %base %ud 1] ~]  ::  TODO: remove this fallback?
  =/  dos  (~(get by dos.rom.ruf) q.bem)
  ?~  dos
    !!  ::  fire next in queue
  =^  mos  ruf
    =/  den  ((de now rof hen ruf) our q.bem)
    abet:(into:den s.bem all.req fis.req)
  [mos ..^$]
::
    %merg                                     ::  direct state up
  ?:  =(%$ des.req)
    ~|(%merg-no-desk !!)
  ?.  ((sane %tas) des.req)
    ~|([%merg-bad-desk-name des.req] !!)
  =^  mos  ruf
    =/  den  ((de now rof hen ruf) our des.req)
    abet:(start-merge:den her.req dem.req cas.req how.req)
  [mos ..^$]
::
    %fuse
  ?:  =(%$ des.req)
    ~|(%fuse-no-desk !!)
  ?.  ((sane %tas) des.req)
    ~|([%fuse-bad-desk-name des.req] !!)
  =^  mos  ruf
    =/  den  ((de now rof hen ruf) our des.req)
    abet:(start-fuse:den bas.req con.req)
  [mos ..^$]
::
    %mont
  =.  hez.ruf  ?^(hez.ruf hez.ruf `[[%$ %sync ~] ~])
  =^  mos  ruf
    =/  den  ((de now rof hen ruf) p.bem.req q.bem.req)
    abet:(mount:den pot.req r.bem.req s.bem.req)
  [mos ..^$]
::
    %dirk
  ?~  hez.ruf
    ~&  %no-sync-duct
    [~ ..^$]
  ?.  (~(has by mon.ruf) pot.req)
    ~&  [%not-mounted pot.req]
    [~ ..^$]
  [~[[u.hez.ruf %give %dirk pot.req]] ..^$]
::
    %ogre
  ?:  =(~ hez.ruf)
```

```
~&  %no-sync-duct
[~ ..^$]
=*  pot  pot.req
=/  bem=(list [pot=term beam])
  ?@  pot
    ?~  got=(~(get by mon.ruf) pot)
      ~&  [%not-mounted pot]
      ~
    [pot u.got]~
  %+  skim  ~(tap by mon.ruf)
  |=  [=term =beam]
  =(pot beam)
|-  ^-  [(list move) _..^^$]
?~  bem
  [~ ..^^$]
=^  moves-1  ruf
  =/  den  ((de now rof hen ruf) p.i.bem q.i.bem)
  abet:(unmount:den pot.i.bem r.i.bem s.i.bem)
=^  moves-2  ..^^$  $(bem t.bem)
[(weld moves-1 moves-2) ..^^$]
::
    %park
?.  ((sane %tas) des.req)
  ~|([%park-bad-desk des.req] !!)
=^  mos  ruf
  =/  den  ((de now rof hen ruf) our des.req)
  abet:(park:den | & [yok ran]:req)
[mos ..^$]
::
    %pork
=/  [syd=desk =yoki]  (need pud.ruf)
=.  pud.ruf  ~
=^  mos  ruf
  =/  den  ((de now rof hen ruf) our syd)
  abet:(park:den & & yoki *rang)
[mos ..^$]
::
    %prep
[~ ..^$(lat.ran.ruf (~(uni by lat.req) lat.ran.ruf))]
::
    %perm
=^  mos  ruf
  =/  den  ((de now rof hen ruf) our des.req)
  abet:(perm:den pax.req rit.req)
[mos ..^$]
::
    %rein
=^  m1  ruf
  =/  den  ((de now rof hen ruf) our des.req)
  abet:(set-rein:den ren.req)
=^  m2  ruf  abet:goad:(lu now rof hen ruf)        :: [goad] >
[(weld m1 m2) ..^$]
::
    %stir
?+    arg.req  ~|(%strange-stir !!)
    [%verb @]  [~ ..^$(veb.bug.ruf +.arg.req)]
    [%mass @]  [~ ..^$(mas.bug.ruf +.arg.req)]
    [%goad ~]
```

```
=^  mos  ruf  abet:goad:(lu now rof hen ruf)
[mos ..^$]
  ::
    [%rise =desk =dude:gall on=(unit ?)]
  =^  m1  ruf
    =/  den  ((de now rof hen ruf) our desk.arg.req)
    abet:(rise:den dude.arg.req on.arg.req)
  =^  m2  ruf  abet:goad:(lu now rof hen ruf)          ::  [goad] <
  [(weld m1 m2) ..^$]
  ::
    [%stay =desk ver=(unit weft)]
  =^  moves  ruf
    =/  den  ((de now rof hen ruf) our desk.arg.req)
    abet:(stay:den ver.arg.req)
  [moves ..^$]
  ::
    [%trim ~]
  =:    fad.ruf        *flow
        dos.rom.ruf
      %-  ~(run by dos.rom.ruf)
      |=  =dojo
      dojo(fod.dom *flue)
      ::
        hoy.ruf
      %-  ~(run by hoy.ruf)
      |=  =rung
      %=    rung
          rus
        %-  ~(run by rus.rung)
        |=  =rede
        rede(fod.dom *flue)
      ==
    ==
  [~ ..^$]
  ::
    [%fine ~]
  ~&  "clay: resetting fine state.  old:"
  ~&  sad.ruf
  `..^$(sad.ruf ~)
  ==
::
  %tire
?~  p.req
  =.  tyr.ruf  (~(del in tyr.ruf) hen)
  `..^$
=.  tyr.ruf  (~(put in tyr.ruf) hen)
:_  ..^$
[hen %give %tire %& tore:(lu now rof hen ruf)]~
::
  %tomb  (tomb-clue:tomb hen clue.req)
  %trim  [~ ..^$]
  %vega
::  wake all desks, then send pending notifications
::
=^  wake-moves  ..^$
  =/  desks=(list [=ship =desk])
    %+  welp
      (turn ~(tap by dos.rom.ruf) |=([=desk *] [our desk]))
```

```
5103          %-    zing
5104          %+    turn    ~(tap by hoy.ruf)
5105          |=    [=ship =rung]
5106          %+    turn    ~(tap by rus.rung)
5107          |=    [=desk *]
5108          [ship desk]
5109      |-    ^+    [*(list move) ..^^$]
5110      ?~    desks
5111          [~ ..^^$]
5112      =^    moves-1  ..^^$  $(desks t.desks)
5113      =^    moves-2  ruf  abet:wake:((de now rof hen ruf) [ship desk]:i.desks)
5114      [(weld moves-1 moves-2) ..^^$]
5115    [wake-moves ..^$]
5116  ::
5117      ?(%warp %werp)
5118  ::  capture whether this read is on behalf of another ship
5119  ::  for permissions enforcement
5120  ::
5121  =^  for  req
5122    ?:    ?=(%warp -.req)
5123      [~ req]
5124    ::  ?:  =(our who.req)
5125    ::    [~ [%warp wer.req rif.req]]
5126    :-  ?:(=(our who.req) ~ `[who.req -.rif.req])
5127    [%warp wer.req riff.rif.req]
5128  ::
5129  ?>  ?=(%warp -.req)
5130  =*  rif  rif.req
5131  =^  mos  ruf
5132    =/  den  ((de now rof hen ruf) wer.req p.rif)
5133    =<  abet
5134    ?~  q.rif
5135      cancel-request:den
5136    (start-request:den for u.q.rif)
5137  [mos ..^$]
5138  ::
5139      %wick
5140  =^  mos  ruf
5141    abet:wick:((de now rof hen ruf) our %base)            ::  [wick]
5142  [mos ..^$]
5143  ::
5144      %zeal
5145  =^  m1  ruf
5146    =|  mos=(list move)
5147    |-  ^+  [mos ruf]
5148    ?~  lit.req
5149      [mos ruf]
5150    =/  den  ((de now rof hen ruf) our desk.i.lit.req)
5151    =^  mos-new  ruf  abet:(set-zest:den zest.i.lit.req)
5152    $(mos (weld mos mos-new), lit.req t.lit.req)
5153  =^  m2  ruf
5154    abet:wick:((de now rof hen ruf) our %base)
5155  =^  m3  ruf  abet:goad:(lu now rof hen ruf)
5156  [:(weld m1 m2 m3) ..^$]
5157  ::
5158      %zest
5159  =^  m1  ruf
5160    =/  den  ((de now rof hen ruf) our des.req)
```

```
    ::  [wick] could be suspending the last blocking desk
    ::
    abet:wick:(set-zest:den liv.req)
  =^  m2  ruf  abet:goad:(lu now rof hen ruf)
  [(weld m1 m2) ..^$]
::
    %plea
  =*  her  ship.req
  =*  pax  path.plea.req
  =*  res  payload.plea.req
  ::
  ?:  ?=([%backfill *] pax)
    =+  ;;(=fill res)
    =^  mos  ruf
      =/  den  ((de now rof hen ruf) our desk.fill)
      abet:(give-backfill:den -.fill lobe.fill)
    [[[hen %give %done ~] mos] ..^$]
  ?>  ?=([%question *] pax)
  =+  ryf=;;(riff-any res)
  :_  ..^$
  :~  [hen %give %done ~]
      =/  =wire
        [%foreign-warp (scot %p her) t.pax]
      [hen %pass wire %c %werp her our ryf]
  ==
  ==
::
++  load
  =>  |%
      +$  raft-any
        $%  [%14 raft-14]
            [%13 raft-13]
            [%12 raft-12]
            [%11 raft-11]
            [%10 raft-10]
            [%9 raft-9]
            [%8 raft-8]
            [%7 raft-7]
            [%6 raft-6]
        ==
      ::  We redefine the latest raft with * for the the ford caches.
      ::  +clear-cache upgrades to +raft
      ::
      +$  raft-14
        $+  raft-14
        $:  rom=room-13
            hoy=(map ship rung-14)
            ran=rang
            fad=*
            mon=(map term beam)
            hez=(unit duct)
            cez=(map @ta crew)
            tyr=(set duct)
            tur=rock:tire
            pud=(unit [=desk =yoki])
            sad=(map ship @da)
            bug=[veb=@ mas=@]
        ==
```

```
5219        +$  rung-14
5220          $:  rus=(map desk rede-14)
5221          ==
5222        +$  rede-14
5223          $:  lim=@da
5224              ref=(unit rind-14)
5225              qyx=cult
5226              dom=dome-13
5227              per=regs
5228              pew=regs
5229              fiz=melt
5230          ==
5231        +$  rind-14
5232          $:  nix=@ud
5233              bom=(map @ud update-state)
5234              fod=(map duct @ud)
5235              haw=(map mood (unit cage))
5236          ==
5237        ::
5238        +$  raft-13
5239          $+  raft-13
5240          $:  rom=room-13
5241              hoy=(map ship rung-13)
5242              ran=rang
5243              fad=*
5244              mon=(map term beam)
5245              hez=(unit duct)
5246              cez=(map @ta crew)
5247              tyr=(set duct)
5248              tur=rock:tire
5249              pud=(unit [=desk =yoki])
5250              bug=[veb=@ mas=@]
5251          ==
5252        +$  room-13
5253          $:  hun=duct
5254              dos=(map desk dojo-13)
5255          ==
5256        +$  dojo-13
5257          $:  qyx=cult
5258              dom=dome-13
5259              per=regs
5260              pew=regs
5261              fiz=melt
5262          ==
5263        +$  dome-13
5264          $:  let=aeon
5265              hit=(map aeon tako)
5266              lab=(map @tas aeon)
5267              tom=(map tako norm)
5268              nor=norm
5269              mim=(map path mime)
5270              fod=*
5271              wic=(map weft yoki)
5272              liv=zest
5273              ren=rein
5274          ==
5275        +$  rung-13
5276          $:  rus=(map desk rede-13)
```

```
                ==
        +$  rede-13
          $:  lim=@da
              ref=(unit rind-11)
              qyx=cult
              dom=dome-13
              per=regs
              pew=regs
              fiz=melt
          ==
        ::
        +$  raft-12
          $+  raft-12
          $:  rom=room-11
              hoy=(map ship rung-11)
              ran=rang
              fad=*
              mon=(map term beam)
              hez=(unit duct)
              cez=(map @ta crew)
              pud=(unit [=desk =yoki])
              bug=[veb=@ mas=@]
          ==
        +$  raft-11
          $+  raft-11
          $:  rom=room-11
              hoy=(map ship rung-11)
              ran=rang
              fad=*
              mon=(map term beam)
              hez=(unit duct)
              cez=(map @ta crew)
              pud=(unit [=desk =yoki])
          ==
        +$  room-11
          $+  room-11
          $:  hun=duct
              dos=(map desk dojo-11)
          ==
        +$  dojo-11
          $+  dojo-11
          $:  qyx=cult
              dom=dome-11
              per=regs
              pew=regs
              fiz=melt
          ==
        +$  dome-11
          $+  dome-11
          $:  let=aeon
              hit=(map aeon tako)
              lab=(map @tas aeon)
              tom=(map tako norm)
              nor=norm
              mim=(map path mime)
              fod=*
          ==
        +$  rung-11
```

```
5335        $+  rung-11
5336        $:  rus=(map desk rede-11)
5337        ==
5338    +$  rede-11
5339      $+  rede-11
5340      $:  lim=@da
5341          ref=(unit rind-11)
5342          qyx=cult
5343          dom=dome-11
5344          per=regs
5345          pew=regs
5346          fiz=melt
5347      ==
5348    +$  rind-11
5349      $+  rind-11
5350      $:  nix=@ud
5351          bom=(map @ud update-state-11)
5352          fod=(map duct @ud)
5353          haw=(map mood (unit cage))
5354      ==
5355    +$  update-state-11
5356      $+  update-state-11
5357      $:  =duct
5358          =rave
5359          need=(list lobe)
5360          nako=(qeu (unit nako))
5361          busy=_|
5362      ==
5363    +$  raft-10
5364      $+  raft-10
5365      $:  rom=room-10
5366          hoy=(map ship rung-10)
5367          ran=rang-10
5368          mon=(map term beam)
5369          hez=(unit duct)
5370          cez=(map @ta crew)
5371          pud=(unit [=desk =yoki])
5372          dist-upgraded=_|
5373      ==
5374    +$  rang-10
5375      $:  hut=(map tako yaki)
5376          lat=(map lobe blob-10)
5377      ==
5378    +$  blob-10
5379      $%  [%delta p=lobe q=[p=mark q=lobe] r=page]
5380          [%direct p=lobe q=page]
5381          [%dead p=lobe ~]
5382      ==
5383    +$  room-10
5384      $:  hun=duct
5385          dos=(map desk dojo-10)
5386      ==
5387    +$  dojo-10
5388      $:  qyx=cult-10
5389          dom=dome-10
5390          per=regs
5391          pew=regs
5392          fiz=melt-10
```

```
5393          ==
5394      +$  dome-10
5395        $:  ank=ankh-10
5396            let=aeon
5397            hit=(map aeon tako)
5398            lab=(map @tas aeon)
5399            mim=(map path mime)
5400            fod=*
5401        ==
5402      +$  ankh-10  (axal [p=lobe q=cage])
5403      +$  rung-10
5404        $:  rus=(map desk rede-10)
5405        ==
5406      +$  rede-10
5407        $:  lim=@da
5408            ref=(unit rind-10)
5409            qyx=cult-10
5410            dom=dome-10
5411            per=regs
5412            pew=regs
5413            fiz=melt-10
5414        ==
5415      +$  rind-10
5416        $:  nix=@ud
5417            bom=(map @ud update-state-10)
5418            fod=(map duct @ud)
5419            haw=(map mood (unit cage))
5420        ==
5421      +$  update-state-10
5422        $:  =duct
5423            =rave
5424            have=(map lobe blob-10)
5425            need=(list lobe)
5426            nako=(qeu (unit nako-10))
5427            busy=_|
5428        ==
5429      +$  nako-10
5430        $:  gar=(map aeon tako)
5431            let=aeon
5432            lar=(set yaki)
5433            bar=(set blob-10)
5434        ==
5435      +$  melt-10
5436      [bas=beak con=(list [beak germ]) sto=(map beak (unit dome-clay-10))]
5437      +$  dome-clay-10
5438        $:  ank=ankh-10
5439            let=@ud
5440            hit=(map @ud tako)
5441            lab=(map @tas @ud)
5442        ==
5443      +$  cult-10  (jug wove-10 duct)
5444      +$  wove-10  [for=(unit [=ship ver=@ud]) =rove-10]
5445      +$  rove-10
5446        $%  [%sing =mood]
5447            [%next =mood aeon=(unit aeon) =cach-10]
5448            $:  %mult
5449                =mool
5450                aeon=(unit aeon)
```

```
5451              old-cach=(map [=care =path] cach-10)
5452              new-cach=(map [=care =path] cach-10)
5453          ==
5454          [%many track=? =moat lobes=(map path lobe)]
5455      ==
5456    +$  cach-10  (unit (unit (each cage lobe)))
5457    +$  raft-9
5458      $+  raft-9
5459      $:  rom=room-10
5460          hoy=(map ship rung-10)
5461          ran=rang-10
5462          mon=(map term beam)
5463          hez=(unit duct)
5464          cez=(map @ta crew)
5465          pud=(unit [=desk =yoki])
5466      ==
5467    +$  raft-8
5468      $+  raft-8
5469      $:  rom=room-8
5470          hoy=(map ship rung-8)
5471          ran=rang-10
5472          mon=(map term beam)
5473          hez=(unit duct)
5474          cez=(map @ta crew)
5475          pud=(unit [=desk =yoki])
5476      ==
5477    +$  room-8
5478      $:  hun=duct
5479          dos=(map desk dojo-8)
5480      ==
5481    +$  rung-8
5482      $:  rus=(map desk rede-8)
5483      ==
5484    +$  dojo-8
5485      $:  qyx=cult-10
5486          dom=dome-8
5487          per=regs
5488          pew=regs
5489          fiz=melt-10
5490      ==
5491    +$  dome-8
5492      $:  ank=ankh-10
5493          let=aeon
5494          hit=(map aeon tako)
5495          lab=(map @tas aeon)
5496          mim=(map path mime)
5497          fod=*
5498          fer=*  ::  reef cache, obsolete
5499      ==
5500    +$  rede-8
5501      $:  lim=@da
5502          ref=(unit rind-10)
5503          qyx=cult-10
5504          dom=dome-8
5505          per=regs
5506          pew=regs
5507          fiz=melt-10
5508      ==
```

```
5509      +$  raft-7
5510        $+  raft-7
5511        $:  rom=room-7
5512            hoy=(map ship rung-7)
5513            ran=rang-10
5514            mon=(map term beam)
5515            hez=(unit duct)
5516            cez=(map @ta crew)
5517            pud=(unit [=desk =yoki])
5518        ==
5519      +$  room-7
5520        $:  hun=duct
5521            dos=(map desk dojo-7)
5522        ==
5523      +$  rung-7
5524        $:  rus=(map desk rede-7)
5525        ==
5526      +$  dojo-7
5527        $:  qyx=cult-10
5528            dom=dome-8
5529            per=regs
5530            pew=regs
5531        ==
5532      +$  rede-7
5533        $:  lim=@da
5534            ref=(unit rind-10)
5535            qyx=cult-10
5536            dom=dome-8
5537            per=regs
5538            pew=regs
5539        ==
5540      +$  raft-6
5541        $+  raft-6
5542        $:  rom=room-6
5543            hoy=(map ship rung-6)
5544            ran=rang-10
5545            mon=(map term beam)
5546            hez=(unit duct)
5547            cez=(map @ta crew)
5548            pud=(unit [=desk =yoki])
5549        ==
5550      +$  room-6  [hun=duct dos=(map desk dojo-6)]
5551      +$  dojo-6
5552        $:  qyx=cult-10
5553            dom=dome-6
5554            per=regs
5555            pew=regs
5556        ==
5557      +$  dome-6
5558        $:  ank=ankh-10
5559            let=aeon
5560            hit=(map aeon tako)
5561            lab=(map @tas aeon)
5562            mim=(map path mime)
5563            fod=*
5564            fer=*
5565        ==
5566      +$  rung-6
```

```
      $:  rus=(map desk rede-6)
      ==
    +$  rede-6
      $:  lim=@da
          ref=(unit rind-10)
          qyx=cult-10
          dom=dome-6
          per=regs
          pew=regs
      ==
    --
|=  old=raft-any
|^
=?  old  ?=(%6 -.old)    7+(raft-6-to-7 +.old)
=?  old  ?=(%7 -.old)    8+(raft-7-to-8 +.old)
=?  old  ?=(%8 -.old)    9+(raft-8-to-9 +.old)
=?  old  ?=(%9 -.old)    10+(raft-9-to-10 +.old)
=?  old  ?=(%10 -.old)   11+(raft-10-to-11 +.old)
=?  old  ?=(%11 -.old)   12+(raft-11-to-12 +.old)
=?  old  ?=(%12 -.old)   13+(raft-12-to-13 +.old)
=?  old  ?=(%13 -.old)   14+(raft-13-to-14 +.old)
?>  ?=(%14 -.old)
..^^$(ruf (clear-cache +.old))
::
::  We clear the ford cache so we don't have to know how to upgrade
::  the types, which are complicated and eg contravariant in +hoon.
::  Also, many of the results would be different if zuse is different.
::
++  clear-cache
  |=  raf=raft-14
  ^-  raft
  %=    raf
      fad  *flow
      dos.rom
    %-  ~(run by dos.rom.raf)
    |=  doj=dojo-13
    ^-  dojo
    doj(fod.dom *flue)
  ::
      hoy
    %-  ~(run by hoy.raf)
    |=  =rung-14
    %-  ~(run by rus.rung-14)
    |=  =rede-14
    ^-  rede
    rede-14(dom dom.rede-14(fod *flue))
  ==
::  +raft-6-to-7: delete stale ford caches (they could all be invalid)
::
++  raft-6-to-7
  |=  raf=raft-6
  ^-  raft-7
  %=    raf
      dos.rom
    %-  ~(run by dos.rom.raf)
    |=  doj=dojo-6
    ^-  dojo-7
    doj(fod.dom **)
```

```
    ::
        hoy
    %-  ~(run by hoy.raf)
    |=  =rung-6
    %-  ~(run by rus.rung-6)
    |=  =rede-6
    rede-6(dom dom.rede-6(fod **))
  ==
::  +raft-7-to-8: create bunted melts in each dojo/rede
::
++  raft-7-to-8
  |=  raf=raft-7
  ^-  raft-8
  %=    raf
      dos.rom
    %-  ~(run by dos.rom.raf)
    |=  doj=dojo-7
    ^-  dojo-8
    [qyx.doj dom.doj per.doj pew.doj *melt-10]
    ::
        hoy
    %-  ~(run by hoy.raf)
    |=  =rung-7
    %-  ~(run by rus.rung-7)
    |=  r=rede-7
    ^-  rede-8
    [lim.r ref.r qyx.r dom.r per.r pew.r *melt-10]
  ==
::  +raft-8-to-9: remove reef cache
::
++  raft-8-to-9
  |=  raf=raft-8
  ^-  raft-9
  %=    raf
      dos.rom
    %-  ~(run by dos.rom.raf)
    |=  =dojo-8
    ^-  dojo-10
    =/  dom  dom.dojo-8
    dojo-8(dom [ank.dom let.dom hit.dom lab.dom mim.dom *flow])
    ::
        hoy
    %-  ~(run by hoy.raf)
    |=  =rung-8
    %-  ~(run by rus.rung-8)
    |=  =rede-8
    ^-  rede-10
    =/  dom  dom.rede-8
    rede-8(dom [ank.dom let.dom hit.dom lab.dom mim.dom *flow])
  ==
::  +raft-9-to-10: add .dist-upgraded
::
++  raft-9-to-10
  |=  raf=raft-9
  ^-  raft-10
  raf(pud [pud.raf dist-upgraded=|])
::
::  +raft-10-to-11:
```

```
5683      ::
5684      ::    add tom and nor to dome
5685      ::    remove parent-mark from delta blobs
5686      ::    change blobs to pages
5687      ::    remove have from update-state
5688      ::    remove bar from nako
5689      ::    remove ankh
5690      ::    set cases in mon to ud+0
5691      ::    add fad
5692      ::    change fod type in dom
5693      ::    change bom type in dom
5694      ::
5695      ++  raft-10-to-11
5696        |=  raf=raft-10
5697        |^
5698        ^-  raft-11
5699        %=    raf
5700          dos.rom
5701        %-  ~(run by dos.rom.raf)
5702        |=  =dojo-10
5703        ^-  dojo-11
5704        %=    dojo-10
5705          fiz  *melt
5706          qyx  (cult-10-to-cult qyx.dojo-10)
5707          dom
5708        :*  let.dom.dojo-10
5709            hit.dom.dojo-10
5710            lab.dom.dojo-10
5711            ~
5712            *norm
5713            mim.dom.dojo-10
5714            [~ ~]
5715        ==
5716      ==
5717      ::
5718          hoy
5719        %-  ~(run by hoy.raf)
5720        |=  =rung-10
5721        %-  ~(run by rus.rung-10)
5722        |=  =rede-10
5723        ^-  rede-11
5724        %=    rede-10
5725          fiz     *melt
5726          qyx     (cult-10-to-cult qyx.rede-10)
5727          dom
5728        :*  let.dom.rede-10
5729            hit.dom.rede-10
5730            lab.dom.rede-10
5731            ~
5732            *norm
5733            mim.dom.rede-10
5734            [~ ~]
5735        ==
5736      ::
5737            ref
5738        ?~  ref.rede-10
5739            ~
5740        %=     ref.rede-10
```

```
            bom.u
    %-  ~(run by bom.u.ref.rede-10)
    |=  =update-state-10
    ^-  update-state-11
    %=    update-state-10
        |2
      ^-  [(list lobe) (qeu (unit nako)) _|]
      %=    |3.update-state-10
          nako
        %-  ~(gas to *(qeu (unit nako)))
        %+  turn  ~(tap to nako.update-state-10)
        |=  nak=(unit nako-10)
        ?~  nak  ~
        `u.nak(bar ~)
      ==
    ==
  ==
  ==
  ::
    lat.ran
  %-  ~(gas by *(map lobe page))
  %+  murn  ~(tap by lat.ran.raf)
  |=  [=lobe =blob-10]
  ^-  (unit [^lobe page])
  ?-  -.blob-10
    %delta   ((slog 'clay: tombstoning delta!' ~) ~)
    %dead    ~
    %direct  `[lobe q.blob-10]
  ==
  ::
    |3
  ^+  |3:*raft-11
  :-  *flow
  %=  |3.raf
    mon  (~(run by mon.raf) |=(=beam beam(r ud+0)))
    |3   pud.raf
  ==
==
::
++  cult-10-to-cult
  |=  qyx=cult-10
  ^-  cult
  =/  qux=(list [=wove-10 ducts=(set duct)])  ~(tap by qyx)
  %-  malt
  |-  ^-  (list [wove (set duct)])
  ?~  qux
    ~
  :_  $(qux t.qux)
  %=    i.qux
      rove-10.wove-10
    ?-    -.rove-10.wove-10.i.qux
      %sing  rove-10.wove-10.i.qux
      %many  rove-10.wove-10.i.qux
      %next
    %=  rove-10.wove-10.i.qux
      cach-10  (cach-10-to-cach cach-10.rove-10.wove-10.i.qux)
    ==
    ::
```

```
5799              %mult
5800          %=  rove-10.wove-10.i.qux
5801            old-cach  (caches-10-to-caches old-cach.rove-10.wove-10.i.qux)
5802            new-cach  (caches-10-to-caches new-cach.rove-10.wove-10.i.qux)
5803            ==
5804        ==
5805      ==
5806    ::
5807    ++  cach-10-to-cach
5808      |=  =cach-10
5809      ^-  cach
5810      ?~  cach-10
5811        ~
5812      ?~  u.cach-10
5813        [~ ~]
5814      ?-  -.u.u.cach-10
5815        %&  ``p.u.u.cach-10
5816        %|  ~
5817      ==
5818    ::
5819    ++  caches-10-to-caches
5820      |=  caches-10=(map [=care =path] cach-10)
5821      ^-  (map [=care =path] cach)
5822      (~(run by caches-10) cach-10-to-cach)
5823    --
5824  ::  +raft-11-to-12: add bug
5825  ::
5826  ++  raft-11-to-12
5827    |=  raf=raft-11
5828    ^-  raft-12
5829    raf(pud [pud.raf 0 0])
5830  ::  +raft-12-to-13:
5831  ::
5832  ::    add .liv and .ren to $dome's
5833  ::    add .tyr and .tur to $raft
5834  ::
5835  ++  raft-12-to-13
5836    |=  raf=raft-12
5837    |^  ^-  raft-13
5838    ::  turn on %base desk  ::  TODO handle other desks somehow
5839    ::                      ::  maybe have kiln send one-time list of desks
5840    ::
5841    =;  rof
5842      rof(dos.rom (~(jab by dos.rom.rof) %base |=(d=dojo-13 d(liv.dom %live))))
5843    ^-  raft-13
5844    %=  raf
5845      dos.rom  (~(run by dos.rom.raf) dojo-11-to-13)
5846      hoy      (~(run by hoy.raf) rung-11-to-13)
5847      |6       [&7.raf ~ ~ |7.raf]
5848    ==
5849    ::
5850    ++  dojo-11-to-13
5851      |=  doj=dojo-11
5852      ^-  dojo-13
5853      doj(dom (dome-11-to-13 dom.doj))
5854    ::
5855    ++  rung-11-to-13
5856      |=  rug=rung-11
```

```
5857        ^-    rung-13
5858        rug(rus (~(run by rus.rug) rede-11-to-13))
5859      ::
5860    ++  rede-11-to-13
5861      |=  red=rede-11
5862      ^-  rede-13
5863      red(dom (dome-11-to-13 dom.red))
5864      ::
5865    ++  dome-11-to-13
5866      |=  dom=dome-11
5867      ^-  dome-13
5868      dom(fod [fod.dom ~ liv=%dead ren=~])
5869      --
5870    ::
5871    ::  +raft-13-to-14: add sad, change busy
5872    ::
5873    ++  raft-13-to-14
5874      |=  raf=raft-13
5875      ^-  raft-14
5876      %=    raf
5877        bug   [~ bug.raf]
5878      ::
5879          hoy
5880      %-  ~(run by hoy.raf)
5881      |=  =rung-13
5882      %-  ~(run by rus.rung-13)
5883      |=  =rede-13
5884      ^-  rede-14
5885      %=    rede-13
5886          ref
5887        ?~  ref.rede-13
5888          ~
5889        %=    ref.rede-13
5890            bom.u
5891          %-  ~(run by bom.u.ref.rede-13)
5892          |=  update-state-11
5893          ^-  update-state
5894          =/  busy  ?:(busy `%ames ~)
5895          [duct rave ~ need nako busy]
5896        ==
5897      ==
5898    ==
5899    --
5900    ::
5901    ++  scry                                  ::  inspect
5902    ~/  %clay-scry
5903    ^-  roon
5904    |=  [lyc=gang pov=path car=term bem=beam]
5905    ^-  (unit (unit cage))
5906    =*  scry-loop  $
5907    |^
5908    =*  ren  car
5909    =/  why=shop  &/p.bem
5910    =*  syd  q.bem
5911    =/  lot=coin  $/r.bem
5912    =*  tyl  s.bem
5913    ::
5914    ?.  ?=(%& -.why)  ~
```

```
5915    =*  his  p.why
5916    ::
5917    ?:  &(?=(%x ren) =(tyl //whey))
5918      ``mass+!>(whey)
5919    ::
5920    ::  ~&  scry+[ren `path`[(scot %p his) syd ~(rent co lot) tyl]]
5921    ::  =-  ~&  %scry-done  -
5922    =+  luk=?.(?=(%$ -.lot) ~ ((soft case) p.lot))
5923    ?~  luk  [~ ~]
5924    ?:  =(%$ ren)
5925      [~ ~]
5926    =+  run=((soft care) ren)
5927    ?~  run  [~ ~]
5928    ::TODO  if it ever gets filled properly, pass in the full fur.
5929    ::
5930    =/  for=(unit ship)  ?~(lyc ~ ?~(u.lyc ~ `n.u.lyc))
5931    ?:  &(=(our his) ?=(?(%d %x) ren) =(%$ syd) =([%da now] u.luk))
5932      ?.  =([~ ~] lyc)  ~
5933      ?-  ren
5934        %d  (read-buc-d tyl)
5935        %x  (read-buc-x tyl)
5936      ==
5937    =/  den  ((de now rof [/scryduct ~] ruf) his syd)
5938    =/  result  (mule |.(-:(aver:den for u.run u.luk tyl)))
5939    ?:  ?=(%| -.result)
5940      %-  (slog >%clay-scry-fail< p.result)
5941      ~
5942    p.result
5943    ::
5944    ++  read-buc-d
5945      |=  =path
5946      ^-  (unit (unit cage))
5947      ?^  path  ~&(%no-cd-path [~ ~])
5948      [~ ~ %noun !>(~(key by dos.rom.ruf))]
5949    ::
5950    ++  read-buc-x
5951      |=  =path
5952      ^-  (unit (unit cage))
5953      ?~  path
5954        ~
5955      ?+    i.path  ~
5956        %sweep   ``[%sweep !>(sweep)]
5957        %rang    ``[%rang !>(ran.ruf)]
5958        %tomb    ``[%flag !>((tomb t.path))]
5959        %cult    ``[%cult !>((cult t.path))]
5960        %flow    ``[%flow !>(fad.ruf)]
5961        %domes   domes
5962        %tire    ``[%tire !>(tore:(lu now rof *duct ruf))]
5963        %tyre    ``[%tyre !>(tyr.ruf)]
5964      ==
5965    ::
5966    ++  domes
5967      =/  domes
5968        %-  ~(gas by *cone)
5969        %+  turn  ~(tap by dos.rom.ruf)
5970        |=  [=desk =dojo]
5971        [[our desk] dom.dojo]
5972      =.  domes
```

```
%-  ~(uni by domes)
%-  ~(gas by *cone)
^-  (list [[ship desk] dome])
%-  zing
^-  (list (list [[ship desk] dome]))
%+  turn  ~(tap by hoy.ruf)
|=  [=ship =rung]
^-  (list [[^ship desk] dome])
%+  turn  ~(tap by rus.rung)
|=  [=desk =rede]
[[ship desk] dom.rede]
``[%domes !>(`cone`domes)]
::
++  cult
  |=  =path
  ^-  (set [@p rave])
%-  %~  run  in
    %~  key  by
    ?~  path  *^cult
    qyx:(~(gut by dos.rom.ruf) i.path *dojo)
  |=  wove
  :-  ship:(fall for [ship=our @ud])
  ?-  -.rove
    %sing  rove
    %next  [%next mood.rove]
    %mult  [%mult mool.rove]
    %many  [%many [track moat]:rove]
  ==
::
:: True if file is accessible
::
++  tomb
  |=  =path
  ^-  ?
  =/  bem  (de-beam path)
  ?~  bem        %|
  =/  cay  scry-loop(car %y, bem u.bem)
  ?~  cay        %|
  ?~  u.cay      %|
  =+  !<(=arch q.u.u.cay)
  ?~  fil.arch   %|
  (~(has by lat.ran.ruf) u.fil.arch)
::
:: Check for refcount errors
::
++  sweep
  ^-  (list [need=@ud have=@ud leak])
  =/  marked=(map leak [need=@ud have=@ud])
    (~(run by fad.ruf) |=([refs=@ud *] [0 refs]))
  =.  marked
    =/  items=(list [=leak *])  ~(tap by fad.ruf)
    |-  ^+  marked
    ?~  items
      marked
    =/  deps  ~(tap in deps.leak.i.items)
    |-  ^+  marked
    ?~  deps
      ^$(items t.items)
```

```
=.  marked
  %+  ~(put by marked)  i.deps
  =/  gut  (~(gut by marked) i.deps [0 0])
  [+(-.gut) +.gut]
$(deps t.deps)
::
=/  spills=(list (set leak))
  %+  welp
    %+  turn  ~(tap by dos.rom.ruf)
    |=  [* =dojo]
    spill.fod.dom.dojo
  %-  zing
  %+  turn  ~(tap by hoy.ruf)
  |=  [* =rung]
  %+  turn  ~(tap by rus.rung)
  |=  [* =rede]
  spill.fod.dom.rede
::
=.  marked
  |-
  ?~  spills
    marked
  =/  leaks  ~(tap in i.spills)
  |-
  ?~  leaks
    ^$(spills t.spills)
  =.  marked
    %+  ~(put by marked)  i.leaks
    =/  gut  (~(gut by marked) i.leaks [0 0])
    [+(-.gut) +.gut]
  $(leaks t.leaks)
::
%+  murn  ~(tap by marked)
|=  [=leak need=@ud have=@ud]
?:  =(need have)
  ~
`u=[need have leak]
--
::
:: We clear the ford cache by replacing it with its bunt as a literal,
:: with its singleton type.  This nests within +flow and +flue without
:: reference to +type, +hoon, or anything else in the sample of cache
:: objects.  Otherwise we would be contravariant in those types, which
:: makes them harder to change.
::
++  stay
  ^-  raft-any:load
  =/  flu  [~ ~]
  =+  `flue`flu
  =/  flo  ~
  =+  `flow`flo
  :-  ver
  ^-  raft-14:load
  %=    ruf
      fad  flo
      dos.rom
    %-  ~(run by dos.rom.ruf)
    |=  =dojo
```

```
      dojo(fod.dom flu)
    ::
        hoy
      %-  ~(run by hoy.ruf)
      |=  =rung
      %=    rung
          rus
      %-  ~(run by rus.rung)
      |=  =rede
      rede(fod.dom flu)
      ==
    ==
  ::
++  take                                        ::  accept response
  ~/  %clay-take
  |=  [tea=wire hen=duct dud=(unit goof) hin=sign]
  ^+  [*(list move) ..^$]
  ?^  dud
    ?+    tea
      ~|(%clay-take-dud (mean tang.u.dud))
    ::
        [%drip ~]
      %.  [~ ..^$]
      %-  slog
      ^-  tang
      :*  'clay: drip fail'
          [%rose [": " "" ""] 'bail' mote.u.dud ~]
          tang.u.dud
      ==
    ==
  ::
  ::  pseudo %slip on %drip
  ::
  ?:  ?=([%drip ~] tea)
    ?>  ?=([?(%behn %clay) ?(%writ %wris) *] hin)
    [[`move`[hen %give +.hin] ~] ..^$]
  ::
  ?:  ?=([%lu %load *] tea)
    ?>  ?=(%unto +<.hin)
    ?>  ?=(%poke-ack -.p.hin)
    ?~  p.p.hin
      [~ ..^$]
    =+  ((slog 'clay: reloading agents failed' u.p.p.hin) ~)
    !!
  ::
  ?:  ?=([%merge @ @ @ @ ~] tea)
    ?>  ?=(%writ +<.hin)
    =*  syd  i.t.tea
    =/  ali-ship  (slav %p i.t.t.tea)
    =*  ali-desk  i.t.t.t.tea
    =/  germ  (germ i.t.t.t.t.tea)
    =^  mos  ruf
      =/  den  ((de now rof hen ruf) our syd)
      abet:(merge:den ali-ship ali-desk germ p.hin)
    [mos ..^$]
  ::
  ?:  ?=([%fuse @ @ @ @ ~] tea)
    ?>  ?=(%writ +<.hin)
```

```hoon
6147      =*  syd  i.t.tea
6148      =/  ali-ship=@p  (slav %p i.t.t.tea)
6149      =*  ali-desk=desk  i.t.t.t.tea
6150      =/  ali-case  (rash i.t.t.t.t.tea nuck:so)
6151      ?>  ?=([%$ *] ali-case)
6152      =^  mos  ruf
6153        =/  den  ((de now rof hen ruf) our syd)
6154        abet:(take-fuse:den [ali-ship ali-desk (case +.ali-case)] p.hin)
6155      [mos ..^$]
6156    ::
6157    ?:  ?=([%park-held @ ~] tea)
6158      ?>  ?=(%wake +<.hin)
6159      =*  syd  i.t.tea
6160      =^  mos  ruf
6161        =/  den  ((de now rof hen ruf) our syd)
6162        abet:(take-park-held:den error.hin)
6163      [mos ..^$]
6164    ::
6165    ?:  ?=([%wick ~] tea)
6166      ?>  ?=(%wake +<.hin)
6167      =^  mos  ruf
6168        =/  den  ((de now rof hen ruf) our %base)
6169        abet:(take-wick:den error.hin)
6170      [mos ..^$]
6171    ::
6172    ?:  ?=([%foreign-warp *] tea)
6173      ?:  ?=(%wris +<.hin)  ~&  %dropping-wris  `..^$
6174      ?>  ?=(%writ +<.hin)
6175      :_  ..^$
6176      [hen %give %boon `(unit rand)`(bind `riot`p.hin rant-to-rand)]~
6177    ::
6178    ?:  ?=([%warp-index @ @ @ ~] tea)
6179      ?+    +<.hin  ~|  %clay-warp-index-strange  !!
6180          %done
6181        ?~  error.hin
6182          [~ ..^$]
6183        ::  TODO better error handling
6184        ::
6185        ~&  %clay-take-warp-index-error^our^tea^tag.u.error.hin
6186        %-  (slog tang.u.error.hin)
6187        [~ ..^$]
6188      ::
6189          %lost
6190        %-  (slog leaf+"clay: lost warp from {<tea>}" ~)
6191        [~ ..^$]
6192      ::
6193          %boon
6194      =/  her=ship  (slav %p i.t.tea)
6195      =/  =desk     (slav %tas i.t.t.tea)
6196      =/  index=@ud  (slav %ud i.t.t.t.tea)
6197      ::
6198      =^  mos  ruf
6199        =+  ;;(res=(unit rand) payload.hin)
6200        =/  den  ((de now rof hen ruf) her desk)
6201        abet:(take-foreign-answer:den index res)
6202      [mos ..^$]
6203      ==
6204    ::
```

```
?:  ?=([%back-index @ @ @ *] tea)
  ?+    +<.hin  ~|  %clay-backfill-index-strange  !!
      %done
    ?~  error.hin
      [~ ..^$]
    ::  TODO better error handling
    ::
    ~&  %clay-take-backfill-index-error^our^tea^tag.u.error.hin
    %-  (slog tang.u.error.hin)
    [~ ..^$]
  ::
      %lost
    %-  (slog leaf+"clay: lost backfill from {<tea>}" ~)
    [~ ..^$]
  ::
      ?(%boon %tune)
    =/  her=ship    (slav %p i.t.tea)
    =/  =desk       (slav %tas i.t.t.tea)
    =/  index=@ud   (slav %ud i.t.t.t.tea)
    ::
    =/  fell=(unit fell)
      ?:  ?=(%boon +<.hin)  `;;(fell payload.hin)
      ?~  roar.hin  ~
      ?~  q.dat.u.roar.hin  ~
      `[%1 `u.q.dat.u.roar.hin]
    ::
    =^  mos  ruf
      =/  den  ((de now rof hen ruf) her desk)
      ?~  fell
        ::  We shouldn't get back null on any of the fine requests we
        ::  make unless they're out of date
        ::
        %-  (slog leaf+"clay: got null from {<her>}, falling back to ames" ~)
        abet:(retry-with-ames:den %back-index index)
      =?  den  ?=(%tune +<.hin)
        (cancel-scry-timeout:den index)
      abet:abet:(take-backfill:(foreign-update:den index) u.fell)
    [mos ..^$]
  ::
      %wake
    ?^  error.hin
      [[hen %slip %d %flog %crud %wake u.error.hin]~ ..^$]
    =/  her=ship    (slav %p i.t.tea)
    =/  =desk       (slav %tas i.t.t.tea)
    =/  index=@ud   (slav %ud i.t.t.t.tea)
    =^  mos  ruf
      =/  den  ((de now rof hen ruf) her desk)
      abet:(retry-with-ames:den %back-index index)
    [mos ..^$]
  ==
::
?:  ?=([%seek @ @ ~] tea)
  ?+    +<.hin  ~|  %clay-seek-strange  !!
      %done
    ?~  error.hin
      [~ ..^$]
    %-  (slog leaf+"clay: seek nack from {<tea>}" u.error.hin)
    [~ ..^$]
```

```
6263      ::
6264          %lost
6265        %-  (slog leaf+"clay: lost boon from {<tea>}" ~)
6266        [~ ..^$]
6267      ::
6268          %boon
6269        =+  ;;  =fell  payload.hin
6270        ::
6271        =/  her=ship  (slav %p i.t.tea)
6272        =/  =desk     (slav %tas i.t.t.tea)
6273        =^  mos  ruf
6274          =/  den  ((de now rof hen ruf) her desk)
6275          abet:(take-fell:den fell)
6276        [mos ..^$]
6277      ==
6278    ::
6279    ?:  ?=([%sinks ~] tea)
6280      ?>  ?=(%public-keys +<.hin)
6281      ?.  ?=(%breach -.public-keys-result.hin)
6282        [~ ..^$]
6283      =/  who  who.public-keys-result.hin
6284      ?:  =(our who)
6285        [~ ..^$]
6286      ::  Cancel subscriptions
6287      ::
6288      =/  foreign-desk=(unit rung)
6289        (~(get by hoy.ruf) who)
6290      ?~  foreign-desk
6291        [~ ..^$]
6292      =/  cancel-ducts=(list duct)
6293        %-  zing  ^-  (list (list duct))
6294        %+  turn  ~(tap by rus.u.foreign-desk)
6295        |=  [=desk =rede]
6296        ^-  (list duct)  %-  zing  ^-  (list (list duct))
6297        %+  turn  ~(tap by qyx.rede)
6298        |=  [=wove ducts=(set duct)]
6299        ::  ~&  [%sunk-wove desk (print-wove wove) ducts]
6300        ~(tap in ducts)
6301      =/  cancel-moves=(list move)
6302        %+  turn  cancel-ducts
6303        |=(=duct [duct %pass /drip %b %drip !>([%writ ~])])
6304      ::  delete local state of foreign desk
6305      ::
6306      =.  hoy.ruf  (~(del by hoy.ruf) who)
6307      [cancel-moves ..^$]
6308    ::
6309    ?-    -.+.hin
6310        %public-keys  ~|([%public-keys-raw tea] !!)
6311      ::
6312          %mere
6313      ?:  ?=(%& -.p.+.hin)
6314        ~&  'initial merge succeeded'
6315        [~ ..^$]
6316      ~>  %slog.
6317        :^  0  %rose  [" " "[" "]"]
6318        :^    leaf+"initial merge failed"
6319            leaf+"my most sincere apologies"
6320          >p.p.p.+.hin<
```

```
        q.p.p.+.hin
      [~ ..^$]
    ::
        %wake
      ::  TODO: handle behn errors
      ::
      ?^  error.hin
        [[hen %slip %d %flog %crud %wake u.error.hin]~ ..^$]
      ::
      ?.  ?=([%tyme @ @ ~] tea)
        ~&  [%clay-strange-timer tea]
        [~ ..^$]
      ::  [wake] when requested time passes, call +wake
      ::
      =/  her  (slav %p i.t.tea)
      =/  syd  (slav %tas i.t.t.tea)
      =^  mos  ruf
        =/  den  ((de now rof hen ruf) her syd)
        abet:wake:den
      [mos ..^$]
    ::
        ::  handled in the wire dispatcher
        ::
        %boon  !!
        %tune  !!
        %lost  !!
        %unto  !!
        %wris  ~&  %strange-wris  !!
        %writ
      %-  (slog leaf+"clay: strange writ (expected on upgrade to Fusion)" ~)
      [~ ..^$]
    ::
        %done
      ?~  error=error.hin
        [~ ..^$]
      %-  (slog >%clay-lost< >tag.u.error< tang.u.error)
      [~ ..^$]
    ==
  ::
  ++  rant-to-rand
    |=  rant
    ^-  rand
    [p q [p q.q]:r]
  ::  +whey: produce memory usage report
  ::
  ++  whey
    ^-  (list mass)
    ?:  (gth mas.bug.ruf 0)
      =/  domestic
        %+  turn  (sort ~(tap by dos.rom.ruf) aor)
        |=  [=desk =dojo]
        :+  desk  %|
        :~  mime+&+mim.dom.dojo
            flue+&+fod.dom.dojo
            dojo+&+dojo
        ==
      :~  :+  %object-store  %|
          :~  commits+&+hut.ran.ruf
```

```
6379                :+  %pages  %|
6380                %+  turn  ~(tap by lat.ran.ruf)
6381                |=  [=lobe =page]
6382                [(scot %uv lobe) %& page]
6383            ==
6384          domestic+|+domestic
6385          foreign+&+hoy.ruf
6386          ford-cache+&+fad.ruf
6387        ==
6388      =/  domestic
6389      %+  turn  (sort ~(tap by dos.rom.ruf) aor)
6390      |=  [=desk =dojo]
6391      :+  desk  %|
6392      :~  mime+&+mim.dom.dojo
6393          flue+&+fod.dom.dojo
6394          dojo+&+dojo
6395        ==
6396    :~  :+  %object-store  %|
6397        :~  commits+&+hut.ran.ruf
6398            pages+&+lat.ran.ruf
6399          ==
6400        domestic+|+domestic
6401        foreign+&+hoy.ruf
6402        ford-cache+&+fad.ruf
6403      ==
6404  ::
6405  ++  tomb
6406    |%
6407    ::  +tomb-clue: safely remove objects
6408    ::
6409    ++  tomb-clue
6410      |=  [=duct =clue]
6411      ^-  [(list move) _..^$]
6412      ?-    -.clue
6413          %lobe  `(tomb-lobe lobe.clue &)
6414          %all
6415        =/  lobes=(list [=lobe =page])  ~(tap by lat.ran.ruf)
6416        |-
6417        ?~  lobes
6418          `..^^$
6419        =.  ..^^$  (tomb-lobe lobe.i.lobes &)
6420        $(lobes t.lobes)
6421      ::
6422          %pick  pick
6423          %norm
6424        =^  mos  ruf
6425          =/  den  ((de now rof duct ruf) ship.clue desk.clue)
6426          abet:(set-norm:den norm.clue)
6427        [mos ..^$]
6428      ::
6429          %worn
6430        =^  mos  ruf
6431          =/  den  ((de now rof duct ruf) ship.clue desk.clue)
6432          abet:(set-worn:den tako.clue norm.clue)
6433        [mos ..^$]
6434      ::
6435          %seek
6436        =^  mos  ruf
```

```
6437        =/  den   ((de now rof duct ruf) ship.clue desk.clue)
6438        abet:(seek:den cash.clue)
6439      [mos ..^$]
6440    ==
6441  ::  +tomb-lobe: remove specific lobe
6442  ::
6443  ++  tomb-lobe
6444    |=  [lob=lobe veb=?]
6445    ^+  ..^$
6446    =/  peg=(unit page)  (~(get by lat.ran.ruf) lob)
6447    ?~  peg
6448      (noop veb leaf+"clay: file already tombstoned" ~)
6449    ::
6450    =/  used=(unit beam)
6451      =/  desks=(list [=desk =dojo])  ~(tap by dos.rom.ruf)
6452      |-
6453      =*  desk-loop  $
6454      ?~  desks
6455        ~
6456      ?:  =(0 let.dom.dojo.i.desks)
6457        desk-loop(desks t.desks)
6458      =/  =yaki
6459        %-  ~(got by hut.ran.ruf)
6460        %-  ~(got by hit.dom.dojo.i.desks)
6461        let.dom.dojo.i.desks
6462      =/  paths=(list [=path =lobe])  ~(tap by q.yaki)
6463      |-
6464      =*  path-loop  $
6465      ?~  paths
6466        desk-loop(desks t.desks)
6467      ?:  =(lob lobe.i.paths)
6468        `[[our desk.i.desks ud+let.dom.dojo.i.desks] path.i.paths]
6469      path-loop(paths t.paths)
6470    ::
6471    ?^  used
6472      (noop veb leaf+"clay: file used in {<(en-beam u.used)>}" ~)
6473    ::
6474    =.  lat.ran.ruf  (~(del by lat.ran.ruf) lob)
6475    (noop veb leaf+"clay: file successfully tombstoned" ~)
6476  ::
6477  ++  noop
6478    |=  [veb=? =tang]
6479    ?.  veb
6480      ..^$
6481    ((slog tang) ..^$)
6482  ::
6483  ++  draw-raft
6484    ^-  (set [norm yaki])
6485    =/  room-yakis
6486      =/  rooms=(list [=desk =dojo])  ~(tap by dos.rom.ruf)
6487      |-  ^-  (set [norm yaki])
6488      ?~  rooms
6489        ~
6490      (~(uni in $(rooms t.rooms)) (draw-dome %& dom.dojo.i.rooms))
6491    =/  rung-yakis
6492      =/  rungs=(list [=ship =rung])  ~(tap by hoy.ruf)
6493      |-  ^-  (set [norm yaki])
6494      ?~  rungs
```

```
6495          ~
6496          %-  ~(uni in $(rungs t.rungs))
6497          =/  redes=(list [=desk =rede])  ~(tap by rus.rung.i.rungs)
6498          |-  ^-  (set [norm yaki])
6499          ?~  redes
6500            ~
6501          (~(uni in $(redes t.redes)) (draw-dome %| dom.rede.i.redes))
6502        (~(uni in room-yakis) rung-yakis)
6503      ::
6504      ++  draw-dome
6505        |=  [domestic=? =dome]
6506        ^-  (set [norm yaki])
6507        =/  =aeon  1
6508        |-  ^-  (set [norm yaki])
6509        ?:  (lth let.dome aeon)
6510          ~
6511        =/  =tako  (~(got by hit.dome) aeon)
6512        =/  yakis=(set [norm yaki])
6513          ?.  &(=(let.dome aeon) domestic)
6514            ~
6515          [[*norm (~(got by hut.ran.ruf) tako)] ~ ~]
6516        %-  ~(uni in yakis)
6517        %-  ~(uni in (draw-tako tom.dome nor.dome tako))
6518        $(aeon +(aeon))
6519      ::
6520      ++  draw-tako
6521        |=  [tom=(map tako norm) nor=norm =tako]
6522        ^-  (set [norm yaki])
6523        ~+
6524        =/  =norm  (~(gut by tom) tako nor)
6525        =/  =yaki  (~(got by hut.ran.ruf) tako)
6526        =/  takos
6527          |-  ^-  (set [^norm ^yaki])
6528          ?~  p.yaki
6529            ~
6530          (~(uni in $(p.yaki t.p.yaki)) ^$(tako i.p.yaki))
6531        (~(put in takos) norm yaki)
6532      ::
6533      ::  +pick: copying gc based on norms
6534      ::
6535      ++  pick
6536        =|  lat=(map lobe page)
6537        =|  sen=(set [norm (map path lobe)])
6538        |^
6539        =.  ..pick-raft  pick-raft
6540        =.  lat.ran.ruf  lat
6541        `..^$
6542        ::
6543        ++  pick-raft
6544          ^+  ..pick-raft
6545          =/  yakis=(list [=norm =yaki])  ~(tap in draw-raft)
6546          |-  ^+  ..pick-raft
6547          ?~  yakis
6548            ..pick-raft
6549          ::  ~&  >  [%picking [norm r.yaki]:i.yakis]
6550          $(yakis t.yakis, ..pick-raft (pick-yaki i.yakis))
6551        ::
6552        ::  NB: recurring tree-wise with the `sen` cache provides
```

```
::  approximately a 100x speedup on a mainnet moon in 4/2022
::
++  pick-yaki
  |=  [=norm =yaki]
  ^+  ..pick-raft
  |-  ^+  ..pick-raft
  ?~  q.yaki
    ..pick-raft
  ?:  (~(has in sen) norm q.yaki)
    ..pick-raft
  =.  sen  (~(put in sen) norm q.yaki)
  =/  peg=(unit page)  (~(get by lat.ran.ruf) q.n.q.yaki)
  ::  ~&  >>  [%picking-lobe ?=(^ peg) +:(~(fit of norm) p.n.q.yaki) n.q.yaki]
  =?  lat  &(?=(^ peg) !=([~ %|] +:(~(fit of norm) p.n.q.yaki)))
    (~(uni by `(map lobe page)`[[q.n.q.yaki u.peg] ~ ~]) lat)
  =.  ..pick-raft  $(q.yaki l.q.yaki)
  $(q.yaki r.q.yaki)
  --
--
--
```

Dill

```
!:
:: dill (4d), terminal handling
::
|=  our=ship
=,  dill
=>  |%                                        :: interface tiles
+$  gill  (pair ship term)                    :: general contact
--                                            ::
=>  |%                                        :: console protocol
+$  axle                                      ::
  $:  %7                                      ::
      hey=(unit duct)                         :: default duct
      dug=(map @tas axon)                     :: conversations
      eye=(jug @tas duct)                     :: outside observers
      ear=(set duct)                          :: syslog listeners
      lit=?                                   :: boot in lite mode
      egg=_|                                  :: see +take, removeme
  ==                                          ::
+$  axon                                      :: dill session
  $:  ram=term                                :: console program
      tem=(unit (list dill-belt))             :: pending, reverse
      wid=_80                                 :: terminal width
  ==                                          ::
+$  log-level  ?(%hush %soft %loud)           :: none, line, full
--  =>                                        ::
|%                                            :: protocol outward
+$  mess                                      ::
  $%  [%dill-poke p=(hypo poke)]              ::
  ==                                          ::
+$  move  [p=duct q=(wind note gift)]         :: local move
+$  note                                      :: out request $->
  $~  [%d %verb ~]                            ::
  $%  $:  %$                                  ::
          $>(?(%verb %whey) waif)             ::
      ==                                      ::
      $:  %c                                  ::
          $>  $?  %merg                       :: merge desks
                  %perm                       :: change permissions
                  %warp                       :: wait for clay hack
                  %zest                       ::
              ==                              ::
          task:clay                           ::
      ==                                      ::
      $:  %d                                  ::
          $>  $?  %crud                       ::
                  %heft                       ::
                  %text                       ::
                  %verb                       ::
              ==                              ::
          task:dill                           ::
      ==                                      ::
      $:  %g                                  ::
          $>(%deal task:gall)                 ::
      ==                                      ::
      $:  %j                                  ::
          $>  $?  %dawn                       ::
```

```
57                    %fake                                 ::
58                ==                                        ::
59            task:jael                                     ::
60    ==  ==                                                ::
61 +$  sign                                                 ::  in result $<-
62    $~  [%dill %blit ~]                                   ::
63    $%  $:  %behn                                         ::
64            $%  $>(%writ gift:clay)                       ::  XX %slip
65                $>(%mere gift:clay)                       ::  XX %slip
66        ==  ==                                            ::
67        $:  %clay                                         ::
68            $>  $?  %mere                                 ::
69                    %writ                                 ::
70                ==                                        ::
71            gift:clay                                     ::
72        ==                                                ::
73        $:  %dill                                         ::
74            $>(%blit gift:dill)                           ::
75        ==                                                ::
76        $:  %gall                                         ::
77            $>(%unto gift:gall)                           ::
78    ==  ==                                                ::
79 ::::::::::                                               ::  dill tiles
80 --
81 =|  all=axle
82 |=  [now=@da eny=@uvJ rof=roof]                          ::  current invocation
83 =>  ~%  %dill  ..part  ~
84    |%
85    ++  as                                                ::  per cause
86      =|  moz=(list move)
87      |_  [hen=duct ses=@tas axon]
88      ++  abet                                            ::  resolve
89        ^-  [(list move) axle]
90        [(flop moz) all(dug (~(put by dug.all) ses +<+>))]
91      ::
92      ++  call                                            ::  receive input
93        |=  kyz=task
94        ^+  +>
95        ?+    -.kyz  ~&  [%strange-kiss -.kyz]  +>
96          %hail  (send %hey ~)
97          %belt  (send `dill-belt`p.kyz)
98          %blew  (send(wid p.p.kyz) %rez p.p.kyz q.p.kyz)
99          %heft  (pass /whey %$ whey/~)
100         %meld  (dump kyz)
101         %pack  (dump kyz)
102         %crop  (dump trim+p.kyz)
103         %verb  (pass /verb %$ kyz)
104       ::
105           %seat
106         %^  pass  /seat  %g
107         :+  %deal  [our our /dill]
108         [%hood %poke %kiln-install !>([desk.kyz our desk.kyz])]
109           ==
110       ::
111      ++  crud
112        |=  [err=@tas tac=tang]
113        =-  +>.$(moz (weld - moz))
114        %+  turn
```

```
115        ~(tap in ear.all)
116      (late %give %logs %crud err tac)
117    ::
118    ++  dump                                  ::  pass down to hey
119      |=  git=gift
120      ?>  ?=(^ hey.all)
121      +>(moz [[u.hey.all %give git] moz])
122    ::
123    ++  done                                  ::  gift to viewers
124      |=  git=gift
125      =-  +>.$(moz (weld - moz))
126      %+  turn
127        ~(tap in (~(get ju eye.all) ses))
128      |=(=duct [duct %give git])
129    ::
130    ++  deal                                  ::  pass to %gall
131      |=  [=wire =deal:gall]
132      (pass wire [%g %deal [our our /dill] ram deal])
133    ::
134    ++  pass                                  ::  pass note
135      |=  [=wire =note]
136      +>(moz :_(moz [hen %pass wire note]))
137    ::
138    ++  from                                  ::  receive blit
139      |=  bit=dill-blit
140      ^+  +>
141      ?:  ?=(%qit -.bit)
142        (dump %logo ~)
143      ::TODO  so why is this a (list blit) again?
144      (done %blit bit ~)
145    ::
146    ++  sponsor
147      ^-  ship
148      =/  dat=(unit (unit cage))
149        (rof [~ ~] /dill j/[[our sein/da/now] /(scot %p our)])
150      ;;(ship q.q:(need (need dat)))
151    ::
152    ++  init                                  ::  initialize
153      (pass /merg/base [%c %merg %kids our %base da+now %init])
154    ::
155    ++  mere                                  ::  continue init
156      ^+  .
157      =/  myt  (flop (fall tem ~))
158      =.  tem  ~
159      =.  ..mere  (pass /zest %c %zest %base %live)
160      =.  ..mere  (show-desk %kids)
161      =.  ..mere  (open ~)
162      |-  ^+  ..mere
163      ?~  myt  ..mere
164      $(myt t.myt, ..mere (send i.myt))
165    ::
166    ++  into                                  ::  preinitialize
167      |=  gyl=(list gill)
168      =.  tem  `(turn gyl |=(a=gill [%yow a]))
169      (pass / [%c %warp our %base `[%sing %y [%ud 1] /]])
170    ::
171    ++  open
172      |=  gyl=(list gill)
```

```
173      ::TODO  should allow handlers from non-base desks
174      ::TODO  maybe ensure :ram is running?
175      =.  +>  peer
176      %+  roll  gyl
177      |=  [g=gill _..open]
178      (send [%yow g])
179    ::
180    ++  send                                 ::  send action
181      |=  bet=dill-belt
182      ^+  +>
183      ?^  tem
184        +>(tem `[bet u.tem])
185      (deal /send/[ses] [%poke [%dill-poke !>([ses bet])]])
186    ::
187    ++  peer
188      (deal /peer/[ses] %watch /dill/[ses])
189    ::
190    ++  pull
191      (deal /peer/[ses] %leave ~)
192    ::
193    ++  show-desk                             ::  permit reads on desk
194      |=  des=desk
195      (pass /show [%c %perm des / r+`[%black ~]])
196    ::
197    ++  take                                  ::  receive
198      |=  [tea=wire sih=sign]
199      ^+  +>
200      ?-    sih
201          [%gall %unto *]
202        ::  ~&  [%take-gall-unto +>.sih]
203        ?-    -.+>.sih
204            %raw-fact   !!
205            %kick       peer
206            %poke-ack   ?~(p.p.+>.sih +>.$ (crud %coup u.p.p.+>.sih))
207            %watch-ack
208          ?~  p.p.+>.sih
209            +>.$
210          (dump:(crud %reap u.p.p.+>.sih) %logo ~)
211        ::
212            %fact
213          ?.  ?=(%dill-blit p.cage.p.+>.sih)
214            +>.$
215          (from ;;(dill-blit q.q.cage.p.+>.sih))
216        ==
217      ::
218          [?(%behn %clay) %writ *]
219        init
220      ::
221          [?(%behn %clay) %mere *]
222        ?:  ?=(%& -.p.sih)
223          mere
224        (mean >%dill-mere-fail< >p.p.p.sih< q.p.p.sih)
225      ::
226          [%dill %blit *]
227        (done +.sih)
228      ==
229    --
230  ::
```

```
++  ax                                            ::  make ++as from name
  |=  [hen=duct ses=@tas]
  ^-  (unit _as)
  =/  nux  (~(get by dug.all) ses)
  ?~  nux  ~
  (some ~(. as hen ses u.nux))
::
++  aw                                            ::  make ++as from wire
  |=  [hen=duct wir=wire]
  ^-  (unit _as)
  %+  ax  hen
  ?+  wir  %$
    [?(%peer %send) @ *]  i.t.wir
  ==
  --
|%                                                ::  poke+peek pattern
++  call                                          ::  handle request
  |=  $:  hen=duct
          dud=(unit goof)
          wrapped-task=(hobo task)
      ==
  ^+  [*(list move) ..^$]
  =/  task=task
    ~|  wrapped-task
    ((harden task) wrapped-task)
  ~|  -.task
  ::  unwrap session tasks, default to session %$
  ::
  =^  ses=@tas  task
    ?:(?=(%shot -.task) +.task [%$ task])
  ::  error notifications "downcast" to %crud
  ::
  =?  task  ?=(^ dud)
    ~|  %crud-in-crud
    ?<  ?=(%crud -.task)
    [%crud -.task tang.u.dud]
  ::
  ::  the boot event passes thru %dill for initial duct distribution
  ::
  ?:  ?=(%boot -.task)
    ?>  ?=(?(%dawn %fake) -.p.task)
    ?>  =(~ hey.all)
    =.  hey.all  `hen
    =/  boot
      ((soft $>($?(%dawn %fake) task:jael)) p.task)
    ?~  boot
      ~&  %dill-no-boot
      ~&  p.task
      ~|  invalid-boot-event+hen  !!
    =.  lit.all  lit.task
    [[hen %pass / %j u.boot]~ ..^$]
  ::  we are subsequently initialized.
  ::
  ?:  ?=(%init -.task)
    ?>  =(~ dug.all)
    ::  configure new terminal, setup :hood and %clay
    ::
    =*  duc  (need hey.all)
```

```hoon
=/  app  %hood
=/  say  (tuba "<awaiting {(trip app)}, this may take a minute>")
=/  zon=axon  [app input=[~ ~] width=80]
::
=^  moz  all  abet:(~(into as duc %$ zon) ~)
=.  eye.all  (~(put ju eye.all) %$ duc)
[moz ..^$]
::  %flog tasks are unwrapped and sent back to us on our default duct
::
?:  ?=(%flog -.task)
  ?~  hey.all
    [~ ..^$]
  ::  this lets lib/helm send %heft a la |mass
  ::
  =?  p.task  ?=([%crud %hax-heft ~] p.task)  [%heft ~]
  ::
  $(hen u.hey.all, wrapped-task p.task)
::  %vega and %trim notifications come in on an unfamiliar duct
::
?:  ?=(?(%trim %vega) -.task)
  [~ ..^$]
::  %knob used to set a verbosity level for an error tag,
::  but dill no longer prints errors itself, so implementing %knob
::  has become a recommendation to error printers (like drum).
::  remove this when %knob gets removed from lull, next kelvin release.
::
?:  ?=(%knob -.task)
  ~&  [%dill %knob-deprecated]
  [~ ..^$]
::  %open opens a new dill session
::
?:  ?=(%open -.task)
  ?:  (~(has by dug.all) ses)
    ::TODO  should we allow, and just send the %yow blits?
    ~|  [%cannot-open-existing ses]
    !!
  =/  zon=axon  [p.task ~ width=80]
  =^  moz  all  abet:(~(open as hen ses zon) q.task)
  =.  eye.all  (~(put ju eye.all) ses hen)
  [moz ..^$]
::  %shut closes an existing dill session
::
?:  ?=(%shut -.task)
  ?:  =(%$ ses)
    ~|  %cannot-shut-default-session
    !!
  =/  nus
    ~|  [%no-session ses]
    (need (ax hen ses))
  ::NOTE  we do deletion from state outside of the core,
  ::      because +abet would re-insert.
  ::TODO  send a %bye blit? xx
  =^  moz  all  abet:pull:nus
  =.  dug.all  (~(del by dug.all) ses)
  =.  eye.all  (~(del by eye.all) ses)
  [moz ..^$]
::  %view opens a subscription to the target session, on the current duct
::
```

```
347    ?:  ?=(%view -.task)
348      =/  nus
349         ::  crash on viewing non-existent session
350         ::
351         ~|  [%no-session ses]
352         (need (ax hen ses))
353      ::  register the viewer and send a %hey so they get the full screen
354      ::
355      =^  moz  all
356         abet:(send:nus %hey ~)
357      :-  moz
358      ..^$(eye.all (~(put ju eye.all) ses hen))
359    ::  %flee closes a subscription to the target session, from the current duct
360    ::
361    ?:  ?=(%flee -.task)
362      :-  ~
363      ..^$(eye.all (~(del ju eye.all) ses hen))
364    ::  %logs opens or closes a subscription to system output
365    ::
366    ?:  ?=(%logs -.task)
367      =.  ear.all
368        ?~  p.task  (~(del in ear.all) hen)
369        (~(put in ear.all) hen)
370      [~ ..^$]
371    ::  if we were $told something, give %logs to all interested parties
372    ::
373    ?:  ?=(?(%crud %talk %text) -.task)
374      :_  ..^$
375      (turn ~(tap in ear.all) (late %give %logs task))
376    ::
377    =/  nus
378      (ax hen ses)
379    ?~  nus
380      ::  session :ses does not exist
381      ::  could be before %boot (or %boot failed)
382      ::
383      ~&  [%dill-call-no-session ses hen -.task]
384      [~ ..^$]
385    ::
386    =^  moz  all  abet:(call:u.nus task)
387    [moz ..^$]
388  ::
389  ++  load                                            ::  import old state
390    =<  |=  old=any-axle
391        ?-  -.old
392          %7  ..^$(all old)
393          %6  $(old (axle-6-to-7 old))
394          %5  $(old (axle-5-to-6 old))
395          %4  $(old (axle-4-to-5 old))
396        ==
397    |%
398    +$  any-axle  $%(axle axle-6 axle-5 axle-4)
399    ::
400    +$  axle-6
401      $:  %6
402          hey=(unit duct)
403          dug=(map @tas axon)
404          eye=(jug @tas duct)
```

```
405          lit=?
406          veb=(map @tas log-level)
407          egg=_|
408      ==
409    ::
410    ++  axle-6-to-7
411      |=  a=axle-6
412      ^-  axle
413      [%7 hey dug eye ~ lit egg]:a
414    ::
415    +$  axle-5
416      $:  %5
417          hey=(unit duct)                      ::  default duct
418          dug=(map @tas axon)                  ::  conversations
419          eye=(jug @tas duct)                  ::  outside listeners
420          lit=?                                ::  boot in lite mode
421          veb=(map @tas log-level)
422      ==
423    ::
424    ++  axle-5-to-6
425      |=  a=axle-5
426      ^-  axle-6
427      ::  [%6 hey `(map @tas axon)`dug eye lit veb |]
428      a(- %6, veb [veb.a &])
429    ::
430    +$  axle-4
431      $:  %4
432          hey=(unit duct)
433          dug=(map duct axon-4)
434          eye=(jug duct duct)
435          lit=?
436          veb=(map @tas log-level)
437      ==
438    ::
439    +$  axon-4
440      $:  ram=term
441          tem=(unit (list dill-belt-4))
442          wid=_80
443          pos=$@(@ud [@ud @ud])
444          see=$%([%lin (list @c)] [%klr stub])
445      ==
446    ::
447    +$  dill-belt-4
448      $%  [%ctl p=@c]
449          [%met p=@c]
450          dill-belt
451      ==
452    ::
453    ++  axle-4-to-5
454      |=  axle-4
455      ^-  axle-5
456      :-  %5
457      =-  [hey nug nay lit veb]
458      %+  roll  ~(tap by dug)
459      |=  [[=duct =axon-4] nug=(map @tas axon) nay=(jug @tas duct)]
460      =/  ses=@tas
461        ~|  [%unexpected-duct duct]
462        ?>(=([//term/1]~ duct) %$)
```

```
463      :-  (~(put by nug) ses (axon-4-to-5 axon-4))
464      %+  ~(put by nay)  ses
465      (~(put in (~(get ju eye) duct)) duct)
466    ::
467    ++  axon-4-to-5
468      |=  axon-4
469      ^-  axon
470      =;  tem  [ram tem wid]
471      ?~  tem  ~
472      %-  some
473      %+  turn  u.tem
474      |=  b=dill-belt-4
475      ^-  dill-belt
476      ?.  ?=(?(%ctl %met) -.b)  b
477      [%mod -.b p.b]
478    --
479  ::
480  ++  scry
481    ^-  roon
482    |=  [lyc=gang pov=path car=term bem=beam]
483    ^-  (unit (unit cage))
484    =*  ren  car
485    =*  why=shop  &/p.bem
486    =*  syd  q.bem
487    =*  lot=coin  $/r.bem
488    =*  tyl  s.bem
489    ::
490    ?.  ?=(%& -.why)  ~
491    =*  his  p.why
492    ::
493    ::  only respond for the local identity, %$ desk, current timestamp, root gang
494    ::
495    ?.  ?&  =(&+our why)
496            =([%$ %da now] lot)
497            =(%$ syd)
498            =([~ ~] lyc)
499        ==
500      ~
501    ::  /%x//whey           (list mass)    memory usage labels
502    ::  /dy/sessions        (set @tas)     all existing sessions
503    ::  /du/sessions/[ses]  ?              does session ses exist?
504    ::
505    ?+  [ren tyl]  ~
506      [%x %$ %whey ~]      =-  ``mass+!>(`(list mass)`-)
507                          [hey+&+hey.all dug+&+dug.all ~]
508    ::
509      [%y %sessions ~]    ``noun+!>(~(key by dug.all))
510      [%u %sessions @ ~]  ``noun+!>((~(has by dug.all) (snag 1 tyl)))
511    ==
512  ::
513  ++  stay  all
514  ::
515  ++  take                                    :: process move
516    |=  [tea=wire hen=duct dud=(unit goof) hin=sign]
517    ^+  [*(list move) ..^$]
518    ?^  dud
519      ~|(%dill-take-dud (mean tang.u.dud))
520    ::
```

```
521    =;  [moz=(list move) lax=_..^$]
522     =?  moz  egg.all.lax
523       ::  dill pre-release (version %5) in some cases ended up in a state
524       ::  where it had both an old-style and new-style subscription open
525       ::  for the default session. here, we obliterate both and establish
526       ::  only the new-style subscription.
527       ::
528       =/  hey  (need hey.all.lax)
529       =/  =sack  [our our /dill]
530       :*  [hey %pass / %g %deal sack %hood %leave ~]
531           [hey %pass [%peer %$ ~] %g %deal sack %hood %leave ~]
532           [hey %pass [%peer %$ ~] %g %deal sack %hood %watch [%dill %$ ~]]
533           moz
534       ==
535     =.  egg.all.lax  |
536     [moz lax]
537   ::
538   =/  nus  (aw hen tea)
539   ?~  nus
540     ::  :tea points to an unrecognized session
541     ::
542     ~&  [%dill-take-no-session tea -.hin +<.hin]
543     [~ ..^$]
544   =^  moz  all  abet:(take:u.nus tea hin)
545   [moz ..^$]
546   --
```

Eyre

```
1   !:
2   ::  lighter than eyre
3   ::
4   |=  our=ship
5   =,  eyre
6   ::  internal data structures
7   ::
8   =>  =~
9   ::
10  ::  internal data structures that won't go in zuse
11  ::
12  |%
13  +$  move
14    ::
15    $:  ::  duct: request identifier
16        ::
17        =duct
18        ::
19        ::
20        card=(wind note gift)
21    ==
22  ::  +note: private request from eyre to another vane
23  ::
24  +$  note
25    $%  [%a $>(?(%plea %keen %yawn) task:ames)]
26        [%b $>(?(%rest %wait) task:behn)]
27        [%c $>(%warp task:clay)]
28        [%d $>(%flog task:dill)]
29        [%g $>(%deal task:gall)]
30    ==
31  ::  +sign: private response from another vane to eyre
32  ::
33  +$  sign
34    $%  [%ames $>(?(%done %boon %lost %tune) gift:ames)]
35        [%behn $>(%wake gift:behn)]
36        [%gall gift:gall]
37        [%clay gift:clay]
38    ==
39  --
40  ::  more structures
41  ::
42  |%
43  ++  axle
44    $:  ::  date: date at which http-server's state was updated to this data structure
45        ::
46        date=%~2023.5.15
47        ::  server-state: state of inbound requests
48        ::
49        =server-state
50    ==
51  ::  +server-state: state relating to open inbound HTTP connections
52  ::
53  +$  server-state
54    $:  ::  bindings: actions to dispatch to when a binding matches
55        ::
56        ::      Eyre is responsible for keeping its bindings sorted so that it
```

```hoon
57        ::      will trigger on the most specific binding first. Eyre should send
58        ::      back an error response if an already bound binding exists.
59        ::
60        ::      TODO: It would be nice if we had a path trie. We could decompose
61        ::      the :binding into a (map (unit @t) (trie knot =action)).
62        ::
63      bindings=(list [=binding =duct =action])
64      ::    cache: mapping from url to versioned entry
65      ::
66      cache=(map url=@t [aeon=@ud val=(unit cache-entry)])
67      ::    cors-registry: state used and managed by the +cors core
68      ::
69      =cors-registry
70      ::    connections: open http connections not fully complete
71      ::
72      connections=(map duct outstanding-connection)
73      ::    auth: state managed by the +authentication core
74      ::
75      auth=authentication-state
76      ::    channel-state: state managed by the +channel core
77      ::
78      =channel-state
79      ::    domains: domain-names that resolve to us
80      ::
81      domains=(set turf)
82      ::    http-config: our server configuration
83      ::
84      =http-config
85      ::    ports: live servers
86      ::
87      ports=[insecure=@ud secure=(unit @ud)]
88      ::    outgoing-duct: to unix
89      ::
90      outgoing-duct=duct
91      ::    verb: verbosity
92      ::
93      verb=@
94    ==
95  ::  channel-request: an action requested on a channel
96  ::
97  +$  channel-request
98    $%  ::    %ack: acknowledges that the client has received events up to :id
99        ::
100       [%ack event-id=@ud]
101       ::    %poke: pokes an application, validating :noun against :mark
102       ::
103       [%poke request-id=@ud ship=@p app=term mark=@tas =noun]
104       ::    %poke-json: pokes an application, translating :json to :mark
105       ::
106       [%poke-json request-id=@ud ship=@p app=term mark=@tas =json]
107       ::    %watch: subscribes to an application path
108       ::
109       [%subscribe request-id=@ud ship=@p app=term =path]
110       ::    %leave: unsubscribes from an application path
111       ::
112       [%unsubscribe request-id=@ud subscription-id=@ud]
113       ::    %delete: kills a channel
114       ::
```

```hoon
        [%delete ~]
    ==
::  clog-timeout: the delay between acks after which clog-threshold kicks in
::
++  clog-timeout     ~s30
::  clog-threshold: maximum per-subscription event buildup, after clog-timeout
::
++  clog-threshold   50
::  channel-timeout: the delay before a channel should be reaped
::
++  channel-timeout  ~h12
::  session-timeout: the delay before an idle session expires
::
++  session-timeout  ~d7
--
::  utilities
::
|%
::  +combine-octs: combine multiple octs into one
::
++  combine-octs
  |=  a=(list octs)
  ^-  octs
  :-  %+  roll  a
      |=  [=octs sum=@ud]
      (add sum p.octs)
  (can 3 a)
::  +prune-events: removes all items from the front of the queue up to :id
::
::      also produces, per request-id, the amount of events that have got acked,
::      for use with +subtract-acked-events.
::
++  prune-events
  =|  acked=(map @ud @ud)
  |=  [q=(qeu [id=@ud @ud channel-event]) id=@ud]
  ^+  [acked q]
  ::  if the queue is now empty, that's fine
  ::
  ?:  =(~ q)
    [acked ~]
  ::
  =/  next=[item=[id=@ud request-id=@ud channel-event] _q]  ~(get to q)
  ::  if the head of the queue is newer than the acknowledged id, we're done
  ::
  ?:  (gth id.item.next id)
    [acked q]
  ::  otherwise, note the ack, and check next item
  ::
  %_  $
    q  +:next
  ::
      acked
    =,  item.next
    %+  ~(put by acked)  request-id
    +((~(gut by acked) request-id 0))
  ==
::  +subtract-acked-events: update the subscription map's pending ack counts
::
```

```
++  subtract-acked-events
  |=  [acked=(map @ud @ud) unacked=(map @ud @ud)]
  ^+  unacked
  %+  roll  ~(tap by acked)
  |=  [[rid=@ud ack=@ud] unacked=_unacked]
  ?~  sus=(~(get by unacked) rid)
    unacked
  %+  ~(put by unacked)  rid
  ?:  (lte u.sus ack)  0
  (sub u.sus ack)
::  +find-channel-mode: deduce requested mode from headers
::
++  find-channel-mode
  |=  [met=method:http hes=header-list:http]
  ^-  ?(%json %jam)
  =+  ^-  [hed=@t jam=@t]
    ?:  ?=(%'GET' met)  ['x-channel-format' 'application/x-urb-jam']
    ['content-type' 'application/x-urb-jam']
  =+  typ=(bind (get-header:http hed hes) :(cork trip cass crip))
  ?:(=(`jam typ) %jam %json)
::  +parse-channel-request: parses a list of channel-requests
::
++  parse-channel-request
  |=  [mode=?(%json %jam) body=octs]
  ^-  (each (list channel-request) @t)
  ?-  mode
      %json
    ?~  maybe-json=(de:json:html q.body)
      |+'put body not json'
    ?~  maybe-requests=(parse-channel-request-json u.maybe-json)
      |+'invalid channel json'
    &+u.maybe-requests
  ::
      %jam
    ?~  maybe-noun=(bind (slaw %uw q.body) cue)
      |+'invalid request format'
    ?~  maybe-reqs=((soft (list channel-request)) u.maybe-noun)
      ~&  [%miss u.maybe-noun]
      |+'invalid request data'
    &+u.maybe-reqs
  ==
::  +parse-channel-request-json: parses a json list of channel-requests
::
::    Parses a json array into a list of +channel-request. If any of the items
::    in the list fail to parse, the entire thing fails so we can 400 properly
::    to the client.
::
++  parse-channel-request-json
  |=  request-list=json
  ^-  (unit (list channel-request))
  ::  parse top
  ::
  =,  dejs-soft:format
  =-  ((ar -) request-list)
  ::
  |=  item=json
  ^-  (unit channel-request)
  ::
```

```hoon
231    ?~  maybe-key=((ot action+so ~) item)
232      ~
233    ?:  =('ack' u.maybe-key)
234      ((pe %ack (ot event-id+ni ~)) item)
235    ?:  =('poke' u.maybe-key)
236      %.  item
237      %+  pe  %poke-json
238      (ot id+ni ship+(su fed:ag) app+so mark+(su sym) json+some ~)
239    ?:  =('subscribe' u.maybe-key)
240      %.  item
241      %+  pe  %subscribe
242      (ot id+ni ship+(su fed:ag) app+so path+(su stap) ~)
243    ?:  =('unsubscribe' u.maybe-key)
244      %.  item
245      %+  pe  %unsubscribe
246      (ot id+ni subscription+ni ~)
247    ?:  =('delete' u.maybe-key)
248      `[%delete ~]
249    ::  if we reached this, we have an invalid action key. fail parsing.
250    ::
251      ~
252  ::  +auth-styling: css for login and eauth pages
253  ::
254  ++  auth-styling
255    '''
256    @import url("https://rsms.me/inter/inter.css");
257    @font-face {
258        font-family: "Source Code Pro";
259        src: url("https://storage.googleapis.com/media.urbit.org/fonts/scp-regular.woff");
260        font-weight: 400;
261        font-display: swap;
262    }
263    :root {
264      --red-soft: #FFEFEC;
265      --red: #FF6240;
266      --gray-100: #E5E5E5;
267      --gray-400: #999999;
268      --gray-800: #333333;
269      --white: #FFFFFF;
270    }
271    html {
272      font-family: Inter, sans-serif;
273      height: 100%;
274      margin: 0;
275      width: 100%;
276      background: var(--white);
277      color: var(--gray-800);
278      -webkit-font-smoothing: antialiased;
279      line-height: 1.5;
280      font-size: 16px;
281      font-weight: 600;
282      display: flex;
283      flex-flow: row nowrap;
284      justify-content: center;
285    }
286    body {
287      display: flex;
288      flex-flow: column nowrap;
```

```css
    justify-content: center;
    max-width: 300px;
    padding: 1rem;
    width: 100%;
}
body.local #eauth,
body.eauth #local {
  display: none;
  min-height: 100%;
}
#eauth input {
  /*NOTE dumb hack to get approx equal height with #local */
  margin-bottom: 15px;
}
body nav {
  background: var(--gray-100);
  border-radius: 2rem;
  display: flex;
  justify-content: space-around;
  overflow: hidden;
  margin-bottom: 1rem;
}
body nav div {
  width: 50%;
  padding: 0.5rem 1rem;
  text-align: center;
  cursor: pointer;
}
body.local nav div.local,
body.eauth nav div.eauth {
  background: var(--gray-800);
  color: var(--white);
  cursor: default;
}
nav div.local {
  border-right: none;
  border-top-right-radius: 0;
  border-bottom-right-radius: 0;
}
nav div.eauth {
  border-left: none;
  border-top-left-radius: 0;
  border-bottom-left-radius: 0;
}
body > *,
form > input {
  width: 100%;
}
form {
  display: flex;
  flex-flow: column;
  align-items: flex-start;
}
input {
  background: var(--gray-100);
  border: 2px solid transparent;
  padding: 0.5rem;
  border-radius: 0.5rem;
```

```
347    font-size: inherit;
348    color: var(--gray-800);
349    box-shadow: none;
350    width: 100%;
351  }
352  input:disabled {
353    background: var(--gray-100);
354    color: var(--gray-400);
355  }
356  input:focus {
357    outline: none;
358    background: var(--white);
359    border-color: var(--gray-400);
360  }
361  input:invalid:not(:focus) {
362    background: var(--red-soft);
363    border-color: var(--red);
364    outline: none;
365    color: var(--red);
366  }
367  button[type=submit] {
368    margin-top: 1rem;
369  }
370  button[type=submit], a.button {
371    font-size: 1rem;
372    padding: 0.5rem 1rem;
373    border-radius: 0.5rem;
374    background: var(--gray-800);
375    color: var(--white);
376    border: none;
377    font-weight: 600;
378    text-decoration: none;
379  }
380  input:invalid ~ button[type=submit] {
381    border-color: currentColor;
382    background: var(--gray-100);
383    color: var(--gray-400);
384    pointer-events: none;
385  }
386  span.guest, span.guest a {
387    color: var(--gray-400);
388  }
389  span.failed {
390    display: flex;
391    flex-flow: row nowrap;
392    height: 1rem;
393    align-items: center;
394    margin-top: 0.875rem;
395    color: var(--red);
396  }
397  span.failed svg {
398    height: 1rem;
399    margin-right: 0.25rem;
400  }
401  span.failed path {
402    fill: transparent;
403    stroke-width: 2px;
404    stroke-linecap: round;
```

```
405      stroke: currentColor;
406    }
407    .mono {
408      font-family: 'Source Code Pro', monospace;
409    }
410    @media all and (prefers-color-scheme: dark) {
411    :root {
412      --white: #000000;
413      --gray-800: #E5E5E5;
414      --gray-400: #808080;
415      --gray-100: #333333;
416      --red-soft: #7F1D1D;
417    }
418    }
419    @media screen and (min-width: 30em) {
420      html {
421        font-size: 14px;
422      }
423    }
424    '''
425  ::  +login-page: internal page to login to an Urbit
426  ::
427  ++  login-page
428    |=  [redirect-url=(unit @t) our=@p =identity eauth=(unit ?) failed=?]
429    ^-  octs
430    =+  redirect-str=?~(redirect-url "" (trip u.redirect-url))
431    %-  as-octs:mimes:html
432    %-  crip
433    %-  en-xml:html
434    =/  favicon  %+
435      weld  "<svg width='10' height='10' viewBox='0 0 10 10' xmlns='http://www.w3.org/2000/svg'>"
436            "<circle r='3.09' cx='5' cy='5' /></svg>"
437    ;html
438      ;head
439        ;meta(charset "utf-8");
440        ;meta(name "viewport", content "width=device-width, initial-scale=1, shrink-to-fit=no");
441        ;link(rel "icon", type "image/svg+xml", href (weld "data:image/svg+xml;utf8," favicon));
442        ;title:"Urbit"
443        ;style:"{(trip auth-styling)}"
444        ;style:"{?^(eauth "" "nav \{ display: none; }")}"
445        ;script:"our = '{(scow %p our)}';"
446        ;script:'''
447                let name, pass;
448                function setup(isEauth) {
449                  name = document.getElementById('name');
450                  pass = document.getElementById('pass');
451                  if (isEauth) goEauth(); else goLocal();
452                }
453                function goLocal() {
454                  document.body.className = 'local';
455                  pass.focus();
456                }
457                function goEauth() {
458                  document.body.className = 'eauth';
459                  name.focus();
460                }
461                function doEauth() {
462                  if (name.value == our) {
```

```
463                         event.preventDefault();
464                         goLocal();
465                       }
466                     }
467                     '''
468           ==
469         ;body
470           =class    "{?:(=(`& eauth) "eauth" "local")}"
471           =onload   "setup({?:(=(`& eauth) "true" "false")})"
472           ;div#local
473             ;p:"Urbit ID"
474             ;input(value "{(scow %p our)}", disabled "true", class "mono");
475             ;+  ?:  =(%ours -.identity)
476                   ;div
477                     ;p:"Already authenticated"
478                     ;a.button/"{(trip (fall redirect-url '/'))}":"Continue"
479                   ==
480             ;form(action "/~/login", method "post", enctype "application/x-www-form-urlencoded")
481               ;p:"Access Key"
482               ;input
483                 =type    "password"
484                 =name    "password"
485                 =id      "pass"
486                 =placeholder  "sampel-ticlyt-migfun-falmel"
487                 =class   "mono"
488                 =required   "true"
489                 =minlength  "27"
490                 =maxlength  "27"
491                 =pattern    "((?:[a-z]\{6}-)\{3}(?:[a-z]\{6}))";
492               ;input(type "hidden", name "redirect", value redirect-str);
493               ;+  ?.  failed  ;span;
494                 ;span.failed
495                   ;svg(xmlns "http://www.w3.org/2000/svg", viewBox "0 0 16 16")
496                     ;path(d "m8 8 4-4M8 8 4 4m4 4-4 4m4-4 4 4");
497                   ==
498                   Key is incorrect
499               ==
500               ;button(type "submit"):"Continue"
501             ==
502           ==
503           ;div#eauth
504             ;form(action "/~/login", method "post", onsubmit "return doEauth()")
505               ;p:"Urbit ID"
506               ;input.mono
507                 =name    "name"
508                 =id      "name"
509                 =placeholder  "{(scow %p our)}"
510                 =required   "true"
511                 =minlength  "4"
512                 =maxlength  "57"
513                 =pattern    "~((([a-z]\{6})\{1,2}-\{0,2})+|[a-z]\{3})";
514               ;p
515                 ; You will be redirected to your own web interface to authorize
516                 ; logging in to
517                 ;span.mono:"{(scow %p our)}"
518                 ; .
519               ==
520               ;input(type "hidden", name "redirect", value redirect-str);
```

```
521              ;button(name "eauth", type "submit"):"Continue"
522           ==
523        ==
524      ;*   ?:   ?=(%ours -.identity)  ~
525           =+   as="proceed as{?:(?=(%fake -.identity) " guest" "")}"
526           ;+   ;span.guest.mono
527                 ; Or try to
528                 ;a/"{(trip (fall redirect-url '/'))}":"{as}"
529                 ; .
530              ==
531      ==
532    ;script:'''
533            var failSpan = document.querySelector('.failed');
534            if (failSpan) {
535              document.querySelector("input[type=password]")
536                .addEventListener('keyup', function (event) {
537                  failSpan.style.display = 'none';
538                });
539            }
540            '''
541    ==
542  ::  +eauth-error-page: render an eauth error reporting page
543  ::
544  ::    optionally redirects the user back to either the login page if we're
545  ::    acting as server, or the host if we're the client.
546  ::
547  ++  eauth-error-page
548    |=  $=  return
549        $?  ~                     ::  no known return target
550            [%server last=@t]  ::  we are the host, return to login
551            [%client goal=@t]  ::  we are the client, return to host
552        ==
553    ^-  octs
554    %-  as-octs:mimes:html
555    %-  crip
556    %-  en-xml:html
557    =/  return=(unit @t)
558      ?-  return
559        ~                        ~
560        [%server *]  %-  some
561                     %^  cat  3  '/~/login?eauth&redirect='
562                     (crip (en-urlt:html (trip last.return)))
563        [%client *]  `goal.return  ::TODO  plus nonce? or abort?
564      ==
565    =/  favicon  %+
566      weld  "<svg width='10' height='10' viewBox='0 0 10 10' xmlns='http://www.w3.org/2000/svg'>"
567            "<circle r='3.09' cx='5' cy='5' /></svg>"
568    =/  msg=tape
569      ?~  return  "Something went wrong!"
570      "Something went wrong! You will be redirected back..."
571    ;html
572      ;head
573        ;*  ?~  return  ~
574            :_  ~
575            ;meta(http-equiv "Refresh", content "5; url={(trip u.return)}");
576        ;meta(charset "utf-8");
577        ;meta(name "viewport", content "width=device-width, initial-scale=1, shrink-to-fit=no");
578        ;link(rel "icon", type "image/svg+xml", href (weld "data:image/svg+xml;utf8," favicon));
```

```hoon
    ;title:"Urbit"
    ;style:'''
            @import url("https://rsms.me/inter/inter.css");
            :root {
              --black60: rgba(0,0,0,0.6);
              --white: rgba(255,255,255,1);
            }
            html {
              font-family: Inter, sans-serif;
              height: 100%;
              margin: 0;
              width: 100%;
              background: var(--white);
              color: var(--black60);
              -webkit-font-smoothing: antialiased;
              line-height: 1.5;
              font-size: 12px;
              display: flex;
              flex-flow: row nowrap;
              justify-content: center;
            }
            body {
              display: flex;
              flex-flow: column nowrap;
              justify-content: center;
              max-width: 300px;
              padding: 1rem;
              width: 100%;
            }
            '''
    ==
  ;body:"{msg}"
  ==
::  +render-tang-to-marl: renders a tang and adds <br/> tags between each line
::
++  render-tang-to-marl
  |=  [wid=@u tan=tang]
  ^-  marl
  =/  raw=(list tape)  (zing (turn tan |=(a=tank (wash 0^wid a))))
  ::
  |-  ^-  marl
  ?~  raw  ~
  [;/(i.raw) ;br; $(raw t.raw)]
::  +render-tang-to-wall: renders tang as text lines
::
++  render-tang-to-wall
  |=  [wid=@u tan=tang]
  ^-  wall
  (zing (turn tan |=(a=tank (wash 0^wid a))))
::  +wall-to-octs: text to binary output
::
++  wall-to-octs
  |=  =wall
  ^-  (unit octs)
  ::
  ?:  =(~ wall)
    ~
  ::
```

```
637    :-  ~
638    %-  as-octs:mimes:html
639    %-  crip
640    %-  zing  ^-  ^wall
641    %-  zing  ^-  (list ^wall)
642    %+  turn  wall
643    |=  t=tape
644    ^-  ^wall
645    ~[t "\0a"]
646  ::  +internal-server-error: 500 page, with a tang
647  ::
648  ++  internal-server-error
649    |=  [authorized=? url=@t t=tang]
650    ^-  octs
651    %-  as-octs:mimes:html
652    %-  crip
653    %-  en-xml:html
654    ;html
655      ;head
656        ;title:"500 Internal Server Error"
657      ==
658      ;body
659        ;h1:"Internal Server Error"
660        ;p:"There was an error while handling the request for {(trip url)}."
661        ;*  ?:  authorized
662              ;=
663                ;code:"*{(render-tang-to-marl 80 t)}"
664              ==
665            ~
666      ==
667    ==
668  ::  +error-page: error page, with an error string if logged in
669  ::
670  ++  error-page
671    |=  [code=@ud authorized=? url=@t t=tape]
672    ^-  octs
673    ::
674    =/  code-as-tape=tape  (format-ud-as-integer code)
675    =/  message=tape
676      ?+  code  "{(scow %ud code)} Error"
677        %400  "Bad Request"
678        %403  "Forbidden"
679        %404  "Not Found"
680        %405  "Method Not Allowed"
681        %500  "Internal Server Error"
682      ==
683    ::
684    %-  as-octs:mimes:html
685    %-  crip
686    %-  en-xml:html
687    ;html
688      ;head
689        ;title:"{code-as-tape} {message}"
690      ==
691      ;body
692        ;h1:"{message}"
693        ;p:"There was an error while handling the request for {(trip url)}."
694        ;*  ?:  authorized
```

```
695                ;=
696                  ;code:"{t}"
697                ==
698              ~
699        ==
700      ==
701  ::  +format-ud-as-integer: prints a number for consumption outside urbit
702  ::
703  ++  format-ud-as-integer
704    |=  a=@ud
705    ^-  tape
706    ?:  =(0 a)  ['0' ~]
707    %-  flop
708    |-  ^-  tape
709    ?:(=(0 a) ~ [(add '0' (mod a 10)) $(a (div a 10))])
710  ::  +host-matches: %.y if the site :binding should be used to handle :host
711  ::
712  ++  host-matches
713    |=  [binding=(unit @t) host=(unit @t)]
714    ^-  ?
715    ::  if the binding allows for matching anything, match
716    ::
717    ?~  binding
718      %.y
719    ::  if the host is ~, that means we're trying to bind nothing to a real
720    ::  binding. fail.
721    ::
722    ?~  host
723      %.n
724    ::  otherwise, do a straight comparison
725    ::
726    =(u.binding u.host)
727  ::  +find-suffix: returns [~ /tail] if :full is (weld :prefix /tail)
728  ::
729  ++  find-suffix
730    |=  [prefix=path full=path]
731    ^-  (unit path)
732    ?~  prefix
733      `full
734    ?~  full
735      ~
736    ?.  =(i.prefix i.full)
737      ~
738    $(prefix t.prefix, full t.full)
739  ::  +simplified-url-parser: returns [(each @if @t) (unit port=@ud)]
740  ::
741  ++  simplified-url-parser
742    ;~  plug
743      ;~  pose
744        %+  stag  %ip
745        =+  tod=(ape:ag ted:ab)
746        %+  bass  256
747        ;~(plug tod (stun [3 3] ;~(pfix dot tod)))
748        ::
749        (stag %site (cook crip (star ;~(pose dot alp))))
750      ==
751      ;~  pose
752        (stag ~ ;~(pfix col dim:ag))
```

```
753        (easy ~)
754      ==
755    ==
756  ::  +host-sans-port: strip the :<port> from a host string
757  ::
758  ++  host-sans-port
759    ;~  sfix
760      %+  cook  crip
761      %-  star
762      ;~  less
763        ;~(plug col (punt dem) ;~(less next (easy ~)))
764        next
765      ==
766      (star next)
767    ==
768  ::  +per-server-event: per-event server core
769  ::
770  ++  per-server-event
771    ~%  %eyre-per-server-event  ..part  ~
772    ::  gate that produces the +per-server-event core from event information
773    ::
774    |=  [[eny=@ =duct now=@da rof=roof] state=server-state]
775    =/  eyre-id  (scot %ta (cat 3 'eyre_' (scot %uv (sham duct))))
776    |%
777    ::  +request-local: bypass authentication for local lens connections
778    ::
779    ++  request-local
780      |=  [secure=? =address =request:http]
781      ^-  [(list move) server-state]
782      ::
783      =/  act  [%app app=%lens]
784      ::
785      =/  connection=outstanding-connection
786        [act [& secure address request] [*@uv [%ours ~]] ~ 0]
787      ::
788      =.  connections.state
789        %.  (~(put by connections.state) duct connection)
790        (trace 2 |.("{<duct>} creating local"))
791      ::
792      (request-to-app [%ours ~] app.act inbound-request.connection)
793    ::  +request: starts handling an inbound http request
794    ::
795    ++  request
796      |=  [secure=? =address =request:http]
797      ^-  [(list move) server-state]
798      =*  headers  header-list.request
799      ::  for requests from localhost, respect the "forwarded" header
800      ::
801      =/  [secure=? host=(unit @t) =^address]
802        =/  host=(unit @t)  (get-header:http 'host' headers)
803        =*  same  [secure host address]
804        ?.  =([%ipv4 .127.0.0.1] address)          same
805        ?~  forwards=(forwarded-params headers)   same
806        :+  (fall (forwarded-secure u.forwards) secure)
807          (clap (forwarded-host u.forwards) host head)
808        (fall (forwarded-for u.forwards) address)
809      ::
810      =/  [=action suburl=@t]
```

```
811      (get-action-for-binding host url.request)
812  ::
813  ::TODO  we might want to mint new identities only for requests that end
814  ::       up going into userspace, not the ones that get handled by eyre.
815  ::       perhaps that distinction, where userspace requests are async, but
816  ::       eyre-handled requests are always synchronous, provides a fruitful
817  ::       angle for refactoring...
818  =^  [suv=@uv =identity som=(list move)]  state
819    (session-for-request:authentication request)
820  =;  [moz=(list move) sat=server-state]
821    [(weld som moz) sat]
822  ::
823  =/  authenticated  ?=(%ours -.identity)
824  :: if we have no eauth endpoint yet, and the request is authenticated,
825  :: deduce it from the hostname
826  ::
827  =?  endpoint.auth.state
828     ?&  authenticated
829         ?=(^ host)
830         ?=(~ auth.endpoint.auth.state)
831     ==
832    %-  (trace 2 |.("eauth: storing endpoint at {(trip u.host)}"))
833    :+  user.endpoint.auth.state
834      `(cat 3 ?:(secure 'https://' 'http://') u.host)
835    now
836  :: record that we started an asynchronous response
837  ::
838  =/  connection=outstanding-connection
839    [action [authenticated secure address request] [suv identity] ~ 0]
840  =.  connections.state
841    :: NB: required by +handle-response and +handle-request:authentication.
842    :: XX optimize, not all requests are asynchronous
843    ::
844    (~(put by connections.state) duct connection)
845  :: redirect to https if insecure, redirects enabled
846  :: and secure port live
847  ::
848  ?:  ?&  !secure
849          redirect.http-config.state
850          ?=(^ secure.ports.state)
851      ==
852    =/  location=@t
853      %+  rap  3
854      :~  'https://'
855          (rash (fall host '') host-sans-port)
856          ?:  =(443 u.secure.ports.state)
857            ''
858          (crip ":{(a-co:co u.secure.ports.state)}")
859          ?:  ?=([[~ ~] ~] (parse-request-line url.request))
860            '/'
861          url.request
862      ==
863    %-  handle-response
864    :*  %start
865        :-  status-code=301
866        headers=[['location' location]~
867        data=~
868        complete=%.y
```

```
869      ==
870  ::  figure out whether this is a cors request,
871  ::  whether the origin is approved or not,
872  ::  and maybe add it to the "pending approval" set
873  ::
874  =/  origin=(unit origin)
875    (get-header:http 'origin' headers)
876  =^  cors-approved  requests.cors-registry.state
877    =,  cors-registry.state
878    ?~  origin                         [| requests]
879    ?:  (~(has in approved) u.origin)  [& requests]
880    ?:  (~(has in rejected) u.origin)  [| requests]
881    [| (~(put in requests) u.origin)]
882  ::  if this is a cors preflight request from an approved origin
883  ::  handle it synchronously
884  ::
885  ?:  &(?=(^ origin) cors-approved ?=(%'OPTIONS' method.request))
886    %-  handle-response
887    =;  =header-list:http
888      [%start [204 header-list] ~ &]
889    ::  allow the method and headers that were asked for,
890    ::  falling back to wildcard if none specified
891    ::
892    ::NOTE  +handle-response will add the rest of the headers
893    ::
894    :~  :-  'Access-Control-Allow-Methods'
895        =-  (fall - '*')
896        (get-header:http 'access-control-request-method' headers)
897      ::
898        :-  'Access-Control-Allow-Headers'
899        =-  (fall - '*')
900        (get-header:http 'access-control-request-headers' headers)
901    ==
902  ::  handle HTTP scries
903  ::
904  ::  TODO: ideally this would look more like:
905  ::
906  ::  ?^  p=(parse-http-scry url.request)
907  ::    (handle-http-scry authenticated p request)
908  ::
909  ?:  =('/_~_/' (end [3 5] url.request))
910    (handle-http-scry authenticated request)
911  ::  handle requests to the cache, if a non-empty entry exists
912  ::
913  =/  cached=(unit [aeon=@ud val=(unit cache-entry)])
914    (~(get by cache.state) url.request)
915  ?:  &(?=([~ @ ^] cached) ?=(%'GET' method.request))
916    (handle-cache-req authenticated request u.val.u.cached)
917  ::
918  ?-    -.action
919      %gen
920    =/  bek=beak  [our desk.generator.action da+now]
921    =/  sup=spur  path.generator.action
922    =/  ski       (rof [~ ~] /eyre %ca bek sup)
923    =/  cag=cage  (need (need ski))
924    ?>  =(%vase p.cag)
925    =/  gat=vase  !<(vase q.cag)
926    =/  res=toon
```

```
927          %-  mock  :_  (look rof [~ ~] /eyre)
928          :_  [%9 2 %0 1]  |.
929          %+  slam
930            %+  slam  gat
931            !>([[now=now eny=eny bek=bek] ~ ~])
932          ::TODO  should get passed the requester's identity
933          !>([authenticated request])
934       ?:  ?=(%2 -.res)
935          =+  connection=(~(got by connections.state) duct)
936          %^  return-static-data-on-duct  500  'text/html'
937          %:  internal-server-error
938            authenticated.inbound-request.connection
939            url.request.inbound-request.connection
940            leaf+"generator crashed"
941            p.res
942          ==
943       ?:  ?=(%1 -.res)
944          =+  connection=(~(got by connections.state) duct)
945          %^  return-static-data-on-duct  500  'text/html'
946          %:  internal-server-error
947            authenticated.inbound-request.connection
948            url.request.inbound-request.connection
949            leaf+"scry blocked on"
950            (fall (bind (bind ((soft path) p.res) smyt) (late ~)) ~)
951          ==
952       =/  result  ;;(simple-payload:http +.p.res)
953       ::  ensure we have a valid content-length header
954       ::
955       ::    We pass on the response and the headers the generator produces, but
956       ::    ensure that we have a single content-length header set correctly in
957       ::    the returned if this has a body, and has no content-length if there
958       ::    is no body returned to the client.
959       ::
960       =.  headers.response-header.result
961         ?~  data.result
962         (delete-header:http 'content-length' headers.response-header.result)
963         ::
964         %^  set-header:http  'content-length'
965         (crip (format-ud-as-integer p.u.data.result))
966         headers.response-header.result
967       ::
968       %-  handle-response
969       ^-  http-event:http
970       :*  %start
971         response-header.result
972         data.result
973         complete=%.y
974       ==
975     ::
976        %app
977     (request-to-app identity app.action inbound-request.connection)
978     ::
979        %authentication
980     (handle-request:authentication secure host address [suv identity] request)
981     ::
982        %eauth
983     (on-request:eauth:authentication [suv identity] request)
984     ::
```

```
985          %logout
986        (handle-logout:authentication [suv identity] request)
987     ::
988          %channel
989        (handle-request:by-channel [suv identity] address request)
990     ::
991          %scry
992        (handle-scry authenticated address request(url suburl))
993     ::
994          %name
995        (handle-name identity request)
996     ::
997          %host
998      %^  return-static-data-on-duct  200  'text/plain'
999      (as-octs:mimes:html (scot %p our))
1000    ::
1001         %four-oh-four
1002     %^  return-static-data-on-duct  404  'text/html'
1003     (error-page 404 authenticated url.request ~)
1004    ==
1005 ::  +handle-name: respond with the requester's @p
1006 ::
1007 ++  handle-name
1008   |=  [=identity =request:http]
1009   ^-  (quip move server-state)
1010   ?.  =(%'GET' method.request)
1011     %^  return-static-data-on-duct  405  'text/html'
1012     (error-page 405 & url.request "may only GET name")
1013   %^  return-static-data-on-duct  200  'text/plain'
1014   =/  nom=@p
1015     ?+(-.identity who.identity %ours our)
1016   (as-octs:mimes:html (scot %p nom))
1017 ::  +handle-http-scry: respond with scry result
1018 ::
1019 ++  handle-http-scry
1020   |=  [authenticated=? =request:http]
1021   |^  ^-  (quip move server-state)
1022   ?.  authenticated  (error-response 403 ~)
1023   ?.  =(%'GET' method.request)
1024     (error-response 405 "may only GET scries")
1025   =/  req  (parse-request-line url.request)
1026   =/  fqp  (fully-qualified site.req)
1027   =/  mym  (scry-mime now rof ext.req site.req)
1028   ?:  ?=(%| -.mym)  (error-response 500 p.mym)
1029   =*  mime  p.mym
1030   %-  handle-response
1031   :*  %start
1032       :-  status-code=200
1033       ^=  headers
1034         :~  ['content-type' (rsh 3 (spat p.mime))]
1035             ['content-length' (crip (format-ud-as-integer p.q.mime))]
1036             ['cache-control' ?:(fqp 'max-age=31536000' 'no-cache')]
1037         ==
1038       data=[~ q.mime]
1039       complete=%.y
1040   ==
1041   ::
1042   ++  fully-qualified
```

```
    |=  a=path
    ^-  ?
    ?.  ?=([%'_~_' @ @ @ *] a)  %.n
    =/  vez  (vang | (en-beam [our %base da+now] ~))
    ?=  [~ [^ ^ ^ *]]  (rush (spat t.t.a) ;~(pfix fas gash:vez))
  ::
  ++  error-response
    |=  [status=@ud =tape]
    ^-  (quip move server-state)
    %^  return-static-data-on-duct  status  'text/html'
    (error-page status authenticated url.request tape)
  --
::  +handle-cache-req: respond with cached value, 404 or 500
::
++  handle-cache-req
  |=  [authenticated=? =request:http entry=cache-entry]
  |^  ^-  (quip move server-state)
  ?:  &(auth.entry !authenticated)
    (error-response 403 ~)
  =*  body  body.entry
  ?-    -.body
      %payload
    %-  handle-response
    :*  %start
        response-header.simple-payload.body
        data.simple-payload.body
        complete=%.y
    ==
  ==
  ::
  ++  error-response
    |=  [status=@ud =tape]
    ^-  (quip move server-state)
    %^  return-static-data-on-duct  status  'text/html'
    (error-page status authenticated url.request tape)
  --
::  +handle-scry: respond with scry result, 404 or 500
::
++  handle-scry
  |=  [authenticated=? =address =request:http]
  |^  ^-  (quip move server-state)
  ?.  authenticated
    (error-response 403 ~)
  ?.  =(%'GET' method.request)
    (error-response 405 "may only GET scries")
  ::  make sure the path contains an app to scry into
  ::
  =+  req=(parse-request-line url.request)
  ?.  ?=(^ site.req)
    (error-response 400 "scry path must start with app name")
  ::  attempt the scry that was asked for
  ::
  =/  res=(unit (unit cage))
    (do-scry %gx i.site.req (snoc t.site.req (fall ext.req %mime)))
  ?~  res    (error-response 500 "failed scry")
  ?~  u.res  (error-response 404 "no scry result")
  =*  mark  p.u.u.res
  =*  vase  q.u.u.res
```

```
?:    =(%mime mark)
  =/    =mime  !<(mime vase)
  %^   return-static-data-on-duct   200
    (rsh 3 (spat p.mime))  q.mime
::   attempt to find conversion gate to mime
::
=/   tub=(unit [tub=tube:clay mov=move])
  (find-tube i.site.req mark %mime)
?~   tub  (error-response 500 "no tube from {(trip mark)} to mime")
::   attempt conversion, then send results
::
=/   mym=(each mime tang)
  (mule |.(!<(mime (tub.u.tub vase))))
=^   cards   state
  ?-   -.mym
    %|   (error-response 500 "failed tube from {(trip mark)} to mime")
    %&   %+  return-static-data-on-duct   200
        [(rsh 3 (spat p.p.mym))  q.p.mym]
  ==
[[mov.u.tub cards] state]
::
++   find-tube
  |=   [dap=term from=mark to=mark]
  ^-   (unit [tube:clay move])
  =/   des=(unit (unit cage))
    (do-scry %gd dap /$)
  ?.   ?=([~ ~ *] des)   ~
  =+   !<(=desk q.u.u.des)
  =/   tub=(unit (unit cage))
    (do-scry %cc desk /[from]/[to])
  ?.   ?=([~ ~ %tube *] tub)   ~
  :-   ~
  :-   !<(tube:clay q.u.u.tub)
  :^   duct  %pass   /conversion-cache/[from]
  [%c %warp our desk `[%sing %c da+now /[from]/[to]]]
::
++   do-scry
  |=   [care=term =desk =path]
  ^-   (unit (unit cage))
  (rof [~ ~] /eyre care [our desk da+now] path)
::
++   error-response
  |=   [status=@ud =tape]
  ^-   (quip move server-state)
  %^   return-static-data-on-duct   status   'text/html'
  (error-page status authenticated url.request tape)
--
::   +request-to-app: subscribe to app and poke it with request data
::
++   request-to-app
  |=   [=identity app=term =inbound-request:eyre]
  ^-   (quip move server-state)
  ::   if the agent isn't running, we synchronously serve a 503
  ::
  ?.   !<(? q:(need (need (rof [~ ~] /eyre %gu [our app da+now] /$))))
    %^   return-static-data-on-duct   503   'text/html'
    %:   error-page
      503
```

```
1159          ?=(%ours -.identity)
1160          url.request.inbound-request
1161          "%{(trip app)} not running"
1162        ==
1163      ::  otherwise, subscribe to the agent and poke it with the request
1164      ::
1165      :_  state
1166      :~  %+  deal-as
1167            /watch-response/[eyre-id]
1168          [identity our app %watch /http-response/[eyre-id]]
1169        ::
1170          %+  deal-as
1171            /run-app-request/[eyre-id]
1172          :^  identity  our  app
1173          :+  %poke  %handle-http-request
1174          !>(`[@ta inbound-request:eyre]`[eyre-id inbound-request])
1175      ==
1176    ::  +cancel-request: handles a request being externally aborted
1177    ::
1178    ++  cancel-request
1179      ^-  [(list move) server-state]
1180      ::
1181      ?~  connection=(~(get by connections.state) duct)
1182        ::  nothing has handled this connection
1183        ::
1184        [~ state]
1185      ::
1186      =.  connections.state  (~(del by connections.state) duct)
1187      ::
1188      ?-    -.action.u.connection
1189          %gen  [~ state]
1190          %app
1191        :_  state
1192        :_  ~
1193        =,  u.connection
1194        %-  (trace 1 |.("leaving subscription to {<app.action>}"))
1195        (deal-as /watch-response/[eyre-id] identity our app.action %leave ~)
1196      ::
1197          ?(%authentication %eauth %logout)
1198        ::NOTE  expiry timer will clean up cancelled eauth attempts
1199        [~ state]
1200      ::
1201          %channel
1202        on-cancel-request:by-channel
1203      ::
1204          ?(%scry %four-oh-four %name %host)
1205        ::  it should be impossible for these to be asynchronous
1206        ::
1207        !!
1208      ==
1209    ::  +return-static-data-on-duct: returns one piece of data all at once
1210    ::
1211    ++  return-static-data-on-duct
1212      |=  [code=@ content-type=@t data=octs]
1213      ^-  [(list move) server-state]
1214      ::
1215      %-  handle-response
1216      :*  %start
```

```
1217        :-  status-code=code
1218        ^=  headers
1219          :~  ['content-type' content-type]
1220              ['content-length' (crip (format-ud-as-integer p.data))]
1221          ==
1222        data=[~ data]
1223        complete=%.y
1224    ==
1225  ::  +authentication: per-event authentication as this Urbit's owner
1226  ::
1227  ::    Right now this hard codes the authentication page using the old +code
1228  ::    system, but in the future should be pluggable so we can use U2F or
1229  ::    WebAuthn or whatever is more secure than passwords.
1230  ::
1231  ++  authentication
1232    |%
1233    ::  +handle-request: handles an http request for the login page
1234    ::
1235    ++  handle-request
1236      |=  [secure=? host=(unit @t) =address [session-id=@uv =identity] =request:http]
1237      ^-  [(list move) server-state]
1238      ::  parse the arguments out of request uri
1239      ::
1240      =+  request-line=(parse-request-line url.request)
1241      =/  redirect     (get-header:http 'redirect' args.request-line)
1242      =/  with-eauth=(unit ?)
1243        ?:  =(~ eauth-url:eauth)   ~
1244        `?=(^ (get-header:http 'eauth' args.request-line))
1245      ::  if we received a simple get: show the login page
1246      ::
1247      ::NOTE  we never auto-redirect, to avoid redirect loops with apps that
1248      ::        send unprivileged users to the login screen
1249      ::
1250      ?:  =('GET' method.request)
1251        %^  return-static-data-on-duct  200  'text/html'
1252        (login-page redirect our identity with-eauth %.n)
1253      ::  if we are not a post, return an error
1254      ::
1255      ?.  =('POST' method.request)
1256        %^  return-static-data-on-duct  405  'text/html'
1257        (login-page ~ our identity with-eauth %.n)
1258      ::  we are a post, and must process the body type as form data
1259      ::
1260      ?~  body.request
1261        %^  return-static-data-on-duct  400  'text/html'
1262        (login-page ~ our identity with-eauth %.n)
1263      ::
1264      =/  parsed=(unit (list [key=@t value=@t]))
1265        (rush q.u.body.request yquy:de-purl:html)
1266      ?~  parsed
1267        %^  return-static-data-on-duct  400  'text/html'
1268        (login-page ~ our identity with-eauth %.n)
1269      ::
1270      =/  redirect=(unit @t)  (get-header:http 'redirect' u.parsed)
1271      ?^  (get-header:http 'eauth' u.parsed)
1272        ?~  ship=(biff (get-header:http 'name' u.parsed) (cury slaw %p))
1273          %^  return-static-data-on-duct  400  'text/html'
1274          (login-page redirect our identity `& %.n)
```

```
1275          ::TODO  redirect logic here and elsewhere is ugly
1276          =/  redirect  (fall redirect '')
1277          =/  base=(unit @t)
1278            ?~  host  ~
1279            `(cat 3 ?:(secure 'https://' 'http://') u.host)
1280          (start:server:eauth u.ship base ?:(=(redirect '') '/' redirect))
1281          ::
1282        =.  with-eauth  (bind with-eauth |=(? |))
1283        ?~  password=(get-header:http 'password' u.parsed)
1284          %^  return-static-data-on-duct  400  'text/html'
1285          (login-page redirect our identity with-eauth %.n)
1286        ::  check that the password is correct
1287        ::
1288        ?.  =(u.password code)
1289          %^  return-static-data-on-duct  400  'text/html'
1290          (login-page redirect our identity with-eauth %.y)
1291        ::  clean up the session they're changing out from
1292        ::
1293        =^  moz  state
1294          (close-session session-id |)
1295        ::  initialize the new session
1296        ::
1297        =^  fex  state  (start-session %local)
1298        ::  associate the new session with the request that caused the login
1299        ::
1300        ::    if we don't do this here, +handle-response will include the old
1301        ::    session's cookie, confusing the client.
1302        ::
1303        =.  connections.state
1304          %+  ~(jab by connections.state)  duct
1305          |=  o=outstanding-connection
1306          o(session-id session.fex)
1307        ::  store the hostname used for this login, later reuse it for eauth
1308        ::
1309        =?  endpoint.auth.state
1310            ::  avoid overwriting public domains with localhost
1311            ::
1312            ?&  ?=(^ host)
1313            ?|  ?=(~ auth.endpoint.auth.state)
1314                !=('localhost' (fall (rush u.host host-sans-port) ''))
1315            ==  ==
1316          %-  (trace 2 |.("eauth: storing endpoint at {(trip u.host)}"))
1317          =/  new-auth=(unit @t)
1318            `(cat 3 ?:(secure 'https://' 'http://') u.host)
1319          =,  endpoint.auth.state
1320          :+  user  new-auth
1321          ::  only update the timestamp if the derived endpoint visibly changed.
1322          ::  that is, it's not hidden behind a user-provided hardcoded url,
1323          ::  and the new value is different from the old.)
1324          ::
1325          ?:(|(?=(^ user) =(new-auth auth)) time now)
1326        ::
1327        =;  out=[moves=(list move) server-state]
1328          out(moves [give-session-tokens :(weld moz moves.fex moves.out)])
1329        ::NOTE  that we don't provide a 'set-cookie' header here.
1330        ::      +handle-response does that for us.
1331        ?~  redirect
1332          (handle-response %start 204^~ ~ &)
```

```
1333      =/  actual-redirect  ?:(=(u.redirect '') '/' u.redirect)
1334      (handle-response %start 303^['location' actual-redirect]~ ~ &)
1335  ::  +handle-logout: handles an http request for logging out
1336  ::
1337  ++  handle-logout
1338    |=  [[session-id=@uv =identity] =request:http]
1339    ^-  [(list move) server-state]
1340    ::  whatever we end up doing, we always respond with a redirect
1341    ::
1342    =/  response=$>(%start http-event:http)
1343      =/  redirect=(unit @t)
1344        %+  get-header:http  'redirect'
1345        args:(parse-request-line url.request)
1346      :*  %start
1347          response-header=[303 ['location' (fall redirect '/~/login')]~]
1348          data=~
1349          complete=%.y
1350      ==
1351    ::  read options from the body
1352    ::  all: log out all sessions with this identity?
1353    ::  sid: which session do we log out? (defaults to requester's)
1354    ::  hos: host to log out from, for eauth logins (sid signifies the nonce)
1355    ::
1356    =/  arg=header-list:http
1357      ?~  body.request  ~
1358      (fall (rush q.u.body.request yquy:de-purl:html) ~)
1359    =/  all=?
1360      ?=(^ (get-header:http 'all' arg))
1361    =/  sid=(unit @uv)
1362      ?.  ?=(%ours -.identity)  `session-id
1363      ?~  sid=(get-header:http 'sid' arg)  `session-id
1364      ::  if you provided the parameter, but it doesn't parse, we just
1365      ::  no-op. otherwise, a poorly-implemented frontend might result in
1366      ::  accidental log-outs, which would be very annoying.
1367      ::
1368      (slaw %uv u.sid)
1369    =/  hos=(unit @p)
1370      ?.  ?=(%ours -.identity)  ~
1371      (biff (get-header:http 'host' arg) (cury slaw %p))
1372    ?~  sid
1373      (handle-response response)
1374    ::  if this is an eauth remote logout, send the %shut
1375    ::
1376    =*  auth  auth.state
1377    ?:  ?=(^ hos)
1378      =^  moz  state  (handle-response response)
1379      :-  [(send-plea:client:eauth u.hos %0 %shut u.sid) moz]
1380      =/  book  (~(gut by visiting.auth) u.hos *logbook)
1381      =.  qeu.book  (~(put to qeu.book) u.sid)
1382      =.  visiting.auth  (~(put by visiting.auth) u.hos book)
1383      state
1384    ::  if the requester is logging themselves out, make them drop the cookie
1385    ::
1386    =?  headers.response-header.response  =(u.sid session-id)
1387      :_  headers.response-header.response
1388      ['set-cookie' (session-cookie-string session-id |)]
1389    ::  close the session as requested, then send the response
1390    ::
```

```
1391        =^  moz1  state  (close-session u.sid all)
1392        =^  moz2  state  (handle-response response)
1393        [[give-session-tokens (weld moz1 moz2)] state]
1394    ::  +session-id-from-request: attempt to find a session cookie
1395    ::
1396    ++  session-id-from-request
1397      |=  =request:http
1398      ^-  (unit @uv)
1399      ::  are there cookies passed with this request?
1400      ::
1401      =/  cookie-header=@t
1402        %+  roll  header-list.request
1403        |=  [[key=@t value=@t] c=@t]
1404        ?.  =(key 'cookie')
1405          c
1406        (cat 3 (cat 3 c ?~(c 0 '; ')) value)
1407      ::  is the cookie line valid?
1408      ::
1409      ?~  cookies=(rush cookie-header cock:de-purl:html)
1410        ~
1411      ::  is there an urbauth cookie?
1412      ::
1413      ?~  urbauth=(get-header:http (crip "urbauth-{(scow %p our)}") u.cookies)
1414        ~
1415      ::  if it's formatted like a valid session cookie, produce it
1416      ::
1417      `(unit @)`(rush u.urbauth ;~(pfix (jest '0v') viz:ag))
1418    ::  +request-is-logged-in: checks to see if the request has non-guest id
1419    ::
1420    ++  request-is-logged-in
1421      |=  =request:http
1422      ^-  ?
1423      ?~  session-id=(session-id-from-request request)
1424        |
1425      ?~  session=(~(get by sessions.auth.state) u.session-id)
1426        |
1427      &(!?=(%fake -.identity.u.session) (lte now expiry-time.u.session))
1428    ::  +request-is-authenticated: checks to see if the request is "us"
1429    ::
1430    ::    We are considered authenticated if this request has an urbauth
1431    ::    Cookie for the local identity that is not expired.
1432    ::
1433    ++  request-is-authenticated
1434      |=  =request:http
1435      ^-  ?
1436      ::  does the request pass a session cookie?
1437      ::
1438      ?~  session-id=(session-id-from-request request)
1439        %.n
1440      ::  is this a session that we know about?
1441      ::
1442      ?~  session=(~(get by sessions.auth.state) `@uv`u.session-id)
1443        %.n
1444      ::  does this session have our id, and is it still valid?
1445      ::
1446      &(?=(%ours -.identity.u.session) (lte now expiry-time.u.session))
1447    ::  +start-session: create a new session with %local or %guest identity
1448    ::
```

```
1449   ++    start-session
1450     |=    kind=?(%local %guest [%eauth who=@p])
1451     ^-    [[session=@uv =identity moves=(list move)] server-state]
1452     =;    [key=@uv sid=identity]
1453       :-    :+    key    sid
1454           ::    if no session existed previously, we must kick off the
1455           ::    session expiry timer
1456           ::
1457           ?^    sessions.auth.state    ~
1458           [duct %pass /sessions/expire %b %wait (add now session-timeout)]~
1459       =-    state(sessions.auth -)
1460       %+    ~(put by sessions.auth.state)    key
1461       [sid (add now session-timeout) ~]
1462     ::    create a new session with a fake identity
1463     ::
1464     =/    sik=@uv    new-session-key
1465     :-    sik
1466     ?:    ?=(%local kind)        [%ours ~]
1467     ?:    ?=([%eauth @] kind)    [%real who.kind]
1468     :-    %fake
1469     ::    pre-scramble our ship name into its displayed value, and
1470     ::    truncate it to be at most moon-length, so that we can overlay
1471     ::    it onto the end of a comet name for visual consistency.
1472     ::    to prevent escalation, make sure the guest identity isn't ours.
1473     ::
1474     |-
1475     =;    nom=@p
1476       ?.    =(our nom)    nom
1477       $(eny (shas %next-name eny))
1478     %+    end    3^16
1479     %^    cat    3
1480       (end 3^8 (fein:ob our))
1481     (~(raw og (shas %fake-name eny)) 128)
1482   ::    +session-for-request: get the session details for the request
1483   ::
1484   ::      creates a guest session if the request does not have a valid session.
1485   ::      there is no need to call +give-session-tokens after this, because
1486   ::      guest session do not make valid "auth session" tokens.
1487   ::
1488   ++    session-for-request
1489     |=    =request:http
1490     ^-    [[session=@uv =identity moves=(list move)] server-state]
1491     =*    new    (start-session %guest)
1492     ?~    sid=(session-id-from-request request)
1493       new
1494     ?~    ses=(~(get by sessions.auth.state) u.sid)
1495       new
1496     ?:    (gth now expiry-time.u.ses)
1497       new
1498     [[u.sid identity.u.ses ~] state]
1499   ::    +close-session: delete a session and its associated channels
1500   ::
1501   ::      if :all is true, deletes all sessions that share the same identity.
1502   ::      if this closes an %ours session, the caller is responsible for
1503   ::      also calling +give-session-tokens afterwards.
1504   ::
1505   ++    close-session
1506     |=    [session-id=@uv all=?]
```

```hoon
1507      ^-  [(list move) server-state]
1508      ?~  ses=(~(get by sessions.auth.state) session-id)
1509        [~ state]
1510      ::  delete the session(s) and find the associated ids & channels
1511      ::
1512      =^  [siz=(list @uv) channels=(list @t)]  sessions.auth.state
1513        =*  sessions  sessions.auth.state
1514        ::  either delete just the specific session and its channels,
1515        ::
1516        ?.  all
1517          :-  [[session-id]~ ~(tap in channels.u.ses)]
1518          (~(del by sessions) session-id)
1519        ::  or delete all sessions with the identity from :session-id
1520        ::
1521        %+  roll  ~(tap by sessions)
1522        |=  $:  [sid=@uv s=session]
1523                [[siz=(list @uv) caz=(list @t)] sez=(map @uv session)]
1524            ==
1525        ^+  [[siz caz] sez]
1526        ?.  =(identity.s identity.u.ses)
1527          ::  identity doesn't match, so re-store this session
1528          ::
1529          [[siz caz] (~(put by sez) sid s)]
1530        ::  identity matches, so register this session as closed
1531        ::
1532        [[[sid siz] (weld caz ~(tap in channels.s))] sez]
1533      ::  close all affected channels and send their responses
1534      ::
1535      =|  moves1=(list move)
1536      |-  ^-  (quip move server-state)
1537      ?^  channels
1538        %-  %+  trace  1
1539            |.("{(trip i.channels)} discarding channel due to closed session")
1540        =^  moz    state
1541          (discard-channel:by-channel i.channels |)
1542        $(moves1 (weld moves1 moz), channels t.channels)
1543      ::  lastly, %real sessions require additional cleanup
1544      ::
1545      ?.  ?=(%real -.identity.u.ses)  [moves1 state]
1546      =^  moves2  visitors.auth.state
1547        %+  roll  ~(tap by visitors.auth.state)
1548        |=  [[nonce=@uv visa=visitor] [moz=(list move) viz=(map @uv visitor)]]
1549        ?^  +.visa  [moz (~(put by viz) nonce visa)]
1550        :_  viz
1551        %+  weld  moz
1552        ?~  duct.visa  ~
1553        [(send-boon:server:eauth (duct u.duct.visa) %0 %shut nonce)]~
1554      [(weld `(list move)`moves1 `(list move)`moves2) state]
1555    ::  +code: returns the same as |code
1556    ::
1557    ++  code
1558      ^-  @ta
1559      =/  res=(unit (unit cage))
1560        (rof [~ ~] /eyre %j [our %code da+now] /(scot %p our))
1561      (rsh 3 (scot %p ;;(@ q.q:(need (need res)))))
1562    ::  +session-cookie-string: compose session cookie
1563    ::
1564    ++  session-cookie-string
```

```
1565      |=  [session=@uv extend=?]
1566      ^-  @t
1567      %-  crip
1568      =;  max-age=tape
1569        "urbauth-{(scow %p our)}={(scow %uv session)}; Path=/; Max-Age={max-age}"
1570      %-  format-ud-as-integer
1571      ?.  extend  0
1572      (div (msec:milly session-timeout) 1.000)
1573    ::
1574    ::
1575    ++  eauth
1576      =*  auth  auth.state
1577      |%
1578      ++  server
1579        |%
1580        ::  +start: initiate an eauth login attempt for the :ship identity
1581        ::
1582        ++  start
1583          |=  [=ship base=(unit @t) last=@t]
1584          ^-  [(list move) server-state]
1585          %-  (trace 2 |.("eauth: starting eauth into {(scow %p ship)}"))
1586          =/  nonce=@uv
1587            |-
1588            =+  n=(~(raw og (shas %eauth-nonce eny)) 64)
1589            ?.  (~(has by visitors.auth) n)  n
1590            $(eny (shas %try-again n))
1591          =/  visit=visitor  [~ `[duct now] ship base last ~]
1592          =.  visitors.auth  (~(put by visitors.auth) nonce visit)
1593          :_  state
1594          ::  we delay serving an http response until we receive a scry %tune
1595          ::
1596          :~  (send-keen %keen ship nonce now)
1597              (start-timeout /visitors/(scot %uv nonce))
1598          ==
1599        ::  +on-tune: receive a client-url remote scry result
1600        ::
1601        ++  on-tune
1602          |=  [ship=@p nonce=@uv url=@t]
1603          ^-  [(list move) server-state]
1604          %-  (trace 2 |.("eauth: %tune from {(scow %p ship)}"))
1605          ::  guarantee the ship still controls the nonce
1606          ::
1607          =/  visa=visitor  (~(got by visitors.auth) nonce)
1608          ?>  &(?=(^ +.visa) =(ship ship.visa))
1609          ::  redirect the visitor to their own confirmation page
1610          ::
1611          =.  visitors.auth  (~(put by visitors.auth) nonce visa(pend ~))
1612          %-  handle-response(duct http:(need pend.visa))
1613          =;  url=@t  [%start 303^['location' url]~ ~ &]
1614          %+  rap  3
1615          :~  url
1616              '?server='  (scot %p our)
1617              '&nonce='  (scot %uv nonce)
1618          ==
1619        ::  +on-plea: receive an eauth network message from a client
1620        ::
1621        ++  on-plea
1622          |=  [=ship plea=eauth-plea]
```

```
1623          ^-  [(list move) server-state]
1624          %-  (trace 2 |.("eauth: {(trip +<.plea)} from {(scow %p ship)}"))
1625          =;  res=[(list move) server-state]
1626            =^  moz  state  res
1627            [[[duct %give %done ~] moz] state]
1628          ?-  +<.plea
1629              %open
1630            ::  this attempt may or may not have been started in +start yet
1631            ::
1632            =/  visa=visitor
1633              %+  ~(gut by visitors.auth)  nonce.plea
1634              [~ ~ ship ~ '/' ~]
1635            ?>  ?=(^ +.visa)
1636            ?>  =(ship ship.visa)
1637            ::NOTE  that token might still be empty, in which case the http
1638            ::       client will probably signal an abort when they return
1639            ::
1640            =.  duct.visa      `duct
1641            =.  toke.visa      token.plea
1642            =.  visitors.auth  (~(put by visitors.auth) nonce.plea visa)
1643            ::  if the eauth attempt was started on our side, we may know the
1644            ::  specific base url the user used; make sure they go back there
1645            ::
1646            =/  url=@t
1647              %-  need
1648              ?~  base.visa  eauth-url
1649              eauth-url(user.endpoint.auth base.visa)
1650            [[(send-boon %0 %okay nonce.plea url)]~ state]
1651          ::
1652              %shut
1653            ::  the visitor wants the associated session gone
1654            ::
1655            ?~  visa=(~(get by visitors.auth) nonce.plea)  [~ state]
1656            =.  visitors.auth  (~(del by visitors.auth) nonce.plea)
1657            =?  sessions.auth  ?=(@ +.u.visa)
1658              (~(del by sessions.auth) sesh.u.visa)
1659            [[(send-boon %0 %shut nonce.plea)]~ state]
1660          ==
1661        ::  +cancel: the client aborted the eauth attempt, so clean it up
1662        ::
1663        ++  cancel
1664          |=  [nonce=@uv last=@t]
1665          ^-  [(list move) server-state]
1666          ::  if the eauth attempt doesn't exist, or it was already completed,
1667          ::  we cannot cancel it
1668          ::
1669          ?~  visa=(~(get by visitors.auth) nonce)  [~ state]
1670          ?@  +.u.visa  [~ state]
1671          ::  delete the attempt, and go back to the login page
1672          ::
1673          %-  (trace 2 |.("eauth: cancelling login"))
1674          =.  visitors.auth  (~(del by visitors.auth) nonce)
1675          =^  moz  state
1676            =/  url=@t
1677              %^  cat  3  '/~/login?eauth&redirect='
1678              (crip (en-urlt:html (trip last)))
1679            (handle-response %start 303^['location' url]~ ~ &)
1680          :_  state
```

```
%+  weld  moz
?~  duct.u.visa  ~
[(send-boon(duct u.duct.u.visa) %0 %shut nonce)]~
::  +expire: host-side cancel an eauth attempt if it's still pending
::
++  expire
  |=  nonce=@uv
  ^-  [(list move) server-state]
  ?~  visa=(~(get by visitors.auth) nonce)
    [~ state]
  ?@  +.u.visa  [~ state]
  %-  (trace 2 |.("eauth: expiring"))
  =^  moz  state
    ?~  pend.u.visa  [~ state]
    %-  return-static-data-on-duct(duct http.u.pend.u.visa)
    [503 'text/html' (eauth-error-page %server last.u.visa)]
  =?  moz  ?=(^ pend.u.visa)
    [(send-keen %yawn ship.u.visa nonce keen.u.pend.u.visa) moz]
  =.  visitors.auth  (~(del by visitors.auth) nonce)
  :_  state
  %+  weld  moz
  ?~  duct.u.visa  ~
  [(send-boon(duct u.duct.u.visa) %0 %shut nonce)]~
::  +finalize: eauth attempt was approved: mint the client a new session
::
::    gives the http response on the current duct
::
++  finalize
  |=  [=plea=^duct nonce=@uv =ship last=@t]
  ^-  [(list move) server-state]
  %-  (trace 2 |.("eauth: finalizing login for {(scow %p ship)}"))
  ::  clean up the session they're changing out from,
  ::  mint the new session,
  ::  associate it with the nonce,
  ::  and the finalization request,
  ::  and send the visitor the cookie + final redirect
  ::
  =^  moz1  state
    (close-session session-id:(~(got by connections.state) duct) |)
  =^  [sid=@uv * moz2=(list move)]  state
    (start-session %eauth ship)
  =.  visitors.auth
    %+  ~(jab by visitors.auth)  nonce
    |=(v=visitor v(+ sid))
  =.  connections.state
    %+  ~(jab by connections.state)  duct
    |=  o=outstanding-connection
    o(session-id sid)
  =^  moz3  state
    =;  hed  (handle-response %start 303^hed ~ &)
    :~  ['location' last]
        ['set-cookie' (session-cookie-string sid &)]
    ==
  [:(weld moz1 moz2 moz3) state]
::  +on-fail: we crashed or received an empty %tune, clean up
::
++  on-fail
  |=  [=ship nonce=@uv]
```

```
1739        ^-  [(list move) server-state]
1740        ::  if the eauth attempt doesn't exist, or it was already completed,
1741        ::  we can no-op here
1742        ::
1743        ?~  visa=(~(get by visitors.auth) nonce)  [~ state]
1744        ?@  +.u.visa  [~ state]
1745        ::  delete the attempt, and go back to the login page
1746        ::
1747        %-  (trace 2 |.("eauth: failed login"))
1748        =.  visitors.auth  (~(del by visitors.auth) nonce)
1749        =^  moz  state
1750          ?~  pend.u.visa  [~ state]
1751          %-  return-static-data-on-duct(duct http.u.pend.u.visa)
1752          [503 'text/html' (eauth-error-page %server last.u.visa)]
1753        :_  state
1754        %+  weld  moz
1755        ?~  duct.u.visa  ~
1756        [(send-boon(duct u.duct.u.visa) %0 %shut nonce)]~
1757      ::
1758      ::TODO  +on-request?
1759      ::
1760      ++  send-keen
1761        |=  [kind=?(%keen %yawn) =ship nonce=@uv =time]
1762        ^-  move
1763        %-  (trace 2 |.("eauth: %{(trip kind)} into {(scow %p ship)}"))
1764        ::  we round down the time to make it more likely to hit cache,
1765        ::  at the expense of not working if the endpoint changed within
1766        ::  the last hour.
1767        ::
1768        =/  =wire        /eauth/keen/(scot %p ship)/(scot %uv nonce)
1769        =.  time         (sub time (mod time ~h1))
1770        =/  =spar:ames  [ship /e/x/(scot %da time)//eauth/url]
1771        [duct %pass wire %a ?-(kind %keen keen+[~ spar], %yawn yawn+spar)]
1772      ::
1773      ++  send-boon
1774        |=  boon=eauth-boon
1775        ^-  move
1776        %-  (trace 2 |.("eauth: sending {(trip +<.boon)}"))
1777        [duct %give %boon boon]
1778      --
1779    ::
1780    ++  client
1781      |%
1782      ::  +start: as the client, approve or abort an eauth attempt
1783      ::
1784      ::    assumes the duct is of an incoming eauth start/approve request
1785      ::
1786      ++  start
1787        |=  [host=ship nonce=@uv grant=?]
1788        ^-  [(list move) server-state]
1789        =/  token=@uv  (~(raw og (shas %eauth-token eny)) 128)
1790        ::  we always send an %open, because we need to redirect the user
1791        ::  back to the host. and we always set a timeout, because we may
1792        ::  not get a response quickly enough.
1793        ::
1794        :-  :~  (send-plea host %0 %open nonce ?:(grant `token ~))
1795                (start-timeout /visiting/(scot %p host)/(scot %uv nonce))
1796            ==
```

```
1797        ::  make sure we aren't attempting with this nonce already,
1798        ::  then remember the secret so we can include it in the redirect
1799        ::
1800        =/  book  (~(gut by visiting.auth) host *logbook)
1801        ?<  (~(has by map.book) nonce)
1802        =.  visiting.auth
1803          %+  ~(put by visiting.auth)  host
1804          :-  (~(put to qeu.book) nonce)
1805          (~(put by map.book) nonce [`duct ?:(grant `token ~)])
1806        state
1807      ::  +on-done: receive n/ack for plea we sent
1808      ::
1809      ++  on-done
1810        |=  [host=ship good=?]
1811        ^-  [(list move) server-state]
1812        %-  %-  trace
1813            ?:  good
1814              [2 |.("eauth: ack from {(scow %p host)}")]
1815              [1 |.("eauth: nack from {(scow %p host)}")]
1816        =/  book  (~(gut by visiting.auth) host *logbook)
1817        ?~  ~(top to qeu.book)
1818          %.  [~ state]
1819          (trace 0 |.("eauth: done on empty queue from {(scow %p host)}"))
1820        =^  nonce=@uv  qeu.book  ~(get to qeu.book)
1821        ?:  good
1822          =.  visiting.auth
1823            ?:  =([~ ~] book)
1824              (~(del by visiting.auth) host)
1825            (~(put by visiting.auth) host book)
1826          [~ state]
1827        =/  port  (~(get by map.book) nonce)
1828        ?~  port  [~ state]
1829        ::  delete the attempt/session, serve response if needed
1830        ::
1831        =.  visiting.auth
1832          =.  map.book
1833            (~(del by map.book) nonce)
1834          ?:  =([~ ~] book)
1835            (~(del by visiting.auth) host)
1836          (~(put by visiting.auth) host book)
1837        ::
1838        ?@  u.port            [~ state]
1839        ?~  pend.u.port  [~ state]
1840        %^  return-static-data-on-duct(duct u.pend.u.port)  503  'text/html'
1841        (eauth-error-page ~)
1842      ::  +on-boon: receive an eauth network response from a host
1843      ::
1844      ::    crashes on unexpected circumstances, in response to which we
1845      ::    should abort the eauth attempt
1846      ::
1847      ++  on-boon
1848        |=  [host=ship boon=eauth-boon]
1849        ^-  [(list move) server-state]
1850        %-  (trace 2 |.("eauth: %{(trip +<.boon)} from {(scow %p host)}"))
1851        ?-  +<.boon
1852            %okay
1853          =/  book  (~(got by visiting.auth) host)
1854          =/  port  (~(got by map.book) nonce.boon)
```

```
1855        ?>  ?=(^ port)
1856        ?>  ?=(^ pend.port)
1857        ::  update the outgoing sessions map, deleting if we aborted
1858        ::
1859        =.  visiting.auth
1860          ?^  toke.port
1861            %+  ~(put by visiting.auth)  host
1862            :-  qeu.book
1863            ::NOTE  optimistic
1864            (~(put by map.book) nonce.boon now)
1865          =.  map.book
1866            (~(del by map.book) nonce.boon)
1867          ?:  =([~ ~] book)
1868            (~(del by visiting.auth) host)
1869          (~(put by visiting.auth) host book)
1870        ::  always serve a redirect, with either the token, or abort signal
1871        ::
1872        =;  url=@t
1873          %-  handle-response(duct u.pend.port)
1874          [%start 303^['location' url]~ ~ &]
1875        %+  rap  3
1876        :*  url.boon
1877            '?nonce='  (scot %uv nonce.boon)
1878            ?~  toke.port  ['&abort']~
1879            ~['&token='  (scot %uv u.toke.port)]
1880        ==
1881      ::
1882        %shut
1883      ::  the host has deleted the corresponding session
1884      ::
1885      =.  visiting.auth
1886        =/  book
1887          (~(gut by visiting.auth) host *logbook)
1888        =.  map.book
1889          (~(del by map.book) nonce.boon)
1890        ?:  =([~ ~] book)
1891          (~(del by visiting.auth) host)
1892        (~(put by visiting.auth) host book)
1893      [~ state]
1894    ==
1895  ::
1896  ++  expire
1897    |=  [host=ship nonce=@uv]
1898    ^-  [(list move) server-state]
1899    =/  book  (~(gut by visiting.auth) host *logbook)
1900    =/  port  (~(get by map.book) nonce)
1901    ::  if the attempt was completed, we don't expire it
1902    ::
1903    ?~  port  [~ state]
1904    ?@  u.port  [~ state]
1905    ::  delete pending attempts, serve response if needed
1906    ::
1907    %-  %+  trace  1
1908        |.("eauth: attempt into {(scow %p host)} expired")
1909    =.  visiting.auth
1910      =.  map.book
1911        (~(del by map.book) nonce)
1912      ?:  =([~ ~] book)
```

```
1913              (~(del by visiting.auth) host)
1914            (~(put by visiting.auth) host book)
1915        ::
1916        ?~  pend.u.port  [~ state]
1917        %^  return-static-data-on-duct(duct u.pend.u.port)  503  'text/html'
1918        (eauth-error-page ~)
1919      ::
1920      ++  send-plea
1921        |=  [=ship plea=eauth-plea]
1922        ^-  move
1923        ::NOTE  no nonce in the wire, to avoid proliferating flows
1924        =/  =wire  /eauth/plea/(scot %p ship)
1925        %-  (trace 2 |.("eauth: {(trip +<.plea)} into {(scow %p ship)}"))
1926        [[/eyre/eauth/synthetic]~ %pass wire %a %plea ship %e /eauth/0 plea]
1927      ::
1928      ++  confirmation-page
1929        |=  [server=ship nonce=@uv]
1930        ^-  octs
1931        %-  as-octs:mimes:html
1932        %-  crip
1933        %-  en-xml:html
1934        =/  favicon  %+
1935          weld  "<svg width='10' height='10' viewBox='0 0 10 10' xmlns='http://www.w3.org/2000/svg'>"
1936                "<circle r='3.09' cx='5' cy='5' /></svg>"
1937        ;html
1938          ;head
1939            ;meta(charset "utf-8");
1940            ;meta(name "viewport", content "width=device-width, initial-scale=1, shrink-to-fit=no");
1941            ;link(rel "icon", type "image/svg+xml", href (weld "data:image/svg+xml;utf8," favicon));
1942            ;title:"Urbit"
1943            ;style:"{(trip auth-styling)}"
1944            ;style:'''
1945                  form {
1946                    border: 1px solid var(--black20);
1947                    border-radius: 4px;
1948                    padding: 1rem;
1949                    align-items: stretch;
1950                    font-size: 14px;
1951                  }
1952                  .red {
1953                    background: var(--black05) !important;
1954                    color: var(--black60) !important;
1955                    border: 1px solid var(--black60) !important;
1956                  }
1957                  code {
1958                    font-weight: bold;
1959                    font-family: "Source Code Pro", monospace;
1960                  }
1961                  button {
1962                    display: inline-block;
1963                  }
1964                  '''
1965          ==
1966          ;body
1967            ;form(action "/~/eauth", method "post")
1968              ; Hello, {(scow %p our)}.
1969              ; You are trying to log in to:
1970              ;code:"{(scow %p server)}"
```

```hoon
                      ;input(type "hidden", name "server", value (scow %p server));
                      ;input(type "hidden", name "nonce", value (scow %uv nonce));
                      ;button(type "submit", name "grant", value "grant"):"approve"
                      ;button(type "submit", name "reject", class "red"):"reject"
                    ==
                ==
            ==
        --
    ::  +on-request: http request to the /~/eauth endpoint
    ::
    ++  on-request
      |=  [[session-id=@uv =identity] =request:http]
      ^-  [(list move) server-state]
      ::  we may need the requester to log in before proceeding
      ::
      =*  login
        =;  url=@t  (handle-response %start 303^['location' url]~ ~ &)
        %^  cat  3  '/~/login?redirect='
        (crip (en-urlt:html (trip url.request)))
      ::  or give them a generic, static error page in unexpected cases
      ::
      =*  error  %^  return-static-data-on-duct  400  'text/html'
                 (eauth-error-page ~)
      ::  GET requests either render the confirmation page,
      ::  or finalize an eauth flow
      ::
      ?:  ?=(%'GET' method.request)
        =/  args=(map @t @t)  (malt args:(parse-request-line url.request))
        =/  server=(unit @p)  (biff (~(get by args) 'server') (cury slaw %p))
        =/  nonce=(unit @uv)  (biff (~(get by args) 'nonce') (cury slaw %uv))
        =/  token=(unit @uv)  (biff (~(get by args) 'token') (cury slaw %uv))
        =/  abort=?           (~(has by args) 'abort')
        ::
        ?~  nonce  error
        ::
        ?^  server
          ::  request for confirmation page
          ::
          ?.  ?=(%ours -.identity)  login
          =/  book  (~(gut by visiting.auth) u.server *logbook)
          =/  door  (~(get by map.book) u.nonce)
          ?~  door
            ::  nonce not yet used, render the confirmation page as normal
            ::
            %^  return-static-data-on-duct  200  'text/html'
            (confirmation-page:client u.server u.nonce)
          ::  if we're still awaiting a redirect target, we choose to serve
          ::  this latest request instead
          ::
          ?@  u.door          error
          ?~  pend.u.door     error
          =.  map.book        (~(put by map.book) u.nonce u.door(pend `duct))
          =.  visiting.auth   (~(put by visiting.auth) u.server book)
          %-  return-static-data-on-duct(duct u.pend.u.door)
          [202 'text/plain' (as-octs:mimes:html 'continued elsewhere...')]
        ::  important to provide an error response for unexpected states
        ::
        =/  visa=(unit visitor)  (~(get by visitors.auth) u.nonce)
```

```
2029        ?~  visa          error
2030        ?@  +.u.visa      error
2031        =*  error  %^  return-static-data-on-duct  400  'text/html'
2032                 (eauth-error-page %server last.u.visa)
2033        ::  request for finalization, must either abort or provide a token
2034        ::
2035        ::NOTE  yes, this means that unauthenticated clients can abort
2036        ::        any eauth attempt they know the nonce for, but that should
2037        ::        be pretty benign
2038        ?:  abort  (cancel:^server u.nonce last.u.visa)
2039        ?~  token  error
2040        ::  if this request provides a token, but the client didn't, complain
2041        ::
2042        ?~  toke.u.visa  error
2043        ::  verify the request
2044        ::
2045        ?.  =(u.token u.toke.u.visa)
2046          %-  (trace 1 |.("eauth: token mismatch"))
2047          error
2048        ?~  duct.u.visa  error
2049        (finalize:^server u.duct.u.visa u.nonce ship.u.visa last.u.visa)
2050      ::
2051      ?.  ?=(%'POST' method.request)
2052        %^  return-static-data-on-duct  405  'text/html'
2053        (eauth-error-page ~)
2054      ?.  =(%ours -.identity)  login
2055      ::  POST requests are always submissions of the confirmation page
2056      ::
2057      =/  args=(map @t @t)
2058        (malt (fall (rush q:(fall body.request *octs) yquy:de-purl:html) ~))
2059      =/  server=(unit @p)   (biff (~(get by args) 'server') (cury slaw %p))
2060      =/  nonce=(unit @uv)   (biff (~(get by args) 'nonce') (cury slaw %uv))
2061      =/  grant=?            =(`'grant' (~(get by args) 'grant'))
2062      ::
2063      =*  error   %^  return-static-data-on-duct  400   'text/html'
2064                 (eauth-error-page ~)
2065      ?~  server  error
2066      ?~  nonce   error
2067      =/  book    (~(gut by visiting.auth) u.server *logbook)
2068      ?:  (~(has by map.book) u.nonce)  error
2069      (start:client u.server u.nonce grant)
2070    ::
2071    ++  eauth-url
2072      ^-  (unit @t)
2073      =/  end=(unit @t)  (clap user.endpoint.auth auth.endpoint.auth head)
2074      ?~  end  ~
2075      `(cat 3 u.end '/~/eauth')
2076    ::
2077    ++  start-timeout
2078      |=  =path
2079      ^-  move
2080      [duct %pass [%eauth %expire path] %b %wait (add now ~m5)]
2081      --
2082  --
2083  ::  +channel: per-event handling of requests to the channel system
2084  ::
2085  ::    Eyre offers a remote interface to your Urbit through channels, which
2086  ::    are persistent connections on the server which can be disconnected and
```

```
2087    ::      reconnected on the client.
2088    ::
2089    ++  by-channel
2090      ::  moves: the moves to be sent out at the end of this event, reversed
2091      ::
2092      =|  moves=(list move)
2093      |%
2094      ::  +handle-request: handles an http request for the subscription system
2095      ::
2096      ++  handle-request
2097        |=  [[session-id=@uv =identity] =address =request:http]
2098        ^-  [(list move) server-state]
2099        ::  parse out the path key the subscription is on
2100        ::
2101        =+  request-line=(parse-request-line url.request)
2102        ?.  ?=([@t @t @t ~] site.request-line)
2103          ::  url is not of the form '/~/channel/'
2104          ::
2105          %^  return-static-data-on-duct  400  'text/html'
2106          (error-page 400 & url.request "malformed channel url")
2107        ::  channel-id: unique channel id parsed out of url
2108        ::
2109        =+  channel-id=i.t.t.site.request-line
2110        ::
2111        ?:  =('PUT' method.request)
2112          ::  PUT methods starts/modifies a channel, and returns a result immediately
2113          ::
2114          (on-put-request channel-id identity request)
2115        ::
2116        ?:  =('GET' method.request)
2117          (on-get-request channel-id [session-id identity] request)
2118        ?:  =('POST' method.request)
2119          ::  POST methods are used solely for deleting channels
2120          (on-put-request channel-id identity request)
2121        ::
2122        ((trace 0 |.("session not a put")) `state)
2123      ::  +on-cancel-request: cancels an ongoing subscription
2124      ::
2125      ::    One of our long lived sessions just got closed. We put the associated
2126      ::    session back into the waiting state.
2127      ::
2128      ++  on-cancel-request
2129        ^-  [(list move) server-state]
2130        ::  lookup the session id by duct
2131        ::
2132        %-  (trace 1 |.("{<duct>} moving channel to waiting state"))
2133        ::
2134        ?~  maybe-channel-id=(~(get by duct-to-key.channel-state.state) duct)
2135          ((trace 0 |.("{<duct>} no channel to move")) `state)
2136        ::
2137        =/  maybe-session
2138          (~(get by session.channel-state.state) u.maybe-channel-id)
2139        ?~  maybe-session
2140          ((trace 1 |.("{<maybe-session>} session doesn't exist")) `state)
2141        ::
2142        =/  heartbeat-cancel=(list move)
2143          ?~  heartbeat.u.maybe-session  ~
2144          :~  %^  cancel-heartbeat-move
```

```
2145              u.maybe-channel-id
2146            date.u.heartbeat.u.maybe-session
2147          duct.u.heartbeat.u.maybe-session
2148        ==
2149      ::
2150      =/  expiration-time=@da  (add now channel-timeout)
2151      ::
2152      :-  %+  weld  heartbeat-cancel
2153        [(set-timeout-move u.maybe-channel-id expiration-time) moves]
2154      %_    state
2155          session.channel-state
2156        %+  ~(jab by session.channel-state.state)  u.maybe-channel-id
2157        |=  =channel
2158        ::  if we are canceling a known channel, it should have a listener
2159        ::
2160        ?>  ?=([%| *] state.channel)
2161        channel(state [%& [expiration-time duct]], heartbeat ~)
2162      ::
2163          duct-to-key.channel-state
2164        (~(del by duct-to-key.channel-state.state) duct)
2165      ==
2166  ::  +update-timeout-timer-for: sets a timeout timer on a channel
2167  ::
2168  ::    This creates a channel if it doesn't exist, cancels existing timers
2169  ::    if they're already set (we cannot have duplicate timers), and (if
2170  ::    necessary) moves channels from the listening state to the expiration
2171  ::    state.
2172  ::
2173  ++  update-timeout-timer-for
2174    |=  [mode=?(%json %jam) =identity channel-id=@t]
2175    ^+  ..update-timeout-timer-for
2176    ::  when our callback should fire
2177    ::
2178    =/  expiration-time=@da  (add now channel-timeout)
2179    ::  if the channel doesn't exist, create it and set a timer
2180    ::
2181    ?~  maybe-channel=(~(get by session.channel-state.state) channel-id)
2182      ::
2183      %_    ..update-timeout-timer-for
2184          session.channel-state.state
2185        %+  ~(put by session.channel-state.state)  channel-id
2186        [mode identity [%& expiration-time duct] 0 now ~ ~ ~ ~]
2187      ::
2188          moves
2189        [(set-timeout-move channel-id expiration-time) moves]
2190      ==
2191    ::  if the channel has an active listener, we aren't setting any timers
2192    ::
2193    ?:  ?=([%| *] state.u.maybe-channel)
2194      ..update-timeout-timer-for
2195    ::  we have a previous timer; cancel the old one and set the new one
2196    ::
2197    %_    ..update-timeout-timer-for
2198        session.channel-state.state
2199      %+  ~(jab by session.channel-state.state)  channel-id
2200      |=  =channel
2201      channel(state [%& [expiration-time duct]])
2202      ::
```

```
2203            moves
2204        :*  (cancel-timeout-move channel-id p.state.u.maybe-channel)
2205            (set-timeout-move channel-id expiration-time)
2206            moves
2207        ==
2208      ==
2209    ::
2210    ++  set-heartbeat-move
2211      |=  [channel-id=@t heartbeat-time=@da]
2212      ^-  move
2213      :^  duct  %pass  /channel/heartbeat/[channel-id]
2214      [%b %wait heartbeat-time]
2215    ::
2216    ++  cancel-heartbeat-move
2217      |=  [channel-id=@t heartbeat-time=@da =^duct]
2218      ^-  move
2219      :^  duct  %pass  /channel/heartbeat/[channel-id]
2220      [%b %rest heartbeat-time]
2221    ::
2222    ++  set-timeout-move
2223      |=  [channel-id=@t expiration-time=@da]
2224      ^-  move
2225      [duct %pass /channel/timeout/[channel-id] %b %wait expiration-time]
2226    ::
2227    ++  cancel-timeout-move
2228      |=  [channel-id=@t expiration-time=@da =^duct]
2229      ^-  move
2230      :^  duct  %pass  /channel/timeout/[channel-id]
2231      [%b %rest expiration-time]
2232    ::  +on-get-request: handles a GET request
2233    ::
2234    ::    GET requests connect to a channel for the server to send events to
2235    ::    the client in text/event-stream format.
2236    ::
2237    ++  on-get-request
2238      |=  [channel-id=@t [session-id=@uv =identity] =request:http]
2239      ^-  [(list move) server-state]
2240      ::  if the channel doesn't exist, we cannot serve it.
2241      ::  this 404 also lets clients know if their channel was reaped since
2242      ::  they last connected to it.
2243      ::
2244      ?.  (~(has by session.channel-state.state) channel-id)
2245        %^  return-static-data-on-duct  404  'text/html'
2246        (error-page 404 | url.request ~)
2247      ::
2248      =/  mode=?(%json %jam)
2249        (find-channel-mode %'GET' header-list.request)
2250      =^  [exit=? =wall moves=(list move)]  state
2251        ::  the request may include a 'Last-Event-Id' header
2252        ::
2253        =/  maybe-last-event-id=(unit @ud)
2254          ?~  maybe-raw-header=(get-header:http 'last-event-id' header-list.request)
2255            ~
2256          (rush u.maybe-raw-header dum:ag)
2257        =/  channel
2258          (~(got by session.channel-state.state) channel-id)
2259        ::  we put some demands on the get request, and may need to do some
2260        ::  cleanup for prior requests.
```

```
2261      ::
2262      ::  find the channel creator's identity, make sure it matches
2263      ::
2264      ?.  =(identity identity.channel)
2265        =^  mos  state
2266          %^  return-static-data-on-duct  403  'text/html'
2267          (error-page 403 | url.request ~)
2268        [[& ~ mos] state]
2269      ::  make sure the request "mode" doesn't conflict with a prior request
2270      ::
2271      ::TODO  or could we change that on the spot, given that only a single
2272      ::        request will ever be listening to this channel?
2273      ?.  =(mode mode.channel)
2274        =^  mos  state
2275          %^  return-static-data-on-duct  406  'text/html'
2276          =;  msg=tape  (error-page 406 %.y url.request msg)
2277          "channel already established in {(trip mode.channel)} mode"
2278        [[& ~ mos] state]
2279      ::  when opening an event-stream, we must cancel our timeout timer
2280      ::  if there's no duct already bound. else, kill the old request,
2281      ::  we will replace its duct at the end of this arm
2282      ::
2283      =^  cancel-moves  state
2284        ?:  ?=([%& *] state.channel)
2285          :_  state
2286          (cancel-timeout-move channel-id p.state.channel)^~
2287        =.  duct-to-key.channel-state.state
2288          (~(del by duct-to-key.channel-state.state) p.state.channel)
2289        =/  cancel-heartbeat
2290          ?~  heartbeat.channel  ~
2291          :_  ~
2292          %+  cancel-heartbeat-move  channel-id
2293          [date duct]:u.heartbeat.channel
2294        =-  [(weld cancel-heartbeat -<) ->]
2295        (handle-response(duct p.state.channel) [%cancel ~])
2296      ::  flush events older than the passed in 'Last-Event-ID'
2297      ::
2298    =?  state  ?=(^ maybe-last-event-id)
2299      (acknowledge-events channel-id u.maybe-last-event-id)
2300    ::TODO  that did not remove them from the channel queue though!
2301    ::        we may want to account for maybe-last-event-id, for efficiency.
2302    ::        (the client _should_ ignore events it heard previously if we do
2303    ::        end up re-sending them, but _requiring_ that feels kinda risky)
2304    ::
2305    ::  combine the remaining queued events to send to the client
2306    ::
2307    =;  event-replay=wall
2308      [[| - cancel-moves] state]
2309    %-  zing
2310    %-  flop
2311    =/  queue  events.channel
2312    =|  events=(list wall)
2313    |-
2314    ^+  events
2315    ?:  =(~ queue)
2316      events
2317    =^  head  queue  ~(get to queue)
2318    =,  p.head
```

```
2319          ::NOTE  these will only fail if the mark and/or json types changed,
2320          ::        since conversion failure also gets caught during first receive.
2321          ::        we can't do anything about this, so consider it unsupported.
2322       =/  said
2323         (channel-event-to-tape channel request-id channel-event)
2324       ?~  said  $
2325       $(events [(event-tape-to-wall id +.u.said) events])
2326     ?:  exit  [moves state]
2327     ::  send the start event to the client
2328     ::
2329     =^  http-moves  state
2330       %-  handle-response
2331       :*  %start
2332           :-  200
2333           :~  ['content-type' 'text/event-stream']
2334               ['cache-control' 'no-cache']
2335               ['connection' 'keep-alive']
2336           ==
2337           (wall-to-octs wall)
2338           complete=%.n
2339       ==
2340     ::  associate this duct with this session key
2341     ::
2342     =.  duct-to-key.channel-state.state
2343       (~(put by duct-to-key.channel-state.state) duct channel-id)
2344     ::  associate this channel with the session cookie
2345     ::
2346     =.  sessions.auth.state
2347       %+  ~(jab by sessions.auth.state)
2348         session-id
2349       |=  =session
2350       session(channels (~(put in channels.session) channel-id))
2351     ::  initialize sse heartbeat
2352     ::
2353     =/  heartbeat-time=@da  (add now ~s20)
2354     =/  heartbeat  (set-heartbeat-move channel-id heartbeat-time)
2355     ::  record the mode & duct for future output,
2356     ::  and record heartbeat-time for possible future cancel
2357     ::
2358     =.  session.channel-state.state
2359       %+  ~(jab by session.channel-state.state)  channel-id
2360       |=  =channel
2361       %_  channel
2362         mode        mode
2363         state       [%| duct]
2364         heartbeat   (some [heartbeat-time duct])
2365       ==
2366     ::
2367     [[heartbeat :(weld http-moves moves)] state]
2368   ::  +acknowledge-events: removes events before :last-event-id on :channel-id
2369   ::
2370   ++  acknowledge-events
2371     |=  [channel-id=@t last-event-id=@u]
2372     ^-  server-state
2373     %_    state
2374         session.channel-state
2375       %+  ~(jab by session.channel-state.state)  channel-id
2376       |=  =channel
```

```
2377          ^+  channel
2378          =^  acked  events.channel
2379            (prune-events events.channel last-event-id)
2380          =.  unacked.channel
2381            (subtract-acked-events acked unacked.channel)
2382          channel(last-ack now)
2383        ==
2384    ::  +on-put-request: handles a PUT request
2385    ::
2386    ::    PUT requests send commands from the client to the server. We receive
2387    ::    a set of commands in JSON format in the body of the message.
2388    ::    channels don't exist until a PUT request is sent. it's valid for
2389    ::    this request to contain an empty list of commands.
2390    ::
2391    ++  on-put-request
2392      |=  [channel-id=@t =identity =request:http]
2393      ^-  [(list move) server-state]
2394      ::  if the channel already exists, and is not of this identity, 403
2395      ::
2396      ::    the creation case happens in the +update-timeout-timer-for below
2397      ::
2398      ?:  ?~  c=(~(get by session.channel-state.state) channel-id)  |
2399          !=(identity identity.u.c)
2400        %^  return-static-data-on-duct  403  'text/html'
2401        (error-page 403 | url.request ~)
2402      ::  error when there's no body
2403      ::
2404      ?~  body.request
2405        %^  return-static-data-on-duct  400  'text/html'
2406        (error-page 400 %.y url.request "no put body")
2407      ::
2408      =/  mode=?(%json %jam)
2409        (find-channel-mode %'PUT' header-list.request)
2410      ::  if we cannot parse requests from the body, give an error
2411      ::
2412      =/  maybe-requests=(each (list channel-request) @t)
2413        (parse-channel-request mode u.body.request)
2414      ?:  ?=(%| -.maybe-requests)
2415        %^  return-static-data-on-duct  400  'text/html'
2416        (error-page 400 & url.request (trip p.maybe-requests))
2417      ::  check for the existence of the channel-id
2418      ::
2419      ::    if we have no session, create a new one set to expire in
2420      ::    :channel-timeout from now. if we have one which has a timer, update
2421      ::    that timer.
2422      ::
2423      =.  ..on-put-request  (update-timeout-timer-for mode identity channel-id)
2424      ::  for each request, execute the action passed in
2425      ::
2426      =+  requests=p.maybe-requests
2427      ::  gall-moves: put moves here first so we can flop for ordering
2428      ::  errors: if we accumulate any, discard the gall-moves and revert
2429      ::
2430      =|  gall-moves=(list move)
2431      =|  errors=(map @ud @t)
2432      =/  og-state  state
2433      =/  from=ship
2434        ?+(-.identity who.identity %ours our)
```

```hoon
    |-
    ::
    ?~  requests
      ?:  =(~ errors)
        ::  everything succeeded, mark the request as completed
        ::
        =^  http-moves  state
          %-  handle-response
          :*  %start
              [status-code=204 headers=~]
              data=~
              complete=%.y
          ==
        ::
        [:(weld (flop gall-moves) http-moves moves) state]
      ::  some things went wrong. revert all operations & give 400
      ::
      %-  (trace 1 |.("{<channel-id>} reverting due to errors"))
      =.  state  og-state
      =^  http-moves  state
        %^  return-static-data-on-duct  400  'text/html'
        %-  as-octs:mimes:html
        %+  rap  3
        %+  turn  (sort ~(tap by errors) dor)
        |=  [id=@ud er=@t]
        (rap 3 (crip (a-co:co id)) ': ' er '<br/>' ~)
      [(weld http-moves moves) state]
    ::
    ?-    -.i.requests
        %ack
      ::  client acknowledges that they have received up to event-id
      ::
      %_  $
        state    (acknowledge-events channel-id event-id.i.requests)
        requests  t.requests
      ==
    ::
        ?(%poke %poke-json)
      =,  i.requests
      ::
      ?.  |(=(from our) =(ship our))
        =+  [request-id 'non-local operation']
        $(errors (~(put by errors) -), requests t.requests)
      ::
      =.  gall-moves
        =/  =wire  /channel/poke/[channel-id]/(scot %ud request-id.i.requests)
        :_  gall-moves
        ^-  move
        %+  deal-as
          /channel/poke/[channel-id]/(scot %ud request-id)
        :^  from  ship  app
        ^-  task:agent:gall
        :+  %poke-as  mark
        ?-  -.i.requests
          %poke       [%noun !>(noun)]
          %poke-json  [%json !>(json)]
        ==
      ::
```

```
2493        $(requests t.requests)
2494    ::
2495        %subscribe
2496    =,  i.requests
2497    ::
2498    ?.  |(=(from our) =(ship our))
2499      =+  [request-id 'non-local operation']
2500      $(errors (~(put by errors) -), requests t.requests)
2501    ::
2502    ::TODO  could error if the subscription is a duplicate
2503    =.  gall-moves
2504      :_  gall-moves
2505      ^-  move
2506      %-  (trace 1 |.("subscribing to {<app>} on {<path>}"))
2507      %+  deal-as
2508        (subscription-wire channel-id request-id from ship app)
2509      [from ship app %watch path]
2510    ::
2511    =.  session.channel-state.state
2512      %+  ~(jab by session.channel-state.state)  channel-id
2513      |=  =channel
2514      =-  channel(subscriptions -)
2515      %+  ~(put by subscriptions.channel)
2516        request-id
2517      [ship app path duct]
2518    ::
2519        $(requests t.requests)
2520    ::
2521        %unsubscribe
2522    =,  i.requests
2523    ::
2524    ?.  |(=(from our) =(ship our))
2525      =+  [request-id 'non-local operation']
2526      $(errors (~(put by errors) -), requests t.requests)
2527    ::
2528    =/  usession  (~(get by session.channel-state.state) channel-id)
2529    ?~  usession
2530      $(requests t.requests)
2531    =/  subscriptions  subscriptions:u.usession
2532    ::
2533    ?~  maybe-subscription=(~(get by subscriptions) subscription-id)
2534      ::  the client sent us a weird request referring to a subscription
2535      ::  which isn't active.
2536      ::
2537      %.  $(requests t.requests)
2538      =*  msg=tape  "{(trip channel-id)} {<subscription-id>}"
2539      (trace 0 |.("missing subscription in unsubscribe {msg}"))
2540    ::
2541    =.  gall-moves
2542      :_  gall-moves
2543      ^-  move
2544      =,  u.maybe-subscription
2545      %-  (trace 1 |.("leaving subscription to {<app>}"))
2546      %+  deal-as
2547        (subscription-wire channel-id subscription-id from ship app)
2548      [from ship app %leave ~]
2549    ::
2550    =.  session.channel-state.state
```

```
2551            %+  ~(jab by session.channel-state.state)  channel-id
2552            |=  =channel
2553            %_  channel
2554              subscriptions  (~(del by subscriptions.channel) subscription-id)
2555              unacked        (~(del by unacked.channel) subscription-id)
2556            ==
2557        ::
2558        $(requests t.requests)
2559      ::
2560          %delete
2561      %-  (trace 1 |.("{<channel-id>} discarding due to %delete PUT"))
2562      =^  moves  state
2563        (discard-channel channel-id |)
2564      =.  gall-moves
2565        (weld gall-moves moves)
2566      $(requests t.requests)
2567      ::
2568    ==
2569  ::  +on-gall-response: sanity-check a gall response, send as event
2570  ::
2571  ++  on-gall-response
2572    |=  [channel-id=@t request-id=@ud extra=wire =sign:agent:gall]
2573    ^-  [(list move) server-state]
2574    ::  if the channel doesn't exist, we should clean up subscriptions
2575    ::
2576    ::    this is a band-aid solution. you really want eyre to have cleaned
2577    ::    these up on-channel-delete in the first place.
2578    ::    until the source of that bug is discovered though, we keep this
2579    ::    in place to ensure a slightly tidier home.
2580    ::
2581    ?.  ?&  !(~(has by session.channel-state.state) channel-id)
2582            ?=(?(%fact %watch-ack) -.sign)
2583            ?=([@ @ *] extra)
2584        ==
2585      (emit-event channel-id request-id sign)
2586    =/  =ship     (slav %p i.extra)
2587    =*  app=term   i.t.extra
2588    =*  msg=tape   "{(trip channel-id)} {(trip app)}"
2589    %-  (trace 0 |.("removing watch for non-existent channel {msg}"))
2590    :_  state
2591    :_  ~
2592    ^-  move
2593    =/  [as=@p old=?]
2594      ?+  t.t.extra  ~|([%strange-wire extra] !!)
2595        ~        [our &]
2596        [@ ~]    [(slav %p i.t.t.extra) |]
2597      ==
2598    =/  =wire  (subscription-wire channel-id request-id as ship app)
2599    %+  deal-as
2600      ::NOTE  we previously used a wire format that had the local identity
2601      ::        implicit, instead of explicit at the end of the wire. if we
2602      ::        detect we used the old wire here, we must re-use that format
2603      ::        (without id in the wire) for sending the %leave.
2604      ?:(old (snip wire) wire)
2605    [as ship app %leave ~]
2606  ::  +emit-event: records an event occurred, possibly sending to client
2607  ::
2608  ::    When an event occurs, we need to record it, even if we immediately
```

```
2609      ::    send it to a connected browser so in case of disconnection, we can
2610      ::    resend it.
2611      ::
2612      ::    This function is responsible for taking the event sign and converting
2613      ::    it into a text/event-stream. The :sign then may get sent, and is
2614      ::    stored for later resending until acknowledged by the client.
2615      ::
2616      ++  emit-event
2617        |=  [channel-id=@t request-id=@ud =sign:agent:gall]
2618        ^-  [(list move) server-state]
2619        ::
2620        =/  channel=(unit channel)
2621          (~(get by session.channel-state.state) channel-id)
2622        ?~  channel
2623          :_  state  :_  ~
2624          [duct %pass /flog %d %flog %crud %eyre-no-channel >id=channel-id< ~]
2625        ::  it's possible that this is a sign emitted directly alongside a fact
2626        ::  that triggered a clog & closed the subscription. in that case, just
2627        ::  drop the sign.
2628        ::  poke-acks are not paired with subscriptions, so we can process them
2629        ::  regardless.
2630        ::
2631        ?:  ?&  !?=(%poke-ack -.sign)
2632                !(~(has by subscriptions.u.channel) request-id)
2633            ==
2634          [~ state]
2635        ::  attempt to convert the sign to json.
2636        ::  if conversion succeeds, we *can* send it. if the client is actually
2637        ::  connected, we *will* send it immediately.
2638        ::
2639        =/  maybe-channel-event=(unit channel-event)
2640          (sign-to-channel-event sign u.channel request-id)
2641        ?~  maybe-channel-event  [~ state]
2642        =/  =channel-event  u.maybe-channel-event
2643        =/  said=(unit (quip move tape))
2644          (channel-event-to-tape u.channel request-id channel-event)
2645        =?  moves  ?=(^ said)
2646          (weld moves -.u.said)
2647        =*  sending  &(?=([%| *] state.u.channel) ?=(^ said))
2648        ::
2649        =/  next-id  next-id.u.channel
2650        ::  if we can send it, store the event as unacked
2651        ::
2652        =?  events.u.channel  ?=(^ said)
2653          %-  ~(put to events.u.channel)
2654          [next-id request-id channel-event]
2655        ::  if it makes sense to do so, send the event to the client
2656        ::
2657        =?  moves  sending
2658          ^-  (list move)
2659          :_  moves
2660          ::NOTE  assertions in this block because =* is flimsy
2661          ?>  ?=([%| *] state.u.channel)
2662          :+  p.state.u.channel  %give
2663          ^-  gift
2664          :*  %response  %continue
2665          ::
2666              ^=  data
```

```
        %-  wall-to-octs
        (event-tape-to-wall next-id +:(need said))
    ::
        complete=%.n
    ==
  =?  next-id  ?=(^ said)  +(next-id)
  ::  update channel's unacked counts, find out if clogged
  ::
  =^  clogged  unacked.u.channel
    ::  only apply clog logic to facts.
    ::  and of course don't count events we can't send as unacked.
    ::
    ?:  ?|  !?=(%fact -.sign)
            ?=(~ said)
        ==
      [| unacked.u.channel]
    =/  num=@ud
      (~(gut by unacked.u.channel) request-id 0)
    :_  (~(put by unacked.u.channel) request-id +(num))
    ?&  (gte num clog-threshold)
        (lth (add last-ack.u.channel clog-timeout) now)
    ==
  ::  if we're clogged, or we ran into an event we can't serialize,
  ::  kill this gall subscription.
  ::
  =*  msg=tape  "on {(trip channel-id)} for {(scow %ud request-id)}"
  =/  kicking=?
    ?:  clogged
      ((trace 0 |.("clogged {msg}")) &)
    ?.  ?=(~ said)  |
      ((trace 0 |.("can't serialize event, kicking {msg}")) &)
  =?  moves        kicking
    :_  moves
    ::NOTE  this shouldn't crash because we
    ::        - never fail to serialize subscriptionless signs (%poke-ack),
    ::        - only clog on %facts, which have a subscription associated,
    ::        - and already checked whether we still have that subscription.
    =+  (~(got by subscriptions.u.channel) request-id)
    %-  (trace 1 |.("leaving subscription to {<app>}"))
    %+  deal-as
      (subscription-wire channel-id request-id identity.u.channel ship app)
    [identity.u.channel ship app %leave ~]
  ::  update channel state to reflect the %kick
  ::
  =?  u.channel  kicking
    %_  u.channel
      subscriptions  (~(del by subscriptions.u.channel) request-id)
      unacked        (~(del by unacked.u.channel) request-id)
      events         %-  ~(put to events.u.channel)
                     :+  next-id
                       request-id
                     (need (sign-to-channel-event [%kick ~] u.channel request-id))
    ==
  ::  if a client is connected, send the kick event to them
  ::
  =?  moves  &(kicking ?=([%| *] state.u.channel))
    :_  moves
    :+  p.state.u.channel  %give
```

```hoon
2725        ^-  gift
2726        :*  %response  %continue
2727        ::
2728            ^=  data
2729            %-  wall-to-octs
2730            %+  event-tape-to-wall  next-id
2731            +:(need (channel-event-to-tape u.channel request-id %kick ~))
2732        ::
2733            complete=%.n
2734        ==
2735    =?  next-id  kicking  +(next-id)
2736    ::
2737    :-  (flop moves)
2738    %_    state
2739        session.channel-state
2740      %+  ~(put by session.channel-state.state)  channel-id
2741      u.channel(next-id next-id)
2742    ==
2743  ::  +sign-to-channel-event: strip the vase from a sign:agent:gall
2744  ::
2745  ++  sign-to-channel-event
2746    |=  [=sign:agent:gall =channel request-id=@ud]
2747    ^-  (unit channel-event)
2748    ?.  ?=(%fact -.sign)  `sign
2749    ?~  desk=(app-to-desk channel request-id)  ~
2750    :-  ~
2751    [%fact u.desk [p q.q]:cage.sign]
2752  ::  +app-to-desk
2753  ::
2754  ++  app-to-desk
2755    |=  [=channel request-id=@ud]
2756    ^-  (unit desk)
2757    =/  sub  (~(get by subscriptions.channel) request-id)
2758    ?~  sub
2759      ((trace 0 |.("no subscription for request-id {(scow %ud request-id)}")) ~)
2760    =/  des=(unit (unit cage))
2761      (rof [~ ~] /eyre %gd [our app.u.sub da+now] /$)
2762    ?.  ?=([~ ~ *] des)
2763      ((trace 0 |.("no desk for app {<app.u.sub>}")) ~)
2764    `!<(=desk q.u.u.des)
2765  ::  +channel-event-to-tape: render channel-event from request-id in specified mode
2766  ::
2767  ++  channel-event-to-tape
2768    |=  [=channel request-id=@ud =channel-event]
2769    ^-  (unit (quip move tape))
2770    ?-  mode.channel
2771      %json  %+  bind  (channel-event-to-json channel request-id channel-event)
2772             |=((quip move json) [+<- (trip (en:json:html +<+))])
2773      %jam   =-  `[~ (scow %uw (jam -))]
2774             [request-id channel-event]
2775    ==
2776  ::  +channel-event-to-json: render channel event as json channel event
2777  ::
2778  ++  channel-event-to-json
2779    ~%  %eyre-channel-event-to-json  ..part  ~
2780    |=  [=channel request-id=@ud event=channel-event]
2781    ^-  (unit (quip move json))
2782    ::  for facts, we try to convert the result to json
```

```
2783        ::
2784        =/  [from=(unit [=desk =mark]) jsyn=(unit sign:agent:gall)]
2785          ?.  ?=(%fact -.event)          [~ `event]
2786          ?:  ?=(%json mark.event)
2787            ?~  jsin=((soft json) noun.event)
2788              %.  [~ ~]
2789              (slog leaf+"eyre: dropping fake json for {(scow %ud request-id)}" ~)
2790            [~ `[%fact %json !>(u.jsin)]]
2791          ::  find and use tube from fact mark to json
2792          ::
2793          ::
2794          =*  have=mark  mark.event
2795          =/  convert=(unit vase)
2796            =/  cag=(unit (unit cage))
2797              (rof [~ ~] /eyre %cf [our desk.event da+now] /[have]/json)
2798            ?.  ?=([~ ~ *] cag)  ~
2799            `q.u.u.cag
2800          ?~  convert
2801            ((trace 0 |.("no convert from {(trip have)} to json")) [~ ~])
2802          ~|  "conversion failed from {(trip have)} to json"
2803          [`[desk.event have] `[%fact %json (slym u.convert noun.event)]]
2804        ?~  jsyn  ~
2805        %-  some
2806        :-  ?~  from  ~
2807            :_  ~
2808            :^  duct  %pass  /conversion-cache/[mark.u.from]
2809            [%c %warp our desk.u.from `[%sing %f da+now /[mark.u.from]/json]]
2810        =*  sign  u.jsyn
2811        =,  enjs:format
2812        %-  pairs
2813        ^-  (list [@t json])
2814        :-  ['id' (numb request-id)]
2815        ?-    -.sign
2816            %poke-ack
2817          :~  ['response' [%s 'poke']]
2818              ::
2819              ?~  p.sign
2820                ['ok' [%s 'ok']]
2821              ['err' (wall (render-tang-to-wall 100 u.p.sign))]
2822          ==
2823        ::
2824            %fact
2825          :+  ['response' [%s 'diff']]
2826            :-  'json'
2827            ~|  [%unexpected-fact-mark p.cage.sign]
2828            ?>  =(%json p.cage.sign)
2829            !<(json q.cage.sign)
2830          ::
2831          ?~  from  ~
2832          ['mark' [%s mark.u.from]]~
2833        ::
2834            %kick
2835          ['response' [%s 'quit']]~
2836        ::
2837            %watch-ack
2838          :~  ['response' [%s 'subscribe']]
2839              ::
2840              ?~  p.sign
```

```
2841                    ['ok' [%s 'ok']]
2842                    ['err' (wall (render-tang-to-wall 100 u.p.sign))]
2843            ==
2844        ==
2845      ::
2846      ++  event-tape-to-wall
2847        ~%  %eyre-tape-to-wall  ..part  ~
2848        |=  [event-id=@ud =tape]
2849        ^-  wall
2850        :~  (weld "id: " (format-ud-as-integer event-id))
2851            (weld "data: " tape)
2852            ""
2853        ==
2854      ::
2855      ++  on-channel-heartbeat
2856        |=  channel-id=@t
2857        ^-  [(list move) server-state]
2858        ::
2859        =/  res
2860          %-  handle-response
2861          :*  %continue
2862              data=(some (as-octs:mimes:html ':\0a'))
2863              complete=%.n
2864          ==
2865        =/  http-moves  -.res
2866        =/  new-state  +.res
2867        =/  heartbeat-time=@da  (add now ~s20)
2868        :_  %_    new-state
2869                session.channel-state
2870            %+  ~(jab by session.channel-state.state)  channel-id
2871            |=  =channel
2872            channel(heartbeat (some [heartbeat-time duct]))
2873        ==
2874        (snoc http-moves (set-heartbeat-move channel-id heartbeat-time))
2875      ::  +discard-channel: remove a channel from state
2876      ::
2877      ::    cleans up state, timers, and gall subscriptions of the channel
2878      ::
2879      ++  discard-channel
2880        |=  [channel-id=@t expired=?]
2881        ^-  [(list move) server-state]
2882        ::
2883        =/  usession=(unit channel)
2884          (~(get by session.channel-state.state) channel-id)
2885        ?~  usession
2886          [~ state]
2887        =/  session=channel  u.usession
2888        ::
2889        :_  %_    state
2890                session.channel-state
2891              (~(del by session.channel-state.state) channel-id)
2892            ::
2893                duct-to-key.channel-state
2894            ?.  ?=(%| -.state.session)  duct-to-key.channel-state.state
2895            (~(del by duct-to-key.channel-state.state) p.state.session)
2896        ==
2897        =/  heartbeat-cancel=(list move)
2898          ?~  heartbeat.session  ~
```

```
:~  %^  cancel-heartbeat-move
      channel-id
      date.u.heartbeat.session
    duct.u.heartbeat.session
  ==
=/  expire-cancel=(list move)
  ?:  expired  ~
  ?.  ?=(%& -.state.session)  ~
  =,  p.state.session
  [(cancel-timeout-move channel-id date duct)]~
%+  weld  heartbeat-cancel
%+  weld  expire-cancel
::  produce a list of moves which cancels every gall subscription
::
%+  turn  ~(tap by subscriptions.session)
|=  [request-id=@ud ship=@p app=term =path duc=^duct]
^-  move
%-  (trace 1 |.("{<channel-id>} leaving subscription to {<app>}"))
%+  deal-as
  (subscription-wire channel-id request-id identity.session ship app)
[identity.session ship app %leave ~]
--
::  +handle-gall-error: a call to +poke-http-response resulted in a %coup
::
++  handle-gall-error
  |=  =tang
  ^-  [(list move) server-state]
  ::
  ?~  connection-state=(~(get by connections.state) duct)
    %.  `state
    (trace 0 |.("{<duct>} error on invalid outstanding connection"))
  =*  connection  u.connection-state
  =/  moves-1=(list move)
    ?.  ?=(%app -.action.connection)
      ~
    :_  ~
    =,  connection
    %-  (trace 1 |.("leaving subscription to {<app.action>}"))
    (deal-as /watch-response/[eyre-id] identity our app.action %leave ~)
  ::
  =^  moves-2  state
    %^  return-static-data-on-duct  500  'text/html'
    ::
    %-  internal-server-error  :*
        authenticated.inbound-request.connection
        url.request.inbound-request.connection
        tang
    ==
  [(weld moves-1 moves-2) state]
::  +handle-response: check a response for correctness and send to earth
::
::    All outbound responses including %http-server generated responses need to go
::    through this interface because we want to have one centralized place
::    where we perform logging and state cleanup for connections that we're
::    done with.
::
++  handle-response
  |=  =http-event:http
```

```
^-  [(list move) server-state]
::  verify that this is a valid response on the duct
::
?~  connection-state=(~(get by connections.state) duct)
  ((trace 0 |.("{<duct>} invalid outstanding connection")) `state)
::
|^  ^-  [(list move) server-state]
    ::
    ?-    -.http-event
    ::
        %start
      ?^  response-header.u.connection-state
        ((trace 0 |.("{<duct>} error multiple start")) error-connection)
      ::  extend the request's session's + cookie's life
      ::
      =^  response-header   sessions.auth.state
        =,  authentication
        =*  session-id   session-id.u.connection-state
        =*  sessions     sessions.auth.state
        =*  inbound      inbound-request.u.connection-state
        =*  headers       headers.response-header.http-event
        ::
        ?.  (~(has by sessions) session-id)
          ::  if the session has expired since the request was opened,
          ::  tough luck, we don't create/revive sessions here
          ::
          [response-header.http-event sessions]
        :_  %+  ~(jab by sessions)  session-id
            |=  =session
            session(expiry-time (add now session-timeout))
        =-  response-header.http-event(headers -)
        =/  cookie=(pair @t @t)
          ['set-cookie' (session-cookie-string session-id &)]
        |-
        ?~  headers
          [cookie ~]
        ?:  &(=(key.i.headers p.cookie) =(value.i.headers q.cookie))
          headers
        [i.headers $(headers t.headers)]
      ::
      =*  connection  u.connection-state
      ::
      ::  if the request was a simple cors request from an approved origin
      ::  append the necessary cors headers to the response
      ::
      =/  origin=(unit origin)
        %+  get-header:http  'origin'
        header-list.request.inbound-request.connection
      =?  headers.response-header
          ?&  ?=(^ origin)
              (~(has in approved.cors-registry.state) u.origin)
          ==
        %^  set-header:http  'Access-Control-Allow-Origin'        u.origin
        %^  set-header:http  'Access-Control-Allow-Credentials'  'true'
        headers.response-header
      ::
      =.  response-header.http-event  response-header
      =.  connections.state
```

```
?:  complete.http-event
  ::  XX  optimize by not requiring +put:by in +request
  ::
  (~(del by connections.state) duct)
::
%-  (trace 2 |.("{<duct>} start"))
%+  ~(put by connections.state)  duct
%=  connection
  response-header  `response-header
  bytes-sent  ?~(data.http-event 0 p.u.data.http-event)
==
::
pass-response
::
  %continue
?~  response-header.u.connection-state
  %.  error-connection
  (trace 0 |.("{<duct>} error continue without start"))
::
=.  connections.state
  ?:  complete.http-event
    %-  (trace 2 |.("{<duct>} completed"))
    (~(del by connections.state) duct)
  ::
  %-  (trace 2 |.("{<duct>} continuing"))
  ?~  data.http-event
    connections.state
  ::
  %+  ~(put by connections.state)  duct
  =*  size  p.u.data.http-event
  =*  conn  u.connection-state
  conn(bytes-sent (add size bytes-sent.conn))
::
pass-response
::
  %cancel
::  todo: log this differently from an ise.
::
((trace 1 |.("cancel http event")) error-connection)
==
::
++  pass-response
  ^-  [(list move) server-state]
  [[duct %give %response http-event]~ state]
::
++  error-connection
  ::  todo: log application error
  ::
  ::  remove all outstanding state for this connection
  ::
  =.  connections.state
    (~(del by connections.state) duct)
  ::  respond to outside with %error
  ::
  ^-  [(list move) server-state]
  :_  state
  :-  [duct %give %response %cancel ~]
  ?.  ?=(%app -.action.u.connection-state)
```

```
3073        ~
3074      :_  ~
3075      =,  u.connection-state
3076      %-  %+  trace  1
3077          |.("leaving subscription to {<app.action>}")
3078      (deal-as /watch-response/[eyre-id] identity our app.action %leave ~)
3079      --
3080  ::  +set-response: remember (or update) a cache mapping
3081  ::
3082  ++  set-response
3083    |=  [url=@t entry=(unit cache-entry)]
3084    ^-  [(list move) server-state]
3085    =/  aeon  ?^(prev=(~(get by cache.state) url) +(aeon.u.prev) 1)
3086    =.  cache.state  (~(put by cache.state) url [aeon entry])
3087    :_  state
3088    [outgoing-duct.state %give %grow /cache/(scot %ud aeon)/(scot %t url)]~
3089  ::  +add-binding: conditionally add a pairing between binding and action
3090  ::
3091  ::    Adds =binding =action if there is no conflicting bindings.
3092  ::
3093  ++  add-binding
3094    |=  [=binding =action]
3095    ^-  [(list move) server-state]
3096    =^  success  bindings.state
3097      ::  prevent binding in reserved namespaces
3098      ::
3099      ?:  ?|  ?=([%'~' *] path.binding)      ::  eyre
3100              ?=([%'~_~' *] path.binding)  ::  runtime
3101              ?=([%'_~_' *] path.binding)  ::  scries
3102          ==
3103        [| bindings.state]
3104      [& (insert-binding [binding duct action] bindings.state)]
3105    :_  state
3106    [duct %give %bound & binding]~
3107  ::  +remove-binding: removes a binding if it exists and is owned by this duct
3108  ::
3109  ++  remove-binding
3110    |=  =binding
3111    ::
3112    ^-  server-state
3113    %_    state
3114        bindings
3115      %+  skip  bindings.state
3116      |=  [item-binding=^binding item-duct=^duct =action]
3117      ^-  ?
3118      &(=(item-binding binding) =(item-duct duct))
3119    ==
3120  ::  +get-action-for-binding: finds an action for an incoming web request
3121  ::
3122  ++  get-action-for-binding
3123    |=  [raw-host=(unit @t) url=@t]
3124    ^-  [=action suburl=@t]
3125    ::  process :raw-host
3126    ::
3127    ::    If we are missing a 'Host:' header, if that header is a raw IP
3128    ::    address, or if the 'Host:' header refers to [our].urbit.org, we want
3129    ::    to return ~ which means we're unidentified and will match against any
3130    ::    wildcard matching.
```

```
3131      ::
3132      ::      Otherwise, return the site given.
3133      ::
3134  =/  host=(unit @t)
3135    ?~  raw-host
3136      ~
3137      ::  Parse the raw-host so that we can ignore ports, usernames, etc.
3138      ::
3139      =+  parsed=(rush u.raw-host simplified-url-parser)
3140      ?~  parsed
3141        ~
3142      ::  if the url is a raw IP, assume default site.
3143      ::
3144      ?:  ?=([%ip *] -.u.parsed)
3145        ~
3146      ::  if the url is "localhost", assume default site.
3147      ::
3148      ?:  =([%site 'localhost'] -.u.parsed)
3149        ~
3150      ::  render our as a tape, and cut off the sig in front.
3151      ::
3152      =/  with-sig=tape  (scow %p our)
3153      ?>  ?=(^ with-sig)
3154      ?:  =(u.raw-host (crip t.with-sig))
3155        ::  [our].urbit.org is the default site
3156        ::
3157        ~
3158      ::
3159    raw-host
3160  ::  url is the raw thing passed over the 'Request-Line'.
3161  ::
3162  ::      todo: this is really input validation, and we should return a 500 to
3163  ::      the client.
3164  ::
3165  =/  request-line  (parse-request-line url)
3166  =/  parsed-url=(list @t)  site.request-line
3167  =?  parsed-url  ?=([%'~' %channel-jam *] parsed-url)
3168    parsed-url(i.t %channel)
3169  ::
3170  =/  bindings  bindings.state
3171  |-
3172  ::
3173  ?~  bindings
3174    [[%four-oh-four ~] url]
3175  ::
3176  ?.  (host-matches site.binding.i.bindings raw-host)
3177    $(bindings t.bindings)
3178  ?~  suffix=(find-suffix path.binding.i.bindings parsed-url)
3179    $(bindings t.bindings)
3180  ::
3181  :-  action.i.bindings
3182  %^  cat  3
3183    %+  roll
3184      ^-  (list @t)
3185      (join '/' (flop ['' u.suffix]))
3186    (cury cat 3)
3187  ?~  ext.request-line  ''
3188  (cat 3 '.' u.ext.request-line)
```

```
3189  ::    +give-session-tokens: send valid local session tokens to unix
3190  ::
3191  ++  give-session-tokens
3192    ^-  move
3193    :-  outgoing-duct.state
3194    :+  %give  %sessions
3195    %-  sy
3196    %+  murn  ~(tap by sessions.auth.state)
3197    |=  [sid=@uv session]
3198    ?.  ?=(%ours -.identity)  ~
3199    (some (scot %uv sid))
3200  ::    +new-session-key
3201  ::
3202  ++  new-session-key
3203    |-  ^-  @uv
3204    =/  candidate=@uv  (~(raw og (shas %session-key eny)) 128)
3205    ?.  (~(has by sessions.auth.state) candidate)
3206      candidate
3207    $(eny (shas %try-again candidate))
3208  ::
3209  ++  deal-as
3210    |=  [=wire identity=$@(@p identity) =ship =dude:gall =task:agent:gall]
3211    ^-  move
3212    =/  from=@p
3213      ?@  identity  identity
3214      ?+(-.identity who.identity %ours our)
3215    [duct %pass wire %g %deal [from ship /eyre] dude task]
3216  ::
3217  ++  trace
3218    |=  [pri=@ print=(trap tape)]
3219    ?:  (lth verb.state pri)  same
3220    (slog leaf+"eyre: {(print)}" ~)
3221    --
3222  ::
3223  ++  forwarded-params
3224    |=  =header-list:http
3225    ^-  (unit (list (map @t @t)))
3226    %+  biff
3227      (get-header:http 'forwarded' header-list)
3228    unpack-header:http
3229  ::
3230  ++  forwarded-for
3231    |=  forwards=(list (map @t @t))
3232    ^-  (unit address)
3233    ?.  ?=(^ forwards)  ~
3234    =*  forward  i.forwards
3235    ?~  for=(~(get by forward) 'for')  ~
3236  ::NOTE  per rfc7239, non-ip values are also valid. they're not useful
3237  ::      for the general case, so we ignore them here. if needed,
3238  ::      request handlers are free to inspect the headers themselves.
3239  ::
3240    %+  rush  u.for
3241    ;~  sfix
3242      ;~(pose (stag %ipv4 ip4) (stag %ipv6 (ifix [sel ser] ip6)))
3243      ;~(pose ;~(pfix col dim:ag) (easy ~))
3244    ==
3245  ::
3246  ++  forwarded-secure
```

```hoon
3247    |=  forwards=(list (map @t @t))
3248    ^-  (unit ?)
3249    ?.  ?=(^ forwards)  ~
3250    =*  forward  i.forwards
3251    ?~  proto=(~(get by forward) 'proto')  ~
3252    ?+  u.proto  ~
3253      %http   `|
3254      %https  `&
3255    ==
3256  ::
3257  ++  forwarded-host
3258    |=  forwards=(list (map @t @t))
3259    ^-  (unit @t)
3260    ?.  ?=(^ forwards)  ~
3261    (~(get by i.forwards) 'host')
3262  ::
3263  ++  parse-request-line
3264    |=  url=@t
3265    ^-  [[ext=(unit @ta) site=(list @t)] args=(list [key=@t value=@t])]
3266    (fall (rush url ;~(plug apat:de-purl:html yque:de-purl:html)) [[~ ~] ~])
3267  :: +insert-binding: add a new binding, replacing any existing at its path
3268  ::
3269  ++  insert-binding
3270    |=  $:  new=[=binding =duct =action]
3271            bindings=(list [=binding =duct =action])
3272        ==
3273    ^+  bindings
3274    ?~  bindings  [new]~
3275    =*  bid  binding.i.bindings
3276    ::  replace already bound paths
3277    ::
3278    ?:  =([site path]:bid [site path]:binding.new)
3279      ~>  %slog.[0 leaf+"eyre: replacing existing binding at {<`path`path.bid>}"]
3280      [new t.bindings]
3281    ::  if new comes before bid, prepend it.
3282    ::  otherwise, continue our search.
3283    ::
3284    =;  new-before-bid=?
3285      ?:  new-before-bid  [new bindings]
3286      [i.bindings $(bindings t.bindings)]
3287    ?:  =(site.binding.new site.bid)
3288      (aor path.bid path.binding.new)
3289    (aor (fall site.bid '') (fall site.binding.new ''))
3290  ::
3291  ++  channel-wire
3292    |=  [channel-id=@t request-id=@ud]
3293    ^-  wire
3294    /channel/subscription/[channel-id]/(scot %ud request-id)
3295  ::
3296  ++  subscription-wire
3297    |=  [channel-id=@t request-id=@ud as=$@(@p identity) =ship app=term]
3298    ^-  wire
3299    =/  from=@p
3300      ?@  as  as
3301      ?+(-.as who.as %ours our)
3302    %+  weld  (channel-wire channel-id request-id)
3303    ::NOTE  including the originating identity is important for the band-aid
3304    ::      solution currently present in +on-gall-response, where we may
```

```
3305      ::          need to issue a %leave after we've forgotten the identity with
3306      ::          which the subscription was opened.
3307      /(scot %p ship)/[app]/(scot %p from)
3308  ::
3309  ++  scry-mime
3310      |=  [now=@da rof=roof ext=(unit @ta) pax=path]
3311      |^  ^-  (each mime tape)
3312      ::  parse
3313      ::
3314      =/  u=(unit [view=term bem=beam])
3315        ?.  ?=([@ @ @ @ *] pax)    ~
3316        ?~  view=(slaw %tas i.t.pax)    ~
3317        ?~  path=(expand-path t.t.pax)  ~
3318        ?~  beam=(de-beam u.path)        ~
3319        `[u.view u.beam]
3320      ?~  u  [%| "invalid scry path"]
3321      ::  perform scry
3322      ::
3323      ?~  res=(rof [~ ~] /eyre u.u)  [%| "failed scry"]
3324      ?~  u.res                     [%| "no scry result"]
3325      =*  mark   p.u.u.res
3326      =*  vase   q.u.u.res
3327      ::  convert to mime via ext
3328      ::
3329      =/  dysk  (conversion-desk u.u)
3330      ?:  ?=(%| -.dysk)  [%| p.dysk]
3331      =/  ext   (fall ext %mime)
3332      =/  mym   (convert vase mark ext p.dysk)
3333      ?:  ?=(%| -.mym)  [%| p.mym]
3334      =/  mym   (convert p.mym ext %mime p.dysk)
3335      ?:  ?=(%| -.mym)  [%| p.mym]
3336      [%& !<(mime p.mym)]
3337      ::
3338      ++  expand-path
3339        |=  a=path
3340        ^-  (unit path)
3341        =/  vez  (vang | (en-beam [our %base da+now] ~))
3342        (rush (spat a) (sear plex:vez (stag %clsg ;~(pfix fas poor:vez))))
3343      ::
3344      ++  conversion-desk
3345        |=  [view=term =beam]
3346        ^-  (each desk tape)
3347        ?:  =(%$ q.beam)  [%& %base]
3348        ?+  (end 3 view)  [%& %base]
3349            %c
3350          [%& q.beam]
3351            %g
3352          =/  res  (rof [~ ~] /eyre %gd [our q.beam da+now] /$)
3353          ?.  ?=([~ ~ *] res)
3354            [%| "no desk for app {<q.beam>}"]
3355          [%& !<(=desk q.u.u.res)]
3356        ==
3357      ::
3358      ++  convert
3359        |=  [=vase from=mark to=mark =desk]
3360        ^-  (each ^vase tape)
3361        ?:  =(from to)  [%& vase]
3362        =/  tub  (rof [~ ~] /eyre %cc [our desk da+now] /[from]/[to])
```

```
3363      ?.  ?=([~ ~ %tube *] tub)
3364        [%| "no tube from {(trip from)} to {(trip to)}"]
3365      =/  tube  !<(tube:clay q.u.u.tub)
3366      =/  res  (mule |.((tube vase)))
3367      ?:  ?=(%| -.res)
3368        [%| "failed tube from {(trip from)} to {(trip to)}"]
3369      [%& +.res]
3370    --
3371  --
3372  ::  end the =~
3373  ::
3374  .  ==
3375  ::  begin with a default +axle as a blank slate
3376  ::
3377  =|  ax=axle
3378  ::  a vane is activated with current date, entropy, and a namespace function
3379  ::
3380  |=  [now=@da eny=@uvJ rof=roof]
3381  ::  allow jets to be registered within this core
3382  ::
3383  ~%  %http-server  ..part  ~
3384  |%
3385  ++  call
3386    ~/  %eyre-call
3387    |=  [=duct dud=(unit goof) wrapped-task=(hobo task)]
3388    ^-  [(list move) _http-server-gate]
3389    ::
3390    =/  task=task  ((harden task) wrapped-task)
3391    ::
3392    ::  XX handle more error notifications
3393    ::
3394    ?^  dud
3395      :_  http-server-gate
3396      ::  always print the error trace
3397      ::
3398      :-  [duct %slip %d %flog %crud [-.task tang.u.dud]]
3399      ^-  (list move)
3400      ::  if a request caused the crash, respond with a 500
3401      ::
3402      ?.  ?=(?(%request %request-local) -.task)  ~
3403      ^~
3404      =/  data  (as-octs:mimes:html 'crud!')
3405      =/  head
3406        :~  ['content-type' 'text/html']
3407            ['content-length' (crip (a-co:co p.data))]
3408        ==
3409      [duct %give %response %start 500^head `data &]~
3410    ::  %init: tells us what our ship name is
3411    ::
3412    ?:  ?=(%init -.task)
3413      ::  initial value for the login handler
3414      ::
3415      =.  bindings.server-state.ax
3416        =-  (roll - insert-binding)
3417        ^-  (list [binding ^duct action])
3418        :~  [[~ /~/login] duct [%authentication ~]]
3419            [[~ /~/eauth] duct [%eauth ~]]
3420            [[~ /~/logout] duct [%logout ~]]
```

```
3421          [[~ /~/channel] duct [%channel ~]]
3422          [[~ /~/scry] duct [%scry ~]]
3423          [[~ /~/name] duct [%name ~]]
3424          [[~ /~/host] duct [%host ~]]
3425        ==
3426      [~ http-server-gate]
3427  ::  %trim: in response to memory pressure
3428  ::
3429  ::    Cancel all inactive channels
3430  ::    XX cancel active too if =(0 trim-priority) ?
3431  ::
3432  ?:  ?=(%trim -.task)
3433    =*  event-args  [[eny duct now rof] server-state.ax]
3434    =*  by-channel  by-channel:(per-server-event event-args)
3435    =*  channel-state  channel-state.server-state.ax
3436    ::
3437    =/  inactive=(list @t)
3438      =/  full=(set @t)  ~(key by session.channel-state)
3439      =/  live=(set @t)
3440        (~(gas in *(set @t)) ~(val by duct-to-key.channel-state))
3441      ~(tap in (~(dif in full) live))
3442    ::
3443    ?:  =(~ inactive)
3444      [~ http-server-gate]
3445    ::
3446    =/  len=tape  (scow %ud (lent inactive))
3447    ~>  %slog.[0 leaf+"eyre: trim: closing {len} inactive channels"]
3448    ::
3449    =|  moves=(list (list move))
3450    |-  ^-  [(list move) _http-server-gate]
3451    =*  channel-id  i.inactive
3452    ?~  inactive
3453      [(zing (flop moves)) http-server-gate]
3454    ::  discard channel state, and cancel any active gall subscriptions
3455    ::
3456    =^  mov  server-state.ax  (discard-channel:by-channel channel-id |)
3457    $(moves [mov moves], inactive t.inactive)
3458  ::
3459  ::  %vega: notifies us of a completed kernel upgrade
3460  ::
3461  ?:  ?=(%vega -.task)
3462    [~ http-server-gate]
3463  ::  %born: new unix process
3464  ::
3465  ?:  ?=(%born -.task)
3466    ::  close previously open connections
3467    ::
3468    ::    When we have a new unix process, every outstanding open connection is
3469    ::    dead. For every duct, send an implicit close connection.
3470    ::
3471    =^  closed-connections=(list move)  server-state.ax
3472      =/  connections=(list [=^duct *])
3473        ~(tap by connections.server-state.ax)
3474      ::
3475      =|  closed-connections=(list move)
3476      |-
3477      ?~  connections
3478        [closed-connections server-state.ax]
```

```
3479        ::
3480        =/  event-args
3481          [[eny duct.i.connections now rof] server-state.ax]
3482        =/  cancel-request  cancel-request:(per-server-event event-args)
3483        =^  moves  server-state.ax  cancel-request
3484        ::
3485        $(closed-connections (weld moves closed-connections), connections t.connections)
3486      ::  save duct for future %give to unix
3487      ::
3488      =.  outgoing-duct.server-state.ax  duct
3489      ::  send all cache mappings to runtime
3490      ::
3491      =/  cache-moves=(list move)
3492        %+  turn  ~(tap by cache.server-state.ax)
3493        |=  [url=@t cache-val=[aeon=@ud val=(unit cache-entry)]]
3494        [duct %give %grow /cache/(scot %u aeon.cache-val)/(scot %t url)]
3495      ::
3496      :_  http-server-gate
3497      :*  ::  hand back default configuration for now
3498          ::
3499          [duct %give %set-config http-config.server-state.ax]
3500          ::  provide a list of valid auth tokens
3501          ::
3502          =<  give-session-tokens
3503          (per-server-event [eny duct now rof] server-state.ax)
3504          ::
3505          (zing ~[closed-connections cache-moves])
3506      ==
3507  ::
3508  ?:  ?=(%code-changed -.task)
3509    ~>  %slog.[0 leaf+"eyre: code-changed: throwing away local sessions"]
3510    =*  event-args  [[eny duct now rof] server-state.ax]
3511    ::  find all the %ours sessions, we must close them
3512    ::
3513    =/  siz=(list @uv)
3514      %+  murn  ~(tap by sessions.auth.server-state.ax)
3515      |=  [sid=@uv session]
3516      ?:(?=(%ours -.identity) (some sid) ~)
3517    =|  moves=(list (list move))
3518    |-  ^-  [(list move) _http-server-gate]
3519    ?~  siz
3520      [(zing (flop moves)) http-server-gate]
3521    ::  discard the session, clean up its channels
3522    ::
3523    =^  mov  server-state.ax
3524      (close-session:authentication:(per-server-event event-args) i.siz |)
3525    $(moves [mov moves], siz t.siz)
3526  ::
3527  ?:  ?=(%eauth-host -.task)
3528    ?:  =(user.endpoint.auth.server-state.ax host.task)
3529      [~ http-server-gate]
3530    =.  user.endpoint.auth.server-state.ax  host.task
3531    =.  time.endpoint.auth.server-state.ax  now
3532    [~ http-server-gate]
3533  ::
3534  ::  all other commands operate on a per-server-event
3535  ::
3536  =/  event-args  [[eny duct now rof] server-state.ax]
```

```
3537  =/  server  (per-server-event event-args)
3538  ::
3539  ?-    -.task
3540    ::  %live: notifies us of the ports of our live http servers
3541    ::
3542      %live
3543  =.  ports.server-state.ax  +.task
3544  ::  enable http redirects if https port live and cert set
3545  ::
3546  =.  redirect.http-config.server-state.ax
3547    &(?=(^ secure.task) ?=(^ secure.http-config.server-state.ax))
3548  [~ http-server-gate]
3549    ::  %rule: updates our http configuration
3550    ::
3551      %rule
3552  ?-    -.http-rule.task
3553      ::  %cert: install tls certificate
3554      ::
3555        %cert
3556    =*  config  http-config.server-state.ax
3557    ?:  =(secure.config cert.http-rule.task)
3558      [~ http-server-gate]
3559    =.  secure.config  cert.http-rule.task
3560    =.  redirect.config
3561      ?&  ?=(^ secure.ports.server-state.ax)
3562          ?=(^ cert.http-rule.task)
3563      ==
3564    :_  http-server-gate
3565    =*  out-duct  outgoing-duct.server-state.ax
3566    ?~  out-duct  ~
3567    [out-duct %give %set-config config]~
3568      ::  %turf: add or remove domain name
3569      ::
3570        %turf
3571    =*  domains  domains.server-state.ax
3572    =/  mod=(set turf)
3573      ?:  ?=(%put action.http-rule.task)
3574        (~(put in domains) turf.http-rule.task)
3575      (~(del in domains) turf.http-rule.task)
3576    ?:  =(domains mod)
3577      [~ http-server-gate]
3578    =.  domains  mod
3579    :_  http-server-gate
3580    =/  cmd
3581      [%acme %poke `cage`[%acme-order !>(mod)]]
3582    [duct %pass /acme/order %g %deal [our our /eyre] cmd]~
3583    ==
3584  ::
3585      %plea
3586  ~|  path.plea.task
3587  ?>  ?=([%eauth %'0' ~] path.plea.task)
3588  =+  plea=;;(eauth-plea payload.plea.task)
3589  =^  moves  server-state.ax
3590    (on-plea:server:eauth:authentication:server ship.task plea)
3591  [moves http-server-gate]
3592  ::
3593      %request
3594  =^  moves  server-state.ax  (request:server +.task)
```

```
3595      [moves http-server-gate]
3596  ::
3597        %request-local
3598      =^  moves  server-state.ax  (request-local:server +.task)
3599      [moves http-server-gate]
3600  ::
3601        %cancel-request
3602      =^  moves  server-state.ax  cancel-request:server
3603      [moves http-server-gate]
3604  ::
3605        %connect
3606      =^  moves  server-state.ax
3607      %+  add-binding:server  binding.task
3608      [%app app.task]
3609      [moves http-server-gate]
3610  ::
3611        %serve
3612      =^  moves  server-state.ax
3613      %+  add-binding:server  binding.task
3614      [%gen generator.task]
3615      [moves http-server-gate]
3616  ::
3617        %disconnect
3618      =.  server-state.ax  (remove-binding:server binding.task)
3619      [~ http-server-gate]
3620  ::
3621        %approve-origin
3622      =.  cors-registry.server-state.ax
3623        =,  cors-registry.server-state.ax
3624        :+  (~(del in requests) origin.task)
3625          (~(put in approved) origin.task)
3626        (~(del in rejected) origin.task)
3627      [~ http-server-gate]
3628  ::
3629        %reject-origin
3630      =.  cors-registry.server-state.ax
3631        =,  cors-registry.server-state.ax
3632        :+  (~(del in requests) origin.task)
3633          (~(del in approved) origin.task)
3634        (~(put in rejected) origin.task)
3635      [~ http-server-gate]
3636  ::
3637        %spew
3638      =.  verb.server-state.ax  veb.task
3639      `http-server-gate
3640  ::
3641        %set-response
3642      =^  moves  server-state.ax  (set-response:server +.task)
3643      [moves http-server-gate]
3644    ==
3645  ::
3646  ++  take
3647  ~/  %eyre-take
3648  |=  [=wire =duct dud=(unit goof) =sign]
3649  ^-  [(list move) _http-server-gate]
3650  =>  %=    .
3651           sign
3652        ?:  ?=(%gall -.sign)
```

```
?>    ?=(%unto +<.sign)
    sign
  sign
==
::  :wire must at least contain two parts, the type and the build
::
?>  ?=([@ *] wire)
::
|^  ^-  [(list move) _http-server-gate]
    ::
    ?:  ?=(%eauth i.wire)
      eauth
    ?^  dud
      ~|(%eyre-take-dud (mean tang.u.dud))
    ?+    i.wire
        ~|([%bad-take-wire wire] !!)
    ::
      %run-app-request    run-app-request
      %watch-response     watch-response
      %sessions           sessions
      %channel            channel
      %acme               acme-ack
      %conversion-cache   `http-server-gate
    ==
::
++  run-app-request
  ::
  ?>  ?=([%gall %unto *] sign)
  ::
  ::
  ?>  ?=([%poke-ack *] p.sign)
  ?>  ?=([@ *] t.wire)
  ?~  p.p.sign
    ::  received a positive acknowledgment: take no action
    ::
    [~ http-server-gate]
  ::  we have an error; propagate it to the client
  ::
  =/  event-args  [[eny duct now rof] server-state.ax]
  =/  handle-gall-error
    handle-gall-error:(per-server-event event-args)
  =^  moves  server-state.ax
    (handle-gall-error u.p.p.sign)
  [moves http-server-gate]
::
++  watch-response
  ::
  =/  event-args  [[eny duct now rof] server-state.ax]
  ::
  ?>  ?=([@ *] t.wire)
  ?:  ?=([%gall %unto %watch-ack *] sign)
    ?~  p.p.sign
      ::  received a positive acknowledgment: take no action
      ::
      [~ http-server-gate]
    ::  we have an error; propagate it to the client
    ::
    =/  handle-gall-error
```

```hoon
3711        handle-gall-error:(per-server-event event-args)
3712      =^  moves  server-state.ax  (handle-gall-error u.p.p.sign)
3713      [moves http-server-gate]
3714    ::
3715    ?:  ?=([%gall %unto %kick ~] sign)
3716      =/  handle-response  handle-response:(per-server-event event-args)
3717      =^  moves  server-state.ax
3718        (handle-response %continue ~ &)
3719      [moves http-server-gate]
3720    ::
3721    ?>  ?=([%gall %unto %fact *] sign)
3722    =/  =mark  p.cage.p.sign
3723    =/  =vase  q.cage.p.sign
3724    ?.  ?=  ?(%http-response-header %http-response-data %http-response-cancel)
3725        mark
3726      =/  handle-gall-error
3727        handle-gall-error:(per-server-event event-args)
3728      =^  moves  server-state.ax
3729        (handle-gall-error leaf+"eyre bad mark {(trip mark)}" ~)
3730      [moves http-server-gate]
3731    ::
3732    =/  =http-event:http
3733      ?-  mark
3734        %http-response-header  [%start !<(response-header:http vase) ~ |]
3735        %http-response-data    [%continue !<((unit octs) vase) |]
3736        %http-response-cancel  [%cancel ~]
3737      ==
3738    =/  handle-response  handle-response:(per-server-event event-args)
3739    =^  moves  server-state.ax
3740      (handle-response http-event)
3741    [moves http-server-gate]
3742  ::
3743  ++  channel
3744    ::
3745    =/  event-args  [[eny duct now rof] server-state.ax]
3746    ::  channel callback wires are triples.
3747    ::
3748    ?>  ?=([@ @ @t *] wire)
3749    ::
3750    ?+    i.t.wire
3751        ~|([%bad-channel-wire wire] !!)
3752    ::
3753        %timeout
3754      ?>  ?=([%behn %wake *] sign)
3755      ?^  error.sign
3756        [[duct %slip %d %flog %crud %wake u.error.sign]~ http-server-gate]
3757      =*  id  i.t.t.wire
3758      %-  %+  trace:(per-server-event event-args)  1
3759          |.("{(trip id)} cancelling channel due to timeout")
3760      =^  moves  server-state.ax
3761        (discard-channel:by-channel:(per-server-event event-args) id &)
3762      [moves http-server-gate]
3763    ::
3764        %heartbeat
3765      =/  on-channel-heartbeat
3766        on-channel-heartbeat:by-channel:(per-server-event event-args)
3767      =^  moves  server-state.ax
3768        (on-channel-heartbeat i.t.t.wire)
```

```
3769        [moves http-server-gate]
3770      ::
3771          ?(%poke %subscription)
3772      ?>   ?=([%gall %unto *] sign)
3773      ~|   eyre-sub=wire
3774      ?>   ?=([@ @ @t @ *] wire)
3775      ?<   ?=(%raw-fact -.p.sign)
3776      =*   channel-id  i.t.t.wire
3777      =*   request-id  i.t.t.t.wire
3778      =*   extra-wire  t.t.t.t.wire
3779      =/   on-gall-response
3780        on-gall-response:by-channel:(per-server-event event-args)
3781      ::   ~&  [%gall-response sign]
3782      =^   moves  server-state.ax
3783        %-  on-gall-response
3784        [channel-id (slav %ud request-id) extra-wire p.sign]
3785      [moves http-server-gate]
3786    ==
3787  ::
3788  ++  sessions
3789    ::
3790    ?>   ?=([%behn %wake *] sign)
3791    ::
3792    ?^  error.sign
3793      [[duct %slip %d %flog %crud %wake u.error.sign]~ http-server-gate]
3794    ::NOTE  we are not concerned with expiring channels that are still in
3795    ::       use. we require acks for messages, which bump their session's
3796    ::       timer. channels have their own expiry timer, too.
3797    ::  remove cookies that have expired
3798    ::
3799    =*   sessions  sessions.auth.server-state.ax
3800    =.   sessions.auth.server-state.ax
3801      %-  ~(gas by *(map @uv session))
3802      %+  skip  ~(tap in sessions)
3803      |=  [cookie=@uv session]
3804      (lth expiry-time now)
3805    ::  if there's any cookies left, set a timer for the next expected expiry
3806    ::
3807    ^-  [(list move) _http-server-gate]
3808    :_  http-server-gate
3809    :-  =<  give-session-tokens
3810        (per-server-event [eny duct now rof] server-state.ax)
3811    ?:  =(~ sessions)  ~
3812    =;  next-expiry=@da
3813      [duct %pass /sessions/expire %b %wait next-expiry]~
3814    %+  roll  ~(tap by sessions)
3815    |=  [[@uv session] next=@da]
3816    ?:  =(*@da next)  expiry-time
3817    (min next expiry-time)
3818  ::
3819  ++  eauth
3820    =*   auth  auth.server-state.ax
3821    =*   args  [[eny duct now rof] server-state.ax]
3822    ^-  [(list move) _http-server-gate]
3823    ~|  [wire +<.sign]
3824    ?+  t.wire  !!
3825        [%plea @ ~]
3826      =/  =ship  (slav %p i.t.t.wire)
```

```
3827      ::
3828      ?:  |(?=(^ dud) ?=([%ames %lost *] sign))
3829        %-  %+  trace:(per-server-event args)  0
3830          ?~  dud  |.("eauth: lost boon from {(scow %p ship)}")
3831          |.("eauth: crashed on %{(trip +<.sign)} from {(scow %p ship)}")
3832        ::NOTE  when failing on pending attempts, we just wait for the timer
3833        ::        to clean up. when failing on live sessions, well, we should
3834        ::        just be careful not to crash when receiving %shut boons.
3835        ::        (we do not want to have the nonce in the wire, so this is the
3836        ::        best handling we can do. the alternative is tracking)
3837        [~ http-server-gate]
3838      ::
3839      ?:  ?=([%ames %done *] sign)
3840        =^  moz  server-state.ax
3841          %.  [ship ?=(~ error.sign)]
3842          on-done:client:eauth:authentication:(per-server-event args)
3843        [moz http-server-gate]
3844      ::
3845      ?>  ?=([%ames %boon *] sign)
3846      =/  boon  ;;(eauth-boon payload.sign)
3847      =^  moz  server-state.ax
3848        %.  [ship boon]
3849        on-boon:client:eauth:authentication:(per-server-event args)
3850      [moz http-server-gate]
3851    ::
3852        [%keen @ @ ~]
3853      =/  client=@p  (slav %p i.t.t.wire)
3854      =/  nonce=@uv  (slav %uv i.t.t.t.wire)
3855      ::
3856      ?^  dud
3857        =^  moz  server-state.ax
3858          %.  [client nonce]
3859          on-fail:server:eauth:authentication:(per-server-event args)
3860        [moz http-server-gate]
3861      ::
3862      ?>  ?=([%ames %tune *] sign)
3863      ?>  =(client ship.sign)
3864      =/  url=(unit @t)
3865        ?~  roar.sign  ~
3866        ?~  q.dat.u.roar.sign  ~
3867        ;;((unit @t) q.u.q.dat.u.roar.sign)
3868      =^  moz  server-state.ax
3869        ?~  url
3870          %.  [client nonce]
3871          on-fail:server:eauth:authentication:(per-server-event args)
3872        %.  [client nonce u.url]
3873        on-tune:server:eauth:authentication:(per-server-event args)
3874      [moz http-server-gate]
3875    ::
3876        [%expire %visiting @ @ ~]
3877      ?>  ?=([%behn %wake *] sign)
3878      =/  server=@p  (slav %p i.t.t.wire)
3879      =/  nonce=@uv  (slav %uv i.t.t.t.wire)
3880      =^  moz  server-state.ax
3881        %.  [server nonce]
3882        expire:client:eauth:authentication:(per-server-event args)
3883      [~ http-server-gate]
3884    ::
```

```
3885          [%expire %visitors @ ~]
3886      =/  nonce=@uv  (slav %uv i.t.t.t.wire)
3887      =^  moz   server-state.ax
3888      (expire:server:eauth:authentication:(per-server-event args) nonce)
3889      [moz http-server-gate]
3890    ==
3891  ::
3892  ++  acme-ack
3893    ?>  ?=([%gall %unto *] sign)
3894    ::
3895    ?>  ?=([%poke-ack *] p.sign)
3896    ?~  p.p.sign
3897    ::  received a positive acknowledgment: take no action
3898    ::
3899    [~ http-server-gate]
3900  ::  received a negative acknowledgment: XX do something
3901  ::
3902  [((slog u.p.p.sign) ~) http-server-gate]
3903  --
3904  ::
3905  ++  http-server-gate  ..$
3906  ::  +load: migrate old state to new state (called on vane reload)
3907  ::
3908  ++  load
3909    =>  |%
3910        +$  axle-any
3911        $%  [date=%~2020.10.18 server-state=server-state-0]
3912            [date=%~2022.7.26 server-state=server-state-0]
3913            [date=%~2023.2.17 server-state=server-state-1]
3914            [date=%~2023.3.16 server-state=server-state-2]
3915            [date=%~2023.4.11 server-state-3]
3916            [date=%~2023.5.15 server-state]
3917        ==
3918        ::
3919        +$  server-state-0
3920        $:  bindings=(list [=binding =duct =action])
3921            =cors-registry
3922            connections=(map duct outstanding-connection-3)
3923            auth=authentication-state-3
3924            channel-state=channel-state-2
3925            domains=(set turf)
3926            =http-config
3927            ports=[insecure=@ud secure=(unit @ud)]
3928            outgoing-duct=duct
3929        ==
3930        ::
3931        +$  server-state-1
3932        $:  bindings=(list [=binding =duct =action])
3933            =cors-registry
3934            connections=(map duct outstanding-connection-3)
3935            auth=authentication-state-3
3936            channel-state=channel-state-2
3937            domains=(set turf)
3938            =http-config
3939            ports=[insecure=@ud secure=(unit @ud)]
3940            outgoing-duct=duct
3941            verb=@                                      ::  <-  new
3942        ==
```

```
3943      ::
3944      +$  server-state-2
3945      $:  bindings=(list [=binding =duct =action])
3946          cache=(map url=@t [aeon=@ud val=(unit cache-entry)])  ::  <- new
3947          =cors-registry
3948          connections=(map duct outstanding-connection-3)
3949          auth=authentication-state-3
3950          channel-state=channel-state-2
3951          domains=(set turf)
3952          =http-config
3953          ports=[insecure=@ud secure=(unit @ud)]
3954          outgoing-duct=duct
3955          verb=@
3956      ==
3957      +$  channel-state-2
3958      $:  session=(map @t channel-2)
3959          duct-to-key=(map duct @t)
3960      ==
3961      +$  channel-2
3962      $:  state=(each timer duct)
3963          next-id=@ud
3964          last-ack=@da
3965          events=(qeu [id=@ud request-id=@ud channel-event=channel-event-2])
3966          unacked=(map @ud @ud)
3967          subscriptions=(map @ud [ship=@p app=term =path duc=duct])
3968          heartbeat=(unit timer)
3969      ==
3970      +$  channel-event-2
3971      $%  $>(%poke-ack sign:agent:gall)
3972          $>(%watch-ack sign:agent:gall)
3973          $>(%kick sign:agent:gall)
3974          [%fact =mark =noun]
3975      ==
3976      ::
3977      +$  server-state-3
3978      $:  bindings=(list [=binding =duct =action])
3979          cache=(map url=@t [aeon=@ud val=(unit cache-entry)])
3980          =cors-registry
3981          connections=(map duct outstanding-connection-3)
3982          auth=authentication-state-3
3983          channel-state=channel-state-3
3984          domains=(set turf)
3985          =http-config
3986          ports=[insecure=@ud secure=(unit @ud)]
3987          outgoing-duct=duct
3988          verb=@
3989      ==
3990      +$  outstanding-connection-3
3991      $:  =action
3992          =inbound-request
3993          response-header=(unit response-header:http)
3994          bytes-sent=@ud
3995      ==
3996      +$  authentication-state-3  sessions=(map @uv session-3)
3997      +$  session-3
3998      $:  expiry-time=@da
3999          channels=(set @t)
4000      ==
```

```
+$  channel-state-3
  $:  session=(map @t channel-3)
      duct-to-key=(map duct @t)
  ==
+$  channel-3
  $:  mode=?(%json %jam)
      state=(each timer duct)
      next-id=@ud
      last-ack=@da
      events=(qeu [id=@ud request-id=@ud =channel-event])
      unacked=(map @ud @ud)
      subscriptions=(map @ud [ship=@p app=term =path duc=duct])
      heartbeat=(unit timer)
  ==
  --
|=  old=axle-any
^+  http-server-gate
?-    -.old
::
::  adds /~/name
::
    %~2020.10.18
  %=  $
      date.old  %~2022.7.26
  ::
      bindings.server-state.old
    %+  insert-binding
      [[~ /~/name] outgoing-duct.server-state.old [%name ~]]
    bindings.server-state.old
  ==
::
::  enables https redirects if certificate configured
::  inits .verb
::
    %~2022.7.26
  =.  redirect.http-config.server-state.old
    ?&  ?=(^ secure.ports.server-state.old)
        ?=(^ secure.http-config.server-state.old)
    ==
  $(old [%~2023.2.17 server-state.old(|8 [|8 verb=0]:server-state.old)])
::
::  inits .cache
::
    %~2023.2.17
  $(old [%~2023.3.16 [bindings ~ +]:server-state.old])
::
::  inits channel mode and desks in unacked events
::
    %~2023.3.16
::
::  Prior to this desks were not part of events.channel.
::  When serializing we used to rely on the desk stored in
::  subscriptions.channel, but this state is deleted when we clog.
::  This migration adds the desk to events.channel, but we can not
::  scry in +load to populate the desks in the old events,
::  so we just kick all subscriptions on all channels.
  %=  $
      date.old  %~2023.4.11
```

```
4059      ::
4060            server-state.old
4061      %=  server-state.old
4062          session.channel-state
4063        %-  ~(run by session.channel-state.server-state.old)
4064        |=  c=channel-2
4065        =;  new-events
4066          :-  %json
4067          c(events new-events, unacked ~, subscriptions ~)
4068        =|  events=(qeu [id=@ud request-id=@ud =channel-event])
4069        =/  1  ~(tap in ~(key by subscriptions.c))
4070        |-
4071        ?~  1  events
4072        %=  $
4073          1              t.1
4074          next-id.c  +(next-id.c)
4075          events       (~(put to events) [next-id.c i.1 %kick ~])
4076        ==
4077      ==
4078    ==
4079    ::
4080    ::  guarantees & stores a session for each request, and a @p identity for
4081    ::  each session and channel
4082    ::
4083      %~2023.4.11
4084    %=  $
4085      date.old  %~2023.5.15
4086      ::
4087          connections.old
4088      %-  ~(run by connections.old)
4089      |=  outstanding-connection-3
4090      ^-  outstanding-connection
4091      [action inbound-request [*@uv [%ours ~]] response-header bytes-sent]
4092      ::
4093          auth.old
4094      :_  [~ ~ [~ ~ now]]
4095      %-  ~(run by sessions.auth.old)
4096      |=  s=session-3
4097      ^-  session
4098      [[%ours ~] s]
4099      ::
4100          session.channel-state.old
4101      %-  ~(run by session.channel-state.old)
4102      |=  c=channel-3
4103      ^-  channel
4104      [-.c [%ours ~] +.c]
4105      ::
4106          bindings.old
4107      %+  insert-binding  [[~ /~/host] outgoing-duct.old [%host ~]]
4108      %+  insert-binding  [[~ /~/eauth] outgoing-duct.old [%eauth ~]]
4109      bindings.old
4110    ==
4111    ::
4112      %~2023.5.15
4113    http-server-gate(ax old)
4114  ==
4115  ::  +stay: produce current state
4116  ::
```

```
4117  ++    stay  `axle`ax
4118  ::    +scry: request a path in the urbit namespace
4119  ::
4120  ++    scry
4121  ~/  %eyre-scry
4122  ^-  roon
4123  |=  [lyc=gang pov=path car=term bem=beam]
4124  ^-  (unit (unit cage))
4125  =*  ren  car
4126  =*  why=shop  &/p.bem
4127  =*  syd  q.bem
4128  =/  lot=coin  $/r.bem
4129  =*  tyl  s.bem
4130  ::
4131  ?.  ?=(%& -.why)
4132    ~
4133  =*  who  p.why
4134  ::
4135  ?.  ?=(%$ -.lot)
4136    [~ ~]
4137  ?.  =(our who)
4138    ?.  =([%da now] p.lot)
4139      ~
4140    ~&  [%r %scry-foreign-host who]
4141    ~
4142  ::
4143  ?:  ?=([%eauth %url ~] tyl)
4144    ?.  &(?=(%x ren) ?=(%$ syd))  ~
4145    =*  endpoint  endpoint.auth.server-state.ax
4146    ?.  ?=(%da -.p.lot)  [~ ~]
4147    ::  we cannot answer for something prior to the last set time,
4148    ::  or something beyond the present moment.
4149    ::
4150    ?:  ?|  (lth q.p.lot time.endpoint)
4151            (gth q.p.lot now)
4152        ==
4153      ~
4154    :^  ~  ~  %noun
4155    !>  ^-  (unit @t)
4156    =<  eauth-url:eauth:authentication
4157    (per-server-event [eny *duct now rof] server-state.ax)
4158  ::
4159  ?:  ?=([%cache @ @ ~] tyl)
4160    ?.  &(?=(%x ren) ?=(%$ syd))  ~
4161    =,  server-state.ax
4162    ?~  aeon=(slaw %ud i.t.tyl)          [~ ~]
4163    ?~  url=(slaw %t i.t.t.tyl)          [~ ~]
4164    ?~  entry=(~(get by cache) u.url)  ~
4165    ?.  =(u.aeon aeon.u.entry)          ~
4166    ?~  val=val.u.entry                 ~
4167    ?:  &(auth.u.val !=([~ ~] lyc))     ~
4168    ``noun+!>(u.val)
4169  ::  private endpoints
4170  ?.  ?=([~ ~] lyc)  ~
4171  ?:  &(?=(%x ren) ?=(%$ syd))
4172    =,  server-state.ax
4173    ?+  tyl  ~
4174      [%$ %whey ~]              =-  ``mass+!>(`(list mass)`-)
```

```
                              :~  bindings+&+bindings.server-state.ax
                                  cache+&+cache.server-state.ax
                                  auth+&+auth.server-state.ax
                                  connections+&+connections.server-state.ax
                                  channels+&+channel-state.server-state.ax
                                  axle+&+ax
                              ==
    ::
    [%cors ~]                 ``noun+!>(cors-registry)
    [%cors %requests ~]       ``noun+!>(requests.cors-registry)
    [%cors %approved ~]       ``noun+!>(approved.cors-registry)
    [%cors %rejected ~]       ``noun+!>(rejected.cors-registry)
    ::
      [%cors ?(%approved %rejected) @ ~]
    =*  kind  i.t.tyl
    =*  orig  i.t.t.tyl
    ?~  origin=(slaw %t orig)  [~ ~]
    ?-  kind
      %approved  ``noun+!>((~(has in approved.cors-registry) u.origin))
      %rejected  ``noun+!>((~(has in rejected.cors-registry) u.origin))
    ==
    ::
      [%authenticated %cookie @ ~]
    ?~  cookies=(slaw %t i.t.t.tyl)  [~ ~]
    :^  ~  ~  %noun
    !>  ^-  ?
    %-  =<  request-is-authenticated:authentication
        (per-server-event [eny *duct now rof] server-state.ax)
    %*(. *request:http header-list ['cookie' u.cookies]~)
    ::
      [%'_~_' *]
    =/  mym  (scry-mime now rof (deft:de-purl:html tyl))
    ?:  ?=(%| -.mym)  [~ ~]
    ``noun+!>(p.mym)
    ==
?.  ?=(%$ ren)  ~
?+  syd  ~
  %bindings               ``noun+!>(bindings.server-state.ax)
  %cache                  ``noun+!>(cache.server-state.ax)
  %connections            ``noun+!>(connections.server-state.ax)
  %authentication-state   ``noun+!>(auth.server-state.ax)
  %channel-state          ``noun+!>(channel-state.server-state.ax)
  ::
    %host
  %-  (lift (lift |=(a=hart:eyre [%hart !>(a)])))
  ^-  (unit (unit hart:eyre))
  =.  p.lot  ?.(=([%da now] p.lot) p.lot [%tas %real])
  ?+  p.lot
    [~ ~]
  ::
      [%tas %fake]
    ``[& [~ 8.443] %& /localhost]
  ::
      [%tas %real]
    =*  domains  domains.server-state.ax
    =*  ports  ports.server-state.ax
    =/  =host:eyre  [%& ?^(domains n.domains /localhost)]
    =/  port=(unit @ud)
```

```
    ?.  ?=(^ secure.ports)
      ?:(=(80 insecure.ports) ~ `insecure.ports)
      ?:(=(443 u.secure.ports) ~ secure.ports)
    ``[?=(^ secure.ports) port host]
  ==
==
--
```

Gall

```
!:
::   ::  %gall, agent execution
!?  163
::
:::::
|=  our=ship
::  veb: verbosity flags
::
=/  veb-all-off
  ::  TODO: add more flags?
  ::
  :*  odd=`?`%.n  ::  unusual events
  ==
=,  gall
=>
|%
+|  %helpers
::  +trace: print if .verb is set and we're tracking .dude
::
++  trace
  |=  [verb=? =dude dudes=(set dude) print=tang]
  ^+  same
  ?.  verb
    same
  ?.  =>  [dude=dude dudes=dudes in=in]
      ~+  |(=(~ dudes) (~(has in dudes) dude))
    same
  (slog print)
::
::  $bug: debug printing configuration
::
::    veb: verbosity toggles
::    dudes: app filter; if ~, print for all
::
+$  bug
  $:  veb=_veb-all-off
      dudes=(set dude)
  ==
::
+|  %main
::
::  $move: Arvo-level move
::
+$  move  [=duct move=(wind note-arvo gift-arvo)]
::  $state-16: overall gall state, versioned
::
+$  state-16  [%16 state]
::  $state: overall gall state
::
::    system-duct: TODO document
::    outstanding: outstanding request queue
::    contacts: other ships we're in communication with
::    yokes: running agents
::    blocked: moves to agents that haven't been started yet
::    bug: debug printing configuration
::    leaves: retry nacked %leaves timer, if set
```

```hoon
::
+$  state
  $+  state
  $:  system-duct=duct
      outstanding=(map [wire duct] (qeu remote-request))
      contacts=(set ship)
      yokes=(map term yoke)
      blocked=(map term (qeu blocked-move))
      =bug
      leaves=(unit [=duct =wire date=@da])
  ==
:: $routes: new cuff; TODO: document
::
+$  routes
  $:  disclosing=(unit (set ship))
      attributing=[=ship =path]
  ==
+$  brood  [=coop =hutch]
::  $yoke: agent runner state
::
::      control-duct: TODO document
::      run-nonce: unique for each rebuild
::      sub-nonce: app-wide global %watch nonce
::      stats: TODO document
::      bitt: incoming subscriptions
::      boat: outgoing subscriptions
::      boar: and their nonces
::      code: most recently loaded code
::      agent: agent core
::      beak: compilation source
::      marks: mark conversion requests
::      sky: scry bindings
::      ken: open keen requests
::
+$  yoke
  $%  [%nuke sky=(map spur @ud) cop=(map coop hutch)]
      $:  %live
          control-duct=duct
          run-nonce=@t
          sub-nonce=_1
          =stats
          =bitt
          =boat
          =boar
          code=*
          agent=(each agent vase)
          =beak
          marks=(map duct mark)
          sky=farm
          ken=(jug spar:ames wire)
          pen=(jug spar:ames wire)
          gem=(jug coop [path page])
  ==  ==
::
++  of-farm
  |_  =farm
  ++  key-coops
    |=  pos=path
```

```
115      ^-  (list coop)
116      =/  frm  (get-farm pos)
117      ?~  frm  ~
118      =.  farm  u.frm
119      |-
120      ?:  ?=(%coop -.farm)
121        ~[pos]
122      %-  zing
123      %+  turn  ~(tap by q.farm)
124      |=  [seg=@ta f=^farm]
125      ^-  (list coop)
126      ^$(pos (snoc pos seg), farm f)
127    ::
128    ++  match-coop
129      =|  wer=path
130      |=  =path
131      ^-  (unit coop)
132      ?:  ?=(%coop -.farm)
133        `(flop wer)
134      ?~  path
135        ~
136      ?~  nex=(~(get by q.farm) i.path)
137        ~
138      $(wer [i.path wer], path t.path, farm u.nex)
139    ::
140    ++  put
141      |=  [=path =plot]
142      ^-  _farm
143      ?:  ?=(%coop -.farm)
144        farm(q (~(put by q.farm) path plot))
145      ?~  path
146        farm(p `plot)
147      =/  nex  (~(get by q.farm) i.path)
148      =/  res  $(path t.path, farm ?~(nex *^farm u.nex))
149      farm(q (~(put by q.farm) i.path res))
150    ::
151    ++  put-grow
152      |=  [=path =plot]
153      ^-  (unit _farm)
154      ?:  ?=(%coop -.farm)
155        ~
156      ?~  path
157        `farm(p `plot)
158      =/  nex  (~(get by q.farm) i.path)
159      =/  res
160        $(path t.path, farm ?~(nex *^farm u.nex))
161      ?~  res  ~
162      `farm(q (~(put by q.farm) i.path u.res))
163    ::
164    ++  put-tend
165      |=  [=path =plot]
166      ^-  (unit _farm)
167      ?:  ?=(%coop -.farm)
168        `farm(q (~(put by q.farm) path plot))
169      ?~  path
170        `farm(p `plot)
171      ?~  nex=(~(get by q.farm) i.path)
172        ~
```

```
173      =/  res
174        $(path t.path, farm u.nex)
175      ?~  res  ~
176      `farm(q (~(put by q.farm) i.path u.res))
177    ::
178    ++  grow
179      |=  [=spur now=@da =page]
180      =/  ski  (gut spur)
181      %+  put   spur
182      =-  ski(fan (put:on-path fan.ski -< -> &/page))
183      ?~  las=(ram:on-path fan.ski)
184        [?~(bob.ski 1 +(u.bob.ski)) now]
185      :_  (max now +(p.val.u.las))
186      ?~(bob.ski +(key.u.las) +((max key.u.las u.bob.ski)))
187    ::
188    ++  germ
189      |=  [=coop =hutch]
190      ^-  (unit _farm)
191      ?~  coop
192        ?.  |(=(%coop -.farm) =([%page ~ ~] farm))
193          ~
194        `[%coop hutch ~]
195      ?:  ?=(%coop -.farm)
196        ~
197      ?~  nex=(~(get by q.farm) i.coop)
198        ~
199      $(coop t.coop, farm u.nex)
200    ::
201    ++  tend
202      |=  [=coop =path =plot]
203      ^-  (unit _farm)
204      ?~  coop
205        ?.  ?=(%coop -.farm)
206          ~
207        `farm(q (~(put by q.farm) path plot))
208      ?.  ?=(%plot -.farm)
209        ~
210      ?~  nex=(~(get by q.farm) i.coop)
211        ~
212      $(coop t.coop, farm u.nex)
213    ::
214    ++  del
215      |=  =path
216      ^+  farm
217      ?:  ?=(%coop -.farm)
218        farm(q (~(del by q.farm) path))
219      ?~  path
220        farm(p ~)
221      ?~  nex=(~(get by q.farm) i.path)
222        farm
223      $(path t.path, farm u.nex)
224    ::
225    ++  gut
226      |=  =path
227      ^-  plot
228      (fall (get path) *plot)
229    ::
230    ++  put-hutch
```

```
|=  [=path =hutch]
^-  (unit _farm)
?~  path
  ?:  ?=(%coop -.farm)
    `farm(p hutch)
  ?.  =([%plot ~ ~] farm)
    ~
  `[%coop hutch ~]
?:  ?=(%coop -.farm)
  ~
=/  nex  (~(gut by q.farm) i.path *^farm)
=/  res  $(path t.path, farm nex)
?~  res  ~
`farm(q (~(put by q.farm) i.path u.res))
::
++  get-hutch
  |=  =path
  ^-  (unit hutch)
  ?~  path
    ?.  ?=(%coop -.farm)
      ~
    `p.farm
  ?:  ?=(%coop -.farm)
    ~
  ?~  nex=(~(get by q.farm) i.path)
    ~
  $(path t.path, farm u.nex)
::
++  get-farm
  |=  =path
  ^-  (unit ^farm)
  ?:  ?=(%coop -.farm)
    ?~  (~(get by q.farm) path)
      ~
    `farm
  ?~  path  ~
  ?~  nex=(~(get by q.farm) i.path)
    ~
  $(path t.path, farm u.nex)
::
++  get
  |=  =path
  ^-  (unit plot)
  ?:  ?=(%coop -.farm)
    (~(get by q.farm) path)
  ?~  path
    p.farm
  ?~  nex=(~(get by q.farm) i.path)
    ~
  $(path t.path, farm u.nex)
::
++  tap-plot
  =|  wer=path
  |-  ^-  (list [path plot])
  =*  tap-plot  $
  ?:  ?=(%coop -.farm)
    %+  turn  ~(tap by q.farm)
    |=  [=path =plot]
```

```
289        [(welp wer path) plot]
290      %+  welp  ?~(p.farm ~ [wer u.p.farm]~)
291      %-  zing
292      %+  turn  ~(tap by q.farm)
293      |=  [seg=@ta f=^farm]
294      ^-  (list [path plot])
295      tap-plot(wer (snoc wer seg), farm f)
296    ::
297    ++  run-plot
298      |*  fun=gate
299      %-  ~(gas by *(map path _(fun)))
300      %+  turn  tap-plot
301      |=  [=path =plot]
302      [path (fun plot)]
303    ::
304    ++  gas-hutch
305      |=  =(list [=coop =hutch])
306      ^-  (unit _farm)
307      ?~  list
308        `farm
309      =/  nex
310        (put-hutch i.list)
311      ?~  nex  ~
312      $(farm u.nex, list t.list)
313    ::
314    ++  tap-hutch
315      =|  wer=path
316      %-  ~(gas in *(set [=coop =hutch]))
317      |-  ^-  (list [=coop =hutch])
318      =*  loop  $
319      ?:  ?=(%coop -.farm)
320        [wer p.farm]~
321      %-  zing
322      %+  turn  ~(tap by q.farm)
323      |=  [seg=@ta f=^farm]
324      ^-  (list [=coop =hutch])
325      loop(wer (snoc wer seg), farm f)
326    --
327  ::
328  ++  on-path  ((on @ud (pair @da (each page @uvI))) lte)
329  ::  $blocked-move: enqueued move to an agent
330  ::
331  +$  blocked-move  [=duct =routes move=(each deal unto)]
332  ::
333  ::  $fine-request: key exchange request for $coop
334  ::
335  +$  fine-request
336    [%0 =path]
337  ::
338  ::  $fine-response: key exchange response for $coop
339  ::
340  +$  fine-response
341    [%0 bod=(unit brood)]
342  ::
343  +$  ames-response
344    $%  [%d =mark noun=*]
345        [%x ~]
346    ==
```

```
347  ::
348  ::    $ames-request: network request (%plea)
349  ::
350  ::      %m: poke
351  ::      %l: watch-as
352  ::      %s: watch
353  ::      %u: leave
354  ::
355  +$  ames-request-all
356    $%  [%0 ames-request]
357    ==
358  +$  ames-request
359    $%  [%m =mark noun=*]
360        [%l =mark =path]
361        [%s =path]
362        [%u ~]
363    ==
364  ::  $remote-request: kinds of agent actions that can cross the network
365  ::
366  ::    Used in wires to identify the kind of remote request we made.
367  ::    Bijective with the tags of $ames-request.
368  ::
369  +$  remote-request
370    $?  %watch
371        %watch-as
372        %poke
373        %leave
374        %missing
375    ==
376  ::  |migrate: data structures for upgrades
377  ::
378  +|  %migrate
379  ::
380  ::  $spore: structures for update, produced by +stay
381  ::
382  ::  remember to duplicate version tag changes here to $egg-any:gall in lull
383  ::
384  +$  spore
385    $:  system-duct=duct
386        outstanding=(map [wire duct] (qeu remote-request))
387        contacts=(set ship)
388        eggs=(map term egg)
389        blocked=(map term (qeu blocked-move))
390        =bug
391        leaves=(unit [=duct =wire date=@da])
392    ==
393  +$  spore-16  [%16 spore]
394  --
395  ::  adult gall vane interface, for type compatibility with pupa
396  ::
397  =|  state=state-16
398  |=  [now=@da eny=@uvJ rof=roof]
399  =*  gall-payload  .
400  ~%  %gall-top  ..part  ~
401  |%
402  ::  +mo: Arvo-level move handling
403  ::
404  ::    An outer core responsible for routing moves to and from Arvo; it calls
```

```
::      an inner core, +ap, to route internal moves to and from agents.
::
++  mo
  ~%  %gall-mo  +>  ~
  |_  [hen=duct moves=(list move)]
  ::
  ++  trace
    |=  [verb=? =dude print=tang]
    ^+  same
    (^trace verb dude dudes.bug.state print)
  ::
  ::  +mo-abed: initialise state with the provided duct
  ::  +mo-abet: finalize, reversing moves
  ::  +mo-pass: prepend a standard %pass to the current list of moves
  ::  +mo-give: prepend a standard %give to the current list of moves
  ::  +mo-talk: build task to print config report or failure trace
  ::
  ++  mo-core  .
  ++  mo-abed  |=(hun=duct mo-core(hen hun))
  ++  mo-abet  [(flop moves) gall-payload]
  ++  mo-emit  |=(=move mo-core(moves [move moves]))
  ++  mo-give  |=(=gift (mo-emit hen give+gift))
  ++  mo-talk
    |=  rup=(each suss tang)
    ^-  [wire note-arvo]
    :+  /sys/say  %d
    ^-  task:dill
    ?-  -.rup
      %&  [%text "gall: {(t q)}ed %{(t p)}":[t=trip p.rup]]
      %|  [%talk leaf+"gall: failed" (flop p.rup)]
    ==
  ++  mo-pass  |=(p=[wire note-arvo] (mo-emit hen pass+p))
  ++  mo-slip  |=(p=note-arvo (mo-emit hen slip+p))
  ++  mo-past
    |=  =(list [wire note-arvo])
    ?~  list
      mo-core
    =.  mo-core  (mo-pass i.list)
    $(list t.list)
  ::  +mo-jolt: (re)start agent
  ::
  ++  mo-jolt
    |=  [dap=term =ship =desk]
    ^+  mo-core
    =/  =wire  /sys/cor/[dap]/(scot %p ship)/[desk]
    ..mo-core
    ::  XX  (mo-pass wire %c %jolt dap ship desk)
  ::  +mo-doff: kill all outgoing subscriptions
  ::
  ++  mo-doff
    |=  [prov=path dude=(unit dude) ship=(unit ship)]
    ^+  mo-core
    =/  apps=(list (pair term yoke))
      ?~  dude  ~(tap by yokes.state)
      (drop (bind (~(get by yokes.state) u.dude) (lead u.dude)))
    |-  ^+  mo-core
    ?~  apps  mo-core
    ?:  ?=(%nuke -.q.i.apps)  $(apps t.apps)
```

```
463    =/  ap-core  (ap-yoke:ap p.i.apps [~ our prov] q.i.apps)
464    $(apps t.apps, mo-core ap-abet:(ap-doff:ap-core ship))
465  ::  +mo-rake: send %cork's for old subscriptions if needed
466  ::
467  ++  mo-rake
468    |=  [prov=path dude=(unit dude) all=?]
469    ^+  mo-core
470    =/  apps=(list (pair term yoke))
471      ?~  dude  ~(tap by yokes.state)
472      (drop (bind (~(get by yokes.state) u.dude) (lead u.dude)))
473    |-  ^+  mo-core
474    ?~  apps  mo-core
475    ?:  ?=(%nuke -.q.i.apps)  $(apps t.apps)
476    =/  ap-core  (ap-yoke:ap p.i.apps [~ our prov] q.i.apps)
477    $(apps t.apps, mo-core ap-abet:(ap-rake:ap-core all))
478  ::  +mo-receive-core: receives an app core built by %ford.
479  ::
480  ::    Presuming we receive a good core, we first check to see if the agent
481  ::    is already running.  If so, we update its beak in %gall's state,
482  ::    initialise an +ap core for the agent, install the core we got from
483  ::    %ford, and then resolve any moves associated with it.
484  ::
485  ::    If we're dealing with a new agent, we create one using the result we
486  ::    got from %ford, add it to the collection of agents %gall is keeping
487  ::    track of, and then do more or less the same procedure as we did for the
488  ::    running agent case.
489  ::
490  ++  mo-receive-core
491    ~/  %mo-receive-core
492    |=  [prov=path dap=term bek=beak =agent]
493    ^+  mo-core
494    ::
495    =/  yak  (~(get by yokes.state) dap)
496    =/  tex=(unit tape)
497      ?~  yak  `"installing"
498      ?:  ?=(%nuke -.u.yak)  `"unnuking"  ::TODO good message here?
499      ?-    -.agent.u.yak
500        %|  `"reviving"
501        %&
502      ?:  =(code.u.yak agent)
503          ~
504        `"reloading"
505      ==
506    =+  ?~  tex  ~
507        ~>  %slog.[0 leaf+"gall: {u.tex} {<dap>}"]  ~
508    ::
509    ?:  ?=([~ %live *] yak)
510      ?:  &(=(q.beak.u.yak q.bek) =(code.u.yak agent) =(-.agent.u.yak &))
511        mo-core
512      ::
513      =.  yokes.state
514        (~(put by yokes.state) dap u.yak(beak bek, code agent))
515      =/  ap-core  (ap-abed:ap dap [~ our prov])
516      =.  ap-core  (ap-reinstall:ap-core agent)
517      =.  mo-core  ap-abet:ap-core
518      (mo-clear-queue dap)
519    ::
520    =.  yokes.state
```

```
521        %+  ~(put by yokes.state)  dap
522        %*    .  *$>(%live yoke)
523          control-duct  hen
524          beak          bek
525          code          agent
526          agent         &+agent
527          run-nonce     (scot %uw (end 5 (shas %yoke-nonce eny)))
528        ::
529            sky
530        ?~  yak  *farm
531        =|  =farm
532        =.  farm  (need (~(gas-hutch of-farm farm) ~(tap by cop.u.yak)))
533        =/  sky=(list [=spur bob=@ud])  ~(tap by sky.u.yak)
534        |-
535        ?~  sky  farm
536        =.  farm  (need (~(put-grow of-farm farm) spur.i.sky [`bob.i.sky ~]))
537        $(sky t.sky)
538      ==
539      ::
540    =/  old  mo-core
541    =/  wag
542      =/  ap-core  (ap-abed:ap dap [~ our prov])
543      (ap-upgrade-state:ap-core ~)
544    ::
545    =/  maybe-tang  -.wag
546    =/  ap-core  +.wag
547    ?^  maybe-tang
548      =.  mo-core  old
549      (mo-pass (mo-talk %.n u.maybe-tang))
550    ::
551    =.  mo-core  ap-abet:ap-core
552    =.  mo-core  (mo-clear-queue dap)
553    =/  =suss  [dap %boot now]
554    (mo-pass (mo-talk %.y suss))
555  ::  +mo-send-foreign-request: handle local request to .ship
556  ::
557  ++  mo-send-foreign-request
558    ~/  %mo-send-foreign-request
559    |=  [=ship foreign-agent=term =deal]
560    ^+  mo-core
561    ::
562    =.  mo-core  (mo-track-ship ship)
563    ?<  ?=(?(%raw-poke %poke-as) -.deal)
564    =/  =ames-request-all
565      :-  %0
566      ?-  -.deal
567        %poke      [%m p.cage.deal q.q.cage.deal]
568        %leave     [%u ~]
569        %watch-as  [%l [mark path]:deal]
570        %watch     [%s path.deal]
571      ==
572    ::
573    =/  wire
574      /sys/way/(scot %p ship)/[foreign-agent]
575    ::
576    =/  =note-arvo
577      =/  =path  /ge/[foreign-agent]
578      [%a %plea ship %g path ames-request-all]
```

```
579        ::
580        =.  outstanding.state
581          =/  stand
582            (~(gut by outstanding.state) [wire hen] *(qeu remote-request))
583            (~(put by outstanding.state) [wire hen] (~(put to stand) -.deal))
584        (mo-pass wire note-arvo)
585    ::  +mo-track-ship: subscribe to ames and jael for notices about .ship
586    ::
587    ++  mo-track-ship
588      |=  =ship
589      ^+  mo-core
590      ::  if already contacted, no-op
591      ::
592      ?:  (~(has in contacts.state) ship)
593        mo-core
594      ::  first contact; update state and subscribe to notifications
595      ::
596      =.  contacts.state  (~(put in contacts.state) ship)
597      ::  ask ames to track .ship's connectivity
598      ::
599      =.  moves  [[system-duct.state %pass /sys/lag %a %heed ship] moves]
600      ::  ask jael to track .ship's breaches
601      ::
602      =/  =note-arvo  [%j %public-keys (silt ship ~)]
603      =.  moves
604        [[system-duct.state %pass /sys/era note-arvo] moves]
605      mo-core
606    ::  +mo-untrack-ship: cancel subscriptions to ames and jael for .ship
607    ::
608    ++  mo-untrack-ship
609      |=  =ship
610      ^+  mo-core
611      ::  if already canceled, no-op
612      ::
613      ?.  (~(has in contacts.state) ship)
614        mo-core
615      ::  delete .ship from state and kill subscriptions
616      ::
617      =.  contacts.state  (~(del in contacts.state) ship)
618      ::
619      =.  moves  [[system-duct.state %pass /sys/lag %a %jilt ship] moves]
620      ::
621      =/  =note-arvo  [%j %nuke (silt ship ~)]
622      =.  moves
623        [[system-duct.state %pass /sys/era note-arvo] moves]
624      mo-core
625    ::  +mo-breach: ship breached, so forget about them
626    ::
627    ++  mo-breach
628      |=  [prov=path =ship]
629      ^+  mo-core
630      =.  mo-core  (mo-untrack-ship ship)
631      =.  mo-core  (mo-filter-queue ship)
632      =/  agents=(list [name=term =yoke])  ~(tap by yokes.state)
633      =.  outstanding.state
634        %-  malt
635        %+  skip  ~(tap by outstanding.state)
636        |=  [[=wire duct] (qeu remote-request)]
```

```
=(/sys/way/(scot %p ship) (scag 3 wire))
::
|-  ^+  mo-core
?~  agents
  mo-core
=?  mo-core  ?=(%live -.yoke.i.agents)
  =/  =routes  [disclosing=~ attributing=[ship prov]]
  =/  app  (ap-abed:ap name.i.agents routes)
  ap-abet:(ap-breach:app ship)
$(agents t.agents)
::  +mo-handle-sys: handle a +sign incoming over /sys.
::
::    (Note that /sys implies the +sign should be routed to a vane.)
::
++  mo-handle-sys
  ~/  %mo-handle-sys
  |=  [=wire =sign-arvo]
  ^+  mo-core
  ::
  ?+  -.wire  !!
    %lyv  ..mo-core  ::  vestigial
    %cor  ..mo-core  ::  vestigial
    %era  (mo-handle-sys-era wire sign-arvo)
    %lag  (mo-handle-sys-lag wire sign-arvo)
    %req  (mo-handle-sys-req wire sign-arvo)
    %way  (mo-handle-sys-way wire sign-arvo)
  ==
::  +mo-handle-sys-era: receive update about contact
::
++  mo-handle-sys-era
  |=  [=wire =sign-arvo]
  ^+  mo-core
  ?>  ?=([%jael %public-keys *] sign-arvo)
  ?>  ?=([%era ~] wire)
  ?.  ?=(%breach -.public-keys-result.sign-arvo)
    mo-core
  (mo-breach /jael who.public-keys-result.sign-arvo)
::  +mo-handle-sys-lag: handle an ames %clog notification
::
++  mo-handle-sys-lag
  |=  [=wire =sign-arvo]
  ^+  mo-core
  ::
  ?>  ?=([%lag ~] wire)
  ?>  ?=([%ames %clog *] sign-arvo)
  ::
  =/  agents=(list [=dude =yoke])  ~(tap by yokes.state)
  |-  ^+  mo-core
  ?~  agents  mo-core
  ::
  =?  mo-core  ?=(%live -.yoke.i.agents)
    =/  app  (ap-abed:ap dude.i.agents [~ our /ames])
    ap-abet:(ap-clog:app ship.sign-arvo)
  ::
  $(agents t.agents)
::  +mo-handle-sys-req: TODO description
::
::    TODO: what should we do if the remote nacks our %pull?
```

```
695  ++  mo-handle-sys-req
696    |=  [=wire =sign-arvo]
697    ^+  mo-core
698    ::
699    ?>  ?=([%req @ @ ~] wire)
700    =/  him  (slav %p i.t.wire)
701    =/  dap  i.t.t.wire
702    ::
703    ?>  ?=([?(%gall %behn) %unto *] sign-arvo)
704    =/  =unto  +>.sign-arvo
705    ::
706    ?-    -.unto
707        %raw-fact  ~|([%gall-raw-req wire] !!)
708        %poke-ack
709      =/  err=(unit error:ames)
710        ?~  p.unto  ~
711        `[%poke-ack u.p.unto]
712      (mo-give %done err)
713    ::
714        %fact
715      =+  [mark noun]=[p q.q]:cage.unto
716      (mo-give %boon %d mark noun)
717    ::
718        %kick
719      (mo-give %boon %x ~)
720    ::
721        %watch-ack
722      =/  err=(unit error:ames)
723        ?~  p.unto  ~
724        `[%watch-ack u.p.unto]
725      (mo-give %done err)
726    ==
727  ::  +mo-handle-sys-way: handle response to outgoing remote request
728  ::
729  ++  mo-handle-sys-way
730    |=  [=wire =sign-arvo]
731    ^+  mo-core
732    ?>  ?=([%way @ @ $@(~ [@ ~])] wire)
733    =/  =ship           (slav %p i.t.wire)
734    =/  foreign-agent   i.t.t.wire
735    ::
736    ?+    sign-arvo  !!
737        [%ames %done *]
738      =/  err=(unit tang)
739        ?~  error=error.sign-arvo
740          ~
741        `[[%leaf (trip tag.u.error)] tang.u.error]
742      =^  remote-request  outstanding.state
743        ?~  t.t.t.wire
744          =/  full-wire  sys+wire
745          =/  stand
746            (~(gut by outstanding.state) [full-wire hen] ~)
747          ::
748          ::  default is to send both ack types; should only hit if
749          ::  cleared queue in +load 3-to-4 or +load-4-to-5
750          ::
751          =?  stand  ?=(~ stand)
752            ~&  [%gall-missing wire hen]
```

```hoon
          (~(put to *(qeu remote-request)) %missing)
        ~|  [full-wire=full-wire hen=hen stand=stand]
        =^  rr   stand  ~(get to stand)
        :-  rr
        ?.  =(~ stand)
          (~(put by outstanding.state) [full-wire hen] stand)
        ::  outstanding leaves are only deleted when acked;
        ::  a nacked %leave is flagged with a %missing request
        ::  we add to the outstanding queue that is only checked
        ::  in the nacked-leaves timer to skip dead-flow %leave(s)
        ::
        ?.  &(?=(^ err) ?=(%leave rr))
          (~(del by outstanding.state) [full-wire hen])
        %-  ~(put by outstanding.state)
        [[full-wire hen] (~(gas to stand) ~[%leave %missing])]
      ::  non-null case of wire is old, remove on next breach after
      ::  2019/12
      ::
      [;;(remote-request i.t.t.t.wire) outstanding.state]
    ::  send a %cork if we get a %nack upon initial subscription
    ::
    =?  mo-core
        &(?=(^ err) |(?=(%watch-as remote-request) ?=(%watch remote-request)))
      (mo-pass sys+wire %a %cork ship)
    ::
    ?-  remote-request
      %watch-as  (mo-give %unto %watch-ack err)
      %watch     (mo-give %unto %watch-ack err)
      %poke      (mo-give %unto %poke-ack err)
      %missing   ~>(%slog.[3 'gall: missing'] mo-core)
      ::
        %leave
      ::  if we get an %ack for a %leave, send %cork. otherwise,
      ::  the /nacked-leaves timer will re-send the %leave eventually.
      ::
      ?~  err
        (mo-pass sys+wire %a %cork ship)
      ::  if first time hearing a %nack for a %leave, after upgrade
      ::  or if all outstanding %leaves have been handled, set up timer
      ::
      =?  mo-core  ?=(~ leaves.state)
        (mo-emit [/gall]~ %pass /nacked-leaves %b %wait `@da`(add now ~m2))
      =?  leaves.state  ?=(~ leaves.state)
        `[[/gall]~ /nacked-leaves `@da`(add now ~m2)]
      mo-core
    ==
  ::
    [%ames %boon *]
  ?^  t.t.t.wire
    ::  kill subscriptions which use the old wire format
    ::
    !!
  =/  =ames-response  ;;(ames-response payload.sign-arvo)
  ::  %d: diff; ask clay to validate .noun as .mark
  ::  %x: kick; tell agent the publisher canceled the subscription, and
  ::      cork; tell ames to close the associated flow.
  ::
  ?-  -.ames-response
```

```
811        %d  (mo-give %unto %raw-fact mark.ames-response noun.ames-response)
812        %x  =.  mo-core  (mo-give %unto %kick ~)
813            =/  key  [[%sys wire] hen]
814            =?  outstanding.state  =(~ (~(gut by outstanding.state) key ~))
815              (~(del by outstanding.state) key)
816            (mo-pass [%sys wire] %a %cork ship)
817      ==
818    ::
819        [%ames %lost *]
820      ::  note this should only happen on reverse bones, so only facts
821      ::  and kicks
822      ::
823      ::  TODO: %drip %kick so app crash can't kill the remote %pull
824      ::
825      =.  mo-core  (mo-send-foreign-request ship foreign-agent %leave ~)
826      =.  mo-core  (mo-give %unto %kick ~)
827      mo-core
828    ==
829  ++  mo-handle-key
830    ~/  %mo-handle-stub
831    |=  [=(pole knot) syn=sign-arvo]
832    ?.  ?=([agent=@ nonce=@ rest=*] pole)
833      ~&  [%mo-handle-key-bad-wire wire]
834      !!
835    =*  dap   agent.pole
836    =/  yoke  (~(get by yokes.state) agent.pole)
837    ?.  ?=([~ %live *] yoke)
838      %-  (slog leaf+"gall: {<`@t`dap>} dead, got %stub" ~)
839      mo-core
840    ?.  =(run-nonce.u.yoke nonce.pole)
841      %-  (slog leaf+"gall: got old stub for {<dap>}" ~)
842      mo-core
843    =/  =routes  [disclosing=~ attributing=[our /]]
844    =/  ap-core  (ap-abed:ap agent.pole routes)
845    ?+    rest.pole  ~|(mo-handle-key-bad-wire/wire !!)
846        [%pug rest=*]
847      ?>  ?=([%ames %stub *] syn)
848      ap-abet:(ap-stub:ap-core rest.rest.pole [num key]:syn)
849    ::
850        [%bod rest=*]
851      ap-abet:(ap-take-brood:ap-core rest.rest.pole syn)
852    ==
853  ::  +mo-handle-use: handle a typed +sign incoming on /use.
854  ::
855  ::  (Note that /use implies the +sign should be routed to an agent.)
856  ::
857  ::  Initialises the specified agent and then performs an agent-level
858  ::  +take on the supplied +sign.
859  ::
860  ++  mo-handle-use
861    ~/  %mo-handle-use
862    |=  [=wire =sign-arvo]
863    ^+  mo-core
864    ::
865    ?.  ?=([@ @ @ *] wire)
866      ~&  [%mo-handle-use-bad-wire wire]
867      !!
868    ::
```

```
869      =/  dap=term  i.wire
870      =/  yoke  (~(get by yokes.state) dap)
871      ?.  ?=([~ %live *] yoke)
872        %-  (slog leaf+"gall: {<dap>} dead, got {<+<.sign-arvo>}" ~)
873        mo-core
874      ?.  =(run-nonce.u.yoke i.t.wire)
875        %-  (slog leaf+"gall: got old {<+<.sign-arvo>} for {<dap>}" ~)
876        mo-core
877      ::
878      ?.  ?=([?(%gall %behn) %unto *] sign-arvo)
879        ?:  ?=(%| -.agent.u.yoke)
880          %-  (slog leaf+"gall: {<dap>} dozing, dropping {<+<.sign-arvo>}" ~)
881          mo-core
882        =/  app
883          =/  =ship  (slav %p i.t.t.wire)
884          =/  =routes  [disclosing=~ attributing=[ship /[-.sign-arvo]]]
885          (ap-abed:ap dap routes)
886        ::
887        =.  app  (ap-generic-take:app t.t.t.wire sign-arvo)
888      ap-abet:app
889    ?>  ?=([%out @ @ *] t.t.wire)
890    =/  =ship  (slav %p i.t.t.t.wire)
891    =/  other-agent  i.t.t.t.t.wire
892    =/  prov=path  ?.(=(ship our) *path /gall/[other-agent])
893    =/  =routes  [disclosing=~ attributing=[ship prov]]
894    =/  =unto  +>.sign-arvo
895    ?:  ?=(%| -.agent.u.yoke)
896      =/  blocked=(qeu blocked-move)
897        =/  waiting  (~(get by blocked.state) dap)
898        =/  deals  (fall waiting *(qeu blocked-move))
899        =/  deal  [hen routes |+unto]
900        (~(put to deals) deal)
901      ::
902      %-  (slog leaf+"gall: {<dap>} dozing, got {<-.unto>}" ~)
903      %_  mo-core
904        blocked.state  (~(put by blocked.state) dap blocked)
905      ==
906    =/  app  (ap-abed:ap dap routes)
907    =.  app
908      (ap-specific-take:app t.t.wire unto)
909    ap-abet:app
910  ::  +mo-clear-queue: clear blocked tasks from the specified running agent.
911  ::
912  ++  mo-clear-queue
913    |=  dap=term
914    ^+  mo-core
915    ?.  (~(has by yokes.state) dap)
916      mo-core
917    ?~  maybe-blocked=(~(get by blocked.state) dap)
918      mo-core
919    =/  blocked=(qeu blocked-move)  u.maybe-blocked
920    |-  ^+  mo-core
921    ?:  =(~ blocked)
922      =.  blocked.state  (~(del by blocked.state) dap)
923      mo-core
924    =^  [=duct =routes blocker=(each deal unto)]  blocked
925      ~(get to blocked)
926    ?:  ?=(%| -.blocker)  $
```

```
=/  =move
  =/  =sack  [ship.attributing.routes our path.attributing.routes]
  =/  card   [%slip %g %deal sack dap p.blocker]
  [duct card]
$(moves [move moves])
::  +mo-filter-queue: remove all blocked tasks from ship.
::
++  mo-filter-queue
  |=  =ship
  =/  agents=(list [name=term blocked=(qeu blocked-move)])
    ~(tap by blocked.state)
  =|  new-agents=(map term (qeu blocked-move))
  |-  ^+  mo-core
  ?~  agents
    mo-core(blocked.state new-agents)
  =|  new-blocked=(qeu blocked-move)
  |-  ^+  mo-core
  ?:  =(~ blocked.i.agents)
    ?~  new-blocked
      ^$(agents t.agents)
    %=  ^$
      agents      t.agents
      new-agents  (~(put by new-agents) name.i.agents new-blocked)
    ==
  =^  mov=blocked-move  blocked.i.agents  ~(get to blocked.i.agents)
  =?  new-blocked  !=(ship ship.attributing.routes.mov)
    (~(put to new-blocked) mov)
  $
::  +mo-idle: put agent to sleep
::
++  mo-idle
  |=  [prov=path dap=dude]
  ^+  mo-core
  =/  yoke=(unit yoke)  (~(get by yokes.state) dap)
  ?:  |(?=(~ yoke) ?=(%nuke -.u.yoke))
    ~>  %slog.0^leaf/"gall: ignoring %idle for {<dap>}, not running"
    mo-core
  ap-abet:ap-idle:(ap-abed:ap dap [~ our prov])
::  +mo-nuke: delete agent completely
::
++  mo-nuke
  |=  [prov=path dap=dude]
  ^+  mo-core
  =/  yoke=(unit yoke)  (~(get by yokes.state) dap)
  ?:  |(?=(~ yoke) ?=(%nuke -.u.yoke))
    ~>  %slog.0^leaf/"gall: ignoring %nuke for {<dap>}, not running"
    mo-core
  ~>  %slog.0^leaf/"gall: nuking {<dap>}"
  =.  mo-core  ap-abet:ap-nuke:(ap-abed:ap dap [~ our prov])
  =-  mo-core(yokes.state -)
  %+  ~(jab by yokes.state)  dap
  |=  =^yoke
  ?:  ?=(%nuke -.yoke)  yoke
  :+  %nuke
    %-  ~(run-plot of-farm sky.yoke)
    |=  plot
    (fall (clap bob (bind (ram:on-path fan) head) max) 0)
  ~(tap-hutch of-farm sky.yoke)
```

```
985     ::   +mo-load: install agents
986     ::
987     ++  mo-load
988      |=  [prov=path agents=(list [=dude =beak =agent])]
989      =.  mo-core
990        |-  ^+  mo-core
991        ?~  agents  mo-core
992        =/  [=dude =desk]  [dude q.beak]:i.agents
993        ::  ~>  %slog.0^leaf/"gall: starting {<dude>} on {<desk>}"
994        $(agents t.agents, mo-core (mo-receive-core prov i.agents))
995      ::
996      =/  kil
997        =/  lol
998          (skim ~(tap by yokes.state) |=([* y=yoke] &(?=(%live -.y) -.agent.y)))
999        =/  mol  (~(gas by *(map term yoke)) lol)
1000       =/  sol  ~(key by mol)
1001       =/  new  (silt (turn agents head))
1002       ~(tap in (~(dif in sol) new))
1003     |-  ^+  mo-core
1004     ?~  kil  mo-core
1005     ~>  %slog.0^leaf/"gall: stopping {<i.kil>}"
1006     $(kil t.kil, mo-core (mo-idle prov i.kil))
1007   ::
1008   ++  mo-authorized-coop
1009    |=  [lyc=(set ship) =farm dap=term =path =coop]
1010    %-  ~(all in lyc)
1011    |=  =ship
1012    =/  cag  (mo-peek | dap [~ ship path] %c (snoc coop (scot %p ship)))
1013    ?.  ?=([~ ~ ^] cag)
1014      %.n
1015    ?~  res=((soft ,?) q.q.u.u.cag)
1016      %.n
1017    u.res
1018   ::
1019   ++  mo-authorized
1020    |=  [lyc=gang =farm dap=term =path]
1021    ^-  ?
1022    ?:  =([~ ~] lyc)
1023      %.y
1024    ?~  (~(get-hutch of-farm farm) path)
1025      %.y
1026    ?:  ?=(~ lyc)
1027      %.n
1028    ?~  coop=(~(match-coop of-farm farm) path)
1029      %.n
1030    (mo-authorized-coop u.lyc farm dap path u.coop)
1031   ::  +mo-peek:  call to +ap-peek (which is not accessible outside of +mo).
1032   ::
1033   ++  mo-peek
1034    ~/  %mo-peek
1035    |=  [veb=? dap=term =routes care=term =path]
1036    ^-  (unit (unit cage))
1037    ::
1038    ?.  ?=([~ %live *] (~(get by yokes.state) dap))  [~ ~]
1039    =/  app  (ap-abed:ap dap routes)
1040    (ap-peek:app veb care path)
1041   ::
1042   ++  mo-apply
```

```
|=  [dap=term =routes =deal]
^+  mo-core
?-    -.deal
    ?(%watch %watch-as %leave %poke)
  (mo-apply-sure dap routes deal)
::
    %raw-poke
  ::  don't validate %noun pokes, for performance
  ::
  ?:  =(%noun mark.deal)
    (mo-apply-sure dap routes [%poke %noun %noun noun.deal])
  =/  =case  da+now
  =/  yok  (~(got by yokes.state) dap)
  =/  =desk  q.beak:?>(?=(%live -.yok) yok)  ::TODO acceptable assertion?
  =/  sky  (rof [~ ~] /gall %cb [our desk case] /[mark.deal])
  ?-    sky
      ?(~ [~ ~])
    =/  ror  "gall: raw-poke fail :{(trip dap)} {<mark.deal>}"
    (mo-give %unto %poke-ack `[leaf+ror]~)
  ::
      [~ ~ *]
    =+  !<(=dais:clay q.u.u.sky)
    =/  res  (mule |.((vale:dais noun.deal)))
    ?:  ?=(%| -.res)
      =/  ror  "gall: raw-poke vale fail :{(trip dap)} {<mark.deal>}"
      (mo-give %unto %poke-ack `[leaf+ror p.res])
    =.  mo-core
      %+  mo-pass  /nowhere
      [%c %warp our desk ~ %sing %b case /[mark.deal]]
    (mo-apply-sure dap routes [%poke mark.deal p.res])
  ==
::
    %poke-as
  =/  =case         da+now
  =/  =mars:clay  [p.cage mark]:deal
  =/  mars-path  /[a.mars]/[b.mars]
  =/  yok  (~(got by yokes.state) dap)
  =/  =desk  q.beak:?>(?=(%live -.yok) yok)  ::TODO acceptable assertion?
  =/  sky  (rof [~ ~] /gall %cc [our desk case] mars-path)
  ?-    sky
      ?(~ [~ ~])
    =/  ror  "gall: poke cast fail :{(trip dap)} {<mars>}"
    (mo-give %unto %poke-ack `[leaf+ror]~)
  ::
      [~ ~ *]
    =+  !<(=tube:clay q.u.u.sky)
    =/  res  (mule |.((tube q.cage.deal)))
    ?:  ?=(%| -.res)
      =/  ror  "gall: poke-as cast fail :{(trip dap)} {<mars>}"
      (mo-give %unto %poke-ack `[leaf+ror p.res])
    =.  mo-core
      %+  mo-pass  /nowhere
      [%c %warp our desk ~ %sing %c case /[a.mars]/[b.mars]]
    (mo-apply-sure dap routes [%poke mark.deal p.res])
  ==
==
::
++  mo-apply-sure
```

```hoon
1101      |=  [dap=term =routes =deal]
1102      ^+  mo-core
1103      =/  app  (ap-abed:ap dap routes)
1104      =.  app  (ap-apply:app deal)
1105      ap-abet:app
1106    ::  +mo-handle-local: handle locally.
1107    ::
1108    ::    If the agent is not running or blocked, assign it the supplied
1109    ::    +deal.  Otherwise simply apply the action to the agent.
1110    ::
1111    ++  mo-handle-local
1112      |=  [prov=path =ship agent=term =deal]
1113      ^+  mo-core
1114      ::
1115      =/  =routes  [disclosing=~ attributing=[ship prov]]
1116      =/  running  (~(get by yokes.state) agent)
1117      =/  is-running  &(?=([~ %live *] running) ?=(%& -.agent.u.running))
1118      =/  is-blocked  (~(has by blocked.state) agent)
1119      ::  agent is running; deliver move normally
1120      ::
1121      ?.  |(!is-running is-blocked)
1122        (mo-apply agent routes deal)
1123      ::
1124      =/  blocked=(qeu blocked-move)
1125        =/  waiting  (~(get by blocked.state) agent)
1126        =/  deals  (fall waiting *(qeu blocked-move))
1127        =/  deal  [hen routes &+deal]
1128        (~(put to deals) deal)
1129      ::
1130      %-  (slog leaf+"gall: not running {<agent>} yet, got {<-.deal>}" ~)
1131      %_  mo-core
1132        blocked.state  (~(put by blocked.state) agent blocked)
1133      ==
1134    ::  +mo-handle-key-request: handle request for keys
1135    ++  mo-handle-key-request
1136      |=  [=ship agent-name=term =path]
1137      ^+  mo-core
1138      =/  yok=(unit yoke)  (~(get by yokes.state) agent-name)
1139      ?.  ?=([~ %live *] yok)
1140        (mo-give %done ~)
1141      =/  ap-core  (ap-abed:ap agent-name [~ our /gall])
1142      =^  bod=(each (unit brood) tang)  mo-core
1143        (ap-serve-brood:ap-core ship path)
1144      ?:  ?=(%| -.bod)
1145        (mo-give %done `keys/p.bod)
1146      =/  =fine-response  [%0 p.bod]
1147      =.  mo-core  (mo-give %boon fine-response)
1148      (mo-give %done ~)
1149    ::  +mo-handle-ames-request: handle %ames request message.
1150    ::
1151    ++  mo-handle-ames-request
1152      |=  [=ship agent-name=term =ames-request]
1153      ^+  mo-core
1154      ::
1155      =.  mo-core  (mo-track-ship ship)
1156      ::
1157      =/  yok=(unit yoke)  (~(get by yokes.state) agent-name)
1158      ?~  yok
```

```
          (mo-give %flub ~)
    ?:    ?=(%nuke -.u.yok)
          (mo-give %flub ~)
    ?:    ?=(%.n -.agent.u.yok)
          (mo-give %flub ~)
    ::
    ::    %u/%leave gets automatically acked
    ::
    =?  mo-core    ?=(%u -.ames-request)
        (mo-give %done ~)
    =/  =wire  /sys/req/(scot %p ship)/[agent-name]
    ::
    =/  =deal
      ?-   -.ames-request
        %m   [%raw-poke [mark noun]:ames-request]
        %l   [%watch-as [mark path]:ames-request]
        %s   [%watch path.ames-request]
        %u   [%leave ~]
      ==
    (mo-pass wire %g %deal [ship our /] agent-name deal)

  ::  +mo-spew: handle request to set verbosity toggles on debug output
  ::
  ++  mo-spew
    |=  verbs=(list verb)
    ^+  mo-core
    ::  start from all %.n's, then flip requested toggles
    ::
    =.  veb.bug.state
      %+  roll  verbs
      |=  [=verb acc=_veb-all-off]
      ^+  veb.bug.state
      ?-  verb
        %odd  acc(odd %.y)
      ==
    mo-core
  ::  +mo-sift: handle request to filter debug output by agent
  ::
  ++  mo-sift
    |=  dudes=(list dude)
    ^+  mo-core
    =.  dudes.bug.state  (sy dudes)
    mo-core
  ::
  ++  mo-handle-nacked-leaves
    |=  =wire
    ^+  mo-core
    ?>  ?=([%sys %way @ @ ~] wire)
    (mo-pass wire %a %plea (slav %p &3.wire) %g /ge/[&4.wire] %0 %u ~)
  ::
  ::  +ap: agent engine
  ::
  ::    An inner, agent-level core.  The sample refers to the agent we're
  ::    currently focused on.
  ::
  ++  ap
    ~%  %gall-ap  +>   ~
    |_  $:  agent-name=term
```

```
          agent-routes=routes
          agent-duct=duct
          agent-moves=(list move)
          agent-config=(list (each suss tang))
          =$>(%live yoke)
      ==
  ::
  ++  trace
    |=  [verb=? print=tang]
    ^+  same
    (^trace verb agent-name print)
  ::
  ++  ap-nonce-wire
    |=  [=wire =dock]
    ^+  wire
    =/  nonce=@  (~(got by boar.yoke) wire dock)
    ?:  =(0 nonce)  wire
    [(scot %ud nonce) wire]
  ::
  ++  ap-core  .
  ::  +ap-abed: initialise state for an agent, with the supplied routes.
  ::
  ::    The agent must already be running in +gall -- here we simply update
  ::    +ap's state to focus on it.
  ::
  ++  ap-abed
    ~/  %ap-abed
    |=  [dap=term =routes]
    ^+  ap-core
    %^  ap-yoke  dap  routes
    =<  ?>(?=(%live -) .)
    (~(got by yokes.state) dap)
  ::  +ap-yoke: initialize agent state, starting from a $yoke
  ::
  ++  ap-yoke
    |=  [dap=term =routes yak=$>(%live ^yoke)]
    ^+  ap-core
    =.  stats.yak
      :+  +(change.stats.yak)
        (shaz (mix (add dap change.stats.yak) eny))  ::  TODO: so bad, use +og
      now
    =.  agent-name  dap
    =.  agent-routes  routes
    =.  yoke  yak
    =.  agent-duct  hen
    ap-core
  ::  +ap-abet: resolve moves.
  ::
  ++  ap-abet
    ^+  mo-core
    ::
    =/  running  (~(put by yokes.state) agent-name yoke)
    =/  moves
      =/  talker  |=(report=(each suss tang) [hen %pass (mo-talk report)])
      =/  from-suss  (turn agent-config talker)
      :(weld agent-moves from-suss moves)
    ::
    %_  mo-core
```

```
yokes.state  running
moves        moves
==
++  ap-request-brood
  |=  [=wire =ship =(pole knot)]
  ^+  ap-core
  ?.  ?=([%g %x cas=@ app=@ rest=*] pole)
    %.  ap-core
    %+  trace  odd.veb.bug.state
    [leaf+"gall: {<agent-name>}: brood request {<pole>} invalid, dropping"]~
  =.  pen.yoke  (~(put ju pen.yoke) [ship pole] wire)
  =/  =fine-request  [%0 rest.pole]
  =/  =plea:ames  [%g /gk/[app.pole] fine-request]
  =/  out=^wire  (welp /key/[agent-name]/[run-nonce.yoke]/bod/(scot %p ship) pole)
  (ap-move [hen %pass out %a %plea ship plea]~)
::
++  ap-take-brood
  |=  [=wire syn=sign-arvo]
  ^+  ap-core
  ~|  ap-take-brood/wire
  ?>  ?=([@ *] wire)  :: TODO: strip crash semantics
  =/  =ship  (slav %p i.wire)
  =/  wis=(list ^wire)  ~(tap in (~(get ju pen.yoke) [ship t.wire]))
  ?+    syn  ~|(weird-sign-ap-take-brood/-.syn !!)
      [%ames %boon *]
    =/  bud  (fall ((soft fine-response) payload.syn) *fine-response)
    |-
    ?~  wis
      =.  pen.yoke  (~(del by pen.yoke) [ship t.wire])
      ap-core
    ?~  bod.bud
      =.  ap-core  (ap-generic-take i.wis %ames %near [ship t.wire] ~)
      $(wis t.wis)
    =.  ap-core  (ap-pass i.wis %arvo %a %keen `[idx key]:hutch.u.bod.bud ship t.wire)
    $(wis t.wis)
  ::
      [%ames %done *]
    ?~  error.syn
      ap-core
    |-
    ?~  wis
      =.  pen.yoke  (~(del by pen.yoke) [ship t.wire])
      ap-core
    =.  ap-core
    %.  (ap-generic-take i.wis %ames %near [ship t.wire] ~)
    %+  trace  odd.veb.bug.state
    [leaf/"gall: {<agent-name>} bad brood res {<ship>} {<t.wire>}"]~
    $(wis t.wis)
  ==
::
++  ap-serve-brood
  |=  [=ship =(pole knot)]
  ^-  [(each (unit brood) tang) _mo-core]
  ?.  ?=([%$ ver=@ rest=*] pole)
    :_  ap-abet
    |+[leaf/"gall: {<agent-name>} bad brood req {<ship>} {<pole>}"]~
  =/  ver  (slav %ud ver.pole)
  ?.  =(1 ver)
```

```
1333        :_  ap-abet
1334        |+[leaf/"gall: {<agent-name>} bad brood ver {<ver>} {<ship>} {<rest.pole>}"]~
1335      ?~  cop=(ap-match-coop rest.pole)
1336        %.  [&+~ ap-abet]
1337        %+  trace  odd.veb.bug.state
1338        [leaf/"gall: {<agent-name>} no coop match {<ship>} {<rest.pole>}"]~
1339      =/  cag=(unit (unit cage))
1340        (ap-peek %| %c (snoc u.cop (scot %p ship)))
1341      =/  has-perms=?
1342        ?.  ?=([~ ~ ^] cag)
1343          |
1344        ?~  res=((soft ,?) q.q.u.u.cag)
1345          |
1346        u.res
1347      =/  =hutch  (need (~(get-hutch of-farm sky.yoke) u.cop))
1348      ?.  has-perms
1349        %.  [[%.y ~] ap-abet]
1350        %+  trace  odd.veb.bug.state
1351        [leaf/"gall: {<agent-name>} no perms for {<coop>} {<ship>} {<rest.pole>}"]~
1352      =/  =brood  [u.cop hutch]
1353      [[%.y `brood] ap-abet]
1354    ::
1355    ++  ap-yawn-all
1356      ^-  (list card:agent)
1357      %-  zing
1358      %+  turn  ~(tap by ken.yoke)
1359      |=  [=spar:ames wyz=(set wire)]
1360      %+  turn  ~(tap in wyz)
1361      |=  =wire
1362      [%pass wire %arvo %a %yawn spar]
1363    ::
1364    ++  ap-idle
1365      ^+  ap-core
1366      ?:  ?=(%| -.agent.yoke)  ap-core
1367      =>  [ken=ken.yoke (ap-ingest ~ |.([ap-yawn-all p.agent.yoke]))]
1368      ap-core(ken.yoke ken, agent.yoke |+on-save:ap-agent-core)
1369    ::
1370    ++  ap-nuke
1371      ^+  ap-core
1372      =/  inbound-paths=(set path)
1373        %-  silt
1374        %+  turn  ~(tap by bitt.yoke)
1375        |=  [=duct =ship =path]
1376        path
1377      =/  will=(list card:agent)
1378        ;:  welp
1379          ?:  =(~ inbound-paths)
1380            ~
1381          [%give %kick ~(tap in inbound-paths) ~]~
1382        ::
1383          %+  turn  ~(tap by boat.yoke)
1384          |=  [[=wire =dock] ? =path]
1385          [%pass wire %agent dock %leave ~]
1386        ::
1387          ap-yawn-all
1388        ==
1389      =^  maybe-tang ap-core  (ap-ingest ~ |.([will *agent]))
1390      ap-core
```

```
++  ap-match-coop
  |=  =path
  ^-  (unit coop)
  (~(match-coop of-farm sky.yoke) path)
::
++  ap-keen
  |=  [=wire secret=? =spar:ames]
  ^+  ap-core
  ?:  secret
    (ap-request-brood wire spar)
  =.  ken.yoke  (~(put ju ken.yoke) spar wire)
  (ap-pass wire %arvo %a %keen ~ spar)
::
::
::  +ap-tend: bind path in namespace, encrypted
++  ap-tend
  |=  [=coop =path =page]
  ?~  cop=(~(get-hutch of-farm sky.yoke) coop)
    ?.  (~(has by gem.yoke) coop)
      %.  ap-core
      %+  trace  &
      [leaf+"gall: {<agent-name>} no such coop {<coop>}, dropping %tend at {<path>}"]~
    =.  gem.yoke  (~(put ju gem.yoke) coop path page)
    ap-core
  =.  sky.yoke  (~(grow of-farm sky.yoke) (welp coop path) now page)
  ap-core
::
++  ap-germ
  |=  =coop
  =/  pen  (~(get by gem.yoke) coop)
  =/  exists  !=(~ (~(get of-farm sky.yoke) coop))
  =?  gem.yoke  &(!exists ?=(~ pen))
    (~(put by gem.yoke) coop ~)
  =/  =wire  (welp /key/[agent-name]/[run-nonce.yoke]/pug coop)
  (ap-move [hen %pass wire %a %plug [%g %x agent-name %$ '1' coop]]~)
::
++  ap-stub
  |=  [=coop num=@ud key=@]
  ^+  ap-core
  =/  =hutch
    ?^  h=(~(get-hutch of-farm sky.yoke) coop)
      u.h
    *hutch
  =.  hutch  [.+(rev.hutch) num key]
  =.  sky.yoke
    ?^  new-sky=(~(put-hutch of-farm sky.yoke) coop hutch)
      u.new-sky
    sky.yoke
  =/  gem  ~(tap in (~(get ju gem.yoke) coop))
  |-  ^+  ap-core
  ?~  gem  ap-core
  $(gem t.gem, ap-core (ap-tend coop i.gem))
::
++  ap-snip
  |=  =coop
  ap-core
  :: ap-core(cop.yoke (~(del by cop.yoke) coop)) :: TODO: fix
  :: +ap-grow: bind a path in the agent's scry namespace
```

```
1449        ::
1450        ++  ap-grow
1451          |=  [=spur =page]
1452          ^+  ap-core
1453          ::  check here, and no-op, so that +need below does not crash
1454          ?:  ?=(^ (ap-match-coop spur))
1455            %.  ap-core
1456            %+  trace  &
1457            [leaf+"gall: {<agent-name>}: grow {<spur>} has coop, dropping"]~
1458          =-  ap-core(sky.yoke -)
1459          (~(grow of-farm sky.yoke) spur now page)
1460        ::  +ap-tomb: tombstone -- replace bound value with hash
1461        ::
1462        ++  ap-tomb
1463          |=  [=case =spur]
1464          ^+  ap-core
1465          =-  ap-core(sky.yoke -)
1466          =/  yon  ?>(?=(%ud -.case) p.case)
1467          =/  old  (~(get of-farm sky.yoke) spur)
1468          ?~  old  ::  no-op if nonexistent
1469            %.  sky.yoke
1470            %+  trace  odd.veb.bug.state
1471            [leaf+"gall: {<agent-name>}: tomb {<[case spur]>} no sky"]~
1472          =/  val  (get:on-path fan.u.old yon)
1473          ?~  val  ::  no-op if nonexistent
1474            %.  sky.yoke
1475            %+  trace  odd.veb.bug.state
1476            [leaf+"gall: {<agent-name>}: tomb {<[case spur]>} no val"]~
1477          ?-    -.q.u.val
1478              %|  ::  already tombstoned, no-op
1479            %.  sky.yoke
1480            %+  trace  odd.veb.bug.state
1481            [leaf+"gall: {<agent-name>}: tomb {<[case spur]>} no-op"]~
1482          ::
1483              %&  ::  replace with hash
1484            %+  ~(put of-farm sky.yoke)  spur
1485            u.old(fan (put:on-path fan.u.old yon u.val(q |/(shax (jam p.q.u.val)))))
1486          ==
1487        ::  +ap-cull: delete all bindings up to and including .case
1488        ::
1489        ::    Also store .case as the high water mark for .spur
1490        ::    to prevent any deleted cases from being re-bound later.
1491        ::
1492        ++  ap-cull
1493          |=  [=case =spur]
1494          ^+  ap-core
1495          =-  ap-core(sky.yoke -)
1496          =/  yon  ?>(?=(%ud -.case) p.case)
1497          =/  old  (~(get of-farm sky.yoke) spur)
1498          ?~  old  ::  no-op if nonexistent
1499            %.  sky.yoke
1500            %+  trace  odd.veb.bug.state
1501            [leaf+"gall: {<agent-name>}: cull {<[case spur]>} no-op"]~
1502          ?~  las=(ram:on-path fan.u.old)
1503            %.  sky.yoke
1504            %+  trace  &
1505            [leaf+"gall: {<agent-name>}: cull {<[case spur]>} no paths"]~
1506          =/  fis  (need (pry:on-path fan.u.old))
```

```
    ?.  &((gte yon key.fis) (lte yon key.u.las))
      %.  sky.yoke
      %+  trace  &
      :_  ~
      :-  %leaf
      %+  weld
        "gall: {<agent-name>}: cull {<[case spur]>} out of range, "
      "min: {<key.fis>}, max: {<key.u.las>}"
    %+  ~(put of-farm sky.yoke)  spur  ::  delete all older paths
    [`yon (lot:on-path fan.u.old `yon ~)]
::  +ap-from-internal: internal move to move.
::
::    We convert from cards to duct-indexed moves when resolving
::    them in Arvo.
::
::    We accept %huck to "fake" being a message to a ship but
::    actually send it to a vane.
::
+$  carp  $+  carp  (wind neet gift:agent)
+$  neet  $+  neet
    $<  ?(%grow %tomb %cull %tend %germ %snip %keen)
    $%  note:agent
        [%agent [=ship name=term] task=[%raw-poke =mark =noun]]
        [%huck [=ship name=term] =note-arvo]
    ==
::
++  ap-from-internal
  ~/  %ap-from-internal
  |=  card=carp
  ^-  (list move)
  ::
  ?-    -.card
      %slip  !!
  ::
      %give
    =/  =gift:agent  p.card
    ?:  ?=(%kick -.gift)
      =/  ducts=(list duct)  (ap-ducts-from-paths paths.gift ship.gift)
      %+  turn  ducts
      |=  =duct
      ~?  &(=(duct system-duct.state) !=(agent-name %hood))
        [%agent-giving-on-system-duct agent-name -.gift]
      [duct %give %unto %kick ~]
    ::
    ?.  ?=(%fact -.gift)
      [agent-duct %give %unto gift]~
    ::
    =/  ducts=(list duct)  (ap-ducts-from-paths paths.gift ~)
    =/  =cage  cage.gift
    %-  zing
    %+  turn  ducts
    |=  =duct
    ^-  (list move)
    ~?  &(=(duct system-duct.state) !=(agent-name %hood))
      [%agent-giving-on-system-duct agent-name -.gift]
    =/  =mark  (~(gut by marks.yoke) duct p.cage)
    ::
    ?:  =(mark p.cage)
```

```
1565            [duct %give %unto %fact cage.gift]~
1566        =/  =mars:clay  [p.cage mark]
1567        =/  =case       da+now
1568        =/  bek=beak    [our q.beak.yoke case]
1569        =/  mars-path   /[a.mars]/[b.mars]
1570        =/  sky  (rof [~ ~] /gall %cc bek mars-path)
1571        ?-    sky
1572            ?(~ [~ ~])
1573          %-  (slog leaf+"watch-as fact conversion find-fail" >sky< ~)
1574          (ap-kill-up-slip duct)
1575        ::
1576            [~ ~ *]
1577        =+  !<(=tube:clay q.u.u.sky)
1578        =/  res  (mule |.((tube q.cage)))
1579        ?:  ?=(%| -.res)
1580          %-  (slog leaf+"watch-as fact conversion failure" p.res)
1581          (ap-kill-up-slip duct)
1582        :~  :*  duct %pass /nowhere %c %warp  our  q.beak.yoke  ~
1583                %sing  %c  case  mars-path
1584            ==
1585            [duct %give %unto %fact b.mars p.res]
1586        ==
1587      ==
1588      ::
1589          %pass
1590        =/  =duct  system-duct.state
1591        =/  =wire  p.card
1592        =/  =neet  q.card
1593        ?:  ?=(%pyre -.neet)
1594          %:  mean
1595            leaf/"gall: %pyre from {<agent-name>}, killing event"
1596            leaf/"wire: {<wire>}"
1597            tang.neet
1598          ==
1599        =.  wire
1600          :^  %use  agent-name  run-nonce.yoke
1601          ?-  -.neet
1602            %agent  [%out (scot %p ship.neet) name.neet wire]
1603            %huck   [%out (scot %p ship.neet) name.neet wire]
1604            %arvo   [(scot %p ship.attributing.agent-routes) wire]
1605          ==
1606        ::
1607        =/  =note-arvo
1608          =/  prov=path  /gall/[agent-name]
1609          ?-  -.neet
1610            %arvo   ?.  ?=([[%l *] +.neet)
1611                      +.neet
1612                    ?+  +.neet
1613                      ~|(%nope !!)
1614                      [%l ?(%spin %shut) *]  +.neet(name [agent-name name.+.neet])
1615                      [%l %spit *]           +.neet(name [agent-name name.+.neet])
1616                    ==
1617            %huck   note-arvo.neet
1618            %agent  [%g %deal [our ship.neet prov] [name task]:neet]
1619          ==
1620        [duct %pass wire note-arvo]~
1621      ==
1622  ::  +ap-breach: ship breached, so forget about them
```

```
1623        ::
1624        ++  ap-breach
1625          |=  =ship
1626          ^+  ap-core
1627          =/  in=(list [=duct =^ship =path])  ~(tap by bitt.yoke)
1628          |-  ^+  ap-core
1629          ?^  in
1630            =?  ap-core  =(ship ship.i.in)
1631              =/  core  ap-load-delete(agent-duct duct.i.in)
1632              core(agent-duct agent-duct)
1633            $(in t.in)
1634          ::
1635          =/  out=(list [=wire =^ship =term])
1636            ~(tap ^in ~(key by boat.yoke))
1637          |-  ^+  ap-core
1638          ?~  out
1639            ap-core
1640          =?  ap-core  =(ship ship.i.out)
1641            =/  core
1642              =.  agent-duct  system-duct.state
1643              =.  wire.i.out  (ap-nonce-wire i.out)
1644              =/  way          [%out (scot %p ship) term.i.out wire.i.out]
1645              (ap-specific-take way %kick ~)
1646            core(agent-duct agent-duct)
1647          $(out t.out)
1648        ::  +ap-clog: handle %clog notification from ames
1649        ::
1650        ::    Kills subscriptions from .ship in both directions:
1651        ::      - notifies local app that subscription is dead
1652        ::      - gives remote %quit to notify subscriber ship
1653        ::    TODO: %drip local app notification for error isolation
1654        ::
1655        ++  ap-clog
1656          |=  =ship
1657          ^+  ap-core
1658          ::
1659          =/  in=(list [=duct =^ship =path])  ~(tap by bitt.yoke)
1660          |-  ^+  ap-core
1661          ?~  in  ap-core
1662          ::
1663          =?  ap-core  =(ship ship.i.in)
1664            =/  core  ap-kill-up(agent-duct duct.i.in)
1665            core(agent-duct agent-duct)
1666          $(in t.in)
1667        ::  +ap-agent-core: agent core with current bowl and state
1668        ::
1669        ++  ap-agent-core
1670          ?>  ?=(%& -.agent.yoke)
1671          ~(. p.agent.yoke ap-construct-bowl)
1672        ::  +ap-ducts-from-paths: get ducts subscribed to paths
1673        ::
1674        ++  ap-ducts-from-paths
1675          |=  [target-paths=(list path) target-ship=(unit ship)]
1676          ^-  (list duct)
1677          ?~  target-paths
1678            ?~  target-ship
1679              ~[agent-duct]
1680            %+  murn  ~(tap by bitt.yoke)
```

```hoon
    |=  [=duct =ship =path]
    ^-  (unit ^duct)
    ?:  =(target-ship `ship)
      `duct
    ~
  %-  zing
  %+  turn  target-paths
  |=  =path
  (ap-ducts-from-path path target-ship)
::  +ap-ducts-from-path: get ducts subscribed to path
::
++  ap-ducts-from-path
  |=  [target-path=path target-ship=(unit ship)]
  ^-  (list duct)
  %+  murn  ~(tap by bitt.yoke)
  |=  [=duct =ship =path]
  ^-  (unit ^duct)
  ?:  ?&  =(target-path path)
          |(=(target-ship ~) =(target-ship `ship))
      ==
    `duct
  ~
::  +ap-apply: apply effect.
::
++  ap-apply
  |=  =deal
  ^+  ap-core
  ?-  -.deal
    %watch-as  (ap-subscribe-as +.deal)
    %poke      (ap-poke +.deal)
    %watch     (ap-subscribe +.deal)
    %raw-poke  !!
    %poke-as   !!
    %leave     ap-load-delete
  ==
::  +ap-peek: peek.
::
++  ap-peek
  ~/  %ap-peek
  |=  [veb=? care=term tyl=path]
  ^-  (unit (unit cage))
  ::  take trailing mark off path for %x scrys
  ::
  =^  want=mark  tyl
    ?.  ?=(%x care)  [%$ tyl]
    =.  tyl  (flop tyl)
    [(head tyl) (flop (tail tyl))]
  ::  call the app's +on-peek, producing [~ ~] if it crashes
  ::
  =/  peek-result=(each (unit (unit cage)) tang)
    (ap-mule-peek |.((on-peek:ap-agent-core [care tyl])))
  ?:  ?=(%| -.peek-result)
    ?.  veb  [~ ~]
    ((slog leaf+"peek bad result" p.peek-result) [~ ~])
  ::  for non-%x scries, or failed %x scries, or %x results that already
  ::  have the requested mark, produce the result as-is
  ::
  ?.  ?&  ?=(%x care)
```

```
1739            ?=([~ ~ *] p.peek-result)
1740            !=(want p.u.u.p.peek-result)
1741         ==
1742      p.peek-result
1743    ::  for %x scries, attempt to convert to the requested mark if needed
1744    ::
1745    =*  have  p.u.u.p.peek-result
1746    =*  vase  q.u.u.p.peek-result
1747    =/  tub=(unit tube:clay)
1748      ?:  =(have want)  `(bake same ^vase)
1749      =/  tuc=(unit (unit cage))
1750        (rof [~ ~] /gall %cc [our q.beak.yoke da+now] /[have]/[want])
1751      ?.  ?=([~ ~ *] tuc)  ~
1752      `!<(tube:clay q.u.u.tuc)
1753    ?~  tub
1754      ((slog leaf+"peek no tube from {(trip have)} to {(trip want)}" ~) ~)
1755    =/  res  (mule |.((u.tub vase)))
1756    ?:  ?=(%& -.res)
1757      ``want^p.res
1758    ((slog leaf+"peek failed tube from {(trip have)} to {(trip want)}" ~) ~)
1759  ::  +ap-move: send move
1760  ::
1761  ++  ap-move
1762    |=  =(list move)
1763    ap-core(agent-moves (weld (flop list) agent-moves))
1764  ::  +ap-give: return result.
1765  ::
1766  ++  ap-give
1767    |=  =gift:agent
1768    (ap-move (ap-from-internal %give gift))
1769  ::  +ap-pass: request action.
1770  ::
1771  ++  ap-pass
1772    |=  [=path =neet]
1773    (ap-move (ap-from-internal %pass path neet))
1774  ::  +ap-construct-bowl: set up bowl.
1775  ::
1776  ++  ap-construct-bowl
1777    ^-  bowl
1778    :*  :*  our                           ::  host
1779            ship.attributing.agent-routes     ::  guest
1780            agent-name                        ::  agent
1781            path.attributing.agent-routes     ::  provenance
1782        ==                                ::
1783        :*  wex=boat.yoke                 ::  outgoing
1784            sup=bitt.yoke                     ::  incoming
1785            ^=  sky                           ::  bindings
1786            %-  ~(run-plot of-farm sky.yoke)
1787            (bake tail ,plot)
1788        ==                                ::
1789        :*  act=change.stats.yoke         ::  tick
1790            eny=eny.stats.yoke                ::  nonce
1791            now=time.stats.yoke               ::  time
1792            byk=beak.yoke                     ::  source
1793    ==  ==
1794  ::  +ap-reinstall: reinstall.
1795  ::
1796  ++  ap-reinstall
```

```hoon
1797        ~/  %ap-reinstall
1798        |=  =agent
1799        ^+  ap-core
1800        =/  old-state=vase
1801          ?:  ?=(%& -.agent.yoke)
1802            on-save:ap-agent-core
1803          p.agent.yoke
1804        =?  ap-core  &(?=(%| -.agent.yoke) ?=(^ ken.yoke))
1805          =-  +:(ap-ingest ~ |.([+< agent]))
1806          %-  zing
1807          %+  turn  ~(tap by `(jug spar:ames wire)`ken.yoke)
1808          |=  [=spar:ames wyz=(set wire)]
1809          (turn ~(tap in wyz) |=(=wire [%pass wire %arvo %a %keen ~ spar]))
1810        =^  error  ap-core
1811          (ap-install(agent.yoke &+agent) `old-state)
1812        ?~  error
1813          ap-core
1814        (mean >%load-failed< u.error)
1815      ::  +ap-subscribe-as: apply %watch-as.
1816      ::
1817      ++  ap-subscribe-as
1818        |=  [=mark =path]
1819        ^+  ap-core
1820        =.  marks.yoke  (~(put by marks.yoke) agent-duct mark)
1821        (ap-subscribe path)
1822      ::  +ap-subscribe: apply %watch.
1823      ::
1824      ++  ap-subscribe
1825        ~/  %ap-subscribe
1826        |=  pax=path
1827        ^+  ap-core
1828        =/  incoming   [ship.attributing.agent-routes pax]
1829        =.  bitt.yoke  (~(put by bitt.yoke) agent-duct incoming)
1830        =^  maybe-tang  ap-core
1831          %+  ap-ingest  %watch-ack  |.
1832          (on-watch:ap-agent-core pax)
1833        ?^  maybe-tang
1834          ap-silent-delete
1835        ap-core
1836      ::  +ap-poke: apply %poke.
1837      ::
1838      ++  ap-poke
1839        ~/  %ap-poke
1840        |=  =cage
1841        ^+  ap-core
1842        =^  maybe-tang  ap-core
1843          %+  ap-ingest  %poke-ack  |.
1844          (on-poke:ap-agent-core cage)
1845        ap-core
1846      ::  +ap-error: pour error.
1847      ::
1848      ++  ap-error
1849        |=  [=term =tang]
1850        ^+  ap-core
1851        =/  form  |=(=tank [%rose [~ "! " ~] tank ~])
1852        =^  maybe-tang  ap-core
1853          %+  ap-ingest  ~  |.
1854          (on-fail:ap-agent-core term (turn tang form))
```

```
        ap-core
    ::  +ap-generic-take: generic take.
    ::
    ++  ap-generic-take
      ~/  %ap-generic-take
      |=  [=wire =sign-arvo]
      ^+  ap-core
      =?  sign-arvo  ?=([%lick *] sign-arvo)
        ?+  sign-arvo
          ~|(%nope !!)
        ::
            [%lick %soak *]
          =-  sign-arvo(name -)
          ?>  &(?=(^ name.sign-arvo) =(agent-name i.name.sign-arvo))
          t.name.sign-arvo
        ==
      =^  maybe-tang  ap-core
        %+  ap-ingest  ~  |.
        (on-arvo:ap-agent-core wire sign-arvo)
      =?  ken.yoke  ?=([%ames %tune spar=* *] sign-arvo)
        (~(del ju ken.yoke) spar.sign-arvo wire)
      ?^  maybe-tang
        (ap-error %arvo-response u.maybe-tang)
      ap-core
    ::  +ap-specific-take: specific take.
    ::
    ++  ap-specific-take
      |=  [=wire =unto]
      ^+  ap-core
      ~|  wire=wire
      ?>  ?=([%out @ @ *] wire)
      =/  other-ship  (slav %p i.t.wire)
      =/  other-agent  i.t.t.wire
      =/  =dock  [other-ship other-agent]
      =/  agent-wire  t.t.t.wire
      =/  nonce=@  0
      ::
      =^  =sign:agent  ap-core
        ?.  ?=(%raw-fact -.unto)
          [unto ap-core]
        =/  =case  da+now
        ?:  ?=(%spider agent-name)
          :-  [%fact mark.unto !>(noun.unto)]
          ap-core
        =/  sky  (rof [~ ~] /gall %cb [our q.beak.yoke case] /[mark.unto])
        ?.  ?=([~ ~ *] sky)
          (mean leaf+"gall: ames mark fail {<mark.unto>}" ~)
        ::
        =+  !<(=dais:clay q.u.u.sky)
        =/  res  (mule |.((vale:dais noun.unto)))
        ?:  ?=(%| -.res)
          (mean leaf+"gall: ames vale fail {<mark.unto>}" p.res)
        :-  [%fact mark.unto p.res]
        %-  ap-move  :_  ~
        :^  hen  %pass  /nowhere
        [%c %warp our q.beak.yoke ~ %sing %b case /[mark.unto]]
      |^  ^+  ap-core
          ::  %poke-ack has no nonce; ingest directly
```

```
1913            ::
1914            ?:  ?=(%poke-ack -.sign)
1915              ingest-and-check-error
1916            ::  if .agent-wire matches, it's an old pre-nonce subscription
1917            ::
1918            ?:  (~(has by boat.yoke) sub-key)
1919              run-sign
1920            ::  if an app happened to use a null wire, no-op
1921            ::
1922            ?:  =(~ agent-wire)
1923              on-missing
1924            =/  has-nonce=(unit @ud)  (slaw %ud (head agent-wire))
1925            ?:  &(?=(~ has-nonce) ?=(%kick -.sign))
1926              on-weird-kick
1927            ::  pop nonce off .agent-wire and match against stored subscription
1928            ::
1929            ?>  ?=(^ has-nonce)
1930            =:  nonce        u.has-nonce
1931                agent-wire  (tail agent-wire)
1932              ==
1933            ?~  got=(~(get by boar.yoke) sub-key)
1934              on-missing
1935            ?:  =(nonce.u.got nonce)
1936              run-sign
1937            (on-bad-nonce nonce.u.got)
1938        ::
1939    ++  sub-key  [agent-wire dock]
1940    ++  ingest   (ap-ingest ~ |.((on-agent:ap-agent-core agent-wire sign)))
1941    ++  run-sign
1942      ?-    -.sign
1943          %poke-ack  !!
1944          %fact
1945        =^  tan  ap-core  ingest
1946        ?~  tan  ap-core
1947        =.  ap-core  (ap-kill-down sub-key)
1948        (ap-error -.sign leaf/"take %fact failed, closing subscription" u.tan)
1949        ::
1950          %kick
1951        =:  boar.yoke  (~(del by boar.yoke) sub-key)
1952            boat.yoke  (~(del by boat.yoke) sub-key)
1953          ==
1954        ingest-and-check-error
1955        ::
1956          %watch-ack
1957        ?.  (~(has by boat.yoke) sub-key)
1958          %.  ap-core
1959          %+  trace  odd.veb.bug.state  :~
1960            leaf+"{<agent-name>}: got ack for nonexistent subscription"
1961            leaf+"{<dock>}: {<agent-wire>}"
1962            >wire=wire<
1963          ==
1964        =?  boar.yoke  ?=(^ p.sign)  (~(del by boar.yoke) sub-key)
1965        ::
1966        =.  boat.yoke
1967          ?^  p.sign  (~(del by boat.yoke) sub-key)
1968          ::
1969          %+  ~(jab by boat.yoke)  sub-key
1970          |=  val=[acked=? =path]
```

```
        %.  val(acked &)
        %^  trace  &(odd.veb.bug.state acked.val)
        leaf/"{<agent-name>} 2nd watch-ack on {<val>}"  ~
      ::
      ingest-and-check-error
    ==
  ::
  ++  on-missing
    %.  ap-core
    %+  trace  odd.veb.bug.state  :~
      leaf+"{<agent-name>}: got {<-.sign>} for nonexistent subscription"
      leaf+"{<dock>}: {<[nonce=nonce agent-wire]>}"
      >wire=wire<
    ==
  ::
  ++  on-weird-kick
    %.  run-sign
    %+  trace  odd.veb.bug.state  :~
      leaf+"{<agent-name>}: got %kick for nonexistent subscription"
      leaf+"{<dock>}: {<agent-wire>}"
      >wire=wire<
    ==
  ::
  ++  on-bad-nonce
    |=  stored-nonce=@
    %.  ap-core
    %+  trace  odd.veb.bug.state  :~
      =/  nonces  [expected=stored-nonce got=nonce]
      =/  ok  |(?=(?(%fact %kick) -.sign) =(~ p.sign))
      leaf+"{<agent-name>}: stale {<-.sign>} {<nonces>} ok={<ok>}"
      ::
      leaf+"{<dock>}: {<agent-wire>}"
      >wire=wire<
    ==
  ::
  ++  ingest-and-check-error
    ^+  ap-core
    =^  tan  ap-core  ingest
    ?~(tan ap-core (ap-error -.sign leaf/"take {<-.sign>} failed" u.tan))
  --
::  +ap-install: install wrapper.
::
++  ap-install
  |=  old-agent-state=(unit vase)
  ^-  [(unit tang) _ap-core]
  ::
  =^  maybe-tang  ap-core  (ap-upgrade-state old-agent-state)
  ::
  =.  agent-config
    :_  agent-config
    ^-  (each suss tang)
    ?^  maybe-tang
      |/u.maybe-tang
    &/[agent-name ?~(old-agent-state %boot %bump) now]
  ::
  [maybe-tang ap-core]
::  +ap-upgrade-state: low-level install.
::
```

```
2029      ++  ap-upgrade-state
2030        ~/  %ap-upgrade-state
2031        |=  maybe-vase=(unit vase)
2032        ^-  [(unit tang) _ap-core]
2033        ::
2034        =^  maybe-tang  ap-core
2035          %+  ap-ingest  ~
2036          ?~  maybe-vase
2037            |.  on-init:ap-agent-core
2038          |.  (on-load:ap-agent-core u.maybe-vase)
2039        [maybe-tang ap-core]
2040      ::  +ap-silent-delete: silent delete.
2041      ::
2042      ++  ap-silent-delete
2043        ^+  ap-core
2044        ap-core(bitt.yoke (~(del by bitt.yoke) agent-duct))
2045      ::  +ap-load-delete: load delete.
2046      ::
2047      ++  ap-load-delete
2048        ^+  ap-core
2049        ::
2050        =/  maybe-incoming  (~(get by bitt.yoke) agent-duct)
2051        ?~  maybe-incoming
2052          ap-core
2053        ::
2054        =/  incoming   u.maybe-incoming
2055        =.  bitt.yoke  (~(del by bitt.yoke) agent-duct)
2056        ::
2057        =^  maybe-tang  ap-core
2058          %+  ap-ingest  ~  |.
2059          (on-leave:ap-agent-core q.incoming)
2060        ?^  maybe-tang
2061          (ap-error %leave u.maybe-tang)
2062        ap-core
2063      ::  +ap-kill-up: 2-sided kill from publisher side
2064      ::
2065      ++  ap-kill-up
2066        ^+  ap-core
2067        ::
2068        =>  ap-load-delete
2069        (ap-give %kick ~ ~)
2070      ::  +ap-kill-up-slip: 2-sided kill from publisher side by slip
2071      ::
2072      ::  +ap-kill-up is reentrant if you call it in the
2073      ::  middle of processing another deal
2074      ::
2075      ::  Should probably call +ap-error with error message
2076      ::
2077      ++  ap-kill-up-slip
2078        |=  =duct
2079        ^-  (list move)
2080        ::
2081        =/  =sack  [our our /gall/[agent-name]]
2082        :~  [duct %slip %g %deal sack agent-name %leave ~]
2083            [duct %give %unto %kick ~]
2084        ==
2085      ::  +ap-kill-down: 2-sided kill from subscriber side
2086      ::
```

```
::    Must process leave first in case kick handler rewatches.
::
++  ap-kill-down
  |=  [sub-wire=wire =dock]
  ^+  ap-core
  =.  ap-core
    ::  we take care to include the nonce in the "kernel-facing" wire
    ::
    (ap-pass (ap-nonce-wire sub-wire dock) %agent dock %leave ~)
  (ap-pass sub-wire %huck dock %b %huck `sign-arvo`[%gall %unto %kick ~])
::  +ap-doff: kill old-style outgoing subscriptions
::
++  ap-doff
  |=  ship=(unit ship)
  ^+  ap-core
  =/  subs  ~(tap in ~(key by boat.yoke))
  |-  ^+  ap-core
  ?~  subs  ap-core
  =+  [wyr dok]=i.subs
  ?:  &(?=(^ ship) !=(u.ship ship.dok))
    $(subs t.subs)
  ::  if we haven't created new-style (nonced) subscriptions yet,
  ::  kick the old-style (nonceless) one that's in use right now.
  ::
  ::NOTE  yes, still safe for pre-release ships with nonce=1,
  ::        this makes a new flow but cleans it up right away.
  ::
  =?  ap-core  (gte 1 ~(got by boar.yoke) wyr dok))
    (ap-pass wyr %agent dok %leave ~)
  $(subs t.subs)
::  +ap-rake: clean up the dead %leave's
::
++  ap-rake
  |=  all=?
  =/  subs  ~(tap in ~(key by boat.yoke))
  |^  ^+  ap-core
  ?~  subs  ap-core
  =/  [=wire =dock]  i.subs
  =/  non  (~(got by boar.yoke) wire dock)
  ?:  &(!all =(0 non))
    $(subs t.subs)
  ?~  per=(scry-peer-state p.dock)
    $(subs t.subs)
  ::
  =/  dud=(set duct)
    =/  mod=^wire
      :*  %gall  %use  agent-name  run-nonce.yoke
          %out  (scot %p p.dock)  q.dock
          '0'  wire
      ==
    %-  ~(rep by by-duct.ossuary.u.per)
    |=  [[=duct =bone] out=(set duct)]
    ^+  out
    ?.  ?&  ?=([* [%gall %use @ @ %out @ @ @ *] *] duct)
            =(mod i.t.duct(i.t.t.t.t.t.t.t '0'))
        ==
      out
    ?:  (~(has in closing.u.per) bone)  out
```

```
2145        ~>  %slog.0^leaf+"gall: rake {<i.t.duct>}"
2146        (~(put in out) duct)
2147      ::
2148      %-  ap-move
2149      (turn ~(tap in dud) |=(d=duct [+.d %pass -.d %a %cork p.dock]))
2150      ::
2151    ++  scry-peer-state
2152      |=  her=ship
2153      ~+  ^-  (unit peer-state:ames)
2154      =/  sky  (rof [~ ~] /gall %ax [our %$ da+now] /peers/(scot %p her))
2155      ?:  |(?=(~ sky) ?=(~ u.sky))
2156        ~
2157      =/  sat  !<(ship-state:ames q.u.u.sky)
2158      ?>(?=(%known -.sat) (some +.sat))
2159      --
2160    ::  +ap-mule: run virtualized with intercepted scry, preserving type
2161    ::
2162    ::    Compare +mute and +mule.  Those pass through scry, which
2163    ::    doesn't allow us to catch crashes due to blocking scry.  If
2164    ::    you intercept scry, you can't preserve the type
2165    ::    polymorphically.  By monomorphizing, we are able to do so
2166    ::    safely.
2167    ::
2168    ++  ap-mule
2169      |=  run=_^?(|.(*step:agent))
2170      ^-  (each step:agent tang)
2171      =/  res  (mock [run %9 2 %0 1] (look rof [~ ~] /gall/[agent-name]))
2172      ?-  -.res
2173        %0  [%& !<(step:agent [-:!>(*step:agent) p.res])]
2174        %1  [%| (smyt ;;(path p.res)) ~]
2175        %2  [%| p.res]
2176      ==
2177    ::  +ap-mule-peek: same as +ap-mule but for (unit (unit cage))
2178    ::
2179    ++  ap-mule-peek
2180      |=  run=_^?(|.(*(unit (unit cage))))
2181      ^-  (each (unit (unit cage)) tang)
2182      =/  res  (mock [run %9 2 %0 1] (look rof [~ ~] /gall/[agent-name]))
2183      ?-  -.res
2184        %0  [%& !<((unit (unit cage)) [-:!>(*(unit (unit cage))) p.res])]
2185        %1  [%| (smyt ;;(path p.res)) ~]
2186        %2  [%| p.res]
2187      ==
2188    ::  +ap-ingest: call agent arm
2189    ::
2190    ::    Handle acks here because they need to be emitted before the
2191    ::    rest of the moves.
2192    ::
2193    ++  ap-ingest
2194      |=  [ack=?(%poke-ack %watch-ack ~) run=_^?(|.(*step:agent))]
2195      ^-  [(unit tang) _ap-core]
2196      =/  result  (ap-mule run)
2197      =^  new-moves  ap-core  (ap-handle-result result)
2198      =/  maybe-tang=(unit tang)
2199        ?:  ?=(%& -.result)
2200          ~
2201        `p.result
2202      =/  ack-moves=(list move)
```

```
2203      %-  zing
2204      %-  turn  :_  ap-from-internal
2205      ^-  (list carp)
2206      ?-  ack
2207        ~          ~
2208        %poke-ack   [%give %poke-ack maybe-tang]~
2209        %watch-ack  [%give %watch-ack maybe-tang]~
2210      ==
2211    ::
2212    =.  agent-moves
2213      :(weld (flop new-moves) ack-moves agent-moves)
2214    [maybe-tang ap-core]
2215  ::  +ap-handle-result: handle result.
2216  ::
2217  ++  ap-handle-result
2218    ~/  %ap-handle-result
2219    |=  result=(each step:agent tang)
2220    ^-  [(list move) _ap-core]
2221    ?:  ?=(%| -.result)
2222      `ap-core
2223    ::
2224    =.  agent.yoke  &++.p.result
2225    =^  fex  ap-core  (ap-handle-sky -.p.result)
2226    =.  ken.yoke    (ap-handle-ken fex)
2227    =/  moves        (zing (turn fex ap-from-internal))
2228    =.  bitt.yoke   (ap-handle-kicks moves)
2229    (ap-handle-peers moves)
2230  ::  +ap-handle-sky: apply effects to the agent's scry namespace
2231  ::
2232  ++  ap-handle-sky
2233    =|  fex=(list carp)
2234    |=  caz=(list card:agent)
2235    ^+  [fex ap-core]
2236    ?~  caz  [(flop fex) ap-core]
2237    ?-  i.caz
2238      [%pass * %grow *]  $(caz t.caz, ap-core (ap-grow +.q.i.caz))
2239      [%pass * %tomb *]  $(caz t.caz, ap-core (ap-tomb +.q.i.caz))
2240      [%pass * %cull *]  $(caz t.caz, ap-core (ap-cull +.q.i.caz))
2241      [%pass * %tend *]  $(caz t.caz, ap-core (ap-tend +.q.i.caz))
2242      [%pass * %germ *]  $(caz t.caz, ap-core (ap-germ +.q.i.caz))
2243      [%pass * %snip *]  $(caz t.caz, ap-core (ap-snip +.q.i.caz))
2244      [%pass * %keen *]  $(caz t.caz, ap-core (ap-keen p.i.caz +.q.i.caz))
2245      [%pass * ?(%agent %arvo %pyre) *]  $(caz t.caz, fex [i.caz fex])
2246      [%give *]  $(caz t.caz, fex [i.caz fex])
2247      [%slip *]  !!
2248    ==
2249  ::  +ap-handle-ken
2250  ::
2251  ++  ap-handle-ken
2252    |=  fex=(list carp)
2253    ^+  ken.yoke
2254    %+  roll  fex
2255    |=  [=carp ken=_ken.yoke]
2256    ?+  carp  ken
2257      [%pass * %arvo %a %keen @ spar=*]  (~(put ju ken) [spar.q p]:carp)
2258      [%pass * %arvo %a %yawn spar=*]  (~(del ju ken) [spar.q p]:carp)
2259    ==
2260  ::  +ap-handle-kicks: handle cancels of bitt.watches
```

```
2261        ::
2262        ++  ap-handle-kicks
2263          ~/  %ap-handle-kicks
2264          |=  moves=(list move)
2265          ^-  bitt
2266          =/  quits=(list duct)
2267            %+  murn  moves
2268            |=  =move
2269            ^-  (unit duct)
2270            ?.  ?=([* %give %unto %kick *] move)
2271              ~
2272            `duct.move
2273          ::
2274          =/  quit-map=bitt
2275            (malt (turn quits |=(=duct [duct *[ship path]]))))
2276          (~(dif by bitt.yoke) quit-map)
2277        ::  +ap-handle-peers: handle new boat.watches
2278        ::
2279        ++  ap-handle-peers
2280          ~/  %ap-handle-peers
2281          |=  moves=(list move)
2282          ^-  [(list move) _ap-core]
2283          =|  new-moves=(list move)
2284          |-  ^-  [(list move) _ap-core]
2285          ?~  moves
2286            [(flop new-moves) ap-core]
2287          =/  =move  i.moves
2288          ?:  ?=([* %pass * %g %deal * * %leave *] move)
2289            =/  =wire  p.move.move
2290            ?>  ?=([%use @ @ %out @ @ *] wire)
2291            =/  =dock            [q.p q]:q.move.move
2292            =/  sys-wire=^wire  (scag 6 `^wire`wire)
2293            =/  sub-wire=^wire  (slag 6 `^wire`wire)
2294            ::
2295            ?.  (~(has by boat.yoke) sub-wire dock)
2296              %.  $(moves t.moves)
2297              %^  trace  odd.veb.bug.state
2298              leaf/"gall: {<agent-name>} missing subscription, got %leave"  ~
2299            =/  nonce=@  (~(got by boar.yoke) sub-wire dock)
2300            =.  p.move.move
2301              %+  weld  sys-wire
2302              (ap-nonce-wire sub-wire dock)
2303            =:  boat.yoke  (~(del by boat.yoke) [sub-wire dock])
2304                boar.yoke  (~(del by boar.yoke) [sub-wire dock])
2305              ==
2306            ::  if nonce = 0, this was a pre-nonce subscription so later
2307            ::  subscriptions need to start subscribing on the next nonce
2308            ::
2309            =?  sub-nonce.yoke  =(nonce 0)  +(sub-nonce.yoke)
2310            $(moves t.moves, new-moves [move new-moves])
2311          ?.  ?=([* %pass * %g %deal * * ?(%watch %watch-as) *] move)
2312            $(moves t.moves, new-moves [move new-moves])
2313          =/  =wire  p.move.move
2314          ?>  ?=([%use @ @ %out @ @ *] wire)
2315          =/  sys-wire=^wire  (scag 6 `^wire`wire)
2316          =/  sub-wire=^wire  (slag 6 `^wire`wire)
2317          =/  [=dock =deal]  [[q.p q] r]:q.move.move
2318          ::
```

```
2319      ?:  (~(has by boat.yoke) sub-wire dock)
2320        =.  ap-core
2321          =/  =tang
2322            ~[leaf+"subscribe wire not unique" >agent-name< >sub-wire< >dock<]
2323          =/  have  (~(got by boat.yoke) sub-wire dock)
2324          %-  (slog >out=have< tang)
2325          (ap-error %watch-not-unique tang)  ::  reentrant, maybe bad?
2326        $(moves t.moves)
2327      ::
2328      ::NOTE  0-check guards against pre-release bug
2329      =?  p.move.move  !=(0 sub-nonce.yoke)
2330        (weld sys-wire [(scot %ud sub-nonce.yoke) sub-wire])
2331      %_    $
2332        moves            t.moves
2333        new-moves        [move new-moves]
2334        sub-nonce.yoke  +(sub-nonce.yoke)
2335      ::
2336          boat.yoke
2337        %+  ~(put by boat.yoke)  [sub-wire dock]
2338        :-  acked=|
2339        path=?+(-.deal !! %watch path.deal, %watch-as path.deal)
2340      ::
2341          boar.yoke
2342        (~(put by boar.yoke) [sub-wire dock] sub-nonce.yoke)
2343      ==
2344    --
2345  --
2346 ::  +call: request
2347 ::
2348 ++  call
2349   ~%  %gall-call  +>  ~
2350   |=  [=duct dud=(unit goof) hic=(hobo task)]
2351   ^-  [(list move) _gall-payload]
2352   ?^  dud
2353     ~|(%gall-call-dud (mean tang.u.dud))
2354   ::
2355   ~|  [%gall-call-failed duct hic]
2356   =/  =task  ((harden task) hic)
2357   =/  prov=path
2358     ?:  ?=(%deal -.task)
2359       ?.(=(p.p.task our) *path r.p.task)
2360     ?.  ?&  ?=([^ *] duct)
2361             ?=  $?  %ames  %behn  %clay
2362                     %dill  %eyre  %gall
2363                     %iris  %jael  %khan
2364                 ==
2365             i.i.duct
2366         ==
2367       *path
2368     /[i.i.duct]
2369   ::                          .
2370   =/  mo-core  (mo-abed:mo duct)
2371   ?-  -.task
2372     %deal
2373   =/  [=sack =term =deal]  [p q r]:task
2374   ?.  =(q.sack our)
2375     ?>  =(p.sack our)
2376     mo-abet:(mo-send-foreign-request:mo-core q.sack term deal)
```

```
2377        mo-abet:(mo-handle-local:mo-core prov p.sack term deal)
2378    ::
2379        %init  [~ gall-payload(system-duct.state duct)]
2380        %plea
2381    =/  =ship  ship.task
2382    =/  =path  path.plea.task
2383    =/  =noun  payload.plea.task
2384    ::
2385    ?:  ?=([%gk @ ~] path)
2386      =/  agent-name  i.t.path
2387      =+  ;;(=fine-request noun)
2388      =<  mo-abet
2389      (mo-handle-key-request:mo-core ship agent-name path.fine-request)
2390    ?>  ?=([%ge @ ~] path)
2391    =/  agent-name  i.t.path
2392    ::
2393    =+  ;;(=ames-request-all noun)
2394    ?>  ?=(%0 -.ames-request-all)
2395    =>  (mo-handle-ames-request:mo-core ship agent-name +.ames-request-all)
2396    mo-abet
2397    ::
2398        %sear  mo-abet:(mo-filter-queue:mo-core ship.task)
2399        %jolt  mo-abet:(mo-jolt:mo-core dude.task our desk.task)
2400        %idle  mo-abet:(mo-idle:mo-core prov dude.task)
2401        %load  mo-abet:(mo-load:mo-core prov +.task)
2402        %nuke  mo-abet:(mo-nuke:mo-core prov dude.task)
2403        %doff  mo-abet:(mo-doff:mo-core prov +.task)
2404        %rake  mo-abet:(mo-rake:mo-core prov +.task)
2405        %spew  mo-abet:(mo-spew:mo-core veb.task)
2406        %sift  mo-abet:(mo-sift:mo-core dudes.task)
2407        %trim  [~ gall-payload]
2408        %vega  [~ gall-payload]
2409    ==
2410 ::  +load: recreate vane; note, only valid if called from pupa
2411 ::
2412 ++  load
2413    |^  |=  old=spore-any
2414        =?  old  ?=(%7 -.old)   (spore-7-to-8 +.old)
2415        =?  old  ?=(%8 -.old)   (spore-8-to-9 +.old)
2416        =?  old  ?=(%9 -.old)   (spore-9-to-10 +.old)
2417        =?  old  ?=(%10 -.old)  (spore-10-to-11 +.old)
2418        =?  old  ?=(%11 -.old)  (spore-11-to-12 +.old)
2419        =?  old  ?=(%12 -.old)  (spore-12-to-13 +.old)
2420        =?  old  ?=(%13 -.old)  (spore-13-to-14 +.old)
2421        =?  old  ?=(%14 -.old)  (spore-14-to-15 +.old)
2422        =?  old  ?=(%15 -.old)  (spore-15-to-16 +.old)
2423        ?>  ?=(%16 -.old)
2424        gall-payload(state old)
2425    ::
2426    +$  spore-any
2427    $%  [%16 spore]
2428        [%7 spore-7]
2429        [%8 spore-8]
2430        [%9 spore-9]
2431        [%10 spore-10]
2432        [%11 spore-11]
2433        [%12 spore-12]
2434        [%13 spore-13]
```

```
          [%14 spore-14]
          [%15 spore-15]
      ==
  +$  spore-15
    $+  spore-15
    $:  system-duct=duct
        outstanding=(map [wire duct] (qeu remote-request))
        contacts=(set ship)
        eggs=(map term egg-15)
        blocked=(map term (qeu blocked-move))
        =bug
        leaves=(unit [=duct =wire date=@da])
    ==
  +$  spore-14
    $:  system-duct=duct
        outstanding=(map [wire duct] (qeu remote-request))
        contacts=(set ship)
        eggs=(map term egg-15)
        blocked=(map term (qeu blocked-move))
        =bug
    ==
  ::
  +$  spore-13
    $:  system-duct=duct
        outstanding=(map [wire duct] (qeu remote-request))
        contacts=(set ship)
        eggs=(map term egg-15)
        blocked=(map term (qeu blocked-move-13))
        =bug
    ==
  +$  blocked-move-13  [=duct routes=routes-13 move=(each deal unto)]
  +$  routes-13
    $:  disclosing=(unit (set ship))
        attributing=ship
    ==
  +$  spore-12
    $:  system-duct=duct
        outstanding=(map [wire duct] (qeu remote-request))
        contacts=(set ship)
        eggs=(map term egg-12)
        blocked=(map term (qeu blocked-move-13))
        =bug
    ==
  +$  egg-12
    $%  [%nuke sky=(map spur @ud)]
        $:  %live
            control-duct=duct
            run-nonce=@t
            sub-nonce=@
            =stats
            =bitt
            =boat
            =boar
            code=~
            old-state=[%| vase]
            =beak
            marks=(map duct mark)
            sky=(map spur plot)
```

```
      ==  ==
  +$  spore-11
    $:  system-duct=duct
        outstanding=(map [wire duct] (qeu remote-request))
        contacts=(set ship)
        eggs=(map term egg-11)
        blocked=(map term (qeu blocked-move-13))
        =bug
    ==
  +$  egg-11
    $:  control-duct=duct
        run-nonce=@t
        sub-nonce=@
        =stats
        =bitt
        =boat
        =boar
        code=~
        old-state=[%| vase]
        =beak
        marks=(map duct mark)
    ==
  +$  spore-10
    $:  system-duct=duct
        outstanding=(map [wire duct] (qeu remote-request))
        contacts=(set ship)
        eggs=(map term egg-10)
        blocked=(map term (qeu blocked-move-13))
        =bug
    ==
  +$  egg-10
    $:  control-duct=duct
        run-nonce=@t
        sub-nonce=@
        live=?
        =stats
        =bitt
        =boat
        =boar
        old-state=(each vase vase)
        =beak
        marks=(map duct mark)
    ==
  +$  spore-9
    $:  system-duct=duct
        outstanding=(map [wire duct] (qeu remote-request-9))
        contacts=(set ship)
        eggs=(map term egg-10)
        blocked=(map term (qeu blocked-move-13))
        =bug
    ==
  ::
  +$  remote-request-9  ?(remote-request %cork)
  ::
  +$  spore-8
    $:  system-duct=duct
        outstanding=(map [wire duct] (qeu remote-request-9))
        contacts=(set ship)
```

```
      eggs=(map term egg-8)
      blocked=(map term (qeu blocked-move-13))
  ==
+$  egg-8
  $:  control-duct=duct
      run-nonce=@t
      live=?
      =stats
      watches=watches-8
      old-state=(each vase vase)
      =beak
      marks=(map duct mark)
  ==
+$  watches-8  [inbound=bitt outbound=boat-8]
+$  boat-8  (map [wire ship term] [acked=? =path])
+$  spore-7
  $:  wipe-eyre-subs=_|  ::NOTE  band-aid for #3196
      system-duct=duct
      outstanding=(map [wire duct] (qeu remote-request-9))
      contacts=(set ship)
      eggs=(map term egg-8)
      blocked=(map term (qeu blocked-move-13))
  ==
::
++  spore-7-to-8
  |=  old=spore-7
  ^-  spore-any
  :-  %8
  ^-  spore-8
  =.  eggs.old
    %-  ~(urn by eggs.old)
    |=  [a=term e=egg-8]
    ::  kiln will kick off appropriate app revival
    ::
    e(old-state [%| p.old-state.e])
  +.old
::
++  spore-8-to-9
  |=  old=spore-8
  :-  %9
  ^-  spore-9
  =-  old(eggs -, blocked [blocked.old *bug])
  %-  ~(run by eggs.old)
  |=  =egg-8
  ^-  egg-10
  =/  [=bitt =boat =boar]  (watches-8-to-9 watches.egg-8)
  :*  control-duct.egg-8
      run-nonce.egg-8
      sub-nonce=1
      live.egg-8
      stats.egg-8
      bitt  boat  boar
      [old-state beak marks]:egg-8
  ==
::
++  watches-8-to-9
  |=  watches-8
  ^-  [bitt boat boar]
```

```
    [inbound outbound (~(run by outbound) |=([acked=? =path] nonce=0))]
::
::  remove %cork
::
++  spore-9-to-10
  |=  old=spore-9
  :-  %10
  ^-  spore-10
  =-  old(outstanding -)
  %-  ~(run by outstanding.old)
  |=  q=(qeu remote-request-9)
  %-  ~(gas to *(qeu remote-request))
  %+  murn  ~(tap to q)
  |=(r=remote-request-9 ?:(?=(%cork r) ~ `r))
::
::  removed live
::  changed old-state from (each vase vase) to [%| vase]
::  added code
::
++  spore-10-to-11
  |=  old=spore-10
  :-  %11
  ^-  spore-11
  %=    old
      eggs
    %-  ~(urn by eggs.old)
    |=  [a=term e=egg-10]
    ^-  egg-11
    e(|3 |4.e(|4 `|8.e(old-state [%| p.old-state.e])))
  ==
::
::  added sky
::
++  spore-11-to-12
  |=  old=spore-11
  :-  %12
  ^-  spore-12
  %=    old
      eggs
    %-  ~(urn by eggs.old)
    |=  [a=term e=egg-11]
    ^-  egg-12
    live/e(marks [marks.e sky:*$>(%live egg-12)])
  ==
::
::  added ken
::
++  spore-12-to-13
  |=  old=spore-12
  :-  %13
  ^-  spore-13
  %=    old
      eggs
    %-  ~(urn by eggs.old)
    |=  [a=term e=egg-12]
    ^-  egg-15
    ?:  ?=(%nuke -.e)  e
      ::!!
```

```
2667        e(sky [sky.e ken:*$>(%live egg-15)])
2668      ==
2669  ::
2670  ++  spore-13-to-14
2671    |=  old=spore-13
2672    :-  %14
2673    ^-  spore-14
2674    %=    old
2675        blocked
2676      ^-  (map term (qeu blocked-move))
2677      %-  ~(run by blocked.old)
2678      |=  q=(qeu blocked-move-13)
2679      %-  ~(gas to *(qeu blocked-move))
2680      %+  turn  ~(tap to q)
2681      |=  blocked=blocked-move-13
2682      ^-  blocked-move
2683      %=  blocked
2684        attributing.routes  [ship=attributing.routes.blocked path=/]
2685      ==
2686    ==
2687  ::  added nacked-leaves timer
2688  ::
2689  ++  spore-14-to-15
2690    |=  old=spore-14
2691    :-  %15
2692    ^-  spore-15
2693  old(bug [bug.old ~])
2694  ::  convert to versioned sky
2695  ::
2696  ++  spore-15-to-16
2697    |=  old=spore-15
2698    ^-  spore-16
2699    :-  %16
2700    %=    old
2701        eggs
2702      %-  ~(urn by eggs.old)
2703      |=  [=term e=egg-15]
2704      ^-  egg
2705      ?:  ?=(%nuke -.e)  [%nuke ~ ~]
2706      %=    e
2707        ken  [ken.e ~ ~]
2708      ::
2709        sky
2710      =|  =farm
2711      =/  ski  ~(tap by sky.e)
2712      |-  ^+  farm
2713      ?~  ski
2714        farm
2715      =/  [=spur p=plot]  i.ski
2716      =;  new
2717        ?~  nex=(~(put-grow of-farm farm) spur new)
2718          ~&  %weird
2719          !!  :: shouldn't continue else loss of ref integrity
2720          :: $(ski t.ski)
2721        $(farm u.nex, ski t.ski)
2722      :-  ~
2723      =/  m  ~(val by fan.p)
2724      %+  gas:on-path  *_fan.p
```

```
2725          %+  turn
2726            ^-  (list @)
2727            =/  wit  ~(wyt by fan.p)
2728            ?:  =(0 wit)  ~
2729            (gulf 1 wit)
2730          |=  a=@ud
2731          [a (snag (dec a) m)]
2732        ==
2733      ==
2734    --
2735  ::  +scry: standard scry
2736  ::
2737  ++  scry
2738    ~/  %gall-scry
2739    ^-  roon
2740    |=  [lyc=gang pov=path care=term bem=beam]
2741    ^-  (unit (unit cage))
2742    =*  ship  p.bem
2743    =*  dap  q.bem
2744    =/  =coin  $/r.bem
2745    =*  path  s.bem
2746    ::
2747    ?:  ?&  ?=(%da -.r.bem)
2748            (gth p.r.bem now)
2749        ==
2750      ~
2751    ::
2752    ?.  ?=([%$ *] path)  ::  [%$ *] is for the vane, all else is for the agent
2753      ?.  ?&  =(our ship)
2754              =([%$ %da now] coin)
2755              =([~ ~] lyc)
2756          ==                      ~
2757      ?.  (~(has by yokes.state) dap)  [~ ~]
2758      ?.  ?=(^ path)                    ~
2759      =/  =routes  [~ ship pov]
2760      (mo-peek:mo & dap routes care path)
2761    ::
2762    =>  .(path t.path)
2763    ::
2764    ?:  ?&  =(%u care)
2765            =(~ path)
2766            =([%$ %da now] coin)
2767            =(our ship)
2768            =([~ ~] lyc)
2769        ==
2770      =;  hav=?
2771        [~ ~ noun+!>(hav)]
2772      =/  yok=(unit yoke)  (~(get by yokes.state) dap)
2773      &(?=([~ %live *] yok) -.agent.u.yok)
2774    ::
2775    ?:  ?&  =(%d care)
2776            =(~ path)
2777            =([%$ %da now] coin)
2778            =(our ship)
2779            =([~ ~] lyc)
2780        ==
2781      =/  yok=(unit yoke)  (~(get by yokes.state) dap)
2782      ?.  ?=([~ %live *] yok)
```

```
2783        [~ ~]
2784      [~ ~ desk+!>(q.beak.u.yok)]
2785    ::
2786    ?:  ?&  =(%e care)
2787            =(~ path)
2788            =([%$ %da now] coin)
2789            =(our ship)
2790            =([~ ~] lyc)
2791        ==
2792      :+  ~   ~
2793      :-  %apps  !>  ^-  (set [=dude live=?])
2794      =*  syd=desk   dap
2795      %+  roll  ~(tap by yokes.state)
2796      |=  [[=dude =yoke] acc=(set [=dude live=?])]
2797      ?.  ?&  ?=(%live -.yoke)
2798              =(syd q.beak.yoke)
2799          ==
2800        acc
2801      (~(put in acc) [dude -.agent.yoke])
2802    ::
2803    ?:  ?&  =(%f care)
2804            =(~ path)
2805            =([%$ %da now] coin)
2806            =(our ship)
2807            =([~ ~] lyc)
2808        ==
2809      :+  ~   ~
2810      :-  %nonces  !>  ^-  (map dude @)
2811      %-  malt  %+  murn  ~(tap by yokes.state)
2812      |=  [=dude =yoke]
2813      ?:  ?=(%nuke -.yoke)  ~  `[dude sub-nonce.yoke]
2814    ::
2815    ?:  ?&  =(%n care)
2816            ?=([@ @ ^] path)
2817            =([%$ %da now] coin)
2818            =(our ship)
2819            =([~ ~] lyc)
2820        ==
2821      =/  yok  (~(get by yokes.state) dap)
2822      ?.  ?=([~ %live *] yok)
2823        [~ ~]
2824      =/  [=^ship =term =wire]
2825        [(slav %p i.path) i.t.path t.t.path]
2826      ?~  nonce=(~(get by boar.u.yok) [wire ship term])
2827        [~ ~]
2828      [~ ~ atom+!>(u.nonce)]
2829    ::
2830    ?:  ?&  =(%v care)
2831            =([%$ %da now] coin)
2832            =(our ship)
2833            =([~ ~] lyc)
2834        ==
2835      =/  yok  (~(get by yokes.state) dap)
2836      ?.  ?=([~ %live *] yok)
2837        [~ ~]
2838      =/  =egg
2839        %=    u.yok
2840            code    ~
```

```
        agent
    :-  %|
    ?:  ?=(%| -.agent.u.yok)
      p.agent.u.yok
    on-save:p.agent.u.yok
  ==
  ``noun+!>(`egg-any`[-:*spore-16 egg])
::
?:  ?&  =(%w care)
        =([%$ %da now] coin)
        =(our ship)
        ?=([%'1' *] path)
    ==
  =>  .(path t.path)
  =/  yok  (~(get by yokes.state) q.bem)
  ?.  ?=([~ %live *] yok)              [~ ~]
  ?~  ski=(~(get of-farm sky.u.yok) path)  [~ ~]
  ?~  las=(ram:on-path fan.u.ski)      [~ ~]
  ?.  (mo-authorized:mo lyc sky.u.yok q.bem path)
    ~
  ``case/!>(ud/key.u.las)
::
=?  path  =(/whey path)  /1/whey
?:  &(?=(%x care) ?=([%'1' *] path))
  =>  .(path t.path)
  ?.  =(p.bem our)  ~
  ::
  ?:  ?=(%$ q.bem)  :: app %$ reserved
    ?+    path  ~
        [%whey ~]
      ?.  ?=([~ ~] lyc)  ~
      =/  blocked
        =/  queued  (~(run by blocked.state) |=((qeu blocked-move) [%.y +<]))
        (sort ~(tap by queued) aor)
      ::
      =/  running
        %+  turn  (sort ~(tap by yokes.state) aor)
        |=  [dap=term =yoke]
        ^-  mass
        =/  met=(list mass)
          =/  dat  (mo-peek:mo | dap [~ ship pov] %x /whey/mass)
          ?:  ?=(?(~ [~ ~]) dat)  ~
          (fall ((soft (list mass)) q.q.u.u.dat) ~)
        ?~  met
          dap^&+yoke
        dap^|+(welp met dot+&+yoke ~)
      ::
      =/  maz=(list mass)
        :~  [%foreign %.y contacts.state]
            [%blocked %.n blocked]
            [%active %.n running]
        ==
      ``mass+!>(maz)
    ==
  ::
  ?~  yok=(~(get by yokes.state) q.bem)  ~
  ?:  ?=(%nuke -.u.yok)  ~
  ?~  ski=(~(get of-farm sky.u.yok) path)
```

```
2899          ~
2900      ?.  (mo-authorized:mo lyc sky.u.yok q.bem path)
2901          ~
2902      =/  res=(unit (each page @uvI))
2903        ?+    -.r.bem  ~
2904          %ud  (bind (get:on-path fan.u.ski p.r.bem) tail)
2905          %da
2906        %-  head
2907        %^    (dip:on-path (unit (each page @uvI)))
2908            fan.u.ski
2909            ~
2910        |=  [res=(unit (each page @uvI)) @ud =@da val=(each page @uvI)]
2911        ^-  [new=(unit [@da _val]) stop=? res=(unit _val)]
2912        :-  `[da val]
2913        ?:((lte da p.r.bem) |/`val &/res)
2914        ==
2915      ?.  ?=([~ %& *] res)  ~
2916      ``p.u.res(q !>(q.p.u.res))
2917  ::
2918  ?:  ?&  =(%t care)
2919          =([%$ %da now] coin)
2920          =(our ship)
2921          ?=([%'1' *] path)
2922        ==
2923      =>  .(path t.path)
2924      =/  yok  (~(get by yokes.state) q.bem)
2925      ?.  ?=([~ %live *] yok)  ~
2926      =/  keys=(list coop)  (~(key-coops of-farm sky.u.yok) path)
2927      =/  authorized=?
2928        ?:  =([~ ~] lyc)  %.y
2929        |-
2930        ?~  keys  %.y
2931        ?<  ?=(~ lyc)
2932        ?.  (mo-authorized-coop:mo u.lyc sky.u.yok q.bem path i.keys)
2933          %.n
2934        $(keys t.keys)
2935      ?.  authorized  ~
2936      :^  ~  ~  %file-list  !>  ^-  (list ^path)
2937      %+  skim  (turn ~(tap-plot of-farm sky.u.yok) head)
2938      |=  =spur
2939      ?&  =(path (scag (lent path) spur))
2940          !=(path spur)
2941        ==
2942  ::
2943  ?:  ?&  =(%z care)
2944          =(our ship)
2945          ?=([%'1' *] path)
2946        ==
2947      =>  .(path t.path)
2948      =/  yok  (~(get by yokes.state) q.bem)
2949      ?.  ?=([~ %live *] yok)             ~
2950      ?~  ski=(~(get of-farm sky.u.yok) path)  ~
2951      ?.  (mo-authorized:mo lyc sky.u.yok q.bem path)
2952          ~
2953      =/  res=(unit (pair @da (each noun @uvI)))
2954        ?+  -.r.bem  ~
2955          %ud  (get:on-path fan.u.ski p.r.bem)
2956          %da  ?.(=(p.r.bem now) ~ (bind (ram:on-path fan.u.ski) tail))
```

```
2957          ==
2958      ?+  res   ~
2959        [~ @ %| *]   ``noun/!>(p.q.u.res)
2960        [~ @ %& *]   ``noun/!>(`@uvI`(shax (jam p.q.u.res)))
2961      ==
2962    ~
2963  ::  +stay: save without cache; suspend non-%base agents
2964  ::
2965  ::    TODO: superfluous? see +molt
2966  ::
2967  ++  stay
2968    ^-  spore-16
2969    =;  eggs=(map term egg)  state(yokes eggs)
2970    %-  ~(run by yokes.state)
2971    |=  =yoke
2972    ^-  egg
2973    ?:  ?=(%nuke -.yoke)  yoke
2974    %=  yoke
2975        code  ~
2976        agent
2977      :-  %|
2978      ?:  ?=(%| -.agent.yoke)
2979        p.agent.yoke
2980      on-save:p.agent.yoke
2981    ==
2982  ::  +take: response
2983  ::
2984  ++  take
2985    ~/  %gall-take
2986    |=  [=wire =duct dud=(unit goof) syn=sign-arvo]
2987    ^-  [(list move) _gall-payload]
2988    ?^  dud
2989      ~&(%gall-take-dud ((slog tang.u.dud) [~ gall-payload]))
2990    ?:  =(/nowhere wire)
2991      [~ gall-payload]
2992    ?:  =(/clear-huck wire)
2993      =/  =gift  ?>(?=([%behn %heck %gall *] syn) +>+.syn)
2994      [[duct %give gift]~ gall-payload]
2995    =/  mo-core  (mo-abed:mo duct)
2996    ?:  ?=([%key *] wire)
2997      ~|  [%gall-take-key-failed wire]
2998      mo-abet:(mo-handle-key:mo-core t.wire syn)
2999    ::
3000    ?:  ?=([%nacked-leaves ~] wire)
3001      =;  core=_mo-core:mo
3002        ::  next time a %leave gets nacked, the state and timer will be set again.
3003        ::
3004        mo-abet:core(leaves.state ~)
3005      %-  ~(rep by outstanding.state)
3006      |=  [[[=^wire =^duct] stand=(qeu remote-request)] core=_mo-core:mo]
3007      ?:  =(~ stand)  core
3008      =^  rr  stand  ~(get to stand)
3009      ::  sanity check in the outstanding queue:
3010      ::  if there's a %leave that was nacked, there should be a %missing request
3011      ::  otherwise %leave is the only request in the queue, and we haven't heard
3012      ::  anc %ack or a %nack, so %ames is still trying to send it.
3013      ::
3014      ~?  >>>  ?&  ?=(%leave rr)
```

```
        =(^ stand)
        =^(rr stand ~(get to stand) !=(%missing rr))
      ==
  "extraneous request outstanding [{<wire>} {<duct>} {<stand>} {<rr>}]"
=?  core  ?&  ?=(%leave rr)
        =(^ stand)
        =^(rr stand ~(get to stand) &(=(%missing rr) =(~ stand)))
        ==
  =+  core=(mo-handle-nacked-leaves:(mo-abed:core duct) wire)
  ::  make sure that only the %leave remains in the queue
  ::
  %_    core
      outstanding.state
    %+  ~(put by outstanding.state)  [wire duct]
    (~(put to *(qeu remote-request)) %leave)
  ==
  core
::
~|  [%gall-take-failed wire]
?>  ?=([?(%sys %use) *] wire)
=<  mo-abet
%.  [t.wire ?:(?=([%behn %heck *] syn) syn.syn syn)]
?-  i.wire
  %sys  mo-handle-sys:mo-core
  %use  mo-handle-use:mo-core
==
--
```

Iris

```
1   !:
2   ::  http-client
3   ::
4   |=  our=ship
5   =,  iris
6   ::
7   ::
8   ::  internal data structures
9   ::
10  =>  =~
11  ::
12  ::  internal data structures that won't go in zuse
13  ::
14  |%
15  +$  move
16    ::
17    $:  ::  duct: request identifier
18        ::
19        =duct
20        ::
21        ::
22        card=(wind note gift)
23    ==
24  ::  +note: private request from light to another vane
25  ::
26  +$  note
27    $%  ::  %d: to dill
28        ::
29        $:  %d
30            ::
31            ::
32        $%  [%flog =flog:dill]
33    ==  ==  ==
34  --
35  ::  more structures
36  ::
37  |%
38  +$  axle
39    $:  ::  date: date at which light's state was updated to this data structure
40        ::
41        date=%~2019.2.8
42        ::
43        ::
44        =state
45    ==
46  ::  +state:client: state relating to open outbound HTTP connections
47  ::
48  +$  state
49    $:  ::  next-id: monotonically increasing id number for the next connection
50        ::
51        next-id=@ud
52        ::  connection-by-id: open connections to the
53        ::
54        connection-by-id=(map @ud [=duct =in-progress-http-request])
55        ::  connection-by-duct: used for cancellation
56        ::
```

```
57          connection-by-duct=(map duct @ud)
58          ::  outbound-duct: the duct to send outbound requests on
59          ::
60          outbound-duct=duct
61      ==
62  ::  +in-progress-http-request: state around an outbound http
63  ::
64  +$  in-progress-http-request
65    $:  ::  remaining-redirects: http limit of number of redirects before error
66        ::
67        remaining-redirects=@ud
68        ::  remaining-retries: number of times to retry the request
69        ::
70        remaining-retries=@ud
71        ::  response-header: the response headers from the %start packet
72        ::
73        ::      We send the response headers with each %http-progress, so we must
74        ::      save them.
75        ::
76        response-header=(unit response-header:http)
77        ::  chunks: a list of partial results returned from unix
78        ::
79        ::      This list of octs must be flopped before it is composed as the
80        ::      final response, as we want to be able to quickly insert.
81        ::
82        chunks=(list octs)
83        ::  bytes-read: the sum of the size of the :chunks
84        ::
85        bytes-read=@ud
86        ::  expected-size: the expected content-length of the http request
87        ::
88        expected-size=(unit @ud)
89      ==
90  --
91  ::
92  |%
93  ::  +combine-octs: combine multiple octs into one
94  ::
95  ++  combine-octs
96    |=  a=(list octs)
97    ^-  octs
98    :-  %+  roll  a
99        |=  [=octs sum=@ud]
100       (add sum p.octs)
101   (can 3 a)
102 ::  +per-client-event: per-event client core
103 ::
104 ++  per-client-event
105   |=  [[eny=@ =duct now=@da rof=roof] =state]
106   |%
107   ::  +request: makes an external web request
108   ::
109   ++  request
110     |=  [=request:http =outbound-config]
111     ^-  [(list move) ^state]
112     ::  if there's already a request on this duct, abort
113     ::
114     ?:  (~(has by connection-by-duct.state) duct)
```

```
115      ~&  %cant-send-second-http-client-request-on-same-duct
116      [~ state]
117  ::  get the next id for this request
118  ::
119  =^  id  next-id.state  [next-id.state +(next-id.state)]
120  ::  add a new open session
121  ::
122  =.  connection-by-id.state
123    %+  ~(put by connection-by-id.state)  id
124    =,  outbound-config
125    [duct [redirects retries ~ ~ 0 ~]]
126  ::  keep track of the duct for cancellation
127  ::
128  =.  connection-by-duct.state
129    (~(put by connection-by-duct.state) duct id)
130  ::  start the download
131  ::
132  ::  the original eyre keeps track of the duct on %born and then sends a
133  ::  %give on that duct. this seems like a weird inversion of
134  ::  responsibility, where we should instead be doing a pass to unix. the
135  ::  reason we need to manually build ids is because we aren't using the
136  ::  built in duct system.
137  ::
138  ::  email discussions make it sound like fixing that might be hard, so
139  ::  maybe i should just live with the way it is now?
140  ::
141  :-  [outbound-duct.state %give %request id request]~
142  state
143  ::  +cancel: client cancels an outstanding request
144  ::
145  ++  cancel
146    ^-  [(list move) ^state]
147    ::
148    ?~  cancel-id=(~(get by connection-by-duct.state) duct)
149      ~&  %iris-invalid-cancel
150      [~ state]
151    ::
152    :-  [outbound-duct.state %give %cancel-request u.cancel-id]~
153    (cleanup-connection u.cancel-id)
154  ::  +receive: receives a response to an http-request we made
155  ::
156  ::    TODO: Right now, we are not following redirect and not handling retries
157  ::    correctly. We need to do this.
158  ::
159  ++  receive
160    |=  [id=@ud =http-event:http]
161    ^-  [(list move) ^state]
162    ::  ensure that this is a valid receive
163    ::
164    ?~  connection=(~(get by connection-by-id.state) id)
165      ~&  [%eyre-unknown-receive id]
166      [~ state]
167    ::
168    ?-    -.http-event
169        %start
170      ::  TODO: Handle redirects and retries here, before we start dispatching
171      ::  back to the application.
172      ::
```

```
173          ::   record data from the http response that only comes from %start
174          ::
175          =.  connection-by-id.state
176            %+  ~(jab by connection-by-id.state)  id
177            |=  [duct=^duct =in-progress-http-request]
178            ::
179            =.  expected-size.in-progress-http-request
180              ?~  str=(get-header:http 'content-length' headers.response-header.http-event)
181                ~
182              ::
183              (rush u.str dum:ag)
184            ::
185            =.  response-header.in-progress-http-request
186              `response-header:http-event
187            ::
188            [duct in-progress-http-request]
189          ::
190        ?:  complete.http-event
191          (send-finished id data.http-event)
192        ::
193        (record-and-send-progress id data.http-event)
194      ::
195          %continue
196        ?:  complete.http-event
197          (send-finished id data.http-event)
198        ::
199        (record-and-send-progress id data.http-event)
200      ::
201          %cancel
202        ::  we have received a cancel from outside; pass it on to our requester
203        ::
204        :_  (cleanup-connection id)
205        ^-  (list move)
206        :_  ~
207        :*  duct.u.connection
208          %give
209          %http-response
210          %cancel
211          ~
212        ==
213    ==
214  ::  +record-and-send-progress: save incoming data and send progress report
215  ::
216  ++  record-and-send-progress
217    |=  [id=@ud data=(unit octs)]
218    ^-  [(list move) ^state]
219    ::
220    =.  connection-by-id.state
221      %+  ~(jab by connection-by-id.state)  id
222      |=  [duct=^duct =in-progress-http-request]
223      ::  record the data chunk and size, if it exists
224      ::
225      =?    chunks.in-progress-http-request
226          ?=(^ data)
227        [u.data chunks.in-progress-http-request]
228      =?    bytes-read.in-progress-http-request
229          ?=(^ data)
230        (add bytes-read.in-progress-http-request p.u.data)
```

```hoon
    ::
    [duct in-progress-http-request]
  ::
  =/  connection  (~(got by connection-by-id.state) id)
  :_  state
  ^-  (list move)
  :_  ~
  :*  duct.connection
      %give
      %http-response
      %progress
      (need response-header.in-progress-http-request.connection)
      bytes-read.in-progress-http-request.connection
      expected-size.in-progress-http-request.connection
      data
  ==
::  +send-finished: sends the %finished, cleans up the session state
::
++  send-finished
  |=  [id=@ud data=(unit octs)]
  ^-  [(list move) ^state]
  ::
  =/  connection  (~(got by connection-by-id.state) id)
  ::  reassemble the octs that we've received into their final form
  ::
  =/  data=octs
    %-  combine-octs
    %-  flop
    ::
    ?~  data
      chunks.in-progress-http-request.connection
    [u.data chunks.in-progress-http-request.connection]
  ::
  =/  response-header=response-header:http
    (need response-header.in-progress-http-request.connection)
  ::
  =/  mime=@t
    ?~  mime-type=(get-header:http 'content-type' headers.response-header)
      'application/octet-stream'
    u.mime-type
  ::
  :_  (cleanup-connection id)
  :~  :*  duct.connection
          %give
          %http-response
          %finished
          response-header
          ?:(=(0 p.data) ~ `[mime data])
  ==  ==
::
++  cleanup-connection
  |=  id=@ud
  ^-  ^state
  ?~  con=(~(get by connection-by-id.state) id)
    state
  %_    state
      connection-by-id    (~(del by connection-by-id.state) id)
      connection-by-duct  (~(del by connection-by-duct.state) duct.u.con)
```

```
289      ==
290    --
291  --
292  ::  end the =~
293  ::
294  .  ==
295  ::  begin with a default +axle as a blank slate
296  ::
297  =|  ax=axle
298  ::  a vane is activated with current date, entropy, and a namespace function
299  ::
300  |=  [now=@da eny=@uvJ rof=roof]
301  ::  allow jets to be registered within this core
302  ::
303  ~%  %http-client  ..part  ~
304  |%
305  ++  call
306    |=  [=duct dud=(unit goof) wrapped-task=(hobo task)]
307    ^-  [(list move) _light-gate]
308    ::
309    =/  task=task  ((harden task) wrapped-task)
310    ::
311    ::  XX handle error notifications
312    ::
313    ?^  dud
314      =/  moves=(list move)
315        [[duct %slip %d %flog %crud [-.task tang.u.dud]] ~]
316      [moves light-gate]
317    ::  %trim: in response to memory pressure
318    ::
319    ?:  ?=(%trim -.task)
320      [~ light-gate]
321    ::  %vega: notifies us of a completed kernel upgrade
322    ::
323    ?:  ?=(%vega -.task)
324      [~ light-gate]
325    ::
326    =/  event-args  [[eny duct now rof] state.ax]
327    =/  client  (per-client-event event-args)
328    ?-    -.task
329    ::
330        %born
331      ::  create a cancel for each outstanding connection
332      ::
333      ::    TODO: We should gracefully retry on restart instead of just sending a
334      ::    cancel.
335      ::    TODO  we might not want to do that though!
336      ::
337      =/  moves=(list move)
338        %+  turn  ~(tap by connection-by-duct.state.ax)
339        |=  [=^duct @ud]
340        ^-  move
341        [duct %give %http-response %cancel ~]
342      ::  reset all connection state on born
343      ::
344      =:  next-id.state.ax             0
345          connection-by-id.state.ax    ~
346          connection-by-duct.state.ax  ~
```

```
347          outbound-duct.state.ax         duct
348      ==
349      ::
350      [moves light-gate]
351    ::
352        %request
353      =^  moves  state.ax  (request:client +.task)
354      [moves light-gate]
355    ::
356        %cancel-request
357      =^  moves  state.ax  cancel:client
358      [moves light-gate]
359    ::
360        %receive
361      =^  moves  state.ax  (receive:client +.task)
362      [moves light-gate]
363    ==
364  ::  http-client issues no requests to other vanes
365  ::
366  ++  take
367    |=  [=wire =duct dud=(unit goof) sign=*]
368    ^-  [(list move) _light-gate]
369    ?<  ?=(^ dud)
370    !!
371  ::
372  ++  light-gate  ..$
373  ::  +load: migrate old state to new state (called on vane reload)
374  ::
375  ++  load
376    |=  old=axle
377    ^+  ..^$
378    ::
379    ~!  %loading
380    ..^$(ax old)
381  ::  +stay: produce current state
382  ::
383  ++  stay  `axle`ax
384  ::  +scry: request a path in the urbit namespace
385  ::
386  ++  scry
387    ^-  roon
388    |=  [lyc=gang pov=path car=term bem=beam]
389    ^-  (unit (unit cage))
390    =*  ren  car
391    =*  why=shop  &/p.bem
392    =*  syd  q.bem
393    =*  lot=coin  $/r.bem
394    =*  tyl  s.bem
395    ::
396    ?.  ?=(%& -.why)  ~
397    =*  his  p.why
398    ?:  &(?=(%x ren) =(tyl //whey) =([~ ~] lyc))
399      =/  maz=(list mass)
400        :~  nex+&+next-id.state.ax
401            outbound+&+outbound-duct.state.ax
402            by-id+&+connection-by-id.state.ax
403            by-duct+&+connection-by-duct.state.ax
404            axle+&+ax
```

```
405      ==
406    ``mass+!>(maz)
407  [~ ~]
408  --
```

Jael

```
1   !:                                              ::  /vane/jael
2   ::                                              ::  %reference/0
3   !?  150
4   ::
5   ::
6   ::  %jael: secrets and promises.
7   ::
8   ::  todo:
9   ::
10  ::    - communication with other vanes:
11  ::      - actually use %behn for expiring secrets
12  ::      - report %ames propagation errors to user
13  ::
14  ::    - nice features:
15  ::      - scry namespace
16  ::      - task for converting invites to tickets
17  ::
18  |=  our=ship
19  =,  pki:jael
20  =,  jael
21  =,  crypto
22  =,  jael
23  =,  ethereum-types
24  =,  azimuth-types
25  =,  point=point:jael
26  ::                                              ::::
27  ::::                    # models                ::  data structures
28    ::                                            ::::
29  ::  the %jael state comes in two parts: absolute
30  ::  and relative.
31  ::
32  ::  ++state-relative is subjective, denormalized and
33  ::  derived.  it consists of all the state we need to
34  ::  manage subscriptions efficiently.
35  ::
36  =>  |%
37  +$  state-2
38    $:  %2
39        pki=state-pki-2                           ::
40        etn=state-eth-node                        ::  eth connection state
41    ==                                            ::
42  +$  state-pki-2                                 ::  urbit metadata
43    $:  $=  own                                   ::  vault (vein)
44        $:  yen=(set duct)                        ::  trackers
45            sig=(unit oath)                       ::  for a moon
46            tuf=(list turf)                       ::  domains
47            fak=_|                                ::  fake keys
48            lyf=life                              ::  version
49            step=@ud                              ::  login code step
50            jaw=(map life ring)                   ::  private keys
51        ==                                        ::
52        $=  zim                                   ::  public
53        $:  yen=(jug duct ship)                   ::  trackers
54            ney=(jug ship duct)                   ::  reverse trackers
55            nel=(set duct)                        ::  trackers of all
56            dns=dnses                             ::  on-chain dns state
```

```
          pos=(map ship point)              ::    on-chain ship state
        ==                                  ::
  ==                                        ::
+$  message-all
  $%  [%0 message]
  ==
+$  message                                 ::    message to her jael
  $%  [%nuke whos=(set ship)]               ::    cancel trackers
      [%public-keys whos=(set ship)]        ::    view ethereum events
  ==                                        ::
+$  message-result
  $%  [%public-keys-result =public-keys-result]   ::    public keys boon
  ==
+$  card                                    ::    i/o action
  (wind note gift)                          ::
::                                          ::
+$  move                                    ::    output
  [p=duct q=card]                           ::
::                                          ::
+$  note                                    ::    out request $->
  $~  [%a %plea *ship *plea:ames]           ::
  $%  $:  %a                                ::      to %ames
          $>(%plea task:ames)               ::    send request message
      ==                                    ::
      $:  %b                                ::      to %behn
          $>(%wait task:behn)               ::    set timer
      ==                                    ::
      $:  %e                                ::      to %eyre
          [%code-changed ~]                 ::    notify code changed
      ==                                    ::
      $:  %g                                ::      to %gall
          $>(%deal task:gall)               ::    talk to app
      ==                                    ::
      $:  %j                                ::      to self
          $>(%listen task)                  ::    set ethereum source
      ==                                    ::
      $:  @tas                              ::
  $%  $>(%init vane-task)                   ::    report install
  ==  ==  ==                                ::
::                                          ::
+$  sign                                    ::    in result $<-
  $~  [%behn %wake ~]                       ::
  $%  $:  %ames                             ::
          $%  $>(%boon gift:ames)           ::    message response
              $>(%done gift:ames)           ::    message (n)ack
              $>(%lost gift:ames)           ::    lost boon
      ==  ==                                ::
      $:  %behn                             ::
          $>(%wake gift:behn)               ::
      ==                                    ::
      $:  %gall                             ::
          $>(%unto gift:gall)               ::
      ==                                    ::
  ==                                        ::
--  ::                                      ::
::                                          ::::
::::                          # light       ::    light cores
  ::                                        ::::
```

```
115  =>  |%
116  ::                                                    ::  ++ez
117  ::::                        ## ethereum^light          ::  wallet algebra
118   ::                                                    ::::
119  ++  ez
120   ::  simple ethereum-related utility arms.
121   ::
122   |%
123   ::
124   ::  +order-events: sort changes by block and log numbers
125   ::
126   ++  order-events
127    |=  loz=(list (pair event-id diff-azimuth))
128    ^+  loz
129    %+  sort  loz
130    ::  sort by block number, then by event log number,
131    ::TODO  then by diff priority.
132    |=  [[[b1=@ud l1=@ud] *] [[b2=@ud l2=@ud] *]]
133    ?.  =(b1 b2)  (lth b1 b2)
134    ?.  =(l1 l2)  (lth l1 l2)
135    &
136   --
137  --
138  ::                                                    ::::
139  ::::                        #  heavy                   ::  heavy engines
140   ::                                                    ::::
141  =>
142  ~%  %jael  ..part  ~
143  |%
144  ::                                                    ::  ++of
145  ::::                        ## main^heavy              ::  main engine
146   ::                                                    ::::
147  ++  of
148   ::  this core handles all top-level %jael semantics,
149   ::  changing state and recording moves.
150   ::
151   ::  logically we could nest the ++su core within it, but
152   ::  we keep them separated for clarity.  the ++curd and
153   ::  ++cure arms complete relative and absolute effects,
154   ::  respectively, at the top level.
155   ::
156   ::  XX doc
157   ::
158   ::  a general pattern here is that we use the ++et core
159   ::  to generate absolute effects (++change), then invoke
160   ::  ++su to calculate the derived effect of these changes.
161   ::
162   ::  for ethereum-related events, this is preceded by
163   ::  invocation of ++et, which produces ethereum-level
164   ::  changes (++chain). these get turned into absolute
165   ::  effects by ++cute.
166   ::
167   ::  arvo issues: should be merged with the top-level
168   ::  vane interface when that gets cleaned up a bit.
169   ::
170  =|  moz=(list move)
171  =|  $:  $:  ::  now: current time
172              ::  eny: unique entropy
```

```
            ::
            now=@da
            eny=@uvJ
        ==
      ::    all vane state
      ::
        state-2
  ==
:: lex: all durable state
:: moz: pending actions
::
=*  lex  ->
|%
::                                        ::  ++abet:of
++  abet                                  ::  resolve
  [(flop moz) lex]
::                                        ::  ++sein:of
++  emit
  |=  =move
  +>.$(moz [move moz])
::
++  poke-watch
  |=  [hen=duct app=term =purl:eyre]
  %-  emit
  :*  hen
      %pass
      /[app]/poke
      %g
      %deal
      [our our /jael]
      app
      %poke
      %azimuth-poke
      !>([%watch (crip (en-purl:html purl)) %default])
  ==
::
++  sein                                  ::  sponsor
  |=  who=ship
  ^-  ship
  ::  XX save %dawn sponsor in .own.sub, check there
  ::
  =/  pot  (~(get by pos.zim.pki) who)
  ?:  ?&  ?=(^ pot)
          ?=(^ sponsor.u.pot)
      ==
    u.sponsor.u.pot
  (^sein:title who)
::                                        ::  ++saxo:of
++  saxo                                  ::  sponsorship chain
  |=  who=ship
  ^-  (list ship)
  =/  dad  (sein who)
  [who ?:(=(who dad) ~ $(who dad))]
::                                        ::  ++call:of
++  call                                  ::  invoke
  |=  $:  ::  hen: event cause
          ::  tac: event data
          ::
```

```hoon
              hen=duct
              tac=task
        ==
^+  +>
?-    -.tac
::
:: boot from keys
    $:  %dawn
        =seed
        spon=ship
        czar=(map ship [=rift =life =pass])
        turf=(list turf)
        bloq=@ud
        node=purl
    ==
::
    %dawn
  ::  single-homed
  ::
  ~|  [our who.seed.tac]
  ?>  =(our who.seed.tac)
  ::  save our parent signature (only for moons)
  ::
  =.  sig.own.pki  sig.seed.tac
  ::  load our initial public key
  ::
  =/  spon-ship=(unit ship)
    =/  flopped-spon  (flop spon.tac)
    ?~(flopped-spon ~ `ship.i.flopped-spon)
  =.  pos.zim.pki
    =/  cub  (nol:nu:crub:crypto key.seed.tac)
    %+  ~(put by pos.zim.pki)
      our
    [0 lyf.seed.tac (my [lyf.seed.tac [1 pub:ex:cub]] ~) spon-ship]
  ::  our initial private key
  ::
  =.  lyf.own.pki  lyf.seed.tac
  =.  jaw.own.pki  (my [lyf.seed.tac key.seed.tac] ~)
  ::  XX save sponsor in .own.pki
  ::  XX reconcile with .dns.eth
  ::  set initial domains
  ::
  =.  tuf.own.pki  turf.tac
  ::  our initial galaxy table as a +map from +life to +public
  ::
  =/  spon-points=(list [ship point])
    %+  turn  spon.tac
    |=  [=ship az-point=point:azimuth-types]
    ~|  [%sponsor-point az-point]
    ?>  ?=(^ net.az-point)
    :*  ship
        continuity-number.u.net.az-point
        life.u.net.az-point
        (malt [life.u.net.az-point 1 pass.u.net.az-point] ~)
        ?.  has.sponsor.u.net.az-point
          ~
        `who.sponsor.u.net.az-point
    ==
```

```
=/  points=(map =ship =point)
  %-  ~(run by czar.tac)
  |=  [=a=rift =a=life =a=pass]
  ^-  point
  [a-rift a-life (malt [a-life 1 a-pass] ~) ~]
=.  points
  (~(gas by points) spon-points)
=.  +>.$
  %-  curd  =<  abet
  (public-keys:~(feel su hen now pki etn) pos.zim.pki %full points)
::
:: start subscriptions
::
=.  +>.$
  %^  poke-watch  hen  %azimuth
  %+  fall  node.tac
  (need (de-purl:html 'http://eth-mainnet.urbit.org:8545'))
::
=.  moz
  %+  weld  moz
  :: order is crucial!
  ::
  ::   %dill must init after %gall
  ::   the %give init (for unix) must be after %dill init
  ::   %jael init must be deferred (makes http requests)
  ::
  ^-  (list move)
  :~  [hen %slip %e %init ~]
      [hen %slip %d %init ~]
      [hen %slip %g %init ~]
      [hen %slip %c %init ~]
      [hen %slip %a %init ~]
  ==
  +>.$
::
:: boot fake
::   [%fake =ship]
::
    %fake
  :: single-homed
  ::
  ?>  =(our ship.tac)
  :: fake keys are deterministically derived from the ship
  ::
  =/  cub  (pit:nu:crub:crypto 512 our)
  :: our initial public key
  ::
  =.  pos.zim.pki
    %+  ~(put by pos.zim.pki)
      our
    [rift=0 life=1 (my [`@ud`1 [`life`1 pub:ex:cub]] ~) `(^sein:title our)]
  :: our private key
  ::
  ::   Private key updates are disallowed for fake ships,
  ::   so we do this first.
  ::
  =.  lyf.own.pki  1
  =.  jaw.own.pki  (my [1 sec:ex:cub] ~)
```

```
347          ::   set the fake bit
348          ::
349          =.  fak.own.pki  &
350          ::   initialize other vanes per the usual procedure
351          ::
352          ::     Except for ourselves!
353          ::
354          =.  moz
355            %+  weld  moz
356            ^-  (list move)
357            :~  [hen %slip %e %init ~]
358                [hen %slip %d %init ~]
359                [hen %slip %g %init ~]
360                [hen %slip %c %init ~]
361                [hen %slip %a %init ~]
362            ==
363          +>.$
364        ::
365        ::   set ethereum source
366        ::     [%listen whos=(set ship) =source]
367        ::
368            %listen
369        ::  %-  (slog leaf+"jael: listen {<whos.tac>} {<source.tac>}" ~)
370          %-  curd  =<  abet
371          (sources:~(feel su hen now pki etn) [whos source]:tac)
372        ::
373        ::   cancel all trackers from duct
374        ::     [%nuke whos=(set ship)]
375        ::
376            %nuke
377          =/  ships=(list ship)
378            %~  tap  in
379            %-  ~(int in whos.tac)
380            (~(get ju yen.zim.pki) hen)
381          =.  ney.zim.pki
382            |-  ^-  (jug ship duct)
383            ?~  ships
384              ney.zim.pki
385            (~(del ju $(ships t.ships)) i.ships hen)
386          =.  yen.zim.pki
387            |-  ^-  (jug duct ship)
388            ?~  ships
389              yen.zim.pki
390            (~(del ju $(ships t.ships)) hen i.ships)
391          =?  nel.zim.pki  ?=(~ whos.tac)
392            (~(del in nel.zim.pki) hen)
393          ?^  whos.tac
394            +>.$
395          %_  +>.$
396            yen.own.pki  (~(del in yen.own.pki) hen)
397          ==
398        ::
399        :: update private keys
400        ::
401            %rekey
402          %-  curd  =<  abet
403          (private-keys:~(feel su hen now pki etn) life.tac ring.tac)
404        ::
```

```
    ::  resend private key to subscribers
    ::
        %resend
      %-  curd  =<  abet
      %-  ~(exec su hen now pki etn)
      [yen.own.pki [%give %private-keys [lyf jaw]:own.pki]]
    ::
    ::  register moon keys
    ::
        %moon
      ?.  =(%earl (clan:title ship.tac))
        ~&  [%not-moon ship.tac]
        +>.$
      ?.  =(our (^sein:title ship.tac))
        ~&  [%not-our-moon ship.tac]
        +>.$
      %-  curd  =<  abet
      (~(new-event su hen now pki etn) [ship udiff]~:tac)
    ::
    ::  rotate web login code
    ::
        %step
      %=  +>.$
        step.own.pki  +(step.own.pki)
        moz           [[hen %pass / %e %code-changed ~] moz]
      ==
    ::
    ::  watch public keys
    ::     [%public-keys ships=(set ship)]
    ::
        %public-keys
      %-  curd  =<  abet
      (~(public-keys ~(feed su hen now pki etn) hen) ships.tac)
    ::
    ::  seen after breach
    ::     [%meet our=ship who=ship]
    ::
        %meet
      +>.$
    ::
    ::  XX should be a subscription
    ::  XX reconcile with .dns.eth
    ::  request domains
    ::     [%turf ~]
    ::
        %turf
      ::  ships with real keys must have domains,
      ::  those with fake keys must not
      ::
      ~|  [fak.own.pki tuf.own.pki]
      ?<  =(fak.own.pki ?=(^ tuf.own.pki))
      +>.$(moz [[hen %give %turf tuf.own.pki] moz])
    ::
    ::  learn of kernel upgrade
    ::     [%vega ~]
    ::
        %vega
      +>.$
```

```
463      ::
464      ::  in response to memory pressure
465      ::    [%trim p=@ud]
466      ::
467        %trim
468      +>.$
469      ::
470      ::  watch private keys
471      ::    [%private-keys ~]
472      ::
473        %private-keys
474      (curd abet:~(private-keys ~(feed su hen now pki etn) hen))
475      ::
476      ::  authenticated remote request
477      ::    [%west p=ship q=path r=*]
478      ::
479        %plea
480      =*  her  ship.tac
481      =+  ;;(=message-all payload.plea.tac)
482      ?>  ?=(%0 -.message-all)
483      =/  =message  +.message-all
484      ?-    -.message
485      ::
486      ::  cancel trackers
487      ::    [%nuke whos=(set ship)]
488      ::
489        %nuke
490      =.  moz  [[hen %give %done ~] moz]
491      $(tac message)
492      ::
493      ::  view ethereum events
494      ::    [%public-keys whos=(set ship)]
495      ::
496        %public-keys
497      =.  moz  [[hen %give %done ~] moz]
498      $(tac message)
499      ==
500    ::
501    ::  pretend ships breached
502    ::    [%ruin ships=(set ship)]
503    ::
504      %ruin
505    ::NOTE  we blast this out to _all_ known ducts, because the common
506    ::        use case for this is comets, about who nobody cares.
507    =/  dus  (~(uni in nel.zim.pki) ~(key by yen.zim.pki))
508    =/  sus  ~(. su hen now pki etn)
509    =/  sis  ~(tap in ships.tac)
510    |-
511    ?~  sis  (curd abet:sus)
512    =.  sus  (exec:sus dus %give %public-keys %breach i.sis)
513    $(sis t.sis)
514    ==
515  ::
516  ++  take
517  |=  [tea=wire hen=duct hin=sign]
518  ^+  +>
519  ?-  hin
520      [%ames %done *]
```

```
521      ?~   error.hin  +>.$
522      ~&  [%done-bad tag.u.error.hin]
523      %-  (slog tang.u.error.hin)
524      ::TODO  fail:et
525      +>.$
526    ::
527        [%ames %boon *]
528      =+  ;;  [%public-keys-result =public-keys-result]  payload.hin
529      %-  curd  =<  abet
530      (public-keys:~(feel su hen now pki etn) pos.zim.pki public-keys-result)
531    ::
532        [%ames %lost *]
533      ::  TODO: better error handling
534      ::
535      ~|  %jael-ames-lost
536      !!
537    ::
538        [%behn %wake *]
539      ?^  error.hin
540        %-  %+  slog
541            leaf+"jael unable to resubscribe, run :azimuth|listen"
542          u.error.hin
543        +>.$
544      ?>  ?=([%breach @ ~] tea)
545      =/  =source-id  (slav %ud i.t.tea)
546      =/  =source  (~(got by sources.etn) source-id)
547      =/  ships  (~(get ju ship-sources-reverse.etn) source-id)
548      %-  curd  =<  abet
549      (sources:~(feel su hen now pki etn) ships source)
550    ::
551        [%gall %unto *]
552      ?-    +>-.hin
553        %raw-fact  !!
554      ::
555        %kick
556      ?>  ?=([@ *] tea)
557      =*  app  i.tea
558      ::NOTE  we expect azimuth-tracker to be kill
559      ?:  =(%azimuth-tracker app)  +>.$
560      ~|([%jael-unexpected-quit tea hin] !!)
561      ::
562        %poke-ack
563      ?~  p.p.+>.hin
564        +>.$
565      %-  (slog leaf+"jael-bad-coup" u.p.p.+>.hin)
566      +>.$
567      ::
568        %watch-ack
569      ?~  p.p.+>.hin
570        +>.$
571      %-  (slog u.p.p.+>.hin)
572      ~|([%jael-unexpected-reap tea hin] +>.$)
573      ::
574        %fact
575      ?>  ?=([@ *] tea)
576      =*  app  i.tea
577      =+  ;;(=udiffs:point q.q.cage.p.+>.hin)
578      %-  curd  =<  abet
```

```hoon
579            (~(new-event su hen now pki etn) udiffs)
580        ==
581      ==
582    ::                                              ::  ++curd:of
583    ++  curd                                        ::  relative moves
584      |=  $:  moz=(list move)
585              pki=state-pki-2
586              etn=state-eth-node
587          ==
588      +>(pki pki, etn etn, moz (weld (flop moz) ^moz))
589    --
590  ::                                                ::  ++su
591  ::::                    ## relative^heavy         ::  subjective engine
592    ::                                              ::::
593  ++  su
594      ::  the ++su core handles all derived state,
595      ::  subscriptions, and actions.
596      ::
597      ::  ++feed:su registers subscriptions.
598      ::
599      ::  ++feel:su checks if a ++change should notify
600      ::  any subscribers.
601      ::
602    =|  moz=(list move)
603    =|  $:  hen=duct
604            now=@da
605            state-pki-2
606            state-eth-node
607        ==
608  ::  moz: moves in reverse order
609  ::  pki: relative urbit state
610  ::
611  =*  pki  ->+<
612  =*  etn  ->+>
613  |%
614  ++  this-su  .
615    ::                                              ::  ++abet:su
616  ++  abet                                          ::  resolve
617    [(flop moz) pki etn]
618    ::                                              ::  ++exec:su
619  ++  emit
620    |=  =move
621    +>.$(moz [move moz])
622    ::
623  ++  exec                                          ::  mass gift
624    |=  [yen=(set duct) cad=card]
625    =/  noy  ~(tap in yen)
626    |-  ^+  this-su
627    ?~  noy  this-su
628    $(noy t.noy, moz [[i.noy cad] moz])
629    ::
630  ++  emit-peer
631    |=  [app=term =path]
632    %-  emit
633    :*  hen
634        %pass
635        [app path]
636        %g
```

```hoon
        %deal
        [our our /jael]
        app
        %watch
        path
    ==
  ::
  ++  peer
    |=  [app=term whos=(set ship)]
    ?:  =(~ whos)
      (emit-peer app /)
    =/  whol=(list ship)  ~(tap in whos)
    |-  ^+  this-su
    ?~  whol  this-su
    =.  this-su  (emit-peer app /(scot %p i.whol))
    $(whol t.whol)
  ::
  ++  public-keys-give
    |=  [yen=(set duct) =public-keys-result]
    |^
    =/  yaz  %+  skid  ~(tap in yen)
      |=  d=duct
      &(?=([[%ames @ @ *] *] d) !=(%public-keys i.t.i.d))
    =/  yez  (weld p.yaz (sort q.yaz sorter))
    |-  ^+  this-su
    ?~  yez  this-su
    =*  d  i.yez
    =.  this-su
      ?.  &(?=([[%ames @ @ *] *] d) !=(%public-keys i.t.i.d))
        %-  emit
        [d %give %public-keys public-keys-result]
      %-  emit
      [d %give %boon %public-keys-result public-keys-result]
    $(yez t.yez)
    ::
    ::  We want to notify Ames, then Clay, then Gall.  This happens to
    ::  be alphabetical, but this is mostly a coincidence.
    ::
    ++  sorter
      |=  [a=duct b=duct]
      ?.  ?=([[@ *] *] a)
        |
      ?.  ?=([[@ *] *] b)
        &
      (lth (end 3 i.i.a) (end 3 i.i.b))
    --
  ::
  ++  get-source
    |=  who=@p
    ^-  source
    =/  ship-source  (~(get by ship-sources.etn) who)
    ?^  ship-source
      (~(got by sources) u.ship-source)
    ?:  =((clan:title who) %earl)
      [%& (^sein:title who)]
    (~(got by sources) default-source.etn)
  ::
  ++  get-source-id
```

```
695    |=  =source
696    ^-  [source-id _this-su]
697    =/  source-reverse  (~(get by sources-reverse) source)
698    ?^  source-reverse
699      [u.source-reverse this-su]
700    :-  top-source-id.etn
701    %_  this-su
702      top-source-id.etn      +(top-source-id.etn)
703      sources.etn            (~(put by sources) top-source-id.etn source)
704      sources-reverse.etn    (~(put by sources-reverse) source top-source-id.etn)
705    ==
706  ::
707  ++  new-event
708    |=  =udiffs:point
709    ^+  this-su
710    =/  original-pos  pos.zim.pki
711    |-  ^+  this-su
712    ?~  udiffs
713      this-su
714    =/  a-point=point  (~(gut by pos.zim.pki) ship.i.udiffs *point)
715    =/  a-diff=(unit diff:point)  (udiff-to-diff:point udiff.i.udiffs a-point)
716    =?  this-su  ?=(^ a-diff)
717      =?    this-su
718        ?&  =(our ship.i.udiffs)
719            ?=(%keys -.u.a-diff)
720            (~(has by jaw.own) life.to.u.a-diff)
721        ==
722      ::  if this about our keys, and we already know these, start using them
723      ::
724      =.  lyf.own  life.to.u.a-diff
725      ::  notify subscribers (ames) to start using our new private keys
726      ::
727      (exec yen.own [%give %private-keys [lyf jaw]:own])
728    ::
729    (public-keys:feel original-pos %diff ship.i.udiffs u.a-diff)
730    $(udiffs t.udiffs)
731  ::
732  ++  subscribers-on-ship
733    |=  =ship
734    ^-  (set duct)
735    ::  union of general and ship-specific subs
736    ::
737    %-  ~(uni in nel.zim)
738    (~(get ju ney.zim) ship)
739  ::
740  ++  feed
741    |_  ::  hen: subscription source
742        ::
743        hen=duct
744    ::
745    ::  Handle subscription to public-keys
746    ::
747    ++  public-keys
748      |=  whos=(set ship)
749      ?:  fak.own.pki
750        (public-keys:fake whos)
751      ::  Subscribe to parent of moons
752      ::
```

```
=.  ..feed
  =/  moons=(jug ship ship)
    %-  ~(gas ju *(jug spon=ship who=ship))
    %+  murn  ~(tap in whos)
    |=  who=ship
    ^-  (unit [spon=ship child=ship])
    ?.  =(%earl (clan:title who))
      ~
    ?:  (~(has by ship-sources) who)
      ~
    `[(^sein:title who) who]
  =/  moonl=(list [spon=ship ships=(set ship)])
    ~(tap by moons)
  |-  ^+  ..feed
  ?~  moonl
    ..feed
  ?:  =(our spon.i.moonl)
    $(moonl t.moonl)
  =.  ..feed  (sources:feel ships.i.moonl [%& spon.i.moonl])
  $(moonl t.moonl)
::  Add to subscriber list
::
=.  ney.zim
  =/  whol=(list ship)  ~(tap in whos)
  |-  ^-  (jug ship duct)
  ?~  whol
    ney.zim
  (~(put ju $(whol t.whol)) i.whol hen)
=.  yen.zim
  %-  ~(gas ju yen.zim)
  %+  turn  ~(tap in whos)
  |=  who=ship
  [hen who]
=?  nel.zim  ?=(~ whos)
  (~(put in nel.zim) hen)
::  Give initial result
::
=/  =public-keys-result
  :-  %full
  ?:  =(~ whos)
    pos.zim
  %-  my  ^-  (list (pair ship point))
  %+  murn
    ~(tap in whos)
  |=  who=ship
  ^-  (unit (pair ship point))
  =/  pub  (~(get by pos.zim) who)
  ?~  pub  ~
  ?:  =(0 life.u.pub)  ~
  `[who u.pub]
=.  ..feed  (public-keys-give (sy hen ~) public-keys-result)
..feed
::
::  Handle subscription to private-keys
::
++  private-keys
  %_  ..feed
    moz      [[hen %give %private-keys [lyf jaw]:own] moz]
```

```
811            yen.own   (~(put in yen.own) hen)
812        ==
813      ::
814      ++  fake
815        ?>  fak.own.pki
816        |%
817        ++  public-keys
818          |=  whos=(set ship)
819          =/  whol=(list ship)  ~(tap in whos)
820          =/  passes
821            |-  ^-  (list [who=ship =pass])
822            ?~  whol
823                ~
824            =/  cub  (pit:nu:crub:crypto 512 i.whol)
825            :-  [i.whol pub:ex:cub]
826            $(whol t.whol)
827          =/  points=(list (pair ship point))
828            %+  turn  passes
829            |=  [who=ship =pass]
830            ^-  [who=ship =point]
831            [who [rift=0 life=1 (my [1 1 pass] ~) `(^sein:title who)]]
832          =.  moz  [[hen %give %public-keys %full (my points)] moz]
833          ..feel
834        --
835      --
836    ::
837    ++  feel
838      |%
839      ::
840      ::  Update public-keys
841      ::
842      ++  public-keys
843        |=  [original=(map ship point) =public-keys-result]
844        ^+  ..feel
845        ?:  ?=(%full -.public-keys-result)
846          =/  pointl=(list [who=ship =point])
847            ~(tap by points.public-keys-result)
848          |-  ^+  ..feel
849          ?~  pointl
850            ..feel(pos.zim (~(uni by pos.zim) points.public-keys-result))
851          ::  if changing rift upward and we already had keys for them,
852          ::  then signal a breach
853          ::
854          =?    ..feel
855              =/  point
856                (~(get by pos.zim) who.i.pointl)
857              ?&  (~(has by original) who.i.pointl)
858                  ?=(^ point)
859                  (gth rift.point.i.pointl rift.u.point)
860              ==
861            =.  ..feel
862            %+  public-keys-give
863              (subscribers-on-ship who.i.pointl)
864            [%breach who.i.pointl]
865          =/  sor  (~(get by sources-reverse) %& who.i.pointl)
866          ?~  sor
867            ..feel
868          ::  delay resubscribing because Ames is going to clear any
```

```
869      ::   messages we send now.
870      ::
871      (emit hen %pass /breach/(scot %ud u.sor) %b %wait now)
872    ::
873    =.  ..feel
874      %+  public-keys-give
875        (subscribers-on-ship who.i.pointl)
876      [%full (my i.pointl ~)]
877    $(pointl t.pointl)
878  ::
879  ?:  ?=(%breach -.public-keys-result)
880    ::  we calculate our own breaches based on our local state
881    ::
882    ..feel
883  =*  who  who.public-keys-result
884  =/  a-diff=diff:point  diff.public-keys-result
885  =/  maybe-point  (~(get by pos.zim) who)
886  =/  =point  (fall maybe-point *point)
887  ::  if changing rift upward and we already had keys for them, then
888  ::  signal a breach
889  ::
890  =?    ..feel
891      ?&  (~(has by original) who)
892          ?=(^ maybe-point)
893          ?=(%rift -.a-diff)
894          (gth to.a-diff rift.point)
895      ==
896    =.  ..feel
897      %+  public-keys-give
898        (subscribers-on-ship who)
899      [%breach who]
900    =/  sor  (~(get by sources-reverse) %& who)
901    ?~  sor
902      ..feel
903    ::  delay resubscribing because Ames is going to clear any
904    ::  messages we send now.
905    ::
906    (emit hen %pass /breach/(scot %ud u.sor) %b %wait now)
907  ::
908  =.  point
909    ?-  -.a-diff
910        %spon  point(sponsor to.a-diff)
911        %rift  point(rift to.a-diff)
912        %keys
913      %_  point
914        life  life.to.a-diff
915        keys
916      %+  ~(put by keys.point)
917        life.to.a-diff
918      [crypto-suite pass]:to.a-diff
919      ==
920    ==
921  ::
922  =.  pos.zim  (~(put by pos.zim) who point)
923  %+  public-keys-give
924    (subscribers-on-ship who)
925  ?~  maybe-point
926    [%full (my [who point]~)]
```

```
[%diff who a-diff]
::
:: Update private-keys
::
++  private-keys
  |=  [=life =ring]
  ^+  ..feel
  ?:  &(=(lyf.own life) =((~(get by jaw.own) life) `ring))
    ..feel
  :: only eagerly update lyf if we were behind the chain life
  ::
  =?  lyf.own
      ?|  ?=(%earl (clan:title our))
          ?&  (gth life lyf.own)
              ::
              =+  pon=(~(get by pos.zim) our)
              ?~  pon  |
              (lth lyf.own life.u.pon)
      ==  ==
    life
  =.  jaw.own  (~(put by jaw.own) life ring)
  (exec yen.own [%give %private-keys lyf.own jaw.own])
::
:: Change sources for ships
::
++  sources
  |=  [whos=(set ship) =source]
  ^+  ..feel
  =^  =source-id  this-su  (get-source-id source)
  =.  ..feed
    ?~  whos
      ..feed(default-source.etn source-id)
    =/  whol=(list ship)  ~(tap in `(set ship)`whos)
    =.  ship-sources.etn
      |-  ^-  (map ship ^source-id)
      ?~  whol
        ship-sources.etn
      (~(put by $(whol t.whol)) i.whol source-id)
    =.  ship-sources-reverse.etn
      %-  ~(gas ju ship-sources-reverse.etn)
      (turn whol |=(=ship [source-id ship]))
    ..feed
  ::
  ?:  ?=(%& -.source)
    %-  emit
    =/  =message-all  [%0 %public-keys whos]
    [hen %pass /public-keys %a %plea p.source %j /public-keys message-all]
  (peer p.source whos)
  --
::
:: No-op
::
++  meet
  |=  [who=ship =life =pass]
  ^+  +>
  +>.$
  --
--
```

```
985   ::                                                         ::::
986   ::::                          #  vane                      ::  interface
987    ::                                                        ::::
988   ::
989   ::  lex: all durable %jael state
990   ::
991   =|  lex=state-2
992   |=  $:  ::  now: current time
993           ::  eny: unique entropy
994           ::  rof: namespace resolver
995           ::
996           now=@da
997           eny=@uvJ
998           rof=roof
999       ==
1000  ^?
1001  |%
1002  ::                                                         ::  ++call
1003  ++  call                                                   ::  request
1004  |=  $:  ::  hen: cause of this event
1005          ::  hic: event data
1006          ::
1007          hen=duct
1008          dud=(unit goof)
1009          hic=(hobo task)
1010      ==
1011    ^-  [(list move) _..^$]
1012    ?^  dud
1013     ~|(%jael-call-dud (mean tang.u.dud))
1014    ::
1015    =/  =task  ((harden task) hic)
1016    =^  did  lex
1017     abet:(~(call of [now eny] lex) hen task)
1018    [did ..^$]
1019  ::                                                         ::  ++load
1020  ++  load                                                   ::  upgrade
1021    =>  |%
1022        ::
1023        +$  any-state  $%(state-1 state-2)
1024        +$  state-1
1025         $:  %1
1026             pki=state-pki-1
1027             etn=state-eth-node
1028         ==
1029        +$  state-pki-1
1030         $:  $=  own
1031             $:  yen=(set duct)
1032                 sig=(unit oath)
1033                 tuf=(list turf)
1034                 boq=@ud
1035                 nod=purl:eyre
1036                 fak=_|
1037                 lyf=life
1038                 step=@ud
1039                 jaw=(map life ring)
1040             ==
1041             $=  zim
1042             $:  yen=(jug duct ship)
```

```
1043                    ney=(jug ship duct)
1044                    nel=(set duct)
1045                    dns=dnses
1046                    pos=(map ship point)
1047            ==      ==
1048        --
1049    |=  old=any-state
1050    ^+  ..^$
1051    =?  old   ?=(%1 -.old)
1052      %=  old
1053        -              %2
1054        own.pki  own.pki.old(+>+ +>.+>+.own.pki.old)
1055      ==
1056    ?>  ?=(%2 -.old)
1057    ..^$(lex old)
1058 ::                                                    ::  ++scry
1059 ++  scry                                              ::  inspect
1060    ^-  roon
1061    |=  [lyc=gang pov=path car=term bem=beam]
1062    ^-  (unit (unit cage))
1063    =*  ren   car
1064    =*  why=shop  &/p.bem
1065    =*  syd   q.bem
1066    =*  lot=coin  $/r.bem
1067    =*  tyl   s.bem
1068    ::
1069    ::  XX review for security, stability, cases other than now
1070    ::
1071    ?.  &(=(lot [%$ %da now]) =([~ ~] lyc))   ~
1072    ::
1073    ?:  &(?=(%x ren) =(tyl //whey))
1074      =/  maz=(list mass)
1075        :~  pki+&+pki.lex
1076            etn+&+etn.lex
1077        ==
1078      ``mass+!>(maz)
1079    ::
1080    ?.  =(%$ ren)  [~ ~]
1081    ?+    syd
1082        ~
1083    ::
1084        %step
1085      ?.  ?=([@ ~] tyl)  [~ ~]
1086      ?.  =([%& our] why)
1087        [~ ~]
1088      =/  who  (slaw %p i.tyl)
1089      ?~  who  [~ ~]
1090      ``[%noun !>(step.own.pki.lex)]
1091    ::
1092        %code
1093      ?.  ?=([@ ~] tyl)  [~ ~]
1094      ?.  =([%& our] why)
1095        [~ ~]
1096      =/  who  (slaw %p i.tyl)
1097      ?~  who  [~ ~]
1098      =/  sec  (~(got by jaw.own.pki.lex) lyf.own.pki.lex)
1099      =/  sal  (add %pass step.own.pki.lex)
1100      ``[%noun !>((end 6 (shaf sal (shax sec))))]
```

```
::
    %fake
?.  ?=(~ tyl)  [~ ~]
?.  =([%& our] why)
    [~ ~]
``[%noun !>(fak.own.pki.lex)]
::
    %life
?.  ?=([@ ~] tyl)  [~ ~]
?.  =([%& our] why)
    [~ ~]
=/  who  (slaw %p i.tyl)
?~  who  [~ ~]
::  fake ships always have life=1
::
?:  fak.own.pki.lex
    ``[%atom !>(1)]
?:  =(u.who p.why)
    ``[%atom !>(lyf.own.pki.lex)]
=/  pub  (~(get by pos.zim.pki.lex) u.who)
?~  pub  ~
``[%atom !>(life.u.pub)]
::
    %lyfe                                :: unitized %life
?.  ?=([@ ~] tyl)  [~ ~]
?.  =([%& our] why)
    [~ ~]
=/  who  (slaw %p i.tyl)
?~  who  [~ ~]
::  fake ships always have life=1
::
?:  fak.own.pki.lex
    ``[%noun !>((some 1))]
?:  =(u.who p.why)
    ``[%noun !>((some lyf.own.pki.lex))]
=/  pub  (~(get by pos.zim.pki.lex) u.who)
?~  pub  ``[%noun !>(~)]
``[%noun !>((some life.u.pub))]
::
    %rift
?.  ?=([@ ~] tyl)  [~ ~]
?.  =([%& our] why)
    [~ ~]
=/  who  (slaw %p i.tyl)
?~  who  [~ ~]
::  fake ships always have rift=0
::
?:  fak.own.pki.lex
    ``[%atom !>(0)]
=/  pos  (~(get by pos.zim.pki.lex) u.who)
?~  pos  ~
``[%atom !>(rift.u.pos)]
::
    %ryft                                :: unitized %rift
?.  ?=([@ ~] tyl)  [~ ~]
?.  =([%& our] why)
    [~ ~]
=/  who  (slaw %p i.tyl)
```

```
1159      ?~  who  [~ ~]
1160      ::  fake ships always have rift=0
1161      ::
1162      ?:  fak.own.pki.lex
1163        ``[%noun !>((some 0))]
1164      =/  pos  (~(get by pos.zim.pki.lex) u.who)
1165      ?~  pos  ``[%noun !>(~)]
1166      ``[%noun !>((some rift.u.pos))]
1167    ::
1168        %vein
1169      ?.  ?=([@ ~] tyl)  [~ ~]
1170      ?.  &(?=(%& -.why) =(p.why our))
1171        [~ ~]
1172      =/  lyf  (slaw %ud i.tyl)
1173      ?~  lyf  [~ ~]
1174      ::
1175      ?~  r=(~(get by jaw.own.pki.lex) u.lyf)
1176        [~ ~]
1177      ::
1178      [~ ~ %noun !>(u.r)]
1179    ::
1180        %vile
1181      =*  life  lyf.own.pki.lex
1182      =/  =seed  [our life (~(got by jaw.own.pki.lex) life) ~]
1183      [~ ~ %atom !>((jam seed))]
1184    ::
1185        %deed
1186      ?.  ?=([@ @ ~] tyl)  [~ ~]
1187      ?.  &(?=(%& -.why) =(p.why our))
1188        [~ ~]
1189      =/  who  (slaw %p i.tyl)
1190      =/  lyf  (slaw %ud i.t.tyl)
1191      ?~  who  [~ ~]
1192      ?~  lyf  [~ ~]
1193      ::
1194      ?:  fak.own.pki.lex
1195        =/  cub  (pit:nu:crub:crypto 512 u.who)
1196        :^  ~  ~  %noun
1197        !>  [1 pub:ex:cub ~]
1198      ::
1199      =/  rac  (clan:title u.who)
1200      ?:  ?=(%pawn rac)
1201        ?.  =(u.who p.why)
1202          [~ ~]
1203        ?.  =(1 u.lyf)
1204          [~ ~]
1205        =/  sec  (~(got by jaw.own.pki.lex) u.lyf)
1206        =/  cub  (nol:nu:crub:crypto sec)
1207        =/  sig  (sign:as:cub (shaf %self (sham [u.who 1 pub:ex:cub])))
1208        :^  ~  ~  %noun
1209        !>  [1 pub:ex:cub `sig]
1210      ::
1211      =/  pub  (~(get by pos.zim.pki.lex) u.who)
1212      ?~  pub
1213        ~
1214      ?:  (gth u.lyf life.u.pub)
1215        ~
1216      =/  pas  (~(get by keys.u.pub) u.lyf)
```

```
1217      ?~  pas
1218         ~
1219      :^   ~   ~   %noun
1220      !>  [u.lyf pass.u.pas ~]
1221  ::
1222        %earl
1223      ?.  ?=([@ @ ~] tyl)  [~ ~]
1224      ?.  =([%& our] why)
1225        [~ ~]
1226      =/  who  (slaw %p i.tyl)
1227      =/  lyf  (slaw %ud i.t.tyl)
1228      ?~  who  [~ ~]
1229      ?~  lyf  [~ ~]
1230      ?:  (gth u.lyf lyf.own.pki.lex)
1231        ~
1232      ?:  (lth u.lyf lyf.own.pki.lex)
1233        [~ ~]
1234      :: XX check that who/lyf hasn't been booted
1235      ::
1236      =/  sec  (~(got by jaw.own.pki.lex) u.lyf)
1237      =/  moon-sec  (shaf %earl (sham our u.lyf sec u.who))
1238      =/  cub  (pit:nu:crub:crypto 128 moon-sec)
1239      =/  =seed  [u.who 1 sec:ex:cub ~]
1240      ``[%seed !>(seed)]
1241  ::
1242        %sein
1243      ?.  ?=([@ ~] tyl)  [~ ~]
1244      ?.  =([%& our] why)
1245        [~ ~]
1246      =/  who  (slaw %p i.tyl)
1247      ?~  who  [~ ~]
1248      :^   ~   ~   %atom
1249      !>   ^-  ship
1250      (~(sein of [now eny] lex) u.who)
1251  ::
1252        %saxo
1253      ?.  ?=([@ ~] tyl)  [~ ~]
1254      ?.  =([%& our] why)
1255        [~ ~]
1256      =/  who  (slaw %p i.tyl)
1257      ?~  who  [~ ~]
1258      :^   ~   ~   %noun
1259      !>   ^-  (list ship)
1260      (~(saxo of [now eny] lex) u.who)
1261  ::
1262        %subscriptions
1263      ?.  ?=([@ ~] tyl)  [~ ~]
1264      ?.  =([%& our] why)
1265        [~ ~]
1266      :^   ~   ~   %noun
1267      !>([yen ney nel]:zim.pki.lex)
1268  ::
1269        %sources
1270      ?.  ?=(~ tyl)  [~ ~]
1271      :^   ~   ~   %noun   !>
1272      etn.lex
1273  ::
1274        %turf
```

```
    ?.  ?=(~ tyl)  [~ ~]
    [~ ~ %noun !>(tuf.own.pki.lex)]
  ==
::                                              ::  ++stay
++  stay                                        ::  preserve
  lex
::                                              ::  ++take
++  take                                        ::  accept
  |=  $:  ::  tea: order
          ::  hen: cause
          ::  hin: result
          ::
          tea=wire
          hen=duct
          dud=(unit goof)
          hin=sign
      ==
  ^-  [(list move) _..^$]
  ?^  dud
    ~|(%jael-take-dud (mean tang.u.dud))
  ::
  =^  did  lex  abet:(~(take of [now eny] lex) tea hen hin)
  [did ..^$]
--
```

Khan

```
::    %khan, thread runner
::
::    this vane presents a command/response interface for running
::    threads. two modes are supported: %fard for intra-arvo
::    requests (i.e. within the same kernel space) and %fyrd for
::    external requests (e.g. from the unix control plane.)
::
::    both modes take a thread start request consisting of a
::    namespace, thread name, and input data; they respond over the
::    same duct with either success or failure. %fard takes its
::    input arguments as a cage and produces %arow, which contains
::    a cage on success (or tang on failure). %fyrd takes an output
::    mark and input page; it produces %avow, which contains a page
::    on success.
::
::    threads currently expect input and produce output as vase,
::    not cage. %fard/%arow use cage instead since this is the
::    eventual desired thread API; however, the input mark is
::    currently ignored, and the output mark is always %noun. (for
::    forward compatibility, it is safe to specify %noun as the
::    input mark.)
::
::    %fyrd does mark conversion on both ends, and additionally
::    lifts its input into a $unit. this second step is done
::    because threads conventionally take their input as a unit,
::    with ~ for the case of "no arguments".
::
::    n.b. the current convention for threads is to use !< to
::    unpack their input vase. !< imposes the requirement that the
::    input type nests within the specified type. this limits %fyrd
::    to threads with inputs for which a named mark exists; it is
::    impossible to use %noun in general since it does not nest.
::    threads written against the current vase-based API could use
::    ;; instead of !< to unpack their input, thus allowing the
::    use of %fyrd with %noun. however the eventual solution is
::    probably to make threads consume and produce cages, and do
::    mark conversion where appropriate.
!:
!?  164
::
=,  khan
|=  our=ship
=>  |%
    +$  move  [p=duct q=(wite note gift)]
    +$  note                                        ::  %khan types
      $~  [%g %deal *sack *term *deal:gall]          ::
      $%  $:  %g                                      ::    out request $->
              $>(%deal task:gall)                     ::    to %gall
          ==                                          ::    full transmission
          $:  %k                                      ::
              $>(%fard task)                          ::    to self
      ==  ==                                          ::    internal thread
    +$  sign                                          ::
      $%  $:  %gall                                   ::    in response $<-
              $>(%unto gift:gall)                     ::    from %gall
          ==                                          ::    update
```

```
        $:  %khan                             ::      from self
            $>(?(%arow %avow) gift)           ::   thread result
      ==  ==                                  ::
    +$  khan-state                            ::
    $:  %0                                    ::      state v0
        hey=duct                              ::   unix duct
        tic=@ud                               ::   tid counter
    ==                                        ::
    --                                        ::
=>
|%
++  get-beak
  |=  [=bear now=@da]
  ?@(bear [our bear %da now] bear)
::
++  get-dais
  |=  [=beak =mark rof=roof]
  ^-  dais:clay
  ?~  ret=(rof [~ ~] /khan %cb beak /[mark])
    ~|(mark-unknown+mark !!)
  ?~  u.ret
    ~|(mark-invalid+mark !!)
  ?>  =(%dais p.u.u.ret)
  !<(dais:clay q.u.u.ret)
::
++  get-tube
  |=  [=beak =mark =out=mark rof=roof]
  ^-  tube:clay
  ?~  ret=(rof [~ ~] /khan %cc beak /[mark]/[out-mark])
    ~|(tube-unknown+[mark out-mark] !!)
  ?~  u.ret
    ~|(tube-invalid+[mark out-mark] !!)
  ?>  =(%tube p.u.u.ret)
  !<(tube:clay q.u.u.ret)
::
++  make-wire
  |=  [=beak =mark]
  ^-  wire
  [%fyrd (en-beam beak mark ~)]
::
++  read-wire
  |=  =wire
  ^-  (pair beak mark)
  ~|  khan-read-wire+wire
  ?>  ?=([%fyrd ^] wire)
  =/  =beam  (need (de-beam t.wire))
  ?>(?=([@ ~] s.beam) beam(s i.s.beam))
::
++  poke-spider
  |=  [hen=duct =cage]
  ^-  move
  [hen %pass //g %g %deal [our our /khan] %spider %poke cage]
::
++  watch-spider
  |=  [hen=duct =path]
  ^-  move
  [hen %pass //g %g %deal [our our /khan] %spider %watch path]
--
```

```
115  =|    khan-state
116  =*    state  -
117  |=    [now=@da eny=@uvJ rof=roof]
118  =*    khan-gate  .
119  ^?
120  |%
121  ::  +call: handle a +task request
122  ::
123  ++  call
124    |=  $:  hen=duct
125            dud=(unit goof)
126            wrapped-task=(hobo task)
127        ==
128    ^-  [(list move) _khan-gate]
129    ::
130    =/  =task  ((harden task) wrapped-task)
131    ?^  dud
132      ~|(%khan-call-dud (mean tang.u.dud))
133    ?+    -.task  [~ khan-gate]
134        %born
135      [~ khan-gate(hey hen, tic 0)]
136    ::
137        %fard  (bard hen 'khan-fyrd--' bear.p.task %| [name args]:p.task)
138        %lard  (bard hen 'khan-lard--' bear.task %& shed.task)
139        %fyrd
140      =*  fyd         p.task
141      =/  =beak       (get-beak bear.fyd now)
142      =/  =wire       (make-wire beak p.args.fyd)
143      =/  =dais:clay  (get-dais beak p.q.args.fyd rof)
144      =/  =vase
145        (slap (vale.dais q.q.args.fyd) !,(*hoon [~ u=.]))
146      =-  [[hen %pass wire -]~ khan-gate]
147      [%k %fard bear.fyd name.fyd p.q.args.fyd vase]
148    ==
149  ::
150  ++  bard
151    |=  [hen=duct prefix=@ta =bear payload=(each shed [name=term args=cage])]
152    ^-  [(list move) _khan-gate]
153    =/  =tid:rand  (cat 3 prefix (scot %uv (sham (mix tic eny))))
154    =/  =beak      (get-beak bear now)
155    =/  =cage
156      ?-  -.payload
157        %&  [%spider-inline !>([~ `tid beak p.payload])]
158        %|  [%spider-start !>([~ `tid beak [name q.args]:p.payload])]
159      ==
160    =.  tic  +(tic)
161    :_  khan-gate
162    :~  (watch-spider hen /thread-result/[tid])
163        (poke-spider hen cage)
164    ==
165  ::
166  ::  +load: migrate an old state to a new khan version
167  ::
168  ++  load
169    |=  old=khan-state
170    ^+  khan-gate
171    khan-gate(state old)
172  ::  +scry: nothing to see as yet
```

```
::
++  scry
  ^-  roon
  |=  [lyc=gang pov=path car=term bem=beam]
  ^-  (unit (unit cage))
  ~
++  stay  state
:: +take: handle responses.
::
++  take
  |=  [tea=wire hen=duct dud=(unit goof) hin=sign]
  ^-  [(list move) _khan-gate]
  ?^  dud
    ~|(%khan-take-dud (mean tang.u.dud))
  :_  khan-gate
  ?-    -.hin
      %gall
    ?+    -.p.hin  ~
        ?(%poke-ack %watch-ack)
      ?~  p.p.hin  ~
      %-  (slog 'khan-ack' u.p.p.hin)
      [hen %give %arow %| -.p.hin u.p.p.hin]~
    ::
        %fact
      =*  cag  cage.p.hin
      ?+    p.cag  ~&(bad-fact+p.cag !!)
          %thread-fail
        =/  =tang  !<(tang q.cag)
        ::  %-  (slog 'khan-fact' tang)
        [hen %give %arow %| p.cag tang]~
      ::
          %thread-done
        [hen %give %arow %& %noun q.cag]~
      ==
    ==
  ::
      %khan
    ?.  ?=(%arow +<.hin)    ~
    ?.  ?=([%fyrd *] tea)   ~
    =*  row  p.hin
    ?.  ?=(%& -.row)
      [hen %give %avow row]~
    =/  [=beak =mark]  (read-wire tea)
    =/  =tube:clay     (get-tube beak p.p.row mark rof)
    =/  =vase          (tube q.p.row)
    [hen %give %avow %& mark q.vase]~
  ==
--
```

Lick

```
::  %lick
!:
!?  164
::
=,  lick
|=  our=ship
=>  |%
    +$  move   [p=duct q=(wite note gift)]
    +$  note   ~                                  :: out request $->
    +$  sign   ~
    ::
    +$  lick-state
      $:  %0
          unix-duct=_`duct`[//lick ~]
          owners=(map name duct)
      ==
    ::
    +$  name    path
    --
::
~%  %lick  ..part  ~
::
=|  lick-state
=*  state  -
|=  [now=@da eny=@uvJ rof=roof]
=*  lick-gate  .
^?
|%
::  +register: Create a move to register an agent with vere
::
++  register
  |=  =name
  ^-  move
  [unix-duct.state %give [%spin name]]
::  +disconnect: Create Move to send a disconnect soak to am agent
::
++  disconnect
  |=  =name
  ^-  move
  =/  =duct  (~(get by owners) name)
  [+.duct %give [%soak name %disconnect ~]]
::  +call: handle a +task:lick request
::
++  call
  |=  $:  hen=duct
          dud=(unit goof)
          wrapped-task=(hobo task)
      ==
  ^-  [(list move) _lick-gate]
  ::
  =/  =task  ((harden task) wrapped-task)
  ?+    -.task  [~ lick-gate]
      %born      :: need to register devices with vere and send disconnect soak
    :-  %+  weld
          (turn ~(tap in ~(key by owners.state)) register)
          (turn ~(tap in ~(key by owners.state)) disconnect)
```

```
57      lick-gate(unix-duct hen)
58      ::
59        %spin      :: A gall agent wants to spin a communication line
60      :-  ~[(register name.task)]
61      lick-gate(owners (~(put by owners) name.task hen))
62      ::
63        %shut      :: shut down a communication line
64      :-  [unix-duct.state %give [%shut name.task]]~
65      lick-gate(owners (~(del by owners) name.task))
66      ::
67        %soak      :: push a soak to the ipc's owner
68      =/  ner=duct  (~(get by owners.state) name.task)
69      :_  lick-gate
70      [+.ner %give [%soak name.task mark.task noun.task]]~
71      ::
72        %spit      :: push a spit to ipc
73      :_  lick-gate
74      [unix-duct.state %give [%spit name.task mark.task noun.task]]~
75    ==
76  ::  +load: migrate an old state to a new lick version
77  ::
78  ++  load
79    |=  old=lick-state
80    ^+  lick-gate
81    lick-gate(state old)
82  ::  +scry: view state
83  ::
84  ::  %a  scry out a list of all ipc ports
85  ::  %d  get the owner of an ipc port
86  ++  scry
87    ^-  roon
88    |=  [lyc=gang pov=path car=term bem=beam]
89    ^-  (unit (unit cage))
90    |^
91    ::  only respond for the local identity, current timestamp, root gang
92    ::
93    ?.  ?&  =(our p.bem)
94            =(%$ q.bem)
95            =([%da now] r.bem)
96            =([~ ~] lyc)
97        ==
98      ~
99    ?+  car  ~
100     %a  read-a
101     %d  read-d
102     %u  read-u
103   ==
104   ::  +read-a: scry our list of ports
105   ::
106   ++  read-a
107     ^-  (unit (unit cage))
108     =/  ports=(list name)  ~(tap in ~(key by owners))
109     ``[%noun !>(ports)]
110   ::  +read d: get ports owner
111   ::
112   ++  read-d
113     ^-  (unit (unit cage))
114     =/  devs=(unit duct)  (~(get by owners) s.bem)
```

```
115      ?~  devs  [~ ~]
116        ``[%noun !>(devs)]
117    ::  +read u: does a port exist
118    ::
119    ++  read-u
120      ^-  (unit (unit cage))
121        ``[%noun !>((~(has by owners) s.bem))]
122    ::
123    --
124  ::
125  ++  stay
126    state
127  ++  take
128    |=  [tea=wire hen=duct dud=(unit goof) hin=sign]
129    ^-  [(list move) _lick-gate]
130    ?^  dud
131      ~|(%lick-take-dud (mean tang.u.dud))
132    ::
133    [~ lick-gate]
134  --
```